International Directory of
COMPANY
HISTORIES

International Directory of

COMPANY HISTORIES

VOLUME 35

Editor
Tina Grant

ST. JAMES PRESS

AN IMPRINT OF THE GALE GROUP

DETROIT • NEW YORK • SAN FRANCISCO
LONDON • BOSTON • WOODBRIDGE, CT

STAFF

Tina Grant, *Editor*

Miranda H. Ferrara, *Project Manager*

Michelle Banks, Erin Bealmear, Joann Cerrito, Jim Craddock, Steve Cusack, Kristin Hart,
Melissa Hill, Margaret Mazurkiewicz, Carol Schwartz, Christine Thomassini,
Michael J. Tyrkus, *St. James Press Editorial Staff*

Peter M. Gareffa, *Managing Editor, St. James Press*

Library of Congress Catalog Number: 89-190943

British Library Cataloguing in Publication Data

International directory of company histories. Vol. 35
I. Tina Grant
338.7409

ISBN 1-55862-394-9

Printed in the United States of America
Published simultaneously in the United Kingdom

St. James Press is an imprint of The Gale Group

Cover photograph: Oslo Stock Exchange
(courtesy of Oslo Børs)

10 9 8 7 6 5 4 3 2 1

CONTENTS

Company Histories

PREFACE _____

The St. James Press series *The International Directory of Company Histories (IDCH)* is intended for reference use by students, business people, librarians, historians, economists, investors, job candidates, and others who seek to learn more about the historical development of the world's most important companies. To date, *IDCH* has covered over 4,700 companies in 35 volumes.

Inclusion Criteria

Most companies chosen for inclusion in *IDCH* have achieved a minimum of US$50 million in annual sales and are leading influences in their industries or geographical locations. Companies may be publicly held, private, or nonprofit. State-owned companies that are important in their industries and that may operate much like public or private companies also are included. Wholly owned subsidiaries and divisions are profiled if they meet the requirements for inclusion. Entries on companies that have had major changes since they were last profiled may be selected for updating.

The *IDCH* series highlights 10% private and nonprofit companies, and features updated entries on approximately 45 companies per volume.

Entry Format

Each entry begins with the company's legal name, the address of its headquarters, its telephone, toll-free, and fax numbers, and its web site. A statement of public, private, state, or parent ownership follows. A company with a legal name in both English and the language of its headquarters country is listed by the English name, with the native-language name in parentheses.

The company's founding or earliest incorporation date, the number of employees, and the most recent available sales figures follow. Sales figures are given in local currencies with equivalents in U.S. dollars. For some private companies, sales figures are estimates and indicated by the abbreviation *est.* The entry lists the exchanges on which a company's stock is traded and its ticker symbol, as well as the company's NAIC codes.

Entries generally contain a *Company Perspectives* box which provides a short summary of the company's mission, goals, and ideals, a *Key Dates* box highlighting milestones in the company's history, lists of *Principal Subsidiaries, Principal Divisions, Principal Operating Units, Principal Competitors,* and articles for *Further Reading.*

American spelling is used throughout *IDCH*, and the word "billion" is used in its U.S. sense of one thousand million.

Sources

Entries have been compiled from publicly accessible sources both in print and on the Internet such as general and academic periodicals, books, annual reports, and material supplied by the companies themselves.

Cumulative Indexes

IDCH contains two indexes: the **Index to Companies**, which provides an alphabetical index to companies discussed in the text as well as to companies profiled, and the **Index to Industries**, which allows researchers to locate companies by their principal industry. Both indexes are cumulative and specific instructions for using them are found immediately preceding each index.

Suggestions Welcome

Comments and suggestions from users of *IDCH* on any aspect of the product as well as suggestions for companies to be included or updated are cordially invited. Please write:

The Editor
International Directory of Company Histories
St. James Press
27500 Drake Rd.
Farmington Hills, Michigan 48331-3535

ABBREVIATIONS FOR FORMS OF COMPANY INCORPORATION _____

A.B.	Aktiebolaget (Sweden)
A.G.	Aktiengesellschaft (Germany, Switzerland)
A.S.	Atieselskab (Denmark)
A.S.	Aksjeselskap (Denmark, Norway)
A.Ş.	Anomin Şirket (Turkey)
B.V.	Besloten Vennootschap met beperkte, Aansprakelijkheid (The Netherlands)
Co.	Company (United Kingdom, United States)
Corp.	Corporation (United States)
G.I.E.	Groupement d'Intérêt Economique (France)
GmbH	Gesellschaft mit beschränkter Haftung (Germany)
H.B.	Handelsbolaget (Sweden)
Inc.	Incorporated (United States)
KGaA	Kommanditgesellschaft auf Aktien (Germany)
K.K.	Kabushiki Kaisha (Japan)
LLC	Limited Liability Company (Middle East)
Ltd.	Limited (Canada, Japan, United Kingdom, United States)
N.V.	Naamloze Vennootschap (The Netherlands)
OY	Osakeyhtiöt (Finland)
PLC	Public Limited Company (United Kingdom)
PTY.	Proprietary (Australia, Hong Kong, South Africa)
S.A.	Société Anonyme (Belgium, France, Switzerland)
SpA	Società per Azioni (Italy)

ABBREVIATIONS FOR CURRENCY _____

DA	Algerian dinar	Dfl	Netherlands florin
A$	Australian dollar	Nfl	Netherlands florin
Sch	Austrian schilling	NZ$	New Zealand dollar
BFr	Belgian franc	N	Nigerian naira
Cr	Brazilian cruzado	NKr	Norwegian krone
C$	Canadian dollar	RO	Omani rial
RMB	Chinese renminbi	P	Philippine peso
DKr	Danish krone	PLN	Polish Zloty
E£	Egyptian pound	Esc	Portuguese escudo
EUR	Euro Dollars	Ru	Russian ruble
Fmk	Finnish markka	SRls	Saudi Arabian riyal
FFr	French franc	S$	Singapore dollar
DM	German mark	R	South African rand
HK$	Hong Kong dollar	W	South Korean won
HUF	Hungarian forint	Pta	Spanish peseta
Rs	Indian rupee	SKr	Swedish krona
Rp	Indonesian rupiah	SFr	Swiss franc
IR£	Irish pound	NT$	Taiwanese dollar
L	Italian lira	B	Thai baht
¥	Japanese yen	£	United Kingdom pound
W	Korean won	$	United States dollar
KD	Kuwaiti dinar	B	Venezuelan bolivar
LuxFr	Luxembourgian franc	K	Zambian kwacha
M$	Malaysian ringgit		

International Directory of
COMPANY
HISTORIES

Aaron Rents, Inc.

Aaron Rents, Inc.

309 East Paces Ferry Road, N.E.
Atlanta, Georgia 30305-2377
U.S.A.
Telephone: (404) 231-0011
Fax: (404) 240-6584
Web site: http://www.aaronrentsfurniture.com;
      http://www.shopaarons.com

Public Company
Incorporated: 1962
Employees: 3,600
Sales: $437.4 million (1999)
Stock Exchanges: NASDAQ
Ticker Symbol: ARONA ARONB
NAIC: 337122 Nonupholstered Wood Household
   Furniture Manufacturing; 337124 Metal Household
   Furniture Manufacturing; 337121 Upholstered
   Household Furniture Manufacturing; 337211 Wood
   Office Furniture Manufacturing; 337214 Office
   Furniture (Except Wood) Manufacturing; 44211
   Furniture Stores; 443111 Household Appliance Stores;
   53221 Consumer Electronics and Appliances Rental;
   53231 General Rental Centers; 532299 All Other
   Consumer Goods Rental; 53242 Office Machinery &
   Equipment Rental & Leasing

Aaron Rents, Inc. rents and sells residential and office furniture, household appliances, consumer electronics, and accessories to both individual and corporate customers. In addition to being one of the largest companies in its industry, Aaron is distinguished as the only rental company that manufactures and reconditions its own furniture. Aaron's Rental Purchase division focuses on providing durable household goods to lower to middle income consumers with limited or no access to traditional credit sources such as bank financing, installment credit, or credit cards. The company operated more than 475 company-operated and franchised stores in 40 states at the end of 1999 and was enjoying its eighth consecutive year of record growth.

Steady Growth from the Late 1950s

Aaron Rents is the creation of entrepreneur R. Charles Loudermilk. Loudermilk was born in Atlanta, Georgia, in 1927—"on the wrong side of the tracks," by his admission. He attended Georgia Tech, had a tour in the Navy, and earned his business degree from the University of North Carolina, before accepting a job with Pet Milk Company and, later, the pharmaceutical and chemical giant Pfizer. While working for Pfizer during the early 1950s, Loudermilk came across a small North Carolina store that rented furniture and other merchandise. Eager to strike out on his own, Loudermilk drew on the concept and started a rental business in 1955, borrowing $500 from Trust Company Bank, while a partner invested another $500.

Loudermilk's first order was for 300 chairs. He and his partner rushed to an army surplus store and purchased 500 chairs. They delivered 300 of them to an auction in Atlanta and charged ten cents per chair per day. "It was a hot day and the chairs didn't stack well," Loudermilk recalled in company annals. "My partner decided he didn't want to be in the rental business anymore." After his partner bailed out, Loudermilk stuck with his idea and continued to buy and rent furniture. Because he had little money to invest in the business, he worked at his mother's restaurant and poured virtually every nickel back into his rental venture for seven straight years. Later, Loudermilk was able to rent a small storefront and hire a woman to answer the telephone; he named the company Aaron Rents to ensure top billing in the Yellow Pages.

Loudermilk gave his receptionist a catalog from a California company and told her to buy rental equipment from it. When a customer called or came in to rent some item, she would simply let that person select pieces from the catalog. If an order came in for a table or bed, for example, Loudermilk would drive down to Sears, buy a piece similar to the one in the catalog, and deliver it himself. Thus Loudermilk got into renting party equipment and sickroom gear, later moving into office and residential furniture. "People said it was a gamble," Loudermilk recalled in the November 21, 1983 issue of *Forbes*. "It really wasn't. We never bought the second item until the first one was rented."

Company Perspectives:

The Company believes it possesses a valuable brand name in the rental business, as well as operating characteristics which differentiate it from its competitors. For instance, the Company's rental purchase concept is unique in offering 12-month rental purchase agreements, larger and more attractive store showrooms and a wider selection of merchandise. In the rent-to-rent business, the Company believes that its ability to deliver residential and office furniture and equipment to its customers quickly and efficiently gives the Company an advantage over furniture retailers who often require several weeks to effect delivery. By having its own manufacturing capabilities, an extensive distribution network and sophisticated management information systems, the Company is well-positioned to meet the distinct needs of its rent-to-rent and rental purchase customers.

Expansion in the 1960s to Mid-1970s

Loudermilk spent the late 1950s nurturing the business at his original Buckhead area store before branching out in the 1960s with a second shop. A third store was opened in 1964 and rented only furniture. By that time, inventory had grown to include large outdoor tents. Loudermilk rented four tents to civil rights marchers when they made their famous trek from Selma to Montgomery, Alabama in 1965. Two years later, the company opened an outlet in Baltimore, its first outside of Atlanta. By 1969, Aaron Rents was generating a healthy $2 million annually from an inventory of about $3 million.

Aside from furniture and party-related supplies, eventually Aaron Rents outlets were renting everything from corkscrews and pillowcases to sofas and executive desks. The business was relatively simple and straightforward. Loudermilk would purchase goods, rent them out, and depreciate them down to a value of zero. Tax laws during the early 1970s allowed him to depreciate the entire value of the item over a period of three years; the depreciated value was written off against income to reduce taxes. Everything that he could get in rent or resale of the item after that was pure profit.

Aaron Rents prospered during the 1960s and 1970s. By the mid-1970s, in fact, the operation had expanded to include nearly 20 showrooms that were generating annual sales of about $10 million. That sales figure made Aaron the largest private company operating in the burgeoning U.S. furniture rental business. Although Aaron's steady growth prior to the 1980s was admirable, it was meager in comparison with the rampant expansion the company would achieve in the following 15 years. Several factors contributed to that expansion. Significantly, in the late 1970s, Loudermilk decided to focus his efforts on the residential and office markets, rather than his traditional party and sickroom segment. That decision resulted in a rapid climb in sales. Therefore, in 1982, Loudermilk sold off his party and sickroom equipment operations and dumped the proceeds into his residential and business division.

In addition to shifting the company's focus, Loudermilk achieved growth during the late 1970s and early 1980s through new financing strategies. Rather than waiting until his goods had depreciated to reap his profits, he began taking less depreciation during the rental period and then barely breaking even on the resale of the furniture. A $200 desk, for instance, would be depreciated down to $100 and then marked up to $130 for resale. Simply put, he found a way to take his profits earlier. When the furniture was no longer rentable, Loudermilk would sell it alongside value-oriented new furniture in warehouse-style stores—they were called Aaron Sells Furniture—next to his rental shops. That way, he was able to attract customers who did not want to rent but did not have cash for expensive new furniture.

The overall strategy helped to boost the company's net income to a record $4.7 million in 1983 from sales of $55.4 million. By the end of that year, Aaron Rents was operating a total of 92 stores in 14 mostly southern states. It was servicing 50,000 rental contracts worth an average of $48 monthly, giving Aaron roughly 15 percent of the $350 million furniture rental market. Loudermilk had become a multimillionaire. He spent his weekends on his 3,700-acre south Georgia plantation, where he tended his herd of purebred limousin cattle and perused his corn and soybean fields. When not at the plantation, he might be found hunting geese in Alaska or Scotland. Otherwise, Loudermilk worked to enlarge his rental empire.

Growth Through Acquisitions in the 1980s

Another important factor in Aaron Rents' tremendous expansion during the early 1980s was Loudermilk's strategy to add to the company's growth through acquisition. Loudermilk took Aaron Rents public in 1982 to raise expansion capital—although he had retained 42 percent of the company's stock as of 1983, which was valued at about $38 million. He used part of the money from the public offering to buy a few of his biggest private competitors. Most notable were the acquisitions of leading private rental companies Metrolease (Metropolitan Furniture Leasing), of North Carolina, and the Houston-based Modern Furniture Rental. Loudermilk bought Modern Furniture in July of 1983 for $6.5 million in cash before plunking down $4.5 million for Metrolease the following summer. Meanwhile, the rental industry in general was expanding, adding fuel to Aaron Rents' growth. Aaron Rents' annual revenues surged to a whopping $84 million in 1984, making it the largest rental company in the nation. Indeed, Aaron Rents surpassed the venerable industry leader GranTree, which had doubled its revenues from $41 million in 1977 to $82 million in 1984.

At the same time, Aaron Rents' bottom line was benefiting from in-house manufacturing operations. The company had started producing its furniture out of necessity in 1971 when Lockheed Corp. brought employees to Atlanta from all over the world to build a new plane.

Manufacturers simply could not meet Aaron's demand for furniture to rent to the influx of workers, so Loudermilk decided to begin building the furniture himself. He purchased a local manufacturer called MacTavish Furniture Industries and was instantly in the furniture-making business. The decision to manufacture proved fruitful, and Aaron became the only company in the rental industry to exclusively build its furniture. The benefits were multifold. Not only did Aaron benefit from a

Key Dates:

1955: R. Charles Loudermilk starts Aaron Rents.
1964: Aaron Rents opens its first furniture rental store.
1971: Aaron Rents acquires MacTavish Furniture Industries.
1982: Aaron rents sells off its party and sick room equipment and goes public.
1983: Aaron Rents acquires Modern Furniture.
1984: The company acquires Metrolease and becomes the largest rental outfit in the United States.
1987: The company purchases Ball Stalker and enters the rent-to-own business.
1988: The company purchases furniture rental operations from Furniture Enterprises, Powell Furniture Rental, and Cort Furniture Rental Corp.
1990: Aaron Rents begins to offer franchise options.
1998: The company acquires Lamps Forever.

dependable, low-cost furniture source, but it also saved money and time related to the repair and reconditioning of its old furniture. In addition, Aaron was able to control both styling and price to suit the specific needs of its targeted customers.

Aaron continued to pursue acquisitions and to expand its furniture making operations during 1984 and 1985. By early 1986, the chain had grown to include 154 stores in 20 states and annual revenues were topping a fat $100 million. Despite sales gains, however, earnings growth had stalled. The problem was primarily the result of the fast store expansion. New stores typically took 12 to 18 months to achieve profitability; many of Aaron's outlets were still dragging down the bottom line. Loudermilk decided to slow the company's expansion and to focus on consolidating and streamlining existing operations. During 1986 and 1987, the company closed some Aaron Sells outlets, beefed up its management team, and launched a drive to cut costs and improve profit margins. Loudermilk took a break from day-to-day management of the company during those years, devoting much of his time to his duties as chairman of the Metro Atlanta Rapid Transit Authority and to his political interests.

The effects of management efforts at Aaron seemed apparent by 1988. Sales rose to $119 million and $132 million in 1987 and 1988, respectively, while net earnings climbed to $4.79 million and $5.54 million. The sales gains, however, were partially the result of Loudermilk's October 1987 purchase of Ball Stalker Inc., an Atlanta-based manufacturer and distributor of upscale office furniture. Similarly, the profit increase was generated primarily by a cut in Aaron's effective corporate tax rate from 46 percent to 34 percent; the tax cut was ushered in with the renowned Tax Reform Act of 1986 (TRA). The TRA eliminated many of the depreciation benefits that Aaron had enjoyed previously, however. So, although earnings rose between 1987 and 1988, they were still low compared with previous projections, and the TRA promised to hurt future profits as well. Evidencing investor discontent with the situation, Aaron's stock price skidded from a high of $25.75 in 1984 to just $12 before the 1987 stock market crash, after which it plummeted to a low $6.50.

Realizing that his company was struggling, Loudermilk returned to day-to-day control of the company in 1987. He renewed the company's efforts to overhaul operations, cut costs, and boost margins. At the same time, Loudermilk continued to expand the Aaron network of stores. Early in 1988, in fact, he purchased furniture rental operations in Florida from Furniture Enterprises and Powell Furniture Rental, as well as a Jackson, Mississippi store from competitor Cort Furniture Rental Corp. By late 1988, the company was operating 183 stores in 31 states. Before the end of the year, however, that number would be reduced as a result of the consolidation of several Aaron Sells outlets with adjacent Aaron Rents stores.

Significantly, Aaron followed in the footsteps of its chief competitors, GranTree and the highly successful Rent-A-Center, in 1987 when it entered the rent-to-own business. Under that program, customers were allowed to make regular payments over a pre-determined period—usually 18 or 24 months—to use furniture, appliances, electronics, and other goods. These payments differed from usual rent payments by being applied to the purchase price, and the consumer could own the item at the end of the rental period. By late 1988, Aaron was offering rent-to-own at 18 of its store locations, introducing a 12-month ownership plan, and Loudermilk was planning to expand the successful program throughout his network. The rent-to-own initiative was part of Loudermilk's push to focus on renting rather than selling furniture.

Reorganization and Franchising in the Late 1980s and 1990s

Facing flat market growth in the furniture rental industry, Loudermilk stepped up reorganization efforts in 1989 by eliminating distinctions between the rental, sales, and combination-store divisions. He replaced them with six geographical regions, each with a vice-president responsible for ten to 20 outlets; previously, a single manager had been placed in charge of about 60 stores. Similarly, the office furniture rental division, which consisted of about 47 stores going into 1990, was reorganized into six geographical regions, each of which was headed by a vice-president. Finally, Loudermilk initiated a franchising campaign designed to increase Aaron's regional coverage with minimal capital cost to the company.

The reorganization was slow to take hold. In fact, Aaron suffered three consecutive years of declining sales and earnings beginning in 1989. Eventually, though, the company's financial performance recovered. Among Loudermilk's successful moves during the early 1990s was renting office equipment, not just office furniture. He had hesitated to rent equipment for several years because he felt that Aaron lacked the management expertise to handle that market segment. That move contributed to Aaron's turnaround, however, which began in 1992. Indeed, although Aaron's sales for 1992 grew marginally to about $145 million, the company posted a profit of about $3.1 million—Aaron's first profit gain since 1988.

Encouraged by success with the Aaron Rental Purchase stores, which made up Aaron's rent-to-own business, Loudermilk began expanding the chain through both franchises and company-owned stores. As a result, revenues sailed to $158 million in 1993 before rocketing to about $186 million in 1994.

Throughout the fiscal 1994 year, the second-ranked company on *Franchise* magazine's Gold 100 list added rental-purchase stores to its chain at a rate of one per week. Growth continued during 1995. By September 1995, in fact, Aaron was operating a total of 206 company-owned outlets and 33 franchised stores, and sales were booming. Revenues swelled 24 percent in fiscal 1995 to nearly $230 million as net income vaulted to a record $11.33 million. By 1998, the number of stores had increased to about 300 (368 by 1999) and revenues were at $380 million, $200 million of which came from the rental purchase business. Aaron also continued to benefit from its five furniture manufacturing plants in Georgia and Florida.

Aaron was selective about to whom it would sell franchise rights and where its franchises were located. "We don't want to be hidden in the middle of a shopping center. We want locations comparable to Blockbuster Video. You never see a Blockbuster store that is not very, very visible," Loudermilk was quoted as saying in the October/November 1995 issue of *Progressive Rentals*. Aaron's stores were on average 10,000 to 12,000 square feet, larger and more attractive than the competition, usually suburban in location, and serving customers with a higher income than other rent-to-own businesses. When he could not find a large enough store, Loudermilk would build a stand-alone unit marked by Aaron's unique design. Aaron's franchise support center provided assistance to franchisees in selecting store location and training in management and operation.

In the late 1990s, the company commanded approximately 30 percent of the estimated $600 rent-to-rent market in the United States and was branching out into the corporate relocation and small office/home office markets. Apartment management companies represented another expanding segment of its rent-to-rent customer base. Aaron Direct, the company's warehouse concept, had a presence in six markets serving national customers that provided interim housing for companies relocating employees. In 1998, the company acquired Lamps Forever, a manufacturer of designer lamps, tables, and matching accessories. The following year, in a major expansion of its national advertising, Aaron acquired rights to the NASCAR Busch Grand National Car Race. Beginning in 2000, the "Aaron's 312" campaign played off the longest race of the season, a 312-mile run, while reminding sports fans, whose demographic profile exactly matched the company's target customer base, of Aaron's three forms of purchasing—cash or check, credit card, or its Lease Plus 12-month lease program.

In 1999, Aaron also was added to the S&P SmallCap 600 Index. That year, for the second time straight, the company was named one of the 200 best small companies by *Forbes*. The company fixed its strategic focus on expansion for the years 2000 and beyond. Adding stores in established markets, targeting the growing office furniture rental segment, accelerating franchised rental purchase store openings, and adding company-operated stores in major markets, Aaron Rents sought to continue growing.

Principal Subsidiaries

Aaron Investment Company.

Principal Divisions

Aaron Rents' Rent-to-Rent; Aaron's Rental Purchase; Mac-Tavish Furniture.

Principal Competitors

Rent-A-Center; Renters Choice; Rent-Way, Inc.; CORT Business Services Corporation.

Further Reading

Bork, Robert H., "Money in the Mattress," *Forbes,* November 21, 1983, p. 108.

Danielson, Gilbert L., "Aaron Rents, Inc., Names Ken Butler and Brian Stahl Division Presidents," *PR Newswire,* February 2, 1995.

Gilligan, Gregory J., "Rent-to-Own Delivers to Aaron a New Direction, Higher Sales," *Richmond Times-Dispatch,* Bus. Sec., July 31, 1993.

Hallem, Jeanie Franco, " 'Cooling It' Is New Motto for Aaron Rents," *Atlanta Business Chronicle,* February 24, 1986, p. 2B.

Massey, John, "Check Out Charlie," *Progressive Rentals,* October/November 1995, p. 23.

Robertshaw, Nicky, "Aaron Rents Expanding with Six-Eight Stores," *Memphis Business Journal,* November 21, 1994, p. 3.

Schonbak, Judith, "Aaron Rents Bounces Back," *Business Atlanta,* September 1988, p. 32.

——, "Aaron Rents Launches New Venture," *Business Atlanta,* July 1992, p. 8.

Weiner, Daniel P., "Aaron Rents Inc.," *Fortune,* November 25, 1985, p. 40.

Welch, Mary, " 'Radical' Shift for Aaron Rents," *Atlanta Business Chronicle,* December 19, 1988, p. 6.

—Dave Mote
—updated by Carrie Rothburd

Abercrombie & Fitch Co.

Abercrombie & Fitch Co.

4 Limited Parkway East
Reynoldsburg, Ohio 43068
U.S.A.
Telephone: (614) 577-6500
Fax: (614) 577-6980
Web site: http://www.abercrombie.com

Public Company
Incorporated: 1904
Employees: 9,500
Sales: $1.04 billion (2000)
Stock Exchanges: New York
Ticker Symbol: ANF
NAIC: 44811 Men's Clothing Stores; 44812 Women's
 Clothing Stores; 44813 Children's and Infants'
 Clothing Stores

Abercrombie & Fitch Co. is a retailer of casual clothing marketed toward young people, predominantly college students. The company oversees about 250 stores nationwide, mostly in shopping malls, and also markets its clothing on the Web and in catalogues. The company's style has become identified with the more risqué aspects of upper-middle-class youth culture, lifestyle, attitudes, and music. In the year since gaining independence from its erstwhile parent, The Limited, Abercrombie has continued its gently provocative ways. This brand image represents a drastic change from the company's origins. During the first half of the 20th century Abercrombie & Fitch Co. was the definitive store for America's sporting elite, outfitting big-game hunters, fishermen, and other adventurers ala Ernest Hemingway. After the chain went bankrupt in 1977, Oshman's Sporting Goods revived the Abercrombie & Fitch name but shifted its focus to more contemporary sporting goods and a wider array of apparel for men and women. The Limited, Inc., after acquiring the company in 1988, eliminated sporting goods entirely.

The Early Years

Abercrombie & Fitch Co. was founded in 1892 in New York City by David T. Abercrombie and Ezra H. Fitch. Abercrombie, a former prospector, miner, trapper, and railroad surveyor or engineer, owned a small shop and factory producing camping equipment in lower Manhattan. Fitch, one of his customers, was a successful lawyer in Kingston, New York, but the outdoors was his chief interest.

The men opened a sporting goods store. Fitch was the visionary of the two, anticipating a clientele far broader than merely those who camped out in the course of earning a living. The partners proved ill-matched, and both men were hot-tempered. Following the latest of many long and violent arguments, Abercrombie resigned in 1907 to return to manufacturing camping equipment. Retaining the company name, Fitch continued with other partners. In 1909 he mailed out 50,000 copies of a 456-page catalogue. Since they cost a dollar each to produce, the catalogues almost bankrupted the company, but the subsequent flood of orders justified the expense. In 1917 Abercrombie & Fitch moved into a 12-story building on Madison Avenue at East 45th Street, a location the advertising department described as "Where the Blazed Trail Crosses the Boulevard." It included a luxuriously furnished log cabin that Fitch made his town house, with an adjoining casting pool.

By this time Abercrombie & Fitch's reputation as purveyor to the sporting elite already was well established. It had equipped Theodore Roosevelt for an African safari and also outfitted, or was soon going to outfit, polar expeditions led by Roald Amundsen and Admiral Richard Byrd and flights made by Charles Lindbergh and Amelia Earhart. Ernest Hemingway was a customer. Every president from Roosevelt to Gerald Ford eventually would buy something from the store.

Roaring 1920s and Depression 1930s

Fitch retired in 1928, selling his interest in the company to his brother-in-law, James S. Cobb, who became president, and an employee, Otis L. Guernsey, who became vice-president. In his first year at the helm, Cobb acquired a similar New York business, Von Lengerke & Detmold, respected for its European-made sporting guns and fishing tackle, and Von Lengerke & Antoine, the Chicago branch, which became a subsidiary of Abercrombie & Fitch but continued until 1959 under its own name. In 1930 Cobb bought Griffin & Howe, a gunsmith shop. The merchandise that Von Lengerke & Detmold and Griffin & Howe had in stock was added to the Madison Avenue store.

By this time Abercrombie & Fitch was selling outdoor and sporting equipment not only for hunting, fishing, camping, and exploration, but also for skating, polo, golf, and tennis. The store also carried a variety of outdoor clothing, boots, and shoes for both men and women, as well as cameras, pocket cutlery, and indoor games. In the 1920s Abercrombie & Fitch became the epicenter of the burgeoning mah-jongg craze and the place in New York to thumb one's nose at Prohibition by purchasing a hip flask. Also during the 1920s, Abercrombie & Fitch opened a summer-only store in Hyannis, Massachusetts, for the yachting set. Net sales and income, rising steadily in this decade, reached a record $6.3 million and $548,000, respectively, in 1929.

These figures would not be topped in the next decade. Sales in the grip of the Great Depression fell to $2,598,925 in fiscal year 1933, when a loss of $521,118 was recorded, on top of a loss of $241,211 the previous year. During this period, Guernsey's negotiations with the firm's creditors probably saved it from collapse. Subsequent years were profitable, and in 1938 Abercrombie & Fitch resumed paying dividends. It also established golf and shooting schools in the store.

By 1939 Abercrombie & Fitch was calling itself "The Greatest Sporting Goods Store in the World." It boasted the world's largest and most valuable collection of firearms and the widest assortment of fishing flies obtainable anywhere (15,000 in all) to accompany its array of rods, reels, and other fishing tackle. Riders, dog fanciers, skiers, and archers all found every conceivable type of gear. Guns and camping and fishing equipment accounted for 30 percent of the New York store's sales volume in 1938. Sales of clothing, shoes, and furnishings accounted for 45 percent. Inventory on hand was valued at about 40 percent of annual sales, an extremely high ratio that reflected Abercrombie & Fitch's readiness to meet its customers' demands. Catalogue mail orders accounted for about ten percent of business.

Abercrombie & Fitch at Mid-Century

Net profit during the 1940s was highest in fiscal year 1947, when it reached $682,894, which turned out to be an all-time

record. In 1958 Abercrombie & Fitch opened a store in San Francisco. Soon thereafter, it added small winter-only stores in Palm Beach and Sarasota, Florida, and summer stores in Bayhead, New Jersey, and Southampton, New York. Guernsey, who had succeeded Cobb as president, explained his firm's mission at this time in frankly elitist terms: "The Abercrombie & Fitch type does not care about the cost; he wants the finest quality."

The New York store remained, of course, the company's flagship. At the close of the 1950s the main floor sported heads of buffalo, caribou, moose, elk, and other big game, stuffed fish of spectacular size, and elephant's-foot wastebaskets. Here were sold a variety of contraptions for indoor and outdoor pursuits. One corner held dog and cat items. The basement was given over to the shooting range, while the mezzanine contained paraphernalia for skindiving, archery, skiing, and lawn games. Floors two through five were reserved for clothing suitable for any terrain or climate. On floor six was a picture gallery and bookstore concentrating on sporting themes, a watch repair facility, and the golf school, complete with a resident pro. On the seventh floor, the gun room, besides more stuffed game heads, held about 700 shotguns and rifles, constituting the most lavish assemblage of sporting firearms on earth. The eighth floor was devoted to fishing, camping, and boating, and reserved a desk for the company's fly- and bait-casting instructor, who gave lessons at the pool on the roof. He also handled mail and telephone inquiries on fishing, hunting, and skiing. The fishing section alone stocked about 48,000 flies and 18,000 lures.

In fiscal 1960, net sales rose to a record $16.5 million, but net profits fell for the fourth straight year, to $185,649. The next year net sales fell below $15.5 million, and net profit dropped again, to $124,097. Nevertheless, Guernsey's successor as president, John H. Ewing, saw no cause for alarm, rejecting the idea of a budget shop or "splash ads for storewide sales." He told a *Business Week* interviewer in 1961 that Abercrombie & Fitch enjoyed a special niche "by sticking to our knitting; by not trying to be all things to all people."

A Disastrous Decade: 1968–77

During the 1960s Abercrombie & Fitch opened new stores in Colorado Springs; Short Hills, New Jersey; Bal Harbour, Florida; and Troy, Michigan, a suburb of Detroit. It also opened small shops in other stores. In 1968, a year in which city riots, protests against the war in Vietnam, and the assassinations of Martin Luther King and Robert Kennedy seemed to be tearing the country apart, Abercrombie & Fitch was finally ready to shake up its way of doing business by holding a warehouse sale. More than 90,000 bemused customers sifted through the Manhattan store one summer day for bargains that included pop-up tents bought so far in the past that no one remembered how to pop them up, boots made of long-haired goatskin hide, miniature antique cannons, leather baby elephants, and Yukon dog sleds.

In early 1970 the store held another sale. A horde of hopefuls turned up to seize such bargains as a 15-foot inoperative hovercraft for $3 and eight $100 surfboards for $17 each. An offbeat newspaper advertising campaign followed, featuring a single item, such as hunting shoes, accompanied by diagrams and copy that overwhelmed the reader with product information. If these antics indicated a measure of desperation, it was because Abercrombie & Fitch had recorded a loss of more than $500,000 in the latest fiscal year. In October 1970 William Humphreys, the new company president, said the ads would be changed and sales would cease because the people who showed up were not Abercrombie & Fitch's kind of customer.

In the ensuing years, Humphreys, a former Lord & Taylor executive, concentrated on cutting the company budget, improving inventory control and credit practices, and expanding into the suburbs. A new Abercrombie & Fitch store opened in Oak Brook, Illinois, north of Chicago. To win a broader range of clientele, the New York store moved its expensive sailboats upstairs from the main floor, expanded its gift and sportswear lines, added a discount clothing shop on the tenth floor, and hired new buyers for women's wear. Nevertheless, the company continued to lose money under Humphreys and his successor, Hal Haskell, its chief stockholder.

In August 1976, after a year in which the company had lost $1 million, Abercrombie & Fitch filed for Chapter 11 bankruptcy. When it closed its doors for good in November 1977, post-mortems pointed out the obvious: the company had failed to make the transition from supplying fat-cat sportsmen of the old school to the skiers, bikers, and backpackers of the 1970s. One advertising man described management as "ossified," and another said company officers had no faith in television's ability to draw in customers even after its first TV commercials, in 1969, filled the store.

The Oshman Decade: 1978–87

Oshman's Sporting Goods, a Houston-based chain, bought the Abercrombie & Fitch name, trademark, and mailing list in 1978 and opened a store in 1979 under the Abercrombie & Fitch name in Beverly Hills, California. With a 52-page catalogue and eclectic merchandise, including exercise machines, Harris-tweed jackets, and $70 pith helmets, the company also outfitted actor Jack Lemmon for an Alaskan fishing trip and Dodger baseball star Steve Garvey for grouse hunting in Minnesota. A bigger Dallas store opened in 1980, complete with $40,000 elephant guns and an Abercrombie Runabout sports convertible for $20,775.

Abercrombie & Fitch returned to New York City in 1984, opening in the renovated South Street Seaport area of lower Manhattan. By the end of 1986 the chain had grown to 26 stores, including a second Manhattan outlet in midtown's glitzy Trump Tower. Net sales reached an estimated $40 million to $45 million in 1985. The Oshman-owned Abercrombie & Fitch chain stocked relatively few hunting and fishing supplies or exotic items, concentrating on exercise machines, tennis rackets, golf clubs, and other paraphernalia of more contemporary interest, much of it designed exclusively for the chain. Men's and women's clothing departments featured business and casual dress as well as sportswear, and the gift departments offered an array of goods, including gourmet edibles.

An upbeat assessment of the new Abercrombie & Fitch by *Chain Store Age Executive* in September 1986 was followed by a more skeptical appraisal by *Forbes* six months later, which described the chain's merchandise as a hodgepodge of unrelated items and concluded, "Sometimes it is better to bury the dead than to try reviving them." *Forbes* estimated sales for fiscal 1986 at $48 million and profits at "a so-so $1.5 million."

Expansion and Independence in the 1990s

In January 1988 The Limited, Inc. acquired 25 of the existing 27 Abercrombie & Fitch stores from Oshman's for about $45 million in cash. The organization was moved to corporate headquarters in Columbus, Ohio, and the inventory was cleared out. A stronger emphasis was placed on apparel, with 60 to 65 percent of the merchandise men's sportswear and furnishings, 20 to 25 percent women's wear, and the remaining 15 to 20 percent gifts, including grooming products and nature books. "We can't get caught up in guns and fishing rods," the chain's president, Sally Frame-Kasaks, a former women's-wear executive, told a *Daily News Record* reporter. Nearly all the goods were mid-priced and bore an Abercrombie & Fitch label.

When Frame-Kasaks left to head Ann Taylor in February 1992, she was succeeded as president of Abercrombie & Fitch by Michael Jeffries, an executive at Paul Harris Stores. At this time the chain had 36 stores credited with annual sales of about $50 million. Jeffries oversaw spectacular growth, with sales increasing to $85 million in 1992, $111 million in 1993, and $165 million in 1994. There were 67 Abercrombie & Fitch stores at the end of January 1995, compared to 49 a year earlier. Moreover, the Abercrombie & Fitch division established new records for merchandise margin rate and profitability for its parent, The Limited, in 1994.

From the outset, Jeffries focused on transforming Abercrombie & Fitch into the retailer of choice for American youth, a demographic said to be growing the fastest during that time. He replaced conservative clothing lines, primarily for men, with casualwear, of a fairly high price point, for both young men and women. Soon, Abercrombie & Fitch had a corporate and retail culture all its own, one dedicated to youth, good looks, and fun. Jeffries ensured that the company kept in touch with the demands of young America by hiring executives and designers in tune with their preferences in clothing, music, and entertainment. Abercrombie & Fitch began publishing its own catalog/magazine, *A&F Quarterly,* which featured the company's clothing lines as well as articles on pop culture, sex, music, and other teen favorites. The company's ad agency, and photographer Bruce Weber, typically imbued Abercrombie & Fitch ads with a sexiness that appealed to target customers and concerned some parents and their legislators.

When The Limited spun off Abercrombie & Fitch in February 1999, headquarters moved from Columbus to nearby Reynoldsburg, and Jeffries continued to helm the operation. Heretofore a huge success, Abercrombie & Fitch began to draw comments from industry analysts on the likelihood of its staying-power; they suggested that, like all clothing retailers, Abercrombie & Fitch was bound to fall from favor someday, and they watched for the signs. Competition for the market had heated up, particularly from American Eagle Outfitters, which began offering similar merchandise, marketed in a similar manner, and for lower prices. The summer of 1999 saw Abercrombie & Fitch bring a lawsuit against American Eagle, claiming the latter had violated its trademarks. The suit was eventually thrown out, however, as a judge determined that clothing style and image were not copyrightable. Amid reports that the company's growth might be slowing, its stock dropped but rebounded again after the 1999 holiday selling-season produced satisfactory results.

Continuing its provocative advertising methods, Abercrombie & Fitch issued a Christmas catalogue that year that featured nude models and overt sexual content; a predictable outrage ensued, and proof of age was required to purchase it thereafter. This approach may have impressed more male than female customers, who, some suggested, were shopping more often at competitors Urban Outfitters and The Gap. Still, as it headed into a new millennium Abercrombie & Fitch was reporting record sales and a loyal following of young customers. According to one survey by Teenage Research Unlimited, reported on in *Time,* American kids ranked the company sixth on a list of cool brands, ahead of Nintendo and Levis. Broadening the scope of its clientele somewhat, Abercrombie & Fitch opened a children's store, abercrombies, in 1999 and planned to introduce a store geared toward West Cost surfer types in 2000.

Principal Competitors

The Gap, Inc.; The Limited, Inc.; American Eagle Outfitters, Inc.; The Buckle, Inc.; Urban Outfitters Inc.

Further Reading

"Abercrombie & Fitch," *Fortune,* July 1939, pp. 124 + .

"Abercrombie's Misfire," *Time,* August 23, 1976, p. 55.

"Caterer to the Outdoor Man," *Business Week,* December 16, 1961, pp. 84–86, 89.

Goldstein, Lauren, "The Alpha Teenager," *Fortune,* December 20, 1999, pp. 201 + .

Lockwood, Lisa, "Edgy Ads: Reaching the Limit?," *WWD,* January 14, 2000, p. 16.

Marcial, Gene G., "Shoppers Bonanza at the Limited," *Business Week,* September 23, 1996, p. 142.

Palmieri, Jean E., "Abercrombie & Fitch Aim: 100 Units; $300M Sales," *Daily News Record,* June 14, 1991, p. 7.

Paris, Ellen, "Endangered Species?," *Forbes,* March 9, 1987, pp. 136–37.

Perman, Stacy, "Fashion Forward: Abercrombie's Beefcake Brigade," *Time,* February 14, 2000.

Sayre, Joel, "The Twelve-Story Game Room," *Holiday,* December 1959.

Stringer, Kortney, "Abercrombie & Fitch Best of Best in Plain Dealer 100," *Cleveland Plain Dealer,* June 22, 1999, p. 1C.

Wells, Melanie, "Anticlimax," *Forbes,* March 20, 2000.

—Robert Halasz
—updated by Mark Swartz

Ace Hardware

Ace Hardware Corporation

2200 Kensington Court
Oak Brook, Illinois 60523-2100
U.S.A.
Telephone: (630) 990-6600
Fax: (630) 573-4894
Web site: http://www.acehardware.com

Private Company
Incorporated: 1928
Employees: 5,180
Sales: $3.18 billion (1999)
NAIC: 44413 Hardware Stores; 42171 Hardware
    Wholesalers

Ace Hardware Corporation is the second largest dealer-owned cooperative in the United States. The co-op pools buying and promotions for its 5,100 local hardware, home center, and lumber stores located in all fifty of the United States as well as in 65 foreign countries and territories. Ace's emphasis on service and modern retailing techniques has helped locally owned and operated Ace retail stores confront intense competition from such home improvement powerhouses as Home Depot and Builders Square. The co-op manufactures its own line of paints and also supplies other products under the Ace brand.

The 1920s–70s: Ace's Years as a Wholesale Buying Cooperative

The Ace Hardware organization was founded in the early 1920s, when Richard Hesse, Frank Burke, Oscar Fisher, E. Gunnard Linquist, and William Stauber united to form a purchasing and advertising partnership among their Chicago-area hardware stores. Their combined buying power enabled the store owners to negotiate lower prices on merchandise purchased from wholesalers. The partners adopted the Ace name in 1927, and incorporated the following year.

Within two years, Ace had evolved into a wholesaling organization, purchasing directly from manufacturers and storing merchandise in its own Chicago warehouse. This move further reduced costs by cutting out the "middlemen" wholesalers, thereby giving Ace members the choice of a competitive edge (they could reduce retail prices) or fatter margins (They could maintain their prices and enjoy higher profits). Frank Burke served briefly as president of the organization, and was succeeded by Richard Hesse in 1930. Hesse served in that capacity for more than four decades, until the end of 1973.

For its first half-century of operation, Ace was essentially a conventional wholesale group, and its profits were shared by its shareholders. The group's low-cost purchasing and distribution methods quickly attracted new members and some franchisees. During its early years, use of the Ace name was recommended but optional; it would later become mandatory for new affiliates. President Hesse expanded services to associates, including a semi-annual dealer convention featuring products and promotions available through the wholesaler. Those meetings continued through the 1990s. By the mid-1930s, the organization had 41 dealer/members and sales of more than $650,000. Growth was so strong, in fact, that the expanding roster of affiliates necessitated doubling warehouse capacity during that decade.

The postwar era saw the dawn of America's "do-it-yourself" (DIY) revolution. Industry analysts have attributed the spectacular growth of this market to several factors. First, the generally high cost of new homes drove consumers into widely available, but sometimes neglected, existing homes. The high charges exacted by repairmen and contractors impelled homeowners to attempt home repair and improvement projects on their own. Also, the emergence of new tools and products that were easy to use furthered the trend. Finally, some observers of the DIY movement have credited the more intangible, but undoubtedly strong, sense of satisfaction attained by consumers who completed a project themselves while saving money at the same time.

On the strength of growing DIY sales, Ace's nationwide revenues increased to $25 million by the end of the 1950s. The organization opened its first distribution centers beyond the bounds of Chicago in 1969. A California facility served the expanding West Coast membership, and an Atlanta warehouse promoted growth in the south. These were the first of 14 retail support centers that came into being across the country by 1994.

Before he retired in 1973, co-founder and long-time president Richard Hesse sold Ace to its member-dealers, thereby forming a dealer-owned hardware cooperative. Purchase of a minimum stake in Ace was required for membership, and dealers contributed a percentage of their co-op purchases to a national advertising fund. Under this new scheme, Ace's profits were returned to its dealer-owners through cash or stock rebates at year's end. The company opened its fourth distribution center in Toledo, Ohio, and moved its expanded corporate headquarters to Oak Brook, Illinois (a western suburb of Chicago) that same year. By 1976, when ownership of Ace had passed completely to its dealers, the organization's sales volume had reached $382 million. From that point on, Ace's board of directors was always made up of dealers.

The Growth of the DIY Movement in the 1970s and 1980s

Arthur Krausman succeeded Hesse as president in January 1974 and advanced to chairman of the board in 1980. During the ensuing years, Ace's member services expanded to include training and education, merchandising, computerized inventory control, insurance, and store layout. The continuous addition of new members during the 1970s necessitated the establishment of new warehouses and distribution centers. By the end of the decade, the organization had added five facilities in the Midwest and Southeast. This diffusion of distribution points helped save freight costs, since many manufacturers were willing to ship freight-paid within a given distance.

The company achieved national penetration in 1978, when it signed on members in the eastern United States. Ace's growth coincided with a six-fold increase in the DIY market, from just under $6 billion in 1970, to $35 billion in 1980, to more than $100 billion by the end of the 1980s. Traditional hardware stores, such as those owned by Ace members, soon found their competition growing too, as mass merchandisers like the "category killer," Home Depot, Inc., began to get in on the profitable DIY trend. Even supermarkets, discount stores, and drug stores began carrying profitable hardware lines during the decade.

While drugstores and grocery stores were overtaken by the chain store revolution in the 1970s, the hardware segment continued to be dominated by independents through the mid-1980s. By 1984, 85 percent of the 23,500 retail hardware stores in the United States were affiliated with co-ops. Those groups held the top share—48 percent—of annual hardware sales. Some observers credited this phenomenon to dealer-owned cooperatives (or "voluntary chains," as they were termed by the National Retail Hardware Association). Others credited the personalized service offered by independent retailers. In a 1980 interview with *Hardware Age*, Ace Chairman Krausman credited the success to flexibility, inventory depth, and advertising of independent operators.

By 1984, Ace's national advertising budget topped $10 million, most of which was spent on television spots. Ace capitalized on its members' reputation for having knowledgeable personnel with the slogan "Ace is the place with the helpful hardware man." This slogan was later modified to include the gender-neutral "helpful hardware folks." Television spots often featured celebrities, including singer Connie Stevens and actress Suzanne Somers in the 1970s and 1980s, and football commentator John Madden in the 1990s. The company continued to emphasize service in advertisements that showcased "helpful" Ace dealers around the country through the middle of the decade. Ace sales more than doubled during the 1980s, from $801 million in 1983 to more than $2 billion in 1993.

Competing with the "Big Boxes" in the 1990s

Following a trend that began in retail foods, Ace introduced a line of private label products in the early 1990s. Private label products enable retailers to offer their customers a consistently low-priced product while generating higher profit margins for themselves. One of Ace's first private label goods was paint, which it began manufacturing in 1984 in a state-of-the-art facility in Illinois (Ace paint had been manufactured by the Valspar Corp. beginning in the 1930s). Although paint is generally considered a low-growth commodity, it is a do-it-yourself mainstay. Low brand loyalty and high price sensitivity made it an ideal private label product. By the early 1990s, Ace's paint division was expanding faster than the rest of the paint industry, and had become the foundation of a private-label program of nearly 7,000 items. In 1991, the paint facility expanded, and in 1995, a second paint facility was acquired in Chicago Heights, Illinois. From 1988 to 1993, private label sales grew at an average annual rate of 12.9 percent, to $350 million. The group planned to transform its private label into a national brand through extensive promotions in the mid-1990s.

While Ace manufactured many of its own paints, the company also purchased some paints (particularly aerosols) from other producers, including Sherwin-Williams, DAP, and ITW Devcon. The company became involved in a product labeling suit with the Attorney General of the state of California for neglecting to warn consumers that several of Sherwin-Williams' paints contained toluene, a known carcinogen. Although Sherwin-Williams' settlement cost it more than $1 million, Ace was simply required to add appropriate warnings on its toluene-based paints.

In October 1994, the Ace officers and board of directors launched a strategic plan known as "The New Age of Ace." This plan was an acceleration of a previous strategic process called "Ace 2000," which focused on improving business for the co-op's top-line members. The board laid out four primary objectives to be achieved by the year 2000: improved retail performance, more efficient operations, international growth, and a faster pace for new store openings. A key aspect of Ace's plan involved incentives for dealers to meet certain standards or risk losing full retail support from the corporation. These requirements included relinquishing connections with any other buying organizations, making at least 80 percent of merchandise purchases through Ace (including and especially Ace paint), using Ace signage, and participating with vendors on special purchases. By late 1994, about 1,500 of Ace's 5,000 dealers did not comply with these minimum requirements. One Ace executive noted that this list of noncompliant retailers would gradually be reduced, as they either joined the majority of dealers or dropped from the organization.

As part of its plan to improve retail performance, Ace also announced that it would open its own stores in the Chicago area to test retail concepts, an objective it achieved in by 1995. The purpose of these stores was to fine-tune retailing practices for all Ace stores. A new store prototype called the "solutions concept store" catered to the do-it-yourselfer, and was pioneered in 1999. Although the company assured its members that it was not planning to acquire or build a significant number of group-owned stores, this aspect of "Ace 2000" disturbed some dealers, according to a December 1994 article in *Do-It-Yourself Retailing*. In fact, the strategic plan called for dealers themselves to generate nearly $500 million in new sales and open 1,000 new stores in underserved markets by the turn of the century. Ace planned to deploy consultants to help retailers identify potential new store sites.

Ace's strategic plan also called for improvements in its warehousing operation through technological advances and increased cooperation with vendors. Goals included vendor consolidation; enhanced electronic data interchange between vendors, warehouses, and retailers; and the expansion of vendor-managed inventory systems to control up to one-fourth of inventory.

The company planned to quadruple its international sales to $400 million by 2000, with a special focus on South America. The passage of the North American Free Trade Agreement (NAFTA) in 1994 prompted Ace to plan a paint plant in Texas. This was done in order to meet anticipated demand from the 70 Mexican Ace stores that were open by that time, and the 26 more that were expected to open. Sales overseas had increased by nearly one-third overall from 1992 to 1993, and by more than 60 percent in Mexico alone. Other areas of concentration included the Middle East, Eastern Europe, Latin America, and the Pacific Rim. According to *Do-It-Yourself Retailing,* Ace hoped to "evolve from being only an exporter to becoming a true world trading company," by offering international affiliates the services enjoyed by dealers in the United States. Licensing was seen to play an important role in the organization's overseas expansion.

The New Age of Ace: Changes in the Mid-1990s

The promulgation of the goals of Ace 2000 and The New Age of Ace exemplified two fundamental changes in the organization and the retail hardware industry. First, by the 1990s, Ace had clearly expanded its expectations of and responsibilities to its affiliates. Second, it demonstrated the organization's determination to survive and grow in the face of increasingly intense competition from what one industry journal called "the big boxes"—mass home improvement merchants, such as Home Depot, Builders Square, and Lowe's.

As CEO Roger Peterson, who retired in May 1995, told *Do-It-Yourself Retailing* in December 1994, "Such growth is necessary if Ace is to remain a major player in the hardware industry, capitalize on the Ace name and reputation, and establish footholds in markets before competition gains a strangle hold." Between 1994 and 1999, wholesale sales at Ace increased more than 37 percent. By the late 1990s, however, the co-op felt itself increasingly challenged by the rollout of Home Depot's small-store format, Villager's Hardware, designed to capitalize on the "convenience" hardware market in which Ace specialized.

The company responded with new initiatives and new ventures. In 1995, it established a subsidiary—National Hardlines Supply—to sell to non-traditional retail customers, increase Ace's buying power, and continue to provide support to its dealers. In 1998, it debuted a new strategic plan called "Encore Growth," and, a year later, "Vision 21." Encore Growth developed programs to improve dealers' gross margins, while Vision 21 aimed to make Ace number one in the "non-big box" sector by getting dealers to embrace the merchandising, marketing, and operational tactics employed by the co-op's best dealers. Vision 21 posited Ace's effectiveness as a co-op upon how well its employees supported dealers' efforts to sell what they bought from Ace profitably, not upon how much inventory moved out of its distribution centers yearly.

Also in 1998, Ace Hardware and the American Rental Association (ARA) formed a comprehensive buying group program called the Member Buying Alliance. The alliance relied upon Ace's National Hardlines Supply (NHS) to provide ARA members a source for commercial rental products and equipment. NHS also became the supplier in 1998 to the largest non-cooperative buying group for lumber and building materials in the United States. This buying group was formed through a merger of Ace's lumber, building materials, and millwork division, and Builders Marts of America.

In November 1999, Ace launched its first venture in cyberspace with its web site, OurHouse.com, which offered products for sale online and project-related information. In April 2000, Ace placed in-store kiosks in more than 1,000 stores, allowing customers immediate access to the web site. This stronger focus on project-oriented merchandising was a response to the growing market of female shoppers undertaking their own home improvement. Also that fall, Ace opened its first Store 21 in Washington state, a technology-intensive merchandising format designed to accommodate the customer and featured salespeople wearing radio headsets.

Still an ongoing problem at Ace was the sizable minority of dealers whose stores were not sufficiently computerized, whose inventory mix generated inconsistent profits, and whose retail presentation did not fit the homogeneous image Ace desired. Many smaller dealers felt that aligning themselves more closely with the co-op diluted their independence as entrepreneurs. By the company's 75th anniversary in 1999, according to an article in *National Home Center News,* only one fifth of the co-op's members shared information with Ace via computer. Furthermore, only about half its 5,100 stores were linked electronically to its buying group through its AceNet 2000 e-commerce system, which had been instituted in 1997.

Ace's board of directors spoke of a ''disconnect'' between the buying group and members, citing programs that generated sales for Ace but didn't necessarily make dealers' stores more productive. To deal with this, a plan was promulgated to leverage the co-op's wholesale side while reducing costs on its retail side. The co-op hoped to take over management of the routine part of individual store operations centrally, checking in merchandise and handling accounts receivables. It also hoped to cultivate a retail chain image to make individual stores more competitive, and to develop programs for merchandising, operations and training. Once members became more profitable, the hope was that they would consider investing in their stores' expansion and opening more stores.

Principal Subsidiaries

Ace Hardware Canada Limited; National Hardlines Supply.

Principal Competitors

The Home Depot Inc.; Lowe's Companies Inc.; TruServ Corporation; Cotter & Company; ServiStar Coast to Coast Corporation; Hardware Wholesalers Inc.

Further Reading

''California Labeling-Suit Settlement Tops $1 Million,'' *Hardware Age,* May 1994, p. 17.

Caulfield, John, ''Visions 21 Puts Co-op and Members in Sync,'' *National Home Center News,* December 13, 1999.

Cory, Jim, ''On the Road,'' *Hardware Age,* April 1994, p. 73.

Davis, Jo Ellen, ''Hardware Wars: The Big Boys Might Lose This One,'' *Business Week,* October 14, 1985, pp. 84–86.

Goldman, Tamara, ''Nailing Down the Home Improvement Market,'' *Marketing Communications,* October 1988, pp. 49–52.

''Hardware Supplement—Hardware Sales: Healthy but Not Spectacular,'' *Discount Merchandiser,* August 1987, pp. 79–96.

Holtzman, M. Jay, ''New Blood, Old Values,'' *Hardware Age,* October 1980, pp. 95–101.

''Home Improvement Booms in 1993,'' *Chain Store Age Executive,* August 1994, pp. 14A-16A.

Jensen, Christopher A., ''The New Age of Ace,'' *Do-It-Yourself Retailing,* December 1994, pp. 57–58.

Pellet, Jennifer, ''No Paint, No Gain,'' *Discount Merchandiser,* March 1992, pp. 74–75.

Reda, Susan, ''DIYers Daunted by Paint Choices,'' *Stores,* August 1994, pp. 52–53.

Uihlein, Reven, ''Co-Ops Stave off Hard Times for Hardware,'' *Advertising Age,* August 30, 1984, pp. 16–17.

—April Dougal Gasbarre
—updated by Carrie Rothburd

Acxiom Corporation

1 Information Way
P.O. Box 8180
Little Rock, Arkansas 72203-8180
U.S.A.
Telephone: (501) 342-1000
Toll Free: (800) 922-9466
Fax: (501) 342-3913
Web site: http://www.acxiom.com

Public Company
Incorporated: 1969 as Demographics, Inc.
Employees: 5,600
Sales: $964.5 Million (2000)
Stock Exchanges: NASDAQ
Ticker Symbol: ACXM
NAIC: 51114 Database and Directory Publishers; 54186 Direct Mail Advertising; 541611 Administrative Management and General Management Consulting Services

Acxiom Corporation—Acxiom is a registered trademark—is a leading provider of information management services and solutions to large corporations dependent upon consumer and business databases stored and managed through computer technology. The company identifies its ''core competencies'' as customer data integration, innovative database marketing services, infrastructure management, premier data content, and integration technologies. Structurally, Acxiom is made up of four operating divisions: Data Products, Services, and Financial Services, based in Arkansas; and Outsourcing, based in Downers Grove, Illinois. Other major business locations include Phoenix; Paris; London; Sydney, Australia; and Sunderland, England. Within this framework, the company maintains an expanding network of operations with several locations in the United States and abroad. Among other things, it provides access to information on all but a small percentage of households in the United States. Its primary client base has been and remains Fortune 1000 companies in the financial, insurance, information service, retail marketing, publishing, healthcare,

media, automotive, and telecommunications fields. Numbered among these corporate clients are AT&T, Advance Publications, Allstate Insurance, Bank of America, Citigroup, Conseco, Federated Department Stores, First USA Bank, General Electric Capital Corp., IBM, The Polk Company, Proctor & Gamble, Sears, Trans Union LLC, and Wal-Mart Stores.

1969–75: Founding and Early Development

Acxiom's history may be traced to 1969, when Charles Ward, an industrialist, founded Demographics, Inc., in Conway, Arkansas. One of his main purposes was to develop a mailing list parity with the Republican Party for the Democrats. In its early years of development, Demographics was primarily a data processing company, serving, among other clients, the local bus manufacturing company. Both physically and financially, it was a small operation, housed in a 6,000 square-foot building that contained the company's single computer and printing press.

In 1975, when his business investments were faring poorly, Ward sold Demographics to the company's management, which was then under the leadership of Charles D. Morgan, who had joined the company in 1972. Morgan succeeded Ward as president and CEO. At the time, the company's revenue was $1.2 million. In order to grow into what Morgan hoped would be a $10 million operation, the company took on any and all jobs, no matter how small. It processed the payrolls for most Conway businesses of any size and handled the billing of the local utility company, Conway Corp. It continued to support campaign and fund-raising efforts of the Democratic Party, the main focus of its enterprise. The only year-round direct marketing customer was Diamondhead, a Hot Springs, Arkansas, land developer.

1976–85: Changing Focus and Going Public

The new owners faced serious problems. Loss of income due to changes in election laws and the near shutdown of Diamondhead compelled Morgan and his associates to take salary cuts and reconsider what Demographics should do, not just to recover but to prosper and grow. Their decision was to concentrate on one specialty: nationwide direct-mail marketing. Morgan went to New York, where he met with David Florence, the

Company Perspectives:

Acxiom Corporation recognizes that to enjoy the freedoms of our society, one also must embrace its responsibilities. For instance, the free flow of information is a cornerstone of our society and has contributed to tremendous consumer benefits and economic prosperity. Yet, this freedom must be accompanied by respect for the laws and regulations that protect consumer privacy. It is this belief that has driven Acxiom to be a leader in addressing consumer privacy concerns and earning the trust of the public—while preserving the open system that has served the best interests of our country and its citizens for more than two centuries.

founder of Direct Media, Inc. DMI's operation inspired Morgan to create what would emerge as the List Order Fulfillment System (LOFS), the country's first fully-automated, on-line system used to generate mailing lists. When David Florence, LOFS's sole customer, decided to sell Direct Media's yellow pages business, the company had no choice but to buy it.

In the early 1980s, Demographics was still very much a company discovering itself, trying to determine what paths to take in what was an exciting, wide-open field: computer-based, information management. Reflecting a kind of strategy shadow boxing, in 1980, the company changed its name to Conway Communications Exchange, Inc., then changed it again in 1983, when it went public, to CCX Network, Inc.

Its necessary dependence on an ever-changing computer technology simply drove the company's continuing need to reassess its opportunities and redesign itself. The volatile nature of that technology made it a tough task and occasionally led to some poor results. For example, in 1983 the company spent about $1 million exploring the possibilities of electronic mail, money that was finally written off as wasted.

1986–91: Acquisitions and Changing Strategies in Economic Turndown

The earnest growth of CCX began in 1986, after Phil Carter, joined the company as president. Morgan and Carter, who was previously a regional manager for IBM, put it on the fast growth track through acquisitions and new tactics. Until that time, the company had only its regional identity, confined to Conway. By July of 1988, it had branches in Ocean, New Jersey, and Philadelphia, plus two locations in the United Kingdom, and it had tripled its workforce. Its activity and bustle through the 1980s repeatedly gained it recognition by *Forbes* as one of "The 200 Best Small Companies in America."

During the economic slump of the late 1980s, Acxiom put into place its chief marketing strategy of aggressively seeking major corporate clients that could benefit from shifting their database management tasks to an external agency in order to concentrate on their core businesses. Acxiom hoped to expand its traditional sales base with long-term contracts offering both stability and high yields. First, however, it had to weather some problems, including the poor performance of its BSA, Inc., the full-service catalog company in Ocean that it had purchased in

1986. After three years, and a $6 million investment in BSA's warehouse, Acxiom decided to close down the operation. The company also faced other problems. Notably, one of its major financial services clients, was suffering financial woes and cut back on Acxiom's services. Rising costs, including postal rates, and recession-caused cutback in clients' advertising budgets also took their toll. By 1991, Acxiom was reeling, cutting back on its own operations and paring its workforce. The worst period was during the early part of 1991, when the company's stock plummeted to a low, at one point, of $11 per share.

1992–2000: Recovery and Further Rapid Growth and Expansion

The core-based strategy of seeking major corporate clients and long-term contracts started paying off in the mid-1990s. After a financial revival between 1993 and 1995, Acxiom began a period of phenomenal growth in both size and earnings. Its revenue grew from $89.7 million in 1990 to $964.5 million in the fiscal year ending in March 2000. Much of the increase came in the last two years, when the company's revenue doubled. Although the company recorded a loss in 1999, its net income between 1998 and 2000 rose from $35.6 million to $90.4 million. Acquisitions in the second half of the decade accounted for some of the increase, but most of it was generated from internal growth. Its surging profits started in 1993, after the company overcame a couple of lean years by securing major long-term contracts with Trans Union Corp. and Allstate Insurance Co.

In 1996, Acxiom made two significant purchases, both of which became effective in April of that year. It bought all the assets and assumed some of the liabilities of its old corporate friend, Direct Media Inc., which, by that time, had become the largest list management and brokerage firm in the world. Besides managing and brokering lists, DMI offered various list-consulting services to its mail marketing clients. Acxiom would later, in 2000, become a minority owner of DMI. Acxiom also purchased all of the outstanding capital stock of Pro CD, Inc., a Massachusetts-based company that provided a variety of reference data on CD-ROM, batch, and on-line, notably information taken from U.S. and Canadian telephone directories and maps. The purchase of Pro CD provided Acxiom with entry to two new markets: Small Office/Home Office (SOHO) and the Internet.

In addition to the company's acquisitions, 1996 saw Acxiom enter an agreement with Oracle Corporation. The arrangement joined Acxiom's consumer-based data warehousing and decision support abilities with Oracle's database and on-line analytical processing (OLAP) prowess. The venture illustrated Acxiom's strategy of partnering with other companies for their mutual benefit through combining their complementary capabilities. According to CEO Morgan, Oracle's OLAP technology added "a multi-dimensional view to the customer knowledge" that Acxiom provided to marketers, making data accessible and usable in any or all departments. Such partnering arrangements, at times temporary, have made Acxiom's corporate identity an ever-shifting phenomenon.

Acxiom's acquisitions and partnering arrangements continued over the next three years. Among other purchases made in

Key Dates:

1969: Company is incorporated in Arkansas as Demographics, Inc.
1975: Demographics begins processing for the direct mail industry.
1980: Company name is changed to Conway Communications Exchange, Inc.
1983: Company is reincorporated as CCX Network, Inc. and makes first public offering.
1986: CCX acquires Southwark Computer Services, Ltd., UK.
1988: Name of company is changed to Acxiom Corporation.
1995: Acxiom begins strategic alliance with The Polk Company for providing data center management.
1996: Company enters agreement with Oracle Corporation adopting Oracle's OLAP to its data warehousing and decision-making methods.
1999: *Fortune* for the second straight year places Acxiom on its list of "100 Best Companies to Work For."

1997, the company bought Buckley Dement, L.P., a marketer of direct mail services for the health care and pharmaceutical industries. It also bought the assets of that company's affiliate, KM Lists, Inc. Other purchases included Normadress, a small French company, and two other direct media companies: National List Protection and MultiNational Concepts. It also formed an alliance with American Business Information, selling ABI its retail portion of Pro CD, Inc.

In 1998, Acxiom acquired May & Speh Inc., its chief competitor. Purchase of that Illinois-based company for about $625 million in stock greatly enhanced Acxiom's ability to analyze marketing data that throughout its history it had been mining for its corporate customers. It also made the company the world's leading database marketing service provider. In addition, the move improved Acxiom's recruitment potential, giving it a major data center in the Chicago suburb, Downer's Grove. May & Speh's "Quiddity" system combined with Acxiom's Data Network promised to give Acxiom's customers the ability to access and interpret data over the Internet, a service capability that provided the company with "the missing piece of its corporate puzzle."

In fact, Acxiom's Data Network and its associated linking technology was one of the company's chief initiatives in the late 1990s. The Data Network was designed to provide Acxiom's clients with cost-effective "real-time desktop access to actionable information over the Internet," allowing it to add middle market companies to its client base. The purchase of both Pro CD and May & Speh had been significant steps in that direction.

A major problem that Acxiom had to confront in the 1990s was a growing, nationwide movement to protect consumer privacy, a concern exacerbated by the increasingly invasive and aggressive actions of both corporate interests and governmental agencies. Because the company provided much of the data and analysis marketers use, it faced potential problems, including the curtailment of its business through legislative action. In fact, it got some bad press over the fact that it had stored information about consumers who had attempted to protect their privacy by not listing their telephone numbers. Acxiom was sensitive to the issue, however, and diligently sought a balance between providing marketers with their desired data and safeguarding consumer rights to privacy. Among other things, Acxiom has worked with the Direct Marketing Assn. (DMA) to help ensure consumer approval of how some data are used. It has also protected consumers through its insistence on "opt out" clauses that allow consumers the right to have their names removed from marketing databases.

In 1999, the company also had special charges associated with the May & Speh acquisition, which resulted in a fairly large net loss and, in August, a fairly sharp drop in its stock price that prompted a law suit on behalf of its shareholders. The drop was in part driven by an article in *Barron's* critical of the company's supposed flaws in its financial practices and its tardiness in collecting payment from its clients. Another contributing factor was the company's announced layoff of over 200 of its "lowest contributors." Short sellers may also have had a hand in driving the stock price down.

The problems did not deter Acxiom's growth, however. Excluding the special charges associated with the May & Speh acquisition, Acxiom established a pattern of delivering record revenues and earnings every quarter beginning in June 1991. Before the stock decline, the company had purchased Computer Graphics, Inc., a private, Phoenix-based firm with a database of 120 million households. During the year it also purchased Horizon Systems Inc., and Marketing Technology, S.A. in Spain. In addition, it entered new alliances, including a strategic partnership with Dun & Bradstreet. Under the agreement, Acxiom would provide its InfoBase for D&B's clients and acquire business marketing information in return. That arrangement came on the heels of other alliances with Abacus Direct Corp. of Broomfield, Colorado and E.piphany of Palo Alto, California. Moreover, the green light was still on for Acxiom's physical expansion, including its planned construction of a $25 million complex in downtown Little Rock to be completed in 2002. By the year's end it had already completed two other Little Rock projects—a building on the west side of town that accommodated abut 270 employees and its new headquarters, Acxiom Plaza, housing another 75 associates.

If Acxiom stumbled a bit in 1999, by 2000 it was back on track and running harder than ever. Its revenue and net profits for the fiscal year ending in March shot up dramatically, allaying concerns over its corporate health. Its robust recovery was also reflected in its stock price, which climbed to $35 per share in early March. New technologies, including the AbiliTec customer data integration technology, and new alliances promised even brighter prospects. For example, in January 2000, the company formed a strategic alliance with Active Software Inc. that would allow it to provide its clients with instant, real-time access to their customers' data through its eCRM solution, Solvitur Enterprise. This and other moves argued that Acxiom was going to remain a very resourceful and growing operation for years to come. A unique, team-oriented culture also resulted in Acxiom being named by *Fortune* as one of the best places to work in America in 1998 and 1999. Moreover, in 2000 *Computerworld* recognized Acxiom as one of the 100 best places to work for in information technology.

Principal Competitors

Experian Information Solutions Inc.; Harte-Hanks, Inc.

Further Reading

Haman, John, ''Acxiom to Pay $625 Million for Chief Rival,'' *Arkansas Business*, June 1, 1998, p. 1.

Novack, Janet, ''The Data Miners,'' *Forbes,* February 12, 1996, p. 96.

Olberding, Sara, ''What Makes Acxiom Corporation Such a Success,'' *The Journal for Quality and Participation,* November/December 1997, p. 46.

Parham, Jon, ''Did Short Sellers Help Push Down Acxiom Stock?'' *Arkansas Business*, September 6, 1999, p. 16.

Parham, Jon, ''Record Revenues Fail to Deter Acxiom Suits,'' *Arkansas Business*, January 31, 2000, p. 10.

''Pro CD, Inc. Acquired by the Acxiom Corporation,'' *Information Today,* May 1996, p. 39.

Reagor, Catherine, ''Arkansas-Based Acxiom Corp. Acquires Phoenix-Based Computer Graphics Inc.,'' *Knight-Ridder/Tribune Business News*, June 18, 1999.

Waldon, George, ''Acxiom's Turnaround—Will It Continue?,'' *Arkansas Business,* November 16, 1992, p. 1.

Walker, Wythe, Jr., ''Acxiom's Growing Pains,'' *Arkansas Business*, February 4, 1991, p. 28.

—John W. Fiero

AEI Music Network Inc.

900 East Pine Street
Seattle, Washington 98122
U.S.A.
Telephone: (206) 329-1400
Toll Free: (800) AEI-MUSIC
Fax: (206) 329-9952
Web site: http://www.aeimusic.com

Private Company
Incorporated: 1971 as Audio Environments, Inc.
Employees: 650
Sales: $100 million (1998)
NAIC: 334612 Prerecorded Compact Disc (Except
Software), Tape and Record Reproducing; 51229
Other Sound Recording Industries; 51334 Satellite
Telecommunications

AEI Music Network Inc. brings consumers and retailers together through music. Using original artists' music to convey specific moods, AEI pioneered the use of ''foreground music'' to engage customers. Red Lobster, Gap, Starbucks, and Hyatt Hotels are among the well-known corporate chains that have used AEI's programming to harmonize with the lifestyle of their patrons. AEI provides in-flight entertainment for 30 commercial airlines; the company also programs video content and sells sound systems. With 260 affiliates serving 130,000 businesses in 50 countries, AEI is the world's largest music service business.

Origins

Mike Malone was a 26-year-old securities analyst at US Investment Services when he started Audio Environments, Inc. (AEI). According to *Fortune* magazine, the stereo at the Hindquarter Leschi, Malone's main hangout, kept breaking. Malone, something of an audiophile, suggested the restaurant install a reel-to-reel tape player. He also offered to record tapes for the club himself.

Malone convinced hairstylist Gene Juarez to be his first customer to the tune of $32 a month. (Juarez subsequently started a successful salon chain, remaining a loyal customer.) Emboldened by this success, Malone quit his job and set up shop in a cramped Seattle office in 1971. Unable to find adequate financing for his novel idea, he went through $100,000 of his own savings in the first year and a half.

At the time, Muzak dominated the use of music in commercial environments. According to *Forbes,* however, Malone noticed that while doctors' offices and the like were constantly awash in ''elevator music''—toned down, instrumental versions of popular songs and standards—more progressive restaurant and shop owners were playing rock'n'roll the way it was recorded. They got customers' attention by playing the music they liked, rather than simply masking silence with background music. Malone later told CNNfn that this concept of ''foreground music'' was simply an offshoot of the popular music explosion of the late 1960s.

Airborne in the 1980s

Prices began at $40 to $75 a month for a four-hour-long tape (in a proprietary format) of customized programming. AEI paid fees and royalties to the music publishers and performing rights societies (ASCAP and BMI) for permission to use the songs. In its early years, AEI targeted fast-growing chains such as The Limited clothing stores and TGI Friday's restaurants. The company established an in-flight division to bring programming to commercial airlines in 1982.

AEI's established rival, Muzak, changed hands in 1972 and 1981; Malone himself tried to buy it in 1986 but was leery of taking on debt to do so. It instead went to Marshall Field V, who later relocated it from New York to Seattle after buying Yesco, Inc. Yesco, another commercial music supplier, had been founded by a former AEI associate.

AEI's headquarters moved to a restored Chrysler showroom a few blocks from its original location in 1987. The company also opened several other offices across the United States as national retail chains drove its growth.

In the fall of 1988, Malone bought the Seeburg Music Satellite Network, acquiring an important new technology. The

Company Perspectives:

The pioneering spirit that was born twenty-nine years ago has now come full circle in 2000 to a new era of progress and innovation on the AEI horizon. Fusing the arts of music and video with technology, our ProFusion Digital Delivery System sets a new standard for business entertainment. By combining the best features from current platforms, it promises to revolutionize the industry. And just as we've seen our horizons expand, the world suddenly seems smaller. With travel between nations and a mobility of people and cultures like never before, our concept of borders and limits has been redefined. Our global programming studios are now being linked digitally across oceans and time zones to share and exchange content, creativity and resources—bringing the world closer still.

Raleigh, North Carolina company, previously a jukebox manufacturer, had developed the capacity to broadcast high-fidelity music programming directly to subscribers via satellite. Most of AEI's programming was delivered via tapes, although it also used a hybrid FM radio/satellite system in some cases. Satellite transmissions were not limited to music. AEI also beamed trailers to show on televisions in the lobbies of United Artists theaters. Voice and fax transmissions were also possible.

In 1989, *Forbes* recounted this impressive list of AEI clients: Wolfgang Puck's Spago restaurant in Los Angeles, Victoria's Secret stores, Gap clothing stores, Wendy's Hamburgers, Bennigan's restaurants, more than a dozen airlines, and the U.S. Navy, which piped in music to its submarines. Air Force One was also a client, subcontracting through United Airlines. The service had more than 55,000 subscribers in all; its programming reached 24 million people a day. Revenues were about $35 million a year.

By the late 1980s, Muzak also was playing contemporary music by the original artists. It had 200 franchisees around the world (most in the United States). Roughly three times the size of AEI, Muzak reached 80 million people a day. For its part, AEI had begun offering elevator-style background music.

Malone owned about three-quarters of AEI. Its success allowed him to build an impressive antique car collection and buy a majority share in the restored Sorrento Hotel in Seattle. He was also a partner in a restaurant in La Jolla, California (George's at the Cove). His "corporate art collection" included early guitars from Bill Haley, Elvis, and John Lennon.

New Frontiers in the 1990s

AEI Music Network Inc. was formed in 1992. A National Service Center was established the same year. By this time, the Systems Division, which installed audio systems in businesses, had become the largest contractor of its kind in the United States. In 1993, AEI paid £18 million ($25 million) for Rediffusion Music, the British market leader in business music. The German subsidiary Reditune Thorsen also was included. Rediffusion had annual revenues of about £160 million. The transac-

tion made AEI the world's largest music service company, operating in about 40 countries.

AEI's sales were about $90 million in 1994; its daily listenership of 35 million was second only to MTV. Still, only between five and ten percent of American businesses used commercial music in the mid-1990s, leaving the market open. While AEI and Muzak (with 70,000 and 200,000 subscribers, respectively) had shared the field with the much smaller 3M Sound Products for years, in 1994 the industry saw its first new entrant in two decades. Digital Music Express (DMX), a service operated by Los Angeles-based International Cablecasting Technologies Inc. (later known as Liberty Digital), offered both CD-quality sound and the capability for clients to change stations from their own sites. The cable-based system offered 60 channels, although a Muzak representative quipped that their programming was not designed specifically for businesses, most of which were not wired for cable anyway. Another new entrant, PlayNetwork, was launched in Redmond, Washington in 1996.

AEI estimated the international music programming industry to be worth $1 billion; it continued to grow by acquisition overseas. The company bought the 6,000 accounts of Philips Media Systems B.V. in April 1997. AEI had entered European joint ventures with Strengholt B.V. (AEI Reditune Music) and Sony Music and Warner Music Group (Music Choice Europe). Its Australian joint venture with Sontec Group bought Soundcom Australia from East Coast Television in October 1997.

AEI was averaging nearly 20 percent growth a year. In July 1998, WavePhore Networks announced that it would be supplying 10,000 satellite receivers to AEI and its affiliates in the next two years. It had already sold AEI 30,000 units in the decade.

The *Wall Street Journal* noted that at the trendiest restaurants it was not uncommon for loud funk to be playing while patrons dined on très chic gourmet fare. While it was long known that faster, louder music turned tables, the programmer's art was becoming increasingly sophisticated. The advent of direct broadcast satellites led to a proliferation of programming concepts as stores and restaurants fine-tuned their environments to suit their respective niches. This "lifestyle programming" targeted specific emotional responses through the music rather than merely following genre categories. Programmers visited stores and analyzed demographics, traffic, and style to come up with distinctive sounds to help differentiate one location from another. The Limited required signature sounds for each of its more than a dozen different divisions.

In the late-1990s, many retailers were packaging their own CDs of their in-store music for shoppers to take home. Victoria's Secret pioneered this in 1988; in fact, five of the best-selling classical albums in U.S. history were collections assembled by the lingerie shop. Old Navy, Pottery Barn, and Starbucks were others hopping on the trend, each featuring its own genre of music. Many hired AEI to package the collections, which fostered brand awareness and were usually profitable in their own right.

AEI Music Markets was created in 1999 to help clients bolster their brands with their own CD compilations, licensed music for advertising campaigns, and multimedia content for

Key Dates:

1971: Audiophile/financial analyst Michael Malone starts compiling music for local businesses.
1982: AEI establishes a division for in-flight entertainment on commercial airlines.
1988: AEI acquires direct satellite transmission technology.
1993: Purchase of Rediffusion Music makes AEI world's largest music service company.
1999: Purchase of Sight & Sound Entertainment bolsters AEI's video imaging business.

web sites. AEI helped the Northwest AIDS Foundation develop its own compilation of popular favorites covered by contemporary artists in 1999.

AEI bought Sight & Sound Entertainment, based in Redmond, Washington, in September 1999. The deal made AEI the world's largest provider of video imaging content for businesses. Sight & Sound was servicing more than 6,000 retail locations in the United States at the time of the acquisition.

AEI Music Network announced a joint venture, AEI Music Latin America, with Cisneros Television Group in October 1999. Cisneros was the leading pay television content provider in Latin America. The new enterprise was to focus on regional programming; it soon debuted 20 channels of music on the DIRECTV direct-to-home satellite television service.

In 2000, AEI was pushing its ProFusion Digital Delivery System, which could store either 160 hours of music or eight hours of MPEG 2 video. Clients received updates either through CD-ROMs or on-line and could broadcast it to hundreds of locations.

Principal Divisions

AEI Music Network; AEI Music Markets-Worldwide; AEI Music Inflight.

Principal Competitors

Liberty Digital; Muzak, Inc.; PlayNetwork.

Further Reading

Beauchamp, Marc, "Mike Malone and the Slumbering Giant," *Forbes,* February 20, 1989, pp. 90, 92.
Coolidge, Shelley Donald, "You Can Whistle a Tune at Work with New Digital Music Express," *Christian Science Monitor,* March 25, 1994, p. 11.
Curtis, James, "Talk About POP Music," *Marketing,* October 22, 1998, p. 34.
Ferraro, Cathleen, "Music Makes Cash Registers Sing for Retailers," *Denver Rocky Mountain News,* April 19, 1994, p. 31A.
Guida, Tony, interview with Michael Malone, *Entrepreneurs Only,* broadcast on the CNNfn cable network on April 6, 1999.
Hartnett, Michael, "Digital Delivery System Increases Power of Store Music and Video," *Stores,* April 2000, pp. 100–02.
Martin, Justin, "Music Man to Air Force One," *Fortune,* September 5, 1994, p. 120.
Paskiet, Amanda, "The Sound of Music," *Restaurant Hospitality,* September 1998, p. 40.
Petersen, Andrea, "Restaurants Bring In da Noise To Keep Out da Nerds," *Wall Street Journal,* December 30, 1997, p. B1.
Reda, Susan, "Targeted Store Music Programs Strengthen Ties Between Sounds and Sales," *Stores,* October 1998, pp. 54–56.
Schuch, Beverly, and Donald Van de Mark, "Improving Elevator Music," interview with Michael Malone, CNNfn's *Biz Buzz,* June 8, 1998.
Smith, Joyce, "Music Moving Up Front," *Kansas City Star,* November 10, 1994, p. B1.
Tomkins, Richard, "Why Customers Are Rocking in the Aisles," *Financial Times,* Marketing and Media, January 19, 1998, p. 15.

—Frederick C. Ingram

Alpharma Inc.

1 Executive Drive
P.O. Box 1399
Fort Lee, New Jersey 07024
U.S.A.
Telephone: (201) 947-7774
Toll Free: (800) 645-4216
Fax: (201) 947-4879
Web site: http://www.alpharma.com

Public Company
Incorporated: 1975 as A.L. Laboratories Inc.
Employees: 3,300
Sales: $742.2 million (1999)
Stock Exchanges: New York
Ticker Symbol: ALO
NAIC: 325411 Medicinal and Botanical Manufacturing;
   325412 Pharmaceutical Preparation Manufacturing

Alpharma Inc. (known until 1995 as A.L. Pharma Inc.) is an international pharmaceutical company involved in manufacturing and marketing specialty generic and branded pharmaceuticals for human as well as animal health products. Formed in 1975 as A.L. Laboratories, a wholly owned subsidiary of the Norwegian pharmaceutical and animal health company, Apothekernes Laboratorium, the company initially focused on producing animal feed antibiotics, particularly bacitracin, then increasingly became involved in manufacturing and marketing human pharmaceuticals. By the mid-1990s, A.L. Pharma's U.S. and international presence in the human pharmaceutical and animal products markets had increased considerably from the company's modest beginnings, positioning it as one of the emerging companies in the global pharmaceutical market.

Origins in the Late 1970s

A.L. Laboratories was formed in 1975 as a wholly owned subsidiary of Apothekernes Laboratorium A.S., a Norwegian manufacturer and marketer of pharmaceutical and health products for humans and animals. Founded in 1903, Apothekernes Laboratorium had been involved for years in the manufacture of bacitracin, an antibiotic for animal feed use. Initially, when Apothekernes Laboratorium began manufacturing bacitracin at its production facility in Oslo during the early 1950s, the substance was marketed as a pharmaceutical grade bulk antibiotic. Shortly thereafter, the applications for bacitracin broadened, and by the late 1950s Apothekernes Laboratorium began marketing the product as an animal feed additive. Bacitracin became the mainstay product for the newly-formed A.L. Laboratories when it established its headquarters in Englewood, New Jersey, in 1975.

Instrumental in the formation of A.L. Laboratories was I. Roy Cohen, who, along with Einer W. Sissener, figured prominently in the company's history for roughly the next 20 years. Under Cohen's and Sissener's stewardship, A.L. Laboratories experienced dramatic growth, evolving into a well-rounded pharmaceutical company that, like its progenitor, Apothekernes Laboratorium, enjoyed considerable presence in the pharmaceutical markets for both humans and animals. Initially, however, Cohen, who served as A.L. Laboratories' president, steered the company toward further growth in the bacitracin field. With annual revenues totaling $6 million shortly after formation, the full development of the company into other segments of the pharmaceutical market was a matter of time.

The expansion of A.L. Laboratories' size and scope was facilitated by its relationship with Apothekernes Laboratorium. With its parent company's backing, A.L. Laboratories received more favorable terms on bank credit than competitor companies of commensurate size. This was an invaluable asset during the company's formative years, particularly when it came to acquiring other companies.

The 1979 acquisition of the chemical and fermentation businesses of Dawe's Laboratories, Inc. was an important step toward increasing the company's U.S. and European presence in the bacitracin field. Located in Chicago Heights, Illinois, these facilities included chemical, fermentation, and blending installations that provided A.L. Laboratories with its entry into organic chemical production and augmented its bacitracin manufacturing capabilities. Ground was broken the following year for a multi-million dollar expansion of the Chicago Heights facilities that, as Cohen related to *Chemical Marketing Reporter*

Company Perspectives:

We operate in a rapidly growing and changing industry. As a leading provider of human generic pharmaceuticals, we stand to benefit as governments worldwide seek to curb skyrocketing health care costs. As a global supplier of animal pharmaceuticals that foster good health and robust growth, enhance reproductive efficiency, and treat and prevent disease, we also stand to benefit as consumers worldwide increase their demand for safe foods—from poultry to livestock to farmed fish. All of these factors position Alpharma for improved growth and profitability. But our greatest strength at Alpharma is our people. Our management team is loyal, experienced and highly qualified. They have run the Company sensibly, making decisions as a team and taking prudent and judicious risk when it made sense to do so. They are supported by our 3,300 people who work diligently to further our success. Each Alpharma employee, at every level of our organization, contributes to our corporate culture with his or her team-oriented, entrepreneurial spirit. We also share a commitment to serving our customers. At the same time we share a passion for sustainable results—results that enhance shareholder value. Most of all, we share a dedication to one clear mission—to build Alpharma into an outstanding organization that makes a meaningful contribution to affordable medicine and safe food supplies on a global scale.

at the time, would "greatly increase antibiotic production capacity [and] multiply our output of feed grade bacitracin." With the bacitracin manufactured at these facilities, A.L. Laboratories marketed its primary product, "Bacitracin-MD," a feed supplement, used for disease prevention, growth promotion, and feed efficiency in the poultry and swine industries.

In the late 1970s, the FDA, responding to the complaints by meat and poultry producers that many of the products marketed as animal feed antibiotics were found to cause pernicious side effects, stepped in and began closely scrutinizing the production of animal feed antibiotics. Excluded from these charges of product inferiority was A.L. Laboratories' Bacitracin-MD, a product meat and poultry producers favored because it did not develop tissue residues in animals. Demand for Bacitracin-MD, and its companion product, "Solu-tracin 50", consequently shot up, providing a boost to A.L. Laboratories' business and creating a need for increased production, a need the expansion of the Chicago Heights facilities was designed to meet.

With business steadily growing, A.L. Laboratories entered the early 1980s propelled by the increasing popularity of bacitracin. By 1983, the company's Bacitracin-MD had been renamed as BMD. That year, A.L. Laboratories completed a major transaction, perhaps the most pivotal purchase in the company's early history, when it acquired a Danish health concern named A/S Dumex. Based in Copenhagen, Dumex was a manufacturer of branded pharmaceuticals, fermentation antibiotics, and nutritional beverage products, which the company sold in more than 40 countries. Included in the deal were manufacturing facilities that, along with Dumex' product line,

complemented A.L. Laboratories' business in the United States and in Norway and gave the company access to important markets in Africa and Asia, where historically it had maintained only a nominal presence.

Entering the Human Pharmaceuticals Market in the 1980s

The following year, A.L. Laboratories became a publicly-held corporation, as Apothekernes Laboratorium gradually began to cede a part of its stake in its formerly wholly owned U.S. subsidiary. The year of A.L. Laboratories' initial public offering also marked the first full year that the company's 1983 acquisition of Dumex contributed to annual revenue. For the year, A.L. Laboratories generated $85.9 million and posted $4.3 million in net income, a laudable increase in nine years.

Broadening Product Line in the 1980s

Such growth prompted A.L. Laboratories' management to desire to become a much larger company. To this end, A.L. Laboratories increasingly became involved in the manufacture and marketing of pharmaceuticals for humans and less aggressively pursued its interests in the animal antibiotic market. This new business strategy was manifested in 1987, when A.L. Laboratories acquired Baltimore, Maryland-based Barre-National from Revco D.S. Inc. for $95 million. The largest U.S. manufacturer of generic cold medicines, Barre-National manufactured more than 200 prescription and over-the-counter drugs, giving A.L. Laboratories a substantial stake in the pharmaceutical market. But, the greatest asset the acquisition gave the company was Barre-National's commanding lead in the liquid (as opposed to tablets or capsules) generic drug market. In this expanding niche of the more broadly defined pharmaceutical market, Barre-National controlled 40 percent of the U.S. market, an entirely new market for A.L. Laboratories that represented the company's future.

Before being acquired by A.L. Laboratories, Barre-National had produced $45 million in annual revenues; by the end of 1988, the first full year under A.L. Laboratories' corporate umbrella, Barre-National's revenues jumped to $65 million, pushing A.L. Laboratories' revenue total for the year to $236.4 million. The growth of Barre-National (which, like Dumex, operated as a subsidiary of A.L. Laboratories) and the initial success recorded in the company's new market validated the decision by A.L. Laboratories' management to seek expansion through the manufacture and marketing of liquid generics, which promised to increase in popularity in the coming years. From 1989 to 1994, the liquid generics market was projected to nearly triple in dollar volume to reach $400 million, a substantial portion of which A.L. Laboratories expected to garner through Barre-National's tight grip on the market. Moreover, there was a relative paucity of competition in the field; only 12 percent of branded (non-generic) liquid pharmaceuticals had generic counterparts, while 25 percent of the branded pharmaceutical tablet and capsule products competed against generic equivalents. With these encouraging signs pointing toward potentially dramatic growth, Cohen gave the rest of the company's management a formidable goal. Cohen expected A.L. Laboratories to be a $1 billion company by the end of the 1990s.

Key Dates:

1975: A.L. Laboratories is formed as a wholly owned subsidiary of Apothekernes Laboratorium.
1979: The company acquires the chemical and fermentation businesses of Dawe's Laboratories, Inc.
1983: The company acquires Dumex and completes its initial public offering.
1987: The company acquires Barre-National.
1994: A.L. Laboratories purchases the pharmaceutical, animal health, aquatic animal health, and bulk antibiotics businesses of its former parent and changes its name to A.L. Pharma.
1995: The company changes its name to Alpharma.
1996: The company becomes the largest producer of fish vaccines internationally.
1998: Alpharma purchases Cox Pharmaceuticals.
1999: Alpharma purchases I.D. Russell Laboratories, Southern Cross Biotech and Jumer Laboratories.

In late 1989, pharmaceutical sales composed 65 percent of the company's business, while animal health products contributed 20 percent. Although A.L. Laboratories had shifted its focus to pharmaceuticals for human use, the company still held an enviable position in the animal antibiotic industry, which continued to suffer from allegations that many of the products contained harmful residues. A.L. Laboratories had avoided these charges and earned a profitable reputation as one of the few reliable animal antibiotic manufacturers. Barre-National, by now in its second full year under A.L. Laboratories management, continued to grow, contributing $85 million, or 30 percent, to its parent company's revenue total. Shortly after Cohen made his prediction that A.L. Laboratories would reach the $1 billion plateau by the end of the decade, the company recorded $266.2 million in revenue. Although still a long way from the target figure, Cohen had plans to help A.L. Laboratories achieve the goal.

Under New Leadership in the 1990s

The most expeditious path was through the acquisition of pharmaceutical and animal antibiotic companies, a course of action for which Cohen prepared. Also during this time, Cohen, then in his late 60s, began looking for a suitable replacement for himself. This would be the first change in leadership in the company's history. After months of discussions in 1990, a suitable replacement was found in Richard P. Storm, an executive with 30 years of experience in the pharmaceutical industry. Of British and Norwegian descent, Storm was born in Argentina, where he later worked for Pfizer Inc., spending 19 years at the Argentinean operations of the giant pharmaceutical company. After leaving Pfizer, Storm moved to the United States in 1980 to join Abbott Laboratories, where he spent another four years before joining Rorer Group, a Fort Washington, Pennsylvania-based pharmaceutical manufacturer.

Selected as A.L. Laboratories' president and chief executive officer in January 1991, Storm left his position as executive vice-president at Rorer Group and immediately set himself to the task of achieving his new company's financial goal. The year of A.L. Laboratories predicted ascension to the $1 billion level had been formally pushed back to 2000, but Storm, nevertheless, approached its fulfillment with a sense of urgency. Several months before Storm assumed stewardship of A.L. Laboratories, the company had purchased NMC Laboratories Inc., a Glendale, New York-based manufacturer and marketer of prescription creams and ointments. The acquisition of NMC added $14 million to A.L. Laboratories annual revenue total, but, by the time Storm came aboard, Cohen had much more to offer his protégé.

In the months leading up to Storm's selection, Cohen had arranged the financing to launch a series of acquisitions, obtaining $220 million from a consortium of 11 European banks led by Union Bank of Norway. Accordingly, Cohen not only handed Storm the reins of the company in January 1991, but also a considerably fattened corporate wallet. Storm took both, clearly elated by the opportunity before him. In an article for the *Business Journal of New Jersey,* Storm related, ''It has been my objective to be a CEO of a NYSE-listed company. This is a major move; hopefully, the last in my career.'' To the *New York Times*, Storm succinctly related that becoming chief executive of A.L. Laboratories ''fulfills all my ambitions.''

Six months later, however, Storm was gone, leaving without explanation at the end of July 1991. In response to Storm's departure, company officials stated that his background at large pharmaceutical companies did not conform to A.L. Laboratories entrepreneurial style. To fill the void left by Storm's exit, the company created a three-member office of the chief executive comprising Jeffrey E. Smith, A.L. Laboratories' chief financial officer since 1984, Cohen, and Sissener, who had been and continued to be the board's chairperson.

Two months after Storm left, A.L. Laboratories acquired the entire feed additive line of Solvay Animal Health Inc., a $12 million company that fleshed out A.L. Laboratories' animal health product line. The following year, in 1992, a story of significant importance to A.L. Laboratories appeared in the *Wall Street Journal*, announcing the possibility that the company was intending to combine some or all of its businesses with Apothekernes Laboratorium, which by this point held a less than 40 percent stake in the company. Actually, talk of somehow combining the complementary businesses of Apothekernes Laboratorium and A.L. Laboratories first began in the mid-1980s, but, by the early 1990s, these discussions had become much more purposeful and explicit. After several years of negotiations, it was agreed in October 1994 that A.L. Laboratories would purchase the pharmaceutical, animal health, aquatic animal health, and bulk antibiotics businesses of its former parent, Apothekernes Laboratorium.

Sissener asserted that the combined operations would help the company position itself for global competition in the specialized industry of human pharmaceutical and animal health products. Beyond the material assets gained, the acquisition led to a name change for A.L. Laboratories to A.L. Pharma Inc., which the company's management felt better reflected the scope of the company's operations and its greater interest in pharmaceuticals. A.L. Pharma also shifted its management structure to encompass five divisions, each consisting of a number of individual companies: U.S. Pharmaceuticals, International Pharmaceuticals, Fine Chemicals, Animal Health and Aquatic Animal Health. The reorganization entailed staff reductions totaling more than one hundred, product line and facility rationalizations, and the discontinuance of some outside research and development projects. Almost exactly one year later, the company changed its name again, to Alpharma Inc., and began to use this name for all its activities and on all its product packaging.

By 1996, Alpharma's attractive "niche focus" had enabled it to prosper. In addition to the 40 percent of its sales that were still in cough and flu products, it had become the world's largest producer of vaccines for farmed fish, controlling 70 percent of the world market for fish vaccines. The move into aquatic animal health had come about with the 1994 merger; A.L. Laboratories brought with it Biomed, which had helped develop one of the first commercially available fish vaccines that made widespread use of antibiotics unnecessary in fish farming. As aquaculture represented a rapidly growing industry—worldwide demand for fish protein was increasing at the same time that the wild fish harvest was declining—this market specialty represented a potential boon for Alpharma. In another promising venture, the company also began to market a generic version of the widely popular Rogaine product to combat hair loss in 1996.

By 1997, Alpharma had more than 170 prescription and over-the-counter products and pulled in revenue of $500 million. Intent upon broadening its market leadership positions through geographical expansion, it established a new subsidiary, Alpharma do Brasil Ltda., bringing its international market presence to 50 countries. As an increasing number of governments in Europe began to encourage generic drug substitution for branded drugs, the company focused on capturing lead market share on that continent as well. It also purchased the decoquinate business of Rhone-Poulenc Animal Nutrition, and, in the next several years, began to sell Decox worldwide. (Decoquinate is an anticoccidial feed additive developed for poultry and used in beef cattle and calves.) The company also purchased Cultor Food Sciences' non-core polymyx (an antibiotic) business and, in December, undertook an alliance with Xactdose, a packaging company specializing in oral liquid unit-dose medications, that would enable it to take a run at the managed care and hospital markets. In 1998, as the drug industry saw continued consolidation of its customer base—chains and wholesalers becoming bigger while partnering with generics companies—Alpharma repackaged many of its popular medications in unit doses.

In 1999, Alpharma entered the emerging French generic drug market through the acquisition of Jumer laboratories. It subsequently broadened its presence in Germany with the purchase of the Isis Pharma Group, the fifth largest generic firm in that country. These acquisitions, combined with the 1998 purchase of Cox Pharmaceuticals from Hoechst A.G., which allowed Alpharma to expand into Britain, established it as the second largest generics supplier in the United Kingdom and one of Europe's largest generics manufacturers. They solidified Alpharma's position as a leading generic manufacturer and supported its strategic agenda of moving into higher-margin generic items and branded generics.

Internal reorganization continued in 1998 with the appointment of Gert Munthe to the newly established position of president and chief operating officer. Munthe became CEO in June 1999, preparing to take over when Sissener stepped down in 1999. Munthe resigned, however, citing personal reasons for his withdrawal from company affairs in late 1999 and was replaced by Ingrid Wiik, who had been president of the company's International Pharmaceuticals Division as next in line for Sissener.

Under Wiik, who was elected president and chief executive officer in January 2000, Alpharma continued its strategic move into the higher margin market of branded products. It entered into an alliance with Ascent Pediatrics, Inc., a company that provided branded pharmaceutical products to the $3.5 billion pediatric market. It expanded its animal product line by acquiring I.D. Russell Laboratories, privately held manufacturer of therapeutic animal health products, and Southern Cross Biotech, manufacturer of a product that aids in the cost-effective production of lean pork. It also obtained exclusive rights to worldwide distribution of a high technology sperm analyzer and became the first generics manufacturer to market Minoxidil Topical Solution. Wiik, in her preface to the company's 1999 annual report, stated that Alpharma would remain competitive by anticipating and responding to its rapidly changing market environment, including the evolution of biotechnology and e-commerce, and that the company remained committed to meeting the growing demand for affordable medicine and safe food.

Principal Subsidiaries

Barre Parent Corp.; Barre-National, Inc.; Dumex; G.F.Reilly Co.; ParMed Pharmaceuticals, Inc.; Biomed, Inc.; NMC Laboratories, Inc.; Able Acquisitions, Inc.

Principal Divisions

U.S. Pharmaceuticals Division (USPD); International Pharmaceuticals Division (IPD); Fine Chemicals Division (FCD); Animal Health Division (AHD); Aquatic Animal Health Division (AAHD).

Principal Competitors

Johnson & Johnson; Merck & Co., Inc.; Watson Pharmaceuticals, Inc.; KV Pharmaceutical Co.; IVAX Corporation; Perrigo Co.

Further Reading

"A.L. Laboratories Buys Danish Drug Concern," *Chemical Marketing Reporter,* September 12, 1983, p. 9.
"A.L. Laboratories Buys Dawe's Laboratories; Vitamin Line Is Included," *Chemical Marketing Reporter,* October 22, 1979, p. 4.
"A.L. Laboratories Inc.," *Drug and Cosmetic Industry,* August 1991, p. 62.
"A.L. Laboratories Inc.," *Fortune,* December 5, 1988, p. 140.
"Bacitracin, Other Drugs Expanded with New Plant," *Chemical Marketing Reporter,* July 28, 1980, p. 5.
Byrne, Harlan S., "A.L. Laboratories Inc.: It Steers Clear of Generic Drug Troubles," *Barron's,* November 20, 1989, p. 58.

Cuff, Daniel F., "Chief Executive Named for A.L. Laboratories," *New York Times,* January 15, 1991, p. D4.

Gwinn, Mary Ann, "Vaccines Catch On—Alpharma is Hooking a Growing Market on Farmed-Fish Inoculations," *Seattle Times*, September 8, 1996, p. E1.

Morrow, David, "Old Drugs, New Labels," *New York Times*, June 13, 1998, p. D1.

Peaff, George, Jr., "Super CEOs," *Business Journal of New Jersey,* April 1991, pp. 24–25.

Roller, Kim, "Analysts Predict Solid Growth for Generics During Remainder of 1999," *Drug Store News*, August 30, 1999, p. 44.

"Skin Deep," *Business Journal of New Jersey,* October 1990, p. 16.

"Storm Resigns as Head of Drug Maker A.L. Labs," *Wall Street Journal,* July 31, 1991, p. B4.

—Jeffrey L. Covell
—updated by Carrie Rothburd

AMC Entertainment Inc.

106 West 14th Street
Kansas City, Missouri 64105
U.S.A.
Telephone: (816) 221-4000
Fax: (816) 480-4617
Web site: http://www.amctheatres.com

Public Company
Incorporated: 1968
Employees: 8,000
Sales: $1.02 billion (1999)
Stock Exchanges: American
Ticker Symbol: AEN
NAIC: 512131 Motion Picture Theaters (Except Drive-In); 512132 Drive-In Motion Picture Theaters

AMC Entertainment Inc., through its American Multi-Cinema, Inc. subsidiary, is the largest theatrical exhibition company in the world in terms of revenues and one of the largest motion picture exhibitors in the United States in terms of number of theater screens operated. In 1999, AMC was running 200 theaters with 2,800 screens in 23 states. An industry leader in the development and operation of multi-screen cinemas, AMC generated annual ticket sales of nearly $1,030 million in 2000.

Kansas City Beginnings

AMC was incorporated by Stanley H. Durwood (formerly Dubinsky) in 1968, but the business was actually started by Durwood's father in 1920. The elder Durwood had previously been a struggling actor working for a traveling tent show. In 1920, he bailed out of his acting career and leased a movie theater in downtown Kansas City. Also in 1920, Durwood's wife gave birth to Stanley, who would grow the start-up business into a small theater empire before the end of the century. During the 1920s and 1930s, Durwood was successful enough to open a few more theaters in the Kansas City area. He was also did well enough to help send Stanley to Harvard during the early 1940s.

Stanley Durwood graduated from Harvard in 1943 with a Bachelor of Arts degree. He joined the U.S. Air Force after college and served during World War II, eventually attaining the rank of lieutenant. After the war, Stanley returned to Kansas City and joined the family business—Durwood Theaters. During the 1950s, Stanley, along with his father and younger brother and sister, slowly expanded the business into a chain of ten local movie houses and drive-in theaters. It was during this period that Stanley contrived an ingenious idea for a new kind of cinema—a single complex with multiple theater screens. Although he was never able to realize his vision while his father was in control of the operation, he kept the idea alive in his mind.

Stanley's father died in 1960, and Stanley and his siblings continued to run the business, with Stanley in charge of operations. By the time Stanley took control of the business, the theater industry was rapidly evolving into a regional, and even national, industry. Because they owned only ten theaters, the Durwoods were under pressure from larger operators with more and bigger complexes. The market reach of such operations was often much greater, so they were usually able to lasso the choice releases, leaving the Durwoods to choose from the less popular motion pictures.

"I had to beg and plead for an Abbott and Costello picture," Durwood recalled in the March 25, 1994 *Kansas City Business Journal.* When Durwood finally got the comedy from the movie distributors, he hated it, but it was a big-name film, and his theaters were packed. Durwood noted, "I thought, what a crummy picture. Now if I could get two crummy pictures in here, I could double my gross and the rent would be the same." Seeking to boost attendance without increasing operating costs, Durwood believed that his multi-screen concept could be the solution.

The Birth of the Multiplex in the 1960s

In 1963, Durwood realized his vision when he built the first multiscreen theater. The concept was unheard of at the time and seemed extravagant; critics wondered why anyone would need two different screens. However, the multiscreen theater, located in a suburban shopping mall, was a success. Durwood quickly began to reconfigure some of his existing facilities into multiple screen, or "multiplex," cinemas. In 1965, Durwood bought out his brother's and sister's ownership interests. Then, in 1968, he incorporated the business as American Multi-Cinema Inc. (the name was shortened in 1983 to AMC). At the time of incorporation, AMC consisted of a local chain of 12 theaters with a total of 22 screens. AMC boosted that figure in 1969 when it opened its first six-screen theater.

AMC took advantage of industry gains during the 1970s, but was also able to consistently strengthen its competitive position in relation to its peers. It achieved those market share gains mostly through construction of new multi-screen cinemas, many of which were adjoined to, or located near, shopping malls.

Despite AMC's success, many of the company's competitors sat on the sidelines during the popularization of multiplex theaters, failing to recognize the long-term nature of the trend. A few competitors, particularly General Cinemas, also built some multi-screen theaters. However, Durwood led the charge. The AMC chain included more than 500 screens in theaters scattered mostly around the Midwest by 1981. And AMC's most rampant period of growth was yet to come.

The success of AMC's multi-screen concept was rooted in Durwood's penchant for efficiency. One prominent studio executive even referred to Durwood as the "father of modern theater exhibition" and the "inventor of professional theater management." Despite its novelty, the multiplex philosophy was relatively straightforward. By putting several screens under one roof, AMC was effectively combining several separate theater facilities. The chief benefit was that the theaters were able to share infrastructure and employees, thus spreading costs over a higher revenue base. For example, by staggering starting times of the movies, one (or a few) employees could staff the box office, while twice as many workers would be needed at two separate theaters. Likewise, only one or two concession stands were needed, parking area requirements were minimized, and costs related to air-conditioning, the lobby, and other infrastructure elements were significantly reduced.

A corollary benefit of multi-cinema theaters, which Durwood especially recognized when he began building complexes with more than two or three screens, was increased market reach. By offering different types of movies, one facility could simultaneously appeal to several segments of the movie-

going population. In addition, AMC could maximize profits on selected features by extending the run of movies that turned out to be very popular. Finally, multiple screens complemented other AMC technical and marketing innovations during the 1970s and 1980s. For example, the company was credited with introducing automated projection systems. AMC introduced the industry's first cupholder armrest in 1981.

Continued Growth in the 1980s

AMC's biggest growth spurt occurred during the 1980s. Although annual movie attendance throughout the decade remained near the one billion mark, the theater industry in general succeeded in steadily boosting ticket prices faster than inflation, thus increasing margins. More importantly, AMC continued to parlay its multi-screen concept into a competitive advantage and was able to significantly boost its share of box office receipts. During 1982 and 1983, AMC increased its total number of screens by more than 200, to about 700. Still eager to speed up expansion, the 63-year-old Durwood took his company public in 1983. Until that year, the company had been 100 percent owned by Durwood and his family. He reluctantly sold about 12 percent of AMC's stock in 1983 in a bid to raise expansion capital.

By 1986, AMC's total number of theater complexes had bolted past 200 with more than 1,100 screens in the United States. Furthermore, Durwood stepped up expansion in western Europe, Australia, and Singapore. By 1990, he planned to be operating 2,500 screens in the United States and 1,500 more overseas.

AMC's strategy represented a slight departure from, or perhaps an amplification of, the growth tactics it had utilized in the past. Instead of building complexes with five or six screens, most of its new facilities during the early and mid-1980s housed eight to 12 screens. Furthermore, Durwood was targeting smaller cities in sunbelt states, especially Florida, Texas, and California. However, to achieve the stellar growth, Durwood was forced to take on a massive load of debt. He hoped to pay the debt off in the long term from strong profit gains.

As the U.S. theater industry expanded unchecked during the mid- and late 1980s, some critics feared that the market was becoming increasingly overbuilt as theater demand was declining. AMC's holdings, alone, had reached 1,500 screens by 1988, and a lot more construction was on the design boards. Furthermore, several of its competitors were hurriedly adding more screens to their existing complexes in what became a trend to "add value" to their theaters. In AMC's case, critics also cited a lack of a market presence in key metropolitan areas like New York, Chicago, and Boston. Moreover, some observers felt that AMC, unlike other theater industry leaders, had made a mistake by not diversifying into movie-related industries during the 1980s.

The criticism about AMC's lack of diversification was prompted by the fact that the theater industry had felt increasing pressure from an onslaught of other channels for movie viewing since the 1970s. Indeed, home videos and cable television, particularly, had been vying for consumer entertainment dollars. In response, AMC's competitors had diversified out of the

Key Dates:

1920: The company's first theater is leased.
1963: The first multiscreen theater is built.
1968: AMC is incorporated as American Multi-Cinema Inc.
1981: AMC introduces the industry's first cupholder armrest.
1988: AMC's holdings reach 1,500 screens.
1995: The first "megaplex" is built.
1999: Longtime chairman and CEO Stanley H. Durwood dies.

theater business. United Artists, the industry leader, had invested heavily in cable television and telecommunications. Similarly, General Cinemas had become active in soft-drink and retail industries. However, to AMC's delight, the movie industry continued to raise ticket and concession prices throughout the 1980s. AMC boosted both its ticket and concession revenues during 1988 and 1989 to bring its gross sales to more than $456 million during 1989. Part of that growth was attributable to specific blockbuster releases that buoyed earnings during the period.

Despite record sales during the late 1980s, AMC was having financial trouble that intensified during the early 1990s. Notwithstanding a history of extremely sound management of its theaters—Durwood himself was known for always flying coach class, buying his suits off the rack, and driving an economical Honda Civic—AMC had let is operating costs escalate during its rapid expansion. Furthermore, the company's cash flow was being devoured by a crushing debt load. AMC lost money every year between 1988 and 1992, with the exception of one year in which it gleaned $567,000 in earnings from its operations. To combat slumping profits, AMC reined in its growth efforts beginning in the late 1980s and concentrated on whipping existing operations into shape. The company added a string of new theaters in 1988, bringing its total number of screens to nearly 1,700, but then stopped expanding and started slashing costs.

Of its 276 theaters, AMC closed 40 of the least profitable, reducing its total number of screens to about 1,600 by 1994. It also cut its work force by about 1,000. As it scrambled to meet its debt obligations, industry revenues picked up. Although AMC's sales wavered barely above the $400 million mark, its operating costs declined and the company posted a $1.3 million net profit in 1993. Although the company was more than $300 million in debt, analysts were optimistic, and it appeared as though Durwood's long-term strategy might pay off after all.

Having overseen a period of great expansion, Stanley Durwood's son Edward left the presidency of AMC in 1995, and Philip M. Singleton, chief operating officer, moved into the post. A former Marine Corp captain and fighter pilot, Singleton had been with AMC since 1974. He was joined by Peter C. Brown, who was appointed chief financial officer.

The Birth of the Megaplex in the 1990s

In the mid-1990s, founder Stanley Durwood was laying new plans to begin building a string of vast complexes with as many as 24 screens under the same roof. This concept was realized in Dallas in 1995 and quickly duplicated in other major markets. As with the multiplex, megaplexes consolidated operations costs and broadened its reach across more market sectors. Moreover, such tremendous spaces also permitted other revenue-generating efforts to flourish, such as restaurants, video-game parlors, and CD and book sales. Despite the million dollar pricetag for the construction of every megaplex, AMC was generally able to recoup its losses, although at the turn of the century the company did curtail its ambitions slightly, building more 20-plexes than 30-plexes. The comforts ushered in by megaplexes made any venues constructed before the 1990s seem old-fashioned.

Durwood died in 1999 of esophageal cancer, and Brown took over as chief executive officer and president. Meanwhile, AMC was busy going international, with a 13-plex in Fukuoka, Japan, and a 20-plex in Portugal, among other locations in Canada, England, and Spain. A joint venture with the Planet Hollywood theme restaurants, Planet Movie, was also planned, but stalled amidst the restaurant company's ongoing financial troubles. More promising, AMC and Hollywood.com, Inc., a web site for movies and entertainment, joined forces to sell movie tickets over MovieTickets.com in 2000.

Principal Subsidiaries

American Multi-Cinema, Inc.

Principal Competitors

Loews Cineplex Entertainment Corporation; Carmike Cinemas, Inc.; Regal Cinemas, Inc.

Further Reading

"AMC's New Chief Fine-Tunes Theater Chain's Strategy," *Wall Street Journal,* July 23, 1999, p. B6.

Bacha, Sarah Mills, "Movie Theater with 24 Screens Part of Project," *Columbus Dispatch,* August 10, 1994, p. G1.

Block, A. B., "What Makes Stanley Borrow? Stan Durwood's AMC Entertainment is Loaded with Debt and Costly Leases. So Why Does the Stock Sell for 27 Times Earnings?," *Forbes,* September 22, 1986.

Cardenas, Gina, "Movie Theater Economics," *New Miami,* September 1993, p. 18.

Gold, Howard, "Screen Gem?," *Forbes,* September 10, 1984, p. 194.

Graham, Sandy, "From Multi to Mega," *Colorado Bizz,* January 2000, p. 50.

Grove, Christopher, "Durwood Legacy Packs 'Em In," *Variety,* May 16–22, 1999, p. 42.

Harris, Kathryn, "AMC Theater Empire Playing Real-Life Drama," *Los Angeles Times,* March 27, 1988, Sec. 4, p. 1.

Henderson, Barry, "AMC Bets on Theater Allure Over Couch," *Kansas City Business Journal,* March 25, 1994, p. 3.

—Dave Mote
—updated by Mark Swartz

American Bar Association

750 North Lake Shore Drive
Chicago, Illinois 60611
U.S.A.
Telephone: (312) 988-5000
Fax: (312) 988-6081
Web site: http://www.abanet.org

Professional Association
Founded: 1878
Employees: 800
Sales: $140 million (1998)
NAIC: 81392 Professional Organizations

The American Bar Association is a voluntary professional association that includes practicing attorneys, judges, law professors, court administrators, and nonpracticing attorneys involved in journalism or other occupations. Although it has no formal authority to discipline lawyers who break the ABA's ethical code, it influences state bars that do have that power. Likewise, the ABA plays a significant role in proposing state and federal laws, reforming the court system, accrediting law schools, and evaluating individuals nominated by the president to be federal judges. It also is a major publisher, with about 90 periodicals such as the *American Bar Association Journal* and many others on various legal specialties. Although the ABA is the major legal association, only about half of the nation's attorneys are members. It competes with numerous other associations based on ethnicity or legal specialty. This large and complex organization, with numerous committees and sections, deals with trends in the legal profession, such as the increased use of paralegals and the effects of Information Age technology, as well as legal controversies such as abortion, the death penalty, improved legal access for all persons, and the litigation explosion.

Origins and Early Activities

Lawyers played a crucial role in founding the United States; most of the men at the Constitutional Convention in 1787 were lawyers. Many early American presidents and other government leaders were lawyers, yet in the early and mid-1800s popular reaction against lawyers and other professionals mounted as part of Jacksonian Democracy. The prevailing complaint at the time was that just about anyone could become a doctor or lawyer without much training. In 1851, for example, the Indiana state constitution mandated that any citizen and voter of good character could begin a law practice. Medical licensing also ended during that era. The emphasis was on equality, at least for white males.

Attitudes began changing after the Civil War as lawyers in New York City formed a city bar association in 1870, followed by state associations in Kentucky in 1871, New Hampshire in 1873, Iowa in 1874, Connecticut in 1875, and Illinois in 1877. At that time many elite lawyers in New York City and other big cities began counseling big businesses, rather than serving primarily as courtroom litigators. In the post-Civil War period, corporations expanded in size and influence, resulting in huge smokestack industries and also an increasing demand for attorneys.

Although others had pushed for the creation of a national professional society for lawyers, Simeon E. Baldwin, a leading Connecticut attorney, played the key role in starting the ABA.

Following Baldwin's invitation, on August 21, 1878, a group of 100 lawyers from 21 states and the District of Columbia met in Saratoga Springs, New York, to organize their profession's first national association. Most of the men who formed the ABA were elite corporate lawyers. Author Jethro K. Lieberman described early ABA membership: "You could become an invitee to membership if you were white, Protestant and native born, preferably with a British surname, and attended the elite law schools such as Harvard, Yale and Columbia; only then did you have a chance of prospering. Catholics, Jews, women and blacks were automatically excluded from membership. This exclusion was necessary to the elite bar's sense of identity. Any fraternity is defined not only by whom it accepts but also by whom it excludes. The Association also pinned the stigma of immorality on the lower class of lawyers as shysters who talked, dressed and acted differently."

The elitist nature of the ABA was not unique for the time. The American Federation of Labor, the nation's major union formed in 1885, did not allow women, African Americans, and

Company Perspectives:

The mission of the American Bar Association is to be the national representative of the legal profession, serving the public and the profession by promoting justice, professional excellence and respect for the law.

unskilled workers to join. Likewise, few women and minorities practiced medicine or most other professions.

The ABA's organization was part of a major professionalization trend in the late 1800s. Scientific medicine began with the adoption of the germ theory of disease and new medical schools based on the German model. The engineering professions started, as did the university-based social sciences of sociology, psychology, and anthropology. The American Economic Association was started in 1885.

Although many have argued that the early ABA was a conservative organization aligned with big business interests, other legal scholars have pointed out that Baldwin and other founders of the bar engaged in various reform efforts. For example, Baldwin pushed for electoral and constitutional reforms in Connecticut, while other ABA founders fought corruption both in politics and business.

The original 1878 ABA Constitution outlined five goals: 1) to advance jurisprudence, 2) to encourage uniform state laws, 3) to strengthen the administration of justice, 4) to uphold the legal profession's honor, and 5) to encourage friendly interaction among bar members. Formation of the ABA stimulated the organization of more local and state bar associations. By 1900 most state bar societies had been started, although they remained unconnected to the ABA in any formal way.

Although the ABA generally had little early success promoting uniform state laws, three states (Minnesota, Missouri, and New Hampshire) approved marriage and divorce laws based on an ABA suggestion in the early 1880s. Starting in 1892, the National Conference of Commissioners on Uniform State Laws held its meetings with the ABA. Working together after 1900, the two organizations suggested several laws that states adopted.

The ABA also proposed federal laws. An early example was the Bankruptcy Act passed by Congress shortly before 1900. "The Bankruptcy Act, as it stands today as amended, is practically the work of this Association," stated a 1903 ABA document.

The ABA's influence on American courts was also seen in the late 1800s. For over ten years the ABA pushed for special federal courts for handling appealed cases before reaching the U.S. Supreme Court. Around 1890, Congress created the U.S. Circuit Courts of Appeal, which followed ABA guidelines.

The ABA in the Early 20th Century

The ABA remained a small organization of just 1,718 members in 1902. Nonetheless, it had made some notable contributions to the legal profession. "Perhaps the most important

accomplishment of the early ABA," wrote Bernard Schwartz, "was its sponsorship of the meetings that led in 1900 to the organization of the Association of American Law Schools." The ABA and the new AALS struggled to upgrade legal educational standards. In the 19th century most attorneys were trained through an apprenticeship system, similar to the informal expectations of the medical profession. However, shortly after the turn of the century, the three-year model for law school was adopted. Likewise, the ABA and the AALS successfully promoted the case method of instruction in law schools.

In 1902 the ABA quit meeting regularly at Saratoga Springs; from that point to 1936 it met in different cities as a means to attract new members. Thus ABA membership grew to 29,008 in 1936. Other statistics demonstrated the same story. The bar went from just two sections, each with two officers, to 14 sections with 960 officers in 1935. The number of committees rose from 18 in 1902 to 27 in 1935. Membership revenues in those years increased from $8,255 to $197,877.66.

In 1921 North Dakota passed a state law that required practicing attorneys to pay dues and become members of the state bar association, the two key features of the so-called "integrated bar," or what critics would call the involuntary or compulsory bar. In 1927 California became the first large state to integrate its bar. These developments were praised by the ABA, which soon strengthened its formal ties to the state bar associations.

A key turning point came in 1936 when the ABA created its House of Delegates, which became the body responsible for making bar policy. Each state bar association was allowed representatives in the ABA House of Delegates, thus linking state and national associations. Although the legal profession was regulated by state governments and state bar societies, the ABA heavily influenced what happened without having any formal authority.

Shortly after the turn of the century reformers in most states passed laws limiting child labor. Moreover, state laws mandating school attendance led to more children going to school rather than work. After the U.S. Supreme Court declared unconstitutional both the federal Child Labor Law and a federal tax on goods made by children, in 1924 an amendment to the U.S. Constitution was proposed to prohibit child labor. The ABA in 1933 voted to oppose that amendment, stating that opposition to the "admitted evil" of child labor should be overseen by states and families. Strangely, just a few moments later the ABA voted against amending the ABA constitution to allow it to take sides on public policy matters.

During the 1930s, the ABA opposed many New Deal laws and reforms pushed by President Franklin Roosevelt, several of which were declared unconstitutional by the Supreme Court. Ironically, the expansion of the federal government during the Great Depression led to an increased need for lawyers. For example, corporations needed more legal advice to make sure they complied with the rules and regulations of the U.S. Securities and Exchange Commission.

The ABA's fight against the New Deal led more liberal attorneys to start their own society called the National Lawyers Guild. A mixture of populists, Marxists, and progressive attor-

Key Dates:

1878: Lawyers at Saratoga Springs, New York, organize the American Bar Association (ABA).

1902: The American Association of Law Schools is started with support from the ABA.

1915: First issue of the *American Bar Association Journal* is published.

1921: North Dakota becomes first state to require all practicing attorneys to be state bar members.

1930s: ABA opposes most New Deal laws and programs.

1936: ABA creates its House of Delegates that ties state bar associations with the ABA.

1957: ABA's office in Washington, D.C., is opened.

1996: ABA dedicates its Museum of Law in Chicago.

neys, mostly on the East Coast, formed the guild in 1937. This move was also motivated by the fact that the ABA represented a largely elite base of lawyers associated with big business while ignoring the legal needs of the lower classes and minorities.

In the late 1800s a few women joined state bar associations for the first time, though very few women practiced law. In 1870 only five American women were working as lawyers, compared to a reported 40,731 male lawyers. By 1900 the number of female lawyers had risen to 1,010 while male lawyers numbered 113,693. More women became lawyers in the 1920s and 1930s, but most did so by attending smaller part-time law schools that resisted ABA efforts to raise educational standards. Corporate lawyers and the ABA elite tried in vain to purge the legal profession of part-time schools that allowed women, minorities, and immigrants to become lawyers. Decades passed before women and minorities joined the legal profession in any significant numbers.

Postwar Developments

After World War II, the federal government and others were concerned about the possible subversive activities of Communists. In response to this Second Red Scare, often known as McCarthyism, the ABA in 1950 voted to expel all ABA members who were members of the Communist Party or supported Marxism-Leninism. Although that vote was consistent with the bar's general reputation as a conservative association, not all lawyers agreed with the ABA. For example, the Association of the Bar of the City of New York opposed this ABA resolution.

The ABA became increasingly politicized, as did the American culture of the 1960s and 1970s. Issues impacting the legal profession during this time included those surrounding the civil rights and women's movements and then a host of new environment and work place safety laws and regulations. Attorneys specializing in such new areas of the law formed new ABA committees to address the issues and influence law-making.

The law as profession also began to change, starting in the late 1970s when many major law firms, the source of most bar leaders, began expanding into huge firms with hundreds of attorneys. Before that time, most law firms were run more or less like secret societies, with little public information available

about their partners or clients. However, the U.S. Supreme Court ruled that professional societies could not restrict advertising by their members because it violated the First Amendment right to free speech and also was a violation of antitrust laws. At that point lawyers, dentists, doctors, and other professionals began advertising their services instead of simply waiting for clients or patients to come to them.

Another significant development that transformed the legal community was the introduction of new publications that featured details on firm management and finances, thus giving lawyers information they needed to compare and possibly change firms. *The National Law Journal* and *The American Lawyer* were the two major periodicals that revolutionized legal journalism. Eventually law firms actually sought to be included in those magazines, which each published lists of the nation's top law firms.

Although the so-called elite lawyers still remained the minority of the nation's attorneys, they received most of the press and continued to dominate state bar associations and the ABA. In fact, when more women and ethnic minorities became attorneys, relatively few joined the ABA that historically had rejected them. In addition, separate associations for women, racial groups, and those practicing in legal specialties competed with membership in the all-purpose ABA.

Another rift in the membership ranks was caused in the early 1990s when the ABA adopted a pro-choice resolution, affirming the right of women to have abortions. Although this was consistent with the 1973 U.S. Supreme Court decision in *Roe v. Wade,* several thousand ABA members left the association because of its stand on such a controversial political question. As Salt Lake City attorney Edward McDonough reflected, in an August 1997 issue of the *Salt Lake Tribune,* the ABA abortion resolution "had no effect on legislation or on court decisions. It had no effect other than to alienate many of the ABA's long-term members and drive them out of the organization."

The resignations came as a blow to the ABA, which was also soon faced with challenges on other fronts. The Massachusetts School of Law sued the ABA in 1993, claiming that the ABA's role in accrediting law schools was unfair. Over the next few years, the ABA was forced to revise its program of accreditation to comply with federal law and preserve the rights of a university to set its own standards. Moreover, the ABA's role in nominating candidates for positions as judges came under fire as the Senate Judiciary Committee announced that it would proceed with its own nominations regardless of ABA input.

During this time, the ABA explored new fronts as well, including the possibility of approving nonlawyer or multidisciplinary partnerships in which lawyers could form businesses with accountants, financial planners, and other professionals. That trend was already underway in Europe and Canada, where consulting divisions of the Big Five accounting firms acquired law firms. Although some American attorneys favored multidisciplinary practices, some were concerned about conflicting professional ethics. For example, attorneys swore to maintain client confidentiality, while accountants were required to report financial problems to the government. In any case, the ABA in 1999 postponed voting on such partnerships.

In the 1990s the ABA offered numerous services to its members and the public. For example, its extensive Web site included information on how to apply for law school, how to find data on disciplined attorneys, and how to contact paralegal associations. It also informed the public about its free Museum of Law in Chicago, its numerous research studies, books, periodicals, and related Web sites. A tremendous amount of information about the legal system, court cases, legal specialties, and other related topics was available on the Internet through the ABA. According to the August 1999 *Profile of the American Bar Association*, the ABA during the 1990s had initiated hundreds of different programs, ranging in topics from child abuse, law practice management, and juvenile crime to the legal problems of the elderly and the high cost of justice. The profiler also observed that ''The legal profession can be viewed as a giant confederation, at the center of which is the American Bar Association.''

The ABA clearly has been one of the nation's most significant organizations, having promoted a society based on the rule of law, not men. Both state and federal governments have passed laws modeled on ABA suggestions. Likewise, the ABA has heavily influenced the court system, law schools, and other aspects of the legal system. Although many Americans have taken the rule of law for granted, many other nations have not enjoyed such stability. On the other hand, the ABA has historically fought for its members' privileges and resisted reforms that would have helped many Americans. As argued by Jerold S. Auerbach and other critics, the bar historically created a system of unequal justice in which the rich could buy access to the law through the best attorneys, while those not so privileged seldom could afford a lawyer. The ABA to its credit recognized the challenge and has tried to promote better access through various *pro bono* programs, with some success. Similarly, the ABA has had limited diversity in its ranks, and in spite of progress, has remained mainly a largely Caucasian organization. ''The data are compelling,'' wrote ABA President William G. Paul in the October 1999 *ABA Journal*, explaining ''Our profession is more than 90 percent white, and enrollment in our law schools is about 80 percent white. But 30 percent of our society is people of color, and in the next few decades it will be 50 percent. These trends put at risk the profession's historic role as the connecting link between our society and the rule of law.'' Thus a major challenge in 2000 for the ABA and the legal profession as a whole was to promote a system of equal justice under the law. The bar and its membership remained optimistic about reaching that goal, while critics alleged that lawyers were more focused on their own pocketbooks.

Principal Divisions

Business Law; Environmental Law; International Law; State and Local Government Law; Antitrust Law; Health Law; Labor and Employment Law; Election Law; Administrative Law; Center for Continuing Legal Education; Commission on Domestic Violence; Commission on Legal Problems of the Elderly; Commission on Mental and Physical Disability Law; Commission on Opportunities for Minorities in the Profession; Commission on Women in the Profession; Coordinating Committee on Gun Violence; Council on Racial and Ethnic Justice; Legislative and Governmental Advocacy.

Principal Competitors

National Bar Association; National Lawyers Association; Bar Association of National Lawyers.

Further Reading

The ABA in Law and Social Policy: What Role?, Washington, D.C.: Federalist Society for Law and Public Policy Studies, 1994.

Auerbach, Jerold, *Unequal Justice: Lawyers and Social Change in Modern America,* New York: Oxford University Press, 1976.

Carson, Gerald, *A Good Day at Saratoga,* Chicago: American Bar Association, 1978.

Chester, Ronald, *Unequal Access: Women Lawyers in a Changing America,* Mass.: Bergin & Garvey Publishers, 1985.

Drachman, Virginia G., *Sisters in Law: Women Lawyers in Modern American History,* Cambridge, Mass.: Harvard University Press, 1998.

Galanter, M. and T. Palay, *Tournament of Lawyers: The Transformation of the Big Law Firm,* Chicago: University of Chicago Press, 1991.

Ginger, Ann Fagan, and Eugene M. Tobin, editors, *The National Lawyers Guild: From Roosevelt Through Reagan,* Philadelphia: Temple University Press, 1988.

Jacobs, Margaret A., ''ABA Puts Off Vote on Nonlawyer Parterships,'' *Wall Street Journal,* August 11, 1999, p. B9.

Linowitz, Sol M., with Martin Mayer, *The Betrayed Profession: Lawyering at the End of the Twentieth Century,* New York: Charles Scribner's Sons, 1994.

McDonough, Edward, ''Not All U.S. Lawyers Condone the American Bar Association,'' *Salt Lake Tribune,* August 3, 1997, p. AA2.

McKean, Dayton David, *The Integrated Bar,* Boston: Houghton Mifflin Company, 1963.

Matzko, John A., '' 'The Best Men of the Bar': The Founding of the American Bar Association,'' in *The New High Priests: Lawyers in Post-Civil War America,* edited by Gerard W. Gawalt, Westport, Conn.: Greenwood Press, 1984, pp. 75–96.

Meserve, Robert W., *The American Bar Association: A Brief History and Appreciation,* New York: Newcomen Society in North America, 1973.

Schwartz, Bernard, *The Law in America: A History,* New York: McGraw Hill Book Company, 1974.

Sunderland, Edson R., *History of the American Bar Association and Its Work,* Ann Arbor: Reginald Heber Smith, 1953.

—David M. Walden

AMERICAN RE
A Member of the Munich Re Group

American Re Corporation

555 College Road East
Princeton, New Jersey 08543-5241
U.S.A.
Telephone: (609) 243-4200
Fax: (609) 243-4257
Web site: http://www.amre.com

Wholly Owned Subsidiary of Munich Re Group
Incorporated: 1917 as American Re-Insurance Company
Employees: 1,600
Sales: $2.96 billion (1998)
NAIC: 52413 Reinsurance Carriers

American Re Corporation is a member of the Munich Re Co., the largest reinsurance company in the world. The third largest provider of property and casualty reinsurance in the United States, American Re operates through primary subsidiary American Re-Insurance, which offers treaty and facultative reinsurance to insurance companies, large businesses, government agencies, pools, and other self-insurers around the world. American Re also provides insurance brokerage and risk management services.

Insuring the Insurers: Early 1900s–1940s

Reinsurance companies, while operating in relative obscurity compared with insurance establishments, play a key role in insurance markets. They provide stability by insuring the insurers. A company that primarily insures homes in California, for example, would likely be bankrupted by a major earthquake. By purchasing reinsurance, the company can protect itself from such catastrophes.

The property/casualty insurance industry, which American Re serves, was in large part a corollary of the Great Fire of London (1666), after which fire insurance was established. In the United States, it was not until early in the 20th century that the hazards of wind, water, damage, personal accident, and explosion were added to established lines of fire insurance. Major British companies, such as Lloyd's of London, provided most reinsurance for American insurers during the early- and mid-1900s.

The American Re-Insurance Company, the first U.S.-owned reinsurer, was founded on March 15, 1917 in Huntington, Pennsylvania. Seven families in that coal mining region formed the enterprise as a vehicle to provide a workers' compensation program for local miners. Because of a dire need by mining families for protection from risks associated with dangerous mining occupations, the company grew quickly. In 1921 the company moved its headquarters to Philadelphia, allowing it to better serve its geographically expanding business. Likewise, the organization transferred its headquarters to New York City in 1933, using the temporary title New York Re-Insurance Company.

American Re continued to expand during the 1930s and 1940s, as property and casualty insurance increased in popularity. During that period, insurance companies were regulated solely by state governments. Therefore, insurance practices varied by region. In 1944, however, the federal government, in *United States v Southeastern Underwriters Association,* made the insurance industry subject to Congressional powers. Growth was particularly brisk after 1948, when states began allowing insurers to write multiple lines of insurance rather than limiting them to just one segment of the market. These changes, combined with strong demand for all types of insurance by burgeoning U.S. corporations, generated an influx of reinsurance activity.

Growth and Expansion: 1950s–80s

American Re broadened its scope in the 1950s by acquiring American Reserve Insurance Company, of New York. In 1963, moreover, it purchased Inter-Ocean Reinsurance Company, of Cedar Rapids, Iowa. The company continued to boost its assets and services throughout the mid-1900s by focusing on customer service, cultivating long-term client relationships, diversifying its products and services, and emphasizing a conservative approach to investing its assets and reserves. In addition to its acquisition activities and straightforward management style, the company broadened its operations through international expansion beginning in the 1950s.

A fundamental goal of the company's overall business strategy during the mid-1900s (and into the late 1900s) was a reduction of the effect of underwriting cycles on its financial performance—the insurance industry, in general, is heavily impacted by inevitable downturns in new insurance underwriting activity. By diversifying globally and across markets, and by securing long-term relationships with healthy clients, American Re was able to weather industry downturns with few financial problems compared with many other reinsurance industry participants. Going into the 1990s, for example, American Re continued to serve clients enlisted shortly after it was founded.

Aetna Life and Casualty Insurance Company, of Hartford, Connecticut, purchased American Re in 1969 in an effort to diversify its holdings. Under Aetna's ownership, American Re continued to attract new clients, boost its reserves, and expand geographically. Indeed, during the 1970s and 1980s the company opened offices across North America—in San Francisco, Kansas City, Chicago, Dallas, Atlanta, Montreal, Minneapolis, and several other cities. It also initiated operations in Mexico City; Bermuda; Bogota, Columbia; Santiago, Chile; Tokyo; Singapore; Melbourne and Sydney, Australia; London; Brussels; Vienna; and Cairo, Egypt.

Although Aetna paid only $340 million for the reinsurer, its new subsidiary proved, over time, to be a major boon to its bottom line. By the early 1980s, in fact, American Re was underwriting about $400 million in reinsurance premiums annually, despite a cyclical industry recess that lingered through 1984. During the mid-1980s, a cyclical upswing propelled American Re-Insurance's underwriting revenues to more than $1 billion by 1987, providing a healthy addition to Aetna's aggregate earnings during that period.

Relatively healthy reinsurance underwriting activity, combined with relaxed regulatory oversight of insurance industry investment practices, induced several new companies to enter both the reinsurance and insurance industries during the mid-1980s. Despite unspectacular profits from insurance underwriting activity during that period, many insurance companies were able to generate fat profits by placing their assets in lucrative, yet risky, investment vehicles, such as real estate and junk bonds. Reinsurers benefited.

In the late 1980s, however, the insurance industry suffered from numerous setbacks. Sloppy management and investment practices caught up with many insurers in the late 1980s, as interest rates and investment returns plummeted during the U.S. economic recession. Worse yet, record losses from catastrophes jolted property/casualty insurers in 1989, 1991, and 1992. Hurricane Hugo, the San Francisco earthquake, the Oakland fires, and hurricanes Andrew and Niki stressed insurance industry reserves with billions of dollars in damage. As property/casualty insurers filed record claims, many reinsurers suffered a significant depletion of their reserves.

Despite general industry turmoil, American Re profited from the conservative investment and management approach that it had practiced throughout most of the century. As the number of establishments competing in the U.S. reinsurance industry plummeted from about 130 in the mid-1980s to approximately 60 by 1992, American Re managed to increase its underwriting revenues, boost its reserves, and increase its annual operating income. For example, American Re-Insurance's combined ratio (a standard industry statistic reflective of financial stability) was the best (lowest) in the reinsurance industry in the early 1990s and had remained significantly below the industry average throughout the 1980s.

American Re-Insurance's stability became increasingly important to the Aetna organization during the U.S. recession. In 1989, for example, the subsidiary contributed $128 million of Aetna's total $676 million in earnings. As Aetna's insurance company investments plummeted in value during the early 1990s, moreover, this ratio ballooned. In 1991, in fact, Aetna's earnings had slipped to $505 million, of which $133 million, or 26 percent, came from American Re Company. Despite its reliance on the reinsurer, Aetna decided to sell the operation in 1992 in an effort to generate much-needed cash to shore up its lagging insurance divisions.

Ownership Changes in the 1990s

Kohlberg Kravis Roberts & Co. (KKR), in the largest leveraged buyout in history of the U.S. insurance industry, purchased American Re Company in 1992 for $1.43 billion. KKR formed a new entity, American Re Corporation, to act as a holding company for American Re-Insurance Company (American Re) and related subsidiaries. Although KKR was taking ownership of the company, it planned to leave direct control of American Re in the hands of existing management. "We'll be a stand alone, separate company and will be totally unrelated to other KKR companies," said Edward Jobe, American Re CEO since 1987, in the June 24, 1992 issue of *Business for Central New Jersey*.

American Re's management strategy following the KKR takeover entailed a four-pronged approach complementary to the organization's legacy of stability and conservatism: Client focus, financial strength, global reach, and commitment to innovation. Client focus was achieved by taking a specialist, or "Whole Account Concept," approach to service and by seeking long-term relationships. Every American Re client received a multidisciplined team of specialists to brainstorm needs and opportunities. "We then respond with customized products and specialized services," explained Jobe in the July 5, 1993 issue of *National Underwriter*. The company augmented its client focus with direct underwriting, long practiced by American Re. By underwriting reinsurance directly, rather than through independent brokers, the company believed it was able to establish better relationships and attract a more stable client base in comparison with most of its competitors.

Key Dates:

1917: American Re-Insurance Company is formed in Huntington, Pennsylvania.
1950: American Re acquires American Reserve Insurance Company.
1969: Aetna Life and Casualty Insurance Company buys American Re.
1992: Leverage buyout firm Kohlberg Kravis Roberts & Co. acquires American Re and forms American Re Corporation, a holding company.
1993: American Re goes public.
1996: Munich Re Co. acquires American Re.

American Re's second management guideline, financial strength, was accomplished through an ongoing emphasis on exceptional cash reserves to back its potential liabilities; high asset quality, which is the result of cautious investments and a conservative asset mix; and a lack of dependence on underwriting cycles. Indeed, in 1993 American Re retained its distinction as having the lowest combined ratio in the industry. In addition, it maintained one of the three largest surpluses in the nation, 94 percent of which was invested in cash and bonds.

Global reach, American Re's third corporate focus, was extended during the early 1990s by providing specialized services to overseas clients and by promoting a reputation for stability. The latter earmark was particularly pivotal in attracting overseas business. ''Every client in the world has access to all of our corporate resources,'' Jobe told *National Underwriter,* ''including our multi-disciplined client teams . . . which partially accounts for the substantial growth in international premium writings we've been experiencing. We have an international network of direct relationships.'' American Re operated ten overseas branches on five continents going into 1994, in addition to its 17 U.S. offices.

American Re was exhibiting its commitment to innovation, its fourth corporate tenet, in the early 1990s through automation, managing environmental risks, and rethinking its catastrophic risk policies. It established computer links among its international offices during the 1980s and early 1990s, for example, allowing the company to efficiently integrate global accounting and currency efforts. The company also had implemented the use of advanced risk analysis software to help it accurately predict damage from natural catastrophes. The company had taken a leading role in the management of environmental risks as well, such as pollution and indoor air quality—an increasingly important sector of the industry in the 1990s.

In addition to its four-pronged management strategy, the company continued to achieve stability through market diversification following the KKR acquisition. The company began decreasing its reliance on conventional underwriting and investment revenues in the early 1990s, instead seeking profits from related fee services. By 1993, in fact, American Re Corporation's new subsidiaries were contributing a significant portion of earnings growth. Am-Re Services, Inc., for example, was established to provide clients with various reinsurance-related

services. Likewise, Am-Re Brokers, Inc., provided client access to worldwide reinsurance resources. Similarly, the Becher + Carlson (B + C) subsidiary specialized in risk management consulting and brokerage for commercial and public entities. Finally, Am-Re Managers, Inc. provided a variety of underwriting and consulting services to noninsurance businesses.

KKR's acquisition of American Re began to pay off in 1993. Company assets grew from $5.89 billion in 1992 to more than $6.23 billion in 1993, a 5.5 percent increase. Total revenue climbed from $1.1 billion in 1992 to an impressive $1.4 billion in 1993, resulting in net 1993 earnings of $75 million. Although company growth slightly lagged behind some industry statistical averages for larger reinsurers, those figures failed to reflect American Re's stability and growth potential. For instance, the company's international division boosted its gross premiums 39 percent in 1993, to $279 million. Furthermore, American Re's debt was significantly reduced and its combined ratio improved a healthy three percentage points. Also in 1993 American Re went public, raising $413.5 million. Its stock traded on the New York Stock Exchange.

Going into the mid-1990s, American Re Corp. expected to continue to benefit most from overseas expansion and growth in fee services. The decline of competing European reinsurers, particularly Lloyd's of London, boded well for international gains. Furthermore, American Re was striving to establish itself in many fast-growth developing markets, such as Russia, China, and Eastern Europe. B + C, for example, secured a consulting contract in 1993 with one of Russia's largest companies, which was also one of the world's largest truck manufacturers. ''The new ownership will create an environment that will make it easier for us to work,'' said Paul H. Inderbitzin, executive vice-president of American Re, in the September 16, 1992 issue of *Business Central New Jersey.* ''We will be aggressive in alternative markets . . . there are no barriers for the future growth of our activities.''

In early 1995 American Re formed a joint venture with Arthur J. Gallagher & Co., a leading U.S. insurance brokerage firm. The new company, called Risk Management Partners Ltd., was based in the United Kingdom and was geared toward providing insurance and risk management services to local U.K. governmental agencies. Under terms of the agreement, American Re agreed to underwrite insurance coverage, while Arthur J. Gallagher agreed to provide risk management services through subsidiary Bassett Services, Inc.

American Re continued to enjoy success, as indicated by the company's results for the first quarter of 1996—reported net income of $49.1 million reflected an impressive 39.5 percent increase over net income during the comparable period a year earlier. In addition, net premiums written by the firm during the first quarter rose 18 percent compared with the same period in 1995.

Although American Re was a strong, profitable performer, talk of a possible sale began to circulate in the insurance industry in mid-1996. Two possible suitors included General Electric Co., and Munich Reinsurance Co. of Germany. Discussion of a sale was generated primarily following the acquisition of National Re Corp. by General Re Corp., which solidified General Re's leading position in the reinsurance market. As consolidation and competition within the reinsurance industry grew, so did speculation about acquisition candidates.

Initially, many were skeptical about the possible sale. KKR had owned American Re only since 1992, and KKR had been increasing its presence in the insurance industry. In 1995 KKR purchased Canadian General Insurance Group Ltd. and attempted to buy the property and casualty operations of Aetna Inc. In early 1996 KKR acquired the four property and casualty businesses of Talegen Holdings Inc. from Xerox Corp., paying about $2.7 billion. Selling American Re would not only lower KKR's earnings, but it would also lessen its authority in the insurance industry.

Skeptics turned out to be wrong, and in August of 1996 KKR announced that it was indeed open to offers for American Re, of which KKR owned 64.1 percent. Although Munich Re, the world's largest reinsurance company, contended early on that it was not interested in buying American Re, the company soon announced it would purchase the reinsurer for about $3.3 billion, or $65 a share. KKR, which paid $1.4 billion for American Re in 1992, stood to make a profit of $1.7 billion. The $3.3 billion was significantly more than American Re's market value, which hovered around $2.5 billion at the time of the announcement. KKR general partner Saul Fox explained the benefits of the sale to reporter Patricia Vowinkel, as published in the *Chicago Sun-Times,* and said, "Given the rapid consolidation of the international insurance community, this transaction will allow American Re to continue as an industry leader, enhancing its ability to provide clients with both service and capacity. ... It is the right move at the right time for both companies, creating a larger, more formidable global competitor." Munich Re greatly expanded its North American operations with the purchase. The company's North American market share of about 7.7 percent, which made it the seventh largest reinsurer in the United States, was significantly enhanced by American Re's share, which was about ten percent. American Re became a wholly owned subsidiary of Munich Re.

In 1997 Edward Noonan was named president and CEO of American Re, and Munich Re's American operations were merged with American Re's businesses. Restructuring commenced, and in June of 1998 the subsidiaries Becher + Carlson Companies, Am-Re Brokers, Inc., and ARB International Ltd., along with Munich Re's International Insurance consultants, were combined into Am-Re Global Services. Just a month later American Re established American Re Capital Markets, Inc., which focused on providing solutions to clients in financial markets. The business planned to start out concentrating on the weather derivatives market. In November American Re renamed its Am-Re Managers, Inc. division Munich-American RiskPartners to reflect its emphasis on globalization.

American Re continued its strategy to strengthen operations in 1999, and the firm's medical cost management program, known as American RePreferred, its alternative risk business, and its Am-Re Global Services division, among others, showed progress. In the summer American Re agreed to buy holding company American Insurance Service Inc., which owned United National Group of Companies, Inc., United National Insurance Co., Diamond State Insurance Co., and Hallmark Insurance Co.

Financial performance in 1999 was not as strong as American Re had hoped, with earnings negatively affected by catastrophic events and price competition within the industry. Although the value of gross premiums written rose from $3.1 billion in 1998 to about $3.5 billion in 1999, net income fell, from $226 million to a net loss of $101 million in 1999. Still, American Re voiced its confidence in future success. CEO Noonan wrote in the company's 1999 annual review, "As part of the Munich Re Group, we make our living taking risk, and we believe there is a good future for those who do so prudently. Difficult times remind us of the great advantage in having a long-term approach to our partners." American Re, with a history of stability stemming from a conservative investment and management approach, stood ready for the unpredictable future with confidence.

Principal Subsidiaries

Munich-American Risk Partners; Am-Re Global Services, Inc.

Principal Competitors

General Re Corp.; Reinsurance Group of America. Incorporated; General Cologne Re.

Further Reading

"Am Re Posts Improved 1993 Results," *National Underwriter,* February 14, 1994.

"American Re Acknowledges Seeking Suitors," *Best's Insurance News,* August 6, 1996.

Darian, Ryan, "100 Largest Groups See Slowdown in Growth," *Best's Review Property/Casualty,* January 1994.

Geet, Carolyn T., "Insurance," *Forbes,* January 3, 1994.

Greenwald, Judy, "Reinsurer Results," *Business Insurance,* April 1, 1996, p. 2.

Howard, Lisa S., "U.S. Cat Losses Not Expected, Says Am Re CEO," *National Underwriter Property/Casualty,* October 18, 1993.

Jennings, John, "Am Re, Independent Again, Shifts Market Focus," *National Underwriter,* July 5, 1993.

——, "Re Quarter Results Continue to Show Strength," *National Underwriter,* May 6, 1996, p. 13.

"Paul Inderbitzin on How That Big American Re and KKR Deal Is Coming Along," *Business for Central New Jersey,* September 16, 1992.

Peltz, Michael, "KKR Market-Times Its Move into Reinsurance," *Institutional Investor,* January 1993.

"Reinsurer Finds New Technologies," *Environmental Manager,* April 1993.

Scism, Leslie, and Steven Lipin, "KKR Holds Talks on American Re Sale—Buyout Firm Is Approached by Units of Munich Re, GE About Possible Deal," *Wall Street Journal,* July 31, 1996.

Scism, Leslie, Steven Lipin, and Greg Steinmetz, "Munich Reinsurance To Buy American Re—KKR Is Expected To See a Profit of $1.7 Billion from $3.3 Billion Deal," *Wall Street Journal,* August 15, 1996, p. A3.

Snyder, John H., "Reinsurance—1992," *Best's Review Property/Casualty,* November 1993.

Taber, George, "KKR Takes Over American Re in a $1.4 Billion Deal," *Business for Central New Jersey,* June 24, 1992.

Vowinkel, Patricia, "Munich Firm To Buy American Re," *Chicago Sun-Times,* August 14, 1996, p. 4.

—Dave Mote
—updated by Mariko Fujinaka

Applebee's International, Inc.

4551 West 107th Street, Suite 100
Overland Park, Kansas 66207
U.S.A.
Telephone: (913) 967-4000
Fax: (913) 341-1694
Web site: http://www.applebees.com

Public Company
Incorporated: 1983
Employees: 18,150
Sales: $669.58 million (1999)
Stock Exchanges: NASDAQ
Ticker Symbol: APPB
NAIC: 72211 Full Service Restaurants; 72241 Drinking
    Places (Alcoholic Beverages); 53311 Lessors of
    Nonfinancial Intangible Assets (Except Copyrighted
    Works)

Applebee's International, Inc. is the leader in the casual dining segment of the United States restaurant marketplace. The company franchises and operates more than 1,100 restaurants under the Applebee's Neighborhood Grill & Bar name, about a quarter of which it owns. The eateries offer moderately priced, high-quality food and drink for all ages in a friendly, informal atmosphere. Applebee's is continuing to expand, with 1,800 outlets the company's stated goal. A smaller restaurant format has been designed for areas with populations under 25,000, to facilitate penetration of previously untapped markets.

Origins

Restaurateur William Palmer and his wife opened the first Applebee's restaurant—named T.J. Applebee's—in Atlanta in November 1980. Offering a unique menu and comfortable atmosphere, the Atlanta eatery was a success. Palmer's goal with Applebee's was to create a neighborhood-like pub and restaurant where patrons could order high-quality food at a relatively low price. Specifically, he hoped to provide an alternative for all ages to fast-food restaurants, steakhouse franchises, and similar chains, which Palmer believed were offering relatively impersonal service and mediocre fare. The concept, while simple, was so successful that T.J. Applebee's began to get the attention of larger food companies. To that end, Creative Food 'N Fun Co. purchased the concept from Palmer in 1983; Creative Food 'N Fun Co. was a subsidiary of the giant holding company W.R. Grace & Co.

W.R. Grace hoped to use its deep pockets to parlay the T.J. Applebee's concept into a large chain of franchised restaurants. Grace, through its wholly owned Creative Food 'N Fun Co. subsidiary, set up a separate Applebee's division in Kansas City to operate the newly incorporated Applebee's. Palmer remained as president of Applebee's. Between 1983 and 1985 Palmer added new Applebee's outlets in the Atlanta area. In addition, Applebee's began franchising the concept to other regional restaurant developers.

Among Applebee's first regional franchisees was Burton ''Skip'' Sack, who purchased the New England franchise rights to Applebee's restaurants in 1984. His experience was representative of other Applebee's franchisees during the late 1980s and early 1990s. Sack had started out as a bus boy at Howard Johnson's, where, over a 22-year-period, he progressed to senior vice-president of the company. He left ''HoJo'' in 1983 and bought the Red Coach Grill chain of eateries. When his first Applebee's restaurant was an instant success, he sold off his Red Coach restaurants and concentrated on developing more Applebee's outlets. During the late 1980s Sack developed a small network of Applebee's outlets in various parts of New England. ''We waited a year and a half to see if it was just a fluke,'' Sack said in the May 3, 1993 *Union Leader,* adding that ''In 1988, we opened our second restaurant in Franklin, Massachusetts, and it did even better.'' By 1993 Sack was operating about 15 outlets that were generating earnings of nearly $18 million annually, and he was planning to open several more stores.

Sack and other Applebee's franchisees generally prospered during the late 1980s and early 1990s. Perhaps the most successful franchisee, however, was Tom E. DuPree, Jr. DuPree opened his first Applebee's restaurant in 1986 and rapidly expanded his chain to become the leading franchisee in the system. "We felt it [the Applebee's concept] hit all the demographic shifts dead center," DuPree explained in the July 5, 1994 *Atlanta Constitution*. "People are tired of plastic drinks and cardboard food," he noted. Dubbed "Apple South," the Atlanta-based company that DuPree created through which to operate his restaurants generated huge sales gains throughout the late 1980s and early 1990s. Indeed, between 1986 and 1991, DuPree opened 52 new outlets. Incredibly, he doubled that number during the next two years by expanding its chain to more than 100 stores. Furthermore, average per-store sales steadily increased.

Sale to Gustin and Hamra

Applebee's major growth spurt began in 1988, after W.R. Grace sold the company. Grace had succeeded in bringing new franchisees into the system but had only achieved moderate growth and profitability. Even by 1986, total revenues from franchise fees and other sources were less than $5 million. In addition, despite the success of individual stores, Applebee's lost money each year between 1985 and 1988, with the exception of a small surplus in 1986. Recognizing that Applebee's had much greater potential were Abe J. Gustin, Jr., and John Hamra. Hamra was serving as chairman of Applebee's board at the time. In 1988 Gustin and Hamra decided to buy the company from W.R. Grace and try their hand at owning and managing the organization. The Applebee's organization was comprised of 54 units at the time, most of which were franchises. That number would surge during the next few years.

Hamra and Gustin were well suited to run Applebee's. Hamra was already acting as chairman, so he had the connections and expertise to pull off the buyout. Gustin, though, would be the driving force behind Applebee's stellar gains during the next five years. He had started his career as a teenager, toiling in his brother's Birmingham, Alabama, barbecue hut. After that, he served a 15-year stint with Schlitz Brewing Co., where he started out driving a beer truck and worked his way up through the marketing side of the company. In a 1993 article in the *Nation's Restaurant News,* Gustin discussed the impact of his mentor at Schlitz, Tom Rupus: "Tom Rupus, vice president of sales when I was at Schlitz, had a huge impact on the direction of my career. . . . He told me, 'I don't care what you're doing; you're gonna look like a businessman.' So I used to ride in the beer trucks and unload beer in a suit and tie."

Gustin was hired away from Schlitz by ABA Distributors, a wholesale beer distributor in Kansas City, where he served as chairman, president, and director. From there, he moved into foodservice as chairman of Juneau Holding Co., a Kansas City-based owner and operator of 18 Taco Bell Restaurants. Gustin wanted to expand his Taco Bell chain but was told that the company was not issuing any more territory rights. At that point he began considering the up-and-coming Applebee's. Gustin

flew to Atlanta, checked out the Applebee's concept, liked what he saw, and worked out a deal to become the organization's third franchisee. Gustin also took the advice of then-chairman John Hamra, and began selling off his Taco Bell holdings. He opened his first Applebee's in 1986. The success of that store prompted him to open six more outlets during the next several months. Then, in January 1988, he teamed up with Hamra to buy Applebee's from W.R. Grace.

Under new ownership, revenues at Applebee's soared 500 percent to more than $24.21 million during 1988. Likewise, net losses for the year plunged from $877 million in 1987 to $47 million in 1988. The increase was largely the result of new restaurants; the Applebee's chain grew to 88 units by the end of 1988 and then to 110 stores by mid-1990. To sustain that growth, Gustin and Hamra had taken Applebee's public early in 1990. Cash from the initial public offering was used to reduce some of the $10 million in debt incurred while acquiring the Applebee's chain from Grace. After the offering, Gustin announced that Applebee's would soon be opening an additional 70 franchise units, news which boosted Applebee's stock price. Unfortunately, the investment capital needed to open the outlets failed to materialize and only 39 of the restaurants were opened.

Expanding in the 1990s

Scrambling in 1990 to raise capital in a recessionary economy, Gustin was finally able to get a loan guarantee from Bell Atlantic, and the cash flow resumed. He recruited new franchisees to add to the company's existing base of about 50, and the Applebee's chain began to sprawl across the United States. In 1990, in fact, Applebee's was selected by *Barron's* as a small company with a five-year high-growth potential because of its management strategy and vision. Adding credence to that assessment was the fact that revenues, which were comprised primarily of franchise-related fees, surged to $38.2 million in 1989, $45.13 million in 1990, and then to $56.5 million in 1991. More importantly, net income rose to $5 million in 1992 from $1.8 million in 1990. Going into 1993, Applebee's was operating about 200 outlets, roughly 85 percent of which were franchised and 15 percent of which were owned by Applebee's International.

The reasons for Applebee's success were several. The foundation of the company's strategy was its neighborhood theme, which influenced all operating decisions in the organization. The Applebee's menu depicted a doormat that read "Welcome to the Neighborhood," on the cover, and the restaurants were designed to project a comfortable, neighborly environment. Franchisees were encouraged to get involved with local charities and neighborhood events, and to personalize their restaurants in some way to keep them from looking like a chain restaurant that could be found in any other city in the nation. The benefit of the neighborhood strategy was that it cultivated repeat business from the local population. In fact, the Applebee's outlets targeted the crowd that would prefer to frequent a local mom-and-pop restaurant than the typical impersonal chain.

As part of the effort to personalize the restaurants, Gustin empowered individual franchisees and restaurant managers to make decisions about how their restaurants operated and even

Key Dates:

1980: T.J. Applebee's Edibles and Elixirs, the brainchild of Bill and T.J. Palmer, opens in Atlanta.
1983: W.R. Grace & Co. purchases the restaurant concept from the Palmers.
1988: Abe Gustin and John Hamra buy Applebee's from Grace.
1989: Applebee's goes public.
1994: 500th Applebee's Neighborhood Grill & Bar opens.
1995: Applebee's buys Rio Bravo Cantina restaurant chain.
1997: Franchisee Apple South announces plans to sell its Applebee's holdings.
1998: Abe Gustin leaves day-to-day management; 1,000th restaurant opens.
1999: Rio Bravo operations are sold to Chevys, Inc.

what type of food they served. Two of the core required menu items were barbecued riblets cut from the tip of the tenderloin, and fajitas. The restaurants also typically offered chicken wings, burgers, lasagna, soup and salad, sirloin steak, apple honey cobbler, and cheesecake. In addition, each restaurant featured a full bar, where Applebee's special apple margaritas were served. Aside from those staples, franchisees were allowed to experiment with their menus and emphasize foods popular in their particular market. Furthermore, Applebee's wait staff was highly trained to respond to customer's specific needs, and staffers were taught a special ten-step serving process. Importantly, the restaurants were set up to ensure that most people were served their meal within 15 minutes of ordering.

Applebee's growth rate accelerated in 1993 and 1994. By exploiting the company's proven management and operating formula, and by attracting new investment capital, Gustin was able to grow the chain at an average pace of more than 100 restaurants annually. During this time, Hamra retired, and Gustin became chairman, chief executive, and president. "My original vision was that there could be as many as 500 Applebee's," Gustin said in the September 20, 1993 *Nation's Restaurant News.* "Now we're targeting 1,200 to 1,500," he added. To help him expand the company, Gustin hired such seasoned executives as Ken Hill, chief operating officer, and George Shadid, chief financial officer. They and other team members rallied going into the mid-1990s to expand the Applebee's chain of eateries to more than 500 going into 1995.

As the number of franchised and company-owned stores rose, so did Applebee's' sales and profits. Indeed, revenues more than doubled in 1993 to $117 million before lurching to $208 million in 1994. For the same years, net income vaulted to $9.5 million before nearly hitting $17 million during 1994. Applebee's continued to expand at a speedy clip in 1995, and by the middle of the year was boasting about 575 outlets in 43 states, one Canadian province, and the island of Curacao. Although the size of the organization had changed, the goals of the individual restaurants had not; "It helps for people to know they can bring the kids, have a drink if they like, and be served their food within 15 minutes of ordering," Gustin said in the July

1995 *Ingram's.* "People also want to walk out without feeling they've left their wallets behind them," he observed.

The year 1995 also saw the acquisition of the 14-store Rio Bravo Cantina Mexican food chain when Applebee's acquired its parent, Innovative Restaurant Concepts of Marietta, Georgia. Wall Street applauded the move, believing Rio Bravo to be a complement to the larger chain, and a concept which had great potential for growth. Rio Bravo offered Mexican food much as Applebee's did American, utilizing a more sophisticated menu than fast-food restaurants and serving beer and wine. The company acquired all of the locations, and it began expansion slowly, deciding to fine-tune the concept before licensing additional outlets. Several franchisees, including Bill Palmer, had been behind the acquisition, and most wholeheartedly supported the move. However, Apple South took an antagonistic tack and bought its own Tex-Mex chain, Don Pablo's. In addition to purchasing Rio Bravo, Applebee's at this time was also developing a new, smaller store prototype for less populous markets.

Apple South Sells Out

A bombshell was dropped on the company at the end of 1997 when Apple South, now the owner of 274 units, decided to sell all of its Applebee's restaurants. In addition to the differences over Rio Bravo, there had been other disagreements between the two partners over the years. The latest flare-up concerned Apple South's Hops Restaurant Bar & Brewery concept, which Applebee's thought too closely resembled its own. Apple South CEO Tom DuPree made the decision to develop the restaurant chains he owned outright rather than pay franchise fees to Applebee's, later making the divorce complete by changing his company's name to Avado Brands, Inc. The restaurants were sold off over the next year and a half to a total of 14 different buyers, with the parent company taking more than ten percent.

The summer of 1998 saw Applebee's open its 1,000th unit. In September the company appointed former Taco Bell franchise and license vice-president Julia Stewart to run the company's restaurant division. Stewart immediately took off on a two-month trip to meet all 58 of the company's franchisees, and announced plans to focus on improving employee morale and brand identity. At the end of the year Abe Gustin stepped down from hands-on management, retaining only the role of board chairman.

In the spring of 1999, Applebee's sold its Rio Bravo Cantina chain—acknowledging that it was not yielding the expected returns—to Chevys, Inc. for $58 million. The company had paid $68 million for the operation in 1995, and had ultimately expanded it to 66 locations. However, the sale did not dampen the mood much at Applebee's, which was now seeing steadily increasing same-store sales.

The company was also ramping up its national advertising, and hired a new ad agency in the summer. The first campaign from Foote, Cone & Belding premiered the next January and featured the slogan, "As American as Applebee's." The ads targeted 21- to 49-year-olds, a narrower segment of the marketplace than before. The budget for network television ads had zoomed from $6 million in 1998 to $16 million in 1999, and was slated to hit $37 million during 2000.

On the heels of its new momentum, Applebee's increased its dividends to shareholders and also implemented a $100 million stock repurchase plan. In the spring of 2000, Abe Gustin stepped down as board chairman, though he continued to own a number of Applebee's franchises. The company also opened its first restaurant in Manhattan, strategically located on 42nd Street near Times Square. Sales totals announced for fiscal 1999 showed an increase of 14 percent, with system-wide revenues a record $2.35 billion.

The company's renewed focus on its core strengths was paying off, and it was continuing to grow steadily. Applebee's had opened more than 100 restaurants annually for seven years running, and anticipated this number to hold steady for the near future. It had already recovered from both the loss of Apple South and the Rio Bravo misfire, proof positive that the company's management was sound and that the American public was well satisfied with what it had to offer.

Principal Subsidiaries

A.I.I. Euro Services (Holland) B.V. (Netherlands); AII Services - Europe, Limited; AII Services, Inc.; Applebee's Neighborhood Grill & Bar of Georgia, Inc.; Applebee's Northeast, Inc.; Applebee's of Michigan, Inc.; Applebee's of Minnesota, Inc.; Applebee's of Nevada, Inc.; Applebee's of New Mexico, Inc.; Applebee's of New York, Inc.; Applebee's of Pennsylvania, Inc.; Applebee's of Texas, Inc.; Applebee's of Virginia, Inc.; Gourmet Systems, Inc.; Gourmet Systems of Arizona, Inc.; Gourmet Systems of California, Inc.; Gourmet Systems of Georgia, Inc.; Gourmet Systems of Kansas, Inc.; Gourmet Systems of Minnesota, Inc.; Gourmet Systems of Nevada, Inc.; Gourmet Systems of Tennessee, Inc.; Rio Bravo International, Inc.

Principal Competitors

Advantica Restaurant Group, Inc.; Brinker International, Inc.; Carlson Restaurants Worldwide, Inc.; CBRL Group, Inc.; Darden Restaurants, Inc.; Lone Star Steakhouse & Saloon, Inc.; Metromedia Company; Outback Steakhouse, Inc.; Ruby Tuesday, Inc.

Further Reading

"Applebee's – Apple South Split Marks Shift in Corporate Parent-Child Relationship," *Nation's Restaurant News*, January 19, 1998, p. 27.

Battaglia, Andy, and Papiernik, Richard L., "Applebee's Core Brand Polishes Off Competition," *Nation's Restaurant News*, March 20, 2000, p. 1.

Carlino, Bill, "Applebee's Takes Root, Bears Fruit in Neighborhoods Across America," *Nation's Restaurant News*, August 5, 1996, p. 50.

Cauley, Lauree, "Applebee's Capitalizing on Pittsburgh's Neighborhoods," *Pittsburgh Business Times & Journal*, June 11, 1990, Sec. 2, p. 15.

Ezell, Hank, "Apple South a Casual Success," *Atlanta Constitution*, July 5, 1994, p. D1.

Kaberlin, Brian, "New Special on Applebee's Table: Buy Big Franchisee," *Kansas City Business Journal*, November 15, 1991, p. 1.

Kaberlin, Brian, and Adam Feuerstein, "Palmer May Rejoin Applebee's International," *Atlanta Business Chronicle*, December 2, 1991, p. 3A.

Keegan, Peter O., "Abe J. Gustin Jr.: 'Risk-Taking' Type of Guy," *Nation's Restaurant News*, September 20, 1993, p. 122.

Mann, Jennifer, "Long Search for the Right President," *Kansas City Star*, December 15, 1998, p. D1.

Papiernik, Richard L., "Applebee's Back on Main Track with Focus on Core Concept," *Nation's Restaurant News*, March 8, 1999.

Plyler, Tami, "Applebee's Recipe for Expansion," *Union Leader*, May 3, 1993.

Romeo, Peter, "What's The Rush? Applebee's Powerful Franchise System Is Eager to Get Its Hands on Rio Bravo, but Headquarters Is Taking It Slow and Steady," *Restaurant Business*, October 10, 1995, p. 36.

Saponar, R. C., "Applebee's to Go Public Wednesday," *Nashville Business Journal*, September 18, 1989, p. 3.

Smith, Margaret, "Corporate Report 100: Serving Success," *Ingram's*, July 1995, p. 45.

Walkup, Carolyn, "Applebee's Nabs Lucrative Slice of Small-Town American Pie," *Nation's Restaurant News*, October 30, 1989, p. 3.

Wishna, Victor, "Ripe for Success," *Restaurant Business*, August 1, 1999, p. 29.

—Dave Mote
—updated by Frank Uhle

Arnold & Porter

Thurman Arnold Building
555 12th Street N.W.
Washington, D.C. 20004-1202
U.S.A.
Telephone: (202) 942-5000
Fax: (202) 942-5999
Web site: http://www.arnoldporter.com

Partnership
Founded: 1946 as Arnold & Fortas
Employees: 1,200
Sales: $218.5 million (1998)
NAIC: 54111 Offices of Lawyers

Arnold & Porter is one of the largest law firms in the United States and in the world. It has a long history of representing corporations in all aspects of modern business law, from taxation and financing to antitrust and mergers and acquisitions. Since the 1950s it has represented Philip Morris Inc. The firm in the past decade has helped its clients organize more than 100 joint ventures in more than 20 nations. Sometimes legislative solutions are necessary, so Arnold & Porter lobbies Congress, state governments, and overseas governments to write new or improved laws. Since the firm began in 1946, it has had a well-earned reputation for helping those with limited resources gain access to legal counsel. Much of that reputation derives from its pro bono defense of those accused of being communists during the McCarthy era and from representing poor convict Clarence Earl Gideon in a landmark 1963 U.S. Supreme Court case that established the right of all to legal counsel. Arnold & Porter is well known for its innovative child care programs and other initiatives that make it easier for working mothers to practice in a large law firm.

Origins of the Law Firm

Thurman Arnold, the founder of Arnold & Porter, was born in Laramie, Wyoming in 1891. The son of a lawyer, Arnold graduated from Harvard Law School in 1914, practiced law until 1917, and then served in the military during World War I.

After the war, he returned to practice law in Laramie. In 1920 he began his government service by being elected as a Democrat to the Wyoming House of Representatives. In 1927 he became the dean of the West Virginia University Law School, and in 1930 he joined the Yale Law School faculty.

In the 1930s Arnold served in the federal Agricultural Adjustment Administration, as an advisor to the U.S. governor general of the Philippines, and as a trial examiner for the newly created Securities and Exchange Commission. From 1938 to 1943 he became well known for his vigorous enforcement of antitrust laws as the head of the U.S. Justice Department's Antitrust Division. Arnold served as a judge in the U.S. Court of Appeals for the District of Columbia from 1943 to 1945.

Arnold had become a well-known critic of social and legal orthodoxy in the 1930s and 1940s. He authored six books, including his best-selling *The Folklore of Capitalism* in 1937. He advocated moral relativism, a philosophy that rejected absolute and universal moral absolutes, and legal realism, a form of judicial activism to meet the needs of society.

Thus in 1945 Arnold was already quite prominent when he decided to return to private law practice. His first partner stayed just a short time. Then in January 1946 Arnold persuaded Abe Fortas to join him to form Arnold & Fortas. Fortas taught at the Yale Law School after he graduated from there. During the Roosevelt presidency, Fortas served as the under secretary in the Department of the Interior led by Secretary Harold Ickes.

In 1947 Paul Porter joined the firm, which was renamed Arnold, Fortas & Porter. Laura Kalman, in her biography of Abe Fortas, argued that the three name partners had little in common. But Norman Diamond, who joined the firm shortly after it was formed, said in his history of the firm that Kalman's conclusion "makes no sense to me . . . [Fortas's] knowledge of Arnold traced to their concurrent service in three different environments. They were colleagues on the Yale Law School faculty. They worked on at least one common project at the Agricultural Adjustment Administration. Both were involved with . . . the Securities and Exchange Commission." Porter had also served at the AAA and was a well-known New Dealer with a common affinity for liberal principles.

The early partnership participated in some major cases after World War II. From 1947 to 1958, it defended without compensation Americans accused of communist loyalties or sympathies during the Second Red Scare or McCarthyism. The firm's defense of State Department employees accused of disloyalty was covered in front-page articles in the *New York Herald Tribune* and later in a Pulitzer Prize-winning book by Bert Andrews. From 1950 to 1958 the law firm aided Owen Lattimore in his fight for civil rights during the excesses of McCarthyism. In the 1955 *Peters v. Hobby* case, the U.S. Supreme Court ruled for Peters, the firm's client, on a technicality and also wrote the only Supreme Court opinion on the loyalty program of the Truman and Eisenhower administrations.

By 1951 the partnership had added Pan American Airways, Lever Brothers, Western Union, Otis Elevator, the American Broadcasting Company, and Sun Oil to its client list. Federated Department Stores hired the firm, and Abe Fortas became a Federated director. Other new clients in the firm's early years included the National Retail Merchants Association, Braniff International, Cyrus Eaton, Investors Diversified Services, Philip Morris, and Unilever.

The firm grew to meet the needs of its growing clientele, from three partners and four associates in 1947 to nine partners and six associates ten years later. In 1960 the entire Washington, D.C. office of the Paul, Weiss, Rifkind, Wharton, and Garrison law firm left to join Arnold, Fortas & Porter. That office previously had done taxation work for Arnold, Fortas & Porter's clients, and in 1960 it became the new tax department—the first time Arnold, Fortas & Porter created separate practice areas. As new laws and regulations proliferated, legal specialization increased at other large law firms as well.

The partnership defended *Playboy* magazine soon after it was started by Hugh Hefner in 1955. Judge Arnold argued that obscenity laws were morality based, not the result of rational thinking. The state of Vermont soon dropped its prosecution without a trial. In 1958 the law firm helped the new publication keep its permit for low-cost second-class mail, a crucial development in *Playboy*'s early financial survival.

In 1963 the U.S. Supreme Court asked Abe Fortas to represent a poor convicted criminal named Clarence Gideon, who had been denied legal counsel by the Florida state court that convicted him. After the Florida Supreme Court upheld his conviction, Gideon himself wrote to the U.S. Supreme Court to appeal his case. Fortas gained a unanimous decision from the court that all persons accused of serious crimes had a constitutional right to legal counsel that would be provided at no cost if they could not afford to hire their own lawyer.

In the late 1940s, Abe Fortas became well acquainted with Lyndon B. Johnson (LBJ), the Texas Democrat, and Fortas in the 1960s was one of President Johnson's closest advisors. For example, Abe's law partner Norman Diamond wrote, "It's common knowledge that Abe was responsible for LBJ's establishment of the National Council on the Arts in 1965 and the selection of Roger Stevens, Abe's friend and client as its head." Although still a law partner, Fortas spent most of his time advising President Johnson on many matters.

Such personal ties to prominent figures like LBJ helped the law firm attract clients. In 1965 LBJ appointed Fortas to the U.S. Supreme Court, a position Fortas never sought and reluctantly accepted. That took Fortas to the top in terms of professional status, but soon it led to his downfall. On May 14, 1969 Fortas resigned from the court because of a scandal in which he agreed to take money from a private client while still sitting on the court. Thurman Arnold and Paul Porter wanted him to return to the law firm, but the younger partners objected. They felt that the firm would be hurt, especially since the American Bar Association had criticized Fortas's behavior that led to his resignation.

With Fortas gone, the partnership soon lost its other two founders. Thurman Arnold died on November 7, 1969 and Porter a few years later. A new generation of leaders accepted the challenge to move forward in the middle of a major transformation in how large law firms operated.

Practice in the Late 20th Century

The late 1970s marked a watershed in the history of America's large law firms. At that time the U.S. Supreme Court said professional associations violated the right to free speech by restricting professional advertising. Soon more professionals began advertising just like other businessmen.

In addition, two new magazines revolutionized legal journalism. The *National Law Journal* and the *American Lawyer* began publishing articles and ratings of the top law firms based on their finances and management. This new information allowed experienced attorneys to seek better offers in rival law firms. Thus lateral hiring increased, as did the demand for new law school graduates, whose beginning salaries gradually increased.

The bottom line was that most large law firms grew by leaps and bounds and changed their traditional ways of operating. By the mid-1980s, said Norman Diamond, Arnold & Porter "had grown into a bureaucracy with some 300 lawyers plus a support staff of close to 1,000 men and women." The company had a formal governing system, a 700-page handbook for partners, and specialists had replaced generalists.

In 1985 the University of California at Irvine sold a group of 100 homes worth $300 million to faculty members. Through its real estate and financial-consulting subsidiaries, Arnold & Porter built and developed this complex. The firm's Myron P. Curzan argued in the November 18, 1985 *Wall Street Journal* that Arnold & Porter's diversification into such new ventures resulted from ''natural evolution'' as a way to provide many services to clients. Other law firms participated in investment banking, advertising, and consulting.

Arnold & Porter in 1987 responded to the increasing number of attorneys who often struggled to balance career and family demands by starting a child care center. Open at nights and on weekends, the center was used just when parents had to work overtime. In 1997 the firm estimated that its child care center allowed an extra $800,000 in annual billable hours. By that time, it claimed the distinction of operating ''the first full-time, on-site child care facility run by a law firm,'' according to a press release dated September 15, 1997. In 1997 *Working Mother* magazine honored Arnold & Porter for the second year in a row as one of the ''100 Best Companies for Working Mothers,'' the only law firm on the list.

In the 1990s Arnold & Porter continued to represent its long-term client Philip Morris Company. Under attack from both the federal government and many state governments, by 1997 the tobacco industry was spending about $700 million annually for defense lawyers to protect it in court.

Arnold & Porter's long history of defending Philip Morris against liability claims helped it gain other clients in similar cases. For example, Wyeth-Ayerst hired the firm to defend itself against class-action lawsuits filed in behalf of alleged victims who had used two popular diet drugs, Redux and fenfluramine, marketed by Wyeth-Ayerst.

Arnold & Porter helped transform former government agencies into private businesses as part of a major worldwide trend of the 1980s and 1990s. For example, in 1996 the law firm helped create U.S. Investigations Services Inc. (USIS), incorporated in Delaware, which replaced the Office of Federal Investigations in the U.S. Office of Personnel Management. This first privatization of a federal agency resulted in USIS becoming North America's largest private investigations firm, in part because it had no significant competitors in serving the federal government.

In 1997 Arnold & Porter built on its 1963 Gideon case by gaining a favorable settlement in the case of *Farmer v. Reno* [Janet Reno, U.S. Attorney General]. The firm represented Dee Farmer, a prison inmate and paralegal. In the end, the federal government issued new prison regulations that allowed so-called ''jailhouse lawyers'' to have access to legal materials in prison law libraries or other areas under the warden's authority. Such cases were ways to make sure that all Americans had access to the legal system, thus strengthening respect for the rule of law in the United States.

In 1997 the Brazilian government honored two Arnold & Porter attorneys for their service to Brazil. The award came after the law firm had served Brazil in financial matters for more than ten years.

Based on Arnold & Porter's 1997 gross revenues of $192 million, the *American Lawyer* in July/August 1998 ranked it as the United States' 41st largest law firm. At that point it had 368 lawyers. The firm's 1997 revenues also earned it a ranking as the world's 49th largest law firm, according to the *American Lawyer* in November 1998.

The following year the firm slipped to 45th largest in America, based on its $218.5 million 1998 gross revenue. The *American Lawyer* in July 1999 also reported that Arnold & Porter had 404 lawyers and that it ranked as the fifth best law firm for its pro bono work.

At the dawn of the new millennium, Arnold & Porter faced competition from several larger law firms. Effective January 2000, the world's largest law firm was London's Clifford Chance, which employed almost 3,000 lawyers after merging with firms in New York City and Germany. Arnold & Porter also faced a rapidly changing economy, with new forms of currency such as the ''euro'' along with the Internet-based electronic economy.

Principal Competitors

Akin, Gump, Strauss, Hauer & Feld LLP; King & Spalding; Skadden, Arps, Slate, Meagher & Flom; Covington and Burling.

Further Reading

Andrews, Bert, *Washington Witch Hunt,* New York: Random House, 1948.

Arnold, Thurman, *Fair Fights and Foul: A Dissenting Lawyer's Life,* New York: Harcourt, Brace & World, 1965.

Carrington, Tim, ''Just When Is a Bank Not a Bank?,'' *Wall Street Journal* (Eastern edition), January 30, 1984, p. 1.

Cottle, Michelle, ''Working 5 to 9,'' *Washington Monthly,* January/February 1997, pp. 40–42.

Diamond, Norman, *A Practice Almost Perfect: The Early Days at Arnold, Fortas & Porter,* Lanham, Md.: University Press of America, 1997.

Kalman, Laura, *Abe Fortas: A Biography,* New Haven, Conn.: Yale University Press, 1990.

Kearny, Edward N., *Thurman Arnold, Social Critic: The Satirical Challenge to Orthodoxy,* Albuquerque: University of New Mexico Press, 1970.

''Live Long and Prosper,'' *Government Executive,* April 1997, pp. 50–53.

Murphy, Bruce Allen, *Fortas: The Rise and Ruin of a Supreme Court Justice,* New York: William Morrow and Company, 1988.

Siconolfi, Michael, ''Law Firms Aren't Simply for Law as Attempts To Diversify Begin,'' *Wall Street Journal* (Eastern edition), November 18, 1985, p. 1.

Stone, Peter H., ''No Tears for Tobacco Lawyers,'' *National Journal,* July 19, 1997, p. 1,465.

Torry, Saundra, ''Lawsuit Binge Follows Diet-Drug Study; Pharmaceuticals: Link to Heart Damage Turns Drugs' Makers, Marketers into Defendants,'' *Los Angeles Times,* October 28, 1997, p. 13.

—David M. Walden

Arthur D. Little, Inc.

25 Acorn Park
Cambridge, Massachusetts 02140-2390
U.S.A.
Telephone: (617) 498-5000
Toll Free: (800) 677-3000
Fax: (617) 498-7200
Web site: http://www.arthurdlittle.com

Private Company
Incorporated: 1909
Employees: 3,500
Sales: $629 million (1999)
NAIC: 54169 Other Scientific and Technical Consulting
   Services; 541611 Administrative Management and
   General Management Consulting Services; 54162
   Environmental Consulting Services; 541618 Other
   Management Consulting Services; 514199 All Other
   Information Services

Arthur D. Little, Inc., based in Cambridge, Massachusetts, is one of the oldest consulting firms in the world. The company specializes in science and technology, offering product development, management consulting, and scientific research services, to corporations and governments worldwide. Arthur D. Little also provides environmental, health, and safety consulting, and its Arthur D. Little Enterprises, Inc., subsidiary commercializes products developed within the company. The firm also oversees a graduate school of management designed to train business executives. Arthur D. Little's international operations grew significantly in the 1990s, and the company has offices and laboratories in more than 30 countries.

Innovative Beginnings: Late 1800s–1940s

Chemists Arthur D. Little and Roger Griffin established Griffin & Little, Chemical Engineers, in Boston in 1886. The venture was a bit of a risk, as chemists and chemistry were viewed rather negatively, but the pair believed there was a market for their consulting services. Hoping to enhance prod-

ucts and processes, Griffin & Little initially became known for its knowledge in papermaking. The firm was able to elevate papermaking from an art to a practical technology, and in 1893 it published *The Chemistry of Papermaking,* a reference work. That same year, however, Griffin was killed in a laboratory accident.

Little kept the business going, and in 1900 the firm patented the first acetate fiber, also known as "artificial silk." The company also worked with cellulose, which eventually led to the creation of nonflammable motion picture film. Also in 1900 Little found a new business partner, William Walker, The firm changed its name to Little & Walker, but Walker remained with the company only five years, leaving to join the faculty at the Massachusetts Institute of Technology (MIT). In 1909 the firm incorporated as Arthur D. Little, Inc. (ADL).

With a goal of offering technological applications to help industry growth, ADL and its corps of leading scientists and researchers worked with a number of companies and organizations. In 1911, for instance, ADL worked with General Motors to set up the automobile company's first research and development laboratory. The firm's other notable clients in the early 1900s included Great Southern Lumber, for which ADL studied the profitability of processing the lumber company's waste products, and Canadian Pacific Railway.

Accomplishments during the 1920s and 1930s were plentiful and noteworthy. In 1921 the firm succeeded in using a bucket of sows' ears to make a silk purse. This revolutionary achievement later became part of the Smithsonian Institute's collection. ADL was involved in the development of an odor classification system, the first of its kind, designed to help in the creation of such products as food, wine, and cosmetics. The firm filed a patent for producing blown glass fibers in 1930; the process paved the way for the creation of Fiberglass. In 1936 ADL was able to make a product that converted sea water into fresh water. Known as the Kleinschmidt vapor compression still, the converter used little fuel and was used extensively by the U.S. Navy during World War II.

Though founder Arthur D. Little died in 1935, his legacy did not, and the firm continued to make progress in the 1940s. ADL

45

Company Perspectives:

Arthur D. Little helps global companies, governments, and emerging ventures with their most pressing business challenges. From more than 40 offices and laboratories in 31 countries, we use business innovation to help our clients set strategy, shape organizational culture, and develop cutting-edge products and technologies. Working with Arthur D. Little, our clients get the performance improvements and breakthrough results that increase top-line growth and bottom-line results. Founded in 1886 by Arthur Dehon Little, we are the world's first consulting firm. Today we are one of the world's premier consulting firms.

worked on "Operation Bootstrap," a technical-economic plan for the industrialization of Puerto Rico, worked with MIT on the production of a low-pressure system to liquefy helium, and came up with an iron blast furnace operation that successfully boosted the production of iron while decreasing consumption of fuel. The system was embraced by the steel industry.

Continued Growth Amid Changes: 1950s–60s

ADL faced some changes in the 1950s, the first involving a change in ownership. By the early 1950s MIT owned 55 percent of ADL, a fact that did not sit well with Royal Little, nephew of the founder. Little thus established the Memorial Drive Trust, a profit-sharing trust for the employees of the firm, in 1953. Little purchased MIT's 55 percent and transferred the shares into the Memorial Drive Trust, hoping to ensure ADL's continued independence.

In terms of business, the company ushered in the 1950s with projects with such large clients as Johnson & Johnson and General Electric. ADL became involved with operations research, the analysis of business operations, and applied the concept to industrial problems. ADL also established Arthur D. Little Enterprises to commercialize in-house inventions and innovations. During the following decade the firm developed the concept of maquiladoras—foreign-owned factories in Mexico where imported materials were assembled by low-wage employees into exportable merchandise—to enhance trade along the U.S.-Mexican border. ADL's laboratories conducted tests of chemical agents to investigate chemotherapy methods for the National Cancer Institute and in the late 1960s patented a process for producing synthetic penicillin. The company worked with computer firm IBM to develop SABRE, a computerized airline ticket reservation system, for American Airlines. In 1964 ADL began a management education program to train managers from developing nations. The program later came to be called the Arthur D. Little School of Management. ADL placed 30 percent of its shares up for public offering in 1969.

Struggles and Changing Times: 1970s–80s

The 1970s and 1980s brought difficult times to ADL. The firm was no longer the only consulting firm specializing in technology but did little to battle competition. Economic conditions across the globe were less than favorable and affected ADL's revenues and growth as well. The firm failed to modernize as its rivals moved into the higher demand fields of business reengineering and management consulting. By the mid-1980s the company's reputation had declined considerably, and ADL's growth was rather dismal—its competitors were growing at about twice the pace, and ADL's profits had changed little in a decade. In addition, many of ADL's mainstays, such as product testing and government contracts, were declining.

Hoping to inject new life into the fifth-largest consulting firm in the United States, CEO John F. Magee hired Charles R. LaMantia as president and chief operating officer in 1986. LaMantia, a former ADL executive, appeared to have his work cut out for him. James H. Kennedy, editor of the trade publication *Consultant's News,* commented on ADL's tired image in *Business Week,* noting, "In the old days you practically genuflected when you heard their name. . . . Now they're not in the mainstream of consulting." Magee, who had headed ADL since 1974, attempted to resurrect the flailing firm by cutting back unprofitable services and putting more energy into such competitive arenas as biotechnology, health care, and information services, but many observers felt the efforts were minimal. One consultant told *Business Week,* "Intellectually, John [Magee] understands the company's problems . . . but he's reluctant to come to terms with them." Another issue plaguing ADL was low morale within the company, caused in some part by perpetually low salaries. Also, because salaries were tied to the firm's performance, employees were making even less than their typically low pay in the 1980s. ADL lost many of its prized employees because of uncompetitive salary packages.

In 1987 ADL was forced to confront a major obstacle when it received a takeover offer from Plenum Publishing Co., a small publishing firm that specialized in marketing English translations of scientific journals from Russia. The company also published scientific books and journals on subjects ranging from metallurgy to physics. Based in New York, Plenum was significantly smaller in size—less than one-sixth—than ADL, but the publishing house was much more profitable; in 1986 Plenum reported earnings of $12.2 million on sales of $38.1 million. Plenum hoped to diversify into consulting and believed ADL, with its scientific bent, would be a good fit. Plenum chairman Martin E. Tash explained to the *Boston Globe,* "They produce information; we publish it. . . . We understand their clients, who are the same as ours, government agencies, research institutions, and industrial companies around the globe."

ADL's board chose to reject Plenum's offer of $128 million, indicating that it believed ADL would fare better as an independent entity. Soon thereafter, Plenum put forth another offer of about $140 million and made it known the amount was negotiable. Plenum's Tash was confident that his offer would be accepted, believing that majority shareholder Memorial Drive Trust would take measures to increase the stock's value. Indeed, Tash's offer of about $55 per share was considerably higher than the stock's trading value, which hovered in the mid-30s range prior to Tash's first takeover attempt. ADL's sagging financial performance further indicated that something needed to be done at the firm. An article in *New England Business* pointed out that despite rising revenues in the 1980s, net income as a percentage of revenue dropped from about five percent in the late 1970s to about half that in the mid-1980s. James

```
┌─────────────────────────────────────────────────┐
│                  Key Dates:                       │
│                                                   │
│  1886:  Chemists Arthur D. Little and Roger Griffin found │
│         Griffin & Little, Chemical Engineers.     │
│  1909:  Company incorporates as Arthur D. Little, Inc. │
│  1935:  Founder Little dies.                      │
│  1953:  The Memorial Drive Trust, an employee trust, is │
│         established.                              │
│  1964:  Arthur D. Little offers a management education │
│         program.                                 │
│  1969:  Thirty percent of the company goes public. │
│  1988:  Company becomes private when the Memorial │
│         Drive Trust buys back the outstanding 30 percent. │
│  1996:  Arthur D. Little School of Management forms part- │
│         nership with Boston College's Carroll School of │
│         Management.                              │
└─────────────────────────────────────────────────┘
```

Kennedy of *Consultant's News* noted that while successful consulting firms aimed for profits of 40 percent prior to taxes, ADL poked along at two percent. Additionally, ADL's utilization rate, which measured billable hours, was about 60 percent, compared to the industry's target average of 80 percent. And with the specialization and consolidation of the consulting industry, many observers felt ADL's diversity was a burden. "Their greatest strength is also one of their greatest weaknesses," Kennedy told *New England Business,* adding "They know about so many industries and subjects. Their breadth is a great strength, yet the trend in consulting is toward specialties and multispecialties . . . toward the boutique instead of the supermarket, and they are a sprawling supermarket."

ADL contended that it had already implemented strategies to streamline operations and fuel profitability. Management structure had been changed, and net income in the fourth quarter of 1986 rose 66 percent compared to the same period in 1985. ADL's LaMantia told *New England Business,* "The place is really on the move. . . . Morale is up, performance is up." ADL demonstrated its self-confidence in 1988 when the Memorial Drive Trust bought back the 30 percent of ADL not owned by the employee trust. Paying $57 a share, the move made ADL a private entity.

Despite the upheavals ADL confronted, the firm continued to make progress in its consulting services. In the 1980s ADL provided technical assistance to the U.S. Postal Service, helping the agency upgrade equipment and systems. The firm also assisted the U.S. Air Force with the production of cryogenic refrigeration systems to be used in space. ADL was involved with studying safety implications of the Eurotunnel, cleaning up the Alaskan oil spill caused by the Exxon Valdez, and conducted an extensive travel plan survey with American Express Travel Related Services.

Strengthening Operations in the 1990s

Magee gave up his position as CEO in July 1988 but retained chairmanship of ADL. LaMantia stepped in as CEO, and the newly private firm began its journey toward, ADL hoped, profitability and success. The firm began by divesting its non-

core businesses, which included Opinion Research Corp., a market research business, and ADL's preclinical pharmaceutical product registration and development business and its industrial and agrochemical registration business. The two divisions were purchased by Biodevelopment Laboratories, Inc., a newly formed company owned in part by two ADL veterans. The spin-offs allowed ADL to concentrate on three core businesses: management consulting; environmental, health, and safety management; and technology and product development.

During the first half of the decade, ADL sought to expand its international presence and to growth through strategic acquisitions. In 1995 the firm purchased The Joyce Institute, an ergonomics consulting agency, and marked its entry into the fast-growing ergonomics field. The Joyce Institute's operations were merged with ADL's environmental, health, and safety consulting division. Also in 1995 ADL acquired Innovation Associates, a training and consulting firm specializing in organizational learning and change, and partnered with Robert Levering, a widely recognized workplace expert. The alliance planned to offer consulting services focused on change management in the workplace.

ADL worked on a number of projects in the early 1990s, many beyond the U.S. border. In 1992 the firm studied the hazards of the transportation and handling of petrochemicals and liquid petroleum gas for Petroleos Mexicanos SA. ADL also researched the use of natural gas for power generation in Asia and conducted an assessment of the need for a second airport for the Massachusetts Aeronautics Commission. The following year, in 1993, ADL won a contract to study the effects of pollution on ocean life and was awarded an environmental contract from the U.S. Army's Chemical Biological Defense Agency. In 1994 ADL began working with Ford Motor Company on the development of hybrid propulsion systems and worked on the privatization of Argentine-owned oil company YPF. Consulting on the privatization of British Rail was on ADL's agenda in 1995, as was training environmental consultants in the former Soviet Union and some countries in central and eastern Europe.

Heading into the latter half of the 1990s, ADL continued to focus on international expansion. The firm announced that it hoped to strengthen its consultancy operations in the Asia Pacific region and was aiming for a growth rate of more than 40 percent. ADL planned to open additional offices, in Thailand and Indonesia, to add to its offices in Malaysia, Singapore, and major metropolitan cities in the region. By the late 1990s ADL's Asia Pacific operations were performing strongly, and revenues in South Asia alone increased 400 percent between 1996 and 1997. ADL reported a growth rate of 33 percent in Asia in 1997.

The firm restructured its management consulting operations in the mid-1990s, and as a result ADL's U.S. financial services activities were shut down. ADL's School of Management formed a partnership with Boston College's Carroll School of Management in 1996, giving ADL's school access to Boston College's educational facilities. In the fall of 1997 the School of Management became an independent entity, no longer functioning as a wholly owned subsidiary of ADL. ADL served as the not-for-profit school's only shareholder. Also in 1997 ADL acquired PRC Aviation and formed a consulting subsidiary, called R. Dixon Speas Associates, focused on the aviation industry. Other strategic acquisitions in the late 1990s included Contactica, a telecommunications consultancy firm with operations all over the world, and the Mountain View Technology Division of ARCADIS Geraghty & Miller, which offered transportation technology, energy systems, and environmental services. In 2000 ADL merged its Epyx fuel cell subsidiary with De Nora Fuel Cells, a subsidiary of Italian company De Nora. The new company was called Nuvera Fuel Cells and focused on the production of fuel cell systems, particularly for the transportation industry. Also in 2000 the firm made plans to take its technology-based businesses, which included telecommunications, media and electronics, and information technology, public. ADL hoped to raise about $150 million in the initial public offering of the newly formed company, called C-Quential Inc.

Though ADL enjoyed happier times in the 1990s than it had during previous decades, the firm continued to face some difficulties. High turnover in the position of North American managing director and conflict between North American and European offices placed ADL on unstable ground. ADL maintained that operations and profits were improving, and that the company was dedicated to furthering growth. CEO LaMantia, who became chairman in 1998, retired in 1999, and ADL brought in two outsiders to run the firm: Lorenzo C. Lamadrid, a veteran of the high-tech industry, was named CEO and president, and Gerhard Schulmeyer became chairman. Within his first month at the helm, Lamadrid cut back staff and restructured North American operations into four business units: strategy consulting, public sector work, environmental health and safety, and technology and product development.

The firm reported sales of $629 million in 1999, with more than 60 percent of revenues coming from outside the nation. Though growth was rather slow—about three percent compared to competitors' growth rates in the double digits—ADL planned to reverse the trend. The firm's new CEO believed ADL was poised to tackle the technology industry by forming strategic alliances with partners to commercialize and market ADL's ideas. "ADL has been developing leading-edge products for decades and has not integrated that particularly well into the global business environment or into the business-creation mode of doing business," Lamadrid told *Business Times* during a trip to Asia. Rather than spinning off the manufacturing of inventions, Lamadrid believed ADL would profit greatly from involving itself in the production process. Indeed, with an unmatched heritage, more than a century of experience, and a history of providing breakthrough innovations, ADL appeared certain to overcome any obstacles.

Principal Subsidiaries

Arthur D. Little Enterprises, Inc.; Arthur D. Little School of Management; Cambridge Consultants Limited; Contactica; Innovation Associates; Nuvera Fuel Cells (Italy).

Principal Competitors

Andersen Consulting; Booz, Allen & Hamilton Inc.; McKinsey & Company; The Boston Consulting Group.

Further Reading

Ackerman, Jerry, "Little Plans Spinoff of Tech Units Cambridge Firm Hopes to Raise up to $150M in IPO," *Boston Globe,* May 11, 2000, p. C8.

Beam, Alex, "Can Arthur D. Little Heal Itself?," *Business Week,* October 20, 1986, p. 56.

Bottorff, Dana, "ADL Buyout Bid Draws Attention to Firm's Ownership and Results," *New England Business,* September 7, 1987, p. 44.

——, "After $55 Bid Termed 'Inadequate' ADL Counters at $57 . . . Then $60 . . . Then . . . ?'', *New England Business,* April 18, 1988, p. 53.

"Despite Upturn, ADL U.S. Leaderless . . . Again," *Consultant's News,* June 1, 1997, p. 1.

James, Kenneth, "Big Plans for Arthur D. Little," *Business Times,* September 17, 1999, p. 10.

Klein, Alec, "ADL to Announce It Picked Lamadrid to Fill CEO Post," *Wall Street Journal,* June 14, 1999, p. B9.

Lenzner, Robert, "Arthur D. Little Takeover Sought," *Boston Globe,* July 14, 1987, p. 1.

Li, Kang Siew, "Arthur D. Little Finds It Pays to Invest in Asia," *Business Times,* February 16, 1998, p. 2.

Mehegan, David, "A.D. Little Rejects $128M Bid," *Boston Globe,* July 25, 1987, p. 33.

Rosenberg, Ronald, "A.D. Little—'A Sleeping Giant' but Some Aren't Sure Takeover a Good Deal," *Boston Globe,* July 14, 1987, p. 53.

——, "Inventing the Inventor: Arthur D. Little Subsidiary Helps with Legal, Product Development and Marketing Expertise," *Boston Globe,* August 15, 1993, p. 80.

—Mariko Fujinaka

Ashley Furniture Industries, Inc.

One Ashley Way
Arcadia, Wisconsin 54612
U.S.A.
Telephone: (608) 323-3377
Fax: (608) 323-3021
Web site: http://www.ashleyfurniture.com

Private Company
Incorporated: 1945
Employees: 4,567
Sales: $816 million (1999)
NAIC: 337121 Upholstered Household Furniture
    Manufacturing; 337122 Nonupholstered Wood
    Household Furniture Manufacturing; 337211 Wood
    Office Furniture Manufacturing; 33791 Mattress
    Manufacturing

Ashley Furniture Industries, Inc. is the fifth largest furniture manufacturer in the United States. It makes a full line of home furnishings, including upholstered living room sets, bedroom furniture and bedding, recliners and other so-called motion furniture with moving parts, and wood furniture. Its wood line is perhaps its best known. The company pioneered tough, shiny tables and cabinets laminated with a virtually indestructible polyester finish in the mid-1980s and stood out in the industry for the daring of its contemporary designs and colors. Ashley maintains manufacturing facilities in Arcadia, Wisconsin and in nearby Whitehall and Independence, Wisconsin, and has warehouses and distribution centers in New Jersey, Florida, and California. Ashley also owns an upholstery plant in Ecru, Mississippi and another facility in Ripley, Mississippi. The company manufactures approximately two-thirds of its products, with the remaining third imported from Asia. Ashley also licenses a chain of stores called Ashley Furniture Homestores, with close to 40 stores operated by independent dealers in areas where the company does not otherwise have strong distribution. Located in the west central portion of Wisconsin, Ashley is far from the hub of furniture manufacturing in the United States, which centers around North Carolina. The firm is privately held by Chief Executive Officer Ron Wanek, Vice-Chairman and co-founder Chuck Vogel, and their sons.

Early Years

Ashley Furniture began as a Chicago corporation, run by a man named Carlyle Weinberger. Weinberger started the company in 1945 as a furniture sales operation. Ashley's specialty was wooden occasional furniture. It bought up goods made by local companies and marketed them in Chicago, which at that time was the main arena of furniture sales. The firm later had a branch in Goshen, Indiana.

In 1970, Ashley Furniture invested in a small, start-up furniture company in Wisconsin. This was Arcadia Furniture, founded that year by Ron Wanek. Wanek grew up on a dairy farm in Winona, Minnesota, and he began his business career working in a furniture factory there. The factory was owned by Eugene Vogel, and wooden cabinetry for stereo speakers and televisions was made there. Wanek moved to Arcadia, a tiny town just across the Mississippi from Winona, to open his own factory. He took with him Eugene Vogel's son Chuck. The two of them began doing production work for Chicago's Ashley Furniture, principally making wooden occasional tables. Arcadia Furniture also produced stereo and television cabinetry, like the factory in Winona. The new company's first facility was a single 35,000-square-foot plant. Vogel was in charge of milling and production, while Wanek oversaw all the other business details. Soon the firm had 35 employees. Its first product line encompassed only 11 simple occasional tables, but the company made money immediately, bringing in $360,000 its first year.

Growth in the 1980s

Although Arcadia started out as a small production plant for Ashley's lines, the Wisconsin company soon became a major producer. In 1976, Wanek and other investors bought out Carlyle Weinberger and took control of Ashley Furniture. At first the two companies kept separate identities, with Arcadia the production arm and Ashley the sales arm. Later they merged officially, using the name Ashley Furniture Industries Inc. Under Wanek's direction, the merged company grew quickly. The

---

Company Perspectives:

Ashley has a rich history of success stories that illustrate its dramatic transition from a "virtual unknown" to a significant force in the industry. For over half of a century, the company has remained committed to its Vision Statement, "We Want To Be The Best Furniture Company." Innovative marketing concepts, quality products and state-of-the-art manufacturing methods have always been driven by the demand for customer satisfaction. At Ashley the stream of satisfied customers continues to grow as Ashley continues to be creative and diversifies to expand business, and improve quality into the next millennium.

---

firm spent $5.5 million in 1979 for a huge addition in Arcadia, enabling it to produce a more varied and sophisticated product line. By 1982, annual sales were $12 million and corporate headquarters moved from Chicago to Arcadia.

Ashley Furniture Industries was something of an anomaly within the furniture industry both for its location and its vigor. The furniture industry in the Midwest gradually moved south, and Ashley was left in a remote, small town in Wisconsin. This gave it high distribution costs, as it was far from major population centers. Ashley, however, had formidable leadership in Ron Wanek. He had a feel for furniture and markets and always approved new designs himself. Ashley's products were aimed at middle-income buyers. The company tried to provide high-quality, durable goods but at an affordable price. To give his company's products a special niche, Wanek moved away from the kind of furniture consumers considered "heirloom pieces"— stodgy, enduring things that would furnish their homes forever— into stylish pieces that had more of an immediate appeal.

To make the kind of furniture Wanek was sure customers would like, Ashley needed to upgrade its technology and find a way to compete on price with imports. Imports began to be a significant factor in the American furniture market in the early 1980s. In 1983 alone, the percentage of imports increased almost 50 percent, according to a profile of Ashley in the April 1986 *Wisconsin Business*. Although the same article describes the furniture industry as a whole at that time as "sleepy," Wanek took notice, and in 1984 he traveled to Taiwan to investigate. He found what is by now a commonplace of the global market—low wages, low cost for facilities, and a tariff of less than three percent for Taiwanese furniture entering the United States. Ashley did begin importing inexpensive parts from Asia to keep its own costs down, but more important, the company moved quickly to build itself an unassailable domestic market.

One change was to branch out from living room furniture to bedroom sets. Company management fixed on the simple fact that American homes had only one living room, but typically three bedrooms. This unassailable logic seemed to dictate bigger markets just waiting for the company. To provide for the new bedroom line, the company invested $4.5 million in its assembly facility and in equipment to streamline its production process. The company started making bedroom furniture in 1983, and by 1986 this accounted for 40 percent of its total sales.

A more significant innovation came in 1986, when Ashley introduced its "Millennium" line. Wanek and his designers had determined that consumers liked shiny furniture. So Ashley came up with a unique polyester finishing technique that gave its wood furniture an impeccable luster. The company produced very shiny black furniture in its occasional and bedroom lines, and then began adding colors like emerald green. These were seen as exciting pieces with contemporary flair. By the mid-1980s, Ashley had a line of approximately 350 different products, most aimed at middle-income consumers. The company had thousands of accounts, the biggest being the wholesaler Levitz Furniture Corporation, which bought $3.7 million worth of Ashley's occasional tables in 1985. Ashley also sold to major mass-market retailers such as Sears, K Mart, and Montgomery Ward, as well as to thousands of smaller stores. Sales climbed rapidly, from about $9 million in 1980 to more than $44 million in 1985.

Innovation in the 1990s

Ashley Furniture had grown from a simple table factory in 1970 to a design leader with huge nationwide sales in the 1980s. The company had worked hard to innovate, incorporating new technology to compete with cheap imports, designing eye-catching furniture that led with style, and moving into new market categories, such as bedroom furniture, to increase its options. Ashley continued to be a quick-moving, vital company in the 1990s, making changes to capture new markets and capitalize on cost-saving equipment. Its great success was its polyester laminate Millennium line, which alone accounted for sales of $100 million in the early 1990s. Although the company had bought expensive new equipment for laminating around 1989, by 1993 Ashley upgraded again, installing a state-of-the-art thermo-laminating press. CEO Wanek was eager to spend money to keep the company on the cutting edge technologically. By the early 1990s, Ashley's investment in equipment for its Millennium line had reached about $55 million.

The company also branched out into new product lines in the early 1990s. Wanek was convinced that Ashley needed to produce furniture that looked totally new and different, to entice customers to give up their old stuff and start fresh with an expensive purchase. In 1993 the company introduced a line of so-called motion furniture—tables with tops and shelves that slide or elevate, beds with nightstands sliding on tracks along each side or heads that moved up to make it more comfortable to watch television. These added features made the Ashley line stand out. At the same time, the company added a line of ready-to-assemble furniture, a market niche where Wanek sensed an opening. Much ready-to-assemble stuff was low-end, and Ashley made more expensive, higher quality goods such as computer desks and hutches. These were meant principally for customers with a home office, a growing demographic. In the mid-1990s the company also introduced its first line of youth bedroom furniture, which included a full range, from bunk beds to computer tables, highlighted with molding in the company's signature polyester finish.

In another major move, Ashley began a new upholstered furniture line in 1994. Because Ashley did not have the equipment in Arcadia to produce upholstered goods, the company bought an existing plant in Ecru, Mississippi from a subsidiary

Key Dates:

1945: Ashley Furniture founded in Chicago.
1970: Arcadia Furniture founded in Arcadia, Wisconsin.
1976: Arcadia owners buy out Ashley.
1986: Introduction of best-selling Millennium line.
1994: Ashley acquires upholstery manufacturer from Sklar-Pepplar.

of a Canadian furniture company, Sklar-Pepplar. Sklar-Pepplar made two product lines at its Ecru plant, called Skyline and Grimson Slater. Ashley took over these lines, selling sofas, loveseats, chairs, ottomans, and such under the name Ashley Upholstery. The products it took over from Sklar-Pepplar sold relatively inexpensively, retailing for around $400 to $700. But Ashley quickly expanded and upgraded the line. By 1995 it was offering Millennium upholstery products, combining its successful polyester laminate with upscale upholstered fabrics. Ashley also moved to upgrade the Ecru plant. At the time of purchase, it stood at 135,000 square feet. By the late 1990s, the plant covered 900,000 square feet and generated at least $200 million in sales of upholstered furniture.

More Successes into the New Millennium

By the late 1990s and into the next century, Ashley showed few signs of slowing down. The company acquired a large plant near Pomona, California, giving it a West Coast presence, and continued to expand in Arcadia and nearby. Ashley also operated assembly and distribution plants in Seattle, Washington, in New Brunswick, New Jersey, and in Orlando, Florida. These plants, in addition to offering distribution to major East and West Coast population centers, took in imported parts from Asia, mainly for tables, and assembled them. With the success of its bedroom line, Ashley decided in the late 1990s to begin to make mattresses and box springs as well. Dealers often sold bedroom furniture sets complete with mattress and box springs, so Ashley believed it could use its existing strength to get in on this market. Its sleep products line was a quick success, as it managed to make something that looked like an old-fashioned mattress but that boasted high-tech construction.

To strengthen its position in motion furniture, Ashley acquired another Mississippi company in 1999. This was Gentry Furniture, of Ripley, Mississippi, a leading maker of reclining sofas and sectionals. Ashley gambled that motion furniture was still a strong growth area. It continued and expanded Gentry's lines and used its plant solely for motion furniture. Its other Mississippi upholstery plant, in Ecru, devoted itself exclusively to stationary furniture. In 1999 the company also branched out into retailing, licensing stores to independent dealers. These

were called Ashley Furniture HomeStores and sold only Ashley goods. The chain grew in its first year to roughly 40 stores.

By the year 2000, Ashley Furniture Industries employed more people in Arcadia than the town's total population of slightly more than 2,100. It had plants in the East, West, and South, and operated several factories in Pacific Rim countries. The plant in Arcadia had grown from 35,000 square feet in 1970 to 1.5 million square feet. Ron Wanek still ran the company, with Chuck Vogel. Wanek's son Todd was a co-owner and chief operating officer, while Vogel's son Ben was another co-owner and vice-president. The company had received offers to take the company public, but its owners preferred to keep it under local control. Ashley continued to offer innovative designs. Its design teams scoured the country for ideas and came up with new products every six months. Its designers tended to look for excitement. For example, the company had pushed its motion furniture since the early 1990s, and by 2000 it had bought up a patented design to allow it to produce elaborate "command center" chairs. The arm of the chair opened up to reveal a telephone, controls for a chair vibrator, and even a small refrigerator. The company's almost restless approach to marketing had paid off. Sales pushed steadily upward. In 1998, Ashley brought in approximately $652 million. By the next year, it had expanded that to more than $800 million. The fifth largest furniture maker in the United States, the company continued to pour out new ideas in the early 21st century.

Principal Competitors

La-Z-Boy Chair Co.; LifeStyle Furnishings International.

Further Reading

"Ashley Sets More Home Office Lines," *HFD,* April 4, 1994, p. 22.
Bednarek, David I., "Building a Future," *Milwaukee Journal Sentinel,* October 11, 1992.
Buchanan, Lee, "Ashley Furniture Buys Gentry," *HFN,* July 12, 1999, p. 1.
Christianson, Rich, "New System Helps Ashley Expand Laminate 'Library'," *Wood & Wood Products,* September 1993, p. 48.
Johnson, Gary, "Ashley Domesticates the Imports," *Wisconsin Business,* April 1986, pp. 20–28.
Klein, Michael, "Fanatic About Making Furniture," *Capital Times* (Madison, Wis.), February 19, 2000, p. 1E.
Kunkel, Karl, "Ashley Keeps It in the Family," *HFN,* June 14, 1999, p. 16.
——, " 'Old-Style' But High-Tech, Ashley's Millennium Is a Hit," *HFN,* May 17, 1999, p. 25.
Marks, Robert, "Ashley Enters Upholstered," *HFD,* April 11, 1994, p. 23.
——, "Ashley Launching RTA Line," *HFD,* October 25, 1993, p. 17.
"Motion Notions: Ashley Puts the Move on Bedrooms," *HFD,* October 18, 1993, p. 15.

—A. Woodward

Astronics Corporation

1801 Elmwood Avenue
Buffalo, New York 14207
U.S.A.
Telephone: (716) 447-9013
Fax: (716) 447-9201
Web site: http://www.astronics.com

Public Company
Incorporated: 1968
Employees: 500
Sales: $50.64 million (1999)
Stock Exchanges: NASDAQ
Ticker Symbol: ATRO
NAIC: 322212 Folding Paperboard Box Manufacturing;
334119 Other Computer Peripheral Equipment
Manufacturing; 334511 Search, Detection, Navigation,
Guidance, Aeronautical, & Nautical System and
Instrument Manufacturing; 335122 Commercial,
Industrial, and Institutional Electric Lighting Fixture
Manufacturing; 335129 Other Lighting Equipment
Manufacturing; 336321 Vehicular Lighting Equipment
Manufacturing

Astronics Corporation is involved in two distinct niches: high-tech electroluminescent lamps and keyboards, and specialty packaging. Astronics supplies various types of lighting for military aircraft and 300 commercial airlines; its Aerospace and Electronics division counts commercial and military clients in 47 countries. Specialty Packaging has 10,000 customers in two dozen countries. Continually investing a hefty portion of earnings into R&D and process improvements, Astronics has placed more than once on the *Forbes* list of the "200 Best Small Companies."

Luminous Origins

French physicist G. Destriau discovered electroluminescence in 1937. In this phenomenon, a cool light emits from an electroluminescent material sandwiched between two elec-

trodes under alternating current (ac power). Scientists spent the next couple of decades making the discovery practical.

In December 1968, Thomas L. Robinson, Sr. established the Astronics Corp., the first company solely dedicated to developing electroluminescent panels. (It was founded independently of the Santa Monica-based Lear Astronics, formed in 1958 by aviation pioneer Bill Lear.) Robinson had been a project engineer at the Cornell Aeronautical Laboratory, where he developed electro-optical devices. He formed Astronics because existing technology was not advanced enough to allow him to complete an electroluminescent flat screen display for the Goddard Space Center while he was at Cornell. (This was completed in 1972.)

Flexible, lightweight, and thin as paper, these solid-state devices produced more light at lower voltage and lower frequencies than conventional incandescent or fluorescent bulbs. They stayed cool and wore out gradually rather than burning out like light bulbs.

The company's first home was the Gardenville Industrial Park in West Seneca, near Buffalo, New York. It later rented space from Moog Inc. at 300 French Road in Cheektowaga. Peter Gombirch, formerly a regional sales manager at Singer Co.'s Industrial Control Division, headed sales and marketing. Its four other employees were all related: Robinson's wife, Bessie, and two sons Thomas, Jr., and Roy.

First year revenues were only $13,000. Sales volume fell to just $1,777 in 1970 as the company devoted its time to research and development. Robinson called on George F. Rand III, chairman of Rand Capital Corp., for financial backing. Rand sent Kevin T. Keane to evaluate the company's business prospects. Keane liked them; he left Maday Body & Equipment Corp. (of which he was part owner) at the end of 1970 to help the inventor's company along. He became president two years later when Robinson retired.

Rand Capital's investment in late 1970 allowed Astronics to document its R&D efforts and gain a contract from NASA via the Singer Co. That project involved making displays for Skylab. The panels also were used in aircraft and sea vessels.

Company Perspectives:

Growth opportunities are targeted that can benefit from our technical and operational superiority. Continuous investment into process and systems technology enables Astronics to provide unique product diversity and performance capabilities, competitive market pricing, and performance with exceptional response standards. Astronics enjoys substantial market share dominance within its selected business areas. In each of its segments, the company aims to be the sole source or the preferred provider for the majority of the business.

Sometimes called Astronics Luminescent Inc., Astronics had about eleven employees and billed $14,000 during 1971. At year end, Keane asked John Kerr, an engineer and Harvard MBA, to join the company as a vice-president. The company filed a stock offering in December 1971 to raise $1.8 million. Before the offering, the Robinson family and Rand Capital Corp. each owned a third of the stock. Half of the money was to fund research and development and establish production facilities. After expenses, however, only about $800,000 was raised; the company decided to use some of it for acquisitions.

Contained Growth in the 1970s and 1980s

Astronics bought A-T-O Inc.'s Scott Aviation Division for $120,000 in May 1972. Scott manufactured panel lighting for Piper and Cessna aircraft. The Scott purchase also gave Astronics entrée into the military market. In December, Astronics bought 90 percent of MOD-PAC Corp., which manufactured paperboard cartons and boxes. It had nearly $2 million in annual sales, more than ten times that of Astronics. Formerly the Cooper Box Co., its history dated back to 1888. Although ostensibly unrelated to the aerospace business, MOD-PAC represented good investment potential; there was also some transferable expertise in its graphics department.

A 14,000-square-foot building at 77 Olean Road in East Aurora was purchased in January 1973. The company relocated its entire electroluminescent operation there. Employment increased to 105 by October 1973. By this time, Astronics was supplying electroluminescent instrument lighting to the Big Three U.S. automakers as well as all levels of aerospace producers including Beech Aircraft and Lear. Military aircraft used exterior lighting strips to facilitate formation flying in low visibility. The company also supplied the nascent copy machine industry.

Profits were $130,340 on sales of $2.7 million in 1974. Sales reached $3.4 million in 1976 and $4.3 million the next, with earnings of $283,000. In November 1977, Astronics bought United Business Equipment Corp. (UBEC) of Buffalo, which sold $1 million of filing systems a year.

Astronics continued to develop printed circuit processes. It worked with Gloucester, Massachusetts-based Flex-Key Corp. to develop a lighted keypad. (Astronics later acquired Flex-Key.) Prototypes of lighted safety vests for park rangers were made for the Park Service; Astronics also was developing applications in ophthalmology and photography and toying with

consumer applications. Eastman Kodak used the lighting strips within its darkened film processing plant in Rochester, New York. They were tinted so as not to mar undeveloped film. Kodak also used special electroluminescent flashlights, which used much less power than ones with conventional bulbs.

By 1979, Astronics was posting annual sales of $8 million a year. MOD-PAC had 90 employees and contributed sales of about $3.5 million. This growth came against a backdrop of layoffs and plant closings among Buffalo's traditional industries such as steel and automobiles. Astronics had created 115 jobs in its first decade.

Although executives were pursuing opportunities for vertical integration, the company acquired Buffalo-based Rodgard Manufacturing Co. in 1981. Rodgard produced industrial plastics products and employed 40 persons. Its annual sales were about $2 million.

Astronics had sales of $125 million in 1986–87. It invested in automating its PC board assembly processes. The company bought the Grimes Electroluminescent Lighting Product Group in 1988. Earnings dwindled to earned $20,000 on sales of $21.9 million in 1988. A $2 million loss on sales of $22.2 million in 1989 prompted Keane to implement a restructuring plan. The company had several more years of declining defense spending to endure.

New Heights in the 1990s

Annual sales held at $7 million in 1991 and 1992. The company began to invest $2 to $3 million a year in capital improvements in the mid-1990s while reducing its debt load. In 1994, Flex-Key operations were moved from Massachusetts to East Aurora, New York, where they were consolidated with those of the E-L Products Co. under the name E-L FlexKey Technologies Inc. Both units had significant military sales. Flex-Key had 40 employees at the time. Astronics had about 300 employees in all. Astronics acquired the assets of Loctite Luminescent Systems Inc. in November 1995 for about $6.5 million, also integrating the new unit, expected to contribute $11 million a year to revenues, into the E-L FlexKey Technologies Inc. subsidiary.

Concerned by its depressed share price, the company began buying back stock in July 1994. Profits rose ten percent to $1.3 million in 1994 on slightly increased sales of $24.9 million. In February 1995, the company announced that it was relocating its headquarters to the MOD-PAC plant as a practical consideration. Keane had been running that packaging subsidiary for the previous four years. That year, MOD-PAC installed the first Heidelberg printing press in the western hemisphere. Its unique coating capabilities won Astronics preferred supplier status to Hershey Foods. In 1996, the company doubled the capacity of its Blasdell, New York specialty packaging facility.

The Rodgard Division was sold to Trenton, New Jersey-based Hutchinson Industries, Inc. (a subsidiary of the French company Hutchinson S.A.) for $2.25 million in late 1996. The sale completed plans to focus Astronics on just two business segments: Specialized Packaging and Printing and Electronic Systems. (The latter was renamed Aerospace and Electronics in 1997.)

Key Dates:

1968: Cornell engineer founds Astronics to develop electroluminescent lamp technology.
1970: Rand Capital provides cash infusion needed to land major Skylab contract.
1972: Astronics enters specialty packaging business through purchase of MOD-PAC Corp.
1989: A $2 million dollar loss prompts a restructuring program.
1994: After reducing debt and investing in process improvements, Astronics begins buying back shares.
1999: Astronics wins a major contract to retrofit F-16s with night vision equipment.
2000: The Specialty Packaging division wins its biggest contract ever, from Tyco Healthcare.

By 1996, the process improvements were paying off as Astronics posted record results: profits increased 51 percent to $2.7 million on sales of $38.4 million, up 35 percent. The company had begun to implement ISO 9001 quality standards throughout the Aerospace and Electronics and Specialty Packaging divisions and picked up the Staples Office Superstore chain as a client.

In April 1999, Astronics officials announced plans for a new $6 million plant for the Luminescent Systems division. A $50 million award to make night vision modification kits for U.S. Air Force F-16s was responsible for half of the 70 new jobs tied to the expansion. Military contracts accounted for less than 30 percent of the division's business, however. In October 1999, Aerospace and Electronics moved into new facilities in Lebanon, New Hampshire, consolidating four locations in the state.

Astronics continued to post record sales and earnings in 1999. Profits were $4.8 million on sales of $50.6 million. Aerospace and Electronics accounted for slightly more than half (52 percent) of total sales. The company had doubled sales in the previous five years, when it averaged compounded annual earnings growth of 22 percent.

Astronics continued to expand its specialty packaging business as well, which had logged more than 25 years of double digit sales growth. It invested nearly 30 percent of 1999 sales in new technology, installing computer to plate technology for made-to-order packaging. In January 2000 MOD-PAC won the largest contract in its history, worth $15 million, to supply printed folding cartons for the Tyco Healthcare Group's northeastern manufacturing plants. The new business prompted plans to hire up to 30 more workers at the Buffalo packaging plant, bringing employment there to 250. MOD-PAC won the contract through its relationship with Graphic Controls Corp., which was acquired by Tyco in 1998. Specialty Packaging contributed about $24 million a year to total sales. The division was also preferred supplier to Hershey Foods and Staples Office Superstores.

As it moved up the defense contractor "food chain" in 1999, Astronics was farming out 75 percent of its F-16-related work. It hoped to take half of that in-house again with its new plants in New Hampshire and East Aurora to double or triple profit margins. In May 2000, Astronics acquired some F-16-related switches and indicators lines from Aerospace Avionics, Inc., a Bohemia, New York-based subsidiary of Smiths Industries. The company bought CRL Technologies of Quebec for CD $4 million in the same month. CRL produced lighted keyboards with applications in the F-16 cockpit and many other places.

Company officials expected sales to rise by 40 percent in 2000, topping $70 million. Commercial and private aircraft manufacturers and operators were ordering more cockpit and exit lighting as well. New aerospace programs included the Lockheed F-22 fighter and Embraer regional jets. The company also was lighting up portable electronic devices such as digital watches and cellular phones through its MaxEL line of high-volume, low-cost electroluminescent devices.

Principal Subsidiaries

Luminescent Systems, Inc.; MOD-PAC Corporation.

Principal Divisions

Aerospace and Electronics; Specialty Packaging.

Principal Competitors

All American Packaging; Field Container Company L.P.; Inductotherm Industries; James River Corp.; Targetti-Tivoli; Universal Packaging Corp.; Westvaco Corp.

Further Reading

Dearlove, Ray, "Small East Aurora Firm Has Glowing Future," *Courier Express,* October 14, 1973, p. 52.
Dodsworth, Terry, "GEC Buys Lear Avionics Arm," *Financial Times,* August 1, 1987, p. 1.
Levy, Michael, "Astronics: A Glowing Business," *Buffalo News,* April 23, 1978, p. B10.
McKeating, Mike, "Astronics Corp.—State-of-the-Art Pioneer," *Buffalo News,* January 20, 1980, p. B4.
Meyer, Brian, "Aircraft Parts Maker Details Plans for New Plant in East Aurora, NY," *Buffalo News,* April 21, 1999.
Robinson, David, "Astronics Moving Unit Here from Massachusetts," *Buffalo News,* Bus. Sec., December 29, 1993.
——, "Astronics Says It's Better Off Than Numbers Show," *Buffalo News,* Bus. Sec., April 30, 1994.
——, "Buffalo, N.Y.-Based Aerospace Manufacturer Expects Sales To Climb," *Buffalo News,* April 21, 2000.
——, "Buffalo, N.Y. Packaging Firm To Add Employees After Winning Big Contract," *Knight-Ridder/Tribune Business News,* March 8, 2000.
——, "Buyback May Help Investors; Earnings Per Share Boosted on the Remaining Stock," *Buffalo News,* Your Money, December 21, 1994, p. 1.
——, "It's Time To Place Bets on Length of Annual Meeting," *Buffalo News,* Bus. Sec., May 8, 1994.
Spies, Tom, "Robots for PC Board Assembly? Think Small," *Production Engineering,* August 1987, pp. 74+.
Sullivan, Margaret, "High Technology Industry Continues To Flourish," *Buffalo News,* January 18, 1981, p. E13.

—Frederick C. Ingram

Auntie Anne's, Inc.

160-A Route 41
PO Box 529
Gap, Pennsylvania 17527
U.S.A.
Telephone: (717) 442-4766
Fax: (717) 442-4139
Web site: http://www.auntieannes.com

Private Company
Incorporated: 1989
Employees: 115
Sales: $168 million (1999 est.)
NAIC: 722213 Snack and Nonalcoholic Beverage Bars

Through its chain of 600 mostly franchised locations, Auntie Anne's, Inc. sells soft, warm pretzels. From its origins in a Pennsylvania farmers' market, the company grew explosively throughout the 1990s. Its stores have become fixtures in malls across the country, where baking aromas, the sight of employees hand-rolling dough, and free samples lure shoppers into buying a softer, sweeter cousin of the prepackaged pretzel. Auntie Anne's has rolled into airports and train stations and has begun pursuing alternate locations such as Wal-Mart. The chain also has expanded into several Asian countries. The secret of its success? "Put people first, profits will follow," founder and CEO Anne Beiler told the CNNfn cable network. Philanthropy has always played a significant part in the company's planning.

Origins

An Italian monk created the first pretzel sometime in the seventh century A.D. Twisting scraps of dough to resemble arms folded in prayer, he gave these *pretiolas*—little rewards—to his students. According to Anne Beiler, founder of Auntie Anne's, the holes in the pretzel represent the Holy Trinity.

A thousand years later, emigrating Germans brought the pretzel to Pennsylvania. As a child in Lancaster County, Pennsylvania, Anne Beiler grew up in the unique world of the Amish—an agrarian society of horse-drawn buggies and con-

servative religious tradition. Her hometown of Gap, Pennsylvania had a population of just 2,000.

Beiler had an early introduction to the world of commerce, baking pies and cakes for the family to sell at age 12, circa 1961. Three years later, she dropped out of school to work at a truck stop, handing her wages to her parents. This was the custom for many Amish girls, whose elders frowned on the secular influences of high schools. At 19, Anne married Jonas Beiler, who also had learned to bake as a youngster. The two then spent several years building churches in Pennsylvania and Texas.

Beiler had her first child at 22 and left the Amish Mennonite church at about the same time because she felt it was too strict. She said that she kept the faith and principles with which she was raised, however. Anne also worked as a waitress and stayed at home to rear two daughters, LaWonna and LaVale.

The Beilers moved back to Pennsylvania in 1987, where Jonas, an auto mechanic by trade, hoped to open a marriage and family counseling center for the Amish community in Lancaster County, who were reluctant to go to outsiders for help. To help raise money for this project, Anne took a $200 a week part-time job managing a concession stand at a farmer's market in Maryland, two hours away. It was there that she began rolling pretzels, which she noticed sold fast and brought in a lot of profit. A 55-cent pretzel used only seven cents worth of ingredients, as *Forbes* later chronicled.

Within a year, she had rented her own 12- by 20-foot pretzel stand in Downingtown, Chester County, Pennsylvania, for $250 a month. She borrowed $6,000 from her in-laws to equip the stall with an oven, mixer, and refrigerator. Beiler, who had 30 nieces and nephews, officially dubbed it "Auntie Anne's" when it opened in February 1988. The first items on the menu were pizza, stromboli, ice cream, and hand-rolled pretzels.

The first pretzels, based on a friend's recipe, were not hot sellers. In fact, according to *Forbes*, she was only bringing in $350 a weekend—barely enough to stay afloat. A bungled delivery of supplies led to a two-month period of pretzel experimentation. With a few extra ingredients suggested by husband Jonas, Anne Beiler came up with a softer, sweeter winner.

Company Perspectives:

Auntie Anne's Promise to Our Customers: Fresh, Hot, Golden-Brown Soft Pretzels; Friendly, Courteous Service; A Sparkling Clean Store.

Pretzel sales quadrupled within a few months, and soon they were all she sold at her booth, rolling them in front of her customers in an entertaining presentation.

Storming the Malls in the 1990s

After raising another $5,000 in capital, Beiler opened a second stand in Harrisburg, Pennsylvania in July 1988. With a winning recipe and soon-to-be-famous name, the stage was set for franchising, which began in early 1989. She agreed to license the first franchise to her brother, construction manager Jake Smucker, who opened a shop in Middletown, Pennsylvania. The Beilers entered their first mall in November 1989. Their seven others had been in farmers' markets.

The enterprise was very much a family affair in those early days and continued to be so. Auntie Anne had a sister making pretzel mix by hand. (She did not give out the recipe to licensees, although an unauthorized version later appeared on the Internet.) Another brother delivered it. Her husband and brother-in-law built the shops, and Anne's two daughters also helped.

Sandy Chandler, who attended Beiler's church, was another early franchisee. So was Ben Lapp, who invested $3,000 in a store in Intercourse, Pennsylvania. Arrangements were quite informal at the beginning. Friends insisted on running their own stores, Beiler says; she simply asked for a percentage of monthly revenues in exchange for use of her name and recipe. (A franchise fee between $2,500 and $5,000 also changed hands.) Beiler sold ten franchises in the first year, but the family had their hands full keeping openings on schedule; the system took in revenues of $1 million in 1990.

A younger brother, Carl Smucker (Beiler had seven siblings), joined the company in August 1990 and recommended a six-month freeze on new franchises. When even he felt overwhelmed, he referred his sister to Francorp, a franchising consultancy based in Olympia Fields, Illinois. Soon, Francorp consultant David Hood helped her devise a policy manual as well as a 100-page contract. To maintain brand integrity, the new agreement banned sales to supermarkets. In addition, the franchise fee was doubled, to $15,000. Hood joined the staff as director of franchising in 1991 and eventually became company president.

Like the original location, the new stores always offered soft, hand-rolled pretzels. By the end of 1989, there were eight stores. A total of 42 stores were added the next year, for the most part in Pennsylvania, New York, and New Jersey. There would be 90 stores by the end of 1991. This string of success did not go unnoticed. *Inc.* magazine named Beiler "Entrepreneur of the Year" in 1992 and again in 1994, when the chain had 279 stores, all but 17 of them franchised. Income was $350,000 on revenues of $8 million.

In 1992, the free counseling center that Jonas Beiler had envisioned opened as the Family Information Center in Lancaster County, but the giving did not end there. Among other groups, Beiler later became involved with the Angela Foundation, named after a daughter who died at 19 months. In all, Auntie Anne's gave $150,000 to charities in 1994, a largesse that frustrated loan officers. Friends, however, referred the Beilers to an "angel" in the form of a chicken farmer, who loaned them $1 million. Auntie Anne was not beyond a few indulgences, though. She bought herself a white $36,000 Cadillac El Dorado. She and her husband also rode cross-country on motorcycles, visiting family-owned stores along the way.

International in 1995

The Auntie Anne's phenomenon steadily worked its way through the malls of America in the mid-1990s. The chain had 344 stores at the end of 1995 and dwarfed competitors such as Pretzel Time and Gretel's Pretzels. Franchisees averaged $300,000 in revenues a year and the entire system took in more than $100 million in revenues. A far cry from Lancaster County, which claimed to produce 80 percent of the world's pretzel supply, Auntie Anne's opened its first international location in Jakarta, Indonesia, where most people had never even heard of pretzels.

At the time, Auntie Anne's offered ten different types of pretzels and several sauces: caramel, sweet mustard, strawberry cream cheese, honey, marinara, and chocolate. Varieties included sour cream and onion, sesame seed, garlic, whole wheat, and caramel almond; they sold for about $1.25 each. For the sweet tooth, there were cinnamon sugar and Glazin' Raisin—two twisted answers to cinnamon buns.

The smell of fresh-baked pretzels proved a powerful calling card; the company also offered free samples. In one case, it sent a pretzel cart dispensing them through a mall in Detroit. To get the name out, Auntie Anne's locations displayed brochures about nutrition facts, locations, and company history.

At the end of 1996, the chain had 408 stores. It continued to play up its Pennsylvania Dutch roots and boasted a considerable number of Amish operators, many of whom were related to each other, although some considered them relatively unsophisticated in business. Beiler conceded in *Restaurant Business:* "It's very un-Amish, what I've done." Interestingly, thanks to a Congressional exemption, Amish franchisees did not have to pay Social Security taxes for their Amish employees. They also did not have to pay into the state workers' compensation fund.

Like bagels, the pretzel concept was catching on as a low-fat alternative to other mall snacks, such as pizza. Auntie Anne's largest competitor, Pretzelmaker, started in 1991, had 200 stores in 1997, and was developing a line of pretzel sandwiches. Gretel's Pretzels, which grew out of the pretzel business of Restaurant Systems, had just 15 stores. Mrs. Fields' Cookies, a master mall marketer, was test-marketing the "Pretzelwich" at a dozen of its 115 Hot Sam stores under the Pretzel Ovens name.

On Tour in 1998

In spite of all the interest in malls, only five percent of mall shoppers ever bought pretzels at the mall. Beiler took her case to

Key Dates:

1989: Anne Beiler opens a booth selling fresh, hot pretzels at a Pennsylvania farmer's market.
1990: Auntie Anne's reaches $1 million in revenues.
1992: The Beilers open a counseling center for Pennsylvania Dutch families.
1995: First international store opens in Jakarta.
2000: Company tests Cookie Farm concept.

the national media to try to reach more of them. Her unique woman's success story made for good copy. The campaign was aimed at women 25 to 54 years old—the bulk of mall shoppers. On the publicity tour, Beiler also offered advice for business owners: "To be successful in life, all you have to do is be a giver rather than a taker," as she was quoted in the *Patriot-News.* "Be a giver and life is full of surprises."

Auntie Anne's grew to 558 stores in 1998, although it accepted only ten out of 6,000 franchise applications that year. The company received 400 inquiries a month. In spite of its success, it remained a family business, with 30 of Anne Beiler's kinfolk working for the company, including yet another brother, Sam Beiler, as chief operating officer. In all, it employed 100 employees at the home office and 35 in regional ones.

The company continued to open stores in enclosed malls, where sales remained strong. It had begun expanding, however, into train and plane terminals and outlet malls. It also dispatched a few trailer units to carnivals.

Auntie Anne's introduced a new taste, the Parmesan Herb pretzel, in November 1998. A year later, it rolled out Auntie Anne's at Home Pretzel Kit in time for the Christmas season. The kits sold for about $10 and contained enough ingredients for ten Original or Cinnamon Sugar pretzels.

By 2000, the stores were selling ten varieties of pretzel, including Cinnamon Sugar and Jalapeño, as well as dipping sauces: three varieties of cream cheese; sweet mustard; marinara; caramel; cheese; and chocolate. Glazin' Raisin offered a low-fat alternative to cinnamon buns. In addition to lemonade, the stores served Dutch Ice, a frozen drink.

Auntie Anne's had nearly 600 locations around the world and was opening seven new ones every month at a cost to franchisees of about $150,000 to $250,000 each. The company now reached into Thailand, Singapore, Indonesia, the Philippines, and Malaysia, and new stores were planned in Venezuela and Hong Kong. The company expected to open up to 20 stores in 2000, mostly in the East. The Pretzel Japan Corporation opened the first Japanese store in Yokohama's new Mosaic Mall in March 2000. This licensee planned to open another 300 stores in the next six years. Systemwide revenues of $200 million were expected for 1999.

In 2000, Auntie Anne's was testing an "interactive" Cookie Farm concept. It used desktop publishing technology to print food coloring images on edible paper. The company disdained the science fiction, "not reality-based" approach of other child-oriented marketing. Instead it decorated its store with farm animals such as a four-foot tall chicken and a purple cow. Inside, a windmill vending machine dispensed prize coupons while illustrating barnyard scenes. The windmill was designed to educate children about "the spirit of giving" and proceeds went to the Children's Miracle Network, which the company had started supporting in 1999.

Principal Competitors

Pretzelmaker; Gretel's Pretzels; Pretzel Time.

Further Reading

Ballon, Marc, "Pretzel Queen," *Forbes,* March 13, 1995, p. 112.
Carrera, Nora, "Business with Twist Draws Franchisors: Pretzelmaker Is the Second Largest Chain of Soft Pretzel Shops and Growing Fast," *Denver Rocky Mountain News,* March 17, 1997, p. 2B.
Cebrzynski, Greg, "Restaurant Chains Say: Let the Buyer Be Aware," *Nation's Restaurant News,* March 23, 1998, p. 16.
Hollister, Danielle C., "Founder of Auntie Anne's Pretzels Builds Franchise Operation," *Patriot-News,* April 5, 1998.
Kochak, Jacqueline, "A New Twist," *Restaurant Business,* September 15, 1998, pp. 80–81.
Kraybill, Donald, *Amish Enterprise: From Plows to Profits,* Baltimore, Md.: Johns Hopkins University, c1996.
Lion, Deborah, "Linda's Little Rewards," *Franchising World,* January/February 1996, p. 48.
Lisovicz, Susan, "Auntie Anne's CEO and Co-Founder," *Entrepreneurs Only,* CNNfn, October 13, 1999.
Mehegan, Sean, "The Modest Merchants," *Restaurant Business,* April 10, 1996, p. 57.
"A New Twist," *Restaurant Business,* June 15, 1997, pp. 71–75.
Prewitt, Milford, "Auntie Anne's Promo Showcases Sweet Smell of Success," *Nation's Restaurant News,* February 27, 1995, p. 12.
Reinan, John, "Doing the Twist and It Goes Like This . . .," *Tampa Bay Tribune,* Business & Finance Sec., April 16, 1999, p. 1.
Rohland, Pamela, "It's Twisted," *QSR—The magazine of Quick Service Restaurant Success,* March/April 1999.
Strauss, Karyn, "Breaking the Cookie-Cutter Image: Auntie Anne's Tests Interactive Units," *Nation's Restaurant News,* January 10, 2000, pp. 8, 72.
Thierry, Lauren, and Bill Tucker, "Auntie Anne's CEO," *Entrepreneurs Only,* CNNfn, May 18, 1999.

—Frederick C. Ingram

BEN&JERRY'S.

Ben & Jerry's Homemade, Inc.

30 Community Drive
South Burlington, Vermont 05403-6828
U.S.A.
Telephone: (802) 846-1500
Fax: (802) 846-1555
Web Site: http://www.benjerry.com

Wholly-Owned Subsidiary of Unilever United States, Inc.
Incorporated: 1978 as Ben & Jerry's Homemade
Employees: 850
Sales: $237.04 million (1999)
NAIC: 31152 Ice Cream and Frozen Dessert
    Manufacturing

Ben & Jerry's Homemade, Inc. produces superpremium ice cream, frozen yogurt, and ice cream novelties in rich and original flavors, loaded with big chunks of cookies and candy. The company uses natural ingredients almost exclusively and insists its diary suppliers not use bovine growth hormone on their herds. The company's plant in Waterbury, Vermont, is the single most popular tourist attraction in the state.

Ben & Jerry's has been distinguished by a corporate philosophy that stresses social action and liberal ideals in addition to profit making. Its innovative and creative marketing devices have further expressed this unorthodox spirit. When confronted with a declining market for superpremium ice cream, its founders turned increasingly to professional managers and finally sold out to Unilever, which promised to maintain Ben & Jerry's traditional values while taking the brand to new heights.

Earthy Origins

Ben & Jerry's was founded in May 1978, when Ben Cohen and Jerry Greenfield opened an ice cream shop in Burlington, Vermont. Cohen had been teaching crafts, and Greenfield had been working as a lab technician when the two decided that "we wanted to do something that would be more fun," as Greenfield later told *People* magazine. In addition, the two wanted to live in a small college town. In 1977, they moved to

Burlington, Vermont, and completed a five dollar correspondence course in ice cream making from Pennsylvania State University. With $12,000 in start-up money, a third of which they borrowed, the two renovated an old gas station on a corner in downtown Burlington and opened Ben & Jerry's Homemade.

The first Ben & Jerry's store sold 12 flavors, made with an old-fashioned rock salt ice cream maker and locally produced milk and cream. Initially, ice cream production ran into some glitches. "I once made a batch of rum raisin that stretched and bounced," Greenfield told *People*. With time, however, the pair's rich, idiosyncratic, chunky offerings such as Dastardly Mash and Heath Bar Crunch gained a loyal following. In the summer of 1978, Ben & Jerry inaugurated the first of the many creative marketing ploys that would help drive the growth of their company when they held a free summer movie festival, projecting films onto a blank wall of their building.

By 1980, Ben & Jerry had begun selling their ice cream to a number of restaurants in the Burlington area. Ben delivered the products to customers in an old Volkswagen squareback station wagon. On his delivery route, he passed many small grocery and convenience stores and decided that they would be a perfect outlet for their products. In 1980, the pair rented space in an old spool and bobbin factory in Burlington and began packaging their ice cream in pint-size cartons with pictures of themselves on the package. "The image we wanted was grass roots," Cohen later told *People*.

The popularity of Ben & Jerry's products brought the company growth, despite the laissez-faire attitude of its two proprietors. At one point, the two were forced to close the doors of their store for a day to devote themselves to sorting out paperwork. In 1981, Ben & Jerry's expanded its pint-packing operations to more spacious quarters behind a car dealership. Shortly thereafter, the company opened its second retail outlet, a franchise on Route 7 in Shelburne, Vermont.

Going National in 1982

Despite its exclusively local operations, Ben & Jerry's first gained national attention in 1981 when *Time* magazine hailed its products as "the best ice cream in the world" in a cover story on ice cream. In the following year, Ben & Jerry's began to expand its distribution beyond the state of Vermont. First, an out-of-state store opened, selling Ben & Jerry's products in Portland, Maine. Then, the company began to sell its pints in the Boston area, distributing their goods to stores through independent channels. At the same time, Ben & Jerry's continued its policy of promoting itself through unique and whimsical activities. In 1983, for instance, the company took part in the construction of the world's largest ice cream sundae in St. Albans, Vermont.

With its continuing expansion, Ben & Jerry's developed a need for tighter financial controls on its operations, and the company's founders brought in a local nightclub owner with business experience to be chief operating officer. As sales grew sharply, Cohen and Greenfield slowly came to realize that their small-scale endeavor had exceeded their expectations. They were not entirely happy about this unexpected success. "When Jerry and I realized we were no longer ice cream men, but businessmen, our first reaction was to sell," Cohen told *People* magazine. "We were afraid that business exploits its workers and the community."

Ultimately, Cohen and Greenfield did decide to keep the company, but they vowed not to allow the growth of their enterprise to overwhelm their ideas of how a business could be a force for positive change in a community. "We decided to adapt the company so we could feel proud to say we were the businessmen of Ben & Jerry's," Cohen concluded. Among the stipulations they made to ensure that their company would be different from other parts of corporate America was a salary cap, limiting the best-paid people in the company to wages just five times higher than those of the lowest-paid employees. As Ben & Jerry's grew, this unusual limitation would complicate the company's high-level staffing.

To finance further growth, Greenfield and Cohen decided to raise capital to expand by selling stock to the public. However, in an effort to maintain a sense of local accountability in the company, they limited the stock offering to residents of Vermont, utilizing a little-known clause of the state law governing stocks and brokering. With the proceeds from this sale of stock, the company began construction of a new plant and corporate headquarters in Waterbury, Vermont, about half an hour away from Burlington.

As Ben & Jerry's products continued to garner attention, its prime competitor in the premium ice cream market, Häagen-Dazs, took steps to protect its own share of the market. In 1984, Pillsbury, Häagen-Dazs's corporate parent, threatened to withhold its products from distributors who also sold Ben & Jerry's ice cream. Ben & Jerry's retaliated by filing suit against Pillsbury, and also by launching a publicity campaign with the slogan "What's the Doughboy Afraid Of?" Pillsbury took steps to restrict distribution again in 1987, when it threatened to stop selling its ice cream to retailers who also sold Ben & Jerry's products. In both cases, legal action brought the restrictive practices to an end. By the end of 1984, sales of Ben & Jerry's products had exceeded $4 million, a figure more than twice as large as the previous year's revenues.

In 1985, Ben & Jerry's expanded distribution of its products dramatically, starting up sales of its pints in New York, New Jersey, Pennsylvania, Virginia, Washington, D.C., Georgia, Florida, and Minnesota. To supply these new markets, the company completed work on a modern manufacturing plant. Among the new offerings that year was New York Super Fudge Chunk, created at the suggestion of a customer from New York City. Throughout 1985, sales of Ben & Jerry's products continued at a break-neck pace. By the end of the year, revenues had reached $9 million, an increase of 143 percent from 1984. As part of their program to remain true to their ideals, Cohen and Greenfield established the Ben & Jerry's Foundation to fund community-oriented projects. In addition to the Foundation's initial capitalization, the two pledged 7.5 percent of the company's annual pre-tax profits to the charity.

Farming Out in 1986

In 1986, facing demand for its products that its one Vermont plant was unable to meet, Ben & Jerry's contracted with Dreyer's Grand Ice Cream, an ice cream company located in the Midwest, to manufacture Ben & Jerry's ice cream in its plants and distribute its products in most markets outside the Northeast. In addition, the company introduced its newest pint flavor, Coffee Heath Bar Crunch.

To promote this and other flavors, as well as the corporate identity, Ben & Jerry's began conducting tours of its Waterbury, Vermont, plant in 1986. In addition, the company launched its "Cowmobile," a converted mobile home that Cohen and Greenfield set out to drive across the country, distributing free scoops of ice cream as they went. Four months into the trip, the Cowmobile burned to the ground outside Cleveland without causing any injuries, bringing the planned expedition to a premature end. These efforts had pushed company sales to $20 million by the end of 1986, as Ben & Jerry's continued to post a remarkable rate of growth.

Cohen and Greenfield's original plan for a cross country trip was brought to fruition in 1987, when "Cow II" made its maiden voyage, also dispensing free scoops of ice cream along the way. After the October 1987 stock market crash, Cow II appeared on Wall Street to hand out scoops of "That's Life" and "Economic Crunch" ice cream to financial industry workers. Along with these highly topical creations, Ben & Jerry's introduced pints of "Cherry Garcia," named for the long-time lead guitarist of the rock group Grateful Dead. In addition, the company began to market its first ice cream novelty, the Brownie Bar. This product consisted of a square of French Vanilla ice cream, sandwiched between two brownies.

At their manufacturing plant in Vermont, Ben & Jerry's also took steps to keep the company in compliance with its ideal of being a socially responsible enterprise. To reduce its impact on the environment, Ben & Jerry's began using its ice cream waste to feed pigs being raised on a farm in Stowe, Vermont. In addition, to keep plant employees happy, the company instituted a variety of gestures, including Elvis day and Halloween costume celebrations, to break the monotony of life in a factory. By the end of 1987, company revenues had increased again, to reach $32 million.

International in 1988

In 1988, Ben & Jerry's opened its first outlets outside the United States when ice cream shops began operating in Montreal, Quebec, and in St. Maarten in the Caribbean. By the end of the year, more than 80 "scoop shops" were flying the Ben & Jerry's banner across 18 different states. At this time, the company decided to hold back on further franchising to make sure that product quality and service in its existing stores met its standards.

Also in 1988, Ben & Jerry's responded to continuing growth in demand for the company's products by opening its second manufacturing facility in Springfield, Vermont. This plant was used to make ice cream novelties, including the "Peace Pop," a chocolate covered ice cream bar on a stick. The name of this product referred to "One Percent for Peace," a nonprofit group founded in part by Cohen and Greenfield that was dedicated to redirecting national resources towards peace.

Together with their employees, Cohen and Greenfield formulated a three-part statement of mission that was designed to sum up the company's unique corporate philosophy. Relying on a theory of "linked prosperity," the mission statement asserted that Ben & Jerry's had a product mission, a social mission, and an economic mission. The company hoped to use this credo to enhance the lives of individuals and communities through its

actions. As part of its philosophy of linked prosperity, Ben & Jerry's introduced several new flavors of ice cream that incorporated ingredients from special sources. Rainforest Crunch, marketed in 1989, used nuts produced by rain forest trees. Chocolate Fudge Brownie, brought out in February 1990, used brownies made at a bakery in New York where formerly unemployed and homeless people worked.

Beginning in the late 1980s, Ben & Jerry's joined the trend toward producing low-fat ice cream and yogurt. Ben & Jerry's Light, introduced in 1989, had reduced levels of fat and cholesterol compared to the regular Ben & Jerry's ice cream but no less fat than other "regular" products then on the market. "It was sort of an oxymoron," the company's chief financial officer admitted to the *Wall Street Journal*. Sales of the products never exceeded about $9 million, and in December 1991 the line was declared a mistake and phased out.

Ben & Jerry's frozen yogurt proved far more successful. Boasting a butterfat content between one and five percent—as opposed to the 17 percent butterfat levels in the regular ice cream—Ben & Jerry's yogurt was selling in 13 cities around the United States in 1992. Within five months, yogurt sales were accounting for 15 to 18 percent of the company's revenues, and by the end of the year, it had become the leader in the superpremium yogurt market. In addition, Ben & Jerry's introduced a pint version of one of its most popular scoop shop offerings, chocolate chip cookie dough. The company had spent five years finding a way to get the chunks of dough into pints of ice cream without having them stick together and gum up the packaging machines. The product was an immediate hit, and soon became the company's best-selling flavor. Finally, the company began to market its ice cream novelties, Peace Pops and Brownie Bars, in "multi-paks" in supermarkets.

In response to continuing demand for its new products, Ben & Jerry's moved to increase its output in Vermont. The company added a pint production line at its Springfield plant, and also borrowed space at the St. Alban's Cooperative Creamery to open another temporary production facility. To increase its capacity over the long term, Ben & Jerry's broke ground on a third ice cream factory in St. Alban's in late 1992. Financed through an additional stock offering, this plant was scheduled to be functional in 1994. In addition, the company completed a new distribution center in Bellows Falls, Vermont. Ben & Jerry's also renewed its co-packing agreement with Dreyer's Grand Ice Cream, Inc., its midwestern partner. By the end of 1992, Ben & Jerry's sales overall had reached $132 million, up from $77 million in 1989.

Further from home, Ben & Jerry's opened two ice cream shops in the Russian cities of Petrozavodsk and Kondopoga. With two Russian partners, the company had spent three years navigating the Soviet bureaucracy and finding supplies for the venture, which Cohen and Greenfield hoped would promote friendship between Russians and Americans. After importing equipment and lining up reliable sources for cream, the company was able to open a combination ice cream plant and parlor, which was blessed by a Russian Orthodox priest on its first day.

As Ben & Jerry's moved into the mid-1990s, it could look back on a streak of extraordinary growth. From one small shop in downtown Burlington, Vermont, it had grown to include a chain of nearly 100 franchised shops, and a line of products sold in stores across the country. Company leaders were aware that it was unlikely that this rate of expansion could continue forever, since Ben & Jerry's growth had come in a mature and stable market. With its idiosyncratic corporate culture and its strong track record of introducing innovative flavors that drove ever-stronger sales, however, it appeared that Ben & Jerry's was well positioned to continue its success.

Going Corporate in the 1990s

Unfortunately, sales of superpremium ice cream slipped in the mid-1990s, as increasingly health-conscious consumers cut back on calories. Ben & Jerry's posted its first quarterly loss ever at the end of 1994, it slowest season. In addition, software problems crippled the new plant at St. Albans, draining the company's resources.

Ben & Jerry's had just over 500 employees in late 1994 when Ben Cohen announced his retirement as CEO (he remained chairman). In order to attract the right caliber of management talent to lead the company, Ben & Jerry's controversially dropped the pay formula that had limited the top salary to just five times the lowest. It launched a "Yo! I'm Your CEO" contest which received 20,000 entries from prospective candidates. However, the new CEO, Robert Holland, Jr., was actually chosen by a professional search firm.

Holland had previously become the first African-American partner at the esteemed management consulting firm McKinsey & Co. He applied his manufacturing expertise to developing a new line of sorbets and resolving the costly equipment problems at St. Albans. Developing new markets, however, was the company's top priority.

Ben & Jerry's continued to look abroad for growth. It had but an eight percent market share in Great Britain—a third that of Häagen-Dazs. The company tested the waters in France in late 1995. It soon afterwards began a kind of guerrilla marketing blitz, complete with Cowmobile, aimed at capturing the youngest of the country's ice cream connoisseurs. At home, Ben & Jerry's whipped up hip concoctions honoring the Doonesbury and Dilbert cartoons as well as the Vermont rock band Phish.

After a year and a half on the job, Holland decided that he was not the right person to develop these new markets and new products. Perry Odak was tapped to replace Holland. He had served briefly as COO of U.S. Repeating Arms Co., maker of Winchester rifles. This surprised some, given Ben & Jerry's philanthropic contributions to gun control groups. However, Odak had plenty of the desired consumer marketing experience with such companies as Armour-Dial, Jovan Inc., and Atari.

Ben & Jerry's enjoyed increased sales in the United States and United Kingdom in the late 1990s, when international sales accounted for about 11 percent of the total. The company signed a new Canadian distribution deal in 1998. The next year, it redesigned its U.S. distribution network to become less dependent on Dreyer's, signing on with the newly-created Nestle/Pillsbury joint venture, Ice Cream Partners. The company began using unbleached paperboard pint containers and planned to begin outsourcing its frozen novelties in 2000.

Unilever 2000

In April 2000, Unilever announced it was buying Ben & Jerry's for $326 million in cash. By coincidence, Unilever announced it was also buying diet food maker Slimfast on the same day. Unilever, which had $45 billion in annual sales, boasted such brands as Lipton Tea, Gordon's fish filets, Wisk detergent, and Dove soap—and Breyer's, Good Humor, and Sealtest ice cream. Although Unilever was in the process of cutting 1,200 of its total 1,600 brands worldwide, Unilever offered the power to take Ben & Jerry's, its only superpremium ice cream, to thousands of new consumers.

However, the purchase reminded at least one observer of the expensive, disastrous 1994 acquisition of Snapple Beverage by Quaker Oats. Snapple also had a quirky image and grass roots origins, but it withered under its new owner until finally Quaker Oats sold it at a huge loss.

The Anglo-Dutch corporation promised it would maintain Ben & Jerry's commitment to social causes. Cohen and Greenfield were to retain management roles. Unilever and Meadowbrook Lane Capital had originally planned to help take the company private, until they were outbid in that effort by Dreyer's Grand Ice Cream Co. Interestingly, the man who had persuaded Cohen and Greenfield to sell, Unilever's North American head Richard Goldstein, soon left to become CEO of International Flavors and Fragrances.

Principal Subsidiaries

Ben & Jerry's Homemade Holdings, Inc.

Principal Competitors

Ice Cream Partners; Dreyer's Grand Ice Cream, Inc.; Mars, Inc.; Nestle S.A.; Good Humor-Breyer's.

Further Reading

Ackerman, Jerry, "$326 Million Sale Makes It Ben, Jerry & Unilever but World's Top Consumer Products Company Says Ice Cream Maker's Good Deeds Won't End," *Boston Globe,* April 13, 2000, pp. C1f.

Alexander, Suzanne, "Life's Just a Bowl of Cherry Garcia for Ben & Jerry's," *Wall Street Journal,* July, 1992.

"Ben & Jerry's Looks Toward Life after Holland," *Ice Cream Reporter,* October 20, 1996, pp. 1ff.

Finch, Julia, and Jane Martinson, "Unilever Gorges on Ice Cream and Slimming Foods," *Guardian,* April 13, 2000.

Hays, Constance L., "Ben & Jerry's Deal Takes on Slightly New Flavor," *New York Times,* May 2, 2000, p. C1.

Hubbard, Kim, "For New Age Ice Cream Moguls Ben and Jerry, Making 'Cherry Garcia' and 'Chunky Monkey' Is a Labor of Love," *People,* September 10, 1990.

Kellaway, Lucy, "New Age Rests in Peace, Man: The Socially Responsible Business Ethic Has Now Become a Self-Interested, Cynical PR Message," *Financial Times,* Inside Track, April 17, 2000, pp. 16+.

Larson, Jane, "Founders of Ben & Jerry's Ice Cream Share Ingredients of Success," *Arizona Republic,* December 9, 1998.

McCormick, Jay, "Ben & Jerry's a la Mode," *Business Week,* May 20, 1996, pp. 22+.

Pham, Alex, "Gun Adviser Takes Post at Ben & Jerry's: For Fabled Firm, CEO Reflects Changing Times," *Boston Globe,* January 3, 1997, pp. C1+.

Shao, Maria, "The New Emperor of Ice Cream," *Boston Globe,* Economy Section, February 2, 1995, pp. 35+.

——, "A Scoopful of Credentials: CEO Holland Brings an Activist's Blend to Ben & Jerry's," *Boston Globe,* March 1, 1995, pp. 1+.

Tomkins, Richard, "Takeovers That Lose Their Cool," *Financial Times,* Comment & Analysis, April 15, 2000, pp. 13+.

"Union Wins Decision over Ben & Jerry's," *Boston Globe,* December 16, 1998, p. C5.

—Elizabeth Rourke
—updated by Frederick C. Ingram

Blue Bird Corporation

3920 Arkwright Road
Macon, Georgia 31210
U.S.A.
Telephone: (912) 757-7100
Fax: (912) 474-9131
Web site: http://www.blue-bird.com

Wholly Owned Subsidiary of Henlys Group plc
Incorporated: 1932 as Blue Bird Body Company
Employees: 2,877
Sales: $626.4 million (1998)
NAIC: 336211 Motor Vehicle Body Manufacturing;
  336213 Motor Home Manufacturing

Blue Bird Corporation, based in Macon, Georgia, is the leading manufacturer of school buses in North America. A wholly owned subsidiary of British bus maker Henlys Group plc since 1999, Blue Bird also manufactures high-end recreational vehicles and commercial buses geared toward charter, tour, and commuter usage. The company offers its products to both private and public organizations, including school districts, state governmental agencies, corporations, and churches. The majority of Blue Bird's products are sold through a network of distributors located in the United States and Canada. The company also offers financing packages to school bus customers and manages four manufacturing facilities, located in Georgia, Iowa, Canada, and Mexico.

Entrepreneurial Beginnings: 1920s–40s

Albert L. Luce, Sr., was a dealer of Ford automobiles in Fort Valley, Georgia, located about 25 miles south of Macon. The small, quiet town boasted groves of pecan trees and little else. Luce's foray into the building of buses began one day when he sold a bus to a customer at his dealership. Luce did not consider the bus, which was built on a Model-T frame, to be of high quality, and he informed the customer that he could probably build a better bus himself. The customer retorted that maybe he should try, and this led Luce to build his first bus, completed in 1927. Luce sold the bus that same year to an individual in a nearby town, and it was

put into operation transporting schoolchildren. Luce then went on to build seven additional buses, and in 1932 he sold his car dealership and formally founded Blue Bird.

Much of Luce's inspiration for starting a new company was reportedly attributable to his strong Methodist faith. The economic depression in the United States was causing car sales to decline, and Luce took this as a divine sign that he should manufacture buses and create jobs in his community. The name of the company, on the other hand, was allegedly inspired by a group of schoolchildren. Luce determined that using the family name would most likely be a poor idea, conjuring up bad puns such as "loose bus." Then, while showing a blue and yellow bus model to some school officials, some of the students dubbed the bus a "pretty little blue bird."

Luce was taking somewhat of a leap of faith with his new company, as public education in the United States at that time generally consisted of small, neighborhood schoolhouses within walking distance of most students' homes. Luce predicted, however, that the consolidation of schools into larger units serving a wider geographical range and improvements in the quality of roads, as well as the building of new roads, would increase the demand for school buses.

In 1937 Blue Bird succeeded in manufacturing a bus made entirely of steel, which was more heavy-duty and considerably safer than the wooden counterparts of the day. By the early 1940s Blue Bird buses could be found in a number of states, and by the end of World War II the company ranked seventh in a group of twelve bus manufacturing companies.

A Family Affair: 1950s–80s

Luce built a company that emphasized community and, influenced by his religious beliefs, clean living. Religious services were offered at the factory's lunchroom on a biweekly basis. Luce was also a businessman, however, and he paid keen attention to the bottom line, tolerating no waste. Luce's son George recalled an incident in 1939 that illustrated Luce's resolve to manage costs and make every penny count. Two of the three sons were home for the holidays from college, George told Rita Koselka of *Forbes* in 1986, when Luce began to discuss their study habits. George explained: "My father told us, 'Boys, I can tell you almost to the penny what the sides, windows or bumpers of a bus cost. If we think the costs are too high in any area, we can try to find ways to cut those costs. Now, it costs me $500 to send you to college. From your grades, I don't think you studied more than 100 hours. That means it cost me $5 an hour for you to study. That's way too much'." Luce then proposed a deal: he would lend his sons $500 each at the commencement of the school year. The loans would be repaid by studying, with an hour's worth of studying prior to dinner counting for one dollar and an hour of studying after dinner being worth 75 cents. The discrepancy in the amount was due to Luce's belief that studying before dinner was more productive. The sons were required to report their daily studies via postcard to the company bookkeeper, and amounts unpaid by the end of the school year were worked off during the summer at the Blue Bird plant (at 40 cents per hour).

The lesson Luce taught his sons through his college loan program proved valuable as they all entered the family business, taking over more control after their father began to suffer from a heart condition in the late 1940s. The sons, George, Albert "Buddy," Jr., and Joseph, focused on growth and expansion, eventually opening additional plants in Virginia, Iowa, Guatemala, LaFayette, Georgia, and two in Canada. School bus contracts were secured through a highly competitive and aggressive bidding process, and to stay on top of the competition, the Luce brothers searched through rival companies' regional newspapers for any information that might provide them with an edge. The brothers were also helped by their attention to maintaining high efficiency and low costs, something they learned from their father.

Aware of the possibility of a saturated market, the impending decline of school-age children, and the problems inherent in relying on one product for all sales, diversification was also on the Luce boys' agenda. Over the course of several decades Blue Bird tried out new products, including city buses, soda delivery trucks, and a window fan. The majority of these new product attempts failed, but one succeeded, though it, too, had a rela-

tively inauspicious start; in 1963 Blue Bird introduced the Wanderlodge, a high-end recreational vehicle, and entered the motor home market.

The original Wanderlodge was priced at $12,000, and the company had high hopes, anticipating a growing audience for luxury recreational vehicles. To promote its new product, Blue Bird sent some of its employees on a two-year trip around the country. Their instructions were to drive the Wanderlodge to various motor home camps to increase visibility and create interest, which would then, hopefully, generate sales. The marketing concept failed, however, and Blue Bird began preparing to return to the drawing board. Then, around the same time, in 1965, *House Beautiful* magazine published an article about the Wanderlodge, and orders for the vehicle began to pick up.

The Luce brothers assumed full control of Blue Bird following their father's death in 1962. By then Blue Bird was the fourth-largest school bus company in the nation, battling for market share with four other top competitors. Over the course of two decades Blue Bird climbed to the top spot, its sales increasing 20-fold. Blue Bird began selling buses to foreign customers in the late 1970s and early 1980s as domestic school bus sales started to drop, and in 1984 the company introduced financing services to its customers. By the mid-1980s one out of every three school bus sales was a Blue Bird, and the company sold about 11,000 school buses annually. Blue Bird employees, which numbered about 1,500 in Fort Valley alone, were paid above the local average wage, and the sense of family and community bred by the elder Luce continued—the Luce brothers knew many of their employees by name.

Though business was strong at Blue Bird, the health of the three Luce brothers was not; in the early 1980s the brothers developed heart conditions, and by the mid-1980s they had each undergone heart bypass operations. Taking the advice of a consultant, the brothers opened their family-only board of directors to outsiders in 1984, and two years later they hired Paul Glaske to serve as president and assume daily control of Blue Bird. Glaske left his post as president of heavy equipment manufacturer Marathon LeTourneau of Longview, Texas, to join Blue Bird. The Luce brothers' plan was to eventually pass control of the company to the third generation of Luces who were then in their early thirties and worked for Blue Bird. In the meantime, Glaske would run the company and had no plans to make major changes at Blue Bird; Glaske told *Forbes* shortly after joining the company, "Blue Bird ... is really what an American company should be, the type of company I can be proud to be associated with."

As management shifted, sales of the Wanderlodge continued to rise, and by the late 1980s Blue Bird was selling about 150 to 200 of the recreational vehicles on a yearly basis, accounting for about 20 percent of total company sales. The price had risen considerably since the early 1960s, with the price tag starting at $199,000. The top model fetched $350,000 before options, which were numerous. The motor home industry, according to the Recreation Vehicle Industry Association, enjoyed sales of 379,500 recreational vehicles in 1986, down from the all-time high of 541,100 in 1976 but up from 1980, when only 181,400 were sold. So committed were owners to their Wanderlodges, affectionately called "Birds," that many traveled to Fort Valley

Key Dates:

1927: Albert L. Luce, Sr., builds his first school bus.
1932: Luce forms the Blue Bird Body Company.
1962: Founder Luce dies.
1963: Company introduces the Wanderlodge and enters the luxury recreational vehicle market.
1986: Blue Bird hires its first outsider to run the company.
1992: Management leads a leveraged buy-out of Blue Bird with the help of Merrill Lynch Capital Partners and renames the company Blue Bird Corporation.
1999: Henlys Group plc acquires Blue Bird.

when their Wanderlodges required servicing. Blue Bird offered the owners free camping at Wanderlodge Wayside Park, Blue Bird's mobile home park.

Changing of the Guard: 1990s

Entering the 1990s, Blue Bird was the confirmed leader in the U.S. school bus market, producing nearly half of all school buses sold in North America, and its recreational vehicle business was solid. A slowdown in school bus sales prompted Blue Bird to reduce the workforce from 427 salaried employees to about 300, and three plants, the Guatemalan unit, one in Canada, and the Virginia plant, were sold. Operations were further streamlined, and the factories were computerized to increase productivity.

The third generation of Luce employees left Blue Bird to pursue other interests, leaving the company with no family members to assume leadership. After George Luce died in 1990, brother Buddy approached president Glaske and told him that the brothers planned to put the company up for sale. In the summer of 1991, potential buyers of Blue Bird began visiting the Fort Valley corporate headquarters to inspect the merchandise. Glaske told the *Atlanta Journal and Constitution,* "We were doing dog and pony shows, sometimes a couple a day, with potential buyers, their lawyers and their accountants." Six companies offered bids, all in the price range of just more than $400 million, in November 1991. Glaske wished to secure interest in the company as part of the sale and also hoped to maintain current management strategies and procedures.

Eventually, Merrill Lynch Capital Partners, Inc., a division of Merrill Lynch & Co., agreed to pay $397 million in a management-led leveraged buyout. The firm acquired 82 percent of Blue Bird in 1992, and Glaske, along with 14 other managers selected by the Luce brothers, acquired the remainder. The name of the company was changed from Blue Bird Body Company to Blue Bird Corporation, and existing management continued to run the company. The two Luce brothers formally retired but kept offices at the factory. Buddy Luce voiced confidence in the new ownership structure and said he hoped new management would carry on the Luce family's legacy. Buddy told the *Atlanta Journal and Constitution,* "We've made an impact in this community, put a manufacturing base where there was none. . . . At my retirement party a man came up to me and said, 'You hired me when I was 18 and now I'm 38, and my

first-born is getting ready for college, and every dollar came from this good company.' I hope people will be able to say that for a long time. I think they will.''

With new owners in place, Blue Bird focused on continued success, which included plans to expand into the commercial bus market. In 1992 the company introduced the Q-Bus, its flagship, medium-duty commercial bus that targeted the charter and commuter markets. The 37-foot bus allowed seating for up to 45 passengers and also offered such features as a restroom and option for a 300-horsepower engine. And to maintain its leadership position in the school bus arena, Blue Bird offered technological innovations, such as the first school bus to run on natural gas, introduced in 1992. Blue Bird also forged strategic partnerships with other companies to work with alternative fuels and search for environmentally friendlier options. In 1994, commissioned by the Antelope Valley School District in southern California, the company teamed with Westinghouse Electronic Systems to develop an electric school bus. A year later Blue Bird worked with John Deere, a leading manufacturer of farm equipment, to install a John Deere natural gas engine in a Blue Bird school bus for the Poway Unified School District, located near San Diego, California. The retrofit was one of many promoted by the California Energy Commission, which began a program in 1992 to convert existing school buses in California to more environmentally friendly and efficient systems. In 1996 Blue Bird and Electrosource, Inc., began work on the development of an advanced battery system to power buses and other electric vehicles. Blue Bird's involvement with fuel alternatives was not only influenced by its desire to stay on the cutting edge of technology but also by the company's belief that school districts across the nation would increasingly opt for more economical, clean-burning vehicles.

Blue Bird's performance over the course of the decade continued to improve, with sales climbing each year. In 1995, for instance, sales reached $517.4 million. The following year sales increased 10.2 percent to climb to $570.2 million. In 1997 sales equaled $576.1 million, up only 1 percent, but gross profit rose 6.9 percent. 1998 sales rose 8.7 percent, to $626.4 million. The company continued to head the North American school bus industry, commanding a market share of about 45 percent in 1999, and though Blue Bird's operations in commercial vehicles and motor homes grew, the company still relied for the most part on its school bus business, which accounted for about 77 percent of net sales in 1998.

As the close of the decade approached, Blue Bird headed toward another significant change. In October 1999 Blue Bird was acquired by Henlys Group plc, the United Kingdom's leading manufacturer of bus bodies. The purchase significantly boosted Henlys efforts to expand in North America. Henlys agreed to pay $428 million for Blue Bird and to repay Blue Bird's debt, which totaled about $237 million. The Blue Bird acquisition was a welcome success for Henlys, as an attempt to purchase bus chassis manufacturer Dennis had recently been thwarted by a rival. Swedish car manufacturer AB Volvo held a ten percent stake in Henlys. Henlys planned to take advantage of Blue Bird's leadership position in the United States to expand operations and move more heavily and aggressively into such areas as the recreational vehicle and commercial vehicle markets. The new owner also planned to increase international exports. Henlys chairman Norman Askew announced his pleasure with the acquisition in a prepared statement, stating, ''Blue Bird's market leadership position, proven experienced management team coupled with a strong financial track record will complement Henlys' existing North American activities. Jointly we will capitalise on existing relationships and distribution networks to deliver strong growth in order to enhance shareholder value.''

Principal Subsidiaries

Blue Bird Capital Corporation.

Principal Competitors

Metrotrans Corporation; Navistar International Corporation; Thor Industries, Inc.; Mayflower Corporation plc.

Further Reading

Jordan, Stephanie, ''Few Changes Planned After Blue Bird Buyout,'' *Macon Telegraph,* December 16, 1991.

Kleinfield, N.R., ''On the Road in a $350,000 Home,'' *New York Times,* June 21, 1987, p. 4.

Koselka, Rita, ''It Was Important to Father and Mother, and It's Important to Us,'' *Forbes,* October 6, 1986, p. 88.

Smith, Randall, ''Merrill Lynch Unit Agrees to Buy-Out of Blue Bird Body,'' *Wall Street Journal,* December 11, 1991, p. B3.

Thurston, Scott, ''Georgia's Blue Bird Rolls into New Era,'' *Atlanta Journal and Constitution,* July 19, 1992, p. R1.

—Mariko Fujinaka

CanWest Global Communications Corp.

CanWest Global Communications Corporation

3100 Toronto Dominion Center
201 Portage Avenue
Winnipeg, Manitoba R3B 3L7
Canada
Telephone: (204) 956-2025
Fax: (204) 947-9841
Web site: http://www.canwestglobal.com

Public Company
Incorporated: 1973 as CanWest Capital Corporation
Employees: 2,500
Sales: C$882 million (1999)
Stock Exchanges: New York Toronto
Ticker Symbol: CWG
NAIC: 512110 Motion Picture and Video Production;
  512120 Motion Picture & Video Distribution; 513112
  Radio Stations; 513120 Television Broadcasting;
  513210 Cable Networks

CanWest Global Communications Corporation is Canada's largest private sector television broadcaster. Although it owns several television stations throughout Canada, it has been frustrated several times in its attempt to build a third Canadian network to compete with the government-owned CBC and CTV, Canada's publicly owned consortium of private stations. The company also has an ownership interest in and runs television stations in Australia, New Zealand, the Republic of Ireland, Northern Ireland, and Chile. It is interested in expanding into the United States, United Kingdom, and Western Europe television markets. Its CanWest Entertainment division controls the company's film and television production and distribution subsidiaries.

A Single Television Station in Winnipeg in the 1970s

CanWest Capital Corporation, the forerunner of CanWest Global Communications Corporation, was founded by Israel ("Izzy") H. Asper, a prominent Canadian tax and corporate lawyer, author, business person, and former political leader.

Asper had studied law at the University of Manitoba and practiced law for 13 years before becoming the leader of the Manitoba Liberal party from 1970 to 1975. He formed CanWest Capital Corporation in the early 1970s as a holding company for his business interests.

The CanWest story began in 1974 when the Canadian Radio-Television and Telecommunications Commission (CRTC) approved the company's license application to establish a new independent television station in Winnipeg, Manitoba. Asper and a group of investors then bought KCND-TV, located across the border in North Dakota, and transported the station's equipment back to Winnipeg where they reassembled it in a converted Safeway supermarket. The station, CKND-TV, became active in fall 1975 and was Winnipeg's third television station.

More Stations in the 1980s

Following the launch of CKND-TV, CanWest turned its attention to Toronto, where the recently licensed Global Television Network was having financial difficulties. Global provided programming for CKND-TV, so CanWest had an interest in its survival. Asper saved the near-bankrupt Global by organizing an emergency rescue. Through conservative management and operating strategies, Global became financially sound. By 1989 CanWest had acquired full ownership of Global.

In 1984 CanWest obtained new licenses for start-up television stations in Regina and Saskatoon, which it operated through a newly formed subsidiary, SaskWest Television Inc. In 1987 CanWest gained control of CKVU-TV in Vancouver, British Columbia.

CanWest turned the Global Television Network into a profitable venture by importing popular American shows such as *M*A*S*H* and *The Young and the Restless.* In the 1990s it carried such popular series as *Seinfeld, Friends,* and *NYPD Blue.* Critics such as the Friends of Canadian Broadcasting, though, complained that Global relied too heavily on American programming at the expense of original Canadian programming. In 1992 the CRTC renewed Global's license for only four years, rather than the usual seven, and required Global to make improvements in its Canadian content.

Company Perspectives:

With respect to our corporate development, we continue to seek ways to expand our television presence in the U.S., the U.K., and Western Europe. The latter is a new twist in our strategy, but we believe there are significant growth opportunities in this group of markets. If we are to grow as a company, we must not only seek a presence in established markets but also markets that are less developed.

A Public Company in the 1990s

In 1991 CanWest had a successful initial public offering (IPO) on the Toronto Stock Exchange. Between 1991 and 1995 CanWest quickly grew into a world-class communications company by acquiring broadcast properties around the world. Its strategy was to buy up cheap, poorly run television networks and make them profitable.

The company made its first international expansion by acquiring an interest in TV3 New Zealand. TV3 was losing money at the time, but in its first year under CanWest management it turned a small profit.

Subsequent international growth included the acquisition of an interest in Australia's Network Ten, which owned stations in Sydney, Melbourne, and Brisbane. It, too, was losing money, but CanWest was able to turn the station around and generate substantial operating profits. In fiscal 1994 Network Ten contributed 64 percent of CanWest's consolidated profits. CanWest also took full ownership of TV3 New Zealand and then launched TV4 New Zealand. In 1998 it launched TV3 Ireland, the Republic of Ireland's first private, over-the-air television network. CanWest also acquired a 30 percent interest in Ulster Television in 1998.

In 1994 CanWest held a 24.5 interest in a new commercial radio station for the United Kingdom. Called ''Talk Radio U.K.,'' the owners received permission to launch the station in mid-1994. It would be Britain's third national commercial radio station.

In its first Latin American venture, CanWest acquired 49 percent of the Chilean television station La Red for C$11 million in 1994. La Red was one of five stations broadcasting in Chile. Determined to make La Red the top television station in Chile, CanWest invested heavily in soccer programming and brought in several high-profile personalities. It also brought in several North American shows, but soon found that Chileans preferred locally produced television programs to imported shows dubbed in Spanish. CanWest also cut personnel at La Red from 300 to 174 and made several executive changes. During the first year La Red's audience market share increased from 5.7 percent to 7.9 percent, and CanWest expected further growth in advertising revenues from La Red. For fiscal 1994 ending in August CanWest had C$202 million in revenues and C$32.5 million net income.

In 1995 England's Independent Television Commission (ITC) took bids for analog TV frequency Channel 5, and CanWest submitted the highest bid of US $57.9 million. It was competing against two British-led consortia and Rupert Murdoch's BSkyBled New Century Television, which submitted the lowest bid. At the end of the year, however, British regulators rejected CanWest's bid for Channel 5, citing concerns about programming quality, and awarded the license to a British-led consortium.

By 1995 CanWest had emerged as a powerful new force in Canadian broadcasting. It was the largest private sector television broadcaster in the country, reaching 73 percent of Canada's English-speaking populace and garnering 16.5 percent of audience share. Its market capitalization exceeded C$1 billion for the first time in 1995. Through a series of acquisitions, it was in the process of building a national network in mainland Canada. It also had interests in television networks in New Zealand, Australia, and Chile. It hoped to use its experience as part of a talk-radio consortium in the United Kingdom to enter that country's undeveloped and lucrative private television market. Asper told *Canadian Business* in 1995, ''We have to be affiliated or connected to or own broadcast outlets in the broadest possible geographical territory.'' Asper also hoped to enter the United States television market. In 1995 Asper received the Order of Canada, the country's highest honor.

In 1995 CanWest launched a takeover bid of C$24 a share for Western International Communications (WIC), which owned eight television stations, 12 radio stations, and interests in cable and satellite TV services. The acquisition would make real Asper's goal of creating a third national television network in Canada in addition to the government-owned CBC Network and the privately owned CTV Network. At the time WIC was embroiled in a lawsuit following the death in April 1994 of its founder, Frank Griffiths, that would dilute the Griffiths family's controlling interest in WIC from 62 percent to less than ten percent.

In January 1996 the British Columbia Supreme Court upheld the Griffiths family's controlling position in WIC. As a result, CanWest said it would reconsider its takeover bid. CanWest subsequently announced plans to launch stations in Edmonton, Calgary, Victoria, and Quebec City. In December the CRTC rejected CanWest's application for the last remaining Calgary-Edmonton TV license and awarded it to Craig Broadcasting of Brandon, Manitoba. The rejection made it impossible for CanWest to complete the national network it was trying to build, at least for the time being. As a symbol of its growth, CanWest shares began trading on the New York Stock Exchange in June 1996.

In March 1997 the CRTC approved CanWest's application to take over Quebec City station CKMI-TV, a CBC affiliate. CanWest planned to broadcast English-language programming to Montreal from the station. With its planned takeover of WIC thwarted, CanWest increased its holdings of nonvoting WIC shares from 9.7 percent to 15 percent. CanWest hoped that its increased stake in the company—even though nonvoting—would give it some influence in the company's affairs and future direction. By December 1997 it had increased its holdings to 30 percent, making CanWest the largest nonvoting shareholder in WIC.

Key Dates:

1974: CanWest is licensed as a new independent television station in Winnipeg, Manitoba.
1984: CanWest obtains new licenses for start-up TV stations in Regina and Saskatoon.
1987: Company gains control of CKVU-TV in Vancouver, British Columbia.
1991: CanWest has a successful initial public offering on the Toronto Stock Exchange.
1995: CanWest attempts its first takeover of WIC Western International Communications.
1998: CanWest acquires Fireworks Entertainment Inc. and forms CanWest Entertainment.
1999: CanWest establishes international film distribution arm, Seven Arts International.
1999: CanWest launches its Interactive Media division.

By early 1998 rumors indicated that Emily Griffiths, matriarch of the Griffiths family, was willing to sell her 62 percent controlling interest in WIC. Analysts noted that CanWest would probably gain control of WIC, even if she were to sell to another buyer. That was because WIC had a "poison pill" clause in its shareholder agreement that would turn all nonvoting shares into voting shares once the majority stake in the voting shares was transferred.

On March 14, 1998, Emily Griffiths sold her WIC voting stock for C$91 million to two buyers, Shaw Communications Inc. of Calgary and the Allard family of Edmonton. CanWest responded by announcing that it had increased its holdings of WIC nonvoting stock to 35 percent and offered to buy all remaining WIC stock of either class for C$650 million. It was CanWest's goal to win a ruling from the CRTC to trigger WIC's shareholder clause that would transform nonvoting shares into voting shares, thus giving CanWest control of WIC.

Immediately three provincial securities regulators began investigating WIC's new poison pill clause, which would make additional nonvoting shares available at half-price to investors who already owned the stock if CanWest increased its position in WIC. The poison pill clause was adopted by WIC's board in an attempt to foil CanWest's hostile takeover bid. In short order the regulators struck down the new poison pill provision, thus allowing CanWest to buy a majority of WIC's nonvoting shares. Shaw Communications responded by offering C$975 million in cash and stock, or C$43.50 a share, for WIC's remaining nonvoting stock, compared with CanWest's bid of C$39 a share. CanWest quickly matched Shaw's offer of C$43.50 a share, but it would require an Ontario court to overturn a previous deal between WIC and Shaw.

In August 1998 CanWest and Shaw Communications reached an agreement that gave CanWest control of WIC for C$950 million. The agreement would have to be approved by the CRTC, however, which could take a year or more. Under the terms of the agreement, CanWest would pay Shaw C$150 million in cash, take on C$300 million in WIC debt, and give up its 44 percent stake in WIC to Shaw, which was valued at about C$500 million. In return, CanWest gained 11 television stations, including four in Alberta, three in British Columbia, three in Quebec, and one in Ontario. CanWest also would obtain two existing licenses for specialty channels RoB-TV, which featured business news and a video-on-demand channel. Shaw would get WIC's 12 radio stations and control of two specialty TV channels, Superchannel and Movie Max, half of the Family Channel, and a 40 percent interest in Teletoon. In September 1999 the CRTC ordered public hearings to begin in October on the case. By mid-2000 CanWest was still awaiting CRTC approval to assume control of WIC's nine television stations.

At the same time CanWest was considering spending another C$900 million to acquire NetStar Communications Inc. of Toronto, which owned cable channels The Sports Network, the Discovery Channel, and others in Canada. ESPN Inc. owned a one-third interest in NetStar. Toward the end of 1998 CanWest put its bid for NetStar on hold, citing differences with ESPN. In February 1999 CanWest announced that it would acquire a 68 percent interest in NetStar in a deal estimated to cost C$875 million, with ESPN keeping its 32 percent. ESPN had the option of tendering its shares or selling them to another buyer. Then, at the last minute, rival CTV, a widely held public consortium of privately owned Canadian television stations and Canada's second network, stepped in and signed a deal for the 68 percent of NetStar for which CanWest was negotiating. In March 2000 the CRTC approved CTV's application for control of NetStar.

Meanwhile, CanWest founder Israel Asper was taking steps to ensure an orderly management succession at the company. In July 1997 he relinquished his post of CEO and president to Peter Viner, who was the CEO of Australia's Network Ten. Asper took on the new title of executive chairman. His son, Leonard Asper, was CanWest's executive vice-president. The next month the Australian Broadcasting Authority ordered CanWest to reduce its stake in Network Ten to 15 percent, the maximum allowed to foreign owners. At the time CanWest effectively controlled 76 percent of Network Ten, according to an Australian court ruling. For fiscal 1997 ending August 31 CanWest reported net income of C$142 million on combined revenues of C$835 million. In October 1997 the company launched its cable network in Canada, Prime TV.

Production, Distribution, and the Internet: 1998–2000

In 1998 CanWest began getting involved in film and television production and distribution. It entered the production side of television and film through the acquisition of Fireworks Entertainment Inc., a leading Canadian independent film and television production company. CanWest was the first Canadian broadcaster to become involved in film and television production. It formed the CanWest Entertainment division for its film and television production and distribution interests. In 1999 CanWest Entertainment opened an international distribution office in London, England.

In August 1999 CanWest bought a 20 percent stake in Alliance Atlantis Communications, Canada's largest film and television company, for more than C$13 million. The acquisition gave CanWest a base from which to expand its programming holdings. Alliance had ownership interests in six Canadian channels and was a leading producer and distributor of television programming. In 1999 CanWest also created its international film distribution arm, Seven Arts International.

CanWest launched its Interactive Media division in 1999 by acquiring 20 percent of two U.S.-based Internet content providers: Internet Broadcasting Systems (IBS), the leading developer of local news-based web sites for television stations, and LifeServ, a community-focused Internet provider of content relating to planning weddings, births, and careers. CanWest planned to launch eight web sites related to Global Television in 2000 in association with IBS. CanWest's overall Internet strategy called for developing a number of content sites that would generate e-commerce and advertising revenues.

The planned management succession strategy came to fulfillment in September 1999 when Leonard Asper became president and CEO, replacing past president and CEO Peter Viner, who became vice-chairman.

A Diversified Media Company for the 21st Century

As of mid-2000 CanWest was still awaiting approval of the WIC transaction, which was tying up a C$383 million investment that the company wanted to transform into a productive, cash-generating asset. CanWest planned to continue to find ways to expand its television presence in the United States, the United Kingdom, and Western Europe. It expected moderate growth from its operations in Canada and Australia and expected that TV3 in Ireland would become profitable by 2001.

CanWest had high expectations for its Internet strategy, which president and CEO Leonard Asper called ''an area of significant future growth for CanWest'' in his 1999 Report to Shareholders. The company believed that it was in a strong position to generate e-commerce sales through its ability to attract major retailers to partner with it, and its television marketing power put CanWest in a unique position to generate more advertising on its web sites than its competitors.

Principal Subsidiaries

CanVideo Television Sales; Global Prime TV; Global Ontario; Global Vancouver; Global Quebec; Global Regina; Global Halifax; Global Saskatoon; Global Saint John; Global Winnipeg; TV3 New Zealand; TV4 New Zealand; TV3 Ireland; Ulster TV; More FM (New Zealand); Network TEN (Australia); Internet Broadcasting Systems (20%); Lifeserv Corporation (20%); Fireworks Entertainment; Seven Arts International; CanWest Entertainment International; WIC Western International Communications.

Principal Divisions

Global Television Network; CanWest International; CanWest Entertainment; CanWest Interactive.

Principal Competitors

Baton Broadcasting Corp. (Canada); Shaw Communications Inc. (Canada); CTV (Canada).

Further Reading

Amdur, Meredith, ''CanWest Bids $58 Million for UK's Ch. 5,'' *Broadcasting & Cable,* May 8, 1995, p. 57.

''Asper Stymied,'' *Maclean's,* January 15, 1996, p. 45.

''Asper Tries Again,'' *Maclean's* January 29, 1996, p. 38.

''The Battle for WIC,'' *Maclean's,* April 27, 1998, p. 53.

Berman, David, ''Channel Changer,'' *Canadian Business,* September 1995, p. 46.

——, ''Feeling Oppressed? Call Izzy,'' *Canadian Business,* April 24, 1998, p. 48.

''CanWest Fires Back at WIC,'' *Maclean's,* April 6, 1998, p. 53.

''CanWest Pulls the Plug,'' *Maclean's,* September 21, 1998, p. 63.

''CanWest Targets WIC,'' *Maclean's,* March 17, 1997, p. 33.

Chard, Paul, ''Too Many Gringos,'' *Canadian Business,* September 1995, p. 48.

Chisholm, Patricia, ''Tycoon of the Tube,'' *Maclean's,* November 27, 1995, p. 36.

''Crushing a Poison Pill,'' *Maclean's,* April 20, 1998, p. 35.

Gage, Ritchie, ''Asper Vision,'' *Manitoba Business,* December 1995, p. 5.

''Global Domination: Izzy Asper May Soon Have His National Network,'' *Maclean's,* August 31, 1998, p. 56.

Hunter, Jennifer, ''Plotting a Takeover: CanWest Global Closes in on Griffiths Family's Control of WIC,'' *Maclean's,* January 19, 1998, p. 46.

Mandel-Campbell, Andrea, ''Television South American-Style,'' *Manitoba Business,* May 1995, p. 30.

Miles, Laureen, ''Phone Lines Open,'' *Adweek Eastern Edition,* June 13, 1994, p. 16.

Newman, Peter C., ''Thumbs Down to Izzy Asper's National Dream,'' *Maclean's,* December 23, 1996, p. 40.

''The Rise of a TV Empire,'' *Maclean's,* February 1, 1999, p. 60.

Tillson, Tamsen, ''Webs Tangle for Dominance,'' *Variety,* April 3, 2000, p. 156.

''Unlocking WIC,'' *Maclean's,* September 20, 1999, p. 39.

Wells, Jennifer, ''Izzy's Dream,'' *Maclean's,* February 19, 1996, p. 40.

——, ''Why a Network?,'' *Maclean's,* February 19, 1996, p. 46.

''WIC Takes a Poison Pill,'' *Maclean's* April 13, 1998, p. 43.

Wilson-Smith, Anthony, ''What's Going at Global?,'' *Maclean's,* February 28, 2000, p. 46.

—David P. Bianco

Capital Radio plc

30 Leicester Square
London WC2H 7LA
United Kingdom
Telephone: (+44) 20 7766-6000
Fax: (+44) 20 7766-6100
Web site: http://www.capitalradio.plc.uk

Public Company
Incorporated: 1973
Employees: 1,035
Sales: £105.2 million ($206.4 million) (1999)
Stock Exchanges: London
Ticker Symbol: CAP.L
NAIC: 513112 Radio Stations

London-based Capital Radio plc is one of the United Kingdom's leading radio and media groups. Its holdings include its flagship Capital FM 95.8 station, which, with more than three million listeners in the London area, has captured the largest metropolitan audience of any radio station in the world. Beyond its grip on the London market, Capital Radio owns the licenses for some 20 other commercial radio stations across the United Kingdom, in markets including Kent, Birmingham, and South Wales. Capital also has aggressively pursued licenses in the promising digital radio market, opening at the end of the 1990s. Since late 1999, the company has been awarded digital licenses to more than 20 local markets, as well as multiplex licenses in the Birmingham, Manchester, and London markets through a joint venture with rival media company Emap. Capital Radio also has been rapidly expanding into the Internet arena, operating a variety of commercial and station-related sites. After an aborted attempt to enter the restaurant business in the mid-1990s, Capital Radio has begun to look closer to home for further expansion; in May 2000 the company beat out Scottish Media Group when it reached an agreement to acquire the Border TV television and radio group. Capital Radio is headed by CEO Dave Mansfield.

Commercial Radio Pioneer in the 1970s

Until the 1970s, British radio waves were the exclusive province of BBC Radio. In 1972, however, the British government opened the country's airwaves to the first commercial stations. LBC, with a mandate to provide news and information, began broadcasting in 1973. Two weeks later marked the debut of Capital Radio, which had been given the mandate to provide "general entertainment" programming. Richard Attenborough, who become chairman of the company (and later was named "president for life"), was the station's first broadcaster.

Capital Radio's early years were difficult ones, however. Advertisers were difficult to find, audiences were reluctant to tune into what many considered the "low brow" and at best amateurish nature of commercial radio. Throughout the 1970s, Capital Radio was forced to turn to its major investors for funding to stay on the air. At one point, Attenborough was forced to sell a painting by Degas to pay the company's employees. Nonetheless, the company enjoyed some successes as well, setting up its own Community Affairs Department and organizing the Capital Helpline, the "Help a London Child" charity program. In the late 1970s, the company inaugurated the "Flying Eye," the first airborne traffic reporter over the London area.

The company's big break came in 1984 when Chris Tarrant joined the company as a presenter for the station's lunch-time show. When Tarrant moved to the breakfast slot, however, his popularity soared; Tarrant became a primary force behind Capital Radio's steady audience gains. Toward the end of the decade, Capital Radio began to prepare for much-needed changes in the independent radio market—which by then had reached nearly 200 stations—by going public, making it the first radio station to gain a listing on the London Stock Exchange. The publication of the *Peacock Review of Broadcasting* sparked a number of developments in the commercial radio world. One of the most significant changes was the splitting of the AM and FM programming requirements (radio stations previously had been required to simulcast the same programming on both bands).

As a result, Capital Radio was able to create two stations: 95.8 Capital FM began programming contemporary hit music, while

Company Perspectives:

Capital Radio is the UK's leading radio group. It is our intention to build on our strengths and to embrace digital technology, which we believe will offer significant growth opportunities, as well as establishing a leading Internet presence.

its AM counterpart, 1548 AM Capital Gold, turned to a "classic golden hits" playlist. By 1990, the Capital Gold station had become one of the most successful on the AM band, while 95.8 Capital FM topped previous audience champion BBC1 for the first time. With nearly three million listeners, the FM station became not only the undisputed leader of the London market, but also the world leader in metropolitan audience share.

Expansion in the 1990s

The passage of the Broadcasting Act of 1990 established a new Radio Authority, which was given charge of attributing new local and national licenses. The new legislation helped pave the way for a shakeup in the radio industry, as a number of major groups began to lead a consolidation of the market. Capital Radio joined the resulting acquisition fray in 1993 when it made its first acquisition, paying £18 million for Midlands Radio Plc., giving it that company's two key Birmingham market AM and FM stations. The company also bought stakes in two other radio groups, GWR and Metro Radio.

The following year, Capital bought another radio company, Southern Radio, paying £33 million for that company's stations in Kent, Sussex, Isle of Wight and Hampshire. With its potential audience reaching beyond London to include much of the Southeast, the company hoped to become more competitive against other media, particularly television, in attracting advertisers. At the same time, Capital itself became the subject of takeover rumors. The company nonetheless maintained its independent course. By the end of 1994, commercial radio, which had long been the ugly duckling of Britain's media, had overtaken BBC Radio for the first time on a national scale. This breakthrough gave the entire industry a boost among advertisers and began U.K. radio's long-running leadership in advertising growth rates. Severe government restrictions—which included a market-based point system that restricted the various major radio groups from extending their holdings—were hampering Capital Radio's growth. Nonetheless, the company managed to acquire Oxford's Fox FM by 1996.

Hope for the future appeared on several fronts, however. In 1996, the government prepared the New Broadcasting Act, which opened the way to the first licenses for digital radio transmission, as well as loosening some of the station ownership restrictions. That same year, Capital Radio launched its first Internet site, becoming one of the earliest entrants in what was to become the boom market for the turn of the century. The company also branched out into record production, setting up the joint venture Wildstar Records with Telstar. Meanwhile, Capital Radio began to cast its expansive gaze beyond radio; in November 1996, the company paid £57 million to acquire the

My Kinda Town restaurant group, composed of a number of theme-based restaurants, including the Chicago Pizza Pie Factory, Tacos, Beach Blanket Babylon, and Harry J. Beans. These restaurants joined another company venture in the works, the Capital Radio Café partnership being constructed on the ground floor of the company's headquarters.

The My Kinda Town acquisition was immediately greeted with disapproval on the stock market, which sent Capital Radio's share price plummeting. The following year proved the market right: struggling to integrate the various restaurant concepts, Capital Radio attempted to convert a number of its restaurants to a Latin theme format, which included the Havana restaurant concept, before deciding to focus its restaurant interests wholly on the Radio Café and Havana concepts. By 1999, My Kinda Town continued to provide the company with a bad case of indigestion, and in that year the company sold off the Havana restaurant chain and closed down its restaurant division, keeping only its four Radio Cafes, which were then regrouped directly under the company.

Returning to radio in 1997, Capital Radio's expansion ambitions were thwarted when its attempted £87 million acquisition of the Virgin Radio group—which held one of the rare national commercial radio broadcasting licenses—was referred to the Mergers and Monopolies Commission. The company's file was promptly caught up in red tape. In the meantime, popular Virgin Radio personality Chris Evans—longtime opponent of Chris Tarrant in London radio's "War of the Two Chris' "—managed to find investors willing to back him in a buyout of Virgin Radio. Capital Radio, now led by CEO Dave Mansfield, was forced to content himself with the purchase of the much smaller XFM radio group, set up just nine months earlier, for £4 million. The company followed up that acquisition in 1998 with the purchases of Red Dragon Radio and Touch Radio, both broadcasting in South Wales.

In 1998, the Wildstar joint venture partnership with Telstar led to the formation of a new joint venture, MusicCapital.com, to set up an online retail music service. Operated under Capital Radio's new Digital Interactive subsidiary, the joint venture marked a new phase in the company's Internet expansion. At the same time, the company began preparing for the next revolution in radio broadcasting, setting up another joint venture, now with rival radio and magazine group Emap plc, to form CE Digital to compete for the coming opening of the United Kingdom's digital radio market.

CE Digital won licenses to broadcast digital multiplex radio stations to the London, Manchester, and Birmingham markets, while Capital went off on its own to win the local license to nearly 20 more digital radio markets—including the digital multiplex license for the Cardiff market, a national digital license, and 16 other local market digital licenses. In January 2000, the company realized its long-held ambition to become a national broadcaster when XFM began transmission over the SkyDigital satellite network. Full rollout of its XFM digital radio network was expected to be completed by mid-2000.

With its Internet interests building up steam—in the late 1990s the company constructed a network of music-content web sites—Capital Radio began to look toward a new media

Key Dates:

1972: British government awards commercial radio licenses.
1973: Capital Radio goes on air.
1984: Chris Tarrant debuts on Capital Radio.
1987: Company is listed on London Stock Exchange.
1988: 1548 Capital Gold AM is launched.
1990: 95.8 Capital FM's audience tops that of BBC Radio One in London.
1996: New Broadcasting Act establishes licensing plan for digital radio.
1996: The first Capital Radio Café is opened.
1999: CE digital joint venture awards three digital multiplex licenses.
2000: XFM digital radio is launched.

market. In April 2000, the company beat out the Scottish Media Group in its bid to acquire the Border TV television and radio group. Capital Radio agreed to buy up the television station, a member of the ITV network, and four local radio stations, in a deal worth nearly £150 million. The Border acquisition helped boost Capital Radio's presence in the northeast, west, and Midlands regions.

By mid-2000, Capital Radio had built its coverage to include one third of the United Kingdom's adult population. The company also announced its intention to pursue further acquisitions and license bids to extend its coverage across the United Kingdom. With advertising revenues rising—reflecting the strength of the British economy and the surge of so-called ''dot-com'' companies seeking to establish their brand names—Capital Radio entered the new century on an upbeat note. As CEO Dave Mansfield said, as reported by *Reuters,* ''The good news will continue. Its been an outstanding time for the company, every dimension of our business has worked well, and we're feeling pretty bouncy.''

Principal Subsidiaries

Birmingham Broadcasting Ltd.; Border TV; Bucks Broadcasting Ltd. (63%); Capital Radio Digital Ltd.; Capital Radio Investments Ltd.; Capital Radio Management Ltd.; Capital Radio Telstar Entertainment Direct Ltd. (50%); Cardiff Broadcasting Co. Ltd.; CE Digital Ltd. (50%); First Oxfordshire Radio Co. Ltd. (57%); Independent Radio News Ltd. (46%); Midlands Radio plc; The Ocean Radio Group Ltd.; Prospect Group Holdings Ltd. (20%); Radio Advertising Bureau Ltd. (45%); Radio Invicta Ltd.; Southern Radio Group Ltd.; Southern Radio Ltd.; Wildstar Records Ltd. (50%); Xfm Ltd.

Principal Competitors

Amazon.com, Inc.; British Broadcasting Corporation (BBC); Chrysalis Group plc; Scottish Radio; Emap plc; Virgin Group plc; GWR Group plc.

Further Reading

Barker, Sophie, ''US Media Run Rule Over Digital Capital,'' *Daily Telegraph,* October 28, 1999, p. 40.
Marr, Melissa, ''Capital Radio Pumps Out Rockin' Results,'' *Reuters,* May 9, 2000.
——, ''Capital Radio Wins Border TV Over with New Bid,'' *Reuters,* April 13, 2000.
Rankin, Kate, ''Having an Absolutely Capital Time,'' *Daily Telegraph,* November 14, 1998, p. 33.
Robins, Jane, ''Fury of a Would-Be Venture Capitalist,'' *Independent,* October 6, 1998, p. 14.

—M.L. Cohen

CARNEGIE
CORPORATION
of NEW YORK

Carnegie Corporation of New York

437 Madison Avenue
New York, New York 10022
U.S.A.
Telephone: (212) 371-3200
Fax: (212) 754-4073
Web site: http://www.carnegie.org

Not-for-Profit Foundation
Founded: 1911
Employees: 86
Total Assets: $1.69 billion (1999)
NAIC: 81341 Civic and Social Organizations

Carnegie Corporation of New York (CCNY) was founded in 1911 by the prominent philanthropist Andrew Carnegie, whose principles have guided the organization since its inception. Carnegie believed that it was the moral responsibility of the rich to eschew ostentatious living, to live frugally, and to use their wealth to benefit the public. Carnegie's original endowment of the foundation had a market value of about $135 million—a legacy which had grown to $1.69 billion by the end of June in 1999. The endowment represents a capital fund that allows Carnegie Corporation to award annual grants totaling approximately $60 million. Such grants are typically made in four general areas: education, international peace and security, international development, and democracy/special projects. In all, about 300 grants are made each year. Although Andrew Carnegie's will stipulated that his bequest be used to benefit those of the United States, approximately seven percent of the available funds are used to assist both past and present countries of the British Commonwealth. In addition to making various grants, the corporation has created various study groups and commissions that have been instrumental in effecting social progress and change throughout history.

1835–1911: Andrew Carnegie and His Legacy

Andrew Carnegie, who became one of America's 19th century "captains of industry," was born in Scotland in 1835 as an heir only to relative poverty. His life followed the elusive "rags

to riches" pattern of the Horatio Alger dream, which posited that hard work joined with personal virtue would inevitably lead to material success in the United States. In Carnegie's case, the reality actually fit that much-maligned myth. After his family emigrated to the United States in 1848, young Carnegie started working as a bobbin boy in a cotton mill. A series of jobs with Western Union and the Pennsylvania Railroad followed before the thrifty Carnegie was able to establish his own business. It was then that he began his rise to both fame and fortune as the founder and owner of Carnegie Steel, the company that established the mammoth steel industry in Pennsylvania.

In 1901, after he turned 65, Carnegie sold his interest in his company to J.P. Morgan's United States Steel Company, devoting the remaining years of his life to philanthropy and writing. He created Carnegie Corporation of New York in 1911 as a separate foundation with a trust fund as large as the rest of his trusts combined. In the foundation's charter he also set down the principles that continued to guide Carnegie Corporation's policies and procedures throughout its history. Before his death in 1919, Carnegie followed what he had himself preached in his book, *The Gospel of Wealth* (1889), by giving away a personal fortune of $311 million. Outside of the Carnegie Corporation endowment, much of his wealth went into other endowments for libraries, foundations, educational institutions, and organizations and projects promoting world peace.

1912–54: The Foundation's First Four Decades

Although the initial $135 million endowment of CCNY may seem a fairly slight sum in an age in which corporate CEOs command annual salaries in that range, it was a considerable fortune in 1911. In fact, in 1915 the corporation's endowment exceeded the grand total of all spending for higher education in the United States.

During the first few years, Andrew Carnegie served as both president and a trustee of the corporation. His private secretary—James Bertram—and his financial agent—Robert A. Franks—were also trustees and officers. Along with Carnegie, they constituted the foundation's first executive committee. After Carnegie's death in 1919, the trustees appointed James R.

Angell to serve as both the first salaried president, or CEO, of the corporation and ex-officio member of the board.

Just before Andrew Carnegie's death, the corporation helped fund the Teachers Insurance and Annuity Association (TIAA) through its sister organization, the Carnegie Foundation for the Advancement of Teaching (CFAT). CFAT was created in 1918 to "protect academic mobility and encourage savings by the nation's college professors." In time, TIAA would become the nation's largest private insurance company.

The third president of CCNY was Frederick P. Keppel, who served in the capacity from 1923 to 1941. It was during his tenure that in 1938 CCNY commissioned Swedish social scientist Gunnar Myrdal to undertake a comprehensive study of the American Negro, a seminal work that strongly influenced the direction of race relations in the desegregation era after World War II. Myrdal's study helped dispel the myth that racial equality and civil justice could be achieved through a system of separate but equal education.

Throughout its early history and into the post World War II years, most grants awarded by CCNY reflected the philanthropic philosophy of its founder. Although the priorities shifted somewhat during the tenures of different presidents, significant grants were made under each of them in support of research, education, and the cause of world peace. Major gifts were used to establish libraries and advance higher education in America, as well as to underwrite continuing and non-traditional educational programs.

1955–82: New Strategies under Presidents Gardner and Pifer

Starting in the 1950s, the relative size of CCNY's portfolio began to diminish as larger private foundations came into existence and the federal budget rapidly inflated, driven by both the Cold War arms race and welfare programs. The possibility that the corporation's influence and prestige might wane with this relative reduction in its endowment compelled its board to re-assess its grant-making strategies to achieve more leverage. Between 1955 and 1981, under presidents John Gardner and Alan Pifer, the corporation narrowed its concentration to selected areas in which its strategists believed it could make important, policy affecting differences. Among other things, CCNY began actively seeking partnerships with other agencies and foundations willing to promote innovative ideas and change.

The principal focus was on education. Gardner and the corporation foresaw the postwar wave of students that would strike at all educational levels, as veterans from both World War II and the Korean War returned home to develop occupational skills and raise their families. Under Gardner's leadership, CCNY worked to make sure that programs strove to achieve or maintain excellence in American education. For primary and secondary schools, the corporation advocated the removal of race and gender barriers to educational opportunities and sought methods of enhancing the special skills of all children. For colleges and universities—besides striving to achieve parity in educational opportunity—Gardner and his staff worked to foster international understanding by supporting special area studies programs and research, the findings of which could be transmitted to policy makers in Washington and other world capitals. During Gardner's tenure, there was a "justified tendency to assume that ideas and innovations generated with Carnegie funds could and would be passed on to governmental authority."

In 1965, Alan Pifer succeeded Gardner as the corporation's president. At the time, the country was reeling from a crosscurrent of divisive, implosive movements. This included anti-Vietnam War activism, assassinations, the pursuit of true racial equality, and the counter-culture movement. Pifer worked diligently to promote equal opportunity and social justice. Under Pifer's watch and through its grants and studies, the corporation supported educational research and training. It also underwrote programs and studies advocating social justice and equal opportunity for both racial minorities and women.

It was in Pifer's first year that CCNY established the Carnegie Commission on Educational Television, whose work helped achieve the passage of the 1967 Public Broadcasting Act. Among other things, that commission's study led to the corporation's establishment of the Children's Television Workshop, which—beginning with Sesame Street in the late 1960s—launched a series of quality educational programs for children. Thereafter, these were generously funded by the federal government, which, under the aegis of the Department of Education, also absorbed the National Assessment of Educational Progress, founded by the corporation in 1969.

1982–96: Hamburg's Presidency and CCNY's "Preventive Orientation"

During the 1970s and 1980s, public concern with the national debt and the cost of welfare programs fueled a new conservatism that forced CCNY to reconsider the efficacy of the public-private partnerships it had sponsored in earlier decades. David Hamburg, a physician and research scientist, took on the presidency of CCNY in 1982. A public policy thinker with a background in public health, Hamburg somewhat altered the corporation's focus and method, using a "preventive orientation" to problems. Among other things, the corporation undertook an assessment of the role played by science and technology in global conflict, thereby reviving international programs promoting world peace. Hamburg committed the foundation to that cause, first through the avoidance of nuclear war and, second,

Key Dates:

1911: Andrew Carnegie founds the Carnegie Corporation of New York.
1919: Andrew Carnegie dies and the foundation appoints its first salaried president.
1938: Corporation commissions Gunnar Myrdal to make study of the American Negro.
1955: John Gardner is named corporation president.
1965: Foundation establishes the Carnegie Commission on Educational Television; Alan Pifer becomes corporation president.
1982: David Hamburg assumes presidency of corporation.
1997: Vartan Gregorian succeeds Hamburg as president.

through fostering better relations between the United States and the Soviet Union.

Under Hamburg's watch, the foundation also underwrote new studies and programs dealing with educational reform and child and adolescent problems arising from such social realities as the changing structure of the American family. The corporation's series of task force reports all stressed the need for a stronger commitment to children's development and welfare—both by families and schools as well as by other institutions involved in shaping their lives, including the media and community organizations and services. Hamburg was also very concerned with the undesirable side effects of technological advance, including sophisticated weaponry, rampant urbanization, environmental damage, depletion of natural resources, and disease.

By 1984, when the foundation had $20 million to award in grants, it began investing much of it in four primary areas: the avoidance of nuclear war, education in America, the prevention of harm to children and young adolescents, and the promotion of better ways to improve life in developing countries. Fairly typical of Carnegie-funded study groups were the Carnegie Forum Task Force on Teaching as a Profession and the Council on Adolescent Development. In 1986, the Task Force on Teaching issued a report that painted a dismal picture of the state of education in America and offered some radical recommendations. Among these recommendations: the national certification of teachers, a national teacher-proficiency examination, a required master's degree for all new teachers, and major salary hikes in the profession. It concluded that public education in America was failing and in the process was gravely threatening the nation's future. The Council on Adolescent Development, formed in 1986, focused on teenage pregnancies, suicides, and drug, alcohol and tobacco use, hoping to find ways to reverse their alarming increase among post-adolescent Americans.

The Carnegie Corporation, often tarred with the brush of "liberalism" by those who did not like its task forces' findings, had repeatedly tried to make legislators deal with pervasive problems that were eroding the quality of life in America or threatening world peace. Its approach was largely to recommend preventative measures, using the reports of commissions and study groups to outline necessary steps to solve the problems that reached crisis proportions.

For example, in 1994 while still under Hamburg's watch, CCNY issued a report entitled "Starting Points: Meeting the Needs of Our Youngest Children." The report argued that new, federally-funded welfare programs were needed to deal with the impact of poverty, abuse, and neglect on an appalling number of the nation's children. The report flew in the face of the decade's conventional wisdom, that government welfare was, in fact, a failed system. In any case, as a result of the study, in 1996 CCNY awarded two-year grants in excess of $3 million to sixteen states and cities participating in the new grants program—named Starting Points State and Community Partnerships for Young Children. It was designed to mobilize community action to help effect the reforms recommended in the 1994 report.

Also in 1994, CCNY established the Carnegie Commission on Preventing Deadly Conflict. The commission, co-chaired by Hamburg and former U.S. Secretary of State Cyrus R. Vance, issued a final report in December of 1997 which stressed that deadly conflicts between and within nations could be prevented through an early-warning system, expedient and effective reaction to crises, and a commitment to resolving the underlying causes of violence.

1997–2000: Vartan Gregorian's Presidency

In 1997, Vartan Gregorian succeeded Hamburg as president of CCNY, and the foundation's basic concentration remained in three program areas: the education and healthy development of children and youths; the prevention of violent conflict in the world; and the strengthening of human resources in developing countries. In his first presidential report, Gregorian expressed his "deep concern" over some specific problems: racial and ethnic relations in the United States—particularly their impact on children; the state of scientific and educational institutes in the countries of the former Soviet Union; the impoverished condition of sub-Saharan African nations; and the impact of the Islamic faith on American society. It was thought that new initiatives could well arise from these concerns in the new millennium.

As the turn of another century neared and CCNY undertook and/or sponsored new programs, its old commitments remained intact, reflecting still the philanthropic interests of its founder. In June of 1999, the corporation awarded grants totaling $15 million to public libraries in 23 cities. The awards marked the centennial of Andrew Carnegie's 1899 $5.2 million gift to New York for the establishment of branch libraries throughout the city's five boroughs. Thus, even as it has mapped out new initiatives and programs, the foundation—Janus like—has kept its past in view.

Further Reading

Lagemann, Ellen Condliffe, *The Politics of Knowledge: The Carnegie Corporation, Philanthropy, and Public Policy,* Middletown, Conn.: Wesleyan University Press, 1989.
Morton, Roger, "The Business of Education," *School Product News,* August 1984, p. 72.
Murphy, E. Jefferson, *Creative Philanthropy: Carnegie Corporation and Africa, 1953–1973,* New York: Teachers College Press, 1976.
Oder, Norman, "Carnegie Corporation Gives $15M to 25 Urban Libraries," *Library Journal,* July 1999, p. 14.

Podesta, Jane Sims, ''Years of Wonder—And Risk,'' *People Weekly,* November 13, 1995, p. 113.

''Preschoolers Need Access to High Quality Programs,'' *Knight-Ridder/Tribune News Service,* September 18, 1996.

Rutsch, Horst, ''Carnegie Commission Says 'Mass Violence Is Not Inevitable','' *UN Chronicle,* Spring 1998, p. 36.

Solorzano, Lucia, ''Teaching in Trouble,'' *U.S. News & World Report,* May 26, 1986, p. 52.

Sun, Marjorie, ''Carnegie Plan Promotes Prevention of Nuclear War,'' *Science,* January 20, 1984, p. 256.

Swetnam, George, *Andrew Carnegie,* Boston: Twayne Publishers, 1980.

—John W. Fiero

Carvel Corporation

20 Batterson Park Road
Farmington, Connecticut 06032-2502
U.S.A.
Telephone: (860) 677-6811
Toll Free: (800) 513-7702
Fax: (860) 677-8211
Web site: http://www.carvel.com

Private Company
Incorporated: 1946
Employees: 600+
Sales: $200 million (1998 est.)
NAIC: 31152 Ice Cream & Frozen Dessert
    Manufacturing; 42243 Dairy Products Wholesalers;
    53311 Owners & Lessors of Other Non-Financial
    Assets; 722213 Snack and Nonalcoholic Beverage
    Bars

Carvel Corporation is a wholesaler and retailer of frozen desserts, as well as a franchisor of frozen dessert outlets. Carvel ice-cream and other frozen desserts are available in over 5,000 locations worldwide, including franchise stores, supermarkets, stadiums, and mall kiosks. In addition to producing and selling soft-serve ice cream, Carvel is the largest branded retailer of ice-cream cakes in the world. Carvel products are available in 12 eastern-seaboard states, Puerto Rico, Canada, and Vietnam.

Soft-Serve Ice-Cream Pioneer: 1934–56

Born in Greece (with the surname of Carvelas) and reared, with six brothers and sisters, on a farm in Connecticut, Tom Carvel tried his hand as an auto mechanic and a jazz drummer before becoming a door-to-door salesman of radios in New York City, a job he did not necessarily enjoy very much. He did enjoy taking drives in the country with his girlfriend, Agnes, and they both enjoyed stopping for ice-cream. This simple pleasure was eventually parlayed into a business. One summer day in 1934, Carvel and Agnes loaded an ice-cream freezer stocked with ice cream confections onto a home-built trailer and drove north.

Stopped by a flat tire in suburban Hartsdale, New York, the two set up shop in a vacant lot and quickly sold their stock. Soon Carvel began spending his summers at a small, rented store in the Hartsdale area, selling ice-cream. Carvel and Agnes were soon married, and they continued this part-time business for five years.

Tom Carvel was mechanically inclined, and during this time he plowed back the earnings to develop an electric freezer that would produce ''soft'' ice cream of a custard-like consistency. In 1936 he developed a secret ice-cream formula and patented a no-air-pump, super-low-temperature ice-cream machine; this would mark the first of his 14 patents. By 1939 Carvel had built five such machines and was supervising three ice-cream stores. Soft ice cream was also being developed by the founder of Dairy Queen during this time. The confection, frozen at a higher temperature than conventional ice-cream, contained less air, and could be drawn from a spout into cone or cup.

During World War II Carvel found a receptive audience when he placed 14 of his patented machines in military-post exchanges (PXs). By 1946 there were 50 machines in operation, but operators had fallen so far behind on their royalty payments that he had to reorganize the business. Carvel then founded two companies and sold 49 percent of the stock to employees and friends for $100,000. One was Carvel Corp., charged with making and selling freezers, while the other was Carvel Dari-Freeze Stores, Inc., whose function was to run a franchise operation. Beginning in 1947, Carvel developed a chain of stores, with Carvel Dari-Freeze selecting and leasing the sites, training the franchisees, and helping to finance them, while Carvel Corp. sold them the freezers and flavorings. The 100th store opened in 1951, and by the end of the following year there were some 200 Carvel stores, grossing nearly $3 million for the two companies, with operating income coming to $538,000.

The freezers and flavorings provided most of the revenue for the Yonkers, New York-based Carvel organization, but the enterprise also charged between ten and 25 cents on each gallon of mix for the two million gallons of ice cream sold in 1952. The company also usually required licensees to buy the free-standing stores as well. Carvel had introduced a unique store model, a building with a glass-and-metal facade that inclined forward slightly and a roof that tilted upward toward the street.

Company Perspectives:

Our Mission: Working together, we will make Carvel the leading choice for unique frozen desserts, by consistently exceeding customer expectations. Our Values: 1) Do the right thing; 2) Do everything to the best of your ability; 3) Treat others the way you like to be treated.

On sites chosen by "location engineers," these outlets—brightly lit at night—were designed for high visibility, preferably adjacent to secondary highways where the traffic moved neither too fast or too slow, in an area of sufficient residents for a critical mass of everyday customers. By 1956 there were more than 500 Carvel stores, most of them in the East and at least half open year-round. What Tom Carvel called "the world's first ice-cream supermarket" opened that year in Hartsdale, offering more than 200 items, including 53 flavors of soft ice cream.

Frozen-Dessert Empire: 1956–89

Carvel was now one of the Big Three of soft-serve ice cream, the others being Dairy Queen and Tastee Freez. Carvel franchisees paid more for their businesses than the other two—at least $25,000 in 1956, of which about $10,000 to $12,000 was in cash and the rest financed by the Carvel organization. Carvel claimed that no franchised store had ever failed, but some of its operators chafed at a system that not only required them to pay a high initiation fee but also to purchase the product mix from a limited number of authorized dairies and a variety of other commissary items from Carvel itself. A group of franchisees took the company to court in 1959, charging Carvel with acting in violation of federal antitrust laws.

Carvel Corporation was vindicated after a long and bitter struggle. In 1965 the U.S. Supreme Court rejected the franchisees' appeal of a lower-court decision, and a year later the corporation and affiliated defendants were awarded damages of $10.53 million against four plaintiffs. Also in 1965, the Federal Trade Commission dismissed a complaint against the company filed by a hearing examiner. Carvel's lawyers successfully argued that the enterprise had to restrict its sources of supply in order to protect the secrecy of its formula and also to ensure the uniformity and quality of the end product sold to the consumer under the Carvel name.

Tom Carvel later maintained that every franchise contract in the world contained language devised by himself, and while this claim may have been exaggerated, Bill Carlino of *Nation's Restaurant News* credited him in 1990 with setting "legal precedent in mandating uniform standards for corporate identity, product specifications and distribution." During this period, however, Carvel lost 70 percent of its franchisees, forcing the company to operate its own stores. Consequently, the company went public in 1969, raising $2.45 million by selling a minority of its stock at $11 a share.

Carvel raised its revenues from $9.09 million in 1967 to $16.4 million in 1969; net income rose from $161,788 to $610,267 during this period. The period was characterized by rapid national expansion. By 1971 there were again more than 500 Carvel Ice Cream outlets, in nine Eastern states ranging as far north as Vermont and as far south as Florida, as well as in Illinois. Outlets also opened in Ohio and Virginia in 1971, plus a new Carvel Ice Cream Supermarket, in Chula Vista, California. In addition to soft ice cream, most Carvel stores were offering 36 flavors of hard ice cream and more than 60 varieties of take-home products, including ice-cream cakes and sandwiches, prepackaged sundaes and parfaits, bulk ice cream, and special ice-cream novelties and desserts. Such take-home products were now accounting for about 35 percent of the chain's retail sales.

Carvel Corp. had its headquarters in The Carvel Inn, a facility in Yonkers that not only offered motel accommodations and commercial office space but also housed a new company training center for franchisees, a self-service ice-cream supermarket, and a bakery chain purchased in 1967. Also part of the company was All American Sports City, a subsidiary-owned and -operated 740-acre development in Dutchess County with home sites, a community center, a golf course, and tennis courts.

Carvel revenues reached $27.07 million in 1973. At the time, franchisees were being assessed between $38,000 to $70,000 (depending on store size) to go into business, with a down payment of at least one-third and the rest financed by the company. Carvel lost $996,136 that year, however, partly because the subsidiary enterprises—The Carvel Inn, All American Sports City and Dugan's Bakery—were not thriving. Carvel returned to the black the following year and in 1976 had 701 stores and net income of $1.7 million on revenues of $41.63 million. However, since the stock continued to languish in price, Tom and Agnes Carvel raised their own ownership to 90 percent of the shares in 1978 and took the company private again.

Being his own boss also enabled Tom Carvel to continue, without challenge, broadcasting his own radio commercials, a practice he had begun in 1955. An unrepentant amateur at the trade, he was in the habit of taking a tape recorder on the road and interviewing the franchisees, who, according to an *Advertising Age* reporter, "became as well known to listeners for their nearly unbearable nervousness as for their pride of ownership." Carvel himself spoke in a voice that *New York Times* columnist Francis X. Clines described in 1978 as sounding "like muffled laundry in a footlocker." The 72-year-old tycoon conceded to *Advertising Age* that more than one Carvel dealer had said, "get that senile old goat off the air," but he was not fazed. "Our commercials are for the people who look like us, talk like us, and sound like us," he told Tom Callahan, a business writer who interviewed him for the *New York Times* in 1985.

Carvel estimated the return on his radio spots as better than four dollars to one. By the 1980s television viewers had become accustomed to CEOs such as Wendy's Dave Thomas and chicken tycoon Frank Perdue peddling their wares on the airwaves. Carvel, however, kept his face off the tube. The company's in-house advertising agency, which prepared and placed the radio spots, did the same for its television commercials. By 1981 television accounted for the vast bulk of the company's ad budget.

Carvel had several other successful means of publicizing his enterprise as well. He introduced a toll-free telephone-ordering

Key Dates:

1934: Tom and Agnes Carvel open their first ice-cream store.
1947: Carvel becomes a franchised retail operation.
1969: Carvel begins a nine-year run as a public corporation.
1985: The franchise operation peaks at 865 stores.
1989: The founders sell their 90-percent holding to Investcorp.
1992: Carvel begins selling its products to supermarkets.
1998: Supermarkets are accounting for nearly half Carvel's sales.

service for wedding, birthday, and holiday cakes; a mobile vending operation; a Carvel-sponsored beauty contest for truckers, who often stopped for Carvel ice-cream; promotions handing out premiums such as flying-saucer discs, baseball hats, pens, pencils, and even brandy snifters; and specialty products that included kosher ice cream (introduced in 1969), Lo-Yo frozen yogurt (1972), and Thinny-Thin dietary desserts (also 1972). Standard, since 1959, were character cakes with names like Fudgie the Whale and Cookie Puss. By late 1981 Carvel had gross revenues of $180 million a year and was employing more than 8,000 people. The price for a store franchise was now about $100,000.

By 1985 Carvel had 865 franchise stores, with revenues reaching $300 million the year before. The stores were in 18 states and several foreign countries as well, including Canada, France, Great Britain, Malaysia, Singapore, and Thailand. That year Carvel settled a six-year-old New York state lawsuit charging the company with forcing its franchisees to buy their supplies solely from Carvel at inflated prices. The company agreed that its franchisees could purchase ice-cream cones and soft-drink syrup from other sources.

New Products and Sales Outlets: 1991–98

Tom and Agnes Carvel sold their 90 percent interest in the Carvel Corp. in 1989 for about $80 million to Investcorp, an international investment bank based in Bahrain. Tom Carvel died the following year. At this time the company still had 700 stores and was the third-largest ice-cream operation in the United States. However, the chain was shrinking in both outlets and revenues. Now managed by Steven V. Fellingham, the company moved its headquarters in 1991 to Farmington, Connecticut, and took the name Carvel Ice Cream Bakery to exploit the entire dessert market. (The cake line now accounted for about 60 percent of the chain's $200 million in annual sales.) A new store design included a new logo and a red awning on the front. Plans called for small, limited-menu outlets in shopping malls, and also for large sit-down establishments. By the spring of 1993 Carvel had ceased making its own equipment. The number of stores had fallen to 580, partly because some licensees did not went to spend up to $30,000 to renovate the stores in the way that the company's new management demanded.

One new service during this time was delivery of ice-cream cakes anywhere in the continental United States, with orders placed by a toll free number and shipped by Federal Express. An assortment of ice-cream pies, cakes, and novelties, including canolis, neopolitans, brownies, and blondies was introduced as an alternative to the offerings of conventional bakeries. Club Carvel, the direct-mail division, had almost 275,000 members receiving mailings on their birthdays and other special occasions.

The most visible change was a non-folksy television campaign with a professional voiceover and glitzy sculptures, seemingly made of ice cream, devised by Industrial Light & Magic Co., a special-effects company owned by film producer George Lucas. This "Everything Should Be Made of Ice Cream" spot took an estimated 10,000 person-hours to perfect. Even more important, Carvel was placing hundreds of ice-cream kiosks in major retail outlets, including supermarkets and stadiums. By the fall of 1994 Carvel ice-cream cakes—more profitable than its cups and cones—had been added to the bakery sections of 250 supermarkets in the Philadelphia metropolitan area alone.

By this time the number of Carvel units was 570, including 23 company-owned units, in 13 East Coast states. Moreover, the company's products were also being carried by 935 eastern supermarkets belonging to 15 chains—potential rivals to the retail stores. Licensees were offered five-year contracts to service these outlets, but many opposed the program either because the supermarkets were taking business away from their stores or because they found it more difficult to make money as distributors than first appeared to be the case. By the end of 1994 the number of stand-alone outlets franchised by Carvel had dropped below 500. Owners of some 42 stores filed a lawsuit late in the year, accusing the company of violating "implied" franchise covenants. One former franchisee won a $200,000 jury verdict in 1999.

The number of Carvel franchise stores had fallen to 450 in 1998. Annual sales were between $110 million and $120 million in 1997, according to Fellingham, not counting $82 million from sales in supermarkets. By 1999 the number of outlets had dropped to 400, but Carvel had a retail presence in some 4,500 supermarkets, including several hundred in the Los Angeles metropolitan area. Supermarket sales came to $95 million in 1998, when sales totaled about $200 million. Carvel restored its original ice-cream cone logo during this time and introduced a new product, "Lil' Love," a smaller cake designed to reward children for small milestones, such as good report cards.

As the company entered a new millennium, its reputation for high quality products and innovations in the industry boded well. Regarding franchise opportunities at Carvel, company literature was optimistic that this side of the business would grow, noting that many people had fond memories of Carvel ice-cream and that the company was "working to leverage this emotional bond with Carvel consumers to attract future generations to the brand."

Principal Competitors

Baskin-Robbins Inc.; Ben & Jerry's Homemade, Inc.; International Dairy Queen, Inc.

Further Reading

Bird, David, "State Suit Against Carvel Ends in Settlement," *New York Times,* December 15, 1985, p. 44.

Callahan, Tom, "A Sweet Job With Sour Notes," *New York Times,* December 1, 1985, Sec. 3, p. 7.

Carlino, Bill, "Tom Carvel: Whipped $15 Loan into a Soft-Serve Empire," *Nation's Restaurant News,* pp. 4, 7.

"The Carvel Story," *Ice Cream Trade Journal,* March 1954, pp. 26–28, 119–20.

"Carvel's Mumble Shakes Radio for 20 Years," *Advertising Age,* May 29, 1978, p. R18.

"Carvel's Recipe for Success," *New York Times,* August 26, 1973, Sec. 3, p. 12.

Cebrzynski, Gregg, "Having Its Cake and Ice Cream Too: Carvel Eyes Growth, Revamp," *Nation's Restaurant News,* March 30, 1998, p. 3.

Church, George J., "Soft Ice Cream Shops Do Bustling Business Based on Kids, Cars," *Wall Street Journal,* September 23, 1955, pp. 1, 14.

Clines, Francis X., "A Voice Terrible, Yet Mouthwatering," *New York Times,* July 25, 1978, p. C1.

Diamond, Sidney A., "FTC Dismisses Attack on Franchise System as Unlawful Restraint of Trade," *Advertising Age,* August 10, 1965, p. 80.

Dowling, Melissa, "Carvel Puts Its Ice Cream in the Mail," *Catalog Age,* March 1993, p. 12.

Folsom, Merrill, "Court Gives Carvel $10-Million Award," *New York Times,* April 21, 1966, pp. 57, 60.

Fowler, Glenn, "Tom Carvel, 84, Gravelly Voice Of Soft Ice Cream Chain, Is Dead," *New York Times,* October 22, 1990, p. B9.

Grimm, Matthew, "Ice Cream Mogul Tom Carvel, Retiring, Hasn't Lost His Curmudgeonly Touch," *Adweek's Marketing Week,* December 18, 1989, p. 8.

Howard, Theresa, "Carvel Reinforces Soft-Serve Heritage," *Brandweek,* February 15, 1999, p. 51.

"Ice-Cream Parlay," *Fortune,* July 1953, p. 166.

Kramer, Bernice, "The Emperor of Ice Cream," *New York,* June 14, 1993, pp. 22, 24.

Lansing, Alfred, "Cold Licks and Hot Profits," *Collier's,* pp. 32, 34.

Lelen, Kenneth, "A New Strategy That Takes the Cake," *Philadelphia Inquirer,* September 5, 1994, pp. D1, D11.

Tannenbaum, Jeffrey A., "Carvel Strategy Frosts Many Franchisees," *Wall Street Journal,* December 10, 1994, pp. B1, B10.

Telzer, Ronnie, "Carvel's Commercial Charisma," *Marketing Communications,* November 1981, pp. 52–53, 57.

Wax, Alan J., "Carvel Updates Image, Goes for Sweet Tooth," *Newsday,* April 26, 1991, p. 47.

—Robert Halasz

CBRL Group, Inc.

P.O. Box 787
307 Hartmann Drive
Lebanon, Tennessee 37088-0787
U.S.A.
Telephone: (615) 444-5533
Fax: (615) 443-9399
Web site: http://www.crackerbarrelocs.com

Public Company
Incorporated: 1970 as Cracker Barrel Old Country Store, Inc.
Employees: 49,314
Sales: $1.53 billion (1999)
Stock Exchanges: NASDAQ
Ticker Symbol: CBRL
NAIC: 72211 Full-Service Restaurants; 45322 Gift, Novelty, and Souvenir Stores; 44511 Supermarkets and Other Grocery (Except Convenience) Stores

CBRL Group, Inc., was formed in 1998 as a holding company for Cracker Barrel Old Country Store restaurants, a chain of over 420 restaurants and gift shops located primarily along interstate highways in the Southeast, Midwest, mid-Atlantic, and southwest United States. Cracker Barrel gift shops, considered by management to be an integral part of the restaurant's country atmosphere, sell reproductions of early American crafts and such food items as preserves and old-fashioned candies. CBRL also owns and operates Carmine's Prime Meats, a gourmet food market located in Florida, and Logan's Roadhouse restaurants, which specialize in steaks and are located throughout much of the United States.

Gas and Grits: 1969–80

The first Cracker Barrel Old Country Store was founded in September 1969 by Dan Evins, a Shell gas station operator who felt he could attract more customers if a restaurant and gift shop were located on the station's lot. He borrowed $40,000 and built his first combination gas station/restaurant/store along the inter-state highway just outside Lebanon, Tennessee. Within one month, Cracker Barrel Old Country Store began to make a profit. Evins incorporated the company the following year and sold half of the new business to a group of local businessmen, raising $100,000 to open his second gas station/restaurant/store. By 1974, Cracker Barrel was operating ten units, all located along interstate highways and all making a profit.

Although Cracker Barrel's restaurant and gift shop sales grew, Evins' gasoline business was less profitable. When the gasoline crisis hit in the early 1970s, the company began building new restaurants without gas stations attached. In 1974, Evins ended his distribution contract with Shell Oil. The restaurants did so well without gasoline service that Cracker Barrel had eliminated gasoline service from all its locations soon thereafter.

Growth and Expansion in the 1980s

Cracker Barrel's solid growth began attracting the interest of independent investors, prompting the company to register with the Securities and Exchange Commission in 1974. Rapid expansion continued through the end of the decade. By 1983, the company was operating 27 units along interstate highways in Tennessee, North Carolina, South Carolina, Georgia, Kentucky, Florida, and Alabama. Between 1978 and 1983, net income and revenues had increased at annual rates of 26 percent and 25 percent, respectively, resulting primarily from the addition of new restaurants. In late 1981, when high interest rates threatened the company's expansion, Cracker Barrel went public, selling shares on the NASDAQ exchange.

Despite Cracker Barrel's continued expansion, sales began to slip. In 1985, Evins tried to stem the slide by making some broad management changes. "We had some people in our management who had grown up in this company, and we were growing fairly fast for a small company," Evins told *Restaurant Business* at the time. "We realized that what we needed was some heavier parts in our equipment, so to speak." Changes included the establishment of a new marketing department and the hiring of five executives, all with experience in larger organizations. The impact was immediately positive. Net sales rose 20 percent to $80 million and net income grew 49 percent

Company Perspectives:

Cracker Barrel Old Country Store's mission statement—pleasing people—is short, but it says a lot. It gives all our Employees a flag to rally around as we accept only the highest levels of quality in our Guest hospitality, and in our relations with Employees, Suppliers and Shareholders. A common mission is vital. We have lots of different people in the company located in various places, in different time zones, with different challenges every day. But remembering we all share the same mission—pleasing people—keeps us united in the unique Cracker Barrel culture. We need a common purpose to grab hold of to remember who we are. In today's business world, the words we frequently use are harsh. But pleasing people lets us talk about feelings and attitudes. Pleasing people is about caring, about letting Guests forget about the lousy day they had as they sit down at a table near the fireplace and order up a favorite meal, getting a genuine smile from the server. All that is something special in the Cracker Barrel experience. A walk through the Retail Store is the same kind of experience. It's not a fast hunt, but a slow tour around the displays. Pleasing people fits that experience, too. Pleasing people recognizes that we have four different sets of people in our picture. And it is all of those people that we must strive to please: our Guests, our Employees, our Suppliers and our Shareholders.

in 1986, due in part to improved operating efficiency and higher margins on sales.

Cracker Barrel also began opening restaurants near tourist destinations, including Opryland; Gatlinburg, Tennessee; and Hilton Head, South Carolina. By the end of 1987, the Cracker Barrel chain consisted of 53 stores in eight states, with annual net sales slightly over $99 million.

Analysts cite several reasons for Cracker Barrel's success. According to *Restaurant Hospitality* magazine, "One has been its unrivaled ability to evoke nostalgia without being corny. Cracker Barrel employees are simply warm and friendly. The stores look old-fashioned but are never cute." This atmosphere, reinforced by its inexpensive "country cookin' menu," helped Cracker Barrel carve out a niche for itself in the family restaurant business.

Cracker Barrel also instituted extensive manager and employee training programs in the 1980s, which greatly improved store efficiency and profit margins. Potential managers spent ten weeks in an extensive training session, whereas hourly employees followed an on-the-job course, called the Personal Achievement Responsibility (PAR) program. Rewards, such as increased wages and cheaper benefits, were given for the successful completion of company-set goals. The result was a turnover rate among hourly employees of 160 percent, approximately half the industry average.

Continued Success Amid Change in the 1990s

Cracker Barrel's tight management system helped it weather the recession in 1990 and achieve existing per-unit sales of over

$2.7 million, almost double the per-unit sales of its nearest competitor, Big Boy. Around the same time, however, the company got caught in a controversy when it fired a number of homosexual employees. For a short time, it seemed the controversy would threaten Cracker Barrel's expansion into the northern states. Nationally-televised protests against the firings sprang up in New York City, Atlanta, and a number of other small towns. The City of New York, which held $3.6 million worth of Cracker Barrel shares in a pension fund, threatened to make waves if the company didn't change its policy. Cracker Barrel announced it would no longer fire employees based on their sexual orientation, although protesters claimed that discrimination continued covertly. Despite the controversy (or perhaps because of the publicity it generated), company profits jumped 50 percent in 1991 to $22.8 million. The number of Cracker Barrel units grew to 106.

In the early 1990s, Cracker Barrel opened new restaurants at a rate of over 20 units per year and expanded into states such as Michigan, Wisconsin, and Missouri. For the first time in its history, however, Cracker Barrel faced some direct competition when Bob Evans Farms, Inc., opened seven Bob Evans General Stores with atmosphere and menu items that closely resembled those of Cracker Barrel. Bob Evans also opened the first of a chain of Hometown Restaurants, slated for development in towns with populations of 30,000 or less.

Analysts predicted heavy competition between the two restaurant chains because both intended to pursue the same market of "vacationers hungry for a homey atmosphere and comfort food." Cracker Barrel seemed well prepared for a market share battle. Net income in 1992 rose 48 percent to $33.9 million, and the number of units expanded to 127. A 1992 *Consumer Reports* survey gave the chain the top customer satisfaction rating, while a survey appearing in the February 1, 1994 issue of *Restaurant & Institution* magazine found that Cracker Barrel "has done the job better than all of its family-restaurant competitors."

Heading into the mid-1990s, Cracker Barrel focused on further expansion and diversification. The company introduced a new format called Cracker Barrel Corner Market. The new stores hoped to take advantage of the burgeoning home meal replacement category—full meals prepared and packaged that required no cooking on the part of the busy consumer. Cracker Barrel opened a few Corner Market stores in business areas of Tennessee to test the concept. The stores initially offered prepackaged Cracker Barrel country cooking meals and later added drive-thru windows and a cafeteria-style counter that offered hot meals. Unfortunately for Cracker Barrel, however, the new stores did not meet expectations, and the project was shelved in 1996.

In 1995 Cracker Barrel embraced a significant change when it hired Ronald N. Magruder as president and chief operating officer. Magruder came from Darden Restaurants and was known for taking the Olive Garden from the position of a small, regional restaurant chain to a national presence. Many analysts considered the hiring to be a positive move. Robert Derrington of Equitable Securities said in *Nation's Restaurant News*, "It's a hell of a coup for those guys. . . . There comes a time when a company has to map out a succession plan. His coming on board was exactly the thing the company needed now.''

With new management in place, Cracker Barrel set out on an aggressive expansion plan. For the fiscal year ended August 1, 1997, the company exceeded the $1 billion mark in revenues for the first time in its history. The average Cracker Barrel rang up more than $3 million in sales annually, which was nearly double that of competing chains, such as Bob Evans Farms. Cracker Barrel was certainly among the leaders in the family restaurant industry, but the company was not without some growing pains—although revenues during fiscal 1996 increased 20 percent over 1995's sales, net income declined 4 percent, from $66 million to $63.5 million. The drop in net income was the first Cracker Barrel had suffered since 1985. Much of the decline was attributed to the closure of three under performing stores and the slowing of its expansion into the Midwest, particularly Wisconsin and Minnesota.

Intent on following through with its expansion strategy and eager to learn from its mistakes, Cracker Barrel began adapting menus to reflect regional tastes—a necessary step, considering that Cracker Barrel was planning to open about 70 percent of its new stores outside of its core Southern market. Cracker Barrel learned its lessons the hard way when newly opened restaurants in Minnesota and Wisconsin performed rather poorly, where sales were only about 60 percent of sales at restaurants in the Southeast. The company realized that standard Southern fare, such as grits, was not high on the list of Midwesterners' cravings, and Cracker Barrel began to investigate regional foods. In Wisconsin, for instance, Cracker Barrel began to offer bratwurst. Cracker Barrel also added regional touches in decor. For example, a soapbox car was added to a store in Akron, Ohio, where a national soapbox derby was held each year.

By late 1997, Cracker Barrel was back on its feet, and during fiscal 1997 alone the company opened 50 new restaurants. Over a two-year period, in fact, Cracker Barrel had opened about 100 new units. Same-store sales increased by 4.3 percent in fiscal 1997, and operations had been streamlined and made more efficient through changes such as a new point-of-sale system. ''Cracker Barrel is no longer just a regional family dining format that happens to put up impressive numbers,'' said Merrill Lynch's Peter Oakes at the time in *Nation's Restaurant News*. ''It's now an industry leader—taking [market] share and starting to flex its muscle.''

Continuing Diversification at the Turn of the Millenium

In the spring of 1998, Cracker Barrel acquired Carmine's Prime Meats, Inc., headquartered in Florida. The purchase marked the company's reentry to the home meal replacement category, as Carmine's operated two upscale, gourmet food markets, known as Carmine Giardini's Gourmet Market, as well as an Italian restaurant, La Trattoria Ristorante.

Cracker Barrel demonstrated that it was serious about aggressive expansion in early 1999 when it reorganized as a holding company, CBRL Group, Inc., that owned and operated the Cracker Barrel restaurants, Carmine's, and other businesses. Magruder was promoted to president and chief operating officer of the new CBRL Group, while Dan Evins became its chairman and CEO while also continuing his duties as chairman and CEO of the Cracker Barrel subsidiary. Getting right to the task of expansion, CBRL acquired Logan's Roadhouse, Inc., which operated 45 Logan's Roadhouse restaurants in 12 states, for about $179 million in early 1999. Logan's restaurants offered steaks, chicken, ribs, and seafood. CBRL also opened a retail-only test store in a mall in Nashville, Tennessee, in 1999.

CBRL made headway in its quest for expansion and diversification, but the company continued to face some challenges. In April of 1999 Ronald Magruder resigned, and CBRL's earnings for fiscal 1999, which ended July 30, 1999, were disappointing. Revenues rose to $1.53 billion from $1.32 billion in fiscal 1998, but net income fell from $104.1 million to a shockingly-low $70.2 million. Same-store retail sales grew 2.4 percent, but same-store restaurant sales declined 3.1 percent, partly due to menu price reductions. CBRL cut back its expansion plans to 30 new Cracker Barrel restaurants in 2000 and 25 the following year.

Despite a few hardships, CBRL remained determined to grow and succeed. The company worked on refining its Carmine Giardini's Gourmet Market operations and planned to open a third location in 2000. The process of integrating Logan's Roadhouse restaurants into CBRL continued, and the company opened 12 new restaurants in fiscal 1999, with plans to open an additional 12 in fiscal 2000. CBRL also looked to other opportunities to boost revenue—such as e-commerce and retail-only stores—while focusing on continued improvements at its flagship Cracker Barrel restaurants. Founder Dan Evins commented on CBRL's objectives in the company's 1999 annual report: ''As always, our goal is to execute a controlled long-term growth strategy while providing our guests with high quality food and attractive retail shopping. With the changes in place to improve operations where needed at Cracker Barrel, the addition of the Logan's concept to our holding company structure, and the opportunities to leverage our expertise in areas of strength, we believe the future for CBRL Group is promising.'' With 426 restaurants in 40 states by mid-2000, there seemed to be no stopping the company from achieving its goals.

Principal Subsidiaries

Cracker Barrel Old Country Store, Inc.; Logan's Roadhouse, Inc.; Carmine's Prime Meats, Inc.

Principal Competitors

Advantica Restaurant Group, Inc.; Bob Evans Farms, Inc.; Big Boy; Darden Restaurants, Inc.; Shoney's, Inc.

Further Reading

Carlino, Bill, "Magruder Exits Darden to Join Cracker Barrel," *Nation's Restaurant News,* July 17, 1995, p. 1.

"Cracker Barrel Set the Survey's Standard for Family Dining for the Fourth Straight Year," *Restaurant & Institution,* February 1, 1994.

Farkas, David, "Kings of the Road," *Restaurant Hospitality,* August, 1991, p. 118.

Ganem, Beth Carlson, "My Country, Right or Wrong," *Restaurant Hospitality,* February 1993, p. 73.

Gutner, Todd, "Nostalgia Sells," *Forbes,* April 27, 1992, p. 102.

Harper, Roseanne, "Cracker Barrel Plunges Back into HMR with Carmine's Purchase," *Supermarket News,* April 20, 1998, p. 49.

Hayes, Jack, "After Free Fall Cracker Barrel Rolls As a Top Contender in Family Segment," *Nation's Restaurant News,* November 17, 1997, p. 1.

——, "Cracker Barrel Protesters Don't Shake Loyal Patrons," *Nation's Restaurant News,* August 26, 1991, p. 3.

——, "With New Prexy in Place, CBRL Group Readies Expansion," *Nation's Restaurant News,* October 5, 1998.

Kramer, Louise, "Cracker Barrel Expands Test of Corner Market," *Nation's Restaurant News,* June 5, 1995, p. 7.

Oleck, Joan, "Bad Politics," *Restaurant Business,* June 10, 1992, p. 80.

Papiernik, Richard L., "Cracker Barrel Springs a Leak, Bottom-Line Fix Under Way," *Nation's Restaurant News,* November 25, 1996, p. 11.

Rhein, Liz, "Along the Interstate with Cracker Barrel," *Restaurant Business,* June 10, 1987, p. 113.

Tarquinio, J. Alex, "Restaurants: King of Grits Alters Menu to Reflect Northern Tastes," *Wall Street Journal,* September 22, 1997, p. B1.

Walkup, Carolyn, "Family Chains Beat Recession Blues with Value, Service," *Nation's Restaurant News,* August 5, 1991, p. 100.

Yanez, Luisa, "Food Fight on the Interstate," *Restaurant Business,* September 20, 1992, p. 50.

—Maura Troester
—updated by Mariko Fujinaka

CertainTeed ▣

CertainTeed Corporation

---

750 East Swedesford Road
Valley Forge, Pennsylvania 19482
U.S.A.
Telephone: (610) 341-7000
Fax: (610) 341-7797
Web site: http://www.certainteed.com

Wholly Owned Subsidiary of Compagnie de Saint-Gobain S.A.
Incorporated: 1917 as Certain-teed Products Corporation
Employees: 7,178
Sales: $2 billion (1999)
NAIC: 324122 Asphalt Shingles Coating Materials Manufacturer; 32742 Gypsum Product Manufacturing; 326122 Plastics Pipe and Pipe Fitting Manufacturing; 327123 Other Structural Clay Product Manufacturing; 327993 Mineral Wool Manufacturing; 32511 Plastics Material and Resin Manufacturing; 332321 Metal Window and Door Manufacturing; 326199 All Other Plastics Product Manufacturing

---

CertainTeed Corporation is a leading U.S. manufacturer and distributor of commercial and residential building materials. Specifically, the company designs and manufactures a large variety of materials including: ceiling systems; insulation; roofing shingles; clay roofing tiles and slates; vinyl siding and accessories; vinyl windows; vinyl fencing; decking and railing; ventilation products; fiber-cement siding; injection molded products; PVC pipe and foundation products; and retractable awning and canopy systems. The company also manufacturers fiberglass reinforcements. CertainTeed maintains 45 manufacturing facilities in North America and sells its products in building supply stores nationwide. In 1988 the company became a wholly owned subsidiary of Compagnie de Saint-Gobain, the world's largest manufacturer of building materials.

A Turn-of-the Century Roofing Company

Among the rapidly changing landscape of 20th century America, people were moving to metropolitan areas and manufacturing was replacing farming as the principal source of income. New railroads stretched across the country, and the automobile replaced the horse and wagon. A young man named George M. Brown from East St. Louis, Illinois, predicted that all of this change would lead to a surge in the sale of building materials. With $25,000 in capital, Brown started his own roofing manufacturing business in 1904; he had a military background, and he chose to reflect this status in the new business name: General Roofing Manufacturing Company. Brown spent his first few years in business developing two varieties of asphalt roofing materials: a smooth-roll type and a grit-surface-gravel type. He then gave his roofing material products military-sounding brand names, such as Major, Sergeant, Corporate, and Guard, which he hoped would project quality and strength. With only a few employees, a small roofing plant, and a small dry felt mill, Brown built his business into a success.

Although the U.S. economy had taken a turn for the worse in 1910, General Roofing flourished and Brown decided it was time to expand. He purchased paper mills in Marseilles, Illinois, and York, Pennsylvania, and converted them to felt mills. He then built manufacturing plants near the felt mills and produced his roofing materials there. In 1912 General Roofing published its first annual report; the company reported an impressive $3 million in assets and a net income of $201,949. The report stated that General Roofing aimed ''to secure its place as the world's largest manufacturer of roofing and building papers.'' In 1913 General Roofing began producing asphalt shingles, which cost less than wooden shingles and were more durable and flame resistant.

By the onset of World War I, General Roofing was establishing a sales presence in some foreign countries. While its overseas sales were halted with the outbreak of World War I, its domestic sales rose steadily. By 1914, General Roofing was opening offices throughout the United States, and its factories worked around the clock. Company headquarters were then moved from East St. Louis, Illinois, to St. Louis, Missouri.

Company Perspectives:

Choosing building materials can be quite a challenge. So how do you make the right decisions for roofing, siding, insulation, windows, outdoor living designs, ventilation and foundations without doing months of research? Just choose CertainTeed. All CertainTeed building products are designed and manufactured to offer unmatched style, durability and comfort.

Over the next few years the company continued to expand and began to manufacture paints. By 1917 it had established itself as a leader in the production and distribution of "asphalt roofing, insulating papers, paints, and varnishes." Also in 1917 the company incorporated, reorganized, and changed its name to Certain-teed Products Corporation, forming the name Certain-teed from its motto: "Quality made CERTAIN . . . Satisfaction GuaranTEED." In 1918 the company began trading on the New York Stock Exchange.

Diversification and Great Depression Challenges

The years following World War I were difficult for Certain-teed. For the first time in the company's history, it failed to reach its projected volume and profits. Despite its troubles, management refused to shutter plants or lay off workers, believing that the company would bounce back and eventually profit from its employees' experience. This gamble proved sound. In 1919 Certain-teed's sales reached an all-time high of over $10 million. The next year the company began producing floor coverings using the same felt material it was using to manufacture roofing materials, and in 1923 again expanded its product line when it began manufacturing gypsum wallboard, a type of plasterboard. Around the same time the company moved its headquarters once again, from St. Louis to New York City. Investments of some $1.7 million were made during this time to improve and expand the company's existing facilities and acquire new facilities in Pennsylvania, Oklahoma, Texas, New Mexico, Oregon, Michigan, and Wyoming.

On October 24, 1929, the bottom dropped out of the stock market and, by 1930, one out of every three American workers was unemployed. Like most other companies during this time, Certain-teed was forced to lower prices, cut salaries, and shut down some of its plants. Certain-teed remained determined to weather the storm, however, and the company's managers remained optimistic about its future. The company reported that "compared to its competitors, its products were more popular than ever" during this time. By 1935 Certain-teed had begun to turn a profit once again, and Brown retired from his posts as president and CEO of Certain-teed.

Even during the economic downturns, Certain-teed continued to develop new and innovative building materials. In 1938 the company developed the WOODTEX shingle, a heavy asphalt roofing shingle with a texture similar to real wood. Certain-teed's commitment to research and development had, in fact, helped it become the world's largest manufacturer of roofing materials and the third largest producer of gypsum materials by the late 1930s. In 1938, the year in which company founder Brown died, Certain-teed was acquired by Celotex Corporation of Chicago, which gained control by purchasing a majority of the company's outstanding stock.

National Defense and Postwar Expansion

Under new parentage, Certain-teed continued to pursue innovations in gypsum wallboard construction until, like most manufacturing concerns, it was called upon to assist in the war effort. During World War II Certain-teed manufacturing facilities were converted for wartime equipment production. In 1942 the company was awarded a contract that included its consulting services, equipment procurement, installation inspection, and personnel training. From that time until the end of the war, Certain-teed produced war equipment at its Pantex Ordnance Plant and received the Army Navy "E" Award for its contributions to the war effort.

During the next few years, Certain-teed regained control of its operations from the Celotex Corporation, when a group of investors, led by Rawson G. Lizars, waged a proxy bid for control. Lizars succeeded and was named president and chairperson at Certain-teed. In 1946 the company started paying dividends on its stock, something it had stopped doing during the Depression. Certain-teed also began developing fiberglass insulation, a product that would be a significant part of its operation in the future.

Certain-teed spent more than $11 million for expansion during the 1950s and continued to add new products to its existing product line. In 1951 it introduced "Fire-Stop Gypsum Wallboard," which had a better fire rating than previous gypsum wallboards. The next year Certain-teed opened its first research and development center, in Paoli, Pennsylvania. The research and development center was the highlight of the company's year; intense price competition, a long, costly strike at the Certain-teed's gypsum plant in Texas, as well as a serious flooding of a gypsum mine, resulted in low sales for the company in 1952.

By 1954 the company was back on the expansion track again. It acquired Wm Cameron & Co., a large building supplies wholesaler and retailer with distribution facilities throughout the southwestern United States. During the same year, Certain-teed acquired controlling interest in Valspar Corporation, a manufacturer of house and commercial paints, but divested this interest in 1959. Other acquisitions included the Gold Seal Asphalt Roofing Company of Chicago Heights and a large gypsum deposit in Nova Scotia. The discovery of the gypsum deposit enabled Certain-teed to develop gypsum products on the East Coast. Certain-teed stockholders approved a spin-off of a new company: the Bestwall Gypsum Company.

By the end of 1959, Certain-teed had developed the first fully automatic shingle packaging machine, which helped boost its sales to over $100 million that year. The following year Certain-teed organized the Institute for Essential Housing (IEH), a wholly owned subsidiary that built low-cost homes for Americans. IEH built economy homes under contract through-

Key Dates:

1904: George M. Brown founds the General Roofing Manufacturing Company in East St. Louis.

1917: Company restructures, incorporates, and changes its name to Certain-teed Products Corporation.

1918: Certain-teed begins trading on the New York Stock Exchange.

1935: Brown resigns as president and CEO.

1942: Company is awarded a National Defense contract.

1966: Certain-teed merges with Gustin-Bacon Manufacturing Corporation, a leading producer of fiberglass products.

1967: Certain-teed forms a partnership with Compagnie de Saint-Gobain, the world's largest building materials supplier.

1976: Company changes its name from Certain-teed Products Corporation to CertainTeed Corporation.

1980: Michael Besson becomes president and CEO of CertainTeed.

1988: Saint-Gobain acquires CertainTeed.

1999: CertainTeed unveils its K-21 line.

out the United States and provided special services such as financing. However, in 1962—the year of the Cuban Missile Crisis—a poor economy resulted in many foreclosures, and Certain-teed was left with a surplus of repossessed homes. A few years later it stopped selling housing.

A Focus on Fiberglass in the 1960s

In the 1960s Certain-teed decided to expand the fiberglass portion of its business. Fiberglass was used to make insulation used in pipes, tanks, and walls, and the company's decision to focus on the product was a good one, as energy conservation emerged as an important consideration in the country. In 1964 the company acquired the fiberglass manufacturing facilities of Pall Corporation in Mountaintop, Pennsylvania, and after the acquisition production at that plant tripled.

In 1966 Certain-teed merged with Gustin-Bacon Manufacturing Company, a leading producer of fiberglass products. This merger enabled Certain-teed to enter commercial and industrial markets for fiberglass insulation for homes. The following year, Certain-teed formed a partnership with Compagnie de Saint-Gobain Industries in France, the world leader in glass technology with a long history that included having made windows for King Louis XIV. The two companies formed the Certain-teed Saint-Gobain Insulation Corporation (CSG), a company which combined Saint-Gobain's technical knowledge with Certain-teed's marketing experience. CSG was a strong competitor in the U.S. insulation market.

Other acquisitions during this time included the pipe division of Ambler-Pennsylvania-based Keasbey and Mattison Company, the second largest producer of A/C pipes in the United States. In 1969 Certain-teed acquired the Bowles & Eden Supply Company and the Rohan Company; these acquisitions greatly increased Certain-teed's capacity to produce PVC

pipes. Around the same time Certain-teed began producing vinyl siding and fiberglass reinforced bathroom components.

Changes in Technology and Ownership in the 1970s–80s

During the energy crisis of the 1970s, CertainTeed became known as "The Energy Saving Company" because it focused on producing thermal insulation, roofing, PVC piping, vinyl siding, and acoustical insulation—materials that helped reduce the consumption of fossil fuels. The company enjoyed steady growth during this decade and concentrated on developing new manufacturing and materials technologies.

The year 1971 marked Certain-teed's purchase of Saint-Gobain's American, Canadian, and Mexican patents for fiberglass and foam, as well as the first year Certain-teed earned a profit from its fiberglass insulation. In 1975 Certain-teed began to manufacture PVC resin, a material used in the production of PVC pipe and vinyl siding. The following year the company shortened its name from Certain-teed Products Corporation to CertainTeed Corporation.

During the late 1970s and early 1980s the company's sales and profits slid. Moreover, organizational problems led to a high employee turnover, even among managers. Product quality dropped, and customers complained of poor service. To help turn the company around, Michael Besson was hired as president and CEO of CertainTeed in 1980. Besson was CertainTeed's fourth chief executive in five years. According to an article in the *Philadelphia Business Journal,* Besson realized the company was in trouble, but he knew it had a strong management team. He believed that with effective leadership and quality products his managers could set the company straight once again. Its partnership with Saint-Gobain was both an asset and a liability. Management was split in its loyalties toward the French industrial giant, and Besson hoped to better unite CertainTeed and Saint-Gobain. Prior to becoming president of CertainTeed, Besson—a Frenchman—had run Saint-Gobain's paper and packaging division, so he was on good terms with the company, and he assured management that he would run CertainTeed as an American company. Besson's efforts were successful. The *Philadelphia Business Journal* named Besson, his management team, and CertainTeed's board of directors the corporate winners of its 1986 Enterprise Awards. In 1988 Saint-Gobain acquired all of the remaining shares of CertainTeed. The company stopped trading on the New York Stock Exchange and became a subsidiary.

Diversification in the 1990s

In 1995 the company developed a plan for future growth called "Strategy 2000." Part of the plan included the unveiling of its K-21 line, the world's largest fiberglass insulation manufacturing line. According to an article in *Ceramic Industry,* the K-21 line spanned the length of three football fields and cost the company more than $100 million. Located in CertainTeed's existing Kansas City plant, the K-21 line was unveiled in 1999.

Realizing that windows were a natural extension of its product line in the early 1900s, CertainTeed began contracting vinyl window companies to fabricate windows bearing the CertainTeed name. Then, in the mid-1990s, it began buying these companies, among them B&K Window Manufacturing Inc. of Woodville, Washington, a fabricator of vinyl windows for new construction and remodeling markets that had been fabricating windows for CertainTeed since 1991. CertainTeed also purchased the assets of Fashonwall Products Inc. of Wixom, Michigan, a fabricator of CertainTeed vinyl high-performance vinyl windows, and acquired Bufftech Inc., of Buffalo, New York, a supplier of fabricated and extruded PVC fencing for residential, commercial, and agricultural markets. In 1997 CertainTeed bought the assets of Horizon Windows, of Elizabethtown, Kentucky, another of its window fabricators.

In 2000 the Vinyl Institute recognized CertainTeed Corporation's PVC plant in Sulphur, Louisiana, as one of the industry's top safety and environmental performers for the ninth consecutive year. Winners of the award were honored for their efforts to improve worker safety and protect the environment. With the full support of Saint-Gobain, its parent company, CertainTeed's future seemed secure. In 1999 Saint-Gobain's sales reached $24.5 billion, with CertainTeed contributing some $2 billion to that figure. In 2000 Certain-Teed planned to actively pursue new markets while more extensively penetrating existing markets. CertainTeed hoped, according to company literature, to "gain market share in product areas such as fiber cement and to increase awareness of the Saint-Gobain name in North America."

Principal Competitors

Armstrong Holdings, Inc.; Elcor Corporation; Owens Corning; Lafarge S.A.

Further Reading

"CertainTeed Acquires Fencing Company," company press release, September 4, 1996.

"CertainTeed Acquires Window Company," company press release, August 1, 1996.

"CertainTeed Acquires Window Fabrication Company," company press release, November 18, 1996.

"CertainTeed Fires Up the World's Largest Fiber Glass Insulation Line," *Ceramic Industry,* September 1999, p. 46.

75th Anniversary: CertainTeed 1904–1979, Valley Forge, Penn: CertainTeed Corporation.

Sullivan, Brian P., "Among the Rubble, CertainTeed's Michael Besson Finds a Jewel," *Philadelphia Business Journal,* March 24, 1986, p. 20.

Urey, Craig, "CertainTeed Buys Assets of Horizon," *Plastics News,* August 4, 1997, p. 9.

"Vinyl Institute Recognizes CertainTeed as One of the Industry's Top Safety and Environmental Performers for 1999," company press release, June 7, 2000.

—Tracey Vasil Biscontini

The Charles Stark Draper Laboratory, Inc.

555 Technology Square
Cambridge, Massachusetts 02139-3563
U.S.A.
Telephone: (617) 258-1000
Fax: (617) 258-1131
Web site: http://www.draper.com

Nonprofit Organization
Incorporated: 1973
Employees: 1,158
Revenues: $231.7 million (1999)
NAIC: 54171 Research and Development in the Physical,
    Engineering, and Life Sciences

Originally a unit of the Massachusetts Institute of Technology (MIT), The Charles Stark Draper Laboratory, Inc. established a stellar reputation for its inertial guidance systems. When man wanted to go to the moon, Doc Draper and his MIT Instrumentation Lab pointed the way. Although the lab acts as a design agent for the government, after the Cold War Draper has expanded the range of its work to include medical and commercial applications for its technologies, including ultra high tech micro-electromechanical systems.

Origins

Charles Stark Draper was born in Missouri on October 2, 1901. After earning a degree in psychology at Stanford in 1922, he came to the Massachusetts Institute of Technology (MIT). Four years later, with a bachelor's degree in electrochemical engineering in his pocket, he began working at MIT as a research associate under a Sloan fellowship. He became a professor there after receiving a Ph.D. in physics in 1938—two decades after starting college.

Draper began teaching aircraft instrumentation at MIT in the late 1920s. The subject matter was a natural concern to Draper, a pilot himself. He founded the Confidential Instrument Development Laboratory in 1932, which later became known as the MIT Instrumentation Laboratory. Walter Wrigley, an early student of Draper, described Draper's early inertial navigation experiments in a 1940 thesis.

One of the lab's first widely disseminated products was the Mark 14 Gunsight used by Allied forces in WWII. Developed for the U.S. Navy, the shoebox-shaped optical device used gyros, springs, and linkages to bring an unprecedented level of accuracy to anti-aircraft gunnery. The lab continued to design fire control systems after the war. The FEBE system (named for Phoebus) incorporated celestial references for improved accuracy and was first demonstrated in 1949.

The development of inertial navigation allowed for a truly historic flight in 1953, when the lab's 2,700-pound Space Inertial Reference Equipment (SPIRE) system guided a B-29 bomber from Massachusetts to Los Angeles without the aid of a pilot. Draper himself and several associates flew aboard that 12.5-hour trip. The next year, 1954, saw the introduction of the first self-contained submarine navigation system (SINS).

Cold War

Said Draper, "An inertial system does for geometry . . . what a watch does for time." The lab's precision gyroscopes and accelerometers made possible the new era of ballistic missiles. Further, they could not be jammed like existing radio guidance systems.

The launch of the Sputnik satellite by the Soviet Union in 1957 brought new urgency to the U.S. Air Force Thor intermediate range ballistic missile (IRBM) program. Work began on the Navy's historic Polaris guidance system the same year. Before the end of the decade, the lab had started work on its FLIMBAL (floating inertial measurement ball) inertial guidance system as well as the Mars Probe project.

Draper was a more charismatic figure than most physicists. He tooled around the MIT campus in a Morgan sports car and entertained the press with stories of extracurricular activities on the baseball field and in the boxing ring. He became known for his work on the Apollo space program, and *Time* magazine named him one of its "Men of the Year" in January 1961.

Company Perspectives:

The organization's mission is to serve the national interest in applied research, engineering development, education, and technology transfer by: Helping our sponsors clarify their requirements and conceptualize innovative solutions to their problems; Demonstrating those solutions through the design and development of fieldable engineering prototypes; Transitioning our products and processes to industry for production, and providing follow-on support; Promoting and supporting advanced technical education.

The success of the Titan and Poseidon missile programs in the 1960s validated the lab's inertial guidance systems. Draper also guided a new Deep Submergence Rescue Vehicle (DSRV) for the Navy, first introduced in 1970. The Apollo 11 manned moon landing in 1969, however, brought the lab its greatest fame. The Draper Lab had received NASA's first contract for the Apollo program. It borrowed upon its design work from the unlaunched Mars Probe of the previous decade as well as the Polaris missile program to construct the navigation and guidance system. According to the *New York Times,* Charles Draper "guided the astronauts to the moon."

Subsequent missions brought more high-visibility challenges. The Apollo 12 guidance system was damaged by lightning after takeoff and had to be reset in orbit. When the Apollo 13 crew reported those famous words, "Houston, we have a problem," the Draper Lab recommended the fix. They transmitted a modified computer program to the crew of the Apollo 14, which was dealing with a faulty switch.

Vietnam Era Conflict

The lab employed 2,000 people in the late 1960s. Half of its work came from NASA by this point. NASA issued the lab a contract to work on avionics for the Space Shuttle in 1971. The next year saw the development of the first digital fly-by-wire system. Skylab was launched in May 1973, with Draper supplying the algorithms for its guidance and control system.

Draper occupied 14 buildings on the MIT campus. Protesters against the Vietnam War targeted the lab for its role in developing military weapons. The students and faculty involved in the protests ceased their research activities.

Although the lab was renamed The Charles Stark Draper Laboratory as a result of the controversy, Draper himself was forced into a brief retirement in 1970. He soon returned, however, and the lab was divested from MIT in 1973, becoming a not-for-profit corporation after three years as an independent division of MIT. It remained closely tied to the institution, however, and Draper employees continued to enjoy campus amenities. Robert Duffy, a newly retired Air Force general, was the lab's first president and CEO while Dr. Albert G. Hill, MIT vice-president for research, headed the board of directors. The lab moved into a new headquarters near MIT in late 1976.

Asked by the U.S. Navy to develop a new guidance system for use in the Trident I long-range C-4 missile, the Lab designed a system with a star-tracker, providing the required accuracy at extended ranges. The Trident I became operational in late 1979. During the 1980s, Draper Lab designed the Mk6 guidance system for the Trident II D5 missile. The system provided increased accuracy over the Trident I system. For U.S. Air Force missiles, the Lab designed instruments; Draper's Missile Performance Measurement System (MPMS) Advanced Inertial Reference System (AIRS) flew on a Minuteman III in 1976 and was adopted for the MX in the 1980s.

Hill retired in 1982, to be succeeded by Kenneth McKay as board chair. The lab opened an annex named in Hill's honor two years later. In 1983, Draper Lab helped defeat a referendum to designate Cambridge a Nuclear Free Zone.

In 1984, the lab began its involvement with micro-electromechanical systems (MEMS). The extremely tiny, cheap guidance instruments promised proliferation in many types of equipment. Work on the Space Station program began in 1987.

Ralph Jacobson, a retired Air Force General, succeeded Robert Duffy as president and CEO in 1987, while Joseph Charyk became chairman of the board. Charles Draper died the same year. The lab endowed the Charles Stark Draper Prize in honor of its founder in 1988. Its honorarium was worth $500,000 in 1999.

Adjusting Course in the 1990s

The Cold War appeared to have ended by 1989 and defense cutbacks soon followed. Draper would reduce its work force by almost 50 percent in the next few years. New legislation encouraged competitive bidding on government contracts, although an Omnibus Basic Ordering Agreement, awarded in 1994, simplified the contracting process between government agencies and Draper.

In 1990, Draper integrated GPS (Global Positioning System) in the guidance system of A-10 Warthog attack aircraft. The lab had increasingly begun yoking its technology to civilian applications, however. It designed robots to manufacture clothing in an attempt to help American companies compete with low-cost Asian labor. The PC-driven Draper Knitwear Machine could make three pairs of sweat pants a minute.

Draper turned more and more to automation in its own production as miniaturization to smaller and smaller tolerances became the order of the day. Human beings simply breathed and sloughed too many stray particles into the air to reliably assemble parts measured in micrometers. An effort begun in the 1970s fashioned the gentlest of robot hands to fit parts together.

Low-cost, micromachined silicon MEMS devices began to enter the consumer marketplace in full force. In December 1993, Rockwell International entered a strategic alliance with Draper to bring these inertial sensors into a variety of consumer applications, from camcorders (image stabilization) to antilock brakes.

Significant projects for NASA and the Navy proceeded at the same time. Draper helped configure the Space Shuttle for special missions, such as its historic docking with the Russian *Mir* space station in June 1995. It completed demonstrations

---

Key Dates:

1922: Charles Stark Draper begins undergraduate studies at MIT.
1932: Confidential Instrument Laboratory established.
1942: The Mark 14 gunsight designed by Draper first sees battle.
1953: A B-29 bomber flies cross-country guided only by the SPIRE system.
1957: Sputnik accelerates work on ballistic missiles.
1969: Draper guides Apollo 11 to the moon.
1973: Lab divested from MIT because of political considerations.
1979: Trident I, guided by celestial cues, becomes operational.
1984: Draper begins developing micro-electromechanical systems (MEMS).
1988: Charles Stark Draper Prize created to recognize engineering achievements.
1993: Rockwell contracts to bring MEMS devices into the consumer marketplace.
1997: First digital autopilot for submarines demonstrated.

---

of its Unmanned Undersea Vehicle (UUV) in 1996. Applications for the UUV included mine reconnaissance and oceanography.

Vincent Vitto succeeded Ralph Jacobson as CEO in July 1997. Vitto was a physicist with 32 years of experience at MIT's Lincoln Laboratory. That year, Draper demonstrated the first digital autopilot for submarines. Fitted to the Seawolf class of attack submarines, it paralleled the fly-by-wire systems found in fighter and civil aircraft. The lab also had begun developing controls for a new, small submersible for Navy SEALs.

Other military products in development included gun-launched, guided munitions using MEMS technology. Aside from inertial guidance systems, MEMS could produce 2mm-wide microphones as well as extremely tiny hydrophones, seismic vibration sensors, and chemical sensors. Space projects included the X-33 and X-34 unmanned, reusable launch vehicles, as well as an emergency escape vehicle for the Space Station.

Draper Lab was using the same technology to pioneer new frontiers in medicine. MEMS devices could be used to track surgical instruments inside the body. Engineers were researching the possibilities of implanting inertial sensing devices in the inner ear to improve balance. Retinal implants and improved artificial voiceboxes were also on the drawing boards. Intriguingly, reports surfaced in the spring of 2000 of Draper creating a silicon template on which networks of capillaries could be grown. If successful, the technique would enable the medical community to grow viable organs for transplantation.

Principal Divisions

Strategic Systems; Tactical Systems; Space Systems; Systems Technology; Special Operations and Land Robotics; Biomedicine.

Principal Competitors

Litton Guidance and Control Systems; Honeywell; Aerospace Technology, Inc.

Further Reading

Fairley, Peter, ''Blood from a Chip,'' *Technology Review,* May/June 2000.
Lewis, Diane E., ''Massachusetts' Draper Labs Asks Custodians To Return Wages,'' *Boston Globe,* September 27, 1996.
——, ''The '90s: Era of Broken Promises, Insecurity,'' *Boston Globe,* October 8, 1996, pp. D14ff.
Morgan, Christopher, Joseph O'Connor, and David Hoag, *Draper at 25: Innovation for the 21st Century,* Cambridge, Mass.: The Charles Stark Draper Laboratory, Inc., 1998.
Rosenberg, Ronald, ''Draper's New Niche: Sweats,'' *Boston Globe,* July 6, 1989, pp. 43ff.
Rotman, Laurie, Margaret Spinner, and Julie Williams, ''The Draper Gopher: A Team Approach To Building a Virtual Library,'' *Online,* March 1995, pp. 21ff.
Shepard, Alan, and Deke Slayton, *Moon Shot: The Inside Story of America's Race to the Moon,* Atlanta: Turner, 1994.
Stauffer, Robert N., ''Robotics Research: What the Labs Might Hold in Store,'' *Manufacturing Engineering,* June 1988, pp. 58ff.
Whitney, Daniel, ''When People Are Too Large and Dirty,'' in ''The Flexible Factory: Case Studies,'' *IEEE Spectrum,* September 1993, pp. 39–42.
Wulf, Wm. A., ''Engineering the Modern World,'' *Journal of Commerce,* December 13, 1999, pp. 5f.

—Frederick C. Ingram

Charlotte Russe

Charlotte Russe Holding, Inc.

4645 Morena Boulevard
San Diego, California 92117
U.S.A.
Telephone: (858) 587-1500
Fax: (858) 587-0336
Web site: http://www.charlotte-russe.com

Public Company
Incorporated: 1975 as Lawrence Merchandising Corp.
Employees: 1,992
Sales: $177.5 million (1999)
Stock Exchanges: NASDAQ
Ticker Symbol: CHIC
NAIC: 44812 Women's Clothing Stores

Charlotte Russe Holding, Inc. is a specialty retailer of women's clothes, aimed at women between the ages of 15 and 35. The company operates two different chains of apparel stores, Charlotte Russe and Rampage. The Charlotte Russe stores target women who want established fashions at reasonable prices; Rampage stores offer higher priced, more cutting-edge clothes and accessories. In 1999 the company began testing a third concept, Charlotte's Room, offering accessories and home fashions. As of April 2000, the company operated a total of 113 stores in 17 states and Puerto Rico.

From Brooklyn to San Diego: 1975–89

Dan, Frank, and Larry Lawrence grew up in the clothing business, working in their father's clothing store in Brooklyn. They moved west, formed the Lawrence Merchandising Corp., and in 1975 opened their own store, in Carlsbad, California. They named the 1,500-square-foot store Charlotte Russe after a dessert they remembered from their childhood.

Over the next ten years, the brothers opened six more stores in San Diego County, bringing in sales of $12 million in 1984. They then began to move into other parts of the state. The units grew bigger, to around 5,000 square feet, and continued to be visually dramatic. To attract the trendy young women they wanted as customers, they concentrated on visual displays, location, and packaging. The Lawrences opened stores in heavily shopped malls, taking prime locations and making Charlotte Russe an anchor store. Their windows made the local news, and customers used the distinctive shopping bags, with a psychedelic art deco design of a buxom woman, at the beach and when travelling.

Their first store outside San Diego was huge compared with other Charlotte Russe locations—20,000 square feet. Inside, the decor was dramatic: television monitors showing the latest rock and fashion videos and some 65 mannequins. As had become a tradition, customers on opening day were served charlotte russe, a pastry made of custard, whipped cream, and cherry topping. Although the Lawrences spent $750,000 on that new store, their expansion plans were conservative and growth was financed internally.

Growth of the Company: 1990–96

In 1990, the Lawrences moved outside California, opening three units in Phoenix, Arizona. By 1991, the company had net sales of about $50 million, with a history of annual sales increasing in double digits. In 1992, despite a slowing retail climate, the company opened stores in Las Vegas, Nevada and Los Angeles.

The Lawrences also saw a change in their customer base and moved to respond. Women who had shopped at Charlotte Russe while in their teens and 20s were now bringing their daughters in to shop with them. The company broadened their inventory, adding more classic styles and special occasion dressing as well as gift items and shoes at several locations. "We hold on to our customer longer than our competition," Larry told Michael Marlow of *WWD* in 1995. "We carry a wide range of inventory for ages 14 to 40. We attract women of a certain attitude, not age."

One of the company's strengths, according to wholesales and industry watchers, was that the brothers, especially Danny, who was in charge of buying, kept their focus on their customer and concentrated on clothes and accessories suitable to the southern California and Southwest areas. As one junior manufacturer explained to *WWD (Women's Wear Daily)* in a 1994 article,

93

Company Perspectives:

Through our fashion content, merchandise mix, exciting store layout and design, and striking merchandise presentation, we project fashion attitudes that appeal to customers from a broad range of socioeconomic, demographic and cultural profiles. In addition, our breadth of merchandise enables our customers to assemble coordinated and complete outfits that satisfy many of their lifestyle needs. Our success is dependent upon our ability to anticipate, identify and capitalize upon the fashion preferences of our target customers.

"Charlotte Russe is one of the best. Number one, the stores are very large and give the women a great atmosphere with a comfortable design. Number two, they watch the trends very closely, but don't overdo them. Number three, they watch their selling on a daily basis and number four, their distribution is terrific. . . . Their turnaround time is 24 to 48 hours." California had emerged as a very strong junior retail market, and in 1995, *WWD* identified Charlotte Russe as one of the three most aggressive junior retail concepts, along with Rampage and Wet Seal.

In April 1996, the company hired Bernard Zeichner as president and CEO. Zeichner had been head of the retail division of Guess? and prior to that was president and CEO of Contempo Casuals. In September, Zeichner and two funds managed by investment firm Saunders Karp & Mergue, L.P. bought Charlotte Russe from the Lawrence brothers.

Starting a Retail Company: 1993–95

Larry Hansel, at age 32, was founder and CEO of Rampage Clothing Co., a California manufacturer that made sportswear and dresses for juniors and children. In 1993, he moved into retail, buying Los Angeles-based Judy's Inc., with its 62 stores, as part of a bankruptcy reorganization plan. Hansel paid $2 million in cash for 80 percent of Judy's stock and assumption of its liabilities. Judy's, which was founded in 1946, had been one of the first retailers to give Hansel an order when he started Rampage.

Originally, Hansel planned to keep the Judy's name and expand the chain. But the first revamped stores were not successful, because they were not "special," according to Hansel. In 1994, he decided to keep some 40 of the Judy's stores and convert them into Rampage stores. As Hansel explained to the *Los Angeles Times,* "It's a brand new vision about business. It's done with product and people. The product is more accessible, fresher and presented better. It's more exclusive. We make over half of it ourselves, and we don't sell to other stores." In addition, the stores would reach beyond the junior market of teens and women in their 20s to target women ages 15 to 35.

The first Rampage retail unit opened in Reno in March 1994, quickly followed by stores in Houston and Los Angeles. Inside the stores, wooden floors replaced carpet, the lights were much brighter, and customers could find other merchandise in addition to clothes, including jewelry, shampoo, and vases. Rampage stores, said Hansel, were "urban, raw, sensual, soft" and

"a collection of boutiques" under one roof. He also started another boutique chain, Friends, for girls 4 to 13, which sold Rampage's existing children's lines and were located close to a Rampage store.

From Boom to Bust for Rampage: 1996–97

By 1996, Hansel was talking about taking the company public and had created expansion plans to accomplish that. While the wholesale side of the business was the major contributor to its annual quarter of a million dollars in revenues, the 45 stores (Rampage, Judy's, and Friends) had sales of $65 million, up from $27 million when Hansel bought the 60-store Judy's chain. Plans included closing or converting the remaining Judy's stores; licensing for shoes, lingerie, swimsuits, and jewelry; a Rampage line of cosmetics; and franchising the retail operation worldwide.

However, within a year, according to the March issue of *Chain Store Age,* Hansel was "overextended and plagued by inventory problems, fashion misses, high overhead and over-structuring." Rampage Clothing Co. and its retail affiliate filed for bankruptcy in June 1997 and began closing or selling the retail units. Charlotte Russe, which had been acquired by Sanders Karp & Megrue the year before, bought 16 Rampage stores for $10.5 million.

The Holding Company: 1996–97

In October 1996, Charlotte Russe president and CEO Bernard Zeichner and investment firm Sanders Karp & Megrue (SKM) bought the California-based Charlotte Russe chain of women's retail stores from the Lawrence brothers, who had founded the chain. SKM owned other retailers, including Dollar Tree Stores and Hibbett Sporting Goods. At the time of the sale, Charlotte Russe had 35 stores in California, Arizona, and Nevada, with annual revenues of about $70 million.

SKM and Zeichner planned to take the chain national, hiring top management with extensive retail experience, consolidating the distribution and corporate operations in San Diego, and upgrading the management information systems. During the first year, Charlotte Russe opened its first store in Northern California and moved into the Texas and Florida markets. Net sales for the 1997 fiscal year grew to $81.5 million, an increase of more than 15 percent from fiscal 1996.

Meanwhile, Rampage Clothing Co., a manufacturer of clothing for juniors and children, and Rampage Retailing, its affiliated chain of stores, filed for bankruptcy in June 1997. Rampage closed most of its retail business, including its Judy's and Friends units, and in October sold the remaining 16 Rampage stores to Charlotte Russe for $10.5 million. The purchase gave Charlotte Russe Holding a second, distinctive store concept, which it continued to operate under the Rampage name.

Integration of Rampage: 1998–99

Integrating the Rampage purchase into its operations put a strain on the company for about six months. Once it established separate buying operations for each chain, moved into a new headquarters building, and opened its larger, more automated distribution center, however, things went more smoothly. Even as the internal changes were going on, Zeichner opened 17 new Charlotte Russe stores, including units in new markets of Georgia and South Carolina. The Rampage chain and new stores helped the company increase its sales a whopping 64 percent, to $134.1 million, despite poorer performance in Charlotte Russe stores that had been open at least a year.

The company continued its subsidiaries' focus on a broader customer base than the traditional junior market, targeting women 15 to 35. Each chain had its own strong brand identity, and the company's "test-and-reorder" approach to merchandising allowed the in-store testing of small quantities of merchandise and the placing of larger orders when customers had indicated, with their purchases, what they liked. Unlike most of its competitors, the company dealt primarily with American manufacturers, which made it possible to get the clothes it wanted in a relatively short period of time.

Another difference between Charlotte Russe Holding and other mall-based specialty retailers was store size. The company's stores averaged 7,500 square feet, about twice the space of most of its competitors. The interiors of the two chains aimed to accomplish different objectives. Charlotte Russe, "Where You Fit In," offered distinct and separate areas of "lifestyle collections"—casual, career, and club wear, shoes, lingerie, and accessories—to create a multi-boutique. Dressing rooms have couches and colors are soft and feminine. That arrangement appeared to attract and encourage shopping by both juniors, ages 15–21, and older women, ages 25–35.

At Rampage, whose tag line was "Bold, Sexy, Modern," merchandise was grouped by color and fashion trends. Hardwood floors and metal fixtures stressed the "urban" message under bright lights. Prices in both chains were lower than at competing women's stores, and more than 80 percent of the merchandise carried house labels. The chains turned over their inventory 12 times a year, a rate that was up to three times greater than most of its competitors. A final benefit of this two-pronged approach was that items that proved to be hot at Rampage soon showed up at Charlotte Russe.

2000 and Beyond

In October 1999, without a dot-com or an Internet strategy to its name, Charlotte Russe Holding, Inc. went public. The company had more than doubled its size since 1996 and was operating 96 stores in 15 states and Puerto Rico. Earnings had increased an average 27 percent annually and sales were growing 40 percent a year. The IPO netted about $13.5 million, which was used to pay down debt under the company's revolving credit facility.

A month later, the company introduced a new concept, Charlotte's Room. Two new, 3,500-square-foot stores opened in Los Angeles and Phoenix, aimed at young women ages 12–20. Although the new units offered some clothes and accessories, the focus was on furnishings, including bedding, rugs, bean bags, and lamps. "If it doesn't work, we can just walk away from it," Zeichner told *Investor's Business Daily* at the end of the year. A second new venture was the development of a web site that would, according to the company, create "a unique 'pop-culture' experience for our customer that blends music, fashion and entertainment."

Through mid-2000, Charlotte Russe Holding continued to read the trends right. Zeichner announced that the company would open more stores than originally planned for fiscal 2001, with a more aggressive expansion of Rampage. New stores were important to the company, because they drove additional profits. In an April 2000 *WWW* article, Zeichner explained, "Since our stores do well over $2.2 million each, we are not looking for strong comparable increases, and our new stores open up with a return investment of over 90 percent." With those strong cash flows, a good economy, and continued accurate trend reading, Charlotte Russe Holding was moving to be a 500-store national chain.

Principal Divisions

Charlotte Russe; Rampage.

Principal Competitors

Limited, Inc.; Wet Seal Inc.; Arden B; bebe stores inc.

Further Reading

Allen, Mike, "Charlotte Russe Stores Sold to N.Y. Investors," *San Diego Business Journal,* October 28, 1996, p. 7.

Cox, Michael D., "Chic Charlotte Russe Outlets Planned at Four Valley Malls," *Arizona Business Gazette,* May 4, 1990, p. 15.

Ellis, Kristi, "Charlotte Russe on the Fast Track," *WWD,* April 27, 2000, p. 9.

——, "Rampage in State of Evolution," *WWD,* May 23, 1996, p. 6.

Ginsberg, Steve, "Charlotte Russe Flies High in Orange County," *WWD (Women's Wear Daily),* August 16, 1985, p. S21.

Glover, Kara, "Rampage Hits the Malls as Retailer Repositions Moribund Judy's Chain," *Los Angeles Business Journal,* September 26, 1994, p. 26.

Goldman, Melanie, "Charlotte Russe Prepares for a Rampage," *Shopping Center Business,* May 1999.

Fidelholtz, Sara, "Rampage CEO Hansel Buys Judy's Chain," *WWD,* February 1, 1993, p. 2.

Green, Frank, "Charlotte Russe Is Hip to What Customers Want," *San Diego Union Tribune,* December 5, 1999, p. I6.

"Homespun Hoopla Gives Small Stores High Profile," *WWD (Women's Wear Daily),* October 31, 1983, p. C20.

Johnson, Greg, "Wet Seal Offers To Buy 21 Rampage Stores," *Los Angeles Times,* July 29, 1997, p. D12.

Kletter, Melanie, "Hot Retailers Try To Stay 'Cool'," *WWD,* June 1, 2000, p. 15.

Marlow, Michael, "West Coast Junior Chains: Trend Catchers," *WWD,* June 29, 1995, p. 6.

Much, Marilyn, "Clothier Finds Bigger Stores Mean Better Strategy," *Investor's Business Daily*, December 7, 1999.

Riggs, Rod, "Charlotte Russe, Despite Bad Time, Will Go Forward with Expansion Plans," *San Diego Union,* February 22, 1992, p. C1.

——, "Charlotte Russe Eyes Growth," *San Diego Union,* June 20, 1989, p. E1.

——, "It's Not a Dessert, But a Total Look," *San Diego Union,* February 24, 1985, p. I1.

Turk, Rose-Marie, "An Eye for Style," *Los Angeles Times,* June 2, 1994, p. E1.

Vrana, Debora, and Kara Glover, "Judy's Chain May End Chapter 11 with New Owner," *Los Angeles Business Journal,* January 25, 1993, p. 8.

Welsh, Alice, "Rating the Retailers: The Junior Market," *WWD,* November 17, 1994, p. 8.

"Zeichner Group Buys Charlotte Russe," *WWD,* October 21, 1996, p. 17.

—Ellen D. Wernick

Chemfab Corporation

701 Daniel Webster Highway
Postal Office Box 1137
Merrimack, New Hampshire 03054
U.S.A.
Telephone: (603) 424-9000
Fax: (603) 424-9028
Web site: http://www.chemfab.com

Public Company
Incorporated: 1968 as Chemical Fabrics Corporation
Employees: 738
Sales: $126.48 million (1999)
Stock Exchanges: New York
Ticker Symbol: CFA
NAIC: 313210 Broadwoven Fabric Mills; 313320 Fabric
   Coating Mills; 339991 Gasket, Packing and Sealing
   Device Manufacturing

Chemfab Corporation is an international leader in the design, manufacture, fabrication, and marketing of flexible polymeric composite materials. The company manufactures a broad range of polymer-based, reinforced and unreinforced fluoroplastics, fluoroelastomers, silicone elastomers, and adhesives. Chemfab's products include laminates, films, coated fabrics, tapes, molded polymer products, and finished articles fabricated from roll goods. The company's products usually fit within three major product groups: engineered industrial products, architectural products, and elastomere products. Engineered industrial products are made of woven fiberglass or other high-strength fibrous reinforcement-coated resins. Chemfab's trademarked architectural products include Sheerfill architectural membrane, Ultralux architectural membrane, Fabrasorb acoustical membrane, and Chemglas roof membrane. Chemglas also is used as a protective layer in the space shuttle cargo bay and in covers for critical components on the new international space station. Chemfab elastomer products include a comprehensive product line of elastomeric closures for use in gas and liquid chromatography, environmental testing, and the packaging and storage of sterile biomedical-culture media. The company also markets specialty fluoropolymer films, silicone elastomers, and other silicone-based products. Chemfab has operations in nine countries around the world and operates within three major business segments. The Americas Business Group is responsible for all manufacturing and sales of engineered industrial products made in, and sold to, the Americas as well as for architectural product sales worldwide. The European Business Group is responsible for all manufacturing and sales of engineered industrial products made in, and sold to, Europe, the Middle East, and Africa. The High Performance Elastomer Group manufactures and sells silicone-elastomer products worldwide. Global markets for Chemfab's products are in the electrical, food processing, biomedical, protective clothing, electronics, communications, aerospace, architectural, and other industrial markets and applications. The company also sells to the medical electronics, personal care, health care, and specialty apparel industries. "During the last five years," wrote Chemfab President/CEO John Verbicky in his 1999 Letter to Shareholders, "the company has nearly tripled its revenue and has tripled its earnings per share."

1968–84: Origins and Early Development

Entrepreneur John Ransom Cook and four business associates, on September 30, 1968, founded Chemical Fabrics Corporation and set up shop in a former Volkswagen dealership building in Bennington, Vermont. Previously, in 1947, Cook had established Warren Wire Company—named after his eldest son, Warren—and manufactured electrical wire insulated with a polymer named polytetrafluoroethylene (PTFE). The E.I. du Pont de Nemours and Company (DuPont) had developed PTFE, trademarked the product and taught the world to call it "Teflon." Three years after the sale of Warren Wire to General Cable Corporation, Cook re-entered the Teflon-coated products business; this time, however, he focused on Teflon-coated glass fabrics for diverse industrial applications. Since there were already established markets for standard 60-inch-wide Teflon-coated glass fabrics, the company (which adopted the trade name Chemfab) pioneered the development of equipment that could coat woven fiberglass webs up to 180 inches wide.

At about this time, an event halfway across the world—namely, the 1970 World's Fair held in Osaka, Japan—was

---

Company Perspectives:

Chemfab will be a world-class company (the best at everything we do) that creates and delivers high performance polymer-based products of superior value. We believe that by providing our customers with superior value in product innovation, performance, quality, delivery, and customer service at competitive prices, we can deliver value to our shareholders and employees. We will be a value-driven company in everything that we do. Business activities which fail to add value will be fixed, disposed of or eliminated, and new activities will have clearly defined value benefits.

---

about to influence Chemfab's direction and growth as a company. The U.S. Pavilion and pavilions of many other nations, were constructed of lightweight, membranelike materials, so much so that the fair was billed a "fabric-structure extravaganza." The roof of the U.S. Pavilion, which was fabricated and installed by the Japanese company Taiyo Kogyo Corporation (Taiyo), was made of vinyl-coated woven fiberglass, air-supported, and held in place by steel cables, according to *Our First 25 Years*—a booklet commemorating Chemfab's founding and progress. Cook recognized both the limitations and the weaknesses of the vinyl-based roofing fabric, which would not pass muster for U.S. buildings: the vinyl was not fire-resistant enough to meet building codes. Furthermore, vinyl-based materials discolored rather quickly after outdoor exposure.

Cook worked intensely with DuPont and Owens-Corning Fiberglas Corporation to develop a Teflon-based roofing material that could meet the requirements of U.S. building and fire codes. Roofing material was an ideal product for Chemfab, "the only company in the world that possessed wide-width PTFE-coating capability," wrote the author of *Our First 25 Years*. The result of the cooperative effort was Chemfab's trademarked Sheerfill, a material that could be modified to varying weight, strength, translucency, and reflectivity to fit the design and location of a structure. Sheerfill reflected heat while allowing light to pass through and did not discolor when exposed to extreme temperatures; the strong, durable product's solar and thermal/optical properties were similar to those of reflective glass, but Sheerfill was translucent rather than transparent.

Chemfab developed architectural membrane products to support Sheerfill roofing but still needed specialized engineering, fabrication, and installation techniques, which it obtained from Buffalo, New York-based Birdair Structures, Inc., a firm that specialized in the installation of membrane structures. In 1973 Birdair completed the first project using Sheerfill: a cone-shaped membrane structure spanning 68,000 square feet covering the student and drama center at The University of La Verne, in California. Then, in 1975, came the completion of an air-supported Sheerfill roof on the Pontiac Silverdome in Michigan. During the 1970s, Chemfab also began to use Teflon-coated fiberglass composites to make radomes, globe-shaped structures for housing radar antenna equipment and, eventually, on a worldwide basis, to shelter satellite and microwave communications equipment.

Disaster struck in 1976: John Cook died when his private plane crashed in an ice storm. Expansion had stretched Chemfab's financial resources to the limit and negotiations for a new lease on building space for a weaving operation in Manchester, New Hampshire were a great burden on the company. John's brother, Paul Cook, gave much needed management and financial assistance to the young company and ensured its continuing viability. He became a Chemfab director and brought in Warren Cook, John's son, to serve as president/CEO.

In 1978 Chemfab won a contract to supply coated material for an enormous canopy over the Hajj Terminal at King Abdul Aziz International Airport in Jeddah, South Arabia. This canopy covered 100 acres (the area of 110 football fields) and was designed to shelter nearly one million pilgrims on their annual pilgrimage to Mecca. Then, in 1979, Chemfab acquired Birdair and increased its participation in the building of a growing number of diversified outdoor membrane structures. Chemfab marketed its high-performance fabric composites worldwide. These composites were produced by encapsulating woven glass fiber within a fluoropolymer-resin matrix; the end product, called "engineered material," surpassed the properties of its separate components. Woven fiberglass coated with thermoplastics and elastomers allowed for the fabrication of products having strong thermal, electrical, and chemical resistance. [*Elastomer—elas*(tic) + (poly)*mer* is a rubberlike synthetic polymer, such as synthetic rubber.] The end-users of these products were the defense and communications markets as well as builders of permanent fabric structures.

To serve its expanding overseas markets, in 1980 Chemfab established a Teflon-coating plant in Kilrush, Ireland. This plant manufactured a broad range of Teflon-based composite products and fabricated end-use products for sale in Europe, Africa, the Middle East, India, and Japan. Gradually, sales subsidiaries were established in England, Denmark, and Spain. Chemfab relocated its headquarters to Merrimack, New Hampshire to gain greater accessibility to the Boston metropolitan area and secure additional space for long-term expansion. Chemfab's advances in fabric-composite technology triggered strong growth for the company. To obtain a larger capital base for further expansion, Chemfab went public in the fall of 1983 and was traded on NASDAQ under the symbol CMFB.

Sales of products for fabric structures increased 70 percent in 1984, representing 49 percent of total sales. During the year, nine fabric structures were completed; Chemfab was the major supplier for the International Stadium project in Riyadh, Saudi Arabia. The company's capability to integrate design and installation gave it a strong marketing edge. Chemfab's international business, excluding the International Stadium project, doubled in 1984. An office was opened in West Germany to assist the marketing group in the United Kingdom and the company's manufacturing facilities in Ireland. Through the acquisition of Florida-based Toralon Products Corporation, a PTFE film manufacturer and owner of a technology for a multilayer cast-film process, Chemfab added film production and lamination to its processes. Furthermore, the acquisition of Environmental Structures Pty, Ltd. opened up opportunities for sales, marketing, and installation services for permanent fabric structures in Australia. For fiscal 1984, sales reached $37.12 million, com-

Key Dates:

1968: John R. Cook and four associates form Chemical Fabrics Corporation.

1973: Company's trademarked Sheerfill roofing material is used at the University of La Verne, California.

1978: Chemical Fabrics supplies coated material for a canopy at King Abdul Aziz International Airport in Jeddah, South Arabia.

1980: Company establishes a plant in Ireland.

1983: Chemical Fabric goes public on NASDAQ exchange.

1990: Company introduces its trademarked process for high-output film casting.

1991: Chemical Fabrics Corporation takes Chemfab Corporation as its legal name.

1993: Boeing applies Chemfab's trademarked DF-29X9 tapes to its commercial jets.

1994: Chemfab enters the biomedical market.

1997: Chemfab moves its stock listing from NASDAQ to New York.

2000: Chemfab expands its multisite e-Store on the Internet and launches its e-commerce business capability for worldwide sales of its products.

pared with $27.02 million in 1983; working capital for 1994 rose to $4.26 million, compared with $1.7 million in 1993.

1985–90: Fall and Rise

Substantial increases in costs for a rapid expansion program, strong competition, a sudden collapse in demand for architectural membranes, and an uneven economy in 1985–86 caused revenues and profits to fall below expectations. Costs rose faster than revenues. Chemfab implemented cost controls, reduced the work force, and moved forward by orienting itself toward more stable, recurring, and proprietary businesses. Chemfab partnered with Owens-Corning Fiberglas Corporation (OCF) to form a joint venture, dubbed OC Birdair, Inc. By combining its engineering expertise with OCF's construction experience and applications technology, Chemfab gained a more efficient delivery system.

Furthermore, to cultivate Japanese and Far East markets and acquire a location for manufacturing and distribution in the Pacific Basin, Chemfab partnered with two Osaka, Japan-based companies: Nitto Electric Industrial Company and Taiyo. The Tokyo-based venture, named Nitto Chemfab Company, Ltd. (later merged in Chemfab Japan, Ltd.), was one of the main customers of Chemfab's Sheerfill permanent architectural products. Chemfab also developed a trademarked acoustical liner fabric, Fabrasorb, which absorbed sound typically encountered in large open areas. For fiscal 1986, Chemfab reported net sales of $23.04 million, compared with record net sales of $37.12 million in 1984; fiscal 1986 net income loss amounted to $5.06 million for 1986, compared with a net income profit of $2.01 million in 1984. In June 1986, Warren Cook retired as president/CEO; he was succeeded by Duane C. Montopoli, who had joined Chemfab as chief financial officer in February 1986 and had served as interim president after Warren's retirement.

According to Andrew Wood's "Chemfab" article in the 1997 issue of *Chemical Week,* "In 1986 Chemfab was on the brink of bankruptcy. . . . Montopoli, a financial whiz rather than an expert in composites, set about diversifying Chemfab into other sectors to reduce its dependence on the architectural market." To repair the company's balance sheet, he sold Chemfab's headquarters building and the surrounding 175 acres of land for $10.3 million but retained full use of the facility and the right, over time, to repurchase the building and 21 acres of land. Proceeds of the sale went to pay down bank debt; financial health was restored and Chemfab began a slow, but steady, growth in both domestic and international markets, especially for its trademarked engineered products—for example, Raydel, radomes, coated release sheets and conveyor belts, insulated cables, and Challenge clothing. Raydel, a microwave-transmissive fabric, was used in the manufacture of radomes and electromagnetic windows; this fabric had an exceptionally low signal loss and outstanding hydrophobicity, characteristics that allowed transmission of signals with minimum distortion, even in adverse weather. Chemfab developed commercial cooking-release sheets and conveyor belts coated with Chemfab's trademarked Fiberglass Teflon. Other products were used in high-speed packaging machines and in the molding of the reinforced epoxy components used in the aerospace industry. Challenge chemical-protective clothing (fluoropolymer-laminated textiles) was used by emergency response teams in the cleanup of hazardous materials; protective hoods were used as an emergency breathing device during escape from smoke and fire.

In 1988 Birdair, Inc., Chemfab's joint venture with Japan's Taiyo, completed the manufacture and installation of a fabric roof over Rome's Olympic Stadium for the 1990 World Cup soccer games. During the same year, Birdair fabricated and installed a cable-supported permanent fabric roof on the new Georgia Dome in Atlanta, Georgia. The multipurpose facility was the home of the Atlanta Falcons and the site of the 1994 Super Bowl. Chemfab completed the construction of high-speed, high-capacity, proprietary fluoropolymer-film equipment, the output of which was sold as film products and used in the manufacture of improved-performance laminated composites. Sales for fiscal 1990 grew 23 percent to $48.73 million; net income was $3.7 million, or $.73 per share. International sales—especially in Western Europe and the Far East—comprised 34 percent of all sales.

1991–95: Economic Recession, Expansion into New Markets

During fiscal 1991 domestic sales of certain Chemfab standard products—especially architectural fabrics—slowed down because of a recession-related soft economy. Nevertheless, solid gains were posted in various other product areas, including spherical radomes and electromagnetic windows, food-processing release sheets, fabricated products for the aerospace industry, and industrial products for markets in the Far East. Chemfab bought two of its English distributors and merged them into one facility, named Inert Materials and Components Ltd., thereby establishing direct distribution of Chemfab products in the United Kingdom. In November, Chemfab adopted Chemfab Corporation as its legal name to emphasize its broadened technological base and the diversification of its product lines. In March 1992 Chemfab sold its voting stock interest in Birdair to Japanese Taiyo and entered into a ten-year supply agreement by which Chemfab continued to be Taiyo's and Birdair's principal supplier of architectural membrane products. This sale marked Chemfab's gradual move to a stronger focus on development and distribution of materials rather than on the structures business.

Chemfab, however, remained committed to maintaining its leadership position in the development, manufacture, and sale of permanent architectural membrane products. The company's modest two percent growth in fiscal 1992 was offset by cutbacks in military spending and a decline in government contracts, but "Chemfab exited fiscal 1992 financially stronger than ever and much improved in many key areas," wrote President/CEO Montopoli in the company's 1992 Annual Report. Zeroing in on the fact that commercial aircraft require smaller diameter and lighter weight wire constructions with outstanding performance properties, Chemfab worked with major aerospace wire manufacturers and Boeing to develop a composite material for commercial aircraft; the resulting product, made into thin, lightweight tapes, was applied to wire and became a key component in the airframe wire used by Boeing for its commercial jets. The Chemfilm DF-29X9 product line became an industry standard. Sales to Boeing and a substantial increase of sales in industrial products made for net sales of $50.93 million in fiscal 1993. If the British pound—the currency in which Chemfab's European sales were recorded—had not weakened relative to the U.S. dollar, fiscal 1993 worldwide sales would have increased four percent over those of the previous year. In December 1992, Chemfab purchased its Merrimack headquarters, which had been occupied under lease since 1986, and 21 acres of land.

During the last quarter of 1994 Chemfab entered the biomedical market by acquiring the Canton Bio-Medical Division of Loctite VSI, Inc.; the acquisition became a wholly owned subsidiary under the name Canton Bio-Medical, Inc. and continued its leadership role as a manufacturer and supplier of high-performance elastomeric closures and stoppers used in the packaging and delivery of laboratory test samples. Canton's products protected container contents from contamination. Chemfab supplied 376,000 square feet of Sheerfill architectural membrane to cover the main terminal at the new Denver International Airport, which opened in February 1995. The roof's outer waterproof shell was made of Teflon-coated woven fiberglass and was about as thick as a credit card. The inner membrane was made of uncoated woven fiberglass. Inner and outer roof membranes comprised 15 acres of material. Ten percent of visible light passed through the roof fabric.

In February 1995, Chemfab purchased Courtaulds Aerospace Ltd.'s Tygaflor business (based in Littleborough, Lancashire, England), a leading manufacturer and marketer of fluoropolymer-based composite materials. The addition of the new subsidiary, Tygaflor Ltd., to Chemfab's pre-existing United Kingdom company made Chemfab the world's leading manufacturer and supplier of fluoropolymer-based flexible composites for high-temperature-release and chemical-resistant applications. Worldwide sales for fiscal 1995 rose 30 percent to a record $67.98 million from the $52.2 million sales for fiscal 1994; net income for fiscal 1995 was $5.31 million, compared with $3.5 million for the prior year. The net income for 1995 shares was $.66 per share.

1996–2000: Peak Performances, Global Presence, Diversification

Chemfab's growth continued to accelerate. Sales for fiscal 1996 peaked at $83.88 million and net income rose to $7.71 million. All the business units reported to John W. Verbicky, who had joined the company in 1993 as vice-president for research and development; in 1996 he was promoted to the newly created position of executive vice-president/COO.

In January 1997 the U.S. army awarded Chemfab a $2.4 million contract for chemical warfare shelters made from a fluoropolymer-Kevlar composite developed by the company. In March Chemfab moved its stock listing from NASDAQ to the New York Stock Exchange and chose CFA as its symbol. During the fourth quarter of 1997, Chemfab established Chemfab (Suzhou) Co., Ltd. about 60 miles inland from Shanghai, in the People's Republic of China. There was a rapidly increasing demand in China for fluoropolymer-composite conveyor belts and pressure-sensitive tapes used in the textile, screen printing, garment manufacturing, food processing, and packaging industries. Later, in Sao Paulo, Brazil, the company founded Chemfab do Brasil Indústria e Comércio Ltda. With the repurchase of shares owned by Nitto Denko and Taiyo, Nitto Chemfab became a wholly owned subsidiary (thereafter known as Chemfab Japan) and the distributor of industrial products in that country. Chemfab also won a contract to build the world's largest continuous membrane roof (one million square feet) to cover the Millennium Dome in Greenwich London for the turn-of-the-century celebration. President and CEO Montopoli announced his intention to retire at year-end 1997; the Board of Directors named COO John W. Verbicky to succeed him.

In fiscal 1998 Chemfab passed the $100-million-sales mark to reach $104.46 million, thereby recording the fifth consecutive year of double-digit growth in net income of $10.93 million. Diluted earnings per share increased 20 percent to $1.33, compared with $1.10 in 1997. The company reviewed and redefined its vision, goals, strategies, and values for a future in which it planned to become a world-class company. Chemfab designed Chemglas as a roof membrane to meet the specific demands of the Tent City project in Mina, Kingdom of Saudi Arabia. This project, to be constructed in three phases, utilized Chemglas as the roof membrane for thousands of tent-styled shelters for use during the hajj (annual pilgrimage) to Mecca. During 1999–2000, Chemfab acquired three fabricating distributors in Germany, a company in France, and another in Italy. Chemfab also purchased Gary, Indiana-based UroQuest Medical Corporation and its wholly owned subsidiary, Bivona Medical Technologies. Bivona designed, manufactured, and marketed proprietary disposable products for the health care and personal care industries; it was also a market leader in the design and manufacture of silicone elastomer products for airway management applications. Thus Chemfab enhanced its position in the medical and health care markets.

Chemfab created the High Performance Elastomers Division to launch its Engineered Elastomer Products business. In the fall of 1999, Chemfab streamlined its operation by consolidating its coating operations in Europe into a single plant and by uniting the operation of the three German acquisitions in one location. In April 2000 the company opened the industrial products platform of its e-commerce business over the Internet at www.polymerstreet.com. This web site was linked to the company's other e-store sites; namely, www.fabflow.com, which offered Chemfab's Fabflow, a unique air diffuser product used in air conditioning systems to reduce noise and eliminate drafts in offices; www.pantastic.com, which sold proprietary bakeware liners making all cookware nonstick and microwave-safe; and www.bivona.com, which sold disposable silicone elastomer products and components to health care providers and medical device manufacturers.

During its slightly more than 30 years of existence, Chemfab "converted itself from what used to be primarily an architectural membrane business into an industrial products enterprise" and became "a world leader in polymer-based engineered products and material systems used in specialized and severe-service environments," President/CEO Verbicky told an interviewer for the *Wall Street Transcript* in December 1999. "During the last five years, the company has nearly tripled its revenue and has tripled its earnings per share. . . . The growth came primarily from the industrial products business," Verbicky explained. Net sales for 1999 peaked at $126.48 million and net income at $8.94 million. Diluted net income per share was $1.11.

Judging from Chemfab's strong balance sheet, low debt, and aggressive and dynamic performance during the last five years of the 20th century—annual growth rates of 19 percent in revenues, 25 percent in net income, and tripled earnings per share—the company could look forward to continuous prosperity in the 21st century. In addition, it might be only a few years before football fans could attend a game played on natural turf grown under an Ultralux roof lined with Fabrasorb acoustical membrane to dampen the cheering of the crowd.

Principal Subsidiaries

Bivona, Inc.; Canton Bio-Medical, Inc.; Chemfab do Brasil Indústria e Comércio Ltda (Brazil); Chemfab Europe (Republic of Ireland); Chemfab Germany GmbH; Chemfab Japan, Ltd.; Chemfab (Suzhou) Co., Ltd. (People's Republic of China); Tygaflor, Ltd. (England).

Principal Competitors

Accusil, Inc.; The Kendall Co.; Mallinckrodt Group, Inc.; Medtronic Xomed Surgical Products, Inc.; Mox-Med, Inc.; MRI Devices Corp.; Point Medical Corp.; Saint-Gobain Performance Plastics Corp.; Specialty Silicone Fabricators, Inc.; Specialty Silicone Products, Inc.; Taconic; Vesta, Inc.; West Pharmaceutical Services, Inc.

Further Reading

"Chemfab Corporation (CFA), CEO Interview: John W. Verbicky," *Wall Street Transcript*, December 20, 1999, pp. 1–4.
Our First 25 Years: Chemfab, Merrimack, N.H.: Chemfab Corporation, 1993, pp. 1–4, 6, 9, 12.
Wood, Andrew, "Chemfab," *Chemical Week*, December 24–31, 1997, pp. 29–30.

—Gloria A. Lemieux

Citadel Communications Corporation

7201 West Lake Mead Boulevard
City Center West
Las Vegas, Nevada 89128
U.S.A.
Telephone: (702) 804-5200
Fax: (702) 804-5936
Web site: http://www.citadelcommunications.com

Public Company
Incorporated: 1991 as Citadel Broadcasting Company
Employees: 1,996
Sales: $196.2 million (1999)
Stock Exchanges: NASDAQ
Ticker Symbol: CITC
NAIC: 513112 Radio Stations

Citadel Communications Corporation ranks among the top six owners of U.S. radio stations in terms of both revenue and number of stations owned. The company specializes in mid-size markets and has an ownership presence in nearly every region of the country. Following the passage of the Telecommunications Act of 1996, which raised ownership limits in single markets and eliminated the national ownership limit on radio stations, Citadel spent more than $1 billion to acquire more than 170 radio stations from 1997 through the end of 1999. When all of the company's pending acquisitions are completed as of mid-2000, Citadel will own more than 200 radio stations in mid-size markets throughout the United States.

Predecessor Active in
Arizona and Montana: 1984–92

The predecessor company to Citadel Communications Corporation was a limited partnership called Citadel Associates Limited Partnership (CALP). CALP was founded by Lawrence Ray Wilson in late 1984 with the purchase of two radio stations in Tucson, Arizona, for $5 million. Two-and-a-half years later Wilson sold the same stations for $10.1 million. During the 1970s Wilson was executive vice-president and general counsel

for Combined Communications Corporation, which owned a television station in Little Rock, Arkansas. Before getting into radio, he was a CPA and practicing lawyer. In 1990 Wilson cofounded and was a general partner in Citadel Associates Montana Limited Partnership (CAMLP), which was formed to own and operate radio stations in Montana that were formerly owned by CALP. The next year Citadel Broadcasting Company was incorporated as a Nevada corporation, and in 1992 Citadel acquired all of the radio stations then owned or operated by CALP and CAMLP.

In 1991 Citadel obtained the first "local marketing agreement" (LMA) from the Federal Communications Commission (FCC) in Colorado Springs. Under an LMA, Citadel would buy time from a radio station and resell it, giving Citadel control of the programming but not ownership of the station or its license. LMA's became a popular way for companies to control radio stations while still meeting federal regulations governing station ownership.

Concentrating on Radio Duopolies: 1992–96

Between 1992 and 1996 Citadel concentrated on acquiring radio duopolies, or AM-FM combinations, in mid-size markets. In 1992 Citadel owned eight radio stations. Wilson bought out his limited partners that year and Citadel also acquired eight radio stations from Price Broadcasting Co. for $12.5 million, including AM-FM combinations in Spokane, Washington; Modesto, California; Redding, California; an AM station in Reno, Nevada; and an FM station in Boise, Idaho. The acquisition effectively doubled the size of the company.

Citadel Communications Corporation was formed as the parent company to Citadel Broadcasting Company in 1993. During 1993 Citadel acquired one AM and six FM stations, giving it a total of 26 stations. Sales for 1993 totaled $21 million. In 1994 the company entered the Albuquerque, New Mexico, market with the acquisition of two FM and two AM radio stations. Citadel subsequently expanded its presence in Albuquerque in 1996 with the acquisition of another AM and three FM stations. The company also acquired FM stations in Modesto, California, and Colorado Springs in 1996.

Increasing Pace of Acquisitions: 1996–97

The federal Telecommunications Act of 1996 changed the ownership rules for radio stations, among other things, allowing companies to acquire and own more stations in a given market. It also removed the national limit on how many stations a company could own. Up to this point Citadel's acquisitions had been concentrated in the western United States. Around this time Citadel began to face its first serious competition in mid-size markets when Capstar Broadcasting Partners was formed in May 1996.

Citadel spent about $70 million acquiring stations in mid-size markets in 1996. At the start of 1997 the company owned 81 radio stations. In April 1997 it made its biggest acquisition to date when it purchased 25 stations owned by Tele-Media Communications Corp. for $117 million. The stations were located in Pennsylvania, Rhode Island, Illinois, and California. It was the first time Citadel had acquired stations outside of the West.

Later in the year Citadel attempted to sell four of the stations—all located in Centre County, Pennsylvania—to Talleyrand Broadcasting Inc. However, the sale was blocked by the U.S. Department of Justice in 1998 because it would have given the buyer in excess of 40 percent of the total radio advertising revenue in that market. At this time Wilson was operating out of his ranch in Bigfork, Montana, and Citadel had offices in Tempe, Arizona.

Other 1997 acquisitions included several radio stations in Arkansas and the Arkansas Radio Network for about $25 million from Snider Corporation and Cornerstone Broadcasting. After this deal was completed, Citadel would own 94 radio stations. During 1997 the company had purchased a total of 61 radio stations for about $230 million.

Aggressive Acquisition Strategy: 1998–2000

In 1998 Citadel completed an initial public offering (IPO) on the NASDAQ and raised $106.9 million for debt reduction and future acquisitions. The company's estimated annual sales of $117 million ranked 13th among radio station owners. Citadel noted, with its IPO filing, that it expected to continue to lose money. It lost $5.3 million in 1997, which it attributed to one-time charges related to acquisitions and interest payments on its debt, and expected even larger losses in the future. Principal owners of the company were Wilson, with 19.1 percent, and ABRY Broadcast Partners, with 37.2 percent.

Later in 1998 Citadel acquired nine radio stations in Baton Rouge and Lafayette, Louisiana, from Citywide Communications Inc. for $34 million. In November it acquired its fifth station in the Harrisburg, Pennsylvania, market for $4.5 million from Zeve Broadcasting Co.

Also in November Citadel acquired 16 radio stations from Wicks Broadcast Group for $77 million in cash, including eight stations in Charleston, South Carolina; five in Binghamton, New York; and three in central Indiana. These were the first stations Citadel would own in those markets. In Charleston and Binghamton, the station clusters would exceed the federal limit of 40 percent of the market's radio advertising revenue. Citadel had acquired some 35 stations since its IPO in July. Before the month of November was done, Citadel had obtained antitrust clearances from the Federal Trade Commission (FTC) to purchase six radio stations in Saginaw, Michigan, for $35 million from 62nd Street Holdings LLC.

For 1998 Citadel lost $3.8 million compared to a loss of $5.3 million in 1997. Net revenue was a record $135.4 million, up about 50 percent from 1997. Broadcast cash flow rose 70 percent to $41.9 million.

At the beginning of 1999 Citadel announced it would move its corporate offices from Tempe to Las Vegas. The company agreed to sell 25 radio stations in six small markets to Chicago's Marathon Media LP for $26 million in cash. The stations were located in small markets not in the top 100, including Johnstown, Pennsylvania; Eugene, Oregon; Medford, Oregon; Tri-Cities, Washington; State College, Pennsylvania; and Billings, Montana. In another transaction, Citadel and Capstar agreed to swap radio stations in Spokane, Washington, and Colorado Springs to avoid federal ownership restrictions.

Citadel had launched an Internet service provider (ISP) called eFortress in 1997. By March 1999 eFortress had nearly 25,000 customers. After acquiring 1,500 dial-up customers from one Rhode Island company in early 1997, Citadel gained more customers that year when it acquired two Rhode Island radio stations from Philip Urso. Urso also owned an ISP called Edgenet, which he would advertise on his two radio stations. Under Citadel, Edgenet became eFortress, with Urso as president of the division. In January 1998 eFortress began expanding to other cities. Following Citadel's IPO, the company acquired six ISPs. Its key markets for Internet service were Rhode Island, Salt Lake City, Colorado Springs, and Albuquerque. In March 1999 Citadel acquired the assets and customer base of another Rhode Island ISP called Brainiac Services, giving eFortress just over 10,000 customers in Rhode Island. However, by the end of 1999 Citadel had decided to sell eFortress and its ISP operations, and expected to complete the divestiture by mid-2000.

During 1999 Citadel announced or completed the acquisition of 78 radio stations for a total of $537 million. In August the company purchased its sixth station in Baton Rouge for $9.5 million from KTBT Radio Broadcasting Co. In October it agreed to acquire 36 radio stations from Broadcasting Partners Holdings for $190 million. The deal, which required FCC approval, would give Citadel 161 stations in 34 markets. The 36 stations included five in Buffalo, New York; four in Syracuse, New York; three in Atlantic City, New Jersey; three in Tyler-Longview, Texas; and four in Monroe, Louisiana.

In November Citadel purchased four stations in Lafayette, Louisiana, the 98th ranked market in the United States, from Radio Broadcasting Co. for $8.5 million. The acquisition would give Citadel an eight-station cluster in that market. During the month Citadel also acquired another station in Murray, Utah, serving Salt Lake City, for $104,202.

In December Citadel announced it would acquire nine radio stations in three Michigan markets from Liggett Broadcasting for $120.5 million. The purchase gave Citadel a six-station cluster in Lansing, Michigan, and a strong station in Flint. It also added two stations in Saginaw, Michigan, giving Citadel a total of eight stations there that added up to more than 70 percent of the radio market revenue—well in excess of the federal limit of 40 percent. As a result, Citadel would have to divest some stations in that market. It also acquired two stations in Worcester, Massachusetts, for $24.5 million from Montachusett Broadcasting. Upon completion of these deals, Citadel would own 177 stations, 54 AMs and 123 FMs.

At the end of 1999 Citadel had grown through an aggressive acquisitions program to become the sixth largest radio group based on revenue and the fourth largest in terms of stations owned. Toward the end of the year it filed a $1 billion shelf offering with the Securities and Exchange Commission (SEC) that would allow it to sell stock up to that amount at any time. The company also arranged a $400 million credit facility to help pay for pending acquisitions worth about $250 million. It was clear that Citadel planned to continue acquiring radio stations.

Continuing Losses, Acquisitions: 2000

In January 2000 Citadel announced it would acquire Bloomington Broadcasting Co. of Chattanooga, Tennessee, which owned 20 radio stations, for $176 million in cash. Included in the purchase were four stations in Chattanooga; four in Grand Rapids, Michigan; four in Columbia, South Carolina; five in Johnson City/Kingsport/Bristol, Tennessee; and three in Bloomington, Indiana. All of the cities were new markets for Citadel.

In May Citadel expanded its presence in the South by purchasing 11 radio stations and one local marketing agreement from Dick Broadcasting Co. of Greensboro, North Carolina, for $300 million. The acquisition consisted of five stations in Birmingham, Alabama; two serving Nashville, Tennessee; four serving Knoxville, Tennessee; and one LMA in Knoxville. With this deal Citadel would own or operate more than 200 radio stations.

For 1999 Citadel reported gross broadcasting revenues of $196.2 million, its highest ever. However, the company's net loss increased from $3.9 million in 1998 to $8.9 million in 1999. Citadel had assumed a large amount of debt in making its acquisitions over the past three years, and its interest expense had exceeded its operating income in all three years. Concerns about the company's ability to turn a profit affected its stock price, which in mid-2000 was near its 52-week low.

Principal Competitors

AMFM Inc.; Beasley Broadcast Group Inc.; Big City Radio Inc.; Cox Radio Inc.; Cumulus Media Inc.; Entercom Communications Corp.; Infinity Broadcasting Corp.; Radio One Inc.; Regent Communications Inc.; Saga Communications Inc.

Further Reading

"The Arizona Republic AZ Inc. Column," *Knight-Ridder/Tribune Business News,* November 24, 1998.

Bachman, Katy, "Citadel Adds to Its Mid-Market Cluster," *Mediaweek,* December 13, 1999, p. 22.

——, "Citadel Buys Wicks Stations, Pushes Limits in 2 Markets," *Mediaweek,* November 30, 1998, p. 4.

——, "Citadel Clusters," *Mediaweek,* November 29, 1999, p. 30.

——, "New Acquisitions Make Citadel a Bigger Fortress," *Mediaweek,* November 1, 1999, p. 6.

Barmann, Timothy C., "Internet Providers Connect As Field Shrinks," *Knight-Ridder/Tribune Business News,* March 4, 1999.

"Big Deals of 1999," *Broadcasting & Cable,* February 14, 2000, p. 34.

"Changing Hands," *Broadcasting & Cable,* November 29, 1999, p. 48.

"Changing Hands," *Broadcasting & Cable,* May 15, 2000, p. 56.

"Citadel Adds Eight," *Broadcasting,* August 3, 1992, p. 35.

"Citadel Communications Corp.," *Broadcasting & Cable,* July 6, 1998, p. 64.

"Citadel Communications Corp.," *Broadcasting & Cable,* September 7, 1998, p. 73.

"Citadel Communications Corp. Is Selling out of Six Small Radio Markets to Pay Debt and Concentrate on Medium-Sized Markets," *Broadcasting & Cable,* January 18, 1999, p. 8.

"The Federal Trade Commission Last Wednesday Said It Has Granted 'Early Termination' to Citadel Communications Corp.'s $35 Million Purchase of Six Radio Stations in Saginaw, Mich., from 62nd Street Holdings LLC," *Broadcasting & Cable,* November 30, 1998, p. 136.

Fink, James, "Acquisition of Stations Expands Citadel Empire," *Business First of Buffalo,* November 8, 1999, p. 9.

Flessner, Dave, "Las Vegas-Based Radio Company Buys Four Chattanooga, Tenn., Stations," *Knight-Ridder/Tribune Business News,* January 24, 2000.

Gilbertson, Dawn, "The Arizona Republic Taking Stock in Arizona Column," *Knight-Ridder/Tribune Business News,* May 11, 1998.

Harris, Jim, "Radio Signals Mix with Consolidation," *Arkansas Business,* June 16, 1997, p. 1.

Holmes, Alisa, "Changing Hands," *Broadcasting & Cable,* November 16, 1998, p. 65.

"The Justice Department Has Killed Citadel Communications Corp's Plans to Sell Four Radio Stations in State College, Pa.," *Broadcasting & Cable,* September 28, 1998, p. 76.

"Las Vegas-Based Firm Proposes to Buy Buffalo, N.Y.-Area Radio Stations," *Knight-Ridder/Tribune Business News,* October 29, 1999.

"Quote of the Week," *Crain's Chicago Business,* January 18, 1999, p. 38.

Rathbun, Elizabeth A., "Citadel Bulks Up," *Broadcasting & Cable,* December 13, 1999, p. 88.

——, "Financial Results Roll In," *Broadcasting & Cable,* March 22, 1999, p. 37.

——, "Internet Ads Drive AMFM," *Broadcasting & Cable,* August 9, 1999, p. 24.

——, "Justice-Friendly Radio Deal?," *Broadcasting & Cable,* January 4, 1999, p. 64.

——, "Muncie, Harrisburg Consolidate," *Broadcasting & Cable,* November 16, 1998, p. 66.

——, "Radio Groups Go Public to Grow," *Broadcasting & Cable,* December 20, 1999, p. 46.

——, "Regent Rules with IPO," *Broadcasting & Cable,* January 31, 2000, p. 64.

——, "Robust 10 in Radio," *Broadcasting & Cable,* May 3, 1999, p. 19.

——, "Shooting Straight from a Fortress," *Broadcasting & Cable,* July 28, 1997, p. 89.

Torpey-Kemph, Anne, "Citadel Bulks Up in Baton Rouge," *Mediaweek,* August 9, 1999, p. 32.

Trimble, Stephen, "Talleyrand Broadcasting to Buy Four Pennsylvania Radio Stations," *Knight-Ridder/Tribune Broadcasting News,* October 16, 1997.

—David P. Bianco

Cleary, Gottlieb, Steen & Hamilton

1 Liberty Plaza
New York, New York 10006-1470
U.S.A.
Telephone: (212) 225-2000
Fax: (212) 225-3999

Partnership
Founded: 1946 as Cleary, Gottlieb, Friendly & Cox
Employees: 1,900
Sales: $366 million (1998)
NAIC: 54111 Offices of Lawyers

Although Cleary, Gottlieb, Steen & Hamilton is still a relatively young law firm, it is a major player in the legal profession in the United States and many nations in Europe, Asia, and Latin America. The firm counsels corporations, nonprofit organizations, several sovereign nations, families, and individuals on a wide range of issues, such as financing, litigation, taxation, mergers, acquisitions, bankruptcy, real estate, and intellectual property concerns. Its February 2000 firm booklet stated, ''In 1999, Cleary Gottlieb was one of the leading issuer's counsel in each of the three principal categories of capital market issuances: equity, debt and high yield debt.'' The firm continues to help governments around the world privatize their state-owned enterprises. It helped pioneer mortgage-backed securities and persists in developing innovative forms of financing. Over 200 of its 600 plus attorneys work in its overseas offices in Paris, Brussels, London, Hong Kong, Tokyo, Frankfurt, and Rome.

Origins and Early Practice

In 1946 seven attorneys formed a new law firm with offices organized in New York City and Washington, D.C. Four of the seven founders of Cleary Gottlieb left the Root Clark law firm where they were disappointed in its changing management style and the fact that it was growing too rapidly. A leading tax attorney, George Cleary had graduated from the University of Wisconsin Law School before working at the Bureau of Internal Revenue and then joining the Root Clark firm in 1925. Leo Gottlieb studied engineering at Yale before he attended Harvard

Law School and in 1925 became a Root Clark partner. The other two attorneys who left Root Clark were Henry Friendly, a graduate of the Harvard Law School, and Mel Steen, who graduated from the University of Minnesota Law School. All four graduated as the top students of their respective law schools.

The other three of the seven founders came from government service, including Hugh Cox and Fowler Hamilton from the U.S. Justice Department. George Ball helped plan the new law firm, but he did not formally join as a partner until July 15, 1946, when his resignation as the general counsel for the French Supply Council became effective.

In 1949 the firm opened its Paris office, the first American law firm to open a new office there after World War II. (The Coudert Brothers law firm, which was the first American firm in the late 1800s to open a Paris office, had maintained its office there during the war.) Cleary Gottlieb's Paris branch was the firm's first effort to develop an international practice, one that would eventually involve about one-third of its attorneys.

According to Leo Gottlieb's history, the firm's total fees received during the year ending December 31, 1946 were $296,000, and its net income was $119,500. At the end of 1950, its fifth year in business, total fees received and net income had increased to $837,500 and $446,500, respectively.

Not surprisingly, the founding partners' prior connections helped the new law firm gain its early clients. For example, Henry Friendly while at the Root Clark firm served as Pan American Airways' general counsel; thus, Pan American became an original Cleary Gottlieb client. George Ball's earlier ties helped Cleary Gottlieb acquire such clients as the European Coal & Steel Community and later the European Common Market and the European Atomic Energy agency.

Other initial clients who had some previous association with Cleary Gottlieb founders included Salomon Bros. & Hutzler, Salomon family members, Nathan W. Levin and the Rosenwald family, Royal Typewriter Company and members of the Thomas Fortune Ryan family, Pennsylvania Railroad, A.T.&T. and New York Telephone Company, American Bosch Magneto

Key Dates:

1946: The firm is established with offices in New York City and Washington, D.C.

1949: The Paris office is opened.

1959: Name partners change, resulting in Cleary, Gottlieb, Steen & Hamilton in New York City and Cleary, Gottlieb, Steen & Ball in Paris and Washington, D.C.

1960: The opening of the Brussels office is announced.

1963: The name Cleary, Gottlieb, Steen & Hamilton unites all offices.

1971: London office is opened, and the firm moves its New York office to 1 State Street Plaza.

1971: The firm hires its first paralegal.

1980: Hong Kong office is opened.

1983: Leo Gottlieb publishes a history of the firm's first 30 years.

1987: Firm opens its new Tokyo office.

1991: The firm's office in Frankfurt is started.

1998: The Rome office is established.

Corporation and George Murnane, and Trico Products and the Evans and Oishei families.

The partnership's first new client was movie star/singer Bing Crosby, who was being sued by the Kraft Cheese Company over a contractual dispute over a Kraft-sponsored television series. In this case and later work, the firm "found Crosby to be an intelligent and agreeable client," according to Gottlieb's history.

In 1946 the law firm began providing legal services to Gerard Piel in his founding of *Scientific American*, one of the most important scientific journals of the post-World War II era. May 1948 marked the journal's first issue, and the firm in the 1980s was still counsel to the journal and its publishing subsidiary W.H. Freeman & Co.

In 1959 name partner Henry Friendly left the firm to become a judge of the U.S. Court of Appeals, Second Circuit. So the firm in New York City changed its name to Cleary, Gottlieb, Steen & Hamilton, while in Washington, D.C. and Europe it became Cleary, Gottlieb, Steen & Ball.

Cleary Gottlieb in the 1950s began representing oil companies. In 1951 it gained as a client the Foreign Petroleum Supply Committee, which had been organized by several oil firms, such as Exxon and Gulf, after the leftist Mohammed Mossadegh took over the Iranian government and the huge oil refinery in Abadan, Iran. This work led to representing other oil organizations and companies in the same decade, including Venezuelan Petroleum Company and Standard-Vacuum Oil Company.

The law firm in the 1950s also began serving R.H. Macy & Co., General Instrument Corporation, Monroe Calculating Machine Company, the Venus Pen and Pencil Corporation, and the Woodward Iron Company. When Elihu Root, Jr., joined the law firm in 1954 as "of counsel," he brought one of his clients, the Fiduciary Trust Company, which for many years was a source of both revenues and increased prestige for Cleary Gottlieb. The

firm's international practice was greatly aided by Jean L. Blondeel, who in the 1950s served as special counsel to the World Bank. He later became president of Luxembourg's Kredietbank, S.A. while serving as Cleary Gottlieb's European counsel.

With these and other clients, Cleary Gottlieb's finances improved. At the end of 1960 the firm's 63 lawyers and 92 clerical staff provided services that brought in $2.6 million in total fees, while net income for 1960 was $1.1 million.

Practice in the 1960s and 1970s

Cleary Gottlieb increased its services to the oil industry in the turbulent 1960s and 1970s, mostly from the work of name partner Hamilton. In 1963 the firm first began representing the American Petroleum Institute, the New York City trade association that included virtually all big oil companies. During the 1967 Six Day War between Israel and Egypt, 26 oil companies organized as the Middle East Emergency Committee hired the firm. In December 1974 the firm again was retained by major oil companies, including Gulf, Exxon, Mobil, Texaco, and Standard Oil Company of California, all of which were trying to deal with the Arab oil embargo. The firm's attorneys helped its oil clients in many nations, not just the Middle East. Daniel Yergin's book *The Prize* described the colorful history of the oil industry without much detail of the role of law firms.

Hamilton also brought many non-oil clients to the firm, including the Mutual Life Insurance Company of New York (MONY), The Oil Shale Corporation that later became Tosco Corporation, and the Sherman Fairchild Foundation and estate.

As multinational corporations expanded, they confronted different laws and cultural differences in the countries where they operated. Finding that the French and Belgian bar organizations were becoming less friendly to foreign law firms, some Cleary Gottlieb partners helped work with government and bar representatives in Paris and Brussels to resolve these disputes. Part of that effort involved helping the state of New York develop rules to license foreign lawyers, which in effect was an exercise in reciprocity.

In the 1960s Cleary Gottlieb gained Banque Nationale de Paris, the major French bank, as one of its major European bank clients. The firm also began representing the Asian Development Bank. The firm's international practice benefitted from the public service of two of its name partners. In 1961 President Kennedy appointed George Ball as the Under Secretary of State for Economic Affairs, and later that year Ball was appointed as the Under Secretary of State, the number two position in the U.S. State Department. Fowler Hamilton served as the administrator of the U.S. Agency for International Development from 1961 to 1963.

Beginning in the mid-1960s, the firm increased its Latin American practice, especially in Brazil, working to help Dr. Alberto Jackson Byington develop oil shale projects, an alternative to Brazil remaining so dependent on oil imports. In 1969 the Brazilian government chose Cleary Gottlieb for assistance on a major bond issue. The firm also provided counsel to foreign banks and corporations with business interests in Brazil. For a few years in the mid-1970s the firm partially supported a Rio de Janeiro office used by its attorneys and local Brazilian lawyers, but that was just a temporary arrangement. The firm continued to have a significant practice in Latin America, mainly from its attorneys based in New York City.

George Cleary reported in an interview reproduced in the law firm's July 9, 1970 *Cleargolaw News* that the firm had a general practice, with considerable involvement in international business finance. At that point the firm had 120 lawyers. Cleary also said his firm had no criminal practice, except occasionally defending a client in an antitrust case.

In December 1970 Automobiles Peugeot, S.A. of Paris retained Cleary Gottlieb. Leo Gottlieb would describe this as "a major development in the firm's history," as it accounted for significant firm revenues and enhanced the firm's reputation in international legal practice.

In his history of the firm, Gottlieb also detailed the firm's personnel as of December 31, 1975, after 30 years of practice. The New York office had 295 individuals, including 103 lawyers. Paris was Cleary Gottlieb's second largest office, with 62 persons, including 24 lawyers. Third was the Washington, D.C. office with 49 individuals, including 19 lawyers. The Brussels office employed 40, including 17 lawyers. The firm's smallest and newest office in London had just 13 employees, which included four lawyers.

Late 20th Century History

Two events in the late 1970s significantly influenced the legal profession. First, the U.S. Supreme Court ruled that professional restrictions on advertising violated First Amendment rights of free speech. Soon some lawyers, doctors, dentists, and other professionals began heavily advertising, just like other businesses. Second, two new periodicals, *The National Law Journal* and *The American Lawyer*, began publishing articles on law firm finances and management and began ranking America's largest law firms, based on either their gross revenues or their number of lawyers. That information facilitated experienced lawyers ("rainmakers") moving to more profitable firms. Those legal developments, combined with new federal laws, numerous mergers and acquisitions, new business startups, and a rapidly growing economy in the 1980s, led to the rapid and broad expansion of many U.S. law firms.

As part of those trends, in the 1980s Cleary Gottlieb increased its international practice with its first two Asian offices, first in Hong Kong in 1980 and then in Tokyo shortly after the Japanese government in 1987 first allowed foreign lawyers to practice. Overall, the firm grew from 194 lawyers in 1986 to 243 in 1990, and at the same time hired more paralegals and support staff. It increased its number of women attorneys from 42 in 1986 to 63 in 1990 and minority attorneys from seven in 1986 to 13 in 1990.

Cleary Gottlieb's gross revenues steadily increased from $100.5 million in 1986 to $181 million in 1989. New associates in 1986 received an average salary of $66,000, while in 1990 they earned $83,000. Likewise, profits per partner jumped from $470,000 in 1986 to $775,000 in 1989.

"Cleary Gottlieb is a rarity among New York's more successful law firms in that it is not a conglomeration of superstars," wrote Erwin Cherovsky in his 1991 book that compared New York law firms. He added that its "lawyers have produced a powerful, transaction-driven corporate law firm that has ridden the M&A [mergers and acquisitions] boom and created a boom of its own." Cherovsky's comments were based on Cleary Gottlieb's status as one of the few large law firms that maintained its traditional "lockstep" compensation plan that paid partners on the basis of seniority, not their individual efforts as "rainmakers."

The American Lawyer in July/August 1998 ranked Cleary Gottlieb as America's 11th largest law firm, based on its 1997 gross revenues of $341 million. Its profits per partner were $1,060,000. The following year the firm slipped to number fifteen, with 1998 gross revenues of $366 million and profits per equity partner of $1,075,000.

Cleary Gottlieb played an important role in the increasingly globalized economy of the 1990s. For example, in Europe the firm represented The Walt Disney Company and SVP Finance as they and several other banks and law firms worked together to save EuroDisneyland, the Paris theme park operated by EuroDisney that lost $923.3 million in about 18 months. Cleary Gottlieb also assisted the Khrunichev [Russian] State Research and Production Space Centre that negotiated with Lockheed to build the International Space Station, one of the joint projects between the former Cold War enemies. In 1998 Cleary Gottlieb opened its Rome office, becoming only the third American law firm to have an office in Italy at the time.

Although Cleary Gottlieb did not have a Latin American office, its attorneys based mainly in New York had a significant presence in that area. In 1997 the firm worked on two major Chilean deals involving Linea Area Nacional Chile and Distribucion y Servicio. After years of filing reports for Telebras, the Brazilian holding company that controlled the state-owned telephone system, Cleary Gottlieb in 1998 again represented Telebras as it was split into 12 private phone companies. Along with Davis, Polk & Wardwell, a firm that represented a banking consortium, Cleary Gottlieb then helped the new companies meet the requirements of the U.S. Securities and Exchange Commission so they could gain listing on a stock exchange. Consequently, the *International Financial Law Review* in February 1999 recognized Cleary Gottlieb as its International Equities Team of the Year for Latin America.

In Asia Cleary Gottlieb also was a major player. For example, in the 1990s it started a Korean practice. In 1999 the firm represented Newbridge Capital Limited when that company acquired 51 percent of Korea First Bank, while the remaining 49 percent continued to be held by the Korean Government. The law firm also represented Daewoo, a Korean company that owed $5 billion to foreign creditors. Cleary Gottlieb's lawyers worked from their base in Hong Kong, traveling to South Korea to negotiate these and other deals, unlike some American law firms which opened offices in Seoul.

Not everyone celebrated these international deals and the globalized economy aided by big law firms like Cleary Gottlieb. A strange mixture of labor unions, environmentalists, and human-rights activists protested the influence of multinational corporations and the support given by the World Trade Organization, the World Bank, and the International Monetary Fund. Nonetheless, privatization of former government-owned businesses continued in many nations, as did many mergers and acquisitions. After $2.7 trillion worth of mergers and acquisitions were completed in 1999, *Business Week* on February 28, 2000 ranked Cleary Gottlieb as the tenth major law firm in M&A based on its 89 deals worth $397.5 billion.

As corporations merged and grew larger, so did some law firms, the best example being the merger of London's Clifford Chance with New York City's Rogers & Wells and Germany's Puender, Volhard, Weber & Axster, which created the world's largest law firm with almost 3,000 lawyers. However, Cleary Gottlieb's Managing Partner Peter Karasz in early 2000 said his firm had no plans for any such international merger and probably would reject any offers. With about one-third of his firm's attorneys based overseas, Karasz in the January 4, 2000 *Financial Times* said: "It's hard to say never [to a merger with a European firm] but we don't have any such thing in mind, given the length of time we have been in Europe and our strengths there. We don't anticipate merging with any other firm because we don't know any other firm that would suit us." Thus began the new century and millennium for Cleary, Gottlieb, Steen & Hamilton as it faced plenty of challenges, ranging from competition from other large law firms to the challenges inherent in converting to a new European currency (the Euro) and a fast-paced electronic economy based on the Internet.

Principal Competitors

Simpson Thacher & Bartlett; Skadden, Arps, Slate, Meagher & Flom; Sullivan & Cromwell, Shearman & Sterling.

Further Reading

Cherovsky, Erwin, "Cleary, Gottlieb, Steen & Hamilton," in *The Guide to New York Law Firms,* New York: St. Martin's Press, 1991, pp. 53–56.

"Cleary Gottlieb to Open in Rome," *International Financial Law Review,* December 1997, p. 3.

Darrow, Peter H., "A History of the Firm," *Cleargolaw News,* December 4, 1991, pp. 8–12.

Eaglesham, Jean, and Lisa Wood, "Karasz Takes the Helm at Cleary Gottlieb," *Financial Times,* January 4, 2000, p. 10.

Gottlieb, Leo, *Cleary, Gottlieb, Steen & Hamilton: The First Thirty Years,* self-published by Leo Gottlieb, 1983.

Hoffman, Paul, *Lions of the Eighties: The Inside Story of the Power-house Law Firms,* Garden City, N.Y.: Doubleday, 1982.

"International Equities Team of the Year (Latin America)," *International Financial Law Review,* February 1999, p. 9.

"International Space Station Deal," *International Corporate Law,* April 1995, p. 4.

McGrath, John, "The Lawyers Who Rebuilt EuroDisney," *International Financial Law Review,* May 1994, p. 10.

McNatt, Robert, "Top 10 M&A Law Firms," *Business Week,* February 28, 2000, p. 6.

Mannix, Rob, "UK Firms Lead Interest in Korean Bar Reform," *International Financial Law Review,* February 2000, p. 38.

Richter, Konstantin, "Trio's Merger Will Create World's Largest Law Firm," *Wall Street Journal* (Europe), June 9, 1999, p. 5.

—David M. Walden

Colgate-Palmolive Company

300 Park Avenue
New York, New York 10022-7499
U.S.A.
Telephone: (212) 310-2000
Toll Free: (800) 850-2654
Fax: (212) 310-3405
Web site: http://www.colgate.com

Public Company
Incorporated: 1923 as the Eastern Operating Company
Employees: 37,200
Sales: $9.12 billion (1999)
Stock Exchanges: New York Amsterdam Frankfurt
    London Paris Zurich
Ticker Symbol: CL
NAIC: 325611 Soap and Other Detergent Manufacturing;
    311111 Dog and Cat Food Manufacturing; 32562
    Toilet Preparation Manufacturing; 325998 All Other
    Miscellaneous Chemical Product and Preparation
    Manufacturing; 325612 Polish and Other Sanitation
    Good Manufacturing; 339994 Broom, Brush, and
    Mop Manufacturing; 327212 Other Pressed and
    Blown Glass and Glassware Manufacturing

Colgate-Palmolive Company's growth from a small candle and soap manufacturer to one of the most powerful consumer products giants in the world is the result of aggressive acquisition of other companies, persistent attempts to overtake its major U.S. competition, and an early emphasis on building a global presence overseas where little competition existed. Today the company is organized around five core segments—oral care, personal care, household surface care, fabric care, and pet nutrition—that market such well-known brands as Colgate toothpaste, Irish Spring soap, Softsoap liquid soap, Mennen deodorant, Palmolive dishwashing liquid, Fab laundry detergent, Soupline/Suavitel fabric softeners, and Hill's Science Diet dog food.

Beginnings

In 1806, when the company was founded by 23-year-old William Colgate, it concentrated exclusively on selling starch, soap, and candles from its New York City-based factory and shop. Upon entering his second year of business, Colgate became partners with Francis Smith, and the company became Smith and Colgate, a name it kept until 1812 when Colgate purchased Smith's share of the company and offered a partnership to his brother, Bowles Colgate. Now called William Colgate and Company, the firm expanded its manufacturing operations to a Jersey City, New Jersey, factory in 1820; this factory produced Colgate's two major products, Windsor toilet soaps and Pearl starch.

Upon its founder's death in 1857, the firm changed its name to Colgate & Company and was run by President Samuel Colgate until his death 40 years later. During his tenure several new products were developed, including perfumes, essences and perfumed soap. The manufacture of starch was discontinued in 1866 after a fire destroyed the factory.

In 1873 Colgate began selling toothpaste in a jar, followed 23 years later by the introduction of Colgate Ribbon Dental Cream, in the now familiar collapsible tube. By 1906 the company was also producing several varieties of laundry soap, toilet paper, and perfumes.

While the Colgate family managed its manufacturing operations in New York, soap factories were also opened in 1864 by B.J. Johnson in Milwaukee, Wisconsin, and in 1872 by the three Peet brothers in Kansas City, Kansas. In 1898 Johnson's company introduced Palmolive soap, which soon became the best-selling soap in the world and led the firm to change its name to the Palmolive Company in 1916. The Peets, who sold laundry soap mainly in the Midwest and western states, merged their company with Palmolive in 1926. Two years later the company that resulted from that merger joined with Colgate & Company to form Colgate-Palmolive-Peet, with headquarters in Jersey City.

Although Palmolive's management initially assumed control of the combined organization, the Colgate family regained control of the company after the 1929 stock market crash and installed Bayard Colgate as president in 1933. The firm adopted its present name in 1953 and moved its offices for domestic and international operations to New York City in 1956.

International Expansion

Between 1914 and 1933 the company began establishing international operations, with subsidiaries in Canada, Australia, Europe, and Latin America. It also built upon its strategy of growth by acquisition, buying up a number of smaller consumer product companies over the next two decades. These acquisitions did little to close the gap between Colgate and its arch-rival, Procter & Gamble, a company that had been formed in the 1830s and had by now assumed a commanding lead over Colgate in selling detergent products in the United States.

In 1960 George H. Lesch was appointed Colgate's president in the hopes that his international experience would produce similar success in the domestic market. Under his leadership, the company embarked upon an extensive new product development program that created such brands as Cold Power laundry detergent, Palmolive dishwashing liquid, and Ultra Brite toothpaste. In an attempt to expand beyond these traditional, highly competitive businesses into new growth areas, Colgate also successfully introduced a new food wrap called Baggies in 1963. As a result of these product launches, the company's sales grew between eight and nine percent every year throughout the 1960s.

Lesch assumed the chairmanship of Colgate, and David Foster became president in 1970 and CEO in 1971. Foster was the son of the founder of Colgate-Palmolive's U.K. operations. He joined the company in 1946 as a management trainee and rose through the sales and marketing ranks both in the United States and overseas.

New Strategies for the 1970s

During the 1970s, as environmental concerns about phosphate and enzyme detergent products grew, the company faced additional pressure to diversify beyond the detergent business. In response to this pressure, Foster instituted a strategy that emphasized internal development via a specialized new venture

group; joint ventures for marketing other companies' products; and outright acquisitions of businesses in which Colgate could gain a marketing advantage over Procter & Gamble. In 1971, for example, the company began selling British Wilkinson Sword Company razors and blades in the United States and other countries. In 1972 Colgate-Palmolive acquired Kendall & Company, a manufacturer of hospital and industrial supplies. It was originally hoped that the Kendall acquisition would bolster the pharmaceutical sales of Colgate's Lakeside Laboratories subsidiary, which had been acquired in 1960. The partnership never materialized, however, and Lakeside was sold in 1974. The Kendall business proved to be one of Foster's most successful acquisitions. Within two years, the subsidiary was producing sales and earnings results well above the company's targeted goals.

In 1971 the U.S. Federal Trade Commission enacted restrictions on in-store product promotions, such as couponing. In response to these restrictions, Foster began to employ other tactics designed to enhance Colgate's visibility in the marketplace. Two such programs awarded money to schools and local civic groups whose young people collected the most labels and boxtops from selected Colgate products. Under Foster, Colgate-Palmolive also began to sponsor a number of women's sporting events, including the Colgate-Dinah Shore Winner's Circle, a women's professional golf tournament. Foster chose women's sports in an effort to appeal to Colgate-Palmolive's primarily female customer base. He even went so far as to have Colgate buy the tournament's home course, the Mission Hills Country Club in Palm Springs, California, so that he could supervise the maintenance of the greens.

In 1973 Colgate acquired Helena Rubinstein, a major cosmetics manufacturer with strong foreign sales but a weak U.S. presence. Believing that its marketing expertise could solve Rubinstein's problems, Colgate reduced both the number of products in the company's line and the number of employees in its workforce, increased advertising expenditures, and moved the products out of drugstores and into department stores. The following year the company acquired Ram Golf Corporation and Bancroft Racket Company, and in 1976 it bought Charles A. Eaton Company, a golf and tennis shoe manufacturer.

Although total U.S. sales of consumer products appeared to be slowing by the end of 1974, particularly in soaps and detergents, Colgate's international sales continued to carry the company forward. It maintained its leadership position abroad through new product development geared specifically to local tastes throughout Europe as well as through its involvement in the growing markets of less-developed countries in Latin America, Africa, and Asia.

Setbacks Beginning in the Late 1970s

Foster's diversification strategy initially improved earnings, but Colgate's domestic sales, market share, and profit margins were beginning to soften. This was due, in large part, to an economic recession and an advertising cutback the company had made in an attempt to boost earnings. Colgate was consistently losing the marketing battle in personal care products to Procter & Gamble. It had no leading brands and few successful new product introductions because of reduced spending for

Key Dates:

1806: Company is founded by William Colgate in New York to make starch, soap, and candles.
1873: Toothpaste is first marketed.
1896: Collapsible tubes for toothpaste are introduced.
1898: B.J. Johnson Company (later renamed Palmolive Co.) introduces Palmolive soap.
1910: Colgate moves from original location to Jersey City, New Jersey.
1928: Colgate and Palmolive companies merge.
1947: Fab and Ajax cleansers are introduced.
1956: Corporate headquarters shifts back to New York.
1963: Baggies food storage bags are launched.
1966: Palmolive dishwashing liquid is introduced.
1967: Sales top $1 billion.
1968: Colgate toothpaste is reformulated with fluoride; Ultra Brite is introduced.
1973: Cosmetics maker Helena Rubinstein is acquired.
1976: Hill's Pet Products is purchased.
1992: Mennen Co. is acquired; Total toothpaste is introduced overseas.
1993: Liquid soap brands of Johnson's Wax are purchased.
1995: Company undergoes major restructuring.
1997: Total toothpaste is launched in the United States; Colgate takes lead in domestic toothpaste market.

research and development. In an effort to remedy this problem and broaden its product mix, Colgate moved into food marketing in 1976 with the acquisition of Riviana Foods, a major producer of Texas long-grain rice with its own subsidiaries in the pet food, kosher hot dog, and candies businesses. The Riviana acquisition, however, did not live up to the company's expectations. Along with purchasing a successful rice-milling business, Colgate found that it had also saddled itself with two unprofitable restaurant chains and a low-quality candy company. In 1977 declines in the price of rice seriously eroded Riviana's cash flow.

Helena Rubinstein created additional headaches. Whereas other cosmetic manufacturers had moved their products from department store distribution to higher-volume drugstores, Colgate's management elected to keep Rubinstein products in department stores even though stores' demands for marketing support eroded the company's margins so severely that it lost money on every cosmetic item sold. Colgate finally sold the business in 1980 to Albi Enterprises.

David Foster had become chairman in 1975. In 1979, embattled by a series of marketing failures and the pressures of an acquisition strategy that yielded more losers than winners, Foster suddenly resigned, citing ill health. Colgate President and Chief Operating Officer Keith Crane was appointed as Foster's successor. A 42-year Colgate employee, Crane quickly instituted a new management structure consisting of several group vice-presidents, reunited all domestic operations under one group, and realigned division managers in an attempt to promote a more cohesive organization. Consumer advertising

and product research were given renewed emphasis to support the company's basic detergent and toothpaste lines.

Over the next two years, Crane sold a number of Foster's acquisitions that no longer fit with the company's long-term strategic plan, including Hebrew National Kosher Foods, which had been part of the Riviana purchase; Ram Golf; and the Bancroft Racket Company. Crane also put the Mission Hills Country Club up for sale and withdrew Colgate's sponsorship of the sporting events his predecessor had nurtured.

Also during the late 1970s and the 1980s, Colgate found itself named as a defendant in two lawsuits. In 1981 the company lost a suit brought by United Roasters, who successfully argued that Colgate had violated the terms of a contract between the two firms for Colgate to market Bambeanos, a soybean snack produced by United Roasters, and was awarded $950,000. The following year the company was sued by the federal government for alleged job discrimination. According to a complaint filed with the U.S. Equal Employment Opportunity Commission, Colgate had failed or refused to hire people between the ages of 40 and 70 since 1978 and had also deprived employees in that age group of opportunities for promotion.

By the end of 1982 Crane also experienced problems at Colgate. Several attempts at new product development never made it out of the test-market stage. Increased advertising expenditures for a limited number of major brands produced only temporary gains in market share while slowly killing off other products receiving little or no media support. Even Fresh Start detergent, one of the most successful new products to come out of the Foster era, was having problems retaining market share. Thus while Procter & Gamble's sales and margins were increasing, Colgate's were on the decline. To make matters worse, the strong dollar overseas hurt Colgate's international sales, and changes in Medicare policy weakened Kendall's business.

Turnaround Under Reuben Mark

In 1983 Crane relinquished the title of president to Reuben Mark, one of the company's three executive vice-presidents and a member of Crane's management advisory team. Mark also assumed the position of chief operating officer at that time; one year later he succeeded Crane as CEO. Mark built upon his predecessor's restructuring efforts in an attempt to increase profits and shareholder value. Between 1984 and 1986 several inefficient plants were closed, hundreds of employees laid off, and noncore businesses sold, including the remnants of the Riviana Foods acquisition, except for the Hill's Pet Products subsidiary.

In an attempt to refocus the company's marketing and profitability, Mark developed a set of corporate initiatives intended to address business areas ranging from production-cost reduction to new product development, with a heavy emphasis on motivating employees and involving them in company decision making. In response to the implementation of these ideas, the company's U.S. toothpaste business enjoyed a boost with first-to-the-market introductions of a gel toothpaste and a pump-type dispenser bearing the Colgate brand name. Similar U.S. market share gains were earned by new and improved versions of its Palmolive and Dynamo detergents and Ajax cleaner.

With the company's turnaround firmly underway, business units managed by key executives were formed to develop plans for the company's major product categories. The purpose of each plan was to identify how products under development could be best introduced in domestic and international markets. Two years into this strategic reorganization, coinciding with Mark's appointment as chairman in 1986, Colgate confronted an embarrassing controversy.

Since the early 1920s Hawley & Hazel Chemical Company had marketed a product called Darkie Black and White Toothpaste in the Far East. Colgate had acquired a 50 percent interest in this company in 1985. The following year, the Interfaith Center on Corporate Responsibility, a coalition of Protestant and Roman Catholic groups, demanded that Colgate change what it deemed to be the product's racially offensive name and packaging, which depicted a likeness of Al Jolson in blackface. The company acknowledged the criticism and agreed to make the necessary changes.

Colgate also continued to seek out growth areas in its personal care product and detergent businesses. In 1987 it acquired a line of liquid soap products from Minnetonka Corporation, the first transaction the company had made in the personal care area in several years. Building upon its success in launching an automatic dishwashing detergent in liquid form ahead of its competitors, the company also beat Procter & Gamble to the market with a laundry detergent packaged in a throw-in pouch called Fab 1 Shot, although this product failed to sustain consumer interest or reach sales expectations over the long term.

Buoyed by product development breakthroughs and a renewed commitment to consumer products marketing, Colgate sold its Kendall subsidiary and related healthcare businesses in 1988 to Clayton & Dubilier. The sale enabled Colgate to retire some debt, sharpen its focus on its global consumer products businesses, and invest in new product categories. Moreover, Mark's global approach enabled the company to maintain its overall profitability despite not having a leadership position in the United States. Although Colgate lagged behind Procter & Gamble in the toothpaste category, for example, it held a commanding 40 percent share of the toothpaste market worldwide.

Mark's strategy appeared to pay off handsomely. By the end of the third quarter of 1989 Colgate's international operations performed strongly while the profitability of its U.S. operations rose, due mostly to manufacturing-cost economies and greater control over promotional and sales expenses. Not yet ready to concede the U.S. market for personal care products to Procter & Gamble, though, Colgate acquired Vipont Pharmaceutical, a manufacturer of oral-hygiene products, toward the end of that year. Vipont's products, several of which Colgate had already been marketing overseas, enabled Colgate to strengthen the market position it had recently established with the introduction of a new tartar-control formula toothpaste.

Major Acquisitions in the 1990s

Colgate continued to make significant acquisitions in the early and mid-1990s while it attempted to gear up its product development program, which had been unable to introduce more than a few new products each year. In 1991 Colgate acquired the Murphy-Phoenix Company (whose top brand was Murphy's Oil Soap) to bolster its household care segment. That same year, Mark initiated a restructuring aimed at improving the firm's profitability and gross margins, which lagged behind the industry leaders. A major part of the effort was the elimination or reconfiguration of 25 factories throughout the world and an eight percent reduction in the workforce. Consequently, Colgate took a $243 million charge in September 1991, which reduced significantly the firm's net income for the full year.

Colgate's most dramatic acquisition to date came in 1992 with the $670 million purchase of Mennen Co., which added to its personal care line the top U.S. deodorant brand, Mennen Speed Stick, and the number two baby-care brand, Baby Magic. In addition, Colgate gained footholds in skin-care and hair products, and the Mennen brands gained the power of Colgate's worldwide distribution and marketing reach. This major acquisition was followed in 1993 by the purchase of S.C. Johnson Wax's liquid hand and body soap brands, which enabled Colgate to become the worldwide leader in liquid soap.

Gross margins steadily improved in the early 1990s, reaching 48.4 percent by 1994 (up from 39.2 percent in 1984). This provided Colgate with additional funds for research and development and advertising. The North American sector also experienced gains in gross margins, which resulted in part from pricing increases on Colgate detergents. In turn, this cut into overall North American sales, which declined eight percent from 1993 to 1994. Mark's strategy was to turn North American sales around through new product introductions such as a variant of Irish Spring soap and an extension of the Murphy's Oil Soap brand into a Murphy's Kitchen Care line of all-purpose cleaners. Under the leadership of Lois D. Juliber, who formerly headed up new product development, the North American sector was able to introduce several products within a short span for the first time.

A hidden jewel within the Colgate empire in the 1990s has been its pet foods sector, Hill's Pet Nutrition. The worldwide leader in therapeutic and specialty wellness pet food, Hill's enjoyed a compound annual growth rate of 14.6 percent from 1989 to 1994. During this period the market for premium pet food increased dramatically in Europe and Japan, with Hill's snatching a substantial portion of this growth. Overall, pet foods were one of Colgate's leading profit generators, boasting gross margins of 55 to 60 percent.

Early in 1995 Colgate made another major acquisition with the $1.04 billion purchase of Kolynos Oral Care from American Home Products, which gained it the Kolynos toothpaste brand, the top brand in Brazil and a leader in several other Latin American countries. This purchase pushed Colgate's share of the Latin American oral-care market from 54 percent to 79 percent.

In September 1995 Colgate announced another major restructuring of its operations to close or reconfigure 24 additional factories and cut 3,000 more employees (more than eight percent of the workforce). Mark said the action was necessary to finance new growth initiatives; Colgate took a $369 million charge as a result. The results in 1995 were also affected by a deepening recession in Mexico, which had accounted for 11 percent of sales and 20 percent of profits in 1994.

Boosting Sales with the Introduction of Total

Beginning in the late 1980s, Colgate had begun development of a toothpaste that contained a gingivitis-fighting antimicrobial agent, triclosan. Researchers found a way to use polymers to bind triclosan to teeth for up to 14 hours, allowing users to fight bleeding gums and bad breath continuously with only two brushings a day. The company began marketing the product overseas in 1992 under the name Total, eventually distributing it to 100 countries. The toothpaste was a major success, and enabled Colgate to increase its worldwide share of that market segment.

In the United States, however, introduction of Total was held up by the Food and Drug Administration (FDA), which required extensive tests to prove the product's effectiveness before Colgate could make gingivitis-fighting claims on package labels. After some five years the agency granted final approval, and Total reached store shelves in December 1997. The company backed it with a $100 million marketing blitz, its largest product introduction to date.

The response was even stronger than anticipated, and cemented Colgate's place as leader of the U.S. toothpaste market, a position it had actually reached in the months prior to Total's introduction. This was the first time since 1962 that ACNielsen's rankings had shown Colgate on top. Following the successful launch, the company's profits and stock price climbed steadily. In December 1998 the FDA also approved a variant of Total, Total Fresh Stripe, which reached stores several months later. A year after Total's release it was the number one toothpaste brand in the United States. Competitors such as Procter and Gamble, which already marketed a triclosan-based toothpaste in Canada, were prevented from mounting a quick response by the lengthy FDA approval process. Powered by Total and the strong U.S. economy, Colgate continued to do well in 1999 and into 2000, with record earnings approaching the $1 billion mark.

As the 21st century dawned, Colgate's global presence as a consumer products company extended to over 200 countries, with leading positions for several of its key brands. Colgate will likely continue to aggressively defend these positions, increase market share of its trailing brands whenever possible, and seek additional brands and product types within its primary product sectors through acquisitions and a revitalized product development program.

Principal Subsidiaries

Alexandril S.A (Uruguay); Arkay Pty Limited (Australia); Asia Pioneer Co., Ltd. (Hong Kong); Barbados Cosmetics Products Limited (Barbados); Baser Kimya Sanayii Ve Ticaret Anonim Sirketi (Turkey); Baser Turketim Pazarlama Ve Ticaret Anonim Sirketi (Turkey); Bella, S.A. (France); Cachet Investments Limited (U.K.); Chemtech (BVI) Co. Ltd. (British Virgin Islands); Chet (Chemicals) (Proprietary) Limited (South Africa); CKS, Inc.; Cleaning Dimensions, Inc.; Colgate Flavors and Fragrances, Inc.; Colgate Music Direct; Colgate Oral Pharmaceuticals, Inc.; Colgate Sports Foundation, Inc. (The Philippines); Colgate Venture Company, Inc.; Colgate-Palmolive (America), Inc.; Colgate-Palmolive Canada, Inc. (Canada); Colgate-Palmolive Charitable Foundation; Colgate-Palmolive Development Corp.; Colgate-Palmolive Enterprises, Inc.; Colgate-Palmolive Global Trading Company; Colgate-Palmolive Holding Inc.; Colgate-Palmolive International Incorporated; Colgate-Palmolive Investment Co., Inc.; Colgate-Palmolive Investments, Inc.; Colgate-Palmolive (Research & Development), Inc.; Colgate-Palmolive Transnational Inc.; Consumer Viewpoint Center, Inc.; CPC Funding Company; CPIF, Inc.; Delpha, S.A. (France); DF Soap Co.; Dimac Development Corp.; Direct Development, Inc.; EKIB, Inc.; Empresa de Maquilas, S.A. de C.V (Mexico); Global Trading and Supply Company; Hamol, Ltd.; Hawley & Hazel Chemical Co. (H.K.) Ltd. (Hong Kong); Herrick International Limited (British Virgin Islands); Hill's Funding Company; Hill's Pet Nutrition, Inc.; Hill's Pet Nutrition Sales, Inc.; Hill's-Colgate (Japan) Ltd. (Japan); HL Soap Co.; Hopro Liquidating Corp.; Inmobiliara Hills, S.A. de C.V (Mexico); Innovacion Creativa, S.A. de C.V (Mexico); Inter-Hamol, S.A. (Luxembourg); JG Soap Co.; JP Soap Co.; K.G. Caviar Im-Und Export, GmbH & Co. (Germany); Kolynos Corporation; Lournay Sales, Inc.; Mennen Interamerica Limited; Mennen Investments Inc.; Mennen Limited; Mission Hill's Property Corporation; New Science, Inc.; Norwood International Incorporated; ODOL Sociedad Anonima Industrial y Commercial (Argentina); Olive Music Publishing Corporation; Paramount Research, Inc.; Pet Chemicals Inc.; Princess House de Mexico, S.A. de C.V. (Mexico); Productors Halogenados Copalven, C.A. (Venezuela); Purity Holding Company; Purity Music Publishing Corporation; Refresh Company Limited (Dominican Republic); Samuel Taylor Holdings B.V. (Netherlands); Softsoap Enterprises, Inc.; Somerset Collections Inc.; Southhampton-Hamilton Company; The Lournay Company, Inc.; The Murphy-Phoenix Company; VCA, Inc.; Veterinary Companies of America, Inc.; Village Bath Products, Inc.; Vipont Pharmaceutical, Inc.; XEB, Inc.

Principal Competitors

Alberto-Culver Company; Amway Corp.; Avon Products, Inc.; Block Drug Company, Inc.; Carter-Wallace, Inc.; Chattem, Inc.; Church & Dwight Co., Inc.; The Clorox Company; Cosmair, Inc.; The Dial Corp.; The Gillette Company; H.J. Heinz Company; Henkel KGaA; Herbalife International, Inc.; The Iams Company; Johnson & Johnson; Mars, Inc.; Nestlé S.A.; Nu Skin Enterprises, Inc.; The Procter & Gamble Company; Ralston Purina Company; Reckitt Benckiser plc; S.C. Johnson & Son, Inc.; SmithKline Beecham plc; Unilever plc/ Univlever N.V.; USA Detergents, Inc.; Warner-Lambert Company.

Further Reading

Foster, David R., *The Story of Colgate-Palmolive: One Hundred and Sixty-Nine Years of Progress,* New York: Newcomen Society in North America, 1975.

Grant, Linda, ''Outmarketing P&G,'' *Fortune,* January 12, 1998, p. 150.

Hager, Bruce, ''Can Colgate Import Its Success from Overseas?,'' *Business Week,* May 7, 1990, pp. 114, 116.

——, ''Colgate: Oh What a Difference a Year Can Make,'' *Business Week,* March 23, 1992, pp. 90–91.

Kindel, Stephen, ''The Bundle Book: At Reuben Mark's Colgate, Attention to Small Details Creates Large Profits,'' *Financial World,* January 5, 1993, pp. 34–35.

Morgenson, Gretchen, ''Is Efficiency Enough?,'' *Forbes,* March 18, 1991, pp. 108–09.

Nayyar, Seema, ''Colgate Buys Its Way Back into the Game,'' *Adweek,* February 17, 1992.

Ono, Yumiko, ''Colgate Slates Cuts in Jobs and a Charge,'' *Wall Street Journal*, September 21, 1995, p. A3.

Parker-Pope, Tara, ''Colgate Places a Huge Bet on a Germ-Fighter,'' *Wall Street Journal*, December 29, 1997, p. B1.

——, ''Colgate Puts Lois Juliber in Line for Top,'' *Wall Street Journal*, January 20, 1997, p. B1.

Rudnitsky, Howard, ''Making His Mark,'' *Forbes,* September 26, 1994, pp. 47–48.

Sasseen, Jane A., and Zachary Schiller, ''For Colgate-Palmolive, It's Time for Trench Warfare,'' *Business Week,* September 19, 1994, pp. 56–57.

—updated by David E. Salamie and Frank Uhle

CompUSA, Inc.

14951 North Dallas Parkway
Dallas, Texas 75240
U.S.A.
Telephone: (972) 982-4000
Fax: (972) 982-4276
Web site: http://www.compusa.com

Wholly Owned Subsidiary of Grupo Sanborns S.A. de C.V.
Incorporated: 1984 as Soft Warehouse
Employees: 19,700
Sales: $6.32 billion (1999)
NAIC: 44312 Computer and Software Stores; 45411
  Electronic Shopping and Mail-Order Houses; 811212
  Computer and Office Machine Repair and
  Maintenance

CompUSA, Inc. is a leading operator of computer superstores in the United States, with more than 200 stores in 84 major metropolitan markets. CompUSA stores offer more than 5,000 products, including microcomputer hardware, software, accessories, and related items. The company's operations also include direct sales to corporate, government, and education customers. CompUSA superstores, each of which have approximately 25,000 square feet of retail space, offer technical support to their customers, repair and service of merchandise, and training centers. Sales via the Internet are conducted through a subsidiary named CompUSA Net.com Inc., which operates the web site cozone.com. CompUSA also sells build-to-order desktop and notebook personal computers through a subsidiary named CompUSA PC Inc.

1980s Origins

CompUSA began in Dallas in 1984 under the name Soft Warehouse, a company that initially sold software and hardware directly to corporate customers and within a year had opened its first retail store. During its early years, management explored the idea of opening a superstore, a large facility offering complete lines of low-cost merchandise. While the concept had proved successful for such retailers as Toys 'R' Us, Circuit City, and Office Depot, computer retail was generally thought to require a smaller sales staff expert in the technical nuances of the product. Soft Warehouse, however, speculated that as the public became more familiar with computers, the computer retail operation would broaden in scope, and with a staff and management more skilled in marketing than in computers, the company opened its first superstore in 1988. While retail chains such as ComputerCity and BusinessLand emerged during the early 1980s, Soft Warehouse developed the first chain of superstores in the computer market.

In January 1989, Soft Warehouse was acquired by a group of investors led by Ronald N. Dubin. Late that year, the company hired as its president and chief executive officer Nathan Morton, a former top executive of a leading retail chain called Home Depot. Morton had no background in computers, and he later recalled for a 1993 *New York Times* article that his friends and family were shocked that he took the leadership position at Soft Warehouse, some attributing the move to a mid-life crisis.

Morton, however, had a unique vision for the development of Soft Warehouse, which led to a period of explosive expansion for the company. Along with other new executives, who came to Soft Warehouse from Kmart, Hechingers, and Wickes Lumber, Morton planned the construction of a series of superstores that would provide the lowest prices in the industry and the largest selection available on a national scale. Eighteen superstores were in operation by the end of the 1980s, and sales increased dramatically from $66 million in fiscal 1988 to $600 million in 1990. The company became the largest chain of computer superstores in the country, changing its name to CompUSA in 1991.

The success of CompUSA was due in part to its finely honed system of merchandise flow. Rather than maintaining an expensive network of warehouses and trucking lines, CompUSA management used computer software to help track inventory and anticipate consumer demand, allowing them to stock the right amount of merchandise in the stores.

Through 1990, product lines at the CompUSA superstores consisted largely of IBM clone personal computers, including a private brand line known as Compudyne. In 1991, the company persuaded manufacturer Apple Computer, Inc. to allow the distribution of the Apple Macintosh personal computer through CompUSA. As Apple had never before allowed distribution through discounters, the company regarded this agreement as reflecting its reputation as a national marketing force. Soon thereafter, CompUSA gained the right to sell another major personal computer brand, Compaq.

While 35 percent of CompUSA's sales were to corporate buyers in 1991, a growing market of home computer users also fueled the company's expansion. In the early 1990s, an estimated 75 million Americans were using personal computers, and users were increasingly willing and able to install and maintain their own equipment without deferring to a computer expert. Moreover, dramatic increases occurred in the number of Americans either working from computers in the home or running home-based businesses as their primary occupation. Catering to this new market, CompUSA provided free information pamphlets throughout its stores to help consumers better understand product capabilities, and the stores featured low prices that were particularly appreciated by small business and home users.

Early 1990s: A Rising Giant Suffers Sagging Profits

In December 1991, CompUSA completed an initial public offering of its shares. Trading began at $15 and within a few months reached a high of $40 as investors leaped at the chance to buy into the burgeoning company. Losses reported in the prior year were attributable to control issues, and CompUSA's sales continued to increase. By the end of 1992, CompUSA operated 36 superstores across the country and had plans to add 12 more over the next six months. The company also introduced training centers in most of its stores, offering computer courses to its customers that generated nearly $700,000 a month, most of which was profit, helping offset low profit margins caused by heightened competition in the industry. The company's sales for 1992 reached $820 million.

In 1993, CompUSA decentralized its corporate structure in preparation for future growth. Nathan Morton was promoted from president to chairperson and CEO, replacing Ronald Dubin. Morton divided the company into three operating units responsible for the eastern, western, and central areas of the United States. An international unit was also formed to research expansion into Canada, Mexico, and Europe.

In spite of the company's expanding sales territories, however, profits lagged. Typical quarterly sales increases of 60 percent failed to generate similar increases in net income, and during the first quarter of 1993, CompUSA reported a 65.8

percent increase in sales and overall losses totaling $986,000. Operating expenses associated with opening new stores as well as high interest expenses contributed to the loss. At a board meeting in December 1993, Morton resigned.

Morton's replacement was CompUSA's president and chief operating officer James Halpin, who had come to the company six months earlier from the Home Base home improvement retail chain. Halpin oversaw the last weeks of the fiscal second quarter in which sales surged 65 percent and the company posted a loss of $5.5 million. He agreed that expenses had gotten out of hand. Rather than trimming expenses by slowing the company's growth, Halpin's plan included out-sourcing assembly of Compudyne computers, centralizing inventory management, and consolidating the management structure by eliminating several executive positions. With these measures, Halpin hoped to restore CompUSA to profitability, facilitating his plan to open 30 new stores by June 1995, which would bring the total number of CompUSA superstores to nearly 80.

Late 1990s Roller-Coaster Ride

Halpin quickly asserted himself, orchestrating a remarkable turnaround that soon had industry observers applauding the resurrection of CompUSA. As he had initially announced, CompUSA's corporate structure was trimmed, purged of posts deemed superfluous. Operating costs were slashed and the company's merchandising mix was revamped, marking the exit of products such as ready-to-assemble furniture to make room for higher-profit computer accessories. By mid-1996, the company was preparing to announce record sales of $3.5 billion and, more impressively, record profits. CompUSA's chief operating officer, Hal Compton, described the influence of Halpin's leadership in an interview with *Discount Store News* on May 20, 1996. "In August of 1994," he said, "our stock was at 6¾, we'd lost $20 million in the previous year, and we were completely out of cash. A year and a half later the stock is soaring [nearly $35 per share at the time], we're reporting record profits and we're sitting on $300 million in cash."

Less than two years after insolvency loomed, CompUSA could justify developing ambitious expansion plans. With 105 stores in operation by mid-1996, the company announced it would add 25 units in 1997 and another 35 units in 1998, aiming for a projected total of 200 stores by the end of the decade. An even bolder bid toward expansion had been made earlier in 1996, when CompUSA attempted to purchase Tandy Corporation's 100-unit Computer City chain. The deal fell through, however, only to be revived months later when negotiations resumed. Eventually, in August 1998, CompUSA completed the windfall deal, purchasing one of its most nettlesome rivals for approximately $175 million. The company appeared destined to blanket the nation with its stores, but not long after the Computer City acquisition was completed, Halpin found himself occupying as tenuous a position as he had occupied only a few short years earlier. CompUSA, for the second time in six years, was suffering from profound problems.

By the end of the 1990s, CompUSA was adrift financially again. The company reported an operating loss of $54.2 million in June 1999, with analysts projecting a $22 million loss on declining sales in 2000. In response, the company's stock value

Key Dates:

1984: Soft Warehouse is founded in Dallas.
1985: Company opens its first retail store.
1988: Company opens its first superstore.
1991: CompUSA is adopted as corporate title.
1996: PCS Compleat, Inc. is acquired.
1998: Computer City is acquired.
2000: Grupo Sanborns completes acquisition of CompUSA.

plummeted to where it had stood in 1994, falling to 6¼. Critics leveled the blame for the company's financial atrophy directly at Halpin and his management team. As CompUSA was pursuing Computer City, the prices of personal computers were dropping steadily, eventually creating a new and burgeoning market for computers priced below $1,000. Halpin, industry observers explained, ignored the trend and continued to concentrate on high-end, feature-filled computers, which proved to be a disastrous mistake as his competitors focused on the sub-$1,000 market and achieved strident growth.

By the end of the decade, desperate times had descended on CompUSA. Another miraculous comeback was needed, and the ramifications of its failure were straightforward. ''It's clear this turnaround has to work,'' CompUSA's chairman told *Business Week* on December 20, 1999. ''If it doesn't, the management has to be changed,'' he added. With his back against a wall, Halpin announced his plan for recovery, pinning the company's hopes on an online operation called cozone.com and the alteration of CompUSA's merchandise mix, which was expected to reflect a greater emphasis on expensive consumer electronics products such as digital cameras, handheld computers, smart toys, and cellular phones. As Halpin began implementing his vision, an added twist to the mystery of CompUSA's future occurred in March 2000, when a massive, Mexico-based telecommunications and retail conglomerate, Grupo Sanborns S.A. de C.V., acquired CompUSA. Concurrently, Grupo Sanborns announced it intended to sell 49 percent of CompUSA to a consortium comprising Telefonos de Mexico, San Antonio-based SBC Communications Inc., and Microsoft Corp. As CompUSA charted its course for the beginning of the 21st century, the influence of its new owners remained as unclear as its ability to establish itself as a retail leader.

Principal Subsidiaries

CompUSA PC, Inc.; CompUSA Net.com Inc.

Principal Competitors

Best Buy Co., Inc.; Circuit City Stores, Inc.; Dell Computer Corporation; Gateway, Inc.; Compaq Computer Corporation.

Further Reading

Brammer, Rhonda, ''Not-So-Super Concept? In Long Haul, CompUSA's Strategy May Not Compute,'' *Barron's,* March 9, 1992, p. 12.

Buckler, Arthur, ''CompUSA's Morton Resigns Top Posts Amid Dissatisfaction over Profitability,'' *Wall Street Journal,* December 16, 1993, p. B13.

Collins, Lisa, ''Computer Retailers Hacking Away,'' *Crain's Chicago Business,* July 22, 1991, p. 1.

''CompUSA Inc Streamlines Operations,'' *PR Newswire,* April 7, 2000.

''CompUSA Names Morton Chairman in a Reorganization,'' *Wall Street Journal,* May 14, 1993, p. B9.

''CompUSA Says Sales Have Been Growing, Margins Improving,'' *Wall Street Journal,* December 10, 1992, p. A13.

''Computer Superstores, Sign of the Times,'' *Fortune,* December 16, 1991, p. 48.

Creswell, Julie, ''CompUSA Is Killing Itself—On Purpose,'' *Fortune,* December 20, 1999, p. 279.

Dvorak, John C., ''It's the Selection, Stupid,'' *PC Magazine,* May 23, 2000, p. 95.

Forest, Stephanie Anderson, ''CompUSA's New Boss: Damn the Torpedoes,'' *Business Week,* February 14, 1994, p. 38.

Hisey, Pete, ''CompUSA: Back to the Bottom Line,'' *Discount Store News,* May 20, 1996, p. 15.

Kimelman, John, ''CompUSA: The Yellow Flag Is Out,'' *Financial World,* June 8, 1993, p. 18.

Mullich, Joe, ''CompUSA Seeks Profit Boost,'' *Business Marketing,* January 1994, p. 3.

——, ''CompUSA's Morton Weds Retail, PCS,'' *Business Marketing,* June 1993, p. 26.

Pope, Kyle, ''Compaq Computers Signs Accords with Three Big Retailers of PCS,'' *Wall Street Journal,* September 9, 1992, p. B4.

Strnad, Patricia, ''Europe Enticing for Computer Superstores,'' *Advertising Age,* November 9, 1992, p. S3.

Strom, Stephanie, ''CompUSA Chairman Ousted by Directors,'' *New York Times,* December 16, 1993, p. D4.

——, ''CompUSA Starts Corporate Reorganizing,'' *New York Times,* May 14, 1993, p. D3.

——, ''Will CompUSA, with $1.3 Billion in Sales, Be the Next Toys 'R' Us?'' *New York Times,* May 30, 1993, p. F5.

—A. Woodward
—updated by Jeffrey L. Covell

CoolBrands International Inc.

8300 Woodbine Avenue, 5th Floor
Markham, Ontario L3R 9Y7
Canada
Telephone: (905) 479-8762
Fax: (905) 479-5235
Web site: http://www.yogenfruz.com

Public Company
Incorporated: 1986
Employees: 421
Sales: $75.6 million (1999)
Stock Exchanges: Toronto
Ticker Symbol: YFa.TO
NAIC: 72213 Snack and Non-Alcoholic Beverage Bars;
 31152 Ice Cream and Frozen Dessert Manufacturing

Through nearly 5,000 franchises, CoolBrands International Inc., formerly known as Yogen Fruz World-Wide, Inc. sells frozen yogurt and ice cream in Canada, the United States, and 80 other countries worldwide. The company's brands include I Can't Believe It's Yogurt, Bresler's Ice Cream & Yogurt Shops, Heidi's Frozen Yogurt, Swensen's Ice Cream, Steve's Ice Cream, Larry's Ice Cream & Yogurt Parlors, and its proprietary frozen yogurt brand, Yogen Fruz. The company also franchises Java Coast Fine Coffees. Through licensing agreements, CoolBrands also produces and distributes frozen desserts for retail at grocery stores under the following brands: Tropicana, Yoplait, Trix, Lucky Charms, Yoo Hoo, Colombo, and Betty Crocker. In 2000, CoolBrands announced plans to acquire the U.S.-based Eskimo Pie Corp., an agreement reached only after a takeover attempt that occupied the company for much of 1999.

1980s Origins

The company that would become CoolBrands was founded in 1985 by brothers Aaron and Michael Serruya. Aaron Serruya had witnessed the success of frozen yogurt dessert shops in the United States, while he was operating a bagel shop with an uncle in Miami. With such businesses as The Country's Best Yogurt (TCBY) and I Can't Believe It's Yogurt (ICBIY) as models, the Serruya brothers decided to open a frozen yogurt franchise in Canada. They first approached several U.S.-based yogurt businesses, hoping to establish an American franchise in Canada, but for a variety of reasons were rejected. So Aaron, then age 19, and Michael, then age 20, put their resources together, including a loan from their father, and proceeded to develop their own franchise concept. Aaron worked with a food technician to develop the frozen yogurt flavors, while Michael consulted with a Canadian design firm on the brand concept, named Yogen Fruz.

With Michael as CEO and Aaron as executive vice-president, Yogen Fruz opened its prototype store at a suburban Toronto shopping mall in August 1986. Offering frozen yogurt in cups or cones, as well as in frozen shakes mixed with fresh fruit, made to order, the shop flourished. The brothers repaid the loan from their father within six months, and within a year the first of many franchises opened in London, Ontario. The frozen yogurt dessert shops were soon opening in shopping malls across Canada, and in 1989 Yogen Fruz franchised its 100th store. A younger brother, Simon, joined the company in 1989 at age 18, while their father sold his typesetting business to oversee offices in Europe.

As franchisers, the Serruya brothers could grow the company without large capital outlays or the need for heavy debt. Under the franchise agreements, the franchisee was required to buy equipment and supplies from Yogen Fruz. Equipment included yogurt dispensing machines, display counters, and neon signs; supplies included yogurt, fresh fruit, cups, cones, napkins, and spoons. Canadian franchisees also paid a six percent royalty.

Master franchise agreements for international expansion involved the same conditions, but charged a two percent royalty. International agreements covered an entire country as franchisees obtained the rights to open stores either through direct ownership or through the sale of franchise licenses to others. Local investors in foreign countries paid up to $500,000 for such rights and agreed to open a set number of stores. The Serruya brothers sought expansion overseas rather than compete in the United States, because frozen yogurt dessert shops had already neared market saturation in the United States.

Key Dates:

1987: First Yogen Fruz franchise outlet opens.
1990: One hundredth franchise opens.
1995: Company acquires Bresler's Ice Cream & Yogurt Shops.
1996: The I Can't Believe It's Yogurt chain is acquired.
1997: Serruya brothers are named Canada's Young Entrepreneur of the Year.
1999: Yogen Fruz is first on *Entrepreneur's* Franchise 500.
2000: Company announces name change to CoolBrands International and enters a merger agreement with Eskimo Pie Corp.

A nontraditional method of expansion employed by Yogen Fruz involved co-branding, which provided for the mingling of Yogen Fruz products with other known food services by way of Yogen Fruz mini-counters in established stores. Cobranding cost about 25 percent less than a full-size store, offering a limited selection of three to four yogurt flavors in standard cups only. The company franchised Yogen Fruz mini-counters to Kentucky Fried Chicken, Pizza Hut, and Dunkin Donuts franchisees overseas.

Yogen Fruz also cobranded with Canadian franchises, such as the Country Style Donuts chain. There, consumers could order their coffee and donuts in the morning and arrive later in the day for Yogen Fruz. This boosted sales for the donut chain by extending its sales day. It did likewise for the Country Style Donut kiosks already established at Canadian Tire stores; customers waiting for the completion of work on their cars could get donuts in the morning and frozen yogurt throughout the day. In early 1995 Yogen Fruz franchisees operated 170 outlets in Canada, which comprised an impressive 80 percent of the frozen yogurt food service market in Canada. In total the company had 250 outlets in 30 countries, including Taiwan, Venezuela, United Arab Emirates, Thailand, and Panama.

U.S. Expansion in the Mid-1990s

When the time came for the Serruya brothers to tackle the U.S. market, they decided to expand through acquisition and sought capital through a public offering of stock. Yogen Fruz became a publicly traded company with a listing on the Toronto Stock Exchange in 1995, selling at C$.50 per share. Having raised the needed capital, Yogen Fruz first approached Bresler's Ice Cream and Yogurt Shops of Des Plaines, Illinois, with an offer to purchase. The sale was completed in June 1995, and the acquisition of Bresler's provided Yogen Fruz with a means of expansion into U.S. markets as well as with valuable new brands. Bresler's had recently acquired 40 Larry's Ice Cream & Yogurt Parlors, located in Florida, and 12 Pro*Portion Cafes in Long Island, New York. With 413 stores, including 15 international outlets and four Café Bresler's quick-service restaurants, Bresler's recorded 1994 sales of $45 million. The Serruya brothers planned to add Yogen Fruz mini-counters to 158 stores in the United States within 18 months. The addition of sales

from Bresler's nearly doubled company-wide sales at Yogen Fruz, reported at approximately $50 million in 1994.

A private offering of stock through warrants provided capital for the company's second large acquisition. In March 1996 Yogen Fruz completed the acquisition of ICBIY and Brice Foods Ltd. from The Brice Group for $14 million. The acquisition involved 1,344 frozen dessert shops, including 520 units in Europe, a 35,000 square-foot manufacturing plant in Dallas, and the Java Coast coffee brand with 368 points of sale. The acquisition more than doubled Yogen Fruz's share of the yogurt shop market in the United States and raised the count of the company's units to well over 2,400 in 67 countries. Michael Serruya became co-president and co-CEO of ICBIY.

Master Franchise Agreements and cobranding remained the Yogen Fruz business strategy. Cobranding agreements involved the Canadian chains Taco Time International, Bagel Boy, and Amigos, as well as the sale of hard-pack frozen yogurt cups at 60 Pizza Hut outlets in Canada. Also, some Yogen Fruz and Bresler's stores began offering Mrs. Fields cookies, while Mrs. Fields outlets began offering the Yogen Fruz and Bresler's brands at select locations in the United States. Cobranding accounted for 20 to 30 percent of growth at this time.

Mater Franchise Agreements for Yogen Fruz outlets involved local investors in Australia, Kuwait, China, Korea, Malta, and Lebanon. In October 1996 the company signed an agreement to franchise the Bresler's Ice Cream brand in Israel, Jordon, Egypt, Lebanon, and the West Bank and Gaza Strip territories. The agreement involved opening 65 new stores over ten years. Other agreements added ICBIY franchises in South Africa and Yogen Fruz franchises in Ukraine, Malaysia, and the former Yugoslav republics. Artal Pakistan Ltd., a KFC franchisee, purchased the rights to open Bresler's and Yogen Fruz franchises in Pakistan.

Acquisitions at Yogen Fruz continued without accumulation of debt. During this time, the company acquired Greater Pacific Food Holdings, Inc., maker of the Honey Hill Farms brand of premium nonfat frozen yogurt. Based in Monterey, California, that company annually produced more than a million gallons of frozen yogurt which sold in California grocery stores. The acquisition involved production facilities only and allowed Yogen Fruz to maximize production capacity at its Dallas facility. Yogen Fruz did not acquire the Honey Hill Farms brand itself until later, in 1999. In November 1996 Yogen Fruz acquired the trademark and franchise rights of Paradise Frozen Yogurt and Juice Bar, including 15 outlets in the Toronto area. This was followed in 1997 by the Golden Swirl chain of 71 frozen-yogurt shops and wholesale operations for $5.2 million, which included Golden Swirl's ''smoothie'' concept, a blend of frozen yogurt and customer selected ingredients, Nature's Own Blend.

In October 1997 Yogen Fruz merged with Integrated Brands, Inc. of Ronkonkoma, New York, in a stock transaction. To accommodate the process, Yogen Fruz restructured its stock into two share classes, subordinated and multivoting. The merger caused the company's stock value to double to $C8 per share. One of the principals of Integrated Brands, Richard Smith, became co-chair and co-chief executive of the new concern, along with Michael Serruya. Integrated Brands' 400 frozen dessert outlets included Swensen's Ice Cream, Steve's Ice Cream, Heidi's Frozen Yogurt, and other brands. Yogen Fruz gained the retail distribution rights for some frozen products under name brands, including Tropicana, Yoplait, Colombo, Betty Crocker, Lucky Charms, and Trix. Distribution of Tropicana frozen fruit juice-based dessert bars began in 1997. For three years afterward it was the fastest growing brand product in that category, reaching second place in the market.

In the midst of this rapid growth, the Serruya brothers gained recognition as Canada's Young Entrepreneur of the Year for international franchising. Opening 150 to 300 new units per quarter, the company's 4,000th franchise opened in December 1997. Under various brands Yogen Fruz frozen dessert shops operated in 82 countries, while revenues reached C$45.9 million, up from C$30 million the year before. Profits were also healthy, standing at C$9.9 million. By this time, half of the company's revenues were generated at its U.S. outlets, while 31 percent came from international outlets and 12 percent originated from units in Canada. In 1999 *Entrepreneur* magazine rated Yogen Fruz number one on its Franchise 500, a list of the fastest growing franchisors worldwide.

The next project was to establish Yogen Fruz products at larger mass-merchandise retail environments. In February 1998 Yogen Fruz signed an agreement to distribute Bresler's Premium Frozen Yogurt to all 440 Sam' Club stores in the United States. An agreement with National Amusements expanded Yogen Fruz outlets to 16 movie theaters in the United Kingdom, while KLM Airlines began to offer the ICBIY brand as part of its flight meals.

1999 and Beyond

The year 1999 presented some challenges for the Serruya brothers and Yogen Fruz. Early in the year, profits for the first quarter were lower than expected, and then certain accounting procedures at the company were publicly questioned. As a result, the company saw a decline in its stock value. Michael Serruya attributed the decrease in earnings to lower franchising income, a $250,000 foreign exchange loss, and the rising cost of butterfat; and the accounting issues were soon clarified, in favor of Yogen Fruz. However, the company's stock dropped to C$3.40 per share. Shortly after the merger with Integrated Brands, Yogen Fruz's stock value had peaked at more than C$14.

Nevertheless, growth strategies continued, as Yogen Fruz signed several Master Franchise Agreements in 1999. YF Posadas SRL of Argentina and Julie 'N Superstores of Barbados involved more than 60 new frozen dessert shops, with possible agreements for other Caribbean countries. A May 1999 agreement involved development of 500 stores in Germany over three years. In August 1999 South Pole Foods Company, a franchisee in Taiwan, obtained the rights to develop 390 brand locations in China and Hong Kong. Fruzco South Africa entered into an agreement to open 37 units, beginning in Johannesburg. In February 2000 the company realized further expansion into the United Kingdom as North Pole Investments, Ltd. obtained master franchise rights to 82 outlets under the Yogen Fruz, Bresler's, ICBIY, and Java Coast brands. The company planned to open the first two outlets in Stratford and London.

Financial performance at Yogen Fruz in 1999 sparked tense discussions at the company's 2000 shareholder meeting. While revenues had increased from C$89 million in 1998 to C$112.6 million in 1999, profits had decreased from C$12.9 million to C$3.2 million, causing another decline in the company's stock value, to $1.25 per share. Michael Serruya surprised shareholders and executives when he resigned his position as co-CEO, of his own volition, to focus on new acquisitions and maximizing shareholder value as co-chair of the board. The board then named David Stein, a principal of Integrated Brands, as CEO, while Aaron Serruya remained executive vice-president. In early 2000 the company announced its intention to adopt a new name, CoolBrands International, to better reflect the company's interests.

During this time, the company had attempted to acquire the U.S.-based frozen dessert veteran Eskimo Pie Corp. Eskimo Pie, which had gone public in 1992, had run into financial trouble soon thereafter in the face of increased competition and shrinking profit margins. Its brand name recognition was solid, but sales faltered. CoolBrands approached Eskimo Pie with an offer to buy, but that offer was rejected as Eskimo Pie management hoped to turn the company around on their own. Eventually, late in 1999, the shareholders agreed to the takeover by CoolBrands, and in May 2000, the companies announced their intent to merge. When completed, the new holding would effectively double CoolBrands U.S. operations. Stein regarded Eskimo Pie as "a perfect match with our core consumer products. . . . In addition, our financial and strategic resources will be used to enhance the success of the Eskimo Pie brand name."

Principal Subsidiaries

Yogen Fruz Canada, Inc.; Bresler's Industries, Inc. (United States); I Can't Believe It's Yogurt, Ltd.; Integrated Brands, Inc.; Kayla Foods, Inc.; Eskimo Pie Corp. (United States).

Principal Competitors

TCBY Enterprises, Inc.; International Dairy Queen, Inc.; Allied Domecq plc.

Further Reading

Chu, Showwei, "Freeze Play," *Canadian Business*, December 26, 1997, p. 77.

Clark, Gerry, "Bringing Back the Brand?," *Dairy Foods*, January 2000, p. 19.

Feinberg, Phyllis, "Cold War: Thaw Reached in Frozen Treat Proxy Fight," *Pensions & Investments*, September 20, 1999, p. 8.

Fisk, Holly Celeste, "Just Desserts: Yogurt Is but the Tip of the Iceberg for Yogen Fruz," *Entrepreneur*, September 1996, p. 179.

Hamstra, Mark, "Yogen Fruz Diversifies with ICBIY Buy," *Nation's Restaurant News,* March 25, 1996, p. 3.

——, "Yogen Fruz Is Warming up to U.S. Stock Market," *Nation's Restaurant News,* December 16, 1996, p. 11.

Hanson, Kim, "Earnings Woe Spark Yogen Fruz Meltdown," *Financial Post*, February 6, 1999, p. C3.

——, "Resistance Melts Away at Eskimo Pie: Firm to be Broken; Yogen Fruz Claims Victory, Plans Bid for Core Assets," *Financial Post*, September 9, 1999, p. C3.

——, "Serruya Suddenly Leaves CEO Post at Yogen Fruz: Unexpected Departure," *Financial Post*, March 1, 2000, p. C8.

McHutchion, John, ''Yogen Fruz Takes on Six Countries,'' *Toronto Star*, July 2, 1996, p. D4.

Mulhern, Charlotte, ''The Big Chill,'' *Entrepreneur,* January 1998, p. 190.

Rojo, Oscar, ''Yogen Fruz Expands Chain,'' *Toronto Star,* October 18, 1994, p. D9.

Rubin, Sandra, ''A Cool, Smooth Investment,'' *Hamilton Spectator*, July 29, 1995, p. C11.

Steinhart, David, ''Restructuring Holds Key to Evolution of Yogen Fruz,'' *Financial Post*, February 27, 1998, p. 25.

Tiffany, Laura, ''Freeze Fame: How this Year's No. 1 Franchise, Yogen Fruz, Is Getting its Just Desserts,'' *Entrepreneur*, January 1999, p. 194.

''Yogen Fruz Plans Cool New Name,'' *Calgary Herald*, February 11, 2000, p. E12.

''Yogen Fruz World-Wide,'' *Ice Cream Reporter*, November 20, 1999, p.8.

—Mary Tradii

Crain Communications Inc

Crain Communications, Inc.

740 North Rush Street
Chicago, Illinois 60611-2590
U.S.A.
Telephone: (312) 649-5200
Fax: (312) 280-3179
Web site: http://www.crain.com

Private Company
Incorporated: 1916 as Crain Publishing Company
Employees: 900
Sales: $240 million (1998)
NAIC: 51112 Periodical Publishers

Crain Communications Inc. is an anomaly in the business world—a solid, innovative media conglomerate run with the values of a neighborhood grocery. This small, family operation quietly yet rigorously carved a place for itself among the nation's media titans. Rance Crain has called his family's company "one of the last bastions of caring and humanity" due to its progressive treatment of its employees in an era of downsizing. Crain is headquartered in Chicago, with 15 offices around the world, and publishes primarily trade periodicals, while also providing subscription, direct mail, and custom printing services. Crain's roster of magazines and news weeklies includes industry heavy-hitters *Advertising Age, Automotive News, Business Insurance, Electronic Media, Modern Healthcare, Pensions & Investments, Plastics News,* and *Crain's Chicago Business.* Rounding out Crain's holdings are two 100,000-watt Florida Keys radio stations and new ventures into electronic media, such as the highly successful AdAge.com.

Freelance Origins

Gustavus Dedman Crain, Jr. (known as "G.D.") was born in Lawrenceburg, Kentucky, in 1885, the second of three boys. Raised in Louisville, G.D. delivered newspapers as a boy. After serving as editor of his high school newspaper, he accepted a scholarship to Centre College in Danville, Kentucky, graduating in three years with a masters degree in English. Returning to Louisville, he signed on as a staff reporter with the *Times,*

developing a powerful instinct for breaking news and frequently scooping his rivals, the *Herald* and *Courier-Journal.* While writing for the *Times,* G.D. augmented his income by freelancing for dozens of business papers. Quitting the *Times,* G.D. Crain hired a small staff and started his own editorial service, churning out news and features on a daily basis. Still G.D. Crain hoped to achieve more, to receive the copy, edit it, and actually publish it.

In 1916, 31-year-old Crain put his experience to the test and founded two specialized periodicals, *Hospital Management (HM)* and *Class.* Later that year Crain moved the company, his wife Ailiene, and daughters Jane and Mary to Chicago, a burgeoning hub of the business world. Setting up shop at 608 South Dearborn Street, in what became known as Printer's Row, Crain founded Crain Publishing Company, which revolved around a simple premise: give readers what they want—factual, fairly-reported news written and edited in a professional manner—and they'd keep coming back. G.D. Crain's unbridled enthusiasm and energy became the cornerstone of Crain Publishing Company and its eventual successor, Crain Communications, Inc., while setting the course for a decades-long career in publishing.

Crain's first endeavor, the 36-page, seven-by-ten-inch *Hospital Management,* debuted in February 1916. Directed toward medical administrators, managers and decision-makers, *HM* covered the ever-expanding hospital field, competing with a St. Louis-based magazine called *Modern Hospital.* G.D. Crain's second venture, the smaller-formatted, 32-page *Class* was a business-to-business digest covering the industrial advertising and sales field. It was also a convenient way to advertise its sibling publication, *HM.* To devote himself to selling ads and editing copy for *Class,* Crain hired sportswriter Matthew Foley as editor of *HM.* In 1919, Crain's older brother Kenneth Crain relocated to Chicago and soon became *HM*'s general manager. By 1922, Crain Publishing was thriving. Yet the year also brought two disparate occurrences with long-reaching consequences: the first was the tragic death of Crain's wife, Ailiene, leaving his young daughters motherless; the second, the auspicious appearance of a young man named Sidney R. Bernstein. Under Foley's tutelage, Bernstein was given his first writing opportunity and was named *HM*'s assistant editor, one of many titles he would hold over the next 71 years.

A New Ad Age in 1930

In 1927, *Class* (revamped in the early 1920s as *Class & Industrial Advertising*) was now called *Class & Industrial Marketing* and grew from pocket-sized to a more accepted 8.5-by-11 inches. Also during this time, G.D. Crain, longtime friend Keith Evans, and other colleagues helped create the National Industrial Advertisers Association to address the collective and individual problems of industrial advertisers and marketers. In the months before Black Tuesday, October 29, 1929, G.D. Crain finalized details for a news weekly called *Advertising Age*. On January 11, 1930, without knowing the full extent of the nation's financial quandary, he published the premiere issue of *Ad Age*, promoted as the "national newspaper of advertising." With no advance notice, 10,000 copies of the 12-page edition appeared on the desks of professionals selected from the Standard Advertising Register. Its premise was to print all news related to advertising and marketing and, moreover, to cover what the industry's bible, *Printer's Ink*, deemed unimportant. Many thought Crain made a crucial mistake with the precipitous launch of *Ad Age*; not only was *Printer's Ink* a well-established and respected business periodical, but the risks were phenomenal. However, G.D. Crain's passion would not be quelled, and years later he admitted he probably would have gone ahead with *Ad Age* despite even the worst financial forecasts. (His risks paid off handsomely--*Printer's Ink* folded in 1967 and *Ad Age* has been considered the "publication of record" for decades.) In the lean years of the Depression, the previously healthy *Class* and *HM* suffered losses and wavered in red ink. To the credit of Ellen Krebby, who was hired in 1921 to handle the office and accounting, Crain never realized the tenuity of the company's financial status. In 1933, rather than sacrifice *Class* altogether, it became a special section of *Ad Age* until ad sales and circulation could recover.

Ad Age was not profitable until 1934, four years after its birth. In the interim, Sid Bernstein was named assistant to the publisher in October 1931, and *Ad Age* grew to average 16 pages with a circulation of 9,000, an increase of nearly 1,400 over the previous year. G.D. Crain's younger brother, Murray Crain, became *Ad Age*'s managing editor, and the three brothers made Crain Publishing Company a family affair. In January 1935, tragedy struck when Matt Foley suffered a heart attack and died at the age of 44. Unable or unwilling to run *HM* without Foley's guidance and verve, Crain sold it. Oddly enough, *HM* would eventually return to Crain after its buyers neared bankruptcy. Though the medical magazine would be sold again in 1952, the company would once again delve into the medical field by purchasing *Modern Healthcare* from McGraw-Hill in 1976.

In June 1935, *Class* reemerged from *Ad Age* as *Industrial Marketing,* then underwent its final name change to *Business Marketing* in 1936, its 20th anniversary. Amidst a flurry of retail and advertising agency growth in the area, Crain relocated north to 100 East Ohio Street. This year was also pivotal for G.D. Crain personally: while meeting with a sales executive of the National Broadcasting Company (NBC) in New York City, he met a 25-year-old woman named Gertrude Ramsay, a secretary at NBC's offices in Rockefeller Center. After a whirlwind courtship, the two married, and Gertrude was whisked off to Chicago. The company, meanwhile, known as Advertising Publications, Inc., opened an office in Washington, D.C. in 1939, and Crain relinquished his status as *Ad Age* editor-in-chief by appointing Bernstein (then director of research and promotion) to editor, while moving managing editor Irwin Robinson to New York full-time in 1940. As the United States became embroiled in World War II, Crain declared, "There are many essential services which advertising is called upon to perform in wartime," and set about fulfilling this obligation. On the homefront, Gertrude had given birth to sons Rance (1938) and Keith (1941).

In 1943, Advertising Publications implemented an unheard of concept—an employee profit-sharing plan—fully funded by the company and the first of many employee benefits programs. When World War II ended, Crain and Bernstein rethought priorities in preparation for a postwar society. In a January 7, 1946 editorial, Bernstein announced "Advertising has emerged from the war with a new stature, new tasks and new duties. It will never again be confined only to the sale of goods and services." This year also marked *Ad Age*'s foray into agency profiles, breaking the industry's silence on billings. The 1950s brought the addition of a features section and the launch of the yearly 100 Leading National Advertisers poll; by the end of the decade, circulation hit 48,400 with the purchase of rival Advertising Agency. Once more outgrowing its premises, Advertising Publication moved into a remodeled warehouse at 200 East Illinois Street, its home until April 1962 when operations moved to 740 North Rush Street.

New Endeavors in the 1960s–70s

New developments in the 1960s included the debut of *Advertising Requirements* (later *Advertising & Sales Promotion* then *Promotion* before merging into *Ad Age* and shutting down in May 1974), and what many termed a changing of the guard in 1964. Nearing 80, G.D. Crain stepped down as publisher of *Ad Age*, a post he had held for 34 years, naming Bernstein president and publisher while assuming the newly-created position of chairperson. The next several years marked both growth and loss: a publication for college students, *Marketing Insights,* would fail after a few semesters, but *Business Insurance,* first published in October 1967, and the acquisition of *American Drycleaner, American Laundry Digest, American Co-Op* and *American Clean Car* substantially increased the company's holdings. To better represent its diversity, Advertising Publications became Crain Communications Inc. and created an American Trade Magazines subsidiary with offices at 500 North Dearborn Street, in Chicago.

As Rance and Keith Crain grew up, curiosity in the family business gave way to genuine interest. Generally considered opposites, Rance and Keith familiarized themselves with Crain

Communications through years of Saturday office visits and nightly dinner conversations with their parents. Yet as Rance and Keith chose their divergent paths up the corporate ladder, each faced the daunting task of proving himself to be more than the boss's son. After studying at DePauw University in Indiana for two years (he later received an honorary degree in 1987), Rance Crain attended Northwestern University to study journalism, becoming sports editor of the *Daily Northwestern.* His tenure at Crain began as a cub reporter for the New York and Washington, D.C. bureaus of *Ad Age,* where his peers gave him little support and less chance of succeeding. However, Rance Crain persevered, doggedly tracking stories and proving both his mettle and writing skills. His management expertise and sagacity would prove paramount to the success of his greatest personal triumph, *Crain's Chicago Business,* as well as the continued prosperity of *Ad Age.* ''*Ad Age* would have been bland and faceless had Rance not been there,'' commented Niles Howard, a former *Ad Age* reporter. Lou DeMarco, a former vice-president and retired *Ad Age* publisher, concurred: ''Rance's enthusiasm is limitless; you can't satisfy his hunger for new ideas.''

In 1978, Rance Crain channeled his energy in a new direction. After meeting Bob Gray, publisher of the *Houston Business Journal,* he decided a business weekly about the Chicago area ''would be twice as successful'' as the Houston endeavor. Marking the first public use of the Crain family name, *Crain's Chicago Business* seemed blessed by fate; the *Chicago Daily News* was going under, and several staffers including Dan Miller, Sandy Presman, and Joe Cappo jumped ship to the new Crain publication. The rest, as they say, is history—though not a smooth one. Just as Rance Crain's drive and enthusiasm pushed *Ad Age* and *Crain's Chicago Business* to the forefront, there were misfires as well. Neither *Thursday* (a jazzy, mid-week edition of *Ad Age*), *The Collector-Investor* nor *Crain's Illinois Business* generated sufficient interest, and *Crain's New York Business* faced an uphill battle after its founding in 1985. Yet Rance Crain stated unequivocally that he'd never give up on *Crain's New York Business,* believing it would someday be to the New York area what *Crain's Chicago* was to the Midwest.

As Rance Crain's newshound instincts had propelled his career, so Keith Crain's abiding interest in cars was the back-

bone of his own career. A car enthusiast since his teens, Keith Crain attended Northwestern University then sold ads and worked on a variety of Crain publications before heading to the company's offices in Detroit to indulge his passion. In 1970, on Keith Crain's behalf, Bernstein bid on the downtrodden *Automotive News* (*AN*), a 46-year-old weekly tabloid based in Detroit. Keith Crain was not only familiar with the internal workings of cars, but soon demonstrated an innate sense of how a trade magazine about vehicles should be written, edited, and marketed. Publisher of *AN* at the age of 30, the often brash, always pertinacious Keith Crain won over Detroit's plutocracy and solidified a place among them. Keith's first *AN* issue came out on June 7, 1971; within six months, it was breaking even and eventually secured a 100 percent paid circulation. As the Detroit office boomed, Keith purchased Akron-based *Rubber & Plastics News* in 1976, stipulating that editor and publisher Ernie Zielasko and Lowell (Chris) Chrisman, vice-president of sales, come along. *Rubber & Plastics News's* first issue under the Crain Communications banner appeared in April, signifying an important venture into the Akron/Cleveland area.

In 1977, Keith Crain led the company into virgin territory with the purchase of *AutoWeek,* Crain's first consumer periodical in 61 years of publishing. Overhauling the tabloid into a glossy magazine, management saw *AutoWeek*'s circulation soar from 25,000 to nearly 280,000. Zielasko and Chrisman, the dynamic duo of *Rubber & Plastics News,* were also the driving force behind the formation of *Crain's Cleveland Business* in 1980, which overtook its competition, the *Northern Ohio Business Journal,* to become the area's definitive news weekly. In May 1981, Keith Crain was named vice-chairman, overseeing Crain Communication's daily activities with Rance Crain. Taking over Keith's former duties as secretary-treasurer were his wife, Mary Kay Crain, as treasurer, and Rance's wife, Merilee Crain, as company secretary (both women, along with Gertrude, Rance, and Keith made up Crain's board of directors).

Gertrude Crain began her own pivotal role in the company when the boys were in high school. A graduate of secretarial school in Manhattan, Gertrude's business interests were put aside to raise her sons. Beginning part-time and progressing to full-time, Gertrude Crain mastered a myriad of tasks that included representing the company at conventions worldwide, overseeing the company's extensive benefits program, monitoring expense accounts, scouring accounts payable invoices, and even signing checks. As the 1970s progressed, Gertrude, Rance, and Keith confidently plied their trades, and Crain Communications hit several milestones. G.D. Crain's pet project, *Ad Age,* commemorated its 40th anniversary and reached a circulation of 65,000, while the Crain think-tank developed *Pensions & Investments* in July 1973.

On November 7, 1973, G.D. Crain was felled by a stroke. Though he recovered temporarily, the ebullient patriarch died December 15th at the age of 88. The loss did not send the company into a tailspin, however. In January, Gertrude Crain became chairman of the board; Keith Crain assumed her former duties as secretary-treasurer; Bernstein was named chairman of the executive committee; and Rance Crain became president. Though Gertrude Crain often downplayed her role at the company, under her influence the company more than quadrupled its number of publications, generating revenues of $160 million in 1993, a steep climb from 1974's modest $10 million.

In October 1975, G.D. Crain was posthumously inducted into the American Advertising Federation's Hall of Fame. Fourteen years later, Sid Bernstein, known in the industry as "Mr. Advertising," was finally given his due as well, inducted into the Advertising Hall of Fame on March 28, 1989. Gertrude Crain, meanwhile, was busy too: in 1986, at age 75, she rode shotgun with NASCAR racer Tim Richmond, hitting 185 mph; for her 77th birthday, she went parasailing in Key Largo. She was recognized not only for her spirit of adventure, but for her professional accomplishments as well. In 1987, she was inducted into Working Woman's Hall of Fame; named Chicagoan of the Year by the Boys and Girls Club of Chicago; and selected as one of the Top 60 Women Business Owners by *Savvy* magazine. In 1988, she received Mundelein College's "Magnificat" medal. In 1992, she was inducted into the Junior Achievement Chicago Business Hall of Fame, and in 1993, she was honored with a lifetime achievement award from the Magazine Publishers of America. Gertrude Crain also served on the board of directors for several organizations, including the International Advertising Association, the National Press Foundation, and the Advertising Council of New York.

Called "as near a perfect example of a specialist magazine as is possible to produce" by British journalist Eric Clark, in his book, *The Want Makers, Ad Age* celebrated its 60th anniversary by unveiling a spiffier look and new logo. Rance Crain, after years of commuting, finally moved east to be near Crain's New York offices. On May 29, 1993, another Crain legend, 86-year-old Sid Bernstein, died. "Sid Bernstein has always served as the editorial conscience of our company," Rance said in a tribute published in *Ad Age* shortly after Bernstein's death. The company carried on, expanding in the memory of both G.D. Crain and Bernstein. In 1994, in a joint venture with America On-Line, *Crain's Chicago Business* and *Crain's Small Business* were hooked up to Chicago On-Line. In the fall, Crain staffers laid the groundwork for two new publications, *Franchise Buyer* and *Waste News,* set to debut in the spring of 1995.

In the mid-1990s, with Gertrude Crain well past traditional retirement age, the industry was rife with speculation about who would take the reins of Crain when the time came. "If you ask my mother about succession plans," Keith noted, "she'd probably wonder about how to replace Rance or me, because she plans to outlive both of us." Though Rance and Keith had taken Crain's interests to new highs, some critics had found fault with the brothers' unusual brand of decision-making, such as choosing ventures based on interest and convenience rather than profit. When Gertrude Crain was asked in a 1987 interview what the biggest problems facing the company were in the near future, she quipped "Rance and Keith." One thing was certain: Gertrude, Rance, and Keith would always be united in perpetuating G.D. Crain's vision. As Nancy Millman, who wrote a family profile for *Chicago* magazine in 1993, pointed out: "The last time a Chicago media empire passed to two brothers with very different personalities and interests, Marshall and Ted Field ended up selling the *Chicago Sun-Times* to Rupert Murdoch—a spot of history that isn't lost on the journalists at Crain."

New Frontiers in the Late 1990s

The increasing globalization of the auto industry spurred Crain to launch *Automotive News Europe* in February 1996. The new sister publication to the 70-year old *Automotive News* was based in London. In the United States, local city magazines were receiving declining support from national advertisers, making them less viable as stand-alone publications. In the fall, Crain announced plans to incorporate *Detroit Monthly* as a supplement to *Crain's Detroit Business.*

Gertrude Crain retired as chairman in May 1996. In her 22 years in the role, the company's annual sales increased from $10 million to nearly $200 million. Keith Crain attributed this success to her ability to spot and nurture talent. She was also remembered for bringing a sense of family to the company as she guided it to tremendous growth. She died on Cape Cod on July 20 at the age of 85. Her sons pledged to keep the business family-owned.

Also that year, American City Business Journals bought CityMedia, reducing the number of large players in business journals to only two. Most were locally owned by small, independent operators. American City, owned by Advance Publications and a sister company to Random House, held 34 after the acquisition, six of which had been CityMedia's, while Crain owned four, in Chicago, Cleveland, Detroit, and New York.

Keith Crain became the company's third chairman in February 1997, while Rance Crain remained president. During this time, Keith Crain was known to preach about the importance of maintaining editorial integrity on the lawless World Wide Web. Nothing else could win reader loyalty in the long run, he maintained. The company's own local web sites were sometimes criticized for simply skimming the content of the print products they represented. Still, AdAge.com billed $1 million a year in advertising revenues in the late 1990s; the timeliness of the content was a key selling point. *Ad Age* also sent out stories via a fax service as well as on the profitable Daily World Wire, a subscription-based service for corporate clients. The site also registered 200,000 new subscriptions a year for the print product.

Crain launched the weekly *InvestmentNews* in September 1997. Its audience included investment advisers, financial planners, and attorneys. Another new quarterly was *Automotive Global Quarterly,* the official magazine of the International Federation of Automotive Engineering Societies, which debuted the next year. Crain bought *Media International* from Reed Business Information in March 1999, and the London-based monthly, which had been started in 1974, was soon incorporated into *Advertising Age International.*

Crain grew fast in the late 1990s, prompting a series of hirings and promotions. The company fostered an entrepreneurial outlook in its editors, whom it saw as most responsible for capturing readers' interest. According to one executive, the editor-as-salesperson could lead the ad sales force to a new level. As it approached a new millennium, Crain was relocating its New York offices, where it employed 200 staffers. Keith Crain told *Folio* that integrating the Internet into the company's traditional publishing remained its largest issue.

Principal Subsidiaries

Crain Associated Enterprises Inc.; Crain Broadcasting, Inc.; Crain Communications Europe LLC.

Principal Competitors

Advance Publications Inc. (American City Business Journals); The McGraw-Hill Companies, Inc.; Primedia Inc.; VNU N.V.

Further Reading

Bernstein, Sid, "A Little Book of Proven Truths," *Ad Age,* June 8, 1992, p. 19.

Borden, Jeff, "A 'Quiet Trailblazer' Is Remembered," *Crain's Chicago Business,* July 29, 1996, p. 1.

Crain, Rance, "A Good Idea Can Take Time to Bear Fruit," *Pensions & Investments,* October 19, 1998, p. 52.

——, "If You Can't Beat 'Em, Join 'Em," *Ad Age,* May 25, 1992, p. 28.

——, "Mom Knew: Treat the Staff Like Family," *Ad Age,* May 27, 1996.

——, "New Course in Adopt-A-School," *Ad Age,* October 27, 1986, p. 58.

——, "New Worlds to Conquer," *Ad Age,* January 21, 1991, p. 34.

——, "The Conscience of Our Company," *Ad Age,* June 7, 1993, p. 22.

——, "The Daredevil of Publishing," *Ad Age,* July 19, 1993, p. 17.

——, "Wear-Down School Prevails," *Ad Age,* February, 4, 1991, p. 24.

"Crain Receives Lifetime Achievement Award from Magazine Publishers," *Automotive News,* August 1989, p. 22.

"Crain Remembered by Friends, Family," *Ad Age,* July 29, 1996, pp. 1, 24.

Danzig, Fred, "Sid Bernstein Leaves a Legacy of Ideals, Progress," *Ad Age,* June 7, 1993, p. 1.

——, "Triumphs and Failures: Six Decades of Marketing's Roller Coaster Ride," *Ad Age,* June 18, 1990, p. 50.

Goldsborough, Robert, *The Crain Adventure: The Making & Building of a Family Publishing Company,* Lincolnwood, Ill.: NTC Business Books, 1992.

Love, Barbara, "A Stepping Stone for Editors," *Folio,* November 1, 1993, p. 10.

——, "What Are You Doing to Develop Your Editors as Entrepreneurs?" *Folio,* Folio: Plus, July 1998, p. 9.

Millman, Nancy, "Two Crains Running," *Chicago,* April 1993, p. 73.

"The 1987 Working Woman Hall of Fame," *Working Woman,* November 1987, p. 107.

Silber, Tony, "Business Title Targets Detroit's Foreign Visitors," *Folio,* June 1991, p. 21.

Stell, Jennifer F. "Challenges for the New Year," *Folio,* Outlook 2000, January 2000, p. 92.

Tannenbaum, Jeffrey, "Franchise-News Junkies," *Wall Street Journal,* September 28, 1994, p. B2.

Wilkinson, Stephan, "The Keeper (and Stoker) of the Company Flame," *Working Woman,* October 1987, p. 70.

Yakal, Kathy, "Read (Not Quite All) About It!," *Barron's,* January 20, 1997, pp. 54, 56.

—Taryn Benbow-Pfalzgraf
—updated by Frederick C. Ingram

CSS Industries, Inc.

1845 Walnut Street
Philadelphia, Pennsylvania 19103
U.S.A.
Telephone: (215) 569-9900
Fax: (215) 569-9979

Public Company
Incorporated: 1923 as City Stores Company
Employees: 2,138
Sales: $392.6 million (1999)
Stock Exchanges: New York
Ticker Symbol: CSS
NAIC: 422120 Stationery and Office Supplies
   Wholesaling; 322222 Coated and Laminated Paper
   Manufacturing; 323119 Other Commercial Printing;
   315299 All Other Cut and Sew Apparel
   Manufacturing

CSS Industries, Inc. designs, manufactures, and distributes seasonal and everyday social expressions and novelties. Social expressions include boxed Christmas and everyday greeting cards, Valentine's Day exchange cards for the classroom, gift wrap, gift bags, and trim, including ribbon and bows, gift tags, and tissue paper. CSS is a leading maker of Halloween masks and also creates and distributes costumes, makeup, and related accessories and novelties. Other holiday novelties include Easter egg dye kits and seasonal wall and table decorations. CSS also manufactures and markets everyday vinyl and paper decorations and children's sticker books and educational activity kits. CSS products are displayed in showrooms in New York City, Memphis, Minneapolis, and Hong Kong. Most of the company's customers, primarily mass merchants, are located in the United States and Canada.

Formed Amidst the Changes of the 20th Century

CSS Industries began as City Stores Company, a holding company for established department stores in urban centers. A phenomenon of the 1920s, such ''ownership groups'' took ad-

vantage of the various cost efficiencies accrued from volume purchases of merchandise for resale, benefits reaped by retail chains and cooperative buying groups. The stores within an ownership group operated separately, however, maintaining their original trade names and identities.

Formed in 1923, City Stores started with the acquisition of three department stores: B. Lowenstein, Inc., founded in Memphis in 1855; and Maison Blanche Co., of New Orleans, and Loveman, Joseph & Loeb, of Birmingham, Alabama, both established in 1887. The following year City Stores purchased Kaufman-Straus Co. of Louisville, founded in 1879. To service the merchandising needs of the company, City Stores formed several subsidiaries to operate departments within the stores; these included City Stores Apparel Co.; City Stores Mercantile Co.; City Stores Furniture Co.; and City Stores Millinery Co.

City Stores thrived through the urban growth and prosperity of the 1920s, but suffered the consequences of the Great Depression. In 1928 the company acquired a majority interest (68.6 percent) in Lit Bros. of Philadelphia, established in 1891. City Stores liquidated two department stores acquired shortly before the stock market crash, Goerke Co. of Newark, New Jersey, and Goerke-Kirch Co. of Elizabeth, New Jersey, discontinued in 1932 and 1935, respectively. The company also liquidated its merchandising subsidiaries that sold remaining merchandise to the department stores. In 1934 City Stores reorganized in accordance with the Corporate Bankruptcy Act, which allowed one class A share or 12 old common shares to be exchanged for a new common share. Outstanding promissory notes were paid or exchanged for convertible notes. Through these arrangements Bankers Securities Corporation (BSC) acquired a majority interest in City Stores.

City Stores endured the Great Depression and, at the end of World War II, the company renewed its acquisition strategy. In 1944 City Stores acquired control of R.H. White, a Boston department store, and purchased the remaining interest from BSC two years later. The company also acquired Richard Store of Miami from BSC in 1946. City Stores purchased a majority interest in two women's specialty clothing stores, Oppenheim, Collins & Co. in 1945 and Franklin Simon & Co. of New York in 1949. The company expanded with the acquisition of Wise,

Smith & Co. of Hartford, Connecticut in 1948 and Lansburgh & Bro. of Washington, D.C. in 1951. The company also added four stories to the seven-story Richard Store in Miami.

In the 1950s City Stores sought efficiency through centralized functions and consolidated certain operations through several stock transactions. In 1950 City Stores merged Maison Blanche and Loveman, Joseph & Loeb, since both subsidiaries served markets in the south. The company merged Lit Bros. into City Stores' operations in 1951. Oppenheim, Collins & Co. merged with Franklin Simon, but the two chains continued to operate under separate trade names and as separate divisions under the newly formed City Specialty Stores. City Stores later changed the name of the Oppenheim, Collins & Co. stores to Franklin Simon. Richard Store Co. and Lansburgh & Bro. merged in 1953 and City Stores merged with another subsidiary, Diversified Stores Corp., in 1960.

Except for the liquidation of Wise, Smith & Co. in 1954, City Stores expanded in the 1950s and early 1960s. The proliferation of housing developments led to the opening of new, suburban stores, such as a 75,000-square-foot R.H. White store in Worcester, Massachusetts and a Richard Store in North Miami. Acquisitions included the Bry-Block department store in Memphis and 73 percent of Specialty Stores Co. Inc. which operated the Hearns Department Store in the Bronx. For $3.5 million, an investment subsidiary acquired control of the W & J Sloane chain of furniture stores in 1961, involving more than 30 stores in California, New York, Connecticut, New Jersey, and other states along the east coast. W & J Sloane purchased a 280,000-square-foot building at a prime location on Fifth Avenue in New York City from Franklin Simon. Lit Bros. acquired four department stores in suburban Philadelphia as well as four automobile accessory stores.

The City Stores Company Fades in the 1970s

During this time City Stores experienced a steady increase in sales, from $232.2 million in 1954 to $309.1 million in 1963, but net income declined from $5 million in 1954 to a loss of $1.6 million in 1963. The company took a number of measures to improve its financial situation. In 1966 City Stores formed a new division to provide consumer credit on installment and revolving credit accounts for its various department stores. The division was funded with $3.8 million in capital stock and $1.7 million in debt. City Stores acquired Wolf & Dessauer Co. for $3.9 million in 1966, but sold the company three years later along with Kaufman-Straus. R.H. White opened a second suburban store, a 50,000-square-foot facility, in Leominster, Massachusetts, in 1968. Sales and profits fluctuated, leading to a net loss of slightly less than $1 million in 1971.

The company struggled through the 1970s as urban decay led to a decline in sales at many of the company's urban locations and inflation increased expenses everywhere. The company discontinued operations at Lansburgh's in 1973, garnering $4 million from the sale of property and other assets. The year ended with a $700,000 loss on sales of $367.4 million. In late 1976 City Stores closed the Lit Bros. store at 8th and Market streets in downtown Philadelphia, diverting customers to the company's suburban stores.

In 1975 City Stores sought to ameliorate its problems through new merchandising programs, improved merchandise presentation, and management training and selection. Merchandising involved upgrading customer selection and updating departments to attract consumers from 25 to 40 years of age. The company also increased the amount of merchandise imported from other countries by 40 percent, seeking to provide quality and value at a lower cost. City Stores sought to improve merchandise presentation within its budget constraints by refurbishing three department stores and five Franklin Simon stores, while several W & J Sloan stores were completely renovated. An experimental interior design center opened under the W & J Sloane name in Maryland. The success of the experiment led to the opening of a second unit in Monterey, California.

After several years of low profits or net losses, City Stores filed for Chapter 11 bankruptcy in July 1979. Under the reorganization plan, City Stores discontinued several retail operations, including the 42 Franklin Simon women's specialty stores, Hearns Department Store, and the eight Richard Stores. The six Loveman, Joseph & Loeb and two R.H. White department stores closed in early 1980. The company sold real estate and other assets owned by the divisions to pay debt and for continuing operations. City Stores consolidated the four B. Lowenstein Bros. stores with the seven Maison Blanche stores to form the Maison Blanche Department Stores Group and planned to upgrade merchandise at the B. Lowenstein Bros. stores to match the moderate to better merchandise at Maison Blanche stores. The company also planned to open a new Maison Blanche department store in a new regional shopping center in Memphis. After selling nine clearance centers, the 41 remaining retail operations of W & J Sloane formed the W & J Sloane Home Furnishings Group.

City Stores was dismantled completely through the bankruptcy process after Philadelphia Industries Inc. (PII), a private investment corporation, acquired 54 percent stock ownership of City Stores in November 1979. Jack Farber, president of PII, became chairman of City Stores and was elected CEO in February 1980. Farber closed or discontinued department store operations in 1982 and discontinued west coast operations of W & J Sloane. He sold a portion of W & J Sloane's Fifth Avenue real estate and refurbished the leased portion. The company rebounded from a net loss of $15.9 million in 1981 to a net income of $5.6 million in 1982 due to the sale of real estate, savings from discontinued operations, and a $3.8 million credit from the early payment of long-term debt. In 1984 Farber discontinued some retail operations of W & J Sloane and sold remaining operations to R.B. Furniture. The sale of related real estate and assets, as well as the sale of the Lit Bros. downtown Philadelphia store, which net the company $5 million, provided funds to pay debt and for new acquisitions.

City Stores acquired a 27 percent interest in Seligman & Latz (S&L) in 1984 and 1985 in anticipation of a merger. In addition to the Adrian Arpel cosmetics division, S&L operated nearly 1,000 beauty salons at department stores in the United States and Europe and 400 fine jewelry stores in national department store chains. The merger never transpired as S&L did not meet a number of requirements in the agreement, including goals to improve earnings. City Stores sold its interest in S&L and Farber pursued a series of acquisitions that permanently changed the nature of the company, renamed CSS Industries in 1985.

A New Company with a New Name in 1985

Under Farber CSS Industries developed into a diversified company through the acquisition of established businesses. CSS completed its first acquisition in January 1985 with the purchase of an 86 percent interest in Rapidforms, Inc. of Bellman, New Jersey, from PII for $8 million, including $5 million in convertible preferred stock. Rapidforms designed and manufactured a variety of business forms, with many customers placing orders with their names and addresses printed on the forms. Rapidforms sold office supplies and business forms to manufacturers, wholesalers, retailers, and small businesses nationwide through direct mail catalogs and brochures. In 1986 Rapidforms acquired Russell and Miller, a direct mail distributor of printed paper products, for $3.3 million in cash and consolidated Russell and Miller's Seattle and Los Angeles operations at Los Angeles for cost efficiency.

With the $12.1 million acquisition of Ellisco Co. from PII in 1986, CSS Industries diversified into another area of business. Ellisco manufactured metal containers in standard forms, such as for paint, shoe polish, and food cans, and specialized in the manufacture of metal containers in accordance with customer specifications. The company served small- to medium-sized companies in the United States and Canada and obtained approximately 12 percent of its business from the U.S. government and government agencies. Ellisco's manufacturing locations included sites in Pennsylvania, Maryland, Ohio, and West Virginia. Ellisco also distributed metal and plastic containers manufactured by other companies.

With new acquisitions and internal improvements, sales and net income at CSS continued to grow. In 1986 sales reached $33 million with net income of $4 million. In 1987 sales at Rapidforms increased 40 percent, with 18 percent of the increase originating from the first full year of operations at Russell and Miller under CSS ownership. Overall sales increased 74 percent to $58.8 million, with 58 percent of the increase resulting from acquisitions in 1986. Net income reached $6.3 million in 1987. With the company operating profitably CSS continued to diversify as well as to expand within existing industry groups.

CSS added gift wrap and related products to its line of businesses with the 1988 acquisition of Paper Magic Group. CSS purchased the company for $38 million, acquiring all of the preferred stock and 84.5 percent of the common stock. Paper Magic designed, manufactured, and distributed seasonal and everyday paper products for gift giving and holiday celebrations. Christmas products included gift tags, folded gift boxes, ribbon and bows, and boxed Christmas cards. In addition to seasonal wall and table decorations, the company produced Valentine cards for classroom exchange, everyday greeting cards, stationery supplies, and elementary school supplies. Paper Magic distributed its products under the Artis, Eureka, and Grand Award brands. The company also obtained licenses to produce certain products with imprints of known cartoon characters, including Care Bears, Teenage Mutant Ninja Turtles, and Walt Disney characters.

CSS's other subsidiaries expanded through acquisition. Rapidforms purchased a 75 percent interest in Standard Forms Inc., with printing and distribution operations in Ramsey, England and Le Havre, France. Ellisco acquired the Penn Corp. & Closures, Inc. and Wheeling Closure Corp. for $4.7 million in 1988, followed by the 1990 acquisition of Ballonoff Home Products for $4 million cash in 1990. CSS recorded sales of $159 million in 1990 and net income of $18 million.

CSS continued to grow through acquisition of companies related to its existing areas of operations. Paper Magic acquired Spearhead Industries for $14.8 million in 1991. Based in Eden Prairie, Minnesota, Spearhead was involved primarily in the creation and distribution of Halloween masks, costumes, makeup, and novelties as well as Easter products, such as egg dye kits. Acquisitions by Ellisco included certain assets International Machine and Toll Works and certain assets of Atlantic Cheinco Corp. CSS sold some assets of the latter, resulting in more than $700,000 in profit from the sale.

After Farber merged PII into CSS in 1993, CSS continued to buy and sell businesses and business assets, which eventually settled into two operating divisions, the Consumer Products Group and the Direct Mail Business Products Group. Acquisitions by Rapidforms included particular assets of the Business Envelope Manufacturers and all assets of the Histacount Corporation. Ellisco discontinued its line of can products with the sale of related equipment and inventory. CSS sold the subsidiary to U.S. Can in 1994 for $34 million, providing funds to further existing operations. In 1993 CSS acquired Berwick Industries, Inc., a ribbon and bow manufacturer whose customers included mass merchants, drug store chains, and wholesale floral, craft, and paper markets. Although under financial and managerial duress, CSS stabilized operations at Berwick while being integrated into Paper Magic. CSS added to its line of Halloween products in 1995 with the purchase of certain assets of Topstone Industries and Illusive Concepts; the latter specialized in crafted Halloween masks.

CSS took a major step toward expansion in the field of gift wrap and accessories in 1995 when Paper Magic acquired Cleo, Inc., a leading manufacturer of gift wrap and trim, primarily for the Christmas season. CSS acquired the company at below net book value, for $133 million, including $108.5 million in cash and the balance in a short-term promissory note. Although Cleo's revenues reached $189 million in 1995, the company had operated at a loss for several years. CSS closed five of Cleo's six manufacturing and packaging plants and four of five warehouses and merged production into Paper Magic and Berwick operations. It was after the acquisition of Cleo that CSS organized its subsidiaries into two divisions, the Consumer Products Group and the Direct Mail Business Products Group.

Social Expressions the Company's Focus in the Late 1990s

The Consumer Products Group emerged as CSS's primary focus of operations. In January 1997 Paper Magic acquired Color Clings Inc., designer, manufacturer, and distributor of vinyl home decorations to mass market merchants in the United States and Canada. Sales at Color Clings reached $30 million in 1996. Rapidforms sold its European operations early in 1997 and, in December, CSS sold the Direct Mail Business Products Group for $84.6 million. With a 90 percent ownership in Rapidforms, the ensuing transactions garnered net cash proceeds, after taxes, of approximately $60 million.

CSS instituted a restructuring program in 1997 that involved the sale of real estate, the discontinuation of poorly performing product lines, and integration of certain functions of Berwick and Paper Magic. The sale of inadequately used facilities resulted in net proceeds of $17.3 million in 1998, while the discontinuation of some product lines resulted in a two percent decline in sales, from $400.6 million in 1998 to $392.6 million. The plan to combine Berwick and Paper Magic failed to obtain expected cost or operational efficiency and the company returned to a decentralized structure with new leadership.

CSS divided its product lines into four groups. The Paper Magic Group—Fall Spring and Everyday Product Division, located in Minnesota, encompassed products for Halloween, Easter, and everyday occasions. The Paper Magic Group—Winter Product Division, based in Scranton, Pennsylvania, focused primarily on boxed Christmas cards, gift tags, and children's Valentine exchange cards. Cleo, Inc., in Memphis, concerned itself with Christmas gift wrap and gift bags, and Berwick Industries, Inc. continued to manufacture ribbon and bows. The company also created a new position, corporate vice-president of licensing. David Erskine was named CEO and president in 1999, replacing Jack Farber, who remained as Chairman of the Board.

CSS continued to develop and expand its seasonal product lines in 1999. New Easter egg decorating kits included a speckle kit and decoupage kit with flowers and stripes. In August 1999 CSS acquired Party Professionals Inc., designer and distributor of elaborately crafted latex masks and related costumes and accessories marketed under two brand names, Don Post Studios and The Great Coverup. The company's customer list consisted of party and specialty stores and sales ranged from $5 million to $6 million per year. Paper Magic introduced a new line of boxed Christmas cards called Pine Hollow. The upscale look of the cards featured holographic trim and unusual embossing. The success of the line led to the development of a gift wrap line for Christmas 2000. CSS also planned a line of photographic cards, Holiday Images, and a line of inspirational cards, called Joyful Greetings.

Principal Subsidiaries

Berwick Industries LLC; Cleo, Inc.; The Paper Magic Group, Inc.

Principal Competitors

American Greetings Corporation; CPS Corporation; CTI Industries Corporation; Delaware Ribbon Manufacturers, Inc.; Disguise, Inc.; Equality Specialties, Inc., Fun World, Inc.; Jean Marie Creations, Inc.; Hallmark Cards, Inc.; Hollywood Ribbon, Inc.; Rubie's Costume Co., Inc.; Signature Brands, LLC.

Further Reading

Autry, Ret, "CSS Industries Inc.," *Fortune,* April 8, 1991, p. 82.
"Berwick Industries, Inc.," *Textile World,* August 1993, p. 10.
Briggs, Rosland, "Philadelphia Holiday Goods Firm Awaits Christmas Boost," *Knight-Ridder/Tribune Business News,* October 26, 1998.
"CSS Elects David J.M. Erskine as President and Chief Executive Officer," *Business Wire,* May 13, 1999, p. 1550.
"CSS Industries Inc.," *Philadelphia Business Journal,* December 3, 1990, p. 24.
"CSS Industries Inc.," *Philadelphia Business Journal,* October 21, 1991, p. 35.
"CSS Industries, Inc. Acquires Party Professionals," *Business Wire,* August 18, 1999, p. 1454.
"CSS Industries, Inc. Announces Organizational Changes," *Business Wire,* November 4, 1999, p. 1648.
"CSS Industries Inc.: Company Agrees on Merger with Philadelphia Industries," *Wall Street Journal,* October 28, 1992, p. B4.
"CSS Industries Inc.: Gibson Greetings Cleo Unit Agrees To Be Purchased," *Wall Street Journal,* October 4, 1995, p. B4.
"CSS Industries To Buy Ellisco," *Wall Street Journal,* August 15, 1986, p. 1.
Hendrickson, Robert, *The Grand Emporiums: The Illustrated History of America's Great Department Stores,* New York: Stein and Day, 1979.
"The Low-Risk Way To Play Volatile Small Stocks," *Money,* April 1993, p. 80.
Nulty, Peter, "CSS Industries Inc.," *Fortune,* August 17, 1987, p. 86.

—Mary Tradii

Curtiss-Wright Corporation

1200 Wall Street West
Lyndhurst, New Jersey 07071
U.S.A.
Telephone: (201) 896-8400
Fax: (201) 438-5680
Web site: http://www.curtisswright.com

Public Company
Incorporated: 1929
Employees: 2,300
Sales: $293.26 million (1999)
Stock Exchanges: New York
Ticker Symbol: CW
NAIC: 333995 Fluid Power Cylinder and Actuator Manufacturing; 332811 Metal Heat Treating; 332912 Fluid Power Valve and Hose Fitting Manufacturing; 331491 Nonferrous Metal (Except Copper and Aluminum) Rolling, Drawing, and Extruding

The Curtiss-Wright Corporation (CWC), built on two of the most esteemed names in American aviation history, has evolved from an aircraft manufacturer to a highly diversified conglomerate to a focused engineering firm. Through its Motion Control segment, CWC literally opens doors (and drops flaps) for commercial and military aircraft makers. Metal Treatment makes aircraft wings stronger, and Flow Control produces valves for nuclear submarines and power plants. The company also makes a tool for freeing accident victims from automobile wreckage, and it has made a number of acquisitions to expand its markets and acquire related technologies.

Lofty Origins

Curtiss-Wright Corporation (CWC) was formed in 1929 as a publicly listed holding company for a variety of aviation concerns, when the Curtiss Aeroplane and Motor Corporation and Wright Aeronautical Corporation merged, bringing together 18 affiliated companies and 29 subsidiaries. Bankers had tried for years to bring together the two rival companies, started by aviation pioneers and inventors Orville and Wilbur Wright and Glenn H. Curtiss, and the merger finally put an end to two decades of patent battles between the Wright brothers and Curtiss. Hailed upon its formation by Wall Street financiers as the world's most prodigious aviation concern, the company debuted with total assets of more than $70 million and stock valued at $220 million as it entered an industry battle with the recently created United Aircraft and Transportation Company.

Although its namesakes had little to do with the creation of the new firm, Glenn Curtiss did serve as a member of the company's technical committee prior to his death in 1930, the year the Curtiss Condor—a civilian version of a two-engine bomber plane—was being introduced by some airlines. The Curtiss-Wright Corporation maintained a position of preeminence in aeronautics throughout the 1930s, although the aviation industry remained relatively small and the firm's sales had reached only $49 million by 1939.

In 1940, the company created the Curtiss Propeller Division, a forerunner of the subsidiary Curtiss-Wright Flight Systems, Inc. Serving as a core source of government work after the United States entered World War II, Curtiss Propeller Division became one of the single largest defense contractors in the world. During the war, the company employed 180,000 workers and produced 146,000 aircraft propellers, 143,000 airplane engines, and more than 26,000 planes as Curtiss-Wright became the second largest manufacturer in the United States with annual sales surpassing $1 billion two years running. Curtiss-Wright engines powered the majority of American planes flown in World War II, including the B-29 that dropped the first atomic bomb on Japan and precipitated the close of the global conflict.

Postwar Diversification

After the war, Curtiss-Wright was forced to deal with a rapid decline in military contracts, and enormous operational cutbacks were made as the company began converting military aircraft engines for use in commercial airliners. In 1949, Guy Vaughan, who had long directed the company's operations, was ousted in a management shake-up and replaced by Roy T. Hurley, who became president and chairperson. Hurley brought a reputation as a production cost-cutter to Curtiss-Wright, having served as a vice-president of production at Bendix Aviation Corporation and a director of manufacturing at Ford Motor Company.

With the United States' involvement in the Korean War during the early 1950s the company again benefited from a new round of government contracts for aircraft engines. As a result, Curtiss-Wright remained among the top ten U.S. defense contractors during the first half of the decade, producing ram-jet engines for guided missiles, aircraft engines and propellers, and flight simulators for the military.

During this time, Hurley initiated a massive diversification drive, beginning in 1951 when Curtiss-Wright acquired a plant in Buffalo, New York, where it began a specialized metal extrusion business. The company also purchased another plant in Carlstadt, New Jersey, to serve as foundation for a new electronics division. During the mid-1950s Curtiss-Wright entered the Canadian market with the creation of the subsidiary Curtiss-Wright of Canada Ltd. (later renamed Canadian Curtiss-Wright). The company also established a scientific products and research division and began construction of a research and development center at Quehanna, Pennsylvania, where it established a nuclear materials laboratory to support defense and peacetime applications of atomic energy.

By the end of 1955, Hurley's diversification drive had helped propel Curtiss-Wright's annual sales from $475 million a year to more than $500 million, with commercial sales generating about 40 percent of the company's income. By 1956, Curtiss-Wright had 16 divisions, and the company's stock had risen to a high of 49⅜.

Curtiss-Wright utilized acquisitions and joint developments with other companies to bolster its engine business, acquiring Propulsion Research Corporation and Turbomotor Associates. The company began developing engines in the low- to medium-range power categories for aircraft, helicopters, and missiles. Curtiss-Wright also teamed up with Bristol Aeroplane Company to develop a series of commercial engines. The company's military engine production continued to consist primarily of the J-65, initially licensed from Great Britain, and its principal commercial product was the 3350 Turbo Compound piston engine, used in the fastest commercial propeller airliners of the day.

In 1956, Curtiss-Wright agreed to loan $35 million to financially troubled Studebaker-Packard and provide management services for the automaker. In return, Studebaker-Packard sold Curtiss-Wright its subsidiary, Aerophysics Development Corporation, and leased the aviation concern its facilities in Utica, Michigan, and South Bend, Indiana, where Curtiss-Wright began producing the army's new Dart anti-tank missile, which Aerophysics Development had helped to develop.

The following year, Studebaker-Packard received the rights to manufacture the Daimler-Benz engine from Germany's Mercedes-Benz in exchange for allowing the German automaker to produce a Curtiss-Wright plane. After two years of managing Studebaker-Packard, Curtiss-Wright terminated its management contract with the automaker and acquired the South Bend and Utica plants it had been leasing as well as the rights to manufacture and sell Daimler-Benz's diesel and multifuel engines, fuel injection systems, military vehicles, and buses.

By 1957, about two-thirds of Curtiss-Wright's sales were from government contracts and about two-thirds of its profits stemmed from nonmilitary sales. Seeking to widen its commercial activities and steer clear of government contracts, the company focused on the development of ultrasonic equipment, new products for its Buffalo extrusion business, and new uses for its plastic material, Curon, which had applications as apparel lining, wall and floor coverings, soundproofing, upholstery, auto trim, and cushions.

In 1958, Curtiss-Wright began operating a nuclear research reactor at its Quehanna facility. The company also established a solar research laboratory in conjunction with New York University, resulting in an agreement with Hupp Corporation to jointly explore, develop, and sell devices in the solar energy field, including heat storage and cooking devices. In 1959, Curtiss-Wright also began producing industrial x-ray inspection equipment, which was added to the firm's lines of quality control equipment, inspection equipment, and measurement systems using ultrasonic, radiographic, and nuclear energy technologies. During this time, Curtiss-Wright entered the earth-moving business with the acquisition of a Continental Copper & Steel Industries division that manufactured such equipment.

Curtiss-Wright's experimental developments included a coal-based blacktop road paving material and an "air car" that could travel six to 12 inches above ground, as well as a lightweight internal combustion engine with only two main moving parts. The rotary engine, which became known as the Wankel, was designed to burn gasoline in such a way as to turn a triangular shaped rotor, rather than driving pistons up and down like conventional piston engines. Developed in conjunction with NSU Werke of West Germany, the engine—for which Curtiss-Wright attained exclusive world rights for aircraft uses and exclusive North American rights for all applications—stemmed from an invention by the German firm's Felix Wankel.

A Management Flap in the 1960s

A series of defense cutbacks during the late 1950s hurt Curtiss-Wright's ramjet development business, and the company's earnings began to decline, falling from $25 million in 1958 to $14.3 million in 1959 as sales dropped from $388 to $329

Key Dates:

1929: Curtiss Aeroplane and Motor Corporation merges with Wright Aeronautical Corporation.
1945: World War II lifts annual sales past $1 billion.
1951: Lead by Roy Hurley, CWC begins massive diversification drive.
1960: New chairman Roland Berner orders sale of several divisions.
1967: CWC drops jet engine business in favor of flap actuation systems and metal treatment.
1972: Excitement over CWC's Wankel rotary engine sends stock skyward.
1978: CWC attempts hostile takeover of copper giant Kennecott Corporation.
1981: Truce between CWC and Kennecott leaves Teledyne with 50 percent control of CWC.
1993: CWC attempts to sell three of four divisions but finds no suitable buyers.
1995: CWC opens a European Flight Systems subsidiary and expands overhaul business.
1998: New acquisitions and long-term airliner contracts brighten CWC's outlook.

million. In April 1960 Hurley was confronted by a hostile crowd at the firm's annual meeting and faced criticism over falling earnings, reduced dividends, high officer compensation, and insufficient information regarding the company's experimental developments. Hurley resigned as president and chairperson one month later and was replaced by one of his more vocal critics, T. Roland Berner. An attorney who had become a director at Curtiss-Wright after leading a nearly successful proxy battle against management in 1948, Berner had been instrumental in the 1949 shake-up that initially brought Hurley to power.

Berner quickly divested Curtiss-Wright of several divisions. The company donated its nuclear reactor to Pennsylvania State University and sold its South Bend and Utica facilities, Curon plastics business, West Coast research facilities, and its process for producing paving material from coal. Furthermore, the company's plant in Lawrence, New Jersey, which had been making ultrasonics as well as quality control and testing equipment, was closed, plans for commercial production of the air car were dropped, and operations at Quehanna ceased.

Seeking to return Curtiss-Wright to the status of a leading aircraft engine manufacturer, Berner shifted the firm's emphasis to defense and electronics products. During the early 1960s, Curtiss-Wright landed Air Force contracts for propellers, missile parts, and the modernization of the J-65 engine and began producing steel rocket casings for solid-fuel boosters for Titan III space launch vehicles. During the same period, Curtiss-Wright's electronics business was expanded through the acquisition of companies engaged in the manufacture of radar cameras and automatic timing controls for aircraft and missiles, as well as the manufacture of printed circuit board connectors for aircraft, missile, and computer applications.

Curtiss-Wright also expanded its activities in nuclear fields with the acquisition of an interest—and eventual complete control of—Target Rock Corporation, a manufacturer of hydraulic components and nuclear equipment. Curtiss-Wright also broadened its Canadian operations with the acquisition of companies engaged in the production of hydraulic equipment for oil companies and steel products for the building and mining industries.

In 1962, the company received a Federal Aviation Agency (FAA) contract to study compressor, turbine, and computer technologies for supersonic transport jet engines and began competing for a major government contract to develop and produce a supersonic commercial airliner engine. During the mid-1960s, the company sold its electronic fittings and components division at a time when it was plowing about $15 million of its own funds into the development of a supersonic transport plane engine.

Curtiss-Wright lost its bid to produce the supersonic engine, and, by 1967, the company had abandoned Berner's goal to build complete aircraft engines, opting to become a first-tier supplier, or subcontractor, for other companies involved in aerospace and other fields. By that time, when Curtiss-Wright landed a Boeing contract to provide flight actuators to extend and retract flaps on the wings of the giant Boeing 747 jet airliner, its "power hinge" mechanics were already in use on a North American Aviation supersonic research plane, a General Dynamic's fighter bomber, and a Boeing helicopter. Curtiss-Wright's relations with governmental and commercial customers continued to improve, and, by the late 1960s, Curtiss-Wright was supplying components for Lockheed's air bus and military transport plane and had become for many aerospace firms a preferred supplier of components for jet engines, helicopters, and aircraft, as well as a supplier of nuclear equipment and high-precision products for firms in nonaerospace industrial fields.

In 1968, Curtiss-Wright began an expansion program at its Buffalo extrusion facility, adding new forging and machining equipment for building aircraft and aerospace components. That year, the company acquired Metal Improvement Company, Inc. (MIC), an industry leader in shot peening technology used to create aerodynamic curvatures in aircraft and other products. The company's operations also were expanded through acquisitions of domestic companies involved in the production of aircraft wing ribs and airframe parts and a Canadian manufacturer of metal-working equipment and supplies for the steel processing industry. In 1969, Curtiss-Wright acquired a majority interest in Dorr-Oliver Inc., an engineering firm that made mechanized equipment for airline cargo terminals; Curtiss-Wright eventually acquired complete control of Dorr-Oliver.

Curtiss-Wright entered the 1970s as a producer of components or systems for all new wide-bodied commercial jet airliners and most jet planes, at a time when cutbacks in defense and military spending resulted in fewer government contracts. When automakers and other firms began showing a growing interest in the Wankel rotary engine, Curtiss-Wright began extending licensing agreements for the engine. In 1970, General Motors Corporation (GM) paid $50 million to acquire a five-year nonexclusive license to develop and manufacture the rotary combustion engine in North America. Subsequent license agreements called for royalty payments to Curtiss-Wright for all sales of Wankel engines in addition to a licensing fee. Speculation on the potential for the development of the smaller, lighter, and more powerful Wankel intensified. By 1972, Wankel had become one of the hottest names on Wall Street, and Curtiss-Wright's stock was one of the most volatile and actively traded.

In 1972, Curtiss-Wright granted Wankel development licenses to Brunswick Corporation, a manufacturer of the Mercury line of outboard motors, and Ingersoll-Rand Company, for use in that firm's compressor, pump, and electric generator assemblies. The following year, American Motors Corporation became Curtiss-Wright's seventh Wankel licensee, about the same time that GM announced it would introduce the rotary engine in its 1975 Vega model. GM soon renegotiated its payment agreement with Curtiss-Wright, however, after indefinitely postponing the debut of the Wankel in its vehicles, citing emissions and gas mileage difficulties as motivating factors.

Takeover Battles of the 1970s

As interest in the Wankel declined, because of hydrocarbon emissions concerns, Curtiss-Wright began acquiring the stock of Cenco Inc., a maker of pollution-control equipment and medical supplies and an operator of nursing homes and hospitals. By July 1975, Curtiss-Wright had acquired 16 percent of Cenco's stock. Upon learning that Cenco was entangled in allegations of fraudulent auditors reports and was on the verge of bankruptcy, Curtiss-Wright took control of the firm and placed Shirley D. Brinsfield, president of Dorr-Oliver, as Cenco chairperson. During this time, Teledyne Inc., a diversified firm with interests in electronic and aviation control systems and insurance, began acquiring Curtiss-Wright stock, and, by mid-1976, it held a 12 percent stake.

Also during this time, Curtiss-Wright was producing a wide range of military nuclear components, nuclear handling equipment, and nuclear systems devices, including special valves and regulators and seal weld fitting machines. The company also began actively developing turbine-powered generators, which were sold both domestically and internationally.

In 1978, Berner launched a proxy challenge to gain control of Kennecott Corporation, the nation's largest copper company. Having already acquired a 9.9 percent interest in the mining concern, Berner charged that Kennecott had wasted assets in its $567 million acquisition of the Carborundum Company, and he proposed a dissident slate of directors committed to selling Carborundum and distributing the proceeds among shareholders, including Curtiss-Wright. Kennecott's directors narrowly won the election, but a federal judge ordered a second vote. To stave off a rerun election, Kennecott convinced Thomas D. Barrow, an Exxon Corporation senior executive, to take control of the copper company, and within two weeks Barrow and Berner had agreed to a new Kennecott board, which would serve through the spring of 1981 and would give Berner's faction a voice in the mining firm's affairs.

Over the next two years, Curtiss-Wright boosted to more than 22 percent its stake in Lynch Corporation, a manufacturer of glass-forming machinery and flow instruments that Curtiss-Wright had controlled for about 15 years. Curtiss-Wright also entered the heat treating market in 1980 with the acquisition of Diebel Heat Treating Company, serving the automotive, oil exploration, and agricultural equipment markets.

By November 1980, Curtiss-Wright had increased its stake in Kennecott to 14.3 percent, and its truce with the company was about to expire. Consequently, the copper company made a bid to acquire Curtiss-Wright, setting off a second round of corporate warfare. Curtiss-Wright responded to the Kennecott threat by initiating a buyback of its own stock to block takeover attempts, spurring a Kennecott offer to buy up Curtiss-Wright's outstanding stock. As a result, Kennecott acquired nearly 32 percent of Curtiss-Wright and surpassed Teledyne as the largest Curtiss-Wright stockholder, though falling short of its objective for majority control. In January 1981, Kennecott and Curtiss-Wright signed a ten-year truce agreement and Curtiss-Wright sold Kennecott its Dorr-Oliver subsidiary and its shares of Kennecott stock; in return, Kennecott gave Curtiss-Wright $168 million and the shares of Curtiss-Wright it held, which, along with stock tendered in Curtiss-Wright's self-buyback, helped give Teledyne more than 50 percent control of Curtiss-Wright.

Reconfiguring in the 1980s and 1990s

Curtiss-Wright's sale of Cenco—resulting in $9.8 million in earnings—along with a $52 million gain from the sale of Dorr-Oliver and Kennecott shares helped push Curtiss-Wright's 1981 earnings to $85 million. Next, the company began investing in Western Union Corporation, acquiring a 21.6 percent stake in the telecommunications concern. This investment proved unsuccessful, however; Curtiss-Wright lost $42 million on the company, and as its 1984 total earnings plunged to $1.9 million—down from $18.5 million a year earlier—the company sold its stake in Western Union. Also during this time, Curtiss-Wright abandoned its hopes for the Wankel, selling its rotary combustion engine business to Deere & Company after failing to discover a commercial application for the engines.

In 1986, Curtiss-Wright received an Air Force contract in excess of $40 million to provide wing-flap actuators for the F-16, leading to ongoing F-16 actuator business. The following year, Curtiss-Wright was forced to fire several Target Rock senior executives after discovering an embezzlement scheme that resulted in the indictment of several former employees and suppliers. Considered a victim of the embezzlements, Curtiss-Wright was not charged with criminal misconduct in the matter, although in 1990 the government initiated litigation against Target Rock Corporation related to embezzlements by former Target Rock officials and their alleged mischarging of government subcontracts.

During the late 1980s, Curtiss-Wright's sales and income remained fairly stable, fluctuating between $21 million and $28 million in earnings and $188 million and $212 million in sales. In 1990, the company's revenues climbed to $214 million while earnings sank to $6.8 million, in large part due to a $13.8 million after-tax environmental charge related to soil and ground water contamination at the company's former Wood-Ridge facility. Over the next two years, however, earnings rebounded to more than $21 million.

In March 1990, Berner died and was succeeded by Shirley D. Brinsfield, an outside director and former chairperson of Cenco who pledged to focus Curtiss-Wright's operations on manufacturing rather than investments. Charles E. Ehinger was elected president and Berner's son, Thomas R. Berner, was elected to the company's board. Less than four months after Berner's death, Curtiss-Wright declared a special dividend of $30 a share. The primary beneficiaries were Unitrin Inc., an insurance company once owned by Teledyne with a 44 percent interest in Curtiss-Wright, and Argonaut Group (formerly owned by Teledyne) with an eight percent interest.

In July 1991, Ehinger resigned as president and Brinsfield assumed the duties of president. Curtiss-Wright sold the engine distribution business of its Canadian subsidiary and discontinued its remaining Canadian operations soon thereafter.

In early 1993, Curtiss-Wright announced that it would explore the sale of three of its four business units, including Metal Improvement Company, its Flight Systems Group, and its Buffalo Extrusion Facility. In May 1993, Curtiss-Wright's presidency was turned over to David Lasky, a former senior vice-president, and, two months later, Curtiss-Wright abandoned attempts to sell its Flight Systems subsidiaries, as offers did not meet expectations. By October, Curtiss-Wright had reached an agreement to sell its extrusion business, while depressed conditions in the commercial and military aerospace markets led the firm to abandon the sale of MIC, which had garnered less than favorable offers. At the end of the year, Curtiss Wright's Target Rock subsidiary agreed to pay the government $17.5 million to settle remaining litigation. The Target Rock settlement, coupled with environmental clean-up charges, contributed to an annual loss of $5.6 million on declining sales of $158.9 million.

Curtiss-Wright entered 1994 seeking expanded commercial markets in the area of pollution control, for which its electronic control valves were well suited. The company faced cutbacks in the production of commercial aircraft, a reduction in pricing levels and Air Force procurement of the Lockheed F-16 fighter plane, the termination of valve orders for the Navy's Seawolf program, and reduced production activity in the Navy's nuclear program. The future of Curtiss-Wright, which abandoned the sale of its subsidiaries in 1993 in favor of optimum shareholder value, appeared contingent on both the economics of the company's traditional markets and the company's success in broaching new markets. The company's future also seemed dependent on its ability and desire to maintain its business units under the Curtiss-Wright name in an era of increasing consolidation and cutbacks in the defense and aerospace industries.

Climbing into 2000

After losing $5.6 million in 1993, CWC posted net earnings of $19 million on total revenues of $166 million in 1994. These figures remained flat for 1995. At the time, government contracts accounted for about 35 percent of the company's business. Military cutbacks, primarily for the F-16 program and military valves, affected the Aerospace and Marine segments. The company also weathered development costs relating to the new Lockheed-Martin F-22, McDonnell Douglas F/A-18 E/F, and Bell Boeing V-22 Osprey programs. It also supplied Sikorsky Black Hawk and Seahawk military helicopters.

CWC won some contracts for which it was not the original supplier, as in several lines of Boeing aircraft, while its Metal Improvement Company subsidiary supplied peen-forming services for Airbus and McDonnell Douglas. CWC sold its Buffalo

Extrusion Facility in June 1995. In spite of cost overruns for commercial nuclear valves, the industrial segment showed improvement.

A European subsidiary, Curtiss-Wright Flight Systems/Europe, opened in 1995. Overseas business, growing significantly, accounted for 18 percent of sales and 34 percent of profits in 1996. The company also opened shot-peening facilities in Belgium and Germany. CWC expanded its overhaul and repair business, capitalizing on the trend of airlines keeping planes in service longer. It bought Aviall, Inc.'s Miami-based Accessory Service unit for about $17 million. The company doubled the capacity of its aerospace plant in Shelby, North Carolina.

Sales were $219 million in 1997 and $249 million in 1998. The company announced another ten-year contract with British Aerospace Airbus for treating the metal surfaces of wings. At home, the company consolidated its actuation system operations at its Shelby plant due to military cutbacks, while the plant in Fairfield, New Jersey continued to handle management, engineering, and testing for military programs.

Boeing announced a slowdown in production in late 1998. CWC predicted little immediate fallout, however, and the company soon announced a new eight-year agreement for flight control systems with Boeing. It also was invited to equip two prototypes in Boeing's Unmanned Combat Air Vehicle program. Within months, CWC announced a ten-year contract to provide shot-peening metal treatments for the Bell Boeing V-22 Osprey tiltrotor aircraft and its commercial derivative. (It also joined Milwaukee Electric Tool Corporation in a rescue tool venture.)

Government contracts averaged less than 20 percent of sales in the late 1990s as CWC sought out new technologies and markets. Curtiss-Wright Flight Systems acquired SIG-Antriebstechnik GmbH, the drive technology unit of SIG Swiss Industrial Company Group, in early 1999. Its products were used mainly in commercial marine craft, high-speed trains, and military vehicles. In June, CWC acquired Metallurgical Processing, an automotive and industrial heat-treating company based in Fort Wayne, Indiana. The next month, it bought flow control business from Teledyne Fluid Systems.

Annual sales, at $293 million, were up 18 percent in 1999. Net earnings rose nearly 30 percent to $39 million. Motion Control sales rose 18 percent to $124 million, primarily due to the Drive Technology acquisition and a surge in commercial aircraft production at Boeing. After a banner year in 1998, Metal Treatment sales slipped a bit to $106 million. CWC's Flow Control segment showed the greatest improvement, with sales jumping 71 percent to $65 million.

Forbes named Curtiss-Wright Corporation one of America's 200 best small companies in 1999. David Lasky retired in April 2000 and was succeeded by Martin R. Benante as CEO and chairman. Lasky had been with the company 38 years; Benante had joined in 1978.

Principal Subsidiaries

Curtiss-Wright Flight Systems Inc.; Metal Improvement Company Inc.; Curtiss-Wright Flow Control Corporation; Curtiss-

Wright Flow Control Service Corporation; Curtiss-Wright Flow Control Company Canada; Curtiss-Wright Flight Systems Europe A/S (Denmark); Curtiss-Wright Foreign Sales Corp. (Barbados); Curtiss-Wright Antriebstechnik GmbH (Switzerland).

Principal Divisions

Motion Control; Metal Treatment; Flow Control.

Principal Competitors

Parker Hannifin Corp.; Aeroquip-Vickers Inc.; Telair International Inc.; Rexroth Corp.

Further Reading

Carley, William M., and Tim Metz, ''Proxy Pugilism: Curtiss-Wright's Bid for Kennecott Has David-Goliath Aspects,'' *Wall Street Journal,* April 18, 1978, pp. 1, 39.

Combs, Harry, and Martin Caidin, *Kill Devil Hill: Discovering the Secret of the Wright Brothers,* Boston: Houghton Mifflin, 1979; Englewood, Colo.: TernStyle, 1986.

''Curtiss-Wright Engine Has Only 2 Moving Parts,'' *Wall Street Journal,* November 24, 1959, p. 4.

''Curtiss-Wright Redefines Itself,'' *Aerospace Daily,* December 10, 1998, p. 388.

''Curtiss-Wright Sees Its Earnings Growth Continuing This Year,'' *Wall Street Journal,* February 18, 1969, p. 8.

''Curtiss-Wright, Studebaker-Packard Paths Marked by Mergers in Plane, Auto Fields,'' *Wall Street Journal,* August 6, 1956, p. 4.

Eltscher, Louis R., and Edward M. Young, *Curtiss-Wright: Greatness and Decline,* New York: Twayne, 1998.

''Facing Reality,'' *Forbes,* November 15, 1967, pp. 24–25.

''Hurley Gives Up Curtiss-Wright Posts; Berner, a Director, Is Named Chairman,'' *Wall Street Journal,* May 26, 1960, p. 9.

''Kennecott and Curtiss-Wright End Corporate Battle by Agreeing to 10-Year Truce Involving $280 Million,'' *Wall Street Journal,* January 29, 1981, p. 3.

Lee, Loyd E., review of *Curtiss-Wright: Greatness and Decline,* by Louis R. Eltscher and Edward M. Young, in *Business History Review,* Autumn 1999, pp. 533–35.

Lavelle, Louis, ''Curtiss-Wright To Lay Off 90 Employees from Essex County, NJ Plant,'' *The Record* (Hackensack, New Jersey), November 19, 1998.

Lenckus, Dave, ''Benefit Termination Not Unlawful: Ruling,'' *Business Insurance,* May 18, 1998, pp. 3f.

Martin, Richard, ''Wondrous Wankel: Engine Not Only Drives Vehicles, But It Also Puts Stocks into Orbit,'' *Wall Street Journal,* June 16, 1972, pp. 1, 25.

Shao, Maria, ''Kennecott's Battle with Curtiss-Wright Involves Ambitions, Strategies and Money,'' *Wall Street Journal,* January 5, 1981, p. 19.

Stevens, Charles W., ''Curtiss-Wright Picks Top Officers After Berner Death,'' *Wall Street Journal,* March 23, 1990, p. C18.

Tannenbaum, Jeffrey A., ''Curtiss-Wright Slates Payout of $30 a Share,'' *Wall Street Journal,* July 13, 1990, p. C9.

''The Well-Deserved Decline of Curtiss-Wright,'' *Forbes,* November 15, 1967, pp. 24–26.

—Roger W. Rouland
—updated by Frederick C. Ingram

INVESTMENT SERVICES

INVESTMENT BANKING

Dain Rauscher Corporation

Dain Rauscher Plaza
60 South Sixth Street
Minneapolis, Minnesota 55402-4422
U.S.A.
Telephone: (612) 371-7750
Fax: (612) 371-7933
Web site: http://www.dainrauscher.com

Public Company
Incorporated: 1909 as Kalman & Co.
Employees: 3,700
Sales: $944 million (1999)
Stock Exchanges: New York
Ticker Symbol: DRC
NAIC: 52312 Securities Brokerage

Dain Rauscher Corporation, formerly known as Interra Financial and Inter-Regional Financial Group briefly before that, is a full-service regional brokerage and investment banking company through its subsidiaries Dain Rauscher Inc. and Insight Investment Management Inc. The firm, the product of successive amalgamations of small midwestern brokerage firms, provides investment advice and services to individual investors primarily in the western United States, as well as investment banking services to corporate and government clients nationwide. In terms of its number of brokers, Dain Rauscher is the tenth largest brokerage in the United States.

Company Roots

Dain Rauscher's roots reach back to 1909, when Oscar Kalman started a small brokerage shop in St. Paul, Minnesota. The venture, dubbed Kalman & Co., began selling stocks and municipal bonds to local customers. Kalman's shop was just one of many brokerage businesses that opened in the United States during the early part of the century. In fact, a surging industrial base generated huge markets for stocks and bonds, particularly during the 1920s. Several of the companies created

to serve those markets would eventually be consolidated into the company that would become Dain Rauscher.

Kalman was the earliest of those companies. It was followed in 1916 by a Denver, Colorado, venture named Bosworth, Chanute, Loughridge & Co. That firm was formed by Arthur Bosworth, Octave Chanute, and Paul Loughridge. They created the company to take advantage of, and facilitate, municipal growth during a boom in Denver's economy. Other companies that would later join to form DRC included Quail & Co., which was founded in Davenport, Iowa, in 1922, and Sullivan & Co., another Denver firm that opened in 1927. However, J.M. Dain started the enterprise that would later be credited with engineering the amalgamation of a brokerage network in the western United States in 1929, shortly before the infamous stock market crash that triggered the Great Depression.

J.M. Dain had moved to Minneapolis in 1922 to represent a Chicago investment firm. In 1929 he decided to branch out on his own with J.M. Dain & Co., a municipal bond trading house. He hired a secretary and opened a small office in Minneapolis. His timing couldn't have been worse. The stock market crash and ensuing depression devastated financial markets. Despite tough times, Dain persevered and, unlike many of the more established trading houses, managed to survive. Another company that started and managed to survive during the Depression was an enterprise that would become Rauscher Pierce Refsnes. That venture would become Dain's sister firm in the 1970s.

Growth Through Acquisition: 1960s

Merrill Cohen took control of Dain & Co. in 1933 and helped steer it through the crisis and into the 1940s. Dain & Co.'s growth was relatively slow, but by the late 1950s the organization was employing 75 workers in eight offices. Dain began to expand much more quickly in the 1960s. That progress was largely the result of the efforts of Wheelock Whitney, who became chief executive of Dain in 1963. It was under his direction that Dain launched an aggressive growth and diversification drive. To that end, J.M. Dain & Co. merged with Kalman & Co. in 1967. Shortly thereafter the company purchased Quail & Co. The resultant organization became Dain, Kalman & Quail, Inc.

Company Perspectives:

PURPOSE: We are dedicated to helping our clients achieve their financial goals. VALUES: Clients first. Trust through integrity. Excellent service to clients and each other. Great people, working together to win. Leadership in our communities and industry. VISION: We aspire to be one of the top three performers in each of our chosen market niches.

In addition to the mergers, Dain launched a new real estate affiliate in 1968 (later called Dain Corporation). By the late 1960s Dain, Kalman, & Quail, Inc. was sporting 17 offices in six upper-midwestern and western states including the Dakotas and Wyoming. Its headquarter offices swelled to house 400 employees and the name of its office building, the Rand Tower, was changed to Dain Tower to reflect the prominence of its major tenant. More acquisitions ensued: J. Cliff Rahal & Co. in Nebraska in 1969; Minneapolis-based, Platt, Tschudy & Co. (the forerunner of Investment Advisers Inc.) in 1970; Woodward-Elwood, also of Minneapolis, and Ralph W. Davis of Chicago, both in 1972. By the close of 1972, Dain had become a public company through the sale of 250,000 shares on the New York Stock Exchange.

The IFG Years: 1973–97

In 1973, the company bought out Bosworth, Sullivan & Co., which was the successor to Bosworth, Chanute, Loughridge & Co. and Sullivan & Co. Inter-Regional Financial Group, Inc. (IFG) was then formed as a holding company that effectively existed to own the assets of the new acquisition and Dain, Kalman, & Quail, Inc. The two firms would operate as separate entities until 1979, when they were fused into Dain Bosworth Incorporated. Thus, Inter-Regional had become a major regional broker with offices in the Midwest and the western United States through Dain Bosworth.

As it labored to expand its sprawling brokerage network in the Western United States during the 1970s and early 1980s, IFG simultaneously stepped up its effort to diversify into new markets. Accordingly, the company launched a number of new ventures and initiatives. Besides its Dain Corporation real estate affiliate, IFG started an investment consulting business (Investment Advisers) and even purchased a life insurance company (Midwest Life), among other ventures. In the early 1980s it also laid plans to open up its own savings and loan business, although federal regulators ultimately thwarted that effort.

IFG took note of the synergies that existed between Dain and Rauscher Pierce Refsnes (RPR). Like Dain, RPR had its beginnings during the Depression era; it shared similar values for client service, integrity and quality; and the company had grown through acquisitions. By 1972, RPR occupied offices in Arizona, Colorado, Florida, Illinois, Missouri, New Mexico, New York, Oklahoma and Texas. In 1981, RPR and IFG executives met to explore working arrangements. With IFG's solid upper Midwest presence, an arrangement with RPR would allow it to expand into promising Southwest markets. In early 1982, an agreement was formalized. Rauscher Pierce Refsnes and Dain Bosworth became separate companies under IFG.

The merger allowed both companies to prosper. RPR added offices in lucrative San Antonio, Austin and Oklahoma City markets. New businesses were also added, such as Shatkin Lee Securities of St. Louis, the predecessor to RPR Clearing. Dain began developing a strong presence in the Pacific Northwest, and by the end of the decade, the firm had opened nine new Washington and Oregon offices. In 1988, Dain acquired The Milwaukee Company along with its 12 Wisconsin and Illinois offices. The Rauscher acquisition boded well for IFG's securities-related ventures. Such was not the case for other ventures.

Among IFG's most successful endeavors during the 1970s was IFG Leasing, a subsidiary that derived most of its income from leasing farm and office equipment. The business took off during the mid-1970s and, at its peak, was accounting for roughly 50 percent of IFG's entire earnings base. Unfortunately, IFG Leasing's prosperity began to wane in the late 1970s, signaling a period of misfortune for Inter-Regional Financial Group. Indeed, IFG Leasing's profits started tumbling in the late 1970s and continued to fall into the early 1980s. IFG Leasing finally became such a drag on IFG's bottom line that it almost forced its parent into bankruptcy. Ultimately, the company wrote losses of $157 million.

IFG Leasing's problems began with the recession of the late 1970s and early 1980s. During the mid-1970s, the company profited from heavy leverage; it borrowed money to purchase equipment, which it leased to customers. The profit margin consisted of the spread between the lease rate charged to customers and the interest rate charged by IFG Leasing's lenders. The strategy failed when interest rates exploded under the Carter administration. Furthermore, because of the recession, many customers simply couldn't pay their bills. The net result was that IFG Leasing began hemorrhaging cash, paying high interest rates and generating insufficient cash flow from its troubled customer base.

By the mid-1980s IFG was teetering on the edge of bankruptcy. Augmenting problems with the leasing division was the disappointing performance of the Rauscher Pierce subsidiary and the Midwest Life unit. IFG managed to obscure problems with its leasing division until 1983, when the dilemma began to climax and IFG decided to shutter the subsidiary. As its troubles became more obvious, IFG's stock price plummeted, from about $25 in 1983 to less than $10 in late 1985. By 1985, in fact, the company's long-term debt had climbed to $73 million (from just $10 million in 1981). Furthermore, IFG had lost $60 million between 1983 and 1985. Investors feared that the company was barreling toward bankruptcy. In spite of the company's losses and tarnished reputation, it was able to protect clients and vendors from losses.

Rising to the chief executive post during IFG's management shakeout in the mid-1980s was Richard D. McFarland, who succeeded Thomas Holloran in June of 1985. McFarland had started with Dain as a salesman in the 1960s and had progressed through the ranks before he became president of IFG in 1982. He was moved to the top slot in 1985 by a board of directors that was eager for a turnaround. Among IFG's first moves under McFarland's direction was to put Investment Advisers and Midwest Life on the auction block. Both subsidiaries were profitable at the time. The sale of the money management unit helped

Key Dates:

1929: J.M. Dain & Co. founded in Minneapolis.

1933: Rauscher, Pierce & Co. chartered in Dallas.

1967: J.M. Dain merges with Kalman & Co. and Iowa-based Quail & Co. to form Dain, Kalman & Quail Co.

1968: Rauscher, Pierce & Co. merges with Phoenix bond house Refsnes, Ely, Beck & Co.

1972: Dain, Kalman & Quail goes public.

1973: Inter-Regional is created as a holding company for Dain, Kalman & Quail and Bosworth, Sullivan & Co. of Denver.

1978: Bosworth, Sullivan merges operations with Dain, Kalman & Quail; the firm becomes Dain Bosworth in 1979.

1980: Rauscher, Pierce & Co. changes name to Rauscher Pierce Refsnes, Inc.

1981: Inter-Regional Financial Group acquires Rauscher Pierce Refsnes and goes public.

1994: Dain Bosworth acquires Clayton Brown Holding Company, a Chicago-based bond house; merges operations into Dain Bosworth and Rauscher Pierce Refsnes.

1997: Inter-Regional changes name to Interra Financial.

1998: Interra combines Dain and Rauscher and changes corporate name to Dain Rauscher; company opens its first California brokerage office in San Diego.

2000: Dain Rauscher opens first international office in Paris.

to reduce IFG's debt and allowed management to begin refocusing its attention on its core brokerage businesses.

Management's streamlining efforts were augmented by rebounding trading markets in 1986 and early 1987. Surging stock markets allowed IFG's core trading business to post record revenue and income figures. Meanwhile, new management continued to chip away at past problems. Among other moves, executives fired and successfully sued IFG's auditors, and managed to sell the life insurance business. During the late 1980s, moreover, the company began to reduce its brokerage staff and to improve the average commissions earned per broker. Although IFG posted a net loss in 1988, it appeared as though it had emerged from its crises by the end of the decade.

IFG's rebound during the late 1980s and early 1990s was largely attributable to the efforts of Irving Weiser, the man that McFarland had hired to serve as president of IFG. Weiser had served as an attorney for IFG's outside counsel before McFarland lured him away in 1985. The 38-year-old Weiser, a Polish Jewish immigrant, had experience in the industry, although he had never made a trade. His problem-fixing skills became valuable to IFG. Among other moves, for example, he helped to reorganize the real estate division after that industry collapsed in the late 1980s.

IFG continued to draw on Weiser's management skills during the early 1990s, during which he was promoted to chairman

of the company. Also during that period IFG emphasized its core securities businesses, cut costs, and managed to boost revenue and profits. To that end, Weiser eliminated some poorly performing offices and continued to shrink the company's total work force. Healthy markets helped IFG to grow its revenue from about $312 million in 1990 to more than $500 million in 1993, about $47.6 million of which was netted as income. In 1993, in fact, the company started to expand again.

In late 1993 and 1994 IFG opened 14 new offices for a total of 93 in 23 states. It also started hiring new brokers, bringing the total brokerage staff at its two firms to a record 1,250 by year's end. Furthermore, IFG expanded eastward with the acquisitions of Clayton Brown Holding Company, a privately held, Chicago-based firm specializing in fixed-income securities. By late 1995, IFG was the tenth-largest full-service regional brokerage house in the nation and the leading broker in its region. The company posted record revenues in 1995 and 1996. More industry changes; however, were on the horizon.

Bigger is Better: 1998–99

As a result of regulatory reform undertaken by the Federal Reserve in 1997, a surge of consolidations swept the securities industry as large banking institutions began acquiring securities firms. This trend resulted in cost-prohibitive prices for securities firms, thus interfering with the long-standing IFG acquisition strategy. The company determined the best response to this new and changing environment was to optimize its large firm resources. As a result, IFG, renamed Interra Financial in February 1997, was dissolved and replaced by a new entity—Dain Rauscher Corporation. Under the reorganization, subsidiaries Dain Bosworth and Rauscher Pierce Refsnes combined in January 1998 to create a single, more powerful brand name and one of the largest securities firms west of the Mississippi River. This action also effected a more streamlined management and prudent cost structure for the firm.

The new company wasted little time in further strengthening its competitive position. In March 1998, Dain Rauscher acquired the rival Minneapolis investment bank Wessels Arnold & Henderson for $150 million. Analysts viewed the deal as an excellent, albeit expensive, strategic move. The deal gave Dain Rauscher depth in some areas where it had faltered, especially in underwriting stock for technology companies and then selling such stock to institutional clients. The alliance was also beneficial because it boosted the firm's corporate finance sector; Dain Rauscher trailed the much smaller Wessels in equity issues. As part of the deal, Dain Rauscher restructured its equity capital markets group to become the Dain Rauscher Wessels division, and Kenneth Wessels was named to head the division.

In August 1998, Dain Rauscher opened its first California brokerage office in San Diego; six months later, in January 1999, the company expanded its California presence and gained access to Florida and the Northeast through the purchase of Artemis Capital Group Inc., a national investment bank and Wall Street's first women-owned public finance company, based in New York City. Its strategic locations and strength in municipal bond underwriting would bolster Dain Rauscher, while Artemis would be joining a large firm with greater credibility and resources.

Despite its aggressive response to increased competition, Dain Rauscher company experienced an 84 percent decline in net income in 1998. This severe earnings decline was the result of several factors occurring that year, including expenses associated with the Wessels purchase, litigation expenses to settle the company's alleged involvement in the Orange County, California, bankruptcy, the failure of its former subsidiary, Midwest Life Insurance, a sluggish initial public offering (IPO) market, and increased competition. By 1999, having settled some of the previous year's issues and bolstered by a good economy and strong stock market performance, the company was able to get its earnings progression back on track with an increase in net income of 730 percent over 1998.

On Track for the Future

Dain Rauscher approached a new millennium with heightened focus on improving service to clients and acknowledging the impact of a global economy on its business. For example, Dain Rauscher Wessels, the firm's equity capital division, signed a strategic partnership and cooperative agreement with Israeli investment Bank, Tamir Fishman & Co. Partnering with the prestigious Israeli investment bank would allow Dain Rauscher to sharpen its focus on technology and growth companies, while also significantly expanding its ability to manage international transactions. In May, the Wessels division took the next step in international growth by opening its first international office in Paris. In February 2000, Dain Rauscher announced that it would also roll out a new large venture capital fund. While venture capital was regarded as a riskier investment vehicle, the stock market remained strong, and that boded well for Dain Rauscher.

Principal Subsidiaries

Dain Rauscher Incorporated; Insight Investment Management Inc.

Principal Divisions

Dain Rauscher's Private Client Group; The Fixed Income Capital Markets Group; Dain Rauscher Wessels; Dain Correspondent Services.

Principal Competitors

U.S. Bancorp Piper Jaffray Inc.; The Charles Schwab Corporation; Morgan Keegan, Inc.; Morgan Stanley Dean Witter & Company.

Further Reading

Allen, James C., "School Finance Guru Jumps From First Southwest Ship," *Dallas Business Journal*, December 24, 1993, p. 1.

Birger, Jon, "Women-Owned Underwriter Marries," *Crain's New York Business,* January 25, 1999, p. 10.

Cawley, Rusty, "SEC Sues Dain Rauscher for 1992 Muni Bond Transaction," *Dallas Morning News,* January 23, 1998, p. 5.

"A Commitment to Service, A Tradition of Trust," company document, Minneapolis: Inter-Regional Financial Group, Inc., 1994.

"Dain to Acquire Local Minnesota Rival Investment Bank," *Knight-Ridder/Tribune Business News,* February 10, 1998.

"Dain Rauscher Buys Artemis Capital Unit," *New York Times,* January 5, 1999, p. C20.

"Dain Rauscher Wessels Has Signed a Strategic Partnership with Israeli Investment Bank Tamir Fishman," *New York Times News Release,* February 22, 2000.

Foran, Pat, "Dain Bosworth's Local Foray Was Capital Idea, Observers Say," *Business Journal-Milwaukee,* February 6, 1989, Sec. 2, p. 1.

French, B. J., "David A. Smith to Step Down as CEO of Rauscher Pierce Refsnes Inc.," *PR Newswire,* September 27, 1995.

Hayes, John R., "All's Fair," *Forbes,* November 21, 1994, p. 46.

"Heads of Minneapolis-based Wessels to Lead Dain Unit after Merger," *Knight-Ridder/Tribune Business News*, February 26, 1998.

"An Independent Tradition of Quality & Service: The Story of Dain Rauscher," company document, Minneapolis: Dain Rauscher Corporation, 1999.

Jean, Sheryl, "Merger Spurs Some Dain Execs to Move On," *CityBusiness-Minneapolis,* March 26, 1999, p. 3.

Lowe, Sandra, "Rauscher Pierce Expands Locally," *San Antonio Business Journal,* May 20, 1994, p. 4.

"Minneapolis-Based Brokerage to Launch Second Venture-Capital Fund," *Saint Paul Pioneer Press,* February 3, 2000.

"Minneapolis-Based Interra Financial Makes Changes Amid Rumor of Sale," *Saint Paul Pioneer Press,* October 15, 1997.

Pollack, Andrew, "SEC Accuses Dain Rauscher of Fraud," *New York Times,* August 4, 1998, p. D2.

Rich, Andrew, "IPO Emerges Out of a Deep Hole," *Minneapolis-St. Paul City Business,* July 15, 1987, p. 1.

Schafer, Lee, "Inter-Regional Financial Group," *Corporate Report Minnesota,* February 1990, p. 21.

St. Anthony, Neal, "New IFG Exec's Initial Challenge: Brokerage Merger," *Star Tribune,* May 18, 1992.

Tosto, Paul, "Inter-Regional Financial Executives Reap Bonus Bonanza," *Minneapolis-St. Paul City Business,* April 8, 1991, p. 1.

Walden, Gene, "IFG Finds Diversifications a Dangerous Game," *Minneapolis-St. Paul City Business,* October 9, 1985, p. 1.

—Dave Mote
—updated by Ana G. Schulz

R Dan River Inc.

Dan River Inc.

2291 Memorial Drive
Danville, Virginia 24541
U.S.A.
Telephone: (804) 799-7000
Toll Free: (800) 274-2439
Fax: (804) 799-7216
Web site: http://www.danriver.com

Public Company
Incorporated: 1909 as Riverside and Dan River Cotton
   Mills, Inc.
Employees: 7,300
Sales: $628.9 million (1999)
Stock Exchange: New York
Ticker Symbol: DRF
NAIC: 31321 Broadwoven Fabric Mills; 313311
   Broadwoven Fabric Finishing Mills; 313312 Textile
   and Fabric Finishing (Except Broadwoven Fabric)
   Mills; 313111 Yarn Spinning Mills; 314129 Other
   Household Textile Product Mills

Dan River Inc. manufactures apparel fabrics and home fashion products, such as bedding. Based in Danville, Virginia, the company is the leading U.S. producer of lightweight yarn-dyed fabrics, including oxford cloth, denims, and broadcloth. Dan River's apparel fabric is sold to clothing manufacturers and made into items with brand names including Brooks Brothers, Liz Claiborne, L.L. Bean, and Arrow. The company's home fashions products are sold under the Dan River brand as well as licensed names, ranging from ''Colours by Alexander Julian'' to ''Barbie.'' The goods are sold to high-volume retail chains and department stores, including Wal-Mart Stores, Inc., which accounted for 12 percent of home fashions sales in 1999. Dan River also makes engineered products, such as high-pressure hoses and conveyer belts, for industrial applications.

Early Years as a Cotton Mill: 1880s–1940s

The erection of a cotton mill was an unusual choice for the six men who together founded the Riverside Cotton Mills. Tobacco, not cotton, was the mainstay of industry in the South. The group of businessmen, however—none of whom had previous experience in textiles—believed textile manufacturing could flourish in the region. In 1882 they started the Riverside Cotton Mills, located in Danville, Virginia, on the banks of the Dan River, and began manufacturing fabric and yarn.

Success was rapid, and by 1888 Riverside had built two additional cotton mills. The company made its first acquisition in 1890 when it purchased Morotock Mill, a local producer of sheetings. Riverside continued to expand by building four more mills between 1893 and 1898, and in 1895 a group that included five of the original six founders established the Dan River Power and Manufacturing Company, which also manufactured cotton. Just over a decade later, in 1909, Riverside and Dan River merged to form the Riverside and Dan River Cotton Mills, Incorporated.

Success and growth continued in the early 1900s as the company turned out sheetings, ginghams, and chambrays, but expansion ceased in the mid-1920s when difficult times hit the textile industry. Riverside and Dan River reported a loss for the first time in history in 1924, and the company struggled through the Great Depression of the 1930s with no growth. The advent of World War II changed the course of the company, however, and high demand for fabrics spurred productivity at the Riverside and Dan River mills. The company that had suffered through the 1920s and 1930s with no innovations or expansion suddenly found itself with an abundance of orders and staff positions to fill.

Changes to enhance productivity, such as the formation of a quality control department and new equipment and manufacturing systems, were implemented. In 1942, the company began a research and development department. Four years later, the company name was shortened to Dan River Mills, Incorporated, and strong performance continued through the 1950s as the nation enjoyed the years following the war. At that time, Dan

River was able to make capital improvements to strengthen operations and become more competitive in the textile industry.

Explosive Expansion and Growth: 1950s–1960s

After Dan River integrated new machinery and modern procedures into its operations, it adopted an ambitious expansion strategy during the 1950s and 1960s in order to diversify its product lines. In 1956 the company bought Iselin-Jefferson Company, Inc., a textile sales firm headquartered in New York. The acquisition included several companies run by Iselin-Jefferson, including cloth manufacturer Woodside Mills, based in Greenville, South Carolina; Iselin-Jefferson Financial Company, Inc., located in New York; and fabric producer Alabama Mills, Inc., which operated a number of factories in Alabama and Georgia. The purchase marked Dan River's first foray beyond the Danville, Virginia area and boosted its personnel by nearly 7,000 workers.

The mid-1960s marked a time of aggressive expansion and diversification through acquisitions. In 1964, Dan River entered a new industry when it acquired Kingston Mills, a carpet manufacturing firm. The following year, the company purchased another carpet company—Wunda Weve Carpet Co., located in Greenville, South Carolina. It also entered the knitted fabrics industry with the acquisition of Marco Fabric Manufacturing, Inc., which made velour fabrics, and added to its knitted fabrics operations in 1965 by purchasing Webco Mills, Inc., a maker of knit fabrics used to produce lingerie. Finally, the company also bought Clifton Manufacturing Co., Inc., a maker of greige fabrics that had six manufacturing plants.

In addition to growth through acquisitions, Dan River constructed several new plants to increase its production capacity and invested in the expansion of its carpet division. The company made several more acquisitions at the end of the decade. Crystal Springs Textiles, Inc., added to the company's finishing capabilities, and Morganton Hosiery Mills, Inc., boosted Dan River's presence in the hosiery product market.

Not only did Dan River focus on expansion, but it also concentrated on innovations in the textile world. In 1956, the same year it had acquired Iselin-Jefferson, Dan River launched its "Wrinkl-Shed with Dri-Don" fabric finish, an improvement on its "Wrinkle-Shed" fabric that had been introduced in 1947. "Wrinkl-Shed with Dri-Don" lent fabric a finish that allowed for washing, drying, and wearing without the need for ironing. In the mid-1960s, with its entrance into the knitted fabrics market, the company began to manufacture double-knit fabrics for clothing. The firm also introduced "Dan-Press," which was its own version of permanent press.

Successes and Struggles in the 1970s and 1980s

At the commencement of the 1970s, the company changed its name once again to become Dan River Inc. The climate of the textile industry and the marketplace shifted, and Dan River was forced to alter some of its practices in order to remain competitive. Economic conditions were such that the firm put a halt to its acquisitions program. Many advances had been made in textile equipment, and Dan River realized that if it hoped to remain innovative and on the cutting edge of the industry, it would need to invest significantly in new machinery. In 1973 the company adopted a modernization program to upgrade equipment and increase efficiency, spending more than $200 million between 1973 and 1980 to realize its goals.

The company strived to lead the textile industry in innovations, and in the early 1970s it entered the denim manufacturing market with the construction of a denim plant. In the late 1970s the company introduced its innovative all-cotton fabric that offered the non-wrinkle characteristics of permanent press. Dan River's sales improved through the 1970s, and in 1979 it reported its highest profit to date, with sales of about $580 million.

The 1980s presented many new challenges to Dan River. Entering the decade, the company faced a hostile takeover bid by the Icahn Capital Corp., run by corporate raider and investor Carl C. Icahn. In order to thwart the takeover, in 1983 Dan River became a private, 70-percent employee-owned corporation, with employees voting to give up their pension plans for a stock ownership program. Employees believed jobs would be saved and that they would have more of a say in corporate decisions, but they quickly found this would not be the case.

Over the following two years, about 1,000 employees were laid off and at least five unprofitable plants were closed. Worse still, workers reportedly learned about the plant closings, as well as the return of corporate headquarters from Greenville, South Carolina, to Danville, Virginia, through newspaper reports rather than from management. Management also made the decision to take the company public again without input from employees, but this plan was tabled in 1987, presumably due to the company's poor performance in the mid-1980s. Because Dan River chose not to disclose company earnings after becoming an employee-owned company, employees did not have a solid idea of the company's financial performance, and this left them uninformed about their stock ownership values. Though management contended that the new ownership plan was beneficial to employees, at the time one worker told *Business Week*, "Frankly, I wish Icahn would have taken over Dan River."

Ironically, Dan River began searching for a buyer in the late 1980s and came close to being acquired by Textile Industries

Key Dates:

1882: The Riverside Cotton Mills is established in Danville, Virginia.

1895: Dan River Power & Manufacturing Company forms.

1909: Riverside Cotton Mills and Dan River Power & Manufacturing Company merge to form Riverside and Dan River Cotton Mills, Incorporated.

1946: Company changes its name to Dan River Mills, Incorporated.

1956: Dan River begins an aggressive acquisition program that includes the purchase of Iselin-Jefferson Company, Inc.

1970: Company changes name to Dan River Inc.

1983: Dan River becomes an employee-owned corporation.

1989: Company is acquired by an investment group headed by Joseph Lanier, Jr.

1997: Dan River goes public and acquires The New Cherokee Corporation.

1998: Company acquires the Bibb Company and enters the engineered products industry.

2000: Dan River forms a joint venture with Grupo Industrial Zaga, S.A. de C.V., and makes plans to construct a manufacturing facility in Mexico.

Australia. High interest rates in Australia extinguished the deal, however. In 1989, Dan River was purchased by a United States-based investment group for about $268 million. The group was led by Joseph L. Lanier, Jr., who had been the head of WestPoint Pepperell, Inc., a textile manufacturing company in Georgia. WestPoint Pepperell had been founded in 1886 by Lanier's ancestors, and Lanier himself had joined the family business in 1957, serving as chairman until a successful hostile takeover in early 1989 essentially forced him into early retirement. Retirement did not last long, however, as Lanier joined Dan River in late autumn. Though Dan River and WestPoint Pepperell shared some traits, they were very different in terms of size—Dan River had sales of about $400 million in 1988 while WestPoint Pepperell reported sales of about $2.15 billion.

Soon after ownership changed hands, Dan River president Lester A. Hudson resigned, and Richard Williams—a member of the investor group that acquired Dan River—was named president and chief operating officer. Lanier served as chairman and CEO. The new management team wasted no time increasing operating margins and production efficiency. Though Dan River had reportedly invested more than $200 million on capital improvements during the 1980s, the company was still not completely modernized, relying on outdated equipment in several plants. Lanier planned to double or triple capital expenditures to streamline operations.

In addition to updating machinery, Dan River made plans to alter its product lines and to place greater emphasis on home fashions and higher-end products. Even before Lanier's group came on board, Dan River's home fashions division had been focusing on growth, expanding significantly in the mid- to late 1980s. From 1986 to 1989, the home fashions group sales increased from about 18 percent to 40 percent of Dan River's total revenues. For the 1990s, the company hoped to increasingly cater to department stores, catalog companies, and specialty stores rather than concentrating solely on mass-market retailers where price points tended to be lower.

Dan River signed a number of new licensing agreements in the early 1990s, including such designer labels as high-quality French bedding company Porthault, home furnishings brand Lillian August, Jones New York, and Alexander Julian's "Colours by Alexander Julian" label. The company also acquired children's licenses, including G.I. Joe and Chutes 'n' Ladders. Larry Queen, Dan River's president of home fashions, commented on the importance of licensing agreements to growing the home fashions business and told *HFD*, "The signing of these new licenses represents our next big move for market share . . . We are continuing to upgrade our image, and attempting to capture more business at the upper end. We are looking at niches where we feel we can offer a superior product."

Strengthening Operations in the 1990s

To streamline operations and focus on growing the profitable home fashions business, Dan River started the decade by selling its Wunda Weve Floor Coverings division to a buyer group that included former president Lester Hudson. Dan River then spent more than $50 million to modernize its plants, installing electronic inventory systems, computer equipment, and modern looms. Production capabilities were increased, and the manufacturing process became more efficient. The company also launched in full scale its innovative Bed-in-a-Bag product, which offered a complete comforter and sheet set in one package for one price. By 1992 the company had reportedly sold more than one million Bed-in-a-Bag sets, and plans to carry the concept further and introduce it into major department stores were set in motion.

In early 1993, Larry Queen, who had been responsible for much of the home fashions division's success, left Dan River. He was replaced by Thomas Muscalino, another former WestPoint Pepperell executive. Muscalino voiced his excitement regarding the company's rapidly growing home fashions business and told *HFD*, ". . . the company's gone through a tremendous metamorphosis . . . It went from a tired, undercapitalized, inefficient operation to one of the most low-cost, highly efficient, best quality producers in America, and they did it real fast." Sales of the home fashions division were expected to account for more than half of total 1993 revenues, and in 1995 the group reported record sales of $227 million. Between 1990 and 1996 the company's home fashions business grew more than 60 percent.

The change in emphasis from lower-grade product to higher quality shifted dramatically during the early 1990s, as well. Muslin sheeting accounted for 51 percent of the company's sheeting business in 1990, while 200 thread-count percale—a higher-quality sheeting—accounted for only about 5 percent. In 1995, however, muslin sheeting accounted for less than 15 percent, while luxury percale had increased its production to more than 30 percent of Dan River's sheeting operations.

Emphasis on the home fashions division did not mean Dan River neglected its other operations. Capital improvements were made in the apparel fabrics division as well, and the group focused on upgrading the quality of yarn and yarn dye. Automation and modernization of yarn manufacturing equipment was implemented as well, and the company was the leading U.S. manufacturer of oxford cloth, garnering about half of the market. Dan River sold apparel fabric to such well-known companies and labels as Brooks Brothers, Arrow Shirt, Liz Claiborne, Levi Strauss, and OshKosh. The company also benefited from the popularity of its wrinkle-resistant shirting fabrics, introduced in the mid-1990s; Dan River attributed the 18.8 percent rise in apparel fabric sales in 1994 to increased sales of the shirting fabrics.

Though Dan River seemed to be on track for continued success, the company ran into a few problems in 1995. Sales rose 3.6 percent to reach $384.8 million, but apparel fabric sales declined 3.3 percent. Profits fell 92.7 percent, primarily due to $9 million in restructuring charges, which included a $4.4 million write-off of outmoded assets, $1.6 million to move its New York City offices, and $3 million to terminate its line of velour apparel fabrics. Dan River was not discouraged by the results, however, and planned to continue growing operations and making capital improvements.

In the late 1990s Dan River sought to stave off competition from the Far East, which offered textiles and home fashion goods at much lower costs. The company also strove to maintain its leadership position in the domestic textiles industry. Part of the company's strategy for growth and success included the addition of strategic acquisitions, and in 1997 Dan River purchased The New Cherokee Corp., a maker of woven fabrics for shirting and sportswear manufacturers. Dan River paid about $65 million for Cherokee, which included plants and a finishing facility. Dan River believed the acquisition made it the largest maker of lightweight yarn-dyed woven fabrics in the Western Hemisphere.

The following year Dan River purchased the Bibb Company, a manufacturer of home fashions textiles. The buy, which made Dan River the fourth-largest textile manufacturer in the nation, expanded its juvenile product repertoire by adding several juvenile licenses, including Barbie, Looney Tunes, and Teletubbies. The deal also provided the company access into the hospitality and health care markets, as well as the automotive industry. Bibb's engineered products division produced textiles and hose yarns used for automotive and industrial hoses and conveyor belts. In addition to the Bibb acquisition, Dan River purchased a home fashions sewing plant in North Carolina from Home Innovations Inc.

To raise capital for its expansion program, Dan River finally went public again in 1997, listing its stock on the New York Stock Exchange. Though sales dropped from $384.8 million in 1995 to $379.6 million the following year, they began to climb in subsequent years, reaching $476.5 million in 1997, $517.4 million in 1998, and $628.9 million in 1999. Boosted by the Bibb acquisition, home fashions performed well, with 1999 sales increasing 34 percent over those of 1998. The apparel fabrics division, however, did not fare as well, as competition from Asia put pressure on pricing. To combat this competition,

which was anticipated to continue, Dan River entered a joint venture agreement to construct an apparel fabrics manufacturing plant and sportswear manufacturing facility in Mexico. The move, which would result in the transfer of nearly half of the company's apparel fabrics business to Mexico, marked Dan River's first major overseas investment. Dan River's partner in the venture was Grupo Industrial Zaga, S.A. de C.V. Together they formed DanZa Textil S. de R.L. de C.V. and Zadar S. de R.L. de C.V.

Dan River in the New Millennium

As Dan River entered the new millennium, the company hoped to remain a viable force in the U.S. textiles industry. The company began the century with the acquisition of Import Specialists, Inc., an importer of textile products for the home, such as doormats, blankets, rugs, and decorative pillows. The purchase allowed Dan River to diversify its home fashions offerings. Also in early 2000, Dan River announced its intent to purchase WesTek Inc., a manufacturer of specialty adhesive coated yarns and textiles used in automotive and industrial hose products and conveyer belts. The acquisition expanded Dan River's engineered products division.

For the first quarter of 2000, Dan River reported sales of $164.9 million, a 2.7 percent decline compared to the same period in 1999. Net income was up, however, from $1.6 million during the first quarter of 1999 to $4.9 million in 2000. Though sales in home fashions were down 2.6 percent, apparel fabrics sales were up 8.1 percent, and sales of engineered products continued to strengthen, increasing 14.3 percent. After more than a century in the textiles business, Dan River remained confident that its future held many more years of success.

Principal Subsidiaries

Dan River Factory Stores, Inc.; DanZa Textil S. De R.L. de C.V. (Mexico, 50%); Zadar S. de R.L. de C.V. (Mexico, 50%).

Principal Competitors

Pillowtex Corporation; Springs Industries, Inc.; WestPoint Stevens Inc.

Further Reading

Adler, Sam, "Hot Dan! From Bed in a Bag to D. Porthault, Dan River Covers the Market," *HFD,* August 9, 1993, p. 32.

Bernard, Sharyn K., "Rising Tide: Dan River's Home Fashions Business Swells to More than $180 Million, Backed by Bed in a Bat and Licensing Successes," *HFD,* April 6, 1992, p. 93.

Dan River: Celebrating a Century of Progress 1882–1982, Greenville, South Carolina: Dan River Inc., 1982.

"Dan River Ready to Reap Fruits of $160-Million Capital Program," *Textile World,* May 1, 1995, p. 27.

Engardio, Pete, "At Dan River, 'A Lot of Us Feel that We Got Took,' " *Business Week,* April 15, 1985, p. 97.

Foust, Dean, "How Dan River's ESOP Missed the Boat," *Business Week,* October 26, 1987, p. 34.

Fraser, Mark, "Dan River: Mid-Sized, Flexible and Fashionable," *HFD,* October 16, 1989, p. 12.

Hopper, Kathryn, "Dan River Buyout Stirs Emotions," *Greensboro News & Record,* October 15, 1989, p. 1.

Malone, Scott, "Dan River in Deal to Make Fabrics, Apparel in Mexico," *WWD,* January 13, 2000, p. 22.

Maycumber, S. Gray, "Dan River Buying New Cherokee for $65 Million Cash," *Daily News Record,* January 15, 1997, p. 19.

McAllister, Isaacs, "Dan River Inc. Style with Substance," *Textile World,* June 1, 1996, p. 30.

Schecter, Dara, "Say Lanier Paying $268M for Dan River," *Daily News Record,* October 12, 1989, p. 2.

Schwartz, Donna Boyle, "Dan River Inks More License: Targets High End with Lillian August, Porthault," *HFD,* January 29, 1990, p. 42.

——, "Dan River Sets Course for Market Share," *HFD,* March 19, 1990, p. 34.

—Mariko Fujinaka

Donnelly

Donnelly Corporation

49 West Third Street
Holland, Michigan 49423-2813
U.S.A.
Telephone: (616) 786-7000
Fax: (616) 786-6034
Web site: http://www.donnelly.com

Public Company
Incorporated: 1936 as Donnelly-Kelly Glass Company
Employees: 5,600
Sales: $897.91 million (1999)
Stock Exchanges: New York
Ticker Symbol: DON
NAIC: 327215 Glass Product Manufacturing Made of
Purchased Glass; 327211 Flat Glass Manufacturing;
336321 Vehicular Lighting Equipment Manufacturing;
33637 Motor Vehicle Metal Stamping; 333314
Optical Instrument and Lens Manufacturing

Donnelly Corporation is a supplier of automotive components, ranking as the largest manufacturer of automotive mirrors in the world and as a leader in the production of other components and systems such as door handles and windows. The company supplies automotive parts to every major automobile manufacturer in the world through 15 production plants in 12 countries. Renowned for innovation in design, Donnelly is recognized also for its use of progressive management theories and systems. The company is a leading practitioner of participative management, a management system that shares decision making among executives and rank-and-file employees.

Origins

Donnelly Corporation was founded by Bernard P. Donnelly in 1905 in Holland, Michigan, as a manufacturer of mirrors for the then-thriving Michigan furniture industry. Founded as the Kinsella Glass Company, the company was later renamed the Donnelly-Kelly Glass Company. Donnelly's main products in the early years were engraved mirrors for use on furniture as well as freestanding engraved wall mirrors. These "art" mirrors, featuring scenes from nature as well as ornate decorative motifs, became very popular for home furnishings through the early part of the century and, as a result, Donnelly's business flourished. The engraving of the mirrors was done primarily by hand, but the precision grinding and polishing that this craftsmanship required formed the basis for much of the glass technology that Donnelly would later develop. Being in business in Michigan during the 1920s meant watching the phenomenal growth of the American automobile industry. Although decorative mirrors remained the core of its business, Donnelly also jumped on the automobile bandwagon and began production of rear windows for touring cars.

World War II marked a turning point for Donnelly. As America geared up for the war effort, the company converted its decorative mirror factory into a specialized lens and mirror production facility. These highly precise glass components were needed for military equipment ranging from aerial gunsights to submarine periscopes, and there were few manufacturers who could produce them with speed and accuracy. Donnelly scrambled to refit its factory with the necessary machinery to perform this task and to retrain its craftsmen to measure in microns instead of inches. Among the techniques developed by Donnelly during its wartime experience was the process of vacuum coating glass with a variety of materials to produce mirrors with varying degrees of reflectivity. This technology would prove invaluable during the company's later development of automobile mirrors.

When the war ended, Donnelly found itself with a great deal of new technology and experience, but in search of new markets for glass and mirror products. Not only had decorative mirrors gone out of fashion, but the furniture industry that Donnelly had supplied was moving south to find cheaper labor. The automobile industry in Michigan, however, was booming. Production could not keep up with the demand from product-hungry postwar consumers. Donnelly made the crucial decision to transform what had been a secondary market into a primary source of sales. The company began to manufacture interior and exterior prismatic mirrors for the automobile industry and soon became one of the leaders among automobile parts suppliers. Donnelly's experience in vacuum coating glass became one of its prime assets as the company developed a number of innovative applications in both the automotive and aircraft industries. By the mid 1950s, with new markets and products fully in place, management decided to change the company name to Donnelly Mirrors Inc. to better reflect this more specialized line.

1960s and 1970s: Innovation and Diversification

The 1960s and 1970s constituted a period of major expansion for Donnelly in terms of both the range of products the company manufactured and the number of industries it supplied. One major innovation for the company during this period was the development of the encapsulated mirror, which was delivered to automotive manufacturers as a single unit mirror enclosed in a plastic frame. The plastic mirror housing was not only much safer than the previously standard metal frame, but was also much cheaper for automobile makers to install. Once Donnelly had the technology and equipment to produce the plastic molding, it was able to expand its line to other plastic components and to provide customers with complete interior mirror assemblies, including the bracket used to attach the mirror to the car. This would mark the beginning of the company's expanded line of complete part assemblies.

By the mid-1970s, this new plastic molding technology allowed Donnelly to introduce one of the most important innovations in the car parts industry. Known as the modular window, this new product involved encapsulating window glass in a plastic frame that also incorporated attachment hardware and decorative trim. This new window not only greatly reduced labor costs at the automotive plants by reducing a four-step process to a single quick installation, but also substantially altered the design possibilities of new vehicles. The streamlined look that became so popular in vehicles through the 1980s was in large part made possible by the Donnelly modular window.

In addition to the major developments in product technology that Donnelly undertook during the 1960s and 1970s, the company also began to reach out to markets overseas. Anticipating the growth of the European and Japanese auto industries, Donnelly founded a wholly owned subsidiary, Donnelly Mirrors, Limited, in Naas, Ireland, to supply these expanding industries. The company also expanded its American markets by producing coated glass products for nonautomotive applications, such as copy machines and fluorescent displays.

The 1980s was a demanding period for the American auto industry, as competition from abroad made serious inroads into the American car market. Donnelly survived this critical period by expanding its line of ready-to-install plastic and glass components as well as by increasing its already established relationship with foreign car manufacturers. As American auto manufacturers began to scramble to meet the quality and energy efficiency standards set by Japanese competitors, Donnelly's emphasis on product development and innovation made the company an increasingly attractive supplier.

Donnelly began to experiment with electronic lighting to provide low glare interior lighting in association with its rearview mirrors. The company then branched out into producing integrated lighting systems, including overhead, door, and visor lights. Like the modular window, which was proving increasingly successful for the company, these assemblies integrated a number of components that previously would have been installed separately by the manufacturers. The reduction in labor costs for the automakers was an important factor in increasing Donnelly's share of the auto parts market. To reflect the growing diversity in the company's product line—which by this time ranged from windows to liquid crystal displays (LCDs)—Donnelly Mirrors, Inc. was renamed Donnelly Corporation in 1984.

As Donnelly moved into the 1990s, the relationship between auto manufacturers and auto parts suppliers was undergoing a profound change. Not only were automakers increasingly looking to suppliers as partners in research and development, but they also were fostering more long-term cooperation and commitment between manufacturers and suppliers. Traditionally, American automakers had obtained lowest possible cost components by buying the same part from five or six suppliers, thereby encouraging cutthroat competition among auto parts manufacturers. As hard times during the 1980s forced many parts suppliers out of business, however, automakers were forced to substitute high-volume and long-term contracts for competition in order to reduce costs. Although the early 1990s were lean years for Donnelly, and the auto industry in general, the company did benefit from several large contracts for complete mirror assemblies and modular windows from Honda, Ford, Mazda, and Chrysler. To meet these new large commitments, Donnelly undertook a costly overhaul of its production facilities, including construction of new plants in Michigan, Mexico, and France and of new production lines within older facilities.

During the 1980s and 1990s, Donnelly's extensive experience in coated glass products gave the company an entry into the then-booming electronics industry, as it began to produce electrically conductive coated glass products to be used in LCD applications. These new applications, including touch-sensitive computer screens, became a significant factor in overall sales. In the early 1990s, however, increased market demands for efficiency of operations prompted the company to restructure its nonautomotive ventures. In 1992, Donnelly's display coatings business was transferred to Donnelly Applied Films Corp. (DAFC), a joint venture with Applied Films Laboratory Inc. in which Donnelly maintained a 50 percent share. Other nonautomotive products also were transferred to, or developed in conjunction with, joint ventures operating independently from Donnelly's core automotive businesses.

One of the most promising new technologies developed by Donnelly in the 1980s was the electrochromic coating of automobile mirrors to allow them to adjust automatically to reduce glare. Donnelly, however, became embroiled in an ongoing legal dispute with Gentex Corporation about the patent rights to this technology. Gentex sued Donnelly in 1990 for patent infringement of its electrochromic mirrors. After a lengthy series of suits and countersuits, in 1993 the parties reached a settlement in which Donnelly agreed to pay Gentex $3.6 million in damages, which took a sizable bite out of net income for that year.

Above all else, Donnelly gained a strong reputation in the world of business for its longstanding innovative approach to company management. Donnelly earned numerous awards and citations over the years for its participative management system and was listed as one of the top ten best companies to work for in America. In 1952, when much of Michigan industry was settling down into long-term combative relationships with big unions and top-heavy management systems, Donnelly introduced a system of employee participation and bonuses called the Scanlon Plan. Developed by an MIT professor, Joseph Scanlon, the plan was based on the principle that if employees were informed about the reasons for company decisions and could participate directly in the benefits of these decisions, employee satisfaction and productivity would increase. The core of the plan involved a set of weighted bonuses for all employees calculated as a percentage of the cost/sales ratio.

From the perspective of the 1990s, when Total Quality Management and employee satisfaction became buzzwords, the plan would not appear revolutionary. In the early 1950s, however, the idea of sharing increases in profits with workers was viewed as almost communistic by some in the auto business. John F. Donnelly, a former seminarian and then president of the company, was firmly committed not only to the management position that this type of plan would lead to increased productivity, but also to the philosophical belief that as the head of a company he was responsible for ensuring a decent and fair work environment. Donnelly Corporation management remained firmly committed to these ideals over the course of almost 50 years.

By the 1990s, what had started as a bonus plan for employees had evolved into a complete team approach to all decision making in the company. Although a hierarchy of management teams was retained, with the executive team at the highest level and ultimately responsible for the operation of the company, decisions were made at each level using cooperative decision-making practices that included all members of the work force. In addition, a series of "equity" committees with elected representatives from all levels in the company were responsible for such issues as pay structure, benefit plans, and grievances. This constantly evolving system has made employee satisfaction among the highest in the country, while the constant questioning and feedback about work processes that the committee structure encourages has led to almost no waste in the Donnelly production line. One unexpected result of this participative management system was that when it became crucial for American car parts makers to forge ties with the Japanese auto industry, Donnelly's management style meshed very closely with that employed in Japan. An important contract with Honda in the mid-1980s was, in part, the result of these harmonious corporate cultures.

When World War II temporarily halted the manufacture of decorative mirrors at the Donnelly-Kelly Glass Company, the company had a respectable $1 million worth of annual sales. By 1965, with the company firmly entrenched in the automobile parts industry, sales had quadrupled to almost $4 million, but this still represented only a very small portion of the auto parts market. It was during the 1960s and 1970s that Donnelly's growth began in earnest, with sales mounting to almost $40 million by 1980. This dramatic increase was mainly due to the company's success at garnering an increasingly large portion of the auto interior mirror market, thanks to its plastic-cased "safety" mirrors and complete mirror assemblies. By 1976 Donnelly controlled 70 percent of the rear-view mirror market. By the early 1990s this figure rose to an impressive 90 percent. The domination of the interior mirror market, in addition to strong growth in exterior mirrors and modular windows, created annual sales of some $337 million by 1994.

Crisis Management in the 1990s

Traditionally, the performance of auto parts suppliers has been almost entirely dependent on the state of the automobile manufacturing industry. When the auto industry went into a deep recession in the early 1980s and again in the early 1990s, Donnelly's sales flattened out and income dropped. By 1992, however, earnings had risen once again and Donnelly appeared to be well on its way to a strong recovery. Although sales did rise in 1994 and 1995, the large expenditures involved in renovating and constructing new manufacturing facilities, as well as litigation expenses from the ongoing patent dispute with Gentex, caused net income to drop. In the first quarter of 1995 Donnelly recorded a net loss of $85,000, at a time when the auto industry as a whole was reporting soaring profits.

Viewed against the backdrop of the automobile industry's robust growth, Donnelly's loss in the first quarter of 1995 took on a profound, and alarming, meaning. By the mid-1990s, the company could no longer point to recessive economic conditions as the cause for its own anemic financial performance. The problem, company officials were forced to concede, was rooted internally, rendering the industry's dominant force an almost farcical failure. On more than one occasion, airplanes and helicopters had to be chartered to make deliveries. Quality control became mutually exclusive terms, as the company's defect rate soared. Employee morale was at an all-time low, worn thin by a decade-and-a-half of new management philosophies and productivity improvement programs, which had the cumulative effect of sending Donnelly's manufacturing operations into a near-chaotic state. In one infamous incident, a company vehicle was reported stolen, only to be found later on a factory floor, lost among the mountains of debris that testified to the pervasive disorder and confusion crippling

Donnelly's manufacturing operations. The situation became a crisis in late 1994 and early 1995, when Honda and Toyota, two of the company's largest customers, appeared as if they might sever their ties to Donnelly.

Faced with losing business it could not afford to lose, Donnelly embraced a new management theory in 1995. Ironically, the major cause of the turmoil at Donnelly had been its willingness to experiment with new management ideas as a way to contend with rapid expansion, but when two former Toyota managers, Art Smalley and Russ Scaffede, joined the company in October 1995, meaningful, corrective changes arrived with them. Companywide, the pair implemented a "lean production system" used at Toyota, a program aimed at improving production quality and efficiency.

Department by department and plant by plant, the new measures were put into place, resulting in gradual yet comprehensive improvements. Production lines were streamlined, inventories were reduced, and a visual production scheduling system known as "kanban" was introduced that enabled workers to prioritize production needs by glancing at posted boards displaying kanban cards. In addition, the company announced in 1997 that it was reducing the number of vendors it used, promising to trim its supplier base in half by the end of the decade. Although Scaffede explained that the lean production system would not be fully implemented until 2001—"It's a deep-rooted, slow change," he remarked to *Automotive News* on August 4, 1997—the company's efforts to solve its problems were clearly bearing fruit by the end of the 1990s. Between 1996 and 1998, defects plunged from 1,290 parts per million to 92 parts per million. Equally important, the company ended the decade by registering four successive quarters of record earnings, exceeding analysts' projections.

With order, efficiency, and quality control restored, Donnelly exited the 1990s displaying its formidable strengths. The company's dominant market position—Donnelly controlled 95 percent of the North American market for rear-view mirrors—fueled prolific revenue growth during the 1990s, leading to a threefold increase in annual sales between 1993 and 1999. Large contracts to supply parts for Daimler Chrysler's minivan and Ford Motor Co.'s Expedition sport utility vehicle during the late 1990s were significant contributors to the company's swelling financial stature, but more important was Donnelly's tradition of innovation. The company's engineering and new-product creativity, which a Honda executive described as "out of this world" in the March 8, 1999 issue of *Forbes,* represented its enduring strengths, fueling confidence that Donnelly's record of success would continue in the 21st century.

Principal Subsidiaries

Information Products Inc.; Donnelly Mirrors, Ltd. (Ireland); Donnelly Investments, Inc.; Donnelly Scandinavia A.B. (Sweden); Donnelly Receivables Corporation; Donn-Tech Inc.; Donnelly Vision Systems Europe Ltd. (Ireland); Donnelly Eurotrim Ltd. (Ireland); Donnelly de Mexico, S.A. de C.V.; Donnelly Euroglas Systems, SARL (France); Donnelly Holding GmbH (Germany); Donnelly International, Inc.; Donnelly Technology, Inc.

Principal Competitors

Britax International plc; Gentex Corporation; Siegel-Roberet Inc.

Further Reading

Couretas, John, "Changed Gang," *Automotive News,* August 4, 1997, p. 81.

"Donnelly Corporation Announces Record Earnings for Fourth Quarter," *PR Newswire,* April 7, 2000, p. 1831.

Ewing, David W., and Pamela Banks, "Participative Management at Work—An Interview with John F. Donnelly," *Harvard Business Review,* January–February 1977, pp. 117–27.

Jones, Terril Yue, "Looking for Nirvana," *Forbes,* March 8, 1999, p. 110.

Levering, Robert, and Milton Moskowitz, *The 100 Best Companies To Work for in America,* New York: Doubleday, 1993, pp. 102–07.

Magnet, Myron, "The New Golden Rule of Business: It's Love Thy Supplier," *Fortune,* February 21, 1994, pp. 5–10.

Moskal, Brian S., "Donnelly Manages for the Future," *Industry Week,* February 1, 1993, pp. 27–33.

Rescigno, Richard, "Greater Than the Whole: Auto Parts Suppliers Are Prospering, While the Big Three Lag," *Barron's,* August 12, 1991, pp. 8–9, 26–30.

—Hilary Gopnik
—updated by Jeffrey L. Covell

Dyckerhoff

Dyckerhoff AG

Biebricher Strasse 69
D-65203 Wiesbaden
Germany
Telephone: (49)(611) 676-0
Fax: (49)(611) 676-1040
Web site: http://www.dyckerhoff.com

Public Company
Incorporated: 1864 as Portland-Cementfabrik Dyckerhoff
 & Söhne
Employees: 11,232
Sales: DM 4.3 billion ($2.19 billion) (1999)
Stock Exchanges: Frankfurt/Main Dusseldorf Berlin
 Hamburg
Ticker Symbol: DYK
NAIC: 32731 Cement Manufacturing; 32732 Ready-Mix
 Concrete Manufacturing; 42132 Brick; 327331
 Concrete Block and Brick Manufacturing; 327332
 Concrete Pipe Manufacturing; 32739 Other Concrete
 Product Manufacturing; 32741 Lime Manufacturing;
 32742 Gypsum Product Manufacturing; 44419 Other
 Building Material Dealers

German-based Dyckerhoff AG is the management holding company for one of the world's largest groups of companies engaged in producing construction materials. Cement and concrete make up about 60 percent of its total sales, however the Dyckerhoff product range also includes limestone and mortar products, plastering systems, filler materials, binding agents, facade insulation products, and do-it-yourself hardware. With almost 80 subsidiaries, the Dyckerhoff group's presence extends throughout the world. More than one-third of Dyckerhoff's revenues are generated outside of Germany. The company consists of four independent business divisions: Dyckerhoff Cement, Dyckerhoff Cement International, Dyckerhoff Concrete, and Dyckerhoff finishing products. Dyckerhoff Cement has a 20 percent market share in Germany and cement production plants in Spain, Luxembourg, the Czech Republic, Russia, Poland, and the United States.

The family of the company's founders own about 40 percent of Dyckerhoff.

Origins in the 1800s

Wilhelm Gustav Dyckerhoff, the founder of the Dyckerhoff company, was born on October 16, 1805, in Elberfeld, Germany. Following in his father's footsteps he became a businessman, and from 1835 until 1860 he worked as an independent wholesaler for ceramics products of the German firm Villeroy & Boch. In 1861 he began a new enterprise to manufacture and sell cement together with Carl Brentano, a German engineer.

On June 4 1864, the 59-year-old Dyckerhoff founded his own cement company, together with his two sons Gustav and Rudolf. Twenty six-year-old Gustav Dyckerhoff, who had gained experience in the import/export business in Germany, England, and France, took over responsibility for administrative and financial aspects of the business. His younger brother, Rudolf Dyckerhoff, was 22 years old and had studied machine building and chemistry in Karlsruhe and Heidelberg. Naturally, he took over responsibility for the production plant. The new company took the name Portland-Cementfabrik Dyckerhoff & Söhne (Portland Cement Factory Dyckerhoff & Sons) and was based in Amöneburg, on the right bank of the river Rhine between Wiesbaden and Mainz.

In 1866 the company was incorporated as an Offene Handelsgesellschaft, a private trading company, and the rights and responsibilities of the three founders were put down in writing. Wilhelm Gustav Dyckerhoff's experience as a businessman together with his son's enthusiasm contributed to the company's rapid success. The factory first employed 14 workers. Its main production facility was a huge round oven with 12 compartments in which the ingredients for the cement were heated. The factory was located directly off the shore of the Rhine river; 2,228 tons of cement were shipped to Dyckerhoff's customers from the factory during the company's first year of existence. In 1882 an 18-meter high water tower was erected to generate power for the plant.

The unprecedented wave of political and entrepreneurial optimism that followed the founding of the German Empire in

Company Perspectives:

Claim: *We want to be technically innovative and leaders in our field through intelligent and original solutions to problems concerning all aspects of the building industry.* Staff: *We believe that the basis for success rests in the qualification, commitment, and performance of our staff and their identification with the corporate goals and tasks.* Customers: *We treat our customers fairly and correctly and prefer long-term benefits to short-term gains.* Environment: *We express our responsibility to the environment through an economic use of raw materials and energy, recultivation in accordance with the requirements of modern landscape conservation, and a reduction of environmental impacts through the use of the latest technologies.*

1871 set off an extensive construction boom. Nevertheless, right from the beginning, the Dyckerhoffs looked for business opportunities outside Germany. In 1867 the first Dyckerhoff exports arrived in the Netherlands. A year later they reached the United States for the first time. As early as 1886 Dyckerhoff products were being exported to over 100 countries. The Metropolitan Opera and the Waldorf-Astoria hotel in New York City were among the most prestigious construction projects to use Dyckerhoff cement. In 1886, 8,000 wooden bins of Dyckerhoff cement were ordered for the foundation of the Statue of Liberty.

In addition to his responsibilities as chief production officer, Rudolf Dyckerhoff became involved in setting up new organizations for the growing German cement industry. In 1864 he was a founding member and was later elected vice-president of the German national trade organization for the manufacture of bricks, clay, and lime products and cement. Twelve years later he co-founded a trade organization for Portland cement manufacturers, where, again, he was elected vice-president and became scientific advisor, especially in the area of standardization. He developed technologies that made it possible to balance out the fluctuation in the ratio of raw materials to ensure a high quality end product. In 1907 Rudolf Dyckerhoff was awarded a professorship. Founder Wilhelm Gustav Dyckerhoff remained involved in the management of the family business until a ripe old age, dying in 1894.

Dyckerhoff Thrives Until World War II

The Dyckerhoff production plant was expanded significantly around the turn of the century and new technologies replaced old ones. Electric power replaced huge steam engines. Steel ball mills were introduced that reduced the percentage of water in the raw cement mixture by one-third. Rotating ovens replaced ring ovens and eliminated the hard work of pulling huge chunks of concrete out of the ovens by hand. Finally, machines were introduced that replaced wooden frames for brick stone production. During this time, Rudolf Dyckerhoff spent many hours in his research laboratory, experimenting with different ratios of clay and lime stone until he found the right mixture to produce a Portland cement with excellent characteristics.

In 1911, before brothers Gustav and Rudolf Dyckerhoff retired, they transformed their business into a limited liability corporation, Dyckerhoff & Söhne GmbH. The new legal format enabled them to limit the risk connected with dynamic expansion and ensured continuation as a family business. Rudolf Dyckerhoff died at age 75 in 1917; Gustav Dyckerhoff died at age 85 in 1923.

The company survived the hard times of World War I, German hyperinflation, and the worldwide economic depression of the 1920s. In 1931 the company merged with Westphalian cement maker Wicking AG to form the new Dyckerhoff Wicking AG. Five years later the company was again renamed, Dyckerhoff Portland-Zementwerke AG. In 1939 Tubag, a company that manufactured cement and bricks joined the Dyckerhoff group. Tubag's speciality was Trass, a volcanic rock that had been used by the Romans, mixed as an additive into mortars and plasters. Two of the most prestigious construction projects of the time, in which Dyckerhoff cement was used, were a stadium for 100,000 built in 1928 in Montevideo, Uruguay, and the restoration of the fundament of the dome in Mainz between 1925 and 1928.

In the early 1930s, Dyckerhoff developed a new technology that allowed for its introduction of the first white Portland cement, which had always before been gray. Called Dyckerhoff Weiss, the product could also be mixed with color pigments to make colored concrete. Another innovation of the 1930s was reinforced thin-shell concrete segments, slender curved slabs used in construction projects such as ice arenas and airplane hangars. These were invented by Dyckerhoff & Widmann, another firm founded by Wilhelm Gustav Dyckerhoff.

Expansion and Diversification: 1956–89

During the post-World War II reconstruction years, Dyckerhoff pioneered another new technology. In 1949 the company introduced a new cement: Dyckerhoff Dreifach. It was especially hard and strong and was used for pre-stressed concrete, such as that used in bridge elements. Another innovation debuted in 1949, when Dyckerhoff cement was shipped in bulk silo containers or special trucks rather than sacks. Three years later Dyckerhoff introduced well cements for oil and gas explorations. Able to hold its shape precisely, this product was critical for such well drilling, which could reach 8,000 meters or more into the earth.

In 1953 the Amöneburg plant's output exceeded one million tons of cement. In 1956 the company name was changed to Dyckerhoff Zementwerke AG to reflect the broader variety of cements being made. The year 1959 marked a new technological era for Dyckerhoff. From that year on, ready-mixed concrete was transported in mixer trucks with rotating containers directly to the construction site. The same year, the first dry ovens were introduced which used less energy and were more environmentally friendly. In 1978, for the first time, cement was packed into paper sacks through a fully automated facility. During the 1960s and 1970s, a boom time for the German economy, Dyckerhoff more or less continuously expanded its capacity, range of products, and sales. In 1973, a peak year for cement production, the annual cement output was more than eight times the figure of 1953, or over eight million tons.

Key Dates:

1864: Portland-Cement-Fabrik Dyckerhoff & Söhne founded.
1886: Dyckerhoff cement is exported to over 100 countries.
1911: Dyckerhoff & Söhne GmbH established.
1931: Merger with Wicking AG to form Dyckerhoff Wicking AG, and Dyckerhoff Weiss, the first white Portland cement in Germany, is introduced.
1936: The company is renamed to Dyckerhoff Portland-Zementwerke AG.
1949: Dyckerhoff Dreifach revolutionizes pre-stressed concrete technology.
1952: Dyckerhoff Well Cements for oil and gas explorations are introduced.
1956: Company is renamed to Dyckerhoff Zementwerke AG.
1985: The new name Dyckerhoff AG and a new Logo are introduced.
1991: Dyckerhoff acquires Deuna Zement GmbH.
1994: Dyckerhoff takes over Ciments Luxembourgeois.
1999: Lone Star Industries acquired.

Between 1974 and 1985 the demand for cement dropped, forcing Dyckerhoff to explore other markets. One important field of diversification was the development of products for the reconstruction, remodeling, or renovation of buildings. The year 1985 was marked by three important events for Dyckerhoff. First, the company was renamed Dyckerhoff AG because its activities had long outgrown the production of cement. With the new name came a new corporate identity concept, including a new, modern logo that has been in use ever since. Second, a new business division for finishing products—Dytec—was founded. Dytec was the new umbrella group for all Dyckerhoff's activities in do-it-yourself products, including plaster, paint and varnishes, insulation materials, glue and other chemicals used in construction, and hardware tools. Finally, Dyckerhoff MIKRODUR, a mineral-based binding material, was introduced to fill and strengthen very small cavities. By the end of the 1980s Dyckerhoff had three strong business divisions: cement, ready-mixed concrete, and Dytec, and seven production plants in Germany, one in Spain, and one in Glens Falls, New York. Dyckerhoff's subsidiaries and shareholdings expanded into Austria, Spain, Luxembourg, the Netherlands, Belgium, Turkey, France, Great Britain, and the United States.

Early 1990s: German Reunification and Modernization

The reunification of Germany in 1990 opened new opportunities for Dyckerhoff. In 1991 the company acquired the Deuna Zement GmbH, founded in 1975 and located in the East German state of Thuringia. Deuna Zement had access to extraordinarily homogenous raw materials which made possible the production of many different cement types, including specialty cements of very high quality. However, the production plant was technologically outdated by western standards, and the high number of employees—1,700—significantly lowered profit-

ability. After reconstruction in the early 1990s, Deuna Zement would become one of the most modern plants of its kind.

However, another effect of the fall of the iron curtain was less favorable for Dyckerhoff. Shortly after the East European markets opened, cement from plants in former Czechoslovakia and in Poland, subsidized in part by their national governments, flooded the new German states of Bavaria, Saxony, Berlin, Brandenburg, and Thuringia. The price for this cement was approximately 20 percent below the market price in Germany. In addition to being able to offer government-subsidized low prices for energy and transportation, these competitors were able to take advantage of significantly lower wages.

Because of the tough competition in the cement market, Dyckerhoff was involved in other activities fueled by the construction boom in East Germany. Old production facilities were modernized throughout the country, as old buildings that had suffered from insufficient maintenance during the previous four decades had to be rebuilt or renovated. Numerous graying and damaged facades in East German cities and towns got a new face. There was enough demand for Dyckerhoff's finishing products division to thrive. Another market opened up when sewage systems were modernized all over eastern Germany, and the construction of new single family houses started booming. To address this market Dyckerhoff started producing finished concrete products in 1990. The new product range included decorative concrete stones, slabs, and edging for paving; garden and landscape furnishings; concrete pipes and sewage treatment technology; and pre-fabricated building parts for floors, walls, stairs, balconies, and garages.

At the same time Dyckerhoff established its ready-mixed concrete division and other production facilities in the new German states. An East German Dyckerhoff subsidiary, the Tricosal GmbH, established a new production for grouting tape in Deuna. The ready-mixed concrete division had established a distribution network with ten subsidiaries and 26 plants in the new German states by 1993. Dyckerhoff's finishing products division also expanded its distribution network and opened service centers in bigger East German cities to advise craftsmen and do-it-yourselfers about products. By 1993 there were about 1,000 employees from the new German states on Dyckerhoff's payroll, and the company had invested approximately DM500 million in its new sites in East Germany.

The Late 1990s: Reorganization and International Growth

By 1994 Dyckerhoff was Germany's second largest producer of construction materials with a 20 percent market share in cement and 18 percent in ready-mixed concrete, as well as an annual production capacity of nine million tons per year worldwide. However, after 1994 the construction boom in eastern Germany began to die out. At the same time the German economy slowed, and prospects for the cement industry were uncertain. Therefore, Dyckerhoff's main capital investments during the 1990s focused on modernization of cement kilns, grinding plants, and logistics infrastructure; broadening the product range; reducing energy costs; and the implementation of environmentally-friendly technologies. For example, about 120 filter systems were installed in all Dyckerhoff cement plants, removing the dust from air and gas emissions. The dust from exhaust gases emitted from rotary kilns where the raw material was dried and ground at 1,400 degrees Celsius was removed by large electrostatic precipitators. The buildings with steel ball mills where the cement klinker was ground to a fine powder were sound-proofed and equipped with sound absorbers to cut noise pollution. The dust content of gas emitted into the environment was monitored continually. All together, between 1988 and 1998, Dyckerhoff invested about DM 1.5 billion in its plants.

While it lowered production costs, Dyckerhoff aggressively expanded into new markets abroad. This was reflected in the number of Dyckerhoff employees working outside Germany; by 1995 28 percent of all employees worked abroad, while only one year earlier that figure stood at 20 percent. At the same time, in 1995, the total number of Dyckerhoff employees rose by one-fifth, caused primarily by the expansion of activities in the ready-mixed concrete and finishing products markets. Another factor that contributed to this workforce growth was the acquisition of a majority share in Luxembourg-based Ciments Luxembourgeois, a group of companies active in the cement, concrete, natural stone, and plasters markets with DM 200 million in annual sales.

In 1994 and again in 1997 Dyckerhoff changed its organizational structure. Until then, Dyckerhoff AG oversaw the operative cement business and also functioned as the parent company for its independent subsidiaries. In 1995 Dyckerhoff AG was transformed into a management holding company, while the cement activities were transferred to a new company, Dyckerhoff Zement GmbH. All cement-shareholdings abroad were organized under the newly founded Dyckerhoff Zement International GmbH. In 1996 the Dyckerhoff Baustoffsysteme GmbH was founded to include all activities in the field of construction materials for building contractors, including such products as binding agents, filling compounds, grouting, immobilizing, and injection materials. Dyckerhoff Beton GmbH was founded in 1997 and managed the ready-mixed concrete division, Transportbeton GmbH, as well as all subsidiaries manufacturing and marketing concrete products. Finally, Dyckerhoff Ausbauprodukte GmbH organized all companies of the finishing products and do-it-yourself business division. The reorganization included a change in Dyckerhoff's top management. Industry outsider Peter Rohde, who had extensive experience in the coal mining industry, succeeded Alexander von Engelhardt, who had guided Dyckerhoff through a decade of significant change.

Because of the stagnating markets in Germany and Western Europe Dyckerhoff saw its main growth potential in Eastern Europe, the United States, and even West-Siberia. Consequently, the reorganization was followed by a series of acquisi-

tions that included cement production plants in Nowiny, Poland; in Hranice and Ostrava, Czech Republic; and Sverdlovsk, Russia. In 1999 Dyckerhoff bought Lone Star Industries Inc., an American producer of cement and ready-mixed concrete, for $1.2 billion. In early 2000 the company announced that it was planning for further global expansion.

Principal Subsidiaries

Dyckerhoff Zement GmbH; Dyckerhoff Zement International GmbH; Dyckerhoff Beton GmbH; Dyckerhoff Ausbauprodukte GmbH; Dyckerhoff Luxembourg S.A. (Luxemburg); Anneliese Zementwerke AG (48.8%); NCD Nederlande Cement Deelnemingsmaatschappij B.V. (Netherlands; 45.6%); Deuna Zement GmbH; Intermoselle S.à.r.l. (Luxemburg; 50%); Ciments Luxembourgeois S.A. (Luxemburg; 68.4%); Cementos Hispana S.A. (Spain; 61.6%); Cementownia ''Nowiny'' S.A. (Poland; 87.1%); Cement Hranice a.s. (Czech Republic; 97.5%); Glenns Falls Cement Company Inc. (United States); Lone Star Industries, Inc. (United States; Beton Union GmbH & Co. KG (Germany; 96.2%); Ispo GmbH; Dyckerhoff Ausbauprodukte AG (Switzerland); Isoned B.V. (Netherlands); Dyckerhoff Matériaux S.A. (France).

Principal Competitors

Heidelberger Zement AG; Nordcement AG; Holderbank Financiere Glaris Ltd.; Lafarge S.A.

Further Reading

''Competition: Court Ruling In Cement-Cartel Fines Case Draws Near,'' *European Report*, June 2, 1999.
''Dyckerhoff Acquires Polish Cement Group,'' *European Report*, January 5, 1996.
''Dyckerhoff steht auf festem Fundament,'' *Süddeutsche Zeitung*, July 5, 1995.
''Für Dyckerhoff sind die neuen Länder ein sehr wichtiger Markt,'' *Frankfurter Allgemeine Zeitung*, October 26, 1993, p. 26.
''Germany's Dyckerhoff Completes Purchase of Lone Star,'' *Reuters Business Report*, October 3, 1999.
''Harald Dyckerhoff,'' *Frankfurter Allgemeine Zeitung*, December 20, 1993, p. 16.
''Holzmann to Discuss Accord on Slave Labor Lawsuit,'' Reuters, October 19, 1998.
''Jürgen Lose 65 Jahre,'' *Frankfurter Allgemeine Zeitung*, November 25, 1999, p. 21.
Kirsch, Jürgen, ''Dyckerhoff AG,'' *World Cement*, September 1998, p. 22.
——, ''Dyckerhoff AG,'' *World Cement*, September 1999, p. 42.
''Von Engelhardt 65 Jahre,'' *Frankfurter Allgemeine Zeitung*, September 20, 1996, p. 28.

—Evelyn Hauser

EchoStar Communications Corporation

5701 South Santa Fe Drive
Littleton, Colorado 80120
U.S.A.
Telephone: (303) 723-1000
Fax: (303) 723-1399
Web site: http://www.echostar.com

Public Company
Incorporated: 1993
Employees: 6,000+
Sales: $1.6 billion (1999)
Stock Exchanges: NASDAQ
Ticker Symbol: DISH
NAIC: 513220 Satellite Television Distribution Systems

EchoStar Communications Corporation is perhaps best known for its direct broadcast satellite (DBS) system, DISH Network, which was launched in 1996 and quickly became the fastest growing satellite TV service in the United States. The company also operates three interrelated business units. Satellite Services oversees satellite uplink, transponder space-usage, and other services for television customers and other satellite users. EchoStar Technologies Corporation designs, manufactures, and distributes DBS reception equipment (set-top boxes and antennas). The third unit, EchoStar International Corporation, is headquartered in the Netherlands and provides a range of satellite-related services throughout Europe, Africa, the Middle East, Australia, and Asia.

1980s Origins

The company that became EchoStar was founded by Charles Ergen in 1980 as a small retail store that sold direct-to-home satellite television products and services. During the 1980s it was primarily a manufacturer and distributor of C-band hardware. C-band satellites were used primarily to broadcast shows to cable system operators, not to individuals, because reception equipment cost about $2,500 and included a ten-foot dish antenna. By the mid-1980s the company, known as Echosphere Corp., was a leading supplier of direct-to-home hardware and services worldwide.

Foreseeing changes in the satellite industry, Egren applied to the Federal Communications Commission (FCC) in 1987 for a direct broadcast satellite (DBS) license. In 1992 EchoStar won a license to broadcast from one of three slots within the broadcasting range of the entire continental United States. The slot, among eight set aside by the FCC, was located above the city of Los Angeles. EchoStar Satellite Corp. was established to build, launch, and operate the company's satellites.

Launching the Programming Service: 1993–95

In December 1993 EchoStar Communications was incorporated in Nevada, with headquarters in Englewood, Colorado, as holding company for 13 direct and indirect subsidiaries. EchoStar claimed to lead the U.S. market for home satellite reception products, with a 30 percent domestic market share. The company had an existing distribution network of 5,000 dealers. For 1993 revenues from subsidiaries were $220.9 million, 33.8 percent more than 1992, with net income of $20.4 million, nearly double 1992's net income of $10.8 million.

In January 1994 EchoStar made arrangements with DirectSat Corporation, a subsidiary of SSE Telecom that had also won a license to put a satellite above Los Angeles, to pool their licenses and resources to offer 110 channels of television, 250 audio channels, and data feeds of financial and weather information.

In 1994 EchoStar offered $624 million in senior secured notes along with 3.7 million common stock purchase warrants. Proceeds to the company were about $335 million. These so-called "junk bonds" had an interest rate of nearly 13 percent, with payment deferred until 1999. The proceeds would be used primarily to construct, launch, insure, and operate two direct broadcast satellites to be built by Martin Marietta Corp. (later Lockheed Martin Corp.) for $159 million. The launches were planned to take place in China in 1995 and 1996, with insurance costing $206.3 million.

If successful, the two satellites would be worth $881 million once service was initiated. The two satellites would enable

Company Perspectives:

Positioned as a single, convenient source for equipment distribution, sales, installation, service and programming distribution, EchoStar Communications Corporation is widely recognized in the communications industry for its research and development activities. The company and its subsidiaries deliver direct broadcast satellite (DBS) television products and services to millions of customers nationwide.

EchoStar to begin broadcasting more than 100 channels of television programming to 18-inch receiver dishes that cost an estimated $500 each. The company's target audience would be the 11.5 million American households not wired for cable and 20.4 million households wired for cable but with limited channel capacity.

AT&T would operate EchoStar I and provide tracking, telemetry, control, and maintenance services for the satellite. AT&T would also provide consulting services to Martin Marietta, the satellite's builder. It was unclear at first who would supply the receiving equipment for consumers. At this point, access to the 18-inch satellite receiver was controlled by DirecTV, a subsidiary of General Motors' Hughes Electronics Corp.

In 1995 EchoStar was building a $50 million uplink facility in Cheyenne, Wyoming, that would be operational by August 1995, and EchoStar I was scheduled to launch October 1, 1995. The company was busy lining up programming. Its initial hardware would consist of an 18-inch dish, set-top box, and remote. It intended to compete directly with the Digital Satellite System offered by Thomson Consumer Electronics and DirecTV.

EchoStar issued a prospectus for a four-million share initial public offering (IPO) in July 1995. By August 1995 EchoStar had signed programming deals with Viacom to carry its basic and premium channels, including Showtime, The Movie Channel, MTV, VH1, and Nickelodeon. It also had signed deals with HBO, CNN, The Disney Channel, Turner Classic Movies, ESPN, C-SPAN, and The Learning Channel.

EchoStar's initial satellite launch was delayed because of problems with its Chinese partner, China Great Wall Industry Corp., which had experienced two launch failures in 1995. Meanwhile, DBS competitors DirecTV, which was owned by General Motors' Hughes Electronics Corp., and Primestar, which was owned by a consortium of cable operators that included TCI Inc. and Time Warner, were mounting extensive marketing campaigns to gain market share.

The company's first satellite was launched from China on December 28, 1995. EchoStar also acquired more channels by purchasing the 22 channel assignments of Direct Broadcast Satellite Corporation (DBSC) for $8 million. EchoStar had acquired a 40 percent interest in DBSC in 1994 and in 1996 acquired the remaining 60 percent for an estimated $23 million.

EchoStar's DBS service would be called the DISH TV Network, with DISH standing for Digital Sky Highway. The service was scheduled to launch in February 1996 with 100 channels. It would compete directly with DirecTV and less directly with Primestar, which required a larger dish and had fewer channels.

The Launch in 1996

At the beginning of 1996 the FCC auctioned two blocks of DBS channels, one of which went to MCI and the other to EchoStar. EchoStar's slot was too far to the west to be able to service the east coast, while MCI purchased the last DBS slot with full coverage of the continental United States. MCI and News Corp. were planning a joint satellite venture to be called American Sky Broadcasting Co. (ASkyB).

When EchoStar began offering DBS service in spring 1996, there were three competitors already offering similar services: DirecTV, United States Satellite Broadcasting, and Primestar. EchoStar was the only DBS service to have the capacity for two national DBS systems. Its receivers would be made by the French manufacturer Groupe Sagem and American company, SCI Systems. Philips would market EchoStar DBS dishes under its Philips and Magnavox brands.

EchoStar previewed its DISH TV Network at a trade show in March 1996, and by May the service was rolled out to consumers, who could chose from five programming packages with monthly fees ranging from $19.99 to $59.99. At the same time the company launched a $40 million advertising campaign to promote the DISH Network. By June 1996 EchoStar claimed to have 50,000 subscribers. The company would continue to offer various price promotions to gain subscribers. EchoStar was adding about 1,500 subscribers per day and forecast up to 400,000 subscribers by the end of 1996. DISH Network reached 100,000 subscribers by August 1996. EchoStar was offering its satellite dish and programming for low prices, and the competitors were soon forced to lower their prices as well.

EchoStar II launched on September 10, 1996, from French Guiana, doubling EchoStar's channel capacity from 80 to 160. The company added two new basic packages: America's Top 40, which consisted of 40 basic networks for $19.95 a month, and America's Top 50, which included a 30-channel audio feed plus ten more channels, for $24.99.

In November 1996 EchoStar introduced a new promotion with computer manufacturer Gateway Inc. Customers who purchased certain Gateway computers would receive a coupon for a free satellite receiver system with the purchase of one year of DISH Network programming. The company would continue to use free dish promotions as an integral part of its marketing programs to attract new subscribers to DISH Network TV.

The company added 65,000 subscribers in December 1996, its strongest month, giving the DISH Network 350,000 subscribers by year's end. Meanwhile, DirecTV added 165,000 subscribers in December, giving it 2.3 million subscribers at year's end.

Subscriber Growth in 1997

Seeking to expand its services beyond DBS, the company began entering into agreements for more satellites, and fixed

Key Dates:

1987: EchoStar founder Charles Ergen files for a direct broadcast satellite license with the FCC, and gets one five years later.

1995: The company's first satellite, EchoStar I, is launched from China.

1996: The company's DBS service, DISH TV Network, is launched.

1997: DISH TV reaches one million subscribers.

1998: EchoStar acquires the assets of American Sky Broadcasting.

1999: Company introduces the first satellite TV receiver/Internet browser; Congress passes the Satellite Home Viewers Act, allowing DBS providers to broadcast local programming in local markets.

satellites. The fixed satellite business required a higher degree of capitalization than EchoStar could command, and the company was admittedly seeking financial partners, among them TCI Satellite Entertainment. By February 1997 the company had $800 million of debt on its balance sheet. Its stock hit a 52-week high of $37 in February 1996, but a year later was worth about 60 percent less. It reached a 52-week low of $15 on January 29, 1997.

By the end of February 1997 it appeared that EchoStar had found its financial partner in Rupert Murdoch and News Corporation Limited. Murdoch was in the process of building an uplink center in Arizona for his proposed joint venture with MCI Worldcom, American Sky Broadcasting (ASkyB). Murdoch's News Corp. planned to buy a 40 percent stake in EchoStar for about $1 billion. The deal would give EchoStar seven satellites able to deliver 500 channels, including the capacity to carry local stations. As part of the deal, MCI would own ten percent of EchoStar. The remaining 50 percent of EchoStar would be retained by the company's shareholders. Under the terms of the agreement, Ergen would continue as CEO of EchoStar, and Murdoch would become chairman. EchoStar quickly announced it would invest $500 million to build eight regional uplink centers with the capability of delivering local broadcast channels. Analysts agreed that DBS service, which included local stations, would be the first really serious threat to cable television.

The proposed merger with News Corp.'s satellite business was soon running into opposition. News Corp. had failed to obtain permission from broadcasters to retransmit their signals, and the FCC was being asked to deny the ASkyB-EchoStar merger. When Murdoch insisted on management control over the merged company, the deal came undone. With News Corp. and EchoStar disagreeing on several technical issues, EchoStar went to court to force News Corp. to make good on a $200 million interest-free loan that was part of the merger agreement. Murdoch countered by insisting that Ergen resign as CEO and give up management of the venture. On May 9, EchoStar sued News Corp. for breach of contract, claiming $5 billion in damages, with News Corp. filing a countersuit the next month. Meanwhile, News Corp. and Primestar reached an agreement in

principle to merge their DBS operations, but that proposed merger was also subsequently called off by federal regulators.

EchoStar continued to seek financial partners and filed with the SEC for a $378 million debt offering, in part to raise an additional $305 million to cover the costs of four planned satellites. As it negotiated with Lockheed Martin to reschedule its payments, the company's debt reached $1.2 billion.

The company began a new promotion on June 1, 1997, whereby consumers could purchase EchoStar hardware for $199 without buying an annual subscription, subscribing on a monthly basis instead. By mid-1997 EchoStar had 590,000 subscribers and was adding nearly 50,000 new subscribers a month. EchoStar III launched in October 1997 from Cape Canaveral, Florida, and would serve primarily the east coast of the United States. The company also purchased 32.2 acres and a 190,000-square-foot building in Littleton, Colorado, for its new campus-style corporate headquarters for $7.5 million.

A $99 installation promotion resulted in 105,000 new subscribers in September. By the end of October EchoStar had 895,000 subscribers and was warning that a shortage of receivers would temporarily limit the number of new subscribers. However, the company had met its financing needs by raising more than $650 million through debt and equity offerings since its proposed merger with News Corp. fell through. The company reached an agreement with Sears, Roebuck & Co. to offer its $199 package in 800 Sears outlets.

For 1997 net losses rose 210 percent to $321.3 million on revenues of $477.4 million, up 140 percent. The company ended the year about $1.4 billion in debt after raising $750 million in debt during the year. The company also ended the year with 1.2 million subscribers.

More Channel Capacity in 1998

In January 1998 EchoStar began beaming the local signals of the top four networks' broadcast affiliates into their respective markets in New York, Chicago, Boston, Washington, Atlanta, and Dallas, with additional cities to follow. Ten more Western cities would be added after the launch of EchoStar IV in the spring, according to EchoStar's plan to reach more than 40 percent of U.S. television households. EchoStar asked the Library of Congress to determine whether copyright law allowed the retransmission of local network signals into their market of origin by DBS satellites.

The company introduced a new Top 60 programming package in May for $28.99 per month to replace the Top 50 package, adding such channels as American Movie Classics, Bravo, and the SportsChannel, among others. New subscribers were offered a $60 credit if they submitted a copy of their latest cable bill.

EchoStar IV launched May 8, 1998, from Kazakhstan. Following the launch, the company encountered problems deploying the solar panels on the satellite. It subsequently found that one primary and one back-up transponder on EchoStar IV failed. Additional capacity was gained through an alliance with Loral Skynet to deliver niche programming through one of Loral's satellites. EchoStar was also preparing to deliver data to consumers. It was already supplying data to niche markets through AgCast, an agricultural report, and Signal, a stock report. It began competing more directly with DirecTV by offering a $100 bounty to any DirecTV subscribers who switched to EchoStar. DirecTV responded by doubling the bounty for DISH TV subscribers who switched to DirecTV.

EchoStar received permission from the FCC to broadcast local network signals to "unserved" homes in Denver, Phoenix, San Francisco, and Salt Lake City from its EchoStar IV satellite. Industry periodical *Broadcasting & Cable* noted that the political climate was good for moving "local-to-local" service ahead, because it was seen as providing competition to cable television and possibly reducing cable subscriber rates. By September it was clear that Congress was working to pass legislation that would permit satellite TV companies to deliver local broadcast signals.

In October EchoStar announced a three-month promotion to new subscribers, giving them a $249 rebate on the cost of receiving hardware in exchange for a one-year subscription to the DISH Network's America's Top 100 CD programming package. DirecTV and Primestar, which each had their own promotions going, declined to match the offer. At the beginning of the month DISH TV had about 1.6 million subscribers, compared to four million for DirecTV and 2.6 million for Primestar. EchoStar also announced that it planned to offer interactive television nationally in 1999—including e-mail and home banking—using software from OpenTV Inc. of Mountain View, California.

Seeking to clarify which households qualified to legally receive imported network signals via satellite, EchoStar brought lawsuits against the top four broadcast networks. The FCC was currently considering new rules for determining such eligibility. The four networks—ABC, CBS, NBC, and Fox—countered by filing suit against EchoStar, claiming the company sold network programming to ineligible customers.

In November 1998 DISH TV introduced BBC America as part of its America's Top 100 CD package. It was the first satellite carriage of the channel, a joint venture between the BBC and the Discovery Networks. EchoStar was also negotiating with cable operators to provide them with a digital satellite supplement to their regular cable offerings. Targeted were small cable operators with largely rural systems.

In December 1998 News Corp. agreed to sell its satellite television assets to EchoStar, which would increase EchoStar's channels from 200 to 500. Under terms of the agreement, EchoStar would pay $1.25 billion to buy the DBS assets of the MCI Worldcom-News Corp. venture, American Sky Broadcasting (ASkyB). The stock deal would give MCI and News Corp. a 37 percent interest in EchoStar and end the litigation over the failed merger attempt in 1997. EchoStar would receive AskyB's uplink center in Gilbert, Arizona, as well as a license to operate at another orbital location, and two satellites then under construction. EchoStar also got a three-year retransmission deal to carry Fox Network's local signals and agreed to carry the Fox News Channel. Following the merger, EchoStar would control more than half the satellite slots over the United States. With FCC approval of ASkyB's license transfer to EchoStar, the deal

closed in June 1999, with EchoStar issuing 8.6 million shares of Class A stock.

Competitor DirecTV responded by acquiring its longtime partner, U.S. Satellite Broadcasting Co., for $1.3 billion in December 1998. The acquisition gave DirecTV an improved programming package and 200,000 new subscribers. In January DirecTV announced it would acquire rival Primestar for $1.82 billion, leaving DirecTV and EchoStar as the number one and two DBS providers. subscribers. EchoStar saw an opportunity to pick up Primestar's old subscribers and offered a $200 bounty to its dealers for every Primestar customer they could switch to DISH TV. Analysts estimated that as many as 1,000 Primestar customers per day were switching to DISH TV.

The Top Two Satellite TV Services in 1999

In an effort to provide interactive television services, EchoStar announced a partnership with Microsoft's WebTV to include the WebTV Network Plus Internet TV service in a new generation of EchoStar integrated receiver/decoders that would be available in spring 1999. The service would deliver Web page content to viewers and allow them to pause a program for up to 30 minutes before resuming it. In June EchoStar rolled out its DISHPlayer, a satellite receiver with an integrated WebTV service that allowed users to surf the Internet, send e-mail, and play video games. The DISHPlayer was priced at $199, plus a subscription fee for programming service and another extra fee for Internet access.

In March EchoStar surpassed the two million subscriber mark for DISH TV. With federal cable rate regulations expiring in March 1999, lawmakers were seeking to find ways to increase competition for cable, rather than extend the rate regulations. In May a House bill on satellite reform passed that would allow DBS companies to provide a programming package that included local programming. For the rest of the year the Satellite Home Viewer Act (SHVA) would be the subject of intense lobbying on the part of satellite providers, cable operators, television station owners, and cable and broadcast networks. Hurdles to offering local-into-local service included passage of appropriate legislation, FCC approval of orbital license transfers, and retransmission deals with every local broadcaster.

In June EchoStar was recognized by President Bill Clinton for providing satellite dishes and 40 hours of school safety programming to school districts across the country. The company's stock reached a 52-week high of $142.63 and later rose to more than $176 before settling around $151.

By the end of August 1999 EchoStar had 2.84 million DISH TV subscribers. EchoStar V was launched on September 23, 1999, from Cape Canaveral. Following a stock split EchoStar's stock was trading at a 52-week adjusted high of $88.25.

In November SHVA passed Congress and was signed into law by President Clinton. It gave DBS providers like EchoStar and DirecTV permission to offer local broadcast channels to their subscribers in those local markets. As a result, satellite TV subscriptions were expected to grow by 2.5 million subscribers in 2000. Local delivery in the top 30 markets was expected to begin as soon as possible. EchoStar was immediately able to provide full market coverage in 13 cities covering 31 million homes, with other cities to follow, while DirecTV offered local broadcast affiliate programming to nearly 12 million households in New York and Los Angeles with other markets to follow. In December 1999 EchoStar had nearly 3.5 million subscribers, and by April 2000 that number had reached four million. For 1999, the company reported a record $1.6 billion in revenues.

Plans for 2000 included up to six new satellites, as well as plans to market set-top boxes capable of recording live television programs without the use of tape. Although EchoStar had yet to show a profit since becoming a DBS provider, the company was positioned to take advantage of the new regulatory climate of the 21st century. Following passage of SHVA in 1999, DBS companies would be able to compete more effectively with cable television operators. Industry consolidation left EchoStar the number two satellite television operator, behind industry leader DirecTV. Both would be competing for market share in the years to come.

Principal Subsidiaries

EchoStar Technologies Corporation; EchoStar International Corporation (Netherlands).

Principal Operating Units

DISH TV Network; Satellite Services.

Principal Competitors

DirecTV.

Further Reading

Albiniak, Paige, and Bill McConnell, "EchoStar Loses One, Wins Another at FCC," *Broadcasting & Cable,* June 21, 1999, p. 19.

Albiniak, Paige, "At Long Last, Local," *Broadcasting & Cable,* November 29, 1999, p. 4.

Bloomfield, Judy, "EchoStar's Big Sky," *HFN—The Weekly Newspaper for the Home Furnishing Network,* March 3, 1997, p. 43.

Brull, Steven V., "Now, Beam up Some Customers," *Business Week,* December 28, 1998, p. 52.

Colman, Price, "Echoes of Slowdown at EchoStar," *Broadcasting & Cable,* February 10, 1997, p. 48.

——, "EchoStar, DirecTV Battle for Eyeballs," *Broadcasting & Cable,* August 31, 1998, p. 43.

——, "EchoStar Unbundles," *Broadcasting & Cable,* June 2, 1997, p. 70.

Dickson, Glen, "Sat TV Goes Interactive," *Broadcasting & Cable,* January 11, 1999, p. 15.

Fehr-Snyder, Kerry, "News Corp.-EchoStar Deal Raises Real Threat for Cable Television Systems," *Knight-Ridder/Tribune Business News,* February 27, 1997.

Fleming, Heather, "Sky's Future Still Cloudy," *Broadcasting & Cable,* April 28, 1997, p. 8.

Hutheesing, Nikhil, "Kamikaze Satellites?," *Forbes,* July 4, 1994, p. 126.

Littleton, Cynthia, and Harry A. Jessel, "Murdoch, Ergen Take to Sky," *Broadcasting & Cable,* March 3, 1997, p. 41.

Locke, Tom, "EchoStar Takes Debt Public," *Denver Business Journal,* March 25, 1994, p. 3A.

Marchand, Nolan, "EchoStar Gets More Customers for Dish," *Broadcasting & Cable,* September 20, 1999, p. 62.

McCarthy, Shira, "EchoStar Shines On," *Telephony,* October 7, 1996, p. 48.

McConnell, Bill, and Paige Albiniak, "Clinton Praises EchoStar," *Broadcasting & Cable,* June 14, 1999, p. 22.

McConville, Jim, "New Bird Boosts EchoStar Capacity," *Broadcasting & Cable,* October 28, 1996, p. 113.

Mundy, Alicia, "EchoStar Woos Rival's Subs," *Mediaweek,* February 1, 1999, p. 5.

Noer, Michael, "Pie in the Sky," *Forbes,* October 9, 1995, p. 12.

Peers, Martin, "Wrapped up in Suits, Echo Grows Fainter," *Variety,* May 19, 1997, p. 24.

Peers, Martin, and Joe Flint, "Rupert Hears an Echo: The Sky is Falling," *Variety,* May 5, 1997, p. 1.

Perman, Stacy, "EchoStar's New Orbit," *Time,* March 10, 1997, p. 56.

Quittner, Joshua, "My Neighbor's Dish," *Time,* June 7, 1999, p. 84.

Roberts, Johnnie L., "Rupert's Death Star," *Newsweek,* March 10, 1997, p. 46.

Stern, Christopher, "EchoStar Banks on Ergen-omics," *Variety,* July 12, 1999, p. 29.

Veilleux, C. Thomas, "EchoStar Beams In," *HFN-The Weekly Newspaper for the Home Furnishing Network,* March 11, 1996, p. 77.

——, "EchoStar DBS Alternative to Bow," *HFN-The Weekly Newspaper for the Home Furnishing Network,* November 14, 1994, p. 84.

—David P. Bianco

EDMC™
Education Management Corporation

Education Management Corporation

300 6th Avenue
Pittsburgh, Pennsylvania 15222-2598
U.S.A.
Telephone: (412) 562-0900
Fax: (412) 562-0598
Web site: http://www.edumgt.com

Public Company
Incorporated: 1962
Employees: 2,780
Sales: $260.8 million (1999)
Stock Exchanges: NASDAQ
Ticker Symbol: EDMC
NAIC: 511519 Other Technical and Trade Schools;
611210 Junior Colleges; 611310 Colleges,
Universities, and Professional Schools; 611410
Business and Secretarial Schools; 611430 Professional
and Management Development Training

The Education Management Corporation (EDMC) owns and operates 22 post-secondary schools nationwide, providing career education to more than 24,000 students from throughout the United States and over 80 foreign countries. The company offers certificates, Associate degrees, or Bachelor's degrees in: culinary arts/management; graphic design; industrial design technology; photography; interior design; computer animation; fashion design/marketing; multimedia and web site design; online media & marketing; interactive multimedia programming; game art & design; and video/audio production. At the National Center for Paralegal Studies in Atlanta, EDMC offers an Associate of Arts degree in legal studies, as well as certificate programs for administrative assistants to the legal profession. EDMC's schools are located in major metropolitan areas in 13 states and Washington D.C. EDMC counts over 100,000 alumni.

1960s Origins

EDMC was founded in 1962, offering professional development education in Pennsylvania. The company's scope and focus then shifted with the 1970 acquisition of the Art Institute of Pittsburgh, founded in 1921. As a post-secondary art school under the parentage of EDMC, the Art Institute of Pittsburgh offered certificate programs in graphic design, interior design, and photography.

Robert B. Knutson joined EDMC in 1969 and became president of the company in 1971. Knutson would oversee a period of expansion through acquisition. Over the next 15 years, EDMC would add to its higher education holdings with eight acquisitions, seven of which would involve commercial arts schools in Denver, Ft. Lauderdale, Atlanta, Philadelphia, Dallas, Houston, and Seattle. The company grouped these, in a national marketing campaign, as "The Art Institutes." The eighth acquisition, of the National Center for Paralegal Training, offered certificates in legal studies. Another driving force behind EDMC's expansion was Knutson's wife, Miryam L. Drucker, who joined the company in 1984 as president of The Art Institute of Dallas, becoming president of The Art Institute of Fort Lauderdale before heading up the Art Institutes umbrella organization in 1988. She and Knutson were married during this time.

Under Knutson, who became EDMC's chairman and CEO in 1986, and Miryam Knutson, who in 1989 was named president and chief operating officer, the company upgraded and expanded the educational capacities of its schools by improving student services, updating the curriculum, upgrading facilities and equipment, and increasing the quality and quantity of faculty members.

Also during this time, the company gave increased attention to implementing technology in the classroom, embarking on a multimillion dollar investment in classroom technology to provide vocational training in computer animation, video production, and desktop publishing. EDMC instituted new programs and restructured several existing programs in order to improve the proportion of students who completed the programs. Some of the schools offering Associate degrees in interior design, industrial design, and graphics design built those programs into Bachelor of Arts degrees in 1993. EDMC also initiated career and employment programs to assist graduates in finding quality entry level positions with higher starting salaries.

160

In the early 1990s, EDMC began developing a culinary arts program, launching its School of Culinary Arts at the Colorado Institute of Art (CIA). Beginning in late 1993, that school offered an Associate of Applied Science degree, an 18-month to two-year program for the instruction of fine food preparation and fine dining restaurant operation. In March 1995 EDMC opened Assignments restaurant, a fully operational, 71-seat restaurant which provided an on-the-job training experience to students. On a rotating five-week schedule, students experienced all facets of restaurant operations, including table service, bar service, preliminary food preparation, and final food preparation for the customer. The facility featured a kitchen modeled after the one at New York's Waldorf-Astoria Hotel, with more than four times the space of an average restaurant kitchen. Through their assignments, students offered American cuisine to the public at lunch and added classic European cuisine for dinner in July.

EDMC pursued growth through the introduction of new schools and the acquisition of existing schools. In 1995 EDMC purchased two schools from the Ray College of Design, for $1.1 million and the assumption of debt, and renamed the schools The Illinois Institute of Art at Chicago and The Illinois Institute of Art at Schaumburg. EDMC also made the culinary arts program, with an Associate of Applied Science degree, an integral part of the Art Institute of Phoenix where classes commenced in January 1996. The following August the company acquired the New York Restaurant School for $9.5 million. Also, EDMC began to offered certificate programs for legal health care specialists and legal administrative assistants at the National Center of Paralegal Training in Atlanta.

In October 1996 the Pittsburgh Art Institute celebrated its 75th anniversary. Distinguished alumni at the festivities included Tom Wilson, creator of the "Ziggy" comic strip, and Mark Stutzman, designer of the U.S. Postal Service's best-selling "Elvis" stamp.

1996: Going Public and Continued Growth

EDMC funded further growth with an initial public offering of stock in October 1996. The company offered 5.4 million shares at $15 per share on the NASDAQ exchange and garnered approximately $45 million. The proceeds funded debt reduction and working capital as well as acquisitions and new schools. EDMC added the Lowthian College in Minneapolis to its chain in January 1997, renaming The Art Institutes International Min-

nesota. At the Colorado Institute of Art, EDMC expanded the Associate degree programs in interior design, industrial design, and graphic design into Bachelor of Science degree programs. The school also introduced an 18-month certificate program in web site administration, which involved existing multimedia and design classes as well as new programming classes staffed by three new faculty members. The Art Institute of Los Angeles opened for classes in October 1997.

For the fiscal year ending June 30, 1997, EDMC reported revenues of $182.8 million, an increase of 23 percent, while income reached $10 million, an increase of 46 percent. The company attributed the rise in income and revenues to increased enrollment and a 5.5 percent tuition increase during the fall 1996 quarter. Student enrollment had increased nearly 20 percent overall, averaging 14,490 students per quarter, while same-school enrollment at schools owned by EDMC for two or more years increased approximately 14 percent.

A secondary offering of stock in November 1997 raised $79.8 million for growth and improvement. Two acquisitions followed closely after the stock offering: the Louise Salinger Academy of Fashion in San Francisco and Bassist College in Portland, Oregon, renamed The Art Institutes International at San Francisco and The Art Institutes International at Portland, respectively. The Portland school offered Associate and Bachelor's degrees in apparel design, merchandising management, and interior design and a Bachelor's degree in business administration. EDMC expected its Associate degree recipients at the Art Institute of Seattle to consider Portland as an option for completion of a Bachelor's degree.

In consultation with professionals in computer design technology, EDMC began to formulate new educational programs and launched three new degree programs for Internet marketing and design in June 1999. The company offered a Bachelor of Science degree in online media and marketing, which involved classes on business strategy and online advertising. EDMC launched the program at the Colorado Institute of Art and planned to extend the programs to several other schools after government approval. The Art Institute of Phoenix offered a Bachelor's degree in game art and design, including character animation and complex mapping and modeling. An Associate degree in multimedia and web design involved interactive design and technical elements, such as audio, video animation, still pictures, text, and data. EDMC planned to offer the latter program in Atlanta, Chicago, Dallas, Houston, Ft. Lauderdale, Los Angeles, Minneapolis, Phoenix, Schaumburg, and Seattle.

By the end of fiscal year June 30, 1999, revenues at EDMC reached $260.8 million. Federal funding for student grants and loans comprised approximately 66 percent of revenues. Average quarterly enrollment reached 19,325 students compared to 17,002 students in fiscal 1998. Moreover, the company's stock, initially offered at $15 a share, had more than doubled to trade around $33 per share in early 1999. EDMC attributed growth in the student body to new educational programs, expanded degree programs, and more evening degree programs. Approximately 25 percent of the increase in enrollment stemmed from evening classes. Tuition increased six percent in 1999, while net income increased 30.9 percent, to $18.8 million. EDMC also reported that 91 percent of 1998 graduates found employment in their areas of study within six months of graduation. Starting salaries averaged $24,200 per year, a 7.2 percent increase over 1997 graduates.

Culinary arts education continued to be a major focus of growth, with three new programs initiated during the fiscal year. In January 1999 EDMC introduced a new culinary arts school at the Philadelphia Art Institute; facilities included Suburban Soup, a take-out restaurant at the Suburban Station transit center. EDMC also initiated plans for a culinary arts program at The Art Institute of Chicago which began in January 2000 with facilities expected to be fully operational for fall 2000.

EDMC's strategy for further growth involved the addition of two new schools per year. In August 1999 EDMC acquired the American Business and Fashion Institute in Charlotte. With 135 students, degree programs included interior design, fashion merchandising, and retail management. EDMC renamed the North Carolina school The Art Institute of Charlotte. A second acquisition involved the Massachusetts Communications College in Boston, with 450 students. The school offered Internet communications and technology; multimedia technology; and recording arts and broadcasting programs.

EDMC continued to improve educational programs at existing schools. In October 1999 the State of Pennsylvania approved EDMC to offer Bachelor of Arts degrees in computer animation, interior design, and industrial design technology at The Art Institutes in Pittsburgh and Philadelphia and a graphic design program at Pittsburgh. The new curriculum added management classes and other field-related courses. The New York Restaurant School, renamed the Art Institute of New York City, received approval to offer an Associate of Occupational Studies in art and design Technology. The program was slated to begin in January 2001. EDMC also planned to expand the culinary arts program there. The Art Institute of Phoenix initiated a Bachelor of Science degree program in online media and marketing.

EDMC sought to strengthen brand recognition for its educational programs among prospective students and corporate employers. A new marketing program promoted The Art Institutes as ''America's Leader in Creative Education.''

Planning for Future Growth

In fall 1999 EDMC introduced the Art Institute Online which offered 12 courses in graphic design. The pilot project was introduced through the Art Institutes of Phoenix and Ft. Lauderdale. The company intended the online courses as a precursor to an online Bachelor of Arts degree in graphic design, the first of its kind. The Socrates Distance Learning Technologies Group of Phoenix, acquired by EDMC in 1998, designed the courses.

EDMC established corporate partnerships to enrich student education with access to Internet infrastructure and functions. First Regional Telecom (FRT) and Tut Systems, Inc. provided students at the Art Institute of Philadelphia with email services, intranet, and access to the company's private label Web Neighborhood port. While FRT designed the port specifically for Art Institute students, allowing for interactive capabilities and possibilities for e-commerce, Tut Systems provided the infrastructure for high-speed access. MarketingCentral.com offered web-based capabilities for collaboration and management of creative projects to students at the Art Institute of Atlanta.

Growth in student enrollment required EDMC to relocate some schools to new facilities. In May the Colorado Institute of Art, renamed the Art Institute of Colorado, completed a move to a 100,000 square-foot, ten-story building near the site of the original school. The move allowed the school to consolidate offices and classrooms into one building, while adding more student-teacher conference rooms and a larger library. New technology involved the addition of a digital darkroom to the traditional photographer's darkroom and fully networked computer labs.

The Art Institute of Pittsburgh, renamed The Design Alliance, moved to a new facility in summer 2000. The $20 million project involved internal demolition of a historic landmark downtown. Renovation of the 170,000 square-foot building included up-dated electrical wiring and fiber optics, providing the infrastructure for 15 state-of-the-industry computer labs with 400 computers and Internet access for faculty and students alike. New technological capabilities included a digital darkroom, an industrial design technology shop, and video production and post-production facilities. EDMC projected enrollment at The Design Alliance to increase 30 to 40 percent during the 2000–2001 school year.

EDMC received approval by an accrediting organization to offer several new degree programs at the Art Institute International of Minnesota. With 700 students, the school planned to offer Associate of Applied Science and Bachelor of Science degrees in graphic design; interior design; media arts and animation; and Internet marketing and advertising. Associate degrees were also available in culinary arts, as well as in multimedia and web design. Also, the National Center for Paralegal Training received approval from the state of Georgia to offer an Associate of Arts in legal studies.

EDMC expanded into new markets with its 21st and 22nd schools. Classes commenced at The Art Institute of Washington in Roslyn, Virginia, in summer 2000. The Art Institute of Los Angeles-Orange County, where classes began in July 2000, offered Bachelor of Science programs in media arts and animation and in Internet marketing and advertising. Associate degree programs included graphic design and multimedia design, with the Culinary Arts school scheduled to open in summer 2001.

Principal Divisions

The Art Institutes; The Art Institutes International.

Principal Competitors

Apollo Group, Inc.; DeVry, Inc.; ITT Educational Services, Inc.

Further Reading

''Art Institute Holds Public Offering,'' *Pittsburgh Post-Gazette,* November 1, 1996, p. B5.

''Education Management Corporation Named to Forbes 200 Best Small Companies List,'' *PR Newswire*, October 25, 1999, p. 7,367.

''Matter of Degree For-Profit Schools Can Now Hand Out a Better Sheepskin,'' *Pittsburgh Post-Gazette,* June 30, 1997, p. A10.

Gammil, Marion, ''Art Institute Takes to the Street to Celebrate 75th Anniversary,'' *Pittsburgh Post-Gazette,* October 25, 1996, p. C3.

Gannon, Joyce, ''He Found a Career By Chance After Training to Work Internationally,'' *Pittsburgh Post-Gazette,* August 1, 1999, p. F5.

Parker, Penny, ''Students Grilled on Cooking Culinary Talents Tested at Restaurant,'' *Denver Post*, March 31, 1995, p. C1.

Schwab, Robert, ''Parent Company of Colorado Institute of Art plans $76 Million Offering,'' *Denver Post*, October 23, 1996, p. C2.

Tascarella, Patty, ''Art Schools' Degree OK'd,'' *Pittsburgh Business Times*, October 22, 1999, p. 3.

——, ''Education Management Corp. Studies Market for Acquisitions,'' *Pittsburgh Business Times*, February 17, 1997, p. 4.

——, ''N.Y. Fund Snaps Up Bargain-Priced Education Management Shares,'' *Pittsburgh Business Times*, November 19, 1999, p. 5.

Walker, Judy, ''A Better Belgian Batter for B. Battis?,'' *Arizona Republic, Phoenix Gazette*, April 17, 1996, p. FD3.

''Work Begins at New Site for Art Institute,'' *Pittsburgh Post-Gazette,* September 11, 1999, p. C12.

Zeiger, Dinah, ''Colorado Institute of Art Trains Future Web Gurus,'' *Denver Business Journal,* August 22, 1997, p. 9B.

—Mary Tradii

EMAP plc

One Lincoln Court, Lincoln Road
Peterborough PE1 2RF
United Kingdom
Telephone: (+44) 1733 568-900
Fax: (+44) 1733 312-115
Web site: http://www.emap.com

Public Company
Incorporated: 1947 as East Midland Allied Press
Employees: 6,388
Sales: £880.1 million ($1.41 billion) (1999)
Stock Exchanges: London
Ticker Symbol: EMA.L
NAIC: 51112 Periodical Publishers; 513112 Radio
   Stations

EMAP plc is a world-leading publisher of specialty and business-to-business magazines, with such titles as *FHM, Smash Hits, Hot Rod,* and *Motor Trend,* and *New Woman,* acquired in 2000, among some 600 titles in all. EMAP's magazines provide 86 percent (circulation and advertising revenues combined) of the company's sales of £880 million. In addition to EMAP's publishing wing, the company is one of the United Kingdom's major private radio companies, including Kiss FM, Magic 105.4, and Metro Radio among its 20 U.K.-based AM and FM radio stations. EMAP has ventured into television as well, with its own music channel, The Box, in the United Kingdom; its EMAP usa division also produces a number of specialty channels. The company has built a strong presence on the World Wide Web, owning all or part of a variety of web sites for which it provides content from its magazine portfolio. Apart from its media interests, EMAP also serves as host to more than 40 trade shows and other specialty events. The strength of EMAP's portfolio—and the weakness of its share price in 2000—has made it the subject of various takeover rumors, particularly by giants such as AOL and others eager to leverage EMAP's extensive content holdings. Chairman Robin Miller and CEO Kevin Hand have consistently insisted on EMAP's desire to remain independent.

Building a Magazine Empire in the 1950s

EMAP traced its origins to the late 19th century. In 1887, Sir Richard Winfrey purchased the *Spalding Guardian,* a local newspaper that provided the basis for the Winfrey family's newspaper interests. The family added three more local newspaper titles in the early part of the 20th century. In 1947, Pat and Richard Winfrey led a consolidation of the family's newspaper titles, merging the Northampshire Printing and Publishing Co. Ltd., the Petersborough Advertiser Co. Ltd., the West Norfolk and King's Lynn Newspaper Co. Ltd., and Bury St. Edmunds, together with the commercial printing operations at Rushden, King's Lynn, and Bury St. Edmunds, to form the East Midland Allied Press. By the beginning of the 1950s, East Midland Allied Press owned 17 newspaper titles.

In the early 1950s, however, East Midland Allied Press became interested in branching out into the magazine market. Eager to fill up its spare printing capacity, the company—by then led by Richard Winfrey—launched its first magazine title, *Angling Times,* in 1953. That magazine found immediate success, building a circulation of more than 50,000 by the end of its first year. *Angling Times* more than doubled its circulation over the next two years. By then, East Midland Allied Press had launched its second magazine, *Trout and Salmon.* In 1956, the company bought up *Motor Cycle News* for just £100. That title went on to take over its segment's lead and became one of the company's biggest and most consistent earners. The company completed the decade with a launch into a new direction, *Garden News.*

Through the 1960s, East Midland Allied Press continued to build up its magazine portfolio, adding five more titles, while increasing its newspaper titles to 19. The company also had taken on a new employee, Robin Miller, who initially joined *Motor Cycle News* as a cub reporter and then rose to editor of that magazine by 1970. But by the end of that year, Miller received a promotion, to the position of editorial manager. Two years later, Miller was joined by David Arculus. Together, Miller and Arculus developed a strategy for East Midland Allied Press's growth, built around its specialist magazine offerings, as well as its local newspaper titles. Miller was named CEO and, later, chairman in the mid-1980s.

Company Perspectives:

EMAP's corporate objective is to create one of the world's most highly rated media businesses in terms of people, products and services, growing faster than our competitors and with operating margins of 20%. To obtain and maintain our market leading positions we will run our business aggressively, investing in our leading brands whilst innovating in both product and process. High margins and good cash flows are a measure of our success, but also enable the company to have a strong and stable platform for growth. Thus the profits generated will go to both reward our shareholders and to continued investment in launch and acquisitions in growth markets. Growth will also demand that we recruit, retain and reward the best people, and in return the quality of their enthusiasm and pride in their products will enable the company's objectives to be met. Together we are building the most exciting media company in the world.

The company's biggest break came, however, in the late 1970s. In 1978, the company was approached by editor Nick Logan, who had covered the punk scene for the *New Musical Express*. Logan had an idea for his own music magazine, a glossy that would print the lyrics to hit songs, as well as offering photos, posters, and pinups—and fulsome praise—of the day's pop stars. The resulting magazine, *Smash Hits,* took the market by storm, becoming a smash hit of its own.

The success of *Smash Hits* propelled East Midland Allied Press onto a new publishing level and encouraged the company to step up its addition of new titles, resulting in the purchasing of titles such as *Which Computer* and *Fleet News,* as well as the launching of its own titles. The company, which changed its name to EMAP in 1985, also began to diversify, buying up business publications company MacClaren in that year. The following year, EMAP, which had already begun organizing the Fleet News Motor Show in the early 1980s, acquired Trade Promotions Services, expanding the company into the exhibitions market as well. In 1990, the company added to its business-to-business publications portfolio with the acquisition of Maclean Hunter. The downturn in the economic climate provided the opportunity for EMAP to go on a buying spree, and the company greatly expanded its magazine and newspaper titles in the early years of the decade.

Global Media Powerhouse in the 1990s

EMAP also made the move into the radio market in 1990, having agreed to back Gordon McNamee's effort to transform his pirate radio station into a legitimate commercial station. McNamee's success in winning a broadcast license gave EMAP a major stake in the station—Kiss FM—and a taste for more. By the end of that year, the company had purchased another radio group, Metro Radio.

EMAP also made its first move overseas—or at least, across the Channel—when it joined with joint venture partner Bayard Press to acquire the magazine title *Le Chasseur Francais* (the French Hunter). Placed in charge of building the company's

French base was Kevin Hand, who took over as CEO of the company in the late 1990s. Back in England, EMAP continued buying into the British radio market in 1991, acquiring the Liverpool-based Radio City group and purchasing a stake in Transworld Communications (acquiring full control in 1994), giving the company four more stations: Red Dragon in Cardiff, Red Rose in Preston, Piccadilly in Manchester, and Aire in Leeds.

In 1992, EMAP turned its attention to building its French position, launching its first wholly owned French title, *Reponses Photo*. Two years later, the company acquired a major stake in the French magazine market when its simultaneously acquired Editions Mondiale and Hersant, giving EMAP control of ten percent of the French market. After completing its acquisition of Transworld Communications, EMAP took over another major radio company, Metro Group, giving the company stations in Newcastle, Hull, Sheffield, and Teesside, and placing it among the United Kingdom's leading commercial radio groups.

The company continued to build up its magazine portfolio, buying 14 titles from Canadian publisher Thompson, and a variety of other magazines, including several golf titles from the New York Times. Whereas most of its magazine titles met with strong success, the company was struggling with *Smash Hits,* which was finding itself outmoded during a time when the British youth market was itself a rapidly dwindling population (down more than 20 percent compared with the early 1980s). Successive revamping of the *Smash Hits* formula helped to win back some of the title's former success.

Meanwhile, EMAP had continued to build its portfolio of local and regional newspapers. By the mid-1990s, the company's titles had reached more than 65 and included the *Stamford Mercury,* one of the world's oldest newspapers. By the mid-1990s the company's other media interests had taken the forefront of the company's future growth plans. Tight restrictions on the local and regional newspaper market in the United Kingdom also had made it difficult for the company to pursue further growth for that division. EMAP, therefore, decided to sell off its newspaper division, to Johnston Press, for £200 million in 1996. The sale enabled EMAP to continue a new round of acquisitions and growth in its other divisions, including the purchase of France's CLT, giving it a number of French television listings magazines, including *Tele Star,* which, at two million copies each week, became EMAP's biggest selling magazine and allowed the company to claim that one in every two French adults reads an EMAP publication.

EMAP also was finding success with another of its magazines, *FHM*. Originally a staid men's fashion magazine, EMAP revamped the magazine's format—keeping only the title—and transformed it into one of the United Kingdom's fastest-growing men's magazines, joining such titles as *Esquire* and *Loaded*. EMAP determined to use *FHM* as its flagship to go global—rolling out country-specific *FHM* magazines in Australia and Singapore. In 1998, also, EMAP began building its Internet presence, launching the EMAP Digital division

By the end of the 1990s, EMAP began to turn its attention to the United States market. In December 1998, the company made its entry in a big way, paying nearly £1 billion for Petersen Publisher Inc., a leading publisher of such titles as

Key Dates:

1887: Sir Richard Winfrey acquires *Spalding Guardian.*
1947: East Midland Allied Press is established.
1948: Robert Petersen launches *Hot Rod* magazine.
1953: *Angling Times* debuts.
1956: *Motor Cycle News* is acquired.
1957: Petersen launches *Teen* magazine.
1978: *Smash Hits* debuts.
1985: Company changes name to EMAP; MacClaren is acquired.
1990: Company acquires Maclean Hunter and Metro Radio, and launches commercial Kiss FM.
1996: EMAP sells newspaper holdings to Johnston Press.
2000: Comany announces a £250 million digital enterprises investment plan.

Hot Rod, Motor Trend, Sport, Teen, and many more titles. The addition of the U.S. company—renamed EMAP Petersen, then EMAP usa in 1999—made EMAP the world's leading publisher of specialist magazines.

Petersen had been founded by Robert Petersen in 1948, a motor racing enthusiast who began selling his own magazine, *Hot Rod,* outside of track meets for a quarter a copy. The following year, Petersen launched another title—initially dedicated to the custom car market, but later transformed into a new car magazine, *Motor Trend.* While continuing to cater to the automotive and then sports markets, Petersen also splashed onto the youth market, with the launch of *Teen* magazine in the late 1950s. *Teen* continued to sell in the million-copy range into the next century. By the 1990s, Petersen—whose two sons had been killed in an airplane crash—sought to retire, and he sold his company to a consortium for US $450 million in 1996; it was taken public the following year.

At the end of 1999, newly named CEO Kevin Hand led EMAP on a reorganization, grouping its business around markets instead of by medium. As such the company formed several new "networks," including EMAP Performance, grouping the company's music-related activities, including its radio stations and *Smash Hits* and other music magazines; EMAP Automotive, grouping all of the company's car, motorcycle, and related magazines, events, and exhibitions; EMAP Active, which focused on sports and outdoor activities; EMAP Elan, which formed an umbrella for the group's various lifestyle interests, themselves formed under subdivisions EMAP Mens, EMAP Wagadon, EMAP Esprit, EMAP Womens, EMAP Youth, EMAP Metro, and EMAP Fashion; and EMAP Health Network, including the company's *Here's Health, Slimming, Nursing Times,* and related activities.

The reorganization followed on the heels of a good year for EMAP; the company launched a French version of *FHM,* which itself followed on the strong-selling Australian version. EMAP determined to deploy *FHM* as an international brand, with further market-specific editions—including a Spanish-language version—planned for the early years of the 21st century.

The newly reorganized company started the new century with a bit of a hangover. Flagging advertising revenues in the United States had worked to depress EMAP's stock price after the first quarter. The low share price—considered greatly undervalued by analysts—quickly led to speculation that EMAP could become a subject of an acquisition attempt, possibly by heavyweights such as content-hungry AOL or rival IPC, the magazine subsidiary of Reed Elsevier, which EMAP had unsuccessfully attempted to acquire in 1998. Nonetheless, Miller and Hand maintained their resolve to lead an independent EMAP into the new century.

By mid-year, 2000 was looking to become another successful year for the company: the February 2000 launch of the U.S. version of *FHM* had sold some 450,000 copies and steadied out at a respectable 130,000 copies per month. The company also made moves to increase its share of the worldwide women's market with the purchase of *New Woman* and the rollout of "new" women's titles such as *minx* magazine. The company also boosted its position in the U.K. radio market with the acquisition of the Melody radio station, renamed Magic 105.4. At the same time, EMAP moved to increase its stake in the booming market for Internet and other digital content, pledging to invest £75 million in 2000, and up to £250 million over three years, in building its digital enterprises portfolio. EMAP's collection of magazines, radio stations, and exhibitions, as well as its growing collection of web sites and dot.com investments, gave it a head start toward achieving its plans to become one of the world's dominant media groups in the 21st century.

Principal Divisions

EMAP Performance Network; EMAP Automotive; EMAP Elan; EMAP Esprit; EMAP Health Network; EMAP usa; EMAP Digital.

Principal Competitors

Advance Publications Inc.; The Hearst Corporation; Axel Springer Verlag AG; International Data Group, Inc.; British Broadcasting Corporation (BBC); IPC Magazines Ltd.; Bertelsmann AG; News Corporation Ltd.; Capital Radio plc; Pearson; Crain Communications, Inc.; Time Warner Inc.; Daily Mail and General Trust plc; The Times Mirror Company; United News & Media plc; VNU N.V.; Hachette Filipacchi Medias S.A.

Further Reading

Beckett, Andy, "Can Smash Hits Survive the End of Take That?," *Independent on Sunday,* February 18, 1996, p. 8.1
Healey, James R., "Publishing Legend Doesn't Stay Retired Long," *Edmonton Sun,* April 14, 2000, p. 26.
Marr, Melissa, "EMAP Piling Up Profits, US Drags Heels," *Reuters,* May 30, 2000.
Potter, Ben, "EMAP Bid Talk Refuses To Die," *Reuters Business Report,* April 19, 2000.
——, "EMAP Considers French Edition of Lads' Title," *Daily Telegraph,* June 2, 1998.
——, "EMAP Has Design on Major US Purchases," *Daily Telegraph,* October 9, 1998.

—M.L. Cohen

ERIE INDEMNITY COMPANY

Erie Indemnity Company

100 Erie Insurance Place
Erie, Pennsylvania 16530
U.S.A.
Telephone: (814) 870-2000
Fax: (814) 870-2095
Web site: http://www.erieinsurance.com

Public Company
Incorporated: 1925
Employees: 3,107
Sales: $530.37 million (1999)
Stock Exchanges: NASDAQ
Ticker Symbol: ERIE
NAIC: 524126 Direct Property and Casualty Insurance
Carriers

Erie Indemnity Company is the attorney-in-fact and manager of the Erie Insurance Exchange, which in turn pools resources from Erie Insurance Company, Erie Insurance Company of New York, Flagship City Insurance Company, Erie Insurance Property and Casualty Company, and Erie Family Life Insurance Company. As manager of these companies, Erie Indemnity charges management fees, of about 25 percent, to each partner and subsidiary. With over 2.8 million policies in force, Erie has nearly 1,500 independent insurance agencies in nine states—Pennsylvania, New York, Maryland, West Virginia, Virginia, Indiana, Illinois, Tennessee, and North Carolina—and the District of Columbia. The company's main product is personal automobile insurance policies, but it also sells commercial automobile, homeowners, multi-peril, and workers compensation coverage policies. Erie is the 12th largest automobile insurer in the United States and the 25th largest property and casualty insurer. Celebrating its 75th anniversary in 2000, Erie maintains a strong presence in the Erie, Pennsylvania, community in which it was founded. In 1986, for example, the company initiated a program wherein it donates Thanksgiving dinners to needy families in the area. The company has also branched out beyond its Pennsylvania roots into the eastern and midwestern states and plans to establish a presence in Wisconsin.

Building a Legacy: 1925–95

Erie Indemnity Company, commonly called "The Erie" by its employees, began as an idea scratched in pencil on a ten-cent tablet. In 1925 Henry Orth (H.O.) Hirt and O.G. Crawford, two Pennsylvanian entrepreneurs, founded the company. Quoted in an article for *PR Newswire,* Hirt recalled that he never anticipated building a future in insurance. "There aren't too many kids that say, 'I want to be an insurance man,' like they say 'I want to be a policeman' or a fireman or an electrician or dentist, engineer or anything of that sort," he related, adding "As many of you have, I got into this business by pure chance."

The insurance industry was extremely competitive at the time, and Erie faced challenging market conditions from the onset, particularly as the country neared the Great Depression years. The company prided itself on outstanding customer service, however, which it felt set it apart from competitors. Even in these early days, Erie began providing 24-hour service for policyholders, with one claims manager, in 1927, reportedly having a telephone installed in his rooms at the YMCA just for that purpose.

Crawford retired in 1933 and Erie came under the full control of Hirt, who was well-respected by both employees and customers. Stephen A. Milne, the fifth president and CEO of Erie, would later attribute much of the company's success to Hirt. "I knew and worked with founder H.O. Hirt and I understand what he wanted to accomplish with this business. As he wrote to agents in the original Agents' Handbook, 'The Erie is committed and dedicated to giving Erie policy holders as near perfect protection, as near perfect service, as is humanly possible, and doing so at the lowest possible cost'," Milne said in an article for *PR Newswire.*

Hirt was reportedly involved in every aspect of the company from the early days. He would keep agents abreast of important news with the "Erie App-a-Week Bulletin," a weekly publication begun in 1931 that gave employees marketing tips and industry news. According to *PR Newswire* Hirt would "pepper the publication with tongue-in-cheek drawings of himself spouting words of wisdom to agents." The bulletin would continue as a tradition at Erie into the 1990s, modernized in

---

Company Perspectives:

Our founder, H.O. Hirt, said it in four words: We are the competition. The key to our stability and growth is the continued development of competitively priced, quality insurance products that are delivered by an exceptional network of independent Agents. In addition to our superior products and service, we've powered our vessel by aggressively recruiting Agents and providing them with valuable marketing tools. Because of our efforts, we're staying in front of our competitors and have earned high praise from top industry analysts. Fast and efficient claims response is a hallmark of our operation. Our customers know that if they have a loss, they will be working personally with someone who is knowledgeable, confident and committed to giving superior service. It's one of our chief competitive advantages. In fact, since our founding, we have proclaimed that The Erie is Above All In Service. It's not a slogan—it's our standard.

---

format and content but still arriving on employee desks every Monday.

Hirt believed that the secret of his success was his stubbornness. "I recommend the virtue of stubbornness to my friends," he said. "The easiest thing in the world to do is to fail, but if you stubbornly refuse to fail, you won't fail, and if you live long enough, you will have succeeded in some degree." He also fostered an attitude that would become the company's motto when he replied to questions regarding the company's ability to face competition with the words "You don't understand. We *are* the competition."

Hirt's son, F. William Hirt, joined his father's business, working his way up the corporate ladder to become an executive with subsidiaries Erie Family Life and Erie Insurance. In 1965, he was elected to the board of directors of Erie Indemnity. The founder's daughter, Susan Hirt Hagan, founded her own consulting firm in Erie, Pennsylvania, and was elected to Erie Indemnity's board of directors in 1980. Hirt passed away in 1982, at the age of 95, after working 37 years at Erie, but his legacy within the company lived on.

Erie Indemnity worked hard to make sure its employees were well trained and happy in their jobs. Many maintained that the company treated employees like family—as of the year 2000 the company had never laid off a single person—and Erie boasted a low employee turnover. Moreover, employees were offered tuition incentives and flexible schedules. Everyone at the company—including the CEO—was on a first-name basis, and it also made it a practice to promote from within the company.

New Leadership in 1996

In 1996 Stephen A. Milne was named president and CEO of Erie Indemnity Corporation. The 47-year-old Milne had worked for the company since 1973 and had thus worked with founder Hirt, taking very seriously his mentor's commitment to insurance as a service industry.

Erie sited Hurricane Floyd—a devastating hurricane that ravaged the East Coast in 1999—as an example of its commitment to customer service. "Erie Insurance literally stunned people with its level of service," said Erie agent David Purinai in the company's 1999 annual report. "Hurricane Floyd struck on a Thursday and nearly all Policyholders who were affected by the storm met with Erie claims representatives by Saturday night. As an Agent, it was gratifying to see the company and its Employees follow up with their promise of service. They showed a tremendous amount of dedication, compassion, and expertise." Hurricane Floyd caused $25 million in damage to Erie Insurance policyholder property.

During this time, the company strove to develop and incorporate better technology to enhance its exceptional customer service. With nearly 1,500 agencies in six states and the District of Columbia, the company depended on technology for good communication. In 1991 it developed a Data Sharing system that allowed agents to submit new applications and policy changes directly to the main office. In 1999 the company introduced a new version of Data Sharing, called DSpro. The new system was Window-based and offered additional tools to assist agents in performing their jobs. Moreover, the company provided its claim adjusters with up-to-date technology, including digital cameras and high-speed computers and modems, to help them perform their jobs efficiently.

In 1998 Erie introduced a private Intranet Web site for its agents. Via the Web site, agents have access to industry and company news and trends, sales, and market tools. Agents could also print up-to-date forms via the Web site, which allowed them to access forms from their homes and other off-site locations.

The company also launched a Web site for its customers. Its Web site contained an agent locator and personalized Web pages for more than 1,200 Erie agencies. The Web site also included excerpts from the Policyholder's magazine *In Sync,* an Insurance library that provided patrons with links to many helpful insurance Web sites, and tips on home and automobile safety such as "What to Do if Your Windshield Cracks." One of the site's most popular features was Erie's "Safe Car Guide," which included a list of vehicles that had passed tough safety standards. The company had begun producing its "Safe Car Guide" in 1996 to help customers decide what kind of car to purchase. In 2000 the Safe Car Guide listed cars in different categories that had passed eight tough safety standards.

Since its inception, Erie continuously competed with thousands of property/casualty insurers for market share. At the end of the century more competitors emerged from direct writers who sold insurance over the phone, over the Internet, and through the mail. Banks also began selling insurance. All of these competitors formed what Erie management described as "crowded seas in an aggressive battle for market share." The private automobile insurance market—Erie's main market—was especially competitive. Nevertheless, Erie continued to prosper. It reduced rates in Virginia, West Virginia, Indiana, Ohio, Maryland, and Pennsylvania, in an effort to retain customers and attract new ones. It offered a "Superior Customer" discount of up to 15 percent, and in 1999 the company reported that it filed with nine jurisdictions to lower rates for married drivers between the ages of 45 and 69.

The married driver rate decrease reportedly cost the company approximately $25 million.

1999 and Beyond

On the brink of a new millennium most analysts viewed Erie Indemnity as sound and secure even with its ever-emerging competitors. Despite rate decreases, Erie's net income increased 6.4 percent to $143.1 million in 1999, up from $134.6 million in 1998. Earnings per share were $1.95 in 1999 compared to $1.81 in 1998. Erie planned to expand in 2000 and hoped to begin writing policies in Wisconsin. The company considered its many agents a key to its future success. In the late 1990s, Erie continued to add new agents to its team—it had over 6000 agents by the end of 1999 and had increased its total number of agents by 375 in three years. In 1999 Ward Financial Group included the Erie Insurance Group in its list of the top 50 property/casualty insurers for overall industry, safety, consistency, and performance. Weiss Rating Inc. gave the Erie Exchange its A (Excellent) Rating, and Erie was among the top 4.7 percent of the more than 2200 property/casualty insurers to earn such a rating from Weiss. In 1999 the company reported that

Erie was one of only two companies commended by the New York State Insurance Department for having no consumer complaints filed against it regarding personal automobile insurance. During the same year, Erie was recognized by *Fortune* magazine as being one of the top 100 Best Companies to Work for in America.

Principal Subsidiaries

Erie Insurance Company; Erie Insurance Exchange; Erie Insurance Company of New York; Erie Insurance Property & Casualty Company; Flagship City Insurance Company; Erie Family Life Insurance Company (21.63%).

Principal Competitors

Alfa Corporation; EMC Insurance Group, Inc., United Fire & Casualty Corporation.

Further Reading

"Erie Insurance Celebrates 75 years of Service," *PR Newswire,* April 20, 2000.

"Erie Insurance Named A Consumer Friendly Company in New York State." company press release, December 22, 1999.

"Erie Insurance Reports Losses From Hurricane Floyd," company press release, September 28, 1999.

"Erie Insurance Seeks to Reduce Rates for Married Drivers," company press release, April 22, 1999.

"Erie Insurance to Expand," *Best's Review—Life-Health Insurance Edition,* May 1999, p. 89.

"Financial World Ranks Erie Insurance Exchange Number Two," company press release, August 12, 1996.

"Meet Steve Milne, our President and Chief Executive Officer," company press release, February 13, 1996.

—Tracey Vasil Biscontini

Esporta plc

Trinity Court
Molly Millars Lane
Wokingham
Berkshire, RG412PY
United Kingdom
Telephone: (+44) 118 912 3500
Fax: (+44) 118 912 3600
Web site: http://www.esporta.co.uk

Public Company
Incorporated: 1982 as First Leisure Corporation plc
Employees: 1,740
Sales: £64 million ($96 million) (1999)
Stock Exchanges: London
Ticker Symbol: ESP.L
NAIC: 71394 Fitness and Recreational Sports Centers

Berkshire, United Kingdom-based Esporta plc was formed from the breakup of First Leisure Corporation plc in 1999. Esporta now comprises that company's health and fitness club holdings (previously held under First Leisure's Health and Fitness Division). Esporta expects to increase its operations from 26 clubs in 2000 to 46 clubs or more by 2002, with much of this growth to be achieved organically. The company's clubs, typically oriented to the family and high-end brackets, operate under the Esporta brand name, but also under the Riverside, Racquets and Health, and Espree brands, with the latter targeted specifically at the corporate fitness segment. While Esporta itself was dormant in 1999, its pro forma revenues as First Leisure's Health and Fitness division totaled £64.0 million for the year, with net profits of £4.7 million. Esporta is led by chairman J.K. Grieves and CEO Graham Coles. The company is listed on the London Stock Exchange.

From Rags to Riches in Postwar London

Esporta was the offshoot of the activities of one of the United Kingdom's entertainment industry's most influential families. Olga and Isaac Winogradsky arrived in London's East End at the turn of the century, after fleeing the pogrom of Tsarist Russia. Settling in the Stepney neighborhood, the Winogradsky family became rag merchants. Growing up in poverty, the three Winogradsky children—Boris (later Bernard), Lew, and Leslie—slept on the floor and all left school before the age of 14 to pursue their careers. The Winogradsky boys all gravitated toward the entertainment business. Both Boris and Lew began their careers as Charleston dancers—with Lew changing his last name to Grade and Boris changing his name to Bernard Delfont. Leslie followed suit, taking the name of Grade.

All three went on to achieve great success in the United Kingdom's entertainment world. As Lew Grade, by then Lord Grade of Elstree, told the *Independent on Sunday:* "None of us Grades knew how we came to do the things we did. Show business came to us naturally." Leslie Grade turned to artist representation, making his early mark by bringing such stars as Bob Hope and Danny Kaye to the damaged theaters of London's West End, as England emerged from the Second World War. Leslie Grade's agency—the Grade Organization, set up with brothers Lew and Bernard—remained one of the country's most prominent until well through the 1960s. The Grade Organization also ran theaters, in addition to becoming one of Europe's largest theatrical agents. Leslie Grade was forced into early retirement after a number of strokes—his place in the agency was taken by son Michael in 1966.

If Leslie Grade had made his parents proud, his brothers made themselves rich. After ending his dancing career and a stint working with Leslie in his theatrical agency, Lew Grade went off on his own—into the newly developing television industry. In 1955, Grade founded the ITC television and film production company, which became one of the country's most important broadcasters through its Midlands-based ATV franchise, part of the ITV independent television network. Under Grade, ITC produced such world-renowned television series as "The Saint," "The Persuaders," and "The Muppet Show," as well as the highly popular mid-60s show, "Sunday Night at the Palladium."

Grade also produced a number of highly successful films and miniseries. His role in building Britain's postwar entertainment industry earned him a life peerage in 1976. The newly

Company Perspectives:
Esporta aims to be the leading operator of health clubs at the premium end of the market by offering superior levels of service and facilities which help people feel good about their lives.

ennobled Lord Grade of Elstree then led ITC into a new venture that was to prove the company's undoing. In the mid-1970s, ITC sunk the then-unheard-of sum of US $30 million into the production of a film called *Raise the Titanic*. As Lew reportedly said afterward, "It would have been cheaper to lower the Atlantic." The film proved a worldwide disaster, toppling ITC's financial position and ultimately leading to the company's loss of its ITV television franchise and the company's sale to rising Australian magnate Robert Holmes.

By then, brother Bernard Delfont was just getting started on a new career. After his stint as a dancer, Delfont had entered the booking side of the entertainment business. Delfont hit the big time at the start of the 1950s when, spending some £40,000, he brought the famed showgirls of Paris's Folies Bergere for a theater run in London. The Folies Bergere show lasted for more than 2,000 performances, earning Delfont more than 600,000 pounds. Delfont used part of these proceeds to fund his brothers' new agency, the Grade Organization, which quickly built up a powerful position in London's theater world.

Leslie Grade's retirement in 1966 led to the sale of the Grade Organization—for £6 million to EMI in 1967. Delfont joined EMI as part of the deal, taking over as head of the company's film and cinema division and, for a time, served as chief executive officer for EMI itself. After EMI had been acquired by Thorn Industries in 1979, its leisure and gambling operations were sold off to Trusthouse Forte. Delfont took over as head of the Trusthouse Forte Leisure division. The following year, however, Delfont—known as "Sir Delfont" since his ennoblement in 1976—was forced into retirement.

At the age of 70, however, Delfont was preparing to start a new career in the entertainment industry. By 1982, he had gathered the resources to perform a buyout of Trusthouse Forte's leisure division. Renaming his new company First Leisure, Delfont set out to build a new empire.

Shaping Up for the 21st Century

Among First Leisure's holdings was the Blackpool Tower, the landmark amusement center in the famed and long-time favorite resort destination for Britain's holiday-goers, bought by Delfont for £6 million. First Leisure's operations extended to encompass a wide variety of entertainment venues, including one of the United Kingdom's leading chains of bowling alleys, seaside amusement piers, squash clubs, bars, theaters, and nightclubs.

Through the 1980s, Delfont built First Leisure into a diversified entertainment conglomerate, boosting especially its numbers of bowling alleys and discotheques. The company also bought up holdings in such varied areas as marinas and caravan

parks. By 1991, Delfont, at the age of 81, was beginning to feel ready for retirement—at least, partial retirement. In that year, Delfont stepped down from his chairman position. He retained his position as president of First Leisure, however, until his death in 1994.

After weathering the severe recession of the early 1990s, First Leisure set out to expand its holdings in new directions, adding the Riva chain of seven bingo parlors in 1993. Through the rest of the decade, the company invested strongly in its bingo wing, building up the Riva chain to 22 bingo parlors. By the end of the 1990s, with the introduction of the National Lottery, the bingo industry found itself under extreme pressures, with revenues dwindled throughout the market. By then, however, First Leisure already had begun building an interest in another area, one that promised explosive growth. In 1994, First Leisure bought up a 75 percent share of the Royal County of Berkshire Racquets and Health Club. More health and fitness-related acquisitions followed, including that of ISK Leisure, bringing the company's total holdings in that market to 26 by century's end.

Another area of focus for First Leisure was the bar and discotheque market. By the middle of the 1990s, First Leisure had become one of the United Kingdom's leading discotheque operators, with more than 20 large-capacity clubs and theme bars grouped under its Dancing division. This division had quickly become one of First Leisure's largest revenue producers, responsible for more than £57 million of the company's £158 million revenues in 1995. By then, however, First Leisure was facing widespread criticism for its diversified (some called them unrelated) interests.

This sentiment was shared by Michael Grade, son of Leslie Grade, who joined the company as chairman and chief executive in 1997. Michael Grade had long blazed his own path in the United Kingdom's entertainment industry. After starting a career as a reporter with the *Daily Mirror* at the age of 17, Grade moved to Hollywood in the 1970s, joining Embassy Television to produce the long-running hit "Who's the Boss" and other hit series. Back in England, Grade joined BBC1 as director of programs in 1984, before taking over as head of Channel Four in 1988.

Grade's arrival at First Leisure was greeted enthusiastically by his uncle, the sole surviving Winogradsky brother, who told the *Independent on Sunday:* "I'm very proud of Michael. He is the only person in the British entertainment business with creative ability and business ability. The two rarely go together." By the middle of 1999, Grade received harsh criticism from Lady Delfont, widow of First Leisure's founder, who said, as reported by the *Daily Telegraph:* "At no time did we understand that Michael Grade's job was to asset-strip a thriving company."

Grade faced criticism from another front. Stockholders revolted over Grade's hefty pay package, while complaining about the company's slipping share price. In response, Grade stepped down as company chairman, while retaining the CEO spot. He also vowed to conduct a review of the company's operations.

Grade's review reached a conclusion that many analysts saw as inevitable: the breakup of the company. In early 1998, Grade sold off First Leisure's failing bingo division, vowing to refocus

Key Dates:

1955: Grade Organization is established.
1967: Grade Organization is sold to EMI.
1979: EMI is acquired by Thorn Electrical Industries and its Leisure division is sold to Trusthouse Forte.
1982: Bernard Delfont leads buyout of Trusthouse Forte Leisure and founds First Leisure plc.
1993: Riva bingo parlors are acquired.
1994: Acquisition of Royal County of Berkshire Racquets and Health Club and ISK Leisure.
1997: Michael Grade is named chairman and CEO.
1998: Bingo division is sold.
1999: Bars and nightclubs division is sold.
2000: Health and fitness division reformed as Esporta PLC.

the company around three remaining divisions: night clubs and bars; health and fitness; and family entertainment centers. At the same time, First Leisure hinted at its interest in entering the restaurant business as well.

By early 1999, however, Grade seemed to have thrown in the towel in his effort to bring together the company's disparate holdings. In May 1999, First Leisure shocked the financial community when it announced that it had entered talks for the sale of the company to the Cannons Group fitness center and entertainment group. Despite the reported purchase price of £530 million, the two sides broke off negotiations less than a week later, claiming an inability to agree on a price for the two companies' merger.

Grade quickly quelled further rumors that First Leisure was looking to sell out to a single buyer. By August 1999, the company had agreed to sell its 31-strong Superbowl chain of bowling alleys to the Allied Leisure-backed acquisition vehicle Moatdale for £111.5 million. The acquisition gave Allied Leisure, itself only recently formed from a merger between Allied and European Leisure, control of 59 bowling alleys in the United Kingdom. After disposing of First Leisure's 50 percent share of the Delfont Mackintosh Theatres group, Grade turned his carving knife to First Leisure's prime asset, selling its nightclub and bars division to a buyout team led by former First Leisure deputy director of operations Paul Kinsey. The cash price for the sale reached £210 million and included the sale of the company's name and Soho Street headquarters.

Grade had successfully pared the now nameless company down to just its health and fitness assets—a division that had been undergoing strong growth in the late years of the 1990s. Instead of incorporating as a new company, Grade revived a

shell company, Just So Fashions, renamed it Esporta Limited, then re-registered the company as Esporta plc. After transferring the former health and fitness holdings to Esporta plc in January 2000, Esporta formally began trading on the London Stock Exchange in February 2000. By then, Grade had stepped down as head of the company—to return to the film and television production world—making way for new chairman JK Grieves and CEO Graham Coles.

The "new" company had steadily expanded its fitness division, acquiring the Espree and Riverside branded clubs. The company also began building its own clubs—its new smaller-scale clubs were branded under the Esporta name—while larger country club-type facilities modeled after the company's original Berkshire acquisition were branded under the Racquets and Health brand name.

Esporta reported (pro forma) revenues of £64 million for the 1999 year, with net profits of nearly £5 million. The company also announced ambitious growth plans, expecting to bring its total number of fitness centers to 26 by the end of 2000 and to 46 by 2002. With the fitness boom only just beginning in the United Kingdom, Esporta's future looked healthy indeed.

Principal Operating Units

Cookridge Hall Golf & Country Club; Dorset Racquets and Health Club; Esporta Health and Fitness; Espree Leisure; Riverside Racquet Centre; Royal County of Berkshire Racquets and Health Club; Surrey Tennis & Country Club; Warwickshire Racquets and Health Club.

Principal Competitors

Cannons Group; Holmes Place; De Vere Group; Dragons Health Clubs; Whitbread.

Further Reading

Baker, Lucy, "First Leisure Strikes Pounds 111m Cash Deal Over Bowling Alleys," *Independent,* August 17, 1999, p. 15.
Bennett, Neil, "Grade's Hard Graft," *Daily Telegraph,* May 2, 1999, p. 4.
Halstead, Richard, "Making of the Grades: Profile: The Grade Dynasty," *Independent on Sunday,* February 2, 1997, p. 4.
Osborne, Alistair, "First Leisure To Sell Off Bars Division for Pounds 210m," *Daily Telegraph,* October 30, 1999.
Reece, Damian, "Pumping Profits," *Sunday Telegraph,* January 9, 2000, p. 10.
Yates, Andrew, "Bid War on the Cards as Sector Giants Stalk First Leisure," *Independent,* August 18, 1997, p. 18.
——, "Bingo Is Out as Michael Grade's Shake-up of First Leisure Begins," *Independent,* January 23, 1998, p. 24.

—M.L. Cohen

Ferrellgas Partners, L.P.

One Liberty Plaza
Liberty, Missouri 64068
U.S.A.
Telephone: (816) 792-1600
Fax: (816) 792-7985
Web site: http://www.ferrellgas.com

Public Company
Incorporated: 1954
Employees: 4,463
Sales: $524.1 million (1999)
Stock Exchanges: New York
Ticker Symbol: FGP
NAIC: 454312 Liquified Petroleum Gas (Bottled Gas)
   Dealers

Ferrellgas Partners, L.P. is the largest retail propane marketer in the United States, with annual sales nearing one billion gallons and a customer base of over one million in 45 states and the District of Columbia. The company sells, distributes, markets, and trades propane and other natural gas liquids largely in rural America, where propane is used for residential heating, cooking, and clothes drying, as well as for agricultural crop drying, space heating, and irrigation. A growing industrial/commercial customer base uses propane for forklift power, temporary construction heat, manufacturing, and cogeneration. In addition, Ferrellgas manages a transportation fleet consisting of 168 transport trucks and 222 railcars, as well as barges and ships on every U.S. liquefied petroleum gas (LPG) pipeline. Ferrellgas owns and operates three large underground storage facilities and an LPG fractionater, which separates LPG from other gases.

Early History

In 1939, A.C. Ferrell Butane Gas Company opened its doors in Atchison, Kansas, as a family-owned and operated gas business. A.C. Ferrell opened his business in the devastating Dust Bowl and during the Great Depression. Facing strong odds that his new venture would fail, he nevertheless forged ahead with

confidence. The fortitude shown by the company's founder established a precedent for intelligent risk-taking that the company would come to regard as its hallmark. Of course, Ferrell's maternal grandfather, E.E. Samson, was a Skelgas bottle dealer in the early days of the Skelgas era, and that influence may have informed his decision as well. Ferrell and his wife embarked on a new future outside of their familiar origins; initially, they had set out to make their livelihood through farming in Valley Falls, Kansas, but moved to the city with the hopes of securing a better standard of living.

According to their son, Jim Ferrell, in the Winter 1999 Ferrell company publication, *Flame,* the husband and wife team optimized their individual talents to make the business work. A.C. Ferrell acted as salesman, and Mabel ran the business operations. She managed the money, collected the bills, kept the books and ran the business out of the home from 1939 until the end of World War II. To make ends meet, A.C. Ferrell took on second and even third jobs. During the war, he worked as a part-time fireman, a part-time police officer, and for the railroad.

Post World War II Prosperity

The end of World War II generated a rebirth of business. Americans were weary of rations and lean times, and pent–up demand made consumers hungry for modern conveniences. This translated into opportunity for the Ferrells. The founder began selling gas refrigerators, floor furnaces, and electric milking machines during this time, and even used a trailer outfitted with a complete kitchen as a marketing tool. He would back the trailer up close to a prospective buyer's back door and leave it there for the buyer to become familiar with and use. The notion worked; the consumer became hooked. When Ferrell returned, he managed to sell a whole new kitchen, similar to the one the consumer had been using in the trailer.

The business grew, and the Ferrells purchased a building in Atchison to house their first office. Mabel Ferrell continued to run the business while A.C. Ferrell drove the company truck, delivered propane, and handled sales. In 1947, the company established its first plant, located across the river in Missouri and on land leased from the railroad. By 1952, the company had

Company Perspectives:

We own our business with a focus on achievement and accountability. Through our individual and collective actions, we define our ownership. We take pride in our efforts and share in the rewards of ownership. We care enough to make a difference and operate our business with excellence that surpasses the competition. When challenged, we defend our business. We step up to every opportunity to serve our Customers. Constant improvement, with continuous dedication to finding and fixing problems describes our owner pride!

approximately 12 employees, primarily comprised of farmers and men returning home from the war. That same year, Mabel died leaving A.C. Ferrell without a business partner and creating a significant gap in the business operations.

Business Struggles: Mid-1950s Through Mid-1960s

A.C. Ferrell continued the business, however, incorporating in 1954 as Ferrell Companies, Inc. He attempted to diversify the business by selling furniture and televisions, but that proved unsuccessful, and by 1965 the business focused solely on the sale of propane and some related equipment. The employee count dwindled to less than four, and only a slight positive cash flow due to depreciation kept the business going.

In 1963, Jim Ferrell, the founder's son, received a degree in business from the University of Kansas and returned home to help his father stabilize the business. This was only to be temporary, as he was in the Army and intended to make the military his career. However, Ferrell found that the company's problems would involve more time to resolve than he originally had anticipated. Giving up his military aspirations in 1965, he devoted himself wholeheartedly to the propane business his parents had started. Not satisfied with merely stabilizing and managing a small company, Ferrell was determined to grow the business. The latter determination marked the beginning of a growth era for the company that would continue through to the next millennium.

Initial Growth: Mid-1960s Through 1970s

In 1965, Jim Ferrell changed the company's name to the more modern moniker Ferrellgas. Within two years, he had borrowed $14,000 from a propane supplier, in return for a contract to purchase all his propane from that company, and used the money to purchase J & J Propane in Rushville, Missouri, located just over the state line from Atchison. Ferrell quickly recognized that in order to grow, he needed a bigger market. Therefore, in 1969, he formed Propane Industrial to serve the larger Kansas City industrial market. Around this time, Coffey Oil & Gas, in Platte City, Missouri, went on the auction block, and Ferrell seized the opportunity, purchasing Coffey and moving his office to that location, just outside of Kansas City. The Coffey Oil & Gas acquisition alone doubled sales for Ferrellgas.

In 1973, the next growth opportunity presented itself with the acquisition of Leavitt Propane in Kearney, Missouri. The com-

pany once again more than doubled sales and once again moved its main office to the new location. This acquisition was significant for two reasons: first, Leavitt operated in three states—Iowa, Kansas, and Missouri—and, second, with Leavitt, Ferrellgas entered the wholesale business. During this time, Ferrell employed the husband-and-wife team approach so successfully initiated by his parents; Ferrell's wife, Zibbie, came to work at Ferrellgas, keeping the books and working on collections.

Ferrellgas was faced with a significant challenge in the early 1970s. During the OPEC oil embargo, U.S. oil prices skyrocketed, and the U.S. government reacted with legislative controls that distorted the marketplace. Ferrellgas's response was to avoid traditional supply sources in favor of small producers and to enter the storage business to help offset flagging sales.

In 1977 Ferrellgas purchased Kathol Petroleum, renaming it Indian Wells Oil Company. This acquisition gave the company a natural gas liquids extraction plant, a field of gas wells, and an introduction to Wall Street, the latter being the result of Indian Wells's involvement in several drilling partnerships designed to fund the drilling necessary to feed the plant. Indian Wells was sold three years later for a profit.

Unprecedented Growth in the 1980s and 1990s

Proceeds from the Indian Wells sale helped the company acquire portions of Buckeye Gas Products Company in Nebraska and Iowa in 1984. Two years later, in 1986, Ferrellgas purchased the remainder of Buckeye and converted the company from a regional propane supplier to a national company. The Little River storage facility closed several years after the Buckeye acquisition due to the much larger Kansas storage fields that were acquired.

The success of the business resulted in the company outgrowing its offices in Kearney. Therefore, in 1981, company headquarters moved to the Building One site in Liberty, Missouri. Ferrell chose Liberty because of its proximity to Kansas City and the 35 office employees at that time. Building Two was constructed in 1983 and by 1986 both buildings were occupied to capacity.

In 1994, after several more large and small acquisitions, Ferrellgas converted from a privately owned company to a Master Limited Partnership (MLP) traded on the New York Stock Exchange. Such a partnership organization combined features of general and limited partnerships with those of publicly traded corporations. Specifically, with most limited partnerships, one group of partners, the general partners, managed a business or investment while another group, the limited partners, raised any capital required by the business. With MLPs, one could issue publicly traded securities to raise capital. For tax purposes, these securities were referred to as partnership units rather than corporate shares even though they were traded like stock. The move to form an MLP was unprecedented in the propane gas industry, giving the company greater financial flexibility and enhancing its capacity to grow. After the MLP's formation, the company acquired 50 high-quality independent retail propane companies. Among these deals was the 1996 purchase of Skelgas, for which Ferrell's grandfather had been a bottle dealer in the 1920s.

Key Dates:

1939: A.C. Ferrell Butane Gas Company opens for business in Atchison, Kansas.
1965: Founder's son, Jim Ferrell, steps in to help stabilize and then expand the company; company is renamed Ferrellgas.
1981: New headquarters are established in Liberty, Missouri.
1998: Company initiates an Employee Stock Ownership Plan.
1999: Ferrellgas acquires Thermogas, making it the nation's largest propane retailer.

In 1997, Ferrellgas purchased the North Carolina Propane Gas Co. Inc., the second largest propane dealer in North Carolina. Also vying, unsuccessfully, for that purchase was Ferrellgas competitor Thermogas Co., a subsidiary of Mapco Inc. and The Williams Cos. Inc., both based in Tulsa. Soon after the acquisition, Ferrellgas brought a lawsuit against Thermogas, alleging that the latter had hired away employees from the North Carolina propane dealer in an attempt to learn proprietary information about Ferrellgas. The lawsuit was quickly settled out of court, and Ferrellgas would eventually be on friendlier terms with Thermogas.

In 1998, Ferrellgas became the first in its industry to form an Employee Stock Ownership Plan (ESOP) when Ferrell sold parent Ferrell Companies, Inc. to employees, resulting in approximately 50 percent ownership. Approved by Congress in 1974, and regulated by the U.S. Department of Labor and the Internal Revenue Service, the ESOP was a form of a long-term savings plan that gave tax breaks to business owners in return for assisting employees in purchasing company stock. The Ferrellgas ESOP distinguished itself from other company plans by not requiring employees to make payroll deductions to participate. The company arranged a $160 million financing package to purchase its 50 percent stake in the enterprise. The decision to enact an ESOP at Ferrellgas was Ferrell's. He was preparing to retire and had no heirs to groom for the leadership role. He recalled in a 1999 interview for the company magazine *Flame:* "I knew I would much rather have the ownership changed in this way, with an ESOP, rather than see it merged into another company. It was the right thing to do."

In late 1999, Ferrellgas became the nation's largest propane marketer in terms of retail volume when it purchased its Tulsa-based competitor Thermogas for $432.5 million. The company's largest acquisition to date, Thermogas added 1,400 employees and 330,000 residential, industrial/commercial, and agricultural customers to the company's client base, while also giving Ferrellgas a presence in Michigan and other upper Midwest states. Before the acquisition, Ferrellgas had been ranked as the nation's second-largest propane retailer; thereafter, it was first, with a workforce of 6,000 in more than 700 retail locations in 45 states and the District of Columbia.

As the company looked forward to continued years of growth, a new management team began to take over. With Jim Ferrell less involved in the day-to-day operations of the company, serving as chairman of the board, the role of president and CEO was held by Danley K. Sheldon, who had been instrumental in taking the company public in 1994, when he was chief financial officer at Ferrellgas. Rounding out the management team in June 2000, Ferrellgas brought in Patrick Chesterman as vice-president and chief operating officer. All agreed that the company's plan for the future focused on continued growth. Such growth would be achieved, according to company literature, through a combination of acquisitions, efforts to bolster client base, and retaining the loyalty of long-standing customers through superior products and service.

Principal Subsidiaries

Ferrellgas L.P.; Ferrellgas Partners Finance Corporation.

Principal Competitors

AmeriGas Partners, L.P.; MDU Resources Group, Inc.; Suburban Propane Partners, L.P.

Further Reading

Kovski, Alan, "Warm Winter Chills Sellers of Heating Fuels," *Oil Daily,* February 26, 1998, p. 1.
Meyer, Gene, "Ferrellgas Says It Has Settled Lawsuits," *Kansas City Star,* September 21, 1999, p. D6.
——, "Ferrellgas Workers Act As If They Own the Business. And They Do," *Kansas City Star,* September 22, 1998, p. E19.
"Risks Pay Off for A.C. Ferrell," *Flame: A Quarterly Publication for All Ferrell Employees and Their Families,* Winter 1999, pp. 6+.
"Transformation," *Truck Fleet Management,* November 1999, p. 16.

—Ana Garcia Schulz

Florida Crystals Inc.

316 Royal Poinciana Plaza
Palm Beach, Florida 33480
U.S.A.
Telephone: (561) 655-6303
Fax: (561) 659-3206
Web site: http://www.floridacrystals.com

Private Company
Incorporated: 1962
Employees: 3,000
Sales: $89.4 million (1999)
NAIC: 11193 Sugarcane Farming; 11116 Rice Farming;
   311311 Sugarcane Mills; 311312 Cane Sugar
   Refining; 311212 Rice Milling

Florida Crystals Inc. is the umbrella company for the various businesses operated and owned by the Fanjul family of Palm Beach, Florida. In addition to holding about 190,000 acres of land in Florida, the Fanjul family has another 240,000 acres in the Dominican Republic, where it also owns and operates the Casa de Campo, a luxury hotel. Although diversified in its operations, the principal business of Florida Crystals is the production and sale of sugar. It operates three sugar mills, a sugar refinery, and a packaging and distribution facility, making it one of the principal sugar producers in the United States. On a more limited scale, the company also grows, mills, and markets rice, primarily in the southern part of Florida. It sells packaged sugar and rice under the Sem-Chi Rice, Flo-Sun Sugar, and Natural Sugars brand names. Although the Fanjuls have been subjected to much adverse criticism for their labor practices, influence peddling, and Florida Crystals' alleged environmental damage to Florida's Everglades, they have worked hard to convince critics that theirs is an environmentally-sound operation. The company stresses its pioneering of the organic farming of both rice and sugar, its crop-rotation practices, and its use of renewable resources to power its mills. It also takes pride in its support of community projects and charities, to which Florida Crystals has donated extensive funds, time, and energy.

1910–59: Fanjul Family Roots and the Loss of Family Holdings in Cuba

The roots of Florida Crystals Inc. go back over a century to Andres Gomez-Mena's arrival in Cuba from his native Spain. Andres made his fortune by milling sugar cane, the main crop of that island country. At the time of his death in 1910, his family owned four sugar mills and held significant properties in the capital city of Havana. Andres' son, Jose "Pepe" Gomez-Mena, reorganized the family holdings under the New Gomez-Mena Sugar Company name. Pepe became a leading figure in sugar production, both in Cuba and abroad. During the 1930s, he served as Cuba's secretary of agriculture and was president of both the National Association of Sugar Mill Owners and the Cuban Institute for Sugar Stabilization. In 1936, his family formed an alliance with another Cuban family when Pepe's daughter Lillian married Alfonso Fanjul, Sr.

Alfonso was the great nephew of Manuel Rionda, who had founded the Czarnikow-Rionda Company in New York and the Cuban Trading Company in Cuba. These organizations operated six Cuban sugar mills in a family business that was carried on, first by Manuel's nephew Higinio Fanjul Rionda, and then by Alfonso. The combined holdings of the two family businesses included interest in ten sugar mills, three alcohol distilleries, and large real estate properties in Cuba, plus the Czarnikow-Riona Company.

Under the rule of Cuban strong man Fulgencio Batista y Zaldivar, the joint-family ventures fared well, growing in size and wealth throughout the 1940s and 1950s. However, when Fidel Castro seized power in 1959, the two families lost all their Cuban properties. The communist dictator's government confiscated the Fanjul and Gomez-Mena holdings and forced Alfonso Fanjul and his family to seek political asylum in the United States.

1960–69: Starting over in the United States

Settling in Palm Beach, Florida, Fanjul began working to restore his family's fortunes. In 1960, he and some associates, also Cuban refugees, raised $640,000 to buy Osceola Farms, consisting of 4,000 acres of land located near Lake Okeechobee. The investors paid $160 per acre for the property. They also bought sections of three Louisiana sugar mills, which were dismantled, barged to Florida, and there reassembled. Fanjul and his oldest son, Alfonso "Alfy" Fanjul, Jr., managed the earliest operations, including the land clearing and soil preparation as well as the building of the Osceola sugar mill constructed using the mill sections imported from Louisiana.

Initially, the sole focus of the business was its cane growing and milling. Osceola, with its daily grinding capacity of 13,500 tons, was more than adequate to handle the sugar cane harvested from the original acreage controlled by the Fanjuls.

In their early years, the Fanjuls and other sugar growers were helped by the U.S. government, which, taking punitive aim at Castro, was determined to destroy the Cuban sugar industry. U.S. trade officials embargoed all Cuban sugar and, through major incentives, encouraged the growth of the industry in the United States. In South Florida, as engineers drained swamps, the U.S. Sugar Corporation and its rivals, including the forerunner of Florida Crystals, quickly bought the available acreage for cane farming. By the middle of the 1960s, Florida's cane acreage was 10 times what it had been when the Fanjuls first started their Floridian operation.

1970–89: Expansion, Problems, Industry Stagnation

After the death of Alfonso Fanjul, Sr., in 1980, managerial control passed to his two eldest sons, Alfonso Fanjul, Jr., and Jose Pepe Fanjul. The latter became the company's chairman and CEO, the former, its president. The company then had reached $30 million in sales, and it was looking for new expansion opportunities.

A major one came in 1985. In that year, the Fanjuls increased their holdings when, leading a group of allied investors, they completed the purchase of Gulf + Western Industries Inc.'s sugar and tourist operations in the Dominican Republic and Florida. The founder and former CEO of Gulf + Western, Charles G. Bluhdorn, who had died two years earlier, had been deeply committed to the social and cultural development of the Dominican Republic, putting over $25 million into programs designed to improve the health, nutrition, agricultural skills and working conditions of that country's sugar cane harvesters. Although many Dominicans feared the new owners would not support Bluhdorn's social programs, the Fanjuls left the Dominican operations intact, including its management team. The purchase increased the cane acreage of Florida Crystals by about 90,000 acres, bringing its total to about 180,000 acres.

Expansion of its operations in the 1970s and 1980s brought Florida Crystals many problems, including legal entanglements and some adverse and at times excoriating press coverage. The whole sugar industry in Florida came under the scrutiny of environmentalists concerned with the destruction of wetlands

and the threat of cane farming to the water supply of the state's southern counties. Although hotly disputed by Florida's cane growers, the environmentalists' claims resulted in serious scrutiny of the industry. Matters would come to a head in the mid-1990s.

The industry was also the subject of attacks from labor activists and consumer groups. These often singled out Florida Crystals because, in its labor-intensive operations, the Fanjuls continued to hire migrant cane cutters to harvest their sugar crop by hand. The company thus bore the brunt of the criticism and resulting legal action. In 1989, arguing that sugar companies failed to pay agreed upon wages, cane cutters brought a major suit against the industry in an attempt to gain unpaid money. Because the Fanjuls then employed about 6,500 of the 8,000 Caribbean cane cutters who migrated to Florida each year, they were the principal target of the $136 million suit.

Added to these problems was the fact that during the 1980s and early 1990s sugar farmers and millers were not faring well. Sugar consumption in the United States was increasing at the comparatively low rate of two percent per year. A major factor keeping the growth flat was the health-fad promotion of sugar substitutes. Nevertheless, by 1990, the company had beaten out U.S. Sugar as the nation's biggest cane grower. It had also become the most powerful force in sugar politics.

1991–2000: Bitter Fight to Survive and Sugar Industry Resurgence

In 1991, the Wilderness Society reported that Florida's sugar farms used two-thirds of their region's water to achieve a paltry one-fiftieth of its economic output while paying less than one-fiftieth of its property taxes, a claim that the industry energetically disputed. By then, too, a $400 million Save-the-Everglades cleanup plan, which would restore almost 70,000 acres of farm land to wilderness, worked to exact much of its cost from Florida's sugar industry. Under duress, but after much resistance, the industry finally agreed to put over $300 million into the Everglades' restoration project, with much of the cost being borne by Florida Crystals.

In the 1990s, the Fanjul family itself came under hostile scrutiny in the media, partly because of the way they managed their business and partly because of their bald political leveraging. In 1995 they were branded as "greedy and ruthless" in articles in *Forbes* and lambasted for their alleged violation of Rule G-37 of the Securities & Exchange Commission. Under that regulation, companies underwriting minority municipal bonds, such as the Fanjuls' faic Securities, were barred from making political contributions. The Fanjuls were in fact trying to defend their economic turf and survive, mustering all the political clout they could in a particularly bitter fight that pitted Florida's cane farmers and processors against fervid environmentalists and their odd bedfellows—corporate sugar-using giants such as Coca-Cola and Hershey. At issue was the price support program of the federal government, then under review by Congress. In 1996, legislators in the House of Representatives and Senate debated a farm bill measure that would have phased price supports out completely. Corporate interests wanted the program killed, thereby driving the price of sugar

Key Dates:

1936: The Gomez-Mena and Fanjul families are allied through the marriage of Alfonso Fanjul, Sr., and Lillian Gomez-Mena.
1959: The Fanjul family takes political refuge in America.
1960: Alfonso Fanjul, Sr., and associates purchase acreage near Lake Okeechobee in Palm Beach County, Florida, and barge in sections of three Louisiana sugar mills.
1962: Florida Crystals Inc. begins as a sugar cane farming operation.
1980: Alfonso Fanjul, Sr., dies; Alfonso, Jr., becomes company CEO.
1985: Fanjuls purchase Gulf and Western Industries' holdings in the Dominican Republic and Florida.
1997: Company's planned merger with Savannah Foods & Industries Inc. collapses.
1998: Company acquires 50 percent interest in Refined Sugars Inc.

down and their profits up. For their part, the environmentalists were simply trying to make sure that sugar cane farming did not "turn the Everglades into a lifeless cesspool." In the end, the price support program remained, at least for the time being.

The acridness of both environmentalists and media watchdogs made the Fanjuls mindful of a need to improve both their family and their company image. They mounted a campaign to convince the public that Florida Crystals was both a good steward of its land and its natural resources and a good neighbor. The company began stressing the idea that it continually sought new ways "to farm in harmony with the environment" and that in such practices as crop rotation it worked diligently to conserve the soil's fertility and to guard against erosion. It also put a 4,000 acre parcel of land aside for growing organic rice and cane, meeting the strict standards required by Organic Crop Improvement Association.

Through its "Florida Crystals Cares" initiatives, the company has also worked diligently to enhance its good-neighbor image. Among other things, it funded the startup of New Hope, a grassroots, not-for-profit agency serving needy families in the Florida Glades and surrounding regions. It has also funded scholarships for Glades-area students at Florida Atlantic University in Boca Raton and has helped fund grants through SUGARCANE (Statewide Urban Grants and Rural Community Assistance Effort), which primarily benefits African-American communities throughout Florida.

Apart from improving its image, Florida Crystals had to cope with the aforementioned industry-wide problem of flat sugar sales. What saved the Florida sugar industry in general and Florida Crystals in particular from taking a fatal blow was the industry's partial resurgence from its 1980s doldrums. Among other things, throughout the 1990s, health addicts leveled their heaviest guns at the consumption of fat, taking some of the heat off sugar. With profits again on the rise, and government price supports still in place, the company again turned to expansion moves and further diversification.

In July 1997, Florida Crystals and Savannah Foods & Industries Inc. announced plans to merge. The Georgia-based company, a public entity, in addition to refining sugar cane, manufactured other food products, including beet sugar. As Alfonso Fanjul noted, if the merger had been completed, it would have made the combined companies "the premier sugar company in the country;" but three months later the deal floundered when a rival bid by Texas-based Imperial Holly Corp. forced Florida Crystals, unwilling to counter Imperial's $18.75 per share offer, to withdraw from the merger.

In 1998, Florida Crystals and the Sugar Cane Growers Cooperative of Florida jointly bought Refined Sugars Inc., a refinery located in Yonkers, New York. The move put the two Florida concerns in the business of making white table sugar. The $65 million cost was shared equally by the Florida companies, giving each a 50 percent share in the plant. What the purchase meant for Florida Crystals was that it finally had a stake in the final stage of sugar production, the packaging and distribution of refined sugar for home consumption.

In 1999, Florida Crystals began growing cane on an additional 25,000 acres in western Palm Beach County, with plans to increase its total annual production of sugar from 750,000 to 800,000 tons. The land was part of a 50,000 acre plantation owned by the Talisman Sugar Corporation, which had earlier agreed to sell it to the federal government for future Everglades restoration. In the meantime, the acreage was leased to Florida's remaining sugar growers.

In order to store the additional sugar cane, Florida Crystals purchased a 92,000 square-foot warehouse in Riviera Beach once used by Curtis Mathes, an appliance and electronics retailer. The selling price was $2.65 million. Clearly, Florida Crystals and the Fanjuls planned to weather whatever environmental, political, or economic storms they encountered and continue to grow.

Principal Subsidiaries

Okeelanta Corp.

Principal Competitors

Imperial Sugar Co.; Tate & Lyle Inc.; United States Sugar Corporation.

Further Reading

Fiedler, Tom, "Battle Rages in Media and Congress over Everglades Sugar," *Knight-Ridder/Tribune News Service*, October 27, 1995.
Lunsford, Darcie, "Florida Crystals Plows East for Storage Space," *South Florida Business Journal*, November 26, 1999, p. 3.
McNair, James, "Florida Crystal Cos. Won't Rival's Bid for Savannah Foods," *Knight-Ridder/Tribune News Service*, September 12, 1997.
Nelson-Horchler, Joani, "G + W Says ' Adios,' " *Industry Week*, January 21, 1985, p. 21.
Resnick, Rosalind, "Nothing Sweet About Sugar; With Everything Working Against Them, Sugar Growers See No Choice: Higher Costs, Lower Profits," *Florida Trend*, March 1991, p. 40.
Roberts, Paul, "The Sweet Hereafter," *Harper's Magazine*, November 1999, p. 54.

—John W. Fiero

FLOWERS INDUSTRIES

Flowers Industries, Inc.

1919 Flowers Circle
Thomasville, Georgia 31757
U.S.A.
Telephone: (912) 226-9110
Fax: (912) 225-3823
Web site: http://www.flowersindustries.com

Public Company
Incorporated: 1919 as Flowers Baking Company
Employees: 18,000
Sales: $4.2 billion (1999)
Stock Exchanges: New York
Ticker Symbol: FLO
NAIC: 311812 Commercial Bakeries; 311821 Cookie and
Cracker Manufacturing; 311919 Other Snack Food
Manufacturing; 311813 Frozen Cakes, Pies, and Other
Pastries Manufacturing; 311412 Frozen Specialty
Food Manufacturing; 311411 Frozen Fruit, Juice and
Vegetable Manufacturing

Flowers Industries, Inc. produces fresh and frozen baked foods and is the third largest wholesale baker in the United States. The company operates three primary businesses: Flowers Bakeries makes fresh baked goods and markets the products to retailers, mostly in the South and Southeast. The Flowers Bakeries division includes such brands as Nature's Own, a leading national bread brand, Cobblestone Mill, and BlueBird. The company's Mrs. Smith's Bakeries division makes frozen breads and desserts, including the nation's leading brand of frozen pie. Pet-Ritz, Stilwell, and Oregon Farms are among the brands in the Mrs. Smith's Bakeries group. Flowers Industries also owns 55 percent of Keebler Foods Company, the number two producer of cookies and crackers in the United States.

Roots in Ice Cream and Bread: Early 1900s–20s

Flowers Baking Company was founded in 1919 in Thomasville, Georgia, by William Howard Flowers. A native of Blakely County, Georgia, Flowers attended school in Pough-

keepsie, New York, before returning to his home state to marry. He moved his new family to Thomasville in 1909. In 1914 Flowers and his brother, Joseph Hampton Flowers, opened Flowers Ice Cream Company to cater to wealthy families from the North who vacationed in Thomasville.

Just before World War I, Thomasville was a small town known primarily as a popular winter resort destination. While the Flowers Ice Cream Company was moderately successful, the brothers soon discovered an even more promising opportunity in that Thomasville had no bakery. The town had to arrange for all of its bread to be shipped in from other locations, and there was no large bakery within 200 miles. Seizing the opportunity, William and Joseph opened a bakery in November 1919. The first modern bakery in the area, Flowers Baking Company was soon flourishing.

During the 1920s, Joseph remained in charge of the ice cream company while William directed the operations of the bakery, which grew rapidly under his leadership. Soon local newspapers were lauding the bakery as having the most modern and sanitary machinery available, and noting that the company was able to produce thousands of loaves of bread each day. (They sold for nine cents a loaf.) In 1928 the company expanded its product line to include sweet rolls and cakes. By the end of the decade, as Flowers Baking Company garnered a reputation for high-quality baked goods, William Flowers began shipping the firm's products to customers throughout the region.

Persevering During Difficult Times: 1930s–40s

With the onset of the Great Depression in the 1930s, many small businesses throughout the United States either collapsed or significantly scaled back their operations. Earnings for Flowers Baking Company fell precipitously; however, bread, being a staple, still sold at a brisk pace. In 1934, at the height of the Depression, Flowers Baking Company reported $90,000 in sales, counted 25 employees, and operated seven wholesale routes. During the same year, William Howard Flowers died, leaving his 20-year-old son Bill in charge of the bakery. Bill Flowers guided the company through its most difficult years. In 1937 he purchased a bakery located in Tallahassee, Florida,

Company Perspectives:

Flowers Industries' mission is to create shareholder value as the nation's leading producer and marketer of fresh and frozen baked foods. Flowers operates efficient bakeries, develops quality products and brands, and provides outstanding customer service. Flowers firmly believes in the long-term growth of baked foods. Baked foods are a staple of the human diet today and are consumed at every eating occasion. With its production flexibility, well-established direct-store-door delivery of fresh products, efficient distribution network for frozen products, and its outstanding team of experienced employees and associates, Flowers will continue to expand in every market where baked foods are sold. To our customers, we pledge to provide you with the quality products you want, when you want them, and where you want them for a good value. To our consumers, we pledge to offer the finest quality baked foods available. To our shareholders, we pledge our continued best efforts to enhance the value of your company.

initiating a growth-through-acquisition strategy that served the company for many years.

When World War II began, Bill Flowers sought to join the U.S. Armed Services, but the federal government required him to remain at home and contribute his share to the war effort by running his bakeries at full capacity. Flowers's ovens proceeded to bake bread on a hectic schedule of 24 hours a day nearly seven days a week in order to meet the demand of American military bases in the Southeast. In 1942 Flowers Bakery joined the Quality Bakers of America, a baking industry cooperative. It was Quality Bakers that created the popular Little Miss Sunbeam trademark that member bakeries, like Flowers, could use to market their products. The trademark was an immediate hit with homemakers and helped Flowers Bakery sell large quantities of its bread. Like many other bakeries during the war, Flowers Bakery distributed small recipe pamphlets that showed how to cook healthy meals at a time when food rationing was common. The pamphlet included such culinary inventions as "Pigs in Clover," "Bologna Blitz," and "Peasant Sandwich."

In 1946 Flowers Bakery purchased a bakery in Jacksonville, Florida. In 1947 Bill's younger brother, Langdon S. Flowers, joined the company after serving in the U.S. Navy. Langdon Flowers sought to develop marketing strategies that would increase sales and foster growth. The Little Miss Sunbeam trademark became a prominent part of the Flowers Bakery marketing program, with the emblem adorning the uniforms of the company's sales force, loaves of bread, and delivery trucks. Little Miss Sunbeam became the company's highly popular "spokesgirl," and revenues skyrocketed. By the end of the 1940s, Flowers Bakery Company was ready to embark upon a period of enormous growth.

Growth and Success: 1950s–80s

The Flowers Bakery Company expanded rapidly during the 1950s. In 1959 the baking industry introduced batter-whipped bread. According to company literature, batter-whipped bread was made by a new process that was "roughly comparable to what a housewife uses in preparing cake batter with an electric mixer." With a softer texture and no holes, the bread was immediately popular, and by the start of the new decade Flowers reported that 18 million loaves had been baked in its ovens.

In the early 1960s, annual sales for the company jumped to over $6 million, and employees numbered around 500. To inspire and honor its sales force, Flowers Bakery initiated annual award ceremonies such as the Outstanding Service award and Salesman of the Year award. The company arranged a televised "Media Appreciation Day" to strengthen its ties to local communities around Thomasville. In order to promote batter-whipped Sunbeam bread, the company conducted "Miss Batterwhip" contests across its entire marketing territory. During the mid-1960s, Flowers Bakery purchased bakeries in Panama City, Florida, and Opelika, Alabama. In 1965 the company opened a new bakery in Jacksonville, Florida, and two years later Flowers acquired the Atlanta Baking Company in Atlanta, Georgia. In 1968 the company changed its name to Flowers Industries, Inc., and went public, trading shares on the OTC exchange. One year later, the company was listed on the American Stock Exchange.

Entering the 1970s, Flowers was not only the preeminent bakery in the Southeast, but also one of the fastest-growing companies in the United States. In 1970 the company had 2,600 employees and annual revenues of $54 million. Flowers's office staff had outgrown its small building in Thomasville, and in 1975 the company relocated its corporate headquarters to a new building on the outskirts of the city. More like a country estate than the home of a *Fortune* 500 company, the administrative offices were set among 15 acres of pine trees populated by quail, deer, and fox.

In 1976 Flowers entered the frozen food business by acquiring Stilwell Foods of Stilwell, Oklahoma, along with its subsidiary Rio Grande Foods of McAllen, Texas. Stilwell had a strong reputation for high-quality frozen foods, which included vegetables, fruits, desserts, and a variety of baked goods. Flowers aggressively pursued success in its new market, implementing a comprehensive capital expenditure program to retool Stilwell and Rio Grande production facilities, upgrade equipment and technology, improve cost-effectiveness, and promote better employee training methods.

The company also continued to grow its fresh bakery business. In 1977 Flowers brought out a new line of variety breads called Nature's Own. These variety breads quickly became one of the best-selling variety breads in the southeastern United States. Besides Nature's Own, Flowers was selling many different kinds of bread, including Sunbeam Rye, Sunbeam Wheat, Sunbeam French, Hollywood Diet, Sunbeam Low Sodium, Sunbeam Batter-Whipped Enriched, and Sunbeam Thin-Sliced Sandwich.

During the 1970s and 1980s, Flowers purchased bakeries in Texas, Tennessee, West Virginia, and Kentucky, and other states, including such well-known regional companies as El Paso Baking Company in El Paso; Griffin Pie Company in London, Kentucky; Kralis Brothers' Foods in Mentone, Indiana; European Bakers, Ltd., in Tucker, Georgia; and Bunny Bread, Inc., in New Orleans. In the late 1980s Flowers acquired

Key Dates:

1914: William Howard Flowers and Joseph Hampton Flowers open Flowers Ice Cream Company.

1919: The Flowers brothers form the Flowers Baking Company.

1934: William Howard Flowers dies, leaving control of the bakery to son Bill.

1942: Flowers Baking Company joins the Quality Bakers of America, a baking industry cooperative.

1947: Bill Flowers's younger brother, Langdon S. Flowers, joins the company.

1967: Company makes its first acquisition when it purchases Atlanta Baking Company.

1968: Flowers goes public and changes its name to Flowers Industries, Inc.

1975: Company relocates its corporate headquarters.

1976: Flowers enters the frozen food market with the acquisition of Stilwell Foods.

1977: Flowers launches a new brand of variety breads called Nature's Own.

1991: Company enters the frozen foodservice dessert market with the purchase of Pies, Inc.

1996: Flowers buys Mrs. Smith's Bakeries and acquires Keebler Corporation.

1998: Flowers becomes the majority shareholder of Keebler; Keebler goes public.

the bakery operations of supermarket chain Winn-Dixie, Inc., and entered the retail in-store bakery arena. In 1983 Flowers introduced Cobblestone Mill, a premium brand of specialty breads, which soon developed into a diverse product line including sandwich buns and English muffins.

Also in 1983, William Flowers retired as chairman of the board after nearly 50 years of directing the company. For the next two years the company was run by Langdon Flowers, until he also retired. The position of CEO was filled by Amos R. McMullian, who had worked in a number of different positions at the company since 1963.

Continued Expansion in the 1990s

During the early 1990s, Flowers continued to grow. The company embarked on a capital improvement plan, allotting $377 million over a six-year period to modernize its bakery equipment. Flowers expanded its frozen bakery business and specialty bakery product line, while continuing to acquire firms that enhanced its traditional bakery business. In 1991 Flowers purchased Pies, Inc., marking its entrance into the frozen foodservice dessert market. The company expanded its Our Special Touch product line for deli-bakery supermarkets and other in-store foodservice operations. Having discovered that the Nature's Own brand of premium bread was one of the company's best sellers, management continued to add such new products as 100% Whole Grain and Light Sourdough to the product line.

In the mid-1990s, management at Flowers planned to continue its strategy of growth through acquisition while also ex-

panding its extensive variety of breads, pastries, desserts, and frozen goods. To maintain its momentum in an extremely competitive industry, Flowers implemented a ''new generation'' of bakeries to help guarantee the highest quality control for its entire product line. With state-of-the-art computerized equipment, a well-trained staff of technicians, and an extremely efficient, high-technology operation, Flowers was poised to take the frozen food and bakery industries by storm.

Flowers began its assault on the nation's fresh and frozen baked foods industries in 1995 when the company acquired five businesses, including bread bakeries and sweet product operations. It was not until 1996, however, that Flowers put its expansion and growth strategy into high gear; Flowers formed a joint venture with Artal Luxembourg Corporation SA's U.S. subsidiary Invus Group Ltd., and the newly formed unit, known as INFLO Holdings Corporation, acquired Keebler Corporation for about $487 million. The major acquisition greatly strengthened Flowers' position in the baked foods industry and instantly transformed Flowers from a regional baked goods firm to a national one.

Keebler then acquired Sunshine Biscuits, Inc., the third largest producer of cookies and crackers in the United States, from G.F. Industries, Inc., for about $171.6 million, solidifying Keebler's number two position in the cookie and cracker market. Prior to the acquisition, Keebler had a market share of about 16 percent and sales of about $1.5 billion in 1995. The buy boosted Keebler's market share to about 23 percent and increased its sales to more than $2 billion a year. Though Keebler still lagged behind market leader Nabisco Biscuit Co., which boasted a market share of 36 percent and annual sales of more than $3 billion, Keebler felt confident that the acquisition would strengthen operations considerably.

Not only did Flowers acquire Keebler in 1996, but the company also bought Mrs. Smith's Inc., expanding Flowers' reach in the frozen baked foods market. The purchase of Mrs. Smith's from J.M. Smucker Co. included the top-selling frozen pie brand in the United States, and Flowers hoped to increase sales of frozen pies, desserts, and baked goods with the aid of Mrs. Smith's strong brand image and extensive distribution network.

Fiscal 1996 proved to be a strong year for Flowers, and the company reported revenues of $1.2 billion, a ten percent increase compared to fiscal 1995 sales, which marked the first time in the company's history that sales exceeded $1 billion. Not only did Flowers benefit from the Keebler and Mrs. Smith's acquisitions, but the company also worked to strengthen existing operations. Flowers added new routes for its fresh bakery lines, launched its Nature's Own and Cobblestone Mill brands into new markets, and invested $75 million in capital improvements during fiscal 1996. A new bread line, construction of a new baking facility, new frozen pie line, and automation of shipping departments were among the improvements.

In 1997 Flowers bought Allied Bakery Products, a maker of frozen breads for the foodservice industry in the Northeast. Later that year INFLO was merged into Keebler, and Keebler changed its name to Keebler Foods Company. In 1998 Keebler launched its initial public offering, and Flowers increased its ownership of the company to 55 percent, becoming a majority shareholder. Also that year Keebler acquired President International, Inc., the fifth largest cookie producer in the nation and best known for making Girl Scout cookies. President's other brands included Famous Amos and Murray.

In late 1998 Flowers began a one-year modernization project at its Mrs. Smith's Bakeries division. Flowers hoped to take advantage of the industry-wide increase in foodservice sales by maximizing production efficiencies and updating equipment at Mrs. Smith's facilities. The company began by shutting down five bakeries and restructuring the remaining plants to focus on specific types of production. New technology and equipment were introduced, and Flowers planned to increase production by about 50 percent to make 200 million pies annually with half the existing workforce. Unfortunately, however, the transition period proved more difficult than Flowers had anticipated—the plants were plagued with equipment problems, which caused low production levels and unusually high operating costs. In order to fulfill orders, primarily for the critical winter holiday season, Flowers hired hundreds of temporary workers to prepare and pack the pies and also shipped pies directly to stores to meet deadlines.

Though Flowers contended that the problems at Mrs. Smith's Bakeries were solved, 1999 earnings were negatively affected. Net income for the year was $7.3 million, an 82.6 percent drop compared to fiscal 1998. Luckily for Flowers, Keebler had a stellar year, reporting record sales of $2.7 billion, up 20 percent from 1998 sales of $2.2 billion. Keebler's retail sales of cookies, crackers, and brownies increased 17 percent, and its specialty division, which included sales to foodservice businesses and to the Girl Scouts of the U.S.A., enjoyed a 33 percent rise in sales. Keebler, which had proved to be a successful investment for Flowers, bought Austin Quality Foods, Inc., a maker of single-serve baked snacks, such as cracker sandwiches, in early 2000, again strengthening its cracker operations. Flowers Bakeries had sales of $961.7 million in 1999, a two percent rise from 1998. The division sought to improve production equipment in order to increase production and made two strategic acquisitions during 1999; Flowers Bakeries purchased Home Baking Co., a provider of baked goods to foodservice customers in the Southeast, and the Memphis bakery operations of supermarket chain Kroger Co., which served Kroger stores in Tennessee, southern Missouri, and northern Arkansas.

As Flowers faced the new millennium, the company planned to continue its strategy of long-term growth. The production and equipment problems that affected the company in the late 1990s had been solved, and Flowers prepared to increase its market share in the frozen and fresh baked goods industries. Chairman and CEO McMullian noted in his letter to shareholders in the 1999 annual report, "We will not let one year of disappointing results undermine this [long-term growth] strategy or cloud our vision for our company. You should take comfort in the underlying strengths of Flowers Industries." As a trend of industry consolidation ensued in early 2000, and such conglomerates as Nestle SA and Groupe Danone began looking to purchase, analysts began suggesting that Keebler Foods would make an attractive acquisition or takeover target. The fate of one of Flowers' most valuable subsidiaries was therefore uncertain.

Principal Subsidiaries

Keebler Foods Company (55%); Flowers Bakeries, Inc.; Mrs. Smith's Bakeries, Inc.

Principal Competitors

Interstate Bakeries Corporation; Nabisco Holdings Corp.; Sara Lee Corporation.

Further Reading

Cohen, Deborah L., "Keebler Spinoff Takes Root for Flowers; Owner's Dilemma; Free Company or Risk Takeover," *Crain's Chicago Business,* April 24, 2000, p. 1.

"Flowers Expects Record Year in Fiscal '97 with 'Strong Recovery,' " *Milling & Baking News,* October 1, 1996, p. 14.

"Keebler Adds Sunshine Business," *Milling & Baking News,* June 11, 1996, p. 1.

A Look Back At 75 Years: Flowers Industries, Inc., Thomasville, Ga.: Flowers Industries, Inc., 1994.

Palmer, Eric, "Working over the 'Long Pull,' " *Milling & Baking News,* January 23, 1996, p. 23.

Palmeri, Christopher, "Pie in the Face," *Forbes,* February 21, 2000.

—Thomas Derdak
—updated by Mariko Fujinaka

Fried, Frank, Harris, Shriver & Jacobson

One New York Plaza
New York, New York 10004-1980
U.S.A.
Telephone: (212) 859-8000
Fax: (212) 859-4000
Web site: http://www.ffhsj.com

Partnership
Founded: 1890s as Riegelman and Bach
Employees: 1,050
Gross Revenues: $225 million (1999)
NAIC: 54111 Offices of Lawyers

Fried, Frank, Harris, Shriver & Jacobson is a major international law firm that operates offices in New York City, London, Los Angeles, and Washington, D.C. In 2000 it ranked among the top firms offering legal services to corporate clients, as well as government agencies and associations. Fried Frank serves clients involved in mergers, acquisitions, taxation issues, antitrust, litigation, and most other areas of corporate law. Unlike some firms, Fried Frank has no single historic client that accounts for most of its revenues; its heritage as a law firm of mostly German Jewish attorneys in the early 20th century is also unique. Sometimes described as a liberal law firm, Fried Frank supports minority organizations such as the Mexican American Legal Defense and Educational Fund and the NAACP Legal Defense and Educational Fund.

Origins and Early Practice

Although the names of Fried and Frank would not be reflected in the company's name until the 1950s, the history of Fried Frank may be traced to the 1890s, when a group of German Jewish lawyers began practicing in New York City at a time when few New York-based firms employed attorneys of Jewish or other ethnic heritage. The lead partner was Charles A. Riegelman in the firm of Riegelman and Bach. Later Riegelman joined other attorneys, and by 1929 he was part of a partnership known as Limburg, Riegelman, Hirsch & Hess.

Riegelman's practice in the early 20th century focused on representing Maurice Wertheim and the investment bank he founded called Wertheim Schroder & Company Incorporated. When Wertheim died, Riegelman also served as his executor, a typical practice in the days before specialization.

In 1932 Walter J. Fried joined the firm as an associate. On January 1, 1934 the firm was renamed again, this time to Riegelman, Hirsch & Hess, after name partner Limburg died. In 1938 the firm recruited partner Arthur L. Strasser and thus became Riegelman, Hess, Strasser & Hirsch. By the end of 1939 Hirsch had died, so the firm of eight partners and seven associates became just Riegelman, Hess & Strasser.

Postwar Expansion

With about 15 lawyers in the late 1940s, the firm's name partners were Riegelman, Strasser, Schwarz, and Spiegelberg. The firm practiced general corporate law and litigation for both American and foreign clients, such as retailer Bergdorf Goodman; importer-exporter Stein Hall; Ecusta Paper, a cigarette paper manufacturer; and some Indonesian firms. Spiegelberg, in particular, had risen to prominence as a litigator for both American and British clients, and he was also well known for helping Congress pass "reverse lend-lease" legislation.

A few years before Riegelman died in 1950, the partnership recruited a new generation of young lawyers, including Hans J. Frank who joined in 1943. Frank had left Germany when Hitler's laws forbidding Jews to practice law had been enacted; in the United States his practice emphasized international taxation. Meanwhile, Walter Fried's specialty in real estate law significantly increased the firm's billings. One of Fried's contributions was in helping found New York City's co-oping residential buildings. In 1955 the law firm became Strasser, Spiegelberg, Fried & Frank.

In 1949 the partnership opened its first branch office in Washington, D.C. Felix S. Cohen, former solicitor for the U.S. Bureau of Indian Affairs (BIA), was instrumental in founding the D.C. office, which worked mainly on representing Native Americans who used the new Indian Claims Commission Act in filing claims against the federal government. By the mid-1950s

---

Company Perspectives:

The core values of Fried, Frank, Harris, Shriver & Jacobson include outstanding and creative solutions for a broad base of important clients, integrity, collegiality and community, individual autonomy and institutional focus, and recognition and rewards.

---

the Washington, D.C., office had developed more of a general law practice, under the leadership of Max M. Kampelman, one of the firm's better known attorneys who in 1989 would receive the Presidential Citizens Medal from President Ronald Reagan and in 1991 would publish his memoirs.

According to journalist John Taylor, in the early postwar era "far and away the most dynamic of the younger attorneys at the firm was Sam Harris." Harris had worked for the Securities and Exchange Commission, started during the New Deal era of the 1930s, and had helped the United States prosecute war criminals in the Nuremberg trials before joining Fried Frank in the late 1940s. Moreover, Harris represented uranium magnate Joseph Hirshhorn of Canada and later joined the board of directors of Rio Tinto-Zinc Corporation after Hirshhorn sold his business to RTZ. Harris was also important in recruiting other young lawyers for Fried Frank, especially several who, like Harris, had graduated from Yale Law School. In those early postwar years in particular, Harris helped recruit other Jewish lawyers who had been excluded from most of the nation's largest law firms. He was made a partner in the firm two years after he arrived, in 1949.

Much of Fried Frank's expansion in the postwar era was influenced by Arthur Fleischer, Jr., who joined the firm as an associate after graduating from Yale Law School in 1958. From 1961 to 1964 Fleischer served as the assistant to the chairman of the Securities and Exchange Commission, then returned to Fried Frank. Under his mentor Sam Harris, Fleischer became a major securities lawyer by the late 1960s. In 1969 he helped organize the Practicing Law Institute's first Annual Institute on Securities Regulation to help lawyers stay informed in that specialty. In 1971 the law firm changed its name to Fried, Frank, Harris, Shriver & Jacobson after Sargent Shriver joined the firm. Shriver was well known for directing the Peace Corps when it was started in the early 1960s during President John F. Kennedy's administration.

In the 1970s and 1980s Fleischer led a team of Fried Frank attorneys engaged in building a strong merger/acquisition practice. In 1975 the firm worked on five such projects; that number increased to 87 in 1985, including one in which Fleischer represented General Electric in its $6.28 billion merger with RCA Corporation. In 1984 Fried Frank represented the Getty Oil Company when it was purchased by Texaco for $10 billion, and for the year 1986 the law firm participated in 11 of the 33 transactions valued at $1 billion or more.

Thus Fried Frank gained a reputation as having a "transactional" practice, based on case-by-case counsel, instead of having one or a few major long-term clients like some other leading law firms. New York's Milbank, Tweed, Hadley & McCloy, for example, had for decades represented the Rocke-

feller family and Chase Manhattan Bank, while New York's Shearman & Sterling's major client since 1891 was Citigroup and its predecessors.

In 1980 Fried Frank attorneys and many others in the profession were saddened by Harris' tragic suicide. "After his death there was a void," said Harris's colleague and friend, Leon Silverman, in the March 1987 *Manhattan, inc.,* adding "He was the most important force in the firm. But it was the character he gave to the firm that permitted it to withstand his death and go on."

Between 1981 and 1987 Fried Frank grew from 204 lawyers and 67 partners to 325 lawyers and 93 partners. The firm's Washington, D.C., office went from 56 lawyers in 1982 to 93 lawyers just five years later. Harvey Pitt, the SEC general counsel who joined Fried Frank in 1978, was responsible for much of the Washington office's growth.

Much of Fried Frank's rapid expansion came from hiring experienced attorneys from competing law firms. Such lateral hiring or raiding began increasing in the late 1970s, after the U.S. Supreme Court ruled that professional advertising was a First Amendment free-speech right and after *The National Law Journal* and *The American Lawyer* began publishing articles about law firm finances and management. This was part of a major transformation of large law firms from a institutions characterized by long-term loyalty to one's firm, relatively slow growth, and a great deal of collegiality, to more of a business culture emphasizing competition for top attorneys with rapidly increasing salaries, openly advertising for clients, specialization, less collegiality, and new offices both in the United States and abroad.

Although Fried Frank represented noted clients such as Goldman, Sachs & Company, Morgan Stanley, and Lazard Freres in the 1980s, its representation of Ivan F. Boesky probably garnered the most media attention. Fried Frank attorneys had in the 1970s begun representing financier Boesky as he established and operated his various businesses. When Boesky was investigated by the Securities and Exchange Commission, Fried Frank partner Harvey Pitt represented him. Finally, Pitt was Boesky's counselor in 1986, when he was charged with securities fraud, advising Boesky to plead guilty to insider trading. Boesky was allowed to act as a government informant in exchange for shorter prison time (three years), paid $100 million in fines, and was barred for life from the securities business. Journalist John Taylor called this "a superb deal" for Boesky. Boesky also used Fried Frank attorneys to help him liquidate his partnerships; thus, "Fried Frank will have worked him on the way up and then worked him on the way down," wrote Taylor.

This was just one side to what the *Wall Street Journal* on December 21, 1987 called "the largest scandal in Wall Street's history." In 1989 a group of investors represented by the Cadwalader, Wickersham & Taft law firm sued Fried Frank for deceptive statements regarding Boesky's finances. Moreover, in 1991, Fried Frank and the auditing firm Oppenheim, Appel, Dixon & Company agreed to settle a lawsuit out of court by paying $11.2 million to some 42 individual and institutional investors in Ivan F. Boesky & Company. Those investors alleged that the law firm had deceived them in documents pre-

Key Dates:

1890s: Charles Riegelman begins a New York City law practice.
1932: Walter J. Fried joins the firm.
1943: Hans J. Frank joins the firm.
1949: Firm opens its Washington, D.C., office.
1970: The London office is established.
1971: The current firm name is adopted after Sargent Shriver joins the firm.
1986: Los Angeles office is opened.
1993: The Paris office is started.

pared for the Boesky firm's initial offering in 1986. At least two books, in addition to many media accounts, covered these and many other aspects of the Boesky scandal.

Another financial scandal occurred in the late 1980s when savings and loans firms began to collapse, leading to a massive government bailout of billions of dollars. In 1983 Fried Frank attorney Thomas Vartanian, as general counsel for the Federal Home Loan Bank Board, had helped develop new rules that deregulated the savings and loans; unfortunately, many took on irresponsible loans and thus soon failed. By the late 1980s Vartanian returned to Fried Frank, where he helped negotiate 55 thrift mergers and acquisitions of the many failed savings and loans, significantly increasing the firm's billings.

Practice in the 1990s

In July 1992 the law firm announced it had formed a representative office in Budapest, Hungary, in cooperation with the locally prominent law firm of Burai-Kovacs, Buki & Partner. With the collapse of communism in Eastern Europe, many American law firms established offices to help foreign firms invest in Hungary, Russia, and other former Eastern Bloc nations. However, this Fried Frank office was shuttered after a few years.

In the late 1990s Fried Frank literature proclaimed, "Over the past several decades, we have represented every one of the major investment banking firms and broker-dealers, each of the Big Six accounting firms and the major insurance companies of the world in securities regulation, compliance and corporate governance matters. And during the same period, we have been involved in nearly every high-profile securities enforcement matter."

Fried Frank's merger/acquisition (M/A) practice in 1998 included representing Kirk Kerkorian, a top Chrysler shareholder, when Chrysler merged with Germany's Daimler-Benz, a $39 billion deal. Other clients included Dow Jones, Loews, GTE, Northrup Grumman. From 1985 to the late 1990s Fried Frank represented Proctor & Gamble during its acquisition of public companies.

Fried Frank's practice in the late 1990s included most other aspects of corporate law. It was involved in major initial public offerings (IPOs), including its 1998 representation of the underwriters in Republic Services's $1.5 billion IPO. One of the

firm's major Latin American clients was Mexico's Grupo Televisa. In 1997 Fried Frank, in a joint venture with the London law firm Simmons & Simmons that later was discontinued, worked on the $8 billion privatization of Endesa, the largest electric company in Spain. Litigation also played a big part in the firm's practice; the firm successfully represented Lloyd's of London, for example, when it was accused of breaking U.S. securities laws. Numerous specific discussions of the firm's clients and their roles in antitrust, intellectual property, and other areas were detailed in Fried Frank literature, a candor not usually seen in the brochures and Web sites of major law firms.

Based on its 1997 gross revenues of $200 million, Fried Frank ranked as the 39th largest law firm in the United States, according to *The American Lawyer* of July/August 1998. The same magazine in November 1998 ranked Fried Frank as the world's 47th largest law firm. The July 1999 *American Lawyer* rankings featured Fried Frank as number 42 among the country's largest law firms, based on its 1998 revenues of $225 million, and 19th in terms of its average partner compensation of $760,000.

At the end of the century law firms continued to expand globally, perhaps the best example being London's Clifford Chance, which had about 3,000 lawyers after mergers with one American and one German law firm. Fried Frank faced plenty of competition from other major law firms operating in the globalized economy. Moreover, employing their own workforce of attorneys, mostly specializing in tax law, large accounting firms also competed with law firms. Finally, with the growth of the so-called "new economy" or Information Age, in which electronic commerce boomed, the entire legal profession, Fried Frank included, faced new and unforeseen opportunities to help corporate clients.

Principal Competitors

Cleary, Gottlieb, Steen & Hamilton; Davis Polk & Wardwell; Simpson Thacher & Bartlett

Further Reading

Cohen, Laurie P., "Boesky Lawyers Call 'Outrageous' Net Worth Claims," *Wall Street Journal*, March 22, 1989, p. 1.

Fleischer, Arthur, Jr., Geoffrey C. Hazard, Jr., and Miriam Z. Klipper, *Board Games: The Changing Shape of Corporate Power,* New York: Little, Brown, 1988.

"Fraud Case Is Dismissed," *Wall Street Journal*, January 3, 1996, p. B2.

"Fried, Frank, Harris, Shriver & Jacobson," in *The Insider's Guide to Law Firms*, special edition, Mobius Press, 1999.

"Fried, Frank, Harris, Shriver & Jacobson," in *Inside Track,* 1984, pp. 336–44.

"Fried, Frank, Harris, Shriver & Jacobson," in *Law Firm Highlights from Vault.com,* New York, 1999.

"Fried, Frank, Harris, Shriver & Jacobson Forms Cooperative Relationship with Hungarian Law Firm," *PR Newswire*, July 20, 1992.

Galanter, Marc, and Thomas Palay, *Tournament of Lawyers: The Transformation of the Big Law Firm,* Chicago: University of Chicago Press, 1991.

Hagedorn, Ann, "Boesky Lawyers Agree to Settle," *Asian Wall Street Journal*, July 10, 1991, p. 19.

Hertzberg, Daniel, ''Milken and 26 Other Drexel Employees Owned Stake in Boesky Arbitrage Firm,'' *Wall Street Journal*, August 15, 1988, p. 1.

Kampelman, Max M., *Entering New Worlds: The Memoirs of a Private Man in Public Life*, New York: HarperCollins, 1991.

Kang, Grace M., ''Suit Tests Continuing Obligation of Law Firms on Advising Clients,'' *Wall Street Journal*, July 20, 1992, p. B6.

''The Legal Masterminds Behind Merger Mania,'' *Business Week*, August 13, 1984, p. 122.

Pollock, Ellen J., ''Legal Beat: Slump Hits Elite Firms, Survey Shows,'' *Wall Street Journal*, June 29, 1993, p. B1.

Radigan, Joseph, ''Getting Sued on the Internet,'' *US Banker*, June 1997, p. 19.

Rice, Robert, ''Leading Law Firms in Joint Venture,'' *Financial Times* (London), August 1, 1997, p. 11.

Slater, Robert, and Jeffrey A. Krames, *The Titans of Takeover*, Beard Group, 1999.

Stewart, James B., and Daniel Hertzberg, ''Boesky Sentence Ends Chapter in Scandal—But Many More Are Thought to Be Implicated,'' *Wall Street Journal*, December 21, 1987, p. 1.

Taylor, John, ''Brief Encounters,'' *Manhattan, Inc.*, March 1987.

—David M. Walden

Frisch's Restaurants, Inc.

2800 Gilbert Avenue
Cincinnati, Ohio 45206
U.S.A.
Telephone: (513) 961-2660
Fax: (513) 559-5160
Web site: http://www.frischs.com

Public Company
Incorporated: 1947
Employees: 5,500
Sales: $159.6 million (1999)
Stock Exchanges: American
Ticker Symbol: FRS
NAIC: 72211 Full Service Restaurants

Frisch's Restaurants, Inc., an Ohio corporation engaged in the food service and lodging business, is probably best known for its midwestern chain of Frisch's Big Boy restaurants. Frisch's operates a total of 88 family-style restaurants—in Ohio, Kentucky, and Indiana—under the Big Boy name, while another 38 are licensed to outside operators. The company also operates five Golden Corral grill buffet restaurants and plans to expand that chain, particularly in Dayton, Cincinnati, and Louisville. In addition, the company operates two high-rise hotels with restaurants, in metropolitan Cincinnati, a Clarion Hotel and a Quality hotel. In 1999, CEO Craig Maier was at the helm of the company, while his parents, Jack and Blanche Maier, were chairman and corporate director, respectively, and sister Karen Maier served as vice-president of marketing. Forced to restructure by a dissident faction on its board, Frisch's has sold many of its non-core holdings, such as a 6.6 percent stake in the Cincinnati Reds. The company also plans to divest the company's Clarion Riverview Hotel and the Quality Central Hotel to strengthen its focus on its core restaurant business.

Early 20th Century Beginnings

The history of Frisch's Restaurants may be traced to 1905, when Samuel Frisch opened a small restaurant on Freeman Avenue in Cincinnati, Ohio. The venture lasted only five years;

when Frisch was earning just enough money to support his growing family, in 1910, he was also ready to find something more profitable. Frisch moved his wife and ten children to the Cincinnati suburb of Norwood to begin a new career in the grocery business. However, he soon returned to the service side of the food industry, opening a café in Norwood. Business was good, and by 1915 Frisch was ready to try a larger operation.

Frisch constructed a new restaurant in Norwood, known as Frisch's Stag Lunch, and this became one of the town's most popular gathering places. By the early 1920s, Frisch's Stag Lunch had moved into a larger building, and Frisch had been joined in the business by three sons, Dave, Irving, and Reuben. Sam Frisch died in 1923, and his son Dave, then only 20 years old, took over the restaurant. The Frisch brothers would continue to work together at Frisch's Stag Lunch for several years.

Dave Frisch Ventures Out in the 1930s

In 1932, Dave Frisch sold his interest in the Stag Lunch to his brothers and opened his own restaurant, Frisch's Café, also in Norwood. The new venture was quickly successful, garnering a loyal customer base, particularly among the local autoworkers who lunched there. Soon Frisch opened another location. However, in the aftermath of the Great Depression, he was forced into bankruptcy and closed both restaurants in 1938.

Fortunately, Frisch soon received some much-needed moral and financial support in the form of investor Fred Cornuelle, a local businessman. With Cornuelle's backing, Frisch again opened a restaurant in Norwood, this one called the Mainliner, one of the first year-round, drive-in restaurants in the Cincinnati area. The Mainliner was so successful that Frisch and Cornuelle were able to construct a second Frisch's restaurant in 1944. Located in Cincinnati, the new restaurant was designed to recall the historic Mt. Vernon home of George Washington.

At an industry convention in California in 1946, Frisch met Bob Wian, who introduced Frisch to the Big Boy, a double-decked hamburger made of two thin patties that cooked faster than one larger patty. Frisch secured Wian's permission to adopt the concept and began offering the Big Boy at his restaurant in Cincinnati. However, he personalized the sandwich by dressing it with a specially formulated tartar sauce rather than the thousand island sauce that Wian used. The recipe was unique to Frisch's and became a big hit with Frisch's customers.

Shortly after their initial meeting, Frisch and Wian entered a franchise agreement under which Frisch would become the exclusive franchisor of Frisch's Big Boy restaurants in Ohio, Kentucky, Indiana, and Florida. Frisch incorporated his business in 1947 and the following year opened his first Big Boy restaurant in Cincinnati. During the same time period, Frisch's new son-in-law, Jack Maier, began working at the Mainliner.

The 1950s–70s

The double-decked Big Boy hamburgers, served at drive-in restaurants, were an instant hit. Over the following three decades Frisch's business grew steadily. The Big Boy concept was becoming immensely popular throughout the Midwest and South, with other restaurateurs establishing Big Boy chains of their own and generations growing up recognizing the front entrance statue of the chubby Big Boy character with jet-black hair and checkered overalls. New Frisch's Big Boy restaurants were constructed and franchised at a rapid pace.

Frisch's went public in 1960, its common stock selling for $12.75 a share on the over-the-counter market. By 1961, the Frisch's chain had expanded to 140 locations, including franchises, which offered Big Boy hamburgers, Brawny Lad steak sandwiches, and Buddie Boy ham and cheese sandwiches. In 1966, Frisch opened a more formal restaurant in the Cincinnati area, called Annette's, after his wife.

In the late 1960s, the Big Boy concept was acquired by the Marriott Corporation, and most of its franchisors enjoyed remarkable growth. Another industry-wide trend among the Big Boy owners was to enter the hotel business as a complement to the restaurant holdings. In 1967, Frisch's entered the lodging business with the opening of Quality Hotel Central in Norwood, across the street from the original Stag Lunch. Five years later, a second hotel was built in Covington, Kentucky, featuring a revolving restaurant on its top floor.

Dave Frisch died in 1970 leaving behind a company with $30 million in annual sales. Jack Maier, who had by this time had been with the company for 23 years and had worked his way up to become executive vice-president, was named president and chairman.

Continued Growth through the 1980s

Under Maier, the company experienced another period of remarkable growth, expanding its Big Boy holdings to Texas, Oklahoma, and Kansas through the purchase of the Kip's Big Boy franchise. Frisch's also entered the fast-foods market during this time, adding another Marriot Corp. franchise to its holdings, that of Roy Rogers Roast Beef restaurants. With the economic slowdown of the early 1980s and consequent high interest rates, Frisch slowed its expansion plans somewhat. However, by 1986, the company owned 105 Big Boy restaurants, 19 Roy Rogers restaurants, and three Prime 'n Wine restaurants. In 1987, it acquired the rights to develop Big Boys in parts of Georgia and Tennessee in addition to the rights already secured in Florida, Indiana, Kentucky, Ohio, Oklahoma, Texas, and parts of Kansas.

In 1989, Craig Maier was tapped as president and CEO of Frisch's. The younger Maier had started with the business as a manager trainee at a restaurant; he had gone on to own and operate a franchise in New Richmond, Ohio, before being named a divisional vice-president for both Frisch's and Kip's Big Boys. During the period from 1989 to 1991, under Craig Maier's leadership, Frisch's sold or reorganized company-operated restaurants in Florida, Oklahoma, and Texas, preferring to focus on Ohio and neighboring states for restaurant expansion. Moreover, Frisch's began phasing out its fast-food holdings. In 1990, when Marriott Corp. sold Roy Rogers to Hardee's, all but one of Frisch's Cincinnati area Roy Rogers outlets was converted to a Hardee's restaurant. By mid-year, Frisch's had reduced its Hardee's restaurants to seven. The company continued to operate 101 Big Boys, two Prime 'n Wine restaurants, and two Quality Hotels.

As it reduced some food service holdings, Frisch's also began to diversify, acquiring stakes in a wide variety of businesses, including a horse farm in Kentucky and a stake in the major league baseball team the Cincinatti Reds. In the meantime, critics alleged, the company took on a debt burden and neglected its restaurants.

Restructuring in the 1990s

Between 1993 and 1996, Frisch's opened 30 restaurants in Ohio and in neighboring states. During this time, however, the company experienced a huge decline in net income, which management attributed to increased labor costs and overly rapid growth.

In 1996, two non-management investors, calling themselves Wolverine Partners, launched a proxy fight to gain themselves and two other non-management investors seats on the board of directors of Frisch's Family Restaurants. Their goal, according to industry analysts, was to break the hold of the Maier family on the chain, which they claimed was dragging down the company's profitability. In the ensuing battle, stock prices dropped below their 1960 initial public offering price, and Jerry L. Ruyan and Barry S. Nussbaum, together owning an eight percent stake in the chain, drafted a management plan that required Frisch's to pay off its debts through the sale of its non-restaurant assets. The Wolverine Partners claimed that the immediate sale of those holdings could generate $20 million to $30 million,

Key Dates:

1905: Samuel Frisch opens a restaurant in Cincinnati.
1921: Frisch manages a chain of three restaurants and his sons join the business.
1946: Dave Frisch is introduced to the Big Boy double-decked hamburger.
1947: Frisch's Restaurants is incorporated.
1960: Company goes public.
1970: Upon Dave Frisch's death, son-in-law Jack Maier is named president and chairman.
1989: Jack Maier's son, Craig, is named president and CEO.
1998: Company begins divesting its non-core assets in order to refocus on restaurants.

which could then be used to eliminate Frisch's long-term debt (approximately $20 million), invest in restaurant improvements, and buy back stock. Wolverine also proposed revamping the company's board of directors, giving the majority voice to non-management directors and requiring the entire eight-member board to be reelected annually.

Frisch's management maintained that many of the changes proposed by Wolverine Partners had already been considered by the company. Restaurant improvements, a computer system in particular, had been slow in development; the Cincinnati Reds investment was once profitable and could become so again; the farm and hotels operated at a profit and would be sold upon receipt of a suitable offer. Management was also non-receptive to the board restructuring recommendations. Moreover, the Maier family alleged, the goal of the Wolverine Partners was only to realize short-term gains on their investments.

Frisch's management firmly held that the loss of profitability over the previous few years was due to overzealous expansion in a competitive environment. The company had opened 30 restaurants, primarily in Indianapolis and in Columbus, Ohio, which overextended their management resources. Frisch's also pointed out that it had indeed been receptive to selling its peripheral assets, and had done so with the Hardee's and Prime 'n Wine chains.

Nussbaum and Ruyan were elected to Frisch's board in 1996 for two-year positions (though shareholders would vote to replace them at the company's 1998 annual meeting). During their tenure, the company sold its horse farm, 15 under-performing Big Boy restaurants in Indiana, and its 6.6 percent share of the Cincinnati Reds baseball team. Moreover, Frisch's reached a development agreement with Golden Corral Restaurants to oper-

ate more than 20 of the casual steak-buffet restaurants in Cincinnati, Dayton, and Louisville. Golden Corral gave Frisch's the opportunity to expand without extending outside its geographic parameters. During this time, Frisch's also began installing point-of-sale computer systems for its 88 Big Boy restaurants, thereby finally introducing computerized workstations at the drive-thru windows, carryout counters, and dining areas. At the end of 1999, the company's board of directors announced the approval of an additional repurchase of up to 200,000 shares of its common shares. This approval supplemented a previous authorization in 1998 to purchase up to 500,000 shares.

Frisch's performed strongly as it closed out the 1990s, with reports of record sales. On March 14, 2000, Frisch's announced that its board had voted to divest the company's Clarion Riverview Hotel and the Quality Central Hotel. This decision, Maier asserted, was consistent with earlier declarations made by the company to maintain focus on Frisch's core restaurant business.

Principal Subsidiaries

Frisch Kentucky, Inc.; Frisch Indiana, Inc.; Frisch Germantown Road, Inc.; Frisch Florida, Inc.; Kip's of Oklahoma, Inc.; Frischs Ohio, Inc.

Principal Competitors

Shoney's Inc.; Advantica Restaurant Group, Inc.

Further Reading

"Frisch's Restaurants, Inc.," *Cincinnati Business Courier*, September 7, 1987, p. 25.
Hamstra, Mark, "Frisch's Eyes Expansion, Inks Golden Corral Pact," *Nation's Restaurant News*, January 19, 1998, p.1.
——, "Investors Launch Proxy Fight at Frisch's Family," *Nation's Restaurant News*, September 30, 1996, p. 3.
Hayes, Jack, "Profits Plus Reds' Stake Sale Puts Frisch's on 'Golden' Trail," Nation's *Restaurant News*, February 1, 1999, p. 11.
Lawley, Lauren, "Frisch's Hopes Riding High with Golden Corral," *Business Courier Serving Cincinnati—Northern Kentucky*, December 18, 1998, p. 30.
Milstead, David, "Big Boy Faces Big Challenges," *Cincinnati Business Courier*, April 17, 1995, p. 1.
Monk, Dan, "Frisch's: Some Assets for Sale," *Cincinnati Business Courier*, August 19, 1996, p.1.
Schaber, Greg, "Roy Rogers Restaurant Chain Ready to Ride Off into Sunset," *Cincinnati Business Courier*, August 5, 1991, p. 4.
Schor, Adam, "Frisch's New Strategy: Add New Stores, Franchise," *Cincinnati Business Courier*, September 7, 1987, p. 1.
Zuber, Amy, "Frisch's Seeks to Nix 2," *Nation's Restaurant News*, September 7, 1998, p. 1.

—Ana Garcia Schulz

"The Difference Is Our Family Pride"℠

Genuardi's Family Markets, Inc.

301 East Germantown Pike
Norristown, Pennsylvania 19401
U.S.A.
Telephone: (610) 277-6000
Toll Free: (800) 660-2400
Fax: (610) 277-7783
Web site: http://www.Genuardis.com

Private Company
Founded: 1920
Employees: 5,000
Sales: $650 million (1999)
NAIC: 44511 Supermarkets and Other Grocery (Except Convenience) Stores

Genuardi's Family Markets, Inc. is a family-owned grocery store chain based in the Norristown, Pennsylvania, area. Long a family owned enterprise, Genuardi's offers a full line of groceries and specializes in prepared foods. Some of the company's stores feature coffee bars, pizza bars, and sandwich stations, and some stores offer delicacies such as imported pasta, polpettes, and cappuccino cake. Genuardi's also owns Zagara's Inc., an upscale grocery store chain in New Jersey. The company was recognized in 1999 as "Family Business of the Year" by the Wharton School of Business and the Pennsylvania Small Business Development Council. More than 7,000 Genuardi employees operate 33 stores in Pennsylvania, New Jersey, and Delaware.

The Huckster Begins a Tradition in the 1920s

Genuardi's Family Markets, Inc. began when Gaspare Genuardi and his wife Josephine started growing vegetables on their small farm in Norristown, Pennsylvania. Gaspare began selling his home-grown produce to his neighbors out of the back of his horse-drawn wagon. He became known for his high-quality produce, integrity, and loyalty to his customers, who affectionately referred to him as "The Huckster." While other grocers were cutting back the size of their portions, Gaspare was throwing in an extra head of lettuce now and then to show his appreciation. Gaspare eventually hired several drivers to

deliver his produce, first by horse and wagon and later by Model T truck.

Gaspare and Josephine Genuardi had nine children, five of whom became involved in the business at an early age. After opening a string of small stores, their sons—Charlie, Frank, Joe, Tom, and Jim—opened the first Genuardi's market on Main Street in Jeffersonville in 1954, the first independently owned supermarket in the area.

The first Genuardi's market was a success and the family quickly set its sights on expansion. The Genuardis used the profits from the first store to open others in the Norristown area during the 1950s. The company was a major family affair; by the 1960s Gaspare's grandsons also worked in the stores "pushing carts, bagging groceries, and running countless errands" according to the *Philadelphia Business Journal*.

Postwar Expansion

In the 1960s and 1970s Genuardi's became the largest and most respected grocery-store chain in the Greater Philadelphia area. Genuardi employees were well trained and dedicated. The Genuardis initiated a program known as the "Legacy," in which current employees and managers mentored new employees and taught them Gaspare Genuardi's original company philosophies, such as the importance of providing customers with outstanding service. "The Genuardi culture was always there for us and as we moved into management roles, we wanted to maintain that. We do that today by meeting regularly with both our personnel and customers," recalled Dave Genuardi in the *Philadelphia Business Journal*.

Genuardi's was also committed to the communities in which its stores were located. In 1976 it established the Community Cash Back Program in which it awarded cash rebates to local nonprofit groups. Under the program, nonprofit groups collected Genuardi's receipt tapes and exchanged them for cash rebates or credit toward the purchase of computer hardware and software. By 2000 the Community Cash Back Program had awarded more than $20 million to 3,500 nonprofit organizations. Genuardi's also operated Genuardi's Children's Charities, which donated funds to organizations that benefit children.

Company Perspectives:

"Genuardiness" describes our philosophies, our culture, and the way we do business. Although the word is new, "Genuardiness" began in 1920, when Gaspare and Josephine Genuardi started what is now Genuardi's Markets.

There are basically twelve characteristics that set Genuardi's apart from other supermarkets. Twelve advantages that, together, create something called "Genuardiness." It's these twelve points that keep customers coming back, assuring a strong, successful future for Genuardi's Family Markets and everyone who works here. (1) Genuardi's food is better; (2) We're known for superior freshness; (3) We're a value-added food store; (4) We're fashionable, yet not upscale; (5) We offer no-hassle shopping; (6) We deliver satisfaction; (7) Our goal is "Legendary Service" that goes beyond what customers expect; (8) Customers enjoy shopping at Genuardi's; (9) We offer "Genuardi's Value"; (10) We're part of the community; (11) Our "Family Pride Makes the Difference"; (12) We play to win and never forget that we're in a tough, competitive business.

Change in the 1990s

In the 1990s Genuardi's was faced with stiff competition from a bevy of supermarket chains as well as indirect competitors such as Kmart, Sam's Club, and many convenient-store chains. Genuardi's restructured to better compete with its competitors. It eliminated unprofitable stores and remodeled others. For the first time since the company's inception, it hired managers from outside the family to oversee its day-to-day operations. The new managers allowed the Genuardis to spend more time interacting with customers, something they considered very important.

Genuardi's also changed the way it brought customers into its stores. While it had focused heavily on promoting its low prices, in the 1990s the company promoted its restaurant-like atmosphere and its many product line choices. "We want to give customers so many choices that they'll have no reason to go anywhere else" Roy Taglialatela, director of perishables and merchandising, explained in *Supermarket News*. Genuardi's built its new stores in middle- and upper-class family neighborhoods, wherein the average household consisted of dual incomes.

The company expanded it private label brands to include over 900 items under the "Genuardi's," "Up Country," and "Fresh from the Farm" labels. Private-label items ran the gamut from canned and frozen groceries to soda, cereal, and fresh meats. The company maintained that its private label products "equaled or exceeded the quality of national brands, but were offered at substantially lower prices."

By 1990 the original Genuardi brothers—Charlie, Frank, Joe, Tom, and Jim—had turned the company over to a new generation of Genuardis. The new family members—Larry, Skip, David, Jim Jr., Joe Jr., Tom Jr., Anthony, and Michael Genuardi—were led by Genuardi's President Charles A. Genuardi, son of Charlie Genuardi. All of the cousins were

shareholders who had worked in Genuardi's markets nearly all of their lives. As of 2000, Charles A. remained president of the company.

In 1997 Genuardi's launched an interactive Web site that featured an online nutritionist, live cooking classes, and interactive chat sessions. Customers could also order groceries via Genuardi's Web site. "We entered into this new medium to help us get a better connection with our customers," said Alan Tempest, Genuardi's director of marketing, in *Supermarket News*. He added: "Using the Internet has become a way of life for people. We feel that eventually this will be an extensive medium of commerce and a strong selling tool for us."

Upscale Focus in the late 1990s

Genuardi's made customer convenience a top priority in its markets. In 1997 it surveyed its customers and found convenience to be extremely important. "They were adamant about it," said Roy Taglialatela in *Supermarket News*. "They said it came near to being an insult to ask them to walk across a huge store to buy milk and eggs." To make some of their markets more user-friendly, Genuardi's placed refrigeration units stocked with milk, eggs, and other essentials near checkout lines, so customers needing only essentials could enter and exit the store quickly. The company also created a separate entrance into the fresh-and-prepared foods isle and gave this area its own cash register. It even installed a portable cash register in this area to help keep lines short during the lunch rush. The biggest change, however, was in the amount of prepared foods offered in the markets. Genuardi's wanted to be more than just a grocery store; it hoped to take business away from the fast-food chains as well. The company quadrupled the space for self-service prepared food and increased the variety of these foods by over 20 percent. Some of Genuardi's newer markets had coffee cafes with hanging lamps and high-backed wooden stools; these markets were equipped with espresso machines and floor-to-ceiling windows. Genuardi's offered Italian specialties such as poplette, meat lasagna bolognese, stuffed hot peppers, colorful roasted vegetables, ricotta pie, and cappuccino cake. Imported pasta was available at a pasta station. Employees working at a pizza station could be seen tossing pizza dough in the air. Lunching customers could dine at a sandwich station or select a piece of cooked meat from a carving station.

Genuardi's prided itself on the freshness of its foods. "While the emphasis here is on prepared foods, produce is a good messenger of 'fresh'. Whether it's a deli sandwich or a meal, it's freshness the customer is buying. And it all comes back to produce," explained Bill Chidley, the vice-president of Design Forum, a firm that helped Genuardi's conceptualize its new stores.

During this time, in 1997, Genuardi's made its first major acquisition, purchasing Zagara's Inc., an upscale grocery chain in New Jersey. Zagara's was known for its deli, bakery, seafood, and high-quality meats. The stores also carried a large variety of vitamins, herbs, and nutritional products. Analysts concluded that the Zagara acquisition demonstrated Genuardi's plans to move into an upscale market. Genuardi's decided against changing the Zagara name and planned to open additional Zagara markets in 2000.

The Genuardi family said it was impressed with the amount and quality of prepared foods Zagara's offered its customers. "They do an incredible job at preparing foods, so this gives us an edge over our competitors Acme and Superfresh," said Larry Genuardi in the *Philadelphia Business Journal.* "We're following the trend in society where people are so time-sensitive; it's driving fast foods and restaurants of all kinds all over the country. With our Zagara's products people get fresh quality food and they get it very quickly. It's just another way of reinventing ourselves" explained Larry Genuardi in the *Philadelphia Business Journal.*

At the Genuardi stores, the company opened its first *glatt* kosher deli department in 2000, featuring a full line of smoked fish and specialties salads, kosher meats, poultry, lunch meats and breads. The kosher deli was certified kosher by the Organized Kashruth Laboratories (OK Labs). Moreover, believing atmosphere to be very important, the company planned to remodel many of its stores in 2000. Genuardi's newer stores boasted glass towers with sculptures of fruit and vegetables so large they could be seen from major highways. The company hoped the sculptures would remind customers of Genuardi's commitment to freshness.

In 2000 Genuardi's announced its position regarding genetically modified organisms (GMOs), food irradiation, and organic standards, becoming the first grocer in the United States to take a stand on the issue. Specifically, company management decided to make efforts to eliminate irradiated ingredients—food exposed to radiation to kill bacteria—from its product line. The company also stepped up efforts to inform its customers about food content through more thorough labeling. "We believe consumers have the basic right to know relevant information that will affect their personal food choices. We also recognize the significance of individual food preferences, and therefore, we want to guarantee choices for our customers to the best of our ability," explained Charles Genuardi in a company press

release. Genuardi's had begun selling organic food in the early 1990s. In 1998 Genuardi's was awarded the "Big O" award by the Organic Trade Association for excellence in promoting organic foods.

As they approached a new century, Genuardi's markets were known for the integrity, quality, and low prices. The company operated 33 stores in Pennsylvania, New Jersey, and Delaware, and the Genuardi family was still closely involved in the company's operations. Genuardi's planned to open five additional stores in the year 2000. Genuardi's Markets was recognized as Pennsylvania's "Family Business of the Year" by the Wharton School of Business and the Pennsylvania Small Business Association in 1999, when it also received a "Salute to Excellence" from the Private Label Manufacturers Association for its private brand product line. In 2000 the company received the Purple Aster Award from the Sons of Italy. The Genuardis were proud of their company's success but also careful not to take it for granted. With the supermarket business being extremely competitive and with the growing popularity of online grocery services, all players in the industry faced challenges. As Larry Genuardi explained in the *Philadelphia Business Journal,* one of the company's biggest challenges was in dealing with nine distinct owners—meaning Charles A. Genuardi and his eight cousins. "We're constantly trying to keep our unity and so far, it's worked," said Larry Genuardi, adding "You hear all these horror stories from other large family businesses, where it turns into people looking out for their own personal interest. Here the company comes first, the individual owners don't. We understand our strengths and weaknesses and the leadership comes from Charles."

Principal Subsidiaries

Zagara's Inc.

Principal Competitors

Acme; Super Fresh; Pathmark Stores, Inc.

Further Reading

Conway, Terry, "Producing Profits at Genuardi's; Building a Legacy, One Generation After the Next," *Philadelphia Business Journal,* 28 May 1999, p. B1.
"Family Businesses of the Year Named by the Pennsylvania Small Business Development Centers," *PR Newswire,* March 20, 2000.
"Genuardi's Glatt Kosher," *Progressive Grocer,* January 2000, p. 14.
Harper, Roseanne, "Happy to Oblige," *Supermarket News,* March 10, 1997, p. 29.

—Tracey Vasil Biscontini

Girl Scouts of the USA

420 Fifth Avenue
New York, New York 10018-2798
U.S.A.
Telephone: (212) 852-8000
Toll Free: (800) GSUSA 4 U
Fax: (212) 852-6514
Web Site: http://www.girlscouts.org/

Nonprofit Organization
Incorporated: 1915 as The Girl Scouts, Inc.
Employees: 500
Sales: $48.20 million (1999)
NAIC: 81341 Civic and Social Organizations

Girl Scouts of the USA takes girls and young women ages 5 to 17 and attempts to prepare them for life as responsible adults. Its founder, Juliette Low, helped take American girls beyond narrow 19-century social expectations by putting them in uniforms and teaching them about such "unfeminine" things as hiking and first aid. As with the organization's older male counterpart, the Boy Scouts of America, civic duty and outdoor recreation have always been part of the program, which has been updated with new activities through the decades in order to stay vital. Numerous professional women in America have been Girl Scouts, and the organization fields 860,000 adult volunteers in addition to its 2.7 million girl members. They move 175 million boxes of cookies a year in their famous annual sale.

Anglo Origins

Magdelaine de Verchères, who defended a French fort with her brothers against the Iroquois in Canada, has been called the "first girl scout." Another early model was Sacajawea ("Bird Woman"), who guided Lewis and Clark through the Pacific Northwest. However, the group now known as the Girl Scouts of the USA took its first cues from a British organization.

Juliette "Daisy" Low (née Gordon) was born in Savannah, Georgia, on October 31, 1861. Born to a genteel family with connections on both sides of the Mason-Dixon line, she recalled sitting on General Sherman's lap on Christmas Day, 1864, after his capture of the city. She also survived the yellow fever epidemic of 1876; however, a botched earache treatment in her twenties left her nearly deaf, and a stray grain of rice thrown at her wedding ruined the rest of her hearing as well as her honeymoon.

She married Willy Low on December 21, 1886 and moved to the storied countryside of Warwickshire, England. Since Willy Low had inherited millions, it may have seemed like the beginning of a fairy tale; however, the two were at odds by 1899. Drinking himself to madness, Willy Low took up with another woman, and ugly divorce proceedings stretched out until his death in June 1905.

In 1911, Daisy Low met Sir Robert Baden-Powell, the Boer War hero who had organized the Boy Scout movement in Great Britain. He introduced her to the Girl Guides, the British group headed by his sister, Agnes Baden-Powell. Like the Boy Scouts, the Guides sought to "Do a Good Turn Daily" and learned all manner of domestic and camping skills.

With Baden-Powell's encouragement, Low started her own Girl Guides company in the lonely valley of Glen Lyon in Scotland. There were just seven girls at first; they hiked, had tea parties, and, of course, tied knots. Proper hygiene was also stressed, and the girls learned to make an economic contribution to their families in the form of raising chickens and spinning wool. Low started more Guide companies after returning to London in October 1911. In January, she sailed for America on the same ship as Baden-Powell and his fiancée Olave Soames.

Juliette Low started an American version of the Girl Guides in Savannah in 1912. She and her friend Nina Pape organized about 20 girls into two troops that first met on March 12. Low's esteemed position in Savannah society helped persuade doubtful parents to entrust their girls to her care to learn useful survival skills and first aid practices. Thus, Low brought something of a social revolution to the United States and helped American girls advance beyond the traditional social roles of the nineteenth century. As imitation diamonds and fur coats were inferior to the original, so should girls not try to imitate boys, the first handbook said.

Company Perspectives:

The Girl Scout Program is girl-driven. It reflects the interests and needs of participating girls. Provides girls with a variety of experiences. Offers age-appropriate activities at each age level. Encourages a progression of skill development and responsibility through the different age levels (Daisy, Brownie, Junior, Cadette, and Senior Girl Scouts). Promotes the development of leadership and decision-making skills. All Program Activities are based on the Four Program Goals. The four goals are: 1) Developing Self-Potential; 2) Relating to Others; 3) Developing Values; 4) Contributing to Society

Soon the city had half a dozen troops. The Guides marched in uniform: dark blue skirts, light blue sateen ties, long black cotton stockings, and enormous black bows in their hair. However, the dust of Georgia clay soon prompted them to replace dark blue with khaki.

On her way to becoming a national celebrity, Low rented an office in the Munsey Building in Washington in June 1913. While there, she negotiated with the Campfire Girls about merging their organizations; however, the Campfire Girls did not want to adopt the Girl Scout laws.

Incorporated in 1915

A talented artist, "Miss Daisy" was a driven and energetic woman. She sold an $8,000 pearl necklace to fund the movement. She had the trefoil and tenderfoot badge patented and in 1915 received a charter in Washington, D.C. for The Girl Scouts, Incorporated. It held its first national convention the same year. Low continued to travel between England and the United States and was named a commissioner for the growing Girl Guide movement in the west central division of London in 1916.

Headquarters were moved to New York City in the spring of 1916. By this time, 7,000 girls had registered. Black troops soon began to form. An official magazine, *The Rally* (later *The American Girl*), was launched in 1917.

During World War I, the Girl Scouts raised gardens, mended homes, and offered comfort; the Surgeon General used 60 of them as messengers. A feature film, *The Golden Eaglet,* was filmed around 1922. It focused on the girls as patriotic heroes and included Low herself in a cameo.

Spacious headquarters at 670 Lexington Avenue in New York City opened in 1924. The World Camp of the Girl Guides and Girl Scouts, a gathering of scouts from many different countries, met at Camp Edith Macy outside New York City in May 1926. Chief Scout Sir Robert Baden-Powell himself attended. Juliette Low died on January 17, 1927; the organization she founded then had more than 150,000 members.

Herbert Hoover was elected president of the United States in 1928. His wife had been president of the Girl Scouts since 1922, and this started the association of first ladies with the role of president or honorary president. By the end of the 1920s, the Girl Scouts had begun registering Native American troops. Membership exceeded 200,000 in 1929, the year the organization first adopted a green uniform.

Selling Cookies in the Depression

During the Great Depression, Girl Scouts collected food, clothing, and toys for the needy. They held their first official cookie sale in Philadelphia in 1934, although the 1928 handbook had suggested cookie sales as a means for individual troops to raise funds. Half a dozen individuals claimed credit for originating the idea, including Bella Spewack, a journalist who later co-wrote the book for the musical "Kiss Me Kate."

The Philadelphia council contracted a private bakery to make the cookies; the next year other councils joined in the order. The first national sale of Girl Scout cookies was in 1936; the group sold 10 million cookies in 1938. By 1940, the Brownie Scouts category for ages seven to ten was added.

World War II again found Girl Scouts in their gardens. They also collected strategic materials for the war effort and came up with alternatives for their own copper and silk medallions and aluminum camping gear, introducing canteens made of galvanized iron and enameled pots and cups. The Girl Scouts had been using ten tons of copper a year for their award pins. A new wartime unit of older scouts was created and given duties in child care, food service, transportation and communication, shelter, clothing, and recreation.

The Girl Scouts began the 1950s with 1.8 million members. The record number brought the need for more adult volunteers and professional staff. The national organization bought the Juliette Gordon Low Birthplace in 1953, and opened it to visitors in 1956. It was the first registered national historic monument in Savannah. The group became congressionally chartered as the Girl Scouts of the USA in 1950. Construction of a new, $3.7 million national headquarters on Third Avenue in New York began in June 1956.

Fighting Prejudice in the 1960s and 1970s

New York troops celebrated 50 years of scouting in March 1961 through "Daisy Days" skill demonstrations. The organization added the Cadette age level in 1963. Cookie sales continued to progress, reaching 58 million boxes in 1965.

The organization had become a strong advocate of the civil rights movement. Black Cadettes from low-income families camped in a Newark gymnasium, watched over by police, in 1966. There they learned community relations as well as camping rudiments, roasting marshmallows over buddy burners—tuna cans stuffed with rolled milk cartons. The Girl Scouts launched the ACTION '70 initiative against racial prejudice in 1969.

One woman started a troop for young cancer patients at a New York hospital in the early 1970s. The qualifications for its unique merit pin centered around making their stay "as pleasant as possible for us, our parents, our doctors and our nurses."

Key Dates:

1911:	Juliette Low meets Sir Robert Baden-Powell and becomes involved in the Girl Guides.
1912:	Juliette Low starts Girl Guides troops in Savannah, Georgia.
1915:	National headquarters established in Washington, D.C.; Girl Scouts incorporated.
1916:	Headquarters moves to New York City.
1934:	Philadelphia council holds first official Girl Scout cookie sale.
1950:	Girl Scouts of the USA chartered by Congress.
1972:	Original Girl Scout laws reworded to reflect social awareness.
1994:	Media scrutiny prompts greater disclosure of cookie revenue disbursement.

The original Girl Scout laws were reworded in 1972, for example, changing "A Girl Scout is clean in thought, word, and deed" to a command to "show respect for myself and others through my words and actions." Leaders strove to combine self-realization with service in the girls' training. There were 3.5 million Girl Scouts in the mid-1970s. The group stressed "Eco-Action," and the organization's first African American president, Gloria D. Scott, was sworn in during the decade.

A total of 105 million boxes of Girl Scout cookies were sold in 1980. Sales reached new heights in 1981, when United Air Lines bought two million shortbread Trefoil cookies for $50,000—packaging them in pairs for in-flight service. The sales provided girls an introduction to the world of commerce, a field in which some excelled. One girl sold 11,000 boxes of cookies in 1985.

National headquarters received a royalty of one cent per box. They allowed no artificial ingredients or preservatives and were supplied by six bakeries: Little Brownie Bakers in Louisville, Kentucky; Famous Foods of Richmond, Virginia; Mother's Cookie Company in Marietta, Oklahoma, and Salerno-Megowen Biscuit Company in Chicago; Interbake in Battle Creek, Michigan, baker since 1939; and Burry of Elizabeth, New Jersey, which had been baking them since 1944.

Worldly-Wise in the 1980s and 1990s

The Girl Scouts program broadened in scope in the early 1980s. The Daisy Girl Scouts level for kindergartners was added while scout publications began addressing such issues as child abuse and suicide. In the late 1980s, the Girl Scouts rebuilt the training center at Camp Edith Macy into a modern facility for adult leadership training and renamed it the Edith Macy Conference Center. In 1989, the group hired its first outside advertising agency (Chiat/Day/Mojo) to advertise a more active image.

After flirting with Atlanta, Baltimore, Cleveland, and St. Louis in 1991, the Girl Scouts organization decided to keep its headquarters in New York City. It had a staff of 500 at the time. In 1992, the Girl Scouts bought some Manhattan office space from Ted Turner, who ironically, had started his media empire in Atlanta. In 1993, the Girl Scouts initiated a Gulf of Mexico patch in conjunction with the U.S. Fish and Wildlife Service's "Year of the Gulf."

Connie Chung's "Eye to Eye" television program aired an exposé on the distribution of funds from the Girl Scout cookie program in January 1994. A Girl Scout leader in the Connecticut Trails Council had brought charges to the state's attorney general, whereupon she was fired. In response, the Girl Scouts began displaying pie charts at their sales locations illustrating where the money went.

Cookies then retailed for $2.50 a box. About a third went to the bakers. Troops kept 33 cents. Councils kept the largest portion, spending it to maintain camps. The list of suppliers had thinned to two: Little Brownie Bakery and ABC Interbake. They made similar cookies under different names: Little Brownie's Tagalongs, Samoas, and Trefoils versus Interbake's Peanut Butter Patties, Caramel deLites, and Shortbread.

Girl Scouts emphasized physical fitness in the mid-1990s, launching the GirlSports initiative in 1996, which featured such robust activities as cliff rappelling. By this time, the girls were also learning about AIDS and teen pregnancy. They had to learn another new tune, as the American Society of Composers, Authors and Publishers (ASCAP) leaned on the group to cease directing troops to sing copyright-protected songs at their meetings.

In 1998, the Girl Scouts hired Siegle & Gale to update its image through a brand identity program. Local troops were also becoming more sophisticated. One in New York City brought in corporate sales coaches to help girls refine their cookie sales pitches. Another in Philadelphia organized "Operation Cookie Lift" to ship cookies to U.S. military personnel in Bosnia. Still others set up web sites. Total sales were around 275 million boxes a year in the late 1990s. Keebler bought Atlanta-based President Baking from a Taiwanese company in 1998, becoming the leading Girl Scout cookie supplier.

There were 2.7 million Girl Scouts in 2000. Some of the new badges they could earn included "Exploring the 'Net," "Desktop Publishing," and "From Stress to Success," which offered training in meditation, massage therapy, and other relaxation techniques. As adults, most would juggle careers and family life, giving such lessons lasting relevance.

Principal Competitors

Boys and Girls Clubs of America; Campfire Boys and Girls; 4H.

Further Reading

Carroll, Jon, "Spawn of Satan Goes Door to Door," *San Francisco Chronicle,* March 28, 1994, p. E10.

Choate, Anne Hyde, and Helen Ferris, eds., *Juliette Low and the Girl Scouts: The Story of an American Woman 1860–1927,* New York: Girl Scouts Incorporated, 1928.

Curley, Suzanne, "Girl Scout Badges Reflect Modern Times," *The State,* April 16, 2000, pp. E1, E4.

Dornbusch, Jane, "What Happened to the Tagalongs & Samoas? Best-Loved Girl Scout Cookies Have New Identities," *Boston Herald,* Arts & Life Sec., January 7, 1994, p. 41.

Ferretti, Fred E., "The Selling of the Girl Scout Cookie, 1981," *New York Times,* March 11, 1981, p. C1, C18.

Garfield, Bob, "Liz Is Cookie Coquette," *Advertising Age,* March 10, 1986, p. 82.

Giordano, Maria, "Girl Scouts' Goals Change with Times," *Times-Picayune,* April 13, 1995, p. F1.

"Girl Scouting, 64 Years Old, Is Changing," *New York Times,* March 8, 1976, p. 29.

"Girl Scouts Give Up Scarce Materials," *New York Times,* October 23, 1941, p. 18.

"Girl Scouts Open Savannah Jubilee," *New York Times,* October 13, 1937, p. 29.

"Girl Scouts Plan 'Daisy Days' Fete," *New York Times,* March 23, 1961, p. 27.

Gross, Esther, "Giving Doughgirls Perfect Sales Pitch: For Scouts, Sweet Taste of Success," *Daily News* (New York), November 12, 1998, Bus. Sec., p. 35.

Haddad, Charles, "Atlanta Doesn't Get Girl Scouts; US Headquarters to Stay in New York," *Atlanta Journal and Constitution,* June 4, 1991, p. C1.

"Keeps Tabs on Sweet Sales: Portable Terminals Scout Council's Cookies," *Computerworld,* January 31, 1983.

McLaughlin, Kathleen, "Scouts Will Study Polish Camp Oaths: Girls' Leaders to Visit Germany to Observe Units That Have Sworn Anti-Soviet Action," *New York Times,* June 9, 1946, p. 34.

Oliver, Myrna, "Bella Spewack: Writer, Scout Cookie Inventor," *Los Angeles Times,* April 29, 1990, p. A40.

Schultz, Gladys Denny, and Daisy Gordon Lawrence, *Lady From Savannah: The Life of Juliette Low,* Philadelphia and New York: Lippincott, 1958.

Scouting for Girls, New York: Girl Scouts Incorporated, 1920.

Shavert, Katherine, "Girl Scouts Respond to Cookie Flap; Campaign Reveals How Pie Is Divided," *Star Tribune* (Minneapolis), April 3, 1994, p. 11E.

Waggoner, Walter H., "Girl Scouts Camp in Police Gym in Newark Neighborhood Project," *New York Times,* March 7, 1966, p. 19.

Warren, Virginia Lee, "When a Girl Scout Pin Is Something Special," *New York Times,* March 8, 1971, p. 43.

—Frederick C. Ingram

Glacier Bancorp, Inc.

Glacier Bancorp, Inc.

49 Commons Loop
Kalispell, Montana 59901
U.S.A.
Telephone: (406) 657-4200
Toll Free: (800) 735-4371
Fax: (406) 756-3518
Web site: http://www.glacierbank.com

Public Company
Incorporated: 1955 as First Federal Savings and Loan of
   Kalispell
Employees: 434
Total Assets: $800 million (1999)
Stock Exchanges: NASDAQ
Ticker Symbol: GBCI
NAIC: 52211 Commercial Banking; 551111 Offices of
   Bank Holding Companies

With assets of more than $950 million, Glacier Bancorp, Inc. is one of the largest financial institutions in Montana. A multibank holding company, Glacier Bancorp operates in western and central Montana through five principal subsidiaries—Glacier Bank, Glacier Bank of Whitefish and Glacier Bank of Eureka, First Security Bank of Missoula, Valley Bank of Helena, and Big Sky Western Bank. In 1999, Glacier Bancorp ventured outside its traditional Montana markets when it acquired Mountain West Bank of Idaho; it now runs five banking offices in Idaho. With 23 branches, Glacier Bancorp offer a full range of retail and commercial banking products and services.

A Small Town Thrift: 1955–80

Glacier Bancorp's roots date back to 1955, when several business leaders in Kalispell, Montana joined together to establish First Federal Savings and Loan of Kalispell. Among the founders were Alton Pierce (who operated a Kalispell drug store), Owen Sowerwein, Milt Mercord, and Ruben Nordem (the owner of a local shoe store). Bob Gattis was recruited to be the new savings and loan's first managing officer. In 1977,

Charles Mercord replaced Gattis as managing officer and chief executive.

Like other savings and loan associations (also known as "thrifts"), First Federal Savings and Loan was a federally chartered bank. Although federal regulations gave such institutions special privileges, including lower capital requirements than their commercial bank counterparts, these same regulations limited the types of services thrifts could offer. While empowered to make real estate loans, savings and loans could not make consumer or commercial loans. Furthermore, thrifts were required to rely solely on individual deposits for their funds. For these reasons, First Federal operated for most of its early history simply as a depository and real estate loan center for the Kalispell area.

Deregulation and Growth in the 1980s

First Federal's outlook changed drastically in 1980, when Congress began to overhaul the regulations governing the banking industry as a whole. By the end of the 1970s, the industry had become considerably more complex, with unregulated financial institutions entering into traditional banking activities. Moreover, depository institutions—such as savings and loans—had sought ways to outmaneuver the regulations that barred them from offering banking services, such as checking accounts. For instance, many thrifts began to tout Negotiable Order of Withdrawal (NOW) accounts. These interest-bearing savings accounts were a near substitute for checking accounts.

In 1980, Congress passed the Depository Institutions Deregulation and Monetary Control Act. This legislation approved NOW accounts and broadened the sphere of thrifts' permissible activities. With the passage of the Garn-St Germain Depository Institutions Act of 1982, savings and loans gained "new investment, deposit, and lending powers, including the ability to make commercial and consumer loans," according to the *Dallas Morning News*. The restrictions on the interest rates thrifts could offer were loosened, as were those that forbade thrifts from borrowing from other financial institutions.

First Federal immediately used its new powers, and it began to offer checking accounts and consumer loans. While many of the

Key Dates:

1955: First Federal Savings and Loan of Kalispell is founded.
1982: Federal legislation expands the kinds of services thrifts can offer consumers.
1984: First Federal Savings and Loan of Kalispell becomes a publicly held company.
1989: First Federal acquires Glacier National Bank.
1990: Glacier Bancorp Inc. is established as a holding company for First Federal.
1992: Evergreen Bancorp. is acquired.
1996: Glacier Bancorp purchases Missoula Bancshares, Inc.
1997: Company converts all of its banks to state-chartered commercial banks.
1998: Glacier Bancorp acquires HUB Financial Corporation.
1999: Company purchases Big Sky Western Bank and Mountain West Bank of Idaho.

nation's savings and loan associations, however, overindulged in the wake of deregulation—making rafts of bad loans and nearly causing the collapse of the American banking industry in the late 1980s—First Federal remained "focused on stability and profits," John MacMillan, the company's future chief executive later told *U.S. Banker.* "We've always believed that a good, strong bottom line protects the company from bad loan decisions."

As First Federal strove both to expand and to diversify its loan mix to include small consumer loans, the company needed to raise additional capital. In an effort to do so, First Federal opted to become a publicly held company in 1984, starting with an initial offering of 550,000 shares. According to the *Missoulian,* going public "positioned the bank for purchases." At the same time, First Federal insured that its employees retained a significant stake in the thrift by rewarding all staff with stock options after they had worked one year with the company. "We have consistently tried to make all employees owners in the bank," MacMillan later explained, adding "It just wasn't our philosophy to reward only the top four or five people."

Bolstered both by its conservative lending policies and loyal employees, First Federal grew during the mid-1980s—despite the fact that Montana's core industries of mining and lumber were mired in a deep slump. The company's assets rose from $140 million in 1986 to $148 million in 1988, while its net income increased from $1.7 million to $1.9 million during the same period. The efficacy of First Federal's approach was further underscored by the failure of other savings and loans. As the *Billings Gazette* reported, across the county thrifts lost a total of $5.8 billion in 1987 and an astounding $11.1 billion the following year. Meanwhile, First Federal held the distinction of being Montana's most profitable thrift in 1988, a fact that led *Barron's* to proclaim that the company was "nestle[d] like a rose among the thorns of the thrift industry."

In 1989, First Federal continued its pursuit of expansion, when it acquired Glacier National Bank of Columbia Falls,

Montana for $150,000. In the process, First Federal became one of the first thrifts in the United States to acquire a bank. With more than $16 million in deposits and a low loan-to-deposit ratio of 37 percent, Glacier offered First Federal clear advantages. When the purchase was completed, First Federal's assets exceeded $165 million. To reflect its wider geographic reach, First Federal changed its name to First Federal Savings Bank of Montana. More important, First Federal altered its structure to became a Federal Reserve holding company, a move that it made to increase its flexibility.

Expansion in the 1990s

First Federal's fortunes received a dramatic boost in 1990, when *Money Magazine* named Kalispell as one of the best places to live in the United States. According to the *Missoulian,* this laudatory article helped "kick off a housing and population boom" in western Montana. Those who flocked to the area's scenic vistas only a few miles from Glacier National Park were often affluent and in search of a second home. First Federal was uniquely poised to capitalize on the growth, as it controlled approximately 15 percent of all mortgages in the area. The company quickly devised tools to serve these wealthier newcomers, offering short-term loans in addition to conventional fixed-rate loans. "We have many unique loans on larger properties," MacMillan would later explain to *Real Estate Finance Today.*

While the Kalispell area around First Federal buzzed with new arrivals, the company made a number of internal changes as well. In October 1990, First Federal once again took a new name. The holding company was redesignated Glacier Bancorp, Inc., and the First Federal branches became Glacier Bank. Still intent on increasing its assets, the company announced in December 1991 that it would acquire Evergreen Bancorp, a privately held corporation that controlled First National Bank of Whitefish and First National Bank of Eureka (both in Montana). When the purchase was completed in 1992, Glacier Bancorp gained $46.2 million of assets, as well as new bank branches.

Soon after the Evergreen acquisition was finalized, chief executive Charles Mercord retired. His post was filled by company veteran John MacMillan. The change at the helm did little to affect Glacier's growth. Between 1992 and 1993, the company's net income surged from $4.10 million to $5.12 million, and by the close of 1993, Glacier had 13 bank branches—all located in northwest Montana. The national press took notice of Glacier's stellar performance. An analyst reporting to *Barron's* in 1992 praised Glacier as a "first-class bank," and *Kiplinger's Personal Finance Magazine* called it "a growth company in a red-hot state's hottest sector." In 1994, Glacier's net income rose again to $5.13 million.

After a record year in 1995, in which Glacier's net income surpassed $5.68 million, the company once again sought to expand its network of banks. In August 1996, Glacier announced that it planned to acquire Missoula Bancshares, Inc.—the Montana-based parent company of First Security Bank of Missoula. The deal, which was completed in December 1996, offered Glacier several clear advantages. First Security brought more than $110 million of assets to Glacier, boosting Glacier's combined assets to more than $520 million. Along with this heightened liquidity, the move bolstered the company's position in the marketplace, as the combined institution controlled 16 offices in ten western Montana communities. Even more impressive was First Security's sound financial record. As MacMillan said in a press release, "First Security has consistently been one of the strongest performing banks in the whole country in recent years." Furthermore, the acquisition provided Glacier access to the burgeoning Missoula market. About two hours south of Kalispell, Missoula was one of the fastest-growing regions in Montana. Unlike Kalispell, Missoula had a multifaceted economy, rooted in government services, medical care, forestry, technology, education, tourism, and trade, making it more adaptable to the vicissitudes of local economic conditions. Finally, the acquisition of First Security allowed Glacier to balance its loan portfolio. The bulk of Glacier's loans were in real estate, and thus "First Security's commercial and consumer loans . . . mesh[ed] nicely," MacMillan explained in a press release. With stronger commercial and consumer loans, Glacier would be protected from any future fluctuations in the Montana real estate market.

Upon completing its purchase of Missoula Bancshares in December 1996, Glacier allowed First Security to retain its autonomy, local management, and local decision-making. This policy quickly became the centerpiece of Glacier's strategy in subsequent acquisitions. As Michael Blodnick—who would later become Glacier's chief executive—noted to the *Northwestern Financial Review* that the "main reason we're buying the banks is because of the talents those banks have in their senior management teams." He emphasized that Glacier's operating philosophy was "to find excellent performers, fast-growing banks with reputations, and [let] those people keep doing their things."

As it sought to integrate its new holdings, Glacier took the unconventional step of converting all of its banks from federal charters to state commercial charters in 1997. Although First Security was chartered as a commercial bank by the state of Montana, Glacier's other holdings still had been operating as federal thrifts. "It becomes time consuming having to deal with all the different agencies," a Glacier executive told *American Banker*. By simplifying this web of regulations and thereby having each bank subsidiary report to the same authority, Glacier hoped to create efficiencies and cut costs. As it streamlined its operations, Glacier also changed the names of First National Bank of Whitefish and First National Bank of Eureka to Glacier Bank of Eureka and Glacier Bank of Whitefish to "more clearly identify the tie with Glacier Bank and expand customer recognition," MacMillan explained in a press release.

Yet while working to integrate its diverse subsidiaries, Glacier also continued to expand in terms of both its geographical reach and the services it offered. In 1997, Glacier launched a partnership with Robert Thomas Securities to provide full-service brokerage and investment services at many of the company's branch banks. Later in the year, Glacier announced its acquisition of HUB Financial Corporation, a holding company that controlled Valley Bank in Helena, Montana. With two offices in Helena (and an additional branch under construction), Valley Bank provided Glacier with $70 million in assets and access to the market in Montana's capital city. Consistent with its general philosophy, Glacier pledged that Valley Bank would retain its autonomy, as well as its decision-making authority.

In 1998, Glacier purchased Big Sky Western Bank, a commercial bank with about $40 million in assets and banking offices in Big Sky and Bozeman, Montana. "We believe this acquisition significantly enhances our banking franchise by giving us access to another rapidly growing market area in Montana," Michael Blodnick announced in a press release. Blodnick had succeeded MacMillan as president and chief executive officer of the company in April 1998. MacMillan, who had served at Glacier for 31 years, remained chairman of the board.

Despite the raft of changes implemented in the late 1990s, Glacier continued to enjoy record growth. In 1997, Glacier's assets increased by six percent, to more than $580 million, and its loans jumped by nine percent. The year 1998 was even more successful. Glacier had expanded its empire to 23 offices in 16 Montana communities, and its assets topped $710 million. As its first full year under state commercial charters, Glacier ranked fourth in *U.S. Banker's* mid-sized bank ranking. Glacier had extended its loan portfolio beyond real estate as well. According to the *Missoulian*, by 1999, the company's loan portfolio consisted of a balanced 42 percent commercial loans, 36 percent real estate, and 22 percent consumer loans. Although the company had achieved an unprecedented compounded annual earnings growth of more than 17 percent between 1988 and 1998, Glacier kept its perspective. "We're just aggressive community bankers who are taking advantage of the changes occurring in this industry," MacMillan told *U.S. Banker.*

But even with its stunning successes, Glacier did not overlook the communities it served. In May 1995, three of the company's banks had been recognized by the Federal Home Loan Bank of Seattle for contributing to the revitalization of the rural Flathead Valley. Specifically, the company was credited with pioneering innovative ways to create homeownership opportunities for low- and moderate-income families. In 1997, Glacier created the Glacier Affordable Housing Foundation, which in one year dispersed more than $2 million in grants and helped 70 families purchase homes.

1999 and Beyond

Glacier completed another acquisition in 1999, when it purchased two bank branches in Butte, Montana from Washington Mutual Inc. "Butte adds a key location that helps expand our strong western Montana banking franchise," Blodnick told the *Associated Press*. As with its other acquisitions, Glacier left control to local management.

Soon after completing its acquisition in Butte, Glacier announced in September 1999 that it would make its initial foray beyond Montana with the purchase of Mountain West Bank of Idaho. This commercial bank with $87 million in assets had offices in Coeur d'Alene, Hayden Lake, Post Falls, and Boise, Idaho. The advantages Glacier stood to accrue by purchasing Mountain West were significant. Most important was the fact that Glacier would no longer be dependent solely on Montana's growth. Mountain West provided Glacier with access to two of the fastest-growing markets in the United States—Idaho's Coeur d'Alene and Kootenai counties. According to *Northwestern Financial Review,* the population in these areas had exploded during the late 1990s. "Our hope is to use this merger as a springboard into Idaho and eastern Washington," Blodnick told the *Spokesman Review.* Moreover, Mountain West's strengths mirrored Glacier's own in the arenas of real estate and commercial loans. Therefore, rather than venture into new spheres (such as agriculture loans), Glacier could continue to focus on what it already did so well.

Glacier's flurry of activity paid off, as 1999 proved to be a banner year. The company's record earnings increased 11.6 percent to reach $12.18 million. At the same time, Glacier's assets grew 25 percent, while commercial loans and consumer loans rose 33 percent and 25 percent, respectively. With more than $950 million in assets, Glacier was one of the largest commercial banks in Montana, and with its plans to expand westward (especially into flourishing Idaho markets), Glacier's future prospects looked exceedingly bright.

Principal Subsidiaries

Glacier Bank; Glacier Bank of Whitefish and Glacier Bank of Eureka; First Security Bank of Missoula; Valley Bank of Helena; Big Sky Western; Mountain West Bank.

Principal Competitors

BancWest Corporation; Wells Fargo & Company; WesterFed Financial Corporation.

Further Reading

"Banking on the West," *Missoulian,* August 15, 1999.

"Barron's Roundtable 1992: Super Stockpicker—Part 1," *Barron's,* January 27, 1992.

Byrne, Harlan, "First Federal Savings Bank of Montana," *Barron's,* September 4, 1989.

Darsa, Deidra, "Sky Is the Limit for Montana's Glacier," *Real Estate Finance Today,* May 1, 1998.

Engen, John, "It's a Wonderful Formula," *U.S. Banker,* June 19, 1998.

"Glacier Bancorp Expands into Butte; More Acquisitions Eyed," *Associated Press Newswires,* May 26, 1999.

"Great Investments in Your Own Backyard," *Kiplinger's Personal Finance Magazine,* July 1, 1993.

Harlan, Christi, "Savings and Loans Cling to Powers in the Face of Re-Regulation," *Dallas Morning News,* August 20, 1984.

Holley, Paul, "Montana S&Ls Held Own in '88," *Billings Gazette,* April 8, 1989.

Kline, Alan, "Montana Company Swapping Charters," *American Banker,* November 18, 1997.

Kramer, Becky, "Mountain West Bank Gets New Parent," *Spokesman Review,* September 11, 1999.

Olmsted, Monte, "Glacier Bancorp Goes West with Idaho Purchase," *Northwestern Financial Review,* October 9, 1999.

—Rebecca Stanfel

Groupe SEB

Chemin du Petit Bois
Les 4 M - BP 172
69132 Ecully Cedex
France
Telephone: (33) (0) 4 72 18 18 18
Fax: (33) (0) 4 72 18 16 55
Web site: http://www.seb.com

Public Company
Incorporated: 1926 as Société d'Emboutissage de
    Bourgogne
Employees: 14,214
Sales: FFr 11.11 billion (EUR 1.69 billion) ($1.7 billion)
    (1999)
Stock Exchanges: Paris
Ticker Symbol: SEB
NAIC: 335211 Cooking Appliances (Except Convection,
    Microwave Ovens); 33521 Small Electrical Appliance
    Manufacturing

France's Groupe SEB is one of the world's leading manufacturers of small appliances and other products for the home. Under its international brands Tefal (also known as T-Fal) and Rowenta, as well as local brands including SEB, Calor (Belgium and France), and Arno (Brazil), SEB markets products in over 120 countries, manufactured from 16 production sites worldwide. More than 75 percent of SEB's sales of FFr 11.11 billion (EUR 1.69 billion) in 1999 came from outside of France. Europe continues to represent the largest portion of SEB's sales, at more than 60 percent, while the North American and Asian markets each contribute around 15 percent of sales. Since the late 1990s, SEB has also begun expanding its South American presence, particularly with the acquisition of Arno in 1997, and that market now contributes ten percent of annual sales. These sales come from a focused product range targeting four specific families in which SEB has gained worldwide leadership positions: electrical cooking appliances, including electric fryers, steam cookers, food processors, toasters, etc.; small domestic equipment, including irons and vacuum cleaners; household goods, especially non-stick cookware under the Tefal/T-Fal brand, and pressure cookers; and personal care equipment, such as electric toothbrushes, scales, depilatories, and massage devices. SEB is led by Thierry de La Tour d'Artaise, who succeeds Jacques Gairard, architect of SEB's international expansion through the 1990s. The founding family, the Lescures, still holds more than 60 percent of SEB's voting rights.

Birth of an Appliance Giant in the 19th Century

If SEB became one of the world's leading manufacturers of small appliances by the end of the 20th century, its origins were on a much humbler scale. In 1857, Antoine Lescure opened a small tinplating workshop in Selongey, in the Burgundy region of France. The company initially specialized in producing tin buckets and watercans, then began to expand its handmade products to include kitchen utensils and zinc washbowls and tubs. Towards the close of the century, Lescure's company began to add mechanical production techniques, a process accelerated at the start of the 20th century, when Lescure acquired one of the first bottle-capping machines.

Three of Lescure's descendants, brothers Jean, Frédéric, and Henri Lescure, took over the family business in 1925, renaming it a year later as the Société d'Emboutissage de Bourgogne. The Lescure family company remained nonetheless a purely regional concern until the mid-1950s. At that time, the Lescure brothers determined to set the company on a new course.

After examining some 40 different cooking products available on the market, the Lescure brothers began to develop their own invention—one that was to prove something of a revolution to the French cook. In 1953, Société d'Emboutissage de Bourgogne introduced the world to the pressure cooker. Known as the "cocotte minute" (minute cooker) in France, the pressure cooker quickly proved popular, transforming the company from a regional concern to a truly national company.

Société d'Emboutissage de Bourgogne's products remained mechanical devices, and continued to target the home utensils market. In 1967, however, the company made its first move into the booming array of electric household products, when it introduced its own electric deep-fryer. The following year, flush with its success, Société d'Emboutissage de Bourgogne made its first acquisition, that of fellow French company Tefal. By then, Tefal had secured for itself the position as the world's leading manufacturer of non-stick cookware—a category the company had invented.

Tefal had been founded in 1956 by scientist Marc Grégoire. At his wife's suggestion, Grégoire developed a patented process for applying the recently discovered PTFE non-stick coating to aluminum frying pans. Grégoire at first sought to interest established manufacturers in his process, but found no takers. Instead, he formed his own company, Société Tefal, and took his product on the road, making demonstrations at stores and trade shows. Tefal quickly found success among French consumers and, by the end of the decade, Grégoire sought to take his invention overseas. The U.S. debut of the company's products—renamed T-Fal for the U.S. market—came during the holiday season of 1960, at New York City's Macy's department store. Success was immediate and the company sold out of its imported stock within weeks. By the end of January 1961, the company was booking orders of nearly 5,000 per week; by the summer of 1961, the company was shipping more than a million pans each month.

The Lescure family company quickly followed the Tefal acquisition with that of Calor, another French company, based in Lyon, specializing in irons, portable heaters, and hair dryers. The Calor acquisition gave the company not only the leadership of France's nonstick cookware and pressure cookers markets, but also of the market for irons. Following the Calor acquisition, the company changed its name to the more modern SEB S.A., which became the holding company for its Tefal and Calor subsidiaries.

International Expansion in the 1990s

By the mid-1970s, SEB had firmly established itself as a leader in the French small appliances market. The company had also begun to turn its attention to the international marketplace, notably through the Tefal/T-Fal brand. Fueling the company's expansion was a listing on the Paris stock exchange, in 1975. The Lescure family remained, however, majority shareholders with control of the company's voting rights. A year after the public offering, Emmanuel Lescure, who had begun his career with the family-run company, took over as the company's president.

The company created a new subsidiary, T-Fal Corp., for its international expansion efforts, which targeted particularly the U.S. and Japanese markets. Through T-Fal, SEB began its policy of internationalization, establishing local bases in order

best to respond to the particular needs of various markets. In this way, the company introduced unique, target-specific products, including square-shaped frying pans in Japan; flat pans in India; and rice cookers designed for the Asian market.

The company remained, however, largely a French company, with the majority of sales coming from its domestic marketplace. The 1980s did little to change this situation; indeed, SEB found itself struggling through much of the early part of the decade. SEB also made a strategic decision to avoid the new and promising market for microwave ovens—unlike its chief French rival Moulinex, which later found strong success in this market. By the end of the 1980s, with its absence from the microwave market, SEB's reliance on ''traditional'' houseware products seemed to place it in a difficult position.

Nevertheless, the company remained firm in its decision to avoid the microwave market. As CEO Jacques Gairard told *L'Expansion*, investing in microwaves offered ''the assurance of seeing one's short-term margins massacred, and, in the long-term, seeing one's position flattened by the countries of Southeast Asia.''

If SEB remained uninterested in microwaves, it nevertheless sought to increase its international presence. The company took a big step in accomplishing this objective when it acquired Germany's Rowenta, in 1988. Founded in 1884, Rowenta had long been at the forefront of ironing technology, introducing the world's first lightweight, thermostat-controlled electric irons in the first half of the 20th century. Rowenta also developed the first steam irons, revolutionizing ironing boards worldwide in 1957. By the late 1980s, Rowenta had captured the worldwide lead in a number of its product groups, which by then included toasters, electric coffee makers, and vacuum cleaners. With factories in both Germany and France, the Rowenta purchase, which cost SEB some US$170 million, significantly enhanced both its production capacity and its worldwide reach. Rowenta's market position in particular placed SEB in a strong position for entry into the rapidly opening Eastern European markets.

SEB's expansion had been guided by Emmanuel Lescure. In 1990, however, at the age of 61, the descendant of founder Antoine Lescure handed over the direction of the company to Jacques Gairard, the first outsider to lead the company. Gairard took the company on a renewed drive to build its international position.

One of SEB's first international moves was the opening of a factory for the assembly of electric fryers in Toluca, Mexico. The implantation of production facilities in Mexico gave the company a stronger position in the North American market and the benefit of lower Mexican wage rates. At the same time, the company made investments in a production site in soon-to-be renamed Saint Petersburg (known as Leningrad under Soviet rule). The Saint Petersburg plant was soon joined by commercial subsidiaries targeting the newly redefined Russian consumer market. As the other countries in the former Eastern bloc began to adopt free market policies, SEB began to establish marketing subsidiaries and local partnerships in these countries as well, including Hungary, Poland, Slovakia, the Czech Republic, and Ukraine, a process largely completed by 1993. In that year, the company also opened a commercial subsidiary in Turkey.

<table>
<tr><td colspan="2">Key Dates:</td></tr>
<tr><td>1857:</td><td>Company is founded by Antoine Lescure.</td></tr>
<tr><td>1926:</td><td>Business is reincorporated as Société d'Emboutissage de Bourgogne.</td></tr>
<tr><td>1953:</td><td>Company introduces the first pressure cooker.</td></tr>
<tr><td>1956:</td><td>Société Tefal is launched.</td></tr>
<tr><td>1967:</td><td>Electric fryer is introduced; company enters into electric small appliance market.</td></tr>
<tr><td>1968:</td><td>Société Tefal is acquired.</td></tr>
<tr><td>1972:</td><td>Calor S.A. is acquired.</td></tr>
<tr><td>1973:</td><td>Company reincorporates as SEB S.A.</td></tr>
<tr><td>1975:</td><td>SEB attains listing on Paris stock exchange.</td></tr>
<tr><td>1988:</td><td>Rowenta is acquired.</td></tr>
<tr><td>1996:</td><td>Enters into joint venture to acquire Red Heart brand of irons (China).</td></tr>
<tr><td>1997:</td><td>Takeover of Arno (Brazil) is effected.</td></tr>
<tr><td>1998:</td><td>Company acquires Volmo (Colombia).</td></tr>
<tr><td>2000:</td><td>Thierry de La Tour d'Artaise is named president of company.</td></tr>
</table>

By then, SEB had clearly defined its plans to become a leading force in its international small appliance markets, launching its Ambition 2000 program outlining the company's strategy for international development. Into the late 1990s, the company opened a series of subsidiaries and branch offices in its targeted international markets, including Ireland, India, and China in 1995; Dubai, Kiev, Bucharest, and Miami in 1996; and Cairo, Oslo, Greece, and South Korea in 1997. The company also formed a joint venture in China in 1996, and acquired a leading Chinese iron manufacturer, Red Heart. At the same time, SEB doubled production at its Mexican plant, as it made steady increases in the North American markets. Nonetheless, Europe—by then still only slowly recovering from an extended economic downturn—continued to produce the majority of SEB's sales.

SEB looked for ways to develop its overseas markets as a means to reduce its reliance on the European markets. In 1997, the company took over 44 percent of Arno, Brazil's leading small appliances producer, with a product range embracing food processors, washing machines, irons, fans, and vacuum cleaners. For a price of more than FFr 1.2 billion, SEB gained not only Arno's five production facilities, but strong access to the booming Brazilian and South American markets. In keeping with SEB's long tradition, the company vowed to maintain the Arno brand name and also introduce its international T-fal and Rowenta brand names.

After completing the Arno acquisition in 1998, for a total position of 97.6 percent, Arno boosted its South American position with the acquisition of Volmo, the leader in the Colombian and Venezuelan home appliance markets, adding that company's product specialties of irons, fans, mixers, and blenders. The company's gains in the South American region were particularly impressive, jumping from just FFr 100 million in the early part of the decade to top FFr 1.7 billion by 1998. In the United States, the opening of a new US$15 million operations and distribution center in Millville, New Jersey, boosted the company's T-Fal subsidiary logistics base for North America.

SEB's South American acquisitions left the company exposed to the economic collapse of most of its South American markets in the late 1990s. The company was similarly exposed to the growing financial chaos in Russia. Adding to the company's burdens was the devastating earthquake in Turkey, which severely cut down on its otherwise booming sales in that country. By 1999, the company saw its sales slip, from EUR 1.76 billion in 1998 to just EUR 1.69 billion in 1999.

SEB responded by cutting some ten percent of its international workforce, and reducing its advertising budget as well. The company also dropped a number of products in which it had been unable to gain worldwide leadership positions, such as heating and air conditioning appliances. Meanwhile, SEB continued to build its presence elsewhere, taking 100 percent control of its Chinese joint venture. The company's presence in the Asia-Pacific region was also boosted by the creation of a subsidiary in Australia, and branch offices in New Zealand and Thailand. In Africa, the company opened a subsidiary in Johannesburg. At the same time, SEB celebrated the sale of its 50 millionth pressure cooker.

Jacques Gairard retired in May 2000 and was succeeded by former company Vice-President Thierry de La Tour d'Artaise, who vowed to continue reinforcing SEB's international standing in the new century. De La Tour d'Artaise also began hinting at the company's willingness to make new acquisitions in what might become a consolidation of the global small appliances market.

Principal Subsidiaries

Calor S.A.; Rowenta Invest B.V.; SA SEB; SEB Développement S.A.; SEB Internationale S.A.; Tefal S.A.

Principal Competitors

Applica; Newell Rubbermaid Inc.; Conair Corp.; Philips Electronics N.V.; Electrolux AB; Salton, Inc.; The Gillette Company; Sanyo Electric Company, Ltd.; Holmes Group; Sunbeam Corporation; Matsushita Electric Works, Ltd.; Whirlpool Corporation; Moulinex S.A.; WKI Holding; NACCO Industries, Inc.

Further Reading

Beaufils, Vincent, "Jacques Gairard," L'Expansion, May 18, 1989, p. 33.
Brothers, Caroline, "France's SEB Warns of Plunge in 1999 Profits," Reuters, August 31, 1999.
Leboucq, Valérie, "Le groupe SEB repart de l'avant," Les Echos, March 3, 2000.
——, "SEB va acheter le leader brésilien du petit électromenager," Les Echos, March 24, 1997, p. 11.

—M. L. Cohen

Groupe Zannier®

Groupe Zannier S.A.

6 bis, rue Gabriel Laumain
75010 Paris
France
Telephone: (+33) 1 44 83 45 45
Fax: (+33) 1 44 83 45 30
Web site: http://www.groupezannier.fr

Public Company
Incorporated: 1962
Employees: 1,662
Sales: FFr 2.32 billion ($343.84 million) (1999)
Stock Exchanges: Lyon Paris
Ticker Symbol: 12472.PA
NAIC: 44813 Children's and Infants' Clothing Stores

Groupe Zannier S.A. of France is one of the world's leading designers and distributors of children's clothing and footwear. Through some ten brand names, Zannier has captured the full scale of children's clothing, from budget-priced clothing, including the brands Z, 3 Pommes, Alphabet, and MDP to upscale clothing, through brand names Confetti, Floriane, Absorba, Lili Gaufrette, and Chipie. Zannier also owns the brand name Kickers, which in April 2000 was spun off into a joint venture partnership, Kickers Worldwide, with the United Kingdom's Pentland Group (one of the largest Kickers franchisees and owners of brand names Speedo and Ellesse, as well as holder of the worldwide license for Lacoste Shoes). Apart from its collection of brand names, the company also operates and/or franchises several retail chain concepts, including its flagship chain of nearly 300 Z retail stores, as well as 25 Confetti boutiques and 26 La Boutique de Floriane stores in France, Switzerland, Belgium, and Saudi Arabia. In May 2000, Zannier increased its worldwide status through the acquisition of Génération Y2K, the Barclays Private Equity vehicle holding children's clothing brands Catimini, IKKS, and Jean Bourget. The completion of that merger, with a total cost to Zannier of nearly FFr 330 million, will boost Zannier's international organization to more than 700 stores and annual sales of more than FFR 4 billion. Groupe Zannier continues to be led by founder and chairman Roger Zannier and his sister, co-founder and company chief operating officer Josette Redon. The Zannier family continues to hold more than 24 percent of the company, which trades on the Paris stock exchange.

Children's Clothing Specialist in the 1960s

Roger Zannier was just 17 years old in 1962 when, together with sister Josette, he founded a small hosiery workshop in Saint-Chamond in the Loire region of France. The company distributed its production of women's and children's goods to local and regional retailers. By the middle of the decade, the company began to focus its production more and more on the children's market, and by 1966 had transformed itself into a children's clothing company. At that time, Zannier began distributing its production on the wholesale circuit.

Zannier's sales built steadily through the end of the decade and into the 1970s. By 1976, its annual sales had topped FFr 30 million. At that time, the company turned to a relatively new—and booming—market, that of the hypermarchés, combining grocery stores with department stores in a single large surface. Zannier reached agreement with several of the country's large hypermarché groups, starting with Paridoc buyer's central, and then adding the groups Continent and Carrefour to its client list.

In the early 1980s, Zannier underwent a new transformation. Rather than invest in the additional production capacity needed to supply its new large-scale customer base, Zannier decided to abandon its own production and instead turn to third-party contractors for manufacture of its clothing designs. The company also acted as a buyer for nonbranded clothing, which it in turn sold to its retailer clients. In 1983, Zannier boosted this element of its business with the acquisition of Stan, based in Lyon.

At the same time that it abandoned production—joining a trend in the clothing industry worldwide, as the countries of the Far East, with lower wages and less strict regulations, offered low-cost production alternatives; Zannier also joined another growing trend, that of the emphasis on brand name, begun with so-called "designer clothing" in the late 1970s. Zannier launched its own brand name, "Z" (pronounced "Zed" in French) in 1983. The launch of Z was quickly followed by a

Company Perspectives:

Groupe Zannier, created by Roger Zannier and his sister Josette Redon, is the world leader in children's clothing, thanks to the balanced presence of its brands in all market segments and all channels of distribution. Through the diversity and the complementary nature of its brands, Groupe Zannier offers its customers a comprehensive range.

move into the retail world. In 1984, Zannier opened its first six Z boutiques, while also launching a parallel franchise network. Toward the mid-1980s, the company emphasized franchising over own-store construction for building the Z network. To support the launch of its retail chain, Zannier spent some FFr 6 million on a nationwide advertising campaign.

Zannier's retail wing grew quickly. By 1986 the number of franchised Z stores reached more than 80, a number that topped 135 one year later. To support its growing clothing empire, Zannier moved to new headquarters—and moved again the following year to a 14,000-square-meter facility, yet remaining in its Saint Chamond base. From there, the company launched its first public offering, selling ten percent of its shares on the Lyon stock exchange. To support its rapidly growing network of franchises, company-owned stores, and brands, Zannier stepped up its advertising investments, launching television and print campaigns, while also becoming a prominent sports event sponsor (one of the company's most well-known sponsorships was that of its own bicycle racing team, which raced from 1986 to 1992).

Building a Children's Leader in the 1990s

The public offering enabled Zannier to start to build its clothing empire. The company began multiplying its collection of brand names—in the early years of the 1990s, Zannier included some 23 brand names. Among these was the Kickers brand of children's shoes, which Zannier acquired in 1988, adding that company's annual sales of FFr 150 to Zannier's own—which was growing by as much as 50 percent per year and more during the late 1980s.

Kickers itself had earned a primary position among French shoemakers. The brand had first been introduced in 1970. At that time, its parent company, Raufast et Fils, had been struggling to maintain its sales. The company had long specialized in high-end babies' and children's shoes under the brands Bébé Souple and Doisouple. But Raufast's shoes, so-called "Sunday shoes," because they were often reserved for the French family's Sunday outings, suddenly saw its market collapse at the end of the 1960s. The social revolution of the period—and the massive adoption by the world's youth of more informal attire—spelled the end of the "dress-up" shoes that had been the Raufast specialty.

Nearly bankrupt, the Raufast company searched for a means to save its business. The turnaround came when Danial Raufast, driving one day, spotted a billboard for the musical *Hair,* with the actors portrayed in colorful clothing and jeans and barefoot. Raufast recognized a need to develop shoes to match the new

fashion of the day, and he set to work creating colorful shoes and boots. If retailers were initially wary, sales of the new Raufast shoes—dubbed Kickers—soon took off and established the company, which later adopted the Kickers name as its own, as a preeminent maker of children's shoes not only in the French market, but on the international scene as well. By 1974, the Kickers brand was seeing sales in 70 countries; the company began building its own retail network, expanding its empire to include more than 90 stores by 1980, nearly half of which were located outside of France.

Kickers' initial years as part of the growing Zannier group were disappointing; by 1989, however, Kickers had been successfully absorbed into its parent company's operations and began producing net profits. It also gave Zannier the opportunity to expand the Kickers concept and link it with its own clothing creations, launching its "Mode de Vie Kickers" ("Kickers Way of Life") line of clothing and accessories.

With Kickers showing strong sales growth (with sales rising more than 40 percent of its previous year), Zannier turned to the acquisition market again, buying struggling Duguy Créations, a specialist in high-end children's clothing based in Nantes. Duguy added some FFr 200 million to Zannier's annual sales—which, by the 1990s, topped the FFr 1 billion mark for the first time and made Zannier the leading children's clothing specialist in Europe. To provide capacity for its growing distribution needs (by the beginning of the 1990s, Zannier was handling some 100,000 clothing items every day), the company opened a new 10,000-square-meter warehouse facility in its Saint Chamond home base.

By the start of the 1990s, Zannier held at least two strong brand names, Z and Kickers, both of which were successfully evolving international recognition as well. To extend its brand name reach, Zannier began licensing its brands to third parties, such as eyewear manufacturer Esiilor and Henon, while purchasing the licenses from others, such as Warner Brothers' cartoon characters and Disney characters, for use in its clothing lines. One of Zannier's brands, Floriane, took the licensing concept still further, using its licensed characters to define their various collections, for example, featuring the Peter Rabbit character on its clothing for the birth to three years old set, while boys from age two and older could choose clothing from the "Goofy" collection.

Despite the rapidly growing economic crisis of the early 1990s, Zannier continued to see strong growth and to pursue an extensive investment program. The company continued to expand its network of Z franchises, which now neared 200 stores, including a growing international contingent. Zannier also boosted the number of Kickers stores, using the same franchising formula that had brought success to the Z name. A rapid turnaround of Duguy enabled that subsidiary's operations to return to profitability. An expansion of its capitalization brought the company the financial leverage to begin eyeing its next major acquisition.

To prepare for future growth, Zannier underwent a thorough reorganization in 1990, putting into place the Groupe Zannier holding company, which in turn oversaw the activities of seven autonomous subsidiaries, including the Z and Kickers chains.

Key Dates:

1962: Roger Zannier and sister Josette Remond open clothing workshop.

1966: Zannier company specializes in children's clothing and begins wholesale distribution.

1976: Distribution agreements are made with Paridoc, Carrefour, and Continent.

1983: Company exits production and launches Z brand name and store format.

1984: Zannier opens six Z stores and begins building Z franchise network.

1986: Listing is gained on the Lyon stock exchange.

1988: Zannier acquires Kickers International.

1990: Sales top FFr 1 billion.

1991: Company launches La Boutique de Floriane, and takes over Groupe Poron.

1992: Sales top FFr 2 billion.

1993: Kickers licensing agreements for Germany and the United States are effected.

2000: Company forms joint venture Kickers Worldwide and acquires Génération Y2K.

With the reorganization complete, the company could return to its expansion plans.

In 1991, Zannier established a new store concept—La Boutique de Floriane, which the company launched in France, and then in Belgium, Switzerland, and other countries. Zannier also boosted its Z network, opening stores in Canada, Portugal, Greece, and Poland and expanding across the whole of the now-unified Germany. Next, Zannier launched a takeover of rival French company Groupe Poron, which with FFr 750 million in annual sales, added that company's Absorba brand and gave Zannier the world leadership position in the children's clothing market.

The takeover of Poron enabled Zannier's annual sales to top FFr 2 billion by 1992. By then, Zannier had begun a thorough reorganization of Poron, including selling off production facilities in France and Tunisia, slashing Poron's payroll from 2,400 employees to just 400, and trimming its number of brands back to just ten. Meanwhile, Zannier, which reorganized its business structure as a limited liability company, began a revamping of the Z store concept, launching a more modern style, while promoting a policy of pursuing new store openings in the centers of towns and cities. Many—if not most—of Zannier's new store openings were now company-owned branches. By 1994, the number of the company's own stores had topped the number of its franchisees.

If Zannier was becoming disenchanted with the franchise format, its ranks of franchisees were starting to revolt against the company. Among franchisee complaints was the burden of outstanding debt imposed upon each of the stores (reaching an average of some FFr 500,000 per store), a burden created, franchisees claimed, by Zannier's method of stocking the stores, which, as reported by *Les Echos,* was claimed to be Zannier "destocking its production and transferring the burden onto the network." Zannier's response was that much of the store chain's problems were due to the economic recession that had taken on the level of a crisis in France and through much of Europe in the early 1990s.

Indeed, Zannier itself had begun to struggle by 1993. With the major acquisitions of Kickers, then Duguy and Poron, and smaller acquisitions, including that of Baby Relax, from Total subsidiary Hutchinson and Hutchinson, made in 1993, Zannier debt load had begun to topple the company, just as its revenues and net income were slipping in the poor economic climate. The company stepped up its brand licensing, forming a licensing agreement with France's Allemand Industrie, a leading French children's shoe manufacturer, for that company to commercialize Zannier's Kickers and Solaria brands in Germany. A similar arrangement with the Pentland Group, based in the United Kingdom, transferred commercialization and distribution of the Kickers brand for the United States market.

By 1994, Zannier's financial problems had forced it into a restructuring of its holdings, which was to last until the late 1990s and see the company's brand names pared down from its high of 23. Among the brand names the company sold was its Kickers subsidiary, which the company bought back just six months later. The implications of these moves led company chairman Roger Zannier into legal difficulty, when, in June 2000, the company's founder was formally charged with misusing company property, spreading misleading information on the market, and releasing inaccurate company accounts.

The company's reorganization and financial difficulties notwithstanding, Zannier continued to invest in its brands, investing some FFr 115 million in developing its network of Z branch stores, as well as continuing the modernization of its existing branches, carrying out renovations on nearly 50 of its stores in 1993.

By 1996, Zannier had succeeded in reducing part of its debt load, which had soared to nearly FFr 700 million in 1995. The company had also pared down its brand names to just five major brands—Z for the low end, Confetti and Absorba at the mid-range, and Kickers and Floriane covering the high end. The company also pursued its strategy of licensing for international expansion, signing up licensees in Taiwan, the Benelux countries, Afghanistan, Pakistan, Lebanon, Korea, Australia, Japan, Turkey, Brazil, Egypt, and other markets. The company also granted the Pentland group the Kickers license for the Canadian market. Meanwhile, Zannier itself continued to pursue the development of its company-owned Z stores, opening more than 20 stores in 1996, half of which were outside of France, as well as a number of Kickers stores.

By the end of 1997, Zannier had succeeded in regaining profitability, posting FFr 88 million in profits on revenues of FFr 1.98 billion for the year, while pushing its debt down to FFr 311 million. Zannier's turnaround continued through 1998, when its sales topped FFr 2.3 billion—including FFr 1.32 billion from Kickers alone—and its net profits climbed to FFr 115 billion. The company once again began looking to build up its portfolio of brands. An attempt to acquire clothing maker Jaccadi failed, in part because that company's franchisees proved wary of Zannier's reputation among its own franchisees.

Instead, Zannier launched a new brand, Lili Gaufrette, targeted at the upscale market, and then, in mid-1999, picked up the Chipie brand—based in the town of Carcassonne in the south of France—for some FFr 200 million, making it one of Zannier's largest acquisitions ever. The company promptly set about redeveloping the Chipie image, stating its intention to build up its new brand to the international size of Kickers.

The development of Kickers' international activity had by then grown to such an extent that the company decided to spin off its holdings. In May 2000, Zannier announced that it had agreed with the Pentland Group, which held licensing rights worth some 50 percent of all Kickers sales, to form the joint venture Kickers Worldwide. While Zannier retained ownership of the Kickers brand, Pentland took over its marketing and development, ensuring continuity across its international range.

Just weeks after the Kickers spin-off, Zannier announced a new acquisition, that of the Génération Y2K holding company, organized by Barclays to group French companies Catimini and IKKS and their portfolio of mostly upscale brands. With a shares-and-cash deal valued at more than FFr 300 million, the Y2K acquisition boosted Zannier to a world-leading company with annual sales of more than FFr 4 billion produced through an internationally operating network of more than 700 stores. Despite the legal troubles of company founder Roger Zannier, which hit the news in June 2000, Zannier remained focused on its powerful collection of brand names and committed to its position as one of the world's foremost children's clothing companies.

Principal Subsidiaries

Kickers Worldwide (50%).

Principal Divisions

Chipie; Z; Floriane; Lili Gaufrette; Confetti; 3 Pommes; Alphabet; Absorba.

Principal Competitors

Du Pareil au Meme; The Gap, Inc.; Kids 'R' Us.

Further Reading

Epinay, Bénédicte, ''Turbulences dans le réseau,'' *Les Echos,* June 28, 1994, p. 14.
Lecoeur, Xavier, ''Le groupe Zannier cherche à relancer son enseigne Z,'' *Les Echos,* December 12, 1999, p. 18.
Tieman, Ross, ''Le president du Groupe Zannier mis en examen,'' *Le Figaro,* June 13, 2000.
——, ''Zannier's Latest Baby Chipie Set To Kick In,'' *Evening Standard,* February 15, 2000.

—M.L. Cohen

Grupo Herdez, S.A. de C.V.

215 Monte Pelvoux
Mexico City, D.F. 11000
Mexico
Telephone: (525) 201-5655
Fax: (525) 576-6929
Web site: http://www.grupoherdez.com.mx

Public Company
Incorporated: 1923 as Compañia Comercial Herdez, S.A.
Employees: 4,000
Sales: 3.23 billion pesos ($337.87 million) (1998)
Stock Exchanges: Mexico City
Ticker Symbol: HERDEZ B
NAIC: 311421 Fruit and Vegetable Canning; 311423
    Dried and Dehydrated Food Manufacturing; 311711
    Seafood Canning; 31193 Flavoring Syrup and
    Concentrate Manufacturing; 311492 Spice and Extract
    Manufacturing; 32562 Toilet Preparation
    Manufacturing; 42247 Meat and Meat Product
    Wholesalers; 42249 Other Grocery and Related
    Products Wholesalers

Grupo Herdez, S.A. de C.V. is the holding company for a group of Mexican subsidiaries engaged in the manufacture, distribution, sale, and import/export of food products, including canned fish, fruits, juices, vegetables, and condiments. Herdez is Mexico's principal canning company and also manufactures, distributes, and sells toiletries, cosmetics, and other personal-hygiene products. Herdez's products were being sold in 25 countries in 1999.

Manufacturer and Distributor: 1914–82

The enterprise that became Grupo Herdez was founded in 1914 in Monterrey, Mexico. In 1923, the food distributor adopted the name Compañia Comercial Herdez S.A. and moved its headquarters from Monterrey to Mexico City. By 1929, the company's line of accounts included the international favorite Quaker Oats oatmeal. The company had also become involved in the packaging of brand name kitchen utensils and some cosmetics products.

Ignacio Hernandez del Castillo, sales director since 1929, purchased the company in 1941 and assumed the presidency. Among the products the company was distributing at this time were Carter's liver pills, a tonic known as Ner-Vita, Forhan toothpaste, and Zonite, an antiseptic mouthwash.

Under Castillo's management, however, the company began to broaden the scope of its product line, bringing more popular American products to Mexico. The year 1945 marked an important development for the company as it began distributing the line of McCormick & Co. spice products in Mexico as well as some General Foods Corp. products, including Maxwell House and Sanka coffees, Log Cabin syrup, Jell-o, and Kool Aid. To help organize its stock and transportation, the company opened distribution centers in Guadalajara, Merida, and Monterrey that year.

In 1947 Herdez teamed with McCormick de Mexico, S.A. de C.V., to manufacture some products—mustard, mayonnaise, and marmalade—as well as to distribute the U.S.-manufactured products in Mexico. The company opened more distribution centers in Guadalajara, San Luis Potosi, Tijuana, and Torreon in 1956. Herdez began producing its own line of canned goods in 1961, including salmon and tuna, tomato juice and puree, chiles, and vegetable salad. Herdez was still acting as distributor of U.S. personal-care products, including (in 1968) Dial soap and Hind's cream. That year it acquired Productos Marpe, S.A., producer of Doña Maria food products in San Luis Potosi.

In 1970 Herdez, with a partner firm, formed Armour de Mexico, which later became Arpons S.A. de C.V. For many years this company would produce some of the more popular Armour Co. products that had originated in the United States—Jergens products, Brylcream, and Scott Emulsion—with distribution overseen by Herdez. The Armour plant also began producing Dial soap in 1973. In that year Herdez opened a research facility in Los Robles, Veracruz, and began distributing Campbell soups.

Hernandez del Castillo died in 1972 and was replaced as head of Herdez by Ignacio Hernandez Pons. When Pons died shortly thereafter, in 1976, his role was filled by his son,

Company Perspectives:

Grupo Herdez's mission is to continue being the leaders in the market of food products by maintaining a real rate of growth, by continuously improving quality, productivity and the profitability of our organization, our people and our products.

Key Dates:

1914: Hernandez-family firm is founded in Monterrey.
1947: Herdez begins making McCormick & Co. products.
1961: Herdez begins producing canned foods.
1993: Purchase of Grupo Bufalo expands Herdez's line.
1996: Hormel Foods Corp. begins U.S. marketing of Herdez goods.
1997: Herdez has acquired two seafood-processing companies.

Enrique Hernandez Pons. A new Doña Maria plant was opened in San Luis Potosi in 1981. The company was reincorporated as Herdez, S.A. de C.V. the following year.

Expansion in the 1990s

Herdez acquired full control of Armour de Mexico in 1988 and purchased a share in Miel Carlota, S.A. de C.V., a producer of honey, in 1989, acquiring the remainder in 1994. In 1991 the firm became a public company under the name Grupo Herdez, S.A. de C.V. In that year the firm had revenues of 770.86 million new pesos ($255.59 million). Its net earnings came to 95.37 million pesos ($31.62 million). Also that year, the company began sponsoring a CART-race competition team.

By this time Grupo Herdez held 80 percent of the Mexican market for prepared *mole,* a popular Mexican sauce made from chocolate and chiles. The company also held 30 percent of the market for canned fruits and 20 percent for canned vegetables. In October 1991 the company also opened a second Ensanada, Baja California, plant—the first was built in 1987—processing chiles, salsa, onions, and other foods only a short drive from its distribution center in La Jolla, California.

Although exports to the United States comprised only four percent of sales at the time, a Herdez executive saw great possibilities for expansion. "Americans haven't even tasted real Mexican food yet," he told Matt Moffett of the *Wall Street Journal.* Grupo Herdez opened a new plant in San Luis Potosi for McCormick teas, spices, food colorings, mustard, and mayonnaise in 1992. The following year it acquired three new distribution centers in Chihuahua, Puebla, and Tijuana, and it purchased Grupo Bufalo, S.A. de C.V., a producer of salsa and packager of olives, capers, and cherries.

The collapse of the peso in late 1994 resulted in both opportunities and challenges for Grupo Herdez. Although exports to the United States became cheaper, about 60 percent of the company's costs—for cans, cartons, and jars, for example—had to be paid in increasingly expensive U.S. dollars. Herdez's profits fell, but the company remained in the black and in early 1996 formed Herdez Corp., a U.S. joint venture, with Hormel Foods Corp. Hormel's grocery-products division began distributing Grupo Herdez's salsas, refried beans, *mole,* and other products under the Herdez, Bufalo, and Doña Maria names, as Mexican food became increasingly popular in the United States. In 1995 a Mexican joint venture had begun distributing Hormel's spam, chile, stew, deviled ham, vienna sausage, and other meat products in Mexico

Grupo Herdez purchased a 40-percent share of Champinones los Altos, a mushroom processor, in 1995. By this time

Herdez was distributing soy sauces and marinades for the Japanese firm of Kikkoman. The following year Herdez completed the acquisition of Alimentos Deshidratados de Bajio, S.A. de C.V., a company producing dried foods and herbs. At the close of 1996 Herdez acquired Yavaros Industrial, S.A. de C.V. This company had seafood and tomato-paste plants, plus a sardine-boat fleet to which Herdez subsequently added two tuna boats, reducing its own costs for procuring seafoods by 30 percent.

Grupo Herdez also acquired another seafood processing and packaging company, Pescado de Chiapas, S.A. de C.V., in 1997, and renamed it Herdez Chiapas. The parent company began marketing shares of stock on the U.S. over-the-counter market that year. Herdez also launched a line of seven types of juices and eight kinds of nectars in 1997. The following year Grupo Herdez introduced a Soften line of creams, deodorants, soaps, and other personal-care products, adding it to the existing Tami and Pons lines. The Doña Maria line included at this time desserts, *mole,* beans, salsa, and a pumpkin-seed-flavored stew called *pipian.*

In late 1999 Herdez announced that it would begin producing consomme with the acquisition of a company named Apel. Also that year, the joint venture with Hormel introduced four dry-sausage products: pepperoni, hot pepperoni, Italian salami, and Genoa salami, as well as three new flavors of Spam spread—mushroom, jalapeno, and red peppers.

In addition to its Mexico City headquarters, Grupo Herdez was maintaining offices in Ensenada, San Luis Potosi, and Veracruz in 1998. There were 12 plants in eight Mexican cities, warehouses in 17 cities, and distribution centers in nine cities. The company was also active in agricultural research, seeking, for example, to perfect various species of chiles. Herdez had recently acquired a guava-tree plantation in the state of Zacatecas for research purposes and was supplying pineapple farmers in Veracruz with tractors and irrigation equipment. "Poor productivity in the countryside was the major limitation to our sales growth," Hernandez Pons had earlier told Moffett.

Established in 1992, the Herdez Foundation took as its focus the investigation and promotion of Mexican cuisine. Funding was extended to the National Autonomous University of Mexico for research on this subject dating from the pre-Columbian era to the present. The foundation moved into its own building in Mexico City, complete with a library for students and scholars, in 1996.

The program entitled Herdez Viva Mexico! was established during this time to sponsor Mexican athletes engaged in international sporting competitions.

Grupo Herdez's revenues grew from 2.53 billion pesos ($319.44 million) in 1997 to 3.23 billion pesos ($353.39 million) in 1998. Exports accounted for six percent of the latter, with sales to the United States comprising 81 percent of that total. Net earnings, however, fell from 208.34 million pesos ($26.3 million) to 148.51 million pesos ($16.25 million), which the company attributed to unfavorable exchange rates. Herdez's total debt was 1.08 billion pesos ($118.16 million) at the end of 1998, of which 39 percent was long-term.

Principal Subsidiaries

Alimentos Deshidratados de Bajio, S.A. de C.V.; Almacenadora Harpons, S.A. de C.V.; Champinones los Altos, S. de R.L. de C.V. (40%); Grupo Bufalo, S.A. de C.V.; Herdez, S.A. de C.V.; Herdez Corp. (United States; 50%); Hormel Alimentos, S.A. de C.V. (50%); McCormick de Mexico, S.A. de C.V. (50%); Miel Carlota, S.A. de C.V.; Yavaros Industrial, S.A. de C.V.

Principal Competitors

Grupo Corvi S.A. de C.V.; Desc S.A. de C.V.; Authentic Specialty Foods, Inc.

Further Reading

Kraul, Chris, ''For Baja Exporters, No Boost from Lower Peso,'' *Los Angeles Times,* January 22, 1995, pp. D1, D3.

Lazarus, George, ''Hormel Joins Forces with Mexican Salsa Maker,'' *Chicago Tribune,* February 26, 1996, Sec. 4, p. 4.

''Mexico Concern's Products to be Marketed in U.S.,'' *Wall Street Journal,* July 11, 1996, p. B4.

Moffett, Matt, ''U.S. Appetite for Mexican Food Grows, Cooking Up Hotter Sales for Exporters,'' *Wall Street Journal,* February 5, 1992, p. A8.

—Robert Halasz

Hanover Foods Corporation

1486 York Street
Hanover, Pennsylvania 17331
U.S.A.
Telephone: (717) 632-6000
Fax: (717) 637-2890
Web site: http://www.hanoverfoods.com

Public Company
Incorporated: 1924 as Hanover Canning Company
Employees: 1,856
Sales: $287.2 million (1999)
Stock Exchanges: OTC
Ticker Symbol: HNFSA
NAIC: 311421 Fruit and Vegetable Canning; 311411
    Frozen Fruit, Juice, and Vegetable Manufacturing;
    311919 Other Snack Food Manufacturing

Hanover Foods Corporation is the largest fully-integrated and independent food processor in the United States. The company grows, processes, packages, markets, and distributes a variety of food products under several different brand names. In addition to the Hanover brand—which is the leading brand in frozen and canned vegetables and beans in Pennsylvania, New Jersey, Maryland, Virginia, and Delaware—the company also markets its products under the labels of regional food companies it has acquired—including Bickel's, Superfine, Spring Glen Fresh Foods, Dutch Farms, Gibbs, Mitchell's, Myers, Bonton Foods, Draper King Cole, Casa Maid, Sunny Side, Sunwise, Phillip's, York Snacks, and L.K. Bowman. Hanover Foods Corporation is also a significant player in the lucrative private label business. The company operates plants in Pennsylvania, Delaware, New Jersey, and Guatemala, producing over 40 million cases of glass-pack, canned, frozen, refrigerated, freeze-dried, and snack food products each year. Since 1995, however, Hanover Foods has been troubled by internecine strife, as different members of the Warehime family (who founded the company and still control some 60 percent of it) have been embroiled in legal struggles for control of the business.

Early Years

In the early years of the 20th century, Harry Virgil Warehime moved from Carroll County, Maryland, to Hanover, Pennsylvania. After settling there and supporting his family as a farmer, Warehime set out to expand beyond his fields and founded the Hanover Canning Company in 1924. The fledgling company canned peas, beans, and tomatoes grown by Warehime and other local farmers during the summer season, and processed sauerkraut in the winter.

Harry Warehime's son, Alan R. Warehime, joined the family business in 1934, after graduating from Pennsylvania State University with degrees in agriculture and economics. With Alan on board, the Hanover Canning Company grew at a steady pace throughout the 1940s. But true success arrived in the 1950s, as the company expanded tremendously, hiring large numbers of new employees. In 1954, Hanover Canning added frozen vegetables to its established line of canned products.

After Harry Warehime died in 1955, his son succeeded him as president and chief executive officer. As the *Harrisburg Patriot* explained on March 28, 1990, it was "under [Alan's] leadership [that] the company grew to become a national distributor and one of the leading independent food processors in the United States." Unlike other executives, Alan Warehime was known for his active involvement in the day-to-day operations of the company. Indeed, rather than isolate himself in his office, he was fond of walking the plant floors.

Perhaps it was his strolls through the Hanover Canning Company that led Warehime to formulate his food-processing innovations. Shortly after Hanover Canning introduced its line of frozen foods, it became the first company to produce pre-made salads in glass jars. These convenient, ready-to-eat items proved very popular with consumers, particularly Hanover Canning's glass-packaged 3-Bean Salad, which debuted in 1955. In the early 1960s, Warehime oversaw the development of "individually quick frozen" (or IQF) vegetables. Prior to this breakthrough, frozen vegetables were packaged in cumbersome block frozen bags which consumers needed to defrost entirely or otherwise break apart on their own. IQF vegetables, on the other hand, could be poured out with ease in simple-to-measure quantities.

Alan Warehime also presided over Hanover Canning's ini- tial acquisitions. In the mid-1950s, Hanover Canning purchased Gibbs and Phillip's—two regional companies whose lines of canned and frozen vegetables complemented Hanover's prod- ucts. In 1961, Hanover Canning entered into new territory when the company acquired nearby Snyder's Pretzels and Chips— which it rechristened Snyder's of Hanover. With annual sales exceeding $2 million in 1960, this snack food company pro- vided Hanover Canning with clear advantages. Founded in 1923, Snyder's enabled its new parent firm to expand beyond the vegetable business, which—though booming—was charac- terized by low margins. Even more enticing was the fact that Snyder's had built an extensive distribution network which could assist Hanover Canning in its efforts to extend into new geographic regions. After its spate of acquisitions, Hanover Canning opted to change its name to convey its new breadth. In 1962, it officially became Hanover Brands Inc.

In the late 1960s, Hanover Brands again broadened its prod- uct lines when it began to compete in the growing private label business. With private-label brands, Hanover Brands created food products for various retail stores and direct-home delivery distributors. The products were then sold under those brand names—not its own—sparing Hanover the costs it accrued when marketing its own brand.

Hanover Brands continued to enjoy soaring sales in the 1960s and 1970s. In 1975, the company made a significant strategic move when it launched a new division—Alcosa— located in Guatemala City, Guatemala. By opening a plant in the warmer climes of Central America, Hanover Brands was seeking to regularize its vegetable business. Certain crops— especially broccoli, cauliflower, and brussels sprouts (so-called "cold crops")—were difficult to produce consistently in the company's fields in Pennsylvania and Delaware. However, these crops could be grown virtually year-round in Guatemala, enabling Hanover Brands to produce a steady stream of frozen and canned cold crops.

Growth in the 1980s and Early 1990s

As it integrated Alcosa into its operations, Hanover Brands also continued to bolster its regional presence in the mid-Atlan- tic states. In the early 1980s, Hanover Brands made two key acquisitions that meshed with its strengths. With the purchase of

Superfine in 1980, the company strengthened its position in the frozen and canned vegetable market. The addition of Myers to the Hanover stable of brands in 1982 made Hanover one of the leading vegetable processors in the region.

As part of an effort to focus on its core frozen vegetable business, Hanover Brands began to retreat from the snack-food market. To this end, the company spun off Snyder's of Hanover into an independent company in 1981. Although the subsidiary had performed reasonably well, Hanover Brands had over- extended the Snyder's brand in the 1970s—dabbling in snack foods experiments such as peanuts and soft sugar cakes. Newly independent, Snyder's of Hanover refocused on its pretzel and potato chip sales. The smaller company did remain closely connected with Hanover Brands, though, as members of the Warehime family continued to preside over it.

During the mid- and late-1980s, Hanover Brands made a series of acquisitions that reinforced its dominance in the canned and frozen vegetable market. In March 1989, Hanover Brands announced its purchase of F.O. Mitchell & Bro. Inc.—a leader in the canned corn niche. Soon thereafter, Hanover Brands made Aunt Kitty's Soup Company a member of its empire.

A Changing of the Guard

The company suffered a tremendous loss in 1990, when Alan Warehime died on March 24. "He knew every facet of the business," John Miller, the vice-chairman of Hanover Brands' board of directors, told the *Harrisburg Patriot*. Succeeding his father at the helm was Alan Warehime's eldest son, John A. Warehime. Alan Warehime's other children were integral to the family's empire as well. Son Michael headed Snyder's of Hano- ver, while daughter Sally Warehime Yelland served on Hanover Brands' board of directors.

In his new capacity as chairman and CEO, John Warehime instituted a bold new strategy. While the company had long held a powerful position in the frozen and canned vegetable market, Hanover Brands was subject to the low margins of that busi- ness. Consequently, John Warehime sought to enter more lucrative sectors of the food processing industry. In keeping with this significant shift, Hanover Brands acquired Spring Glen Fresh Foods in 1990. Spring Glen was a leading producer of fresh foods, such as puddings, salads, deli items, meat loaf, pot pies, and lasagna, which were all hand-made and hand- packaged. Soon after finalizing the acquisition, the company underwent yet another name change, becoming Hanover Foods Corporation.

Hanover Foods involved itself in the "value-added" foods sector in other ways as well. While integrating Spring Glen into its operations, the company also began to expand the product offerings sold under the Hanover brand to include "meal start- ers." In 1991, Hanover launched a line of Stir Fry products that included pre-prepared vegetables and sauce packets. Con- sumers needed only to add meat to the mix to concoct a quick dinner. Soon thereafter, Hanover Foods purchased a food pro- cessing facility in Clayton, Delaware, which allowed the com- pany to handle meat and seafood.

Legal Troubles Casting a Shadow

As John Warehime presided over Hanover Foods' rapid diversification into new areas of food processing, though, he suffered a loss of credibility in 1992, when he and his wife, Patricia, were charged with federal income tax evasion at a separate company in which they were the sole shareholders. The couple had founded Food Services East, Inc., which operated The Cannery—a chain of 14 food stores in Pennsylvania and Delaware. Although Patricia Warehime was sentenced to only a month in jail, and John Warehime received 100 hours of community service work as his punishment, the scandal created "a year of embarrassment and humiliation" for the Warehimes, the couple's attorney told the *York Daily Record* on October 22, 1992.

The event was only the first in a series of costly legal battles that would plague the Warehime family and Hanover Foods for the remainder of the 1990s. In 1993, Michael Warehime—the president of Snyder's of Hanover and a shareholder and board member at Hanover Foods—discovered that John Warehime had made unauthorized loans worth $4.1 million to his ailing Food Services East Inc. using Hanover Foods capital. Michael Warehime and his sister Sally Yelland drafted resolutions prohibiting such loans in the future and requiring John Warehime to provide collateral for the loans. According to the April 24, 1997 edition of the *York Daily Record*, John Warehime was outraged by this maneuver and referred to the proposals as "the coup."

At an October 1994 meeting, the Hanover Foods board of directors eliminated cumulative voting—a mechanism that empowered shareholders to combine their votes in electing board members. John Warehime then used his power as the sole trustee of the Alan R. Warehime Voting Trust to remove his siblings from the board. (In 1988, Alan Warehime had established the Voting Trust as a means of ensuring stability, and had named John Warehime as its trustee. Although the Trust expired in 1998, it gave John Warehime the right to vote a majority of

common stock, including some shares owned by Michael Warehime.) New board members were nominated and approved in place of the ousted ones. Soon thereafter, the board voted to increase John Warehime's compensation package from $482,000 to $1.34 million. During the same period, Hanover Foods' pre-tax earnings plummeted from $10.2 million to $2.68 million, the *York Daily Record* reported on April 26, 1997. "He certainly got very rich last year in a bad year for the company," an irate attorney for Michael Warehime told *York Daily Record* on November 30, 1995.

A web of lawsuits ensued. In February 1995, Michael Warehime filed suit against his brother, claiming that John Warehime had "used the family business to enhance his own financial status, with little regard for the members of the voting trust under his charge," as the *York Daily Record* explained on November 30, 1995. In September 1996, 12 shareholders filed a civil suit on behalf of the company against John Warehime and the directors.

The already grim situation continued to worsen. In 1997, Michael Warehime filed another suit to block his brother from amending the company's charter to create another class of stock. Michael Warehime alleged that the effort was a thinly disguised attempt by John Warehime to solidify his control since the Voting Trust was due to expire the following year. John Warehime countered that the new "Class C" stock would be used to raise $30 million in capital to fund future acquisitions to keep the company solvent. In any event, John Warehime also acceded to the recommendations of an executive compensation firm hired by the board in 1997 to retroactively diminish his salary. The various lawsuits remained unresolved in 2000.

Further Expansion in the Late 1990s

While the family's squabbles were tied up in the courts, John Warehime continued to oversee operations. In the late 1990s, he guided the company in its acquisition of a tomato-processing plant near Sacramento, California. With its capacity to create tomato paste and an array of derivative products (such as spaghetti sauce, vegetable juice, and puree) the plant would allow Hanover Foods to stabilize costs and strengthen its position in the tomato products market. In 1998, Hanover Foods also returned to its former business of snack foods when it acquired the Manheim, Pennsylvania-based Bickel's Snack Foods. Seeking to capitalize on the higher margins of this food category, Hanover Foods purchased other snack foods concerns in 1999, namely York Snacks and Bonton Foods. Despite these changes, Hanover Foods also remained committed to its core of frozen and canned vegetables. To this end, the company acquired L.K. Bowman, a leading producer of canned mushrooms, in 1999.

Principal Operating Units

Alcosa; Bickels; Dutch Farms; Gibbs; Mitchell's; Myers; Bonton Foods; Spring Glen Fresh Foods; Sunny Side; Sunwise; Superfine.

Principal Competitors

Del Monte Foods Company; Pro-Fac Cooperative, Inc.; Seneca Foods Corporation.

Further Reading

Goulet, Neal, "Feud Risks Foods' Future," *York Daily Record*, April 24, 1997.

——, "Hanover Foods Head: 'Pay for Performance'," *York Daily Record*, April 26, 1997.

——, "Sentencings End Year of 'Humiliation,' " *York Daily Record*, October 22, 1992.

Hayman, Rik, "Brother Responds to Lawsuit," *York Daily Record*, November 30, 1995.

"Memorial Service Set for Alan Warehime," *Harrisburg Patriot*, March 28, 1990.

—Rebecca Stanfel

HCA - The Healthcare Company

One Park Plaza
P.O. Box 550
Nashville, Tennessee 37203
U.S.A.
Telephone: (615) 344-9551
Fax: (615) 320-2331
Web site: http://www.hcahealthcare.com

Public Company
Incorporated: 1987 as Columbia Hospital Corp.
Employees: 168,000
Sales: $16.7 billion (1999)
Stock Exchange: New York
Ticker Symbol: HCA
NAIC: 62211 General Medical and Surgical Hospitals

HCA - The Healthcare Company owns and operates approximately 200 hospitals and other healthcare facilities in 24 of the United States, as well as in England and Switzerland. HCA combines past industry leaders Galen Health Care—the hospital network spin-off of Humana—acquired by Columbia in 1993; Hospital Corporation of America (HCA), merged in 1994; Medical Care America, also acquired in 1994; and Healthtrust, merged in 1995.

Birth of a Healthcare Giant in the Late 1980s

The beginnings of HCA - The Healthcare Company can be traced to 1987, when Richard Scott teamed up with Richard Rainwater to form the Columbia Healthcare Corporation. At the time, the 34-year-old Scott was a native of Kansas City, Missouri, and a graduate of both the University of Missouri and Southern Methodist University Law School. Rainwater was a Fort Worth financier.

Prior to his connection with Rainwater, Scott had been trying to start up a hospital operation, with his goal being to create a national healthcare provider network. His initial approaches to hospital executives, however (including the Hospital Corporation of America's Dr. Thomas Frist, who later took

Scott's place at HCA) were rebuffed. Then Scott teamed up with Rainwater, who served as a director on the Hospital Corporation of America's board, and whose credentials also included acting as the Bass family financial advisor. Operating out of Rainwater's investment company, the duo's first move was to purchase two El Paso, Texas hospitals for $60 million. Scott and Rainwater each put up $125,000 and financed the purchase with $65 million from Citicorp. The new venture was named Columbia Healthcare Corporation.

Both of the newly-purchased hospitals were poorly managed and in need of repair. Scott and Rainwater set out to reform the hospitals' operations and complete renovations; along the way, they earned the goodwill of the hospitals' physicians. Next, Columbia and a group of physician investors formed El Paso Healthcare System, Ltd. (EPHS) as a limited partnership. EPHS acquired the two hospitals from Columbia, along with two other physician-owned diagnostic centers, in exchange for partnership shares. The physician partnership would eventually gain a 40 percent share in EPHS, setting a pattern for much of Columbia's future dealings.

Five months after its formation, Columbia moved aggressively to consolidate its El Paso operations. EPHS purchased two new facilities—the general medical/surgical Landmark Medical Center and the adjacent Stanton Medical Building. Landmark, operating in the over bedded El Paso market, had 355 beds but only a 54-bed average daily census. EPHS's response was to close Landmark and transfer its patients and equipment to EPHS's existing hospitals. Landmark and the adjacent building were then sold to a local real estate developer. From this move, EPHS increased the average daily census at its other facilities by 35 patients, bringing an earnings (EBDIT) increase of $3.5 million, to $8.9 million EBDIT on 1988 revenues of $43 million.

In December 1988, Columbia and EPHS moved closer to the goal of becoming a full-service system when EPHS opened its Sun Towers Behavioral Health Center, an 80-bed free-standing psychiatric facility. The behavioral health program from Sun Towers Hospital was transferred to the new facility, expanding the hospital's bed count. In its first year of operation, the psychiatric facility recorded a $2.5 million EBDIT; within two years, its average daily census increased from 11 patients to 45 patients.

Company Perspectives:

Above all else, we are committed to the care and improvement of human life. In recognition of this commitment, we strive to deliver high quality, cost effective healthcare in the communities we serve. In pursuit of our mission, we believe the following value statements are essential and timeless. We recognize and affirm the unique and intrinsic worth of each individual. We treat all those we serve with compassion and kindness. We act with absolute honesty, integrity and fairness in the way we conduct our business and the way we live our lives. We trust our colleagues as valuable members of our healthcare team and pledge to treat one another with loyalty, respect and dignity.

EPHS continued to expand its system, opening its Lifecare Center, which combined a cardiopulmonary rehabilitation facility with an outpatient wellness center. In 1989, EPHS introduced its One Source medical services program—marketing to major area employers—which provided discounts at EPHS system facilities. Within a year, One Source grew to nearly 15,000 members, and generated $6.5 million in revenues.

Between 1988 and 1990, EPHS's system wide average daily census grew from 174 patients to 303 patients. Revenues jumped to $113 million in 1989, and to nearly $135 million in 1990. EBDIT for 1990 was $27.7 million.

The Early 1990s

In 1990, EPHS continued to consolidate its El Paso position, by acquiring two diagnostic imaging centers, beginning construction on a 296,000-square-foot medical office building, and initiating plans for a 29,000-square-foot oncology center. Both new facilities were connected to the Sun Towers Hospital by glass-enclosed skywalks.

That year, however, EPHS formed only part of Columbia's growing empire. Scott had already begun to conquer new markets, purchasing the nearly bankrupt 300-bed Victoria Hospital in Miami in 1988, and expanding this new operation to four Miami hospitals by 1990. That year, Columbia moved into the Corpus Christi, Texas market as well. In these new markets, Scott continued his successful El Paso strategy of creating a full-service healthcare network of facilities, while creating limited partnerships with physician investors.

These partnerships would generate a lot of criticism about Columbia's strategy. Such partnerships risked the danger of physician-partners over-treating their patients in an effort to drive up their own profits. Even so, these partnerships instead seemed to predict the rise of HMOs that would sweep the U.S. health insurance industry by the mid-1990s, by encouraging physicians toward greater efficiency and lower costs of treatment.

Columbia's total revenues were already approaching the half-billion mark in 1990. Scott next engineered two important deals. The first was the merger acquisition of Smith Laboratories and its subsidiary, Sutter Corp., in a stock swap of 3.3 million shares. The deal led Columbia to go public. The second

deal was a landmark joint venture with Medical Care America of Dallas—then the largest surgery center network in the country—to build a $50 million hospital in Corpus Christi.

Scott continued on the acquisition trail. In 1990, Columbia also made a $22 million cash purchase of HEI Corporation, Inc. (which it sold off again the following year), bringing the company into the Houston market. In September of that year, the company, through a limited partnership, acquired Coral Reef Hospital for nearly $18 million in cash and notes. One month later, it acquired Southside Community Hospital for nearly $4.5 million, bringing Columbia's network to 11 hospitals. The company's emphasis on full-service systems proved successful, and revenues grew not only by adding new hospitals to the chain, but also by attracting higher numbers of patients.

More acquisitions followed over the next two years, including the $185 million acquisition of Indianapolis-based Basic American Medical, with four hospitals in the Ft. Lauderdale market. By the end of 1992, Columbia's network had grown to 24 hospitals and over $1 billion in assets. Revenues passed $800 million, with EBITDA of $136 million.

The Mega-Mergers of the Mid-1990s

By 1993, Scott, known to keep a paperweight on his desk reading "If you are not the lead dog, the view never changes," was ready to launch Columbia as a national healthcare provider. In June of that year, Columbia announced its intention to merge with Galen Health Care, increasing its total number of hospitals by four times, and catapulting its revenues past $5 billion. Scott remained in control of the newly renamed Columbia Healthcare Corporation.

Galen, with 74 hospitals in 1993, had formerly been part of Humana. Founded in 1968, Humana had been an earlier success story in the hospital network field, building the second largest hospital chain operation in the United States by 1979. During the 1980s, Humana entered the health insurance business, and by the late 1980s, was forced to divide its operations. At that time, its hospitals and insurance business began competing with each other, especially as rival insurance agencies began directing their customers to other providers. By the early 1990s, Humana's hospital network was faltering, and in early 1993 the hospitals were spun off as Galen Health Care.

Under the terms of the merger—a stock swap worth $3.2 billion—Galen's stockholders received 0.775 shares of Columbia stock for each Galen share they held. The addition of Galen brought the number of Columbia hospitals to 94, and added 15 new markets—primarily metropolitan areas—to the chain. It also gave Columbia a presence in 19 states, as well as in England and Switzerland. With 22,000 licensed beds, Columbia became the largest non-governmental hospital chain in the United States, and was second only to the Veteran's Affairs Department's 64,700-bed system.

In October 1993, one month after the Galen merger was consummated, Scott shook up the industry again by announcing an agreement to merge Columbia with the Hospital Corporation of America (HCA). HCA had been formed by the Frist family and Kentucky Fried Chicken founder Jack Massey in 1968, and had grown steadily. HCA had been made up of 50 hospitals by 1973,

Key Dates:

1987: Richard Scott and Richard Rainwater join together to form Columbia Healthcare Corporation; form El Paso Healthcare System (EPHS), along with a group of physician investors.

1989: EPHS introduces One Source medical services program, which provides discounts at EPHS system facilities, by marketing to major area employers.

1992: Columbia's network has grown to include 24 hospitals and over $1 billion in assets.

1993: Columbia acquires Galen Health Care.

1994: Columbia merges with Hospital Corp. of America and is renamed Columbia/HCA Healthcare Corporation.

1995: Columbia/HCA acquires Healthtrust.

1997: Company merges with Value Health, Inc., and later becomes the subject of a federal healthcare fraud investigation. Scott resigns, and is replaced by Dr. Thomas Frist.

1998: Columbia/HCA completes a series of divestitures.

2000: Company reaches an understanding with the Department of Justice to recommend an agreement to settle its civil claims actions, paying $745 million in fines; later, changes its name to HCA - The Healthcare Company.

and 376 hospitals by 1983, including holdings in seven countries. When changes in Medicare payments and the rise of HMOs began to depress its per-bed census rates, HCA moved to trim its hospital count, spinning off 102 hospitals to physician investors. These hospital spin-offs became Healthtrust, Inc. in the late 1980s. In 1989, Frist, Jr., took control of the company in a leveraged buyout, and continued to sell off hospitals for the next three years before taking the company public again in 1992. By the time the Columbia merger came into being, HCA had grown to include 96 hospitals, which were added to Columbia's 94 and thus helped create the largest hospital chain in the United States.

Renamed Columbia/HCA Healthcare Corporation, the company formally merged in February 1994 in a stock swap worth $5.7 billion. This created a $10 billion company with operations in 26 states. Scott was named chief executive officer, while Frist became chairman.

Meanwhile, HMOs—already notorious for their emphasis on tight cost control—achieved dominance in the private insurance industry. Similarly, government agencies were also beginning to tighten their reimbursement policies. Columbia/HCA moved to consolidate its formerly regional and local operations—including payroll, marketing, and purchasing—into its Louisville, Kentucky, corporate headquarters. This move created, in effect, a national organization. Scott's initial $125,000 investment was by then worth $200 million.

Scott continued to eye new acquisitions and joint ventures, turning to the non-profit hospital market. This market included acquisition of the 585-bed Cedars Medical Center of Miami, as well as joint ventures with university medical schools and

teaching hospitals such as the University of Miami, the University of Louisville, Tulane University, Emory University, the Medical College of Virginia, and the Medical University of South Carolina. Scott's next step was the $860 million purchase in May 1994 of Medical Care America, Inc., the largest provider of outpatient surgery services.

Scott was not yet finished, though. In September 1994, news broke that National Medical Enterprises planned to purchase Healthtrust and American Medical International, in a deal reported to be worth $10 billion that would have given NME a strong second place behind Columbia/HCA. In October 1994, however, Healthtrust instead agreed to be acquired by Columbia for $5.6 billion. Healthtrust's 116 hospitals brought the Columbia chain to 311 facilities, making it the 12th-largest employer in the United States and the 45th-largest in revenues—$14.5 billion for the 1994 fiscal year. Importantly, the Healthtrust acquisition and its concentration of rural hospitals expanded Columbia beyond its traditionally urban base.

The Healthtrust merger was completed in April 1995, with Healthtrust stockholders receiving 0.88 Columbia shares for each share of Healthtrust stock. By then, Columbia had already completed several more acquisitions, including Colorado-based Rose Healthcare System, St. Francis Hospital of Charleston, West Virginia, and Angelo Community Hospital of San Angelo, Texas. Following the Healthtrust acquisition, Columbia also announced acquisitions of The Family Clinic Ltd. of Little Rock, Arkansas, and a number of other hospitals, including three in metropolitan Chicago.

By the beginning of 1996, Columbia/HCA had grown to 340 hospitals, 125 outpatient surgery centers, and a range of other healthcare facilities. These facilities included 182 home health agencies, with 70,000 licensed beds in 36 states, England and Switzerland. Revenues had topped $17 billion, and the company held more than $18 billion in assets. The company's growth continued throughout the remainder of 1996 and into 1997. In November of 1996, Columbia/HCA acquired the Atlanta-based Central Health Services, Inc. Central Health was one of the largest home health providers in the United States, with 29 locations in Georgia, Florida, and Tennessee. Columbia/HCA also acquired ownership interests in several individual medical facilities in various locations, including Tennessee, Ohio, Virginia, West Virginia, and Barcelona, Spain.

In January of 1997, Columbia/HCA announced a planned merger with Value Health, Inc., a $1.9 billion specialty healthcare services company. Value Health provided specialty care benefit programs to large corporations, managed care organizations, insurance companies, and governments at the local, state, and federal level. The merger was completed in August of 1997.

1997–99: Scaling Back

Meanwhile, however, Columbia/HCA had run into serious trouble. In March, 1997, the company's facility in El Paso, Texas, became the subject of a federal healthcare fraud investigation. The investigation was dramatically broadened in scope in July, when approximately 500 federal agents raided Columbia/HCA facilities in seven states. Focusing on Medicare-billing practices and home health operations, the investigation alarmed both investors and the company's board members. Near the end of July, at the urging of the company's board of directors, Scott resigned. At the same time, the company's president and COO, David Vandewater, also resigned. Scott was replaced as chairman and CEO by Dr. Thomas Frist, Jr., who had been at the helm of HCA when Scott acquired it.

Frist, who had been growing increasingly displeased with Scott's tactics, immediately steered the company in a new direction. Rather than attempt to develop a national brand, which had been Scott's focus, Frist instead adopted a local, community focus. His new strategy, announced in August of 1997, included the sale of Columbia/HCA's home care division, changes in laboratory billing procedures, increased reviews of Medicare coding, and the discontinuation of existing contracts with physicians that allowed them to invest in the company's hospitals. This last point, particularly, had been a source of concern for Frist, who believed that giving physicians ownership interest induced them to refer money-making patients to Columbia, while referring less profitable ones to competitors.

Operating under its new strategy, Columbia/HCA set about becoming smaller and more focused. In January of 1998, the company entered into an agreement to sell its Value Behavioral Health subsidiary—one of the operating groups obtained in its Value Health acquisition. A month later, the company agreed to sell ValueRx, another Value Health operating group. A flurry of divestitures followed. Between July 1998 and January 1, 1999, Columbia/HCA sold 33 of its surgery centers, more than 40 of its hospitals, and all home care operations in 19 states. The company continued to prune its operations in 1999, although at a slower pace.

2000 and Beyond

In early 2000, Columbia/HCA announced that it had reached an understanding with the Civil Division of the U.S. Department of Justice to recommend an agreement to settle, subject to certain conditions, civil claims actions against the company. These claims related to the company's coding, outpatient laboratory billing, and home health issues. The understanding called for Columbia to pay a $745 million fine.

In an effort to further its new image, the company also changed its name to HCA - The Healthcare Company. "Returning the company's name to HCA is an affirmation of the culture and values of our more than 168,000 employees," Frist explained in a May 25, 2000 press release. "We have restructured this company based on the principles on which the company was originally founded and our name reflects that change." With its new direction firmly established, and the end of its

3-year federal investigation finally within sight, it appeared that HCA was prepared to face the future. Whether Frist's vision would prove to be feasible or not remained to be seen; if so, it would almost surely result in a company that differed greatly from the aggressive healthcare giant it had previously been.

Principal Subsidiaries

Birmingham Outpatient Surgical Center, Inc.; Columbia/HCA Montgomery Healthcare System, Inc.; Galen Medical Corporation; Montgomery Regional Medical Center, Inc.; Surgicenters of America, Inc.; HCA Health Services of California, Inc.; Kingsbury Capital Partners, Inc.; MCA Management Partnership, Ltd.; Psychiatric Company of California Inc.; Surgical Centers of Southern California, Inc.; Sutter Corporation; Colorado Healthcare Management Inc.; HCA Health Services of Colorado, Inc.; Health Care Indemnity, Inc.; MOVCO, Inc.; AlternaCare Corp.; Amedicorp, Inc.; CHC Holdings, Inc.; Critical Care America, Inc.; Galen Health Care, Inc.; HCA Investments, Inc.; HCA International.

Principal Operating Groups

Eastern Group; Western Group; National Group.

Further Reading

Bell, Julie, "Scott Ignited Firestorm in Health Care," *Gannett News Service,* July 25, 1997, p. S12.

Bell, Julie, and Pinkston, Will, "With Dr. Thomas Frist at the Helm, It's Back to the Future at Columbia/HCA," *Gannett News Service,* July 25, 1997, p. S11.

Galewitz, Phil, "Columbia/HCA Agrees to Settle Fraud Allegations for $745 Million," *San Francisco Examiner,* May 19, 2000.

Hundley, Kris, "Columbia Picks New Name for New Start," *St. Petersburg Times,* May 26, 2000, p. 1E.

Lipin, Steven, Sharpe, Anita, and Jaffe, Greg, "Columbia Board Weighs CEO Departure," *The Wall Street Journal,* July 25, 1997, p., A3.

Lutz, Sandy, "Columbia/HCA Nabs Healthtrust," *Modern Healthcare,* October 10, 1994, p. 2.

——, "Columbia Keeps on Growing," *Modern Healthcare,* March 6, 1995, p. 2.

——, "Columbia on the Fast Track," *Modern Healthcare,* September 6, 1993, p. 10.

——, "Industry Follows, Fears the Leader," *Modern Healthcare,* February 14, 1994, p. 23.

Lutz, Sandy, and Gee, Preston, *Columbia/HCA: Healthcare on Overdrive,* 1998, New York: McGraw-Hill.

Walsh, Matt, "More Patients, Please," *Forbes,* October 10, 1994, p. 72.

—M.L. Cohen
—updated by Shawna Brynildssen

Hispanic Broadcasting Corporation

3102 Oak Lawn Avenue, Suite 215
Dallas, Texas 75219
U.S.A.
Telephone: (214) 525-7700
Fax: (214) 525-7750
Web site: http://www.hispanicbroadcasting.com

Public Company
Incorporated: 1992 as Heftel Broadcasting Corporation
Employees: 828
Sales: $197.9 million (1999)
Stock Exchanges: New York
Ticker Symbol: HSP
NAIC: 513111 Radio Networks; 513112 Radio Stations

Hispanic Broadcasting Corporation (HBC) is the largest Spanish-language radio broadcasting company in the United States. As of mid-2000 it owned and programmed 45 radio stations in 13 markets. The company's stations were located in 12 of the 15 largest Hispanic markets in the United States, including Los Angeles, New York, Miami, San Francisco/San Jose, Chicago, Houston, San Antonio, Dallas/Fort Worth, Mc-Allen/Brownsville/Harlingen in Texas, San Diego, Phoenix, and El Paso. HBC also operates the HBC Radio Network, one of the largest Spanish-language radio broadcast networks in the United States in terms of audience size.

From a Single Radio Station in Hawaii: 1960s–1995

The Heftel family owned and operated a radio station in Hawaii, KSSK-AM, beginning in the mid-1960s and continuing through the 1970s and 1980s. In 1979 the Heftel family added a second station, KSSK-FM. Cecil Heftel was a Democrat representing Hawaii in the U.S. Congress from 1977 to 1986. In 1986 he left Congress and began concentrating on Hispanic radio, acquiring KLVE-FM in Los Angeles. Both of the Hawaii stations were sold in 1990 to allow the company to focus on its mainland stations in Los Angeles and other media-related ventures in Los Angeles and Miami.

Heftel Broadcasting Corporation, which would change its name to Hispanic Broadcasting Corporation in 1999, was incorporated in Delaware in 1992. Initially, Heftel owned an AM-FM combination in Los Angeles, KTNQ-AM, and KLVE-FM. Cecil Heftel was also a partner with Amacio Suarez in a dominant AM-FM combination in Miami, WRTO, and WAQI.

In 1993 Heftel announced plans to merge with the Spanish Radio Network to create the largest Spanish-language radio company in the United States. The Spanish Radio Network owned four radio stations: WQBA-AM-FM in Miami, WADO-AM in New York, and WGLI-AM in Babylon, New York.

In 1994 Heftel signed an agreement with Mexico's Grupo Radio Centro to acquire its U.S. network, Cadena Radio Centro. In exchange, Grupo Radio Centro would invest $20 million in Heftel, which would make an initial public offering (IPO) of stock. Cadena Radio Centro had 64 affiliates in the United States and 12 in Puerto Rico. At this time Heftel owned two radio stations in Los Angeles and was part owner of two in Miami. With the acquisition of Cadena Radio Centro for $6.5 million, Heftel reached approximately 88 percent of the U.S. Hispanic population.

In mid-1994 Heftel announced plans to expand and become the largest radio station group of Hispanic formatted stations in the United States. It planned to acquire another station in Miami, three in Dallas, and one in New York. The company planned to offer four million shares of stock in its IPO to raise about $47 million. By the end of 1994 Heftel had acquired KCYT-FM in Dallas/Fort Worth for $1.9 million.

Clear Channel Communications Inc. As Minority Owner: 1995–2000

In May 1995 Clear Channel Communications Inc. purchased $30 million of Heftel nonvoting stock. Heftel by this time owned 15 Spanish-language radio stations in the United States. The purchase gave Clear Channel a 20 percent interest in Heftel, but less than five percent of its voting stock. At the beginning of 1996 Heftel and its subsidiary Cadena Radio Centro radio network obtained the exclusive sales, marketing, and

distribution rights to CNN Radio Noticias, a Spanish-language
radio news service.

In mid-1996 Heftel was involved in a three-way deal with
Clear Channel Communications and Tichenor Media System
Inc. that made Heftel the largest radio broadcaster to Hispanics
in the United States. Through a tender offer totaling about $206
million, Clear Channel increased its holdings of Heftel stock to
63 percent and installed its own board of directors. Heftel
chairman and founder Cecil Heftel gave up his position, and
Clear Channel president Lowry Mays became president of
Heftel temporarily. Clear Channel would maintain Heftel as an
independent, publicly traded company.

The second part of the deal involved a merger of Tichenor,
which owned about 20 Spanish-language radio stations, and
Heftel into a new company that would own 39 Hispanic stations
and cover all of the top ten Hispanic markets. Head of the new
company, which continued as Heftel Broadcasting Corporation,
would be McHenry T. Tichenor, Jr., president of Tichenor
Media System. The merger between Tichenor and Heftel was
completed in February 1997, leaving Clear Channel with about
43 percent ownership of the new company. The merger-acquisi-
tion made Clear Channel the second largest owner of radio
stations in the United States at the time, with about 100 radio
stations in addition to 18 TV stations. As a result of the merger,
Heftel's assets nearly tripled from $164 million to $479 million.

At the end of 1996 Heftel owned the top-rated Hispanic
radio station in the United States: KLVE-FM of Los Angeles,
which played a mix of Spanish ballads and English-language
songs aimed at Hispanic listeners. Heftel had acquired the station in 1986, and as of 1994 when Heftel went public it was
pulling only about a three percent share of the Los Angeles
market. At the time the station was broadcasting a broad mix
of international Spanish hits. When research revealed that the
audience preferred romance, it switched to soft Spanish love
ballads. By spring 1995 it was the city's top-ranked radio
station.

Through Heftel, Clear Channel put down $10 million for an
option to buy the low-ranking KCSA-FM of Glendale, California from Gene Autry-owned Golden West Broadcasters and
change its format to Spanish. The station was acquired for
$102.5 million and the format changed in February 1997. Heftel
founder Cecil Heftel's son, Richard Heftel, was president and
general manager of the company's Los Angeles stations.

Reflecting the merger with Tichenor, Heftel turned a profit
of $18.8 million in 1997, a substantial turnaround from a $45.4
million loss in 1996. In 1998 a secondary offering of stock
raised $205.2 million, which would be used to reduce debt and
finance acquisitions.

Expansion Through Acquisitions: 1998–2000

In March 1998 Heftel announced that it would acquire
KKPN-FM of Houston for $54 million from SFX Broadcasting
and change the programming to a Spanish-language format. In
Houston, Heftel also owned two stations, Estero Latino on FM
and KLAT, known as La Tremenda, on AM. SFX had to divest
the station to comply with federal regulations. During the second quarter of 1998 Heftel launched WCAA-FM in New York,
which was formerly WNWK, and changed the call letters of
Houston station KKPN to KLTN after acquiring it.

In August 1998 Heftel acquired two radio stations in San
Diego County for $65 million from Jacor Communications Inc.
The two stations' new call letters would be KEBN, dubbed
''K-Buena,'' and KLQV, which would be marketed as
''K-Love.'' Jacor was required by government regulators to
divest the stations to comply with rules governing another
acquisition.

In February 1999 Heftel acquired KHOT-FM in Phoenix for
$18.3 million in cash from New Century Arizona. Phoenix was
the 12th largest Hispanic market. The acquisition gave Heftel
ownership of 40 stations in the top 15 Hispanic markets, including 20 stations in the top ten.

Around this time Heftel united its radio stations into a
national network to be called the HBC Radio Network. The new
network allowed Heftel to offer advertisers a national Hispanic
audience with local programming. Stations in the network
would not all receive uniform programming. Rather, certain
shows from certain markets would be rebroadcast on them. One
popular morning show originating in Los Angeles was broadcast on Heftel stations in San Francisco, Houston, San Antonio,
Dallas, Chicago, Las Vegas, El Paso, and McAllen, Texas.
Other network programs would include lifestyle news and reports from *People en Espanol,* a program of regional music, and
a sports roundup localized for individual markets. When the
HBC Radio Network launched on February 26, 1999, it was
heard on 39 stations that reached more than 18.5 million people,
or 65 percent of the U.S. Hispanic population.

In March 1999 Heftel acquired KISF-FM in Las Vegas for
$20.3 million from Radio Vision, giving it two Spanish-
language radio stations in that market. Las Vegas's Hispanic
population was growing at the rate of nearly 16 percent a year.

In April 1999 Heftel entered a new national sales and programming alliance with Z-Spanish Media Corp. Radio stations
in 19 of the top 20 Hispanic markets would be packaged jointly
by Heftel and Z-Spanish for network advertisers. Heftel's stations reached 65 percent of the Hispanic population, while
Z-Spanish stations reached another ten percent. Heftel also
swapped its KRTX-FM serving Houston for Z-Spanish station
KLNZ-FM in Phoenix.

Heftel and Z-Spanish Media soon became more closely
related, with Heftel purchasing another 4.1 percent of the company to raise its interest to slightly more than ten percent.
Z-Spanish, in turn, said it would affiliate its 34 radio stations
with Heftel's newly created HBC Radio Network, giving the
new network coverage of 19 of the United States' top 20
Hispanic markets.

Key Dates:

1960s: Heftel family owns and operates a radio station, KSSK-AM, in Hawaii.
1979: Family acquires KSSK-FM in Hawaii.
1986: Heftel acquires KLVE-FM in Los Angeles.
1990: Heftel sells its two Hawaii radio stations.
1992: Heftel Broadcasting Corporation is incorporated in Delaware.
1994: Company goes public.
1995: Clear Channel Communications purchases a 20 percent interest in Heftel for $30 million.
1996: With the help of Clear Channel, Heftel merges with Tichenor Media System Inc. to become the largest radio broadcaster to the Hispanic market.
1999: Heftel launches the HBC Radio Network.
1999: Heftel Broadcasting changes its name to Hispanic Broadcasting Corporation.

In mid-1999 Heftel changed its name to Hispanic Broadcasting Corporation to better reflect the nature of its business. The company had a market capitalization of $2 billion. Hispanic Broadcasting Corporation (HBC) could boast more than seven million listeners for its 42 owned or operated radio stations. The company planned to move into new markets and add stations to its existing bases. Spanish-language advertising was estimated to be growing at two to three times the rate of the general market. Spanish-language radio broadcasting was benefiting from the tremendous growth in the Hispanic population, and the Hispanic Broadcasting Corporation was the leading radio broadcaster to that market.

HBC also was reformatting some of its stations in line with an overall strategy to reach a wider range of Hispanics. In Miami, for example, it altered the format of WQBA-AM—one of four Miami stations owned by the company—from "La Cubanisma," or "the most Cuban," to "La radio que habla," or "the station that talks." Most of HBC's FM stations played music, and the company was in the process of changing all of its AM stations to a news/talk format. The company also put all of its stations online, creating web sites for them, and was considering developing an Internet portal for Hispanics.

In October 1999 HBC acquired two radio stations in Los Angeles—KACE-FM and KRTO-FM—from Cox Radio for $75 million, marking Cox's exit from the Los Angeles market. The acquisition gave HBC a five-station cluster in the city, including the top two stations in the market. KACE-FM was one of the city's last black-owned radio stations, playing rhythm and blues oldies. Under HBC it would be reformatted for Hispanic audiences.

For 1999 HBC's Los Angeles stations accounted for 43.4 percent of the company's broadcast cash flow. For the year HBC reported net revenues of $197.9 million, up from $164.1 million in 1998. Net income was $34.2 million, up from $26.9 million in 1998.

In 2000 HBC introduced a new format, Hispanic oldies, or Recuerdo. It was first played on the company's two newest

Los Angeles stations, KRCD-FM (formerly KACE-FM) and KRCV-FM (formerly KRTO-FM). The new format included different types of Hispanic music from the 1960s.

As part of its proposed merger with AMFM Inc., Clear Channel divested 72 stations in 27 markets in March 2000. HBC planned to pick up new stations from Clear Channel in Austin, Texas; Denver; and Phoenix. The acquisitions were blocked, however, by the U.S. Department of Justice in May 2000. The Department of Justice cited Clear Channel's "passive" stake in HBC and would not allow the purchase of the three stations.

At the time Clear Channel owned all of the Class B non-voting shares in HBC, the equivalent of 26 percent of all of HBC's common stock. As a result, Clear Channel was entitled to a class vote on certain matters, including certain sales of assets, consolidations and mergers, and other items. Another significant owner of the company was McHenry Tichenor, Jr., its chairman, president, and CEO, and his family, which held voting control over approximately 17 percent of HBC's Class A common stock.

In May 2000 HBC announced that Prodigy would become the exclusive co-branded Internet service provider (ISP) for the company and its 45 Spanish-language radio stations. Prodigy en Espanol was the first bilingual English-Spanish-language Internet service created for the Spanish-speaking population. It became the preferred ISP on HBC's stations and web sites in the first half of 2000.

In May 2000 HBC stock moved from the NASDAQ to the New York Stock Exchange, in part to increase its visibility and investor base and reduce trading volatility. Its ticker symbol was changed from HBCCA to HSP. In addition to being the largest Spanish-language radio broadcaster, HBC was the ninth largest radio station owner with 45 stations.

Positioning for Significant Growth

Several trends indicated that Spanish-language radio broadcasting in the United States had significant growth potential in the 21st century. The rapidly growing U.S. Hispanic population was estimated to have grown from 27.3 million at the end of 1995 to more than 31 million in 2000. During this period the Hispanic population grew at a rate estimated to be three times the expected growth rate for the overall U.S. population.

HBC also noted that more than two-thirds of the U.S. Hispanic population was concentrated in 15 markets, making them accessible to advertisers through HBC's Spanish-language radio stations in those markets. Hispanics also represented an attractive market to advertisers, because on average they tend to be younger, have larger households, and routinely spend a greater percentage of their income on many different kinds of goods and services than non-Hispanic households. Total Spanish-language advertising revenues increased from approximately $950 million in 1994 to an estimated $1.9 billion in 1999, representing a higher growth rate than for all advertising during the period.

Principal Competitors

Spanish Broadcasting System Inc.; Z-Spanish Media Corp.; Radio Unica; Rodriguez Communications.

Further Reading

Austin, John, "Spanish-Language Radio Is Booming in Fort Worth, Texas, Area," *Knight-Ridder/Tribune Business News,* September 14, 1999.

Bachman, Katy, "Heftel Doubles Its Bets," *Mediaweek,* March 15, 1999, p. 20.

"By Any Other Name, Heftel's Clout Grows," *Mediaweek,* April 19, 1999, p. 3.

Corzo, Cynthia, "Radio Firm Forms Network of Hispanic Stations," *Knight-Ridder/Tribune Business News,* February 26, 1999.

"Dallas-Based Heftel Broadcasting Corp. to Buy Houston Radio Station," *Knight-Ridder/Tribune Business News,* March 27, 1998.

Foisie, Geoffrey, "Heftel Broadcasting Plans Major Growth," *Broadcasting & Cable,* July 11, 1994, p. 49.

"Hispanic Company Buys One of Los Angeles' Last Black Radio Stations," *Jet,* January 10, 2000, p. 20.

"Huge News from Heftel," *Broadcasting & Cable,* August 18, 1997, p. 30.

Kauffman, Bruce, "San Diego FM Stations Begin Spanish Broadcasting," *Knight-Ridder/Tribune Business News,* August 11, 1998.

Medina, Hildy, "KLVE Rides Silky Spanish Sounds to a No. 1 Ranking," *Los Angeles Business Journal,* October 13, 1997, p. 18.

Petrozello, Donna, "Heftel Acquires Spanish Network," *Broadcasting & Cable,* August 29, 1994, p. 42.

——, "Heftel Allies with CNN Radio Noticias," *Broadcasting & Cable,* January 8, 1996, p. 54.

Rathbun, Elizabeth, "Clear Channel Creates Hispanic Powerhouse," *Broadcasting & Cable,* July 15, 1996, p. 29.

——, "Heftel Takes Talent National," *Broadcasting & Cable,* March 8, 1999, p. 41.

Schneider, Michael, "Radio Groups Hit Divestiture Jackpot," *Variety,* March 13, 2000, p. 39.

"Spanish Giant Buys Phoenix FM," *Mediaweek,* February 1, 1999, p. 3.

"Spanish Radio Network," *Television Digest,* August 22, 1994, p. 6.

Tanner, Lisa, "Riding the Spanish Radio Wave," *Dallas Business Journal,* June 11, 1999, p. 13.

Torpey-Kemph, Anne, "HBC Teams with Prodigy," *Mediaweek,* May 8, 2000, p. 62.

Turner, Dan, "L.A. Radio Station to Get New Owner, New Spanish-Language Format," *Los Angeles Business Journal,* December 23, 1996, p. 8.

Whitefield, Mimi, "Dallas-Based Hispanic Broadcasting Tried to Broaden Its Appeal," *Knight-Ridder/Tribune Business News,* August 10, 1999.

—David P. Bianco

Hunton & Williams

951 East Byrd Street
Richmond, Virginia 23219
U.S.A.
Telephone: (804) 788-8200
Fax: (804) 788-8218
Web site: http://www.hunton.com

Partnership
Founded: 1901 as Munford, Hunton, Williams & Anderson
Employees: 1,450
Gross Revenues: $244 million (1998)
NAIC: 54111 Offices of Lawyers

With almost 700 lawyers operating out of 15 offices, Hunton & Williams is one of the world's largest law firms. Headquartered in Richmond, Virginia, by far the smallest city with a major law firm, Hunton & Williams serves large and small companies, industry associations, government agencies, and other clients. Although it continues to provide legal services to historic clients such as utilities, it also represents high-tech and multinational corporations that are part of the increasingly globalized economy. Hunton & Williams offers expertise in virtually all areas of business law, from taxation and environmental concerns to lobbying, financing, and mergers and acquisitions. The firm's heritage is politically conservative, based on its historic opposition to both the New Deal in the 1930s and school desegregation in the 1950s, as well as its later lobbying for Newt Gingrinch's Revolution Reforms and serving such clients as the Heritage Foundation, a conservative think tank that advised President Ronald Reagan. In the 1980s and 1990s the firm stepped up its efforts at *pro bono* work and community service projects, particularly through a northern Virginia branch office, opened in 1984, at which Hunton & Williams and other firms and corporate legal departments founded the *Pro Bono* Consortium, dedicated to helping poor families in need of legal counsel.

Early 20th Century Origins

At the turn of the century, many Americans still had to travel to New York City if they wanted to hire the best lawyers or obtain financing from a major bank. That situation prompted four lawyers in Richmond, Virginia, to start a law firm "patterned after the larger New York firms and equipped to handle all kinds of legal business," according to the front page of the October 7, 1901 *Richmond News*. Already a part of various smaller practices in Richmond, the men were colleagues and friends intent on offering the city a law firm of sophistication and expertise every bit as professional as a New York City firm.

The partnership's original name was Munford, Hunton, Williams & Anderson. The younger name partners, Henry Watkins Anderson and Edmund Randolph Williams, apparently first posed the idea for the new law firm and were instrumental in bringing all four partners together. The first name partner, Beverley Bland Munford, was a well-known attorney in the area, having served as a Democrat in the Virginia General Assembly. Anderson's partner in practice at the time, Munford respected the goal of the new firm and lent his knowledge, experience, and reputation to the founding efforts. Munford was unable to practice for very long, however; having contracted tuberculosis, he retired in 1906 and died a few years later. Rounding out the group of four lawyers was Eppa Hunton, Jr., from the firm of Hunton & Son. Hunton was a key player in the State Constitutional Convention of 1901–1902 when he accepted an offer to become a senior partner in the new Richmond law firm.

Each of the four attorneys brought their strengths to the table. Hunton, already well-connected politically, became one of the two key lawyers to represent railroads that unsuccessfully fought State railroad reforms during the Progressive Era. Through Williams, the new law firm gained most of its early work from the family banking firm of John L. Williams & Sons, which needed legal services as it backed railroads, power companies, and street railways in many parts of the South still recovering from the Civil War devastation of a generation earlier.

Through the Williams bank representation, the firm eventually gained as important clients Frank Gould, son of tycoon Jay Gould, as well as the Virginia Railway and Power Company. Meanwhile, the law firm gained important bank clients such as the First & Merchants Bank and its predecessors, and it also defended against critics the federal government's choice of

Company Perspectives:

Hunton & Williams provides first class legal services to a wide range of clients. Since our founding in 1901, we have become one of the nation's top 20 law firms, with more than 680 attorneys in offices worldwide. We serve international corporations, financial institutions, closely held companies, tax exempt organizations, and technology-related companies. Our attorneys are recognized as leading experts in many of our 50 distinct practice areas.

Richmond as the site of one of the newly created Federal Reserve banks.

With governmental regulations over railroads increasing during the Progressive Era, the railroads turned to lawyers to help them. In 1914 the Richmond, Fredericksburg & Potomac railroad became a client of the law firm. During World War I, Eppa Hunton counseled the federal government as it assumed control over the operations of the nation's railroads.

The firm's utility work continued during the Great Depression. A new partner, Thomas Justin Moore, presented the utility industry's opposition to the Public Utilities Holding Company Act of 1935 before Congress passed it.

At about the same time, the New York Stock Exchange used the Hunton Williams law firm in congressional hearings discussing federal regulation of stock exchanges. Partner Thomas B. Gay, who joined the firm in the early 1920s, argued that Exchange transactions were not interstate commerce and thus Congress had no constitutional authority to regulate such matters. However, after months of hearings in both the Senate and House of Representatives, Congress passed the much amended Securities Exchange Act in June 1934.

By the start of World War II, the partnership also had developed a labor practice representing clients such as the Virginia Electric and Power Company, Newport News Shipbuilding and Drydock Company, and Allied Chemical. The practice faced much stronger unions after Congress passed the National Labor Relations Act in 1935. Although many law firms received more business because of the unprecedented number of new laws, the profession generally was quite opposed to most of President Franklin Roosevelt's New Deal laws.

During the Depression and beyond, the law firm continued to play a key role in the bankruptcy and reorganization of some large railroads. For example, its representation of the Baltimore and Ohio Railroad Company resulted in an amendment to the federal Bankruptcy Act. In 1935 the Denver and Rio Grande Western Railroad Company filed a reorganization petition. The Richmond law firm represented several insurance company creditors in this reorganization that was finally concluded in 1947 by a ruling of the U.S. Supreme Court.

Postwar Years

After World War II ended, several lawyers returned to the firm after serving in the armed forces. Lewis Franklin Powell,

Jr., had joined the firm during the Great Depression, and then after the war became a prominent Richmond attorney, heading the city's bar association, Chamber of Commerce, and school board in the 1950s. In 1954 the law firm changed its name to Hunton, Williams, Gay, Moore & Powell.

From just 11 in January 1950, the firm almost tripled its number of lawyers by the end of the decade. Moreover, the new attorneys picked up new clients such as Albemarle Paper, the Chesapeake Corporation, and Miller & Rhoads. The firm also drew up a new partnership agreement and for the first time organized formal practice groups for taxation, litigation, and labor lawyers. Specialization was replacing the general law practice.

In 1949 the law firm participated in its first utilities rate case when it represented The Chesapeake & Potomac Telephone Company of Virginia. The state's regulatory commission in 1950 accepted the telephone's company's request for revised rates that had been opposed by local and county governments in Virginia.

In the early 1950s, Hunton Williams, together with New York City's Davis Polk law firm, argued in vain to preserve school segregation. The Richmond firm represented the defendant, the school board, in the case of *Dorothy E. Davis v. the County School Board of Prince Edward County, Virginia.* Heading up this case was partner Justin Moore, and he received a favorable decision of sorts when the courts upheld the segregation law of *Plessy v. Ferguson* (''separate but equal'') but found the black and white schools in question were indeed separate but were not equal and called for an improvement program. On appeal, that case became one of the five cases grouped together in the famous U.S. Supreme Court case of *Brown v. Board of Education of Topeka, Kansas* that overturned the 1896 *Plessy v. Ferguson* ruling. Reaction from scholars of legal history was mixed, with some censuring the firm's support of segregated public schools, and others lauding Lewis Powell, who was also head of the Richmond School Board, for helping bring about desegregation in Richmond with relatively little difficulty compared to other southern school districts.

Lewis Powell clearly was the leader of the law firm by the 1960s. The American Bar Association chose him in 1964 to be its new president. Soon thereafter Powell was introduced to FBI Director J. Edgar Hoover, and the two would maintain close relations during the next few years, as Powell, like Hoover, was a staunch anticommunist during the Cold War years. Powell also served as the president of the American Bar Foundation and president of the American College of Trial Lawyers. In 1971 President Richard Nixon asked Powell to serve on the U.S. Supreme Court. Other Hunton Williams lawyers helped prepare Powell, and he had few challenges during his Senate confirmation hearings. Although Powell resigned from the firm in 1972, his presence on the Supreme Court until 1987 was a huge boost to the firm's name and reputation.

The year 1966 saw the debut of the firm's Washington, D.C. branch office, and in 1976, the firm adopted its final name change, shortening the moniker to simply Hunton & Williams.

Key Dates:

1901: The firm is founded by four lawyers in Richmond, Virginia.
1913: Offices move to Richmond's new Electric Building.
1950: The firm consists of some 30 attorneys.
1966: An office is opened in Washington, D.C.
1972: Hunton & Williams attorney Lewis Powell is named to the U.S. Supreme Court.
1976: Firm adopts the permanent name of Hunton & Williams.
1983: New offices are opened in New York and Knoxville, Tennessee.
1989: A Brussels, Belgium, office is established.
1992: The firm expands into Poland with a Warsaw branch.
1994: The law firm opens its Hong Kong office, its first in Asia.
1999: New offices in Miami and London begin operations.

Practice in the 1980s and 1990s

Realizing that many memories of the firm's history were fading quickly, in 1982 Hunton & Williams started an oral history program that yielded over 55 oral histories from the aging descendants of the original founders. This work proved a vital resource for Anne Hobson Freeman in her 1989 book *The Style of a Law Firm: Eight Gentlemen from Virginia,* which focused on the firm's four founders and four key partners of the second generation.

In 1983, the firm established offices in New York City as well as in Knoxville, Tennessee, and the following year an office was set up in McLean, Virginia. By the end of the decade, Hunton & Williams would also boast a new office in Atlanta. Moreover, a significant step towards becoming an international concern was taken in 1989 with Hunton & Williams's new office in Brussels, Belgium. Over the next five years, this would be followed by branches in Warsaw and in Hong Kong.

Following the 1994 Republican victory that gave the GOP control of Congress, lobbying firms such as Hunton & Williams gained more clout. Writer Gareth Cook pointed out that Senator Majority Leader Bob Dole chose former Hunton & Williams lawyer Kyle McSlarrow as his "point man on regulatory legislation" and that the firm both drafted and explained Dole's regulatory reform bill.

The mid-1990s brought some internal legal challenges to the firm, when two lawsuits were filed against Hunton & Williams by investors who charged that the firm's former partner Scott J. McKay Wolas had defrauded them of over $100 million while working out of the firm's New York office. Two Hunton & Williams associates also sued the law firm for allegedly forcing them to leave because they had criticized Wolas' overbilling. Although one suit was settled in late 1998, these events brought some unwelcome media exposure to the Richmond law firm.

Nevertheless, big business continued to look to Hunton & Williams for counsel. The North Carolina Pork Council in 1999 hired Hunton & Williams to defend it in a national controversy concerning the growing number of factory hog farms. Continuing its long tradition of serving utility firms, Hunton & Williams represented 40 different utilities that fought an Environmental Protection Agency plan to reduce urban smog.

Although Hunton & Williams had some smaller, high-tech clients, such as EarthLink Network Inc., in 1999 the firm lost 12 lawyers—its entire technology practice according to the *Washington Post* on December 9, 1999—when they left to join the Palo Alto-based Cooley Godward law firm at its new office near Washington, D.C.

High profile corporate representation continued; on June 25, 2000, Philip Morris Companies Inc., represented by Hunton & Williams and Wachtell, Lipton, Rosen & Katz, announced an agreement to acquire all outstanding shares of Nabisco Holdings Corporation. The agreement also stipulated that Nabisco would merge with Kraft Foods, Inc. owned by Philip Morris to "become the world's most profitable food company," according to a Hunton & Williams press release.

According to *American Lawyer* in its July/August 1998 issue, Hunton & Williams ranked as the country's 28th largest law firm based on its 1997 gross revenues of $220 million. Amidst stiff competition and rapid expansion of law firms around the country, its ranking slipped slightly, to 32nd, based on increased 1998 revenues of $244 million. Also during this time, *American Lawyer*, in cooperation with London's *Legal Business*, came out with its first ranking of the world's 50 largest law firms, among which Hunton & Williams was listed 35th in terms of revenues and 38th based on its workforce, which had swelled to 568 lawyers, 11 percent of whom were based outside the United States.

In 1999 the firm opened a small London office that focused mainly on project finance and securities work, particularly in eastern Europe. About the same time, it opened its Miami office to take advantage of opportunities in American health care litigation and Latin American project finance. Clearly, Hunton & Williams had come a long way from its modest roots back in 1901, when its practice concentrated on local and regional clients. In 2000 it had a major national and international practice and was larger than some of the New York City law firms that it had hoped to measure up to back in 1901.

Principal Competitors

Milbank, Tweed, Hadley & McCloy; Morgan, Lewis & Bockius LLP; Skadden, Arps, Slate, Meagher & Flom; Baker & McKenzie.

Further Reading

Bryson, W. Hamilton, and E. Lee Shepaarfd, "The Virginia Bar, 1870–1900," in *The New High Priests: Lawyers in Post-Civil War America,* edited by Gerard W. Gawalt, Westport, Conn.: Greenwood Press, 1984, pp. 171–85.

Cook, Christopher D., "Pork Council Roots Out Researchers," *Progressive,* September 1999, p. 31.

Cook, Gareth, "Laws for Sale," *Washington Monthly,* July 1995, p. 44.

Davis, Ann, "Legal Beat: Firm's Handling of Allegations of Overbilling Brought Out in Suit," *Wall Street Journal*, June 16, 1997, p. B6.

Fialka, John J., "Court of Appeals Upholds EPA Plan That Would Curb Smog in 19 States," *Wall Street Journal*, March 6, 2000, p. B14.

Freeman, Anne Hobson, *The Style of a Law Firm: Eight Gentlemen from Virginia,* N.C.: Algonquin Books of Chapel Hill, 1992.

Gay, Thomas B., *The Hunton Williams Firm and Its Predecessors, 1877–1954,* Richmond, Va.: Lewis Printing Company, 1971.

Gilliam, George H., "Making Virginia Progressive: Courts and Parties, Railroads and Regulators, 1890–1910," *Virginia Magazine of History and Biography*, Spring 1999, pp. 189–222.

Henry, Shannon, "Call Him PI Tech," *Washington Post*, December 9, 1999, p. E1.

"Hunton & Williams Opens in London," *International Financial Law Review*, April 1999, p. 5.

"Hunton & Williams Settles Suit Involving Former Partner Wolas," *Wall Street Journal*, December 23, 1998, p. B11.

Murphy, Sean D., "Status of the U.S.-USSR Anti-Ballistic Missile System Treaty," *American Journal of International Law*, October 1999, pp. 910–912.

Rehnquist, William H., et. al., "A Tribute to Lewis F. Powell, Jr.," *Washington and Lee Law Review*, Winter 1999, pp. 2 +.

Willing, Richard, "Good Idea to be on Hoover's Good Side, Historian Says Powell Was Wise to Assist the Powerful FBI Chief," *USA Today*, May 1,2000, p. 3A.

—David M. Walden

Infogrames Entertainment S.A.

82-84, rue du 1er Mars 1943
69628 Villeurbanne Cedex
France
Telephone: (+33) 4.72.65.50.00
Fax: (+33) 4.72.65.50.01
Web site: http://www.infogrames.com

Public Company
Incorporated: 1983
Employees: 2,000
Sales: FFr 3.5 billion ($850 million) (1999)
Stock Exchanges: Paris NASDAQ
Ticker Symbol: 5257.PA
NAIC: 339932 Electronic Toys and Games
  Manufacturing; 511210 Software Publishers

France's Infogrames Entertainment S.A. is on the fast-track to global domination of the world's video game market. Infogrames creates, publishes, and distributes video game titles across all of the major video game platforms, including for the Sony Playstation, Nintendo 64, and Sega Dreamcast consoles, the Nintendo Game Boy, PC, and Macintosh computer platforms, and the forthcoming X-Box, Playstation2, Dolphin, and other "next-generation" gaming consoles. Among Infogrames' titles are such international successes as Driver, Ronaldo, and the Alone in the Dark series. The company's catalog extends to some 1,000 titles in all. The company has stepped up production of its own in-house titles since the late 1990s, with more than 80 games in development each year. The company also boasts a strong catalog of licensed products, including the Warner Bros. Looney Tunes characters; video game development rights for the television and film series *Mission Impossible*; Nickelodeon's "Blues Clues" ; and the Harley Davidson and Dodge Viper licenses. One of the leaders in the growing consolidation of the international video game industry—which topped the film industry in revenues for the first time in 1999—Infogrames took a giant step into the big leagues with the acquisition of GT Interactive Software in 1999. Since renamed Infogrames Inc., that acquisition gave Infogrames the number two position worldwide, behind leader Electronics Arts. Infogrames, led by founders Bruno Bonnell and Christophe Sapet, has since snapped up a number of other primary games-market players, including Accolade Inc. and Paradigm Entertainment. Infogrames remains dedicated to the games market, but has nonetheless begun to develop interests in other platforms, such as the mobile telephone network, internet gaming—through the creation of online subsidiary Infogrames.com—and television, with its partnership with Canal Plus to form the Europeanwide Game One satellite channel. Following the GT Interactive acquisition, Infogrames' annual sales shot up to US$850 million, well on the way towards the company's target of US$1 billion in revenues by 2002.

Software Pioneer in the 1980s

Infogrames Entertainment was founded in the early 1980s by Bruno Bonnell and high-school friend Christophe Sapet. Both Bonnell and Sapet, who later went on to university studies in chemical engineering, had been interested in the newly developing computer industry, and while still in school worked as salesmen for an early personal computer system. Bonnell and Sapet quickly recognized the market for personal computers and saw the need for software, especially family-oriented software.

In 1982, Bonnell and Sapet wrote a book designed to teach home users to program using the BASIC computer language. The book achieved modest success, earning the pair some US$10,000. With their book earnings, Bonnell and Sapet founded Infogrames Entertainment in Villeurbanne, outside Lyon, in June 1983. Bonnell and Sapet were joined by Thomas Schmider, and the trio set out to write software. While the company's earliest efforts leaned toward writing programming software, their interests quickly turned toward developing video games.

Infogrames was quick to make a name for itself among the small circle of video game developers of the period. One of the earliest efforts was the title Autoroute Highway, in which players were required to help a frog cross a busy highway. Another title, Le Cube Informatique, also helped establish the company's name as a game developer.

Company Perspectives:

Entertainment is the key to Infogrames' products, but a big part of Infogrames' philosophy is that all of the company's games should give something more to the consumer. Our products are about growth and reward as well as entertainment. The best games are designed to facilitate growth in the person who is playing, whether that growth is hand-eye coordination, logic skills or simply a sense of wonder and inspiration, it should be integral within the game.

Making money proved more difficult. The market for video games remained relatively restrained throughout the 1980s. Video games were seen as a children's toy, and few expected the market to expand far beyond a core five- to 13-year-old audience. Infogrames met with a great deal of skepticism from investors as the company sought to finance its growth. The company, which attempted to expand beyond video games to provide other family-oriented software, such as budgeting software, soon found itself strapped for cash. Yet France's banking community was not about to invest in the untested software market. As Bonnell told *Time International:* "It was not a dotcom world then. It was like, 'Are you serious?'" At last, though, the company found financial backing.

By the end of the 1980s, Infogrames had weathered the worst of its start-up pains, and had refocused its development efforts entirely on video games. Infogrames had bought the rights to produce video game titles using the popular comic character Tintin. In 1988, the company released one of its first big successes, Tintin on the Moon. That title helped pushed the company's sales to the FFr 100 million mark by the beginning of the 1990s.

Games Take off in the 1990s

In large part, Infogrames' development remained linked to the technological developments made in the computer industry. The appearance of new types of gaming platforms—notably the first Nintendo consoles and the related Game Boy devices—were to give a strong boost to Infogrames fortunes. Recognizing the potential of the new platforms, Infogrames quickly began developing games for the Nintendo and Game Boy systems. At a time when purchasing a computer system already represented a major investment—particularly for consumers interested primarily in playing games—the console-type systems had the advantage of working with existing television sets. Nonetheless, Infogrames remained equally devoted to developing for the fast-growing computer industry, especially as the personal computer market consolidated around the PC and Macintosh platforms.

In order to keep up with the changing technology, Infogrames began boosting its own research and development efforts, designing tools that the company used for creating its games. Research and development was to remain a strong component of the company's success through the 1990s, accounting for as much as FFr 300 million of its annual budget. Nonetheless, with the explosion of graphics and sound technologies in the second half of the 1990s, Infogrames began to limit its own efforts on developing the video games themselves, rather than the tools.

As computer technology increased, enabling more and more sophisticated games, development times also increased—by the mid-1990s, games required on average two years of development work. Indeed, one of Infogrames' earliest hits—and the game that put the company on the world's video game map—had been begun in 1990 and was released only in 1992. That game, Alone in the Dark, became an instant success worldwide, and marked the beginning of a long-running series of sequels.

The success of Alone in the Dark encouraged Infogrames in its ambitions to become one of the world's top video game developers. While continuing to develop its own games, the company began to look forward to acquiring other games developers and the distribution rights to third-party efforts, a practice which became common in the video game industry in the 1990s. In order to fuel its ambition, Infogrames went public in 1993, with a listing on the Paris stock exchange. The public offering brought in a number of major shareholders, including the Chargeurs group, and Philips Media, the video game development division of the Dutch conglomerate. Infogrames and Philips Media soon began to collaborate on a number of titles, including such successful games as Asterix, Marco Polo, and Shaolin Road.

The video game industry was seeing a number of important breakthroughs at the time. The addition of CD-ROM drives to most new personal computer systems enabled vast increases in computer game content. The appearance of sound standards, and rapid increases in graphics technology, particularly in the appearance of the first 3D graphics cards, were also adding new possibilities to the gaming experience. The worldwide success of such titles as Doom and Duke Nukem and especially Myst not only established new, more personalized video game genres, but also highlighted the fast-growing market for video games in general. On the console front, the release of the Nintendo 32 system, adding 32-bit graphics, brought a new level of graphics possibilities to video games.

Infogrames had been quick to adopt the new technologies, and joined with other French developers, including Cryo, to lead the video industry in new graphics triumphs. The company had also begun its international expansion, moving first to the Belgian market and then striking a deal with Compagnie Luxembourgeois de Telecommunication to form Infogrames Entertainment GmbH, in order to enter the German market. If the French computer market remained relatively restrained—with only an estimated 30,000 "multimedia-ready" personal computers—the German personal computer market was already in full expansion.

Acquiring Greatness for the 21st Century

By the end of June 1994 (the close of Infogrames' financial year), the company's annual sales had risen to FFr 260 million, and its profits had more than quadrupled over the previous year to near FFr 14 million. The company was on its way to securing its position as France's number one games developer, ahead of

Key Dates:

1983: Infogrames Entertainment is founded.
1985: Company releases Autoroute Highway and Le Cube Informatique.
1988: Acquires license to Tintin characters.
1992: Infogrames releases Alone in the Dark.
1993: Company is listed on the Paris stock exchange.
1996: Acquires Ocean Software Ltd.
1997: Merges with Philips Media.
1999: Company acquires Psygnosis, Accolade, Interplay, and GT Interactive.
2000: Paradigm Entertainment is acquired; GT Interactive is reformed as Infogrames Inc.

Cryo and Ubisoft. Yet Infogrames remained tiny in comparison to industry heavyweights Electronic Arts and Broderbund.

Acquisitions were to provide Infogrames' greatest growth through the second half of the decade, though the company continued to develop its own games, including such international successes as Test Drive. In 1996, Infogrames broke into the international big leagues when it acquired U.K.-based Ocean Software Ltd., giving Infogrames not only that company's strong catalog of video game titles including Jurassic Park, Terminator 2, Robocop, and Batman, but also an entry into the American market through Ocean's U.S. subsidiary. By the end of 1996, more than 70 percent of Infogrames' sales came from beyond France.

The following year, Philips Media merged into Infogrames, boosting Infogrames to the lead in Europe's video game industry. This placed the company in a strong position to take advantage of the true explosion in video game sales in the late 1990s. If the global video game market represented some US$4 billion in total sales in 1996, by the turn of the century, video game sales worldwide topped US$20 billion. By 1999, sales of video games had beat out cinema receipts. Aiding this development were new generations of video console systems, starting with the Sega, continuing with the Nintendo 64, and culminating with the wildly popular Sony Playstation. At the same time, falling computer prices had brought more and more computers into the world's homes, while steady increases in graphics technology and processor speeds had made possible more and more realistic graphics and effects. Among Infogrames' major successes were its Mission: Impossible game and Independence War.

The Ocean and Philips Media acquisitions, and its various video game hits helped the company boost its annual sales to FFr 1.4 billion by the end of its June 1998 year. By then, however, Infogrames, which continued to nourish its ambition to become the world's leading video game publisher, was looking for a new acquisition to boost its position. The highly fragmented video game industry of the late 1990s was ripe for consolidation. Intense competition among game developers, the continually growing output of new games, and the high costs of new game development—with many new games costing up to US$10 million to produce and still more to market—were placing many games developers in increasingly fragile positions.

One such developer was the United Kingdom's Eidos, which had slipped into trouble despite the massive international success of its Tomb Raider series. Infogrames was rumored to be interested in acquiring Eidos. However, that acquisition never materialized. Instead, the company made a series of smaller acquisitions, including Paris-based Psygnosis, a recognized leader in graphics design, a friendly takeover of the United Kingdom's Gremlin Interactive, the United States' Interplay, and, in April 1999, the acquisition of Accolade Inc. That last acquisition gave Infogrames a huge boost to its U.S. distribution circuit, adding Accolade's 18,000-store distribution network.

Infogrames, which remained relatively debt-free, was preparing its next coup for the end of that year. In December 1999, the company surprised the industry with its announcement that it was acquiring U.S.-based GT Interactive (GTI), a company roughly twice Infogrames' size. The GTI purchase, for a total of US$135 million, boosted Infogrames to the rank of number two in the worldwide video game industry, and sent the company's annual sales soaring to some US$850 million—with revenues expected to top the US$1 billion mark by the end of the company's 2001 fiscal year.

By June 2000, Infogrames proved that it was not yet ready to rest in its quest for domination of the world video game market. In a share exchange, the company announced its acquisition of Dallas, Texas-based Paradigm Entertainment. Meanwhile, Infogrames was ramping up for a new series of "next-generation" gaming consoles, featuring 128-bit graphics and Internet access. The first of these, the Sega Dreamcast, appeared at the end of 1999, while the international gaming community awaited the arrival of the Sony Playstation 2 and the Nintendo Dolphin, as well as a new entry by Microsoft, the X-Box.

Even as Infogrames remained committed to maintaining its position as a world leader in video game publishing, it had also made strong moves toward diversifying its activities while remaining focused around its video game core. In the late 1990s, the company joined with Canal Plus to launch a video-game dedicated satellite television station, Game One. The company also sought entry into the booming Internet market, launching its online activities subsidiary Infogrames.com in 2000. At the same time, Infogrames took steps to succeed in the expanding mobile telephony market, particularly with the roll-out of new-generation Internet-ready telephones. With its revenues topping FFr 3.5 billion by June 2000, Infogrames had proved that gaming is serious business.

Principal Subsidiaries

Infogrames Inc. (U.S.).

Principal Divisions

Game One; Infogrames.com.

Principal Competitors

3DO Inc.; Acclaim Entertainment Inc.; Activision, Inc.; Broderbund Software, Inc.; Eidos; Electronic Arts Inc.; Hasbro, Inc.; Havas, SA; id Software; Interplay Entertainment; The Learning Company Inc.; LucasArts; Maxis; Microsoft Corporation; Nintendo Co., Ltd.; Sega of America, Inc.; Sony Corporation; Symantec Corporation; THQ.

Further Reading

Chang, Greg, and John Lyons, "French Firm Gains Control of GT Interactive," *Seattle Times*, November 16, 1999.

Horsburgh, Susan, "The People: Let the Games Begin," *Time International,* June 19, 2000, p. 72.

Hyland, Anne, "Master of the Beautiful Game," *Guardian Unlimited*, February 23, 2000.

Judge, Paul, "A Master of Europe's Video-Game Market," *Business Week*, March 30, 2000.

Kirkman, Alexandra, "Demolition Racer," *Forbes,* November 1, 1999, p. 388.

Mauriac, Laurent, "Super mariolle," *Liberation*, January 21, 2000.

——, "Young Ones Shaping the Future," *European*, February 1, 1997, p. 22.

Strage, Claudia, "Infogrames Plays the Big Boys and Wins," *European*, April 14, 1995, p. 23.

——, "The Stars of Europe: Innovators: Bruno Bonnell," *Business Week*, June 19, 2000, p. 170.

—M. L. Cohen

Interep National Radio Sales Inc.

100 Park Avenue
New York, New York 10017
U.S.A.
Telephone: (212) 916-0700
Fax: (212) 916-0772
Web site: http://www.interep.com

Public Company
Incorporated: 1982 as The Interep Radio Store
Employees: 650
Sales: $103.4 million (1999)
Stock Exchanges: NASDAQ
Ticker Symbol: IREP
NAIC: 541840 Media Representatives

Interep National Radio Sales Inc., formerly the Interep Radio Store, specializes in representing radio stations and selling broadcast time for national spot advertising, which is separate from local advertising and network advertising, which is broadcast simultaneously in network-affiliated stations. According to Interep, national spot advertising typically accounts for 20 percent of a radio station's revenues. It is usually purchased by advertising agencies or media buying services on behalf of their clients. Interep is organized as the parent company of eight radio representation firms that in total represent more than 2,000 radio stations. In 1999 Interep founded Interep Interactive to focus on selling and marketing online advertising on the World Wide Web. In addition to representing radio stations, Interep provides a variety of marketing support services to advertisers and advertising agencies. Among other things, it conducts industry studies designed to promote the use of radio as an advertising medium, and over the years Interep has positioned itself as a company that is concerned with the long-term health of radio as an advertising medium.

From Regional to National Rep Firm: 1953–90

Interep National Radio Sales Inc. has its roots in the 1950s, when Darren McGavren purchased Western Radio, a regional advertising representation firm with client stations throughout California and the Pacific Northwest, in 1953. The Darren McGavren Company grew steadily in the 1950s and 1960s. In the 1960s the company took on a partner, Ralph Guild, and the company was renamed McGavren Guild Radio. To handle its growth, the company was restructured into regional offices to serve major advertising agencies. In the 1970s McGavren Guild Radio became an employee-owned company through an Employee Stock Ownership Plan (ESOP) that would remain in effect into the year 2000.

During the early 1980s ad rep firms began to consolidate. National spot radio advertising revenues were growing at double-digit rates. In 1982 The Interep Radio Store was established as the parent company of McGavren Guild and began acquiring smaller rep firms. Between 1982 and 1984 Interep purchased the firms Weiss & Powell, Major Market Radio, and others to form a "nonwired network" of about 1,000 client radio stations. Such networks made it easier for advertising agencies to purchase national spots in several markets at once for their clients.

Interep continued to acquire other firms throughout the 1980s. Toward the end of the 1980s it created Group W Radio Sales, a firm that represented all Westinghouse radio stations. This marked the first time that a rep firm was dedicated solely to one broadcast group. Dedicated rep firms subsequently became more widespread in the 1990s.

In 1986 and 1987 national spot radio revenues were flat. In 1988 and 1989 they increased by about seven to eight percent. Interep changed its internal structure in order to develop more national sales, creating Marketing Service Teams (MSTs) and Account Management Teams (AMTs). An MST consisted of one person from each of Interep's six companies. Together, the team would call on major advertising agencies, targeting different levels such as the media department, account management, and the creative department. The AMTs would then follow up and work with the client to develop new business ideas.

Innovative Programs in the 1990s

In 1990 and 1991 Interep Radio Store announced its Radio 2000 strategy, a long-term marketing initiative designed to increase radio advertising. Among the goals of Radio 2000 were

---

Company Perspectives:

Interep is the nation's largest independent advertising sales and marketing company specializing in radio, the Internet and new media. We offer the most innovative marketing solutions designed to help national and regional advertisers achieve their business goals utilizing radio, the Internet and other emerging media technologies.

---

to increase radio's share of overall advertising revenue from seven percent to nine percent by targeting national advertisers who were potential users of radio. Such an increase in market share would represent a 28 percent increase in radio's annual advertising revenue. The overall radio advertising market was estimated at $8.8 billion, of which $2.1 billion (24 percent) was from national sales and $6.7 billion (76 percent) came from local advertising. Radio 2000 later became the Interep Marketing Group and was headed by Marc Guild, son of Interep's co-founder, chairman, and CEO Ralph Guild.

As part of its Radio 2000 industry-wide campaign, Interep released the results of its study of the teen market's media and spending habits. The study revealed that teens were heavy radio users. Another Interep study claimed that radio advertising was the best way to reach the growing market of black consumers, suggesting that the Urban Contemporary format, with its 69 percent black audience, represented one of the strongest growth markets in radio for the coming decade.

By 1991 Interep represented more than 2,000 radio stations and accounted for about half of national advertising sales. Its primary competitor was the Katz Radio Group, which accounted for the other half. Interep launched a national sales and marketing network called the Country Radio Format Network to draw advertisers into country radio. Interep convened the first meeting of the network in New York City in November 1991. At this meeting, representatives from individual country music stations developed a plan to promote the use of country radio to advertising agencies and their clients.

The outlook for national spot radio advertising looked flat for 1992 after national spot radio sales for the fourth quarter of 1991 declined as much as 15 percent. National spot radio sales for 1991 fell by about seven percent compared to 1990. Advertisers appeared to be spending more in the top ten markets, and within the top ten only Los Angeles, New York, Chicago, San Francisco, and Dallas showed increases in spot radio ads in 1991. Another factor affecting spot radio sales was network radio, which offered an inexpensive alternative to spot radio. Later in 1992 both Katz and Interep joined to urge the presidential candidates Bill Clinton and George Bush to use spot radio advertising in their campaigns.

As part of a strategic reorganization, Interep dropped 200 stations it represented and combined two of its seven companies into a single entity in 1992. Interep president Les Goldberg noted that with the increasing consolidation of station ownership, there would be fewer station owners to represent in each market. The moves left Interep with about 1,200 stations that it represented.

One concept that Interep marketed in 1993 was called Coupon Radio. Although it never caught on, the system envisioned an electronic memory card that listeners could insert into specially made radios during commercials. Listeners would then take the card to a participating retailer and insert it into a machine there that would print out a discount coupon. The coupon would also serve to demonstrate the commercial's results to the advertiser.

Also in 1993 Interep developed a software package called BrandNet for advertising agencies and advertisers. The system would match a brand's consumer profile with radio station format profiles to determine which stations' audiences had the highest purchase potential for the brand. Interep claimed the software was not biased toward stations that Interep represented, but many buyers remained skeptical.

Many of Interep's efforts, such as conducting industry studies and developing special software systems, were designed to position the company as a forward-looking firm concerned with the long-term future of radio, not just with making a sale. In 1992 Interep began a training program for its sales people and researchers to make them radio marketing specialists. The program included a Harvard Business School course in marketing. Interep claimed the program led to $14 million in new radio business in one year.

In 1994 Interep expanded its Format and Demographic Network program, which was launched in 1992 to change the way that radio advertising was sold. By 1994 the marketing program had four networks: News-Talk Radio, Country Radio, Urban Radio, and 12–24 Radio. Interep claimed that the program resulted in $10 million in new radio advertising. Under the program, Interep sales reps would determine which format best suited the needs of the client and then book time on the appropriate stations, whether or not the stations were represented by Interep.

Early in 1994 the company planned to add Hispanic, direct response, and infomercial format networks to the program. Each network was designed to promote the strength of a particular format to advertisers. Later in 1994 it added more formats, including classic rock, "mature music," oldies, album rock, and interactive radio promotion. Ad revenues for the first half of 1994 grew by 11 percent over the same period in 1993, signaling a comeback after years of flat or declining advertising revenue. At the start of 1995 Interep launched Best of Oldies Music (BOOM), a marketing network of 110 stations that had contracted with Interep to represent their national ad sales.

In October 1994 Interep signed an exclusive agreement with radio station owner Infinity Broadcasting that gave Interep sole representation of national advertising sales for 24 Infinity-owned stations. As part of the agreement Interep would create a new company, Infinity Radio Sales, in January 1995 with 50 sales representatives, headquarters in New York City, and offices in eight other cities. Previously, Katz Radio and its affiliates had represented 11 of the 24 stations, and Interep and its affiliates the other 13 stations. As a result of its agreement with Infinity, Interep pulled ahead of Katz as the leading U.S. radio advertising rep firm.

In another deal similar to the one with Infinity, Interep announced in January 1995 that it would form a new company,

Key Dates:

1953: Darren McGavren acquires Western Radio, a regional advertising representation firm, and forms the Darren McGavren Company.

1960s: Ralph Guild becomes McGavren's partner, and the firm is renamed McGavren Guild Radio.

1982: The Interep Radio Store is formed as the parent company of McGavren Guild and begins acquiring other ad rep firms.

1990: Interep launches Radio 2000, a long-term marketing plan.

1999: Interep changes its name to Interep National Radio Sales Inc. and completes its initial public offering.

Shamrock Radio Sales, dedicated to representing national advertising sales for Shamrock Broadcasting's 19 major-market radio stations. Previously, the majority of Shamrock's stations had been represented by Katz Radio Group and its affiliates. Once Shamrock was acquired by Chancellor Broadcasting in fall 1995, however, Shamrock Radio Sales ceased to exist.

Later in 1995 Caballero Spanish Media merged with Interep to become the company's ninth national advertising rep firm. Caballero represented national advertising sales for 140 Spanish-language radio stations and had an estimated $30 million in annual billings.

Around this time Interep announced it would debut a new interactive services division in 1996 to offer radio stations and advertisers more information about their markets and interactive communications involving the World Wide Web. The company also planned to expand its RadioSite, which developed and maintained web pages for its client stations. As online advertising grew over the next few years, Interep created Interep Interactive in 1999 to focus on selling and marketing online advertising on the World Wide Web.

In February 1996 Interep and station owner Clear Channel Communications formed Clear Channel Radio Sales to handle national advertising sales for Clear Channel's 36 stations in 12 markets. Clear Channel was expected to add about $35 million in gross annual billings for Interep. Interep signed two other exclusive representation agreements early in 1996, one with Philadelphia-based Entercom covering 11 radio stations and another with Keymarket Radio.

In May 1996 Interep adjusted its organizational structure by combining three managed rep firms—Major Market Radio Sales, Torbet Radio Group, and Concert Music Broadcast Sales—into Allied Radio Partners. The new group would allow account executives to represent national ad sales for multiple stations in a single city.

At the beginning of 1997 Interep became the exclusive national sales representative for all 79 CBS radio stations, including the former Infinity Broadcasting stations and those owned by Westinghouse Electric Corp. As a result, CBS folded its CBS Radio Representatives and Group W Radio Sales, which were two of the last major company-owned national advertising rep firms. The 79 stations represented about $250 million in annual advertising sales. With the CBS stations added to its roster, Interep now accounted for about half of the $1.6 billion national radio revenue market, with Katz accounting for the other half.

Later in 1998 Interep was hired by the Theater Radio Network to place its service in theaters. It was only the second non-broadcast client for Interep. Theater Radio Network was launched in 1997 and provided audio programming in 15-minute blocks for movie theaters.

Interep completed its initial public offering (IPO) of 5.4 million shares at $12 a share on December 9, 1999. At the time of its IPO Interep, which changed its name to Interep National Radio Sales Inc., was the exclusive advertising rep firm for more than 2,000 radio stations. The company had 15 offices in the major advertising cities in the United States as well as six satellite locations in other key locations.

For the future, Interep's strategy was to build on its position as the leading independent national spot radio advertising rep firm in the United States. It planned to expand its market share through new clients and strategic alliances with the leading radio station groups. Interep was in a good position to benefit from the consolidation of station ownership that was taking place in the radio industry and already represented several large groups of stations.

Principal Divisions

ABC Radio Sales; Allied Radio Partners; Caballero Spanish Media; Cumulus Radio Sales; D&R Radio; Infinity Radio Sales; McGavren Guild Radio; McGavren Guild/Susquehanna.

Principal Competitors

Katz Media Group, Inc.

Further Reading

Boehlert, Eric, "Interep Targets Advertisers," *Billboard,* August 20, 1994, p. 93.

Bunzel, Reed E., "Interep Country Stations Meet," *Broadcasting,* November 4, 1991, p. 51.

——, "Interep Reveals Radio 2000 Strategy," *Broadcasting,* January 28, 1991, p. 32.

"CBS Radio Goes Solo with Interep," *Mediaweek,* January 27, 1997, p. 3.

Cobo, Lucia, "Study Details Teens' Heavy Use of Radio," *Broadcasting,* July 1, 1991, p. 37.

Cooper, Jim, "Expanding Interep," *Broadcasting & Cable,* March 7, 1994, p. 48.

——, "Interep Uses Software to Focus Buying," *Broadcasting & Cable,* September 20, 1993, p. 45.

Dreyfack, Madeleine, "Non-Wired Radio: Whose Best Deal?," *Marketing & Media Decisions,* February 1984, p. 70.

Heuton, Cheryl, "Interep Unit Could be Industry Harbinger," *Adweek Eastern Edition,* October 10, 1994, p. 12.

"Interep Going a Little Bit Country with Sales Net," *Mediaweek,* October 28, 1991, p. 37.

"Interep Promotes CouponRadio," *Broadcasting & Cable,* September 13, 1993, p. 39.

"The Interep Radio Store," *Mediaweek,* March 18, 1996, p. 8.

''Interep Study Pushes Value of Urban Format,'' *Broadcasting,* August 26, 1991, p. 29.

''Les Goldberg,'' *Broadcasting & Cable,* November 22, 1993, p. 53.

Miles, Laureen, ''Industry Response Cool to Interep's New Radio Unwired-Network Software,'' *Mediaweek,* November 1, 1993, p. 6.

Petrozzello, Donna, ''Clear Channel Gets Dedicated Rep,'' *Broadcasting & Cable,* February 12, 1996, p. 43.

——, ''Interep Creates Allied Radio Partners,'' *Broadcasting & Cable,* May 20, 1996, p. 52.

——, ''Interep Merges with Caballero,'' *Broadcasting & Cable,* October 16, 1995, p. 36.

——, ''Shamrock Deal Blossoms for Interep,'' *Broadcasting & Cable,* January 30, 1995, p. 38.

''Radio's Megareps Lead the Way into the 90's,'' *Broadcasting,* January 15, 1990, p. 110.

Stark, Phyllis, ''Infinity, Interep Join Forces, Create Full-Service Rep Firm,'' *Billboard,* October 8, 1994, p. 97.

Viles, Peter, ''Interep Drops 200 Stations,'' *Broadcasting,* September 21, 1992, p. 14.

Viles, Peter, ''Katz, Interep Team for Political Dollars,'' *Broadcasting,* August 10, 1992, p. 26.

Wilke, Mark, ''New Service Vies for Ears of Filmgoers,'' *Advertising Age,* November 2, 1998, p. 8.

—David P. Bianco

Inter Parfums Inc.

551 Fifth Avenue
New York, New York 10176
U.S.A.
Telephone: (212) 983-2640
Fax: (212)983-4197
Web site: http://www.inter-parfums.com

Public Company
Incorporated: 1985
Employees: 84
Sales: $87.14 million (1999)
Stock Exchanges: NASDAQ
Ticker Symbol: IPAR
NAIC: 325620 Toilet Preparation Manufacturing

Inter Parfums, Inc., formerly known as Jean Philippe Fragrances, is a New York City-based manufacturer and distributor of fragrances and cosmetics. The company's brand name and licensed designer fragrance lines, including Burberry, Ombre Rose, S.T. DuPont, and others, are marketed and sold through independent distributors, in-house executives, and international agents and importing companies. The company also produces so-called alternative or ''knockoff'' fragrances (imitations of expensive designer fragrances) in perfume or cologne forms as well as in skin creams, body sprays, and deodorants. These are sold for low prices through mass merchandisers, supermarkets, and drug stores. Substantially all Inter-Parfums products are produced in the United States or France, in leased factories or plants using subcontractors for production requirements, in conjunction with its 79-percent owned French subsidiary, Inter Parfums S.A.

1980s Origins

The history of Inter Parfums may be traced to the 1985 founding of Jean Philippe Fragrances. Using a contraction of their first names to christen their new company, Jean Madar and Philippe Benacin set out to produce knockoff or inexpensive fragrances that imitated such higher priced designer fragrances as Passion and Calvin Kline's Obsession. Three years following

incorporation, the company went public. In 1989, the company formed a subsidiary, Elite Parfums, Ltd., for its more upscale products. The following year, Jean Philippe bought fragrance and cosmetic rights from Jordache Enterprises along with the exclusive rights to the Jordache trademark. This move focused on the strength and awareness of the Jordache trademark, a brand name once hugely successful during the 1980s designer jeans craze.

In 1991, Jean Philippe acquired two French companies that also served as its major suppliers. Inter Parfums made fragrances that the company distributed exclusively in the United States and Canada. The other company, Selective Industrie, produced Regine perfume, among others, which Jean Philippe also sold in the United States. Since the two suppliers were enterprises under the control of Jean Philippe, their acquisition removed conflict-of-interest questions that had been aimed at the company.

In 1993, Jean Philippe's French subsidiary, Inter Parfums, S.A., acquired the license and inventory of the Ombre Rose fragrance brand from Alfin Inc. Jean Philippe regarded the Ombre Rose brand as complementing its existing line of fragrances, thereby allowing the use of existing distribution channels without incurring significantly greater costs. Also that year Jean Philippe's French subsidiary acquired the selective Burberry fragrance from the Royal Brands division of Brigade International, pursuant to a ten-year license agreement. This acquisition was the stepping-stone used by the company to build a portfolio of luxury brands through direct acquisition of existing brand names.

Building the Business: 1994–96

The perfume fragrance market at the time could be divided into two categories: selective lines, consisting of brand name products with luxury imaging, were distributed through perfumeries and department stores; while mass lines, consisting of moderately priced products, were distributed to a broad customer base with limited purchasing power via mass merchandisers. After the acquisition of the selective Burberry fragrance, Jean Philippe continued to aggressively expand its markets and prod-

Company Perspectives:

When we started this Company . . . we laid the foundation for the legacy of Jean Philippe Fragrances, a company that makes high quality products affordable for the benefit of millions of people around the world. As time went on we met with our employees and customers and it became apparent that what we were building was a world of opportunity— opportunity to provide our customers with quality products, opportunity to create value for our shareholders and opportunity for our employees. Our job was to take this company and move it forward; to make sure that future growth would define us, new products would enrich us and our operating culture would energize us year after year. In recent years, not every opportunity taken has produced the expected results. However, we have learned from these experiences and our flexibility enables us to overcome them.

uct lines through licensing agreements or through direct acquisition of existing product lines. Licensing agreements allowed the right to use brand names, create and package new fragrances, and determine product positioning and distribution, in exchange for payment of royalties proportional to the brand's net sales.

The company purchased the Molyneux and Weil brand names in early 1994 from Cosmetiques et France-I.D., S.A. for approximately $3.6 million in cash and 200,000 shares of the company's common stock valued at approximately $2.2 million. The Molyneux brand name was originally created in the early 1900s by the fashion designer Edouard Molyneux. The Molyneux name enjoyed ranking among the institutional brand names of French perfumery, it had been well established in other Western European countries, and it enjoyed a very prominent market position in South America, especially through the "Quartz" line for women. The company was also attracted to the synergies between the Molyneux name and the Burberry brand name.

In March 1994, Jean Philippe acquired the worldwide trademark for the Intimate and Chaz fragrance lines from Revlon Consumer Products Corp.; in June of the same year it acquired the worldwide trademarks for Aziza from Chesebrough-Pond's USA, an operating unit of Unilever N.V. Aziza was a hypoallergenic eye cosmetic line that at its peak was distributed in approximately 22,000 mass-market outlets with an estimated wholesale volume of $60 million. Aziza was also the first mass-market brand that focused solely on the eyes and the first brand of hypoallergenic makeup on the market. Chesebrough-Pond's discontinued the line in 1992 in the face of plummeting sales. For Jean Philippe, however, the AZIZA acquisition was a strategic move to expand into the mass-market fragrance and cosmetics industry. The company followed the acquisition with two years of extensive market research and product development with the goal of reintroducing the product line.

By August 1994, Jean Philippe had also obtained from Chesebrough-Pond's the rights to manufacture and distribute Cutex nail and lip color in the United States and Puerto Rico. Chesebrough, which had been marketing Cutex, retained ownership of the Cutex trademark and continued to distribute the

Cutex nail polish removers. The licensing agreement fit into each company's strategic plans. Chesebrough planned to focus on skin care, oral care, and deodorants, while Jean Philippe intended to continue its focus on cosmetics and fragrances as well as expand into mass markets. According to trade publications, the Cutex nail care and lip color products division had a wholesale volume in excess of $20 million in 1993.

While the company had an impressive stable of alternative designer fragrances from other distribution channels, the company had no mass market entries until March 1995 when it introduced A Man & A Woman, a knockoff version of Calvin Klein's, CK One. Jean Philippe was keenly aware of the vast potential of the alternative designer fragrance market and wanted a piece of that pie. In 1995, after ten years of growth, the alternative market had grown from a $95 million retail business into a $275 million business. In July, the company advanced its participation in the mass market with the launching of Romantic Illusions, a collection of 12 imitations of department store perfumes packed in cartons designed to look like romance novels. That project allowed the company to differentiate itself from its competitors. Recognizing that romance novels represented a billion dollar industry and comprised nearly 40 percent of the paperbacks sold in the mass market, Jean Philippe decided to capitalize on women's interest in these books to create a new niche.

To appeal to the younger, trendy mass market consumer, the company introduced Jordache Denim, a group of three knockoffs. The collection consisted of Red Denim, a version of Giorgio's Red; White Denim, a knockoff of Vanilla Fields by Coty; and Blue Denim, an imitation of Elizabeth Arden's Sunflowers. This line not only imitated popular scents but also borrowed a marketing concept from the prestigious designer, Gianni Versace, who one year earlier introduced Red Jeans and Blue Jeans, a woman's and man's scent, respectively. The company planned to continue the trend with additional line extensions under the Jordache brand name.

By February 1996, Jean Philippe was ready to relaunch the Aziza hypoallergenic eye cosmetic line. The Aziza brand name recognition provided Jean Philippe the opportunity to introduce a new line of products to an existing loyal customer base. The line was developed to incorporate the 38 best selling eye care products to meet the needs of the 1990s consumer. The primary distribution channels for the new line were mass-market merchandisers, drug chains, and supermarkets.

Refocus and Restructure: 1996–98

In the mid-1990s, Jean Philippe began restructuring in an effort to focus its resources on its profitable core fragrance business in the United States and abroad. An integral part of that process was to relinquish the Cutex lip and nail product license and to begin expanding its prestige portfolio. It achieved the latter by signing an exclusive 11-year license agreement with S.T. Dupont for the creation, manufacture, and global distribution of S.T. Dupont perfumes.

Economic turbulence in Eastern Europe and Brazil resulted in sales declines during this time, and Jean Philippe was forced to close its Brazilian subsidiary, Jean Philippe Do Brazil in 1998. Still, Jean Philippe continued to market products in Brazil and entered into a distribution agreement with a well-known Brazilian fragrance distributor, which included the purchase of existing inventory. This action embodied the company's philosophy on the risks and benefits of global marketing, enumerated in the company's 1998 annual report: ''The Company's worldwide position, which makes it subject to global economic turbulence, should also benefit the Company in the future, as countries emerge from their economic troubles. The economic conditions in a number of markets during 1998, such as Eastern Europe and Brazil, certainly dampened the Company's short-term results. However, the Company's long-term focus will not allow it to abandon these markets, as the company would lose the opportunity to capitalize on the potential resurgence of these countries.'' Jean Philippe did successfully weather the tumultuous periods brought on by its international markets by streamlining the sales and administrative structure of its U.S. operations.

Building the Luxury Brand Portfolio: 1998–99

In April 1999, the company launched the Parfums Deja New fragrance line that aimed to appeal to a wide range of consumers in an emerging middle market and compensate for a relatively flat alternative-fragrance market. The goal of this action was to blur the distinction between prestige and mass market fragrances. Moreover, Jean Philippe introduced two successful S.T. Dupont fragrance lines in 1998. A line of complementary bath products was introduced in the first half of 1999, further enhancing the brand's image.

A 12-year exclusive license agreement with internationally renowned British designer Paul Smith, in December 1998, added to the build-up of the company's prestige fragrance portfolio. The agreement allowed for the creation, manufacture, and worldwide distribution of Paul Smith perfumes and cosmetics. The company's international launch of its first line of Paul Smith perfumes was scheduled for July 2000.

In March 1999, the company entered into an exclusive license agreement with the Christian Lacroix Company, a division of LVMH Moet Hennessy Louis Vuitton S.A. (LVMH) to enable the worldwide development, manufacture and distribution of perfumes. The new alliance with a prestigious fashion label that bottled such luxury fragrances as Christian Dior and Givenchy, was designed to further strengthen the company's position in the prestige fragrance industry.

In August 1999, LVMH acquired a 6.3 percent stake, some 467,000 shares, in Jean Philippe, which during this time changed its name to Inter Parfums, Inc. The stock transaction was valued at $4.2 million. LVMH disclosed in a Securities and Exchange Commission filing that they considered the Inter Parfums business portfolio complementary to their own and intended to open negotiations with Inter Parfums about increasing its ownership to a ''significant minority'' position. LVMH also stated in the filing that it intended to increase its participation on a friendly basis coincident with the execution of a customary strategic minority investment agreement. By November 1999, LVMH had increased its equity investment to approximately 20.5 percent.

The name change from Jean Philippe Fragrances, Inc. to Inter Parfums, Inc. in July recognized the success of its French subsidiary, Inter Parfums, S.A., over the previous five years. For the year ending December 31, 1998, the French subsidiary represented 66 percent of net sales. Since the French subsidiary had helped the company become a formidable competitor in the prestige industry, the company strategy held that the name change would allow even greater industry exposure and open the way for greater license and acquisition opportunities. The company, however, retained the brand name, Jean Philippe Fragrances, for its mass market products.

2000 and Beyond

Among Inter Parfums primary goals for the future were to focus on new product introductions and prestige brand names, as well as keep its U.S. operations profitable in the face of economic downturns abroad. Toward those ends, the company launched a totally new fragrance, Quartz by Molyneux, as well as a new line of S.T. Dupont ''Signature'' perfumes. The company looked forward to the international launch of its first line of Paul Smith perfumes and two new perfume lines under the Burberry name, which continued to be the company's leading selective brand name fragrance. In June 2000, Inter Parfums announced that it would produce and market a new line of fragrances under the FUBU name, a popular American line of fashions for young people. Also, the U.S. debut of Christian Lacroix was made in February 2000 through an exclusive distribution arrangement with Saks Fifth Avenue. Distribution of the Christian Lacroix line in South America was also planned for 2000. On the other end of the market spectrum, Inter Parfums planned a new AZIZA ll line of low priced eye shadow kits, mascaras, colorful lip-gloss products, and pencils created for the ''dollar store'' market.

Principal Subsidiaries

Inter Parfums, S.A. (79%; France).

Principal Competitors

Coty; French Fragrances; Parlux Fragrances.

Further Reading

Brookman, Faye, ''AM Cosmetics Buys Itself a Mass Niche,'' *WWD,* April 11, 1997, p. 9.

Cunningham, Thomas, ''LVMH Buys 6.3 Percent Stake in Inter Parfums,'' *WWD,* August 6, 1999.

——, "LVMH'S Inter Parfums Stake Increasing to 20%," *WWD*, September 29, 1999.

"Jean Philippe Buys Aziza Makeup Mark," *WWD*, June 28, 1994, p. 12.

"Jean Philippe Gets Rights to Cutex," *WWD*, June 3, 1994, p.6.

"Jean Philippe's Numbers," *WWD*, March 29, 1996, p. 12.

"Jean Philippe," *Soap & Cosmetics*, April 1999, p. 22.

Kagan, Cara, "Cutex Enters Chapter 2 With Jean Philippe," *WWD*, March 10, 1995, p. 6.

——, "Jean Philippe Gives 61 Year Old Aziza a Facelift," *WWD*, November 3,1995, p. 8.

——, "Jean Philippe's Launch Strategy: Follow the Alternative Route," *WWD*, March 31, 1995, p. S18.

Marcial, Gene G.," Copycat Scents Are Far From Stale," *Business Week*, February 15, 1993, p. 104.

——, "Knockout Knockoff Scents," *Business Week*, August 16, 1993, p. 94.

——, "Sweet Smells from a Parfumerie," *Business Week*, April 29, 1991, p. 80.

Ozzard, Janet, "October Launch for Lacroix's Second Scent," *WWD*, September 10, 1999.

"Inter Parfums in Burberry's/Ombre Rose Acquisitions," *Cosmetics International*, August 15, 1993, p. 1.

"Parlux Agrees to Buy Famous French Brands," *Knight-Ridder/Tribune Business News*, January 16, 1996.

"Purchasing Power," *WWD*, February 2, 1996, p. 5.

"Taking Charge," *WWD*, April 4,1997, p. 10.

—Ana Garcia Schulz

J·Jill

The J. Jill Group, Inc.

4 Batterymarch Park
Quincy, Massachusetts 02169
U.S.A.
Telephone: (617) 376-4300
Toll Free: (800) 642-9989
Fax: (617) 769-0177
Web site: http://www.jjill.com

Public Company
Incorporated: 1987 as DM Management Company
Employees: 827
Sales: $250.28 million (1999)
Stock Exchanges: NASDAQ
Ticker Symbol: JILL
NAIC: 448120 Women's Clothing Stores; 454110
    Electronic Shopping and Mail-Order Houses

The J. Jill Group, Inc. is an upscale specialty marketer of women's apparel, accessories, and gifts under the J. Jill brand, using multiple distribution channels to market its wares, such as catalogs, retail stores (including its own stores), and its Web site. J. Jill's apparel is almost entirely private label under its own name, with emphasis on natural fibers and unique details. Its target customers are active, affluent women aged 35 to 55.

Selling by Catalog Only: 1987–95

DM Management Co. was founded with venture capital funds in 1987 to build a business by purchasing undervalued and poorly performing catalogs. Carl Lipsky, who founded J. Jill in 1959 (naming it for his wife, Jennifer, and daughter, Jill) sold the company in 1988 to DM Management, which, as its initials implied, was engaged in direct-mail marketing. The company fared poorly in its initial years. In fiscal 1990 (the year ended June 30, 1990), for example, it lost $9.63 million on sales of $23.88 million. Over the next two years, however, DM Management's sales continued to climb and its losses decreased. In fiscal 1993, the company earned $1.55 million on net sales of $47.51 million.

By mid-1993 there were three DM Management apparel catalogs: J. Jill Ltd., The Very Thing!, and Nicole Summers. The first was described by the company as featuring "comfortable and easy-to-wear clothing," the second as "refined apparel for women with discerning tastes," and the third as for "women whose style is distinct but eclectic." Typically, they were mingled and mailed together, with a unique offer of free overnight shipping and handling with a minimum order of $50 and the slogan, "Call us today, wear it tomorrow." DM Management went public in 1993, offering stock at $9 a share. In fiscal 1994 the company enjoyed its best year to date, earning $3.27 million in net income on net sales of $63.34 million.

DM Management added N.S. Memorandum, a specialty *Nicole Summers* career dress spin-off, in 1993, and Gateway, a specialty resort and vacation wear book of fashions from The Very Thing!, in November 1994. A month later it acquired the trademark, customer list, and certain other assets of Carroll Reed, Inc., a specialty retailer and cataloger of classic women's apparel, for $6.21 million. DM Management described the *Carroll Reed* catalog as featuring "enduring styles with impeccable tailoring and superior value." By mid-1995 the company had added a third specialty catalog, Our Favorites, which featured the most popular items from each of the principal catalogs. Circulation of all DM catalogs came to 44.2 million in fiscal 1995, with Nicole Summers leading The Very Thing! and J. Jill, Ltd. (As a recent acquisition, Carroll Reed was not included in this tabulation.)

DM Management was leasing corporate headquarters and production facilities in Hingham, Massachusetts. It owned a distribution center in Meredith, New Hampshire and had three outlet stores—two in New Hampshire and one in Bedford, Massachusetts. DM was offering both brand-name and private-label dresses, suits, sportswear, swimwear, loungewear, coats, jackets, shoes, and accessories, purchasing merchandise from about 450 different vendors.

Focus on J. Jill: 1996–98

DM Management had disappointing net income of $773,000 on net sales of $72.69 million in fiscal 1995. With the stock

---

Company Perspectives:

J. Jill's mission is to provide you with the simplicity, comfort and satisfaction that comes with clothes you can live in and service you can trust.

---

slumping—it fell below $2 a share late in the calendar year—Gordon R. Cooke was appointed to replace Samuel L. Shanaman as president and chief executive of the company. Cooke, former president of Time Warner Interactive Merchandising, had previously helped start an around-the-clock home-shopping show and presided over Bloomingdale's mail-order operations. Interviewed in 1998 for *Forbes* by Peter Kafka, Cooke recalled, "Every skirt we sold was down to the ankles. All our models had little plastic flowers on their dresses, and it drove me crazy. I said, 'Who are we targeting, the 80- to 100-year-old woman?'" Under his direction, DM Management began appealing to how its mature customers wanted to see themselves rather than as they were, using catalog photos and illustrations to evoke youth and fashion.

To save printing and paper costs, DM Management combined the Nicole Summers and The Very Thing! catalogs in March 1996. The overwhelming majority of the company's customers—chiefly career women between the ages of 45 and 65—were not only receiving both books but often getting several copies of the same catalog. Two months later, the company dropped Carroll Reed because of disappointing sales and the difficulty of integrating its customer list with DM's other catalogs. The company made a small profit in fiscal 1996, excluding a $9.6 million charge for the costs of discontinuing this book.

The transformation of DM Management left the company with two core books: Nicole Summers and J. Jill, which was now targeting a customer about a decade younger and more oriented toward casual clothing than the more corporate, career-minded Nicole Summers buyer. J. Jill began offering more exclusive, private-label merchandise under the J. Jill label, a broader range of sizes, and "total look" ensembles that combined apparel, accessories, shoes, and gifts on a single page. Nearly two-thirds of J. Jill catalogs began to go to new customers.

For the 1996 holiday season, DM increased the proportion of new merchandise offerings to 60 percent, compared with only 15 percent in prior years, when the company was essentially promoting goods the customer had already been offered earlier in the year. DM also added product categories to its holiday catalogs, including accessories, gifts, and home furnishings. Nicole Summers offered Elizabeth Arden cosmetics for the first time and introduced crystal from Baccarat and Waterford. Changing to a calendar-year (except for the week after Christmas) annual accounting, DM posted net income of $3.37 million for 1996—excluding the Carroll Reed charge but including a $1.6 million income tax benefit—on net sales of $84.64 million.

DM's marketing changes were inspired by Cooke's use of database management to learn more not only about the company's own customers but also the buying patterns of other mail-order buyers. The company purchased two million names

in 1997 and mailed half of all copies of J. Jill catalogs to prospective, rather than previous, customers. Rather than rely on scattershot techniques or only on its own internal resources, DM was (in 1998) acquiring lists of prospects in part from Abacus, a database cooperative that was pooling information from more than 1,000 catalogers to identify the most active mail-order buyers.

Business was so good in 1997 that, to fulfill its orders, DM Management had to rent 150,000 square feet of space in Meredith to supplement the activities at its own 93,120-square-foot warehouse, plus additional rented quarters in nearby Laconia. The company, in January 1998, began construction of a 400,000-square-foot operations facility in Tilton, New Hampshire. Sales soared to $135.53 million in 1997, and net income rose to $3.9 million. DM raised $17.45 million that year by issuing an additional 1.41 million shares of stock to the public at $13.50 a share. The company enjoyed an even better year in 1998, earning $8.4 million on sales of $218.73 million.

DM Management entered the home furnishings market by adding a 24-page section of sheets, towels, and other domestic goods to its October 1998 issue of J. Jill. This was followed in March 1999 by a freestanding 48-page home catalog entitled Peopleplacesthings, sent to one million prospective customers and stressing "natural fibers, casual comfort, easy care and lots of spirit," according to Patricia Lee, president of merchandising. Peopleplacesthings items featured a muted color palette, with neutral, washed-out hues. The publication was shelved in mid-1999, when DM decided to concentrate instead on building retail and online ventures.

DM Management continued to lavish attention on the J. Jill catalog. In the April 1999 issue of *Catalog Age,* Lois Boyle wrote, "J. Jill hires many of the same beautiful models with streamlined bodies who appear in other books, but it photographs them with a keen difference. The poses and clothes styling reflect a lifestyle—not just clothes on a model. In a look you might call 'sloppy chic,' many J. Jill photos reflect clothes that are comfortably suited to a woman involved in everyday activities." In a later 1999 *Catalog Age* issue, a J. Jill 1998 holiday catalog cover of a "naked" mannequin adorned with Christmas lights was cited as among the ten best catalog covers of the year.

Launching Retail Stores and E-Commerce in 1999

DM Management was renamed The J. Jill Group, Inc. in June 1999. This action was accompanied by a corporate decision to expand its sales through retail and e-commerce operations as well as mail order. The company announced plans to open ten J. Jill stores in 2000 and up to 50 stores by the end of 2001. These outlets would, ideally, be located in upscale malls and close to chain stores such as Crate & Barrel, Banana Republic, Bloomingdale's, J. Crew, Lord & Taylor, Nordstrom, Restoration Hardware, Saks Fifth Avenue, and Talbot's. They would carry about half the stockkeeping units in the J. Jill catalog and would merchandise apparel, accessories, shoes, and gifts in a "lifestyle presentation." Many of the chairs, armoires, and lighting displaying the goods would also be for sale. "We believe retail will eventually represent three to four times our catalog business," Cooke told Shannon Oberndorf of *Catalog Age.*

Key Dates:

1988: Recently founded DM Management purchases J. Jill.
1993: DM Management becomes a public company.
1994: Company buys Carroll Reed, its fourth regular catalog.
1996: DM Management drops two of its four catalogs.
1998: DM constructs a new warehouse in Tilton, New Hampshire.
1999: Company changes its name to J. Jill, opens its first retail stores, and drops its Nicole catalog.

The first two new J. Jill stores, opened in August 1999, were 5,000-square-foot units in Natick, Massachusetts and Providence, Rhode Island. An interactive Web site, linked to the company's order-taking infrastructure and fulfillment operations, made its debut in August 1999. J. Jill Group moved its headquarters from Hingham to Quincy, Massachusetts before year's end.

The Nicole Summers catalog was renamed Nicole in June 1999, with plans announced to feature loose, less-tailored clothing than in the past. The first issue appeared in August but apparently fared poorly. In September J. Jill Group announced that it would lose money during the third quarter of the year and would discontinue Nicole. The company posted another loss for the last three months of 1999 and registered a deficit of $6.84 million (including charges of about $6 million for discontinuing Nicole) on sales of $250.28 million. Company shares of stock, trading as high as $26.50 in May 1999, closed the year at only slightly more than $3. "J. Jill had a wonderful run," an analyst told Philana Patterson of the *Wall Street Journal* in October, adding "They hit a chord—and they created competition. Talbot's, Coldwater Creek and Lands' End began to . . . put more of that type of merchandise in the marketplace."

Of The J. Jill Group's 1999 net sales, J. Jill merchandise accounted for about 87 percent. Almost all of its offerings were private-label merchandise sold under the J. Jill name. Many of these offerings were being designed by the company itself and were not available in other catalogs or retail stores. Regular sizes ranged from 4 to 20, with a broad assortment of apparel also available in the same styles in petite, tall, and large sizes. Extended size offerings accounted for 47 percent of total J. Jill apparel offerings in 1999. About 32 percent of the company's merchandise came from foreign suppliers or buyers, mainly in Hong Kong, Singapore, and Israel. In all, the company purchased goods from about 630 vendors during the year.

J. Jill Group's catalog circulation reached 94 million, and the number of its catalog customers, 1.21 million, in 1999. The J. Jill customer database contained about 2.6 million names at the end of the year, including about one million individuals who had made a purchase from the J. Jill catalog during the previous 12 months. Fulfillment of orders usually took three to five business days. Of J. Jill's five stores in operation at the end of the year, three were outlet stores run solely for the purpose of liquidating overstocks.

Principal Subsidiaries

Birch Pond Realty Corporation.

Principal Competitors

Bloomingdale's By Mail Ltd.; Brylane LP; Coldwater Creek Inc.; Lands' End Inc.; Patagonia Inc.

Further Reading

Boyle, Lois, "Breaking Away from the Pack," *Catalog Age,* April 1999, pp. 87–88.

Brownlee, Lisa, "Catalog Retailer's Turnaround Goes by the Book, Trumps Stores," *Wall Street Journal,* October 28, 1997, p. B6.

Del Franco, Mark, "J. Jill Home Book Held," *Catalog Age,* July 1999, p. 5.

Dowling, Melissa, "Scrambling for Extra Space," *Catalog Age,* March 1998, p. 51.

Hochwald, Lambeth, "New Look, Better Numbers," *American Demographics,* October 1998, pp. 42–45.

Kafka, Peter, "J. Jill's Rejuvenation," *Forbes,* May 4, 1998, pp. 70, 74.

Kiley, Kathleen, "Resortwear Book Sets Sail," *Catalog Age,* February 1995, p. 24.

Merritt, Jennifer, "Catalog Company Orders Up a Turnaround," *Boston Business Journal,* July 31, 1998, p. 1 and continuation.

Miller, Paul, "J. Jill Joins Crowded Home Market," *Catalog Age,* June 1998, p. 22.

Moin, David, "J. Jill Pushes Up Launch Date for Retail Chain Prototypes," *WWD/Women's Wear Daily,* August 31, 1999, p. 11.

Norris, Floyd, "No News Turns into Bad News at Retailer," *New York Times,* September 21, 1999, pp. C1, C11.

Oberndorf, Shannon, "New and Improved," *Catalog Age,* January 1997, pp. 5, 26.

Patterson, Philana, "Catalog Retailers Are Likely To Post Mixed Results as Competition Increases," *Wall Street Journal,* October 18, 1999, p. A43G.

Reidy, Chris, "DM Management Bucks Woes Facing Other Catalog Retailers," *Boston Globe,* January 7, 1998, p. C5.

Schmiel, Jack, "Stand-Out Offers," *Catalog Age,* July 1993, p. 142.

Sloan, Carole, "J. Jill Is Home at Last," *Home Textile News,* April 5, 1999, p. 8.

—Robert Halasz

Johnston Press plc

Johnston Press plc

53 Manor Place
Edinburgh EH3 7EG
United Kingdom
Telephone: (+44) 131 225-3361
Fax: (+44) 131 225-4580
Web site: http://www.johnstonpress.co.uk

Public Company
Incorporated: 1767 as F Johnston & Co.
Employees: 4,100
Sales: £242.56 million ($363.8 million) (1999)
Stock Exchanges: London
Ticker Symbol: JPR.L
NAIC: 51111 Newspaper Publishing

Edinburgh, Scotland's Johnston Press plc has pressed itself into the ranks of the United Kingdom's top five regional newspaper publishing groups. Johnston Press, which holds more than 200 local newspaper titles, including daily, weekly, evening, and monthly titles and both paid and free titles, has helped lead the ongoing consolidation of the United Kingdom's regional newspaper market. Since its acquisition of the regional newspaper division of EMAP, Johnston Press also has snapped up rival Portsmouth & Sunderland, as well as a host of smaller publishers and individual titles. Nevertheless, Johnston Press was disappointed in early 2000 after losing out in a bidding war (to the United States' Gannett) for the 120-title News Communications & Media plc (Newscom). In addition to its print titles, some of which are 200 years old and more, Johnston Press also has been actively building an Internet publishing presence, with more than 50 web sites in operation in 2000 offering access to the company's local newspaper content, as well as services such as online auctions and free internet access. Johnston Press, which shed such peripheral businesses as stationery, toy distribution, and bookbinding in the late 1990s, continues to operate a printing division for its own titles as well as third-party customers, with presses in Burgess Hill, Northampton, and Peterborough. In 2000, the company committed £15 million for the upgrading of its printing capacity. Nonetheless, newspapers remain the company's bread and butter,

and Johnston has stated its interest in further acquisitions as the consolidation of the United Kingdom's regional newspaper industry appeared far from over. The company, having been led by a member of the Johnston family (which still owns 28 percent of the company), would have its first nonfamily-member chairman after Fred Johnston, architect of the company's major growth, stepped down from the chairmanship in 2000 (he remains a nonexecutive director of the company). Roger Parry was named new company chairman, joining CEO Tim Bowdler.

18th-Century Origins

One of the oldest continuously operating publishing companies in the United Kingdom, Johnston Press origins were in Glasgow in the mid-1700s, when Patrick Mair founded a printing company. In 1767, Mair moved his company to the nearby town of Falkirk, then a growing industrial center between Glasgow and Edinburgh. Mair transferred ownership of the company to son-in-law and head printer Thomas Johnston, and the company became known as F Johnston & Co., a name it was to keep for more than 220 years.

The Johnston company specialized in book printing and publishing, for both religious and secular works. Johnston's interest in newspaper publishing took root toward the middle of the 19th century. In 1846, the company bought the *Falkirk Herald,* the local monthly newspaper. Four years later the *Falkirk Herald* converted to a weekly publishing schedule.

For the next 100 years, Johnston's activities remained limited but profitable. By the end of the 1950s, the company's newspaper wing still held only four newspaper titles. The arrival of the latest generation of the Johnston family was to dramatically change the company's profile. Fred Johnston, great-great-great-grandson of Patrick Mair, joined the company in 1962 at the age of 27.

Under Fred Johnston, F Johnston & Co. began to build up its portfolio of titles, while remaining within its Scottish base. In the mid-1960s the company acquired a number of newspapers, all of which were local newspapers, such as the *East Fife Mail* and the *Milngavie & Beasden Herald.* The company continued its policy of pursuing individual newspaper purchases until well into the 1980s.

Company Perspectives:

Johnston Press Plc is a major publisher of quality local newspapers, basing its publishing philosophy on local service to local communities. Johnston newspapers are local quality newspapers produced by local teams of people who have a dedicated commitment to producing local newspapers that both inform and reflect the important issues of the communities they serve, thus encouraging a loyal, committed and valuable readership.

Meanwhile, the company also began to launch new titles, particularly free advertising-based newspapers, beginning with the *Grangemouth Advertiser* in 1976. The company's move to become a U.K. newspaper publisher came in 1978, when it acquired the *Derbyshire Times,* through its acquisition of publishing company Wilfred Edmunds Ltd. That acquisition also brought the company a series of other local titles, concentrated on the North Midlands region of England. From this purchase, F Johnston slowly built a presence in England, while continuing to build up its portfolio of local Scottish newspapers.

Nonetheless, F Johnston, like the rest of the United Kingdom's local and regional newspaper publishing industry, remained hamstrung by legislation enacted in the early 1960s designed to prevent the formation of local newspaper monopolies—especially given the popularity of the 1,200-title local newspaper market among the United Kingdom's reading public. That same legislation, however, restricted the growth of publishing companies, making investment in new equipment and technology difficult, if not financially impossible. Even into the end of the 1990s, Johnston CEO Tim Bowdler complained, "In an era when AOL and Time Warner can merge, Johnston still had to get clearance to buy the 7000-circulation *Arbroath Herald.*"

By the early 1980s, however, new legislation promised a relaxation of newspaper acquisition procedures. The new rules affected primarily the national newspaper market; the effects were immediate, leading to massive investments in new technology and equipment, which ultimately resulted in higher print quality publications. The local and regional markets, however, remained under tight Mergers and Monopolies Commission scrutiny until well into the mid-1990s.

Johnston remained a small company through the 1980s, with its private status, coupled with government restrictions, making it difficult for the company to raise the capital to pursue further acquisitions. To rectify this position, Fred Johnston brought the company public in 1988, with a listing on the London Stock Exchange. The Johnston family retained a large share of the company's stock, and even into the beginning of the 21st century, the Johnston family's share remained at 28 percent. At the time of the stock offering, the company changed its name to Johnston Press plc.

A Regional Publishing Powerhouse for the 21st Century

The public offering enabled the company to step up its expansion efforts. With acquisitions in the local newspaper market restricted by government policy, the company turned toward outside interests to build up its revenues. In 1990, Johnston bought up Dunn & Wilson, giving it a bookbinding subsidiary, and then Cedric Chivers, adding that company's booksellers business. In 1992, Johnston moved into still more remote waters, when it bought Shoesmith & Etheridge, adding that company's stationery and toy distribution activities. By 1993, these acquisitions, plus the company's continued purchases of single local titles, gave it annual revenues worth more than £86 million. By then, Johnston had built up a portfolio of 70 local newspaper titles, worth some 75 percent of its turnover.

The tide in the United Kingdom's regional and local newspaper industry began to turn toward the mid-1990s. To stimulate investment among the country's small local and regional publishers—many of which were struggling to stay afloat financially—the government indicated its willingness to relax its acquisitions procedures. Johnston Press was among the first to take advantage of the new openness in the market, making its first multititle purchase in 1994, when it paid £29.4 million for the Halifax Courier newspaper group. The purchase gave Johnston not only the *Halifax Courier,* but eight other titles, including the three largest newspapers on the Isle of Man.

By the mid-1990s, however, a number of the industry's largest publishers, frustrated with their inability to make large increases in the regional and local newspaper holdings, began to sell out, sparking a wave of consolidation across the market. Among these publishers was EMAP, which in 1996 agreed to sell its 65 newspaper titles—including the 300-year-old *Stamford Mercury*—to Johnston Press for £111 million. EMAP had originally been founded in 1887, by Sir Richard Winfrey, as the newspaper the *Spalding Guardian.* Winfrey's son Richard took over the company, which by then possessed four newspapers, in 1947, changing the name to East Midlands Allied Press. The company took the name EMAP in 1985. During the 1950s, EMAP had expanded from newspapers into magazines. In the late 1970s, the company met with great success with the launch of its *Smash Hits* music magazine, and continued its success into the 1980s with *Just 17* and *Empire.* During the 1990s, EMAP was able to profit from its recession-troubled competitors, buying up a large number of magazine titles (including 14 from Canadian publisher Thomson) to boost its magazine division. By then, EMAP also had begun to explore an interest in other media, particularly radio, which it entered with the acquisitions of Trans World Communications and Metro Radio Group. EMAP's new focus led it to part with its newspaper division.

The EMAP acquisition bolted Johnston into the top five among the United Kingdom's local and regional publishers. By 1997, the company was ready to pursue more multititle acquisitions—reaching an agreement for £52 million to acquire the Home Counties Newspapers group. As Tim Bowdler told the *Independent* at the time of its initial agreement to buy Home Counties: "This is a continuation of the consolidation of a very fragmented industry. We are looking for more acquisitions."

The Home Counties deal fell through before the end of the year, in part because the extended review process of Mergers and Monopolies Commission approval allowed a rival to top Johnston's bid. Nonetheless, Johnston remained committed to

Key Dates:

1767: F Johnston & Co. is established.
1846: Company acquires *Falkirk Herald.*
1850: *Falkirk Herald* is converted to weekly publishing schedule.
1962: Fred Johnston joins company.
1960s: Company acquires *East Fife Mail* and the *Milngavie & Beasden Herald.*
1978: Wilfred Edmunds Ltd. is acquired.
1988: Company goes public on London Stock Exchange.
1990: Dunn & Wilson and Cedric Chivers are acquired.
1996: Company acquires newspaper division of EMAP plc.
1997: Bookbinding and booksellers operations are divested.
1999: Company acquires Portsmouth & Sunderland, and sells stationery and toy distribution operations.
2000: Johnston acquires 14 newspaper titles from Southnews.

growth through acquisition. With the EMAP acquisition, the company also had decided that it had reached sufficient critical mass to allow it to jettison its nonpublishing activities. In September 1997, the company sold off its bookbinding division, which by then included subsidiaries Dunn & Wilson, with binderies in Falkirk and Huddersfield, as well as operations in Ireland and Australia and in Cedric Chivers, located in Bristol. Next to go was the company's Cedric Chivers booksellers business. By 1999, the company had sold off its stationery and toy distribution subsidiaries as well.

Refocused, Johnston Press began seeking its next big acquisition. In 1998, the company entered into talks with rival Portsmouth & Sunderland, for acquisition of that company's newspaper titles. Talks broke off soon afterward, and, in January 1999, Johnston Press attempted a hostile takeover bid of Portsmouth & Sunderland, building up a holding of nearly 15 percent. Finally, in March 1999, Portsmouth & Sunderland agreed to a renewed offer from Johnston, valued at more than £266 million. The addition of Portsmouth & Sunderland's titles boosted Johnston Press from 155 titles to more than 200, securing the company's number four position among the country's more than 120 local and regional publishers.

By the end of 1999, Johnston Press had expanded its annual sales to more than £240 million. In early 2000, the company's bid for the takeover of the 120-title Newscom was outgunned by Gannett, of the United States, which also had acquired the United Kingdom's Newsquest newspaper group. Instead, Johnston contented itself with the purchase of 14 newspapers, including the *Lincoln Standard* and *Four Counties* newspaper titles, from Southnews for £16.5 million.

In March of 2000, the 65-year-old Fred Johnston announced his decision to retire, relinquishing the chairmanship of the company to Roger Parry, marking the first time in the company's history when it had not been led by a member of the Johnston family. Fred Johnston nonetheless remained with the company in a non-executive director's capacity. In the meantime, Johnston Press had turned toward the booming Internet publishing market for future expansion. With more than 50 web sites—each tailored to specific local markets, but offering nationwide linkups—Johnston Press became one of the United Kingdom's most active Internet publishers. The company also became an Internet access provider, offering free Internet access through a number of its web sites. At the same time, Johnston Press remained committed to maintaining its leadership position in the regional and local newspaper market, which remained highly fragmented and ripe for continued consolidation into the new century.

Principal Operating Units

Banbury Guardian; Bucks Herald; Buxton Advertiser; Derbyshire Times; East Fife Mail; Falkirk, Grangemouth & Linlithgow Advertiser; Falkirk Herald; Fife Free Press; Halifax Evening Courier; Hemel Hempstead Gazette; Hucknall & Bulwell Dispatch; Kirkintilloch & Bishopbriggs Herald; Luton & Dunstable Herald & Post; Mansfield Chad; Milngavie & Beasden Herald; Northampton Chronicle & Echo; Peterborough Evening Telegraph; West Sussex County Times; Worksop Guardian; Worthing Herald.

Principal Competitors

Daily Mail and General Trust plc; Newsquest plc; Hollinger International Inc.; Scottish Media Group plc; Independent Newspapers; The Times Mirror Company; United News & Media plc; News Corporation Ltd.

Further Reading

Daeschner, Jeff, ''Johnston Press Tops Profit Forecasts,'' *Reuters,* March 30, 1999.
Larsen, Peter Thal, ''Johnston Moves in on Newspaper Rival,'' *Independent,* January 23, 1999, p. 19.
Murray-West, Rosie, ''Johnston Chairman Will Not Be One of the Family,'' *Daily Telegraph,* March 22, 2000.
Wright, Melanie, ''Johnston Press Accused of 'Smash and Grab' Tactics,'' *Daily Telegraph,* January 25, 1999.
Yates, Andrew, ''A Great Story in Local News,'' *Independent,* April 2, 1998, p. 24.
——, ''Johnston Press Pulls Out of Newscom Battle,'' *Reuters,* May 9, 2000.

—M.L. Cohen

Katz Media Group, Inc.

125 West 55th Street
New York, New York 10019
U.S.A.
Telephone: (212) 424-6000
Fax: (212) 424-6110
Web site: http://www.katz-media.com

Wholly Owned Subsidiary of AMFM Inc.
Incorporated: 1888 as E. Katz Special Advertising
   Agency
Employees: 1,800
Sales: $2.6 billion (1999 est.)
NAIC: 541840 Media Representatives

Katz Media Group, Inc., a giant in the media representation industry, has a long history that dates back to the 1880s and the very beginning of media representation. It has been at different times a private family-owned business, an employee-owned company, a management-owned company, a publicly-owned company, and a wholly-owned subsidiary. Its parent company, currently known as AMFM Inc., is the largest out-of-home media corporation with ownership of more than 800 radio stations, 19 television stations, and 425,000 outdoor advertising displays. Katz specializes in representing electronic media, including radio stations, cable TV systems, and broadcast television stations. It also has a sports marketing division to represent sports teams and venues. One of its subsidiaries, Katz Millennium Marketing, is dedicated to selling advertising on Internet web sites and other interactive media.

Origins Representing Newspapers: 1888–1930

Katz Media Group can trace its history to the 19th century and the very beginning of the media representation business. The completion of the transcontinental railroad in 1869 enabled manufacturers to sell their products nationally, and the concept of a national brand was born. To develop their brands nationally, manufacturers needed to advertise them in different cities across the country. For the most part, they were unfamiliar with the newspapers and other advertising media in these new markets where they were now selling their products.

Seeing an opportunity to represent advertising media to manufacturers interested in establishing a national presence, Emmanuel Katz, an associate of newspaper publisher William Randolph Hearst, moved from San Francisco to New York to persuade New York-based advertisers to buy ads in Hearst's San Francisco newspapers. The venture proved successful, and in 1888 Katz established the first media representation firm, called the E. Katz Special Advertising Agency, on New York's Park Row, with the Hearst newspapers as its first client. In 1912 George R. Katz, Emmanuel's son, merged his Chicago firm with his father's New York agency. The company soon added offices in San Francisco, Atlanta, Kansas City, and Detroit.

Moving onto Radio and Television: 1930s–70s

In the 1930s the Katz Agency expanded its client list to include radio stations, which were then a new advertising medium. The company remained profitable during the 1930s and 1940s, representing newspapers and radio stations. With the advent of television in the 1940s, the Katz Agency signed up its first television clients in 1949.

From the early 1950s through the early 1970s, the Katz Agency was headed by Eugene Katz, grandson of founder Emmanuel Katz. He had joined the firm in 1928. In 1962 the agency stopped representing newspapers in order to focus on representing electronic media. The agency was organized into two groups, Katz Television and Katz Radio.

An Employee-Owned Company: 1970s and 1980s

In 1972 Katz adopted an Employee Stock Ownership Plan (ESOP). After being a family-owned business for 84 years, the company was sold to its employees for about $3 million. In the mid-1970s Katz was involved with several money-losing subsidiaries and representation ventures. It had an interest in a cable TV system; it collected accounts receivables for television stations; it had an outdoor advertising business; and it represented advertising in the New Orleans Superdome. All of these were losing money when new financial management was brought in; Dick

---

Company Perspectives:

Katz Media Group, Inc., headquartered in New York City, is the only full-service media representation firm in the United States serving multiple types of electronic media, with leading market shares in the representation of radio and television stations, cable television systems and networks of broadcast related Internet Web sites.

Mendelson was hired by Katz chairman and CEO Jim Greenwald as chief financial officer in 1975.

Mendelson concentrated on divesting the money-losing operations while at the same time making strategic acquisitions. In 1976 Katz began its in-house data processing operation, Media Data, which later became an important sales tool by providing online computing services to the radio and television stations that Katz represented. In 1982 Mendelson became president of Katz.

In the mid-1970s Katz reorganized its television group into two divisions, Katz American and Katz Continental, to serve the different needs of large and small markets. In 1980 Katz acquired Field Spot Sales and formed a new division, Katz National, to represent independent television stations and, later, Fox affiliates. In 1983 Katz acquired the in-house representative for Metromedia television stations, Metro TV Sales.

Katz Broadcasting was formed in 1981 when the company purchased four radio stations from Park City Communications for $16 million and another station in Tulsa, Oklahoma, for $3 million from Curtis Communications. By 1986 Katz Broadcasting owned and operated 11 radio stations, which were then sold to an employee group headed by the president of Katz Broadcasting for $68.3 million.

During the 1980s media representation firms were consolidating. Katz Radio acquired two major competitors, Christal Radio and RKO Radio Sales, in 1984. At the time Katz Radio had about $130 million in annual billings, Christal about $70 million, and RKO $20 million. Katz paid an estimated $18 million for Christal and $3.5 million for RKO, which was renamed Republic Radio. Both companies would continue to operate as independent subsidiaries of Katz Communications Inc., as the company was then known.

In 1987 Katz Radio acquired another competitor, Blair Radio, which was renamed Banner Radio. For fiscal 1987 Katz Communications had annual billings of about $1.2 billion for its 200 client television stations and nearly 1,300 radio stations. The company had about 1,300 employees. Between 1975 and the end of the 1980s Katz had tripled in size. It had 65 sales offices across the United States.

In the late 1980s the media representation business suffered a downturn, especially in national TV spot advertising. The standard 15 percent commissions in some cases fell as low as seven percent, due to intense competition for station clients. While the industry had enjoyed double-digit revenue growth for most of the 1980s, national spot TV revenue was projected to be flat or increase by three to five percent for 1989. At the end of the decade Katz had about $1.5 billion in total revenues, about two-thirds of which were national TV spot billings. The company represented 197 local TV stations and 1,400 radio stations. The Katz Radio Group and its primary competitor, The Interep Radio Store, accounted for an estimated 90 percent of national spot radio advertising.

New Opportunities in Cable and TV: 1990–94

Through a leveraged buyout, Katz was purchased in 1990 by an investment group consisting of senior management and other investors. During the year Katz Radio acquired Eastman Radio from Jacor Communications for $11.75 million, making the Katz Radio Group the largest billing radio representative.

At the end of 1991 Peter Goulazian, formerly president of Katz Television Group, succeeded James Greenwald as the CEO of Katz Communications. Goulazian also became president of the company, a post that had been vacant for two years following the departure of Dick Mendelson. Greenwald remained as chairman.

Katz began representing cable TV stations in 1991, when one of its broadcast television clients began operating a regional cable news channel. It formed Katz Cable Sales, which sought to represent the Hearst Corp.'s New England Cable News channel as well as Time Warner's planned New York City cable news channel. By the end of 1991 Katz was representing an all-news cable channel in Washington, D.C., and negotiating with other cable systems. In January 1992 Katz announced it would represent Multimedia Cablevision's Wichita, Kansas, cable system. In February 1992 Katz acquired a minority interest in Cable Media Corp., a Detroit-based cable advertising representative that represented a regional sports cable network, among other clients, together with an option to acquire a 100 percent interest in the company. In June 1992 Katz merged its Katz Cable Sales into Cable Media, which began to expand nationally by opening offices in New York, Chicago, Dallas, and Los Angeles. Cable Media would represent all of Katz's cable TV advertising, while cross-media advertising packages involving a combination of cable TV, radio, and broadcast television would be handled by Katz.

In January 1992 Katz Communications acquired Seltel International Inc., a competing television representative, for about $15 million. The acquisition added 120 TV clients and gave Katz more than 320 client TV stations. In some markets Katz would represent competing stations. Seltel would continue to operate as a separate subsidiary until it was merged with Katz American Television to form Millennium Sales & Marketing.

A public filing for a proposed $100 million debt offering revealed that Katz's 1991 revenues had declined 5.9 percent to $117.5 million, due in part to an economic recession and the Gulf War. The company had 1,600 radio clients with a total of $500 million in billing, about 45 percent of the industry total. Katz also had about 300 TV clients with billings of $1.2 billion, or roughly 25 percent of the industry total.

In 1993 Katz Radio Group established another independent division, Katz Hispanic Radio, to represent Spanish-language radio stations. In September 1993 Katz Hispanic Media began representing the seven radio stations owned by Spanish Broad-

Key Dates:

1888: Emmanuel Katz establishes the first media representation firm, the E. Katz Special Advertising Agency.

1930s: The Katz Agency begins to represent radio stations, a new advertising medium.

1949: The agency begins representing television stations.

1972: Katz becomes an employee-owned company.

1990: Senior management takes control of Katz through a leveraged buyout.

1991: Company begins representing cable TV systems.

1994: Donaldson, Lufkin and Jenrette Securities Corp. acquires a majority interest in Katz.

1995: Katz goes public.

1997: Katz becomes a wholly owned subsidiary of Chancellor Media Group.

1999: Chancellor merges with Capstar Broadcasting to form AMFM Inc.

2000: AMFM and Clear Channel Communications merge to create the world's largest out-of-home media corporation.

casting System. The Hispanic radio market continued to grow in the 1990s, and by 1998 Katz had gained exclusive representation of Heftel Media Broadcasting Corp.'s 34 stations. Katz Hispanic Media claimed to represent a 50 percent share of the Hispanic radio ad market with nearly $100 million in 1997 billings.

Katz also expanded internationally in 1993. Katz and London-based International Media Sales formed Katz International Ltd., with headquarters in London, England, and other offices Frankfurt, Germany, and Paris, France.

Ownership Changes: 1994–2000

Toward the end of 1993 the two investment firms, Sandler Media Partners and 61 K Associates, that together owned about half of Katz's privately-held stock, hired investment firm Lazard Freres ''to review their options.'' In January 1994 Katz's management received, and subsequently rejected, a $250 million buyout offer from the Dallas-based investment firm of Hicks, Muse & Co. Later in 1994 Katz announced it was considering making an initial public offering (IPO) of stock.

Katz's plans for an IPO were put on hold when Donaldson, Lufkin and Jenrette Securities Corp. (DLJ), through its investment fund DLJ Merchant Banking Partners Inc., acquired a majority interest in Katz in July 1994. DLJ agreed to pay $99.6 million in cash and assume Katz's outstanding debt of $187 million, bringing the value of the deal to $287.1 million. DLJ purchased all of the stock in Katz held by Sandler and 61 K Associates, making Katz's senior management DLJ's only partners in the investment. DLJ ended up with about 80 percent of Katz's common stock. Katz's annual billings were estimated to be $2 billion. Tom Olson, president of Katz, replaced Peter Goulazian as CEO. Katz's new chairman would be replaced by DLJ Merchant Banking Partners managing director Thompson Dean. Around this time the company changed its name to Katz Media Group Inc.

Also in 1994 Katz merged its cable sales group, Cable Media Corp., with National Cable Advertising to form National Cable Communications, the single largest cable rep firm in the United States.

In March 1995 Katz gained the national representation contract from Chris-Craft Industries for its eight-station group, United Television Inc. Katz and Chris-Craft set up a new unit, United Sales Enterprises, dedicated to selling only the United stations, which billed about $185 million annually.

Katz completed its IPO in 1995, and for the first time in its 108-year history it became a publicly owned company. The company planned to offer 5.5 million shares at $16 to $18 per share, or about 28.7 percent of the firm's common stock. Also in 1995 Katz formed Katz Millennium Marketing, a rep firm dedicated to selling advertising on Internet web sites and other interactive media.

With $1.6 billion in annual billings, Katz was ranked the third-largest media representation firm, behind Cox Broadcasting Corp. at $2.1 billion and Petry Media with $1.8 billion, according to *Broadcasting & Cable*. With the consolidation of radio and TV station ownership, many owner groups were considering opening their own in-house advertising representation agencies.

Early in 1997 Seltel split into two divisions, Republic and Capitol, to improve service to clients. Each new division included stations from markets of varying sizes. Later in the year Katz put Seltel and the Katz Television Group under a single executive, although the two companies would remain separate. Katz National Television, which represented independent stations, was folded into the Katz Television Group.

In July 1997 Katz became a wholly owned subsidiary of radio station owner Chancellor Media Group. It was sold to Chancellor for $373 million, including $155 million in cash and $128 million in debt. Chancellor Broadcasting and Evergreen Media Corp. had just merged to form the Chancellor Media Group, which owned or operated 98 radio stations in 21 U.S. markets. The acquisition caused concern among some radio station owners that were represented by Katz in markets where there were also stations owned by Chancellor. Most of the stations owned by Chancellor were already represented by Katz. At the time of the sale Katz had estimated gross billings of about $2.6 billion in radio, cable, and broadcast television, making it the single largest rep firm.

When Chancellor made its takeover bid, Katz's stock had fallen from its IPO price of $16 to $4.50 per share. The company had failed to meet Wall Street's earnings expectations, due in part to ownership consolidation of radio and television stations. Through a tender offer that was completed in November 1997, Chancellor offered $11 a share, a price agreeable to DLJ, which owned 49 percent of the company. Katz management indicated that it believed an alliance with a media company was necessary for the company's long-term well-being and stability. Tom Olson would remain as president and CEO of Katz and report to the head of Chancellor Broadcasting.

In mid-1998 Seltel became the rep for 26 TV stations in 16 different markets that were owned or being transferred to

Sinclair Communications. It was estimated the stations accounted for up to $110 million in spot billings annually.

In mid-1999 Katz launched a sports marketing division, Sports Spectrum, to represent athletic teams and sports venues. To start, the division represented MSG Network and the Philadelphia Phillies baseball team.

Katz's parent company Chancellor Media merged with Capstar Broadcasting to form AMFM Inc. in July 1999. The merger created the largest radio station group in the United States with 465 radio stations. Then just a few months later, AMFM Inc. and Clear Channel Communications announced they would merge to create the world's largest out-of-home media company. The merged company, which would continue as AMFM Inc., would own approximately 830 radio stations after anticipated divestitures, as well as more than 425,000 outdoor displays for advertising and 19 television stations. The merger was expected to be completed in the second half of 2000.

With the backing of its parent company, Katz was in a position to enjoy a stable, profitable future. Massive consolidation among radio and television stations owners would mean fewer station groups to represent, so competition was likely to be keen among the remaining rep firms. Nevertheless, Katz enjoyed a leadership position and could offer advertisers a unique combination of advertising opportunities in a variety of electronic media.

Principal Divisions

Katz Radio Group; Katz Television Group.

Principal Operating Units

Christal Radio; Eastman Radio; Katz Radio; Katz Hispanic Media; Sentry Radio; Clear Channel Radio Sales; Continental Television Sales; Eagle Television Sales; Millennium Sales & Marketing; Katz International Ltd. (United Kingdom).

Principal Competitors

Interep National Radio Sales, Inc.; Viacom Inc.

Further Reading

Baldwin, William, "The Myths of Employee Ownership," *Forbes,* April 23, 1984, p. 108.

Brodesser, Claude, "An Absorbing Question: After Sale, Katz Media Seeks Positive Return—As Do Wary Clients," *Mediaweek,* July 21, 1997, p. 8.

Brodesser, Claude, "Katz Consolidates at the Top," *Mediaweek,* June 30, 1997, p. 12.

Cobo, Lucia, "Katz Negotiating to Buy Eastman," *Broadcasting,* July 23, 1990, p. 69.

Collins, Larry, "Katz Change in ESOP Plan Points up Stress in Rep Business," *Adweek Eastern Edition,* March 20, 1989, p. 66.

"DLJ Merchant Banking Partners Inc. Has Completed Its Purchase of Katz Media Corp.," *Broadcasting & Cable,* August 29, 1994, p. 67.

"DLJ Swallows Most of Katz," *Mediaweek,* July 18, 1994, p. 4.

"Done Deal," *Broadcasting,* March 9, 1992, p. 18.

Flint, Joe, "Jacor Sells its Rep Firm to Katz," *Broadcasting,* August 20, 1990, p. 53.

——, "Katz Eyes Seltel," *Broadcasting,* January 13, 1992, p. 6.

——, "Katz Reorganizes," *Broadcasting,* December 23, 1991, p. 6.

Foise, Geoffrey, "Katz Merges Cable Rep into Cable Media," *Broadcasting,* June 22, 1992, p. 32.

——, "Katz to Tap Public Debt Market," *Broadcasting,* August 31, 1992, p. 64.

"Former Katz Media Chairman Dies," *Adweek Eastern Edition,* May 1, 2000, p. 86.

Freeman, Michael, "Potential $110M Gain Seen in Seltel-Sinclair Agreement," *Mediaweek,* June 15, 1998, p. 4.

"Hicks, Muse & Co., the Dallas-based Firm that is Backing Two New Radio Groups, Has Reportedly Made an Offer to Buy All of Katz Communications," *Broadcasting & Cable,* January 10, 1994, p. 85.

"Katz Agrees to Buy Christal, RKO Radio Sales," *Broadcasting,* April 2, 1984, p. 56.

"Katz and Cable," *Broadcasting,* December 23, 1991, p. 34.

"Katz and Seltel Have Finished Negotiations," *Broadcasting,* January 20, 1992, p. 64.

"Katz Communications," *Television Digest,* December 23, 1991, p. 7.

"Katz' Dick Mendelson: Getting Back to Rep Basics," *Broadcasting,* September 26, 1988, p. 103.

"Katz Grabs 50% Hispanic Share," *Broadcasting & Cable,* February 16, 1998, p. 30.

"Katz Looks to Cable to Beef up Business," *Broadcasting,* September 30, 1991, p. 50.

"Katz Media Corp.," *Billboard,* August 27, 1994, p. 124.

"Katz Takes on New Rep Contract," *Adweek Eastern Edition,* March 20, 1995, p. 20.

Littleton, Cynthia, "Megareps Armed for Station Squeeze," *Broadcasting & Cable,* August 12, 1996, p. 46.

McClellan, Steve, "Chancellor Buys Katz Media Group," *Broadcasting & Cable,* July 21, 1997, p. 53.

——, "Katz Media Reorganizes," *Broadcasting & Cable,* June 30, 1997, p. 54.

——, "Katz Takes Stock," *Broadcasting & Cable,* March 27, 1995, p. 55.

Miles, Laureen, "Put out the Katz," *Mediaweek,* July 17, 1995, p. 6.

Moshavi, Sharon D., "Katz Keeps its Toe in Cable Waters," *Broadcasting & Cable,* March 1, 1993, p. 49.

"Peter Goulazian, Tom Olson, and Jim Joyella," *Mediaweek,* January 6, 1992, p. 21.

Petrozello, Donna, "Katz Cancels Public Offering with DLJ Deal," *Broadcasting & Cable,* July 18, 1994, p. 18.

"Radio's Megareps Lead the Way into the 90's," *Broadcasting,* January 15, 1990, p. 110.

Rathbun, Elizabeth A., "Consolidation Hurts Katz," *Broadcasting & Cable,* August 25, 1997, p. 33.

Saxe, Frank, "AMFM on Growth Path as Merger Is Approved," *Billboard,* July 31, 1999, p. 89.

Torpey-Kemph, Anne, "Katz Launches Sports Marketing Unit," *Mediaweek,* July 12, 1999, p. 26.

Viles, Peter, "Katz Hispanic to Rep SBS Stations," *Broadcasting & Cable,* September 27, 1993, p. 49.

—David P. Bianco

Kaufring AG

Kieshecker Weg 100
D-40468 Düsseldorf
Germany
Telephone: (49)(211) 4242-0
Fax: (49)(211) 4242-444
Web site: http://www.Kaufring.de

Public Company
Incorporated: 1921 as ERWEGE
Employees: 3,557
Sales: DM 2.76 billion ($1.4 billion) (1999)
Stock Exchanges: Frankfurt/Main
Ticker Symbol: KFR
NAIC: 42233 Women's, Children's, and Infants' Clothing
and Accessories Wholesalers; 42232 Men's and Boys'
Clothing and Furnishings Wholesalers; 42234
Footwear Wholesalers; 42231 Piece Goods, Notions,
and Other Dry Goods Wholesalers; 42211 Printing
and Writing Paper Wholesalers; 42192 Toy and
Hobby Goods and Supplies Wholesalers; 42162
Electrical Appliance, Television, and Radio Set
Wholesalers; 45211 Department Stores; 45299 All
Other General Merchandise Stores

Kaufring AG is the leading German wholesale organization for mid-sized independent department stores and special interest outlets. Its 558 member retailers represent a sales volume of about $3.5 billion. Kaufring's services include purchasing and warehousing; advertising and event marketing; consulting in logistics, new site planning, product range, interior design, advertising, human resources, and information technology; and financial services. As a result of a fundamental restructuring program initiated in 1999, Kaufring planned to divest about one-third of its business through the sale of all Kaufring's active retail subsidiaries, such as Golden Team Sport, Germany's third largest wholesaler for sporting goods. Some 57 former purchasing departments were reorganized into eight divisions, and Kaufring's Far East purchasing subsidiary Centra Trading Ltd.

ceased operations, being replaced by an agreement to work with a Hong-Kong-based purchasing agency.

Early Years as a Purchasing Cooperative: 1921–45

Kaufring was born three years after the end of World War I, when Germany was going through a severe political and economic crisis. Beginning in 1920 a small group of hardware retailers started meeting regularly at Dusseldorf's Bahnhofshotel to network and exchange ideas about how to improve business. Very soon the get-togethers of the regulars became more than just social gatherings. At a time when competition from the new department stores was threatening their very existence, these independent retailers realized that they had to bundle their purchase orders to achieve better terms and prices from suppliers. In early 1921 retailers from the German states Rhineland and Westphalia loosely organized a nonprofit organization, the Einkaufsverein Rheinisch-Westfälischer Geschäftshäuser, or in short ERWEGE. Every other week members met to figure out their purchase needs, and their bundled purchase orders were handed over to representatives of suppliers who also attended those meetings.

Just before Christmas 1921, on December 22, representatives from 28 retail businesses founded the ERWEGE Großeinkaufsgenossenschaft e.G.m.b.H., a limited liability purchasing cooperative based in Düsseldorf. Their members came from a variety of retail businesses: small crafts-based businesses with their own corner shop and origins stretching back to the second half of the 18th century; pure retail businesses founded primarily in the middle of the 19th century; and retail businesses founded in the 20th century, planned from the very beginning more like department stores but without the long tradition of a Kaufhof, Karstadt, or Hertie, already well known German department stores founded in the 1880s. ERWEGE's first official member directory listed 76 member firms.

The 1920s and 1930s saw ERWEGE thrive. New members from all over Germany joined the organization, and its headquarters moved several times into more spacious offices with more exhibition space for product samples. In areas with many producers of hardware products, ERWEGE hired representatives to work with suppliers, negotiate favorable conditions, and place orders. Beginning in the 1930s, ERWEGE expanded its product range into new areas besides the traditional household goods. By 1937 it included products made from glass, china, porcelain, ceramic, leather, and metal; accessories and luxurious goods; toys; home interior products such as rugs, window coverings, linen, and other home textiles; clothing; and food.

The growing product range could not be managed in the old ways. While purchasing offices in Düsseldorf continued to manage the hardware and grocery areas, new central purchasing houses were set up. In 1931 a new purchasing house for textiles was opened in Berlin, and by 1939 there were 12 central ERWEGE offices in place. They had also replaced the old system of supplier representatives.

In addition to expanding its product range, ERWEGE took on new responsibilities for its members, assisting members with advertising, setting up balance sheets at the end of the business year, and offering group insurance. In 1934 ERWEGE expanded into warehousing. A new subsidiary, the Groß-Impex Großhandels Im- und Export GmbH, based in Berlin, was founded to handle this business.

After the Nazis came to power, ERWEGE's marketplace became more and more restrictive. New laws were passed to put the German economy under Nazi control and prepare the country for a war. Production of household goods and kitchen appliances made from iron or steel was restricted. In 1938 a new law was passed aimed at excluding Jews from all business activities; thus Jews were no longer allowed to be members of a cooperative, and ERWEGE lost about 40 members. Some 20 new Austrian members joined through the new office in Vienna after Germany incorporated Austria in 1938.

Two key decisions made it possible for ERWEGE to survive World War II. First, its decentralized purchasing offices made it easier to secure supplies in times of scarcity. Second, a central fund for future investments in new equipment was set up in 1939. During the war ERWEGE's headquarters and some purchasing houses were completely destroyed.

Becoming a Full Service Agency: 1946–64

In the reconstruction years after World War II ERWEGE became one of 20 major dealers in the newly founded German state of North Rhine-Westphalia, responsible for trading textiles from American army supplies. Due largely to this fact, the cooperative was able to balance out losses caused by the war within only two years. In January 1948 ERWEGE members decided at their annual meeting to give the organization a name more oriented toward the future, one that expressed its purpose. On July 27, 1948 it was officially registered under its new name

Kaufring Gemeinschaftskauf GmbH, loosely translated as "purchasing circle." Kaufring was also registered as a trademark. That same year, a new subsidiary responsible for coordinating advertising activities for Kaufring members was founded in Frankfurt/Main.

The currency reform in the three West German zones on June 20, 1948, marked a new beginning for businesses there. For the first time since the war had ended it was possible to buy goods for cash, following years of scarcity from rationing systems. Soon after the currency reform the first retail trade shows were held again. The first Kaufring textile inspection was held in April 1949. During 1949 and 1950 a new Kaufring building was erected in Düsseldorf which accommodated 29 central purchasing departments, including the ones formerly located in Berlin.

Kaufring greatly benefited from the Germans' increasing thirst for consumer goods during the 1950s. Within ten years, the number of Kaufring members almost doubled, from 250 in 1950 to about 480 a decade later. In fiscal year 1952–53, Kaufring for the first time grossed over DM 300 million, a market share of one percent. In 1961–62 the company passed the DM 1 billion mark for the first time and achieved a respectable third place in Germany's market for consumer goods, succeeded only by two large department store chains. New products were stocked by Kaufring, such as baby products, children's clothing, fashion accessories, auto supplies, and do-it-yourself products. Such volume could only be managed by expanding Kaufring's capabilities. Four new purchasing houses—for knitwear, toys, porcelain, and small furniture—were set up by 1960.

Through this dynamic growth, Kaufring continued to be a member-driven cooperative. Kaufring members were involved in decision making and purchasing politics in different ways. A board of directors was installed after a new law regulating cooperatives was enacted in West Germany in the early 1960s. Another institution was an already-existing committee, members of which worked together in sub-committees specializing in such fields as textiles, hardware, food, or advertising. Kaufring's so-called "Chefs' Conversations at the Round Table" were held for the first time in 1964 in all West German regions, while "Kaufring-Junior Circles" provided a forum for junior managers of member businesses.

In 1956 and again in 1961 Kaufring sent groups of delegates on business trips to the United States to study new developments in the retail industry first-hand. As a result, the first self-service shop for textiles within a German department store was opened at a Kaufring member's site, as were the first two full-fledged self-service housewares departments. Also beginning in the mid-1950s, import and export became more important again, and prewar connections to foreign business partners were reestablished. In 1964 Kaufring's subsidiary Groß-Impex imported products from 23 countries around the world, and new purchasing houses were set up in New York, Tokyo, and Hong Kong. Among Kaufring's first non-German members were the by then independent office in Vienna and the biggest and most modern department store in Persia. To intensify and oversee its international activities, Kaufring founded a new subsidiary, Kaufring International GmbH, in December 1964.

Key Dates:

1921: 28 retailers found the purchasing cooperative ERWEGE in Düsseldorf.
1931: ERWEGE significantly expands its product range and attracts department and textiles stores as members.
1948: The cooperative is renamed Kaufring eGmbH.
1950: Kaufring starts offering other professional services to its members.
1968: Foreign offices in Paris, Milan, Vienna, London, Barcelona, Hong Kong, Tokyo, and New York are established.
1977: Kaufring members get wired with the electronic data processing center in Düsseldorf.
1983: Competitor Grohag GmbH is acquired.
1988: Kaufring goes public.
1995: The company expands into retail business.
1999: A fundamental restructuring program focusing on Kaufring's core business is undertaken.

By this time it had become clear that the mere bundling of purchasing power was not enough to sustain Kaufring's success over the long term. Prewar services such as advertising, accounting, and insurance services were offered again, and Kaufring continually expanded into new areas to serve its member firms, becoming a full-service agency for independent retail businesses. Kaufring consulted its members on architecture and interior design, business administration and database management, and import and export issues. Beginning in 1964 the company offered decorating services and developed training programs for sales personnel and other staff.

Cooperation and Acquisitions: 1965–87

In the second half of the 1960s Kaufring introduced its electronic data processing services. Its first central computer was installed at the Düsseldorf headquarters in 1965. Only eight years later, 119 Kaufring members were using its central electronic accounting system; 121 members used a product tracking program; and 102 members were connected with Kaufring's electronic payroll system. Again Kaufring grew too big for its headquarters. A new piece of real estate was bought from the city of Düsseldorf in a special deal. In exchange for Kaufring's new 120,000 square meter location near the Düsseldorf Airport, the city took over Kaufring's old office building and paid Kaufring an extra sum for the lucrative inner-city property. By 1968 all Kaufring departments had moved into the brand-new office building. Although the new facilities were generously planned in the first place, exhibition halls and warehouses grew too small again and were continuously enlarged during the 1970s.

The 1970s marked a turnaround in Germany's economic climate. The world economy moved into a period of recession, consumer spending in department stores began to decrease, rising wages and oil prices pushed costs up, and the new hypermarkets took business from traditional retail stores. To stay competitive, Kaufring members decided at their 1970 general meeting to work even closer together and to take measures to adapt their organization to the new marketplace. Kaufring moved into a period of cooperation and acquisition activities.

For the first time in its history Kaufring started cooperating with other big organizations. In September 1971 the company entered an agreement of cooperation with Neckermann und Reisen (NUR), a major German player in the travel business, and started selling standardized travel packages at 25 selected member locations. Kaufring also started to cooperate with Europe's two biggest food wholesalers, the German cooperatives EDEKA and REWE. By 1980 Kaufring was working with a total of nine regional cooperatives and wholesalers. As a result the company withdrew step by step from warehousing food products until 1984 when the only product group Kaufring carried was candy.

In January 1983 Kaufring had the rare chance to get rid of its only competitor in the German market of mid-sized independent department and specialty stores. At that time the Grohag GmbH had 248 member firms with 450 stores and grossed approximately DM 500 million annually. In comparison, Kaufring's 650 members were generating over DM 1.5 billion per year in retail sales. In a one-of-a-kind deal Kaufring took over Grohag by depositing DM 20 million as liquid asset capital. The deal also included the takeover of Grohag's Swiss subsidiary Alexia Holding AG. However, soon after the takeover, problems arose between Kaufring and Grohag members who were doing business in the same territory. Consequently, by December 31, 1985, Kaufring ceased all Grohag business activities. Some 51 former Grohag members with around DM 300 million in sales decided to join Kaufring.

In addition to these activities, Kaufring continuously worked on improving its member services and business organization throughout the 1970s and 1980s. In the early 1970s, an incentive system was introduced to increase product purchases by Kaufring members. Kaufring-Kaufhaus-Projektgesellschaft (KKP), a new subsidiary that established and managed new department stores in under-represented territories, was established in 1975. In 1971 Kaufring launched a national image campaign that increased its recognition level among consumers from five percent in 1971 up to 24 percent three years later. Moreover, the product range sold under the Kaufring brand name was significantly expanded. In the mid-1960s it included about 630 articles. A decade later, over 2,000 products carried the Kaufring trademark, and by 1978 that number had more than doubled again. All of Kaufring's traditional purchasing houses had closed by 1982. At the same time, the company expanded its international activities and in 1983 founded Kaufring Far East Ltd. in Hong Kong. A new Kaufring service offered human resources consulting. Kaufring also subsidized advertising and large investments for its members. A new logistics scheme was developed that bundled in-going and outgoing product streams through 13 regional shippers, and a new state-of-the art warehouse complex was completed by 1987. In 1985, member retailers purchased 82 percent of their inventory from Kaufring.

Going Public and Subsequent Challenges: 1988–99

At a general meeting of Kaufring members in June 1988, 98.3 percent of all votes were in favor of transforming the cooperative into a public company. On October 20, 1988, Kaufring AG was officially registered in Düsseldorf. All former members of the cooperative signed agreements to turn their business over to the new company; they were given shares in the new enterprise in exchange for their shares in the cooperative. However, they secured their exclusive influence in the business by not publicly offering any stock. Kaufring continued to be owned by the same shareholders until the company's initial public offering (IPO) in October 1991.

The new corporate format made it easier to look for new potential business partners. In 1989 Kaufring sold 25 percent of its share capital to the German retail group Horten AG, which was also based in Düsseldorf. In the same year the new partners founded a new purchasing subsidiary, the Merkur Einkaufsgesellschaft HORTEN-Kaufring mbH in which each partner held 50 percent. In the following year Kaufring invested with Horten and Hertie, two other major German retail groups, in the Sono Centra Trading Ltd., based in Hong Kong and active in the Asian market. After those partners sold their shares in the mid-1990s, Kaufring would hold 100 percent interest in the company until mid-1996, when it found two new partners—Katag AG and EK Grosseinkaur—based in Bielefeld, which each took over a 15 percent interest in Sono Centra.

Three main factors prompted Kaufring's decision to expand into retail trade. First, the new market was expected to bring in more revenue. Second, Kaufring locations that were given up by shareholders and members could be used to avoid a meltdown in membership. Finally, the unexpected reintegration of East Germany into the domestic market opened up a once in a lifetime chance to win market share quickly by taking over businesses there. However, this endeavor turned out to be an unfortunate one for Kaufring and put the company into serious trouble in the latter half of the 1990s. In 1995, one year before Kaufring turned 75, its annual sales passed the DM 3 billion mark, and for the first time in its history the company showed a net loss. In the following years, its business stagnated and revenues decreased continuously. To stop this development and to win new customers, Kaufring purchased a 49 percent share in the Nuremberg-based Nürnberg Bund Handels GmbH (NBH). However, Kaufring went into the red again in 1998, partly because the inventory taken over from NBH caused immense extra costs. In August 1999 Kaufring's finances were no longer liquid after it failed to acquire additional short-term credit. Bad came to worse when several suppliers canceled their provision

agreements with Kaufring. This in turn made Kaufring customers nervous; many of them financed their purchases with bills of exchange issued by the Kaufring headquarters, and these would be worthless if Kaufring had to file bankruptcy. Consequently, many Kaufring customers began looking for other suppliers.

A radical restructuring program was enacted that year, aimed at selling off all retail businesses and concentrating on Kaufring's core competencies. In spring 2000 the company expected that the program would diminish Kaufring's sales by about one-third and its workforce by 3,000 or about 80 percent. Despite an expected loss of about DM 110 million, the company maintained that it would be able to pay all extra costs from its own reserves and might even be able to pay a dividend in 2001.

Principal Subsidiaries

Kaufring Logistik GmbH; J.Gg. Rupprecht GmbH; Kaufhaus Moses GmbH; Innosys Vertriebsgesellschaft für Handelssysteme mbH; WEKA-Kaufring Kaufhaus GmbH; Nürnberger Bund Handelsgesellschaft mbH; Merkur Einkaufsgesellschaft Kaufring-WOOLWORTH mbH (50%); Planungsring GmbH; Kaufring Handelsbeteiligungs- und Verwaltungsgesellschaft mbH; KVV KONZIS Versicherungs-Vermittlungs-Gesellschaft mbH.

Principal Competitors

Metro AG; Aldi Einkauf GmbH & Co. KG; Spar Handels AG.

Further Reading

"Beim Kaufring brennt es lichterloh," *Lebensmittel Zeitung*, August 6, 1999, p. 6.
"Der Kaufring ist 75 Jahre alt geworden," *Frankfurter Allgemeine Zeitung*, October 7, 1996, p. 24.
Kaufring: Europas größter Verbund selbständiger Kaufhäuser und Fachgeschäfte, Cologne: EuroHandelsinstitut e. V., 1998, 69 p.
"Kaufring sieht wieder Land," *Süddeutsche Zeitung*, March 10, 2000, p. 30.
Maderner, Stephan "Das Ringen um den Kaufring," *TextilWirtschaft*, August 12, 1999, p. 52.
"75 Jahre Kaufring," *Markt + Marke*, Düsseldorf, Germany: Kaufring AG, 1996, 303 p.

—Evelyn Hauser

KB Toys

300 Phillipi Road
Columbus, Ohio 43228-0512
U.S.A.
Telephone: (413) 499-0086
Fax: (413) 499-3739
Web site: http://www.KBkids.com, www.cnstores.com

Division of Consolidated Stores Corporation
Incorporated: 1922
Sales: $1.8 billion (1999)
Employees: 16,000
NAIC: 45112 Hobby, Toy and Game Shops

KB Toys is the second-largest retailer of toys behind Toys 'R' Us and the largest mall retailer of toys in the United States. Unlike the giant free-standing outlets run by its major competitor, KB's chain consists of approximately 1,300 smaller mall-based toy stores in all 50 states, the American Territory of Guam, and the Commonwealth of Puerto Rico. KB stores carry brand name products along with stock from discontinued lines, which are sold at bargain prices at its KB Toys stores, KB Toy Works stores, KB Toy Outlet, KB Toy Express, and online at www.KBkids.com. Due to their smaller retail space, KB stores do not carry sporting goods, choosing instead to focus on video products, which account for 25 percent of overall sales. The company was purchased in 1996 by the retail conglomerate Consolidated Stores Corporation, a leading value retailer specializing in toys and closeout merchandise that also operates closeout stores under the names Odd Lots, Big Lots Furniture, Mac Frugal's, Close-Outs, and Pic 'N' Save.

From Candy Wholesaler to Toy Retailer

KB began as Kaufman Brothers when two brothers in Pittsfield, Massachusetts, opened a wholesale candy business in 1922. Kaufman Brothers provided retailers with candy and soda fountain supplies. The Kaufman brothers got into the toy business by accident. During the 1940s, they acquired a wholesale toy company from a previous client as payment for outstanding debts owed to Kaufman Brothers for purchased candy. It was an opportune moment for Kaufman Brothers to diversify because the cost of producing candy was prohibitive during World War II due to shortages of important ingredients, especially sugar. Kaufman Brothers assumed operation of the toy company, changing its name to Kay-Bee Toy & Hobby Stores. By 1948, the toy business was so much more successful than the confectionary business that the Kaufman brothers decided to focus their energies entirely on toys. Kaufman Brothers opened its first retail toy store in Connecticut in 1959.

It wasn't until 1973 that the Kaufman brothers, who still owned and operated the company, decided to move once and for all from wholesaling to retailing. They discontinued their wholesale business altogether and concentrated on their 26 retail stores. Suburban malls were popping up across the country, and the Kaufmans wanted to take advantage of the boom. By 1976, only three years after making the decision to focus solely on retail, Kay-Bee Toy & Hobby had more than doubled its number of stores from 26 to 65 across New England, New York, and New Jersey. One year later, in 1977, the company changed its name from Kay-Bee Toy & Hobby to Kay-Bee Toy and Hobby Shops, Inc., primarily to distinguish itself from competitors with initials in their names or logos. In 1981, when the company was operating 210 stores, it changed its name again, this time to Kay-Bee Toy Stores, reflecting a de-emphasis on hobby products. The company was purchased in 1981 by Melville Corporation. As a subsidiary of Melville, Kay-Bee acquired Toy World, with 52 stores, in 1982; Circus World, with 330 stores, in 1990; and K&K Toys, with 133 stores, in 1991. These three acquisitions moved Kay-Bee into the upper echelon of U.S. toy retailers.

Although Melville Corporation already had an impressive list of retail names as part of its corporate family before buying Kay-Bee Toys, the purchase price of $64.2 million represented the greatest expenditure that Melville had ever made. After the sale, Howard Kaufman remained president of Kay-Bee Toys, and the company's strategy remained essentially the same, exploiting the niche it had developed in malls.

The toy business itself went through enormous structural changes during the period of Kay-Bee's rise to prominence. The relationship between manufacturers and retailers became much

Company Perspectives:

The Company's goal is to build upon its leadership position in closeout retailing, a growing segment of the retailing industry, toy retailing and children's products by expanding its market presence in both existing and new markets.

closer, to the detriment of wholesalers, distributors, and smaller retailers. Many small retailers were driven out of business during the 1970s and 1980s; however, Kay-Bee was large enough and could buy in enough volume to compete with its major competitors. Kay-Bee could also take advantage of its long-standing policy of buying discontinued stock from manufacturers at a favorable rate and selling it at extremely reduced prices. Kay-Bee's strategy was to pack the entrance of its locations with these bargains to entice shoppers into the store. Once inside, managers reasoned, shoppers would be likely to purchase higher-end products that were priced more conservatively. In this way, Kay-Bee developed a very different strategy from most of its competitors. Kay-Bee's main competitors, Toys 'R' Us and Wal-Mart, were developed as free-standing stores that customers would make a conscious decision to visit with the intention of making purchases. Kay-Bee, on the other hand, realized that having its stores inside large malls meant that most of its customers probably came to the mall for some other reason, and that Kay-Bee needed to draw this mall traffic in. An important part of this plan was store design. All Kay-Bee outlets were designed with bright, eye-catching colors at the front of the store along with neatly arranged stacks of toys at bargain prices.

Kay-Bee's corporate image was just as bright and wholesome as the look of its stores, with the company's public relations philosophy emphasizing family values as much as value for dollars. In 1994, Kay-Bee developed the program Prescribe Reading Early to Kids (Pre-K) to help foster literacy in disadvantaged families, providing grants and free books to the program, which was organized in conjunction with local health care and community organizations. Kay-Bee was also sensitive to issues of violence in children's toys. In 1993, Kay-Bee withdrew the Sega product Night Trap, which was controversial for its violence, despite the fact that Kay-Bee had a close relationship with Sega of America and that video sales were one of Kay-Bee's most important sectors.

Kay-Bee chairman and CEO Ann Iverson took a strong stand against violence when she removed all realistic toy guns from Kay-Bee's stores in 1994. This decision was prompted by an incident earlier that year in New York City in which a 13-year-old boy was shot and killed by a policeman who mistook his toy weapon for the real thing. Almost 300,000 toy weapons were incinerated as a result of Iverson's decision, constituting an undetermined loss in revenue for Kay-Bee Toys, but producing enough electricity to light 48 homes for a month. The company also participated in New York's "Goods for Guns" program, which offered gift certificates to people who surrendered real firearms. Although Ann Iverson left as chairman in 1994, her policy of not selling look-alike guns was continued by

her successor, Alan Fine, who had been senior vice-president before becoming president and CEO.

Restructuring in the Early 1990s

In the early 1990s Kay-Bee began a major restructuring process that paralleled that of many other subsidiaries in the Melville Corporation group. Kay-Bee closed nearly 250 less-profitable stores from 1993 to 1994 in what the company described as a strategic realignment program. While Kay-Bee also opened some new, bigger stores during the same period, the chain nevertheless suffered somewhat in overall sales due to the dramatic number of store closings. After having reached the $1 billion mark in 1990, the company fell below that level for the year 1993 with sales of $919,054. The realignment was well managed, however, and, by 1994, the company was back to $1.01 billion in net sales, despite continued store closings.

However, mall construction in the United States slowed during the early 1990s, and Kay-Bee was finding no attractive new malls in need of its outlet. For this reason, Kay-Bee decided to launch a new string of free-standing stores in 1994, under the name Toy Works. Each of the approximately 75 Toy Works stores had a race course design with colorful markings and category signage to guide shoppers through the wide aisles of stores averaging 15,000 square feet. Kay-Bee hoped to differentiate itself from competitor Toys 'R' Us with this distinctive store design as well as by focusing on improved customer service. At the same time, Kay-Bee began expanding some of its mall-based stores from an average of 3,500 square feet to 5,000 square feet. The bigger stores sold an expanded product line, including sporting goods and toys for adults.

The decision to move into free-standing stores, enlarge floor space, and broaden the product line put Kay-Bee in direct competition with Toys 'R' Us for the first time. Additional competition came from the large discount chains, such as Wal-Mart, Kmart, and Target, which in 1995, grabbed 40 percent of the U.S. toy market. Nevertheless, in 1996 Kay-Bee stores managed to increase sales by 6.4 percent over the previous year, to $1.1 billion.

Joining Consolidated in 1996

In 1996, after an aborted attempt in 1995 to spin off Kay-Bee Toys, the Melville Corporation decided to sell the chain of 1,045 stores to Consolidated Stores Corporation for about $300 million. Consolidated already operated Toys Liquidators, Toys Unlimited, and the Amazing Toy Store close-out stores, as well as general retailers Odd Lots, Big Lots, All for One, and the It's Really $1.00 stores. William Kelley, chief executive officer and chairman of Consolidated's board, said in a *New York Times* article that he expected the combined businesses to offer "a great deal of synergy." Kay-Bee, under the direction of president Michael Glazer, continued to be run as a separate business within Consolidated's new Toy Division despite talk of its merging with their Toy Liquidators chain. Immediately after the sale, the stock of Consolidated surged upward.

Kay-Bee provided a 50 percent return on Consolidated's investment in its first nine months of new ownership. In 1997, Kay-Bee's sales boosted Consolidated's revenue by about 70

Key Dates:

1922: The Kaufman brothers open a wholesale candy business.

1948: The brothers exit the candy business to focus exclusively on their toy stores.

1959: Kaufman Brothers opens its first retail toy store in Connecticut.

1973: The company moves from wholesaling to retailing toys, calling itself Kay-Bee Toy & Hobby.

1981: The company is purchased by Melville Corporation, and becomes a division known as Kay-Bee Toy Stores.

1994: Company launches a new string of free-standing stores under the name Toy Works.

1996: The Melville Corporation sells the chain to Consolidated Stores Corporation.

1998: KBkids.com is started to market KB merchandise online.

percent after the chain achieved double-digit sales growth during the 1996 Christmas season. The chain closed out fiscal 1997, the best year in the company's history, with a ten percent comparable store gain over 1996. In order to meet growing supply needs, Kay-Bee automated its distribution centers and installed a new client/server-based planning system.

Glazer, quoted in *Discount Stores News* in July 1997, attributed the chain's outstanding performance to closing underperforming stores and writing off lots of obsolete inventory prior to the sale to Consolidated. Consolidated also established a specific identity for the 1,200 stores and brushed up the chain's image with a new logo, KB. It integrated Kay-Bee with its core close-out business, and was boosting the chain's higher-margin close-out items from 25 to about 30 percent of its business.

By 1998, KB had annual sales of $1.6 million despite a somewhat difficult year in the toy industry. To combat the slowing trend, KB came up with some creative merchandising alternatives, such as working closely with vendors on promotions and preselling select toys in hot demand. The following June, Consolidated's Toy Division announced the formation of a new subsidiary developed in partnership with BrainPlay.com. KBkids.com LLC took advantage of the well-established KB brand name to launch its online retail business offering toys, video games, software, and videos. That fall, KBkids.com entered into a major partnership agreement with America Online,

Inc., which provided the web toy business access as one of the premier toy retailers featured on AOL. In 1999, KBkids.com received top points from an e-commerce market research firm, the Gomez Advisors, in the categories of customer confidence, overall cost, and bargain shopping. *Softletter* named the site one of the "Ten Best Online Software Stores of 1999" in its October 15th issue. Even the *Wall Street Journal* dubbed the site the "best overall" online toy retailer. In a little more than four months online, KBkids.com increased its business more than 400 percent and twice ranked among the five biggest gainers on the NextCard eCommerce Movers index.

It seemed nothing could stop KB Toys from challenging its rivals in the toy industry. Operating profit for 1999 was up 51 percent from 1998. The company, seeking to capitalize on its growth, decided to hold an initial public offering in the spring of 2000, then postponed trading due to unfavorable market conditions. Notwithstanding this delay, KB was more focused than ever on fine-tuning its position in the very fashion-forward toy industry. With relatively small stores and a knack for innovation and creativity in marketing, KB was ready as ever to make quick adjustments to changing customer and merchandise trends.

Principal Competitors

Toys 'R' Us, Inc.; F.A.O. Schwartz; Wal-Mart Stores, Inc.

Further Reading

Blanton, Kimberly, "Kay-Bee Stores Buy Southern Toy Retailer," *Boston Globe,* September 5, 1991, p. 52.

Daly, Christopher B., "Toy Weapons Will Be Incinerated to Make Electricity, Retailer Says," *Washington Post,* November 9, 1994, p. A5.

Johnson, Jay L., "Face to Face . . . with William G. Kelly," *Discount Merchandiser,* July 1996, p.14.

Liebeck, Laura, "From Kay-Bee to KB, New Image and Focus Revive Chain," *Discount Store News,* July 21, 1997, p. 29.

Mehegan, David, "A Berkshire Toy Empire," *Boston Globe,* October 9, 1990, p. 41.

Neuborn, Ellen, "Melville to Close, Change Some Stores," *USA Today,* December 12, 1992, p. B1.

Stern, Sydney Ladensohn, and Ted Schoenhaus, *Toyland: The High Stakes Game of the Toy Industry,* Chicago: Contemporary Books, 1990, pp. 280–81.

"Toy Retailer Meets Demand with New Conveyor System," *Material Handling Engineering,* October 1996, p.112.

Walters, Donna K. H., "Masters of the Toy Universe," *Los Angeles Times,* September 2, 1993, p. D1.

—Hilary Gopnik and Donald McManus
—updated by Carrie Rothburd

König Brauerei GmbH & Co. KG

Friedrich-Ebert-Strasse 255-263
D-47139 Duisburg
Germany
Telephone: (49) (203) 455-0
Fax: (49) (203) 455-2515
Web site: http://www.koenig.de

Wholly Owned Subsidiary of Holsten Brauerei AG
Incorporated: 1858 as Bayrische Bierbrauerei Theodor
    König
Employees: 400
Sales: DM 350 million ($180 million) (1999)
NAIC: 31212 Breweries

König Brauerei GmbH & Co. KG is one of Germany's large breweries, and, with a profit-to-sales ratio of over five percent, one of the most profitable ones. König Brauerei's König Pilsener and alcohol-free Kelts are among Germany's best known national beer brands. In a shrinking German beer market, König Brauerei invests about DM 50 million or 15 percent of its total sales in advertising. A family business for 142 years König Brauerei was acquired by the Hamburg-based Holsten brewery in early 2000.

Theodor König Founds a Brewery in 1858

Theodor König, the founder of König Brauerei, was born into a wealthy farming family that owned a large estate in Münsterland, in western Germany. He grew up on the family farm and as a boy paid visits to the brewery at a nearby castle. After his military service, the young man worked on a large farm for two years, which also ran a small brewery. Realizing that he was more interested in beer brewing than in farming, König decided to learn the craft from scratch where the best beer was made. At age 25, he began his life as a journeyman, which lasted five years and took him to Munich, the capital of beer brewing at the time, and then to Vienna, where he learned about the Pilsener beers being brewed in Bohemia.

Around 1855 Theodor König returned as an experienced beer brewer. The first job he took was at a local brewery in

Beeck, a small town in the lower Rhine region. At the time an idyllic setting located on the Emscher river, Beeck was soon to become one of Germany's newest industrial centers. In 1856 König purchased a piece of property on Beeck's main thoroughfare and started working on his dream of a brewery of his own. He set up a brick factory at another site and thus, when he was finally granted a brewing concession in 1858, part of his brewery had already been built. The Bayrische Bierbrauerei Theodor König sold its first beer in its own beer hall, a public room that every brewery at that time had. In the first years Theodor König invited his brother Franz, who was also a brewer, to help him set up the business. König's beer hall soon became popular among the workers from nearby factories.

Within a short period of time, Beeck and the surrounding region developed into an important industrial center of the emerging coal, iron, and steel industries. König started delivering his beer to the neighboring towns. German industrialist August Thyssen was a frequent visitor to König's brewery and consulted him about real estate he was planning to buy for new mining sites. In the end, Thyssen persuaded König to sell him his own property—his brick factory in Alsum and a farm and restaurant in Hamborn—which Thyssen developed into one of Europe's largest iron and steel makers, the August Thyssen-Hütte AG.

Meanwhile, for König, sales went up almost steadily, interrupted only by the wars in 1866 and 1870. König expanded and modernized the brewery to keep up with growing demand. In 1888 the first steam engine to power a cooling unit went into operation at the brewery. In 1891 founder Theodor König died at age 66. By that time, beer production volume had increased three-fold over the past ten years, and was at some 70 times the brewery's output during its first year of operation.

The Second Generation Takes Over in 1891

After Theodor König's death, his oldest sons Leo and Hermann König took over the business. Because of the uninterrupted industrial growth that was drawing more and more people into the region, the brewery and its beer production continued to expand at a rapid pace. Given increased demands for new equipment as well as compensation for Theodor König's other heirs, the business was transformed into a public company in 1899. In 1900

Company Perspectives:

The Duisburg-based König Brauerei, with its premium beer König Pilsener and the alcohol-free Pilsener Kelts, is one of the most successful of German breweries. The company, founded in 1858, and the slogan, "Heute ein König" (Today a king), have become well-known far beyond Germany's borders.

beer output reached 50,000 hectoliters (hl) for the first time. (One hectoliter equals about 26.5 gallons.) The only factor that dampened growth was a growing anti-alcohol movement of the time. In 1906 a new steam-powered generator and cooling facility replaced the old one; in 1912 the old brewing tanks were replaced by aluminum and steel tanks. The first delivery automobile was also purchased around this time.

In the first decade of the 20th century, consumer taste in beer began to change. The more well-off beer consumers, in particular, began to shift from heavy, bottom fermenting beers to the lighter Pilsener, which contained more hops. Around 1911 König Brauerei began developing a new specialty beer under the name König Pilsener, which soon became exceedingly popular. When World War I broke out in August 1914, however, the brewery suffered a serious setback. During the war, supplies of raw materials, such as barley, malt, and hops, were rationed by the government. The "war beer" brewed in 1917 contained so little hops and malt that the final product hardly tasted like beer at all. The war was followed by hyperinflation which was finally ended by a currency reform in 1924. During those turbulent times, in autumn 1921, the third generation of the König family first entered the company's management. In 1925 Max König, son of Hermann König, and Leo König's son, Richard, took over the family business.

Expansion in the 1920s

After World War I and the economic depression that followed, the two König brands—König Export and König Pilsener—started regaining their prewar popularity. To take advantage of the trend and to make the company more crisis-proof, the management decided to expand beyond its regional market. The first long-distance König customers were attracted in Cologne and Dusseldorf in 1924 and 1925. Soon thereafter, the König brand became well known throughout all of the Rhineland. The brewery's efficiency was greatly assisted by new delivery trucks, which replaced older horse-drawn wagons. However, König Brauerei limited the area in which the company's own trucks would deliver, so more distant customers traveled to purchase beer directly from the König brewery. The widening demand called for new investments and modernization. In addition to building new production facilities, the company also bought up neighboring real estate. By 1929 the König distributorship network had greatly expanded; more than 100,000 hl of beer left the brewery that year. In 1934 the last wooden keg and the last horses left the brewery.

In 1929 the Great Depression began, spreading from New York City around the world. The industrial region around Duisburg went into a sudden economic downturn, forcing numerous businesses and factories, big and small, to close down. Many citizens lost their jobs, and in 1932 about half of all Duisburg inhabitants subsisted on welfare. At the brewery alone, the workforce was cut in half, as was the output of König beer. As if this were not enough to contend with, the German government increased the beer tax by 46 percent in 1930 and two years later required all breweries to significantly cut beer prices. König Brauerei reacted with a strict cost cutting program as well as a successful expansion into the Netherlands and Belgium. The economy began recovering in 1934 and by 1938, when beer output once again passed 100,000 hl, König Brauerei had become a leading German brewery. In 1937 König Brauerei was transformed into a private company again to preserve its character as a family business. Its new name was König Brauerei K.G. which was managed by Max and Richard König.

The outbreak of World War II in September 1939 brought a lot of soldiers to western Germany, and König beer consumption increased. On the other hand, malt became scarce again. König's master brewer Schüler started experimenting with new ingredients around 1941, discovering that *molke*, a byproduct of dairy factories, could be used as a replacement for malt. The resultant new "war beer" made with *molke* became a bestseller and pushed output up to 170,000 hl. Also during this time, other breweries having transportation or production difficulties began contracting with König Brauerei to serve their Duisburg-based customers. At the same time, 22 subcontracting breweries brewed König "war beer" for distant customers. However, when the war reached inside the borders of Germany, the horizon darkened for König Brauerei. Between October and December 1944 the majority of its production buildings were destroyed in bombing raids. An office was established in the Mühlheim Forest to administer subcontractors and clearing out the wreckage started immediately.

When the American military arrived in Beeck at Easter 1945, a large portion of the rubble was already gone. After the war the company management decided that instead of rebuilding the old facilities it would invest in a completely new state-of-the-art brewery that would significantly increase production capacity and the company's economic efficiency. In the first years after the war, when food was rationed and unavailable, König Brauerei began providing its employees with meals prepared on the company premises from food that was bartered for beer. In February 1946 the first postwar "beer-like beverage" left the König Brauerei. Soon the old König customers could be served again. However, it took until 1948 before the last subcontracts serving far away König customers could be canceled. In the same year a new currency was introduced in West Germany and the economy began to pick up speed again. New wholesale and hospitality customers were added to the existing network of 28 König dealers. Substantial advertising campaigns also promoted sales of König Pilsener. New customers were won all over Germany, and in 1958, the year of König's 100th anniversary, beer output reached 500,000 hl for the first time.

A National Brand in the 1960s

A marketing coup occurred at König Brauerei in the 1960s, as the company attempted to position König Pilsener as a premium quality beer throughout Germany to create a basis for further growth. In theory, marketing beer to Germans was not difficult. In the mid-1960s, beer was a favorite beverage among the German population; they consumed 120 liters of it per capita per year.

Key Dates:

1858: König Brauerei is founded by Theodor König.
1899: The brewery is transformed into a public company.
1911: Brewing of König Pilsener begins.
1924: Brewery expands its reach beyond regional borders.
1937: König Brauerei becomes a private limited liability company.
1944: The brewery is destroyed during bombings.
1967: Output reaches one million hectoliters per year.
1970: König Pilsener becomes a national brand.
1989: The company is transformed into König Brauerei GmbH & Co. KG, and alcohol-free Kelts brand is introduced.
2000: Holsten Brauerei AG acquires majority share in König Brauerei.

Moreover, König Brauerei was at that time West Germany's largest private brewery and was already distributing its beer brands nationally. However, the German beer market was a regional one, and local brands had fiercely loyal followings.

Under the management of Leo König, who had studied business as well as brewing, and his cousin Renate König, the company employed a young ad agency called "Team" to develop a new ad campaign for König Pilsener. On the national level the campaign was aimed at image building, while on a regional level its main purpose was the "hard sell." Team was not happy with the DM 500,000 budget, which was rather lean for a national campaign. However, they decided to take up the challenge.

As the story goes, when young creative Team member Jürgen Scholz visited his client he was surprised by the many happy-faced, good-looking people he saw in the König Brauerei. Asked about this, Leo König declared that in his brewery everybody was happy and "König-treu", that is loyal to the company. This statement became the basis for the brewery's new image campaign. While most other breweries used the taste of their beers as their unique selling proposition, the new König Pilsener campaign sold the experience, tradition, integrity, and joy of the people working for König. The photos used in the advertising campaign were taken in the brewery and showed scenes of the day-to-day business of brewing beer, using the real brewmasters in their traditional work clothes. The ad copy covered themes from the König world, including the German purity law, the importance of tradition, and the beer's taste. Later, popular German politicians and artists gave their testimonials to the beer in ad campaigns as well. With an initial run in two of Germany's major magazines, the campaign was very successful, especially in persuading more upscale restaurants and bars to carry König Pilsener as a specialty beer. By the beginning of the 1970s, the German beer landscape had changed completely; the national brands led the market.

Alcohol-Free Alternatives in the 1990s

In the late 1980s König Brauerei responded to a new trend worldwide—the demand for "light" products—and created an alcohol-free beer called Kelts. To combat the market research showing that alcohol-free beer drinkers were "party poopers," the brewery launched several promotion campaigns using hu-

mor as their main selling point, one of which featured two comic policeman characters, known as The Kelts-Control, who hung out in popular bars. The company considered the campaigns a success and noted that they resulted in more orders from the hospitality industry.

In 1992 Leo and Renate König retired, and a new four-person management team was put into place. Leo König had managed the brewery for some 25 years, during which time total sales at the König Brauerei jumped by 375 percent, from DM 87 million to DM 326 million. During the same time period its beer output increased by 240 percent from one million to 2.4 million hl per year. Most importantly, König Pilsener had been established as one of the best-known and most successful German premium beer brands. One of the new managers was Leo König's daughter, Doris König, at that time 37 years of age, who took over responsibility for marketing. In 1991 König Brauerei spent about 6.5 percent of its total sales on advertising. About two-thirds of this budget was spent on König Pilsener and one-third on KELTS.

In the late 1990s consolidation was speeding up in the shrinking German beer market and higher investments were needed to keep pace with the competition. An Arthur Anderson study on the future of the brewery industry in Germany projected that per-capita beer consumption would drop by one-fifth within ten years. Other projections suggested that only one-third of Germany's 1,283 breweries would be able to survive the increasing process of concentration. König Brauerei's management decided to team up with a strong partner in order to secure the long-term future of the business. In February 2000 König Brauerei gave up its independence when it was sold to Hamburg-based Holsten Brauerei AG. The two companies were a perfect match; while König Pilsener was mainly distributed in northern and western Germany and the bulk of its customers came from the hospitality industry, Holsten's market was mainly Germany's North and East as well as the retail market. As planned, all König brands would be continued and marketed independently by König Brauerei.

Principal Subsidiaries

König Brauerei Verwaltungs GmbH; topGast Gesellschaft für Gastronomieberatung mbH; Vortmann GmbH & Co. KG.

Principal Competitors

Dortmunder Actien Brauerei AG; Warsteiner Brauerei Haus Cramer GmbH & Co. KG; Brauerei Veltins; Binding Brauerei AG; Brauerei Beck & Co.

Further Reading

Bott, Hermann, "Eine Frage der Zeit," *Spiegel*, January 24, 2000, p. 92.
Drohner, Klaus, "Holsten überrascht die Bier-Branche mit König-Deal," Lebensmittel Zeitung, January 21, 2000, p. 12.
"Kelts: Imagewandel mit Humor," *HORIZONT*, October 15, 1993, p. 18.
Latz-Weber, Herbert, "Brauer brauchen starke Marken," *Werben und Verkaufen*, September 2, 1994, p.58.
Leogrande, Joern, "Bilder aus der täglichen Brauarbeit," *Werben und Verkaufen*, May 30, 1997, p. 154.
"Leo König zieht sich in Verwaltungsrat zurück," *HORIZONT*, October 9, 1992, p. 9.

—Evelyn Hauser

Krause Publications, Inc.

700 East State Street
Iola, Wisconsin 54990-0001
U.S.A.
Telephone: (715) 445-2214
Fax: (715) 445-4087
Web site: http://www.krause.com

Private Company
Incorporated: 1964
Employees: 570
Sales: $87.8 million (1999)
NAIC: 51112 Periodical Publishers; 51113 Book
  Publishers

Krause Publications, Inc. an employee-owned enterprise, bills itself as ''the world's largest publisher of hobby periodicals and books.'' The company publishes and circulates 53 magazines and newspapers for special-interest enthusiasts, covering a wide variety of hobbies and trades, including antiques, arts and crafts, classic cars, coins and paper currency, comic books, fishing, guns, hunting, knives, sports memorabilia, stamps, and toys. On such topics, Krause has printed over 650 books, adding over 100 titles per year. In addition, it publishes serials on the rural construction trade and manages hobby shows. In 1999, in a partnership arrangement with eBay, it also began publishing the official eBay magazine. Although the company is headquartered in Iola, Wisconsin, the small rural town in which it was founded, its publications are printed at several different sites throughout the country. Krause maintains a very helpful web site that provides extensive information, including up-to-date news releases and job opportunities as well as information about its extensive publications.

1952–68: Unauspicious Origins Give Way to Necessary Diversification

Krause Publications certainly began humbly enough. Chester Lee (Chet) Krause, an Iola, Wisconsin, carpenter with an interest in coins and firearms, founded the company in the fall of 1952 when, at 27, he began issuing a newsletter entitled *Numismatic News*. Born in 1923 on his family's farm in nearby Helvetia, young Chet had become interested in collecting both stamps and coins while he was attending a one-room schoolhouse on property adjacent to his family's land. After a fire destroyed the farm in 1940, his parents moved the family to Iola. Krause lost his stamp collection in the fire but was able to save his coins.

During World War II, Krause served in the Army, returning home in 1946 to begin working as a carpenter, a trade he would continue to practice until 1957, when he gave it up to devote all his time to his new business. Before making the decision to go exclusively into publishing, Krause worked very hard to gain respectability for his first serial, *Numismatic News*. Initially, the publication consisted of a single page of newsprint printed by the local weekly newspaper. It was in part inspired by *Shotgun News*, a tabloid publication to which Krause then subscribed.

The first issue of *Numismatic News* bore an October 13, 1952 imprint date. For the next 18 months of his new publishing venture, Krause operated out of his house on Iola Street, where, with help from his mother, Cora, he put the work together on the kitchen table. At first it was a losing venture, leaving Krause down $1,342 in out-of-pocket expenses over the first year, but from that single page and mailing list of 600 readers he gradually turned the work into a competitive publication with a respectable number of both subscribers and advertisers.

In the early spring of 1953, Krause rented office space and hired his first employee, a clerk he shared with an insurance agent. *Numismatic News*, which would remain Krause's sole publication for seven more years, grew to 24 pages in 1954, and began turning a profit. Three years later, just before stopping work as a carpenter, Chet Krause constructed a new office building to house his growing operation.

Over the next few years, Krause developed *Numismatic News* into a very durable serial. He was doing well enough by 1961 that he was able to purchase another serial, *Coin Press*, from a publisher in New Jersey. Krause renamed it *Coins,* and in 1962 it first appeared under the new owner's imprimatur.

In the next year, Krause hired Clifford Mishler as associate editor of *Numismatic News*. The young man hailed from Vandalia, Michigan, which, like Iola, was also a small rural town, and like Krause, Mishler was an avid coin collector. He helped Krause expand the publication, which by 1964 had grown to an average issue length of 116 pages. However, just when prospects for greater expansion seemed very good, the company hit a temporary setback. In 1965, inexplicably, interest in coin collecting took a fairly drastic downturn, and the company's sales began to drop.

Although it survived and again began a forward surge by 1968, Chet Krause and his associates realized that diversification was needed. Until then, the entire focus of the company had been on coins minted in America. That was soon to change.

1968–89: Branching Out, Sustaining Strong and Steady Growth

In 1968, the first move towards diversification came when Krause and his staff decided to add book publication and world coins to the company's initial focus on U.S. coins. The result was the 1972 publication of the first edition of the *Standard Catalog of World Coins,* a cornerstone in Krause's book division. By then the company had already begun diversifying. In the fall of 1971, it had begun issuing a monthly tabloid called *Old Cars* and was considering other hobbies and interests suited to coverage in serials and books.

The physical expansion of Krause and the growth of its staff through both the 1970s and 1980s pretty much kept pace with its ever-increasing product line. Once committed to the idea that diversification was necessary to provide a solid buffer against the volatile interest swings of collectors and hobbyists, the company doggedly branched into new interest territories, even some that it suspected, like most fads, would have a limited life. During the same period, in addition to venturing into new fields with serials initiated in-house, Krause grew through the acquisition of existing publications.

In 1975, Krause Publications moved into its State Street plant, a 20,000 square foot facility accommodating the company's 60 employees. Over the next two decades, the plant had to be enlarged five times in order to house the much expanded operation and a workforce that by 1992 had grown to over 300. By the end of 1990s, Krause began further physical expansion scheduled for completion in September 2000.

In 1980, when it first expanded its plant, Krause began publishing a serial on baseball cards, first issued as *Baseball Cards* but later entitled *Sports Cards Magazine and Price Guide.* In the next year, the company purchased an existing serial named *Sports Collectors Digest.* This move into baseball cards and other sports memorabilia proved very timely, spurring sales rapidly upwards through the next dozen years. Still more diversification followed. In 1982, the company bought a publication devoted to comic books and in the next year an additional one on phonograph records.

Further expansion of Krause's operation came in tandem with its burgeoning hobby and trade periodicals and workforce. In 1987, with another plant enlargement, the company began publishing its first serial on firearms, followed by one on toys in 1988. Adding yet more space in 1989, Krause also began issuing works on the outdoors and rural construction.

In the 1980s, in an amicable arrangement, ownership and control of the company shifted from Chet Krause to his employees. A major move came in the fall of 1988, when the company established its Employee Stock Ownership Plan (ESOP). Under its terms, each employee who had worked at Krause for more than one year was credited with some stock, which, when retiring, the employee could sell back to the company. Over the next several years, the ESOP acquired all the stock.

1990s: New Fields, Including E-Commerce

In the 1990s, leadership of Krause Publications passed into the hands, first of president Clifford Mishler and then Roger Case, who succeeded Mishler as president in January 2000. Case had joined the company in 1988 as director of numismatic publications and within six years was named the firm's executive vice-president.

In 1992, the company estimated that about 45 percent of its overall business came from the nation's interest in collecting baseball cards, while coins and cars, the first focus areas of Krause product line accounted for about 15 percent of its sales. Further diversification was still in the works, however. The company started publishing serials on general collectibles in 1993. It added one on knives in 1994, stamps in 1996, and crafts in 1997. In 1996 and early 1997, through some important acquisitions, it also added substantially to its book line, bringing its total of books still in print to 600. First it acquired DBI Books, an Illinois publishing company that added about 50 new titles to Krause's book division line. Most of these dealt with firearms, knives, and outdoor activities. Next, it bought Books Americana from an Alabama publisher, adding about 30 books on a variety of collectibles. Then, in January 1997 Krause doubled its book division product line when it acquired the non-automotive titles of the Pennsylvania-based Chilton Book Co. Finally, in 1999, the company purchased Landmark Specialty Publications, a Norfolk, Virginia-based publisher of books and antique and collectible serials, including the *Antique Trader Weekly.* Among other things, the deal boosted Krause's workforce by about 40 percent. It also involved the acquisition of some online services. Not that the Internet was new to the company. In 1998, Krause had gone online with an auction web site (http://www.collectit.net) designed to attract customers with an interest in all sorts of collectibles. However, it later discontinued that service.

Key Dates:

1952: Chester Krause begins publication of *Numismatic News.*
1961: Company acquires Coin Press.
1963: Clifford Mishler joins Krause as associate editor.
1972: Krause publishes the first edition of the *Standard Catalog of World Coins* and publishes its first non-numismatic offering, *Old Cars.*
1988: Roger Case joins Krause as director of numismatic publications; company establishes Employee Stock Ownership Plan (ESOP).
1991: Mishler becomes Krause's third president.
1995: Company is named ESOP Company of the Year by ESOP Association.
1999: Krause Purchases Landmark Specialty Publications and begins publishing the official eBay magazine in partnership with eBay.
2000: Case succeeds Mishler as Krause's president.

It was also in 1998 that Krause made another important acquisition when it purchased the International Collectible Exposition from McRand International. The Exposition had two annual shows, one in Rosemont, Illinois, and the other at alternate-year locations on the East and West Coasts. Over its history, Krause has sponsored and run many events related to its publications. Some of these, eventually community-sponsored events, it initiated; with others it held an affiliation. Three of these were local affairs: the Iola Old Car Show and Swap Meet, which had been held annually on grounds in back of the company's complex; the Iola Rod and Kustom Weekend; and the Iola Vintage Military and Gun Show. Other affiliated shows occurred across the country, including the Blade Show and International Cutlery Fair in Atlanta; Blade Show West in Costa Mesa, California; Chicago International Coin Fair; Chicago Paper Money Exposition; Kit Young Hawaii Trade Conference and Card Show; MidAmerica Coin Expo; Tuff Stuff Summer Classic; and SportsFest in Chicago. The International Collectible Exposition was a major addition to this program.

Krause Publications managed very well in a tough enterprise. In the late 1990s, estimates indicated that new periodicals hit the national marketplace on an average of two a day, some of which quickly failed. More simply faded away. Even some distinguished, time-honored publications succumbed, such as *Life,* which issued its last number in June 2000. Moreover, Krause published magazines for special interest readers, hobbyists who tended to ride the crest of a national craze one year only to slide into a trough of disinterest the next. The company's quick response to the fickleness of the market and the diversity of its product line helped it both survive and prosper. Its policy was to weather declining circulation in some areas by spreading costs across its whole product line. At various points in its develop-

ment, it relied heavily on the excellent sales of publications appealing to readers enmeshed in a collectible mania, baseball cards, for example, which, as mentioned above, in 1992 accounted for almost half the company's overall business. Because overhead costs were spread over the broad range of its publications, Krause continued to publish some serials even in the ebb tide of public interest, knowing that hobby interests tended to be cyclical and that interest might be rekindled. Tenacity had limits, of course, and over the years the company suspended the publication of some of its titles and consolidated others.

By the end of the 1990s, the company stepped yet further into the world of e-commerce, most importantly in a 1999 partnership arrangement with eBay, the Internet's chief auction site. Under its terms, Krause undertook the publication of the official eBay magazine. In September, the company published and distributed the first issue, anticipating a circulation of 400,000 copies. Although bearing eBay's imprint, the magazine was designed to appeal to anyone with an interest in the Internet, not just online auctions. Early in 2000, Krause also entered a partnership with Shop At Home, Inc. and collectibles.comsm, one of the leaders in e-commerce on both television broadcast channels and the Internet. According to the agreement, both companies would create an online ''newsstand'' selling books and serials for all sorts of hobbyists and collectors. Both of these partnering arrangements demonstrated that Krause Publications was increasingly responsive to the Internet's tremendous potential and that it remained ready to accept the challenge of change, something that not all print media companies have demonstrated.

Principal Competitors

Meredith Corporation; Random House Inc.; The Reader's Digest Association, Inc.; Reed Elsevier plc.

Further Reading

Barrier, Michael, ''Collecting the Collectors,'' *Nation's Business,* October 1992, p. 53.
Eads, Stefani, and Robert McNatt, ''From the Net to the Newsstand,'' *Business Week,* May 3, 1999, p. 6.
Francis, Thomas, ''Krause Publications Buys International Collectible Exposition,'' *Knight-Ridder/Tribune Business News,* August 12, 1998.
Grabatstein, Lisa, ''Let's Make a Web Deal,'' *Mediaweek,* May 17, 1999, p. 70.
Kerwin, Ann Marie, ''Ink and Paper World Clicks with the Online Universe: Wenner, Krause Plan Magazine; Hearst Weighs Women's Guide,'' *Advertising Age,* July 5, 1999, p. 29.
McIntyre, David, ''Iola, Wis., Proves Ideal Setting for Employee-Owned Publisher,'' *Knight-Ridder/Tribune Business News,* March 30, 1999.
Mulholland, Megan, ''Iola, Wis.-Based Publishing Venture Will Step into Online Commerce,'' *Knight-Ridder/Tribune Business News,* May 9, 1999.

—John W. Fiero

Laboratoires de Biologie Végétale Yves Rocher

3, allée de Grenelle CP
92444 Issy Les Moulineaux
France
Telephone: (+ 33) 1 41 08 57 00
Fax: (+ 33) 1 41 08 58 61
Web site: http://www.yvesrocher.fr

Private Company
Incorporated: 1965
Employees: 6,800
Sales: FFr 10.78 billion ($1.79 billion) (1999 est.)
NAIC: 32562 Toilet Preparation Manufacturing

World-renowned Laboratoires de Biologie Végétale Yves Rocher is one of the world's leading producers of plant-based cosmetics and skin care and other personal care products and is one of the pioneers of natural and environmentally friendly beauty products. Marketing more than 300 different products in nearly 90 countries, Yves Rocher operates a—primarily franchised—chain of more than 1,350 "Centres de Beauté" worldwide. More than 70 percent of the private company's more than FFr 10 billion in annual sales is produced outside of the company's French home. Although the company's beauty center network assures a large part of Yves Rocher's sales, it also sells through other retail distribution networks, including sales to large supermarkets and department stores. Yet direct sales and correspondence sales have long been a principal vehicle for Yves Rocher's distribution. The company's catalog sales alone number 15 million clients, resulting in shipments of more than 130 million packages each year. Since 1997, Yves Rocher also has held one of the leading positions worldwide in door-to-door sales, thanks to its acquisition of Stanhome Worldwide Direct Selling, which boasts some 60,000 salespeople hosting in-home sales parties throughout the world. The company continues to be led by founder Yves Rocher, who is joined by sons Daniel and Jacques, and the Rocher family has maintained a tight grip on its voting rights majority, while Elf Aquitaine S.A. subsidiary Sanofi holds 60 percent of the company sales and 40 percent of its voting rights. In 2000, Sanofi, since its merger with Synthlabo and a resulting reorganization of its activities around its core pharmaceuticals base, has indicated its willingness to sell back its share of the company to the Rocher family. Despite a decade of increasingly intense competition—not only from large supermarkets hoping to join in on the natural products bandwagon, but also from such global giants as L'Oreal or catalog sales powerhouse 3 Suisses—Yves Rocher continues to play a leading role in sales of natural beauty products and has declared its expectations to double its sales (to FFr 20 billion) by the early years of the new century.

Rubbing the Right Way in the 1950s

Born and raised in the tiny village of La Gacilly in the Morbihan, Brittany region of France, Yves Rocher remained committed to his birthplace when he began to build his career. Rocher had long held an interest in plants and their properties and their uses in traditional healing techniques. Rocher left school to begin a career as a clothing salesman in the region's markets. But a recipe—for a hemorrhoid salve based on ingredients taken from plants—given to him by an elderly "healer" sent Rocher in a new direction.

Using the attic of his family's La Gacilly home, Rocher set to work preparing the recipe and in 1956 started sales of the hemorrhoid salve, taking out an ad in the magazine *Ici Paris*. Orders for the salve poured in, and Rocher, encouraged, began to extend his range of products, adding cosmetics at the start of the 1960s. Mail order remained Rocher's primary sales channel through that decade. In the meantime, Rocher became mayor of La Gacilly, vowing to stop the erosion of its population, which had been fleeing the village in search of work. Part of Rocher's solution to this problem was to found his own company, creating jobs for the benefit of the community. In this, Rocher was entirely successful; from a population at a low of 1,100 people in 1994, La Gacilly entered the 21st century with a population of nearly 2,350, many of whom were employed in Rocher's business.

Yves Rocher proved equally successful as a businessman. In 1959, the company's sales had grown sufficiently to support the company's own botanical garden and laboratory. Apart from Yves Rocher's own experiments and research, the company began

Company Perspectives:

Nature is man's future. This conviction, inscribed at the heart of the company, opens infinite perspectives for us. As we know, we are far from knowing all of Nature's secrets. Out of the 300,000 plants that have been categorized, only a few hundred are being used for their cosmetic properties. Thanks to 30 years of experience on research trips and in our bio-vegetable research laboratories, we have discovered new active plants and have shown their effectiveness. In return, Nature needs to be respected. This is why our company and all of its employees contribute to its protection through concrete actions. Man's future will be that much more beautiful if Nature is respected. It's all a matter of conviction and feeling.

searching throughout the world for plants susceptible to providing ingredients for a growing list of skin care and beauty products.

If Rocher's business had remained primarily on the cottage-industry level at the start of the 1960s, by the middle of the decade sales had grown large enough to enable Rocher to incorporate his company, as Laboratoires de Biologie Végétale Yves Rocher, and to build his first factory, as well as an expanded botanical garden and laboratory facility specialized in transforming botanical substances into cosmetic ingredients, now given the lofty name of "Le Centre d'Etudes et de Recherche en Cosmetologie" (Center for the Study and Research of Beauty Care). With ingredients such as camomile and lime-blossom, Rocher had anticipated the coming boom of interest in natural products and ecology in general. In 1965, the company produced its first catalog, the "Green Book of Beauty," which remained a hallmark of the company into the 1990s.

Rocher's success in selling beauty care products by mail order—considered a rarity for the time—translated into steadily increasing sales and the need for increased production capacity. In 1969, Yves Rocher opened a new production facility in its La Gacilly home town. The company also eyed a move into the retail arena and opened its first retail store in Paris in 1970. The success of that location led the company to launch a rapid expansion of its retail network, through company-owned stores but especially through selling franchises to the Yves Rocher name and product line. By then, too, the company had begun to move into the international marketplace, expanding its mail order and retail business into the rest of Europe. Germany proved especially susceptible to Rocher's message of affordably priced, natural ingredients-based products, and Rocher soon rose to the lead in that country's market. By the early 1970s, the company's sales had topped FFr 80 million.

To fund its expansion and to enter the global marketplace, Rocher, described by *Le Monde* as "totalitarian and autocratic" chose to avoid a public listing of his company and, instead, sought to form an alliance with a larger partner. In 1973, Rocher sold 60 percent of his company to Elf Aquitaine subsidiary Sanofi, yet Rocher retained the majority—57 percent—of the company's voting rights and, therefore, control of its direction. Sanofi was, in fact, to remain more or less a silent partner throughout the two companies' relationship.

As Rocher continued to build up its retail network as well as increase its mail order catalog customer list, it also sought to launch the company into another direct sales arena, setting up its own in-home party sales service. By 1981, Yves Rocher's three-pronged approached had enabled the company to top FFr 1 billion in annual sales. Mail order remained the company's largest sales channel, accounting for as much as 70 percent of its sales each year. The company, meanwhile, continued to invest in research and development of new products and technologies, now in its own "Center for Applied Research." In 1982, the company released the results of one effort, in which it claimed to have developed a technique to extract the DNA of certain plants and then re-engineer the plants to produce heightened benefits. The company's A.D.N Revitalizing Resource line of skin care products helped boost the company into the top ranks of the world's cosmetics products manufacturers. By 1984, Yves Rocher's sales had reached FFr 2.6 billion.

Refocusing in the 1990s

During the 1980s, Yves Rocher sought to expand its cosmetics empire into other areas. The company began a diversification program that saw it enter into the textiles industry, especially the market for women's and children's clothing. Over the course of the decade, the company made a number of acquisitions of clothing manufacturers, including the brands Jean Chancel, Claverie, Tartine et Chocolat, Sym et Danjean, and Petit Bateau, which the company acquired in 1988, following the counsel of the BNP (Banque Nationale de Paris). Yves Rocher also gave his blessing to a new cosmetics company, Daniel Jouvance, founded by son Daniel, which became an Yves Rocher subsidiary. By the end of the decade, Rocher's clothing division rivaled its cosmetics group with some FFr 1 billion in annual sales. Yet the Petit Bateau acquisition seemed to have given the company a case of seasickness.

By the end of the year, Yves Rocher discovered that its new subsidiary was, in fact, sinking fast, with losses mounting to FFr 178 million for that year alone. In fact, as was later shown in a court-ordered financial review of Petit Bateau pre-acquisition accounts, Petit Bateau had been taking on water for some time. Its accounts had been falsified, however, with its stock overvalued by more than FFr 20 million, its capital holdings inflated by more than FFr 40 million, and accounting errors adding another FFr 3.5 million—on top of underestimated consolidated losses remaining from the 1987 year.

After discovering Petit Bateau's losses in 1988, Yves Rocher promptly accused BNP—which had been the company's counselor, but, in a conflict of interest, not only held ten percent of Petit Bateau, but also represented the interests of that company's former owners—of fraudulent behavior, sparking a legal and publicity battle that was to last throughout the 1990s. The battlelines were drawn when Yves Rocher's employees marched on the BNP headquarters in Paris, shouting, "BNP, give us back our bread!" An amicable settlement, reached in 1989, quickly fell through and the two companies moved to the legal battlefield. There, Yves Rocher filed a number of court complaints against BNP, which countersued—and won—in 1991. Yves Rocher and son and future heir Didier, charged with blackmail and attempted extortion, were required to pay dam-

Key Dates:

1956: Yves Rocher begins home-made production of hemorrhoid cream.
1965: Creation of Yves Rocher brand and incorporation of company.
1969: Opened new production facility.
1970: Launch of first retail magazine in Paris; beginning of European expansion.
1973: Sanofi acquires 60 percent of company's share (43 percent of voting rights).
1980: Launch of in-home party direct sales operation.
1981: Sales top FFr 1 billion.
1988: Acquisition of Petit Bateau.
1992: Shutdown of subsidiary Danjean.
1993: Sell-off of clothing subsidiaries.
1997: Acquisition of Stanhome Worldwide Direct Selling Service.
2000: Proposed acquisition of Sanofi's shares.

ages amounting to one franc. Yet the same court decision ordered a review of Petit Bateau's 1987 books.

Meanwhile, Yves Rocher, which stuck firmly to its private status, was faced with pumping its own capital into raising the Petit Bateau subsidiary. By the mid-1990s, the company had successfully turned around the maker of children's clothing and undergarments, transforming it into its most profitable clothing subsidiary. The rest of Yves Rocher's empire, however, was struggling. Amid a worldwide recession, Yves Rocher was seeing steady erosions in its share of the marketplace as more powerful rivals such as L'Oreal, Estée Lauder, and Unilever, or mail order specialists such as La Redoute and 3 Suisses, moved to enter the natural beauty products business. At the same time, the major retail circuit, eager to participate in the surging demand for natural and plant-based cosmetics, began rolling out their own low-priced alternatives. As a result, Yves Rocher watched its market share tumble; in France alone, its share dropped to just 5.5 percent by 1991. At the same time, its textiles wing was faltering, as its various clothing subsidiaries struggled to fight the tide of declining sales in the depressed European and French marketplaces.

Amid the company's woes, its founder decided to step down, placing in his stead eldest son Didier in 1992. Having been groomed to take over his father's business for some years, Didier Rocher nonetheless inherited a company in dire straits. According to a confidential company memo, as reported by the *Nouvel Observateur,* the company's financial position was such that it could no longer ''assure the financing of its development and therefore the continuity and independence of the company.'' To restore Yves Rocher's financial position, Didier Rocher led the company on a belt-tightening exercise, slashing costs to save some FFr 171 million per year, dropping prices by up to 50 percent on some products, and—most dramatic in a company originally founded to create jobs—the cutting back of some five percent of the company's 4,500 employees, a number that included 35 positions in La Gacilly itself.

In addition, Yves Rocher began to shed much of its textiles division, shutting down its Danjean subsidiary and relinquishing the license to the Tartine and Chocolat brand before finding a buyer for most of its other clothing subsidiaries in Italy's Miroglio Tessile. By 1993, Yves Rocher had trimmed down the division to just Petit Bateau, by then the company's strongest clothing performer.

On the positive side, Yves Rocher worked to modernize its image to compete with its flashier competitors, dropping its Green Book. The company also made a number of product breakthroughs, including its 1993 introduction of the ingredient Retinol, a vitamin A derivative, said to help protect the skin against sun and pollution damage. By the mid-1990s, the company was back on the growth track, building up its customer base to more than 25 million worldwide and extending its network of retail stores to 1,000 locations in 84 companies. Its sales had grown to an estimated FFr 7 billion, with benefits said to have topped FFr 350 million in 1994. In September 1994, the company began preparations to double its production capacity at La Gacilly, boosting its payroll there from 1,200 to 2,200 employees.

Yet the end of 1994 brought tragedy to the company, when Didier Rocher, practicing shooting high-calibre weapons, accidentally shot himself in the head, dying from the wound. At the age of 65, Yves Rocher returned to the helm of the company he had founded, seconded by sons Daniel and Jacques. Rocher remained in charge long enough to restructure the company's executive directorship and named long-time employee Jean-Christian Fandeux as head of the company's operations. One of the company's first acts was to continue the announced construction of the new FFr 100 million production facility that had been announced by Didier Rocher.

Soon after, the simmering war between Yves Rocher and BNP flared up with the release of the report on Petit Bateau's 1987 finances. Yves Rocher, convinced that he had been defrauded, printed and mailed out 23,000 copies of a 12-page account of his version of how BNP allegedly defrauded his company, while at the same time buying advertising space in the country's newspapers and magazines. The Rocher-BNP battle once again wound up in court.

In the meantime, Yves Rocher continued to make gains in rebuilding its international position. By 1997, the company's annual sales neared FFr 8 billion. The company by then boasted five production facilities and another five sites for its clothing production. Although mail order still accounted for more than 50 percent of its annual sales, its network of 1,350 retail stores had risen to represent 19 percent of its sales.

In 1997, the company took a step forward when it acquired Stanhome Inc.'s Stanhome Worldwide Direct Selling subsidiary, adding that company's ''party plan'' sales force of more than 60,000, with sales of FFr 1.3 billion bringing Yves Rocher into the North American, South American, and Asian markets. The company announced its intention to double its sales to secure a position among the world's top ten cosmetics companies and also among the world's top direct sales organizations.

Yves Rocher returned from retirement once again in September 1998, taking over control of the company he had founded. The following year, the company announced its interest in regaining the shares of its company long held by Sanofi, as the company completed its merger with Synthlabo and began a process of shedding its nonchemicals holdings—including the fashion house of Yves Saint Laurent—to refocus on its core pharmaceuticals division. With Yves Rocher back at the company's helm, and sons Daniel and Jacques retaining active roles in the company's operations, the company continued to enjoy both strong sales and high levels of customer loyalty.

Principal Subsidiaries

Daniel Jouvance; Petit Bateau; Le Monde en Parfum.

Principal Competitors

L'Oréal ; The Body Shop International plc; 3 Suisses; Clinique Laboratories; La Redoute S.A.; The Estée Lauder Companies Inc.

Further Reading

Gay, Pierre-Angel, ''Yves Rocher sauve le caractère familial de son groupe,'' *Le Monde,* January 25, 1995, p. 18.
Leparmentier, Arnaud, ''Yves Rocher règle ses comptes avec la BNP dans l'affaire Petit Bateau,'' *Le Monde,* February 25, 1992.
Peyrani, Béatrice, ''Yves Rocher a fait son temps,'' *Nouvel Economiste,* April 30, 1993, p. 69.
Valo, Martine, ''Les dix ans de l'affaire Petit Bateau/Yves Rocher,'' *Le Monde,* March 3, 1998, p. 17.

—M.L. Cohen

Leica Camera AG

Oskar-Barnack-Strasse 11
D-35606 Solms
Germany
Telephone: (49)(6442) 208-0
Fax: (49)(6442) 208-333
Web site: http://www.Leica-camera.com

Public Company
Incorporated: 1849 as Optical Institute C. Kellner, Wetzlar
Employees: 1,472
Sales: DM 265 million ($135 million) (1999)
Stock Exchanges: Frankfurt/Main
Ticker Symbol: G.LCC
NAIC: 333315 Photographic and Photocopying
    Equipment Manufacturing

Leica Camera AG is a manufacturer of high quality equipment for photography, photographic reproduction, and observation. The company, which was the first to successfully market a 35-mm compact camera, is best known for its expensive, highly sophisticated cameras. Leica Camera's product line includes compact cameras, of both rangefinder and single reflex lens system varieties, as well as lenses, projectors, enlargers, and binoculars. Major cornerstones of the company's high price policy are extraordinary quality, product longevity, and system compatibility. Headquartered in Solms, Germany, Leica Camera has three production facilities in Germany and one in Portugal, as well as marketing subsidiaries in the United States, France, and the United Kingdom. Leica products are marketed by over 100 local agents around the world and sold by traditional specialist retailers. The company's largest markets are Germany, with about 34 percent of total sales, and the United States with about 19 percent. Lancet Holding BV, the property of Swiss industrialist Stephan Schmidheiny, holds a 13.6 percent share in the company.

1840s Origins

The roots of Leica Camera go back to 1849, when 23-year-old Carl Kellner, a talented mechanic, founded his own Optical Institute in the German town of Wetzlar. Kellner invented an optical corrected eyepiece with a new combination of lenses that significantly improved the image quality in field glasses and telescopes. The technology was well received by scientists, and, encouraged by this success, Kellner next focused on building a new kind of microscope based on mathematical principles. Kellner's microscopes, which first left his Wetzlar workshop in 1851, generated images of exceptionally high quality and soon earned a him reputation in the scientific community. In 1855 Carl Kellner died of tuberculosis. His widow married Friedrich Belthle, who secured the existence of the Optical Institute.

In 1864 mechanic Ernst Leitz joined the Optical Institute. One year later he became a partner and, after Belthle's death in 1869, the sole proprietor of the company which he renamed E. Leitz, Wetzlar. Leitz's introduction of the more economical serial manufacturing of microscopes also increased their image quality standards and made them more reliable for scientific research. By 1900, the Leitz company had gained a worldwide reputation, employed 400 people and produced about 4,000 microscopes a year. The market for microscopes was growing, and, only a decade later, the Optical Institute produced 9,000 microscopes, the variety of which was also constantly expanding. When Ernst Leitz died in 1920, his second son, Ernst Leitz II, took over the business. Four years later he helped make a new invention commercially successful—the first Leitz Camera, called Leica for short.

Oskar Barnack Creates the Leica Camera in 1914

Up until the first decade of the 20th century photography was more of a hobby than an art form. The plate cameras used by photographers were heavy and needed the support of even bigger and heavier tripods. For that reason photography was limited to highly composed images, most often taken in studios. Several manufacturers were working on a more compact camera using smaller film formats that would allow photographers more mobility and flexibility. Among the models launched were the American models Sept, Sico, Phototank, Tourist Multiple, and Simplex, as well as the French Homeos stereo camera, and the British Centum Film camera, none of which succeeded commercially.

The first 35-mm compact camera was developed and manufactured at the Leitz company. Oskar Barnack experimented with his idea for several years before he finally invented the Leica camera. Apprenticed to a company in Lichterfelde that made astronomical instruments, he became interested in technical instruments, astronomy, and photography. After he finished his training as a precision tool maker, Barnack joined Jena-based optical manufacturer Carl Zeiss. In his spare time, he went on hiking trips and became an amateur photographer. In order to take pictures on his hiking trips, Barnack started experimenting with a plate camera in 1905, which he later modified to take 20 mini-pictures on one plate of film. Later he began experimenting with a device for cinema film, which perforated the edges of film so that it could be moved along mechanically with sprockets. The camera Barnack designed used film twice the size of film used by movie makers, which he found optimal for later enlargement. Barnack showed his invention to a manager at Carl Zeiss, who rejected it.

In 1911 Barnack moved to Wetzlar and became a master machinist at the E. Leitz company. Ernst Leitz II encouraged Barnack to develop his camera idea further and made him a development engineer at the Leitz experimental laboratory. There Barnack constructed two metal-made miniature cameras using 35-mm motion-picture film with single-shutter-speed. The so-called ''Ur-Leica'', or ''original Leica,'' was equipped with the famous Elmar lens which was developed by German microscope expert Max Berek, who had joined E. Leitz in 1912. The pictures Barnack took in 1914 in the countryside around Wetzlar were of exceptionally high quality.

Further development of the Leica camera was interrupted by World War I. Finally, in 1924, Ernst Leitz II decided to mass produce the camera, and in December of the same year the first six Leica cameras were built at E. Leitz. In 1925 the Leica camera was presented to the public for the first time at the Leipzig Spring Fair and became an instant success.

Revolutionizing Photography in the 1930s

The first serial Leica I or model A used an f/3.5 fixed lens in a retracted position, an eye-level viewer, and a focal-plane self-capping shutter with a speed range of 1/25 to 1/500 of a second. The 35-mm film with 36 exposures was advanced by a knob that cocked the shutter at the same time that it wound the film. The Leica was small enough to fit in a coat pocket and enabled photographers to take several pictures in a row without changing film. This ability was instrumental in the development of photojournalism; reporters and artists alike were able to work quickly and be flexible, thus broadening the scope of their subject matter considerably. The Leica camera was soon embraced by photographers around the world and greatly enhanced their ability to capture the world on film. Postwar Germany in the 1920s became the center of a new, dynamic style of photography. Many well-known photographers of the time, including Henri Cartier-Bresson, became loyal Leica users. Recalling the beginning of his career, in an introductory essay for his 1952 collection *The Decisive Moment,* Cartier-Bresson would recall: ''I worked with enjoyment. I had just discovered the Leica. It became the extension of my eye, and I have never been separated from it since I found it.''

Leica users were soon demanding new features, and, encouraged by Leica's success, E. Leitz refined its next generations of cameras in various ways. Lenses could be changed, from wide-angle to telephoto; a viewfinder was built into the camera; a more affordable version of the Ur-Leica was made available, the Leica Compur or Model B, which did not have the focal plane shutter. The Leica II or Model D introduced in 1932 used a lens-coupled range-finder for quick and accurate focusing. Another new model, Leica III or Model F, was introduced a year later with slow shutter speeds. Another field of improvement was the image quality. Up until 1935 Max Berek designed several award-winning lenses, including the fast Hektor, Summar normal, Elmar long-focus, and Thambar. The additional improvements introduced during the 1930s made Leica cameras especially famous for their high optical quality and very quiet shutter. Leitz marketing strategy including using the testimonials of such famous photographers as Margaret Bourke White and Cartier-Bresson, as well as that of adventurers like Admiral Richard Byrd and Charles Lindbergh. The strategy proved very effective.

The growth in popularity of the Leica 35-mm cameras inspired film manufacturers as well as competitors. The introduction in 1931 of Agfa's panchromatic emulsion film, which was sensitive to light of all colors at a speed of ASA 32, made sharper enlargements from 35-mm negatives possible. During this time, One of Leica's main competitors was the Contax, another 35-mm camera introduced by Carl Zeiss in 1932.

World War II interrupted camera development and production at the Leitz Werke. However, Leica cameras were widely used to capture images of the war. After the war, many journalists, artists, and professional and amateur photographers continued to use Leica cameras, and Leitz could hardly keep up with demand. In 1949 the company established a modern glass laboratory which developed specialty glass for optical lenses. In 1951, one year after Ernst Leitz II turned 80, the one-millionth Leica lens was produced at the Leitz Werke. To serve the fast growing North American market, a Leitz subsidiary was founded and a camera production plant built in Midland, Canada. Another legendary Leica model, the Leica M3, was presented to the public at the Cologne Photokina, the world's largest photography fair, in 1954.

Ernst Leitz II died in 1956. His three sons, Ernst Leitz III, Ludwig Leitz, and Günther Leitz took over the management of the company. During this time, competition between Leica and Contax intensified, with each vying for dominance of the professional camera market. The Contax FB, introduced by Zeiss in 1956, would be the last 35-mm model to carry the Zeiss name for many years.

Competition Intensifies in the 1960s

During the 1960s Leitz manufactured custom-made Leica cameras for special uses in addition to its several serial models. For example, the company produced 125 Leica 3G cameras with the three-crowns emblem of Sweden engraved in an all-black case for the Swedish Army. In 1966, 150 Leicas were custom made for the NASA with oversized controls for advancing the film and opening the case so that they could be handled by astronauts wearing gloves on space missions. To keep up with demand, Leitz had to expand production capacity. In 1966 a new production plant for Leica cameras started operations in Oberlahn, near Weilburg, Germany. In 1973 another production plant for Leica cameras went into operation in Vila Nova de Famalicao near Porto in Portugal. In 1968 ten Leica collectors established the Leica Society in the United Kingdom; by the mid-1990s the Society had grown to over 2,100 members. However, the times of unchallenged market leadership came to an end as the 1970s approached.

Both Leica and Contax cameras were very expensive and many aspiring photographers could not afford them. Not surprisingly, several manufacturers attempted as early as the late 1920s to create inexpensive 35-mm cameras for a mass market. Most of them failed to gain an audience, as the Great Depression made purchases of such things as cameras either impossible or frivolous. The first successful attempt at marketing a cheaper 35-mm camera was the Argus, introduced in the United States in 1935 at a price of $12.50.

The real competitive threat, however, came from the other side of the globe. After World War II the Japanese started challenging the world's leading camera manufacturers. At first, the imitation Japanese Leica and Contax cameras, which carried the labels Canon and Nikon, elicited only skepticism. However, when American photojournalists used Japanese cameras to photograph the Korean War, they found that some of the Japanese lenses were of very high quality. During the 1950s and 1960s Japanese camera makers made quality the number one priority for their exports and as a result became more and more successful in competing with rangefinder cameras and lenses made in Germany. Also, the many advantages of single lens reflex cameras, in which the user views his subject directly through the lens rather than through a telescoping mechanism to the side of the lens, became serious competition for the rangefinder systems. In 1965 the first single-lens reflex camera made by Leitz,

the Leicaflex, was introduced. The next models followed in 1968 with the Leicaflex SL, the Leicaflex SL2 in 1974, and the Leica R3 in 1976.

Due to shrinking demand and high development and production costs, by 1970 the Leica product line was no longer profitable. Retail prices could not cover the cost of making the expensive cameras and lenses by hand. Under pressured to make strategic decisions that could turn Leica's fate around, Leitz started looking for suitable strategic partners and for ways to cut costs for camera development and production. In 1972 Leitz signed a partnership agreement with the Japanese camera maker Minolta. However, the old rivalry with Zeiss and its Contax flared up again in 1974, as Zeiss had become part of a group that developed a new model, the Contax RTS, a single lens reflex system. Additional development costs were incurred when Leica's new rangefinder model M5 turned out to be too bulky.

An Independent Company in 1992

During the early 1980s Leitz kept reporting losses with Leica cameras despite the loyalty of numerous professional photographers and world famous collectors such as the Sultan of Brunei and Queen Elizabeth. In 1986, Leica GmbH was founded to manage the Leitz camera division. One year later Ernst Leitz Wetzlar GmbH and Wild Heerbrugg AG merged to form Wild Leitz AG. The new optical concern was headquartered in Switzerland and employed 9,000 people. In 1988 Leica GmbH became an independent division of Wild Leitz and moved headquarters and camera production to a new facility in Solms near Wetzlar. By that time the camera arm had produced losses for over a decade, subsidized by profits from Leitz microscopes and surveying systems.

While Leica had difficulties selling its annual output of just 20,000 cameras retailing at $3,200 to $4000, Japanese camera maker Minolta sold about 2.5 million cameras in 1988. In the United States Leica camera sales reached a peak of about $8 million in 1985 and dropped off sharply afterwards to about half that amount in 1987. Less than eight percent of America's camera dealers carried Leica in 1988. It was a vicious cycle; in order to gain market share Leica needed to aggressively market its product lines, and this required money the company wasn't making. Leitz's decision to move half of the camera production abroad also turned out to be problematic. While it lowered personnel cost by about one-third, this gain could not outweigh endless quality problems with the parts manufactured in Portugal and Canada. The new Leica management decided in summer 1988 to move a great chunk of the lens production and camera assembly back to Germany. Another of the company's strategic mistakes was not pursuing the new technology of autofocus cameras which had first been invented by Leica engineers. The Japanese, however, realized the commercial potential of this new concept and successfully introduced it to the market while Leica was struggling with reorganization.

In 1990 Wild Leitz Holding AG merged with the British optical group Cambridge Instrument Company. Leica Camera GmbH, the camera subsidiary, became Leica Camera AG. Two years later Wild Leitz sold its Canada production plant to Hughes Aircraft, which continued to manufacture some lenses for Leica cameras. In 1992 a team of executives, led by Leica's president Bruno Frey and supported financially by a subsidiary of Deutsche Bank, attempted a management buyout of the camera operations from Wild Leitz, but failed. Two years later another attempt led by former CFO Klaus-Dieter Hofmann was successful. The Leica brand name remained the property of Wild Leitz, which allowed the new independent company to continue using it for their microscopes and other instruments. Wild Leitz also kept a minority share in Leica. Hofmann became CEO of the newly independent Leica Camera AG.

Two years after the management buyout, Leica Camera was ready to make an initial public (IPO) offering of stock. Some 4.5 million shares were floated on the Frankfurt stock exchange, and Hofmann managed to get the company out of the red. In the year of the IPO Leica introduced the ''R'' camera line, its first new series in 30 years. After record profits in 1996, the company was able to report record sales the following year, yet it realized losses rather than profits for 1997 and 1998 amounting to DM 30 million. The acquisition of German miniature camera maker Minox in 1996 turned out to be a major mistake, since the expected synergy between to the two companies did not take place. At the same time Leica camera sales dropped sharply in Asia. In 1998 Leica Camera was also confronted with a lawsuit that accused the company of profiting from slave labor under the Nazi regime. Leica, answering the charges, maintained that its founder, Ernst Leitz, had rescued several Jews from deportation to concentration camps and had been jailed himself by the Nazis for helping Jews.

At the beginning of 1999 Hanns-Peter Cohn became the new CEO of Leica Camera. The new management team developed a strategy for the new millennium, which it referred to as ''Leica 21.'' One of its cornerstones was the brand-new Leica S1 series of digital scanner cameras. This was a first step into another revolution in photography: the age of computer-based image recording and processing that did not require the 35-mm film that made Leica a legend. Whether this new direction would succeed remained to be seen. Regardless, Leica remained one of the most important and influential brands of the 19th and 20th centuries.

Principal Subsidiaries

Leica Camera Inc. (United States); Leica Camera s.a.r.l. (France); Leica Camera Ltd. (United Kingdom); Leica Aparelhos Opticos de Precisao S.A. (Portugal; 91.33%); Leica Projektion GmbH Zett Geräte (Germany); Feinwerktechnik Wetzlar GmbH (Germany); Minox GmbH Optische und Feinmechanische Werke (Germany); VSZ Versand- und Servicezentrum GmbH (Germany).

Principal Competitors

Nikon Corporation; Olympus Optical Co. Ltd.; Canon Inc.; Matsushita Electric Industrial Co., Ltd.; Minolta Co., Ltd.; Carl-Zeiss-Stiftung.

Further Reading

''Aus Wild Leitz wird Leica Heerbrugg AG,'' *Der Rheintaler*, July 1990.

Fuhrman, Peter, ''New Focus at Leica,'' *Forbes*, October 1988, p. 100.

Goldsmith, Arthur, ''The Camera and Its Images,'' The Ridge Press, Inc., 1979, pp. 160–73.

Grehn, J., *125 Jahre Leitz-Mikroskopie*, Wetzlar, Germany: Ernst Leitz Wetzlar GmbH, 1977, 72 p.

Kusch, Sabine, ''Annäherung und die neue Marke Leica,'' *Horizont*, April 20, 2000, p. 84.

''Leica Camera Focuses on Initial Stock Sale,'' *Los Angeles Times*, September 5, 1996, p. 12.

''Leica Sells Majority Stake in Its Camera Division,'' *European Report*, June 15, 1992.

Parkes, Christopher, ''Managers Buy Camera Subsidiary of Leica,'' *Financial Times* (London), June 6, 1992, p. 12.

Reip, Rita, ''The Camera That Captured the World,'' *New York Times*, June 9, 1996, p. 40.

Rhoads, Christopher, ''German Companies Face U.S. Lawsuits Over Slave Labor,'' *Wall Street Journal*, September 1, 1998, p. A14.

Schwarz, Harald, ''Wir haben die Gewinnzone im Sucher,'' *Süddeutsche Zeitung*, February 18, 2000, p. 27.

Shaw, John, ''Leica: Focus on Future,'' *Europe Business Review*, January-March 1999, p. 28.

—Evelyn Hauser

Leica Microsystems Holdings GmbH

Ernst-Leitz-Strasse 17-37
D-35578 Wetzlar
Germany
Telephone: (49)(6441) 29-0
Fax: (49)(6441) 29-2599
Web site: http://www.Leica-microsystems.com

Private Company
Incorporated: 1849 as Optical Institute C. Kellner,
 Wetzlar
Employees: 3,600
Sales: DM 880 million ($449 million) (1999)
NAIC: 334516 Analytical Laboratory Instrument
 Manufacturing

Leica Microsystems Holdings GmbH (LMS) is one of the world's leading manufacturers of microscopes and related scientific equipment for research in the healthcare, semiconductor, and other industries. LMS is based in Wetzlar, Germany, and produces a broad range of optical and opto-electronic instruments in 11 factories in Germany, Switzerland, Austria, England, the United States, China, and Singapore. About 90 percent of the company's sales are generated outside Germany, supported by 18 sales organizations and associated dealers around the world. Light microscopy has been at the core of the LMS's business since the company's founding. LMS is also among the world market leaders for automatic measurement and inspection systems for the inspection of microchips and wafers in the semiconductor industry. Another important business area are confocal microscopes based on laser technology which allows the creation and analysis of 3D images in clinical diagnostics, cytogenetics, and materials science.

Beginnings in 1849

In 1849, in the German town of Wetzlar, 23-year-old Carl Kellner founded his own Optical Institute. Kellner was very talented in detailed mechanics and interested in optical studies, to which he also applied his studies in mathematics. Specifically, Kellner invented an optical corrected eyepiece with a new combination of lenses that significantly improved the image quality in field glasses and telescopes. His invention was a success among scientists, and Kellner decided to use his knowledge to build a new kind of microscope.

In his workshop in Wetzlar, which employed 12 assistants, Kellner started manufacturing microscopes. The first microscope was delivered to Geneva, Switzerland, for testing in 1851. Kellner's microscopes soon earned a reputation among scientists. Because he designed them based on mathematical principles, they generated images of exceptionally high quality. Two years later there were more microscopes leaving the Optical Institute than telescopes. The institute manufactured three types of microscopes with a different number of lenses. As word spread about their high quality, demand grew.

Increased demand presented difficulties for Kellner, as the old-fashioned production techniques of his small workshop limited the number of microscopes that could be produced; in the first five years in business only 130 were manufactured. In 1855 Kellner died at age 29 of tuberculosis; his widow married Friedrich Belthle and secured the existence of the Optical Institute. However, the firm's fortunes went up and down and was seriously threatened when Belthle himself became ill.

In 1864 Ernst Leitz joined the company. A talented mechanic, Leitz had learned his craft as an apprentice for a German company that manufactured laboratory equipment and in Switzerland with a manufacturer of precision instruments such as electric clocks and telegraphs. One year after he joined the Optical Institute, Leitz became a partner and the firm's name was changed to Optical Institute Belthle und Leitz, Wetzlar, vorm. C. Kellner. In 1867 the Optical Institute manufactured its 1000th microscope.

After Belthle's death in 1869 Ernst Leitz—at that time just 26 years old—became sole proprietor of the company and renamed it Optical Institute E. Leitz, Wetzlar. The outbreak of the Franco-Prussian War in 1870 made Leitz's business difficult in its first year. However, his organizational talent and extensive experience together with an expanding market for microscopes led to the growing success of the company. One of the major decisions he made as an entrepreneur was to switch from the slow, labor-

Company Perspectives:

Leica Microsystems' mission is to be the world's first-choice provider of innovative solutions to our customers' needs for vision, measurement, lithography and analysis of microstructures. Leica has developed from five brand names, all with a long tradition: Wild, Leitz, Reichert, Jung and Cambridge Instruments. Leica symbolizes not only tradition, but also innovation.

intensive manufacturing by hand to serial manufacturing, which would soon became the industry standard. In addition to its economical efficiency, the new production techniques improved the quality standards of the microscopes, which in turn made them more reliable for scientific research. Leitz also presented and demonstrated his products at many scientific congresses. In the last decades of the 19th century the use of microscopy increased rapidly with the rising popularity of natural sciences. In 1892 a sales office was opened in New York City which later became E. Leitz, U.S.A. By the turn of the century the Leitz company had gained a worldwide reputation.

By 1900 the Leitz company consisted of several facilities, oversaw 400 employees, and produced about 4,000 microscopes a year. By 1910, the company was manufacturing 9,000 microscopes annually and employing a workforce of 950. From a product line of fewer than 20 different types of microscopes and three different tripods, the company had expanded to produce 34 different microscope types including 21 different microscopes for medical and biological research as well as for scientific education in schools and universities; four different microscopes for geological and mineralogical research; and nine microscope types with distinct tripods for special uses such as for museums, measurement, brain research and other specialties. Also during this time, the 100,000th Leitz microscope was shipped to German bacteriologist and Nobel Prize Laureate Robert Koch. During World War I, between 1914 and 1918, the Leitz company was obliged by the German government to convert to war production.

New Generation of Leitz Leadership in the 1920s

Although Ernst Leitz's eldest son Ludwig had been involved in management of the family business, he died in an accident in 1898. Leitz's second son, Ernst Leitz II who joined his father's company as an apprentice in 1889, was then groomed for leadership, becoming responsible for new business development and management of the production facilities and eventually becoming his father's partner. Leitz II placed a high priority on research and development, adding optical measuring instruments for industrial use to the Leitz product line. When his father died in 1920, Ernst Leitz II took over the business and transformed it into a public limited corporation.

Four years later Ernst Leitz II decided to begin mass production of a new invention, the first Leitz camera, called the Leica. The company had long offered drawing aids for reproducing images seen under microscopes when Leitz II tapped Oskar Barnack to experiment with developing a small-format still camera for that purpose. The result was Barnack's invention of the

world's first 35-mm camera. Barnack's idea of reducing the format of photo negatives and enlarging them after exposure revolutionized photography. The first photos with this new camera taken in 1914 were of exceptional quality. However, the further development of the new technology was interrupted by World War I. The Leica camera was finally offered to the public for the first time at a trade show in 1925 in Leipzig. In 1926 the first Leitz 35-mm projector for slides or film strips was produced. The first auto-focus enlarger followed in 1933. In the field of cameras, lenses, and photography accessories, the Leica set the quality standard for the world until well after World War II.

Leica camera technology provided new inroads to microscopy, merging the two into the new field of photomicrography, in which a camera affixed to a microscope by a connecting tube could capture highly magnified images. Other new Leitz products of the time included a biological polarization microscope and the photometer, a device that measured illumination. The photometer was designed by Max Berek, a microscope expert who had worked for Leitz since 1912 and developed the very successful f/3.5 Elmar lens for the original Leica camera.

After World War II, a new glass research laboratory was established in Germany. In 1951, one year after Ernst Leitz II turned 80, the one-millionth Leica lens was produced at the Leitz Werke. In the same year a Canadian subsidiary was founded, and a camera production plant was built in Midland, Canada. E. Leitz, Canada became a leading lens producer, which in 1961 developed the first lens for underwater photography. Ernst Leitz II died in 1956. His three sons, Ernst Leitz III, Ludwig Leitz, and Günther Leitz, who had been involved in the business as directors from 1930 onward, took over the business.

New Partners and Owners in the 1970s–80s

The Leitz Werke remained in the ownership of the Leitz family and by the 1970s was known as Ernst Leitz Wetzlar GmbH, boasting a workforce of 6,600 employees. With the speed of technological innovation accelerating and globalization of the world economy shifting into high gear, it became necessary for the company to look for a partner. In 1972 Leitz started working with Wild Heerbrugg AG, a large Swiss optical company founded in 1921 by Jacob Schmidheiny, Heinrich Wild, and Robert Helbling. Wild Heerbrugg was known for its surveying instruments, stereo microscopes, tool plotters, and optical systems for industrial and military use. When the share capital of Ernst Leitz Wetzlar GmbH was increased in 1972, Wild Heerbrugg purchased a 25 percent stake in the company, and the two companies agreed to cooperate in product development, production and distribution. Two years later Wild Heerbrugg bought another 26 percent of the Leitz shares.

The year 1986 marked the beginning of a period of company reorganization. After Leitz struggled with financial losses for several years, Dr. Stephan Schmidheiny, from one of Switzerland's wealthiest families, bought out significant Leitz shareholdings and took the company under the wings of his investment group Unotec AG. The Leica camera division was thereafter organized as part of an independent private company, Leica GmbH. Ernst Leitz Wetzlar GmbH and Wild Heerbrugg AG merged to form Wild Leitz AG. The new optical concern was headquartered in Switzerland and employed 9,000 people.

Key Dates:

1849: Carl Kellner founds an Optical Institute in Germany.
1869: Ernst Leitz becomes sole proprietor of the Optical Institute.
1892: A sales office is opened in New York City.
1920: Ernst Leitz II takes over the business, which is transformed into a public limited corporation.
1924: Ernst Leitz II decides to mass produce the Leica camera.
1951: Canadian operations commence.
1971: A production facility for stereo microscopes is established in Singapore.
1972: Wild Heerbrugg buys 25 percent of Leitz.
1986: Ernst Leitz Wetzlar GmbH and Wild Heerbrugg AG merge to form Wild Leitz AG.
1990: Wild Leitz Holding AG merges with The Cambridge Instrument Company; Wild Leitz AG becomes Leica Heerbrugg AG.
1992: Management buyout of the Leica camera business.
1997: Leica group is split into Leica Microsystems and Leica Geosystems.

1990s Mergers and Reorganizations

In 1990 Wild Leitz merged with The Cambridge Instrument Company, a company rich in optical history, founded in 1833. Having struggled in the 1970s, Cambridge had come under the management of Terence J. Gooding, who took it public in Great Britain, made several acquisitions, and returned it to profitability. In 1988 the company was realizing an annual profit of $10 million on $230 million in sales, and CEO Gooding took the next step. He approached Wild Leitz AG, which was three times as big as Cambridge but also producing losses and dealing with a heavy debt load, and suggested a merger of the two famous optical groups. Gooding's endeavor was successful. The Cambridge Instruments group at the time included the German microtome maker R. Jung based in Heidelberg; Austrian optical company C. Reichert of Vienna, which pioneered fluorescence microscopy; the optical systems division of the American Bausch & Lomb group; and American Optical Company, an optical group with a tradition reaching back even further than that of the Leitz company.

The new holding company, Leica Plc, was headquartered in St. Gallen, Switzerland, registered in Bar Hill, England, with shares trading on the London stock exchange. Stephan Schmidheiny's Unotec Holding AG held over 40 percent of Leica Plc stock, while Gooding's investment group owned over eight percent. Other major shareholders of the new Leica group included the Warner Lambert Company, Midland Montagu Equity Ltd., and Anton Schrafl Associates. With combined sales of $800 million the new Leica group became one of the largest producers of optical and scientific instruments in the world. About half of Leica's sales were generated in Europe while 35 percent came from North America. Optical microscopes and surveying instruments each accounted for about one-fourth of total sales. Another 19 percent of Leica's revenues came from defense and other optics; 16 percent from scientific instruments; ten percent from metrology systems; and eight percent from other professional products.

After the merger, the whole group was represented under the Leica name, which had gained widespread recognition in its capacity as the camera brand of choice among photojournalists. Wild Leitz AG, Heerbrugg, the largest of the Leica subsidiaries, was renamed Leica Heerbrugg AG. The second largest Swiss subsidiary of the Leica group, Kern & Co. AG, a manufacturer of industrial measuring systems and specialty optics based in Aarau, became Leica Aarau AG. All products of the Leica group were marketed under their original brand names, including Wild Leitz, Leica, Kern, R. Jung, C. Reichert, and Britain's Cambridge Instruments in Europe, and American Optical in the United States. The merger expanded the distribution networks of the former Wild Leitz group into the United States and the Far East, putting the Leica group in a better position to compete with Japanese firms Nikon and Olympus in Asia.

In 1992 Leica Heerbrugg made headlines when it re-measured the summit height of Mount Everest from the Chinese side with its GPS survey system. The new measurement established that the mountain was some two meters lower than the previous official elevation. That same year, the Leica group sold its camera business to a group of the company's management. Leica Camera was allowed to use the Leica brand name for its products, but the Leica name would remain the property of the former Swiss parent.

In 1997 the remaining companies of the Leica group were split into two independent units: Leica Microsystems and Leica Geosystems. Leica Mikroskopie and Systeme GmbH became Leica Microsystems Holdings GmbH and the management of the group returned from Switzerland to Wetzlar, Germany, where it all began 150 years earlier. In 1998 the Geosystems group was sold to the international investment group Investcorp. The Leica Microsystems group was bought by London-based venture capital firm Schroder Ventures in a $500 million deal in the same year. Schroeder provided financial resources for business development to make Leica Microsystems fit for an initial public offering in the year 2000.

Despite its organization turmoil, Leica Microsystems (LMS) continued to expand its geographical reach and product lines. In 1992 LMS researchers developed a scanning acoustic microscope that was able to image elastic constants of materials and could be used to detect defects below the surface of microchips. In 1993 and 1994 the company launched two joint ventures for specimen preparation instruments and for microscopes in China. A year later, LMS partnered with German competitor Zeiss to establish LEO, a joint venture for electron microscopes, and introduced the first automatic fluorescent microscope. In 1996 LMS bought the E-beam Lithography business from the Jenoptik group; the U.S. National Institutes of Health ranked its laboratory microscope, the Leica DM LB, Top Product for biomedicine. Business partnerships of the late 1990s included a joint distribution alliance with Zymed Laboratories, Inc, a manufacturer of immunochemical reagents and monoclonal antibodies, as well as an alliance with Renishaw PLC, a leading British manufacturer of physical, laser, and video measurement and inspection equipment, as well as spectral analysis systems for new product development. In 1998 LMS acquired Jenoptic Silmetric GmbH from the German Jenoptik group.

Principal Subsidiaries

Leica Mikrosysteme Vertrieb GmbH; Leica Microsystems Ltd. (Hong Kong); Leica Microsystems (Canada) Inc.; Leica Microsystems K.K. (Japan); Leica Microsystems (SEA) Pte Ltd (Singapore); Leica Microsystems Inc. (United States); Leica Microsystems (UK) Ltd; Leica Microsystems AG (Switzerland).

Principal Competitors

Nikon Corporation; Olympus Optical Co. Ltd.; Carl-Zeiss-Stiftung; Jenoptik AG.

Further Reading

"Aus Wild Leitz wird Leica Heerbrugg AG," *Der Rheintaler*, July 1990.

Bauder, Donald C., "Gooding Plans to Buy Wild Leitz and Merge It with Cambridge," *San Diego Union-Tribune*, August 25, 1989, p. D-1.

Bowley, Graham, and Susanna Voyle, "Schroder to Buy Leica Microscopes Business," *Financial Times* (London edition), April 7, 1998, p. 25.

Bridger, Chet, "Owner Takes Depew, N.Y.-Based Maker of Eye-Testing Equipment Off Market," *Knight-Ridder/Tribune Business News*, March 22, 2000.

"Cambridge Instruments is Part of Swiss Company," *Business First of Buffalo*, April 2, 1990, p. 11.

Grehn, J., *125 Jahre Leitz-Mikroskopie*, Wetzlar, Germany: Ernst Leitz Wetzlar GmbH, 1977, 72 p.

"Leica Sells Majority Stake In Its Camera Division," *European Report*, June 15, 1992.

"Nazi-Zwangsarbeiter: Langes Warten auf Entschädigung," *dpa*, December 14, 1999.

"Opting for Optics," *swissBusiness*, September-October 1994, p. 10.

"Schroder Ventures Buys Leica Microsystems in $500 Million Deal," *European Venture Capital Journal*, April-May 1998, p. 27.

"See Interfaces with Acoustics," *R & D*, May 1992, p. 48.

—Evelyn Hauser

LILLIAN VERNON®

Lillian Vernon Corporation

One Theall Road
Rye, New York 10580-1450
U.S.A.
Telephone: (914) 925-1200
Toll Free: (800) 505-2250
Fax: (914) 925-1444
Web site: http://www.lillianvernon.com

Public Company
Incorporated: 1951 as Vernon Specialties
Employees: 5,100
Sales: $241.77 million (2000)
Stock Exchanges: AMEX
Ticker Symbol: Lillian Vernon
NAIC: 45411 Electronic Shopping and Mail-Order
  Houses

The Lillian Vernon Corporation is a mail-order catalog company specializing in household, gardening, and decorative merchandise as well as gifts and children's products. Personalizing these items for free has been one of the company's trademarks since the beginning. Lillian Vernon's catalogs have become a fixture in American popular culture. The company has boasted Hillary Clinton, Tipper Gore, Frank Sinatra, and Loretta Lynn among its clientele.

Over 90 percent of Lillian Vernon's customers are women with an average household income of $53,000. Over half work outside the home and have children living at home. Ninety percent of sales occur during the holidays. The company has one million square feet of warehouse space; more than a dozen outlet stores in the eastern United States help sell $4 million of overstock a year.

Although Lillian Vernon went public in 1987, it remained essentially a family-run company, with its founder Lillian Vernon acting as CEO, and her son David Hochberg acting as vice-president of public affairs. Another son, Fred Hochberg, was president and COO until 1992 when he left, reportedly unwilling to wait for his mother to let loose the reins.

Beginning at Home

Lillian Vernon Corporation was founded in 1951 under the name Vernon Specialties. The name was taken from the founder's adopted home in Mount Vernon, New York; her Jewish family had fled Nazi Germany in 1937, when she was ten years old. At that time, Lilly Menasche Hochberg was 22 years old, recently married, pregnant, and looking for a business she could run from her kitchen table. Hochberg soon changed her first name to the more American-sounding "Lillian," and eventually became known as Lillian Vernon. She formally changed her name after a divorce in the 1990s.

Using part of the $2,000 she and her husband had received as wedding gifts, Vernon took out a $495 advertisement in *Seventeen* magazine offering monogrammed leather handbags and belts for $2.99 and $1.99 each. The leather goods were purchased from Vernon's father, Herman Menasche, who ran a small leather factory. The 24-karat gold monograms were purchased from a distributor and hand-applied on the goods by Vernon herself.

Vernon received $16,000 worth of orders from her first ad. She then used her profits to buy ads in other popular women's magazines. She took in $32,000 for the year; sales grew and, within a few years, the company landed several contracts to manufacture custom-designed products for major corporations, including Max Factor, Elizabeth Arden, Avon, and Revlon. In 1954, Vernon Specialties moved out of Vernon's kitchen and into three facilities in Mount Vernon in order to meet the growing demand for its products.

Two years later, in 1956, Vernon Specialties mailed its first catalog to the 125,000 customers who had responded to the company's magazine ads since 1951. The catalog had sixteen pages of black-and-white photos offering items such as signet rings, combs, cuff links, and blazer buttons—all of which could be personalized through the company's free monogramming service.

In fact, the key to Vernon Specialties' early success in the mail-order business was its offer of free monogramming, which continued as one of the features that distinguished the company from its competitors in the mid-1990s. Within a few years of its debut, the catalog was expanded by Vernon to include products

274

Company Perspectives:

We are totally committed to satisfying our customers. We create value for our shareholders and customers by providing outstanding products and services. We are dedicated to exclusive and value-priced products, helping our customers to live better for less.

for the home. She personally chose every product featured in her catalogs and had an "uncanny knack" for judging the needs and desires of middle-class housewives. Based on her own experiences, she knew that housewives required well-built products at reasonable prices. Although products were bought from a variety of manufacturers, most were customized under the Lillian Vernon name. As proof of the quality of its products Lillian Vernon offered a 100 percent money-back guarantee, which stated that "customers can return a product even ten years after it has been purchased."

Vernon Specialties' catalog was quite successful in its first decade, and sales continued to increase. In 1965, the company changed its name to Lillian Vernon Corporation. Sales were given an added boost in 1968, when Lillian Vernon introduced personalized Christmas ornaments in its catalogs. This product line would grow so popular that over 75 million ornaments would be sold by 1994. In 1970 the company's annual sales hit $1 million.

Sales continued to grow moderately throughout the 1970s. In 1978, as a response to the growing number of catalog customers interested in retailing Lillian Vernon products in their own stores, the company established its Provender wholesale division. Provender provided retailers with Lillian Vernon's own line of imported toiletries, fancy foods, and kitchen textiles, such as towels, aprons, and pot holders. Around that time, the company also opened The New Company, a wholesale manufacturer of brass products headquartered in Providence, Rhode Island.

In 1982, sales jumped again when the company introduced its first sale catalog offering overstocked merchandise at prices up to 75 percent off the original retail prices. Due largely to the success of its sale catalogs, Lillian Vernon posted record revenues of $75 million in 1983. The following year, Lillian Vernon introduced a line of private-label, exclusively designed home organization products in its catalog, a line that grew to represent 25 percent of business within ten years. In 1985, the company streamlined its operations by incorporating its Provender division into the main wholesale division.

The mail-order industry grew by leaps and bounds in the 1980s, with the number of people ordering merchandise by phone or mail increasing 70 percent between 1982 and 1992. Small, specialty catalogs like Lillian Vernon entered the market in full force, taking sales away from traditional mail-order giants like Sears and Montgomery Ward.

Going Public in 1987

By 1987, Lillian Vernon was mailing out 80 million catalogs a year. The company went public that year, with an initial offering of 1.9 million shares on the American Stock Exchange.

Proceeds for the offering were used to construct a state-of-the-art National Distribution Center in Virginia Beach, Virginia. That year, net income totaled $4.4 million on revenues of $115.5 million. The following year, net income grew to $6.9 million on revenues of $126 million.

Expansion continued with the 1989 addition of a computer center at the company's National Distribution Center. That year, Laura Zambano was named to the position of senior vice-president, general merchandise manager, taking over many of the merchandising responsibilities from Vernon. Also that year, the company opened its first outlet store near its Virginia Beach distribution center. The company made an attempt to further diversify its product offerings by introducing a high-end home furnishings catalog, which ultimately was incorporated into the company's other catalogs.

The following year, however, Lillian Vernon introduced the highly successful Lilly's Kids catalogs, specializing in toys, games, and personalized gifts for children. Sales hit $162 million in 1991 with profits of $9.5 million. A new customer service center was opened in Virginia, as were two new outlet stores: one in a suburb of Washington, D.C., and the other in Williamsburg, Virginia.

Lillian Vernon was able to stay on top of the booming catalog industry by constantly introducing new products and by keeping prices reasonable. As the company entered its fourth decade, the average price of a product was $17 and the average customer order totaled $39. In 1992, the company declared its first quarterly dividend of $0.05 per share. That year, it also introduced its Christmas Memories catalog, specializing in Christmas ornaments and holiday decorations for the home. By 1992, Lillian Vernon was adding over 1,000 new products a year to its four catalogs and had three more outlet stores in Virginia and New York state.

In 1993, Lillian Vernon launched its Welcome catalog, offering home organization products and decorative accessories for people who had recently moved to new homes. Net income for 1993 totaled $12.8 million on revenues of $196.3 million. Headquarters were moved from Mount Vernon to New Rochelle, New York.

Although the catalog and direct marketing industry boomed in the 1980s, cyclical downturns are inevitable. Company management regarded increased specialization and diversification of its catalogs as essential to success in this rapidly changing environment. In response to increased competition, Lillian Vernon began test-mailing its catalogs in Canada and also began investigating other foreign markets. The company offered products on television's QVC Shopping Network, and Vernon personally appeared on Joan Rivers's television shopping program in 1994. In another effort to keep on top of trends in the direct marketing industry, Lillian Vernon became one of 39 catalogs to be featured on The Merchant, one of the first CD-ROM shopping discs.

As Lillian Vernon approached its fiftieth anniversary, the company seemed intent on expansion. It launched another specialized catalog in February 1995 offering cookwear, cutlery, table accessories, gourmet gifts, and small electric appliances. Two months later, it launched a special section in its core

---

Key Dates:

1951: Lilly Hochberg starts a home-based mail order business.
1954: Vernon Specialties moves out of Hochberg's home.
1956: First catalog mailed.
1965: Name changes to Lillian Vernon Corporation.
1982: Company introduces first liquidation catalog.
1987: Lillian Vernon lists on the American Stock Exchange.
1989: First outlet store opened.
1993: President Fred Hochberg, the founder's son, departs suddenly.
1995: Offer to buy most of the company falls through; Lillian Vernon goes online.
1996: HarperCollins publishes Vernon's autobiography, *An Eye for Winners*; Lillian Vernon begins mailings to consumers in Japan.
1998: Lillian Vernon enters British market.
2000: Rue de France acquired.

---

catalog featuring luggage and travel accessories. The company began selling its products through the Prodigy online service and was also looking into further growth through acquisitions and expansion of its corporate gift, premium, incentive, and gift certificate markets.

A New Outlook in the 1990s

The sudden departure of her son Fred Hochberg from the president's post in 1992 made Lillian Vernon reevaluate her plans for the company. A French company offered to buy it in 1994, and the next spring, a New York-based investment group, Freeman Spogli & Co. offered $190 million for three-quarters of it. To sweeten the deal, both Vernon and her son David Hochberg were to keep their executive positions for five years; they would also control one-quarter of the company's equity.

Although the Lillian Vernon Corporation posted record revenues of $222.2 million for the fiscal year, a postal rate hike was announced in January and the company had seen paper costs rise 50 percent in the preceding 12 months. Freeman Spogli reportedly ran into problems with its financing due to the tough environment; the cataloger did have 10,000 competitors, after all. When Vernon and Hochberg would not agree to lower the agreed price, the deal was called off.

Also in the spring of 1995, the gourmet Lillian Vernon's Kitchen catalog debuted. It was more organized and more brand-oriented than the company's main catalog. The company also began to make its products available over the Internet via an America Online store.

President Stephen Marks left the company in May 1995. His replacement, Howard Goldberg, was not named until the end of March 1996. Goldberg had formerly been in charge of the Macy's catalog.

In the fiscal year February 1996, Lillian Vernon mailed 179 million catalogs to 18 million people. This garnered nearly five

million orders. Revenues rose slightly to $238.2 million, although profits were halved due to increased costs. There were more auspicious developments in the rest of the year. Harper-Collins published Vernon's autobiography, *An Eye for Winners*, and paper prices came down.

At the time, Lillian Vernon was producing a new catalog every couple of weeks. It began mailings in Japan and expanded its National Distribution Center in Virginia by 335,000 square feet. A new seasonal telemarketing center opened in New Rochelle, New York. The company also test marketed a membership-based buyer's club.

The Lillian Vernon catalog had long included garden-related products when the company launched its first dedicated gardening catalog in March 1998. With more upscale offerings than the core catalogs, it proved instantly profitable. In the fall of 1998, Lillian Vernon began mailing to U.K. consumers in cooperation with Great Universal Stores PLC.

In August 1998, corporate headquarters moved to a seven-acre site in Rye, Westchester County, New York. The company began buying back its stock, which lost almost 20 percent of its value in one year, in October 1998. After takeover rumors caused it to rise in the mid-1990s, investors doubted the company's prospects, even though it managed to stay virtually free of long term debt. One believer in Lillian Vernon—the woman, that is—was fashionable Manhattan hairstylist Paolo Martino, who married her in 1998.

As Vernon noted in an interview, buyers had become more affluent in the previous decades. More could purchase luxuries like Wedgewood china, for example. They still appreciated bargains, however. The annual clearance sale for the Virginia Beach distribution center became something of a tourist attraction, visited by about 16,000 shoppers. The event grossed half a million dollars in four days.

Employment at Lillian Vernon swelled from 600 to 4,000 in the weeks before Christmas. The company faced increased competition for workers at its Virginia Beach call center due to the opening of other, similar businesses in the area. A new online catalog debuted in December 1998. At the time, Lillian Vernon managed 16 outlet stores and eight catalogs.

Lillian Vernon launched the ''Neat Ideas'' catalog in the fall of 1999, featuring kitchenware, a category that accounted for 15 percent of the company's total sales. (Lillian Vernon's Kitchen had been dropped by then.) Lillian Vernon acquired the Rue de France catalog in 2000 and launched a new web site. Revenues for the fiscal year slipped from $255.2 million to $241.8 million as the mailing list was trimmed somewhat to reduce costs: profits doubled to $6.3 million.

As Lillian Vernon prepared to celebrate its fiftieth anniversary in 2001, the company was publishing seven catalog titles: Lillian Vernon, Lilly's Kids, Personalized Gift, Lillian Vernon Gardening, Christmas Memories, Neat Ideas, and Favorites. It had added seasonal call centers in Las Vegas, Nevada, and New Rochelle, New York, and was debuting 3,000 unique products a year.

Principal Subsidiaries

Lillian Vernon International, Ltd.; Lillian Vernon Fulfillment Services, Inc.; Lillian Vernon Retail Corporation.

Principal Competitors

Hanover Direct; Spiegel; Williams-Sonoma.

Further Reading

Belton, Beth, "Catalog Queen Has More up Her Sleeve," *USA Today,* November 29, 1996, p. B7.

Bryan, Marvin, "How a Refugee Created a Mail-Order Empire," *Profit,* March 2000, pp. 12–21.

Burney, Teresa, "The Matriarch of Mail Order," *St. Petersburg Times,* December 23, 1996, p. 8.

Byrne, Harlan S., "Lillian Vernon Corp.: Segmentation Builds Catalog Sales," *Barron's,* June 4, 1990, p. 58.

"Cause of Failed Lillian Vernon Sale Is Disputed," *Mergers & Acquisitions Report,* September 25, 1995, p. 11.

Coleman, Lisa, "I Went Out and Did It," *Forbes,* August 17, 1992, p. 102.

Furman, Phyllis, "Exec Losses, Wrecked Deal Unhinge Lillian Vernon: Tough Catalog Industry Environment Hinders Efforts to Find a New Buyer," *Crain's New York Business,* September 25, 1995, p. 39.

Garbato-Stankevich, Debby, "Lilly's Red-Hot Love Affair," *HFD: The Weekly Home Furnishings Newspaper,* June 21, 1993, p. 52.

——, "Lillian Vernon's Kitchen Catalog Debuts," *HFN,* March 20, 1995, p. 41.

——, "Vernon, Suitor Ax Buyout Agreement," *HFN,* September 25, 1995, p. 49.

Gattuso, Greg, "Lillian Vernon Looks to the Future," *Direct Marketing,* August 1994, p. 33.

Goldbogen, Jessica, "Lillian Vernon's New Green Thumb," *HFN,* March 9, 1998, p. 26.

Kehoe, Ann-Margaret, "The Profits Are in the Mail," *HFN,* September 16, 1996, p. 57.

Lisovicz, Susan, and Bill Tucker, "Lillian Vernon, Founder & CEO," *Entrepreneurs Only* (television program), broadcast on August 26, 1999 on CNNfn.

Peltz, James F., "Lillian Vernon Still the Head of Catalog House," *Los Angeles Times,* June 26, 1995, p. D4.

Simon, Virginia, "A Marketing Maestro Orchestrates," *Target Marketing,* October 1992, p. 16.

Sinha, Vandana, "Catalog Retailer Lillian Vernon Expands Virginia Beach, Va. Clearance," *Norfolk Virginian-Pilot,* August 8, 1998.

——, "Seasonal Help Scarce at Virginia Beach, Va. Catalog Call Center," *Norfolk Virginian-Pilot,* December 22, 1998.

Thau, Barbara, "Lillian's Kitchen: Cataloger Taps E-Commerce, Innovative Products for Growth," *HFN,* August 9, 1999, p. 51.

Vernon, Lillian, *An Eye for Winners: How I Built One of America's Greatest Direct-Mail Businesses,* New York: HarperCollins, 1996.

—Maura Troester
—updated by Frederick C. Ingram

Lions Gate Entertainment Corporation

595 Burrard Street, Suite 3123
P.O. Box 49139
Vancouver, British Columbia V7X 1J1
Canada
Telephone: (604) 609-6100
Fax: (604) 609-6149
Web site: http://www.lionsgate-ent.com

Public Company
Incorporated: 1997
Employees: 342
Sales: $78.4 million
Stock Exchanges: American Toronto
Ticker Symbol: LGF
NAIC: 51211 Motion Picture and Video Production;
    51212 Motion Picture and Video Distribution; 512191
    Teleproduction and Other Postproduction Services

Lions Gate Entertainment Corporation is a leading independent film and television production company based in Canada. Lions Gate has a number of subsidiaries located in both Canada and the United States, and the company is also a partner in several other ventures. Subsidiaries include Lions Gate Films, which produces and distributes motion pictures, Lions Gate Studios, the largest film and television production facility in Canada, Lions Gate Television, which makes TV series and movies, and Avalanche Films, a video distribution company. Lions Gate also has stakes in Peter Guber's Mandalay Pictures, a producer of theatrical films for release through Paramount, Cine-Groupe, which produces animated television programs, and Sterling Home Entertainment, a video distributor. Lions Gate continues to grow by making acquisitions, including video company Trimark Holdings, which it purchased in 2000. The company's founder, Frank Giustra, stepped down as CEO in June of that year and his place was taken by former Sony Pictures executive Jon Feltheimer.

Origins in 1997

Lions Gate Entertainment Corporation was founded by financier Frank Giustra in the summer of 1997. Giustra, the son of a Sudbury, Ontario nickel miner, had served previously as CEO of Yorkton Securities, Inc., an investment bank that specialized in funding mining ventures. During his years as a banker, he also had been involved in the financing of a half dozen films. A lifelong movie fan, Giustra had decided that he wanted to enter the entertainment business when he reached the age of 40. Leaving Yorkton in December of 1996, he set out to assemble a Canadian film company that could compete with Hollywood on its own terms.

To fund the new venture he put up $16 million of his own money and used his banking connections to arrange for $40 million in financing from investors, including Yorkton. Giustra then obtained $64 million when Lions Gate merged with Toronto Stock Exchange listee Beringer Gold Corp. to became a public company. Beringer's mining assets were quickly sold off, and the newly christened Lions Gate Entertainment set out to purchase several existing Canadian film businesses with its new war chest.

One of Lions Gate's first purchases was Cinepix Film Properties, a Montreal-based producer and distributor that had been founded in 1962 by John Dunning and Andre Link, who both still ran the company. Cinepix released both English- and French-language films, and it was one of Canada's leading independent motion picture companies. Cinepix also had a U.S. distribution arm based in New York. The company produced ten to 12 modestly budgeted titles annually and also distributed edgy art-house fare such as grunge rock documentary *Hype,* Vincent Gallo's offbeat *Buffalo 66,* and *Sick: The Life & Death of Bob Flanagan, Supermasochist.* In addition, Cinepix owned 56 percent of Cine-Groupe, a Montreal-based animated film production company. Giustra renamed Cinepix Lions Gate Films after the acquisition, but kept its leadership intact. An offshoot, Lions Gate International, was later formed in Los Angeles to serve as a worldwide distribution branch.

Lions Gate also bought North Shore Studios, located in Giustra's home base of Vancouver, British Columbia. North Shore (subsequently renamed Lions Gate Studios) was Canada's largest film production facility, with six busy sound stages. Because it was cheaper to work there, many American production companies chose Vancouver to shoot their movies and TV shows. The series *The X Files* was shot at North Shore for its first five seasons, and other American shows such as *Millennium* used the studio as well.

Another branch of Lions Gate was Mandalay Television, a California-based producer of made-for-TV movies. Mandalay was acquired in a deal with Hollywood mogul Peter Guber, who was given four percent ownership of Lions Gate. Guber was a controversial figure in the film world, with a string of hit movies such as *Batman* and *Midnight Express* to his credit, but also a reputation for profligate spending. He had run Columbia Pictures for five years starting in 1989, but the company had been forced to write down $510 million in lawsuit and contract settlement expenses following his departure.

Gambling on Guber in 1998

In early 1998 Lions Gate announced a second, larger deal with Guber to form Mandalay Pictures, which would produce feature films costing between $15 and $75 million each. Guber and his partners Paul Schaeffer and Adam Platnick would own 55 percent of Mandalay, and Lions Gate would own the rest. The complicated financial arrangement called for Giustra's company to put up $80 million, with more than $700 million coming from Paramount Pictures and other companies who would share distribution rights. Lions Gate would not earn anything from the deal until after the distributors had recouped their costs. Noting Guber's reputation, Lions Gate declared that it had protective measures in place that would guard against excessive spending. A total of 20 films was to be produced in a five-year period, with the first due in 2000.

In June of 1998, Lions Gate completed another purchase, this time picking up a bankrupt film distributor called International Movie Group, Inc. (IMG). Ten years earlier IMG had received $14 million in financing from Frank Giustra and Yorktown Securities, but the company had gone belly up in 1996. IMG's main asset was its film library, which included such titles as Jean-Claude Van Damme's *Kickboxer*. IMG's holdings were integrated into Lions Gate's other operations, and its former CEO Peter Strauss was named president of newly formed Lions Gate Entertainment, Inc., which would become the American parent company for Lions Gate's U.S. interests. Strauss had put in many years in the movie business, going back to Allied Artists Pictures Corp., where he had overseen production of such classic films as *Cabaret* and *The Man Who Would Be King*. Strauss had been instrumental in bringing Giustra and Guber together.

Lions Gate's newly allied divisions were now beginning to bring home contracts and make production plans. Mandalay Television announced that it would be shooting TV series for ABC (*Cupid*), Lifetime (*Oh Baby*), UPN (*Mercy Point*), and Showtime (*Rude Awakening*). Lions Gate Films also picked up distribution deals for Paul Schrader's *Affliction,* a to-be-titled Ted Demme drama, and several others. Another new subsidiary, Lions Gate Media, was formed at this time to explore additional television production possibilities.

Lions Gate also was drawing attention for two controversial projects with which it was involved. One was the Adrian Lyne-directed remake of Vladimir Nabokov's *Lolita,* which was slated to be released uncut in Canada through Lions Gate Films. The portrait of an obsessive pedophile had received a great deal of negative prerelease publicity, as well as a few critical raves. It eventually was released for a limited run before being broadcast on cable television. A much bigger controversy involved the company's plans to film Bret Easton Ellis's novel *American Psycho,* which depicted a stockbroker who was also a sexual sadist. The company was wooing Leonardo Di Caprio for the lead, his first role after the blockbuster *Titanic*. Despite the offer of a reported $21 million, Di Caprio turned the project down, possibly because his fan base of teenage girls would be unable to view the anticipated R to NC-17 rated film. The company continued with its production plans after Di Caprio dropped out, however, and signed Christian Bale for the role.

Assessing the First Year's Results

At the end of the company's first year in business, a loss of $397,000 U.S. dollars on revenues of $42.2 million was reported. Lions Gate's stock also had fallen to a low of $1.40 a share. The annual loss was far from unexpected for a brand new company, but the slipping share price was bothersome, as it reduced the company's ability to make acquisitions. Purchase of an American reality-based television company, Termite Art Productions, could only be made with the issuance of three convertible promissory notes, rather than a stock swap, because of the low price. The $2.75 million deal brought Lions Gate the maker of a wide spectrum of programs that ranged from History Channel documentaries to tabloid-style fare like "Busted on the Job."

Concern about the low share price finally led Giustra to call a shareholder meeting for October 30, where a vote was made to list Lions Gate on the American Stock Exchange. A two-for-one stock consolidation was effected to bring the share price up to the AMEX minimum. It was hoped that the greater exposure of an AMEX listing would boost the stock's value.

In January of 1999 the company named Roman Doroniuk, formerly with competitor Alliance Communications, to the posts of president and chief operating officer. Giustra remained Lions Gate Entertainment's CEO and chairman. Meanwhile, Lions Gate Films was scoring kudos for the films *Affliction* and *Gods and Monsters,* which were now in theaters, while hockey comedy *Les Boys 2* was breaking box office records in French Canada. Cine-Groupe also signed a deal to produce 26 half-hour episodes of a cartoon series called *Mega Babies,* to premiere on Fox Family TV in the fall of 1999. The previous year Fox Family had purchased a 20 percent stake in Cine-Groupe. A new infusion of $16.5 million also was received when 5.4

million shares of Lions Gate stock were sold on a "bought-deal" basis.

In March, the company received its first Academy Awards when James Coburn won an Oscar for best supporting actor in *Affliction* and *Gods and Monsters* was honored for Bill Condon's adapted screenplay. Lions Gate had reportedly spent $500,000 in a public relations campaign to promote the two films, which were nominated for a total of five awards.

Controversy over *American Psycho* continued to mount in Toronto, where scenes for the movie were being shot. Several antiviolence and victim's rights groups were protesting the film's production, although city officials ultimately issued a permit allowing location shooting. Many Canadians were up in arms about the project because notorious Ontario sex killer Paul Bernardo was found to have a copy of the book at his bedside.

More New Projects in 1999

In April 1999 the company moved its financial operations to Toronto, where new president Doroniuk's offices were located. Giustra and the corporate headquarters remained in Vancouver. New projects on which company divisions were working included TV movies *The First Daughter* and *The Linda McCartney Story,* TV series *Hope Island* and *Cliffhangers,* and animated feature *Heavy Metal 2000,* produced for Columbia Tri-Star.

When the company released its figures for the second fiscal year, it reported losses of $9.3 million on revenues of $78.3 million. The studio and film divisions were the healthiest, with video sales to the United States via new subsidiary Avalanche Films and half-owned Sterling Home Entertainment particularly strong. The biggest chunk of red ink was attributable to the investment in Mandalay Pictures. Because of "accounting rules," in the words of President Doroniuk, Lions Gate was picking up 100 percent of Mandalay's losses. In the summer the company put its 13.8-acre Vancouver studio complex up for sale. The asking price was $28 million, but there were no immediate takers. The company's television division also had been restructured to emphasize hour-long non-network series over the production of more financially risky network shows. Its association with Guber's Mandalay Television had been terminated.

In the summer Lions Gate scored a hit in theaters when the Canadian-produced drama *The Red Violin* took in nearly $10 million on the art-house circuit. The Samuel Jackson-starring film was made by a French- and English-Canadian team and

was financed and shot internationally. In the fall the company announced two more major deals. Lions Gate Television was to produce a miniseries based on author Dean Koontz's novel *Sole Survivor,* and Lions Gate Films would distribute a new low-budget film starring and co-produced by Kevin Spacey entitled *The Big Kahuna.* Spacey reportedly took Lions Gate's $1.5 million offer over several larger ones because he was impressed with the company's track record and its marketing savvy.

Late in the year Lions Gate was seeking still more capital, arranging for a $13.4 million line of credit and filing a preliminary prospectus to sell $30 million in preferred stock shares and common stock purchase warrants. In December the first release from Mandalay Pictures also reached theater screens. *Sleepy Hollow,* directed by Tim Burton, grossed $30 million in its opening weekend despite mixed reviews. Lions Gate also began distributing *Dogma,* which was directed by Kevin Smith and was the company's widest release to date. The film grossed $8.7 million on its opening weekend, and it was expected to earn triple that amount over time. *Dogma* was another controversial project, a satire of Catholicism whose distribution had been switched from Disney-owned Miramax to Lions Gate because of the subject matter.

In January 2000 yet another influx of cash was obtained, this time $33.1 million from a group of investors that included Microsoft co-founder Paul Allen, former Sony executive Jon Feltheimer, German broadcasting company Tele-Munchen, and SBS Broadcasting SA. The money was earmarked to fund more acquisitions.

Giustra Steps Down in 2000

The new financing was quickly followed by dramatic management shifts at the company. Jon Feltheimer took over Giustra's job as CEO, with the founder retaining only his board chairman duties. A short time later President Doroniuk made his own exit, apparently frustrated at having been passed over for Giustra's job. While the dust was clearing, Lions Gate took home its third and fourth Oscars when *The Red Violin* garnered a statuette for best original score and *Sleepy Hollow* won for art direction.

Quickly grabbing the reins, industry vet Feltheimer announced an increase in filmmaking activity, with 15 movies budgeted at $5 to $20 million to be made annually. In addition, the Avalanche video subsidiary would soon start production on several $1 million genre films to help expand its catalog. Acquisition of another independent film company and a film library were also on Lions Gate's agenda. In June the company accomplished the latter, purchasing low-budget film and video distributor Trimark for an estimated $50 million in stock and cash, plus assumption of $36 million in debt. The ten-year-old company specialized in action and genre films and had a 650-title library. Trimark also owned a web site, CinemaNow, which offered broadband streaming capabilities. Lions Gate was expected to begin featuring its own product on the site, which showcased independent films, some available exclusively over the Internet.

After only three short years in business, Lions Gate Entertainment had seen many changes and was still growing rapidly.

The company was expanding on its strengths as a producer and distributor of independent films, while at the same time growing its home video and television production divisions. Lions Gate's long-term prospects were still somewhat hazy, but much effort was being made to establish it as a permanent part of the movie industry landscape.

Principal Subsidiaries

Avalanche Films; Cinepix Animation, Inc.; Cinepix Films, Inc.; LG Pictures, Inc.; Lions Gate Entertainment Inc.; Lions Gate Films Corp.; Lions Gate Films Inc.; Lions Gate Media Corp.; Lions Gate Media Inc.; Lions Gate Television; Trimark Holdings; Distribution International Cine-Groupe J.P. Inc. (56%); Sterling Home Entertainment (50%).

Principal Competitors

Alliance Atlantis Communications, Inc.; Artisan Entertainment, Inc.; Bertelsmann AG; DreamWorks SKG; Metro-Goldwyn-Mayer, Inc.; The News Corporation Ltd.; Overseas Filmgroup, Inc.; Sony Pictures Entertainment; Time Warner, Inc.; Unapix Entertainment, Inc.; Universal Studios, Inc.; Viacom, Inc.; The Walt Disney Company.

Further Reading

Bond, Paul, and Etan Vlessing, "Lions Gate Gets New Partners in $33.1 Mil Deal," *Hollywood Reporter,* January 5, 2000, p. 1.

Bouw, Brenda, "Lions Gate Founder Steps Down as Chief Executive: Frank Giustra To Be Replaced by Jon Feltheimer," *National Post,* March 22, 2000, p. C1.

——, "Two Lions Gate Films Up for Five Oscars," *National Post,* February 11, 1999, p. C8.

Craig, Susan, "Lions Gate Loses Senior Executive," *Globe and Mail,* April 7, 2000, p. B2.

"'Dogma' Converts Audiences," *Hollywood Reporter,* January 6, 2000, p. 37.

Dunkley, Cathy, "Roaring Growth for Lions Gate," *Hollywood Reporter,* May 12, 2000, p. 1.

Eisner, Ken, "Focus—Canada: Lions Gate Opens New Doors," *Variety,* December 8, 1997, p. 107.

Enchin, Harvey, "Former Yorkton Head Creates Entertainment Giant," *Globe and Mail,* September 12, 1997, p. B12.

Harris, Dana, "Trimark Fits Plate of Prowling Lions Gate," *Variety,* June 12, 2000, p. 8.

Kelly, Brendan, "Lions Gate Reveals Mixed Bag for Year," *Daily Variety,* July 30, 1999, p. 4.

Kennedy, Peter, "Securities: Now He's Trying To Sign Leonardo Di Caprio to a Movie Deal. Can Howe Street Chutzpah Work in Tinseltown?," *Financial Post,* June 20, 1998, p. 14.

Lippman, John, "Movies: Rich Film Deal Gives Guber New Partners," *Wall Street Journal,* March 10, 1998, p. B1.

Lyons, Charles, "Lions Gate-Keepers," *Variety,* March 27, 2000, p. 8.

MacDonald, Gayle, "Lions Gate Boss Vows Smoother Ride," *Globe and Mail,* September 15, 1998, p. B16.

——, "Lions Gate Gambles on Hollywood," *Globe and Mail,* September 24, 1998, p. B18.

Mayers, Adam, "The Lions Roar at Hollywood," *Toronto Star,* September 13, 1997, p. E1.

Reguly, Eric, "Lions Gate's Hollywood Gamble," *Globe and Mail,* June 11, 1998, p. B17.

Shecter, Barbara, "Lions Gate Puzzler: Shares Dip Well Below Book Value," *Financial Post,* September 10, 1998, p. 27.

Westell, Dan, and Keith Damsell, "Beringer, Lions Gate To Merge," *Financial Post,* November 11, 1997, p. 36.

—Frank Uhle

Mashantucket Pequot Gaming Enterprise Inc.

Route 2
Mashantucket, Connecticut 06339
U.S.A.
Telephone: (860) 312-3000
Fax: (860) 312-1599
Web site: http://www.foxwoods.com

Private Company
Incorporated: 1992
Employees: 11,500
Sales: $1 billion (1998 est.)
NAIC: 713210 Casinos; 721120 Casino Hotels; 722110,
    Full Service Restaurants; 722213 Snack and Non-
    Alcoholic Beverage Bars; 711310 Promoters of
    Performing Arts, Sports, and Similar Events with
    Facilities; 713910 Golf Courses and Country Clubs

Mashantucket Pequot Gaming Enterprise Inc. operates the Foxwoods Casino Resort, a 4.7 million square-foot complex comprised of five casinos; three hotels; over 55,000 square feet in meeting space; a theater and entertainment district; a health spa; 17 retail shops; five gourmet restaurants; and a variety of casual restaurants, bars, and cafes. The resort's casinos encompass over 315,000 square-feet of gaming space including a non-smoking casino. With over 340 gaming tables, Foxwoods offers poker, blackjack, craps, roulette, baccarat, and several novelty games. Other gaming options include keno, high stakes bingo, and more than 5,800 slot machines, including high-limit slots from $5 to $100. For family entertainment Foxwoods provides theaters, an arcade, Turbo Ride, and the Mashantucket Pequot Museum and Research Center. Gaming and many services are available 24 hours a day, every day of the year. Located on the Mashantucket Pequot reservation at Ledyard, Connecticut, Foxwoods towers above the wooded countryside with its striking turquoise roofs. The resort takes its name from the Mashantucket Pequot Tribal Nation; the Pequot Indians are known as ''the fox people,'' while Mashantucket means ''much-wooded land.''

A Resort Rises Above the Woods

The history of Mashantucket Pequot Gaming may be traced to the efforts of the Pequot Indians to gain national recognition as a Tribe. History books had long held that the Pequots, of what is now southeastern Connecticut, virtually disappeared during the 17th century, following the Pequot War and the Colonial years of hardship and disease. Those who weren't killed, historians maintained, were assimilated into the European culture of the time. Those descended from Pequots of the pre-Colonial area, however, begged to differ. In the 1970s, a man of Pequot descent, Richard ''Skip'' Hayward, led a successful movement for the federal recognition of the Pequot Tribe; Hayward was elected chairman of the Mashantucket Pequot Tribal Nation in 1975, and the government officially recognized the Tribe in 1983. Archeologists would later support the Tribe's claims, as the discovery of artifacts revealed that the Pequots did indeed survive the 1637 war and lived as a Tribe for years to come, striving to maintain their culture. What had dwindled to a small parcel of reservation land was bolstered in the early 1980s by a $900,000 federal grant used to repurchase Pequot land; the Pequot reservation would eventually total some 2,500 acres.

As chairman of the Mashantucket Pequot Tribe, Heyward, who had worked as a pipefitter in the 1970s, announced that the Tribe would begin developing some of the reservation land in order to better the Tribe's economic status. In 1986, they opened a 2,100-seat bingo hall on the reservation. Two years later, with the signing of The Indian Gaming Regulatory Act legalizing gambling on Indian reservations, Heyward and the Tribe decided to build a casino. Typically, Heyward encountered difficulties finding investors for the project, but he was eventually able to secure funds abroad, through a Malaysian developer who reportedly provided around $60 million in start-up capital. To consult in the management and legal issues surrounding the new casino, Heyward tapped G. Michael Brown, who would be named CEO of the company in 1993.

The new Foxwoods High Stakes Bingo & Casino opened in February 1992, offering poker, blackjack, roulette, and other games at 170 game tables. In addition to the 46,000 square-foot gaming casino, the facility included three restaurants, a museum, and a piano bar. The casino proved a success from the first day as charter and tour buses brought senior citizens and tourists from New York, Rhode Island, Massachusetts, and other areas of Connecticut. The Tribe did not originally intend to operate a 24-hour facility but quickly adapted to demand.

Foxwoods began to offer gaming on slot machines in early 1993. The Mashantucket Pequot Tribe and the State of Connecticut agreed that the Tribe would pay to Connecticut a 25 percent state tax on ''net win,'' or a minimum of $100,000 million per year. Foxwoods started with 1,500 machines and quickly reached an average daily win of $585, exceeding expectations. Foxwoods staff and consultants designed many of the slot machines. The Rock 'n Reels quarter slots, based on the Wurlitzer jukebox of the 1940s, proved so popular that Foxwoods decided to manufacture and market the machines to other casinos in partnership with Anchor Game.

Foxwoods introduced the Wampum Club card to measure guest gambling activity and to provide guest discounts. A magnetic swipe code on the back of the card recorded game play and added points accordingly. With a free membership, Wampum Club card holders swiped the card at slot machines, bingo, keno, and table games and redeemed accumulated points toward meals, theater tickets, discounts at the salon or spa, merchandise, or admission to the Cinedrome. Foxwoods also awarded random cash prizes and offered special promotions to club members.

Heyward's hopes for property remained ambitious, and expansion plans were soon realized. In November 1993 Foxwoods completed a $240 million expansion, which transformed the casino into a complete destination resort, renamed Foxwoods Resort Casino. The expansion involved five large gaming areas, offering keno, Racebook, an additional 1,150 slot machines, and an additional 64 game tables. New services included a beauty salon, 17 retail shops, an ice cream parlor, a delicatessen, and a pizza stand. Facilities at the 312-room Great Cedar Hotel included a health spa, a fine dining restaurant, and meeting and conference rooms; the hotel has received the AAA Four-Diamond rating since opening. Moreover, the Mashantucket Pequot Tribe invested in the Two Trees Inn, a 280-room country inn adjacent to Foxwoods, which offered a 24-hour free shuttle service to the casinos.

For family fun and adult entertainment Foxwoods created a theater and entertainment district. The Cinetropolis District included the Cinedrome, a 360-degree video theater featuring family films during the day and high tech videos and live entertainment as a dance club at night, the Cinedrome Niteclub. The Turbo Ride comprised six-direction seats which moved with the action on the oversized video screen. Entertainer Frank Sinatra presided over the opening of the Fox Theater, a 1,400-seat live-performance center.

The spectacular financial success of Foxwoods allowed the Tribe to expand further. In June 1994 a $65 million project added 300,000 square feet and involved the relocation of the bingo hall to a larger space. The new multi-purpose center accommodated over 3,000 bingo players or up to 5,000 people for live performances and boxing events. Foxwoods placed 1,200 slot machines into the former bingo hall, increasing total slots to 3,864 and total gaming space to 190,000 square feet. New family-oriented entertainment included the Fox Arcade, featuring electronic video games, pinball, and other games.

Another $80 million expansion began in April 1995, adding a poker room and a high-limit gaming area with 30 tables. A 200-seat, state-of-the-art Racebook featured a 50-foot high resolution video screen, L.E.D. display boards, individual television carrels, and real-time odds. The second phase of the project involved a new casino for non-smokers, completed in spring 1996.

During this time, competition for Foxwoods emerged in the form of the new Mohegan Sun casino, just ten miles away. However, according to company management, the new casino only affected slot machine revenues temporarily as many gamblers preferred the ample amenities at Foxwoods, while the overall customer base continued to grow. Slot-win per day averages were comparable by fall 1996 as slot business increased 43 percent overall, with 3500 new machines between the two casinos. Foxwoods and Mohegan Sun, operated by the Mohegan Tribe, eventually would come to see themselves as partners in attracting tourism to Connecticut rather than as competitors.

Foxwoods enhanced its services with the implementation of ATM network multimedia applications. Basic applications included interactive information kiosks throughout the resort and in hotel guest rooms. The technology also allowed Racebook patrons to stop and replay videos of horse races at individual television carrels, allowing them to review the last three races. The addition of a photo into the Wampum Card member's record allowed a MagScanCard reader to project the image and name of a bingo winner onto a large video screen along with the winning bingo card.

Conventions and an Upscale Clientele in the Late 1990s

Already attracting 30,000 visitors per day, in December 1995 Foxwoods unveiled a $350 million plan to add 1.4 million square feet of resort facilities. The 18-month project involved a 824-room hotel and over 50,000 square feet of conference and meeting space designed to attract large and small conferences, trade shows, meetings, and special events. In addition to grand views of the Connecticut woods, the Grand Pequot Tower included a three-story atrium, the 25,000 square-foot Grand Pequot Ballroom which featured crystal chandeliers, two gourmet restaurants, and a café. Meeting facilities included rooms ranging from 3,000 square-feet to 6,300 square-feet, while the ballroom provided up to five divided rooms. The Foxwoods Business Center offered office supplies and a variety of business services. The

---

Key Dates:

1986: Pequot Tribe opens a high stakes bingo hall.
1988: U.S. government legalizes reservation gambling.
1992: The Foxwoods High Stakes Bingo & Casino opens for business.
1993: Foxwoods becomes a destination resort with a $240 million expansion.
1995: Tourist traffic reaches 30,000 visitors per day.
1997: Opening of Grand Pequot Tower.
1999: Arrival of one millionth bus passenger.

---

addition of 50,000 square-feet of gaming space included 958 slot machines, 60 game tables as well as high-stakes gaming in the exclusive Club Newport International.

The major portion of the Grand Pequot Tower opened in July 1997. Additional floors were completed in November followed by the opening of additional meeting space in April 1998. By the time the expansion was complete, Foxwoods became the most profitable casino in the Western hemisphere and the slot machines garnered more revenue per day than slots in New Jersey or Nevada.

To complement the resort's upscale image, Foxwoods introduced a private-label fragrance, designed by Georges and Vivian Gotlib, in May 1997. The couple had been seeking new outlets for their fragrances and presented a classic floral fragrance to Foxwoods' merchandising division. The products fit with the resort's fashion-forward boutiques and salons. Promotions involved posters displayed throughout the resort, advertisements on the in-house television channel, and sample and information tables at a Paul Anka concert. The launch of a bath and body care line, Sea and Forest, was planned for July.

Other activities of the Mashantucket Pequot Gaming Enterprises involved a partnership with the Bernard Investment Group. The joint venture acquired two area golf courses, renamed the Foxwoods Golf and Country Club at Boulder Hills, a championship, 18-hole course, and the Foxwoods Executive Golf Club at Lindhbrook, a smaller 18-hole course in nearby Rhode Island. Foxwoods provided a shuttle service for hotel patrons. The Mashantucket Pequot Tribe began development of Fox Navigation, a ferry service from Long Island to New London, Connecticut, with bus transportation to Foxwoods from New London.

The rapid expansion of Mashantucket Pequot Gaming was not without its hitches, however. The company met with resistance from some vocal southeastern Connecticut citizens, who claimed that the casino brought traffic congestion and crime to their towns. Some alleged that organized crime had entered the area as well. Residents of one neighboring town brought a lawsuit against the federal government, hoping to curtail the company's expansion efforts. However, the company prevailed in its efforts to expand and improve the resort. Moreover, it addressed concerns about a possible increase in gambling addiction by working with the Connecticut Council on Problem Gambling. Brochures and posters with a toll-free help line number were distributed throughout the gaming centers. Also during this time, the company brought in a new management team, after suspecting some illegal financial dealings, or at best conflicts of interest, on the part of CEO Brown and another former manager, Alfred J. Luciani. The new management, including Hilton Hotels executive Bud Celey as CEO, set to work improving the company's fiscal accountability.

Bolstering its tourist draw, the Tribe opened a museum near the Foxwoods cite in August 1998. The Mashantucket Pequot Museum and Research Center traced the history and way of life of the Tribe from the Ice Age to the present day reservation. The museum included a life-size 16th-century Pequot village including hand-crafted human figures, and an outdoor living-history museum which recreated an 18th-century two-acre farm. Film and video presentations included a computer-animated production of a caribou kill of 11,000 years ago, projected on a spherical screen 50 feet in diameter. The facility also included a library and archives, available for research by students and scholars.

To streamline its food preparation operations Foxwoods constructed a central kitchen facility to support the preparation of over 40,000 meals per day at 29 restaurants. Equipment included a 50-gallon steam-jacketed kettle for the preparation of soups, stews, and cooking stock and a wood-chip smoking cabinet for seafood and poultry. A warming/steaming table connected to the heating, ventilation and air conditioning system to provide a continual supply of steam while the drainage system for a fish freezer connected to the resort's drainage system. Kitchen facilities included a 2,000 square-foot cook/chill commissary for baking and food preparation.

Foxwoods completed the final phase of the Grand Pequot Tower Hotel in the fall of 1998. The 20,000 square-foot Grand Spa and Salon provided jacuzzis, steamrooms, an exercise room, a heated swimming pool, and beauty and massage services. Accommodations at the hotel included 23 luxury villas for premium players, including the two-story, 5,000 square foot Mashantucket Villa. Located on the 22nd and 23rd floors, the villas featured original artwork, large screen televisions, and gold-plated bathroom fixtures. Services included on-call butlers, available 24 hours a day.

Continued Success at the End of the 1990s

Despite some local opposition, the people of Connecticut were generally satisfied with the effects of reservation gaming on the state. Over $100 million a year in state taxes on slot machines funded economic development in 169 cities and towns throughout Connecticut. Foxwoods became the largest employer in southeastern Connecticut and was significant in recruiting employees from Rhode Island as well. After decreases in defense spending led to massive layoffs in the area around 1990, Foxwoods provided many new jobs to fill the void. While many of the jobs paid less than one could earn in the defense industry, the health care and other benefits were comparable. New positions included technicians for the design and repair of high tech slot machines as well as for the building of ferry boats for Fox Navigation, a high-speed ferry service. The ferry service also sparked economic renewal at New London where terminal facilities were refurbished.

A new advertising campaign launched in May 1999 involved a new slogan. From ''experience the wonder of the

Connecticut woods,'' a tagline that had originated with the bingo hall, Foxwoods adopted ''the wonder of it all'' to reflect its appeal as a resort destination. The print and television campaign targeted residents of New York, Massachusetts, Rhode Island, and Connecticut. At the end of 1999, the campaign focused primarily on New Yorkers as Fox Navigation's ferry service neared implementation.

Foxwoods continued to be a popular gambling destination as 1999 produced record revenues, including a record slot win of $70.4 million for the month of July. The facilities attracted more than 40,000 visitors on an average day in 1999, and for the third year in a row, more than one million people arrived at the resort by tour bus. In December Foxwoods gave the one-millionth passenger over $1,000 in prizes, while all passengers on that patron's bus received gifts and a private party. The December 1999 issue of *Casino Player* magazine named Foxwoods among its ''Best of the Millennium'' list of casinos in the United States and the Caribbean. Of its 33 ratings categories, the magazine commended Foxwoods in several, praising in particular its restaurants, bars and lounges, family attractions, high-limit slot salons, casinos, shopping, and hotel rooms.

Principal Competitors

Trump Hotels & Casino Resorts Inc.; Mohegan Tribal Gaming Authority; Connecticut Lottery Corporation.

Further Reading

Abbott, Elizabeth, ''After 5 Years, Mashantuckets Own an Empire,'' *Providence Journal*, February 23, 1997, p. A1.

Bixby, Lyn, ''Pequots Opening $400 Million Hotel, Casino,'' *Hartford Courant*, July 3, 1997, p. F1.

Coombs, Joe, ''Connecticut Casino Firms View Each Other as Partners, not Rivals,'' *Knight-Ridder/Tribune Business News,* May 10, 1999.

——, ''Ledyard, Conn.-Area Casinos Cash in on Profits.'' *Knight-Ridder/Tribune Business News,* August 23, 1999.

Connor, Matt, ''Rising to the Challenge,'' *International Gaming and Wagering Business*, July 1997, p. S14.

Davis, Paul, ''Job Fair is Latest Example of Casino's Impact on Rhode Island,'' *Providence Journal*, January 11, 1998, p. A1.

''Foxwoods Resort Casino Cited as One of Millennium's Best in Nationwide Roundup by Casino Player Magazine,'' *Business Wire*, December 6, 1999, p. 1,549.

Gianatasio, David, ''Foxwoods Gets 'Restaged' by Trahan,'' *ADWEEK New England Advertising Week*, May 24, 1999, p. 1A.

Hamilton, Robert A., ''Foxwoods Reaches Out to Long Island,'' *New York Times*, March 5, 2000, p. 3.

Jackson, Susan, ''Can the Pequots Stay on a Roll?,'' *Business Week*, July 21, 1997, p. 38.

Larson, Soren, ''Foxwoods Gambles on Fragrance,'' *WWD*, May 23, 1997, p. 6.

Peppard, Donald M., ''In the Shadow of Foxwoods: Some Effects of Casino Development in Southeastern Connecticut,'' *Economic Development Review,* Fall 1995, p. 44.

Rubenstein, Ed, ''Foxwoods Retools, Expands Kitchens to 'Ante Up' Operations, Guest Service,'' *Nation's Restaurant News*, March 2, 1998, p. 22.

Saul, Stephanie, ''Foxwoods Casino Expanding: Last Stand for Small Town?,'' *New Jersey Record*, August 24, 1997, p. A10.

''A Stroke of Luck,'' *Economist*, June 13, 1998, p. 28.

—Mary Tradii

MedImmune, Inc.

MedImmune, Inc.

35 West Watkins Mill Road
Gaithersburg, Maryland 20878
U.S.A.
Telephone: (301) 417-0770
Fax (301) 527-4200
Web site: http://www.medimmune.com

Public Company
Incorporated: 1988
Employees: 664
Sales: $383.4 million (1999)
Stock Exchanges: NASDAQ
Ticker Symbol: MEDI
NAIC: 325412 Pharmaceutical Preparation
Manufacturing; 54171 Research and Development in
the Physical, Engineering, and Life Sciences

MedImmune, Inc. is a biopharmaceutical company that develops and markets products to combat infectious disease and cancer, among other things. In its brief history, the company has developed drugs that help premature infants from succumbing to respiratory syncytial virus (RSV) and that reduce infection in transplant patients. It is also testing drugs that would prevent Lyme disease, cervical cancer, and other infectious diseases. MedImmune's 1999 acquisition of U.S. Bioscience added drugs for treating ovarian cancer, AIDS-related pneumonia, and side effects of chemotherapy and radiation to the company's pharmaceutical portfolio. Since going public three years after its incorporation, the company's fortunes have risen and fallen with the mercurial biotech market. Despite a disastrous first-round rejection of its RSV drug by the Food and Drug Administration (FDA), the company bounced back to become one of the "premier biotech companies in the world," according to the *Washington Post.*

Late 1980s Origins

MedImmune began in 1988 when two doctors at the Walter Reed Army Hospital in Washington, D.C.—Wayne Hockmeyer

and Franklin Top—joined forces to find ways to combat and prevent a variety of modern-day plagues, including AIDS, Lyme disease, and Hepatitis B. Hockmeyer has remained CEO and chairman since the company's inception; Franklin Top was MedImmune's first executive vice-president and medical director.

In one of its first projects, MedImmune forged a research agreement with Connaught Laboratories, a Canadian vaccine manufacturer. MedImmune's quest to develop a vaccine to prevent Lyme disease never came to fruition with Connaught, however, and in 2000, the company was still working to develop an improved U.S. vaccine and a second-generation vaccine in Europe.

During its early years, MedImmune also worked to develop and test CytoGam, a drug that attacks life-threatening cytomegalovirus infections that can occur in patients who have had kidney transplants or AIDS. FDA approval in 1991 won MedImmune international attention.

After that success, the 75-employee company decided to go public, launching it on a roller coaster ride of stock prices and revenues. Early on, profits came rolling into the company, based on arrival of CytoGam in the marketplace, and analysts were enthusiastic. One industry observer, in the Washington Business Journal, wrote: "MedImmune Inc.'s initial public offering for $29 million shows one of the strongest local biotech companies to come down the pike in awhile." In a report in *The Insiders' Chronicle*, a Smith Barney analyst said the company was already "equal in quality to any of the first-tier biotechnology companies." Moreover, when MedImmune announced a pact with Merck to develop new AIDS drugs, a Morgan Stanley analyst told the *Chronicle,* "MedImmune is now the leading contender in the immunotherapy of AIDS area."

The AIDS work was spurred by a MedImmune discovery of a monoclonal antibody, dubbed MEDI-488, that was shown in laboratory tests to be effective in killing many strains of HIV. An antibody is a protein secreted by cells in the blood and is part of the body's natural defense system against viruses. Monoclonal antibodies are antibodies derived from clones, or identical copies, of a single cell. They can be screened in the laboratory and targeted treat a specific disease.

Company Perspectives:

MedImmune is a fully integrated biopharmaceutical company focused on developing and marketing products that address medical needs in areas such as infectious disease, immune regulation and cancer.

Merck and Co. funded research and testing of 40 monoclonal antibodies, spending approximately $13 million on the project over the next three years. This sent MedImmune stock soaring. When the company went public in May 1991, stock was initially offered at $9.25. After the announcement of work with Merck, stock prices shot up to $47.

"It is very promising in the early laboratory stage, but as with any promising compound, it is a long way for the laboratory to the actual drug," MedImmune spokesman Fred Spar told the *Washington Business Journal*. Spar was right; Merck soon balked at disappointing results for testing, which caused MedImmune's stock to drop. The two companies renegotiated, and in 2000 the company was still working with monoclonal antibodies related to AIDS and HIV. Merck also worked with MedImmune to develop an AIDS vaccine based on forms of a bacteria used in a tuberculosis vaccine.

Other work in the early 1990s focused on vaccines for other illnesses, including schistosomiasis, a parasitic disease that affects as many as 200 million worldwide, causing their extremities to swell. Specifically, MedImmune worked to genetically engineer a drug currently used against TB so that it could work against schistosomiasis.

Challenges in the Early 1990s

The company then moved full-speed ahead into developing a vaccine against RSV, which kills about 4,500 infants each year and sends another 90,000 to the hospital. However, in 1993, an FDA panel unanimously rejected the drug, RespiGam, citing sloppy research as its reason for recommending further testing. Within two days, MedImmune's stock dropped almost 50 percent, causing losses, on paper at least, of $140 million. Stock was down by 70 percent a few months later.

Claiming that MedImmune had made misleading statements about the drug's chances for approval by the FDA, stockholders filed two class-action lawsuits. MedImmune denied all allegations in the suit, and the suits were settled out of court in late 1995 for $637,500, which the company took as a charge against earnings.

By late 1993, critics were pondering the erratic performance of MedImmune. One *Washington Post* article explored both the problems the FDA had with the clinical trials and the mutiny by shareholders. The FDA's concerns were apparently based on worries that the test did not randomly select children to try the drug. Because a nurse had knowledge of the children's medical histories and earlier tests of the drug, she may have excluded children who were sicker and less likely to respond to the drug, the FDA alleged. "From the statistical side, the whole thing was amateurish, and that was the tragedy," Paul Meier, a Columbia

University statistician, who was a member of the FDA, told *Washington Post*. In an interview with the *Washington Post* in 1999, MedImmune's CEO Wayne Hockmeyer termed this period the company's "nuclear winter."

Still, because of RespiGam's potential—the director of the National Institute of Allergy and Infectious Disease called it an "important advance"—MedImmune decided that rather than scrap the project, it would begin trials again, this time keeping scrupulous records in a more professional format. In deciding to start from scratch on research for RespiGam, MedImmune had to reinvest two years and tens of millions of dollars. "The strategy we pursued was the one I called 'bet the farm'," Hockmeyer told the *Washington Post*, adding that employees "were tense. They were single-minded. They were focused. The entire organization hummed."

The bet paid off. In 1995, the results of a fresh study were in, showing that RespiGam did work to prevent RSV. The next year, it went on the market, and MedImmune regained footing with investors. However, RespiGam did have a drawback in that it was inconvenient, having to be administered intravenously every month. MedImmune went on to develop a monoclonal antibody as an improved way to fight off the virus. The drug, Synagis, was approved by the FDA in the summer of 1998 and went on the market a few months later. A *Washington Post* article the next year called it "One of the most successful new products in the history of the biotech industry."

To promote Synagis, MedImmune teamed up with Ken and Bobbi McCaughey, parents of septuplets born in 1997. With the help of a public relations firm, they provided the McCaugheys with media training and taped a video news release and public service announcement that were distributed via satellite and aired by 1,600 television stations around the world, including the "Oprah Winfrey Show." Wall Street was enthusiastic. During the first full quarter the drug was on the market, MedImmune's revenues jumped 73 percent from the same quarter the year before. "The Synagis launch appears to be a blowout," a 1999 report from Morgan Stanley Dean Witter & Co. maintained, adding "MedImmune continues to exceed our expectations quarter after quarter."

In 1999, the efficacy of the vaccine was reaffirmed after the first season's use. Of 1,839 patients evaluated at nine U.S. sites, the RSV hospitalization rate was 2.3 percent. In the preapproval trials, 4.8 percent of those using Synagis were hospitalized, and 10.6 percent of babies taking a placebo had to be admitted to the hospital.

In 1997, MedImmune signed a $60-million deal with Abbott Laboratories for the rights to market Synagis. Sales of the drug were expected to reach $270 million in 2000. The same year, CytoGam, the drug for kidney and AIDS patients, began marketing in Canada, Poland and Mexico. On the heels of this success, MedImmune began building a new $65 million, 91,000-square-foot facility in Frederick, Maryland, about 25 miles north of its Gaithersburg headquarters.

Research Horizons: Late 1990s and Beyond

Drug research and development can take years, and thus many MedImmune projects were in the works at once. In the late 1990s, MedImmune began research on several other fronts, including vaccines to prevent cervical cancer and genital warts. The company entered into a strategic alliance with SmithKline Beecham to develop and commercialize human papillomavirus (HPV) vaccines. In 2000, MedImmune was conducting clinical trials of the vaccine, while SmithKline Beecham was responsible for the final development of the product, regulatory issues, manufacturing, and marketing. The vaccines used recombinant DNA technology to imitate the structure of natural papillomarivurs, but were not infectious themselves. The vaccine was already shown to be effective when tested on dogs.

The company was also developing a vaccine to prevent urinary tract infections, a malady that affects about half of all women by the time they are 30. In preclinical studies, MedImmune's vaccine helped produce antibodies that blocked *E. coli*, the main culprit in urinary tract infections, from binding the bladder, thus preventing infections. In 2000, MedImmune was performing clinical trials of the vaccine.

Another vaccine in the works would thwart B19 parovirus, a usually mild virus, but one that can lead to a number of other serious diseases, especially for those with sickle cell anemia or for pregnant women. MedImmune created a virus-like particle that was non-infectious, in an attempt to induce immunity in vaccinated people. The drug was in trials in 2000.

As antibiotic resistance became more prevalent worldwide, MedImmune was also working to develop new preventive therapies for common infections, including those caused by Streptococcus pneumoniae. This bacterium causes a variety of illnesses in both the elderly and the young, from meningitis to middle ear infections to pneumonia. Working with Human Genome Science and St. Jude Children's Research Hospital, MedImmune was researching possible vaccines in 2000.

The company developed and tested a new monoclonal antibody dubbed MEDI-507 in the late 1990s. The immunosuppressive agent, it was hoped, would help during bone marrow transplants, when white blood cells sometimes attack the tissue of the recipient. It was also considered potentially useful in treating psoriasis.

MedImmune's next venture was into the realm of oncology. In 1999, the company formed an alliance with Ixys, Inc., a privately held biopharmaceutical company, to develop new monoclonal antibodies. One, called Vitaxin, was a cancer treatment. The drug, in clinical trials in 2000, appeared to inhibit a key pathway involved in the formation of new blood vessels and could provide a way to combat the growth and spread of tumors. The company's reach into the oncology field was further solidified when it acquired Pennsylvania-based U.S. Bioscience, which it renamed MedImmune Oncology. In the deal, MedImmune gained two oncology drugs already on the market and several in clinical trials.

One of the drugs on the market was Ethyol, which generated worldwide sales of about $70 million in 1999. The drug worked by protecting normal cells from the toxic effects of chemotherapy and radiation, while not protecting the malignant cells. Ethyol was used mainly in combating toxicity of chemo drugs used to treat ovarian and lung cancers. It was also the first FDA-approved therapy to prevent severe dry mouth, a side effect of radiation therapy. The other drug on the market, Hexalen, a chemotherapy drug, was approved in 1990 for treating ovarian cancer.

Neutrexin, approved in over 30 countries and the United States, was also being studied by MedImmune. The drug was marketed to help severely immunocompromised patients fend off potentially deadly pneumonia infections. In 2000 it was undergoing trials to determine if its anti-tumor properties could help patients with colorectal cancer.

As MedImmune's researchers worked to develop new treatments for a gamut of diseases, the biotech market was on a roller coaster ride in the volatile stock market of the new millennium. MedImmune's stock was no exception, trading at a high of $228 a share in early April, then declining to $168 a few weeks later, only to rise again. "For years a laughingstock on Wall Street, the biotech industry is now one of its stars, in every sense," one analyst noted in a June 2000 *Washington Post* article."

MedImmune hoped that one of its ventures, begun in 2000, would pan out and help keep the company's stock up. The company was investigating whether a specific vaccine could stop an addict's craving for cocaine. As a February 2000 *Washington Post* report explained, MedImmune was building a "catalytic antibody that eats cocaine in a lab rat's bloodstream the way Pac Man gobble up the bad guys in a computer maze." According to Frank Vocci, director of treatment research and development at the National Institute on Drug Abuse, MedImmune could potentially produce "an antibody able to reduce cocaine to an inactive substance as fast as people put it into their bodies." The President's Office of National Drug Control Policy had given a researcher, Donald W. Landry, a biochemist at Columbia University's College of Physicians and Surgeons, $2.8 million in research grants beginning in 1994 to develop such a vaccine. In early 2000, Landry teamed up with MedImmune, which would engineer and test thousands of variants of the antibody Landry developed. The company would also work to develop new ones. Although current antibodies were not efficient enough to quell human cravings for cocaine, MedImmune's senior vice-president for research, Scott Koenig, remained optimistic, telling the *Washington Post:* "I don't want to say it's a no brainer. It's challenging, but we have the experience to give it a good shot. If it can be done, we'll do it."

Principal Subsidiaries

MedImmune Oncology, Inc..

Principal Competitors

Biogen, Inc.; Glaxo Wellcome plc; Merck & Co., Inc.; North American Vaccine Inc..

Further Reading

"Biotechs: Catch a Risky Wave," Business Week, April 24, 2000, p. 184.

Escobar, Lousia Shepard, "Breakthrough on AIDS Scored by Med-Immune," *Washington Business Journal,* November 4, 1991, p. 1.

Gillis, Justin, "MedImmune Fights Off a Virus," *Washington Post,* March 22, 1999, p. F12.

Gugliotta, Guy, "Can an Antibody Gobble Up Cocaine Cravings?," *Washington Post,* February 7, 2000, p. A4.

Henderson, Charles W., "Efficacy of Vaccine Reaffirmed after First Season's Use," *Antiviral Week,* November 15, 1999, p. 16.

Southerland, Daniel, "MedImmune: What Went Wrong?," *Washington Post,* December 23, 1993.

The Insider's Chronicle, "Merck pact puts MedImmune Squarely in AIDS picture," Dec. 2, 1991

Washington Business Journal, "MedImmune fast out of the block with quick profit," June 10, 1991, p. 1.

—Barbara Ruben

MTA Metropolitan Transportation Authority

Metropolitan Transportation Authority

347 Madison Avenue
New York, New York 10017-3739
U.S.A.
Telephone: (212) 878-7000
Toll Free: (800) 638-7622
Fax: (212) 878-0186
Web site: http://www.mta.nyc.ny.us

Government-Owned Company
Incorporated: 1965 as Metropolitan Commuter
  Transportation Authority
Employees: 57,551
Sales: \$5.71 billion (1998)
NAIC: 485112 Commuter Rail Systems; 485113 Bus and
  Motor Vehicle Transit Systems; 485119 Other Urban
  Transit Systems

The Metropolitan Transportation Authority (MTA), a public-benefit corporation chartered by the state of New York, operates North America's largest transportation network, serving—in the year 2000—a population of 13.2 million people in a 4,000-square-mile area in and around New York City. MTA subways, buses, and railroads move 1.7 billion people a year—about one in every four users of mass transit in the United States and two-thirds of the nation's rail riders. MTA bridges and tunnels carry more than 250 million vehicles a year—more than any other bridge and tunnel authority in the nation. The MTA is governed by a 17-member board chosen by the governor of the state of New York, the mayor of New York City, and the executives of seven New York counties in the vicinity of the city.

Rescuing a "Collection of Losers": 1965–73

The increasing reliance on the automobile for transportation in the New York City metropolitan area following World War II resulted in a decline of ridership in mass transit. By 1960 it was clear that the remaining privately owned bus and rail lines would not long survive. In 1965 the state of New York established the Metropolitan Commuter Transportation Authority to purchase and operate the bankrupt Long Island Rail Road (LIRR), which was carrying 80,000 commuters to the city each workday. The MCTA purchased this line from the Pennsylvania Railroad for \$65 million in 1966.

By this time, following a strike of New York City's subway and bus lines and a costly labor settlement, political pressure had mounted to integrate the city's Transit Authority into a state-supported system. After voters in late 1967 approved a bond issue yielding \$1 billion for mass transportation, the MCTA was reorganized as the Metropolitan Transportation Authority and given the mandate to direct the operations, financing, coordination, and planning of city and commuter transportation facilities. (Links between the city and New Jersey, however, remained under the jurisdiction of the bistate Port of New York Authority.) The MTA now assumed direction not only of the Transit Authority (including its subsidiary for the bus lines, the Manhattan and Bronx Surface Transportation Operating Authority) and the LIRR, but also the Triborough Bridge and Tunnel Authority, whose surplus toll-generated income from seven bridges and two tunnels could be used to help support the LIRR and the city's subways and buses.

New York Governor Nelson Rockefeller appointed William Ronan, his chief aide, as first chairman of the MTA. They pledged to modernize the city's transit system for \$2.9 billion, and in that year the MTA's first 100 air-conditioned subway cars went into service. In 1969 the state, for the first time, made a direct financial grant to the system, providing one-tenth of the projected \$1 billion needed for the construction of a proposed Second Avenue subway line in Manhattan. The LIRR was receiving the first of a fleet of 620 electric-powered cars. In August 1969 Rockefeller promised to make the trouble-plagued LIRR the "finest commuter railroad in the world"—and proclaimed the goal achieved only two months later, to much derision.

In 1971 the MTA and Connecticut's Department of Transportation took over operation of the commuter lines of the bankrupt Penn Central Transportation Co.'s New Haven division. The MTA, which had already agreed to buy 144 new electric cars for the line, also leased Manhattan's Grand Central Terminal from the Penn Central for 60 years. In 1972 the MTA completed the takeover of the Harlem and Hudson division

Key Dates:

1965: Metropolitan Commuter Transportation Authority is founded.
1968: Reorganized as the MTA, this agency assumes a broad mandate to direct public transportation in the metropolitan area.
1973: MTA network reaches its fullest extent.
1981: First five-year MTA capital budget is adopted.
1990: The system has been extensively overhauled since 1983.
1998: Discount cards and joint passes are being widely used.

commuter lines from the Penn Central but allowed the company to continue operating these lines. The 14.5-mile Staten Island Rapid Transit was purchased by the city from the Baltimore & Ohio Railroad in 1971 and turned over to the MTA to run. In 1972–73 the MTA took over the operation of ten previously private bus lines in Nassau County, establishing the Metropolitan Suburban Bus Authority as a subsidiary. The MTA also took over operation of two commuter lines running between Hoboken, New Jersey, and Port Jervis and Spring Valley, New York, respectively.

Some progress was made during these years. The LIRR sported all air-conditioned cars for the first time and improved its formerly dismal on-time performance. Excavation work also began on the Second Avenue line. But in spite of fare increases—including the first-ever bridge and tunnel toll hike—and nearly $400 million a year in city, state, and federal subsidies for operating expenses by 1974—the MTA's deficit grew from $44 million in 1969 to $325 million in 1973. Ronan called his agency's component parts "the biggest collection of losers ever assembled under one roof," according to Robert H. Connery and Gerald Benjamin, authors of *Rockefeller of New York*. Work on the Second Avenue subway stopped in 1975, as New York City fell into near-bankruptcy.

Back from the Brink: 1976–95

The MTA got a break when the Consolidated Rail Corp. (Conrail), a newly created federal body, assumed responsibility for operating the three former Penn Central commuter lines in 1976. But in 1982 the MTA had to reassume control because Congress had decided Conrail should not be responsible for passenger services. The operation now received the name Metro-North Commuter Railroad. Meanwhile, in 1979, the city's subways and buses reached their nadir, according to one account. Despite a 12-day strike in 1981, followed by two fare increases, the subways and bus lines were in better shape by the time Richard Ravitch ended a four-year tenure as MTA chairman in 1983. Ravitch said he was most proud of assembling about $8.5 billion in federal, state, and local financing to rebuild the metropolitan area's mass-transit system. This sum included $6.5 billion for the city's subways and buses over the next five years.

During the succeeding seven-year tenure of Richard Kiley, the city subway and bus fare first reached, and then, exceeded $1. There was a six-week Metro-North strike in 1983 and a two-

week LIRR strike in 1987. All of the LIRR and Metro-North cars, and 90 percent of the MTA's subway cars and buses, were replaced or rebuilt, however, and most of the 2,000 miles of MTA rail and subway track also were replaced. Completion of a tunnel under the East River brought subway service to Roosevelt Island for the first time. The number of subway breakdowns and derailments fell dramatically. After a five-year effort, the entire subway and bus fleet was declared graffiti-free in 1989. Subway ridership—two billion annually in the 1940s—began rising again after dropping to less than one billion in 1983.

New York's legislature appropriated $9.6 billion in 1993 for the MTA's third capital-improvement five-year plan. Although the program called for 184 new LIRR cars, most of the money was allocated for new subway tracks, switches, and signal lights, and to rehabilitate one out of every five subway stations. The riders also were tapped for more money, with the city subway and bus fare reaching $1.50 in 1995, after the state declined to commit any further funds to the capital program. Motorists were hit in 1993 for the seventh toll increase in 13 years, paying as much as $6 to cross the Verrazano-Narrows Bridge between Brooklyn and Staten Island. As a result of a subway crash that killed five people in 1991, the MTA began imposing random testing of its drivers for drug and alcohol use. By the end of 1992 crime seemed a less urgent concern, following 27 straight months of decline in offenses committed. In 1995 subway ridership reached its highest level since 1974.

Converting to Plastic in the Late 1990s

During the MTA's fourth, $13 billion capital-improvement program, the agency committed $1.6 billion for 1,080 subway cars. Deliveries began in 1998 for a $412 million LIRR diesel fleet, consisting of 36 locomotives and 134 coaches. In 1997 all 468 subway stations were able to accept the plastic MetroCard, and the TBTA's E-Z Pass became the world's largest electronic toll-collect system. Also that year, the MTA issued a joint commuter rail pass for LIRR and Metro-North riders and allowed the city's MetroCard users to transfer from bus to subway or subway to bus for free during a two-hour period. In 1998 the MTA issued discount cards allowing riders 11 subway and bus ride fares for the price of 10, and 7- and 30-day unlimited-ride cards (for $17 and $63, respectively). A one-day unlimited pass was priced at $4.

By the summer of 1998, 70 percent of the people using the city's subways and buses were buying MetroCards rather than tokens. Subway ridership rose about 17 percent between mid-1997 and the end of 1998. City buses attracted 20 percent more passengers after reaching a low of 436 million in 1996, following 20 years of declines. The MTA was planning to order more than 600 new buses in 1999.

Also in 1998, the MTA, which had taken out a new 110-year lease on Grand Central Terminal in 1993, completed a $200 million redevelopment of the structure. The agency, which had inherited the New York Coliseum from the TBTA, sold the Columbus Circle site of the now-vacant convention center to The Related Cos. and Time Warner Inc. for $345 million. The developers intended to demolish the Coliseum and an adjacent office tower for a complex that would include a hotel, apartments, offices, a concert hall, and television studios. In another

1998 transaction, the MTA leased a vacant 33-floor building at 2 Broadway, in lower Manhattan, for 49 years, and was planning, after renovation, to make the building its headquarters.

In 2000, the MTA adopted a new $17.1 billion five-year budget for capital improvements, including funds for preliminary engineering work on a Second Avenue subway line from 125th Street to the southern end of Manhattan and a subway link to La Guardia Airport, plus construction of a LIRR connection to Grand Central Terminal. The plan was counting on $1.6 billion from a state transportation bond issue that would need voter approval and $22 billion in new and refinanced bonds, which would put $3 billion into the capital program but saddle the MTA with $10 billion in new debt. A deficit of $2.4 billion for the operating budget was projected over the same-year period, despite an expected state contribution of $847 million during this period.

Of the $5.71 billion received by the MTA in 1998 for operations, 50 percent came from fares, 15.5 percent from tolls, and 23 percent from state and regional taxes, with most of the remainder from state and local subsidies. Almost 62 percent of this revenue was spent on New York City buses and subways, with 25 percent for commuter rail and MTA headquarters, four percent for bridges and tunnels, and two percent for suburban buses and the Staten Island railway. Nearly seven percent went for debt service. In 1999 fares covered about 60 percent of the operating costs of the city's subways and buses but only 43 percent of Metro-North costs and 37 percent of LIRR costs.

Principal Subsidiaries

The Long Island Railroad Company; Metro-North Commuter Railroad Company; Metropolitan Suburban Bus Authority; New York City Transit Authority; Staten Island Rapid Transit Operating Authority; Triborough Bridge and Tunnel Authority.

Principal Competitors

Command Bus Company; Green Bus Lines; Jamaica Buses; Liberty Lines Express; New York Bus Service; Queens Surface; Triboro Coach.

Further Reading

Akst, Daniel, "Where Did All the Griffiti Go?," *Forbes,* May 28, 1990, pp. 328, 330, 332, 334.

Bagli, Charles S., "Sale of Coliseum Site Receives Approval," *New York Times,* July 30, 1998, p. B3.

"Bringing Mass Transit into the 21st Century," *Bond Buyer,* Special Advertising Supplement, November 20, 1997.

Burks, Edward C., "Riders Applaud L.I.R.R. Improvement," *New York Times,* June 3, 1974, p. 62.

"The Commuter Revolt That Conrail Can't Quell," *Business Week,* September 1, 1980, p. 19.

Connery, Robert H., and Gerald Benjamin, *Rockefeller of New York,* Ithaca, N.Y.: Cornell University Press, 1979.

Corry, John, "About New York," *New York Times,* January 28, 1976, p. 30.

Goldman, Ari L., "Accord Is Reached on M.T.A. Operation of 3 Conrail Lines," *New York Times,* August 9, 1982, pp. A1, D8.

Dunlop, David W., "Deal Reached on Restoration of Grand Central Terminal," *New York Times,* December 21, 1993, pp. A1, B4.

Faison, Seth, "$9.6 Billion for M.T.A. Is Crucial To Rebuilding Plans," *New York Times,* April 3, 1993, pp. 1, 26.

"Harlem and Hudson," and "Long Island Rail Road," *New York Times,* July 28, 1969, p. 20.

Jochum, Glenn, "MTA Taking Its Toll on LI," *LI Business News,* December 18, 1995, p. 1 and continuation.

Lardner, James, "Painting the Elephant," *New Yorker,* June 25, 1984, pp. 41–46, 49–52, 57–72.

Levine, Hugh, "Huge Rebuilding Effort Awaits Kiley's Successor," *New York Times,* November 27, 1990, pp. B1, B7.

Lueck, Thomas J., "New York's Bus Ridership Surges After Long Decline," *New York Times,* December 22, 1998, pp. A1, B4.

MacFarquhar, Neil, "Card Halves Cost for Double-Fare Riders," *New York Times,* July 4, 1997, p. B4.

"M.T.A. Takes Over 2 Commuter Lines," *New York Times,* May 27, 1972, pp. 60.

Newman, Andy, "Hop On, Hop Off: The Unlimited Metrocard Arrives," *New York Times,* July 3, 1998, pp. B1, B5.

Perez-Pena, Richard, "Approval Expected for Transit Spending Plan," *New York Times,* May 1, 2000, p. B6.

Prial, Frank J., "Connecticut and New York Take Over the New Haven," *New York Times,* January 1, 1971, p. 46.

Roberts, Sam, "Ravitch Era: Debate and Innovation," *New York Times,* August 30, 1983, p. B4.

"Saving New York from Strangling," *Business Week,* March 9, 1968, pp. 64–66, 68.

Silver, Roy R., "Nassau To Begin Take-Over of Buses," *New York Times,* April 1, 1973, p. 137.

Sims, Calvin, "Ending 10 Years of Rebuilding, M.T.A. Wants 5 More," *New York Times,* August 26, 1991, pp. B1, B4.

—Robert Halasz

Midwest Express Holdings, Inc.

6744 South Howell Avenue
Oak Creek, Wisconsin 53154
U.S.A.
Telephone: (414) 570-4000
Toll Free: (800) 452-2-22
Fax: (414) 570-9666
Web site: http://www.midwestexpress.com

Public Company
Incorporated: 1984
Employees: 3,179
Sales: $447.6 million (1999)
Stock Exchanges: New York
Ticker Symbol: MEH
NAIC: 481111 Scheduled Passenger Air Transportation;
   481112 Scheduled Freight Air Transportation

Midwest Express Holdings, Inc. is the holding company for Midwest Express Airlines. Midwest Express is a small airline carrier, ranked at the beginning of the 21st century as the 17th largest in the United States. Despite its small size, Midwest Express is an industry leader, finding profits where other airlines struggle, and leading the nation in customer service and satisfaction. The airline is geared primarily toward business travelers, who make up approximately 55 percent of its passengers. Midwest Express distinguishes itself by flying direct between many cities underserved by other, larger carriers. Its home base is in Milwaukee, where its planes fly out of that city's Mitchell Field airport. The airline also has a smaller hub in Omaha, Nebraska, and a third hub is in development for the year 2000. Its fares are comparable to those of other airlines, but Midwest Express offers luxurious amenities on its flights, including gourmet food served on china plates with linen napkins, complementary wine and champagne, and planes retrofitted to provide extra foot room. It flies nonstop from Milwaukee to close to 30 cities in the United States and Canada and operates other nonstop routes originating in Omaha and in Kansas City, Missouri. The company also operates a subsidiary, Skyway Airlines, to offer connecting flights from Midwest Express flights, especially to smaller cities.

Beginnings with Kimberly-Clark

Midwest Express Airlines began originally as an air transport service run by the Kimberly-Clark Corporation for the benefit of its employees. Kimberly-Clark was a paper products company, known particularly for its Kleenex brand tissue. Beginning in 1948, it used its own aircraft to fly workers out to mills in difficult-to-reach locations. By 1969, Kimberly-Clark's flight department evolved into a subsidiary, called K-C Aviation. This company ran Kimberly-Clark's small fleet of planes and also provided servicing work on the planes of the parent company's corporate clients. By 1982, Kimberly-Clark's transportation needs increased, as it was having to shuttle employees between its headquarters near Appleton, Wisconsin and a forest products research center in Atlanta. K-C Aviation became a regularly scheduled shuttle airline, serving Appleton, Atlanta, and Memphis. The president of K-C Aviation was Timothy Hoeksema, a former pilot with the company. He oversaw a period of rapid growth at the flight subsidiary, helping it move from a 53-person operation in 1977 to a firm that employed 500 people and brought in $50 million in the early 1980s. Hoeksema had a feel for the airline industry, and he was instrumental in helping K-C Aviation become a full-fledged airline. The airline industry had been deregulated in 1978, allowing many small start-ups to get into the market. K-C Aviation was already doing much of what a small airline did anyway, making regularly scheduled flights for business people. So it was not much of a change to re-christen the company Midwest Express Airlines and begin nonstop service from Milwaukee to Boston, Dallas, Atlanta, and Appleton.

The new airline aimed small, at first wanting only to fill what looked like an available niche. One apparently shrewd business choice was claiming Milwaukee as its home base. Milwaukee's Mitchell Field airport had just undergone major renovations, and it had the advantage of being relatively close to north suburban Chicago. Chicago's O'Hare was both huge and congested, while Mitchell was by comparison much easier to negotiate. So the airline believed customers both in southern Wisconsin and northern Illinois would enjoy the ease of flying out of Milwaukee. Midwest Express also wanted to concentrate on service. In the early 1980s, many small airlines were entering the market hoping to compete on price. People's Express and other small carriers offered cheap, no-frills flying. But Midwest Express wanted to go

---

Company Perspectives:

Midwest Express exists to: provide the highest quality travel experience to our consumers; foster a work environment of mutual respect, caring, pride, continuous improvement and dedication to safety, where employees are valued for their contributions; and increase shareholder value as a means to future growth and success.

---

the opposite route and offer opulent accommodations, friendly service, great food, and the convenience of direct routes without cumbersome layovers. Midwest's fleet was very small, at first only four planes, but it renovated them so that they carried only 60 seats instead of 85 or more. Seats were two-by-two instead of the usual three-seat layout, and the reduced number of seats meant maximum leg room. Instead of spending as little as possible on customer food, Midwest Express went all out. Its meals were served on china, with linen napkins, and typical dinner choices offered flyers were beef Wellington or lobster. Hoeksema was sure this emphasis on service would work out, although to some it seemed a risky business strategy. But because of his long experience with business travelers, Hoeksema felt sure he knew what customers wanted most.

The airline grew slowly, adding new routes each year, and gradually increasing its number of customers served. In 1985, the company suffered a tragic reversal, when one of its planes crashed just after takeoff, killing all 27 passengers on board as well as the four crew members. No wrong-doing was attributed to the airline, but it shook consumer confidence and set the airline back considerably with the loss of one quarter of its fleet. The company operated in the red for its first several years, losing more than $3 million by 1986, according to figures from the Department of Transportation. Yet Midwest's reputation grew. Its percentage of passengers at Mitchell Field increased from less than one percent in its first year to close to ten percent four years later. *Consumer Reports* rated the airline number one for comfort in 1985, an honor it continued to enjoy. By 1988, the company was making a profit, and it was in the black year after year from then on. When it began, Midwest's flights were only 20 percent full, but by 1988 its flights were about 66 percent full, and sales stood at around $54 million. In addition, it still had the deep pockets of parent Kimberly-Clark to help. Kimberly-Clark put $120 million into Midwest's expansion in the late 1980s, allowing the airline to boost its fleet from four planes to 11. By 1989, it was the third largest carrier flying out of Milwaukee, and its direct flights took it to 15 cities.

Exploiting a Niche in the Early 1990s

Midwest Express grew in the 1990s, but it remained a small airline and avoided direct competition with the major airlines. It carefully exploited its niche as it expanded, keeping in mind its core customer group of business travelers. Thus it offered few trips on weekends, and timed flights so that business people could make day trips. While airlines like Northwest and American might offer trips to Washington, D.C. every hour, Midwest Express typically scheduled early morning flights, with an early evening return. Midwest did not offer discounts to people booking several weeks in advance, as other airlines did, because it

depended on the quick trips business travelers made as the need arose. Midwest's standard fares were thus comparable with other airlines' regular fares, though passengers who wanted a cheaper flight might have turned to a bigger carrier to get it. By catering to business travelers, Midwest gave itself another profit advantage. Business travelers rarely checked luggage, but took carry-on bags for their mainly short trips. This freed much of the cargo hold, so Midwest's planes could earn money carrying freight. The company grew and prospered in the early 1990s, though several similar full-service airlines failed. Small full-service airlines that did not make it included Air Atlanta and St. Louis's Air One.

As the airline added more destinations, it looked for a smaller airline that could act as a "feeder," bringing passengers from small cities into Milwaukee to connect with Midwest Express flights. Midwest worked out an agreement with Mesa Airlines of New Mexico, and in 1989 that company inaugurated its new Skyway Airlines, or the Midwest Express Connection, for flights into Milwaukee. At first the companies had no direct financial relationship, but Skyway soon became a subsidiary of Midwest. Skyway ran a fleet of small, 19-seat turboprop airplanes, bringing passengers between Milwaukee and cities like Green Bay, La Crosse, and Stevens Point in Wisconsin, and operating between other Midwestern towns, including Des Moines, Flint, and Cincinnati.

At its ten-year anniversary, Midwest Express was doing very well. The airline industry as a whole had trouble in the early 1990s, especially as customer satisfaction dropped. Out of the entire domestic airline industry, only two carriers were profitable in 1993. One was the no-frills Southwest Airlines, and the other was Midwest Express. Southwest spent on average 20 cents for passenger meals, while Midwest lavished $10 per passenger for food. Other carriers sought to imitate Southwest and cut down on frills as a way of clinging to often elusive profitability. But Midwest never faltered in its mission to provide first-class service and would consider trimming costs only in areas the public would never notice. It was going against the prevailing pattern in the industry, and it was working.

By 1993, Midwest Express was only the 24th largest airline in the United States, with revenues of $165 million. According to interviews with its president, Timothy Hoeksema, the airline did not have plans to expand aggressively. But Hoeksema was confident little Midwest would continue to do well despite troubling trends in the industry. In an article in *Forbes* from October 23, 1995, Hoeksema declared: "When you have an industry with dissatisfied customers, you have a business opportunity." In other words, as things got worse for the larger carriers, Midwest would still make money. Customers often specified they wanted to fly on Midwest. It was one of the few airlines that really had such a recognizable and positive identity. The company baked and served fresh chocolate chip cookies on board. No other carrier could beat that.

Midwest's growth was slow and controlled. In 1994 it opened a hub in Omaha. This gave it easier access to western markets, including flights into Los Angeles. By the mid-1990s the airline ran a fleet of 19 jets, and Skyway, its feeder subsidiary, had 12 smaller planes. Revenues surpassed $200 million for the first time in 1994 and continued to go up. In 1995, parent Kimberly-Clark decided to spin off the airline subsidiary. Midwest Express went public in October 1995. Kimberly-Clark hung on to 30 percent of the airline's shares, while sales of the remainder brought in $81 million. After going public, Midwest did not have the cozy backing of the large paper company, and it had to spend more money on its plane leasings because it lost the paper company's high credit rating. But the new public company was absolutely free of debt, with a comfortable cushion of cash.

Milestones in the Late 1990s and Beyond

Midwest added a few airplanes to its fleet each year, buying slightly used planes from other carriers and renovating and refitting them. The airline grew to be a major player in Milwaukee, with about a 30 percent share of flights from Mitchell Field. It was still possible for the carrier to have an unprofitable quarter, such as a bad period in May and June of 1996, when unusual fogginess around Milwaukee caused the airline to cancel a record 750 flights. But overall, the company steamed ahead, and its stock value was noted on Wall Street. By 1998, Midwest's stock was one of the stars of the market. The booming economy, good weather brought by the warm weather pattern El Nino, and a dip in fuel costs combined to bring the company's stock to an all-time high in February 1998. The company contemplated buying more planes and adding a third hub somewhere in the Midwest.

As the company encountered such good fortune, its employees began to organize. Midwest had operated without union representation through its formative years. In 1997 the Teamsters Union and the Air Line Pilots Association (ALPA) vied with each other to represent Midwest's pilots. ALPA won out after elections in December 1997, and the Association of Flight Attendants (AFA) began organizing roughly a year later. Negotiations between the unions and the company dragged out for some time. Negotiations for the first pilots' contract began in August 1998, and a federal mediator was called in the next March. With no contract imminent, ALPA took a vote on authorizing a strike in July 1999. A strike by pilots was narrowly averted in February 2000. Although the airline had been consistently profitable since the late 1980s, pay for pilots lagged behind other airlines. Other issues in the contract involved retirement pay and health benefits. At least 80 percent of the airline industry was already unionized, and settling its first contract with its pilots represented a major step in Midwest's maturation.

In the late 1990s and into the next century, Midwest continued to stand out among domestic airlines, for the same reasons it always had. Customer complaints were high throughout the industry, and consumers railed about flights inconveniently routed through hubs and planes being overcrowded and delayed. Meanwhile Midwest won awards for its service year after year. Business customers who could afford to pay Midwest's fares chose the airline for its direct flights and its home-baked cookies. Midwest Express was the 17th largest domestic airline carrier in the late 1990s, and it was too small to compete directly with airline giants in many markets. But it had the flexibility to offer what the big fliers could not. The company relentlessly pursued its niche market. Midwest's long history of profitability was quite unusual in the industry, and the little airline made no indications that it would change its winning formula.

Principal Subsidiaries

Skyway Airlines.

Principal Competitors

Northwest Airlines Inc.; Southwest Airlines Co.

Further Reading

Brelis, Matthew, ''Midwest Express's Frills Run Counter to Airline Industry Trend,'' *Knight-Ridder/Tribune Business News*, July 8, 1999.

Byrne, Harlan S., ''Flying High,'' *Barron's*, August 5, 1996, p. 19.

Conant, Jennet, with Monroe Anderson, ''Tragedy Over Milwaukee,'' *Newsweek*, September 16, 1985, p. 38.

Dorsey, Jennifer, ''Midwest Carrier Turns 10, Profitably,'' *Travel Weekly*, July 4, 1994, p. 34.

Gribble, Roger A., ''Teamsters Asks Board To Poll Midwest Pilots on Desire for a Union,'' *Wisconsin State Journal* (Madison), September 24, 1997.

Ivey, Mike, ''Flying High,'' *Capital Times* (Madison, Wis.), June 16, 1994, pp. 1B, 3B.

Lank, Avrum D., ''Midwest Express Shares Soar,'' *Milwaukee Journal-Sentinel*, February 22, 1998, p. 1.

Lank, Avrum D., and Joel Dresang, ''Smooth Landing After Labor Turbulence,'' *Milwaukee Journal-Sentinel*, February 13, 2000, p. 1A.

Leonhardt, David, ''Big Airlines Should Follow Midwest's Recipe,'' *Business Week*, June 28, 1999, p. 40.

Morris, John, ''Midwest Pampers Passengers,'' *Milwaukee Journal*, February 15, 1987, pp. 1D, 6D.

Oliver, Suzanne, ''Niche Airline,'' *Forbes*, October 23, 1995, p. 122.

Parkins, Al, ''Midwest Carves Out Classy Niche,'' *Capital Times*, July 2, 1986, p. 10.

Poole, Claire, ''Air Kleenex,'' *Forbes*, March 20, 1989, p. 10.

Reingold, Lester, ''No Paper Airline, Despite the Kleenex,'' *Air Transport World*, November 1990, p. 68.

Sharma-Jensen, Geeta, ''Midwest's Chief Runs a High-Minded Firm,'' *Milwaukee Journal*, March 4, 1990, pp. 1D, 5D.

Shearer, Lloyd, ''Little Airline with Lots of Comfort,'' *Parade Magazine*, October 15, 1989, p. 20.

Tandon, Shaun, ''Midwest Express, Pilots Reach Late-Night Accord; Strike Is Off,'' *Capital Times*, February 13, 2000.

Wright, M. Eileen, ''No Cheap Seats, Just Top-Flight Air Service,'' *Wisconsin Business Journal*, December 1984, pp. 10–14.

Yenkin, Jonathan, ''Little Airline That Could,'' *Wisconsin State Journal*, June 19, 1989.

—A. Woodward

Motor Cargo Industries, Inc.

845 West Center Street
North Salt Lake, Utah 84054
U.S.A.
Telephone: (801) 292-1111
Fax: (801) 296-5317
Web site: http://www.motorcargo.com

Public Company
Incorporated: 1954 as Barton Truck Line, Inc.
Employees: 1,738
Sales: $125.3 million (1999)
Stock Exchanges: NASDAQ
Ticker Symbol: CRGO
NAIC: 48411 General Freight Trucking, Local; 484122
    General Freight Trucking, Long-Distance, Less Than
    Truckload

Motor Cargo Industries, Inc. is one of the largest regional LTL (less than truckload) trucking and logistics companies that serves customers mainly in ten western states. Its modern fleet of more than 620 tractors and 2,300 trailers provides both dry and refrigerated delivery of food, electronics, clothing, hardware, auto parts, other consumer merchandise, and industrial items. Through its wholly owned subsidiary MC Distribution Services, Motor Cargo offers flexible warehousing and distribution management services. It operates six logistics/warehousing facilities where customers' items can be consolidated to save trailer space and thus reduce shipping costs. Motor Cargo is often cited for using the latest information technology to keep track of its operations and finances, a crucial factor in providing the fastest delivery times possible. Through agreements with other trucking companies, Motor Cargo moves items all over the nation as well as Canada and Mexico.

The Early Years

In 1922 the Barton family started a small firm called the Barton Truck Line in Tooele, Utah, a small town about 25 miles west of Salt Lake City. With its original two trucks, the company remained a modest operation as Utah did not enjoy the prosperity most of the nation enjoyed in the roaring twenties. The worsening depression of the 1930s prevented any significant growth of the Barton Truck Line.

Once the nation entered World War II, the depression ended as the government and the private sector expanded to meet the new demands. During World War II, the military established ten bases and an army hospital in Utah, including some near Tooele and the rest within about an hour's drive. At that time, most of the Barton Truck Line's routes were between Tooele and Ogden defense facilities. In or near Ogden were 1) the Ogden Arsenal, the main depot for supplying ordnance and equipment to the western states after 1943, 2) the Utah General Depot, the nation's largest quartermaster depot after its construction in 1941, 3) Ogden Air Depot, later named Hill Air Force Base, the state's largest employer by 1943, 4) the Clearfield Naval Supply Depot, and 5) the Bushnell Military Hospital in nearby Brigham City. The Tooele Army Depot, completed in 1943, and the Dugway Proving Ground, used to test chemical weapons, were close to the Barton Truck Line's home base.

New Ownership and Expansion After World War II

In 1947 the Barton family sold its partnership to William C. Tate and his son Harold R. Tate. The father had been born and raised in Tooele, Utah and had worked for 20 years on the Tooele Valley Railroad and owned two other small businesses before purchasing the Barton Truck Line.

According to the Utah Division of Corporations, Barton Truck Line, Inc. was incorporated in 1954, with William C. Tate as its president, general manager, and a director. His wife Vera M. Tate was the vice-president and a director, and his son Harold R. Tate was the secretary-treasurer and a director. William C. Tate and Harold R. Tate transferred control of a Peterbilt tractor and two Brown trailers worth $30,000 to the new corporation, in exchange for the father holding about two-thirds and his son one-third of the company's stock.

During the 1950s and early 1960s, the firm continued shipping to and from Tooele and Salt Lake City and Ogden and also expanded to Logan on the northern borders of Utah. In the

Key Dates:

1922: Barton Truck Line is started in Tooele, Utah.
1947: Tate family purchases the partnership.
1954: Barton Truck Line, Inc. is incorporated.
1960s: First interstate shipping is started—to Wells, Nevada.
1973: Barton purchases Bonanza Truck Lines and changes its name to Motor Cargo.
1970s: Shipping to the Los Angeles area is started.
1977: Firm purchases R&R Transportation of Reno and begins intrastate Nevada service.
1981: Begins routes to Phoenix and Tucson.
1982: Deliveries are started to the San Francisco Bay area.
1986: The El Paso Service Center is opened.
1997: The company's IPO is completed.
1998: The firm acquires Las Vegas/LA Express, Inc.
1999: Motor Cargo closes its Chicago office.

mid-1960s the company started shipping to Wells, Nevada, its first interstate route. William C. Tate in 1966 moved to Salt Lake City to be closer to his growing company's main terminal. Then in 1972 he retired and turned over the business to his son Harold Tate, the new president of Barton Truck Line, Inc.

A turning point came on March 19, 1973 when Barton Truck Line, Inc. merged with Bonanza Trucking Company, a unanimous decision by the shareholders of both firms that left Barton as the surviving corporation. Bonanza had been incorporated in Utah in 1959, with Harold R. Tate as its president. In 1968 Bonanza had merged with Colorado Freightways, Inc., incorporated in Nebraska with its general offices in Denver, Colorado. Bonanza in 1968 was the surviving corporation headed by Denver's George R. Cannon, its president, treasurer, and a director.

With the acquisition of Bonanza, Barton became a regional trucking firm with new shipments to and from Utah, Denver, and Los Angeles. In June 1973, just a few months after Barton acquired Bonanza, it changed its name to Motor Cargo, according to the Utah Division of Corporations.

The Trucking Deregulation Era Since 1980

In 1980 the federal government ended its regulation of most interstate trucking. The increased competition that resulted led to the demise of many trucking companies. Motor Cargo survived at least in part by not reducing its rates so far that they could not make a profit, a mistake some competitors made.

Motor Cargo in the 1980s and early 1990s expanded its business with new routes and facilities. For example, in 1981 it opened new service facilities in Tucson and Phoenix, and the following year began shipping to the San Francisco Bay area. Direct routes into the Albuquerque area were increased in 1984, and the company service center in El Paso was established in 1986. In 1991 Motor Cargo opened terminals in Portland, Seattle, and Medford, Oregon.

In 1991 Motor Cargo chose Lou Holdener, its vice-president of operations since 1984, to be its new president, while Harold

R. Tate remained chief executive officer and chairman of the 750-employee firm. In October 1993 the company reported an on-time delivery performance of 98.7 percent, the highest in the western United States. It achieved that level through two-driver sleeper teams that allowed nonstop transportation and direct routes that avoided most satellite terminals and hub-and-spoke systems that hampered other carriers. From 1989 through 1993 Motor Cargo's accident rate consistently was less than the national average. At the same time its revenues increased steadily from $49.1 million in 1989 to $68.7 million in 1993, while the company remained profitable with 1993 net earnings from operations of $5.2 million.

In 1994 Motor Cargo trucks delivered materials among ten states: Washington, Oregon, Idaho, California, Nevada, Idaho, Utah, Colorado, Arizona, and western Texas; the firm also provided intrastate shipping within Arizona, California, Utah, and Nevada. A partnership with Reimer Express provided service throughout Canada. Motor Cargo operated more than 35 service centers from Seattle in the north to El Paso on the Mexican border.

Effective January 1, 1995, a new federal law prohibited states and local governments from regulating prices, routes, and services of intrastate trucking, with the exception of carriers of household items. "The industry has operated with regulation for over 60 years, and now it's a completely new playing field," said Dave Titus of the California Trucking Association in the November 7, 1994 *National Review*.

Thus the deregulation started in 1980 during the Carter administration was completed. The impact was evident from the increased number of trucking entities. *U.S. News & World Report* on September 18, 1995 stated that the number of licensed interstate truckers had increased from 17,000 in 1980 to more than 60,000.

On January 1, 1996 Motor Cargo Industries, Inc. was incorporated in Utah with Marshall Tate as its president and a director. Harold R. Tate and Marvin Freidland were the other two directors. Marshall Tate, Harold R. Tate's son, represented the family's third generation to lead Motor Cargo.

Just a few months later, in July 1996, Arnold Industries Inc. based in Lebanon, Pennsylvania, announced that it planned to purchase the Utah company. In February 1997, however, Arnold decided not to buy Motor Cargo, stating in the *Lancaster New Era*, "Details of the proposed acquisition proved complex and could not be resolved within a reasonable timeframe."

Motor Cargo experienced few union problems in the 1990s. For example, Teamsters briefly picketed the company but did not disrupt company operations. The company in Utah was not unionized because of the state's right-to-work law.

In the 1990s regional carriers like Motor Cargo were forced to upgrade their information technology systems by national carriers that had more resources to invest in high-tech systems. "If a carrier can't do business electronically, it can't do business with many industries," said Rita Moore of American Freightways in the April 1999 *Logistics Management and Distribution Report*. "Retail is a prime example."

Keeping track of shipments was much easier with electronic systems. Bill Mahan, Motor Cargo's chief operating officer, said in 1999, ''We beefed up our call center and added client-specific data to our shipment information. Customers may request information based on a pro number, shipment number, bill-of-lading number, a shipment date, or other information.''

Motor Cargo also shared with its customers a cost-modeling computer program that tracked shipment data such as density, weight, origin, and destination. Such computer programs lowered costs for both the shipper and carrier. For example, Motor Cargo might consolidate shipments from two companies to one destination by using just one trailer instead of two.

Motor Cargo personnel used the latest technology, including cellular phones used by all of its line drivers, satellite-based global positioning systems (GPS), and laptop computers. The bottom line was that investments in computers and advanced telecommunications were necessary to survive in the deregulated trucking industry.

In May 1998 Motor Cargo announced that its subsidiary MC Distribution Services was acquiring the operating assets of Las Vegas/LA Express, Inc. (LVLAX). A Pomona, California firm with $4.8 million in revenues at the end of the fiscal year ending September 30, 1997, LVLAX focused on providing mainly retail operations with assembly, segregation, and distribution services. Motor Cargo President Marshall Tate in a May 28, 1998 *PR Newswire* stated, ''The addition of LVLAX to MCDS provides us with a stronger client base, an enhanced distribution infrastructure, and a dedicated and talented management team. Further, it represents an important first step in implementing MCDS's strategic growth plan.''

Motor Cargo also announced in 1998 that Starbucks Coffee Company had awarded a three-year contract to MC Distribution Services for logistics management services for Starbucks' new stores under construction worldwide. Previously MC Distribution Services served Starbucks in the western United States and the Pacific Rim. Other Motor Cargo customers in the 1990s included 3M Company, NCR Corporation, Sharp Electronics Corporation, Steelcase, Sony, Moen, Pepperidge Farms, American Honda Motor Corporation, Digital Equipment, Kinney Footlocker, Hills Brothers Coffee, and Best Products.

In June 1999 Motor Cargo opened a 120-door terminal in Phoenix, Arizona. In December 1999 the company announced that it had opened a new Reno, Nevada facility that it owned and shut down a leased facility in the same city. The new 50,000-square-foot Reno terminal featured 84 dock doors and modern maintenance capabilities.

''The Nevada market has contributed greatly to our Company's success over the last 50 years,'' said Motor Cargo Industries President/CEO Marshall Tate in a December 21, 1999 *PR Newswire*. ''We operate more facilities in Nevada and serve more of the state's population than any other carrier.'' Motor Cargo's growth in Nevada was due in part to that state's booming population. In December 1999 the U.S. Census Bureau reported that Nevada was the nation's fastest growing state for the fourteenth year in a row. Its population had increased 51 percent since 1990.

With its headquarters in North Salt Lake, a municipality just north of Salt Lake City, Motor Cargo was well positioned geographically to take advantage of free trade agreements between Canada, the United States, and Mexico. Although Canada and the United States historically enjoyed close trade relations, in 1989 they approved the Canada-United States Free Trade Agreement to reduce any barriers to trade. Then the U.S. Senate in 1994 ratified the North American Free Trade Agreement (NAFTA), which lowered barriers between Canada, Mexico, and the United States. ''Trade between Canada and Mexico has increased tremendously since NAFTA,'' said Richard Krott of The Rocky Mountain Trade Corridor in the December 27, 1998 *Salt Lake Tribune*. Located in the so-called Canadian-Mexican trade corridor, Motor Cargo reported that its shipping had increased mainly to Canada, which annually bought more than $400 million in goods and services from Utah, but also to Mexico, which bought more than $70 million annually from Utah.

Motor Cargo had agreements with other truckers that allowed them to transport their customers' merchandise anywhere they desired. For example, one of its strategic partners was Columbia, South Carolina-based Southeastern Freight Lines, which shipped items in the southeast and southwest.

In 1999 and 2000 the entire trucking industry suffered under rising gasoline prices. Prices for regular unleaded gasoline in Utah rose 40 to 50 cents per gallon in 1999 and by the end of February 2000 averaged about $1.51 per gallon statewide. California fuel prices were even higher. According to Motor Cargo President Marshall Tate, fuel accounted for five to six percent of his company's costs. Although Motor Cargo passed some of those costs on to its customers, the firm also absorbed part of the increased fuel costs.

The company recorded 1998 revenues of $114.7 million, an increase of 8.8 percent over its 1997 revenues of $105.4 million. Its net earnings also increased, from $5.6 million in 1997 to $5.8 million in 1998. The year 1999 brought mixed results, with revenues increasing 9.2 percent to $125.3 million, but Motor Cargo's net earnings decreased 19.6 percent to $4.7 million.

After becoming a public corporation in November 1997, Motor Cargo's stock declined from an initial $12 per share to less than $5 per share in late 1999 and remained less than $5 per share in the first four months of 2000. The company's less-than-truckload segment of the trucking industry was a difficult place to make money for it had just a two or three percent annual increase, whereas long-haul carriers enjoyed a five to six percent increase in their segment.

In 1999 Motor Cargo closed its Chicago division, which it had opened in 1998 to gain new customers who wanted items shipped to the western states. President Marshall Tate said the Chicago operation was not profitable, so it was shut down. He emphasized, however, that Chicago was just one of 56 divisions, so its closure was merely a minor setback.

Although Motor Cargo remained a profitable business, it faced numerous challenges in 2000. Stiff competition, rising fuel prices, low stock prices, and increased expectations for speedy delivery in the fast-paced Information Age gave Motor Cargo officials plenty of obstacles to overcome.

Principal Subsidiaries

MC Distribution Services, Inc.

Principal Competitors

Consolidated Freightways Corporation; Roadway Express, Inc.; Yellow Freight Corporation; Con-Way Western Express; Viking Freight.

Further Reading

"Arnold Won't Buy Motor Cargo," *Lancaster New Era* (Lancaster, Penn.), February 13, 1997, p. B5.

Bluth, John F., and Wayne K. Hinton, "The Impact of World War II," in *Utah's History,* Richard D. Poll, general editor, Provo, Utah: Brigham Young University Press, 1978, pp. 481–96.

Cohen, Warren, "Taking to the Highway," *U.S. News & World Report,* September 18, 1995, pp. 84–87.

"Death: Wm. C. (Cec) Tate," *Deseret News,* July 10, 1995, p. C8.

Marshall, Jonathan, "Cheap Truckin'," *National Review,* November 7, 1994, pp. 54–56.

"Motor Cargo Board Elects President," *Deseret News,* July 11, 1991, p. D7.

"Motor Cargo Industries, Inc. Announces Opening of New Reno, Nevada Facility," *PR Newswire,* December 21, 1999.

"Motor Cargo Industries, Inc. Reports Acquisition and New Logistics Contract," *PR Newswire,* May 28, 1998, p. 1.

"Motor Cargo Industries, Inc. Reports 1998 Results," *PR Newswire,* February 10, 1999, p. 1.

"Motor Cargo Industries, Inc. Reports 1999 Results," *PR Newswire,* February 9, 2000.

"Nevada Tops the Nation in Growth—Again," *Salt Lake Tribune,* December 30, 1999, p. A11.

Oberbeck, Steven, "Motor Cargo Shrugs Off Chicago Shutdown," *Salt Lake Tribune,* July 27, 1999, p. C7.

——, "Utah Smack in Middle of North-South Trade . . . ," *Salt Lake Tribune,* December 27, 1998, p. E1.

Richardson, Helen L., "Regional Carriers Grow With Changing Markets," *Transportation & Distribution,* August 1998, pp. 35–42.

Sahm, Phil, "$1.51 a #%!! Gallon? Don't Blame Us, Say Utah Gas Sellers," *Salt Lake Tribune,* March 15, 2000, p. A1.

"Southeastern Freight Lines Announces Strategic Alliance Partnerships for Northeast, Midwest Regions," *PR Newswire,* August 25, 1998, p. 1.

"Teamsters Protest at Motor Cargo Has Little Impact," *Deseret News,* May 16, 1995, p. D7.

Thomas, Jim, "Cyber Carriers," *Logistics Management and Distribution Report,* April 1999, pp. 51–54.

Walden, David M., "Motor Cargo," in *Centennial Utah: The Beehive State on the Eve of the Twenty-first Century,* by G. Wesley Johnson and Marian Ashby Johnson, Encino, Calif.: Cherbo Publishing Group, 1995, pp. 88–89.

—David M. Walden

National Hockey League

1251 Avenue of the Americas
New York, New York 10020
U.S.A.
Telephone: (212) 789-2000
Fax: (212) 789-2020
Web site: http://www.nhl.com

Not-for-Profit Organization
Incorporated: 1917
Employees: 289
Sales: $1.47 billion (1999 est.)
NAIC: 711211 Sports Teams and Clubs

The National Hockey League (NHL) is a nonprofit corporation, based in New York, that serves as a trade association for its 30 franchises; six of its teams are located in Canada and the remaining 24 are U.S.-based. The NHL is unrivaled as a premiere hockey league, attracting the world's best players. Although hockey is Canada's most popular sport, and the NHL enjoyed rapid growth in the United States in the 1990s, hockey still ranks a distant fourth among the four major North American professional team sports in terms of revenues and television ratings.

Origins

While early forms of ice hockey may be traced to 17th-century Holland, the origins of modern ice hockey may were established in the late 1800s, when the sport became especially popular among university students in Ontario, Canada. In fact, Kingston, Ontario, is reputed to be the site of the first amateur hockey league, which consisted of four teams. During this time, the English Governor General of Canada, Lord Stanley of Preston, had a son who was a fan of the growing sport. Stanley was convinced by his son to purchase a silver bowl and donate it as a trophy to be awarded to the winning amateur hockey team in an annual playoff. Thus, the Stanley Cup championship trophy actually predated the NHL. Lord Stanley never attended a championship game, let alone award his cup to the first winners in 1893. He had already returned to his native England.

The Stanley Cup helped drive Canadian interest in hockey. Seeds of the game were then planted by Canadian college students attending Yale and Johns Hopkins, making New Haven and Baltimore the first homes to hockey in the United States. It was the Americans who introduced professionalism into the sport. Adhering perhaps to a British preference for amateur sports, Canadians seemed content to compete for an amateur cup, although a few players were known to accept money under the table. The Americans, however, seemed more interested in turning a profit from the game. The first professional league was formed in Michigan's Upper Peninsula, and the best Canadian talent was imported.

In 1910 the National Hockey Association (NHA) was created out of two rival Canadian "amateur" leagues that were at the time raiding one another's players, offering as much as $1,000 for a single game. The Pacific Coast Hockey Association (PCHA) was soon formed and began luring players away from the NHA. By 1912 the NHA and PCHA champions were playing for the Stanley Cup, and any vestige of the original intent of awarding the trophy to the best amateur team was long forgotten.

World War I Leads to Birth of NHL

World War I disrupted play, especially in the NHA, when a team representing the 228th Battalion of the Canadian Army was ordered overseas. This left five teams in the league and an unbalanced schedule. To rectify the problem—as well as to rid themselves of Eddie Livingstone, the unpopular head of the Toronto franchise—the owners of the NHA hoped to drop the Toronto team and redistribute its players. In the end, however, they adopted a simpler solution; they formed a new league and left the NHA to Livingstone. Thus, on November 22, 1917, in Montreal's Windsor Hotel, the National Hockey League (NHL) was created.

The champions of the NHL and PCHA now vied for the Stanley Cup. By the early 1920s, however, the PCHA was suffering financially and so joined forces with the Western Hockey League. WHL franchises were generally located in cities too small to generate the revenues required to match player salaries offered by the NHL. When the NHL began to expand to wealthy American cities, WHL players were sold to the new franchises, rather than be lost without compensation in the player raids that were sure to come. By 1926 the Stanley Cup had become the exclusive property of the NHL.

The Boston Bruins became the first American-based franchise in the NHL, beginning play in 1924. The following year, the Hamilton franchise was sold and relocated to New York, where it was renamed the "Americans" and rented Madison Square Garden for its games. Another new franchise, named the Pirates, was awarded to Pittsburgh. In 1926 three more American-based franchises were awarded. The owners of the Madison Square Garden, impressed by the success of their tenants, purchased their own franchise and named it the Rangers. Also added were the Chicago Black Hawks and the Detroit Cougars (eventually renamed the Red Wings). By the late 1920s, the NHL consisted of ten teams. With six playing in the United States, the balance of power began a gradual shift to the south.

To accommodate the large crowds necessary to support the growing NHL, the country also saw a golden era of rink construction in the 1920s. In addition to Madison Square Garden, several other storied arenas were built: the Montreal Forum, Boston Garden, Detroit's Olympia Stadium, the Chicago Stadium, and in 1931, Toronto's Maple Leaf Garden.

The league was also bolstered by the growing popularity of radio. A newspaper reporter named Foster Hewitt began doing radio broadcasts of Toronto games, and in 1933 a network of 20 Canadian stations was created to carry NHL games on Saturday nights. By the end of the season this network had grown to include 33 stations. It was estimated that an impressive 72 percent of all radios in Canada were tuned to the weekly game. American-based teams soon began to broadcast their games as well.

The Depression, followed by the uncertainties of World War II, resulted in NHL franchises transferring to other cities, and the eventual abandonment of some teams. Pittsburgh moved to become the Philadelphia Quakers, and the Ottawa Senators became the St. Louis Eagles. Both teams soon folded. Despite winning a Stanley cup, the Montreal Maroons withdrew from the NHL following the 1937–38 season. The New York Americans, at an economic disadvantage to the Madison Square Garden-owned Rangers, moved to Brooklyn, suspended operations for the duration of World War II, and never returned to league play.

The Original Six: An Era of Stability

The era of the "Original Six" teams—consisting of Montreal, Toronto, Boston, Chicago, Detroit, and New York—ran from the 1942–43 season to 1966–67. For most of this period, from 1946 until his retirement in 1977, Clarence S. Campbell headed up the NHL as league president. Despite strong attendance following the war, the NHL resisted expansion, rejecting bids for new franchises from Philadelphia, Los Angeles, and Cleveland. Television initially had an adverse effect on attendance in some of the American cities in the early 1950s, especially in Chicago and Boston. By the end of decade, however, both franchises were again prospering.

NHL hockey was first broadcast on television on October 9, 1952, from the Montreal Forum, where the Canadiens hosted Chicago in the season opener. The following month Foster Hewitt provided the first telecast from Maple Leaf Garden. The popular Saturday night radio broadcasts in Canada were now superceded by the *Hockey Night in Canada* telecasts that quickly became a national obsession. *Hockey Night in Canada* would one day become the longest running television show in North America. While American-based teams began to televise their games locally, success on a national basis in the United States eluded the league. The first attempt was made by CBS with its "Game of the Week" package that began with the 1959–60 season. Several years later, NBC would purchase the rights for slightly more than the $2 million-a-year that CBS had been paying. Hockey ratings were poor, lagging well behind ABC's *Wide World of Sports* and CBS's NBA basketball telecasts. By 1974 no U.S. television network was interested in broadcasting NHL hockey.

After 25 years of maintaining a six-team league, the NHL was more than ready for expansion in 1966 when six additional cities were awarded franchises, at a cost of $2 million each, to begin play in the 1967–68 season. The new teams were the Los Angeles Kings, Minnesota North Stars, Philadelphia Flyers, Pittsburgh Penguins, Oakland Seals, and St. Louis Blues. In one stroke the NHL became a coast-to-coast league. By 1970 two more teams joined: the Buffalo Sabres and Vancouver Canucks.

As more North American cities sought entry into the NHL, the franchise price rose to $6 million. While two additional teams joined the league in 1972, the Atlanta Flames and New York Islanders, a group of Canadian promoters formed the World Hockey Association. They charged only $500,000 for a franchise, a significant savings that the WHA urged its team owners to invest in, enticing established players away from the NHL. Although the NHL did not take the threat seriously at first, it quickly found itself in a war with the WHA, which was preparing to play its first season in 1972–73. The average player salary in the NHL was $25,000, but with competition from the WHA, the numbers quickly escalated, despite efforts to hold the line. When the WHA Winnipeg Jets signed Chicago superstar Bobby Hull, the new league gained instant credibility, which led to more NHL players switching leagues, including Detroit's legendary Gordie Howe. Clarence Campbell assured the NHL Board of Governors that the WHA would fold before the start of the 1973–74 season. He was wrong in that prediction and every one he would make over the next several years about the imminent demise of the rival league. Despite the crippling effects of the league war, the NHL contin-

Key Dates:

1917: National Hockey League organized in Montreal.
1924: The Boston Bruins become the first U.S. team to join the NHL.
1943: NHL teams pared to what becomes known as the ''Original Six.''
1967: Six new franchises granted, doubling size of league.
1972: World Hockey Association begins play and challenges NHL supremacy.
1979: Four World Hockey Association teams join the NHL.
1991: Play suspended ten days because of players' strike.
1993: Gary Bettman is named first NHL Commissioner.
2000: Two new teams join the NHL—the Columbus Blue Jackets and the Minnesota Wild—and the league totals 30 franchises.

ued to expand, adding the Washington Capitals and Kansas City Scouts for the 1975–76 season.

During this period, NHL players met the Soviets in an eight-game Summit Series, which led to the 1976 Canada Cup tournament that featured four European national teams. The EuroSoviet style of play came as a revelation to the North Americans. Although Soviet players were forbidden from leaving their country, the Europeans were eager to sign on, and the WHA was eager to sign them. The NHL was slow to follow suit, but soon its scouts were also searching for talent in Czechoslovakia and Scandinavia.

The war with the WHA lingered on, and one of its casualties was Clarence Campbell. After serving 31 years as president of the NHL, he was eased out, replaced in 1977 by John A. Ziegler, Jr., The most pressing matter for Ziegler to address, of course, was the war with the WHA that was crippling owners in both leagues. Several NHL franchises were forced to relocate and try their chances elsewhere, but it was apparent that North America simply could not support 32 major league hockey teams. After much back-channel negotiating, the war finally came to an end in 1979 when four WHA teams were added to the NHL: the Edmonton Oilers, Hartford Whalers, Quebec Nordiques, and Winnipeg Jets. Although the transaction was called an expansion, the effect was a merger between the two leagues.

The NHL spent the next decade essentially marketing a former WHA player: Wayne Gretzky. His trade from Edmonton to the Los Angeles Kings in 1988 arguably saved that franchise and created the momentum for later expansion of the NHL to the Sun Belt cities of the United States. The rise of in-line skates also served to popularize the game of hockey in warm weather cities. Nevertheless, the NHL still lagged well behind the other major North American team sports, and still had no network television presence in the United States. It was a local broadcast and cable-only product.

New Leadership in the 1990s

The NHL suffered its first labor disruption in April 1992 when a players' strike interrupted play for ten days. Although Ziegler saved the season, the strike cost him his job. He was replaced as league president in October 1992 by Gil Stein. Several months later, in February 1993, Gary Bettman left the NBA to become the first commissioner of the NHL. Because most of the clubs were losing money, Bettman initiated talks with National Hockey League Players' Association executive director Robert Goodenow to negotiate a salary cap in an effort to curb escalating costs. In the meantime, Bettman was forced to deal with a strike by on-ice officials in November 1993. The strike lasted 16 days and was resolved when a Collective Bargaining Agreement was reached on November 30, 1993. The situation with the players reached a head before the 1994 season. At the end of training camp, Bettman announced that the start of the season would be delayed. He and the owners believed that only by depriving the players of their salaries would the NHL be able to gain the relief it felt it so desperately needed. Goodenow and the players assumed that they were being locked out, but Bettman carefully avoided using the term, because the standard player's contract did not give the club the right to lock out a player and not pay him his salary. A player could give notice of default, and if not paid in three weeks become a free agent. According to Gil Stein in his book, *Power Plays*, ''Had the default notices been served, Bettman was prepared with a backup plan. He would try for three weeks to negotiate a new CBA with Goodenow, and then save face by announcing that, since he was satisfied with the progress of talks, the season would start.'' Not realizing he could have bargained from a position of strength, Goodenow made major concessions in order to salvage the season, and Bettman made sure that the standard player's contract was amended so that the NHLPA would not be able to prevent a future lock out.

Bettman aggressively positioned the NHL for the next century. As the league expanded into the West and South with new teams in Colorado, Dallas, Phoenix, Miami, Tampa Bay, the Carolinas, Nashville, and Atlanta, revenues rose rapidly. Annual sponsorships increased from $25 million to $300 million within five years. Grassroots efforts to attract children to the game were also stepped up. Street hockey tournaments were created, and equipment and instruction provided.

After 20 years without a network presence on American television, Bettman landed a five-year, $250 million deal with Fox. Ratings steadily increased, and it appeared that the NHL was poised to attain unprecedented popularity for hockey. The numbers, however, began to slide. In its first season on Fox, the NHL averaged a 2.0 rating, but by 1999 the numbers had dipped to 1.4, prompting Fox to drop hockey from its schedule. ABC, partnered with ESPN, signed a five-year, $600 million deal that began in 1999–2000. Rather than the broad-based marketing approach that Fox employed, ABC targeted hockey's existing core audience. The early ratings showed promise, and the NHL was further encouraged by ABC's willingness to promote hockey on its prime-time schedule, a commitment that Fox had been unwilling to make. The NHL also took an aggressive position with the Internet, becoming the first major profession sports league to bring its Internet business in-house when it bought out partner IBM. According to league studies, hockey fans were more Internet-oriented than those of other sports. Furthermore, the NHL's web site attracted 30 percent of its hits from outside of North America. With the possibility of someday broadcasting its games over the Web, the NHL was unwilling to share future profits with a partner.

As the league continued to expand, adding the Columbus Blue Jackets and Minnesota Wild for the 2000–01 season, to bring the number of franchises to 30, the pool of player talent changed in composition. Once dominated by Canadian players, hockey by the end of the 20th century was truly an international sport. Nearly a quarter of NHL players came from Europe, representing 16 nations. The change in the All-Star Game format was indicative of this shift. Beginning in 1998 the game pitted "North America" versus "the World."

Facilities were upgraded across the league. Not only were expansion teams moving into state-of-the-art arenas, replete with the luxury boxes that generate the income crucial to the economic viability of team sports, but the older franchises also saw a wave of construction. New arenas were opened in Montreal, Toronto, Boston, Chicago, Philadelphia, St. Louis, Buffalo, and Los Angeles.

Despite many promising signs, the NHL faced some serious challenges at the end of the century, mostly involving small-market Canadian franchises that were saddled with a number of economic disadvantages. The U.S.-Canadian exchange rate was crippling, because players insisted on being paid in U.S. dollars, but the clubs' received most of their revenues in weaker Canadian currency. They also had to pay far more in national and local taxes than U.S.-based teams. In fact, the Montreal Canadiens and Vancouver Canucks each paid more in taxes than all of the U.S. teams combined. To help these Canadian franchises, the NHL adopted an assistance plan in 1996. Efforts to provide public assistance, however, received little support from Canadian voters.

To keep pace with rising players' salaries, ticket prices rose steadily across the league, often driving away many traditional fans. To some observers, the economics of hockey entered a rarefied state at the close of the century, as corporations replaced gentleman owners. Although most teams lost money each year, the value of an NHL franchise increased in value. According to former NHL president and CEO, Gil Stein, "The hockey business may not be a money-maker, but the arena business seems to be. And the presence of an NHL hockey team appears to be a necessary component for operating a successful arena. . . . So large corporate entities whose core businesses benefit from a hockey team should continue to covet owning one, provided, of course, that their other businesses (arena, cable TV, beer sales, and so forth) are successful enough to absorb the annual hockey deficits. However, the continued rise in losses generated by NHL clubs does not augur well for the viability of small-market teams where that corporate synergy does not exist."

Principal Divisions

NHL Enterprises, L.P.; NHL Enterprises Canada, L.P.; NHL Europe; NHL Productions.

Principal Competitors

The National Basketball Association; The National Football League; Major League Baseball.

Further Reading

Barry, Allen and Andrew Albanese, "By the Numbers: Who's Watching?," *Wall Street Journal*, June 2, 2000, p. W9.
Beltrame, Julian, "Canada Backs Out of Pledge to Aid Hockey Teams," *Wall Street Journal*, January 24, 2000, p. B10.
Conway, Russ, *Game Misconduct*, Buffalo: London Bridge, 1996, 304 p.
Diamond, Dan, et. al., *Total Hockey*, Kingston, N.Y.: Total Sports, 1998, 1878 p.
Fischler, Stan, *Cracked Ice*, Lincolnwood, Ill.: Masters Press, 1998, 340 p.
Fong, Petti, "Canada: Penny-Wise, Franchise-Foolish," *Business Week*, March 27, 2000, p. 70.
Friedman, Wayne, "Hockey Comeback Tied to Engaging its Core Audience," *Advertising Age*, February 2, 2000, p. 40–41.
National Hockey League Official Guide & Record Book 2000, Kingston, N.Y.: National Hockey League, 2000.
Stein, Gil, *Power Plays: An Inside Look at the Big Business of the National Hockey League*, Secaucus, N.J.: Carol Publishing Group, 1997, 240 p.
Stone, David, "NHL Looks to Cast a Web on the Net," *Hockey Digest*, Summer 2000, p. 12.

—Ed Dinger

NETSCAPE

Netscape Communications Corporation

501 East Middlefield Road
Mountain View, California 94043
U.S.A.
Telephone: (650) 254-1900
Fax: (650) 528-4124
Web site: http://www.netscape.com

Wholly Owned Subsidiary of America Online, Inc.
Incorporated: 1994 as Mosaic Communications
    Corporation
Employees: N/A
Sales: $461 million (1999)
NAIC: 51121 Software Publishers; 541512 Computer
    Systems Design Services

Netscape Communications Corporation, based in Mountain View, California, is one of the leading providers of open software designed for use on the Internet and intranets. Netscape offers a line of client and server software, development tools, and commercial applications to create a complete platform for live online applications. Since spring of 1999, the company has been owned by America Online, Inc., the world's largest online service provider.

Genesis of the Enterprise

James H. Clark, one of Netscape's founders, was born into poverty in 1944 in Plainview, Texas. Although prone to mischief, such as smuggling whiskey on high school band trips, he eventually earned a Ph.D. in computer science from the University of Utah, after first studying physics. Clark had discovered computers during a stint in the Navy, which he joined after dropping out of high school. His first teaching job, at the University of Santa Cruz, soured him on academia, so he began freelancing as a consultant, which seemed even more dismal to him.

Clark turned down an offer from Hewlett-Packard, having developed a dislike for big corporate culture during an earlier stint with Boeing. In 1979 Clark went to work as a professor at Stanford University, where he made three-dimensional graphics

the focus of his research for three years. Finding it difficult to sell his ideas to existing computer companies, Clark founded Silicon Graphics Inc. (SGI), a computer workstation manufacturer, in 1982. That company went public four years later and later garnered popular fame for animating the dinosaurs of the blockbuster movie *Jurassic Park*. Eventually Clark became frustrated at being unable to guide the company into low-cost, network-friendly hardware, and he resigned in February 1994, passing up $10 million worth of stock options. In 1995, SGI's annual revenues were $2.2 billion.

Netscape's co-founder, Mark Andreessen, was born in 1972 in New Lisbon, Wisconsin, to a salesman and his wife, who worked for Land's End. As Andreessen grew up, the personal computer was also coming of age, and he wrote his first BASIC programs—video games—at the precocious age of eight. While a 21-year-old undergraduate who had first leaned toward electrical engineering, Andreessen was assigned to work on three-dimensional visualization software for the prestigious National Center for Supercomputing Applications at the University of Illinois at Champaign-Urbana. While working there for $6.85 per hour, he and six other peers created Mosaic, a graphical interface program for finding interesting Internet sites without the need for specialized programming knowledge. Within its first 18 months, Mosaic was credited with sparking a three-fold increase in the number of Internet users; the number of web sites grew by a factor of 100. After graduation, Andreessen began to work in Silicon Valley for Enterprise Integration Technologies, which produced Internet security products. Appropriately, his first connection with James Clark was electronic.

The future of the "information superhighway"—the theoretical network for carrying interactive video, e-mail, and all types of data—was subject of much speculation in 1993. Existing telephone lines and cable television seemed possible means. Clark had been considering the Internet as a possible carrier for interactive video, so he sent Andreessen an e-mail message the same day he resigned from Silicon Graphics.

After two months of introductions, discussion, and debate about potential products, Clark and Andreessen formed Mosaic Communications in April 1994. Instead of working on 3-D video games or interactive television, Andreessen proposed

Key Dates:

1994: James Clark and Mark Andreessen form Mosaic Communications, which is later renamed Netscape; begin offering software that allows users to browse on the Internet.
1995: Company makes initial public offering; shares more than double in a single day.
1996: Netscape acquires Collabra Software; becomes the most popular PC application in the world, with 38 million users; accuses Microsoft of anticompetitive business practices.
1997: Netscape relaunches its website as Netcenter, in a move toward becoming a major Internet portal.
1999: Netscape is acquired by America Online, Inc.

making Mosaic even better, creating a "killer" program to be known as "Mozilla." Clark supplied $4 million to set up the company's headquarters in Mountain View, California, while Andreessen led the development effort.

In November, the company was renamed Netscape, as the University of Illinois objected to the company's use of the name "Mosaic." Spyglass Inc., started by another U.I. alumnus, Tim Krauskopf, had licensed the name along with the software from the school. Later, Microsoft paid Spyglass for the rights to bundle Mosaic with its Windows 95 operating systems.

Early Growth

To say the Netscape grew exponentially in its first two years would be an understatement. Beginning with the two founders and an assistant, employment grew to over 250. Not surprisingly, the first new hires were five of Andreessen's programming colleagues from the University of Illinois, as well as other programmers, software developers, and cryptographers. Clark also assembled the best management team he could find. In January 1995, the company hired Jim Barksdale away from AT&T's McCaw Cellular division—a $2.3 billion a year business—to be Netscape's CEO. Barksdale had earlier helped organize Federal Express into the state-of-the-art shipping dynamo it was to become. Andreessen served as vice-president of technology, in charge of overseeing product development, while Clark gave himself the job of "Head of PR."

Like the University of Illinois had done with the original Mosaic, Netscape gave away most of its Netscape Navigator browsing software free of charge, which generated goodwill from the community of Internet users. Nevertheless, it was an extremely controversial move for such a new company. Netscape did manage to avoid packaging costs—interested parties simply downloaded the software via modem. It also established an ultimate base of virtual shoppers.

In order to make money, the company charged from $1,500 to $50,000 to supply companies with web servers, the means to establish web sites on the Internet. The most expensive systems could create "virtual" stores in which customers could examine photographs and descriptions of products, order and pay for them with credit cards. This market had plenty of room for growth: in the mid-1990s, less than ten percent of Internet users participated in electronic commerce. By late 1996, it was estimated that more than 24 million North Americans used the Internet.

In December 1994, the company began selling improved versions of its browsing software for $40 per package. Resale partners included Apple, AT&T, Hewlett-Packard, Digital, IBM, Novell, to name only a few. By 1996, Netscape was selling its products in 29 countries. It also brokered arrangements with more than 100 Internet service providers to distribute Navigator to their customers. One of the keys to the system's acceptance was its ability to work with all kinds of computers and operating systems, referred to as "open architecture," a concept, in the form of TCP/IP (Transmission Control Protocol/Internet Protocol), that made the Internet itself possible.

The openness of the company's servers made them attractive for establishing internal corporate networks, dubbed "Intranets," that could also communicate easily with outside networks. Soon, Netscape approached a similar market share in this lucrative arena as it had on the Internet, gaining 70 percent of the Global Fortune 100 companies as customers, including AT&T, Hewlett-Packard, Lockheed Martin, McDonnell-Douglas, Silicon Graphics Inc., CNN, Dow Jones, National Semiconductor, Motorola, and Eli Lilly. MCI was Netscape's first major client.

Preparations for a Secure Future in the 1990s

In April 1995, a consortium of Adobe Systems, International Data Group, Knight Ridder, TCI, and Times Mirror bought an 11 percent share in the company. Netscape's initial public offering (IPO) came in August 1995. The first day market capitalization was worth $2.2 billion. The stock originally sold for $28 a share; after a day of trading, it was worth $75. On December 5, it peaked at $171. Clark owned 32 percent of the company, which made him, according to press reports, the first Internet billionaire. As *Time* noted, the year was a record one for high-tech IPOs in the United States: $8.5 billion in capital was created for these new ventures. IPOs in all industries raised $29 billion. The success of the initial public offering came in spite of the fact that Netscape had not yet posted a significant profit.

Although Bill Gates dryly characterized the excitement over new Internet stocks as "frothy," Microsoft, too, entered the market. Late in 1995, Microsoft offered a version of its own browser, called Internet Explorer 2.0, free for downloading, as well as including a browser with the new Windows 95 operating system. Numerous strategic alliances were subsequently formed. While Netscape teamed with MasterCard to develop Secure Courier encryption standards, Microsoft and Visa announced the development of Secure Transaction Technology. In January 1996, Netscape and VeriFone, the largest credit card transaction processor, announced their plans to develop credit card payment systems for use over the Internet that would use the new Secure Courier technology. Soon afterward, Netscape teamed up with America Online, the largest provider in the United States of on-line services. The deal allowed AOL to offer improved Internet access through the Navigator browser (even though it had earlier spent $41 million to acquire similar technology) and strengthened Netscape's market share. GTE and MCI had earlier agreed to use Navigator in their networks.

In spite of the competition, both Netscape and Microsoft worked with Hewlett-Packard to develop a Hypertext Markup Language (HTML) that could be printed as seen on screen. HTML displays graphics and highlighted words that can be selected with a mouse to access other pages of information. At the same time, however, 28 companies, including IBM and Apple, announced their support for the JavaScript language, a means of imbedding programs within web pages, developed by Sun Microsystems Inc. and Netscape.

Understandably, Netscape put a great deal of effort into making Internet transmissions secure. Nevertheless, in September 1995, two hackers at the University of California at Berkeley managed to undermine the Navigator security code. The company corrected the problem and posted warnings to users on the Internet. Damage to the company's image appeared to be mitigated by the newness of the field, the newness of companies specializing in this area of technology, and the lack of reliable and easy-to-use web software elsewhere.

Netscape's innovative way of attacking the security problem mirrored its marketing strategy; both involved giveaways. To strengthen its new browser software, the company distributed beta versions—test copies disseminated before the product's commercial release. To spur the testers, Netscape, in its "Bugs Bounty" program, offered prizes ranging from coffee mugs to $1,000 for the first people to identify flaws, particularly security lapses.

In January 1996, Netscape purchased its neighbor Collabra Software Inc. for $108.7 million. One of Collabra's main products was Share, a system enabling simultaneous e-mail discussions and document sharing among network users. Subsequent releases of Share combined these facilities with Navigator's Internet access capabilities. In February, Netscape acquired Paper Software, Inc., which had recently developed 3-D programs for the Internet.

The Browser Wars

By June of 1996, Netscape Navigator had 38 million users, making it the most popular PC application in the world. Its fierce competitor, Microsoft, however, was far from giving up the fight. In August, the company released its 3.0 version of Internet Explorer, beating Netscape's release of Navigator 3.0 by just a few days. In addition, Microsoft had enlisted the aid of some very powerful allies in its efforts to promote Explorer; both MCI Communications Corp. and America Online had agreed to offer Explorer 3.0 as their "first choice" browser.

In August 1996, Netscape sent a letter to the U.S. Department of Justice (DOJ), charging Microsoft with anticompetitive practices and urging the DOJ to investigate Microsoft's business practices. Netscape maintained that Microsoft was using its dominance in personal computer operating systems to influence computer manufacturers, Internet service companies, and others into making Microsoft's software the primary choice for accessing the Internet. Netscape also accused Microsoft of charging PC makers less for its Windows 95 operating system if they agreed not to pre-install other Web browser programs. The antitrust investigation of Microsoft would continue for years, and in 2000 a Federal judge would call for the break-up of Microsoft into two smaller companies.

In late 1996, Netscape added to its line of products when it introduced Netscape Communicator. Communicator was an integrated product designed to allow users to communicate, share data, and access information on Intranets and the Internet through open email, groupware, editing, and calendar features. The new product built on, and was intended for use with, only Netscape's Navigator software. Another new product was introduced in early 1997: Visual JavaScript. Visual JavaScript was a programming tool written entirely in Java, which allowed developers to build applications that ran on both intranets and extranets without writing software code. Further product diversification followed, with the introduction of Netscape Publishing Suite, Netscape Netcaster, and other software applications.

In September 1997, Netscape relaunched its website as Netcenter. The new site offered access to Internet software, content, and community resources, grouped into easy-to-navigate categories. Three months later, the company added an online shopping site to Netcenter. These measures helped move Netscape away from being primarily a browser maker to being a significant Internet portal.

Changes in Policy, Focus, and Ownership

In January 1998, Netscape surprised the industry by announcing that it would make the source code for Communicator 5.0 available for modification and redistribution on the Internet. By so doing, the company believed it could benefit from the creative power of programmers on the Internet by incorporating their best enhancements into future versions of the software. As promised, Netscape posted the source code on the Internet on March 31. In the ensuing months, the company also released the code for its Messenger product and its Directory Software Developer's Kit.

1998 was also a year of intensified focus on the Netcenter aspect of the business. In the spring, the company established a new division devoted solely to the development of Netcenter, and subsequently initiated a 60-day campaign to improve the site. The greatest change of the year, however, came in November, when Netscape announced that it had agreed to merge with America Online. The merger, a $4.2 billion stock-for-stock transaction, was completed in February 1999. Netscape co-founder Andreessen was named to the post of chief technology officer at America Online.

2000 and Beyond

Under the parentage of America Online, Netscape continued to build its presence as an Internet portal. Toward that end, the company enhanced its Netcenter site with such features as a Personal Finance channel, an improved Entertainment channel, America Online instant messaging, an Internet Security Center, an expanded Small Business channel, and various other additions. Netscape also continued to broaden its line of software products, with a continuous stream of new Internet-related applications and improved versions of existing applications. As the company moved into the future, it seemed apparent that it had successfully negotiated the transition from a "browser provider" to a multi-faceted Internet and intranet software developer and major Internet portal. With the backing of its parent company and its own strong record of success, Netscape appeared poised for continued growth on many fronts.

Principal Operating Units

United States; Japan; Europe; Latin America.

Further Reading

Baker, Molly, ''Stargazers Abound While Internet Stocks Skyrocket,'' *Wall Street Journal,* December 7, 1995, p. C1.

Bottoms, David, ''Jim Clark: The Shooting Star @ Netscape,'' *IW: The Management Magazine,* December 18, 1995, pp. 12–16.

Clark, Jim, *Netscape Time: The Making of the Billion-Dollar Start-Up that Took On Microsoft,* 1999, New York: St. Martin's Press.

Collins, James, ''High Stakes Winners,'' *Time,* February 19, 1996, pp. 42–47.

Corcoran, Elizabeth, ''Microsoft Opens Battle of the Browsers: Market Leader Netscape Will Follow with Its New Navigator Due Out Monday,'' *The Washington Post,* August 13, 1996, p. D01.

Cusumano, Michael, and David Yoffie, *Competing on Internet Time: Lessons from Netscape and Its Battle with Microsoft,* New York: Free Press, 1998.

Egan, Jack, ''The Net-Net On Netscape,'' *US News & World Report,* August 14, 1995, p. 75.

Elmer-DeWitt, Philip, ''Bugs Bounty,'' *Time,* October 23, 1995, p. 86.

Epper, Karen, ''MasterCard Forms Link to Ensure Security of Transactions on Internet,'' *American Banker,* January 12, 1995, p. 19.

Hadjian, Ani, ''Hackers Find a Chink In Netscape's Armor,'' *Fortune,* October 30, 1995, pp. 20–21.

Hof, Robert D., ''Nothing But Net,'' *Business Week,* December 18, 1995, p. 69.

Holzinger, Albert G., ''Netscape Founder Points, and It Clicks,'' *Nation's Business, January,* 1996, p. 32.

Johnson, Bradley, ''Microsoft, Netscape Vie For 'Net,'' *Advertising Age,* December 11, 1995, p. 4.

Korzeniowski, Paul, *Microsoft vs. Netscape: The Battle for the Internet Infrastructure,* 1997, Charleston, SC: Computer Technology Research Corp.

Krantz, Michael, ''.Com Before the Storm: Microsoft and a Netscape-Sun Alliance Prepare to Battle Over the Spoils of the Web,'' *MEDIAWEEK,* September 4, 1995, p. 20.

Lewis, Jamie, ''Netscape, Share Make Good Partners,'' *PC Week,* October 23, 1995, p. N20.

Lewis, Peter H., ''Will Netscape Be the Next Microsoft, Or the Next Victim of Microsoft?,'' *New York Times,* October 16, 1995.

Miller, Michael J., ''Warfare on the World Wide Web,'' *PC Magazine,* November 7, 1995, p. 75.

Moeller, Michael, ''Netscape's Andreessen Surfs Into Computing's Next Wave,'' *PC Week,* September 25, 1995, p. 18.

Moeller, Michael, and Talila Baron, ''Online Players Vow JavaScript Support,'' *PC Week,* December 11, 1995, p. 8.

''A New Electronic Messiah,'' *Economist,* August 5, 1995, p. 62.

Quittner, Joshua, ''Browser Madness: Crazy for Internet Companies, Wall Street Investors Drove Netscape to the Sky. But Will the Bubble Burst?,'' *Time,* August 21, 1995, p. 56.

Rigdon, Joan E., ''VeriFone and Netscape Plan Software To Ease Internet Credit Card Payments,'' *Wall Street Journal,* January 22, 1996, p. B8.

Rosen, Louise, ''Suit Charges Netscape with Invasion of Privacy,'' *Upside Today: The Tech Insider,* July 10, 2000.

Sandberg, Jared, ''AOL, Netscape Are Discussing an Alliance,'' *Wall Street Journal,* January 22, 1996, p. A3.

Serwer, Andrew, ''Internet-Worth: Why the Frenzy Won't Stop Soon,'' *Fortune,* December 11, 1995, p. 26.

Sprout, Alison L., ''The Rise of Netscape,'' *Fortune,* July 10, 1995, p. 140.

Sullivan, Ed, ''Security On Web Not Quite Ready,'' *PC Week,* October 30, 1995, p. 73.

—Frederick C. Ingram
—updated by Shawna Brynildssen

New Look Group plc

New Look House
Mercey Road
Weymouth
Dorset DT3 5HJ
United Kingdom
Telephone: (+44) 1305 765-000
Fax: (+44) 1305 765-001
Web site: http://www.newlook.co.uk

Public Company
Incorporated: 1969
Employees: 7,677
Sales: £419 million ($628.5 million) (2000)
Stock Exchanges: London
Ticker Symbol: New L.
NAIC: 44812 Women's Clothing Stores

The United Kingdom's New Look Group plc is helping people dress smart for cheap. The Dorset-based group is one of the country's fastest-growing chains, with more than 550 retail stores specializing in women's clothing. New Look's target markets range from the 9- to 15-year-old set, with the company's own 915 label, and the 15 to 35 age set, featuring low-priced fashions often emulating the styles of far higher priced designer labels. New Look has captured a leading share of the discount fashions market, pricing its items as much as 10 to 15 percent lower than competitors such as Etam and Marks & Spencer. Yet the company has faced increasingly stiff competition from a new breed of cut-priced clothiers, such as Matalan and Mark One, while more fashion-oriented labels such as Asda's George and the diversified retail group Arcadia's Dorothy Perkins and Top Shop chains have adopted New Look's value-priced approach. Founded by Tom Singh, New Look owes part of its success to its fast stock rotation, with stores receiving new stock every week, encouraging shoppers to return regularly. The company has increasingly shifted from a relatively small store format to stores of more than 2,000 square feet and an increasing number of its own "mega-stores" featuring an extended range of products to include footwear, lingerie, and accessories, categories that now make up approxi-

mately 20 percent of total sales. While the bulk of New Look's stores are in the United Kingdom, the company has a limited presence on the European continent, notably with some 30 stores in France. Founder Singh, who retains a 33 percent share of the company, remains New Look's managing director commercial. Since May 2000, the company's direction has been guided by CEO Stephen Sunnucks.

Single Store in the 1960s

Tom Singh's grandfather emigrated to the United Kingdom from India's Punjab in the 1930s. Singh's parents followed later, and Singh himself was just a baby when he arrived in England. The elder Singhs opened a drapery store in the Somerset area and, later, built a small chain of retail shops. Despite this retailing background, Tom Singh studied international law and geography while pursuing his university degree. But after graduation, Singh decided to set up his own business. Borrowing £5,000 from his parents, Singh opened his first store in Taunton, in the southwest of England.

The store, named New Look, sold women's garments that Singh bought from suppliers in the Middle and Far East, allowing him to offer a wide range of styles to appeal to his rural customer base and also to maintain low prices. At the start, Singh developed the retail strategy that was to enable him to build New Look into one of the country's leading retail chains. As he told the *Financial Times,* "The idea remains to offer loads of choice, continually changing the merchandise so that the customers keep coming back."

Singh's customers kept coming back—and Singh kept going after new customers, opening new New Look stores. The company initially kept to England's southwestern regions, opening stores in the area's smaller seaside and market towns, rather than enter the larger and more urban markets. Through the 1980s the company's store openings remained modest, with new stores appearing about every nine months. The company itself increasingly had become a family affair, as Singh was joined by his wife and brother-in-law. Singh himself was an entirely hands-on manager, participating in all aspects of the company's operations, from driving to London to buy and pick up new stock, to delivering stock to the New Look stores, to sorting and pricing merchandise, and handling such administrative functions as staff hiring and bill paying.

New Look retained its provincial, value-priced image through the end of the 1980s—even until well into the 1990s, the company's clothing was often looked upon as unfashionable. Yet New Look continued to attract customers and build up its sales. By 1989, the company had built up a chain of 46 stores. In that year, Singh took the first steps toward preparing to step up the company's expansion, hiring Gavin Aldred as joint managing director. Aldred, a close friend of Singh, was the first person from outside the Singh family to take a prominent position in the company.

A Retail Value in the 1990s

Aldred's background—he worked as a retail consultant, but also had been involved in a number of failed companies—was to later haunt New Look when it sought a listing on the London stock exchange. In the meantime, Aldred and Singh put together a new management team, including John Hanna as co-managing director, and then set New Look on a massive expansion drive. The company began looking outside of its southwest base for new locations, while at the same time targeting larger towns and urban areas, with new New Look openings in such towns as Guildford and Haywards Heath. Within a year after Aldred's joining the company, New Look had nearly doubled its retail chain, topping 70 stores.

Within five years, New Look had grown into a nationally operating retail chain of some 200 stores. The company's annual sales had seen growth rates in the range of 50 percent per year in those five years, while its profits growth reached 80 percent in the same period. The company, which had built its expansion primarily in its traditional small market locations, now prepared to take the New Look signage into the United Kingdom's larger markets and urban High Streets. To fuel this expansion—and also to allow Singh's parents to cash in on their initial £5,000 investment, worth 50 percent of the company—Singh prepared to take his company to the stock market.

The company's initial public offering (IPO), scheduled for November 1994, was instead canceled at the last minute. A number of factors were behind the cancellation, not least of which was the poor climate for new stock issues at the time, especially in the retail market hard hit by a lingering recession. The company's aggressive expansion plans—calling for a doubling of its stores in the mid-1990s—also were called into question by analysts. As one analyst told the *Independent,* New Look was "coming to the market when all the easy growth has

already taken place. It is now expanding into larger towns where there is more competition. Its exemplary profit record over the past few years is unlikely to be sustainable."

Stock analysts also were concerned about a series of in-family deals, including the transactions among various companies owned by the Singh family, purchases made by the company of holdings from the Singh family's own pension fund, as well as payments totaling £3.6 million to Singh and his wife made in the year prior to the attempted offering—all of which raised concerns that New Look remained too much of a family-run business to offer institutional investors the necessary confidence in its stock. Meanwhile, the presence of Aldred raised concerns from some potential investors, given his prior involvement with failed companies. Yet, other analysts suggested as well that large investors were reluctant to back a company run by an Indian.

Finally, with the company's stock valued no higher than £130 million, much lower than the hoped-for £180 million, New Look pulled the plug on its IPO, vowing to reconsider its options the following year, while maintaining its expansion plans with or without a public offering. At the same time, Singh claimed that the company had profited already from the build-up to the public offering, telling the *Independent:* "The flotation process has been enormously beneficial to us because we know far more about the company than we did before."

The Singh family was able to realize its investment in 1995, when a team of venture capitalists, including BZW Private Equity and Prudential Venture Managers, paid £170 million for a 70 percent share of New Look. The new capital enabled New Look to continue its expansion drive; by mid-1996, the company had grown to 333 stores. In that year the company, which by then had entered the French market, rapidly building up a network of 19 stores in France, also targeted the women's clothing market in Germany, opening its first store in Essen. The company's German sales proved disappointing, however. After building up its German holdings to three stores by the end of the decade, the company decided to abandon that market.

Joining the company in 1996 was Howard Dyer, chairman of Hamley's, who was named as chairman and charged with building up New Look's executive staff with an eye toward the company's future attempt at gaining a public listing. Seeking to avoid the difficulties of launching a new IPO, New Look attempted to back into the market, by acquiring rival women's clothing chain Etam. Yet that company, which had been struggling with losses for some time, was instead bought up by its French counterpart, which had topped New Look's bid with one of £56 million.

In the meantime, New Look was getting a new look from the British consumer. The company's launch of its new label 915, targeted at the 9-to-15-year-old set, met with strong sales. That label joined with changes in New Look's overall clothing lines, as the company began reacting faster to new clothing trends. Fashion trends themselves were seen as evolving more and more rapidly—the appearance of a celebrity wearing a particular clothing item could easily spark demand across the United Kingdom for that item. New Look capitalized on this development, using its strong network of suppliers and its long-

Key Dates:

1969: Tom Singh opens first women's clothing store.
1970–88: Southwest England expansion to 46 stores.
1989: National growth; recruitment of nonfamily management.
1990: Chain reaches to 70 stores.
1993: Opening of 200th New Look store.
1994: Aborted attempt public stock offering.
1995: Singh family sells 75 percent of New Look to venture capitalists.
1996: Opening of 300th New Look store; entry into French and German markets.
1997: Launch of 915 label; failed attempt to acquire Etam.
1998: Public offering on London stock exchange.
1999: Opening of 500th New Look store; exit of German market.
2000: CEO Jim Hodkinson forced to resign.

held policy of fast stock rotation to tap demand for each new fashion fad. Consumers in turn changed their opinion of New Look, raising the company's reputation.

By 1998, the company was making new preparations for a public offering. Boosting the company's direction now was Jim Hodkinson, who had built up the Kingfisher's B&Q chain of DIY stores, joining the company as chief executive officer, and Stephen Sunnucks, as retail managing director. At the same time, Gavin Aldred agreed to step down from his position on the company's board of directors. These changes, coupled with New Look's sustained ten-year growth record, enabled the company to succeed in its new IPO. Tom Singh, who, through a conversion of shares, now held 33 percent of the company, became one of the United Kingdom's richest retailers, with holdings valued at more than 170 million.

The public offering enabled New Look to continue its expansion drive, as the company topped 500 stores in 1999. New Look also began converting many of its locations to new, larger formats, including the introduction of a mega-store format, allowing the company to extend its range of products to include an increasing share of shoes, lingerie, and accessories. These items, which before had remained limited to around ten percent of sales, came to represent some 20 percent of the company's sales by the turn of the century.

New Look abandoned the German market in 1999. At the same time, the company had boosted its network of French stores, which became profitable in the same year, to nearly 30 stores. The company's international growth became more important to New Look at the turn of the 21st century as the expansion for the company's U.K. store network became increasingly limited. Nonetheless, New Look's long concentration on smaller markets meant that it remained underrepresented in the United Kingdom's 250 largest markets, giving it room for some growth. Yet increasing competition came from not only clothing discounters, but also from higher-end retail fashion rivals, such as Marks & Spencer and others, which began adopting New Look's low-pricing policies. These pressures made New Look a potential acquisition candidate—at the end of 1999, the company reportedly held merger talks with Switzerland's Voegele.

The tightening competitiveness of the United Kingdom's retail market continued to place pressure on New Look as the company entered the 21st century. The company's rapid growth through the 1990s, meanwhile, failed to impress a stock market skeptical of retail stocks in general and concerned that New Look had already reached saturation in its home market. The company also was rocked by scandal, when CEO Jim Hodkinson was forced to step down amid complaints about his conduct at a social function. Hodkinson was replaced by Stephen Sunnucks in May 2000. Despite these clouds, New Look's popularity among British consumers remained steady, and the company looked good to retain its position as one of the United Kingdom's leading women's clothing retailers.

Principal Competitors

Marks and Spencer plc; Debenhams plc; Next plc; Etam; Tommy Hilfiger; Littlewoods Organisation plc; Mark One; Matalan.

Further Reading

Cope, Nigel, ''Flotation Makes Pounds 120m for the Man Who Tailored New Look,'' *Independent,* May 21, 1998, p. 23.
Osborne, Alistair, ''New Look Aims for Higher Volume,'' *Daily Telegraph,* November 26, 1999.
Rankine, Kate, ''A Long, Hard Look at the Head of New Look,'' *Daily Telegraph,* April 18, 1998, p. 31.
Thomson, Richard, ''Chic and Unashamedly Cheap,'' *Independent,* April 26, 2000, p. 9.
——, ''Looking Good on a Budget,'' *Daily Telegraph,* May 26, 2000.
——, ''180m Pounds New Look Float Is Scrapped,'' *Independent,* November 3, 1994, p. 36.

—M.L. Cohen

Noland Company

80 29th Street
Newport News, Virginia 23607
U.S.A.
Telephone: (757) 928-9000
Fax: (757) 928-9170
Web site: http://www.noland.com

Public Company
Incorporated: 1919 as Newport Plumbing & Mill Supply
Company
Employees: 1,512
Sales: $482.8 million (1999)
Stock Exchanges: NASDAQ
Ticker Symbol: NOLD
NAIC: 421720 Plumbing and Heating Equipment and
Supplies Wholesalers; 421730 Air Conditioning
Equipment and Supplies Wholesalers; 421610
Electrical Apparatus and Equipment, Wiring Supplies
and Construction Materials Wholesalers; 421830
Industrial Machinery and Equipment Wholesalers

Noland Company is a wholesale distributor of plumbing, heating, air conditioning, refrigeration, electrical, and industrial supplies. The company's main product line is plumbing fixtures, including jacuzzi bathtubs, fancy sinks, and related supplies. Noland Company serves over 24,000 customers—primarily the construction industry and industrial manufacturing—in 14 southeastern states through its more than 110 branches.

The Early Years: A Self-Made Man Seizes Opportunities

Beginning with his departure from an orphanage at the age of eleven, L.U. "Casey" Noland, founder of Noland Company, was the quintessential self-made man. At a young age, he went to Baltimore, where he worked at various jobs and eventually attained employment at a steelworks. He then found an apprenticeship with a plumber, which led to employment at the New-

port News shipyard. Noland later took a position at an engineering firm, where he became vice-president at just 26 years of age. It was in 1915, however, that he truly began to make his mark. At that time, Noland and T.B. Clifford took advantage of new economic opportunities created by the advent of World War I, and formed a mechanical contracting business called the Noland-Clifford Company.

The Noland-Clifford Company did well, but it had difficulty procuring plumbing supplies. Locally, supplies were scarce and so most had to be shipped from Baltimore. Rather than purchase supplies on an as-needed basis, as most contractors did, the company began to stock an inventory of regularly required materials. It was when other local contractors began to seek supplies from Noland-Clifford's stash that Casey Noland recognized a need for a wholesale distributor in the Newport News area. Thus, the Newport Plumbing & Mill Supply Company was formed in 1919.

By the time the company incorporated as Noland Company in 1922, Noland had opened branches in Roanoke, Virginia, and Goldsboro and Winston-Salem, North Carolina. The company prospered, selling modern bathtubs, sinks, toilets, and related supplies. Thus, it continued to open new branches throughout the southeastern states. Noland's philosophy of strong sales support involved sales training, good employee benefits, and the incentive of a share in the company's profits.

Growth had its obstacles, however, but Noland was always up to the challenge. For example, when a railroad embargo halted shipments of supplies to the West Palm Beach branch during the Florida building boom, Noland resolved the problem by acquiring a 3,000-ton steamship to transport supplies to West Palm Beach. In doing so, Noland Company became the only plumbing, heating and mill supplier in Florida. When the land boom later collapsed, Noland shipped the inventory from Florida to a new branch in Washington, D.C. As the business expanded and became more difficult to manage, Noland purchased a three-seat plane to speed travel to distant company branches.

Noland Company survived—and even thrived—during the Great Depression. In 1930, the company opened four new branches, filling what need existed as other companies failed.

The only year the company experienced a financial loss due to the hard times was in 1932. Later, as President Roosevelt's civil service programs expanded access to electricity, Noland Company started an electrical supply department in 1938 and added refrigeration supplies to its product line in 1940. Company headquarters were moved to a larger facility in downtown Newport News, a few blocks from the original office. During the postwar home-building boom, Noland Company continued to thrive, providing plumbing, electrical and other supplies to construction contractors. By 1952, Noland Company encompassed 25 branch units with 1,000 employees, and annual sales reached $50 million.

Postwar Era

Upon the death of Casey Noland in 1952, L.U. Noland, Jr. took over the company's operations. Thankfully, the company continued to grow as Noland, Jr., emphasized customer service and satisfaction. His efforts, in fact, culminated in *Supply House Times* naming the Noland Company "Wholesaler of the Year" in 1960.

In the early 1960s, the company diversified its wholesale supply offerings, with central air conditioning equipment becoming a significant new source of sales in the hot and humid southern states. The company upgraded its warehousing facilities, transferring operations to new modern buildings that allowed for more efficient operations. Noland included showrooms at many of the new buildings to display luxury plumbing fixtures and home lighting.

Noland Company became a public company with an initial offering of stock in 1967. Proceeds from the sale of stock funded acquisitions and electronic data processing. In the late 1960s, the company began implementation of the computer-based Branch Data System which automated daily paperwork. The move streamlined purchase orders, vendor invoices, price changes, billing, and accounts receivables. After several years of branch level implementation, all branches were linked to a mainframe computer in the late 1970s, enabling accessibility to information from distant branch locations for analysis at the central corporate office. The system provided managers with sales and inventory reports on a daily basis, allowing them to better serve branch units from the supply warehouses. In conjunction with computerized inventory tracking, Noland also implemented the "First In, First Out" inventory method in 1974 to reduce the impact of inflation on profit.

Expansion in the 1970s centered primarily on the states of Tennessee, Arkansas, and Alabama. In 1971, Noland acquired two units of the Amstar Division of American Standard—one located in Knoxville, Tennessee, and the other in Birmingham, Alabama. Soon thereafter came the purchase of Amstar Supply Company in Little Rock, Arkansas in 1972. The company expanded with three more acquisitions and three new branches in 1978: three single-unit wholesale outlets were purchased near existing Noland outlets that had growth potential. The new locations were Superior Supply in West Memphis, Arkansas; Savannah, Tennessee; and Annapolis, Maryland. The new branches were located in Mechanicsville, Maryland; Mountain Home, Arkansas; and Columbus, Mississippi. In early 1979, the company acquired Southern Supply in Jackson, Tennessee. With 61 branches in 11 southeastern states, 1979 sales reached $272 million.

Meanwhile, Noland continued its program to modernize, expand, and renovate its facilities. In 1978, four branch units were replaced by newer, larger facilities, while six others were expanded and a new warehouse-office-showroom opened in Atlanta. Also, a sales and service center opened in Roanoke, Virginia, and the company's new Drilling Equipment Branch completed its first full year of operations in 1978, selling and repairing new and used well drilling rigs. A 70,000 square-foot main branch facility was completed in Norfolk in 1979.

Upgrading branch facilities produced a favorable response from the industry, as a survey of manufacturer's representatives voted 26 of the company's 44 showrooms onto the blue-ribbon list of better plumbing showrooms in *Supply House Times* magazine. Twelve of the 26 showrooms were named "Best in Territory."

The 1980s

The 1980s proved to be financially uncertain years as sales and earnings fluctuated. The high rate of inflation and high interest rates discouraged home building and industrial production, which were Noland Company's key markets. The company took preventive measures and lowered its operating expenses—including staff cutbacks—to offset declining sales in 1980. The company halted capital expenditures for new equipment, branch expansion, and facilities upgrades, with the exception of those already in progress. Luckily, it was around this time that the Branch Data System, in its second full year of operation, began to realize effective stock management and reduced inventory costs.

As economic conditions improved, the company resumed its expansion and improvement programs. The company acquired Tropical Supply Company in 1981, which had five branches in southeast Florida. In 1983, the company expanded its product line to include maintenance and repair parts, and implemented a new advertising program designed to highlight the company's showroom outlets. Noland Company added twelve new branches through both acquisition and new start-ups, but at the same time closed two small stores in 1984.

Noland also resumed its facilities improvement in the mid-1980s, remodeling eight branches in 1984 and seven branches in 1985. The company also built a new 84,000 square-

<table>
<tr><td colspan="2">

Key Dates:
</td></tr>
</table>

Key Dates:

1919: Newport Plumbing & Mill Supply Company is established.
1922: Company name changes to Noland Company.
1938: Company adds electrical supply division.
1952: L.U. Noland, Jr., becomes president.
1960: Noland named ''Wholesaler of the Year'' by Supply House Times.
1978: Implementation of Branch Data System significantly improves inventory control.
1991: Only net loss since the Great Depression.
1995: International expansion into Latin America.
1999: State-of-the-art inventory technology implemented.

foot facility in Frederick, Maryland. New facilities in Richmond included the Pipe, Valve, and Fitting Center and the Virginia Regional Distribution Center/Industrial. The latter facility was designed to serve the special requirements of the DuPont Company, including just-in-time delivery to area factories. This led to improvements in computer tracking of inventory.

The company also implemented a number of new technologies to improve customer service in the mid-1980s. The Customer Direct Order Entry System, a computer-to-computer ordering system, was introduced in 1982 and attracted large industrial customers. To facilitate faster counter service at its branches, the company invested in the Advanced Counter Computer System of electronic cash registers. The Counter Area Merchandising Program added self-service racks for tools, repair parts, and other frequently required items. The company also added industrial automation products to its supply line, primarily for customers in Nashville and Montgomery. The efforts to improve customer satisfaction proved valuable as *Supply House Times* once again named Noland Company ''Wholesaler of the Year'' in 1985.

Expansion continued with the June 1985 acquisition of Mars Plumbing Repair Parts and Mars Plumbing Supply Company; the latter supplied pipe, valves, and fittings to utility and mechanical contractors and industrial manufacturers through nine branches in San Antonio. With 17 new branches overall, Noland recorded its third year of record earnings in 1985, at $6.5 million. Sales at that time reached $380.9 million, representing an increase of 13.4 percent over those of 1984.

A Third Generation Leads Noland into the 1990s

Sales and earnings continued to fluctuate as the third generation of Nolands assumed leadership of the company when L.U. Noland III became chairman of the Board and CEO in 1987. Competitive pricing lowered profit margins and a slowdown in the economy led to a reduction in sales. The company responded by closing its unprofitable units, reducing the total number of branches to 94 in 1989; by laying-off some of its employees; and by decreasing its inventory. Unfortunately, a high rate of bankruptcy among the company's customers in the construction industry led to losses from uncollectible accounts payable. In 1991, Noland Company experienced a 10.3 percent

decline in sales, to $384.5 million, and its first net loss since the Great Depression.

As the 1990s continued, however, modest improvements in the economy resulted in slow growth in the construction and industrial manufacturing industry. Noland lowered operating expenses by reducing its sales staff, thus increasing the average sales per employee and its gross profit margins. In 1992, sales reached $492.1 million. Sales of air conditioners and supplies did well at this time, but business in the company's other departments declined.

In 1994, the company experienced a 15 percent increase in sales of industrial maintenance, repair and operating supplies through a systems-oriented sales and service approach. Noland Company added six new branches through both acquisition and new store openings. While Maryland branches served the company's Pennsylvania markets, it operated for the first time within Pennsylvania with an acquisition in Hanover. Noland Company's conservative control of expenses improved profit margins from 18.7 percent in 1992 to 19.6 percent in 1994. This resulted in an 89 percent rise in net income in 1994, and a 9.2 percent increase in sales to $440.2 million.

The up and down trend of the 1990s continued in 1995, however, as lower-than-expected sales in the company's major markets—housing construction and industrial production—resulted in a 20.5 percent decline in earnings. Although the company's sales had actually risen 6.7 percent that year, excess stock had hurt the company financially. Sales in the air conditioner/refrigeration department made a significant contribution to total revenue. The dramatic increase resulted from Noland Company's entry into the export market in Latin American countries. Operating a new branch in Miami, Noland International sought exclusive distributors in Latin America.

The company continued to expand in profitable markets as the 1990s wore on. Noland Company acquired two plumbing supply houses in Clearwater and Tampa, which increased the number of branches in Florida to 18, and gave Noland a branch in every major market. The acquisition of Raub Supply Company added seven locations in Pennsylvania and Virginia, as well, raising the company's total number of branch locations to 107 in 14 states.

The company again designed a new branch computer system to improve inventory turnover and reduce excess inventory. The new system utilized bar-coding technology instituted at company warehouses and branch units in 1990. With implementation of the new system at 55 branches in 1995, excess inventory declined $1.7 million. The company therefore planned to complete implementation of the system the following year, in 1996.

In the late 1990s, L.U. Noland III implemented a reorganization strategy to stabilize earnings and sales. Reorganization involved changes in staffing at both the sales and management levels. The company altered its approach to sales, shifting to a commission-based program with no salary. The sales staff was reduced from 333 to 250 people, which resulted in relocating employees to other positions in the company. L.U. Noland III also renewed the company's emphasis on employee training for all areas of the company. Its new headquarters included a multimedia training center—Noland University—to provide the continual development of new classes. Four regional management positions were added to address problems early, rather than wait for problems to reach the corporate office. The company also replaced branch credit managers with area credit managers, providing better controls and less bad-credit losses.

Noland Company continued to build on its success through new and time-tested methods. In 1999, the company decided to withdraw from the Texas market, and closed its six unprofitable branches in order to focus instead on the profitable southern and southeastern markets. The company updated and improved its inventory management strategy with state-of-the-art technology for more precise monitoring and forecasting. The system, implemented in 1999 for one-third of the company's branch units, included a Stock Locator System and Systematic Cycle Counting in all warehouses.

The company also instituted an Internet-based catalog to facilitate business-to-business sales, while at the same time, promotions for the company's 35 Bath & Idea Centers resulted in a 22 percent increase in showroom sales. A central Industrial Distribution Center opened in 2000 to improve service to the company's industrial integrated supply accounts.

Principal Subsidiaries

Noland Properties, Inc.

Principal Competitors

Pameco Corporation; Watsco Inc.

Further Reading

Glynn, Matt, ''Virginia-Based Noland Co. Expects an Even Better Year,'' *Knight-Ridder/Tribune Business News,* April 24, 1997.

Noland Company: A Blend of Traditional Strengths and Progressive Changes, Newport News: Noland Company, 1990.

''Noland Company Reports 1993 Earnings of $3.3 Million,'' *PR Newswire,* February 18, 1994.

''Noland Company Reports Lower '95 Earnings,'' *PR Newswire,* February 23, 1996.

''Noland Reports Record Earnings for 1999,'' *PR Newswire,* February 21, 2000.

—Mary Tradii

Norsk Hydro ASA

Bygdoy allé 2,
N-0240, Oslo 2
Norway
Telephone: (47) 22-43-21-00
Fax: (47) 22-43-27-25
Web site: http://www.hydro.com

U.S. Headquarters:
Norsk Hydro Americas, Inc.
100 North Tampa Street, Suite 3350
Tampa, Florida 33602
Telephone: (813) 222-3880
Fax: (813) 222-5741

Public Company (44% owned by Kingdom of Norway)
Incorporated: 1905 as Norsk Hydro-Elektrisk
  Kvaelstofaktieselskab (Norwegian Hydro-Electric
  Nitrogen Corporation)
Employees: 37,900
Sales: NOK 102.43 billion ($12.8 billion) (1999)
Stock Exchanges: New York Oslo Stockholm London
  Paris Frankfurt Dusseldorf Hamburg Amsterdam
  Zürich Geneva Basel
Ticker Symbol: NHY
NAIC: 325311 Nitrogenous Fertilizer Manufacturing;
  32532 Pesticide and Other Agricultural Chemical
  Manufacturing; 331316 Aluminum Extruded Product
  Manufacturing; 211111 Crude Petroleum and Natural
  Gas Extraction; 211112 Natural Gas Liquid Extraction

Norsk Hydro ASA is the largest public industrial company in Norway, with operations in three core areas: oil and energy, light metals, and agriculture, such as agricultural chemicals. Fertilizer ranks as the company's leading product, but revenues from oil and gas contribute almost half of the company's profits. Norsk Hydro's light metals division is involved with the manufacture of aluminum and magnesium, and the company is a leading producer of PVC pipe in Scandinavia and the United Kingdom.

Early Years as a Hydro-Electric Company: 1905–40s

Norsk Hydro was founded in 1905 by Norwegian entrepreneurs Sam Eyde and Kristian Birkeland as Norsk Hydro-Elektrisk Kvaelstofaktieselskap (Norwegian Hydro-Electric Nitrogen Corporation). Originally, the company exploited the hydro-electric resources of waterfalls to generate electricity used in the production of nitrogen fertilizers. Initial output was mostly limited to Scandinavian markets until after World War II, when the Norwegian government took a 48 percent stake in the company and ushered in an era of multinational expansion and diversification. In 1969, the company name changed to Norsk Hydro A.S. By the 1990s, the company's size justified a decentralized organization plan grouping the company into four business segments, each serving as the strategic and financial center for its composite divisions: agriculture, oil and gas, light metals, and petrochemicals. Combining these segments with a growing number of other activities—from alginate production to pharmaceutical research, seafood, and insurance—Hydro proved that its origins in fertilizers laid fertile ground for almost a century of lush business growth.

As early as World War II, Hydro's fertilizer activities fueled widely divergent enterprises; in this case, German occupying forces made use of the company's plant in Rjukan, Norway to produce heavy water (deuterium oxide) for use in nuclear reactor research. The Rjukan plant produced ammonia, which yielded heavy water as a by-product. With its use as an atomic brake fluid, heavy water was a key tool in atomic fission experiments and the development of the atomic bomb, a device that was considered a key determinant for the outcome of the war. Fearing German access to heavy water for their escalating research program, the Allies chose 11 saboteurs, trained them in the British Isles, and on February 1943 parachuted them onto the Hardanger plateau, from where the renowned "Heroes of Telemark" descended to Vemork by combining skiing, treacherous climbing, and sheer willpower to destroy the plant. Though the definitive impact of the sabotage on the outcome of the war remained a point of historical debate, the mission's unquestionable adventure appeal energized numerous books and documentaries and two feature films.

Company Perspectives:

Hydro is an industrial group based on the processing of natural resources to meet needs for food, energy and materials. We must do this in ways that do not diminish the ability of future generations to meet their own needs. The challenge is to find a proper balance between caring for the environment and serving human needs. We want to take our part of this responsibility. So we are designing our products to have the minimum adverse effect on the environment throughout their entire life cycle. We will conduct our business activities in accordance with the demands of the environment and demonstrate openness in environmental questions. By doing this, we hope to prove that we are worthy of our 'licence to operate.'

World War II brought far more change than the destruction of the Rjukan plant. After the bombing of Hydro's Heroya plants in 1944 and the financial losses that resulted, the company moved to consolidate much of its business in Norway and to expand the scope of its interests. While 97 percent of the company's shares were owned by foreigners at the outbreak of World War II, after armistice the Norwegian government seized German holdings and took a 48 percent stake, which along with additional purchases and reparation rose to a 51 percent government stake in the company.

Expansion in the 1950s and 1960s

Starting in the 1950s, Hydro expanded into a number of new businesses, both directly and indirectly related to its core fertilizer production. In 1951, Hydro began production of magnesium metal and polyvinyl. In 1967, the company opened an aluminum reduction plant and semi-fabricating facility at Karmoy, Norway, and constructed the Rldal-Suldal hydro-electric facility to power the Karmoy works. The company also made preliminary steps in seafood with its fish-arming subsidiary, MOWI, in 1969. With Hydro's 1965 and 1967 opening of two Norwegian ammonia plants using naphtha (a liquid mixture of hydrocarbons distilled from petroleum, coal tar, and other hydrocarbon-rich substances) and heavy fuel oil feedstocks in the production process, the company became dependent on outside suppliers of raw materials. Attempting to supply its own hydrogen for ammonia production, Hydro began investigating opportunities in gas and oil production in the late 1960s. These initiatives, paired with a new management strategy starting in the late 1960s, spurred tremendous growth that transformed the company into an industrial group.

Under the leadership of Johan B. Holte (president from 1967 to 1977 and chairman of the board from 1977 to 1985), Hydro restructured not only its policies on employee relations but its overall organizational structure. Holte set new standards for cooperation between management and workforce at all levels of Hydro; and those levels multiplied rapidly, as Holte initiated aggressive moves to expand and diversify core business beyond domestic fertilizers and into light metals, gas and oil, and eventually other segments on an international scale. In a 1990 retrospective article, Holte's successor as president, Odd Narud,

summarized the organizational strategy for Hydro's in-house publication, *Profile Magazine:* ''The company has concentrated on growth in its core areas; agriculture, oil and gas, light metals and petrochemicals. It is the sustained efforts to improve in these areas which have created the basis for serious involvement in new product areas.''

By the early 1970s, oil and gas constituted one such ''new product area.'' In 1965, when Norway granted licenses for offshore petroleum exploration, Hydro obtained concessions and formed partnerships with foreign companies on numerous fields. In 1969, the Phillips Petroleum-operated drilling rig Ocean Viking struck oil in the Ekofisk field, in which Hydro owned a share. The company's success with North Sea oil and gas continued with the Elf-Aquitaine-operated Frigg discovery in 1971. In an attempt to combine Hydro's success with a stronger petroleum policy, the Norwegian government increased its share of Hydro to 51 percent and created Statoil, a state-owned company, in 1972. Hydro began operating its oil refinery at Mongsted, Norway in 1975. Experience from these projects in the 1960s and 1970s would prove extremely beneficial for Hydro's innovative contributions to oil and gas development in the late 1980s and early 1990s.

Growth through Acquisitions in the 1970s and 1980s

Building on its natural gas liquids resources, Hydro began investing large amounts of capital in the petrochemical industry in the early 1970s, with the decision to build the Rafnes petrochemical complex, which began production of ethylene and vinyl chloride in 1978. Falling in the wake of the international oil crises, however, Hydro's petrochemical activity incurred losses until the late 1980s. Nevertheless, the company implemented ongoing growth strategies through the 1980s: in 1982, the company formed Norsk Hydro Polymers Ltd., one of two PVC manufacturers in the United Kingdom, after acquiring BIP Vinyl's Aycliffe facility and the last 50 percent of Vinatex; in 1984 the company acquired KemaNord's facility in Stenungsund, Sweden, and formed Norsk Hydro Plast AB; in 1987 Hydro bought 47 percent of Singapore Polymer to better target Asian markets (increasing its holdings to 60 percent a year later); and in 1989, Hydro Polymères was formed in France to produce PVC and engineering plastics in continental Europe. By 1990, the company announced development of a new PVC plant at Rafnes. And in March 1991, Hydro announced a joint venture with BFGoodrich Company to market vinyl-based injection-molding compounds for use in applications such as business machine components, telecommunications equipment, and construction products.

The company also covered new ground in fertilizers, with the acquisition of NSM, a Dutch firm (1979); 75 percent of the Swedish firm, Supra (1981); a British firm renamed Norsk Hydro Fertilizers Ltd. (1982); a West German company renamed Ruhr Stickstoff AG (1985); and 80 percent of the French Compagnie Francaise de L'Azote (1986), along with the remaining 20 percent the following year. After restructuring its fertilizer division in 1987, the other divisions in Hydro's agriculture segment shifted as well, with sales of industrial gas operations in Finland and Sweden and formation of a new company, Hydrogas AS, the largest company in the industrial chemicals division. By 1990, Hydrogas sold the whole range of

Key Dates:

1905: Norsk Hydro-Elektrisk Kvaelstofaktieselskap is founded.
1951: Company begins production of magnesium metal and polyvinyl.
1969: Company changes name to Norsk Hydro A.S.
1972: Government of Norway increases its share of Hydro to 51 percent.
1999: Hydro acquires Saga Petroleum ASA; the government of Norway's stake in Hydro is reduced to 44 percent.

industrial gases in Norway and held about ten percent of the carbon dioxide market in Europe. In 1991, the agricultural segment continued to acquire fertilizer facilities: one in Rostock, Germany; another in Green Bay, Florida; another in the United Kingdom; and three ammonia plants facilities in Trinidad and Tobago.

Hydro expanded its light metals segment in the 1980s. First it acquired five aluminum extrusion plants in Europe from Alcan Aluminum Limited. Then, in 1986, the group merged with Ardal og Sunndal Verk AS (ÅSV), a government-controlled aluminum company, and consolidated its interests in May 1988, renaming the merged entity Hydro Aluminum AS (ranked as the world's fifth largest aluminum company in 1990, with sales of NOK 15 billion). Hydro positioned its growing aluminum extrusion business to supply growing demand in strategic market segments, such as the automotive industry (a separate automotive aluminum unit was established in Munich, the German automotive capital, in 1990) and tubing for air conditioning systems in the United States. The company's purchase of Bohn Aluminum & Brass in 1990 further strengthened its position in the U.S. extruded products market.

Just as aluminum's light weight and high strength characteristics made it suitable for automotive parts ranging from frames to tires, magnesium was characterized by similarly useful formability and lightness. In addition to the construction of a new magnesium plant in Canada in 1986, Hydro collaborated with the automotive industry in the development of magnesium components. By the early 1990s, these efforts were disrupted by a stagnant economy—which led to depressed prices and high inventories of magnesium—and by reverberations from the United States Commerce Department International Trade Administration's 1991 claim that Canada and Norway were unfairly dumping magnesium in the United States, and its imposition of anti-dumping duties to deter continuation of the practice. That same year, Hydro announced reduction of magnesium production in its Norwegian and Canadian plants, resulting in 1992 levels between 25,000 and 30,000 tonnes less than 1991 levels.

Expansion and internationalization of its core businesses increasingly exposed Hydro to opportunities in the less related, though no less promising spectrum of "other activities," including seafood and salmon farming and processing. While Hydro's involvement in salmon farming began with its 50 per-

cent acquisition of MOWI in 1959, not until the end of the 1970s did Hydro's stake reach 75 percent, and not until 1980 did MOWI operate internationally. In 1980, MOWI acquired 44 percent of the Icelandic ocean ranching company, ISNO, and 75 percent of Fanad Ireland, a near-bankrupt trout farming operation that became a world leader in fish farming. Other developments included the acquisition of Golden Sea Produce (1983), with Sea Life Centre aquariums in Scotland and England; new fish farms at Haveroy and Turoy (1985 to 1986); the establishment of the Prodemar turbot farming facilities, in cooperation with the Bank of Bilbao in Spain (1987); the establishment of Biomar, a joint venture between Norsk Hydro, Dyno Industrier a.s., and KFK (1988); and the acquisition of the Danish fish smoking companies Pescadana and B&H Fish Export (1990).

Starting in the mid-1980s, Hydro also aspired to become a leading company in bio-polymers, fatty acids, and pharmaceuticals. A series of acquisitions toward that end started in 1985, when Hydro bought a majority share (and later acquired over 90 percent) of Carmeda AB, a producer of biologically active surfaces for medical equipment. In 1986, Hydro Pharma AS was established to develop pharmaceutical activities, including the products of drug delivery systems by Biogram AB, diagnostic ultrasound equipment by Vingmed Sound A/S, enzymes by Marine Biochemicals, and fatty acids by Johan C. Martens. In 1987, Hydro Pharma acquired all the shares of NAF Laboratories, a leading Norwegian pharmaceuticals supplier. Hydro's Pharma and Biomarine Divisions were merged into the Biomedical Division in 1988. And in 1989, the company increased its stake in Securus, a company listed on the Oslo stock exchange, to 77.3 percent. By 1990, these diversified activities were all brought under one umbrella with Securus's takeover of Hydro's Biomedical division.

The 1980s represented a period of growth that virtually transformed Hydro into a multinational giant. The company's operating revenue of 14 billion kroner in 1980 soared to over 60 billion in 1990; its 13,000 employees increased to 42,000 over the same period.

Streamlining Operations in the 1990s and Beyond

A picture of Hydro with nothing but such positive growth figures, however, would be misleading; suffering from international economic recession in the late 1980s and early 1990s—compounded by low-priced competition from the changing economies of Eastern Europe and the former Soviet Union in areas such as light metals and fertilizers—Hydro was forced to consolidate operations and manage cost reductions to remain competitive into the 1990s. As early as April 1991, efforts began to pay off, with Moody's upgrading Hydro senior debt ratings to A3 from Baa1, reflecting the company's good positioning in the face of possible economic slowing in Western Europe. In 1992, the company president, Egil Myklebust, announced a two-year plan to reduce fixed costs by NOK 1,500 million. In the third quarter of 1991, the magnesium and fertilizer businesses were extensively restructured, with plant closures and rationalization of Swedish fertilizer interests. In December 1991, Hydro's UK North Sea oil and gas interests were sold to British Borneo Petroleum, and Dutch exploration and production assets were also put up for sale. In June of that year, Japan's Nippon Steel Chemical Co. and Nichimen Corp. jointly took over the resin compound manufacturing division of Hydro's chemical division.

In the early 1990s, Hydro also implemented a strategy of internationalization in its core businesses. In 1992, the company's oil and gas division was made operator for the first offshore license in Namibia. It was also awarded blocks in Vietnam, Angola, and continued to negotiate numerous feasibility contracts in Russia (such as the 1990 gas discovery in Schtockmanskoye in the Barents Sea). In 1993, Hydrogas A.S. negotiated the acquisition of 70 percent of the Polish state-owned Plgaz Gdansk as part of that firm's privatization process. In its agricultural operations, Hydro spent the early 1990s acquiring fertilizer facilities in the United Kingdom, the U.S., and in Germany. Hydro also bought ammonia plants, located in Trinidad and Tobago, from W.R. Grace, and in 1994 Hydro purchased Fisons' NPK fertilizer business.

Major gas and oil development continued to distinguish Hydro as a major technical innovator and a big player in improved petroleum markets projected for the later 1990s. Hydro applied state-of-the-art technology as an operator in the Oseberg field, which quickly became a major source of oil and gas after it began production in 1988. Building on Oseberg's transport system, the Troll-Oseberg gas injection (TOGI) project, and later on the Troll oil project, Hydro demonstrated the advantages of remote-controlled subsea systems to develop and control deep-water projects. Much of the technology was used in the Phillips Petroleum Company's 1993 project to plan and build new facilities called Ekofisk II at the Ekofisk field, of which Hydro held a 6.7 percent share. After acquiring 300 Danish gasoline stations from UNO-X in 1990 and Mobil Oil's Norwegian marketing and distribution system in 1992, Hydro also became a major player in on-land gas and oil marketing. In 1994, Hydro merged its Norwegian and Danish oil and marketing operations with Texaco's.

Despite the company's expansion, sluggish sales caused by a weak global economy prompted Hydro to divest some of its noncore operations in the early 1990s. In 1992 the company sold Hydro Pharma a.s., its pharmaceutical division, and a year later Hydro sold Freia Marabou, a manufacturer of chocolate.

Hydro announced the highest profit in the company's history in 1994, buoyed by higher industry prices in three of Hydro's four core divisions. During 1994, aluminum prices increased about 75 percent, nitrogen fertilizer prices enjoyed a rise of about eight percent, and PVC prices jumped 27 percent. Oil prices fell during the year, and though they were forecast to rise during 1995, the U.S. dollar was expected to weaken, thus bringing oil prices down. Still, Hydro believed its higher production of crude oil would offset low oil prices. Hydro's future seemed promising, but industry analysts remained slightly skeptical, worried that Hydro had cut back costs too severely and thus would be too reliant on commodity prices.

In the mid-1990s Hydro became involved with Canadian oil and gas operations when it partnered with Petro-Canada to work oil and gas fields off of Canada's east coast. In 1996, Hydro further expanded its on-land gas and oil operations when it acquired the Swedish gas station business of UNO-X. In other divisions, Hydro formed a $500 million joint venture with Jor-

dan Phosphate Mines Co. and bought a 30 percent stake in Hulett Aluminium in South Africa in 1997.

Heading into the second half of the 1990s, Hydro faced many challenges as it struggled to succeed in a volatile economy. By 1998 prices of crude oil, aluminum, and fertilizer had dropped, severely affecting Hydro's earnings and operations. Crude oil prices in early 1998 were the lowest since 1994, and not only had fertilizer prices declined, but Hydro suffered from low demand outside of Europe and overcapacity problems. In addition, the outlook for the fertilizer industry was gloomy. In response to poor market conditions and declining earnings—net income was NOK 5.2 billion in 1997, compared to NOK 6.2 billion in 1996—Hydro restructured its operations to focus on three core segments, including oil and energy, agriculture, and light metals. Hydro planned to cut back its investment budget and sell or spin off its noncore operations, such as pharmaceuticals, seafood, and food additives.

In 1999, Hydro made its largest acquisition to date when it purchased Saga Petroleum ASA, the leading independent producer of oil in Norway. Just a year earlier, Hydro had sold a ten percent interest in Saga to Statoil, and talk of Hydro reducing or exiting petrochemicals rose. However, in 1999, Hydro chose to focus on expanding its operations in oil production. With the Saga acquisition, Hydro planned to cut back its work force in oil exploration by about 20 percent in order to lower costs. Saga operated a number of oil fields on the Norwegian shelf, including Snorre, Vigdis, and Tordis, as well as Haltenbanken South. The purchase boosted Hydro's oil exploration and production operations considerably, and oil and gas represented about 65 percent of the company's revenue base, up from about 50 percent prior to the acquisition.

Hydro endeavored to integrate its new business strategy, called "Focus on the Future," in 1999, and the acquisition of Saga was a major step in the right direction for the oil and energy division. In light metals, Hydro made progress by acquiring a 25 percent interest in Brazilian company Alunorte and sealed a long-term agreement for Aluvale, also of Brazil, to supply aluminum. Hydro also invested in a remelting facility in the United States and began construction of another state-of-the-art remelting plant, which would use remelted scrap to produce primary quality aluminum. In early 2000 Hydro acquired Wells Aluminum Corporation, an extrusion company headquartered in the United States. The purchase greatly expanded Hydro's North American operations and made it the fourth-largest extrusion company in North America.

Faced with difficult market conditions, Hydro's agriculture division focused on a turnaround strategy to return to profitability. The strategy included plans to reduce costs by NOK 2 billion during 1999. Three nitrogen fertilizer plants in Europe were closed to strengthen operations, and Hydro merged its Hydro Agri Europe and Hydro Agri International units into a new segment called Plant Nutrition.

Hydro sold several noncore assets during 1999 for a total of NOK 2.4 billion. Divestments in 1999 and 2000 included Pronova Biopolymer, Hydro's share of Dyno, and Hydro Seafood AS. Hydro also sold its oil and gas assets in the United Kingdom to Conoco (U.K.) Limited for $540 million. The sale included exploration licenses and Britannia, Alba, and Gryphon fields, all acquired by Hydro during its purchase of Saga. In June 2000 Hydro sold its Hydro Aluminium Fundo division, which produced aluminum wheels, to Midal Group/Aluwheel of Bahrain.

Net income declined from NOK 3.75 billion in 1998 to NOK 3.42 billion in 1999, but the company remained confident that profitability would soon return. Both operating income and pre-tax income increased, and Hydro announced that improvements resulting from its new "Focus for the Future" corporate strategy exceeded expectations; CEO Egil Myklebust noted in Hydro's 1999 annual report that the company had enjoyed performance improvements of more than NOK 1.3 billion during 1999, surpassing Hydro's target of NOK 1 billion. As Hydro welcomed a new millennium, the company anticipated significant growth and continued expansion. Myklebust reflected on the future and its new business strategy in a prepared statement: "Hydro's history and growth is closely tied to Norway. But to move forward and become a leading global performer in selected businesses, we need greater international presence in terms of market positions, assets and employees. . . . Our base will continue to be in Norway, but we will have global operations in Oil and Energy, Light Metals, and Agri. It is in these areas that we intend to become a leading player."

Principal Subsidiaries

Norsk Hydro Americas, Inc. (United States); Hydro Agri Argentina SA; Hydro Agri Colombia Ltda.; Hydro Agri Costa Rica SA; Hydro Agri Uruguay SA; Ceylon Oxygen Ltd. (67%; Sri Lanka); Hydro Chemicals Norge AS; Hydro Wax AS; Hydrogas AS; Norsk Hydro Chile SA; Norsk Hydro (Far East) Ltd. (Hong Kong); A/S Svaelgfos; Hydro Aluminium AS; Norsk Hydro Kraft OY (Finland); Norsk Hydro Magnesiumgesellschaft mbH (Germany); Hydro Texaco AS (50%); Norsk Hydro Olje (Sweden); AS Pelican (36%); Scancracker (50%).

Principal Competitors

Exxon Mobil Corporation; IMC Global Inc.; Royal Dutch/Shell Group.

Further Reading

Bahree, Bhushan, "Norsk Hydro Bids for Saga Petroleum in Stock Deal Valued at $2.23 Billion," *Wall Street Journal,* May 11, 1999, p. A18.

"BFGoodrich and Norsk Hydro Complete Formation of Joint Venture," *PR Newswire,* March 21, 1991.

"ITA Preliminary Finds Canada and Norway Are Dumping Magnesium," *International Trade Reporter,* February 19, 1992, p. 308.

"Japanese Firms to Buy Resin Division of Norwegian Corp.," *Agence France Presse,* June 14, 1991.

Meland, Marius, "Norsk Hydro Loses Luster Despite Results," *Wall Street Journal Europe,* February 24, 1995, p. 10.

Norsk Hydro a.s., "Hydro Between 80 and 90," *Profile Magazine,* December 1990.

"Norsk Hydro in the Polish Privatization Process," *Warsaw Voice,* July 25, 1993.

"Norsk Hydro Reports Stronger Third Quarter," *Business Wire,* October 25, 1993.

"Phillips Norway Group Submits Plan for Long-term Ekofisk Operation," *Business Wire,* July 1, 1993.

Ribbing, Mark, "Wells to Get Foreign Owner; Aluminum Company Based in Towson Sold to Hydro Norsk," *Baltimore Sun,* January 25, 2000, p. C1.

Tangeraas, Fredrik, "Norsk Hydro's Cyclical Nature May Hurt Shares," *Wall Street Journal Europe,* January 8, 1998, p. 12.

"U.S.S.R. Joint Venturing Offshore Areas," *Offshore,* November 1990, p. 27.

—Kerstan Cohen
—updated by Mariko Fujinaka

Organización Soriana, S.A. de C.V.

Alejandro de Rodas 3102-A
Monterrey, Nuevo Leon 64610
Mexico
Telephone: (528) 329-9000
Fax: (528) 329-9127
Web site: http://www.soriana.com.mx

Public Company
Incorporated: 1971
Employees: 23,730
Sales: 20.65 billion pesos ($2.15 billion) (1999)
Stock Exchanges: Mexico City
Ticker Symbol: SORIANA
NAIC: 445299 Warehouse Clubs & Superstores; 44511
   Supermarkets & Other Grocery Stores; 5551112
   Offices of Other Holding Companies

Organización Soriana, S.A. de C.V. is the holding company for one of the largest self-service retail chains in Mexico, with 89 stores in operation at the end of 1999 in 20 states. Groceries, liquor, fruit, fish, meat products, vegetables, bread, pastries, and tortillas account for about two-thirds of sales, but Soriana also sells general merchandise, including such family and home products as clothing, hardware, personal- and health-care products, pharmaceutical products, electronic goods, and stationery. Soriana's strategy is mainly aimed at serving the middle- and low-income population in urban zones through a flexible store format that combines timely availability of food products with household products and basic services for the family at the same location.

A Family Enterprise Begins in 1905

The history of Soriana may be traced to the 1905 establishment of a fabric store in Torreon, in the state of Coahuila, in northern Mexico. Some 150 miles west of Monterrey, the Torreon area was long a center for cotton farming, while the city was founded in 1888, springing up around the crossing of two major railroads. The manufacture and sale of textiles became a natural extension of the cotton trade in the area.

By the 1930s Pedro Martin, and his sons Francisco Martin Borque and Armando Martin Borgue, expanded the scope of the retail outlet, offering wholesale goods to much of the area. Together, they traveled the Durango, Chihuahua, and Sonora mountain ranges of northern Mexico, providing village retailers with textiles and other wares.

By the mid-1950s, the wholesale trade activities had been discontinued and the enterprise consisted of a self-service store in Torreon. This soon developed into a chain of Soriana discount stores. The discount retail format was becoming widely popular in Mexico and the United States during the 1950s and 1960s; successful businesses could offer household goods and clothing at up to 20 percent below manufacturers suggested retail, while their department store counterparts were marking up prices by as much as 40 percent. Under these conditions, the Soriana concept grew.

In 1968, brothers Francisco and Armando opened the first Soriana hypermarket in Torreon. This store—larger than a supermarket and carrying general merchandise as well as groceries—would become the cornerstone of a Soriana chain. Moreover, this Soriana hypermarket predated the first hypermarket of chief competitor Aurrera S.A. (later known as Cifra) by several years.

A Modern Corporation: 1970s–90s

Soriana began to accelerate its growth in 1971, and for this purpose the business was incorporated, with consequent centralization of its administration. Another hypermarket was opened in Monterrey in 1974, and company headquarters were moved from Torreon to Monterrey in 1989. The chain of events that led to the founding brothers leaving the Soriana management team is unclear; in a 1991 *Wall Street Journal* article, Matt Moffett remarked that the year before "the chief executive officer and majority stockholder bumped himself upstairs, effectively removing members of the founding family from day-to-day management." At the time, however, Francisco Martin Borque remained as Honorary Chairman, while Armando Martin Borque remained on the board of directors. Ricardo Martin Bringas was director general (chief executive officer) of Soriana, while Francisco J. Martin Bringas served as chairman.

Company Perspectives:

Soriana's mission is to retail basic products and services for the family and home at a fair price-quality ratio, and thus help our customers make the most of their family income; to maintain a leading position in the markets in which the Company operates through the use of state-of-the-art technology and quality service, focusing on the customers' needs; to implement optimum financial strategies, allowing us to give added value to our operations and achieve high profitability and continuous growth; to foment stable and mutually beneficial relationships with suppliers and employees, and to contribute in this way to the communities in which we participate.

Members of the Martin family, in fact, made up the majority of the company's board and would become majority stockholders when the company went public.

Net sales were reported at 1.83 billion new pesos ($606.76 million) in 1991, while net income reached 90.02 million new pesos ($29.85 million). By this time, Soriana was Mexico's fifth-largest retailer, and while its overall sales were considerably less than those of Cifra and other top retailers, Soriana maintained a dominant presence in northern Mexico. The company went public during this period, with shares trading on the Bolsa in Mexico City.

Management moved quickly to modernize the Soriana operations, installing automatic price scanners at its checkout lines as well as satellites to help facilitate credit card purchases. Investors were apparently impressed with the aggressive moves of Soriana management; the company's stock rose in value almost 30 percent in 1991. In 1992 Organización Soriana was operating 21 commercial centers, including discount department stores, supermarkets, and hypermarkets, in nine northern Mexican cities in four states.

The Mid-1990s and Beyond

Corporate reorganizations characterized much of the mid-1990s, as subsidiaries were merged and spun off to create a leaner, more efficient organization. At the beginning of 1993 the company incorporated three real-estate subsidiaries. The following year it completed a merger with Grupo Sorimex and Organización de Recursos Financieros. Also that year, subsidiary Soriana Sultana was merged with Soriana del Nazas, the organization's 15-unit hypermarket chain. Soriana del Nazas included a U.S. subsidiary, Gemso Corp., which was handling credit, receiving, warehousing, and shipping for the Mexican operation. Upon merging, Gemso was integrated with Soriana Sultana's U.S. credit, shipping, and warehousing firm MB International Corp.

Organización Soriana grew rapidly in the mid-1990s. There were 48 stores by the end of 1994. During the next three years the company opened six stores per year on the average. The rate of return grew even more dramatically. In 1994 net profits came to 4.6 percent of sales, but in 1995 that figure shot up to 8.8 percent, a ratio that was virtually maintained over the course of the next three years. Similarly, return on equity increased from 5.9 percent in 1994 to 16.9 percent in 1995, and in 1998 this ratio reached 17.9 percent. The number of stores reached 65 in 1997. Net sales came to 13.89 billion pesos ($1.75 billion), up from 8.53 billion pesos ($1.12 billion), in 1996, and net earnings were 1.16 billion pesos ($146.46 million), up from 725.24 million pesos ($94.86 million).

These sterling results were the fruit of a conservative, bottom-line strategy. Organización Soriana began this period with the advantage of having its operations in Mexico's most affluent area, the four Mexican states bordering the United States, which because of their proximity were benefiting more than most from the newly established North American Free Trade Agreement. The company was controlling its costs by sticking to a no-frills warehouse-type format, buying in bulk and selling at price margins only slightly above cost. Moreover, Soriana remained almost debt-free while its rivals borrowed heavily to expand throughout Mexico.

When the value of the peso fell sharply in late 1994, Soriana had no large dollar debt to service. Buyers flocked over the Rio Grande to spend their dollars on Mexican goods that had suddenly become cheaper. The cheap peso also brought many more foreign manufacturers to the border areas where Soriana's stores were concentrated, adding about $1 billion to payrolls in the region between 1995 and 1998. In Ciudad Juarez, Joel Millman of the *Wall Street Journal* wrote in 1998, "Hundreds of Soriana cash registers bang away practically nonstop from 8 a.m., when workers get off the overnight shift at nearby assembly plants, to almost midnight, when the stores shut down."

Organización Soriana was also a technological leader in its field. In 1996 the company began installing computer-based point-of-sale register systems in its large-format Hipermart stores, which had an average of 35 checkout lanes. This system ran a Windows software program placed in more than half the stores by late 1998. It enabled the chain to gather highly specific data to help store managers make inventory and staffing decisions as well as to interface sales data in real time with corporate systems such as inventory control and accounting.

By 1998 Organización Soriana, now Mexico's fourth-largest publicly listed supermarket operator, was being recognized as the nation's best-performing retail chain. The number of its stores reached 76 in 13 states that year, with a total of 629,500 square meters (6.78 million square feet) of selling space. These outlets were in states as distant from Soriana's base as Jalisco in west-central Mexico; Aguascalientes, Guanajuato, Queretaro, San Luis Potosi, and Tlaxcala in central Mexico; and Veracruz in eastern Mexico. In order to achieve economies of scale, the company was pursuing a strategy of building new stores in consolidated geographic blocks, supported by its distribution network and electronic communications systems. Net sales reached 16.31 billion pesos ($1.78 billion) in 1998, and net income 2.27 billion pesos ($248.36 million), both record highs.

Organización Soriana's expansion continued with 13 new stores in 1999, including outlets in the cities of Guadalajara and Puebla and the chain's first presence in the states of Colima, Hidalgo, Michoacan, Puebla, Sinaloa, Sonora, and Tabasco. Total selling space reached 750,711 square meters (8.08 million

---

Key Dates:

1905: Soriana is founded as a Torreon fabric store.
1968: The first Soriana hypermarket, in Torreon, opens.
1992: Soriana has 21 stores in nine cities and four Mexican states.
1994: The Soriana chain has grown to 48 stores.
1998: Soriana is the fourth-largest publicly listed Mexican supermarket operator.
1999: Soriana has 89 stores in 20 Mexican states.

---

square feet). The company had a market value of $2.1 billion in mid-1998, and the Martin family held an 80 percent stake in the business.

Organización Soriana completed installation of point-of-sale terminals equipped with a specialized computer program to enable the creation of customer databases, thereby allowing the company to identify purchasing habits and preferences. New products were being introduced to the firm's private-label line of goods. There was a Soriana credit card, a consumer credit program, and a bank debit card for use with welfare-system programs. The Mexico City warehouse was expanded and modernized in 1999, and the Guadalajara distribution center was expanded. Construction began of a new general goods and grocery supply and distribution center in the Monterrey metropolitan area. Soriana had a fleet of 103 trucks and 154 refrigerated trailer boxes.

These developments were all part of a four-year, $400-million program that included expansion of stores and warehouses and new technology. For 2000, the plan called for expenditure of 1.76 billion pesos to open 11 stores, modernize existing ones, and acquire land for still more outlets. The first new store scheduled to open in 2000 was to be in Leon, followed by two in Monterrey and one in Gomez Palacio, Durango.

Principal Subsidiaries

Centros Comerciales Soriana, S.A. de C.V.; Tiendas de Descuentos Sultana, S.A. de C.V.

Principal Competitors

Wal-Mart de Mexico S.A. de C.V.; Controladora Comercial Mexicana, S.A. de C.V.; Grupo Gigante, S.A. de C.V.

Further Reading

"Checkout," *WWD/Women's Wear Daily,* July 24, 1994, p. 6.
"Hot CEOs," *Latin Trade,* May 1999, p. 58.
"Mexican Grocery Chain Thrives with Microsoft Open System," *Progressive Grocer,* November 1998, Supplement, p. 11.
Millman, Joel, "Mexico's Soriana Outperforms Rivals in Retail Market," *Wall Street Journal,* April 29, 1998, p. A19.
Moffett, Matt, "Mexican Retailers Jockey for Position, Hoping to Win Big as Nation Recovers," *Wall Street Journal,* August 26, 1991, p. A4.

—Robert Halasz

Orthodontic Centers of America, Inc.

5000 Sawgrass Village Circle
Ponte Vedra Beach, Florida 32082
U.S.A.
Telephone: (904) 280-4500
Toll Free: (888) 272-2872
Fax: (904) 285-7406
Web site: http://www.ocai.com

Public Company
Incorporated: 1994
Employees: 2,072
Sales: $226.29 million (1999)
Stock Exchanges: New York
Ticker Symbol: OCA
NAIC: 62121 Offices of Dentists

Orthodontic Centers of America, Inc. (OCA) is the leading provider of practice management services to orthodontic practices in the United States. Although OCA's founder and leader is a certified orthodontist, the company is not involved in the practice of orthodontics. Instead, OCA develops orthodontic centers and manages the business operations of its affiliated orthodontists, who are then free to devote their energies to patient care. OCA-affiliated orthodontists benefit from the economies of scale realized by operating as part of a larger whole and receive marketing and advertising support from OCA. The company manages 537 orthodontic centers located in 43 states, Puerto Rico, Japan, and Mexico. There are 346 orthodontists affiliated with OCA's practice management system.

Origins

Dr. Gasper Lazzara spent more than 25 years practicing as an orthodontist before he decided to embark on a career as an entrepreneur. Like all entrepreneurs, Lazzara was convinced his business venture would succeed, and like most entrepreneurs, he failed to meet his expectations. In 1980, Lazzara joined forces with another orthodontist and two optometrists associated with Pearle Vision Center, a company that was rapidly turning optometry into an efficient, profit-producing enterprise geared for vol-

ume business. Lazzara intended to achieve the same results in orthodontics, and he gathered the financial resources to make his entrepreneurial dream a reality. Pearle Vision invested $700,000 in Lazzara's enterprise, start-up money that was enriched by the contribution of $75,000 from each of the active partners. With $1 million in seed money, Lazzara and his partners opened 16 dental practices in Florida, establishing the offices within shopping malls. The business foundered, forcing the dissolution of the partnership forged to create the enterprise. Lazzara had failed, but he was not willing to let his first mistake dash his dreams of becoming a successful entrepreneur.

Lazzara made his next bid to infuse economies of scale into the practice of orthodontics in 1985. For his second venture, Lazzara enlisted the help of his longtime accountant, Bartholomew Palmisano Sr., whose unwavering attention to fiscal matters would underpin Lazzara's innovative approach to the business of straightening teeth. Lazzara used a combination of his personal savings and bank loans to purchase two orthodontic offices in Jacksonville, Florida, which would serve as the proving ground for Lazzara's business strategy in 1985 and for his company's other orthodontic ventures in the years to come.

At the heart of Lazzara's plan was consolidating the orthodontic industry in which he had labored for decades. The U.S. orthodontic industry was highly fragmented, with 90 percent of the approximately 9,000 practicing orthodontists acting as sole practitioners. Eventually, Lazzara hoped to bring a significant portion of the thousands of offices in operation under the banner of one management company, a company that would later become known as OCA. His plan was based on the theory that if one central organization provided a full range of management services to a host of satellite offices, then the individual offices would realize increased operational efficiency and greater profits, achieving results better than would be achieved as separate businesses. Freed from the responsibilities of managing the business side of their practices, orthodontists, Lazzara concluded, could devote more time to attending to patients, thereby increasing their business volume. Moreover, a systematic approach to dealing with the operational aspects of an orthodontic practice would yield greater efficiency, Lazzara contended, with office design, inventory control, staff bonuses, and other aspects of the business standardized in a fashion similar to successful franchise organizations. Further, with advertising and marketing resources emanating from a central organization, individual orthodontists could expect greater promotional support for their practice than they could provide on their own. Lazzara hoped to prove his point in Jacksonville; if he succeeded, he could begin consolidating the industry, establish his own satellite offices, and create a powerful force in the multibillion dollar U.S. orthodontic industry.

As Lazzara fleshed out the details of his business strategy, the future of his entrepreneurial dream hinged on the results achieved with the pilot Jacksonville practices. Lazzara and Palmisano needed to produce quantifiable results, figures that the pair could use to convince orthodontists of the financial gains to be made by joining a central management organization. Accordingly, Palmisano set up a computer system capable of monitoring the operational functions of the two offices and charting their productivity. With the information gleaned from Palmisano's electronic scrutiny, fundamental changes were made. Inventories were reduced and invoicing procedures were more tightly controlled, causing patients to pay their bills more promptly. Within a year, the partners could point to tangible results. The operating profit margins of the two practices increased from 10 percent to 30 percent; Lazzara and Palmisano were in business.

In contrast to the latter half of the 1990s, Lazzara expanded his network of affiliated orthodontic centers at a measured pace during his first years in business. By the beginning of the 1990s, nine more orthodontic practices had affiliated themselves with Lazzara's management services program. The pace of expansion accelerated from there, with 20 more orthodontic centers joining the fold during the next two years, giving Lazzara a total of 31 centers by the end of 1991. At this point in the company's development, all but five of the orthodontic centers were located within general dentists' offices. During 1992, when 16 more centers became affiliated practices, Lazzara began implementing a strategy to relocate all of the company's affiliated centers to freestanding locations, preferring either shopping centers or professional office buildings as site locations.

Reorganization in 1994 Followed by Rapid Expansion

As Lazzara's organization of affiliated orthodontic centers prepared to enter the mid-1990s, the corporate structure of the

organization underwent significant change. The reorganization, executed on October 18, 1994, marked the debut of OCA as the corporate banner for the affiliated centers. Before October 1994, there were two management entities that oversaw the business operations of the affiliated centers, which, following the reorganization, were referred to as OCA's predecessor entities. In October 1994, OCA was formed to acquire the two predecessor management entities and all of the assets and liabilities of the predecessor operating entities—the orthodontic centers previously affiliated with the two management entities. In the wake of the structural changes, OCA, with Lazzara serving as the company's chief executive officer and Palmisano serving as its chief financial officer, became the single managerial concern governing the business operations of all of the company's orthodontic centers. Two months later, Lazzara completed OCA's initial public offering (IPO), selling 26 percent of the company to the public and netting $18 million from the stock sale.

By the time of OCA's IPO, there were 46 affiliated orthodontists operating 75 OCA offices, each run according to the detailed specifications formulated by Lazzara and Palmisano. OCA mandated a screening process, excluding cases that required elaborate braces attached to the back of teeth or patients with jaw-joint problems. "We only do bread-and-butter orthodontics," Lazzara explained in a May 20, 1996 interview with *Forbes* magazine. In the same interview, Palmisano offered his perspective. "The most expensive cost is an idle staff," he remarked. Within an OCA center, responsibilities were clearly defined for each staff member, enhancing efficiency. If no patients were scheduled for a particular day, the center's staff was trimmed to include only a receptionist who answered incoming telephone calls. OCA specified the layout and design of its orthodontic centers, among myriad other details, and offered staff bonuses, with awards based on how successfully each office controlled inventory and brought in new patients.

In exchange for adhering to the operational criteria dictated by OCA and sharing revenue with OCA, affiliated orthodontists reaped the benefits of OCA's services. For its constituents, OCA developed and implemented an aggressive marketing program that by far exceeded the means of orthodontists who served as sole practitioners. The company utilized local and national television, radio and print advertising, and internal marketing promotions, spending an average of nearly $70,500 per year for each affiliated orthodontist on direct marketing costs and advertising. In comparison, the typical independent orthodontist spent an average of $4,400 per year on marketing and advertising. Because of the considerable gulf separating the marketing budgets of OCA affiliates and independent orthodontists, Lazzara possessed a powerful recruitment tool to induce practicing orthodontists to ally themselves with OCA. On average, an OCA doctor saw 77 patients per day during the mid-1990s versus the industry average of 42 patients per day. Further, affiliated orthodontists in practice for at least a year generated 512 new cases per year, compared with the industry average of 170 new patients per year for non-OCA orthodontists. For the consumer, there was an inducement to use OCA as well. At $2,770, OCA fees during the mid-1990s for straightening teeth were 20 percent below the national average.

The cumulative effect of the perquisites for orthodontists and consumers alike made OCA an attractive alternative to the tradi-

Key Dates:

1985: Dr. Gasper Lazzara acquires two orthodontic offices in Jacksonville, Florida.
1994: Orthodontic Centers of America, Inc. completes its initial public offering of stock.
1998: Company begins expanding into international markets.
1999: Partnership agreement with BriteSmile, Inc. is signed.

tional orthodontic practice. Consequently, the company was poised for national expansion, an inherent aspect of Lazzara's strategy and one that he financed by selling stock in OCA to the public. Following the company's IPO at the end of 1994, Lazzara sold the public another 34 percent in 1995, raising $82 million, and completed another public offering in April 1996, selling 12 percent of OCA for $75 million. Against the backdrop of Lazzara's efforts to raise capital, OCA expanded vigorously. Between the end of 1994 and the end of 1996, the number of OCA centers more than tripled, increasing from 75 to 247, spreading out to cover 28 states. Of the 247 centers composing OCA at the end of 1996, 134 were developed by the company (at an average cost of $230,000) and 113 were existing orthodontic practices whose assets were acquired by the company.

Late 1990s: International Expansion and Diversification

The aggressive pace of expansion during the mid-1990s continued unabated during the late 1990s, elevating OCA to the leadership position in its industry. There were other companies in the orthodontic industry pursuing strategies similar to OCA's business plan, but strident growth kept the company's rivals at bay. In 1997, 1998, and 1999, Lazzara added at least 100 new centers each year to his network, giving the company 537 centers by the end of 1999, more than seven times the total recorded five years earlier. The company's prodigious growth extended its geographic coverage into 43 states, but the most eye-catching aspect of OCA's expansion during the latter half of the 1990s occurred overseas. Beginning in 1998, Lazzara began expanding internationally, developing orthodontic centers in Japan and Puerto Rico. By the end of 1998, OCA managed six centers in Japan and two centers in Puerto Rico. In 1999, the company expanded aggressively in Japan by adding 18 more centers, bolstered it presence in Puerto Rico by developing three additional centers, and completed its entry into Mexico by establishing two centers. By the end of the decade, Lazzara was exploring additional expansion opportunities in Canada, England, and Spain.

OCA's physical expansion during the late 1990s was coupled with the expansion of its operational scope, as Lazzara steered the company in a new business direction. Lazzara signed an agreement with BriteSmile, Inc., a developer and manufacturer of teeth-whitening technology and related products. Under the terms of the agreement, OCA conducted a pilot program in 1999 that incorporated BriteSmile's systems into OCA centers in Jacksonville and in Tucson, Arizona. Pending the success of the trial program, Lazzara intended to provide BriteSmile systems to all affiliated orthodontists wishing to offer teeth-whitening services to their patients. In a related venture, OCA started the trial operation of a cosmetic dental center in Jacksonville in 1999. The experimental center, designed to resemble a boutique or a spa rather than a dental office, offered cosmetic services such as teeth-whitening services and porcelain teeth laminates.

As OCA prepared for the future, the company faced tantalizing expansion opportunities. Despite the prolific growth of OCA and the expansion of other companies similar to OCA, less than ten percent of practicing orthodontists were affiliated with practice management companies. Moreover, among the handful of major practice management companies, OCA was demonstrating an enviable superiority, particularly in relation to one of its main rivals, Apple Orthodontix, Inc. Apple Orthodontix filed for protection from its creditors under Chapter 11 of the U.S. Bankruptcy Code in January 2000. The company's misfortune proved to be OCA's gain, as Lazzara signed a definitive agreement to acquire up to 47 orthodontic practices affiliated with Apple Orthodontix. As Lazzara plotted the company's course beyond the Apple Orthodontix transaction, there was justifiable confidence that the coming years would continue to deliver robust financial growth for OCA.

Principal Subsidiaries

Orthodontic Centers of Alabama, Inc.; Orthodontic Centers of Arkansas, Inc.; Orthodontic Centers of Arizona, Inc.; Orthodontic Centers of California, Inc.; Orthodontic Centers of Colorado, Inc.; Orthodontic Centers of Connecticut, Inc.; Orthodontic Centers of Florida, Inc.; Orthodontic Centers of Georgia, Inc.; Orthodontic Centers of Hawaii, Inc.; Orthodontic Centers of Idaho, Inc.; Orthodontic Centers of Illinois, Inc.; Orthodontic Centers of Indiana, Inc.; Orthodontic Centers of Kansas, Inc.; Orthodontic Centers of Kentucky, Inc.; Orthodontic Centers of Louisiana, Inc.; Orthodontic Centers of Maine, Inc.; Orthodontic Centers of Maryland, Inc.; Orthodontic Centers of Massachusetts, Inc.; Orthodontic Centers of Michigan, Inc.; Orthodontic Centers of Minnesota, Inc.; Orthodontic Centers of Mississippi, Inc.; Orthodontic Centers of Missouri, Inc.; Orthodontic Centers of Nevada, Inc.; Orthodontic Centers of New Hampshire, Inc.; Orthodontic Centers of New Jersey, Inc.; Orthodontic Centers of New Mexico, Inc.; Orthodontic Centers of New York, Inc.; Orthodontic Centers of North Carolina, Inc.; Orthodontic Centers of North Dakota, Inc.; Orthodontic Centers of Ohio, Inc.; Orthodontic Centers of Oklahoma, Inc.; Orthodontic Centers of Oregon, Inc.; Orthodontic Centers of Pennsylvania, Inc.; Orthodontic Centers of Puerto Rico, Inc.; Orthodontic Centers of Rhode Island, Inc.; Orthodontic Centers of South Carolina, Inc.; Orthodontic Centers of Tennessee, Inc.; Orthodontic Centers of Texas, Inc.; Orthodontic Centers of Utah, Inc.; Orthodontic Centers of Virginia, Inc.; Orthodontic Centers of Washington, Inc.; Orthodontic Centers of Washington, DC, Inc.; Orthodontic Centers of West Virginia, Inc.; Orthodontic Centers of Wisconsin, Inc.; Orthodontic Centers of Wyoming, Inc.

Principal Competitors

Castle Dental Centers, Inc.; Apple Orthodontix, Inc.; OrthAlliance, Inc.

Further Reading

Basch, Mark, "Florida-Based Orthodontic Centers of America Sets Goal," *Knight-Ridder/Tribune Business News,* May 21, 1996.
——, "Florida's Orthodontic Centers of America Reports Rise in Earnings," *Knight-Ridder/Tribune Business News,* November 1, 1996.
——, "Three Jacksonville, Fla., Company Stocks Stood Out in 1995," *Knight-Ridder/Tribune Business News,* January 1, 1996.
Dolan, Kerry A., "Braces for the Masses," *Forbes,* May 20, 1996, p. 260.

Freedman, Michael, "Streetwalker," *Forbes,* February 7, 2000, p. 194.
Massingill, Teena, "BriteSmile Teeth-Whitening Centers Move Headquarters to California," *Knight-Ridder/Tribune Business News,* November 1, 1999.
Robertshaw, Nicky, "Orthodontics Centers Moves into Memphis Three Local Offices for Florida MSO," *Memphis Business Journal,* December 1, 1997, p. 1.

—Jeffrey L. Covell

Panda Management Company, Inc.

899 El Cerito Street
South Pasadena, California 91030
U.S.A.
Telephone: (626) 799-9898
Toll Free: (800) 877-8988
Fax: (626) 403-8688
Web site: http://www.pandamgmt.com

Private Company
Incorporated: 1973
Employees: 4,000
Sales: $220 million (1999)
NAIC: 72211 Full-Service Restaurants; 722211 Limited-
Service Restaurants

Panda Management Company, Inc. (PMC), based in South-ern California, has grown dynamically ever since 1983 when it opened its first Panda Express, its most successful operation. As that name suggests, Panda Express units are fast-service Chi-nese restaurants, now found in over 34 states, the District of Columbia, Puerto Rico, and Japan. Altogether, PMC manages over 300 Panda Express Restaurants, six Panda Inn Restaurants, eight Hibachi-San Restaurants, and seven Panda Panda loca-tions. Panda Inns, the first of which opened in 1973, are all located in Southern California, as are the Panda Pandas, upscale, gourmet Chinese food restaurants. The Hibachi-San Restaurants, featuring Japanese cuisine, are located in shopping mall food courts, about half of which are at select sites outside California. The much more ubiquitous Panda Express Restau-rants are located in five basic operating environments: mall food courts; supermarkets and retail chains; shopping centers and key intersections; university and college campuses; and air-ports, casinos, and sports arenas. Their key market focus is the customer in the 18 to 34 age bracket, the upwardly-mobile segment of the working population most likely to adapt to a nouveau, fast-food cuisine. In contrast to the Panda Express units, Panda Inn, Panda Panda, and Hibachi-San restaurants are full-service restaurants. In association with EATertainment In-ternational, the company has also ventured into quick service

Cajun food with Orleans Express. However, it is the tremen-dous success of the Panda Express chain that fuels PMC's accelerating expansion. Its aggressive plans called for the open-ing of from 70 to 80 new units in 2000 alone, including an increasing number of street-level, stand-alone, drive-in units, making them more competitive in a market dominated by ham-burger, fried chicken, and Mexican food chains. None of the restaurants operated by Panda Management is franchised; all are owned by founder Andrew Cherng and his wife, Peggy.

1973–82: Founding and Development of Panda's Full-Service Restaurants

Andrew J.C. Cherng and his father, master Chinese chef Ming-Tsai Cherng, founded what would evolve into Panda Management when, in 1973, they opened the first of seven Panda Inns, full-service restaurants located in Southern Califor-nia. The initial site was in Pasadena, a suburb of Los Angeles, one of America's great ethnic melting pots. The Cherngs had migrated to the United States from Japan in the 1960s after first getting there from their native China by way of Hong Kong and Taipei, and their establishment was one of the first in the area to modify authentic Mandarin and Szechwan dishes to comple-ment the area's Oriental cuisine.

Initially, the Cherngs were determined to expand in the full-service Chinese restaurant market, a tough business in Califor-nia, thanks to its large Asian-American population. Although the new company was able to open additional full service restaurants, the younger Cherng soon saw that fast food, drive-thru restaurants were a national craze in the United States. He also realized that Southern California offered an excellent mar-ket for experimenting with an Oriental food version of that kind of operation. Accordingly, he set out to expand into the quick service restaurant field.

1983–91: Company Steadily Expands with Its Panda Express Chain

In 1983, Cherng launched Panda Express, opening the first unit in a mall in Glendale, California. It proved to be a very successful beginning for what would become PMC's chief chain. Because the Panda Express was one of the few quick-service restaurants to evolve from a full-service concept and because it introduced a new food to that market, it found a good market niche, close to a wide-open field, in fact. It joined authentic Mandarin cuisine to a sector historically dominated by hamburgers and fried chicken. Panda Express sent the company into a growth cycle that by the year 2000 had not abated.

The Panda Express outlets, depending on location, varied in size, assuring some flexibility. Like the first, the early units were usually located in shopping malls, but eventually they spread into other spots where potential customers were to be found, sites where people were on the move: into strip centers, airports, and universities, for example. Starting in 1988, they were also placed in grocery stores when the Cherngs placed a Panda Express in a Vons supermarket.

The dishes featured at the various Panda restaurants originated in three regions of China: Canton, Beijing, and Szechwan. Although less inclusive, the dishes at the Panda Expresses were the same as those served at the original Panda Inns and were prepared on the site of each unit, even the smallest ones. Because few concessions were made to expediency, the food quality remained high and quickly won the new chain a loyal customer base.

Their success led to the company's concentration on expanding its new chain, first in its home base of Southern California, then eastwardly, to the Western states of Nevada, Arizona, Colorado, and Utah and eventually to the East Coast, where it would meet stiffer competition from a rival chain, Toronto-based Manchu Wok, which was already well established East of the Mississippi River.

1992–2000: Accelerated Expansion and New Directions

By the end of 1992, the Panda Express chain numbered just over 50 units. Market indicators were very strong, encouraging rapid expansion. Notably, the National Restaurant Association issued a report indicating that between 1987 and 1990 there was a 31.5 percent gain in the Asian segment of the fast-food business. Overall, Asian restaurant sales in the United States rose from $7.5 billion in 1990 to $8.3 billion by August of 1995.

Panda Management responded the market surge with very quick growth. By April of 1994, it was operating 125 units in 21 states, Washington, D.C., and Japan. Sixty of these were financed by money generated internally from sales that in 1993 had reached $100 million and $112 million by May of the next year. By that time, Panda Express was running neck and neck with Manchu Wok, which, with far more units, was just keeping even in sales. By 1993 it had even fallen far behind Panda Express in the number of its new openings, though it was still the dominate express Chinese food chain in the eastern part of the United States.

One thing contributing to the rapid increase in the number of Panda Express units was the chain's versatility. Its five different footprints, ranging from 400 to 2,000 square feet, allowed it to find unit sites in a wide variety of places and to adjust size to sales that in 1994 ranged from $350,000 to more than $1.5 million per unit.

In 1994, in part to help make its expansion and diversification plans go smoothly, Panda revamped its upper management team. In January of that year, it recruited and hired Joseph Micatrotto as president and chief operating officer. Although Andrew Cherng remained chairman and CEO, he gave Micatrotto considerable latitude in mapping out new directions for the company. Micatrotto, who grew up in a ''little Italy neighborhood'' of Cleveland, came to Panda from a 14-year career at Chi-Chi's, a Louisville, Kentucky-based chain of Mexican restaurants. The company also hired Russell Bendel as senior vice-president of operations. He joined Panda after resigning his post as COO at El Torito, another chain of Mexican restaurants based in Irvine, California. Although neither Micatrotto nor Bendel had knowledge of Oriental cuisine, they had the managerial, organizational, and leadership skills that PMC needed.

At the time Micatrotto took the reins as president, PMC already had an enviable history of minority employment. About 45 percent of the workers were Hispanic and 40 percent Asian. As part of his program, Micatrotto scheduled ''cultural diversity'' lunches, sensitivity training experiences through which workers developed their awareness of their diverse cultures. Considering that the vast majority of Panda Express customers were non-Asian in their heritage, that program had a solid basis.

Although Micatrotto resigned the presidency of Panda Management in 1996, relinquishing it to Peggy Cherng, one of the things that he had recommended was an increase in the number of street-level, freestanding stores offering dine-in, drive-through, and carry-out services. By the end of 1998 these accounted for only about 80 Panda Express units, most of which were located in malls and other, less traditional places. By adding more stand-alone units, the company sought to offer stiffer competition to such fast-food giants as MacDonald's and Taco Bell as well as traditional Chinese restaurants.

In the 1990s, Panda Management also took steps to increase the percentage of takeout orders. In 1995, its 173 Panda Express units were averaging only a 30 percent volume in take-out sales, considered rather low for limited service Chinese food restaurants. In addition to a ''Flavors of China'' campaign, stressing Panda's authentic regional foods, it promoted a home meal replacement family dinner featuring two entrees, rice or chow mein, and appetizers for $12.99. Also, to improve its efficiency,

Key Dates:

1973: Company is established by Andrew and Ming-Tsai Cherng with opening of first Panda Inn.
1983: First Panda Express is opened.
1988: PMC puts first outlet in Vons supermarket.
1994: Company hires Joseph Micatrotto as president and chief operating officer.
1995: Micatrotto becomes CEO.
1996: Micatrotto resigns, and Peggy Cherng assumes presidency.
1999: Company opens 300th Panda Express.

the company modified its distribution channel by changing from using up to 70 dealers to using just a single, central company to distribute its raw products.

By the mid 1990s, Panda Management had begun committing more of its revenue to its advertising budget, which, until then, had been very small. Although it continued to use direct mailings, as it did in its 1995 "Flavors of China" campaign, it began running ads in print and on radio, with the latter as its main media strategy. It also started conducting focus group sessions, using questionnaires and evaluations of the quality of its foods, but it was not until 1999 that it produced its first block of television ads. These were initially limited to the Las Vegas area, where, in a relatively new market for the company, it had 19 Panda Express units. At that time, Peggy Cherng said that the campaign was a test of the medium's ability to bolster sales and "the commercials' ability to deliver the brand message."

Authenticity in Chinese cooking has not been easy for PMC to maintain, especially since some concessions had to be made to American tastes and preference for quick service. Simply put, the fast-food format required a kind of juggling act between quality and speed. Among other things, reflecting health conscious trends in the United States, Panda Express restaurants used no MSG in any of their foods. Basically, in order to preserve the authenticity of their dishes, they also kept recipe modifications to a minimum, using only minor adjustments to suit the American pallette. For example, they cut back on the spice levels in their array of Szechwan dishes, making them much milder than they would be in Asia. Most importantly, even as the chain entered its period of explosive growth in the 1990s, its restaurants continued to prepare their foods from scratch, maintaining what Micatrotto called "a quick service environment with a full-service kitchen."

In 1998, celebrating its 25th anniversary, Panda Management redesigned and reopened its flagship Pasadena Panda Inn,

the first of its restaurants. The renovation was in a way symbolic, reflecting the company's desire to preserve tradition even as it ventured into new culinary and geographic areas. Although the restaurant was one of the first to serve foods from diverse Chinese provinces, its kitchen also produced several original dishes, including Tea Smoked Duck, Creamy Mustard Shrimp, Lotus Leaf, and Sizzling Crispy Garlic Chicken.

Throughout its history, Panda Management has worked diligently to play a significant, good neighbor role in its host communities. Under the rubric "Panda Cares," it has been involved in many initiatives undertaken to improve the quality of life for children in those communities. In addition to contributions of money, the company has urged its employees to volunteer their time and labor, allowing them to initiate their own Panda Cares events that include meals donated by Panda Express. The program has both enhanced Panda's image, creating solid good will, and bolstered the morale of its employees. An example of PMC's commitment occurred in February, 1999, when, in Las Vegas, it opened its 300th restaurant with a gala celebration. PMC donated 20 percent of its opening day profit to the Candlelighters for Childhood Cancer of Southern Nevada.

Prospects for continued growth for PMC's Panda Express chain remained very good at the century's close. The chain was firmly established, had an excellent reputation, and enjoyed a growing brand awareness. It also had barely begun to saturate its markets outside Southern California.

Principal Competitors

Benihana Inc.; McDonald's Corporation; Manchu Wok; P.F. Chang's China Bistro, Inc.; Subway; Taco Bell Corp.; Wendy's International, Inc.

Further Reading

Bernstein, Charles, "Manchu Leads the Working Race," *Restaurants & Institutions*, August 1, 1994, p. 30.
Cebrzynski, Gregg, "Panda Express Breaks TV Ad Campaign as Test to Raise Brand Awareness," *Nation's Restaurant News*, August 9, 1999, p. 11.
Farkas, David, "Fast and Friendly," *Chain Leader*, March 2000, p. 72.
Glover, Kara, "Success on Oriental (Food) Express," *Los Angeles Business Journal*, September 25, 1995, p. 21.
Marchetti, Michele, and Alisson, Lucas, "Creating *Panda*-monium," *Sales & Marketing Management*, January 1996, p. 14.
Martin, Richard, "Panda Express: Bullish about the Bear," *Nation's Restaurant News*, May 16, 1994, p. 86.
——, "Top Chi-Chi's, El Torito Execs Tackle Panda Push," *Nation's Restaurant News*, August 7, 1995, p. 18
Walkup, Carolyn, "Panda Express Promo Targets Takeout Business," *Nation's Restaurant News*, February 28, 1994, p. 7.

—John W. Fiero

Paulaner Brauerei GmbH & Co. KG

Hochstrasse 75
81541 Munich
Germany
Telephone: (089) 480 050
Fax: (089) 480 055 14
Web site: http://www.paulaner.com;
          http://www.paulaner.de

Private Company
Founded: 1634
Employees: 1,177
Sales: DM 532.2 million ($258.58 million)(1998)
NAIC: 31212 Breweries

The Paulaner Brauerei GmbH & Co. KG is one of the oldest beer breweries in Bavaria and one of the richest in tradition. The Paulaner brewery is located in the heart of Munich, the beer capital of Germany, if not the world. The company brews a broad variety of beer types, including pilseners, light and dark lagers, alcohol-free and light beers, and special seasonal beers. Paulaner is the world's second largest producer of Weissbier. The Paulaner Group includes a number of other German brands such as Hacker-Pschorr, AuerBräu, Thurn und Taxis, and Thomasbräu. The Paulaner brand name has come to be known the world over through its affiliate in the United States and its beer pubs in Singapore, Bangkok, Shanghai, Beijing, and Manilla.

17th Century Origins

The roots of the Paulaner Brauerei stretch back into the early 17th century. In 1627 Bavarian Elector Maximilian invited the brothers of the Italian Order of Saint Francis of Paola—the Paulaners—to establish a monastery in Au, a village near Munich. The strict rules of the order forbade the monks most any animal products, including meat, butter, and eggs. While in Italy the monks were able to supplement their meager diet with wine; in Bavaria special heavy beer assumed that role. The order inherited a brewery from widow of a Munich brewer in 1633, and the following year they received royal permission to begin brewing beer themselves.

One of their brews was a beer in celebration of the feast day of their order's founder, St. Francis of Paola. The beer came to be known as Salvator, after a nearby church. Salvator was known as a Starkbier—that is, a strong beer—because of its high herb, spice, and alcohol content. The monks themselves referred to it as the "the holy oil of St. Francis" or "blessed father's beer" and, beginning in 1751, they were officially permitted to invite the public each April 2, St. Francis Day, to the monastery for a glass of Salvator. The popularity of Salvator, soon renowned as "the strongest beer in Munich," increased so quickly that the monks realized they could not continue to simply give it away. However, they sold it below the market price which enraged local brewers and innkeepers who complained of the unfair competition to the royal administration.

A Munich Tradition in the 19th Century

Despite such opposition, the festive celebration of Salvator's first Ausschank—or pouring—became a Munich tradition in which all Munich social classes took part, one which has continued to the present day. So important an event is it that politicians and other figures of national prominence in Germany congregate in Paulaner's Salvatorkeller every March for the first taste of the new batch of Starkbier. Salvator is said to have caused a minor revolution in Munich in 1844. When the price of the beer was increased not long before the March pouring, angry residents stormed the brewery in protest. Only when the old price was restored did the crowds return to their homes.

A wave of anti-clericism finally forced the Paulaner monks to give up of their monastery in 1799. For a short time the brewery was operated as a state enterprise. When it could not turn a profit, it was taken over by the Order of Malta. In 1806, brew master Franz Xavier Zacherl leased the brewery. In 1813, the year Zacherl obtained the business outright, he was also granted the right to sell Salvator at a price higher than the officially regulated rate for other beers. Zacherl's extraordinary privilege again caused discontent among his competition. Finally in March 1837, after years of hearing bitter complaints, King Ludwig I gave his royal approval to the higher price by declaring Salvator a luxury good. Under Zacherl the brewery became a successful operation once again. His Bierkeller was

Company Perspectives:

Whoever considers himself good, has stopped getting better. For this reason Paulaner takes care to insure particularly high quality. While we use innovative technology and most up-to-date brewing facilities, at the same time we have remained faithful to the greatest extent possible to the age-old ways of brewing and the traditional old recipes. Our ingredients include select quality malt, Hallertauer aroma-hops, crystal clear water from our own 240 meter deep wells, and our very own fine yeast. All Paulaner beers are brewed according to the Bavarian Purity Law of 1516. For good reason. Because we know that in the future everyone will agree about one thing: Good, better, Paulaner.

considered the largest in the world and under the management of his wife it became a meeting place for artists, writers and actors. Zacherl was also interested in the most up-to-date brewing techniques and he sent his brew master to England to learn brewing using steam.

Zacherl committed suicide in 1849. Because he had no children of his own, the brewery passed into the hands of his nephews, the Schmederer Brothers. The brothers expanded the business, adding restaurants, increasing the volume of beer brewed annually, and establishing the enterprise on a solid business basis as well. In 1886 the company was organized as an Aktiengesellschaft, a joint share company, called Gebruder Schmederer Actienbrauerei in München. In 1894 the Salvator brand was trademarked. In 1899, the business was reorganized as the Actiengesellschaft Paulanerbrau (zum Salvatorkeller) in München. Their businesses, with the Paulaner Brewery at their core, made the Schmederer brothers and their families wealthy members of Munich society.

Rapid Growth in the 20th Century

The 1920s were a time of intense activity for Paulaner. In 1921 it purchased the Aktienbrauerei zum Ebert-Faber; two years later it set up joint ventures with three other Bavarian breweries, the Hofbrauhaus Coburg AG in Coburg, AuerBräu in Rosenheim, and Thomasbräu in Munich. The latter had taken the step to brew lighter beers, such as pilseners, a bold move in Bavaria where heavier beers were traditional, and northern German pilseners were looked down on. In 1928 the Thomasbräu brewery and Paulaner merged to form Paulaner-Salvator-Thomasbräu AG. The merger gave Paulaner two brewing facilities in Munich. Between 1925 and 1930, Paulaner acquired five other breweries and brewing related firms.

Paulaner continued to expand early during World War II, branching out into the production of mineral water in 1941, with the acquisition of Mineralwasser Buchsbaum & Co. and its absorption into Paulaner's bottling division. However, by the end of the war, the Allied bombing raids on Germany had destroyed more than 70 percent of Paulaner's production facilities. Afterwards, what was left of the Thomasbräu brewery was demolished and new housing built on the land. In the first years after the war, Paulaner's annual beer production dropped to 109,000 hectoliters (2.8 million gallons). Paulaner concentrated on rebuilding its brewery in Munich. Reconstruction lasted from 1951 until about 1967. By then, the company's annual beer production had climbed to over 730,000 hl (19.3 million gallons). It topped one million hl (26.5 million gallons) in 1971.

The 1970s were a period of consolidation for the Bavarian brewing industry as a whole. Paulaner, however, expanded, acquiring various smaller breweries throughout the region. In 1979, Paulaner was itself acquired when Josef Schorghuber purchased more than 96 percent of the company's stock for DM 100 million. Just months before, Schorghuber, an extremely successful airline, construction, and real estate tycoon and one of the most remarkable entrepreneurs in German history, had spent DM 80 million for another major Bavarian brewery, the Hacker-Pschorr brewery. The two acquisitions gave Schorghuber control of more than half of the total beer production in Munich. He continued to add new breweries to his beer empire, which was organized under the Paulaner name, through the 1980s: Rosenheimer AuerBräu, Kulmbacher Reichelbräu, and Monchshofsbräu in 1986, as well as SternquellBräu in 1990.

In the 1990s Schorghuber committed Paulaner to transforming itself from a regional beer, the bulk of whose sales were concentrated in Bavaria, to a brand with a strong market presence throughout Germany. The events that contributed to this decision were the unexpected opening of the borders with the German Democratic Republic (GDR) in late 1989, the monetary union of the Federal Republic of Germany and the GDR in July 1990, and the unification of Germany in October 1990. Suddenly opportunities were abounding: a huge market of new German consumers was open to West German companies, while the privatization of the East German economy made it possible to gain a foothold in eastern Germany by acquiring breweries that had previously been state-owned.

Paulaner entered the East German market aggressively. In 1990 it sold 177,000 hl (4.6 million gallons) of its various brands of beer there, some 152,000 hl (4 million gallons) of which were the Paulaner brand. The company struck a short-lived operating agreement with Sachsenbrau, a brewery in Leipzig. Subsequently it founded a brand new company in the east, Leipzig Brau, which became part of the Paulaner group of breweries; during the same period Paulaner also opened 11 distribution points in eastern Germany. In all, Paulaner invested some DM 92 million in the states of the old GDR in 1990.

The company later admitted that its jump into eastern Germany had been taken without enough careful planning. As a result, the company reported losses of DM 14 million in 1990. Losses would continue to plague Paulaner until 1995. Making matters worse, Paulaner sales in eastern German sales dropped significantly in 1991 and 1992 as the first blush of unification faded and harsher economic realities set in for the residents of the new German states. Paulaner's 1991 acquisition and subsequent modernization of a brewery in the city of Dessau also contributed to the company's losses. In 1991 Paulaner spent DM 15 million on the new subsidiary, renamed Brauhaus Dessau. It sank another DM 13 million in it in 1992, and DM 15 million in 1993, with the plan of developing the brand as a successful regional beer in the state of Sachsen-Anhalt. Despite the introduction of Dessator, Germany's first Starkbier in a can,

Key Dates:

1627: The Brothers of St. Francis of Paola establish a monastery in Au, a Bavarian village near Munich.
1634: The Paulaners begin brewing beer.
1780: The Paulaners are permitted to sell their beer publicly.
1799: A wave of secularization forces the monks out of the monastery, and the brewery is taken over by the state.
1806: Brewmaster Franz Xaver Zacherl leases the Paulaner brewery.
1813: Zacherl purchases the brewery.
1848: Zacherl dies and the brewery passes into the hands of his nephews, the Schmederer brothers.
1886: Paulaner Brewery is organized as a joint stock company, Gebrüder Schmederer Actienbrauerei, in Munich.
1899: Company reorganized as Paulanerbräu (zum Salvatorkeller) in München.
1920s: Paulaner Brewery acquires several Bavarian breweries.
1928: Following a merger with Thomasbräu, company renamed Paulaner-Salvator-Thomasbräu AG.
1940s: Paulaner breweries largely destroyed in bombing raids.
1979: Josef Schorghuber acquires Hacker-Pschorr Brauerei for DM 80 million and Paulaner Brauerei for DM 100 million.
1986: Rosenheimer AuerBräu, Kulmbacher Reichelbräu, and Monchshofbräu are added to the Paulaner group of breweries.
1990: Paulaner enters newly-opened East German market and acquires Brauerei Dessau.
1994: Company reorganized into Paulaner Brauerei AG and Paulaner-Salvator Beteiligungs (PSB).
1995: Josef Schorghuber passes away, and his holdings, including Paulaner, are taken over by his son Stefan Schorghuber.
1998: PSB is restructured as full owner of the Paulaner Brauerei Gruppe.
1999: PSB becomes Bayerische BräuHolding AG.

Brauhaus Dessau was unable to perform as hoped. In 1994 the Dessau brewery was closed down for good.

In the early 1990s, Paulaner took steps to make its production and products more environmentally friendly. The changes were a response to the enormous amounts of water being used by Munich breweries in the production of beer; in 1992 approximately three million cubic meters of water were used, nearly half of which was accounted for by Paulaner. The company invested DM 50 million, introducing state-of-the-art production technologies which reduced water consumption to six liters of water used for every liter of beer brewed. At the same time Paulaner stopped selling its 12-ounce bottles of beer in traditional six packs wrapped in cardboard packaging. Instead, it sold them in returnable plastic 12-packs, which the company hoped would encourage consumers to return the bottles for a deposit.

Schorghuber completely reorganized its brewing interests in May 1994. Paulaner-Salvator-Thomasbräu was split into two new organizations. Paulaner Brauerei comprised the beverage production and sales departments of the old company, including AuerBräu in Rosenheim, Hacker-Pschorr, and Bayerische Frischgetranke, a soft drink company. The other company, Paulaner-Salvator-Beteiligungs (PSB), was a holding company which took care of the old company's properties and domestic shareholdings. The purpose of the reorganization was to bring greater efficiency to company operations and to make them more easily manageable. The reorganization affected the company's stock. PSB continued to be publicly traded on the Munich stock exchange, while Paulaner Brauerei became that company's fully-owned subsidiary. The announcement of the reorganization had an immediate impact on the price of the company's stock: on consecutive days it jumped first DM 70, then DM 100 in value.

In May 1995 75-year old Josef Schorghuber died of a stroke. Control of Schorghuber GmbH—a holding company which in addition to the Paulaner breweries included Bayerische Hausbau, one of the large construction companies in Bavaria, the Arabella hotel chain, the Bavaria Flug airline, along with a number of foreign companies—passed into the hands of his son, Stefan. Stefan, who had previously run the Arabella Hotels, took a personal interest in the brewing companies. He eventually became the chairman of Paulaner's Aufsichtsrat.

Late 1995 saw the conclusion of a court case in which Paulaner had been involved since 1982. That year a German watchdog group for investors, filed a complaint against Schorghuber's holding company for withholding profits to which smaller stockholders were contractually entitled. At the time the complaint was first made, and Schorghuber offered a settlement of DM 1100 a share to Paulaner stockholders. In its 1995 ruling, the Bavarian court awarded the shareholders compensation plus interest amounting to DM 2,721. One German publication calculated that with approximately 30,000 shares outstanding, the total cost to Schorghuber would be DM 81.6 million. A spokesperson for Schorghuber, while not offering details out the financial implications of the ruling, said it would in no way cause financial difficulties for Schorghuber. In 1997 another court ruled that holders of Paulaner and Hacker-Pschorr stock were entitled to DM 228 and DM 185 respectively, for interest they had been denied by Schorghuber's accounting methods.

The German beer industry as a whole experienced a 0.8 percent decline in sales in 1995, while Bavarian brewery sales fell by 4.5 percent. Paulaner, however, bucked the trend and was able finally to reverse its four-year downward spiral. The sales of the Paulaner brand went up by two percent while Hacker-Pschorr increased by 7.5 percent. Paulaner Weissbier became the second best seller in Germany, trailing only Erdinger. Ten percent of Paulaner's revenues came from exports. Those improvements, while not turning a profit, enabled Paulaner to break even. In 1996, however, the company was able to report profits of nearly DM 4 million. Paulaner continued to expand its brewing business in the mid-1990s. In late 1995 it purchased the EKU brewery for an undisclosed price; in late 1996 it acquired the Thurn und Taxis brand.

In November 1998 the PSB was restructured as a strategic holding company for all the group's beverage activities, which included its German breweries, a Chilean brewery (Cervecerias) and the Bavarian bottler Coca-Cola AG. The restructuring was accomplished by an exchange of stock between PSB and the Schorghuber holding company. PSB received a 14.4 percent share in the bottling company in exchange for its 20.9 percent share in Hacker-Pshorr, one of Schorghuber's real estate holding companies, and DM 30 million in cash. Henceforth PSB held 100 percent of the Paulaner Brauerei Gruppe. PSB was reorganized only a year later as Bayerische BräuHolding AG.

In late November 1999, Paulaner's famous Salvatorkeller, the beer hall where the presentation of the year's first batch of Salvator Starkbier took place each March, burned to the ground. Some 400 firefighters fought the blaze from early morning until around noon, but were unable to save the structure. Arson was suspected; at least three times in the hours before sunrise, witnesses found signs that someone was trying to set a fire in the Salvatorkeller's restaurant. No motive for arson could be adduced by the company or police and no suspect was arrested. When the Starkbier season arrived again in 2000, Paulaner held the tasting in a warehouse building on its brewery grounds.

Paulaner reported 1999 results that were better than the rest of the beer industry. The Paulaner group of breweries increased sales by 2.1 percent. The Paulaner brand increased its sales by 4.4 percent, solidifying its position as one of Germany's top ten brewers. Its Weissbier sales jumped a remarkable 10.3 percent.

Principal Subsidiaries

Hacker-Pschorr Bräu GmbH; AuerBräu AG (97.6%); InterDrink GetränkeVertriebsgesellschaft mbH; Automaten Betriebs Gesellschaft Monaco für Spiel und Unterhaltung mbH; Fürsterliche Brauerei Thurn und Taxis Vertriebsgesellschaft mbH. (95%); Paulaner North America Corporation (United States); Thomasbräu GmbH.

Principal Competitors

Privatbrauerei Erdinger Weissbräu Werner Brombach GmbH; Brauerei Beck & Co; Löwenbräu Buttenheim International GmbH; Ottinger Braugruppe.

Further Reading

Heine, Hans-Gerd, "Paulaner besser als die Branche," *Suddeutsche Zeitung,* February 3, 2000.

Hübner, Alexander, "Paulaner-Salvator heisst jetzt Bayerische BrauHolding," *Vereinigte Wirtschaftsdienste,* November 15, 1999.

Melton, Brian, "Out on a Limb with Germany's Paulaner," *Fort Worth Star-Telegram,* March 24, 1994.

"Nachbesserung für Paulaner-Aktionare," *Suddeutsche Zeitung,* November 25, 1995.

"Personalien Josef Schoerghuber 75 Jahre," *Suddeutsche Zeitung,* April 13, 1995.

"Schoerghubers Nachfolge," *Lebensmittel Zeitung,* May 26, 1995.

—Gerald E. Brennan

Petroleum Helicopters, Inc.

2121 Airline Highway, Suite 400
P.O. Box 578
Metairie, Louisiana 70001-5979
U.S.A.
Telephone: (504) 828-3323
Toll Free: (800) 235-2452
Fax: (504) 828-8333
Web site: http://www.phihelico.com

Public Company
Incorporated: 1949 as Petroleum Bell Helicopters, Inc.
Employees: 1,850
Sales: $250.88 million (1999)
Stock Exchanges: NASDAQ
Ticker Symbol: PHEL
NAIC: 481211 Nonscheduled Chartered Passenger Air
  Transportation; 481212 Nonscheduled Chartered Freight
  Air Transportation; 48819 Other Support Activities
  for Air Transportation ; 62191 Ambulance Services

Petroleum Helicopters, Inc. (PHI), based in Louisiana, operates one of the largest fleets of commercial helicopters in the world. It provides a wide and diverse range of transportation services to the petroleum company, principally in the Gulf Mexico. It also has contract operations at various places throughout the world, including spots in South America, Asia, and Africa. The company also provides medical and emergency evacuation services, including a growing air ambulance operation. In addition, PHI conducts extensive pilot and crew training and helicopter-repair services, which in no small measure account for its excellent safety record. Although it is a public company, 51 percent of its stock is owned by CEO Carroll Suggs, widow to Robert Suggs, the company's renowned founder.

1949–59: Starting Out to Fill
Oil Industry Needs in Louisiana

With the close of World War II, a marsh-land and offshore oil and gas industry began emerging in states bordering the Gulf of Mexico, notably Texas and Louisiana. The placement of drilling rigs in remote or difficult to access places posed significant problems. In Louisiana, seismograph crews often had to traverse rugged terrain in four-wheel drive jeeps and trucks, and marshes and swamps in swamp buggies, sometimes getting bogged down. It was a slow and fairly dangerous way to get to potential drilling sites. Jack Lee, who was then president of a seismographic company, was appalled by the situation and anxious to find a viable alternative. Thinking that helicopters could provide both a more efficient and safer mode of transport for his crews, Lee approached Robert L. Suggs and M.M. Bayon with his idea. Under the leadership of Suggs, the new company officially went into business on February 21, 1949, with an initial investment of $100,000, three Bell 47 D model helicopters, and a small workforce of eight employees. The company was initially named Petroleum Bell Helicopters, Inc.

Potential use of PHI's services quickly increased when, in the 1950s, offshore drilling in the Gulf of Mexico started its rapid expansion. The company was already positioned to provide timely transport services to and from drilling rigs and platforms, not just for seismic crews but for other industry offshore workers and equipment. By 1952, it also began expanding its services on an international scale, starting up operations in oil field locations outside up the lower, 48 states of the United States. By the end of the decade, it had operations in Alaska, Canada, Bolivia, Colombia, Puerto Rico, and Greenland.

The changes in the nature of its services required larger aircraft, and in 1955, PHI began using Sirkorsky S-55s. In the same year, the company designed and built offshore refueling facilities in the Gulf of Mexico for its growing fleet of rotary-blade aircraft. By 1959, it had added Sirkorsky S-58s to its fleet and, among other things, used them to transport power poles over mountainous terrain in Puerto Rico. Such special use of its helicopters demonstrated PHI's willingness to adapt to the needs of its customers.

It was also in the 1950s that PHI began taking significant steps towards achieving the industry's premier safety record. At that time there was a paucity of helpful guidelines for helicopter maintenance and operation, reliable ground rules for ensuring the safe and efficient use of the aircraft. In 1956, the company established its own in-house training program, something that

Company Perspectives:

Our mission is to provide worldwide helicopter services that are unsurpassed in safety and customer satisfaction. We are a team dedicated to continuous improvement in an environment that promotes trust, personal growth and mutual respect.

thereafter played a major part in its enviable reputation for safety and high quality of service.

1960s: Continued Expansion and Unique Missions

In the 1960s PHI continued to expand its operations both at home and abroad. Demands for its services were quickly growing. Between 1961 and 1963, its number of flight hours increased from 200,000 to 300,000 hours. Eventually, customer needs would take the company to 42 countries, where it established associations that in some cases lasted to the end of the century. An important step occurred in 1967, when PHI began operating in Africa, in Angola, or what was then Portuguese West Africa. The long range development of Angola's Cabinda Gulf Oil Company has ever since kept a fairly sizable number of PHI aircraft and personnel working there.

Starting even earlier, in the 1950s, PHI also established a reputation for public service, even the extremely dangerous work of saving lives during disasters, notably the great hurricanes that ravaged the Gulf of Mexico and the Carribean. For instance, in 1961, when Hurricane Carla slammed into the Texas coast with winds of 145 mph, PHI pilots rescued 500 people. During the decade, such heroic efforts won several PHI pilots Winged S Awards for rescue work under hazardous conditions. It was in the mid-1960s that PHI also engaged in the first of many unique missions for the U.S. government when one of its pilots undertook the mid-air retrieval of a rocket-launched space module upon its return to earth. Thereafter, PHI often worked for NASA, retrieving objects released from spacecraft. The company was also undertaking some unique assignments for other agencies and businesses, developing a diverse range of uses for its craft and crews outside petroleum industry needs.

By the end of the 1960s, PHI's fleet of aircraft numbered 87. The rapid growth of the offshore oil industry in the Gulf of Mexico fueled PHI's own expansion. As a result, in 1969 PHI built a new facility, the Lake Palourde Heliport at Morgan City, Louisiana, which was then the largest heliport in the world. The growth also required a tracking system that would allow reliable communications between pilots and flight-following facilities throughout their missions. PHI began developing such a system, one that would ultimately become a computerized network allowing effective and dependable communications with airborne pilots from Texas to Florida.

1970s: Oil Boom Leads to PHI's Accelerated Expansion

No decade in the 20th century matched that of the 1970s for the petroleum and related industries in the United States. It was boom time pure and simple. By the time that it began, PHI

already had in place techniques and procedures for ensuring safety and quality service, setting industry standards.

By the decade's first year, PHI had logged over 1 million flight hours, the first commercial helicopter company in the world to achieve that milestone. Two years later, in 1972, PHI placed a major order for new helicopters costing about $5 million. The purchase increased the company's fleet to 233 aircraft by 1974, when PHI was employing almost 1,000 people. The company continued to find diverse uses for its fleet of rotary-winged aircraft. In 1971, in Costa Rica, its pilots fashioned a sling load technique for transporting goods to offshore rigs, including pallets of bananas weighing two tons.

PHI growth was steady and very strong through the entire decade. At the time of its 25th anniversary in 1974, it was maintaining operations at 13 Gulf Coast and 5 foreign bases. By the end of the decade, the company's fleet reached 308 aircraft, the largest non-military fleet of helicopters in the world. Only the fleets of the U.S. and Soviet Union militaries were larger.

1980s: PHI Weathers the Oil Industry's Collapse

Unfortunately for U.S. oil and related industries, the boom did not last, and with the resulting collapse in the early 1980s, PHI faced the prospect of a major decline in the oil field's need for its services. Robert Suggs and his staff knew that the company's continued growth would depend on increasing diversification. An important step was taken in 1981 when, in support of Acadian Ambulance's newly created Air Med Program, PHI put its Aeromedical Services Division into operation. The company quickly became one of the major providers of air medical services, expanding beyond its Louisiana base by mid-decade.

In 1984, it reached another milestone when it logged its five-millionth flight hour. At that time, it was operating a fleet of 417 aircraft. Nationally, it also greatly enhanced its profile through its support of the Los Angeles Olympics and its participation in the Louisiana World's Fair Exposition, where it prominently displayed one of its Sirkorsky S-76 helicopters on the deck of an oil rig erected for the event. It was the same model helicopter that in 1986 PHI put into use for its medical helicopter support of the Cleveland MetroHealth Medical Center's services. It was also in 1986 that PHI introduced innovations in training services with in-house courses focusing on the impact of human factors on pilots and their decision making. Another innovation came in 1988, when the company established PHI Technical Services, a new business providing maintenance services to third-party customers.

When founder Robert Suggs suffered a fatal heart attack in 1989, there was some apprehension about PHI's future, including a possible corporate raid, but Carroll Suggs, his widow, quickly allayed concerns when, in 1990, she took over the company's reins as chairman, president, and CEO. In an industry dominated by males, she demonstrated that she could get the job done, garnering several awards in the process.

1990–2000: PHI Tightens Corporate Belt but Continues to Grow and Diversify

In 1990, PHI had a fleet of 291 copters or one out of every 69 non-military whirlybirds in the world. In its primary use market,

Key Dates:

1949: Company is founded by Robert L. Suggs.
1952: PHI begins its international expansion.
1956: Company begins in-house training program.
1966: Aerospace role begins with work for NASA.
1970: PHI reaches over one million flight hours.
1981: PHI starts up its Aeromedical Services Division.
1982: Oil bust hits industry hard, but diversification helps PHI.
1989: Robert Suggs, PHI's founder, dies.
1990: Carroll Suggs becomes chairman, president, and CEO.
1991: PHI reaches seven million flight hours.
1997: Company acquires Air Evac Services.
1999: PHI opens new heliport facility in Boothville/Venice, Louisiana, and begins construction of new operations and maintenance facility in Lafayette, Louisiana.

that of transporting crews and equipment to and from offshore oil platforms in the Gulf of Mexico, PHI held about a 60 percent share, thrice that of Offshore Logistics, its closest competitor. The company had started a strong turnaround from the dark days of the 1980s, when inexpensive foreign oil wreaked havoc with the American oil industry. For the fiscal year ending in April, 1990, the company had netted almost $10 million from revenues of $188 million, or $1.63 per share, its best performance since just before the oil bust hit in 1982. Still, the profits came in part from some downsizing measures, including the sell-off of some of its assets. Among these were some of its older aircraft. In fact, even with a mild resurgence of the oil industry in the mid-1990s, PHI was forced to continue to take belt-tightening measures: reducing its workforce, selling equipment, and using other cost-cutting measures. The Gulf of Mexico, although remaining PHI's principal source of business, still lagged way behind in its pre-bust rig count through the decade. Also, technological advances in the industry reduced the number of workers needed on rigs, thereby cutting back on transportation needs. As a partial solution to the Gulf oil drilling doldrums, throughout the decade PHI looked for new international markets to tap for potential growth, both in South America and Asia, including countries once forming the Soviet Union.

Despite the U.S. oil industry's stagnation, PHI continued to grow. By 1991, it had logged its seven millionth flight hour. It was also reaching some important milestones. Under Carroll Suggs' leadership, the company attained a new level as a service-orientated and customer-driven organization, one able to customize operations to fit the specific needs of its clients. Suggs also stressed PHI's continued commitment to both safety and diversification. In order to improve its already enviable safety record, the company dedicated a million dollars annually to a safety incentive program. The result was that PHI's accident rate fell to one-seventh of the national average. Its excellent safety record earned the company international recognition and several awards, including, in 1996, the Federal Aviation Administration's High Flyer Award.

Among other new challenges, in 1994, during the Haiti embargo, PHI put some of its craft to use patrolling the Haiti-

Dominican Republic border, making it the first civilian company chosen for such a service. In 1997, it was also selected as the first civilian operator to support the National Science Foundation's Antarctica Program. It was also a landmark year in other ways. Among other important measures, PHI established Acadian Composites, Inc., which repairs and overhauls structural composite panels on helicopters. It also acquired the Arizona-based Air Evac Services, Inc., the country's largest air medical transport service.

Through the decade, PHI continued to play a major role during disasters. For instance, in 1997 it began fighting fires for the U.S. Forestry Service, and in the following year helped transport food and medical supplies to Nicaragua, which had been ravaged by flooding caused by Hurricane Mitch.

A new downturn in oil prices in the late 1990s led to a further reduction in drilling activity in the Gulf of Mexico with disappointing results for PHI. The worst year was 1999, when the Gulf drilling rig count dropped to its lowest on record and, in real dollar terms, the price of crude oil plummeted to lows not posted since the Great Depression. Although the company realized record revenues, its flight hours in the area and income from its transport services declined from the previous year and resulted in some further belt-tightening measures, including the sale of underused assets and a reduction in labor costs. However, a solid increase in revenues from its Aeromedical and Technical Services operations helped offset the impact of the decline in production rigs. Between them, the operations produced an increase in revenue of $14.3 million, a growth, respectively, of 30 and 25 percent over the previous year.

At the close of the century, despite the volatility of the oil market, PHI remained very upbeat. It looked for new ways to use its air fleet and planned for additional growth In August 1999, it ended construction and put into operation a new, state-of-the-art heliport in Boothville/Venice, Louisiana named the Robert L Suggs Heliport in memory of PHI's founder. At year's end, it was also on its way to completing its new operations and maintenance facility in Lafayette, Louisiana.

Principal Subsidiaries

Air Evac Services, Inc.; Acadian Composites, L.L.C.; Evangeline Airmotive, Inc.

Principal Competitors

Offshore Logistics, Inc.; Air Methods Corporation; Rowan Companies, Inc.

Further Reading

Barrett, William P., "Do I Look like a Haggard Cat?," *Forbes*, October 29, 1990, p. 44.
Biers, John M., "Helicopter Firm to Get New Home," *Times-Picayune* (New Orleans), January 5, 1999, p. C1.
Griggs, Ted, "Exec Tells Challenges of Business," *Advocate* (Baton Rouge), November 6, 1999, p. 1C.
Lear, Calvin, "Larger Facility Planned to Keep PHI in Lafayette," *Advocate* (Baton Rouge), October 23, 1996, p. 3B.
"PHI 50th Anniversary," special issue of *The Daily Advertiser* (Lafayette, La.), February 19, 1999, pp. 1–56.

—John W. Fiero

The Pew Charitable Trusts

2005 Market Street, Suite 1700
Philadelphia, Pennsylvania 19103-7017
U.S.A.
Telephone: (215) 575-9050
Fax: (215) 575-4939
Web site: http://www.pewtrusts.org

Not-for-Profit Organization
Founded: 1948
Employees: 125
Total Assets: $4.89 billion (1999)
NAIC: 81341 Civic and Social Organizations

The Pew Charitable Trusts, established in 1948, is one of the nation's largest private foundations. Its over $4.7 billion in assets sustains seven separate trusts, all of which were created by 1979 to provide financial support for a variety of domestic and international charities and services—some of which involve considerable risk but hold the hope of great public benefit. From income generated by its assets, the foundation makes annual grants totaling over $200 million. Over one-fifth of that total is used to underwrite charitable and public service programs in the Philadelphia area, to which, historically, the Pew family and the foundation have maintained close ties. The remaining 80 percent in grants is awarded to widely distributed charities that support educational, cultural, and religious activities; environmental studies; and public health, policy, and resource services. In the 1980s and 1990s, the foundation increasingly used funds for initiating projects in partnering arrangements with external agencies.

1859–1948: The Pew Legacy and Establishment of the Foundation

Joseph Newton Pew (1848–1912), who established his family's fortune, was an enterprising and prescient businessman who saw great promise in the fledgling petroleum industry. The industry first sprang up in his native Pennsylvania, when, at Titusville, the nation's first producing well was dug in 1859. He began his career in the field in 1876, when he helped develop Pittsburgh's initial natural gas service. Just fourteen years later, he founded the Sun Oil Company, which, by the time of his death in 1912, had a solid toehold in an industry that in its early stages was almost completely dominated by John D. Rockefeller's Standard Oil Company.

A devout Christian and highly principled man, Pew was a notable philanthropist who passed his values on to his children. Two of his sons, J. Howard and Joseph Newton, Jr. took on the management of Sun Oil and turned it into a major corporation, greatly adding to the family's wealth. They also became two of the Pew Charitable Trusts' founders when it was established in 1948 as The Pew Memorial Foundation. As the founders, they were joined by their two sisters, Mary Ethel Pew and Mabel Pew Myrin. The four principals, the core of the foundation's board, established the foundation as a memorial to their parents. They were also joined by three other family members: Jno. G. Pew, cousin to the founders and Sun Oil's vice-president in charge of production; Frederick B. Hufnagel, Jr., nephew to J. Howard Pew's wife, Helen; and J.N. Pew III, son of J.N. Pew, Jr.

The board met for the first time on April 3, 1948. Using 880,000 shares of Sun Oil stock, it capitalized the foundation from the annual dividend of $880,000 returned by those shares. Initially, the board members emphasized four major areas of giving: scientific, charitable, religious, and educational. The first six grants awarded by the foundation reflected its priorities, starting with $30 thousand to the American Red Cross and $95 thousand to the Institute for Cancer Research.

1949–55: Expansion under the Original Board

Areas of focus and the number of annual grants made by The Pew Memorial Foundation began expanding quickly. For example, in 1949, at the suggestion of J.N. Pew, Jr., the foundation began a program to assist black colleges and, in 1951, hired Jerome H. Holland as a consultant on interracial concerns. Holland, who would later become president of Delaware State College and Hampton Institute, visited many of the nation's black colleges to help shape the foundation's special program.

In its early days, the foundation worked anonymously and was therefore virtually unheralded and unknown. That was the

---

Company Perspectives:

Stewardship is our most important mandate at The Pew Charitable Trusts. Good stewardship of the seven charitable funds that constitute the Trusts means allocating our resources wisely, effectively and in accord with the intent of our donors and the mandate of our current board. Merely doing or supporting good work is not sufficient. We must do our work well. With finite resources in a world of seemingly infinite problems, we must leverage our resources beyond the comparatively small amount of money we have to invest. By striving to make a discernable difference in a few key areas, the Trusts' staff fulfill their responsibility to the board, and the institution fulfills its responsibility to a 52-year heritage left to us by our donors.

---

choice of the Pew family members, who insisted on following a biblical admonition instructing alms givers to give in secret. Most grants were awarded on the basis of what the Pew family members already knew about recipient organizations, and many reflected their individual interests and concerns—especially those promoting higher education, public-health improvement, emergency response needs, and religion. From the outset, because of the Pew family's close ties to Philadelphia, agencies in that city were major beneficiaries of the foundation's largess. Yet the organization also reached out to help both national and international groups, especially during emergencies. Altogether, between 1948 and 1956, The Pew Memorial Foundation made 181 grants totaling $12.5 million.

1956–70: Growth under the Glenmede Trust Company

A major change in the administration of The Pew Memorial Foundation came in 1956 with the founding of The Glenmede Trust Company. Named after the Pew family estate in Bryn Mawr, Pennsylvania, it was created to provide a professional staff to alleviate the increasing demands on the board members' time that the foundation's grant-making decisions and asset management required.

Initially, The Glenmede Trust's primary responsibility was the administration of the newly created Pew Memorial Trust, plus two others established in 1957: The Mary Anderson Trust and the J. Howard Pew Freedom Trust. Under a twelve-member board of directors, Glenmede began operating with just two staff members, including its first president: Allyn R. Bell, Jr. Board membership was governed by a special succession agreement designed to preserve the vision of the organization's founders. Nine of the twelve board members were major Sun Oil stockholders, and included the four founders and other members of the original board of The Pew Memorial Foundation. These members, comprising the Committee on Grants, Donations, and Contributions, had the primary responsibility for grant-making decisions. The committee grouped its awards under five categories: educational, charitable, medical-hospital, medical-research, and religious grants. It also maintained the founders' policy of anonymity.

Between 1957 and 1969, under the administration of Glenmede, the committee awarded 2,562 grants with a yearly average funding of $5 million, or four times the yearly average granted between 1948 and 1956. Many of the larger grants were made to assist major expansion projects, such as the building of new facilities. Much more numerous were smaller grants made to assist projects in a wide variety of fields and geographical areas. Also, after co-founder J.N. Pew, Jr.'s death in 1963, a memorial trust in his name became the fourth trust administered by Glenmede. A fifth, The Knollbrook Trust, was added in 1965—named after the home of J. Howard Pew.

In 1967, the grants committee permitted the first public recognition of one its gifts. As a tribute to the deceased co-founder, J.N. Pew, Jr., it allowed the J.N. Pew, Jr. Charitable Trust to be listed on a bronze plaque in the lobby of the Lou Henry Hoover Building at Stanford University. In the 1970s, new federal filing requirements would bring a permanent end to the Trusts' policy of anonymous grant making.

1971–79: Changes in Leadership and Accelerated Growth

In a two-month period at the end of 1971 and the beginning of 1972, J. Howard Pew and Mabel Pew Myrin died. Their remaining sister and co-founder of The Pew Memorial Foundation, Mary Ethel Pew, died seven years later. Although their great legacy remained, their loss brought an end to the first era of the foundation, that in which its creators actively chartered its course.

Mabel Pew Myrin's death brought the activation of a memorial trust that had been created in her name in 1957, bringing the number of Pew family trusts administered by The Glenmede Trust Company to six. The Medical Trust, the legacy of Mary Ethel Pew, brought the total to seven upon her death in 1979.

Because J. Howard Pew had been the chairman of Glenmede's Committee on Grants and the foundation's principal guiding hand, his passing compelled the committee to select his replacement. Their choice was Robert G. Dunlop, who had succeeded J. Howard Pew as president of the Sun Oil Company in 1947. Under Dunlop and his successor, R. Anderson Pew, the foundation's grants committee had to cope with a revised federal tax code that, in effect, required Glenmede to sell some stock and re-invest part of its capital at a higher rate of return. The upshot was that the foundation had more money to grant. Between 1970 and 1975, its grant funding increased from $9.4 million to $33 million. By 1978, the figure increased to $49.6 million—nearly as much as its grants total for the entire 1960s decade.

Altogether, between 1970 and 1979, the foundation awarded 3,552 grantees $296 million. In the process, the Committee on Grants addressed some new or broadened concerns, including ecological, political, cultural, and economic interests—both at the local and national levels. The changes also occasioned increases in the size of Glenmede's staff, and its move—twice—into new offices.

1980–90: New Policies for Change

In March of 1979, facing a new decade, the Committee on Grants met to determine the ways in which it could best adapt to

Key Dates:

1948: The Pew Memorial Foundation is founded by the four surviving children of Joseph and Mary Pew.

1956: The Glenmede Trust Company is created to administer the new Pew Memorial Trust.

1957: Foundation establishes The Mary Anderson and The J. Howard Pew Freedom Trusts.

1963: The J.N. Pew, Jr. Charitable Trust is created upon its namesake's death.

1965: Foundation establishes The Knollbrook Trust.

1971: Co-founder J. Howard Pew dies.

1972: The Mabel Pew Myrin Trust, created in 1957, is activated after her death.

1979: The Medical Trust, the legacy of Mary Ethel Pew, is activated upon her death.

the needs of a world undergoing some extraordinary and rapid changes. Its decision was that the committee itself should initiate some projects, partnering with agencies that its members thought capable of implementing them. Thereafter, the foundation played a much more active role in its support of its founders' philosophy and goals. The committee also separated grants into seven categories: American Policy and Values; Conservation; Culture; Education; Health; Religion; and Social Welfare. Later it added two more: Federated Giving and Emergency Needs. In addition, the committee decided to hire consultants in these areas to help guide it.

First hired were consultants in the health field. Among other things, they recommended the creation of the Health Policy Program, which the committee approved in 1981. The next year, under that program, the foundation made four grants totaling $9 million. The program also served as a prototype of the Trusts' TIPs (trust initiated programs), the first of which was the Pew Scholars Program in the Biomedical Sciences, a very successful project that became the working model for future TIPs. Its modus operandi called for identifying an issue, selecting an advisory panel, soliciting proposals, and implementing selected programs under administrating agencies outside the foundation.

In the 1980s, TIPs led to a special emphasis on health professions, providing support to educational projects in primary care, dentistry, nutrition, veterinary medicine, and nursing. At the same time, The Trusts continued to award grants to the various institutions and agencies that the individual Pew family members had supported through the foundation's history. TIPs provided the means of linking past interests to current needs. In addition, the Trusts provided contingency funds for disaster relief, as it had done since its inception.

In 1986, Dr. Thomas W. Langfitt became Glenmede's president. The next year, he administered a reorganization plan in which The Glenmede Trust Company became the sole subsidiary of The Glenmede Corporation and was divided into two divisions: The Trust and Investment Division and The Pew Charitable Trusts Division. At that time the Committee on Grants became the board of the latter.

By 1988, in terms of funds allocated in grants, The Pew Charitable Trusts had become the second leading private foundation in the United States. In the decade's closing year, its board authorized $146 million in grants to 448 agencies, a sum greater than the total amount awarded in the first 25 years of the foundation's existence. In all, between 1980 and 1989, its grants, made to over 5,000 agencies, totaled $1.13 billion.

1990s: New Directions

Throughout its history, The Pew Charitable Trusts endeavored to reverse the decline of religious faith wherever it was occurring, promote the free-market economic system throughout the world, and extend charity where evidence clearly indicated it was needed. While that mission remained intact throughout its history, new and changing problems in the world necessitated an ongoing reassessment of how that mission might best be implemented.

In the late 1980s, as the Trusts' assets continued strong growth, the board adopted four basic principles to guide it through the 1990s: philanthropy as a service, accountability in grant making, open communications, and interdisciplinary programming. It also elected to broaden its geographical scope through grants with both a national and international impact.

In 1991, the Trusts reserved $35 million for special grant-making projects and the creation of a "Dream Team" of advisors to help identify needs that could be served through new grant-funded initiatives. From discussions with the Dream Team, The Trusts' board chose to fund a handful of projects, including, in 1991: The Delta Partnership (for improving the economic condition in the Mississippi Delta region); the Pew Partnership for Civic Change (for redressing problems in small cities); and Earth Force (for promoting an ecological awareness in the nation's youth). In 1992, the Neighborhood Preservation Initiative (for assisting working-class neighborhoods' efforts to maintain their health and viability) was funded as well.

While these initiatives were being implemented, general growth was steady. By 1993, the Trusts' grants, made to 506 organizations, totaled almost $167 million. The foundation was also undergoing some internal changes. In 1992, increases in the size of the staff had caused the Trusts to move once more, this time to One Commerce Square, a new office building in Philadelphia's financial district. Two years later, in 1994, Langfitt resigned his presidency and was replaced by the Trusts' executive director, Rebecca W. Rimel.

Through the mid 1990s, the Pew Partnership for Civic Change addressed several issues. Among other things, it sponsored successful youth and community development projects in several cities. In 1996, the foundation also initiated the Pew Leadership Award for the Renewal of Undergraduate Education, promoting curriculum reform in higher education. It also put considerable effort into the fight to save the nation's forests, one of its longstanding concerns. Furthermore, the trust began addressing new problems, such as the erosion of the democratic process in America. It supported projects designed to boost election turnouts, reform campaign financing, and restore ethical values in politics.

During the remaining years of the decade, while continuing to support its traditional charities, the Trusts remained flexible by using a Venture Fund for exploring needs outside the defined goals of its six program areas: culture; education; environment; health and human services; public policy; and religion. In 1999, 43 grants totaling $83.5 million were made through the Venture Fund program—about 33 percent of the total amount of $250.2 million committed to grants by the Trusts. The figures revealed the foundation's determination to meet the new challenges of a changing world head on.

Further Reading

Cockburn, Alexander, ''PEW: Millions Wasted?,'' *The Nation,* January 31, 1994, p. 117.
Key, Peter, ''Pew Makes a Push into Politics,'' *Philadelphia Business Journal,* March 3, 2000, p. 1.
Kriz, Margaret, ''Call of the Wild,'' *National Journal,* October 23, 1999, p. 3038.
McMillen, Liz, ''Pew Trusts Conclude Sweeping Reorganization of Grant-making Programs and Leadership,'' *The Chronicle of Higher Education,* May 2, 1990, p. A27.
Moran, Mark, ''Easing the 'Cold War' between Managed Care, Academic Med.,'' *American Medical News,* December 8, 1997, p. 3.
Pittman, Karen, ''Proven Strategies to Build Healthy Communities for Youth: Changing Conditions, Changing Odds, Changing Lives,'' *Nation's Cities Weekly,* June 16, 1997, p. 9.
Rottenberg, Dan, ''Town & Country's Generous American Award for 1991: The Pew Charitable Trusts,'' *Town & Country Monthly,* December 1991, p. 137.
Scheinbart, Betsy, ''America's Richest Foundations Give to Arts,'' *Back Stage,* August 27, 1999, p. 2.
Shmavonian, Nadya K., ''The Pew Charitable Trusts,'' *Alcohol Health & Research World,* Winter 1989, p. 75.

—John W. Fiero

Platinum Entertainment, Inc.

2001 Butterfield Road, Suite 1400
Downers Grove, Illinois 60515
U.S.A.
Telephone: (630) 769-0033
Fax: (630) 769-0049
Web site: http://www.platinument.com

Public Company
Incorporated: 1991
Employees: 101
Gross Sales: $48.89 million (1999)
Stock Exchanges: OTC
Ticker Symbol: PTET
NAIC: 334612 Prerecorded Compact Disc (Except
    Software), Tape, and Record Reproducing; 51222
    Integrated Record Production/Distribution

In 1999, Platinum Entertainment, Inc. was the largest independent record company in the United States. The company produces and sells albums through several labels including CGI Platinum, Platinum Nashville, House of Blues, Light Records, and River North Records. Initially a gospel music company, Platinum quickly expanded its roster of artists to include pop, classical, urban, country, and blues performers. The company also developed an innovative business plan. Rather than focus on discovering hit new musicians, Platinum has built its sales steadily by signing contracts with veteran artists, including Peter Cetera, The Beach Boys, and Dionne Warwick. In addition, Platinum Entertainment has been at the forefront of the digital music revolution. The company's PlatinumCD.com allows consumers to purchase compact discs (CDs) and create custom CDs online. Moreover, Platinum's HeardOn.com (now part of LiveOntheNet.com's web site) offers free downloads of Platinum musicians. Financial struggles at Platinum in the late 1990s forced a dramatic decline in the company's net worth and the value of the company's stock. In July 2000 the company moved its shares from NASDAQ to the OTC Bulletin Board, as it sought to address liquidity problems through institutional investors.

From River North Studios to Platinum Entertainment: 1985–93

Platinum Entertainment was the brainchild of Steve Devick, an amateur musician who founded River North Studios in 1985 after a short career as an optometrist. Located in Chicago, River North Studios became popular with the city's influential advertising community, which used River North to record jingles for television and radio commercials. Because of its high-tech equipment, though, River North quickly won the admiration of musicians as well. A consummate businessman, Devick was the first to invest in Platinum Technology Inc., a software company launched by Andrew Filipowski in 1987. (This partnership would endure for over a decade, as Devick and Filipowski fruitfully collaborated on a number of occasions.)

Devick made his next major move in 1990, when he formed Chicago Gospel International (CGI), a record company that produced African American religious music. While many of the major record labels had overlooked gospel music, Devick recognized the genre's money-making potential. Launching CGI set the tone for most of Devick's future transactions. Rather than pursuing mass-market artists, Devick concentrated on finding musical niches such as gospel that were underexplored by the major studios.

While Devick ventured into new territory with CGI, River North Studios continued to perform strongly. In 1991, the company recorded ''I Wanna Be Like Mike,'' a jingle for a Gatorade commercial that featured basketball sensation Michael Jordan. As the commercial and its catchy song proved a hit with audiences across the United States, Devick teamed up with A&M Records to capitalize on the jingle's popularity. Devick founded a new venture—River North Records—which produced a single of the song. A&M distributed the ''I Wanna Be Like Mike'' record, which sold over 100,000 copies.

Buoyed by his successes at both CGI and River North Studios, Devick reorganized his expanding array of businesses as Platinum Entertainment in 1991. CGI, River North Studios, and River North Records retained their individual labels within the Platinum company. Platinum also continued to bolster its gospel offerings, acquiring A&M's gospel division in 1992. In

+---+
| **Company Perspectives:** |
| |
| *It's so simple. Music is perfectly suited for e-commerce* |
| *because like video and software it's electronically transmit-* |
| *table.* |
+---+

early 1993, Platinum bought the bankrupt Light Records, which had a strong gospel catalogue as well as one of contemporary Christian music. By the end of the year, advertising work accounted for only about ten percent of River North Studio's total revenue, as the studio devoted most of its efforts to recording Platinum productions.

Growth and Development: 1993–97

Platinum's fortunes changed dramatically late in 1993, when PolyGram Distribution Group (one of the largest record companies in the United States) agreed to distribute Platinum's CGI and River North labels. PolyGram's decision reflected the growing stature of gospel music in the marketplace. Although religious music overall accounted for only 3.1 percent of the $10 billion in U.S. music sales in 1993, many analysts anticipated that African American gospel music sales would soar in the mid-1990s. ''The potential for gospel is enormous,'' an ebullient Devick told *Billboard* in the wake of his distribution deal with PolyGram, noting, ''The key is that it's good music that can compete in the marketplace not just with gospel, but with R&B as well.'' CGI's gospel music sales bore out Devick's claims. In 1993, Platinum achieved gospel music sales of $1 million per month, according to the October 29, 1993, edition of the *Chicago Tribune*. Moreover, every album ever released by CGI had been ranked on *Billboard*'s Top Gospel chart. By 1994, Platinum was the leading producer of gospel music.

In the months following its distribution agreement with PolyGram, Platinum rapidly diversified its musical offerings. Rather than confine itself solely to gospel, Platinum ventured into the adult contemporary genre as well, most notably when River North Records signed pop singer Peter Cetera (the former lead singer of the hit band Chicago) to a multi-album deal in October 1993. As the *Chicago Tribune* explained, ''Platinum [was] hoping that the Cetera deal w[ould] bring the company as much success with the adult contemporary format as it ha[d] found on the gospel music charts.''

In a similar vein, Platinum sought to enter the competitive sphere of country music. Early in 1994, the company established River North Records Nashville. Headquartered in Tennessee, Platinum's newest label initially departed from the company's usual approach of relying on established artists when it quickly released an album by country newcomer S. Alan Taylor. But River North Nashville reverted to form when it signed its first high-profile artist, Holly Dunn (the recipient of the Country Music Association's 1986 Top Female Vocalist award), in July 1994.

Meanwhile, Platinum formed its own distribution arm in 1994 to complement its agreement with PolyGram. The new entity—Light Distribution—distributed Platinum and other companies' religious music to Christian bookstores. Platinum also continued to hone the innovative marketing strategies that had helped make its gospel albums best-sellers. For example, while most religious music producers had traditionally sold their wares only at concerts and Christian bookstores, Platinum employed television direct-response ads.

Simultaneously, Platinum strove to develop its roster of artists (in 1995, the company signed perennial pop favorites The Beach Boys to a multi-album deal), and also focused on making key acquisitions of other music companies. In an effort to raise capital to pare down its debt and facilitate further acquisitions, Platinum became a publicly traded company in March 1996, raising $32 million in its initial public offering. Platinum then began a spate of acquisitions, including the purchase of the Double J Music Group, a Nashville-based country music publisher that controlled the copyrights to more than 250 country songs, in June 1996. Platinum's CGI also won an exclusive recording contract with the 8.5 million member National Baptist Convention USA, Inc. to record live gospel music on behalf of the group for commercial distribution. Later in 1996, Platinum obtained a 50 percent stake in House of Blues Records, a leading blues music label. With this arrangement, Platinum was empowered to produce and distribute all current and future artists signed to the House of Blues record label.

Platinum's most significant acquisition occurred in November 1996, when it purchased Intersound Inc. for $24 million. Headquartered in Georgia, Intersound was one of the largest independent record companies in the United States, with a solid presence in several music categories, including gospel, adult contemporary, country, urban, dance, and classical. With 1996 sales exceeding $33 million, Intersound controlled its own proprietary distribution system and had signed a stable of artists, including Kansas, Jefferson Starship, The Guess Who, Crystal Gale, and the Bellamy Brothers—much like the proven artists with solid sales Platinum had courted in the past.

Fueled by the company's numerous acquisitions, Platinum's 1996 revenues soared to $25.5 million, though a net loss of $3.7 million was reported for the year. However, since Platinum's future prospects looked bright, it was able to finalize a deal with a consortium of investors that included Maroley Media Group in December 1997. Under the terms of the agreement, the investors took control of 33.8 percent of Platinum's outstanding shares. In return, Platinum gained a considerable influx of cash, which it planned to use to pay down debt and to continue to grow.

At the close of fiscal 1997, Platinum reported record revenues of $42.6 million, a gain of 67 percent from the prior year. The company's loss had shrunk to only $91,000. The year had brought a number of other positive events as well. Platinum's River North Records was ranked tenth among all record labels in terms of total radio play, and the popularity of gospel music (Platinum's stronghold) continued to increase. According to the Recording Industry Association of America, gospel music sales had increased 38 percent in 1997, and the genre exceeded both classical music and jazz in sales. Platinum's gospel division even won a Grammy award in 1997, for Cissy Houston's ''Face to Face'' album. In addition, Platinum gained another venerable performer in 1998, when Dionne Warwick signed with River North Records in February.

Focusing on the Internet: Late 1990s

Platinum's business strategy shifted dramatically in 1998. The company announced in April that it was partnering with Platinum Technology to create an Internet-based music site. Soon thereafter, Platinum Entertainment forged an agreement with Liquid Audio, a developer of secure online music delivery systems. On October 1, 1998, Platinum debuted PlatinumCD .com—a web site where the company made its entire catalogue of recordings available to consumers via Liquid Audio. Consumers could "click" on a desired track from the web site, and the song was then transmitted directly to the computer hard drive of the customer, who paid a set fee per song. The buyer could then record the track onto a compact disc. PlatinumCD.com also allowed consumers who used the web site to create custom CDs online. Platinum would then compile the CD mix and send it to the buyer.

With the launch of PlatinumCD.com, Platinum Entertainment blazed a new path in the music industry. Most of the company's competitors were opposed to the digital transmission of music, fearing that the technology would encourage piracy and erode profits. Devick had a different view. "It's a natural progression for the distribution of music," he told the *Chicago Tribune* on April 30, 1998. With electronic transmission, Platinum also saved on shipping costs, promotional expenses, and manufacturing costs.

Soon after PlatinumCD.com was operational, Platinum Entertainment announced an agreement with The Music Connection Corporation—the parent company of www.MusicMaker .com, the largest custom-music compilation Internet site. Under the terms of the deal, Platinum acquired ten percent of The Music Connection Corporation in exchange for Platinum stock, and the two businesses combined their catalogues of recordings—which could be purchased and downloaded from either company's web site. "This arrangement allows Platinum to create a virtual inventory of our valuable music catalogue without financial risk, and should provide our company with substantial incremental revenues," Devick said in a press release. (Devick's prescience was demonstrated in July 1999, when MusicMaker.com's initial public offering pushed the value of Platinum's holding to over $11 million.)

In November 1998, Platinum once again entered new territory when it decided to offer free promotional tracks for digital download in the popular MP3 file format on both MP3.com and PlatinumCD.com. Platinum planned to post four songs on both web sites every two weeks. Consumers could download the tracks after completing a registration card. MP3—a compression technology that sped the download times of sound files while retaining a high sound quality—was considered to be the bane of the recording industry because it had been used to disseminate unauthorized copies of music. Platinum, on the other hand, believed MP3 could play an important role in promoting its artists and driving retail sales. "Our feeling is people don't really want to buy stolen cars," Devick told *Newsbytes News Network*. "I think you avoid piracy by giving people legal alternatives."

Platinum's efforts to build PlatinumCD.com were successful. Visits to the web site increased from 13,500 in October to 3.8 million in December. Although most were "window shoppers," Platinum felt confident that its web sales would grow, mainly because the company's target customer inhabited the same demographic group that market research revealed as the most likely to make purchases on the Internet. In any event, total sales for the year exceeded $40.6 million, and Platinum artist Otis Rush won a Grammy award for best traditional blues album.

Platinum introduced additional changes in 1999. The company shifted its distribution from a dual system with PolyGram/ Universal to a solely in-house one with its own newly created PED Corp., located in Atlanta. This move was prompted when PolyGram filed a lawsuit against Platinum, claiming that its agreement had barred Platinum from moving recordings through its own distribution channels and that Platinum had violated that agreement.

Platinum focused on maximizing its online sales. Cognizant of the fact that Internet music sales had accounted for only one percent of total sales in 1998, however, Devick cast about for innovative ways to turn a profit. "In the short term, the real increase in profitability going forward on the Internet will be the promotional use of music and the nonmusic sites that will be willing to pay content holders for their use of their catalogues," Devick explained to the *Chicago Daily Herald*. In other words, Devick hoped to sell Platinum's music to other online companies, such as electronic greeting card businesses.

In November 1999, Platinum raised the stakes yet again, when it created a new web site—HeardOn.com. Unlike PlatinumCD.com (which would remain operational), HeardOn.com made Platinum's entire catalogue available for free download. Platinum intended to profit in this venture by attracting online advertisers to HeardOn.com, and also believed that the site would promote the retail sale of the company's records. The new business offered an added bonus. Every visitor to HeardOn.com who downloaded music was required to complete an in-depth registration card that provided a wealth of data. Platinum would eventually collect a powerful marketing database, which the company could use to target customers in specific ways or to sell to other companies.

Platinum also believed that HeardOn.com would bring new talent to the company. Unsigned musicians were encouraged to post their songs on the web site. Every three months, the most frequently downloaded artist would then receive a record contract worth at least $250,000. Moreover, HeardOn.com contained a classical music radio station—with all recording available for free download. While many analysts and industry insiders decried Platinum's venture as the end of the music business, Devick was optimistic. Despite naysayers, Devick observed to the *Chicago Sun-Times*, ''Radio turned out to be the biggest boost for music that ever occurred.'' Devick believed the Internet held out similar potential.

Soon after launching HeardOn.com, Platinum divided its online and ''bricks and mortar'' operations. While the company's digital division would remain in Downers Grove, in November 1999, Platinum moved its traditional operations to Atlanta to join the distribution center. Further changes quickly followed. In January 2000, Platinum announced that HeardOn.com would be folded into LiveOntheNet.com—a web site that offered online music, concerts, and sporting events. LiveOntheNet.com, a member of the divine interVentures, Inc. family of e-commerce companies, paid Platinum a $2 million licensing fee. For Devick, the deal illustrated Platinum's ''emerging role as a business to business Internet content provider,'' as he explained in a press release.

However, the move was also part of an effort to consolidate operations and cut costs. Financial struggles for Platinum in 2000 had intensified when it terminated its distribution contract with PolyGram Distribution. Without PolyGram's services, Platinum was forced to retool, and logistical problems arose when it moved to new distribution facilities of its own. Reportedly, the new facilities were not available on time and the move then had to occur during the company's busiest season, just before the winter holidays. Distribution operations were delayed during the move, and the company experienced excessive customer dissatisfaction in the form of high product returns for 1999. With liquidity problems beginning the new year, the company's primary bank loan came due and could not be paid. The future of the company, so bright a year before, was in question in the new millennium.

Principal Subsidiaries

CGI Records Inc.; Intersound Inc.; Just Mike Music Inc.; Lexicon Music Inc.; Light Records Inc.; Peg Publishing Inc.; Recording Experience Inc.; Royce Publishing Inc.

Principal Competitors

Sony Music Entertainment Inc.; Time Warner Inc.; Universal Music Group.

Further Reading

Collins, Lisa, ''Market for Gospel Sees Growth Spurt,'' *Billboard*, April 9, 1994.
Culloton, Dan, ''Web's Big Hit,'' *Chicago Daily Herald*, August 18, 1999.
Eig, Jonathon, ''Praise the Lord! Gospel Lifts the Other Platinum,'' *Crain's Chicago Business*, June 3, 1996.
Fording, Laura, ''Cyberscope: MP3 Finds a Friend,'' *Newsbytes News Network*,'' November 6, 1998.
''Platinum Entertainment CEO: E-Commerce Perfect for Music,'' *Dow Jones News Service*, July 15, 1998.
''Platinum Entertainment, Inc. Acquires One of the Largest Independent U.S. Record Companies, Intersound Inc.,'' *Business Wire*, November 13, 1996.
Rothschild, David, ''River North Records Lands Peter Cetera,'' *Chicago Tribune*, October 29, 1993.
Scully, Michael, ''Minor Players Could Have Major Impact,'' *Tennessean*, November 24, 1999.
Ward, Angela, ''Only Happy Problems for Platinum's General Counsel,'' *Corporate Legal Times*, November, 1994.
Williams, Elisa, ''Companies Promise to Deliver CD Music to Home Computers via Internet,'' *Chicago Tribune,* April 30, 1998.
Wolinsky, Howard, ''Tapping Digital Music,'' *Chicago Sun-Times*, July 12, 1999.

—Rebecca Stanfel

Plexus Corporation

55 Jewelers Park Drive
P.O. Box 156
Neenah, Wisconsin 54957-0156
U.S.A.
Telephone: (920) 722-3451
Toll Free: (877) 733-7260
Web site: http://www.plexus.com

Public Company
Incorporated: 1979
Employees: 3,150
Sales: $492.4 million (1999)
Stock Exchanges: NASDAQ
Ticker Symbol: PLXS
NAIC: 334412 Bare Printed Circuit Board Manufacturing; 334418 Printed Circuit Assembly (Electronic Assembly) Manufacturing; 541330 Engineering Services; 541710 Research and Development in the Physical, Engineering, and Life Sciences

Plexus Corporation refers to itself as a "product realization service," that is, it helps corporations design and develop and manufacture electronic components and other products. The company is organized into two operating units: Plexus Technology Group and Plexus Electronic Assembly. The Technology Group provides product development engineering, prototyping, and test development services. Electronic Assembly provides manufacturing and after-market support services. Together, these two operating units offer a full range of product realization services, including: hardware and software design; printed circuit board design; prototyping services; new product introduction; material procurement and management; printed circuit board and higher level assembly; functional and in-circuit testing; final system box build distribution; after-market services. Plexus has three types of facilities that are used in the product realization process: design centers, protocenters, and manufacturing centers. The company's major markets include medical (31 percent of 1999 sales), networking/telecommunications (24 percent), industrial (22 percent), computer (14 percent), and avionics/other (nine percent).

In 1999 Lucent Technologies Inc. accounted for 16 percent of Plexus's sales, and General Electric Co. for 12 percent.

1980s Origins

Plexus was incorporated in Wisconsin in 1979 and began operations in 1980. The company was founded by Peter Strandwitz, John Nussbaum, and a group of other entrepreneurs, interested in a venture to design and build computer circuit boards by contract. Located in the eastern Wisconsin city of Neenah, on Lake Winnebago, the new company found the bulk of their early work through contracts with IBM.

The business grew, and by 1987, Plexus reported revenues of $24.5 million. However, the company also reported a net loss of $1.3 million. Turnaround was quick, and the next year the company saw revenues of $53.2 million and net income of $393,000, a dramatic increase in sales of 117 percent. To effect this change, management had cut operating expenses as a percentage of sales by 50 percent. The company's stock, then traded over-the-counter, responded in 1989 by nearly doubling in the first six months. Sales in 1989 again rose substantially to $78.1 million.

By the end of the 1980s Plexus had organized its business among three subsidiaries. One, Technology Group Inc., was headquartered in Neenah, Wisconsin, and focused on electronic product development and testing. The other two subsidiaries were the company's dual contract production units, Electronic Assembly Corp. and Electronic Assembly Inc., with facilities in Neenah as well as in Richmond, Kentucky.

Quality Control Leads to Strong Sales in the 1990s

Strong sales growth continued in the 1990s as Plexus developed a reputation for quality control in producing its electronic circuit boards. With the quality of boards produced in the Far East and the Pacific Rim slipping in recent years, more companies were buying boards made in the United States. Sales in fiscal 1991 reached $120.4 million, representing a five-year growth rate of 26 percent.

By 1991 the two contract production units had been merged into one, Electronic Assembly Corp. The other subsidiary, Technology Group Inc., focused on product design and development. The company's customers ranged in size from giant IBM to a small Wisconsin-based maker of telecommunications devices for the deaf. The company's CEO and founder Peter Strandwitz told *The Business Journal-Milwaukee:* ''Three key factors in Plexus' success are state-of-the-art technology, a high-quality, motivated labor force, and the quality demands of its customer base.'' Analysts agreed that the quality of Plexus' technology was among the industry's best. Due to its board testing equipment, Plexus could test board designs even more thoroughly than some of its customers, according to one analyst.

For 1992 sales rose 32 percent to $157.4 million, while net income jumped 39 percent to a record $5.1 million. In 1993, however, sales were flat at $159.6 million, and net income plunged about 50 percent to $2.6 million. Analysts considered the results predictable and forecast improved sales for 1994. The company had completed work on its new 175,000-square-foot Advanced Manufacturing Center in Neenah. Costs associated with bringing the facility online had affected profits in 1993. The new facility added capacity in anticipation of future business from outsourcing by major electronic manufacturers. Major customers included IBM and GE Medical Systems.

Expansion and Alliances: 1995–2000

In 1995 Plexus expanded by hiring 500 people in the fourth quarter. Some of the new employees were hired through Wisconsin's Department of Vocational Rehabilitation, leading the company to hire workers with physical disabilities primarily for basic assembly jobs. Plexus also developed new training methods and established its Mentor Training Program, wherein volunteer mentors helped new employees through their first days and weeks at the company. Workforce diversity and training objectives became part of the company's strategic plan in 1996, and in 1998 Plexus was given the Governor's Exemplary Employer Award.

In 1997 Plexus gained marketing clout through a design and marketing agreement with Cadence Design Systems Inc., the world's largest software design company. Under the agreement, Cadence's 450-person sales force would market Plexus products and services to its customers. Plexus, with its large staff of engineers, provided the electronics industry with design, manufacturing, and testing services, but had a minimal sales force.

In April 1997 a new assembly plant in Green Bay, Wisconsin, began operations. The $22 million, 110,000-square-foot facility was built by Plexus on an Oneida reservation. Plexus

and the Oneida tribe collaborated on the building and equipment for the facility, which was financed and owned by the Oneidas but operated by Plexus. It was Plexus's third electronic manufacturing services plant in addition to plants in Neenah and Richmond, Kentucky. The Green Bay facility featured five cells; the first became operational in April 1997, and others could be brought on line as business increased. Plexus also opened a design center in Raleigh, North Carolina, in 1997.

To help it land corporate research and design contracts, Plexus formed alliances with other research and design companies. In addition to its alliance with Cadence Design Systems, Plexus formed an alliance with Adaptive Microwave, a digital compression company based in Fort Wayne, Indiana, with expertise in video compression. Another alliance was established with IDEO of Palo Alto, California, the world's largest private firm in industrial design and engineering. Plexus's longest-standing alliance was with Battelle Institute of Columbus, Ohio, a private research and development company with $1 billion in sales. For fiscal 1998 net sales were $396.8 million, with net income of $19.2 million. The company had about 2,400 employees.

In early 1999 Plexus expanded its Raleigh, North Carolina, design center, which was originally opened in September 1997. It also opened its third regional design center in Louisville, Colorado, near Boulder. The 14,000-square-foot facility was designed to house up to 60 engineers. Plexus began by transferring a core team of eight to ten engineers from Neenah, then hired more engineers in Colorado. Overall, Plexus planned to double its engineering staff to 500 nationally over the next three years. The company's geographic expansion was guided in part by a desire to locate in high quality-of-life areas that would attract highly qualified technical candidates. Future expansion plans included the West Coast, Boston, Texas, and Europe. Expansion was seen as necessary to win contracts from global corporations.

In mid-1999 Plexus acquired SeaMED, a medically focused electronic design and manufacturing services provider in the Seattle, Washington, area. The acquisition added 135 engineers and support personnel to the company's Design Center staff. SeaMED's customers included Boston Scientific, Johnson & Johnson, Medtronic, and Novoste. Later in the year Plexus acquired printed circuit board assembly production facilities in the Chicago area from Shure Inc. for the RF/wireless technology market.

In addition to expanding its research, development, and production capabilities, Plexus continued to develop new technologies. Late in 1999 the company announced it had designed an inexpensive radio module that allowed computers to communicate by radio wave from ten miles apart, compared to ten feet permitted by current technology. In addition, the high frequency wireless band used in this new technology could send 10 to 20 times the amount of data that existing systems could handle. The technology also allowed computers within the confines of a building to communicate several hundred feet apart. Using this technology computers would be able one day to communicate directly with one another in real time while bypassing all wired infrastructures.

Plexus has focused on the high-end, low-volume aspect of the electronics business, which has resulted in smaller sales

Key Dates:

1979: Plexus is incorporated as a Wisconsin corporation.
1988: Sales increase 117 percent, and company turns a profit.
1994: A new 175,000-square-foot Advanced Manufacturing Center in Neenah is completed.
1999: Company acquires SeaMED, an electronic design and manufacturing services provider for the medical market.
2000: Company acquires a manufacturing facility in Mexico, the company's first expansion outside the United States.

growth than companies focused on high-volume commodity electronics have realized. As a result Plexus's stock was not given a high valuation by Wall Street and was considered undervalued by investors during 1999. However, by March 2000 the company's stock price had jumped from $34 a year ago to about $56, and Plexus's market capitalization exceeded $1 billion for the first time.

Plexus's high degree of engineering skill made it a leader in supplying contract engineering and manufacturing as well as design and testing services to the electronics industry. As the company sought to expand its capabilities, it hoped to establish an overseas presence; at the end of 1999 all of its facilities were located in the United States. Through acquisitions and internal expansion, the company planned to increase its engineering staff and open facilities in Mexico and Europe. In May 2000 it completed the acquisition of the electronic contract manufacturing operations of Elamex, S.A. de C.V. in Juarez, Mexico, for approximately $54 million. Plexus would operate two facilities there, a newly constructed 210,000-square-foot electronic manufacturing plant and a 40,000-square-foot service center. It was the company's first expansion outside the United States.

Principal Subsidiaries

Plexus Electronic Assembly Corporation; Plexus Technology Group, Inc.; SeaMED Corporation.

Principal Competitors

ACT Manufacturing Inc.; Benchmark Electronics Inc.; Jabil Circuit Inc.; Solectron Corp.

Further Reading

Boardman, Arlen, "Neenah, Wis.-Based Plexus Corp. Develops Computer Radio Module," *Knight-Ridder/Tribune Business News,* November 18, 1999.
——, "The Post-Crescent, Appleton, Wis., Arlen Boardman Column," *Knight-Ridder/Tribune Business News,* March 9, 2000.
——, "Wisconsin-Based High-Tech Firm Needs Mexican Labor for Expansion," *Knight-Ridder/Tribune Business News,* March 5, 2000.
——, "Wisconsin's Plexus Signs Deal with Software Design Giant," *Knight-Ridder/Tribune Business News,* February 13, 1997.
Dries, Michael, "Plexus Corp.," *Business Journal-Milwaukee,* January 29, 1994, p. 9.
Haber, Carol, "Oneida Tribe, Plexus Team on Plant," *Electronic News,* March 24, 1997, p. 46.
Hudson, Kris, "Firm to Open Electronics Design Center in Louisville, Colo., Business Park," *Knight-Ridder/Tribune Business News,* February 16, 1999.
"In Neenah, Wis., Plexus Tells Shareholders to Expect Bigger Projects," *Knight-Ridder/Tribune Business News,* February 13, 1998.
Kueny, Barbara, "Plexus Corp.," *Business Journal-Milwaukee,* July 25, 1992, p. 6B.
"Neenah, Wis.-Based Product Design Firm to Form Division in Colorado," *Knight-Ridder/Tribune Business News,* April 11, 1999.
"Plexus Corp.," *Business Journal-Milwaukee,* December 10, 1990, p. 19.
"Plexus Corp.," *Business Journal-Milwaukee,* July 31, 1989, p. S14.
"Plexus Corp.," *Business Journal-Milwaukee,* February 27, 1989, p. 24.
Schaff, William, "Give Plexus its Due," *InformationWeek,* September 13, 1999, p. 192.
Squires, Susan, "Plexus Wins Wis. Governor's Exemplary Employer Award," *Knight-Ridder/Tribune Business News,* June 4, 1998.

—David P. Bianco

Polaris Industries Inc.

1225 Highway 169 North
425 Lexington Avenue
Minnesota, Minnesota 55441
U.S.A.
Telephone: (612) 542-0500
Toll Free: 1-800-POLARIS
Fax: (612) 542-0599
Web site: http://www.polarisindustries.com

Public Company
Incorporated: 1954 as Hetteen Hoist & Derrick
Employees: 3,350
Sales: $1.32 billion (1999)
Stock Exchanges: New York Pacific
Ticker Symbol: PII
NAIC: 336322 Other Motor Vehicle Electrical and
  Electronic Equipment Manufacturing; 336612 Boat
  Building; 336991 Motorcycle, Bicycle, and Parts
  Manufacturing; 336999 All Other Transportation
  Equipment Manufacturing; 315228 Men's and Boys'
  Cut and Sew Other Outerwear Manufacturing; 315239
  Women's & Girls' Cut and Sew Other Outerwear
  Manufacturing

Polaris Industries Inc. is the largest manufacturer of snow-mobiles in the world and a major competitor in all-terrain vehicles (ATVs) and personal watercraft (PWC). It introduced a line of motorcycles in 1998. A pioneering force in the U.S. snowmobile industry, Polaris has since its inception enjoyed a strong reputation for quality and innovation. In 1989, for instance, the ''MacNeil-Lehrer News Hour'' called Polaris America's version of Mercedes-Benz.

The snowmobile industry leader has had its share of troubles during its history, however. In 1964 it nearly went bankrupt with the failure of the Comet, its first front-engine sled. During the late 1970s and early 1980s—a period of flagging sales and sell-offs that shook the industry as a whole—Polaris's future looked just as grim. A mid-1981 leveraged buyout that took the form of a

limited partnership prevented an otherwise imminent plant shut-down, but it was several years before Polaris was again running smoothly, this time as a revitalized company uniquely situated in a far leaner industry. A decade later, on December 23, 1994, Polaris completed its transformation from a limited partnership to a corporation. Headquartered in Minneapolis, Polaris operated manufacturing facilities in Minnesota, Wisconsin, and Iowa; it sold its products through approximately 2,000 North American dealers and a network of international distributors that marketed Polaris products in 116 countries around the world.

Arctic Origins

Polaris Industries was born in Roseau, a small community within a few miles of the northernmost point in the contiguous 48 states. This relatively remote area, located closer to Winnipeg, Manitoba, than to Minneapolis, inspired a climate of persistent innovation. Hetteen Hoist & Derrick, the forerunner of Polaris, was established in 1945 not for the manufacture of snowmobiles, however, but as a problem-solving job shop that became known for its fabrication of one-of-a-kind machinery for farmers in the region. Metal supply was at a premium at the end of World War II, and Edgar Hetteen was a skilled and inventive metal worker who could help people make do with what they had. Close friend David Johnson bought into the company while he was still serving in the navy, and Edgar's brother Allan Hetteen became a partner in the early 1950s. The company produced farm equipment, including straw choppers, portable grain elevators, and sprayers, but also depended on welding, grinding, and general repair work in the off-season.

Given the area's climate, the seasonal nature of the original business, and the fact that the founders were avid outdoorsmen, it was perhaps inevitable that the idea of snowmobile production would eventually transform the company. At the time, trips to fishing, hunting, and trapping areas in the winter had to be navigated by cross-country skis or snowshoes. Although inventors had been toying with the concept of snow machines since the 1920s, no reliable machine was readily available that could be used for such utilitarian purposes. Not until the 1950s, in large part because of the work of Johnson, did the general notion of creating a snow-going vehicle steered by skis begin to

Company Perspectives:

For almost 50 years, Polaris has been making machines that not only take you out there, they offer you a way out. A break from the routine. An escape from the ordinary. A moment of freedom. Snowmobiles came first in 1954 and quickly established a track record for advanced engineering. All-terrain vehicles followed in 1985, and since their introduction have set the standard for performance and innovation. 1992 saw the arrival of our personal watercraft and their unprecedented combination of power and comfort. Then in 1997, the Polaris RANGER was born, creating a whole new class of off-road utility vehicles. In 1998 we introduced Victory motorcycles and Cycle World *named them ''Best Cruiser''; in 1999* Motorcycle Cruiser *named them ''Cruiser of the Year.'' Of course, there's more to having a great time than just a great ride. So we also make parts and accessories designed to match our machines better than anything off the shelf, and a full line of garments and collectibles to stylishly capture the spirit of Polaris. We even offer financial services to make getting on our machines, and out into the open, easier than ever. Today, we have over $1 billion in sales worldwide, with engineering, manufacturing and distribution facilities all across the Midwest, and wholly-owned subsidiaries in Canada, Australia and New Zealand. It's been a fun ride, but then, after all these years, that's what we're all about.*

take shape as an industry in the United States. The company sold its first machine, a rough, virtually untested model, to an eager Roseau lumberyard owner in 1954. There was then no clear development plan to guide the company in this new area. Indeed, Edgar Hetteen was focused principally on selling the company's mainstay straw choppers and was lukewarm on the idea of snow machines until he saw the considerable interest generated when the company's first snowmobile customer demonstrated his powered sled.

Other orders followed that year and the company, which renamed itself Polaris Industries after the Latin name for ''north star,'' worked on improving the original concept with each consecutive model. Five machines were built in the winter of 1954–55 (all of which sold for less than $800), 75 in the winter of 1956–57, and more than 300 in 1957–58. The earliest models were called Sno-Cats, then Sno-Travelers, and were purchased primarily by outdoorsmen and utility companies. The sleds, propelled by a rear-end four-cycle engine, featured a toboggan-style front with a steering wheel and control levers. The early production line yielded one-of-a-kind machines, with components varying from one vehicle to the next. Skis were fabricated from bumpers of Chevrolets and steering wheels were appropriated from cars and trucks. Not surprisingly, the early machines were heavy and utilitarian. The Ranger rear-engine prototype and the Ranger model, manufactured between 1956 and 1964, formed the basis for Polaris snowmobile development.

When the bulk of the business shifted from fabricating farm equipment to designing, building, and testing snowmobiles, Edgar Hetteen was faced with a marketing problem. The company needed to broaden interest in the machine beyond utilitarian to recreational use. In short, Polaris had to convince people it would be fun to ride around in the middle of winter in a small, open-air vehicle. As Jerry Bassett wrote in *Polaris Partners,* ''Edgar Hetteen, as the first president, had to establish a sales network for a product that could only be sold in places which got snow to people who weren't totally certain that they needed his product.'' During a promotional trip Hetteen made in 1958, according to C.J. Ramstad in *Legend: Arctic Cat's First Quarter Century,* ''Hetteen got a real taste of the enormity of the problem that year when he set up an exhibit at a sport and travel show. Full of enthusiasm, he hustled show goers into his booth and eagerly showed them his new 'snow machine.' The curious public thought the machine somehow produced snow. They wanted to know which end the snow came out!''

Then, inspired by a friend's suggestion, Hetteen decided to make a snowmobile trip across Alaska to demonstrate both the durability and recreation his company's product offered. In March 1960 Hetteen and three others covered more than a thousand miles in about three weeks on one Trailblazer and two Rangers. The adventure yielded national publicity, but Hetteen was shocked to find that it had also created dissension at home. The negative response of some of the company's backers to Hetteen's trip, viewed by them as unnecessary, even frivolous, resulted in his selling out his controlling interest in Polaris. After a trip back up to Alaska he returned to Minnesota, this time west of Roseau to Thief River Falls, where he started the company that became Arctic Enterprises and later Arctco Inc., producer of Arctic Cat snowmobiles. His younger brother Allan, 31 at the time, became president of Polaris.

Running a nearly parallel course to Polaris was another company that contributed to the early industry history. In Canada, Joseph-Armand Bombardier developed and patented the sprocket-and-track assembly in 1937 and developed a one-piece molded rubber track in 1957. In 1958, the first year of Ski-Doo brand manufacturing, his company produced 240 snowmobiles, while Polaris manufactured about 300 that same year. The early 1960s marked the beginning of snowmobiling as a sport with the front-engined Bombardier Ski-Doo. Such vehicles were used for recreation as well as competitive racing. The testing of the first Polaris front-engined machine, the Comet, looked promising, but the 1964 model failed in production. The company's very survival was suddenly at stake.

Polaris co-founder David Johnson later joked, ''We made 400 machines and got 500 back.'' But it was the value of his word and reputation at the time that convinced the creditors to give the company breathing room and a second chance. Johnson and Hetteen redoubled their efforts by converting the Comets to rear-engined machines while they worked on a new front-end model. They hit pay dirt with the front-engined Mustang, which enjoyed successful production from 1965 to 1973 and brought the company into the sporty racing vehicle arena.

Corporate in the 1970s

After its one stumble, the company grew rapidly in the boom years of the 1960s. So pronounced was the growth that it outstripped the management skills of the owners, who had to decide whether to hire professional managers or sell the company. In 1968 Polaris was sold to Textron, a diversified company holding E-Z Go golf carts, Bell helicopters, Talon zippers, and Schaefer pens. The company kept Polaris in Roseau and continued snowmobile manufacturing, but also began limited research and development on watercraft and wheeled turf vehicles. Herb Graves of Textron became president and Johnson stayed on as vice-president to oversee production.

During the 1970s Polaris began to solidify its reputation for high-performance snowmobiles. In pre-Textron years, Polaris had purchased its snowmobile engines from a number of suppliers. With the entry of Textron, Polaris was able to bring on Fuji Heavy Industries as its sole supplier. Fuji engineers went to Roseau to work on building a high-quality engine specifically for Polaris. Increasingly, the Polaris product lines were being noticed. The TX Series set a standard for power and handling in racing and gained popularity with recreational riders. Introduced in 1977, the liquid-cooled TX-L was a strong cross-country racing competitor. Polaris also introduced the RX-L in the mid-1970s, which carried the first Independent Front Suspension (IFS) and produced winners on the racing circuits shortly after its debut. The 1970s also marked the opening of corporate offices in Minneapolis, with product development and production staying up north.

The sport of snowmobiling grew by leaps and bounds in the early 1970s; enthusiasts in the snowbelts of the United States and Canada now numbered more than a million. The growth rate for the industry was 35 percent per year, versus 20 percent for other recreation industry manufacturers. In 1970, 63 companies manufactured snowmobiles in the United States, Canada, Europe, and Japan. Bombardier held 40 percent of the market, with an additional 40 percent shared by Arctic Cat, Polaris, Scorpion, and Sno Jet. About one-third of the machines manufactured in North America in the early 1970s were made in Minnesota.

Factory-backed racing teams found Polaris support in the days of Allan Hetteen and Textron, but the death of a Polaris team member in 1978 effectively ended the program. From 1981 on the company sponsored a modified racing program with independent racers. Hill climbs, stock and modified oval racing, snow and grass drag racing, and cross-country endurance racing tested the limits of the machines and appealed to customers. Racing was an important part of engineering re-

search and development as well as public relations and product marketing.

Yet in the late 1970s, despite everything that favored the industry—including regular improvements in safety and an expanding trail system that would eventually rival the U.S. Interstate Highway System in total miles—the snowmobiling boom was about to go bust. Companies began shutting down or selling off their snowmobile divisions in the face of declining sales. Names such as Scorpion, AM, Harley-Davidson, Johnson & Evinrude, Chaparral, and Suzuki would no longer be seen on snowmobile nameplates. By 1980 even Arctic Enterprises, the number one manufacturer, was in trouble. High energy costs, economic recessions, snowless winters, and overexpansion eventually drove all but three manufacturers of snowmobiles out of business. Industry sales slid downhill from 500,000 units annually in the early 1970s to 316,000 in 1975; 200,000 in 1980; 174,000 in 1981; and 80,000 in 1983.

Management Buyout in 1981

Textron wanted out of the snowmobile business, too. Textron president Beverly Dolan, who had been president of Polaris during its first years with Textron, told Polaris's then-president, W. Hall Wendel, Jr., to sell off the company. A deal to sell the Polaris division to Canada's Bombardier fell through, however, because of the threat of antitrust action by the U.S. Department of Justice. Liquidation was on the horizon. This opened the door for a management group leveraged buyout led by Wendel, who believed that there was a market for snowmobiles and that seasonal snowfalls would rise again. Polaris Industries was created in July 1981, and a shutdown of the Roseau plant was avoided. (Still, the company began production with just 100 workers after the buyout.) Also at this time, plant workers voted the union out and Polaris proceeded to establish a Japanese labor model of worker participation, with a crew that had firsthand knowledge of the machines and their capabilities. Times were still tough, though: the 1982 product line consisted of the 1981 model with some detail changes, and barely more than 5,000 machines were built that season. The same year as the buyout, Polaris attempted to purchase Arctic Cat. When the deal failed, Arctic Cat shut down, leaving Polaris, at least for a while, as the only American snowmobile manufacturer.

The first years following the management buyout from Textron were lean and characterized by a skeleton factory crew and tight budgets. But the Textron debt was paid off ahead of schedule and the snowmobile line was expanded and improved. The company also expanded into Canada to become more price competitive and to create a stronger dealer network. Five years after the buyout the company had reached sales of $40 million and employed 450 people. A Polaris innovation of the early 1980s was the "Snow Check" early deposit program. Polaris encouraged its dealers with incentives to make spring deposits on machines for preseason delivery. For the first time snowmobiles were built to dealer orders rather than manufacturer forecasts, which had been resulting in excess inventory. Other factors helping the industry along at the time were advancements in clothing technology, winter resorts welcoming snowmobilers on winter vacations, and new engineering on the machines producing quieter, more reliable vehicles. By 1984 there were

20 million snowmobilers in the northern snowbelt and mountain regions using the vehicles for rescue and outdoor work as well as recreational and sporting events.

One of the highlights of the 1980s was the introduction of the Indy line of snowmobiles, which became so popular that other high-quality Polaris sleds, such as the Cutlass, were phased out. Good suspension, special features (such as handwarmers and reverse drive), powerful engines, and reliability all pushed Polaris into the number one position in the market. The Indy 500 was named the "sled of the decade" by Snowmobile magazine.

The 1990s and Beyond

Into the 1990s Polaris continued to improve the performance, ride, and reliability of its machines by introducing such features as the triple-cylinder and high-displacement engines, extra-long travel suspensions, and specialized shock absorbers. The machines of the 1990s were a long way from the industry's early noisy, pull-start models, with uncertain braking and questionable reliability. In 1990 Polaris held 30 percent of the snowmobile market, manufacturing 165,000 units. Arctco Inc. held 25 percent of the total market, followed by Yamaha and Ski-Doo (Bombardier, Inc.), both at 22.5 percent.

Just as the snow outside Polaris's doors had provided a proving ground for snowmobiles, the summertime swampland of the far north provided a place for testing wheeled turf vehicles. The company built and sold two-wheel tractor-tired bikes in the middle to late 1960s as it was testing diversification into such areas as lawn and garden products, single and two-person watercraft, and snowmobile-engined go-carts. The Textron acquisition and merger with E-Z Go golf carts ended formal ATV product development, so testing stayed underground until after the buyout. The company then tried but failed to sell private-label ATVs to other large companies. Still hoping to better utilize its manufacturing facilities, the company brought out two ATV designs, a three-wheel and a four-wheel with automatic shifting, which caught the interest and commitment of distributors. Added features such as racks and trailers appealed to farmers, ranchers, and lawn maintenance workers. ATVs made perfect sense for Polaris in that they shared engines and clutches with snowmobiles, could be marketed through the same dealers, and represented a seasonal line manufactured in fall and winter months for sale in the summer, just the opposite of snowmobiles.

When Polaris entered the ATV market all the major manufacturers were Japanese, led by Honda. Polaris ATVs, a combination recreation-utility vehicle, avoided direct competition with the leaders. The majority of the two million ATVs in use in the mid-1980s was in the United States and Canada. The first production run of the Polaris ATVs was a resounding success and quickly sold out to dealers. Eventually, production of three-wheel vehicles would be curtailed by all manufacturers, in response to reports of rising accidents and deaths and action by the Consumer Product Safety Commission. Polaris ceased manufacture of its three-wheel adult version after its first year of ATV production. In 1990 the retail cost of a four-wheel ATV ranged from $2,400 to $4,000 and Polaris controlled about seven percent of a shrinking market. By the end of 1993,

however, ATV sales made up 26 percent of entire sales by product line. ATV manufacture was now year-round, with a dedicated production line, and had the potential to surpass snowmobile production. Because of marketing and distribution that now extended beyond the snowbelt to tractor, lawn and garden, used car, and motorcycle dealers, Polaris had become a key national as well as international player in the broader market of recreational vehicles.

Polaris introduced its first personal watercraft (PWC) in 1990, becoming the first major U.S. company to enter that industry. The recreational vehicle started off with a splash due to its speed and handling. Just as it had in snowmobiles and ATVs, Polaris emphasized machine stability, coming up with an entry in the market that was wider than most and was a sit-down rather than stand-up model, which by then was declining in popularity. In the late 1980s personal watercraft was the growth segment of the marine industry and the trend was toward machines requiring less athletic ability and targeting a broader age range. The recreational vehicle was similar to the snowmobile and the ATVs in terms of engine type and channels of distribution. By testing competitors' products Polaris identified the qualities it wanted in its entry: a machine that was fast and fun to drive, with good handling and stability, as well as better boarding in deep water than the competitors'. The company's first model was a success and drew high-income, first-time buyers. By the end of 1993 PWC made up nine percent of total Polaris sales.

In 1994 Polaris employed 2,400 people companywide, had a sister plant in Osceola, Wisconsin, and was planning another plant in Iowa. Polaris Canada, a wholly owned subsidiary, provided 25 percent of total sales, or about $100 million. Since 1991, $70 million had been spent in plant improvements and new product development. David Johnson, the only person to see Polaris through all its incarnations, commented in Bassett's retrospective, "The biggest strength of Polaris is the people. . . . Everybody who's involved at Polaris, whether it's with the watercraft, or with the ATVs or the snowmobiles, they want to make the best machine they know how." Polaris's partnership with its employees meant not only sharing in making the best product possible, but sharing in the benefits. Profit sharing began in 1982 with an average of $200 per employee. By 1993 employees shared $6.8 million.

In December 1994 Polaris converted from a limited partnership to a public corporation for several reasons, including its desire to maximize shareholder value, its need for greater flexibility, and the approaching 1997 deadline for relinquishing its partnership tax status. The small company that began up along the Canadian border 40 years earlier had since transformed itself, through a series of rebirths, into a worldwide leader, with annual sales of more than $800 million.

Polaris had a great year in 1994: sales rose 56 percent to $826 million and profits climbed 66 percent to $55 million. Its share price fell drastically, however, after Barron's ran an article in January 1995 wondering whether a light snowfall would affect the company. Sympathetic analysts pointed to the new areas of the company's business that were not snow-related, such as ATVs and watercraft, where the company had captured market shares of 20 and 15 percent respectively.

In fact, Polaris had become the perfect diversification success story. In spite of *Barron's* worries, all product segments set records in 1995, leading to total sales of more than $1 billion in 1995. Revenues had more than tripled in five years. Snowmobiles accounted for 40 percent, down from 67 percent in 1990.

Polaris opened its own engine plant in Osceola, Wisconsin in October 1995. The company had previously bought Japanese engines from Fuji Heavy Industries and had set up the Robin ATV engine joint venture in Hudson, Wisconsin in February 1994. The new plant gave Polaris some flexibility in dealing with currency fluctuations.

Another record year followed in 1996, although snowmobile and watercraft sales slipped. Still, snowmobiling was reaching new highs in popularity, revitalizing the economy of sleepy Minnesota resorts that would otherwise have closed for the winter. Other related businesses popped up, supplying snowmobile trailers or hauling the finished goods to market. Demographics and a lack of new trails led some to believe that the boom was coming to an end, however. Concurrent with the rediscovery of the snowmobile was an explosion in personal watercraft sales, which tripled between 1991 and 1996. Makers of larger powerboats felt that they were spoiling their business, though.

As the revitalized Harley-Davidson could not make its famous "hogs" fast enough, Polaris decided to develop its own big, heavy cruiser class motorcycle priced below the Harleys. Made in Iowa, the first Victory V92C rolled off the line on July 4, 1998. Wendel noted that the company had already shown it could compete with the Japanese bike makers in other categories. The Harley mystique would be difficult to approach, although the Victory bikes received generally enthusiastic reviews. Others began making American bikes at the same time: Big Dog Motorcycles of Sun Valley, Idaho, the reborn Excelsior-Henderson Motorcycle Mfg. Co. of Minnesota, and numerous smaller shops.

W. Hall Wendel, Jr., stepped down as CEO in May 1999, remaining a major shareholder as well as board chairman. Thomas Tiller, president and chief operating officer since the previous summer, became the new CEO. Tiller had spent 15 years at General Electric, learning from its legendary leader, Jack Welch. When appointed, Tiller announced plans to double the company's sales within four years.

Polaris had made huge strides growing organically, and several record years gave Polaris plenty of cash for acquisitions. But the company stuck with joint ventures instead. In 2000, it contracted with Karts International Inc. to make a line of Polaris mini-bikes and go-carts for children. It also marketed a child-sized snowmobile to compete with Arctic Cat's Kitty Cat and began developing a snowmobile video game for kids to "burn Polaris into their beautiful little brains," as Tiller put it. Polaris took aim at hunters with a special camouflaged ATV co-branded with Remington firearms. Other promotions with DeWalt Industrial Tool Co. and NASCAR helped publicize the brand in the South.

In March 2000, Edgar Hetteen and David Johnson, joined by current Polaris chief Tom Tiller and seven others, recreated the epic Alaskan journey Hetteen had taken 40 years earlier to promote the snowmobile. This time the trip raised funds for Lou Gehrig disease research.

Dark clouds were just over the horizon: the Department of the Interior banned snowmobiles from most national parks in May 2000. "The snowmobile industry has had many years to clean up their act and they haven't," said an official. Polaris and Arctic Cat countered that both had been working to cut emissions and noise for years, but were waiting for the Environmental Protection Agency to announce a new emissions standard in September 2000 before retooling their production lines. The Park Service also complained of the potential for disturbing wildlife that snowmobiles offered.

Principal Subsidiaries

Polaris Industries Inc. ("Polaris Delaware"); Polaris Real Estate Corporation of Iowa, Inc.; Polaris Real Estate Corporation; Polaris Industries Export Ltd. (Barbados); Polaris Industries Ltd. (Canada); Polaris Acceptance Inc.; Polaris Sales Inc.; Polaris Sales Australia Pty Ltd.

Principal Operating Units

All-Terrain Vehicles; Snowmobiles; Personal Watercraft; Parts, Garments and Accessories.

Principal Competitors

Arctco Inc.; Bombardier Inc.; Honda Motor Co., Ltd.; Suzuki Motor Corp.; Yamaha Corp.

Further Reading

Bassett, Jerry, *Polaris Partners,* St. Paul, Minn.: Recreational Publications, Inc., 1994.
Beal, Dave, "Can Roseau County Keep It Up?," *St. Paul Pioneer Press,* March 4, 1991.
——, "For Snowmobile Makers, Storm of Century Timely," *St. Paul Pioneer Press,* November 11, 1991.
Dapper, Michael, "Snow Pioneers," *Snowmobile,* November 1994, pp. 74–93.
Feyder, Susan, "Making Waves," *Star Tribune* (Minneapolis), January 5, 1998, p. 1D.
Foster, Jim, "Polaris Now a Public Corporation," *Minneapolis Star Tribune,* December 23, 1994, p. 3D.
Geiger, Bob, "What's with Polaris Industries Shifting Among Ad Agencies?," *Star Tribune* (Minneapolis), November 13, 1995, p. 2D.
Hendricks, Dick, "Snowmobiling: The Next Generation," *Snowmobile,* January 1995, p. 13.
Hetteen, Edgar, and Jay Lemke, *Breaking Trail,* Bemidji, Minn.: Focus Publishing, 1998.
Kennedy, Tony, "Polaris Revs Up for Motorcycles," *Star Tribune* (Minneapolis), February 20, 1997, p. 1D.
McCartney, Jim, "Polaris Will Dive into Water Scooter Market Next Year," *St. Paul Pioneer Press,* August 2, 1991.
Opre, Tom, "Snowmobiles at 25," *Outdoor Life,* January 1984, pp. 18–20.
"Polaris Snowmobile Celebrates Birthday," *St. Paul Pioneer Press,* July 17, 1989.
Peterson, Susan, "Nature vs. Noise," *Star Tribune* (Minneapolis), May 15, 2000, p. 1D.
——, "Revving Up Polaris," *Star Tribune* (Minneapolis), May 18, 1999, p. 1D.

Phelps, David, "Toro, Polaris Find Right Product Mix; Two Companies Diversify Successfully While Remaining Strong in Old Lines," *Star Tribune* (Minneapolis), January 8, 1996, p. 1D.

Poole, Wiley, "Built in the U.S.A.," *Trailer Boats,* September 1992, pp. 60–61.

Ramstad, C. J., *Legend: Arctic Cat's First Quarter Century,* Deephaven, Minn.: PPM Books, 1987.

Rubenstein, David, "Wheels of Fortune," *Corporate Report Minnesota,* March 1986, pp. 58–62.

"The Ruckus Over Snowmobiles," *Changing Times,* January 1980, p. 16.

Schonfeld, Erick, "Catching a Killer Wave with Polaris," *Fortune,* May 29, 1995, p. 155.

Skorupa, Joe, "Ski-Doo: 50 Years on Snow," *Popular Mechanics,* January 1992, pp. 94–95.

"Splendor in the Snow," *Corporate Report Minnesota,* April 1977, pp. 10–12.

Stevens, Karen, "That Vroom! You Hear May Not Be a Harley," *Business Week,* October 20, 1997, p. 159.

Taylor, John, "Built in Iowa: Polaris Unleashes Victory, a Cruiser-Class Motorcycle," *Omaha World-Herald,* Bus. Sec., July 10, 1998, p. 18.

"Those Wild Snowmobilers—Expensive Fun in More Ways Than One," *Corporate Report Minnesota,* February 28, 1970, pp. 8–10.

"Those Wild Snowmobilers—Where Do They Go from Here?," *Corporate Report Minnesota,* March 14, 1970, pp. 8–10.

Youngblood, Dick, "He Made Winters Fun and Brought Factories to Roseau, Thief River Falls; Edgar Hetteen Formed Polaris and Arctic Enterprises," review of *Breaking Trail* by Edgar Hetteen and Jay Lemke, *Star Tribune* (Minneapolis), February 4, 1998, p. 2D.

——, "Hetteen's Back in the Driver's Seat; This Times He's Finding Big Demand for New All-Season Vehicle," *Star Tribune* (Minneapolis), October 7, 1996, p. 2D.

—Jay P. Pederson
—updated by Frederick C. Ingram

PR Newswire

810 Seventh Avenue, 35th Floor
New York, New York 10019
U.S.A.
Telephone: (212) 832-9400
Fax: (212) 541-6414
Web site: http://www.prnewswire.com

Wholly Owned Subsidiary of United News & Media plc
Incorporated: 1954
Employees: 1,200
Sales: $100 million (1998 est.)
NAIC: 514110 News Syndicates

PR Newswire is among the world leaders in the electronic delivery of information directly from companies, institutions, and agencies to news media and other organizations throughout the world. A subsidiary of United News & Media plc, PR Newswire operates through 35 worldwide bureaus. It also has an exclusive partnership with Canada NewsWire Ltd. and numerous international affiliates. The company transmits an average of 1,200 news releases per day as well as numerous multimedia broadcasts and other information, using wire, fax, satellite, and Internet technologies to deliver news and information supplied by more than 40,000 client companies, institutions, public relations agencies, and other clients. The firm's clients, which pay an annual membership fee, are able to choose from a variety of distribution options. In the late 1990s, PR Newswire added several services for public relations professionals, including distributing news releases, setting up conference calls on the World Wide Web, providing investor relations web sites, and cybercasting press conferences, annual meetings, and other events. In 2000, PR Newswire began offering clients the capability to track online news release activity, enabling them to monitor hits, rumors, perceptions, and discussions of their companies on the Internet.

Origins as Local Newswire Service: 1950s–60s

PR Newswire was founded in 1954 by Herbert Muschel, the originator of *TV Guide,* to deliver news releases from public and

investor relations practitioners to the news media. Prior to the founding of PR Newswire, delivering news releases to the media was a time-consuming and uncertain process. Each newspaper or periodical had to be serviced individually. PR Newswire enabled public and investor relations professionals to deliver their news items to several publications at once.

At first, PR Newswire delivered news releases from public relations agencies, corporations, and other sources to 12 major news media in New York City over a private teleprinter network. Clients would submit one copy of their news release to PR Newswire, which in turn would provide simultaneous delivery over its newswire for a flat fee of $15 per day.

In the 1960s there was a general newspaper strike in New York City, and during the strike PR Newswire expanded its teleprinter circuit to newspapers in Philadelphia, Washington, and Pittsburgh. The company continued to operate during the 1960s as a public relations wire service, delivering news release content from client companies, institutions, and agencies, to newspapers on its circuit.

Changes in Ownership: 1970s–80s

In 1971 PR Newswire was acquired by Western Union Corporation. For the next ten years it operated as a wholly owned subsidiary of Western Union, during which time its distribution expanded to include the investment community across the United States. Then in 1982 the company was acquired by United News & Media Group plc of London, England. It would continue as a wholly owned subsidiary of this new parent company.

In the mid-1980s PR Newswire began building a national distribution network. It acquired local wire services and opened more bureaus across the United States. At the end of the decade PR Newswire had 17 bureaus and about 15,000 clients. In 1990 it acquired Publicity Central of Minnesota. With the 1997 acquisition of Southwest Newswire in Dallas and Public Relations News Service in Chicago—the two largest remaining wire operations in the United States—PR Newswire had completed its national distribution network. It was able to reach 22,000 media outlets and one million financial institutions directly.

New Services and Technologies: 1990s

NewsFax was one of the new services introduced by PR Newswire at the beginning of the 1990s. The service complemented the company's wire service by using fax transmissions to reach news media and other organizations that were not wire subscribers and did not have access to online wire services. NewsFax saved client companies the trouble of doing their own in-house faxing of news and information.

Another new service introduced late in 1989 was called Entertainet, an entertainment-oriented news and sports network. Entertainet was formed jointly by three companies: PR Newswire, ABC Television Networks, and computer networking company Indesys Inc. The service delivered sports and entertainment news releases from client companies into editorial computers at 16 newspapers. The system utilized both satellite and FM subcarrier channels to broadcast time-sensitive text and data to multiple locations.

Another service introduced in 1991 was called US Bankline. PR Newswire partnered with Federal News Service to transmit the full text of testimony on Capitol Hill in Washington, D.C., regarding major banking reforms. The service provided transcripts of congressional banking hearings as well as all banking-related news releases from banks, financial institutions, and government agencies that were carried on PR Newswire. The US Bankline service also allowed subscribers to post responses and announcements on an electronic bulletin board.

PR Newswire began offering a new clipping service in 1995 called eWatch. This new service gave clients the capability of tracking what was said about them on the Internet, in electronic messages posted in public discussion groups and on commercial bulletin boards. The service proved popular, and in 2000 PR Newswire acquired eWatch, the company that provided the service, from WAVO Corp.

By 1997 PR Newswire had created a web site that could be used by journalists to access corporate news releases. A "Today's News" section contained all news releases from the previous 72 hours. Visitors to the site could search the database by industry, company, stock symbol, and state. Another section, "Company News," offered a searchable database containing one year's worth of corporate news releases. PR Newswire subsequently upgraded its web site and created a journalists-only PRN Press Room site in addition to the PR Newswire home page.

With the exponential growth of the Internet and e-mail in the second half of the 1990s, PR Newswire made a series of acquisitions that enabled it to offer a range of new, interactive services to its clients. These acquisitions included ProfNet in 1996, NEWSdesk International in 1998, Two-Ten Communications in 1999, and eWatch in 2000. ProfNet is a service that connects journalists with experts in different fields. Following its acquisition, ProfNet continued to operate as a wholly owned subsidiary of PR Newswire. The acquisition of eWatch expanded PR Newswire's core business into online measurement and results monitoring. Using eWatch, customers could track hits, rumors, perceptions, and discussions of their companies and products on the Internet.

The acquisition of NEWSdesk International and Two-Ten Communications was part of an international expansion strategy for PR Newswire. NEWSdesk International is a service that allows the tracking of online news release activity. It was merged into PR Newswire's European operations. Two-Ten was the largest distributor of corporate news in the United Kingdom. It gave PR Newswire a base for expanding into the public and investor relations markets in Europe. Following the acquisition of Two-Ten for $27.2 million, it was merged with NEWSdesk into PRN Europe.

In 1999 PR Newswire partnered with two other firms, PR Services Inc. and Computer Directory Service, to offer a quick and inexpensive news release service for smaller companies mainly in high-tech fields. PR Services would provide news release writing services through its online Press Release Factory, where client companies could provide basic information and have their news release written for them. PR Newswire then provided distribution to media and financial companies. Computer Directory Service, an Internet directory of technology companies in Michigan, provided a pool of potential clients.

Also in 1999 PR Newswire added video news release services and launched the investor relations web site service vIRtual IQ. vIRtual IQ allowed companies to provide financial data online on web pages developed and housed by PR Newswire. Traffic was driven to the site through hot links on other high-traffic investment-related web sites.

In March 2000 Charles H. Morin became president and CEO of PR Newswire. He had joined PR Newswire in 1989 as its chief financial officer and had served in 1999 as president of the company's American division. Morin replaced Ian Capps, who had served as president and CEO of PR Newswire since 1991, capping a media career that spanned more than four decades.

According to the 1999 annual report of its parent company, United News & Media, PR Newswire enjoyed good growth in the United States as well as internationally. PR Newswire's revenues increased by 32 percent during 1999. The company was making good progress online and was in the process of establishing a leadership position in Europe. In its nearly 50 years of existence, PR Newswire has evolved from a local wire service based in New York City to an international information distributor and Internet company. As new technologies have impacted the way news and information are distributed to the news media and other organizations, PR Newswire has grown and expanded to offer cutting-edge news services.

Principal Subsidiaries

PRN Europe (United Kingdom).

Principal Competitors

Business Wire; Medialink; Canada NewsWire Ltd.

Further Reading

Bottoms, David, "Who Says What about Your Company," *Industry Week*, November 6, 1995, p. 51.

"Charles Morin to Succeed Ian Capps as CEO of PR Newswire," *PR Newswire*, May 31, 2000.

Davis, Riccardo A., "Fast Facts by Fax: PR Wire Services Expand Business," *Philadelphia Business Journal*, April 2, 1990, p. 17B.

"Ian Capps," *Television Digest*, November 4, 1991, p. 9.

Miles, J.B., "Firms Turn to VSAT for New Broadcasting Network," *PC Week*, June 26, 1989, p. 54.

"New US Bankline Service Covers Proposed Banking Legislation," *Online*, September 1991, p. 12.

Noack, David, "Corporate Press Release Web Sites," *Editor & Publisher*, May 17, 1997, p. 34.

"PR Newswire Acquires Internet Monitor eWatch from WAVO Corp.," *PR Newswire*, January 25, 2000.

"PR Newswire Buys UK News Service," *Editor & Publisher*, June 12, 1999, p. 24.

Smith, Jennette, "Small Firms Can Get PR Power on the Web," *Crain's Detroit Business*, March 15, 1999, p. 13.

—David P. Bianco

Publishers Group, Inc.

1700 Fourth Street
Berkeley, California 94710
U.S.A.
Telephone: (510) 528-1444
Toll Free: (800) 788-3123
Fax: (510) 528-3444
Web site: http://www.pgw.com

Private Company
Incorporated: 1976 as Publishers Group West
Sales: $120 million (1999 est.)
Employees: 250
NAIC: 42292 Book, Periodical and Newspaper
   Wholesalers

Publishers Group, Inc. (PGI) is the largest distributor of books from independent publishers in the United States. The company's two divisions include Publishers Group West (PGW) and Avalon Publishers Group. PGW, originally the company's only business, handles distribution and accounts for three-fourths of revenues. The 150 publishers it represents include Grove/Atlantic, Kelley Blue Book, Feral House, New World Library, and the National Geographic Society. Its sister company, Avalon, was formed in 1994 to invest in companies that PGW distributes. These include Carroll & Graf, Thunder's Mouth Press, and John Muir Publications, which are now wholly owned, as well as a number of others. The privately held company is still run by some of its early investors including president, chairman and CEO Charlie Winton, his brother, COO Michael Winton, and CFO Randall Fleming.

1970s Origins

The origins of PGI date to 1976 when math textbook publisher Page Ficklin Publications, of Palo Alto California, formed a subsidiary called Publishers Group West. PGW's purpose was to distribute books from so-called ''small press'' publishers. One of the new operation's sales representatives was Charlie Winton, a graduate of Stanford University's film school who had first been hired by owner Jerry Ficklin to unload trucks. Winton did well in his new job, and was made sales manager for PGW within six months. After a period of modest growth, PGW was purchased by Winton, Ficklin and two others from Page Ficklin in 1978. One of the company's key strategies was to develop sales through chain bookstores, which were not then well-stocked with small press titles.

In 1979 PGW moved its headquarters to Emeryville, California. Winton's brother Michael and former Stanford classmate Randall Fleming joined the small company's board of directors, also helping with the move, which required only a single U-Haul truck. The company expanded dramatically later in the year when PGW's presentation at the American Booksellers Association meeting in Anaheim, California, brought a number of new publishing clients into the fold. Titles distributed by PGW jumped from 70 to nearly 300. One of these, Bernard Kamoroff's *Small Time Operation: How to Start Your Own Small Business, Keep Your Books, Pay Your Taxes, and Stay Out of Trouble,* proved to be a hit, selling 440,000 copies over the next decade. In 1981 company founder Jerry Ficklin left, selling his stake to the other investors.

The company's sales were continuing to grow rapidly, with revenues for 1982 hitting $2.5 million. At this time PGW's income was drawn equally from chains, such as B. Dalton and Waldenbooks, and independent booksellers. A major new distribution deal was inked in 1983, when Carroll & Graf Publishers came on board. The East Coast-based company, which specialized in mysteries, history, biography and fiction, broadened PGW's profile from that of an exclusively West Coast operation to one of national reach.

Setbacks, Triumphs in 1985

In 1985, PGW experienced a difficult year. Its employees, heretofore generally comprised of laid-back college students, were unionized by the Teamsters, dramatically altering the atmosphere of the workplace. On the sales front, PGW's revenues took a hit when the company was forced to take back abnormally high returns of stock from B. Dalton, which was undergoing its own travails. A saving grace for the year was PGW's first New York Times bestseller, *Diets Don't Work* by Bob

Schwartz, published by Breakthru Books. Sales of this title accounted for 15 percent of the company's $7 million in revenues for the year.

With this high-profile success, the company was able to gain access to more bookstores than ever before, but the book's heavy sales highlighted the need for a more formalized billing procedure. Previously, contracts for distribution were not formulated in a consistent manner, and from this time forward PGW began to charge a percentage of the net billing of each title it distributed. With the new arrangement the company would receive 24 percent of the net, with shipping to PGW's warehouse paid by the publisher, who would also pay for any promotional materials that were used.

The company maintained a sales staff which visited independent bookstores and chain buyers to promote new titles, typically with slide shows and catalogues for each category of books. PGW's publishers produced a wide range of titles, which included fiction, nonfiction, juvenile, travel, computer books and calendars. New Age books were particularly strong sellers. Sales of audiotapes, which PGW began handling in 1980, took off in the latter part of the decade, with Shakti Gawain's Creative Visualization selling more than 150,000 units. Other audiotapes distributed by PGW included those of Minnesota Public Radio, Vital Body, and Source Cassette Learning Systems.

PGW was also becoming more than just a distributor at this time. The company worked with its clients to suggest editorial changes and marketing angles, occasionally coming up with a concept that led to a new publication, such as *Gawain's Reflections in the Light: Daily Thoughts and Meditations*. PGW represented 200 publishers by the end of the 1980s, with ten percent or more of these changing in a typical year as companies were dropped and added. Some went out of business, while others were discontinued if PGW felt their products were not up to the distributor's overall standards.

In 1989, sales hit $25 million, the company having grown almost fourfold in less than ten years. This caused problems in the areas of shipping and order processing, however, and complaints were received from the Northern California Booksellers Association. The company responded by consolidating operations that had previously been in three locations into a single 65,000 square foot facility in the San Francisco Bay Area. New releases were also shipped to the east from Lebanon, Pennsylvania.

Further Growth in the 1990s

PGW's success continued in the early 1990s. Strong sellers included the hit *50 Simple Things You Can Do to Save the Earth,* as well as several books on the John F. Kennedy assassination. Despite the faltering U.S. economy, the company's sales continued to grow, reaching $42 million in 1992. Nonetheless, PGW was trimming its list of clients, moving to a total of 180 by late that same year. The company was marketing a total of some 720 new books and 50 audiotapes annually at this time, in addition to handling a "backlist" of several thousand. Revenues were split evenly between new releases and older titles. The company was also working on building its sales in Canada.

At the same time, PGW was moving toward more direct involvement with its clients. In the summer of 1992, the company purchased a minority interest in Moon Publications, whose books it had been distributing for some time. Within a year, PGW took over majority ownership, and this led to the formation of a new corporate structure for the company. In April 1994, a sister business to PGW was formed, Avalon Publishing Group, with ownership of both now held by a new entity, Publishers Group, Inc. Avalon's purpose was to invest in publishing companies, and those it became associated with were required to use PGW for distribution. This would ideally bring in a double revenue stream, both through the return on Avalon's investment and from PGW's distribution fees. The company's ownership remained private, with the Winton brothers and Randall Fleming still in charge of the company. A major step forward came in 1993 with the signing of a distribution deal with Grove Press and Atlantic Monthly Press, who would bring more general trade books to the company's lineup.

Over the next several years, Avalon began purchasing stakes in a number of other publishers, including Marlowe and Company, Thunder's Mouth Press, and Four Walls Eight Windows. In 1996, the unit purchased 20 percent of Carroll & Graf, which allowed that publisher to more aggressively seek out big new titles. The same year also saw PGW lose two major computer book publishing clients when Peachpit and The Waite Group were acquired by companies with different distribution arrangements.

In 1996 PGI experienced a drop in revenues, the first in its history, but it bounced back in 1997 following layoffs of 15 from its staff of 220 and a reduction in clients to 145. Net sales for the year topped $100 million, up 25 percent. Some of that higher total was due to the wild success of Charles Frazier's *Cold Mountain,* published by Grove/Atlantic, which sold more than 1.5 million copies in hardcover. Also during the year, acquisition funds were bolstered by an investment from outside firm Sycamore Hill.

Early in 1998, Avalon purchased the remaining portion of Carroll & Graf. The division's original description as an investment unit was no longer accurate, as it had become a full-fledged publisher. A new division of Avalon, Avalon Travel Publishing, was established and began issuing titles under the Moon Travel Handbooks and Foghorn Outdoors names, both formerly independent companies that had been acquired. The pending acquisition of John Muir, a Santa Fe-based travel publisher with such popular lines as the Rick Steves and Travel Smart series, was expected to further expand Avalon Travel's reach. Avalon also purchased the assets of Grove founder Barney Rosset's bankrupt Blue Moon Books. The company pledged to continue publishing the imprint, with Rosset remaining involved as a consultant. Blue Moon's focus was described as ''Victorian erotica.''

At this same time, PGW was moving distribution operations yet again, from the Bay area to Reno, Nevada, where a 272,000 square foot facility was established. East Coast distribution continued to be handled out of Lebanon, Pennsylvania. Sales to book chains now accounted for more than two-thirds of PGW's business, up substantially from the 50 percent figure of a decade earlier.

In the spring of 2000, another new publishing venture was announced at Avalon. An imprint, Nation Books, was to be launched by Avalon unit Thunder's Mouth Press, in conjunction with the Nation Institute, publisher of the Nation magazine. Projected subject areas were politics, culture and history. Titles were expected to be a mix of reprints and new books, with the first ones due to appear in the fall of 2000.

As it neared the end of its first quarter-century in business, PGI appeared to be in excellent health. The successful move into publishing in the 1990s had broadened the focus of the company and boosted its revenues, which peaked at $120 million for 1999. One-fourth of sales now came from the Avalon Publishing Group division, and its success enhanced that of distribution arm Publishers Group West, which shipped all Avalon product. Ongoing bookselling trends such as the growth of ''superstore'' chains and online sales sites appeared likely to ensure the company's success for some time to come.

Principal Divisions

Avalon Publishing Group; Publishers Group West.

Principal Competitors

Baker & Taylor Corporation; Ingram Industries, Inc.; National Book Network; Random House, Inc.; Simon & Schuster, Inc.; Time, Inc.

Further Reading

Farmanfarmaian, Roxane, ''Avalon Publishing Acquires John Muir Publications,'' *Publishers Weekly*, November 15, 1999, p. 11.
——, ''Big Year for PGW: Sales Now Top $100 Million,'' *Publishers Weekly*, February 23, 1998, p. 11.
Kinsella, Bridget, ''PGI: Primed for the Future,'' *Publishers Weekly*, February 28, 2000, p. 26.
Milliot, Jim, ''Fewer Clients Bring More Sales for PGW,'' *Publishers Weekly*, April 1, 1996, p. 17.
——, ''PGW Revamps to Align Itself Better With Market Conditions,'' *Publishers Weekly*, June 16, 1997, p. 14.
——, ''The Name of the Game is Distribution,'' *Publishers Weekly*, November 21, 1994, p. 48.
''Publishers Group West Forecasting Major Gains for 1994,'' *Publishers Weekly*, April 25, 1994, p. 15.
Reid, Calvin, ''Avalon, the 'Nation' to Launch Nation Books,'' *Publishers Weekly*, March 27, 2000, p. 14.
''Revenues Up 25% at Publishers Group West,'' *BP Report Simba Information Inc.*, February 3, 1992.
See, Lisa, ''Publishers Group West: Small Press Distributor Hits the Big Time,'' *Publishers Weekly*, May 29, 1989, p. 40–43
Taylor, Sally, ''Bay Area Publishing: 'A Work in Progress','' *Publishers Weekly*, March 27, 1995, p. S4.
Zeitchik, Steven M., ''Patricia Kelly – Publishers Group West,'' *Publishers Weekly*, April 5, 1999.

—Frank Uhle

Puma AG Rudolf Dassler Sport

Würzburger Strasse 13
D-91074 Herzogenaurach
Germany
Telephone: (49)(9132) 812-489
Fax: (49) (9132) 812-356
Web site: http://www.Puma.de

Public Company
Incorporated: 1948 as Puma Schuhfabrik Rudolf Dassler
Employees: 1,424
Sales: DM 1.4 billion ($714.9 million) (1999)
Stock Exchanges: Frankfurt/Main
Ticker Symbol: PUM.FSE
NAIC: 316211 Rubber And Plastics Footwear
   Manufacturing; 316219 Other Footwear
   Manufacturing; 315212 Women's, Girls', and Infants'
   Cut and Sew Apparel Contractors; 315211 Men's and
   Boys' Cut and Sew Apparel Contractors

Puma AG is among the world's leading manufacturers of athletic shoes, sportswear, and accessories. The company is perhaps best known for its soccer shoes and has sponsored such international soccer stars as Diego Armando Maradonna and Lothar Matthäus. The company also offers lines shoes and sports clothing, designed by Lamine Kouyate, Amy Garbers, and others. Since 1996 Puma has intensified its activities in the United States where it has a market share of eight percent. Puma owns 25 percent of American brand sports clothing maker Logo Athletic, which is licensed by American professional basketball and football leagues. The American entertainment group Monarchy/Regency owns 32 percent of Puma.

1920s Origins

In the small town of Herzogenaurach, not far from the German city of Nuremberg, two brothers laid the foundation for what would become the European capital of sportswear. Adolf and Rudolf Dassler were born into a poor family at the turn of the 19th century. Their father, Christoph Dassler, was a worker at a shoe factory, while their mother, Pauline Dassler, ran a small laundry business. At age 15 Rudolf Dassler started working at the same shoe factory as his father and soon showed the qualities of an entrepreneur. He was energetic, persistent, and ambitious, and he saved his hard-earned money instead of spending it right away. However, it was not until after World War I that he had a opportunity to prove himself in business. After the war, Rudolf Dassler took his first positions in business management, first at a porcelain factory and later in a leather wholesale business in Nuremberg.

In the early 1920s Rudolf Dassler decided to go back to Herzogenaurach and team up with his brother Adolf in a business partnership. Their company, which was incorporated as the Gebrüder Dassler Schuhfabrik in 1924, produced slippers and outdoor shoes. Rudolf Dassler ran the business, while Adolf took care of the technical operations and production. Soon they realized that there was not a particularly promising market for their shoes and so switched their focus to the manufacture of track shoes and football boots, a market that was just getting started at that time.

With a great deal of luck the company acquired its first major client, the sports club in Herzogenaurach, which ordered no fewer than 10,000 pairs of athletic shoes in 1925. Thus, despite the ongoing worldwide economic depression in the late 1920s, the Dassler company took off and gained a reputation among athletes and sporting goods companies. Half of all athletes at the Olympic Games in Amsterdam in 1928 wore Dassler shoes. In 1936, African-American track star Jesse Owens brought the company into the public eye when he won four gold medals at the Olympic Games in Berlin wearing Dassler shoes.

Three years later World War II broke out. Although the brothers could have given up for a number of reasons during the war, it was not this world-shattering event that led to the Dassler company's sudden end, but a homemade war of a different kind. In 1948, the two brothers had a serious falling-out, and they stopped talking to each other. Their company was split into two new companies: Adolf Dassler formed his own business named adidas, combining his nickname Adi with the first three letters of his last name; Rudolf Dassler set up his own shop called

Company Perspectives:

We live today in a world that is growing together, that changes ever faster, and that offers information in abundance. Puma is convinced that in such a world a brand's success depends on more than the quality of its products. Behind the products there must be a brand with its own unique personality. Only then will it distinguish itself from the competitor's "white mountains." Puma is determined to be one of those special brands that tackle things in a different way: unmistakable and convincing. In the midst of the white mountains Puma will be the "Blue Mountain." Puma will not be the biggest, but be visible in an unmistakable way, as the alternative sports brand.

Puma Schuhfabrik Rudolf Dassler. The two brothers had become competitors.

A number of world-class athletes, especially runners and soccer players, helped the young Puma brand gain acceptance. In 1950, at the first international soccer match after World War II, several German players wore the Puma "Atom" shoe. The Olympic Games in 1952 in Helsinki were a spectacular success for Puma and opened the British market to the young company. The American Olympic Committee made Puma its official shoe supplier in 1952 and again 1956. In 1952 the American women's 400-meter relay team won the Olympic gold medal in Puma running shoes. Puma's image was also carried around the world by the rising soccer star Pelé, the Brazilian "king of the stadium" who favored Puma's "King" shoes. After some early difficulty, the company's export business began to thrive. Puma shoes were shipped to 55 countries on five continents. The first licensed production line was opened in Austria. In 1959 Rudolf Dassler's firm was transformed into Puma Sportschuhfabriken Rudolf Dassler Kommanditgesellschaft, as Dassler's wife and his two sons, Armin and Gerd, became part owners of the firm. By 1962 Puma shoes were exported to almost 100 countries around the world.

Another Puma hallmark was product innovation. In 1960 Puma introduced a new technology for soccer shoes, using a vulcanization process to join the soles to the uppers. Soon 80 percent of all soccer shoes were manufactured with this technology. In the early 1960s Puma also developed running shoes with a uniquely shaped sole that supported the natural movement of the foot, based on the latest medical research of the time. In the late 1960s Puma was the first company to offer athletic shoes with a Velcro strap.

A Second Generation of Family Leadership in the 1970s

Rudolf Dassler died in 1974, and his son Armin A. Dassler, who since the early 1960s had been managing Puma's first foreign subsidiary in Salzburg, Austria, took his place. Twelve years later Puma went public and was renamed Puma AG Rudolf Dassler Sport. The company continued to introduce innovative products. In the mid-1970s Puma introduced the so-called S.P.A. technology—sport shoes with a higher heel

that relieved strain on the Achilles tendon. In 1982 Armin A. Dassler invented the Puma Duoflex sole, with special slots that increased the foot's mobility. In 1989 the company introduced the new Trinomic sport shoe system with hexagonal cells between sole and shoe that cushioned the runner's foot. Other innovations followed in 1990 and 1991. Inspector Shoes were shoes for kids with a "window" in their soles that allowed parents or trainers to observe whether the shoes were still the perfect fit during those years of rapid foot growth. The high tech Puma Disc System athletic and leisure shoes, which, instead of laces, used a disk that tightened a series of wires.

During the 1970s and 1980s, world famous athletes wore Puma products on their feet and bodies. High-jumper Dwight Stones broke the world record in Puma shoes three times in the years 1973 through 1976. In 1977 tennis player Guillermo Vilas won the French and U.S. Open in Puma shoes. Sprinter Renaldo Nehemia ran three world records in 100-meter hurdles between 1979 and 1981 in Puma spikes. In the early 1980s American football star Marcus Allen of the Oakland Raiders, as well as baseball greats Jim Rice and Roger Clemens, both of the Boston Red Sox, and George Brett of the Kansas City Royals, favored Puma shoes. American sprinter Evelyn Ashford won two gold metals in Puma shoes at the Olympic Games 1984 in Los Angeles. Tennis stars Martina Navratilova and the young German tennis talent Boris Becker won their events at the famous Wimbledon tennis competition in the mid-1980s in Puma shoes.

In 1991 the Swedish conglomerate Proventus AB bought all Puma common stock traded publicly in Frankfurt and Munich. That same year saw the founding of Puma International, a holding company for Puma's divisions in the Far East, Australia, Spain, France, Austria, and Germany, which were organized as independent profit centers. Despite the company's high profile and success, its profits had steadily declined until, in the early 1990s, they were nonexistent. It was not until 1994 that Puma again turned a profit, and Puma shareholders received a dividend for the first time in 1996.

New Management in the 1990s

In 1993 Puma's prospects looked anything but bright. The company had been in the red for almost a decade. In December 1992 parent company Proventus gave Puma a badly needed capital boost of DM 50 million. However, the company was competing in a stagnating market driven increasingly rapid product cycles that resulted in rising research and development and marketing costs, as well as losses through more frequent markdowns of older models. Although Puma scored high in brand name recognition, the company that in the 1980s had generated half of all sales with shoes in the lower price ranges was now struggling with its cheap image. Much like its competitor adidas, Puma tried to succeed by leaving low price markets that allowed only low profit margins; breaking into premium price markets—the traditional territory of American giants Nike and Reebok—became their new goal. It was perhaps too little, too late. This strategy at first resulted in significant losses in sales and market share. Adding to the company's problems was the fact that the successful introduction of the innovative Puma Disc System shoes in 1992 had been an expensive undertaking. By February 1993 it was clear that Puma needed new leadership, and parent company Proventus replaced Puma CEO

Stefan Jacobsson with Niels Stenboej, who came from Abu Garcia, another Proventus subsidiary that made equipment for sports fishing. However, only three month later Stenboej left amidst changes in upper management at the Proventus Helsingborg headquarters.

The arrival of 30-year old Jochen Zeitz hailed better times for Puma. At the time the youngest CEO of a European publicly traded company, Zeitz had an MBA from the European Business School and had traveled the world from Brazil to the United States, making his first mark as a product manager for Colgate Palmolive in New York and Hamburg. In 1990 he joined Puma and as a vice-president of international marketing and sales, where he was responsible for the company's international communications strategy and contributed significantly to the repositioning of the Puma brand. On year after Zeitz became CEO, Puma reported its first profit—DM 25 million—since its initial public offering in 1986. Under Zeitz's leadership the company initiated a fundamental, market-oriented "fitness program" that included rigorous cost cutting and reorganization measures. Inflexible structures were replaced, as was the case when the purchasing and product development departments were merged. Several warehouses were replaced by a central distribution center, and all departments became profit centers.

Puma's restructuring was but one part of its new success story. The other was its innovative marketing plan. At its core was the positioning of the Puma brand as an international performance sports brand for high-quality athletic shoes, sport textiles, and accessories. The company also based its innovative marketing concepts on the latest trend research, earlier ignorance of which had in part caused Puma's past downturns.

As a result, Puma launched the "Puma-Offensive '95," a marketing program with four key areas of activity. The first was based on the revival of the classic Puma suede shoes in the trendy clubs of New York, Los Angeles, and San Francisco. Puma developed a collection of shoe "originals" in various colors and matching textile collections targeting fashion and trend conscious youth. The second element of the marketing

offensive was the Puma "World Team." Top sports figures, such as German soccer star Lothar Matthäus and Jamaican sprinter Merlene Ottey, represented Puma products in an advertising campaign. The third piece in Puma's marketing mix was known as "Replica," a line of "fashions for fans" made available through sports retailers and soccer clubs.

One of the most successful elements of Puma's concerted marketing effort was the Street Soccer Cup, a worldwide street soccer competition first organized in 1994. The idea was developed in cooperation with Leonberg-based advertising agency Godenrath, Preiswerk & Partner (GPP). In 1993 the "street ball" wave had become immensely popular, as kids began storming Germany's courtyards, playgrounds, and parking lots to play pick-up games of basketball. Puma and GPP worked together to popularize street soccer, which was characterized by its favoring of technique and finesse over athleticism, its focus on casual fun rather than club regulations, and its preference for free style dress over uniforms. New rules for the game had to be established as well. Street Soccer was played in the street on a concrete or asphalt surface, not on a grass field. The 20-by-14 meter field was bordered by a fence. Four players plus one reserve player stormed two goals. Street Soccer was played in two age groups: ages 10 to 13 and ages 14 to 16.

The event campaign was carried out in cooperation with the major German sports magazine *Sport-Bild* and was supported by retail sporting goods stores. Other prominent German companies also joined Puma as sponsors. Germany's teenagers embraced the idea. In fact, demand far exceeded supply, and thousands of registrations could not be accepted. About 31,000 youngsters between age 10 and 16 kicked the ball in over 6,000 teams with names like "Magic," "Street Attacks," and "Turkish Brothers." Over 250,000 people watched the games at almost 200 events. The finals were played out in front of the Reichstag building in Berlin. The success of this innovative concept encouraged Puma to continue it on an international scale in 1995. The Street Soccer Cup '95 was also played in France, Hong Kong, and Tokyo. Puma introduced a new line of Street Soccer shoes and a collection of colorful clothing for players and spectators. All told, approximately 800,000 people watched 70,000 kids playing soccer at more than 400 events during this Puma event.

Mid-1990s and Beyond: Conquering Western Europe and North America

The year 1996 marked the end of the restructuring period Puma had been undergoing since 1993. This was followed by a period of new alliances and higher investment in international marketing and new product development. For the first time since the company went public, Puma shareholders saw a dividend in 1996 after the company achieved a three-year sales record in comparison to previous years. A Puma stock offering on the Frankfurt and Munich stock exchanges in June 1996 reduced the holdings of parent company Proventus Handels AB to 25 percent. A few months later the American movie production and distribution firm Monarchy/Regency bought a 12.5 percent stake from Proventus; it obtained the other 12.5 percent in 1997.

In 1999 Monarchy/Regency upgraded its shareholdings to 32 percent. The transaction made Monarchy/Regency Puma's biggest single shareholder. The interests of the new partners complemented one another in that Monarchy/Regency was interested in a platform from which it could build relationships in the sports world to diversify into new markets, while Puma CEO Zeitz believed that the entertainment company could help Puma with its marketing efforts.

In the second half of the 1990s Puma intensified its international activities. A new subsidiary—Puma Italia S.r.l.—began operations in 1997. Two years later Puma opened its new subsidiary Puma UK. However, the most important strategic market for Puma was the United States. In 1997 Puma generated about 80 percent of its sales outside Germany, and this figure shrunk to ten percent if license income was included. Puma's position was especially strong in Japan where ten percent of all license fees were collected. On the other hand, only a tiny fraction—4.5 percent—of Puma sales of approximately $846 million derived from the United States, representing less than one percent market share. A first step toward penetrating the largest sports market was the acquisition of Puma North America and the Puma trademark from Proventus AB in January 1996. In 1998 Puma sealed a long-term contract with the Women's Tennis Association (WTA), making Puma the official supplier of shoes and textiles for the WTA women's tour. In the same year Puma acquired a 25 percent share in Logo Athletic, one of the leading licensed suppliers for the American professional sports leagues. The deal started paying off in the very next year. In 1999 Puma became one of four suppliers of the American National Football League (NFL). Beginning in the 1999/2000 season 13 NFL football teams were wearing Puma, as well as nine National Basketball Association teams. When two Puma teams—the St. Louis Rams and the Tennessee Titans—competed for the Superbowl in January 1999, about 1.3 billion TV watchers worldwide were exposed to the Puma logo. Another novelty was the 1998 contract between Puma and then 16-year-old American tennis talent Serena Williams. The five-year contract included not only promotion activities for Puma-wear but also engagements in movie and music projects of Puma parent Monarchy/Regency. The strategy certainly seemed to be paying off in 1999 when Puma's U.S. sales increased by 60 percent, and, moreover, the company seemed well-positioned for the future.

Principal Subsidiaries

Puma United Kingdom Ltd.; Puma France S.A.; Puma (Schweiz) AG (Switzerland); Austria Puma Dassler GmbH; Puma North America, Inc. (United States); Logo Athletic Inc. (United States; 25%); Puma Benelux B.V. (Netherlands); Puma Canada, Inc.; Puma Italia S. r. l. (Italy); Puma Polska sp.zo.o (Poland); Puma Hungary Kft.; Puma Australia Pty. Ltd.; Puma New Zealand Limited; Puma Chile S. A.; World Cat Ltd. (Hong Kong); Puma Far East Ltd (Hong Kong).

Principal Competitors

adidas-Salomon AG; Nike, Inc.; Reebok International Ltd.; Fila Holding S.p.A.

Further Reading

"30 jähriger wird Vorstands-Chef," *HORIZONT*, May 7, 1993, p. 38.

Diekhof, Rolf, "Eine Katze zeigt die Krallen," *Werben und Verkaufen*, March 24, 1995, p. 102.

Fallon, James, "U.S. Film Producer Buys 12.5% Interest in Puma," *Daily News Record*, November 8, 1996, p10.

"Puma auf einer schwierigen Wegstrecke," *Süddeutsche Zeitung*, February 24, 1993.

Michaelis, Karin, "Puma wetzt die Krallen," *Werben und Verkaufen*, February 4, 2000, p. 106.

Rhymer, Rigby, "The Spat That Begat Two Empires," *Management Today*, July 1998, p. 90.

"Sportliches Comeback," *Werben und Verkaufen*, December 19, 1994, p. 50.

"Wir sind wie David im Kampf gegen Goliath," *Süddeutsche Zeitung*, December 8, 1997.

—Evelyn Hauser

RAG AG

Rellinghauser Strasse 1-11
D-45128 Essen
Germany
Telephone: (49) (201) 177-01
Fax: (49) (201) 177-3475
Web site: http://www.rag.de

Private Company
Incorporated: 1968 as Ruhrkohle AG
Employees: 65,200
Sales: DM 26.7 billion ($13.6 billion) (1999)
NAIC: 212111 Bituminous Coal and Lignite Surface
   Mining; 212112 Bituminous Coal Underground
   Mining; 212113 Anthracite Mining; 213113 Support
   Activities for Coal Mining; 325199 All Other Basic
   Organic Chemical Manufacturing; 42152 Coal and
   Other Mineral and Ore Wholesalers; 42181
   Construction and Mining (Except Oil Well)
   Machinery and Equipment Wholesalers

RAG AG is one of the world's leading hard coal producers and Germany's number one coal producer. Based in Germany, the company consists of an international group of more than 450 companies active in mining, coal trading, engineering, power generation, and chemicals, and has over 220 subsidiaries around the world. RAG's domestic coal and coke mining activities are managed by Deutsche Steinkohle AG. Its international mining activities, including the American coal producer Cyprus Amax Coal and the Australian Burton Coal Mine, are managed by RAG Coal International AG. STEAG AG is an power generation engineering firm. RÜTGERS AG is a producer of plastics, basic organic and specialty chemicals, and a construction firm. RAG's activities in the fields of environment and coal trading are organized through Saarberg AG. About two-thirds of RAG's revenues come from its domestic and international coal subsidiaries and one-quarter of total sales originate outside Germany. The three main RAG shareholders are German energy suppliers VEBA with 37.1 percent, VEW with 30.2 percent, and steel maker Thyssen Stahl AG with 12.7 percent of the share capital.

Origins in 1968

RAG's history is inextricably linked to the postwar history of the German coal industry. It was a history of reducing production of hard coal and closing down coal mines, determined by German economic politics. After World War II, Germany was confronted with a serious shortage of energy, due primarily to the destruction of many power plants and transmission systems during the war. Previously the coal industry was one of Germany's motors of economic growth—but it also fed the German war economy. The formerly powerful coal cartel was put under control of the occupation forces after the war. However, when the Western Allies gave up control over Germany, the German coal industry together with the West German government began making plans for a new coal conglomerate.

Hard coal had fueled German power generation for half a century, and in the mid-1950s the country was faced with a dilemma when coal production had surged so that stockpiles grew and sales plummeted. Three main factors contributed to this development. First, domestic coal had to compete with imported coal which was cheaper due to falling shipping costs. Second, cheap oil from the Middle East was replacing coal as a fuel. Third, the German energy and steel making industries, two of the main consumers of German coal, implemented new, more energy efficient technologies which radically cut the amount of coal needed.

By the middle of the 1960s it became clear that a fundamental structural change in Germany's energy industry was on its way and that, unchecked, it could lead to an economic and social crisis for the country. Most of Germany's coal mines and processing facilities were located in the Ruhr; an unregulated decline could have had serious consequences for the whole region. In 1968 the German government issued legislation aimed at the regulated reorganization of the German coal industry. At its core was the establishment on November 27, 1968 of Ruhrkohle AG—RAG for short—which was owned by 24 companies, including VEBA, Hoesch, Mannesmann, Thyssen, and Klöckner.

RAG became the national umbrella organization for 52 coal mines, 29 coke producers, and five briquette manufacturing plants with combined sales of DM 5.8 billion and 182,650

Company Perspectives:

RAG AG's roots are in domestic mining. It is among the most important driving forces of structural change in the mining regions of the Ruhr and Saar. The tasks connected with this role are diverse as well as demanding. Between our tradition and the demands of the future, RAG takes responsibility for the people in the mining regions. Beyond that, trend-setting innovations create profitable national and international growth. This growth, together with continued efforts to train our employees, create new perspectives and contribute in a major way to secure domestic jobs.

employees. On November 30, 1969, all these plants and employees were reorganized into seven companies, the Bergbau AG Niederrhein, Oberhausen, Gelsenkirchen, Herne/Recklinghausen, Essen, Dortmund, and Westfalen. RAG was thus unique in Germany, operating as a private enterprise yet dependant on support from the state. This support was given mainly in the form of subsidies but also through laws protecting German coal interests in some sectors.

Oil Shocks and Energy Policy: 1970s–80s

In August 1970 RAG enacted a strategy that became the foundation of the gradual transformation of the German coal industry into a leaner but more efficient industrial sector. This strategy included six major points: 1) concentration on the most productive coal mines and an optimized allocation of coal reservoirs to the mines; 2) the creation of combined coal mines as an alternative to closing some of them down completely; 3) to protect the environment, satellite mines would be planned and operated in regions with new coal deposits; 4) downsizing activities were to take into consideration the effects on the regional economies and job markets; 5) job cuts had to be timed in such a way that employees had enough time to prepare for the change by either moving, training for a new job, or retiring; 6) downsized employees had to be supported in this transition through job offers from other companies or early retirement programs.

RAG's basic strategy did not change much during the following decades. However, it had to be modified in response to the economic turbulence that came with the 1970s and 1980s. When the first oil price increases hit the German economy in 1973, they brought an increase in unemployment and a sudden decline of economic growth. The government realized the dangers of dependence on foreign fuel supplies and demanded that German coal production be kept at then-current levels. A second oil price shock followed in 1978 and the government went so far as to request the domestic coal industry to prepare for expansion. Much development work was initiated which resulted in a decline of productivity.

In 1973 RAG consisted of 38 coal mines, 22 coke production plants, and two briquette factories which employed a total of 148,425 people. By 1984 the numbers declined to 23 mines, 12 coke plants, one briquette factory and 122,257 employees. During the same time period, coal production dropped by 22 percent while sales climbed by 50 percent. In the 1980s, after

the oil crises of the 1970s were forgotten, the market for coal started declining again.

In 1985, when Heinz Horn became RAG's new CEO, the German coal industry seemed to have stabilized. However, when the U.S. dollar abruptly lost almost half of its value, energy prices on the world market declined, making German coal far too expensive. To prevent economic disaster, the German government subsidized the German coal industry heavily, despite regulations of the European Community (EC). However, the German public became more and more critical towards this policy. In 1987 a so-called "Kohlerunde" took place, a get-together of government officials and representatives from the industry. The result was an agreement to gradually diminish coal production and the number of employees by about 18 percent by 1995.

Coal Concept 2005 in the Early 1990s

In 1989 the European Community (EC) pressured Germany to reduce subsidies for steam coal. That year government subsidies for the German coal industry amounted to approximately DM 66,000 per employee. The EC formed a Coal Commission to develop a new policy for the German coal industry after 1995. The commission came to the conclusion that the coal industry was a strategic factor in securing Germany's energy supply and that it was not able to survive without government subsidies. However, the industry agreed on reducing the annual output of steam coal from 45 million MT to 40.9 million MT annually. At the end of 1989 RAG reorganized its subsidiaries. The three remaining Bergbau AGs were merged with RAG. At the same time, two new companies were founded to manage RAG's mining business: Ruhrkohle Niederrhein AG and Ruhrkuhle Westfahlen AG.

After East and West Germany were reunified in 1990, coal subsidies became an issue once again, because the high cost of integrating the East German economy was putting the German government under extreme financial pressure. In 1991 a second "Kohlerunde" was held to find a solution. The result was the Coal Concept 2005, a mutual agreement between the coal mining industry, the miner's trade union, the electricity industry, the state governments of coal-producing states, and the federal government. According to Coal Concept 2005, subsidized sales of domestic coal to energy and iron and steel producers was to be reduced from 66 million MT in 1991 to 50 million MT by 2005. Any steam coal output that exceeded this limit would not be subsidized. Existing contracts with power stations to buy domestic coal—the "Jahrhundertvertrag"—were continued but with gradually reduced volumes until 1997 and a fixed volume after that until 2005. Another existing contract with steel mills—the "Hüttenvertrag"—was also extended until 2005. For RAG the Coal Concept 2005 meant reducing coal mining capacity by nine million tons a year. The number of active coal mines was reduced from 17 to 12 by the end of 1991. In connection with those measures, the number of RAG employees would be reduced by 27,000 by the year 2000.

While coal mining was gradually reduced, RAG began transforming itself into a diverse technology concern. Specifically, the company became active in logistics, coal-based chemistry, and environmental technology. One field of activity for environmental services became the clean up, recultivation, and reforestation of areas where coal mines and processing plants had been closed down. The government subsidies were used more and more to strengthen growing markets instead of conserving old structures in declining industries. One of the new areas of activity was logistics. RAG owned a 600-kilometer-long railway system and 140 locomotives which were used to ship 70 million tons of coal across the Ruhr. In addition, Ruhrkohle owned ten harbors and a shipping company at Duisburg harbor on the river Rhine and a share in another shipping company at Rotterdam harbor.

Between 1970 and 1992, the percentage of RAG's total sales generated by activities other than coal jumped from two percent to over 30 percent. By 1992, 27 percent of RAG's 124,000 employees worked in areas other than coal mining and production. In October 1992 the RAG advisory board approved a new company structure. All of RAG's non-coal activities were organized under the umbrella of a new management holding company, the RAG Beteiligungs GmbH. They included the energy division STEAG AG, chemicals producer Rütgerwerke AG, the environmental division Ruhrkohle Umwelt GmbH, the logistics complex RAG Umschlags- und Speditions GmbH and the real estate arm RAG Immobilien AG.

In 1992 and 1993 there was a sudden decline of prices in the steel market, and sales dropped. This in turn led to rising coal reserves, and demand for coal went down. Moreover, cheap coke from countries such as China and Australia flooded the world market. Not surprisingly, the German steel making industry put pressure on RAG to significantly reduce coal prices. The conflict escalated when Klöckner, one of Germany's largest steel makers, was granted the right in 1993 to purchase up to 30 percent of its coal supply abroad in order to avoid bankruptcy. German steel giants Krupp/Hoesch and Thyssen claimed they needed similar consideration. However, while those companies partly relied on their own coke production facilities and bought additional volume only as needed from RAG, Klöckner depended completely on the expensive RAG coke. Finally, in May 1994 an agreement was reached between RAG and the German steel makers. The latter agreed to buy between 3 and 3.5 million tons of coal from

RAG annually until the end of 1997. As a result of the crisis period in the early 1990s, RAG closed down one coke plant and cut the output of the other three from seven million tons in 1991 to 4.2 million tons in 1995. At the end of the same time period, RAG's briquette factory had produced 0.2 million tons of briquettes, only half of the output from 1991.

Diversification and Reorganization After 1995

At the end of 1994, RAG CEO Heinz Horn, who had managed the company through a crucial process of diversification for almost a decade, retired and was succeeded by Gerhard Neipp. Under Horn's leadership, RAG had managed to generate almost half of its total sales in areas other than coal mining. Moreover, a new agreement with the German government reached at the beginning of 1994 had allowed RAG's non-coal subsidiaries to keep 25 percent of their profits instead of transferring them to the parent company. In July 1995 a new company structure was introduced that transformed RAG into a pure management holding company. To express the new, broader focus of its activities, Ruhrkohle AG was renamed RAG AG. A new subsidiary—RAG Vertrieb und Handel AG—was established to better coordinate all activities connected with the distribution and trading of coal, as well as other logistics activities and services.

In 1996 the German electricity lobby finally won its battle against the "Kohlepfennig," a tax on electricity that was collected as a partial funding for the coal subsidies, which diminished the competitiveness of the German electricity industry by keeping the prices at an artificially high level. The highest German court ruled the policy to be against the German constitution, which at the same time voided the "Jahrhundertvertrag," the treaty that had subsidized the German steam coal.

In March 1997 a new "Coal Compromise" was negotiated between the coal industry, the mining trade union, the German federal government, the state governments of North Rhine-Westfalia, and the Saarland. That year total government subsidies for the German coal industry amounted to over DM 9 billion—DM 7 billion to subsidize German steam coal and DM1 billion for the steel industry. According to the new agreement, coal subsidiaries were to be cut gradually until 2005 and the industry would be downsized to about ten coal mines and an annual output of 30 million tons of coal. The 90,000 employees in 1997 would be cut in half by 2005. At the same time a new regulation allowed RAG to use more of its profits derived from its non-coal activities to invest in its non-coal and international business. In the same year RAG Bergbau AG took over the Saarbergwerke AG, a government-owned coal mining company based in Saarbrücken, and was renamed Deutsche Steinkohle AG which included RAG's domestic coal mining activities. Another new subsidiary, the new Saarberg AG, organized all non-coal activities of the former Saarbergwerke, RAG's environmental services and oil trade.

RAG's domestic coal activities were still dominated by closing down coal mines, training the staff that had been laid off in new professions, and making existing coal mines more efficient. At the same time, however, the company expanded its international coal business. In 1996 RAG Coal International was founded to manage all RAG's coal activities abroad, including the exploration and development of new coal reservoirs; the planning, development, and operation of coal mines and processing facilities; and the manufacture of mining equipment. In the fall of 1999, when RAG bought 95 percent of an Australian coal mine, Burton Coal Joint Venture, and the American firm Cyprus Amax Coal Company based in Denver, Colorado, it was suddenly the world's second largest private coal producer. Cyprus-Amax included seven coal mines and two strip mines in Wyoming and Colorado. In 1999 RAG Coal International generated an output of 65 to 70 million tons of coal in 17 coal mines, totaling almost $1 billion in sales. Geographic advantages and more efficient technologies in the United States made the costs for coal mining one-tenth those of Germany. In American strip mines the difference was staggering; while it cost about $137 to produce a ton of coal in Germany, it cost not much more than $5 in an American strip mine. Another new market for RAG was China, with its international coal trading firm RAG EBV AG and its mining equipment arm DBT Deutsche Bergbau-Technik GmbH.

RAG's non-coal activities also became increasingly successful in the late 1990s. STEAG AG invested in a petrochemical power plant in Leuna and was also active in STEAG's Micro Tech division. It was the market leader for wet-process engineering for semiconductor production, serving clients such as IBM, Intel, and Hewlett Packard. Moreover, RÜTGERS AG subsidiary Isola, which was merged with the electro plating business of Allied Signal, became a world market leader in its field.

Principal Subsidiaries

Deutsche Steinkohle AG; RAG Beteiligungs-GmbH; RAG Coal International AG; RAG EBV AG; STEAG AG (72%); RÜTGERS AG (95%); Saarberg AG; Ruhrgas AG (18%); RAG IMMOBILIEN AG (99%); RAG INFORMATIK GmbH; RAG BILDUNG GmbH; Harpen AG (23,5%).

Principal Competitors

The Broken Hill Proprietary Company Limited; Peabody Holding Company, Inc.; CONSOL Energy Inc.

Further Reading

"Building Round Coal," *World Mining Equipment*, September 1995, p. S4.
Garding, Christoph, "Ruhrkohle: Es kommt noch dicker," *Focus*, July 5, 1993, p. 118.
"Heinz Horn 65 Jahre," Sueddeutsche Zeitung, September 15, 1995.
Hessling, M., "German Hard-Coal Industry," *Engineering & Mining Journal*, October 1992, p. 16.
Husemann, Ralf, "Ruhrkohle hat sich vom Bergbau emanzipiert," *Süddeutsche Zeitung*, September 12, 1996.
Knop, Carsten, "Die RAG löst sich langsam aus der politischen Umklammerung," *Frankfurter Allgemeine Zeitung*, September 5, 1998, p. 21.
Pollard, Sidney, "The German Tradition of Organized Capitalism: Self-Government in the Coal Industry," *Business History*, January 1995, p. 127.
Sturm, Norbert, "Von der Kohle zum High-Tech-Konzern," *Süddeutsche Zeitung*, January 30, 1992.
"The Energy to Export," *World Mining Equipment*, September 1999, p. S22.

—Evelyn Hauser

Ralphs Grocery Company

1100 West Artesia Boulevard
Compton, California, 90220
U.S.A
Telephone: (310) 884-9000
Fax: (310) 884-2601
Web site: http://www.ralphs.com

Wholly Owned Subsidiary of Fred Meyer Inc. and
division of The Kroger Company
Incorporated: 1909
Employees: 30,000
Sales: $5.48 billion (1998 est.)
NAIC: 44511 Supermarkets and Other Grocery (Except
Convenience) Stores

Ralphs Grocery Company is the largest food retailer in Southern California, and is showing signs of eventually evolving into one of the largest grocers in the western region of the United States. The company operates over 400 stores throughout California, offering tens of thousands of products to its customers, with many of those products presented under Ralphs private label. Family owned until 1968, Ralphs went through two complicated mergers to arrive at its high profile status within the food retailing industry, eventually becoming a unit of food retailing giant Kroger Company. Ralphs became such a growing force in Southern California, in fact, that it was prevented from further expansion in the greater Los Angeles region until 2003. Though most traditional Ralphs stores operate under the Ralphs moniker, the company also runs several stores in Northern California under the names Cala Foods and Bell Markets, as well as large warehouse stores under the names Food 4 Less, Foods Co, and PriceRite in Nevada. In 2000, the company began transforming some of its stores into markets offering high-quality gourmet food products, known as Ralphs Fresh Fare.

1873–1968: The Evolution of a Family-Owned Grocery Store

In 1873, a young bricklayer named George A. Ralphs was injured in a hunting accident and sought employment at a grocery store in Los Angeles. Within a year, he had saved enough money to purchase his own small store and was soon joined in the enterprise by his brother Walter Ralphs. Together the brothers ran Ralphs Bros. Grocers in downtown Los Angeles, a neighborhood grocer offering regional produce and grains at low prices and priding itself on its customer service. As the area's population boomed over the next few decades, Ralphs' inventory and size increased as well. In 1909 the company was incorporated as Ralphs Grocery Company, and two years later it launched a much larger branch store.

By 1928, the Ralphs chain consisted of ten stores. The Ralphs brothers focused on modernizing these facilities, and home delivery service by horse-drawn wagons eventually made way for self-service and parking lots. In the 1930s, the Ralphs stores began featuring bakeries and creameries in their 25 stores; the 1940s would bring delicatessens and other in-store conveniences.

A new generation of Ralphs took over the company after its founder, George Ralphs, died, and by the middle of the century the family had made Ralphs one of the top grocers in the state. The company focused on marketing themselves as a high quality food retailer, but it was equally dedicated to keeping prices competitive, a combination which helped bring the number of Ralphs locations to over 100 stores by the 1950s.

By the 1960s, the company's growth was strong enough to attract the attention of a national retail giant, which believed Ralphs was ready, with the right backing, to reach beyond the confines of a family-owned business. After steadily expanding throughout the decade, Ralphs was approached in 1968 by Cincinnati-based Federated Department Stores, one of the largest grocery chain store owners in the country. Federated offered to buy the company from the Ralphs family, which had run the business from its inception. By the time Federated entered into negotiations with Ralphs, the family was ready to unload what had evolved into much more than a mom-and-pop operation. So at year's end, Ralphs was sold to Federated for just over $60 million.

1970s–80s: Ups and Downs

Ralphs operated well under its new parent company, with the small but vibrant chain maintaining a forceful and steady

Company Perspectives:

Ralph's mission is to give our customers the very best. That's why Ralphs offers things you won't find at other stores, like our exclusive Member Benefits guide. With you Club Card, you'll get discounts all over California on everything from car rentals to fine dining. You'll also save on your favorite vintages of win with Ralphs Fine Wine Club. And when it comes to a passion for the very best, Ralphs brings you Fresh Fare. It's a brand new type of Ralphs store, which brings you the best the world has to offer.

presence in the rapidly growing Los Angeles region. Throughout the 1970s and early part of the 1980s Federated ran Ralphs smoothly and quietly, and the chain remained centered exclusively in Southern California, with little plan for national or statewide growth. Nevertheless, Ralphs was influential in the industry; the company was among the first to introduce checkout stations with laser price scanners.

After about a decade under Federated, Ralphs had fresh life breathed into it with the arrival of a new and energetic CEO, a man who had been devoted to work within the grocery industry since his childhood. Byron Allumbaugh was appointed CEO of Ralphs in 1976, after having spent two decades working in almost every behind-the-scenes department of the company. Allumbaugh began his career in the food retail industry at the age of 12, when he went to work during World War II at his local grocer's meat department. From then on, Allumbaugh spent most of his time working in produce stores, and by college age had dropped out of school to devote himself to the industry full time. Allumbaugh joined Ralphs in 1958, already a seasoned, knowledgeable executive, and when the company began looking around for a new CEO in the late 1970s, Allumbaugh was the natural choice. He was universally liked by the company, and he aided sales by personally spending a certain amount of time each week on the floor, hearing customer complaints and preferences, and generally getting a sense of what was and was not working. As much as Allumbaugh was appreciated by his employees, however, the CEO's ambitions differed from those of his company's parent in a fundamental sense; he wanted no less than the statewide, and, eventually, national expansion of Ralphs Grocery.

In the middle of the 1980s parent company Federated became vulnerable to a growing number of competitors taking advantage of the new corporate trend of mergers and consolidations. A specific threat came from a Canadian company, Campeau Corporation, which during the 1980s had set its sights on acquiring its powerful rival from the south. In 1988, Campeau launched a $4.2 billion hostile takeover of Federated stock. In the midst of this ordeal, in order to stave off the mounting debt the company had accrued from fighting Campeau's takeover, Federated put some of its more lucrative companies up for sale, among them Ralphs Grocery.

It was at this time that Ralphs faced the most challenging threat to not only the company's success, but its very existence. When the chain was put on the market, several of Ralphs competitors, such as the California-based Lucky and American Stores, came forward with offers. In the end, however, Allumbaugh

convinced his management team to raise over $1 billion in order to buy part of their own company from Federated. Therefore, when Campeau finally prevailed in its takeover of Federated, Ralphs was to be only partly owned by the Canadian corporation and was able to maintain a significant amount of independence via the Allumbaugh shares. Had Allumbaugh failed to buoy his fellow officers to fight for the company, Ralphs in all likelihood would have wound up either a wholly owned subsidiary of Campeau, which eventually filed for bankruptcy, or a nameless addition to the operations of one of its competitors.

Ralphs Grocery came out of its struggles in the late 1980s with its name and management intact, but the battle had cost the company dearly in terms of financial sacrifice. By 1990, the company had lost $51.3 million on revenues of $2.8 billion, and the losses threatened to continue unless some sort of restructuring took place. Allumbaugh, who had seen his company grow five times over during his 15-year tenure, was determined to bring Ralphs out of the red, and proceeded to shut down or relocate some of the chain's less lucrative sites.

Despite the company's setback, however, Allumbaugh and his team had set a stable groundwork for Ralphs, of a sort which would ensure the company's survival during just such a difficult time. The company had kept up with or been ahead of technological trends in the field, and had maintained a good reputation for fine produce and low prices. Most of the stores were cost-efficient, particularly in their use of automated systems, and were well prepared to make a financial comeback in the early 1990s.

1990–99: More Mergers and Further Growth

Campeau's takeover had slowed the company's goal of expanding beyond its Southern California center and had forced Ralphs to focus on strengthening its existing stores. With wise managerial guidance, Ralphs in the early part of the 1990s slowly began to make a comeback despite its own recent misfortunes and California's overall flat economy.

The renewed growth of the company was noticed by one of Ralphs' greatly visible cohorts, the highly successful company Food-4-Less, located in Northern California. At the time, Food-4-Less was larger and more profitable than Ralphs and was owned and funded by the huge Yucaipa Companies, which operated several chain companies around the country. In 1993, only a few years after Ralphs' flirtation with disaster, Food-4-Less approached the company with a friendly merger proposition. The idea was the brainchild of Yucaipa's charismatic and eccentric leader Ronald Burkle. Burkle was known not only in the grocery industry, but throughout the industry of Hollywood as well, as a man devoted to high-profile parties and collecting famous mansions; certainly somewhat of an aberration in the staid field of food retail. Already in possession of the Midwest's Dominick's Finer Foods, as well as the hugely successful Smith Food and Drug Centers, Burkle was looking for ways in which to increase his profits on the West Coast, and a union between Food-4-Less and Ralphs seemed the perfect way to accomplish such a goal.

After a little more than a year of negotiation, the two companies merged, with Burkle's company taking on much of Ralphs' debt, as well as paying Ralphs' shareholders about $525 million.

Key Dates:

1872: George A. Ralphs begins working in a grocery store in Los Angeles.
1874: Ralphs and his brother Walter launch Ralphs Bros. Grocers in downtown Los Angeles.
1909: Company is incorporated as Ralphs Grocery Company.
1911: First branch store is opened.
1928: Ralphs chain consists of ten stores.
1950: Ralphs consists of over 100 locations.
1968: The Ralphs family sells business to Federated Department Stores for $60 million.
1976: Byron Allumbaugh is named CEO.
1988: Ralphs battles for independence through a hostile takeover attempt of Federated Department Stores by Campeau Corporation.
1994: Ralphs merges with Food-4-Less.
1998: Ralphs merges with Fred Meyer, Inc., and those operations are acquired by The Kroger Company, making Ralph's a division of Kroger.

The new company was conjoined under the moniker of Ralphs Grocery Company, with the vast majority of stores operating with the Ralphs title. Directly after the merger, Ralphs Grocery Company was running 280 locations under the Ralphs name and about 80 less traditional warehouse stores through the Food-4-Less title. Allumbaugh retained his place as CEO of the new company, but he now had to answer to Burkle, a man with similar financial goals for Ralphs but with a decidedly different temperament.

Burkle differed from Allumbaugh in several ways, the most noticeable of which was the former's high-profile status within California's business and political community. Host to several fund raising parties for state Democratic leaders as well as for presidential hopeful Bill Clinton, Burkle's name was tied to powerful sources, the nature of which allowed the businessman access to areas beyond the more traditional routes of food retail. Involved with work in grocery stores since childhood, when he worked in his father's Claremont store, Burkle came to represent to the industry a changing trend in the grocery business: the entrepreneur was not only interested in steady growth and profits, he was also at the forefront of creating consolidation and huge chain stores where there were once primarily locally owned operations.

Indeed smaller independent stores were becoming increasingly rare in the middle of the decade, as corporations took advantage of a rapidly growing national trend of merging small companies, such as Ralphs, with other businesses of a similar size to create lower overhead, increased profits, and a smaller behind-the-scenes labor force. For Ralphs, the new partnership with Food-4-Less proved a profitable move and helped to shift the company in directions which were impossible for the business only a few years before. By 1995, the company had become a powerful state-wide presence and the most potent force in Southern California's grocery industry. In 1996 alone, Burkle and his team opened 27 new stores, a number which equaled half of all the new grocery stores in Southern California. Such an increase in activity did not go unnoticed by California's antitrust officials,

however, and by the next year the company was forbidden to open any new locations around Los Angeles until 2003. The partnership between Food-4-Less and Ralphs by the middle of the decade had turned the company into a $5.5 billion business.

The 1990s proved to be the decade of shifting partners and mergers for Ralphs. In 1998, the increasingly powerful national grocery corporation Fred Meyer Inc. (which had recently acquired Yucaipa subsidiary Smiths) showed an interest in the profitable company, which was by this time the oldest and most recognized chain west of the Mississippi. That year, Ralphs was purchased by Fred Meyer, making the latter one of the largest grocers in the country. Those were not all the changes Ralphs saw that year; later in 1998 the most powerful food retailer in the country, Kroger, merged with Ralphs' new parent company, a union which made Kroger by far the largest grocer in the United States.

At decade's end, as a wholly owned subsidiary of Fred Meyer and therefore a division of Kroger, Ralphs continued its upward wave of expansion, having in 1999 over 440 stores in operation and several plans for out-of-state growth, some of which were realized through its acquisition of ten Nevada-based PriceRite stores. Following a long company tradition, the company did not turn its back on its community or, more specifically, the less fortunate members belonging to it. Through The Ralphs/Food-4-Less Foundation, the company gave away thousands of dollars in cash and products every year in an effort to support causes as wide ranging as relief for hurricane victims and abused women to drug prevention programs. Though such involvement of course helped to keep the Ralphs name at the forefront of its customers' minds, the company's efforts also aided in establishing and maintaining a reputation for both financial success and a humanitarianism often lacking in many other large corporations.

Principal Operating Units

Ralphs; Ralphs Fresh Fare; Food-4-Less; Cala Foods; Bell Markets; PriceRite.

Principal Competitors

Albertson's Inc.; Safeway Inc.; Stater Brothers Holdings Inc.; Lucky Stores Inc.; The Vons Companies Inc.

Further Reading

Darlin, Damon, ''Party Boy,'' *Forbes,* November 18, 1996, p. 188.
''Fred Meyer, Quality Food Centers, and Ralphs Grocery Company Mergers Completed,'' *PR Newswire,* March 10, 1998.
Glover, Kara, ''Backseat Driver Steers Ralphs with Style,'' *Los Angeles Business Journal,* September 9, 1991, p. 20.
Knestout, Brian, ''Kroger: A Big Fish Gets Much Bigger,'' *Kiplinger's Personal Finance Magazine,* January 1999, p. 34.
Liebeck, Laura, ''Fred Meyer to Become $15 Billion Player,'' *Discount Store News,* November 17, 1997, p.1.
''Ralphs Provides Disaster Relief to Salvation Army Workers in Port Hueneme,'' *PR Newswire,* February 4, 2000.
Weinstein, Steve, ''The New Ralphs,'' *Progressive Grocer,* November 1995, p. 32.
Zwiebach, Elliot, ''Food-4-Less, Ralphs in $1.5 Billion Pact,'' *Supermarket News,* September 19, 1994.

—Rachel H. Martin

Rentrak Corporation

7700 Northeast Ambassador Place
Portland, Oregon 97220
U.S.A.
Telephone: (503) 284-7581
Toll Free: (800) 929-8000
Fax: (503) 282-9017
Web site: http://www.rentrak.com

Public Company
Incorporated: 1981 as National Video, Inc.
Employees: 275
Sales: $123.78 million (1999)
Stock Exchanges: NASDAQ
Ticker Symbol: RENT
NAIC: 51211 Motion Picture and Video Production;
   541512 Computer Systems Design Services; 53311
   Lessors of Nonfinancial Intangible Assets (Except
   Copyrighted Works); 5699 Miscellaneous Accessories

Rentrak Corporation is the world's largest distributor of pre-recorded videocassettes on a pay-per-transaction basis. In a pay-per-transaction arrangement, video rental store operators lease movie titles rather than purchasing them and share the rental proceeds with the supplier. Rentrak, which processes more than 11 million transactions per week, services retailers throughout the United States and Canada, as well as a number of outlets in Japan and the United Kingdom through affiliated companies. The company also is involved in Internet-related business through three subsidiaries: Blow Out Video, Inc. sells videos and DVD movies over the Internet and at five retail locations; FourMovies.com provides an online database of more than 160,000 movie titles stocked by approximately 10,000 video rental stores; and 3PF.COM, formerly operating as ComAlliance, Inc., processes and fulfills orders for electronic-commerce companies.

Origins

For its formation and development, Rentrak took its direction from Ron Berger. Born in Tel Aviv and raised in New York City, Berger was a 25-year-old college dropout living in Portland, Oregon, when he scored his first success in the franchising business. In 1973, he began franchising a chain of camera shops and quickly amassed a fortune. The chain, named Photo Factory, grew to 54 stores during its first six years in business. By the end of the decade, Berger's net worth had soared to $15 million, but he would lose everything before the 1980s began. Photo Factory was heavily in debt and in a vulnerable financial state. When interest rates rose sharply in mid-1979, Berger's company collapsed, forcing him to declare bankruptcy. Overnight, his fortune was gone.

After liquidating Photo Factory, Berger was still unemployed six months later when he received a telephone call from a friend. Berger's friend offered him a job managing a video rental store in New York City, which he refused, but the offer set Berger's professional life in motion again. He was intrigued by the video store concept, then not far out of its infancy as a retail format. Berger went to the public library in Portland and began looking through stacks of telephone books, searching state by state for all the video rental stores in operation. He identified 900 such stores throughout the country and, with the help of several former Photo Factory employees, began calling each one, endeavoring to create what would become the first national survey of video rental stores. After compiling market research data gleaned from 300 stores on his list, Berger was ready to distribute the information. He paid for a one-inch advertisement in the *Wall Street Journal* and offered his survey for $95 per copy. The response was swift and enlightening. Deluged with requests for his survey, Berger realized he had found a business that was destined to grow. After selling 300 copies and pocketing more than $25,000, he decided to start a chain of franchised video rental stores called National Video.

Unable to obtain any financing because of the financial failure of Photo Factory, Berger was forced to seek alternative means to get his business started. In January 1981, he left Portland and rented an inexpensive hotel room in Las Vegas, which was hosting the Consumer Electronics Show. Berger paid for another advertisement in the *Wall Street Journal,* a simple message that read: ''If you agree the future of video retailing is in franchising, call me.'' Berger submitted the telephone num-

Company Perspectives:

Rentrak celebrated the ten-year anniversary of its Pay-Per-Transaction system in January 1999. Rentrak pioneered the concept of sharing revenue between program suppliers and home video retailers as a way to lower the initial investment retailers make for each videocassette, thereby increasing the number of videocassettes retailers can obtain and expanding the total studio rental revenues generated for a movie title. The company offers videocassettes from the majority of the major studios and independent video suppliers.

ber of his hotel room and waited. The third call he received was from a Waco, Texas, television executive named Jack Hauser, who listened to Berger explain his National Video franchise concept. Berger offered to sell Hauser a franchise for the nominal price of $10, but he insisted the store had to be designed and managed precisely according to his specifications. Hauser agreed. The first National Video unit, established in Waco, was immediately successful, earning $3,500 in profit during its first month in business. Hauser was elated and Berger had proven his point. With a highly successful prototype to point to, Berger began franchising the concept in earnest, asking for far more than the $10 he had charged Hauser.

Development of Rentrak in the Mid-1980s

Berger's second attempt at franchising proved more successful than his first, enabling the rejuvenated entrepreneur to charge as much as $35,000 for an individual National Video franchise. By 1985, there were nearly 600 National Video franchises in operation, generating nearly $8 million in annual sales for Berger's Portland-based company. At this point in its brief history, National Video ranked as the largest franchised chain of rental video stores in North America, having quickly carved a dominant position in a burgeoning industry, but despite the rising financial figures Berger and his franchisers faced a worrisome problem. As more and more people frequented video rental stores, the inventory of each store needed to increase and change more frequently, a burdensome financial task for the mom-and-pop operators who not only composed most of National Video's franchiser ranks but also represented the overwhelming majority of video rental store operators throughout the country. With each movie title costing approximately $70, most National Video operators lacked the capital to consistently refresh their 2,500-title collections and, consequently, were struggling to remain competitive. Realizing the gravity of the problem facing many in the video rental industry, Berger came up with a solution that would enable his franchisers to better compete.

The details of Berger's plan formed the core of what became known as the pay-per-transaction (PPT) system. Instead of purchasing movie titles from movie studios, retailers leased the titles. Berger's leasing system, dubbed Rentrak, divided the rental profits among video rental store retailers, Berger's company, and the movie studios, with the retailers and the movie studios receiving 45 percent each and National Video, the corporation, receiving the remaining 10 percent. The payments were determined by the number of times a particular title was rented. In exchange for

sharing their profits, retailers paid less than $10 for a title, enabling them to buy a larger quantity of popular movies and to increase the breadth of their collections as well.

For those National Video operators with a meager amount of capital, Rentrak represented a viable solution to their problem, but before the effectiveness of the leasing system could be tested, Berger needed some capital of his own. To fully develop Rentrak, including the software needed to keep track of each rental transaction in a more than 600-unit chain, Berger needed money. Bankers continued to shun the Portland-based company because of the failure of Photo Factory, a situation that forced Berger to sell a portion of his company to the public. In November 1986, he completed National Video's initial public offering, selling 30 percent of the company to investors, which raised $5 million. With the proceeds, Berger was able to develop and market his PPT system, at the time unaware of the great importance that Rentrak's debut would represent in the history of his company.

Rentrak proved highly successful, quickly becoming an indispensable tool for National Video franchisers. As franchisers signed up for the system, they were joined by retailers outside the National Video network, creating what became a highly important source of revenue for Berger's company. By the end of the decade, roughly 1,000 video rental stores were connected to Rentrak, each paying $5,000 for the hardware and software needed to manage the revenue-sharing leasing system.

The late 1980s witnessed the encouraging acceptance of Rentrak, but the end of the decade also saw Berger's chain of National Video outlets disappear from the national retail landscape. A new breed of competitor was to blame, specifically the rental video stores rolled out by Wayne Huizenga, who began feverishly expanding his chain of Blockbuster Video stores during the late 1980s. Huizenga's stores, which stocked 10,000 titles, dwarfed the 2,500 title units composing National Video, and true to their name, the Blockbuster units delivered a devastating blow to National Video operators. "Wherever Blockbuster opened a store," Berger remarked in a December 5, 1994 interview with *Forbes* magazine, "they killed us." By 1988, Huizenga had approximately 250 stores in operation, with considerably more soon to open up throughout the country. Berger envisioned a bleak future for National Video, forcing him to make what he later referred to as the most difficult decision in his business career. In 1988, he sold the 746 National Video franchises in operation to Philadelphia-based West Coast Video. In the wake of the divestiture, Berger's business became solely dependent on PPT-derived revenue, which was evinced in the company's new corporate title, Rentrak Corporation.

Although the sale of the National Video franchises represented the loss of a profitable, $100 million business, Berger's strategic decision was in the best interest of his company's long-term future. Blockbuster expanded vigorously—acquiring West Coast Video as it blanketed the nation with stores—and quickly dominated the rental market. Berger, meanwhile, was free to focus his full attention on expanding his leasing system, which remained an attractive alternative to paying upwards of $70 per title. Although unprofitable during its first several years as an exclusively PPT company, Rentrak saw its ranks of subscribers swell nevertheless. By the time the company was able to turn a profit, there were more than 3,000 retail outlets

Key Dates:

1980: Bankrupt entrepreneur Ron Berger begins compiling the first national survey of video rental stores.

1981: Berger sells first franchise of his National Video retail concept.

1986: National Video's initial public offering funds the development of Rentrak, a pay-per-transaction system.

1988: Facing competition from rival Blockbuster Video, Berger sells his 746-unit National Video chain and renames company Rentrak Corporation.

1993: The Pro Image, a 200-store sports memorabilia franchise, is acquired.

1995: The acquisition of Entertainment One and Supercenter Entertainment leads to the formation of BlowOut Entertainment.

1996: The Pro Image and BlowOut Entertainment are divested.

1999: Two new subsidiaries, ForMovies.com and 3PF.COM, Inc., are formed to support the company's pay-per-transaction business.

using Rentrak, enabling Berger's company to register $69 million in revenue in March 1994, the end of its fiscal year, and its first profit for several years, a gain of $813,000. By this point, Berger, who had been hamstrung by the rise of Huizenga's Blockbuster during the late 1980s, had already broken free from his self-imposed confinement. His talents had always realized their greatest success in retailing, which was where Berger directed Rentrak's corporate resources in 1993.

Diversification and Growth during the 1990s

The success of Rentrak had convinced Berger that the system could be altered to create a just-in-time inventory computer system for other types of retail businesses. Accordingly, in 1993 he acquired The Pro Image, a 200-store sports memorabilia franchise. With stores in 45 states, as well as units in Canada, Puerto Rico, Germany, and Japan, Pro Image generated $84 million in revenue in 1992. As the Pro Image acquisition was being concluded, Berger was preparing to re-enter the retail video market, five years after his exit. In November 1993, Rentrak opened a 20,000 title store in Times Square called Blow Out Video that sold videos rather than renting them.

Thanks to the continued growth of its PPT leasing system and the addition of a retail chain and the Blow Out Video concept, Rentrak was able to recoup the revenue lost when Berger was forced to sell the company's National Video franchises. Annual sales had dropped to $11 million immediately following the divestiture, but by 1995 the company was collecting more than $110 million in sales, as the number of stores using the Rentrak leasing system surpassed 5,000. Pro Image was expanding as well, as the 229 store chain announced its intentions to establish units in Malaysia, Singapore, and Brunei. Berger also found time to develop a new business for his rapidly growing enterprise. In May 1995, Berger acquired Entertainment One Inc., followed by the purchase of Supercen-

ter Entertainment Corporation in September 1995. Each of the acquired companies operated video sales and rental operations at supercenters owned by the massive discounter, Wal-Mart. In October 1995, Berger combined his own Supermarket Video entity with his two recent acquisitions to form BlowOut Entertainment. Six months after its formation, BlowOut Entertainment was operating 181 video rental departments in selected Wal-Mart and Kmart supercenters.

Rentrak entered the late 1990s as a multi-faceted enterprise growing in three directions, but the company would soon lose its diversified complexion. In 1996, Berger restructured Rentrak by disposing of the subsidiary businesses that interfered with the company's mainstay PPT revenue sharing system. Citing a need to focus all the company's resources on developing and marketing PPT services, Berger liquidated the money losing Pro Image subsidiary by either selling or closing the more than 200 stores composing the chain. BlowOut Entertainment, unprofitable as well, was spun off to Rentrak shareholders in the form of a special dividend. Meanwhile, the company's PPT business continued to blossom. In 1995, Rentrak signed an agreement with Movie Gallery, a video rental retailer, to install PPT systems in all of Movie Gallery's nearly 900 stores. The deal was expected to be worth between $100 million and $150 million in new business over the course of the ensuing ten years.

Following the 1996 divestitures, Berger focused on expanding the company's PPT business, including a concerted push into the United Kingdom in 1998 and an increase in the company's involvement in Japanese markets. By the end of the decade, the company was continuing to sign up new stores to its leasing system, despite the competitive pressure mounted by movie studios, which began offering revenue sharing leasing programs of their own. During Rentrak's fiscal year ending in March 2000, nearly 2,000 new video outlets were connected to the company's PPT network.

As Rentrak prepared for the 21st century, its consistent progress in PPT services was complemented by promising prospects in a new area of expertise: Internet-related business. Through a subsidiary named FourMovies.com, the company provided web site services for video retailers and consumers through a searchable online database. The database included more than 160,000 movie titles stocked by approximately 10,000 video rental stores. Rentrak's other major electronic-commerce business, 3PF.COM, processed and fulfilled customer orders for Internet businesses. Although these new areas of opportunities had the potential for significant revenue growth, it was Rentrak's dominant position in PPT services that fueled Berger's confidence for the future.

Principal Subsidiaries

Attitude 2 Travel, Inc.; BlowOut Video Holding Company; FourMovies.com, Inc.; LRC Inc.; Mortco Inc.; Orient Link Enterprises; PDF, Inc.; Rentrak Canada; Rentrak Europe BV (Netherlands); Rentrak UK Limited (England, 92%); RTK Kelly Limited; Streamlined Solutions, Inc.; Transition Sports, Inc.; 3PF.COM, Inc.

Principal Competitors

LDI, Ltd.; Ingram Entertainment Inc.; Baker & Taylor Corporation.

Further Reading

Alaimo, Dan, ''Rentrak Mulls Way to Blowout Stake,'' *Supermarket News,* April 8, 1996, p. 43.

Block, Alex Ben, ''First Rewind, Then Fast-Forward,'' *Forbes,* August 12, 1985, p. 112.

Gauntt, Tom, ''Earnings Plunge, but National Video Charges On,'' *Business Journal-Portland,* July 20, 1987, p. 6.

Goldstein, Seth, ''Indies with Extras Won't Be Crushed by Competition, Authoring House Says,'' *Billboard,* August 7, 1999, p. 63.

——, ''Rentrak Sees Long-Term Gains for PPT Business,'' *Billboard,* October 5, 1996, p. 10.

Gubernick, Lisa, ''If at First You Don't Succeed . . . ,'' *Forbes,* December 5, 1994, p. 80.

Paglin, Catherine, ''National Video Lays Out Plan to Take Itself Public,'' *Business Journal-Portland,* September 15, 1986, p. 8.

''Ron Berger: Chairman, President and CEO, Rentrak Corp.,'' *Chain Store Age Executive with Shopping Center Age,* December 1995, p. 64.

—Jeffrey L. Covell

Robert Wood Johnson Foundation

Route 1 and College Road East
Post Office Box 2316
Princeton, New Jersey 08543-2316
U.S.A.
Telephone: (609) 452-8701
Fax: (609) 452-1865
Web site: http://www.rwjf.org

Private Foundation
Incorporated: 1972 as a National Foundation
Employees: 150
Net Assets: $8.04 billion (1999)
NAIC: 813211 Grantmaking Foundations

The Robert Wood Johnson Foundation is one of the largest private philanthropic organizations in the United States and the largest focusing specifically on health issues. Each year, the Foundation provides approximately 1,000 grants totaling in the hundreds of millions of dollars to hospitals and research institutions. At any given time some 2,300 groups across the country are being assisted with Foundation money. The Foundation's philosophy is straightforward: it awards grants for hands-on research and practice initiatives. The focus is on making affordable basic health care available to everyone, but it goes beyond that. Foundation-sponsored research covers such topics as how to treat chronic illness, how to prevent illness associated with substance abuse, and how to educate both the medical profession and the public about health care topics.

Since 1972, when the Foundation was established as a national organization, health care topics have become increasingly complex. In the 1970s it was believed that universal national health care in some form would be implemented over the next several years. At the beginning of the 21st century the debate over national health care was still contentious, and a comprehensive national program was still a dream. Other factors changed the health care picture through the 1980s and 1990s. The advent of AIDS, for example, had a dramatic impact on the social, economic, and political fabric vis-à-vis health care. The increasing elderly population would have a strong long-term impact. Moreover, people were living longer, which meant increased susceptibility to cancer, diabetes, Alzheimer's disease, and a host of other conditions. The Foundation believes that it serves people most effectively by continuing to focus both on health care and on health improvement.

General Johnson: A Life of Civic Duty

Although the Foundation as a national organization was established in 1972, its origins go back some four decades earlier. The best way to understand the Foundation's philosophy is to understand the man who created it—a man who spent his career combining his business acumen with his strong humanitarian beliefs.

Robert Wood Johnson was born in 1893 with what Waldemar Nielsen in his book *The Golden Donors* called "a silver tongue depressor in his mouth." His father and uncles had founded a small medical supply company in the 1880s. The company developed a way to mass produce sterile surgical dressings, and within a decade the company, Johnson & Johnson, was highly successful. Young Robert was educated by tutors and in private schools and was planning to attend college. Upon his father's sudden death in 1910, the 17-year-old boy decided to forego college and instead went to work at Johnson & Johnson's plant in New Brunswick, New Jersey.

He began as a mill hand and worked his way up, gradually learning all the jobs at the plant. By 1918 he was vice-president, and in 1932, he succeeded his uncle as president. Under his leadership, Johnson & Johnson became one of the most widely recognized companies in the world; by the late 1960s the company had sales of over $700 million in some 120 countries.

Johnson's success as a business leader was based in part on his intelligence and his competitive drive. Perhaps to a greater extent, however, it was based on his unwavering belief in the importance of public service. He became involved in local politics in Highland Park, New Jersey, and was elected mayor at the age of 27. (Later he would encourage his employees to participate in civic affairs and even established a "Sound Government" program at Johnson & Johnson to promote this goal.) When the Great Depression hit in 1929, not only did Johnson manage to

---

keep his work force, but he also raised their salaries. During World War II he served as vice-chairman of the War Production Board. (He attained the rank of brigadier general and thereafter was known as General Johnson.) He was a firm believer in promoting dignity and self-worth among his employees; he paid them good wages and encouraged them to voice their opinions about their work environment. A personally fastidious man (he required that corners in his factories be painted white so that dirt could be seen and promptly removed), he was an early pioneer in controlling corporate pollution. He built a model factory community in Gainesville, Georgia, in the 1920s that featured a clean work and living environment—no smokestacks or chemical runoff. It is hardly surprising that such a civic-minded man would choose to earmark his sizable fortune to helping others.

Foundation's Origins in the 1970s

The Robert Wood Johnson Foundation has existed as a national philanthropy since 1972, but its origins actually go back to 1936. General Johnson set up a foundation with the goal of providing support to a variety of humanitarian projects. One of the earliest of these was the establishment of a school of hospital administration at Northwestern University in Evanston, Illinois. As time went on, Johnson desired that his foundation achieve a broader scope. Toward the end of his life he set about plans to establish the foundation as a national organization to which he would bequeath the bulk of his sizable estate.

Despite—or in some cases perhaps because of—their good work, private philanthropic organizations have always been the focus of investigation by the government. Terrence Keenan, the Foundation's special program director, addressed the issue in a booklet published in 1992. He stated bluntly that members of Congress "themselves forever chafing under (and not infrequently flayed by) the Constitution's demands for public accountability of public servants, is very uncomfortable with the foundation as a center of power and wealth which has no such accountability."

Given Congress' attempts to regulate private foundations over the year, Keenan's words are hardly surprising. Since foundations were often created by wealthy and powerful families, the popular belief more often than not was that they were nothing more than elaborate schemes for exempting the rich and their corporations from paying taxes. Congress, no doubt influenced by constituents as well as by its own skepticism toward the wealthy, convened several committees to investigate foundation practices. For much of the 20th century, legislators

sought to restrict private foundations. Sometimes this reached the point of absurdity; in 1952, during the height of anti-Communist hysteria in the United States, a Congressional committee was set up to investigate whether private foundations were promoting "un-American" activities.

There were other concerns, however, that were more legitimate. During the 1960s, the House Select Committee on Small Business, under the leadership of Texas Congressman Wright Patman, investigated private foundations and discovered what appeared to be questionable business practices. Patman's findings led to further action by the government. A U.S. Treasury Department report issued in 1965 mirrored Patman's complaints: inadequate oversight in foundations allowed companies and wealthy families to use foundations as huge tax exemptions while providing little measurable charity.

The debate continued until 1969 when the Tax Reform Act was passed. Among the stipulations was a four percent net excise tax on foundation investment income, and a required annual payout of all net investment income (or a minimum of six percent of the endowment, whichever was greater) within one taxable year.

Not surprisingly, the legislation discouraged the launch of any new foundations and made life unpleasant for existing ones. In the ensuing years, modifications to the 1969 law were enacted; the excise tax was halved and payouts were reduced to a flat 5 percent. Nonetheless, foundations still faced other regulations, as well as the stereotype of being tax havens for the wealthy.

Johnson's belief in what his foundation could do—and what it should do—was so strong that he did not allow congressional activity in the 1960s to deter his mission. When he died in January 1968, his bequest to the foundation totaled some $300 million in Johnson & Johnson stock. (By the time Johnson's will was probated in 1971, those shares were worth $1.2 billion.) Johnson did not make any formal stipulations about the Foundation's mission in his will, but he had made his wishes known to the men who would become its trustees. Johnson chose these men to serve on the Foundation's board based on their business acumen and their sense of ethics. All of them were Johnson & Johnson executives—a move that had caused conflict in similar foundations. The General, however, was obviously as good a judge of character as he was a businessman.

Furthering the Mission of General Johnson

Gustav O. Lienhard, president of Johnson & Johnson, retired from that position to assume the chairmanship of the Foundation. Although he and the other trustees were conservative in their outlook, they were experienced and savvy enough to realize that a stodgy mainstream organization would never be able to meet the General's goals. Their goal was to make the Foundation "productive," and to that end Lienhard had the foresight to hire the well-respected and progressive head of the Johns Hopkins Medical School, Dr. David Rogers.

Rogers put together a staff of talented and progressive health care authorities, and they began to create a plan for shaping the Foundation's mission. Rogers and his staff worked well with the trustees and their mutual respect gave the Foundation a strong framework on which to build.

Key Dates:

1910: Robert Wood Johnson begins career at Johnson & Johnson following his father's death.

1936: Johnson begins private philanthropic foundation to promote improved health care.

1968: Johnson dies, bequeathing bulk of his estate to the foundation.

1969: Congress passes Tax Reform Act that sets new rules for private foundations.

1972: Robert Wood Johnson Foundation established as a national foundation.

1976: Foundation moves from New Brunswick, New Jersey, to Princeton, New Jersey.

1985: Gustav Lienhard retires as chairman and is replaced by Robert Myers.

1987: Foundation revamps mission and goals to reflect changes in health care needs.

1989: Sidney Wentz replaces Robert Myers as chairman.

1999: Wentz retires and is replaced by Robert E. Campbell.

The first mission statement in 1972 stated that the Foundation's goal was "the encouragement of institutions or individuals who are attempting to restructure the American health delivery system to make effective care more available to nonhospitalized patients." Other foundations at the time were donating approximately $100 billion annually to health care, but most of that money was going into research and hospital construction. The Robert Wood Johnson Foundation decided to focus its energies on the actual delivery of health care to the patient—an area that it felt had been unwisely neglected. Specifically, the Foundation would concentrate on three aims: improving access to health care, improving health care services to enhance the quality of care, and developing methods to objectively analyze public health policy.

To this end, the Foundation decided to achieve its goals through the establishment of large-scale field trials of ideas it saw as innovative. The Foundation would fund not only the trials, but third-party objective evaluations. It would also collaborate with medical schools, hospitals, research institutions, government agencies, and other foundations as a means of furthering its goals. By having a national rather than a regional focus, the Foundation could share its knowledge and expertise with a wide range of health care agencies and institutions.

A good example is Clinical Scholars, one of the earliest and most successful Foundation programs. Started in 1973, it provided young physicians the opportunity to study such non-clinical topics as demography, economics, management, and similar fields at the graduate level for two years at major colleges and universities. Giving clinicians a grounding in these non-clinical subjects, the Foundation believed, made them more well-rounded and could improve their ability to deliver quality health care. The Foundation put some 800 men and women through this program from inception through the 1990s. Many of them went on to positions in major medical research institutions, government agencies, and major corporations in the health care field.

Among the early efforts were: a program to help teaching hospitals consolidate health services for high-risk teens and young adults (those vulnerable to substance abuse, teen-age pregnancy, and venereal disease); a training program for dental students focusing on care of handicapped patients; a rural infant care program that allowed medical schools and state health departments to collaborate to reduce infant mortality; and a program to establish emergency medical communications systems.

From the beginning, one element that distinguished the Foundation from similar organizations was that staff members had experience with health care in addition to whatever other skills they brought to the table. This was particularly useful, because staff could make informed decisions about grant proposals. As former Foundation president Leighton E. Cluff, M.D., explained in his book *Helping Shape the Nation's Health Care System,* "This made possible staff review of proposals and programs from the perspectives of health economists, nurses, physicians, and experts in public health, health systems, health services research, finance and accounting, and health policy."

Changing Needs in Health Care

When the Foundation was launched as a national organization, the biggest problem that appeared to plague health care in the United States was the need for greater access to health care. The cost of health care was also at issue, and many experts believed that universal health care in some form was only a matter of time. Because the Foundation's trustees and staff had an understanding of health care, they were able to conduct substantive self-evaluations to determine whether they needed to change their direction. In 1980, for example, the Foundation evaluated such changes in health care as the growth in outpatient services and modified its goals to reflect this and other changes. These goals included improving health care access to under-served populations; finding ways to make health care more affordable; and helping people get the most out of the health care they receive.

A larger such evaluation was conducted in 1986, and the following year the Foundation fashioned a revised set of beliefs and goals. By the mid-1980s, health care issues were quite different from what they had been in the 1970s. Costs were rising, and more people were finding themselves unable to afford even basic health care. Those who could not afford care but who had chronic conditions posed another problem, as did an increase in problems stemming from substance abuse. How to care for those suffering from mental illness was a growing concern, in part the result of de-institutionalization programs that gave many mentally ill individuals more freedom over their own lives. The appearance of AIDS and its epidemic spread was a huge change on the health care horizon. While the basic goals remained essentially the same, the Foundation sought programs and proposals from a broader base than the usual medical institutions and universities. It also began looking toward single-site programs. In the past, the Foundation had funded programs that ran at several sites across the country. Now it would also fund regional programs, which could address concerns in specific regions. Regional programs that were successful could later be replicated on a larger scale.

The scope and variety of programs implemented at the Foundation during the 1980s and 1990s were wide-ranging. Among the larger projects were Faith in Action, a program that helped provide volunteer services to the chronically ill to more than 1,100 interfaith coalitions across the country; Covering Kids, a health care access program for low-income uninsured children that complemented government and private-sector initiatives; A Matter of Degree, which worked to create community-campus partnerships at colleges with the goal of reducing substance abuse; and Chronic Care Initiatives in HMOs, which sought to improve the delivery of health care to chronically ill patients in managed care groups. Smaller programs focused on such issues as creating childhood immunization registries, discouraging smoking among teens and young adults, and palliative care for the elderly and terminally ill.

Strong leadership has always been important to the Foundation. When Gustav Lienhard stepped down in 1985 he was replaced as chairman by Robert Myers, who oversaw the 1987 initiatives and the 1989 expansion of the Foundation's headquarters building. He stepped down in 1990 and was replaced by Sidney Wentz, who guided the Foundation through the major health care changes of the 1990s. Wentz stepped down in 1999 and was replaced by Robert E. Campbell. Regarding the Foundation's presidency, when David Rogers resigned, he was succeeded by Leighton Cluff (who had served as executive vice-president). Upon Cluff's retirement in 1990, Stephen Schroeder, a physician who taught at the University of California-San Francisco, was chosen as his replacement. With sound management, clear goals, and a strong endowment (which increased from $2.6 billion in 1989 to $7.8 billion in 1998), the Foundation remained a strong and influential player in health care as it entered the new century.

Further Reading

Cluff, Leighton E., *Helping Shape the Nation's Health Care System: A Report on the Robert Wood Johnson Foundation's Program Activities, 1972–1989,* Princeton, N.J.: Robert Wood Foundation, 1989.

Keenan, Terrance, *The Promise At Hand: Prospect for Foundation Leadership in the 1990s,* Princeton, N.J.: Robert Wood Foundation, 1992.

Nielsen, Waldemar A., *Golden Donors: A New Anatomy of the Great Foundations,* New York: Truman-Talley, 1985.

"One Billion Dollar Legacy Makes Foundation the Second Biggest," *New York Times,* December 6, 1971, p. 1.

"Robert Wood Johnson," *Current Biography,* New York: H.W. Wilson Company, 1943.

—George A. Milite

Rubio's Restaurants, Inc.

1902 Wright Place, Suite 300
Carlsbad, California 92008
U.S.A.
Telephone: (760) 929-8226
Toll Free: (800) 354-4199
Fax: (760) 929-8203
Web site: http://www.rubios.com

Public Company
Incorporated: 1985
Employees: 2,738
Sales: $67.9 million (1999)
Stock Exchanges: NASDAQ
Ticker Symbol: RUBO
NAIC: 722211 Limited-Service Restaurants

Rubio's Restaurants, Inc. operates a chain of over 100 Rubio's Baja Grill restaurants, most of which are located in Southern California, where the company was founded. In the greater Los Angeles area alone there are over 40 restaurants, but Rubio's has also expanded into four other states: Arizona, Nevada, Colorado, and Utah. In 1999, these accounted for 23 of the company's units. The fast-service restaurants serve over 40 dishes based on the cuisine of the Baja region of Mexico, including a fish taco that was founder Ralph Rubio's first menu item when he opened business at a small stand in San Diego. The chain's menu now features many other seafood items, including lobster burritos and shrimp quesadillas, but each restaurant also serves marinated, grilled steaks and chicken. Although Rubio's provides fast-food service, each chain unit prepares much of its food on a daily basis, ensuring, for example, fresh salsa, guacamole, sauces, beans, rice, and chips. Also, although there is a take-out service, the grills have a casual, Baja-inspired atmosphere which encourages in-house dining. There are aquariums, patio tables shaded by thatched-palm palapa umbrellas, even decorative surfboards. However, without the restaurants' special atmosphere, Rubio's dishes are also sold at other outlets in and near San Diego, including the Del Mar Racetrack and QUALCOMM Stadium.

1982–87: Creating a Market for Rubio's Signature Fish Taco

According to Ralph Rubio's own account, Rubio's Baja Grill resulted from a challenge made by his father Ray (Rafael) "to get off his surfboard and make something of his life." It was 1982, and although Ralph had no business experience of note, he did have a good recipe for making what became the chain's signature menu item—its fish taco. He had gotten the recipe at a taco shop in San Felipe, a fishing village in Baja California, where, in the mid-1970s, he and other student friends from San Diego State University used to take their spring break. After sampling the fare at the shop, Ralph knew that he had found a very tasty and rather unique Mexican dish. He wangled the recipe from Carlos, the obliging counter man, took it home and began making fish tacos for family and friends.

With the financial backing and business acumen of his father and the help of his brother Robert, Ralph Rubio bought a small building in the Mission Bay section of San Diego and, in January of 1983, began making and selling his unique tacos under a sign reading "Rubio's. The Home of the Fish Taco." Before opening that first Rubio's, Ralph Rubio had only limited experience in managing a restaurant. He had starting working as a waiter in 1978, largely to have daytime hours free for the beach, but it was only after making his deal with his father that he got some managerial experience as an assistant manager at the Pier Company restaurant in Seaport Village. Thus Rubio's had an unassuming but fairly risky start for a restaurant chain that by 1999 had sold more than 35 million fish tacos. The family, using Ray Rubio's initial investment of $30,000, bought the building at a "distressed" sale for $16,000. Previously a hamburger grill, it was little more than a stand, but it would do. Not knowing whether the business would take hold, the Rubios started out frugally. In order to save money while learning and building the business, Ralph elected to move back into to his parents' home.

The careful start soon paid off. The fish taco became a favorite treat for the crowd of young surfers in the neighborhood, and the initial unit's success soon encouraged expansion plans. In fact, from the outset the Rubios began reinvesting the company profits, building a chain, first in San Diego, then beyond. However, expansion was slow and cautious at first. It

Company Perspectives:

As we move into 2000, the growth potential for our concept is greater than ever before. Major fast-food Mexican chains have done an excellent job of educating people about Mexican food. In most regions, tacos and burritos are no longer a new or exotic idea. In addition, with the expansion of a number of casual dining Mexican chains, many consumers are also now becoming aware that real Mexican food is not ground beef and reheated beans. We believe that consumers are ready for high quality Mexican food in a quick service format. Our goal is to fill that demand on a national level.

was three years before the company opened its second restaurant, located on College Avenue near San Diego State University. In the next year, 1987, it added another unit. It also reached $1.6 million in sales. By that time, Ralph Rubio had moved out of the kitchen. Though he continued to do his own marketing and advertising, his principal concern was management, making sure that the company in its growth made the right decisions.

1988–91: Expanding into New Markets Despite Decade-End Recession

In 1988, the company added three more Rubio's Deli-Mex restaurants, as they were then called. Although the chain was still relatively small, consisting of just six units, it had started moving into new market areas. Rubio's opened one of its units in San Marcos, an inland community that provided a test of the company's chance of catching on in a locale where residents had no knowledge of Baja cuisine and demographically differed from beach areas where younger and more active people tended to congregate, a group more willing to try novel foods.

Believing that the San Diego market, though very profitable, was almost saturated, Ralph Rubio had adopted a strategy of opening additional units first throughout San Diego County and then in North County, Orange County, and Los Angeles, which offered a much larger market potential than San Diego. Original plans called for buying land for the new units, but Rubio felt that commercial property in promising locales often sold at prohibitive prices, which forced the company to continue leasing land at its new sites. Initially, Rubio's tried to finance its expansion from its profits, but when its rate of growth picked up, it had to rely on bank loans. That slowed growth somewhat, as did the recession of the late 1980s.

1992–2000: Growth of the Chain and Going Public

Growth of Rubio's in the 1990s greatly accelerated, particularly between 1998 and 2000. At the end of 1992, the chain consisted of 16 restaurants employing about 300 people. These had combined sales of $8.9 million. Also, they were still wholly under the family's control, but continued growth was clearly going to make a strict family-management impractical if not impossible. When the chain grew to 26 locations, during 1996, the company began extensive recruiting outside the family.

Over the next four years, the company worked to put together a strong executive team and solid board of directors.

Ralph Rubio remained at the company's helm as president and CEO, and after his father's retirement in 1999, he also became chairman of the company's board. Many new members of the team brought important experience from their previous work at other fast-food and other retail chains. They included chief operating officer, Stephen J. Sather; chief financial officer, Joseph Stein; chief marketing officer, Bruce Frazer; and director of real estate, Ted Frumkin.

Among other things, they faced some stiffening competition from other chains. At least in Southern California, the fish taco was becoming popular enough to attract tough players, even the fast-service, Mexican-food giant, Taco Bell, which started offering its own version of the famous fish taco in mid-decade.

However, the greatest challenge was a happy one—coping with success. In 1995, Rubio's Baja Grill units numbered 23. By the end of the following year, they had increased to 31, in 1997 to 43, and in 1998 to 59. That represented an annual average growth rate of nine units between 1995 and 1998. The strong sales in the same period justified the accelerated expansion. Same-store increases in sales hit double digits in both 1997 (18 percent) and 1998 (10.4 percent). Those figures prompted Rubio's decision to go public, which it did in 1999, when it made its first stock offering of 3.15 million shares of common stock, traded on the NASDAQ, priced at $10.50 per share.

Prior to that, financing had been achieved through private placements of Rubio's stock, made possible because of the company's solid reputation. The fact that in 1993 the U.S. Small Business Administration had named Rubio's California's most successful entrepreneurial business helped. Between 1995 and 1997, the company privately placed convertible preferred stock totaling $17.6 million.

Through its initial public offering in 1999, the company raised an additional $23.4 million, allowing it to finance the opening of 31 new restaurants, giving it a total of 90 Rubio's Baja Grill locations. It also tapped into four new markets: Denver, Salt Lake City, Sacramento, and Tucson. With that single-year 50 percent increase in its total number of units, Rubio's primary challenge was to maintain the quality of its operation. Its special development and operations teams accomplished that feat with no major difficulties.

Rapid growth carried risks, of course. Among other things, the company could not afford to invest in property for its new Baja Grills during its accelerating expansion. As a result, the company continued to lease all of its restaurant locations, with, of course, the sole exception of its initial unit. Its plans for expansion into the next century called for the continued leasing of property. To keep the expense of adding new restaurants down, the company was determined to operate within very specific cost and size limits. Historically, Rubio's restaurants ranged between 1,800 and 3,600 square feet in size, with its smallest units located in food courts. New plans called for selecting sites for units with a footprint ranging between 2,000 and 2,400 square feet, with an average start up cost of about $380,000.

Ways to ensure efficiency and economize without sacrificing quality in food or service became the study of Rubio's growing managerial team throughout the 1990s. For example, in 1998, Rubio's hired Paul Wartenberg as director of information tech-

Key Dates:

1983: Ralph Rubio's family begins business at stand in Mission Bay area of San Diego.
1986: Expansion begins with opening of second restaurant; Rubio's sells its one-millionth fish taco.
1991: Company expands into Orange County.
1995: Rubio's completes a $3.5 million private placement.
1996: Company adds a $4 million private placement.
1997: Restaurants become Rubio's Baja Grills and expand into Phoenix and Las Vegas markets; company also completes another private placement of $10.1 million.
1999: Company goes public.
2000: Rubio's opens its 100th Rubio's Baja Grill.

nology. He joined the company from CKE Restaurants, parent company to two fast-food chains. His job was to ensure that Rubio's, in adapting computer technology to its expansion needs, took no costly false steps. Other moves were made to achieve cost-cutting efficiency. Among other steps, in the winter of 2000, Rubio's signed a contractual agreement with Alliant Foodservice Inc., which provided centralized distribution of all food and paper products to the company's chain of restaurants.

Starting in 2000, the company also initiated a franchise program to help its expansion into new markets. The stratagem called for partnering with other chain operators. Plans also called for opening 36 new restaurants in 2000 and 41 more in 2001, mostly in the company's existing markets, where brand recognition was high and was being regularly reinforced through radio and television advertising. A milestone was reached on March 27, 2000, when, in Pasadena, Rubio's Restaurant Inc. opened it 100th Rubio's Baja Grill. At that time, Ralph Rubio indicated that the achievement was just the beginning of the company's efforts to create a nationwide chain.

Through its development into a chain of 100 plus restaurants, Rubio's has acted like a company that can meet its own expectations, one that will stake a solid nationwide claim to a significant share of a very tough market. Its vitality has been reflected in its upbeat, forward-looking strategies and timely moves. As even its Baja Grill menu suggests, it has been on the go from the beginning, year by year trying new dishes and varying the menu that began simply with its famous fish taco as its centerpiece. Most all additions have been based on the Mexican cuisine of Baja California. Some of the new dishes,

like Rubio's Lobster Burrito, became almost as popular as the original offering. Other favorites included char-grilled steak, chicken and seafood items that became staples on the menu. Like most of the better fast-food chains, Rubio's never stopped experimenting with its menu and frequently offered promotional items that might or might not find a permanent menu slot, depending on their popularity. In 1999, for example, the company introduced a Tequila Shrimp Burrito garnished with a new mango-tequila salsa, Shrimp and Crab Enchiladas topped with a jalapeño cream sauce, and a Grilled Chicken Salad. The trick will be to make those exotic sounding entrees as popular across the land as they have proved to be in Rubio's established markets.

Principal Subsidiaries

Rubio's Restaurants of Nevada, Inc.

Principal Competitors

Del Taco Restaurants Inc.; Prandium Inc.; Taco Bell Corp.; Wahoo's Fish Tacos.

Further Reading

Battaglia, Andy, "Rubio's Growth Plan: Become Biggest Fish Taco Purveyor in Each Pond," *Nation's Restaurant News*, August 23, 1999, p. 11.

Brune, Brett R. R., "Rubio's Deli-Mex Casts Line into Four New Market Areas," *San Diego Business Journal*, September 12, 1988, p. 8.

Casper, Carol, "Fishing for Customers: A Sub-sub-segment Builds Around Signature Fish Tacos," *Restaurant Business*, March 20, 1996, p. 102.

Cebrzynski, Gregg, "It's the Lobster That Got Away and the Tale of the Talking Bag," *Nation's Restaurant News*, July 27, 1998, p. 16.

Disbrowe, Paula, "Tacos of the Sea," *Restaurant Business*, October 1, 1997, p. 145.

Fikes, Bradley J., "No Pesky Problems for the Rubio's Chain," *San Diego Business Journal*, February 22, 1993, p. 8.

Hardesty, Greg, "Orange County, Calif., Market Kings Plan to Take Fish Tacos Nationwide,"
Knight-Ridder/Tribune Business News, September 17, 1997, p. 917.

"IT Director Says Function Always Triumphs over Fashion at Rubio's," *Nation's Restaurant News*, May 24, 1999, p. 16.

Kragen, Pam, "Southern California Fish Taco Chain Expands, Stresses Baja Theme," *Knight-Ridder/Tribune Business News*, June 2, 1997, p. 602.

Spector, Amy, "Rubio's Files for IPO Amid Expansion Push," *Nation's Restaurant News*, April 5, 1999, p. 8.

—John W. Fiero

Ryanair Holdings plc

Corballis Park
Dublin Airport
Co. Dublin
Ireland
Telephone: +353 (1) 812 1212
Fax: +353 (1) 844 4409
Web site: http://www.ryanair.com
         http://www.ryanair.ie

Public Company
Incorporated: 1985
Employees: 1,400
Sales: £370.1 million (2000)
Stock Exchanges: London Dublin NASDAQ
Ticker Symbol: RYAAY
NAIC: 481111 Scheduled Passenger Air Transportation

Ryanair Holdings plc, Europe's largest budget airline, has gone a long way toward making air travel a commodity in the United Kingdom. Operating on the Southwest Airlines formula, Ryanair often causes traffic to double or triple on the routes it enters. It is flown by about seven million passengers a year. The Internet has helped the carrier slash costs on the distribution side. The brash upstart constantly clashes with the Irish airports and advertising authorities and with its state-supported nemesis, Aer Lingus.

Familial Origins

Cathal, Declan, and Shane Ryan formed Ryanair with £1 million from their father, Dr. Tony Ryan, chairman and CEO of Guinness Peat Aviation, the aircraft leasing giant. Ryanair began flying a 15-seat Bandeirante on scheduled routes between Ireland and the United Kingdom in June 1985. It entered the Dublin-London market the next spring, competing with British Airways (BA) and Dan Air as well as Aer Lingus. One million passengers a year flew Dublin-London before Ryanair; that number would triple in the next decade.

To save costs, the airline used secondary airports, including four in the West Country. In the first year, Ryanair had two airplanes and five employees apart from flight crew. An official told *Aviation Week & Space Technology* how the company had borrowed a PC in order to claim its reservations office in Dublin was "computerized." The company broke even its first year, an impressive feat considering the paper-thin margins of the airline industry.

By 1988, Ryanair had grown to 600 employees and was fielding 40 flights a day. On two key international routes, Dublin-Manchester and Dublin-Glasgow, Aer Lingus matched fares and increased frequencies, forcing Ryanair into a hasty retreat from those markets. In addition, the company had reserved planes for European charter work that never materialized, *Aviation Week* reported. It learned the hard way about the costs of maintaining too many different kinds of planes—four types in a fleet of eight.

Ryanair lost IR £7.5 million ($11 million) in 1988. CEO Eugene O'Neill resigned over differences with the board of directors about how to proceed during those rough times. P.J. McGoldrick took his place as CEO, although O'Neill remained on the board of directors. At the time, the company was 90 percent owned by the Ryan family and ten percent by employees.

In November 1989, the Ryans injected another IR £20 million into the airline, allowing it to place an order for ten Aerospatiale/Aeritalia ATR-42 turboprop transports for $100 million. At the time, the airline operated six ATR-42s and eight BAC-111s.

Much as Southwest did in the United States, Ryanair's low fares brought a new class of traveler into the skies. Airline traffic tripled in Ireland between 1986 and 1989. Recognizing the carrier's contribution to tourism and wanting to maximize the use of Irish airline capacity, the Irish government banned competition between Ryanair and Aer Lingus from November 1989 until September 1992. As a result, Ryanair lost the Dublin-Paris route to Aer Lingus but gained time to reorganize.

Company Perspectives:

Ryanair is Europe's Leading Low Fares Airline: This year we expect to carry over 6 million passengers across 34 routes. We have recently added 7 new European routes to our ever expanding network. We operate a low fares, no frills policy, and have the lowest fares on all of the routes we fly whether from Ireland, UK or continental Europe. On Ireland - UK routes, Ryanair is market leader on every route where it competes with Aer Lingus. Ryanair is confident that Europe's high-cost and often state-subsidised airlines will be no match for its low cost, no frills formula. In addition to our routes between Ireland and the UK, 15 European cities now enjoy the benefits of truly low cost air travel and with Ryanair set to grow by 25% each year, and a US $2 billion order for 45 new aircraft in place, millions of European air travellers will feel the 'Ryanair effect' in the years ahead.

(France had not allowed Ryanair to offer fares as low as it had wanted anyway.)

New Management in the 1990s

By 1990, Ryanair was posting IR £40 million in revenues but losing IR £7 million a year. It had accumulated losses of nearly £19 since its founding, and the *Observer* reported that it "came within hours of financial collapse." P.J. McGoldrick quit his position as CEO early in 1992. His replacement, Conor Hayes, resigned as CEO at the end of 1993 and was to be succeeded by his deputy, Michael O'Leary. Formerly accountant for the company, his financial controls were credited with returning it to profitability. He had also been Tony Ryan's assistant. According to the *Sunday Times,* part of his terms were that he and the two other executive directors, Cathal and Declan Ryan, would share half the airline's future profits.

O'Leary was in his early 30s when he took over. A charismatic figure, he played soccer on the baggage handlers' team even as he cut wages 25 percent. He spoke of an unrestrained admiration for Southwest Airlines CEO Herb Kelleher and sought to emulate not only his operational strategies but the spirit he inspired in employees. "We must amuse, surprise, and entertain," he quoted. At Ryanair, like Southwest, managers (including O'Leary himself) helped in other jobs (such as loading baggage and passenger check-in) when needed. *Air Transport World* reported Ryanair was carrying 3,077 employees per passenger, more even than Southwest, which carried 2,443.

Although McGoldrick had wanted to partner with a U.S. airline with sights on Europe, O'Leary did not want to enter a strategic alliance for fear of losing control over costs. He kept the company focused on point-to-point flights, avoiding complicated code-sharing and Fifth Freedom deals. With profits of just 92p per passenger, Ryanair claimed to be the lowest-cost airline in Europe. Margins were so low that on short flights Ryanair made most of its money from duty-free sales. After a couple of years of breaking even, Ryanair posted a pretax profit of £1.7 on turnover of £75 million for the 1993–94 fiscal year. The next year, profits rose to IR £5 million.

In the mid-1990s, Ryanair had 500 staff and 11 Boeing 737s and was carrying more than two million passengers a year. In contrast, Aer Lingus had three times as many aircraft and ten times the staff, but flew only twice the passengers. Ryanair sold round trip tickets from Dublin to the United Kingdom for as little as £59, and its share of the London-Dublin route eventually exceeded Aer Lingus's 40 percent. Both Ryanair and British Midland complained of the Irish state carrier's perceived predatory pricing policies to European Community regulators.

Britain had the most liberalized air market in all Europe, and competition had emerged in the form of EasyJet, which was selling one-way fares between London (Luton) and Glasgow or Edinburgh for £29. EasyJet did not work through travel agents or computer reservation systems. Ryanair, however, relied on travel agents for 70 percent of bookings. Unlike EasyJet, it still issued paper tickets, but did away with assigned seating.

In November 1996, an American investment group lead by David Bonderman bought 20 percent of the carrier. Bonderman, who had been associated with Southwest, also remained a director of Continental Airlines, which he had helped revitalize. In a series of complex transactions, a new company, Ryanair Holdings plc, was formed.

In the 1996–97 fiscal year, the company posted pretax profits of IR £25.6 million on turnover of IR £136.4 million. Ryanair looked to the newly liberalized (deregulated) skies of Europe, aiming for 25 percent a year growth. The continent was a relative stranger to budget air travel. Several factors, however, promised to be particularly costly on short, cheap flights, such as standardized fees for computer reservation systems, hopelessly inefficient air traffic control, and costly landing fees at congested European airports. Ryanair planned to use London's Stansted Airport rather than Dublin as a base for flights to the continent because of its lower costs. Ryanair cut agents' commissions from nine percent to 7.5 percent, following a growing industry trend, while opening its Ryanair Direct telemarketing center, Ireland's largest.

O'Leary had told the *Observer* that while other carriers spent years developing markets into profitability, Ryanair "will not enter a route if we cannot break even in three hours and grow the market by at least 100 percent." In 1997, Ryanair launched routes to Paris (Beauvais) and Brussels (Brussels South) with fares as low as IR £79. It expected to double traffic between Dublin and Paris. It had gained a 37 percent market share on Dublin-London, which in 1997 surpassed Paris-London as Europe's busiest air corridor.

Public in 1997

In the 1997–98 fiscal year, Ryanair flew more than four million people, generating sales of £182.6 million. In May 1997, the company listed shares on the Dublin and Nasdaq stock markets. The Ryan family owned about 40 percent after the offering, worth £100 million; they had pulled £110 million from the company to that point. O'Leary owned 14 percent, and employees received bonuses from £2,500 to £5,000. Through the flotation, Bonderman maneuvered a £1 million investment into a £50 million shareholding, according to the *Sunday Times.*

The timing seemed great: the airline industry as a whole was recovering, and a healthy economy in the British Isles was encouraging more vacationing. The share price doubled within four months of the offering. Another share placement on the London Stock Exchange raised £50 million. Wary analysts, however, remembered how many budget airlines had failed in the United States during the preceding decade.

Ryanair looked for a hub in continental Europe to find respite from Aer Rianta's high costs and threw its support behind a proposal (Huntstown Air Park) to build a second airport in Dublin. Ryanair was pitching proposals to build or fund its own terminal there in exchange for reduced landing fees. Dublin Airport had fees nearly three times higher than average. Aer Rianta, which also owned eight Great Southern hotels, was slated for 2002, and the government seemed wary of doing anything to devalue this asset (via breaking its monopoly) before its sale.

BA launched a low-cost offshoot, called simply "Go," in early 1998. Go had little effect on Ryanair's market share when it entered the London-Rimini and London-Venice routes in the winter of 1998–99. During 1998, Ryanair carried more passengers than Go, EasyJet, and Debonair combined. Regulatory authorities in Europe took a more aggressive stance regarding the predatory pricing tactics that major airlines in the United States had used to eliminate competition from budget carriers. Ryanair continued to open new routes in Germany, France, and Italy, and in the 1998–99 fiscal year, posted after-tax profits of £45.3 million on operating revenues of £232.9 million; both figures were up substantially.

Two U.K. upstarts, Debonair and AB Airlines, folded in late 1999. Both had tried to incorporate traditional perks into a budget fare system. Both KLM and Lufthansa were considering forming low-fare subsidiaries, although Go had already lost £20 million in 17 months and BA posted its first loss in the dozen years since its privatization. Both BA and Aer Lingus had repositioned themselves toward more lucrative business traffic.

In the winter of 1999, an off-peak season, some carriers offered fares as low as £5 or £6 on Dublin-Liverpool and Dublin-London (although taxes brought the final cost up to more than £30). Still, only two percent of Europeans were flying low-fare airlines, compared with 28 percent in the United States, according to the *Irish Times*. Probably Ryanair's most viable competition came from Virgin Express, which began a Shannon-London (Stansted) route in late 1998 and began Shan-

non-Brussels in December 1999. It also was considering routes from Dublin and Cork.

Taking a shot at its old rival Aer Lingus, Ryanair ran a controversial ad reading, "It's not just the Bank of Ireland that gets robbed at Dublin Airport," referring to an event that had in fact just happened. This brought censure from the Advertising Standards Authority.

Ryanair continued to expand its European network, investing $200 million (£124 million) in five new planes and adding 250 jobs in London and Glasgow. It expected to carry seven million passengers, passing Aer Lingus, and hoped to be carrying 12 million passengers a year by 2004. A new hub on the continent was planned by 2002.

Ryanair launched Ryanair.com in January 2000, leapfrogging over Aer Lingus, which had an Internet presence but not online booking. The new web site soon became the busiest one in the country, logging 14 million impressions a month. E-commerce proved to be a low overhead way for the carrier to sell 50,000 tickets a week, more than double the amount sold on Travelocity.com, the next most popular travel site. Ryanair sold $130 million worth of tickets online in the first year. It planned to exploit its potential as a portal to other travel services.

Principal Competitors

Aer Lingus; British Airways plc; Virgin Express Holdings.

Further Reading

Beesley, Arthur, "Ryanair Revises Strategy for Dublin Airport Terminal," *Irish Times,* October 28, 1999, Bus. Sec., p. 18.
Brown, John Murray, "A Streamlined Approach To Beat the Turbulence," *Financial Times,* Companies & Finance Sec., May 10, 1997, p. 18.
Canniffe, Mary, "Ryanair Comes to Market at a Very Opportune Time," *Irish Times,* Business & Finance Sec., May 7, 1997, p. 14.
Dalby, Douglas, "Ryanair Chief Executive To Leave at Year's End," *Irish Times,* June 24, 1993, p. 14.
Gresser, Charis, "Flying High for the Price of a Pair of Jeans," *Irish Times,* Business & Finance Sec., October 23, 1997, p. 19.
Harrison, Bernice, "Devil Is in the Detail in Ryanair Price Promise," *Irish Times,* Business & Finance Sec., January 13, 2000, p. 23.
Harrison, Michael, "P.J. Flies Back into Limelight," *Independent* (London), Business and City Page, February 27, 1992, p. 31.
Kelleher, Rory, "Airlines Book Themselves onto Internet Jet as Market Takes Off," *Irish Times,* Bus. Sec., March 3, 2000, p. 59.
Lowden, Ian J., "Pushy Upstarts," *International Business,* October 1996, p. 12.
McHugh, Fiona, "Ryanair To Move Hub to Europe," *Sunday Times,* Bus. Sec., September 13, 1998.
Murphy, Colm, "Ryanair Soars Above Rivals on the Internet," *Sunday Times,* Bus. Sec., March 19, 2000.
"New Captain at Ryanair as Airline Heads for Europe," *Irish Times,* November 23, 1996, Bus. Sec. p. 16.
O'Connor, Anthony, "Leader of the Pack," *Airfinance Journal,* December 1997, pp. 28–32.
Ott, James, "Ryanair Seeks To Strengthen Position During Reprieve from Competition," *Aviation Week & Space Technology,* November 6, 1989, pp. 58–59.
Reed, Arthur, "Southwest Style in Europe," *Air Transport World,* August 1995, p. 63.

Reeves, Scott, "Offerings in the Offing: Smooth Takeoff," *Barron's,* June 2, 1997, p. 47.

"Ryanair Aims To Spread Wings over Europe; New Strategy Still To Be Revealed," *Irish Times,* November 15, 1994, Bus. Sec., p. 16.

Skapinker, Michael, "Low-Cost, No-Frills Airlines Tighten Seat Belts," *Financial Times,* October 22, 1998, Companies & Finance Sec., p. 23.

——, "There's No Such Thing as a Free Lunch—US-Style No-Frills Airlines with Low Fares Are Trying Their Luck in Europe," *Financial Times,* December 18, 1995, Bus. Travel Sec., p. 12.

"Taking Ryanair to a Higher Plane," *Director,* May 1997, p. 18.

Taylor, Cliff, "Airline Confident Low-Cost Formula Can Continue To Deliver Growth," *Irish Times,* June 17, 1998, Bus. Sec., p. 16.

Walters, Joanna, "Irish Eyes Are Smiling at Ryanair," *Observer,* Bus. Sec., November 27, 1994, p. 6.

——, "Why Irish Aer's Not Smiling," *Observer,* Bus. Sec., August 14, 1994, p. 5.

—Frederick C. Ingram

Saucony Inc.

13 Centennial Drive
Peabody, Massachusetts 01961
U.S.A.
Telephone: (978) 532-9000
Fax: (978) 532-6105
Web site: http://www.saucony.com

Public Company
Incorporated: 1910 as A.R. Hyde And Sons
Employees: 494
Sales: $154.1 million (1999)
Stock Exchanges: NASDAQ
Ticker Symbols: SCNYA SCNYB
NAIC: 316211 Rubber and Plastics Footwear Manufac-
turing; 316219 Other Footwear Manufacturing;
315228 Men's and Boys' Cut and Sew Other
Outerwear Manufacturing; 315239 Women's and
Girls' Cut and Sew Other Outerwear Manufacturing;
336991 Motorcycles, Bicycles, and Parts

Saucony Inc. (under the corporate umbrella of Hyde Athletic Industries, Inc. until 1998 when Hyde reorganized and took the Saucony name), is known primarily as a designer, manufacturer, and marketer of high performance running shoes, in particular for marathon runners and triathletes. During the 1990s, the company expanded its market presence with its walking and hiking shoes, and the reintroduction of "classic" models from the 1980s. Saucony also manufactures Hind brand athletic apparel, high performance bicycles through its Merlin subsidiary, and Spot-Bilt shoes for coaches and officials. In 2000, its products were available in 23 foreign countries and in over 5,500 retail outlets in the United States.

Origins

This history of Saucony is inextricably linked with that of Hyde Athletic Industries, which was founded by Russian immigrant Abraham Hyde, who came to the United States in 1890. At first Hyde, a cobbler, worked in a space he rented in a laundry making slippers from old carpet remnants. In 1910, Hyde was able to move his business to a house in Cambridge, Massachusetts, where he founded the company A.R. Hyde and Sons. Until 1932 he produced his "carpet slippers" and street shoes for women and children. He branched into athletic goods in 1932 with ice skates he called Pleasure Skates. By the end of the 1930s, he was producing a whole line of athletic footwear, including baseball shoes, roller boots, and bowling shoes.

With the outbreak of World War II, production was given over to boots for soldiers. As a result of this work, Hyde was awarded the Army/Navy E Award for Manufacturing Excellence—the only American shoe company so honored. After the war, the company resumed production of athletic shoes and, in 1952, purchased the Illinois Athletic Shoe Company, makers of Spot-Bilt athletic shoes. In 1960 NASA awarded Hyde a contract to produce footwear for America's space program, and as a result, the boots worn by astronauts during the first space walk bore the Hyde label.

In 1968 Hyde purchased the Saucony Shoe Manufacturing Company, a maker of running shoes located in Kurztown, Pennsylvania. In the early 1970s Hyde transferred all development and production activities connected with running shoes to the new subsidiary. Until the late 1960s, Hyde and Sons was a family-owned business. However, in July 1969, the year after the Saucony acquisition, an initial public offering was announced. In October 1969, 350,000 shares were sold; the following year, the company changed its name to Hyde Athletic Industries, Inc.

Slowly Gaining Market Share in the 1970s and 1980s

Hyde had annual sales of approximately $20 million in 1976, and Saucony running shoes remained a little-known niche brand. In 1977, however, a national American magazine gave the shoes an award for "Best Quality." The article established the Saucony brand in the mind of runners throughout the country. It also established the company as a going prospect. In September 1977 Colgate Palmolive offered to acquire the company for 312,690 shares of Colgate stock valued at about $7.7 million. In less than a month, however, the negotiations ended.

Company Perspectives:

Saucony Incorporated's family of companies offers a wide range of technical products for every workout need. We design and market separate lines for men and women within most technical footwear categories. In keeping with our emphasis on performance, we market and sell our technical footwear to athletes who have a high participation rate in their sport of choice. We address this market through our "Loyal to the Sport" advertising campaign. We believe that these consumers are more brand loyal than those who buy athletic footwear for casual use. The Saucony brand is recognized for its technical innovation and performance. As a result of our application of biomechanical technology in the design process, we believe that our Saucony footwear has a distinctive 'fit and feel' that is attractive to athletic users. We design our Saucony technical cross training, women's walking and outdoor technical trail shoes with many of the same performance features and 'fit and feel' characteristics as are found in Saucony technical running shoes.

Saucony expanded its line of running shoes into the 1980s; as marathon runs, and later triathlons, became popular, Saucony won the loyalty of more and more long-distance runners. Still Hyde experienced slow growth during the 1980s—a decade that otherwise saw an explosion in the sale of athletic shoes. Growth was hampered primarily by the company's size, which limited the amount it was able to spend on advertising. "We didn't have the funds for promotion," Hyde's vice-president John Fisher told the *Christian Science Monitor* in 1984, adding "Nike was giving away more shoes than we used to sell. On the way up, it was just word of mouth." However, some industry observers at the time felt that Hyde's slow pace of expansion enabled it to maintain control of production quality that later contributed further to the company's reputation. In 1984 Hyde reported its sales had increased 22 percent over 1983, sales it attributed in large part to its line of Saucony running shoes. In early 1985, the company moved into a new headquarters building in Peabody, Massachusetts. The same year it purchased the Brookfield Athletic Shoe Company, a firm which manufactured roller skates, ice skates, and in-line skates.

Hyde announced in September 1988 plans to re-launch the PF Flyer line of canvas sneakers that had been so popular in the 1950s and 1960s but which had essentially disappeared from the market by the 1980s. The move was made in response to the sudden resurgence of popularity of another canvas shoe, Keds, which were expected to have sales three times higher than 1985 levels. The 1988 version of PF Flyers retailed for between $60 and $70, compared to less than $15 in the 1950s when Flyers were among the most popular gym shoes on the market. Hyde planned to market the shoes for 11 to 18 year old males initially; it held off bringing out adult models for a year hoping they would catch on with younger buyers before their parents made nostalgia purchases.

In December 1988, Hyde announced that it had agreed to be acquired by an investment group called Silvershoe Partners for $8.50 a share, approximately $23.5 million in all. A week later,

Blue Star Holding Inc. a mysterious Cambridge, Massachusetts, company owned, according to the *Boston Globe,* by "publicity-shy Europeans," made a counteroffer of $9.50 a share. Blue Star would only say it had been watching Hyde for some time. Spokespersons for Hyde told the press it was banned by the terms of its agreement with Silvershoe from entering negotiations with any other buyer. In spring 1989, a Hyde shareholder asked a Superior Court judge to block the company from holding its June shareholders meeting at which the acquisition by Silvershoe would be voted on. The shareholder, Roberta Klotz, maintained that the agreement, which gave Silvershoe control of two-thirds of Hyde stock, was against the interests of its stockholders. The Superior Court judge denied Klotz's request. By autumn, however, it looked like a judge's ruling would not be necessary to prevent the deal. Silvershoe's bank refused to provide the levels of financing necessary to make the purchase. The deal did not close by the original July 31 deadline, and another in mid-August also passed. Finally, in late September, Hyde's board of directors approved a request to terminate the merger agreement.

Challenges in the Early 1990s

Hyde could not approach the sales levels of the big players in the field of athletic footwear, in particular Nike, which had the lucrative Michael Jordan basketball shoe franchise. By 1990, however, the company seemed to be in solid shape with annual sales of more than $60 million and a workforce of about 250, up from 150 in 1988. The company also boasted a line of running shoes that were made in the United States, in its Bangor, Maine, factory. In June 1992, Hyde signed a distribution agreement with Tokai Sporting Goods Co, a Japanese company, that introduced Saucony running shoes to the Japanese market. The deal also gave Hyde a Saucony sales office in Tokyo.

In the early 1990s, Hyde's Saucony division was responsible for nearly three-quarters of its total sales. Most of those products were still serving what was a niche market—runners, in particular long-distance runners, including professionals. However, the line had experienced a five-year sales plunge; between 1987 and 1991 sales fell from $55 million to $36 million.

In May 1992, the company's fortunes changed. An article in the magazine *Consumer Reports* gave Saucony's Jazz 3000 shoe its "best buy" rating. As a result of the unexpected publicity, Saucony sales doubled over the next couple months. Industry analysts wondered whether Hyde had the wherewithal or the savvy to capitalize on its new momentum. The company planned to more than double its advertising budget, to place ads in non-running periodicals like *USA Today,* and to initiate a "Made in the USA" campaign. Hyde also estimated it would soon have to boost the output of its Bangor factory, by introducing new equipment and nearly tripling its workforce there. The following year, the company reported that sales of its Saucony line had risen by $11 million to $47 million. The number of stores that carried Saucony shoes had jumped 25 percent, and Hyde's share of the American athletic shoe market had doubled to 6.6 percent.

Consumer Reports helped bring Hyde into the news again in mid-1993, but in a very different light. In July, Reebok International Ltd. sued its rival for falsely implying in its advertising and public relations materials that the Saucony Instep was the magazine's top-rated women's walking shoe. In fact *Consumer Reports* had named Reebok's Avia 382 the top shoe. Hyde told the press it intended to contest the Reebok suit, and ten days later the two companies reached an out-of-court settlement. Hyde agreed to discontinue claims that it produced the top walking shoe.

Hyde Athletic Industries was producing outdoor recreational products for children, its PF Flyer line, Brookfield roller skates, and ice skates for children. However, its line of Saucony athletic footwear, including running, walking, hiking, fitness, and tennis shoes accounted for the lion's share of the company's annual sales, nearly 75 percent. In 1993, noting that the fitness boom of the 1980s was winding down, Hyde expanded the line of walking and hiking shoes it had inaugurated in 1985, adding five new models. At the same time the company offered purchasers of its walking shoes a free membership in the Saucony Walking Club, which included a logbook, training information, and a regular newsletter.

During this time, Hyde expanded its international presence. In September 1993, it opened a sales and marketing office in Heidelberg, Germany, to service Europe, Great Britain, and Ireland. In November it acquired its Australian distributor, S.P. Agencies, for an undisclosed price, renaming it Saucony S.P. That deal gave Hyde an interest in four of its foreign distributors, including Saucony B.V. of the Benelux, Saucony Canada, the company's branch office, and Saucony U.K. in England. Otherwise, Hyde was represented by 15 independent distributors throughout the world.

More unwelcome publicity emerged in the mid-1990s, when the Federal Trade Commission (FTC) charged that Hyde and New Balance Athletic Shoes, another New England manufacturer, had falsely claimed in their advertising that their products were made in the United States. The FTC maintained that although the shoes were assembled domestically, most of their parts were produced overseas. New Balance fought the ruling, claiming the FTC's guidelines were hopelessly outdated. Hyde, on the other hand, to avoid the costs of fighting a court battle,

entered into a settlement with the agency. Under its terms, the company would be allowed to sell what stock it had that bore "Made in U.S.A." labels. It also agreed to affix the label only to products made entirely or virtually entirely in the United States. Hyde and New Balance were the first high-profile cases brought against companies for violation of the FTC's "Made in U.S.A." standards. Some observers noted that the agency seemed to be going after small fish and ignoring much larger, more egregious offenders. Others believed it was looking to set precedents that would give it ammunition in larger cases. In the end, after an administrative review of its guidelines that lasted more than three years, the FTC decided to retain the strict standards it had enforced for nearly 50 years.

Hyde found itself at odds with its competitor Reebok again in 1996. Reebok had signed triathlete Michelle Jones to an endorsement contract early in the year. Hyde sued, claiming that under the terms of its own contract with Jones, they were entitled for a year after the deal's expiration to an opportunity to match any competing offer. Hyde was the first company to go after endorsements in the triathlon, and maintaining its profile in the sport—particularly in the women's event—was seen as important to the company. In March it won an injunction from a Massachusetts Superior Court judge barring Jones from representing Reebok in its advertising and from wearing Reebok products in appearances or competition. The two companies settled out-of-court the following summer. Reebok paid Hyde an undisclosed amount of money in exchange for its immediate release of Jones from all contractual obligations.

Hyde Becomes Saucony in the Late 1990s

In late 1997, Hyde began undergoing a major transformation. In August it spun off Brookfield International Inc., the subsidiary that produced in-line skates, roller skates, skateboards, and protective gear, often under license from companies such as Walt Disney Co., Hasbro Inc., and Mattel Inc. Brookfield's CEO James Buchanan and investment firm Brynwood III bought the company for an undisclosed sum. In January 1998, Hyde completely reorganized the Saucony Footwear division, which, with the sale of Brookfield, accounted for 85 percent of Hyde's total annual sales. The division was split into Saucony International and Saucony North America, with administrative headquarters remaining in Peabody, Massachusetts.

The reorganization was undertaken to help turn Saucony around, as it had reported losses of $4.7 million for 1997. About half of Saucony's employees in Peabody were expected to be relocated or reassigned to make the division's operations more efficient. In spring 1998 Hyde formally changed its name to Saucony Inc.

In a little more than a year, Saucony turned its performance around completely. After hovering around the same price for five years, its stock prices more than tripled. Cause for the turnaround was the Saucony Originals line. Originals were built around the Jazz running shoe, one of the company's popular, long-discontinued, high-performance models of the early 1980s. Jazz were unable to match the technology of the late 1990s, but they were comfortable and attractive, and, with a price tag between $40 and $60, they were very affordable. When it introduced the new line, Saucony also extended its advertising well beyond the running magazine forum, into youth-oriented periodicals such as *Spin* and *Vibe*. When Saucony Originals were featured in a fashion forecast in *Teen People*, the line took off. The fact that the shoes were frequently worn by rock stars only increased their popularity more. With the Originals line accounting for 37 percent of the company's 1999 net sales Saucony planned to introduce other Originals models in 2000.

Despite lackluster performance for the athletic shoe industry as a whole, Saucony's 1999 sales increased 47 percent over 1998. As the millennium turned, Saucony increased its public profile by sponsoring events such as Super Bowl XXXIV and the Los Angeles Marathon, where the company donated 1,900 pairs of its shoes to local students.

Principal Subsidiaries

Hyde International Services, Ltd. (Hong Kong); Hyde Transition Corp.; Hyde, Inc.; Saucony Canada, Inc. (85%); Saucony UK, Inc.; Saucony Sports, B.V. (Netherlands); Saucony SP Pty. Ltd. (Australia); Saucony Deutschland Vertriebs GmbH (Germany); Quintana Roo, Inc.

Principal Competitors

Nike, Inc.; New Balance Athletic Shoe, Inc.; Reebok International Ltd.; Avia Group International, Inc.

Further Reading

"Avia Unit Sues Rival Hyde Over No. 1 Footwear Title," *Wall Street Journal*, July 16, 1993, p. 6B.

"Europeans Make Hyde Bid," *Boston Globe*, December 29, 1988, p. 26.

Gibbs, Alison, "Hyde Reorganizes Saucony Unit," *Boston Herald*, January 22, 1998, p. 32.

"Hyde Athletic Buys Cambridge Bike Maker," *Boston Globe*, February 20, 1998, p. E5.

"Hyde Athletic Makes Strides in Footwear," *Boston Herald*, December 19, 1994, p. 39.

"Hyde Athletic Runs into the Red," *Boston Herald* April 4, 1998, p. 16.

Merl, Jean, "Helping Youths in the Long Run," *Los Angeles Times*, February 9, 2000, p. B1.

Pereira, Joseph, "Hyde Beats Reebok in Endorsement Race," *Wall Street Journal*, March 26, 1996, p. B14.

Reidy, Chris, "Made in the USA; Or is it?," *Boston Globe*, April 4, 1995, p. 43.

——, Picking Up the Pace: Fashions, Broader Base Let New Balance Set a Record, *Boston Globe*, April 12, 2000, p. E1.

Scott, David Clark, "Best Feet Forward: Athletic-Shoe Industry, Stumbling Over Imports, Is Still in the Race," *Christian Science Monitor,* April 12, 1984, p. B1.

Shapiro, Eban, "Getting a Running Shoe in the Door," *New York Times,* August 13, 1992, p. D1.

Strauss, Gary, "Hyde Athletic Is Making Strides," *USA Today,* July 28, 1993, p. 3B.

Syre, Steven, and Charles Stein, "Saucony Finds Shoe that Fits," *Boston Globe*, June 3, 1999, p. D1.

Vartran, Vartanig G., "A Brisk Pace Is Set by Nike," *New York Times*, January 21, 1986, p. D12.

Walsh, Sharon, "FTC Cites 2 Athletic Shoe Makers; Agency Alleges 'Made in the U.S.A.' Labels on Sneakers Are False," *Washington Post*, September 21, 1994, p. F2.

White, George, "Sneaking Back: P.F. Flyers Live—This Time from Head to Toe," *Los Angeles Times*, September 15, 1988, Sec. 4, p. 1.

—Gerald E. Brennan

Sauder Woodworking Company

502 Middle Street
Archbold, Ohio 43502
U.S.A.
Telephone: (419) 446-2711
Toll Free: (800) 523-3987
Fax: (419) 446-3692
Web site: http://www.sauder.com

Private Company
Incorporated: 1940
Employees: 3,400
Sales: $545 million (1999)
NAIC: 337122 Nonupholstered Wood Household
   Furniture Manufacturing; 337214 Office Furniture
   (Except Wood) Manufacturing; 321219 Reconstituted
   Wood Product Manufacturing; 337127 Institutional
   Furniture Manufacturing; 337215 Showcase

Sauder Woodworking Company is the eighth largest furniture manufacturer in the United States and the largest producer of ready-to-assemble (RTA) furniture, a niche of the furniture industry that the company is credited with creating. Sauder Woodworking produces more than 40,000 furniture items each day at its technologically advanced factories, offering more than 30 collections in traditional, contemporary, and transitional styles. The company's furniture is sold in more than 70 countries and is retailed domestically primarily through Sears, K-Mart, and other discount retailers. Through a subsidiary named Sauder Manufacturing, the company is a leader in the production of church furniture, a line of goods that reflects the company's Mennonite roots in Archbold, Ohio, where Sauder Woodworking employs 3,400 of the town's 3,500 residents. Another subsidiary, Archbold Container, manufactures corrugated packaging and displays. The company is privately owned and operated by the Sauder family.

Origins

Sauder Woodworking is the progeny of Erie Sauder, a devout Mennonite cabinetmaker. Erie Sauder had worked at Archbold Ladder Co. in Archbold, Ohio, before he decided to start working for himself in 1934. He initially found work making kitchen cabinets around Archbold. One of his first large orders came from a local hatchery that needed sticks to insert between incubator cages. Erie Sauder and his wife Leona worked together in a small, weather-beaten barn; she sawed the boards while he finished the sticks. Although they earned only $5 per week, it was enough to feed their family.

A few years after he started his business a nearby church burned down. Erie Sauder won the job of building new pews, thus expanding his business into church furniture; Sauder Woodworking eventually become a leading manufacturer of church furniture in the United States. Erie Sauder kept his workers busy during down times by making custom cabinets and taking on other miscellaneous work. For example, he began making small, inexpensive tables from the precious oak, maple, and walnut scraps left on his shop floor at the end of the day, low-priced "leftovers" as he called them.

One day in 1940 a couple of traveling salesmen stopped by Sauder's shop. They were intrigued by his low-priced tables and asked Erie Sauder if they could take some samples to a furniture show in Chicago. They later returned with an order for 25,000 tables. Erie Sauder was stunned by the request and doubted the ability of his modest shop to produce so many pieces. But he was able to secure a loan from a nearby bank that he used to incorporate his business, expand his production facilities, and hire more workers. With the help of friends and relatives, as well as "a lot of luck," according to Erie Sauder, he was able to fill the order. "It's amazing what you can do when you don't know it can't be done," became Erie Sauder's motto.

1951: The First RTA Table

Erie Sauder continued to make his custom cabinets, church pews, and tables throughout the 1940s and 1950s. Sauder Woodworking, like many other manufacturers of the time, benefited from the post-World War II economic expansion that began in the late 1940s. Of import to Sauder Woodworking's success was a request from a furniture retailer in Detroit in 1951. A buyer from the Federal Department Store determined that if he could devise a way to make furniture lay flat in a box, he could significantly reduce shipping and inventory storage costs. He envisioned a sort of snap-together table that customers could set up at home. Erie Sauder designed such a table, and with it the ready-to-assemble industry. The inexpensive tables sold rapidly and strengthened Sauder Woodworking's business.

Erie Sauder retired in 1974, when the company's sales had reached $12 million annually. With only an eighth grade education, Sauder had built his company from a simple shop in a weather-beaten barn to a multimillion dollar furniture manufacturer. Erie Sauder's sons, Maynard and Myrl, took over the company's management. At age 42, Maynard Sauder assumed the chief executive slot when his father stepped aside, and his younger brother, Myrl, was placed in charge of engineering, research, and development. The combination of Myrl Sauder's engineering expertise and Maynard Sauder's business savvy would prove to be a powerful combination during the next two decades.

The majority of Sauder Woodworking's sales in 1974 came from the sale of church furniture and ready-to-assemble pieces. Most of the company's furniture sold through a distributor, who branded the product Foremost Furniture. Although Sauder Woodworking was generally pleased with the distributor's efforts, Sauder Woodworking decided to take on its own sales and marketing efforts in 1974 and continued to sell its products under the Foremost name until it had completely phased in the Sauder Woodworking brand name by the mid-1980s.

Sauder Woodworking emphasized technology during the late 1970s and 1980s as it shifted the focus of its operations to the growing market for ready-to-assemble (RTA) furniture. RTA furniture is usually composed of panels made of particle board (boards fashioned from glue and wood chips or tiny wood particles). The boards are usually laminated to simulate a real wood finish or covered with some other colored protective coating that improves the panel's appearance. The boards typically are pre-drilled and routed to accept accompanying screws, fasteners, and other hardware. The customer assembles the furniture at home, usually needing only a screwdriver and/or hammer to finish the job. Maynard Sauder sought to make Sauder Woodworking's production facilities state-of-the-art, thus improving both quality and productivity. Sauder Woodworking engineers introduced advanced chemical etching techniques, for example, which allowed them to carve ridges into simulated wood grain. They also incorporated new cutting methods to create curved molding and bracket feet from particle board. Significantly, Sauder Woodworking worked to improve assembly instructions and provided consumers with a toll free number that they could call to get help.

As a result, returns to merchants were reduced and the retailer's perceived value of the product increased.

At the same time Sauder Woodworking improved its operations during the 1970s and 1980s, demand for RTA furniture increased. Consumers began to realize the value of RTA furniture; they could purchase an RTA table, desk, dresser, or other furnishing for 25 percent to 50 percent less than they might have to pay for conventional furniture. In addition, because it was easy to ship and store, RTA goods became extremely popular with discount retailers and mass merchandisers. Those distribution channels far outpaced expansion of conventional furniture sales channels throughout the 1980s and early 1990s.

In large part because of the efforts of Sauder Woodworking and its competitors, the public perception of RTA improved significantly during the 1980s and early 1990s. New high-tech laminating processes were developed that made particle board panels nearly indistinguishable from natural wood. Etched paper laminates, for example, closely mimicked both the look and feel of real wood. Improved epoxies eliminated moisture problems and new joints and connections increased the rigidity of RTA pieces. As RTA furniture improved, consumers began using it for everything from kitchen tables and office furniture to living room shelves and stereo cabinets. In fact, Sauder Woodworking sold RTA pieces that were priced as high as $400.

Sauder Woodworking's technological edge made it the United States' largest RTA manufacturer. Myrl Sauder had invented or adapted from other industries a variety of highly efficient machinery that made Sauder Woodworking more efficient than most of its competitors and far more cost effective than traditional furniture makers. For example, hardwood furniture makers often lost about 50 percent of the raw material during the production process. In contrast, Sauder Woodworking used high-tech saw lines to cut parts precisely with minimal waste. Scraps were collected for reuse, and even the sawdust was sold as composting material.

To manufacture its RTA furniture, Sauder Woodworking would take raw particle board and fiber board sheets, laminate both sides with veneer-like paper, and then cut the panels and parts to suit the product being made. The company typically produced different products in lots of 6,000 to 10,000 and stored them until time for packaging. By the early 1990s, Sauder Woodworking was processing 50 truckloads of particle board daily in its Ohio factories. It boasted more than 70 acres of production and warehouse facilities and a work force of 2,500, with about 1,850 engaged in building RTA furniture.

Indeed, because of Sauder Woodworking's strong growth during the 1980s, the shift changes had become the major event in Archbold, a town with a population of 3,500. Sauder Woodworking's production facilities had expanded to employ the large majority of the local residents, and most of those who were not employed at Sauder Woodworking were directly dependent on its workers. The work force, which was all nonunion, operated in three shifts, 24 hours per day, up to six days per week.

Growth of the RTA Industry in the 1990s

During the late 1980s and early 1990s, the U.S. economy dipped into a recession, stifling revenue growth and profits for

---

Key Dates:

1934: Erie Sauder starts his own woodworking company, initially making kitchen cabinets.
1940: Sauder Woodworking Co. is incorporated.
1951: Company makes first snap-together table, thereby creating the ready-to-assemble furniture industry.
1974: Erie Sauder's retirement passes leadership to his son, Maynard; company assumes control over its own sales and marketing efforts.
1990s: Company invests heavily in new production facilities.
2000: First television commercial campaign is launched.

---

much of the furniture industry. In contrast, Sauder Woodworking continued to post solid sales gains in excess of 15 percent annually throughout the early 1990s. Sales topped $300 million in 1992 and reached the $415 million mark by 1994. By that time, the company was employing more than 3,000 workers. To keep pace with demand, Sauder Woodworking had invested tens of millions of dollars in production facilities during the early 1990s, including work on a planned facility that would use the wood scraps it generated for its own energy.

Despite the capital required by rampant growth, Sauder Woodworking remained a family owned and operated company during the 1980s and into the 1990s. During this time, Maynard and Myrl Sauder were gradually passing control of the operation to a new generation of Sauders.

Although family members were welcome into the business, they were expected to meet certain standards. "We've got three rules for family members who want to work here," Maynard Sauder told *Forbes*. "A good education, success working someplace where the family name means nothing, and interest in a real opening at the company." Maynard Sauder's son, Kevin, became vice-president of marketing and sales in the early 1990s. He had worked at Northern Telecom after receiving his M.B.A. from Duke University. Similarly, Maynard Sauder's son-in-law, Garrett Tinsman, was hired to oversee Sauder Woodworking's new production facility scheduled to open in 1994.

At 89 years of age, Erie Sauder continued to return to Archbold every spring from his winter home in Florida. He oversaw Sauder Woodworking's nonprofit Sauder Farm and Craft Village, where visitors could watch craftspeople at work and attend fiddle contests and quilt fairs. "It draws 120,000 people to Archbold a year and still loses money," Maynard Sauder noted in *Forbes*.

Going into the mid-1990s, Sauder Woodworking benefited from continued domestic growth in the demand for RTA. Although church furniture represented an increasingly small percentage of Sauder Woodworking's sales, the company remained a leading manufacturer of church pews. Sauder Woodworking also enjoyed solid success overseas. After only a few years in the export business, by 1994 Sauder Woodworking was exporting $40 million worth of product to more than 60 countries worldwide. In 1993, Sauder Woodworking was named the Ohio Exporter of the Year. The company launched a national RTA advertising campaign in 1994, with a goal of doubling company sales by the turn of the century.

With the exception of one cheerless period, the latter half of the 1990s saw Sauder Woodworking move stridently forward, as the company gained ground on its competitors and realized significant growth. The one painful incident occurred in June 1997, when Erie Sauder, at the age of 92, passed away, but the legacy he left behind was displaying encouraging vitality. Although the company fell well short of doubling its sales during the second half of the 1990s, its stature within the industry increased measurably, thanks in large part to the continued growth of the RTA industry. By the end of the decade, Sauder Woodworking ranked as the eighth largest furniture manufacturer in North America, moving up two positions from the slot it occupied during the mid-1990s. The ascension was attributable to the company's continued leadership of the RTA industry, which gained an appreciable boost in business from the prolific growth of another, much higher profile, industry.

Personal computers rapidly became ubiquitous household fixtures during the latter half of the 1990s, igniting, in turn, the growth of electronic commerce. Few industries were as well suited for shopping via the Internet as the RTA industry, underscoring the importance of Erie Sauder's creation of RTA furniture that could be mailed in a flat box. Although Sauder Woodworking stood to benefit considerably from the increasing growth of electronic commerce, the company achieved more tangible gains from the proliferation of personal computers themselves. During the latter half of the 1990s, both aspects of the digital revolution—the sale of personal computers and the growth of electronic commerce—worked in Sauder Woodworking's favor. The increasing number of homes with computers meant an increasing need for furniture to house the hottest consumer trend of the decade. Sauder Woodworking moved quickly to reap the rewards to be won in the fast-growing market, introducing nearly 100 new products designed for the home office.

By the end of the 1990s, Sauder Woodworking's dominant market position befitted a venerable pioneer in the furniture business. The company's factories, regarded as some of the most technologically advanced in the world, were churning out nine million pieces of furniture, organized into more than 30 collections, each year. As the company entered a new century, its pace of growth internationally and domestically showed no signs of slackening. In 1999, Sauder Woodworking entered the Indian market, establishing exclusive showrooms in Bangalore and Hyderabad, which extended the company's geographic reach into more than 70 countries. In early 2000, the company's firm grasp on the domestic market promised to tighten after the debut of a national television commercial campaign, the first for Sauder Woodworking and the first national campaign for an RTA furniture manufacturer.

Principal Subsidiaries

Archbold Container Co.; Sauder Manufacturing Company Inc.

Principal Competitors

Bush Industries, Inc.; IKEA International A/S; O'Sullivan Industries Holdings, Inc.

Further Reading

Amatos, Christopher A., ''Sawdust Not Gathering at Sauder,'' *Columbus Dispatch,* September 13, 1992, Bus. Sec.

A History of Sauder Woodworking Co., Archbold, Ohio: Sauder Woodworking Co., 1994.

DiFrancisco, Jennifer, ''Wood Works for RTA-Maker Sauder,'' *HFN The Weekly Newspaper for the Home Furnishing Network,* June 14, 1999, p. 26.

Kunkel, Karl, ''Sauder Targets TV Viewers,'' *HFN The Weekly Newspaper for the Home Furnishing Network,* January 3, 2000, p. 28.

McLoughlin, Bill, ''CEO Divulges Growth Strategies,'' *HFN The Weekly Newspaper for the Home Furnishing Network,* October 7, 1996, p. 6.

Waldon, George, ''More Home Work: Office Product Sales Are Booming as Workers Stay Home for a Living,'' *Arkansas Business,* June 8, 1992, p. 14.

Weinberg, Neil, ''Old-Fashioned Ways Still Work,'' *Forbes,* March 14, 1994.

—Dave Mote
—updated by Jeffrey L. Covell

Scottish & Newcastle plc

50 East Fettes Avenue
Edinburgh EH4 1RR
United Kingdom
Telephone: 0131 528 2000
Fax: 0870 333 2121
Web site: http://www.scottish-newcastle.com

Public Company
Incorporated: 1931 as Scottish Brewers Ltd.
Employees: 60,000
Sales: $5.31 billion (1999)
Stock Exchanges: London
NAIC: 31212 Breweries; 72241 Drinking Places
(Alcoholic Beverages); 42281 Beer and Ale
Wholesalers; 44531 Beer, Wine, and Liquor Stores;
72111 Hotels (Except Casino Hotels) and Motels

Scottish & Newcastle plc is the United Kingdom's largest brewer. It produces several brands, including Courage, McEwan's, and Newcastle, which are marketed in approximately 50 countries. Scottish & Newcastle also owns and operates a 2,800-unit chain of branded restaurants and pubs, which serve Scottish & Newcastle beers. The company is in the process of selling two chains of vacation resort villages—Center Parcs and Holiday Club Pontin's. It is also in the process of acquiring a majority interest in Danone Group, a French brewing group with operations in Belgium, Italy, and France.

1700s and 1800s: The Youngers and the McEwans

Scottish & Newcastle's roots begin with the establishment of the William Younger Brewery in Leith in 1749. Its founder left management of the brewery to his wife, Grizell, in 1753 when he became an exciseman. Grizell continued to operate it and another brewery he had purchased in the late 1760s, after her husband died in 1770. Grizell Younger married the original owner of the second brewery, Robert Anderson, in the 1780s; by then her sons had apprenticed under her and the elder, Archibald Campbell Younger, had set up a brewery at Holyrood

Abbey. This generation of Youngers established several other breweries in this area and sold the Leith Brewery in 1801. In 1821, William Younger II, the youngest son, combined the various family interests into William Younger & Co., which prospered in the 1830s and beyond. William Younger II took on his son, William Younger III, and Alexander Smith and his son Andrew as partners in 1836. Smith's son Andrew and several Younger heirs served as partners until 1887, when the company was registered as a limited liability company, two years before its stocks were traded publicly. The previous year, William Younger IV and Andrew Smith had built the Holyrood Brewery after purchasing an additional site next to the company's existing property. This brewery continued to operate for 100 years and was rebuilt by Scottish & Newcastle (partially financed by Guinness for the Harp Lager Consortium) in 1971.

In 1931 William Younger & Co. merged with William McEwan & Co. Ltd., another Edinburgh brewer, forming Scottish Brewers Ltd. Later, Scottish & Newcastle would locate its headquarters in William Younger's Holyrood Abbey Brewery and its production facilities in McEwan's, each on opposite sides of Edinburgh, a brewing center since the monastic breweries of the 12th century.

McEwan's was started by William McEwan, a shipowner's son who established the Fountain Brewery in 1856 at Fountainbridge, Edinburgh, after serving an apprenticeship. McEwan's nephew, James Younger, managed the operation after 1886, when William McEwan entered political life. Three years later the firm was registered as William McEwan & Co. Ltd. Before the merger with Younger, McEwan's acquired the trade of yet another Edinburgh brewer, Alexander Melvin & Co., in 1907. Scottish and Newcastle continued to brew at the Fountain Brewery into the 1990s. McEwan's Export (sometimes identified as ''MacEwan's'' in foreign markets), a light ale, led canned ale sales for Britain in the 1990s.

Mid-1900s: Scottish-Newcastle Merger

Scottish Brewers acquired several more operations after World War II, including Manchester's Red Tower Lager Brewery Ltd. in 1956 and Edinburgh's Thomas & James Bernard

Key Dates:

1749: William Younger establishes the William Younger Brewery in Leith, Scotland.
1821: William Younger II, the founder's youngest son, combines the various Younger family interests into William Younger & Co.
1931: William Younger & Co. merges with William McEwan & Co. Ltd., forming Scottish Brewers Ltd.
1960: Scottish Brewers Ltd. merges with Newcastle Breweries.
1989: Scottish & Newcastle purchase a majority interest in two hotel chains.
1990: Company forms a retail division to manage its pubs and restaurants.
1995: The name of Scottish & Newcastle's beer division is changed to Scottish Courage.
1999: Scottish & Newcastle purchases a line of pubs, restaurants, and lodges.
2000: Company sells its hotel business and acquires majority interest in Danone Group.

Ltd., J & J Morison Ltd., and Robert Younger Ltd. in 1960. In April of that year, Scottish Brewers and Newcastle Breweries merged to form Scottish & Newcastle Breweries Ltd. After the merger, the wines and spirits businesses were combined and the two brewing centers essentially carried on business as before.

Newcastle Breweries Ltd. had incorporated in 1890. Proud of its urban origins, the brewery's logo featured the city's skyline in silhouette against its trademark blue star. The city of Newcastle itself claimed, somewhat tenuously, to be England's first brewing town. Newcastle Breweries was most strongly identified with its Newcastle Brown Ale (in the 1990s, the largest selling bottled ale in Britain), which continued to be produced in the city of its namesake throughout changes in ownership. Nicknamed "The (Brown) Dog," the beer won a top award for bottled beer in London in 1928, a year after it was introduced.

Like Scottish Brewers, Newcastle Breweries was an amalgamation of regional brewers, all family-controlled: John Barras & Co. Ltd. (which dated back to 1770), William Henry Allison & Co., James, John & William Henry Allison, and Carr Brothers & Carr. The Barras company operated the Tyne Brewery, which became the center of the Newcastle Breweries' production and, like the Fountain Brewery, remained operational under Scottish and Newcastle. In Newcastle Breweries' first 30 years other brewers and pubs were acquired, such as John Sanderson & Sons (1898), Fosters' Bishop Middleham Brewery Ltd. (1910), Addison, Potter & Son (1918), and Matthew Wood & Son Ltd. (1919). Between the end of World War II and the creation of Scottish & Newcastle, Newcastle picked up the Northern Corporation (1955), the Duddingston Brewery (from Steel, Coulson & Co. Ltd. in 1954), James Deuchar Ltd. (1956), and John Rowell & Son Ltd. (1959).

In the 1950s and 1960s, many breweries were scrambling to form alliances of one type or another. Some brewers, including

Courage, Barclay, and Newcastle, received some protection from hostile mergers in the form of the Whitbread "Umbrella," investments by the giant brewer in the late 1950s. In return, these associations offered Whitbread certain marketing advantages. Another type of alliance was formed in 1961, when Courage, Barclay & Simonds, Scottish & Newcastle, and Bass, Mitchells, & Butlers all joined Ireland's Guinness firm in the Harp Lager Ltd. consortium, which produced a very successful draught lager, quickly leading its category in sales. The Harp lineup changed considerably over the years, with Courage and Scottish & Newcastle leaving in 1979 but becoming franchisees.

Scottish & Newcastle produced and marketed wine and spirits through Mackinlay-McPherson Ltd., formed in 1962. This division was later known as Waverly Vinters. It sold the products of Glenallchie Distillery Co. Ltd. and Isle of Jura Distillery Co. Ltd. County Hotels & Wine Co. Ltd. was acquired in 1962, Christopher & Co. Ltd. was added in 1972, and wine and spirit distributors Gough Brothers Ltd. was owned from 1979 to 1984.

Expanding into the Leisure Industry: 1966–95

In 1965, the company entered the leisure industry with Thistle Hotels Ltd., which was expanded in 1979 with the purchase of Thorn EMI's hotel group. In 1989, Scottish & Newcastle acquired a majority interest (65 percent) in the Dutch hotelier Center Parcs (founded in 1967), and it sold Thistle Hotels for £645 million. It bought Pontin's Ltd. the same year. In 1991, the rest of Center Parcs was obtained. The Leisure Division achieved turnover of £406.6 million in 1995, when it operated 14 resorts under the Center Parcs name in five countries and 17 Holiday Club Pontin's hotels in the British Isles. By that time, Center Parcs attracted more than three million guests a year to its recreation-oriented, natural settings.

Scottish & Newcastle attempted to buy Cameron in 1984, but the bid was scuttled by government regulators. In 1985, Moray Firth Maltings was acquired. In 1986, when company turnover was £828 million, it acquired Nottingham's Home Brewery (including 450 pubs), and the next year (in its second attempt) Matthew Brown. These purchases gave Scottish & Newcastle the Theakston line of ales and three breweries, which continued to operate in the 1990s. The cost for the Home, Brown, and Theakston breweries was £272 million.

In 1990, a retail division, headquartered in Northampton, was formed to manage pubs and restaurants. Although ownership of bars by brewers was forbidden in the United States, this market could not be ignored, since it accounted for most of the beer sales in Britain. Scottish & Newcastle became the fourth largest pub operator in the United Kingdom after acquiring Chef & Brewer from Grand Metropolitan plc in 1993 for £628 million. Operating more than 2,600 sites in 1995, including those of Inntrepreneur Estates Ltd. acquired in the Courage merger, the division earned operating profits of £142.7 million in 1995 on turnover of £722.7 million. Brands included Chef & Brewer, T&J Bernard, Barras & Co., and Rat 'N' Parrot ale houses; Homespreads and Country Carvery & Grill restaurants; and Vino Veritas bistros. Big Hand Mo, a line of pubs featuring video games, was designed to attract 18- to 24-year-olds.

The forerunners of these establishments were the revived, multi-use pubs introduced by brewers such as Courage and Newcastle in the 1920s and 1930s to meet the demands of competition and public responsibility. The brewers sought to attract middle-class customers with elaborate architecture and restaurants. Barclay Perkins opened one of the most grand, the Downham Tavern, near Bromley in 1930. To promote food sales, it had no bars, but it did have a huge hall where Shakespeare eventually was performed. Nevertheless, the take-home market eroded pub sales so that by 1980 pubs only supplied 63 percent of the beer market, down from 80 percent in 1955. In 1963, Courage, Barclay & Simonds owned 4,800 establishments; Scottish & Newcastle owned 1,700. Scottish & Newcastle's holdings remained between 1,400 and 1,700 houses for the next two decades, but by 1970 Courage owned 6,000, which fell to about 5,000 by 1986. John Smith's owned 1,536 in 1967. Amusement With Prize machines helped brewers dependent on tied estate survive through hard times. In the mid-1970s, Courage received about £2.5 million per year from them. Scottish & Newcastle owned 2,300 pubs in 1990, when it employed 20,000.

Courage Ltd. Acquisition in 1995

The name of Scottish & Newcastle's beer division was changed to Scottish Courage Limited in 1995 after taking over Courage Ltd., a wholly owned subsidiary of Foster's Brewing Group of Australia in a transaction worth the equivalent of £858 million. Based in Bristol and Plymouth, Courage had been traditionally strongest in the southwest of England. John Courage, a shipping agent and a Scot of French Huguenot extraction, founded Courage at a brewhouse he bought in London for £615 in 1787. After his death in 1793, his wife Harriet took over the firm's operation; she was succeeded by John Donaldson, the senior clerk, upon her death in 1797. Within a few years Donaldson had become a partner. Around mid-century, John Courage, Jr., and his sons began to run the business as the Donaldsons assumed a less active role.

Although the company specialized in mild ale, Courage brewed porter (which from the 1700s to the 1830s had been London's main brew) in a London brewery acquired in the late 18th century; production there ceased in 1980. In the late 1800s Courage bought fashionable pale ale from Burton brewers to meet demand in London; in 1903 it bought Hall's Hampshire brewery, rebuilding it.

Courage produced an estimated 10,000 barrels in 1830 and 250,000 in 1880. The company, typical of London brewers, continued to use draught horses to distribute its products locally throughout the 19th century. Courage owned about 80 horses in this period, whereas a larger brewer like Barclay Perkins owned perhaps two to three times as many. After World War I they eventually were displaced.

At the turn of the century, Courage sought ownership of more pubs and bought several brewers: Alton Brewery Co. (1903), Camden Brewery Co. Ltd. (1923), Farnham United Breweries Ltd. (1927), Noakes & Co. Ltd. (1930), C.N. Kidd & Sons Ltd. (1937), and Kingston Brewery Co. Ltd. (1943). In the Edwardian period, Courage was one of the top 20 brewers in Britain, and one of the top 50 industrial concerns. William

McEwan, William Younger, John Smith, and Newcastle Breweries occupied a lower tier.

In 1957, Courage & Barclay Ltd., a limited liability company registered in 1955, took over the brewing rights of both Courage & Co. and Barclay, Perkins & Co. In the postwar years, Courage & Barclay was the country's fourth largest brewer, based on its capital of £15.8 million. A new wave of acquisitions followed: Reffell's Bexley Brewery Ltd. (1956), wine and spirit merchant Charles Kinloch & Co. Ltd. (1957), Nicholsons & Sons Ltd. (1959), and Yardley's London & Provincial Stores (1959). In 1960, H. & G. Simonds Ltd., a brewing concern that itself had expanded rapidly in the 1930s, was bought, whereupon Courage & Barclay Ltd. was renamed Courage, Barclay & Simonds Ltd. and its brewing rights were sold back to Barclay, Perkins & Co. Ltd., which then became known as Courage & Barclay Ltd. The company acquired a league of other breweries after these ownership shuffles, including Bristol Brewery Georges & Co. Ltd. (1961), Clinchy & Co. Ltd. and Uxbridge Brewery Ltd. (1962), Charles Beasley Ltd. (1963), Star Brewery Co. (1965), Plymouth Breweries Ltd. (1969), and John Smith's Tadcaster Brewery Co. Ltd. (1970). Again, in 1970, the company changed its name, to Courage Ltd.

The 1961 takeover of Bristol Brewery Georges came in response to a United Breweries takeover attempt, and outbidding United proved quite expensive: Courage & Barclay paid about £19 million for share capital previously valued at £12 million. It denied United access, however, to Courage's home territory, the South. The same year, a merger with Bass was discussed.

John Smith's brewery in Yorkshire, next door to the Samuel Smith brewery, merged with Courage in 1970. John Smith's dated back to 1847. A new brewery, housing Courage's headquarters, was built in 1883, and another brewhouse was added in 1976; yet another replaced the original in 1984.

In 1972, Imperial Tobacco Group Ltd., continuing a diversification into less controversial products, bought Courage for £320 million, whereupon it became known as Imperial Brewing & Leisure Ltd. Ironically, Scottish & Newcastle also had made a bid for Courage, and observers saw the northern and southern firms as complementary. Courage's wary directors believed, however, that the company would be significantly restructured in such a deal, beginning with a relocation of its headquarters to Edinburgh. In 1986, when Courage's turnover was £839 million, Hanson Trust plc acquired the Imperial Group and sold Courage to Elders IXL (owners of the Foster's brand) for £1.4 billion. Courage held nine percent of the British beer market in 1988. Scottish & Newcastle finally bought it in 1995. The purchase made Scottish & Newcastle Great Britain's largest brewer. Moreover, following the Courage merger, Scottish & Newcastle moved into the ranks of Europe's top six breweries. (Before the merger, only about 15 percent of Scottish & Newcastle's turnover came from Europe, including the United Kingdom.)

Scottish and Newcastle's considerable success from 1960 to 1980 was powered by a few brands—such as Newcastle Brown Ale and McEwan's Export—that led the free trade sector. From 1965 to 1975 its U.K. sales nearly doubled; its free trade sales increased by about 150 percent. In addition to participating in the Harp consortium, Scottish & Newcastle developed its own lager brands—McEwan's and Kestrel—in the mid-1970s. The acquisition of Courage strengthened its brand lineup overall, to the point of possibly overstocking its import lager category.

Focus on Retail and Beer in 1999

In December of 1999, Scottish & Newcastle significantly expanded its retail division with the purchase of Greenall's pubs, restaurants, and lodges. The £1.4 billion acquisition consisted of 531 pubs, 234 pub-restaurants, and 61 lodges. This brought the company's total number of pubs to more than 3,400. Since Scottish & Newcastle was allowed to own no more than 2,739 branded, or "tied" pubs—as mandated by the Department of Trade and Industry—the company was required to sell or "unbrand" more than 700 of the outlets. In early 2000, therefore, Scottish & Newcastle agreed to sell 481 of its pubs to the Royal Bank of Scotland, and another 361 pubs to the Pub Estate Company. Together, the two divestitures generated £280 million.

After the Greenall's acquisition, Scottish & Newcastle restructured its retail division to include four discrete divisions: branded pubs, restaurants, local pubs west, and local pubs east. This restructuring was significant in that it evidenced Scottish & Newcastle's increased emphasis on branded pubs within its retail operations.

In February 2000, Scottish & Newcastle made a strategic decision to get out of the leisure business altogether by offering for sale its Center Parcs and Holiday Club Pontin's chains. The company felt that this divestiture would better allow it to focus on expansion of the beer and retail divisions. This intensified focus on expansion in the beer business was evidenced just a month later, when Scottish & Newcastle announced that it had entered into a merger agreement with Danone Group. Danone was the maker of France's top-selling premium lager. It also operated the second largest brewing operation in Belgium and held a 24 percent interest in Birra Peroni SpA, the second largest such operation in Italy. Under the terms of the deal, Scottish & Newcastle was to pay Danone a first installment of £470 million. In exchange, Scottish & Newcastle was to receive management control. Until May of 2003, Danone would have the option of selling its remaining interest to Scottish & Newcastle for £1.226 billion, or consolidating its holdings into a joint venture, of which it would own no more than 25 percent.

Looking Ahead

With the acquisition of Danone Group, Scottish & Newcastle was poised to become the second largest brewer in Western Europe, surpassed only by Heineken. Meanwhile, consolidation within the European beer market was rampant, with two major players in the U.K market—Bass and Whitbread—selling their brewing operations to larger competitors and fo-

cusing on their interests in the restaurant and hotel industries. It appeared that Scottish & Newcastle, however, would remain independent. In a June 2000 interview with Scotland's *Evening News,* Scottish & Newcastle's chief executive, Brian Stewart, outlined the company's plans: "At the moment, we are satisfied that we can develop the business internationally as a major player. We will be the seventh biggest brewer in the world. We are satisfied we can move ahead from there on our own. We are not looking for partners." It also appeared that Scottish & Newcastle would continue to focus on its beer business, rather than abandoning brewing in favor of pubs and restaurants.

Principal Subsidiaries

Center Parcs N.V. (Netherlands); Cleveland Place Holdings plc; The Chef & Brewer Group Limited; Huggins & Company Limited; Public House Company Limited (50%).

Principal Competitors

Bass plc; The Nomura Securities Co., Ltd.; Heineken N.V.

Further Reading

Foster, Geoffrey, "How Thistle Was Grasped," *Management Today,* June, 1987, pp. 68–69.

Gilbert, David C., and Rachel Smith, "The UK Brewing Industry: Past, Present, and Future," *International Journal of Wine Marketing,* 1992, Vol. 4, No. 1, pp. 19–27.

Gourvish, Terence R., and R.G. Wilson, *The British Brewing Industry, 1830–1980,* Cambridge, England: Cambridge University Press, 1994.

Heller, David, "Scottish & Newcastle Deal Finds Little Cheer," *Daily Express,* March 21, 2000.

Mathias, Peter, *The Brewing Industry in England, 1700–1830,* Cambridge, England: Cambridge University Press, 1959.

Pitcher, George, "A Beerage Made in Heaven?," *Marketing Week,* March 31, 1995, p. 25.

Richmond, Lesley, and Alison Turton, eds., *The Brewing Industry: A Guide to Historical Records,* Manchester, England: Manchester University Press, 1990.

Rock, Stuart, "Scottish & Newcastle: A Brewery on the Hop," *Chief Executive,* June 1986, pp. 34–36.

Slingsby, Helen, "Last Chance Saloon," *Marketing Week,* February 17, 1995, pp. 35–36.

Sigsworth, Eric M., *The Brewing Trade During the Industrial Revolution: The Case of Yorkshire,* York: St. Anthony's Press, 1967.

Snowdon, Ros, "S&N Overhauls Pub Strategies," *Marketing,* July 27, 1995, p. 3.

——, "Takeover Is No Small Beer," *Marketing,* May 25, 1995, p. 12.

Tibbetts, Graham, "Anything by Small Beer," *Evening News-Scotland,* June 7, 2000, p. B4.

Wombwell, David, "Newcastle Brown," *Marketing,* May 18, 1995, p. 10.

—Frederick C. Ingram
—updated by Shawna Brynildssen

SPAR

SPAR Handels AG

Osterbrooksweg 35-45
D-22867 Schenefeld
Germany
Telephone: (49)(40) 8394-0
Fax: (49)(40) 8394-1922
Web site: http://www.spar.de

75% Owned by Intermarché
Incorporated: 1952 as Deutsche Spar
Employees: 24,989
Sales: DM 13.03 billion ($6.64 billion) (1999)
Stock Exchanges: Frankfurt/Main
Ticker Symbol: SPA
NAIC: 44511 Supermarkets and Other Grocery (Except
   Convenience) Stores; 44512 Convenience Stores;
   45211 Department Stores; 42241 General Line
   Grocery Wholesalers

SPAR Handels AG is Germany's seventh largest company active in grocery wholesale and retail with a market share of about ten percent. The German SPAR group consists of five wholesale organizations, 1,350 food and nonfood hypermarkets and discount stores, and approximately 3,850 independent SPAR retailers. About half of SPAR's sales come from wholesale with the independent mid-sized grocery retailers. The other half is generated in SPAR and SUPERSPAR supermarkets, EUROSPAR, Famka, and Attracta hypermarkets, Netto grocery discount markets, and KODI non-food discount stores. SPAR has also introduced Express convenience stores at gasoline stations and has a 25 percent share in the E-commerce site Einkauf24. The French grocery retailer Intermarché, itself a subsidiary of ITM Enterprises S.A., owns 75 percent of SPAR. SPAR supermarkets represent the largest national member of the International SPAR organization, with 100 grocery wholesalers and over 20,000 grocery retailers in 28 countries around the world with total sales of about $30 billion.

SPAR's Origins in the Early 1950s

SPAR's co-op origins were influenced by an existing model in the Netherlands. In 1932 Dutch grocery wholesaler A.J.M. van Well founded the first cooperative grocery chain in Europe. At that time cooperation between wholesale and retail businesses was uncommon. Van Well and his business partners—16 of his retail customers—decided to work together in harmony in order to secure profits on a regular basis. In the reconstruction years after World War II, the concept became popular among German mid-sized grocery wholesalers and retailers. Many of them were concerned about their ability to compete with large conglomerates on one hand and the widespread produce cooperatives at the other end of the market.

At an international wholesale trade meeting on February 16, 1952, the president of the German grocery trade organization VDN, Rolf Knigge, and two state chapter heads, Werner Hagen from North-Rhine Westphalia and Franz Weissbecker from Bavaria, founded the Deutsche SPAR modeled after the Dutch organization. By the end of 1952, 20 wholesalers belonged to the group, loosely organized into northern and southern German groups, which met several times to exchange ideas and experiences. At one such meeting, on October 8, 1952, in Frankfurt, they decided to make their enterprise and the SPAR trademark public.

The idea of about 50 cooperating wholesalers was not well-received by other parts of the industry. Many retailers were afraid they would have their choice of suppliers restricted. Many wholesalers did not sympathize with SPAR, which they saw as a growing new competitor in its own right. The food industry even stopped delivery of goods to one SPAR wholesaler, I.A. Schnell, in the German town of Hohenweststedt. However, other SPAR wholesalers helped out with the goods that were not delivered to the Schnell business, and soon they started looking for ways to jointly purchase certain products for all SPAR members.

To coordinate the group's activities, Centrale der Arbeitsgemeinschaft SPAR was founded in the German city of Münster. At a meeting in January 1953 the foundation was laid for the group's further development. The gathered SPAR mem-

Company Perspectives:

Our goals are 1) the results-based and consumer-oriented optimization of our product mix emphasizing freshness and local specifics; 2) increasing consumer awareness of the SPAR profile (sympathy, freshness, quality and security) by managing neighborhood stores in an exemplary manner and by profile-enhancing consumer marketing; 3) a noticeable improvement of the SPAR prices for the consumer; 4) achieving a delivery standard that guarantees product presence and ''daily freshness,'' and improving delivery modalities according to the needs of retailers at an acceptable cost. In addition, to provide the necessary waste management; 5) development and realization of clear conditions that guarantee profits and the existence of progressive independent SPAR retailers; 6) to offer wholesale services based on retailers' needs and to constantly test and optimize quality and efficiency 7) to expand SPAR's market position through a joint effort of intensified, active market acquisition by securing and developing locations; 8) to significantly improve and strengthen in a sustainable way the motivation, the professional and other training of independent retailers and their employees; 9) to intensify the communication between independent SPAR retailers and wholesalers.

bers agreed on a set of core principles and the first SPAR logo. They decided to transform the Münster-based Handelshof GmbH, a private wholesale business founded in 1949, into SPAR's central purchasing organization. At the same time, the principals of the Handelshof GmbH agreed to sell their capital to the SPAR members and to move the company's headquarters to Frankfurt/Main. On August 19, 1953, the renamed Handelshof SPAR GmbH was officially registered in Frankfurt.

The Handelshof SPAR GmbH was the umbrella organization for all SPAR wholesalers. It purchased products centrally from manufacturers, developed and managed central advertising campaigns, consulted its members on best business practices and issued licenses to new SPAR wholesalers. In 1953 four regional purchasing organizations were set up, serving the German North, South, West, and Southwest. The first SPAR brand products were developed in the same year.

In July 1955 the Deutsche Handelsvereinigung SPAR e.V. was founded to serve as the central committee for all SPAR member businesses. Each regional SPAR group was represented by a wholesaler and a retailer. Delegates had one vote, each representing 100 SPAR retailers, and decisions were made at central delegates meetings. Thus SPAR members were able to influence business politics of the group.

By 1958 the number of SPAR member wholesalers peaked at 55. At the same time there were approximately 12,000 retail stores bearing the SPAR banner. In 1959 the first SPAR supermarket opened in Hersfeld, and the following year the first SPAR mail order catalog was introduced and the first nationwide advertising campaign, worth DM 2.5 million, launched.

By 1964 there were 26 SPAR brand products, and that number would increase to 540 by the end of the decade. During

this time, four subsidiaries were founded to run wholesale businesses and offer services such as electronic data processing, purchasing and bookkeeping. Moreover, the Deutsche SPAR Handels GmbH & Co. (DSH) was founded to purchase primarily non-food products for the whole SPAR group and to centralize invoicing and payment processes for SPAR member firms and the industry suppliers.

The 1970s were characterized by a process of concentration and restructuring of the German retail landscape. The shrinking of Germany's retail food market segment had begun in 1968, and in the ensuing years the number of SPAR wholesalers and delivery districts decreased by about one-third to 33, while the number of SPAR independent retailers shrunk by 40 percent to 6,200 stores. As the number of stores went down, the remaining stores started growing in size. To make up for losses in the grocery segment, the group also started to diversify into non-food markets. As a result, SPAR's wholesale revenues more than doubled during the 1970s and even sales of the traditional SPAR retailers rose by almost 50 percent.

The SPAR principles, which were agreed to by all participating businesses, were the basis for the group's success. While they were regularly interpreted, updated or modified according to changes in business environment, they remained the same in essence, and every member of the SPAR organization had to adhere to them or be excluded from the group. A catalog agreed on by SPAR delegates in November 1972 listed the main obligations and services for SPAR members which remained unchanged up until the 1990s. They included guaranteed minimum sales for SPAR wholesalers and retailers and a minimum sales area size for SPAR retailers; the full product range to be offered; the obligation for retailers to order most products from SPAR wholesalers; exclusive use of the uniform SPAR logo in predefined sizes; participation in all SPAR organs and services; openness of financial statistics; controls on competition between SPAR members by means of assigned territories; and the right of first refusal by the group whenever a SPAR store was put up for sale.

Mid-1980s Formation of SPAR Handels-AG

The 1980s were a decade of stabilization for the German SPAR. The number of SPAR wholesalers remained at about 30. While several wholesale businesses merged during that period, new wholesalers joined the group. The number of SPAR retailers decreased, reaching about 5,400 by the mid-1980s. In 1982 SPAR member company Koch & Sohn, based in Düsseldorf, established a new brand for the group—the KODI non-food discount stores. In 1985 the three leading German SPAR wholesalers Pfeiffer & Schmidt (Schenefeld), Karl Koch & Sohn (Düsseldorf) and Kehrer & Weber (Munich) merged to form the SPAR Handels-AG. The following year the SPAR Handels-AG acquired shares in eight mid-sized German grocers. In 1988 the company's stock was first traded on the stock market.

The second half of the decade saw the number of SPAR retailers rise once again, the result of takeovers and consolidation in the grocery industry. SPAR's strong market position was reflected in increasing sales. Sales of SPAR retailers rose by one-third, from DM 8.9 billion in 1980 to DM 11.7 billion in 1990. The wholesale side of the business grew even faster. In

Key Dates:

1949: Handelshof GmbH, a German wholesale business, is founded.
1952: Deutsche SPAR co-op is founded.
1953: Handelshof and SPAR merge, forming Handelshof SPAR GmbH, which is incorporated in Frankfurt.
1972: SPAR delegates agree on updated SPAR principles.
1982: First KODI non-food discount stores open in Düsseldorf.
1985: The largest SPAR members merge to form SPAR Handels-AG.
1988: Company goes public.
1990: First SPAR supermarket opens in former East Germany.
1995: SPAR logistics center in Mittenwalde near Berlin starts operations.
1997: French trade group Intermarché becomes SPAR's majority shareholder.

1980 30 SPAR wholesalers grossed DM 5 billion; by 1990, though the group had shrunk to include nine SPAR wholesale businesses, sales had jumped by 80 percent up to DM 9 billion.

Expansion in the 1990s

Immediately after the Berlin Wall came down in 1989, SPAR developed a crash program to help about 3,000 East Germans set up their own SPAR neighborhood stores. The first SPAR supermarket on the territory of the former German Democratic Republic opened in March 1990. Designed in the style of markets in the West and stocked with products from the West, by the beginning of April 1991 there were already more than 1,500 retail stores in the new East German states that purchased products from SPAR and were interested in becoming independent SPAR retailers.

To serve the new German states—Saxony, Saxony-Anhalt, Mecklenburg-Vorpommern, and Brandenburg—subsidiary SPAR Nordost was founded. Thuringia, the fifth new state, was served from the SPAR subsidiary in Friedewald near Bad Hersfeld in former West Germany. When the East German centrally administered grocery wholesale and retail industries were privatized, SPAR Nordost took over 400 supermarkets in good locations and 1,600 other grocery stores from the former East German Handelsorganisation (HO). SPAR also acquired warehouses form ten former East German wholesale firms. Thus, with this East German expansion, the number of SPAR wholesale customers suddenly increased significantly; the total number of SPAR retail customers grew by 2,000 between 1990 and 1992, an increase of almost 30 percent.

The next step was the integration and modernization of the new facilities. Before new facilities were available, 86 warehouses taken over by SPAR served the new SPAR retailers. Four central warehouses in Rostock, Magdeburg, Potsdam and Döbeln became key locations. At the beginning of 1992 SPAR Nordost was merged with the SPAR Handels-AG. All of its facilities were organized under the region Nordost. The new wholesale warehouses were transformed into modern logistics centers. Between 1992 and 1995 SPAR invested more than DM 1 billion into modernizing its logistics network in the new German states. In April 1995 a brand-new SPAR logistics center started operations in Mittenwalde near Berlin. The whole Nordost territory was served by three central warehouses in Mittenwalde, Rostock, and Döbeln, as well as two regional and three discount warehouses.

In 1995 there were about 1,340 independent SPAR retailers in the new German states, 11 EUROSPAR hypermarkets, eight self-service department stores, 211 Netto food discount markets, and 18 Kodi nonfood-discounters. In addition SPAR delivered to over 800 other retail customers including 20 food departments of the Karstadt and Hertie department stores.

Combined sales of SPAR wholesale and retail businesses rose by more than 43 percent between 1990 and 1995. In the new German states alone SPAR grossed DM 5.5 billion, a market share of between 13 and 14 percent. In 1993 30 percent of SPAR's net sales derived from the new German states. By the mid-1990s, 1,200 out of 1,600 SPAR neighborhood stores in East Germany were managed by independent retailers.

Recession and Reorganization in the Late 1990s

SPAR's horizon was soon darkened, however, by fierce competition in the grocery retail industry, especially for market share in the new German states, along with a significant drop in fruit, vegetable, and meat prices and increasingly frugal shopping behavior. SPAR, and the industry as a whole, entered a period of ruinous price competition. This was particularly hard on independent SPAR retailers in East Germany, since they had not yet had the time to build a sustainable neighborhood customer base. Already, in the early stage of building their businesses, they were often in the red, their very existence threatened by other grocery chains. Moreover, they had to fight daily for the best purchasing modalities and began to feel that the SPAR wholesale conditions did not meet their needs.

In August 1995 a group of disgruntled SPAR retailers in Saxony-Anhalt, Mecklenburg-Vorpommern and Thuringia founded an interest group called ''Interessengemeinschaft der möglicherweise Spar Geschaedigten e.V.''—the ''Interest Group of those Possibly Harmed by SPAR.'' They accused their regional SPAR wholesalers of unrealistic sales projections, overpriced rents, and unfavorable prices and conditions. The group's story was featured in *Der Spiegel*, Germany's premier news magazine, and the SPAR headquarters then accused those business owners of sub-optimal management practices. In the following internal and external information campaign, SPAR leaders admitted minor problems and promised help to struggling East German SPAR retailers, except for those belonging to the Interest Group. The disputes were eventually more or less settled, at least in public. Membership of the Interest Group fluctuated between 60 and 100 during the late 1990s. One of the several pending lawsuits against SPAR was settled in February 2000 in favor of SPAR.

The increasingly competitive marketplace put SPAR under pressure to find new markets and competent partners for strategic alliances. Beginning in 1995 SPAR stocked the shelves of

50 Hertie grocery departments in addition to the 71 Karstadt grocery departments it had supplied since 1991. One year later it started deliveries to 600 VeGe/Vivo markets formerly owned by Contzen. SPAR's endeavor to find new strategic partners bore fruit in 1997. After an alliance with the Tengelmann Group, another leading German retail supermarket and distribution group, failed in 1995, the French trade group Intermarché became majority shareholder of SPAR through its Swiss subsidiary Intercontessa AG in the summer of 1997. The group, with retail sales of over DM 40 billion, had a structure similar to SPAR's, with 2,200 independent retailers in France, Portugal, Spain, Italy, Belgium, and Poland.

Beginning in 1996 SPAR went on an unprecedented acquisition spree. Between 1996 and 1998 it took over 66 Bolle Markets in Berlin; 36 large Continent self-service department stores from the French Promodès trade group with annual sales of about DM2 billion; the wholesale business of the Kathrainer AG; eight self-service department stores from the Holzer Parkkauf GmbH; the Karlsruhe-based Pfannkuch Group with 212 markets in Southwest Germany and net sales of DM1.1 billion; 152 PRO Hamburg markets in the Hamburg area and 34 markets around Kassel.

However, the weight of those new acquisitions was proving too heavy for SPAR. In particular, venturing into the department store market segment seemed an unfavorable risk. The transformation of the Continent stores into INTERSPAR self-service department stores was costly, and the ongoing price war in Germany diminished sales. SPAR was deep in the red, by over DM 300 million, in 1998. Moreover, since the engagement with Intermarché, SPAR preferred shares lost 80 percent of their value. In 1998 a new strategy was developed, focusing on small and mid-sized grocery and convenience stores. Some 74 large INTERSPAR self-service department stores were sold to U.S. giant Wal-Mart in a $658 million deal, while another 44 stores of the same format were integrated into the EUROSPAR

distribution line. In November 1999 SPAR wholesaler L. Stroetmann GmbH & Co. did not extend its contract with SPAR and joined competitor Edeka Zentrale. As the company approached a new millennium, management was focused on turning the company around.

Principal Subsidiaries

Handelshof SPAR GmbH (82.3%); Deutsche SPAR Handelsgesellschaft mbH & Co. (77.8%); Gerhard Prahm GmbH & Co. KG (50%); L. Stroetmann GmbH & Co. (24.9%); INTERSPAR Warenhandelsgesellschaft mbH & Co. OHG; Offene Handelsgesellschaft NETTO Supermarkt GmbH & Co. (50%); KODI Discountläden GmbH; IQS Institut für Qualitätssicherung und -prüfung im Lebensmittelhandel GmbH (70%); SPAR Finanz AG (77.8%); ''Einkauf 24'' GmbH (50%).

Principal Competitors

Tengelmann Group; Aldi Group; Edeka Zentrale AG; Rewe-Liebbrand; Metro AG; Lidl & Schwarz Stiftung & Co. KG.

Further Reading

''Die Spar Handels-AG spuert die Folgen der Rezession,'' *Frankfurter Allgemeine Zeitung*, June 3, 1994, p. 16.
''Neue Spar,'' *Frankfurter Allgemeine Zeitung*, May 21, 1996, p. 19.
Roessing, Sabine, ''Vom Debattierclub zum Machtfaktor,'' *Lebensmittel Zeitung*, February 16, 1996, p. 38.
SPAR—größte Freiwillige Handelskitte, EuroHandelsinstitut e. V., Cologne, Germany: 1997, 52 p.
''Wal-Mart's Hyper Deal,'' *Grocer*, December 12, 1998, p. 5.
''Wir stehen bei der Spar vor einem Scherbenhaufen,'' *Lebensmittel Zeitung*, July 9, 1999, p. 6.

—Evelyn Hauser

Spelling Entertainment

5700 Wilshire Boulevard
Los Angeles, California 90036-3659
U.S.A.
Telephone: (323) 965-5700
Web site: http://www.viacom.com

Wholly Owned Subsidiary of Viacom, Inc.
Incorporated: 1977 as Aaron Spelling Productions, Inc.
Employees: 400
Sales: $568.1 million (1998)
NAIC: 512110 Motion Picture and Video Production;
   512120 Motion Picture and Video Distribution

Wholly owned by Viacom, Inc., Spelling Entertainment produces and distributes popular television programs for network broadcast and first-run syndication. Known previously as the Spelling Entertainment Group, Inc., the company divested many of its noncore businesses in the late 1990s, and its television operations were then merged into Viacom's Paramount Television Group in 1999. Although founder Aaron Spelling was once referred to as "the king of schlock," there can be no denying his commercial savvy in producing such hit television fare as "Dynasty," "Beverly Hills, 90210," and "Melrose Place."

Company Origins

Aaron Spelling began writing for television in 1956, after serving with distinction in the Army Air Corps during World War II, graduating from Southern Methodist University, and working as an actor for a few years thereafter. As a writer for Four Star Productions, Spelling's first job was with the television show *Dick Powell's Zane Grey Theater,* where he earned $125 a week. By 1959, Spelling was producing the show. When that series ended in 1962, Spelling had already begun producing other series, and in 1968 he teamed up with actor Danny Thomas to form Thomas-Spelling Productions. That year, Spelling introduced a cop show called *The Mod Squad,* which was picked up by the American Broadcasting Company (ABC) and would run for five years. In 1972, Spelling formed a new production company, Spelling-Goldberg Productions, with a

new partner, Len Goldberg. Among that company's hit fare was the police drama *S.W.A.T.,* which gained notoriety for its violent action sequences.

The 1970s were high point in Spelling's career as a producer. During this time, he created and produced a bevy of hit shows, including *Starsky and Hutch, Charlie's Angels, The Love Boat,* and *Fantasy Island.* Indeed, Spelling productions propelled ABC to the top of the television ratings charts throughout the 1970s. In 1976, Spelling also tried his hand at producing a relatively new type of show, the made-for-TV movie. *The Boy in the Plastic Bubble,* starring a young John Travolta, met with popular success.

In 1977, Aaron Spelling Productions, Inc., based in Los Angeles, was incorporated. Under that new corporate organization, Spelling scored another success with the 1981 premier of *Dynasty,* a night-time soap opera that would run for nine years. Spelling's behind the scenes debut in the world of motion pictures came in 1983, when he produced the hit *Mr. Mom,* starring Michael Keaton. Aaron Spelling Productions went public in 1986, while *Dynasty* and another hit series, *Hotel,* continued to garner impressive ratings. However, two new series, *Finder of Lost Loves* and *The Colby's,* the latter a spin off of *Dynasty,* met with lukewarm response and were soon cancelled. During this time Spelling continued to work on major motion pictures, producing three more films, none of which garnered the critical or popular success of *Mr. Mom.*

Challenges in the Late 1980s

By the late 1980s, Spelling appeared to have lost his "Midas touch." Annual revenues were on the decline as the company had just one show on broadcast television and two others in production. The company's stock declined from its initial issue price of $14 per share in 1986 to just $5 per share in 1988, and sales and earnings declined by double-digit percentages.

Spelling foreshadowed a potential merger in a 1988 interview with Mark Frankel of *California Business.* Therein he noted that producing TV shows had become so expensive that independent production companies such as his would "have to branch out and do other things besides just producing for television—become miniconglomerates—in order to make sure that we can keep doing what we do.'' Besides perhaps hoping to secure the resources of a wealthy parent company, the company also targeted the foreign syndication market as an avenue for growth, acquiring Worldvision Enterprises Inc., a global distribution company, in 1989.

Financier Carl Lindner, through his company Great American Communications, had purchased a majority interest in Spelling Entertainment, and in 1991, that 82 percent stake was acquired by the Charter Company, based in Cincinnati, for $189.5 million in cash and notes. Charter completed its acquisition of Spelling with a mid-1992 exchange of stock valued at $44 million. Renamed Spelling Entertainment Group, the merged companies continued to hold on to a few Charter assets through the mid-1990s.

However, Charter was in financial and managerial upheaval, and less than a year would pass before Spelling's corporate ownership structure changed again. In 1993, Charter sold its controlling (now at 53.4 percent) interest to Blockbuster Entertainment Corporation for $141.5 million. By the end of 1994, Viacom Inc. had acquired Blockbuster and announced its intention to sell Blockbuster's stake in Spelling to help settle its own debts. The sale, however, never came to pass.

During this time Spelling Entertainment acquired Republic Pictures Entertainment and merged it with its Woldvision subsidiary in mid-1994, creating a library of 7,000 feature films, made-for-TV movies and miniseries, and 15,000 episodes of Spelling-produced television. Global syndication of these programs proved a steady source of revenue that fueled new production efforts.

Making Hits Again in the 1990s

Spelling's television production business rebounded in a big way in the early 1990s. *Beverly Hills, 90210,* a prime time teen drama that featured among its cast of rich and beautiful teens Aaron Spelling's daughter, Tori, was the first in a string of early 1990s television hits. Spun off from that program was another drama, *Melrose Place,* which was slightly steamier in content and aimed at a slightly older audience. This series become a mainstay of Rupert Murdoch's burgeoning Fox network.

Pursuant to its dealings with Fox, Spelling Entertainment acquired Virgin Interactive Entertainment plc, a producer of such interactive games as ''The 7th Quest'' and ''The Lion King.'' Virgin Interactive provided Spelling with another avenue for diversification in its growing array of businesses. Thus, from its core in television production, Spelling had expanded

into large-scale domestic and international distribution of television, film, and video material, interactive games, and licensing and merchandising. By the end of 1994, the company's domestic television production and distribution contributed less than 25 percent of annual revenues. The diversification strategy was appearing to have paid off in increased sales and net income. Revenues nearly quintupled, from $122.75 million in 1991 to $599.84 million in 1994, and net income almost doubled from $12.96 million to $24.11 million.

Spelling Entertainment pursued television production opportunities for both network broadcast and syndication. In addition to placing reruns of *Beverly Hills, 90201* and *Melrose Place* in syndication, the company formed Big Ticket Television to produce first-run comedies for syndication. In 1996 Big Ticket Television launched *Moesha* and its most successful syndicated show to date, *Judge Judy,* a real-life courtroom series in which a curmudgeonly California judge decided small claims cases and offered advice and opinions along the way. New shows for broadcast on the Warner Brothers WB network included the 1995 launch of *Savannah,* about four young southern women in New York City, and *Club Paradise,* a teen-drama set at a year-round resort. While the family drama *Seventh Heaven* received low marks from the critics, a solid viewer following kept the show in production.

While Viacom had Spelling Entertainment Group up for sale, Spelling's subsidiaries provided mixed results. Virgin Interactive lost money though sales increased annually, showing a $14.8 million loss in 1995 on $212.2 million in revenues. Worldvision acquired the rights for Carolco movies for overseas distribution, supplying a new source of steady revenue to its film library. Following the success of an earlier *Beverly Hills, 90210* novelization and the *Melrose Place Companion Guide,* Hamilton Projects licensed promotional paperback publication rights for *Savannah.*

Merging with Paramount Television Group

When Spelling Entertainment did not attract a satisfactory bid, Viacom took the company off the market and began to restructure. Spelling was refocused on television production as Viacom closed the feature film and direct-to-video production divisions and sold off assets, including TeleUNO, Spelling's entertainment channel in Latin America, which was sold to Sony Pictures in 1998. Moreover, Viacom put Virgin Interactive on the auction block. Overall losses of $52.3 million in 1997 improved to a loss of $7.3 million in 1998 on revenues of $586 million. In addition to improving the financial stability of the Spelling group by divesting noncore businesses, Viacom also sought to make the company fit well into its vast entertainment holdings.

Spelling added several new shows to its production schedule in the late 1990s. New shows for 1997 included *Sunset Beach,* a daytime soap opera, and the syndicated *Love Boat: The Next Wave.* Four new network series in 1998 included *Charmed,* a witchcraft comedy, *Rescue 77,* a paramedic action-drama, *Buddy Faro,* a detective drama, and *Any Day Now,* an odd-couple comedy. Syndicated shows included *TAG-I: Real Heroes,* a reality-based series of real-life heroism produced by Worldvision. Big Ticket Television capitalized on the success tober 1999 Viacom sold its remaining shares of Virgin Interactive. Although its individual corporate structure had changed dramatically, Spelling Entertainment remained a vital production company and legacy of the prolific producer Aaron Spelling, who in 1999 had no plans to retire.

Key Dates:

1956: Aaron Spelling begins writing scripts for television.
1968: Thomas-Spelling Productions is founded; *The Mod Squad* debuts on ABC.
1977: Aaron Spelling Productions, Inc. is founded; the *Love Boat* series premiers.
1981: Debut of popular *Dynasty* television series.
1986: Company goes public.
1990: First teen-drama *Beverly Hills 90210* debuts.
1993: A majority stake in Aaron Spelling Productions is acquired by Blockbuster.
1994: Viacom acquires Blockbuster, including its stake in Spelling Productions.
1999: Viacom completes acquisition of Spelling's outstanding shares, and Spelling operations are merged into Viacom's new Television Group.

---

of *Judge Judy* with a Tennessee-based courtroom series, *Judge Joe Brown,* which began syndication in 1999. While production of *Beverly Hills, 90201* continued into the 2000 season, the final episode of *Melrose Place* aired in May 1999. In a new venture into the world of e-commerce, Spelling Entertainment worked with its web page designer Artist Direct and Amazon.com in offering an online auction of the props and wardrobe used on the set of *Melrose Place.* Proceeds from the auction went to charities.

After a successful restructuring, divestment of 43.9 percent of Viacom's interest in Virgin Interactive, and a return to profitability for Spelling, Viacom decided to acquire the remaining 22 percent interest in Spelling Entertainment. In March 1999, Viacom offered $9 per share when the stock selling at $6.75 per share. After completing the acquisition in June, Viacom placed Spelling Entertainment Inc. and Big Ticket Television under Paramount Television Group. The film libraries and licensing company were merged with Paramount subsidiaries. Viacom discontinued Worldvision as it shifted *Judge Judy* and all off-network production to Paramount Domestic Television. In Oc-

Principal Competitors

Time Warner Inc.; The Walt Disney Company; Fox Entertainment.

Further Reading

Coe, Steve, and David Tobenkin, ''Aaron Spelling: TV's Overachiever,'' *Broadcasting & Cable,* January 23, 1995, pp. 11 + .

Frankel, Mark, ''The Angst of Aaron,'' *California Business,* April 1988, p. 24.

Frook, John Evan, ''Analysts Question Sale of Spelling in Near Future,'' *Los Angeles Business Journal,* March 26, 1990, p. 7.

Littleton, Cynthia, ''Eight Shows Have Spelling Excelling,'' *Variety,* June 29, 1998, p. 17.

——, ''Spelling, New World Courtships Continue,'' *Broadcasting & Cable,* April 22, 1996, p. 34.

McClellan, Steve, ''Spelling on the Block,'' *Broadcasting & Cable,* August 14, 1995, p. 33.

''Parachute Publishing Works Its Magic on Spelling Television's Hit Series Charmed,'' *Business Wire,* September 23, 1999.

Sarkisian, Nola L., ''Melrose Place Props on Block,'' *Los Angeles Business Journal,* May 3, 1999, p. 19.

Schneider, Michael, ''Paramount's Great Big Tent: Spelling and Big Ticket Folded In,'' *Electronic Media,* June 28, 1999, p. 45.

Spelling, Aaron, and Jefferson Graham, *Aaron Spelling: A Prime Time Life,* New York: St. Martin's Press, 1996.

''Spelling Entertainment Group,'' *Billboard,* March 9, 1996, p. 54.

Swertlow, Frank, ''How to Spell Success: A Chat with Prolific TV Producer Aaron Spelling,'' *Los Angeles Business Journal,* May 17, 1999, p. 3.

''Viacom Offers to Buy Spelling Ent.,'' *United Press International,* March 19, 1999.

''Worldvision's Real Heroes,'' *Mediaweek,* November 2, 1998, p. 34.

—April Dougal Gasbarre
—updated by Mary Tradii

STULLER
SINCE 1970

Stuller Settings, Inc.

302 Rue Louis XIV
Lafayette, Louisiana 70508
U.S.A.
Telephone: (337) 837-4100
Fax: (337) 981-1655
Web site: http://www.stuller.com

Private Company
Founded: 1970 as South Central Distributors
Employees: 1,450
Sales: $285.7 million (1999)
NAIC: 339911 Jewelry (Except Costume) Manufacturing;
339913 Jewelers' Material and Lapidary Work
Manufacturing

Stuller Settings, Inc. is the nation's largest wholesale supplier of findings and mountings used by retail jewelers and artisans. Stuller maintains an inventory of over 100,000 jewelry items, each of which falls into one of six major categories: findings; mountings; loose diamonds and colored gem stones; finished jewelry; tools; and supplies. With an account base of over 40,000 independent jewelers throughout North America, the company relies heavily on its catalogs or source books, from which its customers place their orders via telephone, fax, or e-mail. The company has manufacturing facilities in Lafayette, Louisiana and Chattanooga, Tennessee. Its service division—Stuller Service Centers Inc.—maintains key sites in Houston, Los Angeles, Seattle, Miami, Chicago, and Philadelphia. There, it stores its product line in sufficient quantities to assure ''just in time delivery'' of its settings and mountings to retailers throughout the country. The company also has buying offices located in Ramat Gan, Israel; Bangkok, Thailand; and Bombay, India. At these sites, gem dealers provide the company with its needed supply of diamonds and colored stones. Stuller emerged as an industry leader in the 1990s due to the quality of its product line and the company's efficiency, which featured a one-day turn around order service.

1968–81: Part-Time Job into a Successful Business

The company's founder, Matthew Gordy Stuller, began learning the jeweler's trade in 1968, when he started working part time for a local jewelry store in his hometown of Lafayette, Louisiana. At the time, he was just a sophomore at Our Lady of Fatima High School. He worked first at Clark's Jewelers in downtown Lafayette, and then later at a store called the House of Diamonds. There, he was taught the jewelry trade by Jack Stern, a veteran jeweler who befriended Stuller and acted as a mentor to help him get started. Although young Stuller could only work after school, he quickly picked up the essentials of the business, and within just a few months had both learned the craft of jewelry repair and also worked his way into sales. In his senior year, Stuller and Stern started their own business—Hub City Jewelers—a trade shop they opened in a corner office of a suite of offices leased by Stuller's father, an orthodontist. Stern died shortly thereafter, and Stuller decided to shut down the business.

Stuller was just 19 years old when he developed his first wholesale product line and went on the road, operating under the name South Central Distributors. After securing a loan from a Lafayette-area bank, he bought the findings inventory from Jewelmont, a New Orleans company. At first, Stuller drove throughout Louisiana in a Nissan 240Z, selling his line from the back seat and trunk while also making important connections. When his territory soon expanded into two other states, he bought a Winnebago and remodeled the inside by adding store fixtures to display his line of findings, mountings, tools, and supplies.

By 1973, Stuller was able to hire salesmen to cover his territory for him, but the road experience stuck with him. Although slow and cumbersome, the decision to continue working on the road helped to shape some key ideas in his business philosophy—notably his belief that a manufacturer and wholesaler of a jewelry line owed his customers both quality merchandise and quick, efficient service. He had already been one of the first to offer same-day shipment of orders, providing that service from the outset. Over the next several years, refinements in procedures continued to improve the efficiency of his com-

Company Perspectives:

We want to do it right the first time, and that takes people who are dedicated to the details. As a company, we treat our people right. We treat them as individuals. So that's how our staff treats every one of our customers. Enthusiasm and commitment are contagious. Our customers feel it every time they do business with us.

pany. In 1972, while still working the territory himself, Stuller began offering toll-free telephone ordering. Later "Stuller milestones" adopted in the 1980s and 1990s resulted from his earnest conviction that efficiency in getting his company's products to its customers was second only to their quality.

A few years later, Stuller finally left the road work to others in his company, while also changing the name of the company to Stuller Settings, Inc. At that time, the business issued its first catalog and began special-order manufacturing. Within a short time, it also began casting its own findings and mountings—a base product line that became the core of Stuller's future operations.

1982–92: Stuller Thrives during Louisiana Recession

In 1982, Stuller Settings, Inc. moved from its original location into a new, 11,000 square foot manufacturing and distribution center that was constructed to fit the special needs of the firm. In that same year, Stuller began offering automatic second-day air delivery for open accounts and prepaid orders—an industry first. It was also in 1982 that the company issued its initial full-color mountings and findings catalog, which was another manufacturing and wholesale jewelry trade innovation.

Two years later, Stuller Settings began marketing its line nationally, and in 1985 had to break ground on an addition to its plant in order to accommodate the rapidly increasing business. The expansion was completed in 1986 and doubled the size of the facility. By 1989, however, it was already necessary to double the company's main facility's size again. The company was outgrowing itself faster than was imaginable. In 1993, the executive offices and administrative operations were moved to a high-rise office building. In 1994, the company's main facility was again renovated to create more space.

The success of Stuller Settings through the 1980s and early 1990s came at a time when Louisiana's petroleum industry was reeling from an oil bust that sent the state into a deep recession. While many oil-related businesses were closing their doors, Stuller Settings kept widening its own. Its growth in the period remained one of the few bright lights on the area's economic scene. The recession hit South Louisiana particularly hard, including the company's home base of Lafayette. That the company thrived in such an economic climate showed that the state's economic future well-being would depend on the sort of diversification the company represented.

During those years, Matt Stuller repeatedly won recognition—not just as a successful businessman, but as a model of the sort of entrepreneurial spirit that Louisiana desperately needed in its efforts to break away from single-industry dependence. Among other awards, in 1989 the company received the U.S. Senate's Productivity Award for Louisiana for "outstanding achievement in productivity and quality improvement." In 1991 the company also received the Lantern Award from the Louisiana Board of Commerce and Industry for its economic and civic contributions to the state. Individually, Matt Stuller was honored in 1995 with the "Entrepreneur of the Year" award given by *Inc.* magazine in the wholesale distribution category for Louisiana.

Stuller's success cannot be measured merely in quantitative terms, however. The company had always prided itself on the quality of its product line and on its swift service, which assured clients that orders would be shipped on the same day that they were placed. Through its history, it had worked to finely hone its production and delivery system, making it one of the most efficient companies in its particular industry. In 1988, it added toll-free fax ordering to its distribution service. In the next year, it enhanced its automation by implementing a fully computerized order entry, inventory, and manufacturing applications system. The year after that, it began offering automatic second-day air delivery to COD accounts. In 1992, it began providing next-day air delivery to all its customers. During the same period, it pushed the order deadline for guaranteed next-day delivery to continental U.S. accounts to later afternoon hours (3:00 p.m. Central Time). By 1994, Stuller had pushed the order cut-off time to the end of the working day. This "rolling cutoff" allowed jewelers in any of the 48 contiguous states to place an order by 5:00 p.m. of their local time and still be guaranteed next-day delivery.

Hand in hand with its ever increasing efficiency, Stuller enhanced its product line through additions and quality assurance. In 1987, using its own proprietary metal molding technology, it introduced a new line of wire basket settings. Three years later it introduced its in-stock finished diamond and colored stone jewelry program. The introduction of a line of religious jewelry followed in 1992. Also in that year, the company implemented its in-stock platinum product program.

Each of these new lines or programs were supported by a full-color catalog made available to its customers. Stuller also gathered all of its printed source books into an electronic catalog—a single CD-ROM that made them available in an easy-to-access, computerized format. This electronic catalog allowed the company's customers to select images for their own web sites or to display in e-mailings to their own clients; it also included such features as stone maps, allowing jewelers to make selections confidently from Stuller's huge inventory of diamonds and other gem stones.

1993–2000: New Services and Expansion Plans

In 1993, Stuller introduced its "Match and Bag" program, one of the mainstays in its "Have it Your Way" service. Put in place under the company's Diamond and Colored Stone Department, the program allowed customers to reduce their inventories and save considerable time by having Stuller's expert staff select gems to match customer-ordered mountings. Always concerned with both quality and security, in 1998 Stuller also

Key Dates:

1970: Company buys findings inventory from Jewelmont in New Orleans and begins wholesaling its inventory under the name South Central Distributors.
1984: Stuller begins marketing its line nationally.
1985: Company doubles size of facility.
1989: Second expansion again doubles size of plant; company receives U.S. Senate Productivity Award.
1991: Company receives Lantern Award from the Louisiana Board of Commerce and Industry.
1993: Administrative offices move into separate high-rise headquarters.
1994: Third expansion once more doubles manufacturing and distribution facility.
1995: Company introduces its ''Have It Your Way from Stuller'' service.
1999: Construction begins plant addition and new office building.

began offering Gemprint digital registration for diamonds sized at $\frac{3}{8}$ ct. or larger. This laser reflection technology allowed the company's customers an important tool for use in the identification and recovery of stolen diamonds.

In the 1990s, the company also added to its line of special kits for retail jewelers. According to Dr. Charles D. Lein, Stuller's president and COO, these kits offered ''a great way to focus attention on a particular category of jewelry,'' giving jewelers a means of grouping their inventories into discrete and distinct segments. Included among these were family jewelry, gold wedding bands, diamond stud earrings, children's jewelry, and teen jewelry kits.

By 1997, Stuller had plans to use $42 million to further increase the size of its physical operation by 2000 and to double its payroll by 2004. The company briefly considered expanding at a new location but eventually decided to remain in Louisiana. The new projections called for hiring 1,300 more people, bringing the staff to 2,419 and increasing the annual payroll from $21 million to $54 million. Estimated land and building costs totaled about $24 million and equipment purchases another $17 million. Scheduled for completion in June 2000, construction on the large addition to the manufacturing and distribution building commenced in 1999. When finished, it would add 238,000 square feet to that facility, once again doubling its size. Construction was also begun on a new five-floor administration office building adjoining the plant. Also scheduled for release in that summer was the company's newest tools book, a comprehensive guide to the various tools and supplies that the company makes for the bench jeweler.

Facing the new century, company founder Matt Stuller singled out three areas of attention that the company would address in its plans for helping independent jewelers compete successfully with large department store and chain outlets: the industry's increased attention to jewelry branding; the need for jewelers to create unique, customized pieces; and a rapidly expanding e-commerce.

Principal Competitors

M. Fabrikant & Sons; Lazare Kaplan International Inc.; OroAmerica, Inc.

Further Reading

''Business Briefs,'' *Advocate* (Baton Rouge), January 16, 1997, p. 1D.
Guarisco, Tom, ''Fruit of Loom Parent's Taxes Cut—481,382 Request Ok'd; Other Denied,'' *Advocate* (Baton Rouge), December 11, 1997, p. 1C.
Roskin, Gary, ''Stuller Embraces Digital Gemprint,'' *Jewelers Circular Keystone,* October 1998, p. 30.
''Stuller Settings' Specialty: Small Orders for Small Stores,'' *Jewelers Circular Keystone,* January 1987, p. 144.
Theriot, Stella, ''Bringing up Baby,'' *Times of Acadiana,* July 14, 1999, p. 23.
Walowitz, Hedda, ''Stuller Settings: Growth Through Service,'' *Jewelers Circular Keystone,* November 1988, p. 166.

—John W. Fiero

Sylvan Learning Systems, Inc.

1000 Lancaster Street
Baltimore, Maryland 21202
U.S.A.
Telephone: (410) 843-8000
Toll Free: (800) 338-2283
Fax: (410) 843-8065
Web site: http://www.sylvan.net

Public Company
Incorporated: 1979 as Sylvan Learning Corporation
Employees: 7,437
Sales: $338.49 million (1999)
Stock Exchanges: NASDAQ
Ticker Symbol: SLVN
NAIC: 611691 Exam Preparation and Tutoring; 61163
 Language Schools; 61171 Educational Support
 Services

From tutoring school children lagging in the three Rs to building a collection of universities in Europe, Sylvan Learning Systems, Inc. has become the largest private provider of educational services in the world. The company began with a small network of U.S.-based learning centers in 1979 and by 2000 had become a holding company for several subsidiaries overseeing 800 centers franchised across North America as well as 1,000 learning centers in Europe. Through its two English language subsidiaries, the Wall Street Institute and ASPECT, Sylvan offers instruction throughout Europe and Latin American, with new programs beginning in Asia and the Middle East.

Late 1970s Origins—Early 1990s Bargain

The first Sylvan Learning Center was opened in Portland, Oregon, in 1979 by W. Berry Fowler, who started a business tutoring students of all ages and skill levels. His business grew over the next six years to include franchises across the country, where students seeking to bolster their classroom abilities, from ages four and up, typically attended one-hour classes, twice weekly, in small classes of about three. In the mid-1980s,

Fowler sold his private company to KinderCare Learning Centers, an Alabama-based chain of childcare facilities that was expanding the scope of its business. Under the KinderCare system, Sylvan languished, as diversifying beyond its means had dragged down KinderCare's profits until it was forced to file for bankruptcy in 1992.

Sylvan was a bargain when it was purchased from Kinder-Care for $8 million the following year by the young team of Douglas Becker and Christopher Hoehn-Saric. Becker and Hoehn-Saric were friends at prep school and had both worked at a ComputerLand store in the Baltimore area; when they graduated, both decided to skip college in favor of heading straight into the business world. Together with a couple of partners they invented a small, computerized, medical records-storing device called Lifecard, which they were able to sell to Blue Cross and Blue Shield of Maryland, funding further businesses ventures. They next acquired KEE, Inc., an educational software and computer firm, where they gained expertise in software development and were able to land a deal with IBM. Casting about for new opportunities, Becker and Hoehn-Saric were attracted to the Sylvan Learning Center concept, which at the time had 483 centers nationwide, and, through KEE, they purchased a 50 percent interest in the company from KinderCare.

By 1993, they had acquired the other half. At age 23, Becker became Sylvan's chairman and CEO, while Hoehn-Saric, then 27, served as president (a title he held until 1999, when he became chairman and CEO of the new Sylvan Ventures Internet concern).

The two entrepreneurs were already millionaires by the time they took over Sylvan. According to a 1992 article in the *Baltimore Business Journal*, the team's goal was "to make the word 'Sylvan' synonymous with educational services, just as IBM is with computers or World Book with encyclopedias." At the time, a self-assured Becker told the journal, "There's no recognized brand name in this area, and I see no reason why it shouldn't be Sylvan." Hoehn-Saric told *Fortune* in 1994 that "We thought education as an industry was going through pretty dramatic changes. We saw a parallel between education and what health care was like, that the private sector had a greater role to play."

<table>
<tr><td colspan="2">Key Dates:</td></tr>
<tr><td>1979:</td><td>Sylvan is Founded by W. Berry Fowler.</td></tr>
<tr><td>1985:</td><td>Fowler sells Sylvan Learning to KinderCare Learning Systems.</td></tr>
<tr><td>1990:</td><td>KinderCare enters into a joint venture with Douglas Becker and R. Christopher Hoehn-Saric in which the two acquire a 50 percent share of the company.</td></tr>
<tr><td>1991:</td><td>Sylvan enters into a deal making the company the only commercial testing partner for Educational Testing Services.</td></tr>
<tr><td>1993:</td><td>Becker and Hoehn-Saric buy out the other half of Sylvan and take the company public.</td></tr>
<tr><td>2000:</td><td>Sylvan sells its Prometric testing services and refocuses on teaching rather than testing.</td></tr>
</table>

Ambitiously predicting 30 to 40 percent growth for the company each year for the next three to five years, Decker and Hoehn-Saric set about raising Sylvan's profile, running advertisements in *People, Newsweek* and *Good Housekeeping* that touted Sylvan's track record in helping students improve their schoolwork. Actress Sandy Duncan was featured in a radio ad campaign, and Marvel designed a marketing comic book for the company.

From the onset, Decker and Hoehn-Saric recognized a need for greater technology in their learning centers. The company installed computers and testing software that helped the centers pinpoint areas in which a student could use further tutoring. Moreover, the company began installing entire computer labs at Sylvan centers and offering adult computer training courses.

At the same time, Sylvan won a contract from the nonprofit Educational Testing Service which allowed for students to take a computerized version of the Graduate Record Exam (GRE) at Sylvan Centers. "Before, we were just a tutoring firm. Now, we're viewed more as partners by public educators," Becker told *U.S. News and World Report*.

The Early 1990s: Private Company, Public Education

To further Sylvan's push into public education, and effect a spirit of cooperation between Sylvan and public schools, the company initiated a program under which Sylvan centers or teachers were established in a few Baltimore public schools. Decker believed in his company's ability to help students learn more and faster, and he also believed that his company could provide a service to the public schools for less than they were already spending on remediation programs. By 1994, Sylvan was providing programs and teachers for disadvantaged children in several school systems across the country: ten in Baltimore, four in the District of Columbia, and more in Pasadena, Texas. By 1995, the company was serving· more than 4,000 students in 38 schools in the three cities and had also moved into St. Paul, Minnesota, where it tutored about 750 students. "Because Sylvan is not trying to take over public schools outright, teachers unions and other privatization critics have been more receptive to its role," a 1995 *Education Week* article stated. The

in-school tutoring arm of Sylvan had begun just as the company went public in December 1993 at $11 a share.

Sylvan effected successful results for stockholders. In the third quarter of 1994, the first year after it went public, the company posted a net income of $1.42 million, or 15 cents a share on revenue of $12.1 million, record high earnings for the company and more than double 1993's figures.

In 1995, Sylvan acquired Remedial Education and Diagnostic Services, Inc., a Philadelphia-based company providing tutoring to parochial schools, 233 in all, in Pennsylvania, Florida, Ohio, Delaware, Maryland, New Jersey, and the District of Columbia.

At the same time, Sylvan's public school tutoring program had expanded to several Maryland counties, as well as to Chicago, Newark, and Broward County, Florida. In all, Sylvan's School Services programs were serving 7,900 students in 58 public schools.

Another new venue for Sylvan services was found in providing educational services to employees in large workplaces. Through a wholly owned subsidiary called the Pace Group, and using a proprietary program called Sylvan At-Work, Sylvan began serving such corporate clients as Martin Marietta and Texas Instruments.

Sylvan's role as a testing service was enhanced when the company inked a deal with Novell, Inc., at the time one of the world's largest software companies. Novell agreed to have Sylvan conduct certification testing of professionals users of Novell's computer programs. However, the testing side of Sylvan's business also met with some challenges during this time. Competitor Kaplan Educational Service sent 20 of its employees to take the GRE at a Sylvan center. The undercover examinees discovered a way to compromise the security of the computer version of the GRE. Educational Testing Service suspended computer administration of test, and Sylvan's stock dropped from $19.75 to $17.50 after the news.

Nevertheless, Sylvan forged ahead with its testing services and by 1995 Sylvan had entered into a $140 million deal to acquire Minnesota-based Drake Prometric LP, a company with nearly the same amount of annual sales, $42 million, as Sylvan. With that acquisition, Sylvan secured its niche in providing computerized testing services to government agencies, technology companies, and scientific institutions. It renamed the company Sylvan Prometric.

By 1996, Sylvan had outgrown its Columbia, Maryland, headquarters (midway between Washington, D.C. and Baltimore) and had moved into a new facility in downtown Baltimore, erected on 11 acres of land and costing an estimated $350 million. Also during this time, the company became something of a media darling, its founders appearing in stories on all three major network newscasts, as well as on the NBC program "Nightline." Sylvan's successful operations as a franchisor also garnered attention, and the company was named among the top ten on the *Franchise Times* 1996 list of Top 200 Franchises, a list that included McDonald's and General Nutrition Centers. Moreover, Becker and Hoehn-Saric were named Maryland Entrepreneurs of the Year for 1996 by accounting firm Ernst and

Young. In a rather dubious endorsement, Sylvan was referred to in the 35,000-word manifesto of the so-called Unabomber, as having had ''great success'' in controlling the minds of children. ''I guess this means we've become a household name,'' Becker quipped to the *Baltimore Sun.*

Sylvan continued to launch several new ventures. The national Association of Securities Dealers (NASD) hired the company to provide computerized testing for the country's 500,000 registered brokers. Ten months later, however, Sylvan was sued by the American College Testing Service over charges that Sylvan had illegally obtained the NASD deal. Sylvan prevailed in court, and also that year won a $10 million contract to provide computer-based testing for National Council of Architectural Registration Boards.

The Late 1990s: Going Global

A joint venture with MCI Communications Corp. (now MCI WorldCom) helped Sylvan develop an international distribution network of adult professional education services. The company, called Caliber Learning Network, Inc., opened about 50 centers in 1997. International expansion was also pursued through the 1996 acquisition of Wall Street Institute, a provider of English language instruction in Europe and Latin America. Sylvan was thus able to realize its global goals while also making inroads into the adult education marketplace. Of the 170 Wall Street Institute centers, nearly half were in Spain. Sylvan's computerized testing services went abroad during this time as well, to China, where testing centers were developed throughout the vast country. Michael Moe, an analyst who followed Sylvan for Montgomery Securities in San Francisco, called the move a ''significant expansion of Sylvan's testing franchise,'' and observed that Sylvan was rapidly being recognized as a brand name in education internationally.

In 1997, contracts with public school districts were realized in Charleston, South Carolina, Oklahoma City, New Orleans, and Richmond, Virginia. That year, Sylvan also acquired Canter & Associates, a provider of professional development and graduate degree programs for educators with an enrollment of 4,500 students in a master's level distance learning program. At this time, there were nearly 700 Sylvan Learning Centers throughout the United States, and the company also provided tutoring services to 38,000 students in 625 private and parochial schools. Sylvan Prometric had become the largest network of computer-based testing centers in the world, with about 2,000 testing sites servicing 105 countries. The company launched a new ad campaign with the slogan, ''Success is learned.'' ''I'd like to make Baltimore almost a Silicon Valley for corporations in the education business,'' Becker told the *Baltimore Sun.*

Sylvan's hectic pace of activity growth had a price. In the midst of rapid expansion and product development, some problems in customer service had developed. When Sylvan rolled out a computerized version of the GMAT test for students applying to medical schools, the Manhattan site ran short on computer terminals, leaving some test-takers stranded. NASD complained about software glitches, and competition from the Kaplan Educational Centers, a division of the Washington Post Co., began to heat up. ''Sylvan hasn't faced a lot of competition from well-funded competitors,'' Kaplan President and CEO

Jonathan Grayer told *Business Week,* suggesting that his company intended to remedy that situation.

If challenges were surfacing, they weren't necessarily affecting profits, which soared from about $5 million in 1994 to $28 million in 1997. Stock was at a high of $45, and the accolades kept coming, as Becker was named 1998 Businessperson of the Year by the *Baltimore Business Journal.*

In 1998, the company acquired Schulerhilfe, a tutoring business with more than 900 centers across Germany, Austria, and Italy. Sylvan pushed further into Europe in 1999 with plans for a network of overseas colleges. For $29 million, Sylvan acquired a controlling interest in University Europea of Madrid, a private, for-profit university in Spain with an enrollment of over 7,000. Sylvan planned to expand its university network in Europe and Latin America in 2000. ''There is an enormous opportunity for university-level programs in international markets with a rising middle class,'' said Raph Appadoo, president and CEO of Sylvan International Universities, adding ''People want their children to succeed. They want degree programs at the university level. But in many international markets, the slots just aren't available in public universities. That's where private universities come in.''

While Sylvan was growing internationally, problems continued to plague its testing services, and the company decided to jettison that part of its holdings. In 2000, Sylvan finalized the sale of Prometric to the Thompson Corporation, a Canadian firm, for about $775 million. ''It required management capabilities beyond what we were able to bring to the table,'' Becker said in a *Baltimore Sun* interview following the sale of Prometric. ''We could take that same time and those same resources and use them to grow 10 companies. The opportunity to transform the company back into an entrepreneurial vehicle makes me feel much more comfortable.''

As an ''entrepreneurial vehicle'' Sylvan lost no time in launching a $500 million Internet venture designed to invest in and ''incubate'' companies that bring Internet technology solutions to the education and training marketplace. ''We are a big believer in the bricks and clicks economy,'' Becker told the *Baltimore Sun,* signaling the company's move into the realm of the Internet.

Apollo Advisors, which has invested $200 million in both Sylvan and the new Internet ventures, welcomed Sylvan's move. ''There are just dozens of educational Internet companies,'' said Larry Berg, a partner in the New York-based Apollo Advisors, ''But there are no blockbusters yet. What I love about Sylvan is that they are very targeted. They have one of the best brands in the business and an entrepreneurial culture.''

Principal Subsidiaries

Aspect International Language Schools; Canter & Associates; Wall Street Institute; Caliber Learning Network, Inc.; Universidad Europea de Madrid (54%; Spain); Schulerhilfe (Germany).

Principal Operating Units

Sylvan Ventures; Sylvan Learning Group; Sylvan International Universities.

Principal Competitors

Kaplan Education Centers; DeVry Inc.; ITT Educational Services Inc.; Learning Tree International Inc.; Berlitz International Inc.

Further Reading

Barrett, Amy, ''Lessons for the Tutors: Sylvan Learning Systems Fast Rise Leads to Growing Pains,'' *Business Week,* November 17, 1997.

Bowler, Mike, ''Bringing Critical Mass to Baltimore,'' *Baltimore Sun,* January 19, 1997.

Freaney, Margie, ''Sylvan Shoots for 30% to 40% Annual Growth,'' *Baltimore Business Journal,* February 28, 1992, p. 3.

Glanz, William, ''The Education of Doug Becker,'' *Baltimore Business Journal,* October 1998, p. 8.

Luciano, Lani, ''Three Franchisers that Make the Grade,'' *Money,* September 1995.

Rogers, Alison, ''With a Little Help from Their Friends,'' *Fortune,* September 19, 1994.

Somerville, Sean, ''Sylvan's Choice: Bigger Isn't Better,'' *Baltimore Sun,* March 5, 2000.

—Barbara Ruben

Tasty Baking Company

2801 Hunting Park Avenue
Philadelphia, Pennsylvania 19129
U.S.A.
Telephone: (215) 221-8500
Fax: (215) 223-3288
Web site: http://www.tastykake.com

Public Company
Incorporated: 1914
Employees: 1,100
Sales: $226.35 million (1999)
Stock Exchanges: New York Pacific Boston
Ticker Symbol: TBC
NAIC: 311812 Commercial Bakeries

Based in Philadelphia, Tasty Baking Company is one of the country's oldest and largest independent baking companies. A baker of individual snack cakes since 1914, the company manufactures and sells approximately 100 varieties of food products, including breakfast baked goods, single portion cakes, cookies, pies, brownies, snack bars, pretzels, and large family sized cakes and pies under the Tastykake, Dutch Mill, Aunt Sweeties, and Snak n' Fresh brands. From three bakeries, Tasty distributes its products to supermarkets and convenience stores throughout the Mid-Atlantic states, where it is the leading producer of snack cakes. An aggressive national distribution program is seeking to position the Tasty brand as a leader in the Midwest, South, Southwest, West Coast, and the Hawaiian Islands, as well as in Canada and Puerto Rico. While the Tasty Baking brands reach a total of 47 states, Tastykake baked goods are still regarded as a Philadelphia institution, honored alongside such other distinctly local food treats as cheese steaks, hoagies, and scrapple.

A Strong Start in 1914

Tasty Baking was founded in 1914 by Philip J. Baur and Herbert C. Morris. Baur came from a German-American family in the process of selling its large Pittsburgh bakery, while Morris, a Boston egg salesman, was from a well-established Cleveland family. Together, Baur and Morris decided to de-

velop small cakes, pre-wrapped fresh at a bakery plant before distribution to the local grocer, in contrast to the loaf cakes that were handled and cut into portions by the grocers under the unsanitary conditions of the time. Since the sale of the Baur bakery forbade any Baur to open a bakery within 100 miles of Pittsburgh, the two decided to make Philadelphia their base. They found a deserted, burnt-out plant in North Philadelphia with its own railroad siding and set up shop there.

On February 25, 1914, the Tasty Baking Co. was incorporated with capital of $46,000, half provided by Baur and his father, the other half from Morris's father-in-law, Edward K. Sober. Baur was responsible for production, Morris for sales, and Morris's wife came up with the name of the new product, *Tastykake*. From the onset, the company focused on using only the finest ingredients delivered fresh daily to the bakery. This included farm fresh eggs, Grade A creamery butter, real milk, cocoa, spices and natural flavorings. Sugar and flour were sifted by hand. The early cakes were produced in white, yellow, chocolate, raisin, molasses, and sponge cake varieties. After baking—at first in a single oven—the cakes were iced, cut into rectangles, wrapped, packed into boxes, and distributed to retailers who sold them for ten cents each. In its first year the company had impressive gross revenues of $300,000. By 1918, sales had reached $1 million.

By April 1915, Tasty Baking was serving stores as far away as Mt. Carmel and Reading, Pennsylvania; Trenton, New Jersey; and Wilmington, Delaware, as well as 13 Philadelphia routes. Morris would sell an agent only as many cakes as he thought that agent could sell within the two days between visits. The salesman replaced anything that had become stale with a new cake and took the stale one back to the plant, where it was destroyed. All business was transacted in cash. When this system broke down because the agents got behind on their payments, Tasty Baking decided to hire its own distributors and pay them a salary, commission, and car allowance. This arrangement remained in operation until the mid-1980s.

In 1922, Tasty Baking constructed a new, five-story plant on Hunting Park Avenue in North Philadelphia. Two additions were built within three years. The new plant led to new products: the Junior, a lemon sponge cake with icing on top; a chocolate cupcake; and the revolutionary Krimpet, a finger-sized butterscotch sponge cake baked in a fluted pan. The latter two products sold two for a nickel and became the company's best sellers. During this decade the Tastykake horse-drawn wagon was a familiar site on Philadelphia streets. Gasoline-fueled trucks and electric cars and trucks were also used, and Tasty products moved by rail and ship to more distant areas, but the last horse was not retired until 1941.

By 1930 the Hunting Park plant had five buildings and 350,000 square feet of floor space. Annual sales had climbed to $6 million. A lunchbox-size square apple pie, called the Tasty-Pie, proved a quick success. Newspaper advertisements, billboards, streetcar placards, and slides shown in movie theaters displayed Tastykake pastries or depicted children eating the products. The company weathered the Depression without layoffs by cutting its production costs. During World War II, Tasty Baking employed 203 people, and company advertising promoted the sale of war bonds.

The Kaiser Era: 1953–81

After Philip Baur died in 1951, his heirs purchased stock from the holdings of E.K. Sober's daughter (Herbert Morris's wife), giving the Baur family majority control of the private company. Vice-President Paul R. Kaiser became president, and Morris, who had served as president since the company's inception, became chairman of the board. In April 1954, Kaiser was able to report that the Tastykake territory had grown to cover parts of nine states and the District of Columbia. By the end of the decade, annual sales had grown to nearly $22.9 million. Net income first passed the $1 million mark in 1955.

Under the slogan "Automate or Abdicate" Kaiser advanced a program of installing spiral metal chutes, powered conveyor belts, and auxiliary equipment. The baking cycle, which took up to 12 hours in 1935, was cut to as little as 45 minutes in 1956. Acquisition of a Battle Creek wrapping machine began an era of automatic wrapping. A larger and more modern laboratory was completed in 1956.

During the 1950s, Tasty Baking's traditional customers, mom-and-pop retail stores, began to give way to supermarkets. Radio and television were replacing the company's traditional reliance on billboards and posters. Moreover, Tasty Baking began sponsoring Philadelphia Phillies baseball telecasts, featuring commercials starring Joe E. Brown, Betty White, and Shari Lewis with her puppets. Over the next 25 years, the company extended its sponsorship to baseball's Baltimore Orioles and Washington Senators, football's Philadelphia Eagles and hockey's Philadelphia Flyers, adding spokespersons ranging from musical impresario Dick Clark to Philadelphia sports heroes Bobby Clarke, Richie Ashburn, and Bill White.

As the factory's neighborhood changed, the company sought to establish better public relations ties with the surrounding African American community. In 1960, a two-month boycott of Tastykake products, organized by 400 black ministers, ended after Tasty Baking agreed to add African Americans to its sales, clerical, and other positions. Moreover, the company chose organized the Allegheny West Foundation to rehabilitate housing, introduce new businesses, and support other forms of community development in its home of North Philadelphia. Over the years, Tasty Baking remained committed to neighborhood improvement and sponsored numerous rehab projects and new constructions benefiting the North Philadelphia community.

When Tasty Baking went public in 1961, its offered stock sold out the first day, the price rising immediately from $20 a share to over $27 per share. Officers and directors continued to hold nearly half the shares, however. In 1965, the company diversified for the first time by acquiring Phillips & Jacobs, Inc., a producer of industrial chemicals and wholesale printing supplies, for about $2.5 million in stock. The next year it added a Baltimore graphic arts supply business, a potato chip company, and a biscuit business. The following year it added Philadelphia and Atlanta graphic arts companies.

By 1968, Tasty Baking was serving 30,000 stores in 12 states. Sales in 1967, when net income was $2.8 million, reached $67.4 million, of which the baking operations accounted for 57 percent. Graphic arts accounted for 28 percent. The remaining 15 percent came from the acquisition of potato chip and pretzel manufacturers and three Ohio cookie distributors. The Baur family held 58 percent of the company's voting stock by 1968, management held 12 percent, and the public held 30 percent.

In March 1970 Kaiser told a group of Philadelphia financial analysts that the Tastykake division was distributing 35 varieties of small cakes and pies to 28,000 stores in 12 states on a three-day-a-week basis. He also noted that the graphic arts division was supplying 17,000 items to the printing and allied trades in 14 states. The cookie-distribution companies were marketing a complete line of cookies, crackers, and biscuits to 4,000 retail outlets in Ohio and western Pennsylvania. Despite this expansion, the ratio of net profits to sales fell in 1970 for the ninth consecutive year; it was only 2.8 percent, compared to 5.8 percent in 1962.

Concluding that the potato chip and pretzel businesses were a drain on earnings, Tasty Baking sold them in 1970. In the same year, Tasty Baking expanded in a new direction by acquiring Larami Corp., a Philadelphia toy manufacturer, importer, and distributor. By 1972 the company's ratio of net profits to sales had improved slightly, but in the recession year of 1974 it was down to 2.6 percent: $3.5 million in net income on net sales of $132.1 million. In 1976, when net income peaked at $6.7 million on sales of $157 million, Tasty Baking made an unwise $5.5-million acquisition of Ole South Foods Co., a frozen dessert manufacturer. Tasty eventually dissolved Ole South Foods in 1979; that year Tasty lost $2.2 million on net sales of $169.5 million—its first annual loss.

Charting a New Direction: The 1980s

In 1981, Kaiser's last year as chief executive officer, Tasty Baking charted a new direction. The aging population of the Mid-Atlantic states, he said, indicated "a decrease in the number of teens, and they're the big snack and cake eaters.'' The company introduced a chocolate-covered pretzel and also entered the breakfast food market with Danish pastries and muffins. Finger-shaped cakes and cupcakes were packaged singly to attract more unit sales in single person households. Tasty also entered agreements with distributors as far away as California. In a process learned from Ole South Foods, baked goods were frozen in Philadelphia, shipped under refrigeration, and thawed at their destinations. Larami Corp. formed a Hong Kong trading company to import premium non-toy gifts for direct-mail marketing by Tasty Baking.

Kaiser's 28-year reign came to an end in April 1981, when dissident shareholders, upset by three consecutive quarters of losses, forced his resignation. Philip J. Baur, Jr., president of the Tastykake division and Kaiser's brother-in-law, succeeded him as chairman of the board. Nelson G. Harris, the company president since 1979, succeeded Kaiser as chief executive officer. Under new leadership, Tasty Baking retrenched. In October 1981, the company retreated from two of its major expansion projects, selling the toy manufacturer Larami and withdrawing from all but eight of its new markets in 40 states. In an October 1981 *New York Times* article, Harris explained, ''We went too far too fast. The problems of distribution and transportation became prohibitive, and there was the problem of not advertising aggressively enough.''

Although 1982 was a recession year, Tasty Baking halted a five-year decline in unit sales. Net income rose from $1.7 million in 1982 to $2.4 million in 1983 and $2.9 million in 1984, when net sales reached $222.4 million. Long-term debt was reduced from $19 million to $7 million. Tastykake distribution stabilized at 21 states, including California, where the company was sponsoring baseball's San Diego Padres. (California was dropped in 1988, however.) Also during this time, subsidiary Phillips & Jacobs began serving the New York City market.

Tasty Baking reorganized its sales organization in 1985. While delivery persons had typically owned their own trucks

and absorbed the cost of store returns, routes were now offered for sale to the driver-sales reps, who would become independent owner-operators of their territories. The company offered to finance the sales, with no down payment. According to Harris, the deliverymen ''paid $50,000 or $60,000 and got something worth $110,000–$120,000. . . . We had 386 routes, and we sold them all. Today [in 1989] we have about 510 routes, and we've had 50 route splits.''

The sale of its routes raised $16 million for Tasty Baking and made drivers more dutiful in tending their accounts. Such dedication was essential to the company, because most Tasty products contained no preservatives or artificial flavors and thus had shelf lives as short as four days. Sales rose ten percent immediately. Meanwhile, Harris allotted more than $40 million to upgrade the Philadelphia plant. Between 1981 and 1988, Harris' business strategy and initiatives resulted in revenues doubling to $264 million, while profits rose more than sevenfold, from $1.3 million to $9.5 million.

In 1989 Tasty Baking repackaged its Tastykake products in bright yellow instead of the traditional blue and white. The company also began a new line of cakes and pies, in flavors that changed monthly, and introduced a line of honey-graham cookies, called Tasty Bears, aimed at children aged six to 12. The following year the company introduced both Chocolate Royals, oversized cupcakes filled with chocolate mousse and topped with icing, and TastyLights, a low-fat cupcake. Finding that the former sold much better than the latter, leading division president Carl S. Watts concluded: ''There's a segment that may not want a snack cake every day. But when they do, they want it to be as indulgent as can be.'' By the end of 1990, some 30 percent of Tasty's bakery revenues were coming from products introduced since 1982, including Honey Buns and Pastry Pockets. Watts succeeded Harris as chairman and chief executive officer of the company in 1992.

Growth Through New Products: 1991–95

In 1991 Tasty Baking introduced its premium Gold Collection line. Several new products were introduced in 1992, including Tasty Mini Cupcakes, and lemon and jelly filled reduced-fat Krimpets cupcakes. That year carrot cake and chocolate chunk macadamia cookie cupcakes were added to the Gold Collection items. During 1993, new products included Dunkin' Stix, Pound Kake, and Blueberry Mini Muffins. Also in 1993, the company spun off its printing supplies subsidiary, Phillips & Jacobs, to its shareholders, who received two shares of its common stock for every three shares of Tasty Baking common stock.

In 1994, Tasty Baking launched a record six new snack-cake products. These included Kreme Krimpies, a crumpet-shaped, creme-filled sponge cake; Whirly Twirls, a chocolate roll cake with white creme filling and a dark chocolate coating; and P.B. Krunch, a crunchy wafer layered between strips of peanut butter covered with a rippled chocolate coating. The other three were seasonal products: Bunny Trail Treats, Sparkle Kakes, and Kringle Kakes, for Easter, the Memorial Day/Fourth of July period, and Christmas, respectively. St. Patty's Treats were introduced in 1995 to complete the company's holiday coverage. Thirty-four percent of Tasty's snack-cake sales in 1994 came from Tastykake products that did not exist ten years before.

Stripped of Phillips & Jacobs, Tasty Baking had net sales of $142 million in 1994 and net income of $5.8 million from continuing operations. Its long-term debt was $10.3 million in July 1994. Officers and directors controlled about nine percent of the common stock, whereas institutions held 44 percent.

In 1995 Tasty Baking was selling its products in about 30 states. In addition to its approximately 25,000 retail outlets in the Mid-Atlantic states, it was selling through direct alliances with major grocery chains in the Midwest, South, and Southwest. Cakes, cookies, and doughnuts sold for 25 to 69 cents per package, with family packages and jumbo packs ranging from $1.99 to $3.39. Pies, pastries, and brownies typically retailed for 69 cents apiece or per package. Three varieties of English muffins ranged from $1.49 to $1.69 per package. Customers could also order a variety of Tastykake gift packs by calling a toll-free number. By August, the company had acquired Dutch Mill Baking Company.

Also that year, responding to the growing fat-free and low-fat food market, Tasty Baking introduced a new line of eight low-fat snacks. Having failed at an earlier attempt, in 1989, to launch a line of low-fat products, the company spent nearly a year reengineering its product line to eliminate fat without compromising the taste of Tastykake.

Improving and Expanding Operations: 1996–99

In 1996 Tasty Baking stepped up efforts to improve its packaging facilities, seeking to ensure product freshness while increasing the speed at which its products could be boxed or packaged. Also during this time, Tasty Baking acquired a new bakery in Oxford, Pennsylvania, from competitor Keebler Co., and set about refitting it for the production of yeast-raised products, including Danish and sweet rolls.

Seeking to attract new customers and bolster sales, the company entered the lucrative dessert cookie market in 1997 by launching a premium line of chocolate chip and oatmeal raisin cookies. Packaged in 12-ounce boxes, under the brand name of Tasty Collections, the premium cookies retailed at $2.99. The company also introduced its Cream Bars, dark chocolate-covered chocolate cake with vanilla or peanut butter filling. With these new cookie entries and the popularity of its brand name, the company reasoned, it could carve out at least some portion of the then $3.6 billion cookie market. While Tasty Baking held 64 percent of the market for sweet cakes in the Mid-Atlantic states, Entenmann's (a unit of Bestfoods) was the market leader of box-packed homestyle cookies.

Elsewhere, the company continued its expansion efforts. In August 1998, it began selling Tastykake products in the Chicago area. Also, recent deals struck with two distributors, Metz Baking of Deerfield, Illinois, and St. Louis-based Earthgrains Co. expanded the company's distribution to 46 states. In November, Tasty Baking entered yet another market, food service. Through its Oxford facility, the company began selling breakfast foods (Danish pastry, bear claws, coffee, and donuts) in bulk pack containers to college cafeterias, hospitals, and large corporations.

In April 1999, Tasty Baking announced that it would begin offering family-sized packages of sweet baked goods, starting with eight varieties in its core marketing area. Expanding its market range into the dinnertime dessert menu, the move also reflected the company's systematic buildup of product offerings to achieve maximum flexibility in a variety of eating markets.

By moving specifically into the dessert market, the company hoped to boost revenues, which had only experienced modest growth over the two previous years: 1.8% ($149.3 million) between 1996 and 1997 and one percent ($150.7 million) between 1997 and 1998. The company also hoped to effectively compete with Entenmanns's bakeries and increase the productivity at its Oxford plant.

Sales, however, continued to be slow through midyear 1999. A new line of Classic Baked Goods had performed well; however, sales of the company's core product lines were not as healthy. In a company statement, Carl S. Watts, Tasty Baking's president and CEO, attributed the declines to "competitive pressures, combined with our recent realignment and discontinuance of routes in certain sales territories, excessive hot June weather, as well as our concentrated effort to bring promotional cost under more control, resulted in this decrease in gross sales."

During this time, undeterred by sluggish financials, Tasty Baking entered the multi-serve pie market. Large eight-inch in diameter versions of Tasty's four-ounce, single serve apple and lemon pie predecessors were initially introduced, with pumpkin pie set for debut in time for the holiday season. The company planned to make the Oxford plant more profitable and would eventually bake the larger pies at that facility, while continuing to produce the single-serve pies at Hunting Park.

The company's 1999 fourth quarter results increased net sales. Initiatives taken by the company through the first three quarters of 1999 were credited, including improved profitability of route and national sales operations; restructure of promotional efforts; improved operating results from the bakery modernization program; and improved operations at the Oxford facility.

2000 and Beyond

Tasty Baking approached the new millennium boosting its sales opportunities through a national distribution venture with Aramark Corporation. By agreement, the Tastykake brand assumed "preferred vendor" status in Aramark's Refreshment Services division. This enabled the Tastykakes product to be distributed throughout Aramark's refreshment services system that distributed more than 1.5 million cups of coffee to 60,000 business and industry locations throughout the United States.

As market research had indicated that Tasty Baking needed to broaden its Classic Baked Goods line of family-sized cakes and packaged cookies, the company planned two extensions of the line: the Raspberry Danish Strip and Cheese Danish Strip. At least five more extensions, including Danish rings and cinnamon buns, were also planned. Again, the new marketing initiative was designed to capture market share from its chief rival, Entenmann's.

New venues for Tasty Baking during this time were Wal-Mart stores nationwide, and Vons and Ralph's Grocery stores in California. Moreover, the company looked toward the Hawaiian Islands, where it entered into a distribution agreement with Hawaii Baking Company, Hawaii's largest baked goods supplier. In addition to introducing its traditional line of products in California and Hawaii, Tasty Baking planned to add a new product, Tropical Delights, cupcakes filled with tropical flavors such as papaya, guava, pineapple, and coconut.

Principal Subsidiaries

TBC Financial Services, Inc.; Dutch Mill Baking Company, Inc.; Tasty Baking Oxford, Inc.

Principal Competitors

Bestfoods; Interstate Bakeries Corporation; McKee Foods Corporation; Nabisco Holdings Corporation.

Further Reading

Briggs, Rosland, "Pie Company Wants to Take Philadelphia Market Share from Entenmann's," *Knight-Ridder/Tribune Business News,* September 19, 1999.

——, "Snack-Foods Maker Tasty Baking to Serve up New Family-Sized Desserts," *Knight-Ridder/Tribune Business News,* April 14, 1999.

Bullock, Jill M., "Tasty Expects Benefits from New Packaging," Wall *Street Journal,* August 25, 1989, p. 4D.

Desloge, Rick, "Earthgrains Heats Up Hunt for Acquisitions; Philly Bakery Fits, Analysts Says," *St. Louis Business Journal,* March 8, 1999, p. 5.

"Expansion Setback Is Forcing Change at Tasty Baking," *New York Times,* October 22, 1981, p. 4D.

Gardner, Joel R., *Seventy-Five Years of Good Taste: A History of the Tasty Baking Company, 1914–1989,* Philadelphia: Tasty Baking Co., 1990.

Helzner, Jerry, "Local Mystique: Tasty Baking Hopes to Transport It to Most Big Markets," *Barron's,* April 30, 1984, p. 53.

Kaiser, Paul R., "Tasty Baking Company," *Wall Street Transcript,* September 23, 1968.

——, "Tasty Baking Company," *Wall Street Transcript,* May 18, 1970.

Kasrel, Deni, "New Revenue Recipe for Tasty Baking," *Philadelphia Business Journal,* September 11, 1998, pp.1–2.

McCalla, "Tasty's Recovery Too Slow For Some," *Philadelphia Business Journal,* July 30, 1999, pp. 3–4.

Meeks, Fleming, "Junk Food Blitz," *Forbes,* May 27, 1991, pp. 196–98.

Randolph, Deborah A., "Tasty Baking Co. Dissidents Oust Kaiser, Omit Dividend and Cut Officers' Salaries," *Wall Street Journal,* April 27, 1981, p. 22.

Randolph, Deborah A., "Tasty Baking Whips Up New Recipe in Effort to Bolster Its Sluggish Sales," *Wall Street Journal,* January 11, 1981, p. 34.

Reyes, Sonia, "Tasty Baking is Sweet on Classics, Ads," *Brandweek,* May 8, 2000, p. 18.

Rice, Judy, "Changing Donuts to Dollars," *Food Processing,* May 1996, p. 119.

"Tasty Baking Sets Spinoff of Printing Supplies Unit," *New York Times,* July 13, 1993, p. D4.

Warner, Susan, "Philadelphia's Tasty Baking Co. Unveils Low-Fat Cake Snacks," *Knight-Ridder/Tribune Business News,* October 30, 1995.

——, "Tasty Baking to Buy New Bakery in Chester County, Pa.," *Knight-Ridder/Tribune Business News,* April 5, 1996.

—Robert Halasz
—updated by Ana G. Schulz

Tejon Ranch Company

P.O. Box 1000
4436 Lebec Road
Lebec, California 93243
U.S.A.
Telephone: (661) 248-3000
Fax: (661) 248-3100
Web site: http://www.tejonranch.com

Public Company
Incorporated: 1936
Employees: 148
Sales: $55.9 million (1999)
Stock Exchanges: New York
Ticker Symbol: TRC
NAIC: 112111 Beef Cattle Ranching and Farming;
115116 Farm Management Services; 213112 Support
Activities for Oil and Gas Operations; 111335 Tree
Nut Farming; 23311 Land Subdivision and Land
Development

The Tejon Ranch Company, at the southern end of California's Central Valley, is the largest and one of the oldest ranches in the state. The ranch itself is the largest contiguous parcel of land held in private hands in the state. Measuring approximately 270,000 square acres, it is one-third the area of Rhode Island and approximately the size of the city of Los Angeles. Tejon Ranch's close proximity to that city—Los Angeles is only 60 miles to the south—as well as its location on several key highways, including Interstate 5, make parts of its land ripe for lucrative commercial and residential development. In the latter half of the 1990s the company announced an ambitious 30-year real estate development plan, which includes land planning, real estate development, commercial sales and leasing, and income portfolio management. Tejon Ranch's other activities are those in which it has engaged for most of its existence: livestock, farming and resource management. At the end of 1999, it owned about 45,000 head of cattle; its permanent crops included 1,555 acres of wine grapes, 1985 acres of almond trees, 738 acres of pistachio trees, and 295 acres of walnut trees. Tejon Ranch's

resource management activities encompass oil and mineral leases, a game management program that includes recreational hunting, the provision of locations for films, and a quarter horse breeding program. Its $55.9 million in 1999 revenues were an all-time high for the company.

19th Century Origins

The Tejon (pronounced ''TAY-yohn'') Ranch traces its existence back to the late 18th century. Europeans first set foot on the land when the Spanish soldiers crossed the Tehachapi Mountains hunting for deserters. The name ''Tejon''—Spanish for ''badger''—was first reportedly used when troops found a dead badger in the entrance to a canyon in the area. In 1843 the Mexican government made grants for the land that became three ranches: *Rancho los Alamos y Agua Caliente* (Cottonwoods and Hot Water Ranch); *Rancho el Tejon* (Badger Ranch), *Rancho de Castec* (Eye Ranch). A fourth tract, *Rancho la Liebre* (Rabbit Ranch), was granted in 1846. Those four ranches would later be joined together to form the Tejon Ranch.

The Mexican-American War broke out during this time, and in 1848, following Mexico's defeat, the Treaty of Guadalupe Hidalgo gave California its independence; in 1850 it was admitted as the 31st state of the union. Despite pressure from eastern settlers to break up for homesteading some of the enormous spreads of lands granted earlier by Mexico, the U.S. government chose to respect the validity of those grants. As a consequence, tracts of California land that frequently measured 100,000 or more acres—like Tejon Ranch—were held by a few private owners.

Between 1855 and 1866, the four Tejon ranches were acquired by Edward Fitzgerald Beale. Beale was a colorful figure in California history: the naval officer who first announced the discovery of gold in California in 1848, the Superintendent of Indian Affairs in California and Nevada from 1852 to 1854, who established the first Indian reservation in the United States, and eventually, in 1876, the ambassador to the Austro-Hungarian Empire. Finally, in 1880, he retired to the Tejon Ranch and began raising cattle. Author/journalist Charles Nordhoff, who visited the ranch around that time, described it as the most impressive in all California.

Company Perspectives:

Tejon Ranch Company is a diversified, growth-oriented real estate development and agribusiness company committed to increasing shareholder value through creative development of its land holdings and maximizing its earnings.

When Beale died in the spring of 1893, the ranch passed into the hands of his son, Truxtun. The Beale family sold the Tejon Ranch in 1912 for about $3 million to a 70-member group of Southern California investors led by *Los Angeles Times* owner Harry Chandler and Moses Sherman, a wealthy Southern California land developer. Those investors and their heirs would retain control of Tejon Ranch until the late 1990s. The rights to the Ranch's ''Cross & Crescent'' brand, which later served as the company's logo, were officially transferred to the new owners in 1917, five years after the purchase.

The new owners secured the necessary water entitlements and gave the spread over to cattle ranching and farming. Occasionally, more adventurous projects were undertaken, such as an attempt early on to raise ostriches. The venture proved more difficult than anticipated, however, and when the craze for ostrich plumes proved to be short-lived, the idea was given up.

1930s–70s: Weathering Economic Downturns

On February 14, 1936 the Tejon Ranch Co. was incorporated as a California corporation, and 108,000 shares of stock were issued. That same year, oil was discovered on the ranch. That discovery enabled Tejon Ranch to weather difficult financial years in the 1940s and 1950s. Without those revenues, according to Jack Hunt, Tejon's president in the mid-1990s, Tejon would probably not have survived those years in its present form. (Tejon oil took on added significance after the Gulf War, and by 1993 the company had leased more than 9,000 acres to ARCO.) Tejon also leased land for mineral and rock extraction during this time.

In 1967 one of the company's lessees completed a state-of-the-art cement manufacturing plant with a capacity of 600,000 tons of cement per annum. The facility would be the source of significant royalties for Tejon and, in the 1980s, a source of a headache or two.

In the early 1970s, Tejon established a series of subsidiaries: Tejon Development Corp. and Tejon Agricultural Corp. were both founded in 1972, while Tejon Ranch Feedlot, Inc. was established the following year. In 1974 it added another subsidiary when for $1.27 million the company purchased Waterman-Loomis Co., a producer of alfalfa seed in Bakersfield, California. Tejon Ranch was first listed on the American Stock Exchange in 1973. In 1980, the company attempted to reincorporate under Delaware's jurisdiction but gave up the plan when it encountered difficulties registering a new stock offering related to the change with the Securities and Exchange Commission. Tejon was not able to reincorporate in Delaware until June 10, 1987, replacing the original California corporation.

Hard economic times—the result of overproduction, low prices and debt—overtook California farming, in particular the

large agricultural companies, in 1985. To see its way through the crisis, Tejon Ranch underwent restructuring, buying out its limited partners. Using an option in its partnership agreement, Tejon was able to obtain interests from them, for which they had originally paid $18 million. As a result, John Hancock Mutual Life Insurance Co., one of Tejon's big lenders, put a moratorium on Tejon's outstanding debts. ''It let us continue to operate,'' Cal Walters, the company's president at the time, told the *San Diego Union-Tribune,* adding ''If we hadn't [restructured], that option would not have been available to us.''

Despite the downturn in California agriculture, the stock of Tejon Ranch Co. went on a price rampage, increasing in value so much during 1985 and early 1986 that twice the American Stock Exchange froze trading in the company's shares. Tejon's price rose more than 25 points in less than a week in March 1985 and more than 38 points in a week in October. Stock which had sold for just under $100 per share in January 1985 was going for over $245 per share in December, and in January 1986 it would jump another 32 points. The speculation was fueled by the belief that Tejon was about to undertake the major commercial development of part of its vast land holdings.

New Uses for Old Land in the 1980s

As early as 1980 Tejon had announced its intention to begin developing its land at some indefinite point in the future, and the land's strategic location between Los Angeles, Bakersfield, and Edwards Air Force base made such development extremely lucrative. By February 1985, Tejon stock had jumped to $400 a share at which point the American Stock Exchange froze trading once again. Analysts explained that the stock's volatile behavior was rooted in its ''thin float''; more than 50 percent of the company's stock was held by the Times-Mirror Company, and other institutional investors. As a result, fewer than 630,000 shares were available for trading. To ease that shortage, in early February 1986, Tejon's directors approved a ten-for-one split of company stock.

Despite the split, market speculation in Tejon stock continued unabated into 1988. In response to another halt in trading by the Exchange, the company's president Jack Hunt announced that the company was considering the sale of a ''significant'' part of Tejon's business. Two weeks later, it confirmed that it had sold its subsidiary, W-R Research Inc., for $20 million. W-R Research developed new varieties of alfalfa seed. By May 1990, the *Los Angeles Times* could report that Tejon was one of the best performing companies on Wall Street, with a 34.4 percent price to sales ratio nearly ten points higher than any other California company and a market value almost two hundred times higher than its book value.

When the California real estate market took a downturn in 1990, and the development of Tejon's land was no longer such a profitable prospect, the stock suffered. The company was in the fourth year of a serious drought which forced it that year to reduce its cattle herd from 14,000 to 6,000 head. By the time the 1991 season rolled around, Tejon's agricultural operations had been severely impacted as well, and it appeared that because of state cutbacks in water supplies, the company would not have access to sufficient water to produce full crops, a likelihood that signaled significant losses in revenues. Indeed, in August 1991,

Key Dates:

1843: Mexican government begins making land grants of the property that is later joined into Tejon Ranch.
1855: Edward Fitzgerald Beale begins purchasing the four ranches that form the original Tejon Ranch.
1912: Tejon Ranch is purchased by group of investors headed by Harry Chandler and Moses Sherman.
1936: Tejon Ranch Co. is incorporated in California.
1973: Tejon Ranch goes public on the American Stock Exchange.
1980: The company announces its intention to commercially develop parts of its land holdings.
1985: Company restructures.
1986: Directors approve a ten-for-one stock split.
1991: Acclaimed artist Christo installs part of his exhibit—''The Umbrellas''—on Tejon Ranch land.
1995: Storms wipe out 23 percent of Tejon Ranch almond orchards.
1999: Petro Travel Plaza, the first phase of the Tejon Ranch development plan, is completed, and the company is listed on the New York Stock Exchange.

Tejon reported its second quarter profits had dropped 65 percent from the previous year; in November 1991 it reported an 87 percent decline in profits from 1990.

In October 1991, the artist Christo, who gained international renown by literally wrapping public edifices such as the Pont Neuf in Paris and later the Reichstag in Berlin, used Tejon Ranch lands for an art installation entitled ''The Umbrellas.'' As part of the project, which had been in planning stages since 1987, Christo erected on the land 1,760 large, bright yellow umbrellas, each weighing some 448 pounds, along a 19 mile stretch of rugged hillsides. They were exhibited there for three weeks. Tejon agreed to allow its land to be used for ''The Umbrellas'' after being assured by Christo—and sponsors of his earlier work—that the work or its preparations would not damage the ecology of the ranch. ''Our questions had been only with his methods, not his art,'' a Tejon Ranch lawyer told the *Christian Science Monitor,* noting, ''Since then we have become his fans.'' Another set of umbrellas, set up in the hills north of Tokyo Japan, were opened at the same time as those on Tejon Ranch. The entire cost of the project, estimated at over $26 million, was borne by the artist. Christo's work gave Tejon Ranch, a company known to few in California, much less the rest of the country, a higher media profile.

In the early 1990s, Tejon Ranch became embroiled in a controversy surrounding the presence of the cement factory that long leased ranch land. The National Cement Co. plant was licensed to burn hazardous liquid waste, which it did as part of its cement production process. In 1991, after the plant's federal and state operating permits expired, area residents mounted a protest to block new ones from being issued. Independently of the protest, Tejon refused to co-sign National's application for new permits. Because it could not vouch for the accuracy of National's claims on its permit applications, Tejon would not share responsibility for the cement company's actions. Federal

law required the owner of the land on which such a site operated to co-sign for all permits, and as a result, the Environmental Protection Agency (EPA) refused to issue them. State officials then attempted to persuade the EPA to reconsider its ruling, because National was the only facility in California licensed to incinerate hazardous liquid waste. Without it the state would be forced to dispose of such waste in scarce landfills. To extricate itself from the controversy, Tejon considered taking the unprecedented step of selling the land outright to National Cement. In August 1994, a federal judge granted National Cement permission to continue burning hazardous waste in its manufacturing processes while the EPA order to cease burning was appealed. The fight dragged for years thereafter in the courts.

In 1995 Tejon suffered again at the hands of the unpredictable weather brought on by global warming. Sustained winds, blowing in excess of 100 miles an hour toppled some 200 acres of Tejon almond orchards. The loss amounted to about 23 percent of the company's producing almond trees, which accounted for three percent of Tejon's total revenues in 1994. As a result of the storms, Tejon's net income for 1995 was $1.28 million lower than the previous year.

Development Plans in the 1990s

The most important development of the 1990s for Tejon Ranch, by far, was its decision after years of consideration to plunge headfirst into commercial development of its land. The momentous step had been rumored for years, rumors fueled by the company's own public statements. In October 1980, Tejon had announced plans for a community consisting of houses and condominiums, together with a retirement village, but did not offer a timetable for the plan. That remained the case in 1990, when other developers were eyeing land around the ranch. Whether the fault lay with its management team or its corporate owners was unclear; whatever the case, its touch-and-go attitude toward land development won Tejon Ranch a reputation as an extremely cautious company.

In 1992 Tejon seemed to confirm this view of itself when company president Jack Hunt told the *San Francisco Chronicle:* ''We are managing the asset for the long haul only. The fact that such a big ranch so close to L.A. still exists is a miracle. . . . That's largely because the [ownership] group does not depend on the ranch to survive. They have a big sense of stewardship, and they don't have to pull value out of the ranch.'' In 1993 real estate analysts believed that between the faltering Southern California real estate market and Tejon's indecision, decades would pass before anything was built on the company's land.

By 1997, however, a great deal had changed back at the ranch. In March 1995, Jack Hunt, Tejon's president and CEO of nine years, resigned to take over King Ranch in Texas. He was replaced a year later by Robert A. Stine, a San Diego real estate developer, who was given the go-ahead to move Tejon Ranch Co. aggressively toward development. Stine immediately replaced more than half of the company's directors with individuals with backgrounds in land development. In July 1997, the Times-Mirror Company, a publishing company which held the largest single block of Tejon stock—31 percent—sold its four million shares to Third Avenue Trust and Carl Marks Management Co. *Barron's* later reported that the selling price was $13.50 a share, well below the stock's current market price.

At the end of 1997, Tejon made public the first of its plans for developing its property. The first project was called the Tejon Industrial Complex, which was to cover an 350 acre area along its Interstate 5 frontage, the main traffic corridor between Los Angeles and San Francisco. Later plans included the development of a tourist attraction along the highway and a city built for a population of 20,000. The complex would consist of industrial buildings, warehouses, and other commercial structures to service the 50,000 motor vehicles that traveled daily through the Tejon Pass on I-5. Tejon entered a joint venture with Petro Shopping Centers, a company that built and operated highway travel plazas throughout the United States. The Petro Travel Plaza, a 51-acre development at the Tejon Industrial Complex, was the first development project in Tejon's Five Year Plan. Completed in 1999 at a cost of about $25 million, the Petro Travel Plaza was one of the largest in California, consisting of a movie theater and laundry for truckers, showers, a hairstyling salon, ice cream parlor, mercantile store, Internet-access area, and a shoe shine stand, in addition to the obligatory gas station and convenience mart.

Perhaps nothing illustrated Tejon's new direction so well as its sale to Northrop Grumman Corp. for $4.25 million of a site it had leased to the aircraft giant for nearly 20 years. The company's inviolable policy in previous years had been that it would not sell ranch land. With the Northrop-Grumann sale in the summer of 1998, the new management explicitly separated itself from that old policy and showed itself willing to chisel off pieces of Tejon's California empire.

Tejon's plans to move aggressively into real estate led the company to move its stock off the American Stock Exchange. Beginning July 28, 1999, it was traded on the New York Stock Exchange. The changeover was taken to give the company better access to the nation's capital markets, to ease some of the volatile fluctuation in price that the stock had experienced on the American Stock Exchange, and because most publicly traded real estate developers list on the New York Stock Exchange.

Tejon's results for 1999 seemed to confirm the wisdom of the company's new direction. Its $55.9 million in revenues were a record high, up from $48 million in 1998. 1999 was also the third year of increasing revenues—the three years Stine was at the helm. It was also the culmination of a year that saw not only the opening of the Petro Travel Plaza but also the beginning of a partnership with three national home building companies to build a 4,000-acre residential community in north Los Angeles county; a letter of agreement with Enron North America to develop a major power plant on Tejon Ranch to serve the new real estate developments; and a deal with Qwest Communications to route that company's fiber optic network through Tejon Ranch.

Principal Subsidiaries

Tejon Ranchcorp and its subsidiaries Laval Farms Corporation and Laval Agricultural Company; Tejon Marketing Company; Tejon Ranch Feedlot, Inc.; White Wolf Corporation; Tejon Development Corporation; Tejon Industrial Corporation; Champion Feedlot Trading Corp.; Liebre East Texas, Inc.; Tejon Almond Growers, LLC; Pastoria Power Project LLC; Eastquads 3820 LLC; Eastquads 3826 LLC; Eastquads 3832 LLC; RSF 6051 LLC; Tejon Cattle Feeders LLC.

Principal Competitors

Bartlett and Company; King Ranch, Inc.; Koch Industries, Inc.

Further Reading

"California Land Firm's Stock Moves to New York Stock Exchange," *Bakersfield Californian,* July 28, 1999.

Chandler, John, "Waste Plant Is Threatened With Closure," *Los Angeles Times,* March 20, 1992, p. B3.

Christie, Bob, "Aircraft Maker Buys Site from California's Tejon Ranch for Radar Testing," *Bakersfield Californian,* August 23, 1998.

——, "New Roadside Service Center Set to Open in Bakersfield, Calif.," *Bakersfield Californian,* June 25, 1999.

Collier, Robert, "Where Cattle Once Roamed: Spurred by Economic Pressures and Visions of Creating Future Metropolis," *San Francisco Chronicle,* December 20, 1992, p. 7.

"Diverse in Its Landscape and Business Dealings, Tejon Ranch is Branching Out," *Los Angeles Times,* February 8, 1998, p. B2.

Gaw, Jonathan, "As It Turns 150, Tejon Ranch Weighs Development," *Los Angeles Times,* September 19, 1993, p. A3.

Kristof, Kathy M., "The Times 100: The Best Performing Companies In California," *Los Angeles Times,* May 1, 1990, p. D2.

Lindsey, Robert, "Oil, Water and Boom: Will They Mix?," *New York Times,* October 28, 1980, p. A16.

"Major Development Plans Announced by Tejon Ranch Co.," *Business Wire,* December 16, 1997.

"Net Income Drops at California's Tejon Ranch," *Bakersfield Californian,* March 12, 1996.

Sabbatini, Mark, "Antelope Valley; Cement Firm Wins Stay on Order to Stop Burning Waste," *Los Angeles Times,* August 26, 1994, p. B9.

Savitz, Eric J., "For Land's Sake—Wall Street to Contrary, Tejon Hasn't Turned to Dust," *Barron's,* October 29, 1990, p. 16.

——, "High noon: Times-Mirror and the Chandler Family Let Go of Tejon Ranch," *Barron's,* August 25, 1997, p. 19.

"Shares Of Calif. Property Tejon Ranch Soar 44% On Development Hopes," *Dow Jones Online News,* August 25, 1997.

Stavro, Barry, "Times Mirror to Sell Stake in Tejon Ranch," *Los Angeles Times,* July 19, 1997, p. D2.

"Tejon Ranch Assessment Of Storm Damage," *PR Newswire,* January 24, 1995.

"Tejon Ranch Co.'s Directors Approve 10-for-1 Stock Split," *Wall Street Journal,* February 5, 1986.

"Tejon Ranch Mulls Proposal to Sell Part of Its Business Lines," *Wall Street Journal,* March 7, 1988.

"Tough Times Squeezing Some of State's Largest Growers," *San Diego Union-Tribune,* September 30, 1985, p. E1.

Wood, Daniel B., "Umbrella Project Gets Mixed Response," *Christian Science Monitor,* October 7, 1991, p. 11.

—Gerald E. Brennan

TenFold Corporation

180 West Election Road
Draper, Utah 84020
U.S.A.
Telephone: (801) 495-1010
Toll Free: (800) 836-3653
Fax: (801) 495-0353
Web site: http://www.10fold.com

Public Company
Incorporated: 1993 as KeyTex Corporation
Employees: 700+
Sales: $92.4 million (1999)
Stock Exchanges: NASDAQ
Ticker Symbol: TENF
NAIC: 51121 Software Publishers

TenFold Corporation is a major provider of vertical software applications for corporations in the insurance, health care, energy, communications, banking, investment management, and other industries. About 60 percent of its revenues comes from insurance companies. Using its patented Universal Application technology as a foundation, TenFold develops flexible client applications that later are licensed to others. Tenfold made history in 1998 when it became the first company of its kind to offer a money-back guarantee ensuring that its clients would get their Internet-based programs for a fixed fee and on time. TenFold promises its clients a "ten fold" advantage compared to other so-called integrators. One reason for its rapid growth is its ability to complete a project in a few months, while competitors' products can be years in development. TenFold had no clients until 1996, and stock analysts and technology consultants praise this young company for its innovative technology, rapid revenue growth, profitability, and sound management team of mostly former Oracle Corporation executives.

1980s Origins

A graduate mathematician from Brown University, Jeffrey L. Walker founded Walker Interactive Products to develop financial and accounting software before joining Oracle Corporation. Walker started Oracle's application division back in the mid-1980s, developed Oracle Financial and other applications, and played a key role as the firm's chief financial officer when Oracle became a public corporation.

After Walker retired from Oracle, he was prompted to return to the business world to satisfy his desire to automate the development of software applications. He knew companies often spent too much money and time in creating essential applications. So Walker and some other former Oracle personnel started a new firm, originally called KeyTex Corporation, incorporated in Delaware on February 3, 1993.

Walker and his early employees set up a small San Francisco office. "They had to rescue some furniture from a dumpster to start the first office," recalled Liz Tanner, the company's public relations director in a phone interview in May 2000.

For about four years Walker and his small group of about 25 KeyTex employees worked on a new technology they called the "Universal Application." Company literature later described the Universal Application as "our collection of technologies for building large-scale, complex applications quickly and reliably. It supports rapid development and quick maintenance to make enhancing and evolving TenFold applications easy and inexpensive."

In those early days, the company operated in what Liz Tanner referred to as "stealth mode"; its new technology was still in development and secrecy was imperative. Some employees even had to ask to print business cards, so that they could prove to their families that they had real jobs. Walker's personal investments and a few pilot and consulting projects provided the company's initial funding.

In 1996 Walker and his team were ready for business. They tapped as company president Gary Kennedy, another Oracle executive who had hired about 3,000 Oracle workers and had become the president of Oracle USA in 1990. Kennedy was raised in Utah, and he had hoped to return there after several years' absence. With Walker's approval, the company moved its headquarters to Salt Lake City. Soon they relocated the

---

Company Perspectives:

TenFold Corporation's mission is to become the world's premier supplier of vertical software applications.

---

headquarters to Draper, a suburb south of Salt Lake City. Walker remained in San Francisco.

Utah offered TenFold several advantages. The University of Utah, Utah State University, and Brigham Young University trained many software engineers and other high-tech personnel and helped several of the state's approximately 800 software firms get started, including Evans & Sutherland, Novell, and WordPerfect. Moreover, the cost of living was far less than in Utah than it was in the Silicon Valley.

Soon after becoming TenFold's president, Kennedy presented his goals to Walker and other executives. According to Tanner, many were "astounded" by Kennedy's bold vision, and it would eventually be realized. In addition to Walker and Kennedy, other individuals who left Oracle and became TenFold executives included William Conroy, Robert Hughes, Sameer Shalaby, Adam Slovik, Larry Stevens, and Richard VanderDrift. Thus most TenFold's executives were former Oracle leaders, a great example of the risks businesses take when they train leaders who then leave for other opportunities.

Building the Business: 1990s and Beyond

In 1997 one of TenFold's first major customers was Barclays Global Investors, among the world's largest institutional investors. Working with Barclays personnel, TenFold in just six months built the TenFold Revenue Manager program that was then used by Barclays to automate billing invoices and revenue accounting. Barclays used the TenFold application to replace Microsoft Excel, which required considerable manual work to invoice customers.

One of TenFold's key moments came in mid-1998 when it began offering its unique TenFold Guarantee to promise its customers they would receive their applications on time and at the fixed price or else they would be fully refunded their money. As TenFold ads indicated, the firm was committed to "do or die." TenFold ads also stressed that "92% of all large-scale software development projects fail," referring to the results of a 1998 CHAOS study by the Standish Group that found 92 percent of such projects either far exceeded their budget or time projections or were just terminated. Thus in one of its 1999 ads, TenFold invoked the famous William Tell story: "Imagine an archer who hits the bull's eye only eight percent of the time. . . . we don't miss. You might say we have straighter arrows in our quiver." In another 1999 ad, TenFold emphasized that it was a "well-kept secret" that 92 percent of software applications projects failed as companies wasted millions in the process. The final tagline read: "The secret's out. Pass it on."

Thus TenFold made bold promises that it could do something most competitors failed to do. "TenFold has built a reputation in the software industry as both an innovator and something of a maverick," said the Aberdeen Group, a Boston

consulting group that tracked the computer and communications fields.

In 1998 Mercy Health Services and its Michigan Cardiovascular Network (MHS MCN) faced a major problem after Summit Medical Systems ended its data services contract for the Society of Thoracic Surgery (STS) National Database. MHS chose TenFold as its partner to develop software to track outcomes of cardiovascular operations, partly because of TenFold's promise to build a set of applications quicker than its competitors. In December 1998, just six weeks after this project began, TenFold demonstrated the initial version of TenFold CardioTrac for MHS MCN. After CardioTrac was formally launched in early 1999, MHS MCN intended to tailor it to keep track of other clinical outcomes besides those of cardiovascular surgery. The MHS MCN contract was TenFold's first project in the healthcare industry. Later HealthSouth would become another major healthcare client.

In May 1999, TenFold and Perot Systems Corporation formed a strategic alliance. TenFold President Gary Kennedy told *CNN Financial Network,* "it became obvious that there was a wonderful match between our aims and theirs, between our cultures and Perot's cultures." Ross Perot, in turn, noted that TenFold was "one of the most unique companies I have ever encountered." Although the two companies were not directly competing at the time, the agreement created a TenFold partner instead of a potential competitor.

On May 21, 1999 TenFold became a public corporation, with an initial public offering of 5.2 million shares of its stock at $17 per share raising $88 million. In a May 21, 1999 interview on *CNN Financial Network,* TenFold President/CEO Kennedy said, "we probably could have gone public a year or so ago, but it was important to me to make sure that the company was in very stable hands. . . . I didn't want to come here and tell the market what we were going to do; I wanted to describe what we had done. I didn't want to say we were going to be profitable; I wanted to be profitable. I didn't want to say we were going to build a strong management team; I wanted to have one built already. So we've waited."

In 1999 TenFold signed a contract to construct a group of software applications to facilitate energy trading, billing, logistics, and risk control for Southern Company Energy Marketing. Don Jefferis left his position as Southern Company Energy Marketing's vice-president to head up the TenFold Energy Group. TenFold used its EnergyNow! suite of applications to provide integrated and comprehensive software for such energy companies.

Most of TenFold's business came from providing software applications for insurance companies. For example, in 1999 it worked on a fixed-time contract to create and install new programs for Utica National Insurance Group, a $600 million company based in Utica, New York. TenFold contracted to develop applications for Utica's 11 business divisions that eventually would provide all Utica agents with access via the Internet to all company business and customer information. Utica chose TenFold because of its timely services, fixed price instead of the hourly rates charged by competitors, and the fact that TenFold guaranteed its work and prices.

Key Dates:

1993: KeyTex is founded by former Oracle Corporation executives.
1996: Firm relocates to Draper, Utah, a suburb of Salt Lake City.
1997: Name of firm is changed to TenFold Corporation.
1998: The company begins offering its unique TenFold Guarantee.
1999: The firm's IPO is completed.
2000: Company receives a U.S. patent for its trademarked Universal Application technology.

TenFold's other insurance clients in 1999 included Provident Companies, Crawford & Company, TIG Insurance, Trinity (a Unitrin subsidiary), United Casualty (another Unitrin subsidiary), and Westfield Companies. Moreover, TenFold served the following investment management companies: Barclays Global Investors, Dresdner RCM Global Investors, Franklin Templeton, and Loomis, Sayles & Company. Its other clients during this time were Enron, Mercy Health Services, Ameritech, NAI Block, and Nielsen Media Research.

On October 7, 1999 TenFold completed its purchase of LongView Group, Inc. from that company's parent Barclays California Corporation. TenFold reportedly paid $22 million for LongView, while Barclays simultaneously paid $4 million for a TenFold software license and related technical support.

Stock analysts and industry consults gave TenFold high marks in several areas. For example, giving TenFold stock a "buy" rating in September 1999, Deutsche Banc Alex. Brown described the company as "The Best of Buy and Build in Vertical Market Application Software," also noting that "TenFold has put together a top-notch management team . . . and we believe that management has the ability to take the company to $1 billion and beyond over the next three to five years."

Goldman Sachs analysts agreed and on February 4, 2000 placed TenFold on its "U.S. Recommended List," emphasizing that, "We believe that TenFold has an attractive market opportunity, innovative technology and methodology, and solid momentum to support its valuation longer term." The Goldman Sachs analysts were impressed by TenFold's fourth quarter 1999 performance, especially the company's license revenues of $23.7 million, an increase of 265 percent over fourth quarter 1998, which was more than double Goldman Sachs' estimate.

TenFold in 1999 reported annual sales of $92.4 million, up from $40.2 million in 1998 and $14.1 million in 1997. The company's 1999 sales were generated almost evenly between license revenues of $47 million and services revenues of $45.3 million. The largest source of those revenues was insurance services and licenses, although the firm was diversifying into other industries as part of its long-term strategy.

In its 1999 10-K Report, TenFold wrote: "An element of our business strategy involves organizing our business along industry lines, and evolving these business units into separate operating companies." To facilitate that process, its subsidiaries were based in different cities. For example, TenFold Insurance, Inc., was headquartered in Dallas.

Major companies added to the TenFold client base in 1999 and 2000 included SkyTel and Southern Company, as well as investment management customers Chase Manhattan Bank and Oppenheimer Capital, among others. In 2000 TenFold operated a total of 15 offices in the United States and London, including a new office facility in San Francisco where the firm planned to occupy six floors. Thus managing its expanding business operations was one of TenFold's major challenges as the new millennium began.

Principal Subsidiaries

TenFold Healthcare, Inc.; TenFold Energy, Inc.; TenFold Communications, Inc.; TenFold Insurance, Inc.; TenFold Investment Management, Inc.; TenFold Financial Services, Inc.

Principal Competitors

Cambridge Technology Partners; Sapient Corporation; Andersen Consulting; Computer Sciences Corporation; Interim Technology Inc.; Policy Management Systems Corporation; SAP A.G.; PeopleSoft Inc.; Baan Company; Electronic Data Systems Corporation.

Further Reading

Berquist, Thomas P., et. al., *TenFold: Strong Fourth-Quarter Results,* Goldman Sachs Report, February 4, 2000.

Carricaburu, Lisa, "Utah Firm: Y2K Bug Just a Symptom," *Salt Lake Tribune,* November 1, 1998.

"Consultant Killers," *Red Herring Magazine,* August 1, 1998.

Dennis, Kathryn, "Concentra, TenFold Challenge Larger Competitors," *Technology Marketing Intelligence,* September 15, 1998.

"Fixed-Term Contracts: Ready or Not, Here They Come," *Solutions Integrator,* April 1, 1998.

Frye, Colleen, "Shared Risk, Shared Reward," *Software Magazine,* February 1998.

Hoffman, Thomas, "Automated Billing Saves Bank Time," *Computerworld,* September 28, 1998.

Keri, Jonah, "Software Firm Winning Clients With Money-Back Guarantee," *Investor's Business Daily,* July 20, 1999.

King, Julia, "Integrators Get Creative on Project Pricing," *Computerworld,* April 26, 1999.

McGee, Marianne K., "Customized Apps—Tenfold Targets Specific Industries for Custom Software," *Informationweek,* April 13, 1998.

——, "TenFold Development of Critical Apps," *Computer Reseller News,* April 6, 1998.

"Mercy Health Services Chooses Fast Track Partner to Expand CV System," *Cardiovascular Disease Management,* January 1999.

Mortenson, W. Christopher, and Patrick O'Hara, *TenFold Corporation,* Deutsche Banc Alex. Brown Equity Research Report, September 10, 1999.

"A New Wrinkle to an Old Debate: TenFold Pushes Buy and Build," *Insurance & Technology,* January 1999.

"Powerful Minds," *Power Trading Technology,* September 20, 1999.

Shein, Esther, "Prix Fixe Deals," *PC Week Online,* July 27, 1998.

"Trading Places [Interview with Gary Kennedy]," *CNN Financial Network,* May 21, 1999.

"Upside's 1998 Hot 100 Private Companies," *Upside Today,* April 21, 2000.

—David M. Walden

Trans World Airlines, Inc.

515 North 6th Street
St. Louis, Missouri 63101
U.S.A.
Telephone: (314) 589-3000
Toll Free: (800) 221-2000
Fax: (314) 589-3129
Web site: http://www.twa.com

Public Company
Incorporated: 1928 as Transcontinental Air Transport
Employees: 21,000
Sales: $3.31 billion (1999)
Stock Exchanges: American
Ticker Symbol: TWA
NAIC: 481111 Scheduled Passenger Air Transportation

In the 1990s, Trans World Airlines, Inc. (TWA) ranked as the seventh largest U.S. airline company. The firm's history has been influenced by such well-known personalities as Charles Lindbergh, Amelia Earhart, Jack Frye, and Howard Hughes. However, under the late 1980s and early 1990s stewardship of corporate raider Carl Icahn, the company widely known as TWA squandered much of its reputation. It filed for bankruptcy protection twice in the 1990s, losing money ten years in a row even as its rivals logged record profits. Although TWA leads the pack in on-time performance, lingering image problems have prevented it from winning much of the lucrative business travel market.

Origins

TWA was established through the merger of several small airline companies in the 1920s. One of those small companies was Maddux Air Lines, which began a luxury passenger service between Los Angeles and San Diego on July 21, 1927. Maddux and a number of other carriers were organized by a group of investors who sought to establish a transcontinental passenger line using a combination of airplane flights and railroads. The group, Transcontinental Air Transport, hired Charles Lindbergh to survey the route. On July 7, 1929, TAT inaugurated the

"Lindbergh Line," offering coast-to-coast transportation in about 48 hours. The journey departed New York in the evening and crossed the eastern U.S. by the Pennsylvania Railroad. The next morning passengers flew from Columbus, Ohio, to Waynoka, Oklahoma. From there the Santa Fe Railroad took them overnight to Clovis, New Mexico. From Clovis the passengers flew on to either Los Angeles or San Francisco.

In those early days of commercial aviation, airlines made most of their money hauling mail for postal services. The United States Postmaster at the time, Walter Folger Brown, was responsible for assigning three transcontinental airmail routes. American Airlines won the southern route, Northwest Airlines won the northern route, and TAT was awarded the central route, but only on the condition that the company merge with Western Air Express. In 1930, the two companies joined to form Transcontinental and Western Air Lines, or TWA. That October the new company covered the coast-to-coast route completely with airplanes, in light of the failure of the previous scheme. The trip was reduced to 36 hours and then later to 24.

Bill Boeing manufactured what were generally regarded as the best airplanes of the day; however, he refused to sell them to any air transport company except his own. Excluded from the Boeing market, TWA's general manager, Jack Frye, solicited designs from a number of manufacturers. A small California operation run by Donald Douglas proposed an impressive design which outperformed Frye's basic specifications. TWA accepted Douglas's offer, and the first DC-1 was built. The DC-1, however, became obsolete before it could be mass produced, so it was lengthened and otherwise improved. The new plane, the DC-2, was every bit as practical as the DC-1, but more difficult to fly.

New Owners in the 1930s and 1940s

Air travel was a risky business in the 1930s. Breaches in pilot discipline and frequent equipment failures caused a number of TWA airplane crashes. At one point, the airline was losing five percent of its personnel annually to such accidents. The company was further troubled when the Roosevelt Administration decided to cancel all government airmail contracts with private carriers in 1934. Many airlines, including TWA, depended on mail contracts for their profitability. During this crisis TWA was sold to a group led by Lehman Brothers and John Hertz of the Yellow Cab Company. The government decided to restore the airmail contracts a few months later and reopened the bidding. Curiously, companies that had held contracts before were barred from bidding. In order to get around this stipulation, the company responded by merely adding "Incorporated" to its name. It was re-awarded 60 percent of its original airmail system and, over a period of a few years, recovered the rest.

Under the new owners, Jack Frye, a vice-president and former Hollywood stunt pilot, was promoted to president. The new management instituted major improvements in TWA's training and flight efficiency and also upgraded its airport facilities. The airline employed directional "homing" radar and installed runway lights to facilitate night flying. The DC-3 became the company's new workhorse while business improved significantly.

In the 1930s airline companies became especially vulnerable to buyouts. General Motors Corporation acquired Eastern Airlines in 1933 and American Airlines was taken over by the auto magnate E.L. Cord. When General Motors purchased stock in TWA, the airline worried that it would be forcibly merged with some other GM interest. In 1938, when TWA had fully recovered from the airmail fiasco, the Lehman/Hertz group sold the airline to another group of investors. During this time Frye personally convinced millionaire Howard Hughes to invest in TWA. It is very likely that Frye wanted Hughes's interest in the company so that he could help to defend it from any hostile takeover bids, especially from GM.

At the outset, Frye and Hughes respected each other as aviators and businessmen. Frye was a daredevil flier, a man totally enthralled with aviation and its possibilities. Hughes was an equally eccentric young man who was devoted to breaking aviation records. From his father he inherited ownership of the extremely lucrative Hughes Tool Company, the primary supplier of oil well drilling bits. Using this large fortune Hughes purchased 25 percent of TWA's stock. In 1941 he gained a controlling interest in the airline and later increased his share to 78 percent.

One of Hughes's first activities at TWA was to begin development of a new airplane, the L-049 Constellation, in association with Lockheed. While the Constellation was still being

developed, Hughes approved Frye's proposal to buy another new airplane, Boeing's 307 Stratoliner, for the interim. The Stratoliner had a pressurized cabin and was able to reach an altitude of 20,000 feet. As a result, it could fly over bad weather rather than be forced to navigate through it.

Overseas in World War II

TWA was one of the first American airline companies to serve during the Battle of Britain in 1940. Even before the U.S. government had officially committed itself to the war effort, TWA was helping the Army Air Corps assist the British. When the U.S. became fully involved in 1941, TWA was assigned two military supply routes: the North Atlantic route to Prestwick, Scotland, and the South Atlantic route from Brazil to Liberia and points east.

The airline had the distinction of flying President Roosevelt and a number of other government personnel to and from various meeting places during the war, most notably, Casablanca. The war gave TWA the opportunity to upgrade and expand its facilities worldwide in anticipation of the allied victory. The U.S. War Department actively supported the airline's activities during the war. It would be fair to say that TWA served the country well and that it also profited handsomely. When TWA's military service was over it had flown 40 million miles for the Army, and was exposed to hundreds of new destinations.

The major overseas carriers after the war were Pan Am, American, and TWA. All these airlines requested licensing for commercial use of much of their wartime network. TWA was granted two transatlantic routes to Europe, one via the "great circle" near the Arctic, and the other via the Azores to the Mediterranean. From there TWA flew on to India, Southeast Asia, and Japan. The company also enjoyed a government subsidy in the immediate postwar years.

Hughes and Frye had grandiose, but divergent, plans for their company, whose name they had changed to Trans World Airlines. The Constellation they helped to develop first flew in 1944, served briefly during the war, and entered wide commercial use in the postwar era. However, it was at this time that the two men began to disagree. Hughes, who was injured in the crash of a test plane during the war, had developed a very difficult personality and was known to hold up major business decisions for weeks while he agonized over minute details. He even disappeared for several days with a Constellation, only to turn up in Bermuda making endless test landings.

TWA soon found that it did not have enough business on its 21,000 miles of postwar international routes to generate a profit. Frye's efforts to rectify the problem collided with the plans of Hughes's financial manager, Noah Dietrich. Dietrich charged that Frye had mismanaged the airline into a financial crisis and dangerous overexpansion. Hughes offered to provide money for TWA from the Hughes Tool Company, but only on the condition that Frye resign. Thus in January 1947 Frye left TWA.

TWA suspended many of its plans for further expansion. The headquarters was moved from Kansas City to New York. Ralph Damon, who had previously been with American Airlines, was brought in to replace Jack Frye. Damon was an old-school engineer and airplane manufacturer known for his careful attention to detail. Damon's numerous successes at the airline, however, were shrouded by Hughes's continued interference and manipulation. Hughes insisted that the company reduce its advertising and promotion at a time when it was probably most needed. Regardless, TWA went off its postwar government subsidy in 1952, and a year later was healthy enough to declare a ten percent stock distribution. Two years later Damon died at work, a victim of pneumonia and exhaustion. Doctors suggested that his poor health was exacerbated by the unrelenting pressure of running an airline for Howard Hughes.

Mid-1950s Bailout

Damon's successor was Carter Burgess, a former Assistant Secretary of Defense. Burgess lasted only 11 months, during which time he never even met Hughes. TWA's next president was Charles Thomas. Thomas kept a low profile, followed all of Hughes's orders, and kept the company in good financial condition. When Thomas took over in the mid-1950s, all of the airlines were competing to be the first to have jetliners in their fleets. While the other leading companies were laying their plans and placing orders, TWA's order was delayed by Hughes's indecision over which airplane to buy, the Boeing 707 or the DC-8. Weeks later he finally decided to order 76 airplanes from Boeing and Convair. The jetliners would cost $500 million, much more than TWA could afford. Hughes's plan was to have his successful tool company purchase the planes and lease them to the airline. He wanted to keep TWA's profits low, channel money out of the Tool Company, and thereby avoid paying large penalty taxes.

Unfortunately, a world oil glut hurt the Hughes Tool Company so badly that it was unable to pay for the new airplanes. As a result, TWA was forced to turn to a group of Wall Street investment bankers for financial support. The bankers were aware of Hughes's reputation as a successful tycoon, but also recognized that his interests were probably not the same as those of the airline. As a condition for their financial assistance, they required that Hughes's majority voting interest in TWA be placed in a trust under their control. Negotiations lasted until the bankers' deadline, when Hughes finally conceded.

One of the investment group's first actions was to install Charles Tillinghast as president of TWA. Tillinghast, a lawyer, promptly filed an antitrust suit against Hughes, alleging violations of the Sherman Act and the Clayton Anti-Monopoly Act, and accusing him of monopolizing aircraft purchases for his own benefit and to the detriment of TWA. Hughes responded with a countersuit, charging that they swindled him out of his airline. The litigation continued for many years and cost TWA over $10 million. In the end, the courts returned no clear decision.

Tillinghast reorganized the airline quickly and completely. Management was restructured and pared down. TWA placed orders for newer B-727s and French-built Caravelles. In addition, Tillinghast attempted to change the company's public image. In light of its association with Hughes, TWA was regarded as being overly concerned with speed, glamour, and style, and not enough with dependability, efficiency, and safety. TWA emerged from its troubles with stable and consistent profits through 1966, largely due to the direction of Charles Tillinghast. Ironically, the chief beneficiary of TWA's improvement was Howard Hughes. In 1966 he sold his stock in the airline for $546.5 million, or $86 per share. Three years earlier TWA stock had sold for a paltry $7.50.

Diversifying in the 1960s

Aside from the large profits and the Hughes fiasco, the 1960s were important in another way. It was at this time that Tillinghast made perhaps his most important contribution. Hoping to provide the company with protection against the unpredictable and unstable airline business, he initiated a diversification program aimed at strengthening the airline's capital structure and cash flow.

TWA's diversification began in 1964 with a contract to provide base support services to the National Aeronautics and Space Administration at Cape Kennedy. In 1967 TWA purchased Hilton International, the operator of all Hilton Hotels outside the United States. Later, TWA acquired the Canteen Corporation, Spartan Food Services, and Century 21, a real estate firm. The company was the first to diversify into non-airline businesses, and its timing was auspicious, as the industry was suffering from the recession of the early 1970s. TWA's B-747s and L-1011s were flying with nearly empty passenger cabins. The original decision to purchase the jetliners was made in response to Pan Am's huge orders, and not based on TWA's needs. As a result, the airline was plagued with overcapacity; it owned too many big, inefficient planes.

To make matters worse, TWA suffered a crippling six-week flight attendants' strike in 1973. By 1975 several payrolls could only be met with the immediate sale of six 747s to the Iranian Air Force. It was an unfortunate financial transaction for TWA (which sold the jetliners for about one-sixth their actual value), but the airline was desperate for cash. TWA was also losing money on its trans-Pacific route, which had been awarded during Lyndon B. Johnson's presidency. For the first time in its history, TWA's network stretched around the world, but even this would soon come to an end.

Tillinghast retired amid these numerous crises. He was succeeded in January 1976 by Carl Meyer. Meyer navigated the airline through a series of changes in the airline passenger market. Costs were reduced as international traffic expanded. The Airline Deregulation Act of 1978 allowed TWA to establish a more efficient dual hub system: St. Louis for domestic traffic and New York for international traffic. Moreover, under Carl Meyer TWA reduced its fleet and its staff. The company purchased more fuel-efficient airplanes while selling the ''gas-guzzlers'' as soon as their value had completely depreciated.

Raided in the 1980s

On January 1, 1979, TWA created a holding company called the Trans World Corporation, which assumed ownership of the airline and the various subsidiaries. Several years later, facing financial difficulties, Trans World Corporation decided to sell its airline. Thus TWA was acquired by ''corporate raider'' Carl Icahn early in 1986. Icahn's style of ''raiding'' usually involved buying up enough of a company's stock to threaten the other stockholders with a controlling interest or takeover. This drove the price of the stock up to a point where he could decide to sell, usually at a large profit. In his battle with Texas Air Corporation (parent of Eastern Airlines) for control of TWA, Icahn enlisted the support of the target airline's labor unions with pledges to honor their numerous demands. With their support, Icahn was able to hold out with a bid of $18.17 per share and ultimately took over. Icahn fired the airline's popular president, Richard Pearson, and replaced him with Joseph Corr.

Icahn's apparent commitment to TWA and hands-on approach surprised many observers. He launched a new subsidiary, the Travel Channel, acquired Ozark Airlines, pared expenses to the industry's lowest cost-per-available-seat-per-mile (8.5 cents), and turned 1986's loss into a profit for 1987. That success, however, was fleeting. A number of intractable problems—including an insufficient number of hubs and feeder lines, a rapidly declining market presence, heavy debt load, and price wars—plagued the airline.

By the end of 1988, when Icahn took TWA private, the firm's nearly $4 billion debt load gave it a negative net worth and contributed to the growing dissatisfaction of TWA's labor unions. Both the Air Line Pilots Association and the Independent Federation of Flight Attendants filed suits against Icahn alleging poor management. The financier in turn threatened to liquidate the airline in a long, drawn out bankruptcy if he did not obtain wage concessions from the unions and cooperation from creditors.

Losing Money in the 1990s

From 1985 until January 1992, when TWA declared Chapter 11 bankruptcy, its share of the domestic market had slipped from seven percent to 5.5 percent and its slice of the international market was halved from 20.9 percent to 10 percent. The company's bankruptcy reorganization plan called for its 28,000 employees to make 15 percent ($660 million) wage and work rule concessions in exchange for an additional 35 percent stake in the company, raising their share of TWA's equity to 45 percent. Creditors forgave $1 billion of the airline's $1.5 billion debt in exchange for the remaining equity. Icahn gave up his entire 90 percent share of the company, left it $200 million in cash, and paid the federal government's Pension Benefit Guaranty Corporation $240 million to prop up TWA's pension plan, which was underfunded by an estimated $1.2 billion. About 2,000 jobs were eliminated, domestic capacity was reduced by 13 percent, and international volume was cut by 38 percent. The company even relocated its headquarters from Mt. Kisco, New York, to the more centrally located St. Louis, Missouri.

Robin H.H. Wilson and Glenn A. Zander were selected to run the company on an interim basis in the fall of 1992. Wilson had been with TWA for most the 1960s and 1970s, and Zander was a 28-year veteran of the company. In February 1993, the joint chief executives traveled around the United States to explain their plan to bring the company out of bankruptcy, which included a major image overhaul, from low-budget to quality-conscious. A new advertising campaign launched TWA's ''Comfort Class'' seating, with more leg room than any other leading airline. Although the effort raised customer satisfaction, TWA continued to lose money in 1992 and 1993.

TWA emerged from bankruptcy protection months later than it had hoped, in November 1993, after the peak summer season. Wilson and Zander became executive vice-presidents of operations and finance, respectively, and former Piedmont Airlines chief William R. Howard took the airline's helm. Within just two months, however, Howard and Zander resigned after a dismal winter season, leaving TWA with yet another dilemma. Although board member Donald F. Craib, Jr., had no airline experience (he was formerly chairman and CEO of Allstate), he was selected to succeed Howard. Jeffrey Erickson, formerly of Reno Air, became CEO in the spring of 1994, temporarily ending the string of executives passing through the top job.

As new owners, TWA's employees made heroic efforts to sustain their company, improving service and timeliness and donating their own pay to fund advertising and capital expenses. Yet they watched the value of their shares decline by over one-third in the first six months of 1994. That June, two of the airline's three largest unions agreed to another $200 million in concessions to help the company survive yet another harsh winter. The company also started post-bankruptcy negotiations with creditors, including the Pension Benefit Guaranty Corp., offering a swap of about 15 percent in equity for about $800 million of debt. Late in 1994, when the plan was unveiled, Anthony L. Velocci, Jr., of *Aviation Week & Space Technology*, who had long followed the saga, related analysts' general skepticism that the offer would be accepted.

Although revenues rose eight percent to $3.4 billion, TWA posted a $436 million loss for 1994. The company filed for its second Chapter 11 in June 1995 to shed $500 million of its $1.7 billion in debt. This time around, creditors had approved its deal before filing, putting it on track to emerge from its second restructuring in August 1995.

With unprofitable routes already slashed and employee loyalty taxed to the fullest, managers gambled on a new strategy in 1996. They installed a new yield management system (software determining how many seats are sold at what prices) in a plan to emphasize the lucrative business side of the market.

Soon the carrier began to show signs of a turnaround, with some union representatives balking at the generous stock options granted Erickson. TWA began hiring again, planning to increase employment by nearly ten percent in 1996. It announced plans to finally acquire some new planes, 15 leased MD-83s, on July 16.

The next day, Flight 800 to Paris exploded shortly after taking off from New York City, killing all 230 people on board. An extended investigation to determine the cause of the explosion followed. Senior executives were criticized in the press by New York Mayor Rudolph Giuliani for their slow response to the news. However, Erickson had been in London lobbying for a new route and could not charter a return flight until the next morning. Further, two of his top aides had recently resigned.

Ultimately, Erickson resigned after TWA announced a $14 million loss for the third quarter—traditionally the airline's strongest season. Erickson had been struggling with both the board of directors and the pilots' union. The carrier posted a loss of $259 million on $3.6 billion in revenues in 1996.

The board chose Gerald L. Gitner as Erickson's replacement, making the position permanent in February 1997. The selection reportedly infuriated the Machinists' union, although it was later revealed that the union's two representatives on the TWA board had voted in favor of Gitner. Gitner had worked at Texas Air and Pan Am, both of which folded; the Machinists at Eastern Airlines had gone on strike after it was acquired by Texas Air, led by Frank Lorenzo.

The steam that had driven TWA's turnaround, the loyalty of its relatively underpaid workers, was giving out. TWA was the only major U.S. airline to lose money in 1997. By focusing on on-time performance, the carrier tried to capture a bigger percentage of the lucrative business travel market—no other major airline controlled less. To improve reliability, TWA retired its old Lockheed L-1011s in favor of smaller Boeing 757s. International service was also greatly scaled back. In 1997, TWA was second among majors for on-time performance. Pilot William Compton was promoted to president in December 1997 and oversaw the airline's efforts to keep planes moving on time.

However, the strategy failed as planes flew with many unfilled seats that would have otherwise gone to vacation traffic. While other major airlines were posting banner years, TWA again lost money ($121 million) for the tenth straight year in 1998. The company at the end of the year was embroiled in contract disputes and calls for new leadership from unions and shareholders alike. It had recently ordered 125 new jets. Compton was designated TWA's new CEO, effective May 1999, while Gitner remained chairman. The Machinists' union derided the shift as a "manipulative shuffle."

In July 1999, Compton called Boeing's new 717-200 a symbol of where the airline was headed. With AirTran, TWA was the launch customer for the plane, a medium range jet designed by McDonnell Douglas (also known the MD-5) before that manufacturer was acquired by Boeing. TWA ordered 50 of the 717-200s and invested $15 million in a state-of-the-art flight simulator to train pilots in their use.

TWA contracted with Indianapolis-based Chautauqua Airlines to provide feeder services on small, 50-seat regional jets. A new labor agreement made the partnership possible. On regional routes, TWA had previously been using only turboprop aircraft, which were generally less favored by passengers. At least 15 of Chautauqua's Embraer 145 regional jets were to be in service by the end of 2001 in markets around the country.

TWA ranked first in a 1999 J.D. Power and Associates survey of business travelers. It continued to lead the other major airlines in on-time performance. Intriguingly, it also ranked second in the number of passenger complaints to the federal government. Lingering image problems prevented the carrier from charging top rates. TWA had a limited network and faced competition on nearly all of its routes. Once strong in New York, the airline had retained only one hub, the crowded, outdated St. Louis-Lambert International Airport. Since most passengers did not want to travel to the middle of the country every time they flew, TWA was working out agreements so its passengers could earn frequent flier miles on other airlines such as America West.

Principal Subsidiaries

Ambassador Fuel Corporation; Royal Ambassador Insurance Company; Getaway Management Services, Inc.; International Aviation Security, Inc.; International Airport Services; International Aviation Security Gesellschaft; International Aviation Security Italia S.r.l.; International Aviation Security Ltd.; International Aviation Security (UK); International Aviation Security N.V.; Mega Advertising, Inc.; Northwest 112th Street Corp.; Ozark Group, Inc.; TWA Getaway Vacations, Inc.; The Getaway Group (UK), Inc.; The TWA Ambassadors Club, Inc.; Transcontinental & Western Air, Inc.; Trans World Computer Services, Inc.; Trans World Express, Inc.; Trans World Pars, Inc.; TWA Aviation, Inc.; TWA de Mexico S.A. de C.V.; TWA Employee Services, Inc.; TWA Group, Inc.; TWA Nippon, Inc.; TWA Standards & Controls, Inc.; TWA-NY/NJ Gate Company, Inc.; TWA-LAX Gate Company, Inc.; TWA-San Francisco Gate Company, Inc.; TWA-Logan Gate Company, Inc.; TWA-D.C. Gate Company, Inc.; TWA-Omnibus Gate Company, Inc.; TWA-Hangar 12 Holding Company, Inc.; LAX Holding Company, Inc.; TWA Stock Holding Company, Inc.; ConFin Inc.; Constellation Finance LLC; Worldspan, L.P. (26.31%).

Principal Competitors

AMR Corporation; Southwest Airlines Co.; UAL Corporation; Delta Air Lines Inc.

Further Reading

Alexander, Keith L., "TWA Changing 'From Inside Out'," *USA Today,* July 17, 1995, p. 8B.
Biederman, Paul, *The U.S. Airline Industry: End of an Era,* New York: Praeger, 1982.

Carey, Christopher, "Agreement with Indianapolis Carrier Gives TWA Regional Presence; Deal with Chautauqua Airlines Is for 10 Years," *St. Louis Post-Dispatch,* November 4, 1999, p. C1.

——, "Debt Is Gone, But Icahn's Not Forgotten; Financier Still Has the Right to Buy Cheap Airline Tickets," *St. Louis Post-Dispatch,* January 18, 1998, p. E1.

——, "Machinists Did an About-Face in TWA Attack: Acting Officers Had Union's OK," *St. Louis Post-Dispatch,* February 9, 1997, p. 1E.

——, "TWA Demonstrates New $15 Million Flight Simulator," *St. Louis Post-Dispatch,* September 17, 1999, p. C1.

——, "TWA Execs' Pay Blasted by Attendant; Airline Cites Steady Financial Improvement," *St. Louis Post-Dispatch,* May 22, 1996, p. 1C.

——, "TWA Gave Lucrative Deals in CEO Switch," *St. Louis Post-Dispatch,* April 25, 1997, p. 1B.

——, "TWA Tries to Sell Its Best Customers on Its Success," *St. Louis Post-Dispatch,* February 13, 1998, p. C10.

Chandler, Susan, "TWA Is Carrying Some Heavy Baggage," *Business Week,* April 7, 1997, p. 40.

——, "How TWA Faced the Nightmare," *Business Week,* August 5, 1996, p. 30.

Donlan, Thomas G., "Super Pilot or Predator? Zeroing In on What Carl Icahn Has Wrought at TWA," *Barron's,* September 26, 1988, pp. 8–9.

Driscoll, Lisa, "Carl Has 9 Lives, But He's Getting Up to 8½," *Business Week,* February 24, 1992, pp. 56–57.

Field, David, "Financial Turbulence: TWA Loses Millions Despite Robust Year," *USA Today,* February 9, 1999, p. 1B.

——, "TWA Waits for Changes to Pay: Its Flights Are on Time, Its Planes Are Newer, But Fliers Aren't Buying It Yet," *USA Today,* May 9, 2000, p. 5B.

Flannery, William, "TWA Calls Boeing's 717 a Symbol of Airline's Future," *St. Louis Post-Dispatch,* July 2, 1999, p. C10.

Flint, Perry, "Return the Company to Profitability," *Air Transport World,* January 1994, p. 88.

Foster, Vintage, "Detroit Business Turnaround Specialist Puts Himself Out of Work," *Detroit Free Press,* November 10, 1996.

Heaster, Randolph, "Future of TWA at Issue; Resignation of CEO After Troubled Third Quarter Raises Speculation by Analysts," *Kansas City Star,* October 26, 1996, p. B1.

——, "TWA Angers Machinists' Union with Gitner's Selection As CEO; Labor Officials Claim Downsizing in New York Part of Larger Cuts," *Kansas City Star,* February 18, 1997, p. D12.

——, "TWA Machinists Union Faults Airline on Naming of CEO," *Kansas City Star,* March 23, 1999, p. D11.

Icahn, Carl C., "It's Your Captain Speaking: TWA's Corporate Pilot States His Case," *Barron's,* October 31, 1988, pp. 35–38.

Kelly, Kevin, "Can a "Labor of Love' End TWA's Tailspin?," *Business Week,* April 19, 1993, pp. 80–82.

Laing, Jonathan R., "What's the Next Chapter?," *Barron's,* January 3, 1994, pp. 17–19.

Leonhardt, David, "Does TWA Need a New Captain?," *Business Week,* December 28, 1998, p. 58.

——, " 'You're Cleared for Takeoff, Boss'," *Business Week,* May 11, 1998, p. 74.

Petzinger, Thomas, Jr., *Hard Landing,* New York: Times Business, 1995.

Rosato, Donna, "Once Again, TWA Faces Trauma and Uncertainty," *USA Today,* July 19, 1996, p. 4B.

Serling, Robert J., *Howard Hughes' Airline: An Informal History of TWA,* New York: St. Martin's Press, 1983.

Song, Kyung M., "Pilot Faces Challenging Trip at TWA's Helm: New CEO Compton Must Try to End Losses and Achieve Labor Peace," *St. Louis Post-Dispatch,* March 21, 1999, p. E1.

——, "TWA Welcomes New CEO, Reviews New Boeing Jets," *St. Louis Post-Dispatch,* May 26, 1999.

"TWA: The End of the Raid," *Economist,* September 12, 1992, pp. 89–90.

"TWA: Phoenix Arises," *Economist,* February 27, 1993, pp. 70–72.

Underwood, Elaine, "Up, Up and Away," *Brandweek,* September 20, 1993.

Velocci, Anthony L., Jr., "TWA Employees Near Goal of Ending Icahn's Reign, Leaving Chapter 11," *Aviation Week & Space Technology,* August 10, 1992, pp. 30–31.

——, "TWA Plea to Creditors: Take More Equity," *Aviation Week & Space Technology,* October 17, 1994, p. 35.

——, "TWA Taps "Outsider' to Head Ailing Carrier," *Aviation Week & Space Technology,* January 10, 1994, p. 30.

—John Buckvold
—updated by April Dougal Gasbarre
and Frederick C. Ingram

Valley Media Inc.

1280 Santa Anita Court
Woodland, California 95776
U.S.A.
Telephone: (530) 661-6600
Fax: (800) 999-1794
Web site: http://www.valley-media.com

Public Company
Incorporated: 1979 as Valley Record Distributors
Employees: 1,500
Sales: $888.97 million (1999)
Stock Exchanges: NASDAQ
Ticker Symbol: VMIX
NAIC: 421990 Other Miscellaneous Durable Goods
Wholesalers

Valley Media Inc. grew from a single record store in the 1970s to the largest one-stop distributor of CDs, cassettes, videos, and DVDs. It fills orders from retailers through two warehouse facilities located in Woodland, California and in Louisville, Kentucky. At the beginning of 2000 the company carried 260,000 different products and had an inventory valued at some $250 million. It regularly wins the Wholesaler of the Year award for large distributors from the National Association of Recording Merchandisers for its high level of service. Although sales were approaching $1 billion in 2000, the company operates on razor-thin margins; a mishandled move into a new warehouse in Woodland in 1999 resulted in a loss for the company's 1999–2000 fiscal year as costs quickly escalated.

Record Store Origins in the 1970s

Valley Media was founded by Barney Cohen in a warehouse in Davis, California, in the 1970s. Cohen, a graduate of Antioch College in Yellow Springs, Ohio, moved to Woodland, California with his wife. In 1974 he started a music store, Barney's Goodtime Musicstore, with borrowed money. He then opened a second store in Davis, which was more successful. By 1979 he owned four stores and decided to switch from retail to wholesale, calling his new company Valley Record Distributors.

The company initially operated out of the back of one of the record stores in Davis. In 1984 it expanded into a 2,000-square-foot warehouse in Davis. Cohen sold the last of his record stores in 1985. In his first year as a wholesaler he had about 20 customers, all of them within 50 miles of the warehouse. He also helped people open record stores by advising them on what to stock. With two employees, Valley Record Distributors had $2 million in sales in its first year. With its Data General midlevel mainframe, Valley was the first one-stop to have a computerized system. It carried about 30,000 titles.

Steady Growth in the 1980s

Sales doubled every year for the first few years. In 1986 Valley added CDs to its inventory and moved its operations to Woodland. By the end of 1987 Valley's sales had reached $16 million and the company won its first Wholesaler of the Year award from the National Association of Recording Merchandisers (NARM). Valley distinguished itself from its competition by offering special order fulfillment and supplying deep catalog items. Valley also committed to carrying every classic title.

In 1989 Valley moved across the street to a new, 66,000-square-foot warehouse. Its customers included about 1,000 independent stores and 50 chain locations. Orders were taken and fulfilled through electronic data interchange (EDI) for the first time. Cohen told *Billboard,* ''We believe we were the first company to take an electronic order. We've been ahead of the curve with technology all along.''

Increased Competition in the 1990s

In the early 1990s Valley faced competition from other one-stop distributors. When Alliance Entertainment Corp. purchased one-stop Abbey Road, it became a $600 million company, compared with Valley's $100 million size. When Alliance offered Borders Books and Music a better deal, Valley lost one-third of its business. In response, Valley vowed never to let any single account become more than ten percent of its business, and it began acquiring small- to medium-sized one-stop distributors. When Alliance filed for Chapter 11 bankruptcy protection in 1997, all of the business that Valley lost came back.

Valley began distributing independent labels in 1994 through an agreement with Rounder Records of Cambridge, Massachusetts. Together they set up Distribution North America (DNA) as a 50–50 joint venture to distribute Rounder product. In December 1997 Valley bought out Rounder's interest in DNA. By 1999 DNA had 150 suppliers, including several multilabel groups.

In October 1995 Valley installed a new inventory control system that allowed it to ship 95 percent of its orders on the same day they came in. It was designed and built by the Cormer/PCC consortium, which had built hardware/software installations for Kodak and Timex. Called ''a perpetual-inventory system with a random locator,'' the system did not require Valley to store its product in any order. When a new shipment arrives, it is put into the nearest open space, with only the computer keeping track of where the product is located. Orders are held until they total 10,000 units. The pickers are then given a summary of product to pull in the exact order of the items' floor locations, so that no one has to go through the warehouse more than once. The product is then piled into a sorter, which reads the bar codes, adds price stickers, and sorts it into individual orders. This system enables Valley to receive an order as late as 6:00 p.m. one day and get the product to the retailer by 9:00 a.m. the next day.

Online Retailers and Videos: 1995–2000

Valley was one of the first music distributors to supply Internet retailers. Valley became involved in supplying Internet retailers as early as 1994 through a personal relationship, when Cohen's son was a classmate of Internet retailer CDNow's cofounder Jason Olim. Supplying Internet-based retailers soon became a big enough part of Valley's business for it to warrant having its own manager. That business segment initially was called Sound Delivery, then became i.Fill in 1999. By 1999 CDNow was a leading online retailer and Valley was one of the leading Internet fulfillment companies with more than 20,000 orders from Internet retailers a day. As part of its service to Internet retailers, Valley would ship orders in client packaging and was able to reach nearly 70 percent of the United States via ground UPS in two days.

In May 1997 Valley acquired video distributor Star Video Entertainment, based in New Jersey, for $37.9 million. Valley wanted to get into video distribution because of growing demand from Internet retailers. The company also wanted to diversify to stay ahead of other one-stops, and it expected that DVD sales would explode over the next few years. Acquiring Star Video virtually doubled the size of the company, but integrating the culture of video distribution with that of music distribution took two years. Found Barney Cohen told *Billboard* in 1999, ''We had a lot of big integration issues, and one of the reasons that we delayed going public is we wanted to be able to tell the world that we are over the hump of integration, and we feel we are.''

Unlike other video distributors that concentrate on rentals, Valley intended to focus on sell-through, believing that videos were underrepresented and undersold. Valley was able to sell a lot of video to its music accounts and, eventually, its video accounts began taking music. After the acquisition of Star Video in 1997, Valley significantly increased its stock of video titles, carrying every single music video available, 40,000 theatrical videos, and more than 3,000 DVD titles. Valley did not distribute adult-oriented video or DVD product, however.

For fiscal 1998 ending March 30, Valley had sales of $583 million. Of that total, $234 million was from video sales resulting from the acquisition of Star Video. Net income was $2.6 million. In fiscal 1999 video sales accounted for about one-third of Valley's overall sales.

In September 1997 Valley broke ground on its second warehouse in Louisville, Kentucky. It began receiving product on May 1, 1998 and shipped its first order on June 1. The second warehouse gave Valley the capacity it needed to handle the sale of Blockbuster's music stores to Wherehouse Entertainment in 1998, which added 400 stores to Valley's customer base with just a week of preparation.

At the end of 1998 Valley was the top one-stop wholesaler of records, cassettes, and compact discs, and it was one of the top five video distributors in the United States. It carried about 275,000 music titles and 30,000–40,000 video titles. It had about 1,100 employees nationwide, including some 800 at its Woodland headquarters.

Toward the end of 1998 Valley announced plans for an initial public offering (IPO) in 1999. Proceeds were expected to be used to help Valley repay a loan used to finance its 1997 acquisition of Star Video. Valley hoped its New Media division would attract investors interested in electronic commerce. It changed the name of its online fulfillment business from Sound Delivery to i.Fill. Its online customers were retailers who sold over the Internet or through 800 telephone numbers advertised on television. By mid-1999 Valley was fulfilling more than 20,000 orders a day from online retailers. For fiscal 1999 sales to Internet retailers were about $130 million, and it was described by Valley as its fastest growing business.

Going Public: 1999–2000

Valley priced its IPO of 3.5 million shares at $16 a share. In the first day of trading, March 25, 1999, the stock price jumped nearly 26 percent to close at slightly more than $20. The IPO raised $56 million, with substantial trading volume indicating strong investor interest in the company.

After extending its contract with Amazon.com for two years, Valley announced that it had won a contract with Virgin Entertainment to fill all of its audio, video, and DVD orders as well as selected book titles for Virgin E-Commerce.

As part of its New Media initiative, Valley entered into a partnership with Atlanta-based Amplified.com to provide custom CD and downloadable music capabilities to retailers and labels. Under the terms of the agreement, Valley would take an ownership interest in Amplified.com, which would in turn build a custom CD manufacturing facility within Valley Media's warehouse. This capability would allow Valley to offer its suppliers' products in a new format.

Following the IPO, Valley announced that it would expand its operations into a new 260,000-square-foot distribution facility near its corporate headquarters in Woodland. The newly leased facility was about a mile away from the company's 170,000-square-foot distribution center, which would be converted to administrative office space. Another 330,000-square-foot distribution facility was located in Louisville, Kentucky.

Net sales for fiscal 1999 ending April 3 were $889 million, up from $583.5 million in fiscal 1998. Net income increased 69.2 percent from $2.6 million to $4.4 million. The company noted spectacular growth in its online customers. Sales to traditional retail accounts rose 32.4 percent to $178.7 million, and sales from independent distribution increased 20.4 percent to $55 million.

In mid-1999 Valley reported a net loss of $799,000 for the first quarter ending July 3 of its fiscal year 2000. The overall loss was attributed to higher than expected costs associated with opening its new warehouse in Woodland. As a result of problems associated with moving into the new facility, Valley was unable to fill orders on time, and some customers resorted to other distributors. Labor and freight costs rose as the company tried to make up for lost time.

Sales of $185.8 million during the first quarter were 20 percent higher than the $154.4 million of the previous year's first quarter. For the second quarter ending October 3, 1999,

Valley reported net income of $335,000 on sales of $205.2 million. For the six months ending October 3, Valley reported a net loss of $464,000 on sales of $390.9 million, compared with the previous year's six-month loss of $847,000 on sales of $343.3 million.

The slide in profitability during the year resulted in a much lower stock price for Valley Media. In December the company created a new chief operating officer position and promoted senior vice-president Melanie Cullen to the position. The company realized that its senior management was being stretched too far, when earlier in the year the company's IPO and move into a new warehouse coincided. With president and CEO Robert Cain on the road talking to investors about the IPO, the move into the new warehouse ended up costing significantly more than expected. When the problems were revealed in June 1999, the company's stock fell 31 percent in one day, to less than $15 a share. At the beginning of December 1999 it was trading at less than $10 a share.

For fiscal 2000 Valley expected to post a loss as a result of problems associated with moving into its new warehouse and a downturn in its mainstream business. In an effort to cut costs, the company planned to trim its inventory from $250 million to $210 million to reduce borrowing costs. It also planned to merge its Internet division, i.Fill, with Atlanta-based Amplified.com, while retaining a 50 percent ownership in the business. Training issues and implementation of new systems continued to plague the new warehouse facility in early 2000. The company also lost $28 million worth of business from Wherehouse Entertainment when a special contract expired. Other cost-cutting measures included closing a Boston warehouse and trimming some positions at the company's headquarters.

Ultimately, the mishandled warehouse move cost Valley Media president and CEO Robert Cain his job. In May 2000 he resigned from Valley Media and was temporarily replaced by founder Barney Cohen. Cain had joined Valley Media in 1991 as a consultant and replaced Cohen as CEO at the end of 1997. At the time of Cain's resignation, Valley's stock had fallen to $4 a share.

2000 and Beyond

In addition to competition from other large one-stop distributors, Valley Media faced competition from areas such as revenue-sharing programs started by the movie studios. The company acknowledged that it risked losing market share to those distributors who adopted revenue-sharing. Valley decided not to participate in the studios' revenue-sharing programs and was the only major distributor not to participate.

The company also faced risks from retailers, including Amazon.com and Wherehouse Entertainment, who were beginning to buy direct and bypass the wholesale distribution channel. Wherehouse accounted for 15 percent of Valley's sales in 1999.

As a company that has employed the latest technology throughout its history to provide high levels of service, Valley has positioned itself to benefit from the growth of electronic commerce and Internet retailers. It has been supplying Internet merchants since the mid-1990s and was one of the first music distributors to do so. It also has developed new media initiatives and ventures involving the latest music downloading and custom CD technologies.

Principal Subsidiaries

i.Fill; Distribution North America.

Principal Operating Units

Full-line Distribution Group; New Media Group; Independent Distribution Group.

Principal Competitors

Alliance Entertainment Corp.; Anderson Merchandising; BMG Distribution Co.; Handleman Co.; Ingram Entertainment Inc.; Sony Music Distribution.

Further Reading

Barnes, Terry, "Fulfilling Expectations: Picking, Shipping and Doing the Math," *Billboard,* May 29, 1999, p. 60.

Chan, Gilbert, "Woodland, Calif.-Based Music, Video Wholesaler Plans IPO," *Knight-Ridder/Tribune Business News,* December 23, 1998.

Christman, Ed, "The Chairman of the Award-Winning Distributorship Knows a Thing or Two About Music and Moving It," *Billboard,* May 29, 1999, p. 57.

Fitzpatrick, Eileen, "New Media: Valley's Online Activity is Fulfilling Venture," *Billboard,* May 29, 1999, p. 60.

Glover, Mark, "Woodland, Calif.-Based Music, Video Wholesaler Plans To Expand," *Knight-Ridder/Tribune Business News,* April 28, 1999.

Goldstein, Seth, "Valley Media To Take the IPO Plunge," *Billboard,* January 16, 1999, p. 70.

Jeffrey, Don, "Big Valley, From the Beginning," *Billboard,* May 29, 1999, p. 56.

Kasler, Dale, "CEO of Woodland, Calif., Music Wholesaler Resigns After Mishandled Move," *Knight-Ridder/Tribune Business News,* May 23, 2000.

——, "Profits Soar at California-Based Wholesaler Valley Media," *Knight-Ridder/Tribune Business News,* February 25, 1999.

——, "Woodland, Calif.-Based Music Distributor Says It Has Turned the Corner," *Knight-Ridder/Tribune Business News,* December 29, 1999.

Morris, Chris, "DNA's Annual Confab Finds Distributors on the Upswing," *Billboard,* July 10, 1999, p. 61.

——, "The Facts About DNA: Valley's Distribution Unit Has a Life of its Own," *Billboard,* May 29, 1999, p. 58.

"NARM Honors Merchandisers, Suppliers," *Billboard,* March 18, 2000, p. 56.

"Taking Stock: Valley Media Inc.," *Sacramento Business Journal,* November 12, 1999, p. 45.

"Valley To Form New Internet Company," *Supermarket News,* February 21, 2000, p. 76.

—David P. Bianco

Vari-Lite International, Inc.

201 Regal Row
Dallas, Texas 75247
U.S.A.
Telephone: (214) 630-1963
Toll Free: (877) 827-4548
Fax: (214) 630-5867
Web site: http://www.vlint.com

Public Company
Incorporated: 1981 as Vari-Lite, Inc.
Employees: 451
Sales: $91.53 million
Stock Exchanges: NASDAQ
Ticker Symbol: LITE
NAIC: 53249 Other Commercial and Industrial
    Machinery and Equipment Rental and Leasing;
    335122 Commercial, Industrial, and Institutional
    Electric Lighting Fixture Manufacturing

Vari-Lite International, Inc. is a leader in the field of automated lighting systems. The company produces motorized lights that can be controlled with computers to change the direction, size, color, and pattern of light. Vari-Lite systems are used extensively by touring musical groups, Broadway shows, television and movie studios, and at corporate events. Prior to the year 2000, the company's equipment was only available for rental. Now, however direct sales are offered to churches, amusement parks, regional theater groups, and other new markets. Vari-Lite went public in 1997, with the company's founders and early investors (including members of the rock group Genesis) continuing to own slightly less than half its stock. Subsidiaries of Vari-Lite International include Showco, which rents and operates concert sound systems, and IGNITION! Creative Group, which provides lighting for corporate events.

1970s: Formative Years

Vari-Lite's roots go back to the late 1960s, when college friends Jack Calmes and Rusty Brutsche played in a Texas-based blues band. The seeds of a business were sown when they built a sound system for their shows that was so good, other acts began to rent it from them. In March 1970 Calmes and Brutsche joined with engineer Jack Maxson to incorporate Showco, the purpose of which was to provide sound systems for regional rock concerts. The company was started out of Maxson's garage and initially consisted of two trucks and two sound systems. At this time, touring bands typically used different sound gear at every venue, which not infrequently led to technical snafus and disgruntled customers.

A few months into the company's first year, Showco provided such impressive sound for a Three Dog Night concert in Dallas that the band asked for its help at other venues. This job led to others in which the company traveled with touring artists, setting up the sound system for each performance. Showco was soon working with such major acts as Led Zeppelin and James Taylor. In 1972 the company added lighting to its offerings when newly-hired Kirby Wyatt began to use industrial equipment such as lifts and trusses to rig lights above stages.

The company grew throughout the 1970s, though it often had little in the way of cash reserves. Several unsuccessful ventures, such as trucking and disco light businesses, also ate into earnings. Toward the end of the decade, with competition in the concert sound industry growing, the company began looking for a new way to compete. Of particular concern at this time was Showco's now-outdated lighting gear, which the company could not afford to replace.

In 1980 a company engineer, Jim Bornhorst, built an experimental light that could be made to quickly change colors using a dichroic glass filter and a small motor. Not long after this, a casual remark by Jack Maxson at a company brainstorming session led to a conceptual breakthrough. The words, "two more motors and it moves," sent the project in the direction of a color-changing, moveable light, a prototype of which was built over the next several months. However, there were no funds available to refine the concept beyond this stage, a situation that was made even worse when the company's contract for a Led Zeppelin tour was cancelled when drummer John Bonham died.

Genesis Provides Support in the Early 1980s

Seeking backing, Bornhorst and company CEO Brutsche flew to London to meet with longtime clients Genesis, the British rock band. A demonstration was set up at a 500-year-old barn in the English countryside. Shown the capabilities of the new light, the band, their lighting director, and their manager were impressed enough to give Showco the funds to build 50 more for use on their next tour. In exchange for this backing, the rockers were given a sizable ownership stake in the company. Genesis manager Tony Smith came up with the name Vari-Lite, which would be given to both the equipment and the new company which was formed to market it.

The new lights, which were controlled by a computer, made it through the tour despite frequent technical glitches. At this stage they were still seen as a novelty, but when Texans ZZ Top toured using improved versions the following year, many in the industry took notice. Within a short period of time Vari-Lite was the system of choice for such stars as Paul McCartney and Billy Joel. The Vari-Lite VL1 spot luminaire, as it was christened, enabled the lighting operator to change the color, beam size, shape, position and intensity of the light, as well as create patterns (using pre-cut metal "gobos"), allowing for dynamic effects on stage that had heretofore been impossible with fixed lights. The new system also reduced the number of instruments required to light a show, since one moveable light could be programmed to provide the coverage of up to eight fixed ones. Although Vari-Lite equipment cost more to use, the savings in labor and setup time helped offset this.

The company was granted a patent for its new system in 1983 and received a number of others over the years. Vari-Lite hired workers to build the lighting instruments and computer controllers, using components purchased from outside suppliers. The company rented the gear to touring bands and supplied trained staff to program and run the shows, much as was being done with Showco's sound systems. Vari-Lite equipment was not available for purchase, and it did not interface with standard lighting systems, relying as it did on proprietary technology.

In 1986 the company brought out a new system, the Series 200. The new VL2 and VL3 lights it used contained microprocessors which facilitated better communication with the redesigned computer control board. That same year Showco also introduced its PRISM integrated concert sound system, the first of its kind in the industry. Two years later a holding company, Vari-Lite International, Inc., was created to assume ownership of both Vari-Lite and Showco. The company had by now established offices in several major entertainment centers in the United States and abroad from which it could rent equipment and mount tours. Annual revenues were an estimated $20 million.

In 1989 Vari-Lite sued competitor Syncrolite, Inc., alleging patent infringement. Syncrolite had been founded by Jack Calmes, who had resigned as president of Showco in 1980. Calmes countersued, alleging that his former partners had hidden the development of the Vari-Lite system from him when he left, causing him to lose significant profits when he sold his stock. The situation was eventually resolved in Vari-Lite's favor.

Moving Beyond Rock Concerts in the 1990sM

After the company's success with touring rock bands, other entertainment sectors began to make use of Vari-Lite equipment. Broadway shows and television production companies were two early adopters of the new lights. Vari-Lite received a prime time Emmy award in 1991 for Outstanding Achievement in Engineering, in recognition of the Series 200 system. Noise generated by cooling fans on the lights, not a problem at rock concerts, still prevented some uses in these contexts, however. In 1992 the company introduced the Series 300 system and VL5 wash luminaire, which was smaller in size and utilized convection cooling to allow silent operation. This opened up further markets for the company, which was still renting rather than selling its lights. Vari-Lite gear was also being used widely for corporate events. The company's entry into this field dated to Kirby Wyatt's creation of Showco Creative Services in 1980, which later evolved into the Vari-Lite subsidiary IGNITION! Creative Group, Inc.

A new subsidiary, Irideon, Inc. was formed in 1994. Irideon targeted the architectural lighting market, which illuminated outdoor structures at night for dramatic effect. Other new businesses included Brilliant Stages, Inc., and Theater Projects Lighting Services Limited, both U.K.-based theater support companies acquired in 1994. Vari-Lite itself was now reaching a wider range of users than ever before. These included artist David Hockney, who integrated lighting effects into a painting, as well as the 1996 Atlanta Olympic Games and that year's Republican and Democratic conventions.

In the mid-1990s the company also filed another patent infringement suit, this time against top competitor High End Systems, Inc. After several years, the issue was resolved out of court. The settlement reportedly required High End to pay a sum of cash and future licensing fees to Vari-Lite.

The Late 1990s and Beyond

In 1997 Vari-Lite sold two million shares of stock on the NASDAQ exchange, which allowed it to retire almost half its debt. Some 47 percent of the company remained in the hands of Genesis and Vari-Lite management. Following the public offering, the company began to convert its rental offices into what it called Vari-Lite Production Services agencies. The main difference was that the company now offered conventional lighting

Key Dates:

1970: Showco, Inc. is founded in Texas to provide concert sound systems.
1980: First prototype of color-changing, moving light; rock group Genesis funds construction of 50.
1981: Vari-Lite, Inc. founded as sister to Showco; lights debut at a Genesis rock concert.
1983: Company receives its first patent for the original Vari-Lite system.
1988: Vari-Lite International incorporated as holding company for Vari-Lite & Showco.
1991: Vari-Lite wins its first Emmy award for Series 200 lighting system.
1997: Vari-Lite goes public.
1998: Company begins selling off several foreign rental operations as well as Irideon and Brilliant Stages units.
2000: Vari-Lite begins offering lighting products available for purchase.

gear along with programmable Vari-Lite equipment, enabling its customers to do "one-stop" shopping.

The following year the company purchased several overseas concerns which served as leasing agents for Vari-Lite: VLSC-Scandinavia AB of Stockholm, as well as VLB N.V. and EML N.V. of Brussels. The company also published a book of concert photographs by employee Lee Magadini, *A Different Light,* proceeds from which went to the Vari-Lite International Foundation. The Foundation was established to fund AIDS organizations in memory of Kirby Wyatt, who had died of the disease in 1995.

Near the end of 1998 Vari-Lite announced the sale of its Irideon architectural lighting subsidiary to Electronic Theater Controls. Irideon had never really taken off, and the company took a loss on the investment. Business in general for Vari-Lite had fallen off since the initial public offering, and other steps were soon taken to improve the bottom line. In early 1999 the company sold Brilliant Stages to a subsidiary of Tomcat Global Corporation, and it also parted with lighting operations in the Middle East and Australia later in the year. Battling another of its competitors, the company initiated a patent infringement lawsuit against Danish lighting company Martin Gruppen A/S.

Vari-Lite made another dramatic move in 2000 when it announced that it would begin selling a line of automated lights which worked with conventional systems. Heretofore, Vari-Light had only rented its equipment, and it was not compatible with industry standards. The company was optimistic that it would tap into markets that had not previously been reached, including regional theater groups, churches, amusement parks, and restaurants. Vari-Lite also expected to expand its distribution to new geographic areas in the process.

As it neared its 20th year in business, Vari-Lite was still completing changes which were expected to make it more competitive and profitable. The company's reputation for quality and its established relationships with top entertainment and corporate clients put it in a strong position to succeed.

Principal Subsidiaries

Vari-Lite, Inc.; Vari-Lite Asia, Inc. (Japan); Vari-Lite Hong Kong, Ltd. (Hong Kong); Vari-Lite Europe Holdings, Ltd. (United Kingdom); Concert Production Lighting, Inc.; Showco, Inc.; IGNITION! Creative Group, Inc.

Principal Competitors

Audio Analysts USA, Inc.; Clair Brothers Audio Enterprises; Clay Paky SPA; Coemar SPA; Cooper Industries, Inc.; dB Sound, Inc.; General Electric Company; High End Systems, Inc.; Martin Gruppen A/S; Maryland Sound Industries, Inc.; Matthews Studio Equipment Group; Netter Digital Entertainment, Inc.; Production Resource Group PLC; Southern California Sound Image, Inc.

Further Reading

Cashill, Robert, "ETC Purchases Irideon from Vari-Lite," *Lighting Dimensions*, November 30, 1998.
——, "Vari-Lite/Martin Lawsuit Enters New Phase," *Lighting Dimensions*, September 30, 1999.
Hall, Cheryl, "All the World's a Stage for Dallas Lighting Firm," *Dallas Morning News*, January 15, 1995, p. 1H.
Johnson, David, "From Bullrings to Boardrooms," *Lighting Dimensions*, January/February 1997.
——, "Vari-Lite Vs. High End," *TCI*, October 1, 1995, p. 14.
McHugh, Catherine, "Vari-Lite Production Services Gears Up," *Lighting Dimensions*, November 30, 1997.
Tatge, Mark, "Syncrolite Chief Sues Former Showco Partners," *Dallas Morning News*, October 25, 1989, p. 1D.
Weathersby, William, Jr., "Automating Hockney," *Lighting Dimensions*, December 30, 1997.
Wrolstad, Mark, "Former Showco President Loses Case," *Dallas Morning News*, October 8, 1993, p. 1D.

—Frank Uhle

Vector Group Ltd.

100 S.E. Second Street
32nd Floor
Miami, Florida 33131
U.S.A.
Telephone: (305) 579-8000
Fax: (305) 579-8001
Web site: http://www.brookegroup.com

Public Company
Incorporated: 1980 as Brooke Partners L.P.
Employees: 2,200
Sales: $567 million (1999)
Stock Exchanges: New York
Ticker Symbol: VGR
NAIC: 312221 Cigarette Manufacturing

Known through 1999 as the Brooke Group Ltd., Vector Group Ltd. is a holding company for a variety of companies, the most important being the Liggett Group Inc., the successor of the Liggett & Myers Tobacco Company. Liggett is the fifth largest manufacturer of cigarettes in the United States, producing the branded cigarette Eve, as well as the value-price brand Pyramid. Through its subsidiary Liggett-Ducat Ltd., the company also manufactures and markets cigarettes in Russia. In addition to its tobacco holdings, Vector Group also owns interests in an investment banking and brokerage business in the United States, real estate development businesses in the Russia; and various Internet and software-related companies. These are held through the company's majority-owned subsidiary, New Valley Corporation.

Early 1980s: LeBow's Turnaround Candidates

Brooke Partners L.P. was founded in 1980 by financier Bennett S. LeBow as an investment vehicle. Bennett bought troubled companies that he considered undervalued and attempted to turn them around. LeBow had studied engineering, worked as a computer analyst for the U.S. military, and formed his own computer company in 1967. He took that company, DSI

Systems Inc., public in 1969, but then pushed too hard to expand and nearly bankrupted the company. After selling DSI in 1971 he became an advisor to high-tech companies, frequently investing in them as well.

LeBow formed Brooke Partners with the assistance of investment firm Drexel Burnham Lambert Inc., which owned 15 percent. Brooke sold one of its early investments, computer display maker Information Displays Inc., in 1984. In 1985 Brooke bought 54 percent of computer maker MAI Basic Four, which sold software and hardware to small companies in highly specific markets like the hotel business. MAI had been losing money. As it usually did, Brooke quickly sent in its own managers and advisors to cut expenses, pare down the firm's staff, and put a new business strategy in place. MAI was soon making money again.

Brooke also bought the microfilm division of Bell & Howell Co. and Brigham's Inc., an ice cream business. With its MAI success under its belt and a growing portfolio of companies, Brooke turned to a much bigger target; the Liggett Group, once one of the largest U.S. tobacco companies. At the time it was owned by British firm Metropolitan plc.

Mid-1980s: Liggett Acquisition

Liggett began as a manufacturer of snuff in Belleville, Illinois in 1822. In 1873 John Edmund Liggett, grandson of the firm's founder, joined with George S. Myers to form Liggett & Myers, which began producing cigarettes. Liggett eventually produced L&M, Chesterfield, and Lark cigarettes, which were some of the best-known brands in the industry for several decades.

While the firm remained profitable, it made many mistakes over the years. In the 1950s, with the use of filters becoming widespread on cigarettes, Liggett put its money into Chesterfields, which were not filtered. The decision cost Liggett market share in ensuing years. The company also missed opportunities related to the marketing potential of packaging changes. When crush-proof, flip-top boxes were introduced, for example, Liggett ignored the innovation. Likewise, with the health risks of cigarettes increasingly on the public's mind, competitors introduced low-tar cigarettes in 1967. Liggett did nothing as low-tar cigarettes became increasingly prevalent. Finally, in 1976, Liggett introduced Decade, its first low-tar cigarette, nearly ten years after the competition.

Meanwhile, Liggett was diversifying. It bought or created brands in the liquor market including Wild Turkey, a prestigious bourbon put out through its Austin, Nichols & Co. subsidiary. The firm also imported table wines and liqueurs like Campari aperitif from Italy. Its Paddington Corp. subsidiary imported J&B Scotch. Liggett also put out Alpo, the best-selling canned dog food in the United States. Due to the decline of Liggett's tobacco profits, Alpo was one of the firm's biggest profit makers. By the early 1970s the company's president, Raymond J. Mulligan, had come from the Alpo division and had no background in the cigarette business. Liggett had profits of $80.4 million in 1973 on sales of $586 million.

Sales of Liggett's premium brands of alcohol grew at an annual rate of 20 percent over the next five years. In 1978 the company gave up on international cigarette sales, spinning off its foreign cigarette business to Philip Morris for $108 million. Liggett nearly sold its domestic cigarette business too, but could not quite work out a deal. By 1979 cigarettes had shrunk to 20 percent of Liggett's business, while wine and spirits accounted for 30 percent. The firm held only three percent of the cigarette market. Meanwhile, Alpo continued to grow and the company moved into the growing market for dry dog food. Liggett's Diversified Products Corp. was pumping up sales as well, becoming the largest maker of barbells and other physical fitness equipment.

Liggett also bought two leading Pepsi Cola bottling companies; one in Fresno, California, and the other in Columbia, South Carolina. Meanwhile, it cut its advertising for cigarettes by 45 percent, causing many industry observers to believe that the company was preparing for the eventual demise of its cigarette business. The following year, however, Liggett introduced generic cigarettes. Considered a risky move because cigarette marketing was so dependant on brand names, it nevertheless proved a successful one. None of its larger rivals produced generic cigarettes, so Liggett captured the market for them.

Also in 1980, Liggett Group was bought by Grand Metropolitan Ltd., the London-based liquor and entertainment company, for $575 million after a long takeover battle. Grand Metropolitan had already owned 9.5 percent of Liggett, and Liggett had imported Grand Met's J&B Scotch. Liggett initially opposed the purchase, and to dissuade Grand Met sold its Austin, Nichols subsidiary, which made the Wild Turkey bourbon Grand Met wanted to own, for $97.5 million.

With Grand Met, Liggett experienced some success with generic cigarettes over the next several years, but by 1984 larger rivals were challenging it. R.J. Reynolds began selling its Doral brand cigarettes at generic prices, for instance, while Brown & Williamson Tobacco Co. brought out a line of generic and private-label cigarettes. Liggett's management had been considering buying the firm from Grand Met for $325 million, but when Liggett's rivals brought out competing generic products, the group's financing fell through.

Liggett's sales and profits plummeted until it was bought by Brooke Partners in 1986 for $137 million. Brooke installed LeBow's partner William Weksel as chairman. Not content with its move into tobacco, Brooke bought 53 percent of telecommunications firm Western Union Corp. in 1987. Founded in 1851, Western Union had once been a communications giant. But the advent of the telephone slowly strangled the firm. By the time Brooke assumed control, the telegraph accounted for less than ten percent of Western Union's revenue. It made more money from its teletypewriter services, mailgrams, and money order service.

When the British shipbuilding concern that was building LeBow's private yacht went bankrupt, Brooke bought it for less than $5 million. In 1988, moreover, Brooke proposed a buyout of American Brands. When that didn't work, LeBow tried to persuade American Brands to buy the Liggett Group. That effort failed as well. In the meantime, Liggett introduced the Pyramid brand of low-cost cigarettes, which proved to be one of the most successful cigarette introductions of the 1980s. Then, in 1989, Brooke Partners started SkyBox International Inc., a sports trading card company.

1990: Corporate Restructuring

In 1990 the Liggett Group changed its name to Brooke Group Ltd. and announced it would emphasize its push to diversify into sports and entertainment products. Liggett already had a small football and basketball card business, and distributed chocolate mints made in Finland. The cards and candy used the same distribution channels used by the cigarette business. At about the same time, William Weksel resigned and LeBow was elected chair. Liggett's 1989 sales of $572.9 million accounted for the lion's share of Brooke Partners' total sales, but smoking was under increasing legal pressure. So, Liggett changed its name to Brooke Group and split into two subsidiaries; Liggett Group Inc. managed the firm's tobacco business, while Impel Marketing Inc. managed the group's other activities. Impel specialized in the sales and marketing needed to broaden sales of sports and entertainment products.

Later in 1990, LeBow restructured his companies. Brooke Group became the parent of Brooke Partners, which was suffering from the heavy debt it acquired as the result of its many leveraged buyouts. As a result, Brooke Group (formerly Liggett

Group) became responsible for Brooke Partners' $300 million debt. The interest on the bonds paying for Brooke Partners' acquisition of MAI and Western Union came to $45 million a year, severely limiting Brooke Group's cash flow. Some investors were outraged. One portfolio manager told the *Wall Street Journal* that LeBow "took an equity investment and turned it into a junk bond." The price of Brooke Group's shares plummeted.

Brooke Group had been managed by a nominally independent company called Brooke Management Inc., which was owned by LeBow and whose sole client was Brooke Group. In 1991 Brooke Group paid Brooke Management $10.2 million for services and expenses. LeBow decided to fold Brooke Management into Brooke Group, and in 1992 Brooke Group paid LeBow $12 million for Brooke Management, a firm whose assets comprised the managerial expertise of LeBow and his associates. LeBow had not drawn a salary as president of Brooke Group, but he did after the buyout.

In 1992 Brooke Group took a charge to restructure MAI and SkyBox International, its sports and trading card subsidiary. SkyBox lost $80 million in 1991. Brooke Group lost $149.6 million in 1991 and $75.8 million in 1992. Furthermore, its English boat yard, renamed Brooke Yachts International Ltd., went under in 1992, leaving Brooke with a $4.8 million write-off. Liggett's sales were declining, meanwhile, partly because of a decision to place more emphasis on its full-price brands of cigarettes like Chesterfield, Eve, and L&M. Liggett's cigarette market share had sunk to three percent from six percent since its 1986 takeover by Brooke.

Liggett named Edward Horrigan chairman and CEO in 1993. Horrigan, the former chairman of R.J. Reynolds Tobacco, said that Liggett would look again to the overseas market, try to hold market share of its branded cigarettes, and try to expand the market share of its discount cigarettes. At the same time, Philip Morris and RJR were announcing discounts on their leading brands, thus putting pressure on the discount cigarette market. Liggett restructured its headquarters and manufacturing operations in 1993. In 1994 it reduced its sales force by 150, using 300 part time sales people instead. It also cut employee benefits.

In 1993 the Western Union subsidiary (later renamed New Valley) entered Chapter 11 bankruptcy. One of its last remaining profit makers, its telex business, had gone sour as fax technology made it obsolete. Brooke fought with New Valley's debt holders to keep control of New Valley's one remaining profitable business; money transfer. With its U.S. operations in turmoil, Brooke sought to invest in the former Soviet Union. One venture, a joint venture with the Ducat tobacco company in Moscow, took years to produce a cigarette because of disagreements with the Russian government and other problems.

Fed up with the company's problems, a group of shareholders filed suit against LeBow and four other Brooke officers alleging that they had enriched themselves at the expense of the company, which had been stripped of assets. Soon thereafter, the *Wall Street Journal* published an intensely critical article about Brooke Group in which it claimed that LeBow "has increasingly used the company as a kind of personal bank." The shareholder suit was settled in 1994 after LeBow repaid much of the $20 million that

the lawsuit alleged he owed the company. The settlement linked LeBow's future salary to company performance, and required approval by outside directors of any transaction of more than $100,000 between Brooke Group and LeBow.

Despite Horrigan's efforts, the cigarette market share of Liggett continued to decline, falling to 2.3 percent of the U.S. market in 1994; Liggett held .9 percent of the branded market and 5.4 percent of the discount market. Liggett also sold 750 million cigarettes in the Middle East and Eastern Europe, and produced over 300 combinations of brands, lengths, styles and packages. Overall, Brooke had profits of $110.1 million in 1994 on sales of $479.3 million.

In November 1994, New Valley was forced to sell its money transfer services as part of its Chapter 11 bankruptcy reorganization. After it emerged from bankruptcy in 1995, it bought a 28.2 percent interest in Brazilian airplane manufacturer Empresa Brasileira de Aeronautica, S.A., for $12.8 million. In March 1995, Brooke sold its remaining 15 percent stake in SkyBox International. The firm also purchased 6.4 percent of the ShowBiz Pizza Time chain, and Ladenburg Thalmann, a 119-year-old New York securities firm that cost it $26.8 million. By mid-1995 Brooke had improved enough for *Business Week* to conclude that LeBow was "finally paying attention to beefing up Brooke's quarterly performance and bottom-line results."

Late 1990s: Media Attention

In late 1995, LeBow teamed up with Carl Icahn—a former adversary who was known for corporate takeovers—to make a highly publicized effort to take over RJR Nabisco. After purchasing substantial amounts of Nabisco's stock, the two men made repeated attempts to force the company to split into two parts: R.J. Reynolds Tobacco, which produced Winston and Camel brand cigarettes; and the Nabisco Brands division, which produced a variety of foods. Despite encountering some early support among RJR Nabisco shareholders, the would-be corporate raiders failed to effect their plan.

Brooke Group caught the media's attention again in 1996 and 1997—as well as the ire of the tobacco industry. In 1996, LeBow agreed to settle several health-related lawsuits brought by smokers—a first for any cigarette manufacturers. This decision spelled trouble for other cigarette makers, depressing their stock prices and setting a precedent for future settlements and concessions. Again in 1997, LeBow enraged the tobacco industry by testifying in court, as part of another settlement agreement, that smoking was addictive and that it could lead to serious illness. He also agreed to turn over documents providing evidence of tobacco industry duplicity and fraud. LeBow's admitted reasons for cooperating were practical rather than ethical; he merely wanted to avoid lengthy litigation and costly legal fees.

Subsequently, Liggett became the first domestic cigarette maker to place a warning on cigarette packages stating that, "Nicotine is addictive," and to disclose all the ingredients of one of its cigarette brands.

In 1998, Brooke Group agreed to sell three of Liggett Group's cigarette brands to Phillip Morris Inc. The sale of the three brands—L&M, Chesterfield, and Lark—generated $300 million in cash for the company. The agreement included only domestic rights; Phillip Morris already owned international rights to the three brands, which it had purchased in the late 1970s.

On May 24, 2000, the company changed its name to Vector Group Ltd. The following month, Vector announced that it was selling its Russian tobacco subsidiary, Liggett-Ducat Ltd., to Gallaher Group plc for $400 million. The company planned to use the proceeds to retire a portion of its debt.

What's Ahead for Vector Group?

In 1999, a Florida jury found cigarette makers liable for conspiracy, fraud, and the illnesses of 500,000 or more smokers. Liggett, along with several other U.S. cigarette manufacturers, faced potentially massive punitive penalties related to this verdict. Such penalties, if severe enough, were highly likely to drive the company into liquidation. In addition, a substantial number of other individual lawsuits, class action suits, and third-party recovery actions were pending in which Liggett was named a defendant. The outcomes of these cases were likely to have a significant impact upon the company's operations.

If this did not come to pass, it seemed likely that LeBow would continue to pilot his company through the murky and troubled waters of the tobacco industry. In a June 2000 interview with *Reuters,* LeBow said that he planned to stay in the cigarette business, even while cooperating with anti-tobacco lobbyists. He explained this seemingly contradictory stance by saying, "It's very important that we stay in the business, that we be the maverick of the industry, so we can beat up on the rest of the industry and make them do the right thing."

Principal Subsidiaries

BGLS Inc.; Liggett Group Inc.; Liggett-Ducat Ltd.(Russia); New Valley Corp. (55.5%).

Principal Competitors

Phillip Morris Companies Inc.; R.J. Reynolds Tobacco Holdings, Inc.; Gallaher Group plc; B.A.T. Industries plc.

Further Reading

Atlas, Riva, "Blowing Smoke," *Forbes,* March 29, 1993, p. 60.

Cohen, Laurie P., "Ready Credit; Head of Brooke Group Draws on Its Coffers to Tune of Millions," *Wall Street Journal,* July 30, 1993, pp. A1, A4.

"Liggett's New Recipe," *Financial World,* February 1, 1980, pp. 48–49.

Cole, Robert J., "Grand Met Raises Bid for Liggett," *New York Times,* May 15, 1980, p. D1.

Fields, Gregg, "The New Barbarian," *Miami Herald,* November 13, 1995, p. 26BM.

Finch, Peter, "Bennett LeBow: Up from Bottom-Fishing," *Business Week,* December 12, 1988, pp. 108, 110.

Garcia, Beatrice, "Liggett May Break from the Pack," *Miami Herald,* May 2, 1999, p. 1E.

Gloede, William, "L&M Smokes Out Generic Competition," *Advertising Age,* August 13, 1984, pp. 4, 58.

Kansas, Dave, "Brooke Group to Settle Shareholder Suit Over Dealings with Chairman LeBow," *Wall Street Journal,* March 18, 1994.

"L&M Smokes Out Generic Competition," *Advertising Age,* August 13, 1984.

Lowenstein, Roger, "Why Some Holders of Tobacco Firm May Feel Burned," *Wall Street Journal,* November 30, 1990.

Oliphant, Jim, "Was Traitor Betrayed?," *Miami Daily Business Review,* July 7, 1997.

Ramirez, Anthony, "Liggett to Change Its Focus with Shift from Cigarettes," *New York Times,* June 22, 1990, pp. D1–D2.

Schwartz, John, "A Maverick's Complaint: Liggett's LeBow Broke Tobacco's Ranks, But He Says the States Broke a Deal," *Washington Post,* July 24, 1997, p. E01.

Stevenson, Richard W., "Grand Metropolitan Sells Liggett to an Investor," *New York Times,* October 29, 1986.

"Witness Protection: Whistle Blowing Tobacco Company Deserves a Break," *Philadelphia Inquirer,* August 22, 1997.

—Scott M. Lewis
—updated by Shawna Brynildssen

Vedior NV

Jachthavenweg 112
1076 DC Amsterdam
The Netherlands
Telephone: (+31) 20 573-56-00
Fax: (+31) 20 573-56-02
Web site: http://www.vedior.com

Public Company
Incorporated: 1997
Employees: 12,500
Sales: NLG 8.9 billion ($4.29 billion) (1999)
Stock Exchanges: Amsterdam
Ticker Symbol: VDOR
NAIC:

Vedior NV ranks among the world's largest international and temporary staffing services providers, behind leaders Manpower and Adecco. Vedior, which operates more than 2,000 branch locations in more than 26 countries, annually provides short- and long-term positions for more than 1,000,000 people. The acquisition of the United Kingdom's Select Appointments in 1999, for a price of US$ 1.8 billion, has enabled the company to reinforce its position in the British, American, Australian, and South African markets. Europe remains the company's principal market. Until the Select acquisition, France, which is the largest temporary employment market in Europe, accounted for some 50 percent of Vedior's sales. The company's European activities operate primarily under the Vedior Europe and VediorBis brand names. In 2000, the company combined much of its specialist staffing services under the Expectra division. Specialist staffing is one of the company's target markets, accounting for 25 percent of sales. Generalist administrative and light industrial staffing services contribute 75 percent of sales. Since 1999, Vedior, under the direction of CEO Gert Smit, has focused on becoming a "pure play" staffing services provider, after selling off its Abilis cleaning division to Denmark's ISS for nearly US$ 500 million. Strapped for cash after the Select acquisition, Vedior has called a temporary halt to further growth through acquisition. Nonetheless, with chief rivals Kelly and Randstad nipping at its heels,

Vedior remains committed to securing its position among the world's top three international staffing services providers.

Turn-of-the-Century Origins

While Vedior NV came into its full independence as an international staffing specialist at the turn of the 21st century, its origins reached back to the turn of the 20th century. The company's earliest predecessor was a cleaning service established in 1909. One of the company's longest and largest customers signed on in 1927, when this company began providing cleaning services to Unilever. Other large, long-term customers followed, including Solvay Laboratories, based in Belgium and the Netherlands, in 1958 and Renault, of France, in 1976. Another of Vedior's early components was established in 1949 as a temporary employment agency created to meet the needs of the postwar reconstruction of the Netherlands. Among the company's services was manpower provision for the country's agricultural sector. Administrative personnel also became a company focus in the 1950s and 1960s.

By then, another core component of the future Vedior had also begun business. In 1954, Laurent Negro founded Bis S.A. Negro. Born in the Provence region, Negro had studied in Paris until the Second World War. With the Nazi occupation of France, Negro, then 17 years old, joined the French Resistance. After the war, he spent time traveling, first to Asia, and then to the United States. It was in the United States that Negro was introduced to a relatively new market: that of the temporary employment agency. Negro returned to France, bringing the employment agency concept with him. Bis, for a time the sole employment agency in France, held a longtime dominance in what was to become the largest European market for temporary staffing services.

During the 1970s, the predecessors to Vedior came under the sway of the Vroom & Dreesman retail concern. Vroom & Dreesman had built up a position as one of the Netherlands' major retailers, operating a string of Vroom & Dreesman department stores throughout the country. Founded by friends Anton Dreesman and Willem Vroom in 1887, the company had largely completed its initial national expansion by the outbreak of the First World War. Dreesman and Vroom managed to keep their com-

Company Perspectives:

Through its strong market position in the generalist staffing sector, Vedior aims to introduce and develop higher margin speciality staffing services in those markets where the provision of such services remains relatively underdeveloped. Vedior has a balanced organic and acquisitive growth strategy in targeted market segments. The company believes that diversity by geography and industry sector helps to minimize the impact of economic cyclicality thereby promoting a balanced earnings stream. This consistently pursued strategy is also aimed at strengthening the company's market position in Europe and expanding its network in the United States. Vedior also has a key foothold in promising younger growth markets in Asia and South America. The increasing scale of its activities and the company's extensive geographical coverage make Vedior an attractive partner for large international clients, offering them a wide range of staffing services, enhancing flexibility, productivity and quality. Vedior is continuously focused on the development of new supplementary services in order to provide the clients and employees with a "one-stop shop" for their employment-related needs. Such services include permanent placement, outsourcing, training, outplacement, vendor-on-premises services, and mobility centers. To reach its ambitious objectives, Vedior relies on the commitment and talent of its employees, both internal and external, because they are the ones who guarantee the quality and continuity of its services. Vedior offers its employees a stimulating environment, where the development of skills, creativity and self-responsibility are the main focus.

pany and its growing network of stores in the family by convincing family members to operate each new location—in this way, each store maintained a large degree of independence while the company itself remained in the Vroom and Dreesman families.

The decentralized structure of the Vroom & Dreesman chain began to make way for more modern and efficient centralized management in the 1960s, a process that was largely completed by 1973 when the Vroom & Dreesman Group was formed. At the time, Anton Dreesman, grandson of the company's cofounder, was appointed to lead the company. A doctor of economics and law, Dreesman came to the company after holding a position as a professor at the University of Amsterdam. Dreesman quickly reorganized the company and turned the company towards an ambitious expansion drive.

Part of Dreesman's objective was to diversify the company beyond its traditional retail base. While Vroom & Dreesman continued to emphasize retailing—and expanded beyond department stores into specialty retailing—the company now turned toward the business services sector, acquiring a number of cleaning services and employment agencies. Operating under the Vedior name in the 1980s, the business sector operations began to move beyond the Netherlands into other European markets, including Belgium and Germany.

Anton Dreesman's diversification drives led the company to reorganize into a new divisional structure, a reorganization that

continued through much of the 1980s and resulted in a change of name for the company—to Vendex International. Dreesman and his family held most of the company's stock—and thus a tight grip on the company's direction. By the end of the decade, however, Dreesman's health had begun to fail. After suffering a series of strokes, Dreesman turned over the company's direction, at first to Arie van der Zwan, and then, in 1990, to Jan Michiel Hessels.

By then, Vendex had begun to suffer losses due to the steadily declining economic climate of the late 1980s and early 1990s. Hessels, named chairman of the company, began to restructure Vendex, stripping off many of its unprofitable holdings—such as its Brazilian department store and banking businesses and its U.S. chain of Mr. Goodbuys stores, which had declared bankruptcy in 1991—while pursuing new acquisitions to boost its domestic retail position.

Independence for the 21st Century

In the mid-1990s, Vendex International went public. After taking a listing on the Amsterdam stock exchange in 1995, Vendex began to eye the potential of splitting its operations into two separate companies. The proposal of new legislation, which allowed Dutch companies to perform such a de-merger action, and the likelihood of the legislation being passed (as it was in 1997), encouraged Vendex to begin preparations for its Vedior spinoff. At the end of 1996, Vendex took the important step of acquiring Bis S.A., for approximately NLG 830 million.

The purchase of Bis came just 10 days after the death of founder Laurent Negro. By then, Bis, once the dominant temporary staffing agency in France, had fallen behind rivals Manpower and the freshly created Adecco (through the merger of Switzerland's Adia and France's Ecco). Bis's problems had begun during the 1980s, when Negro led the company on its own diversification drive. The collapse of the French economy at the beginning of the 1990s, and the economic crisis that reigned in that country through the first half of the decade, plunged Bis into losses. Meanwhile, the ailing Negro had not been able to find a successor for the company he had built. By 1996, Hessels and Negro had largely reached an agreement for the takeover of Bis's employment agencies by Vendex's employment division. In mid-1996, Vendex acquired 60 percent of Bis. The rest of the French company was acquired after Negro's death in January 1997.

With the Bis acquisition completed, Vendex announced its intention to spin off its business services operations into the newly named Vedior NV, which then took its own listing on the Amsterdam stock exchange. At that time, Vendex sold only 20 percent of its holding—then the legislation was passed that permitted Dutch corporations to de-merge their operations. Vendex shed the rest of its shareholding in Vedior in 1998, through a distribution of its shares to Vendex's shareholders. As Hessels explained to *The European:* "We always realized that there was no real synergy between our retail and temping activities." However, with Bis added to Vedior's staffing services operations, the new company was said to have the "critical mass" to compete as an independent company. The addition of Bis doubled Vedior's employment business, making it one of the world's largest. The acquisition also shifted the largest portion of the company's revenues to the French market.

Key Dates:

1909: Start of cleaning services.
1949: Temporary staffing services are added.
1973: Anton Dreesman named head of Vroom & Dreesman.
1970s: Vroom & Dreesman expands into temporary staffing and cleaning services.
1996: Bis S.A. is acquired.
1997: Vedior NV goes public.
1998: Vedior is spun off as independent company.
1999: Cleaning services division is sold, and Select Appointments (U.K.) is acquired.
2000: Acsys (U.S.) is purchased.

Gert Smit was named head of Vedior NV. The new company grouped its operations under four divisions: VediorBis, for the company's French activities; VediorEurope, for its activities in the Netherlands, Belgium, Germany, Luxembourg and Spain; Abilis, for its cleaning services division; and Miscellaneous Services, which grouped its Markgraaf trademark bureau, and FAA, based in Germany, a provider of vocational and other training courses.

Vedior began to show its promise in its first year, boosting revenues by more than NLG 1 billion to nearly NLG 8.9 billion. The company was also quick to go on an expansion drive, making a series of acquisitions culminating with the US\$ 1.8 billion purchase of Select Appointments in 1999. Among the companies acquired by Vedior were ISU, a temporary employment agency based in Germany; Unitech, of France; Sistemas Servicios y Soluciones and Gropesa ETT, both in Spain; All Clean, a cleaning services company in Belgium; and Newjob2000, in Switzerland. While these acquisitions helped boost Vedior's existing international operations, the company also prepared to enter new European territories, including Italy in 1998, through a joint venture with that country's Aries; and Portugal in 1999, with the purchase of Psico Group, that country's third largest temporary staffing services provider, and More-Recursos Humanos, based in Lisbon.

The company's emphasis on boosting its staffing services operations brought it to reassess its other operations. In May 1999, Vedior announced that it had agreed to sell its Abilis and TMB cleaning services operations to Denmark's ISS, for a total price of some \$500 million. By shedding its cleaning services division, Vedior sought to transform itself into a "pure play" temporary employment company capable of securing its position among the world's top three international staffing companies. The sale of its cleaning services division also helped boost Vedior's war chest to nearly \$1 billion, enabling it to eye a major acquisition in the near future.

That acquisition came in September 1999, when Vedior announced its intention to acquire Select Appointments, based in the United Kingdom and with operations in North America, Australia, and South Africa. For the acquisition, Vedior agreed to pay nearly \$1.8 billion—after paying 25 percent out of its reserves, the company hoped to raise much of the remainder through a new shares issue. A warning on lower profits, however, led to a slump in Vedior's share price, placing the shares issue in jeopardy and leaving the company scrambling for the financial backing needed to finalize the Select acquisition.

Select added £520 million (\$750 million) in sales to Vedior. It also gave the company a strong springboard in the United States market, where Vedior had been largely absent. In order to boost its newfound U.S. position, Vedior made a bid to acquire that country's Acsys, with 40 offices in 22 major U.S. cities. Made in April 2000, the acquisition offer for \$76 million offered the prospect of doubling Vedior's presence in the North American market. The company also looked toward the South American continent for future growth—at the end of April 2000, Vedior acquired a 50 percent share of RH Internacional Limitada, based in Rio de Janeiro.

Despite these acquisitions, Vedior announced its intention to slow down on its expansion, at least its acquisition drive, in favor of increasing its profitability. Among the steps the company took was to roll out a new computer platform to its network of agencies. Vedior also announced its intention to expand its Internet presence and products. At the same time, Vedior began to step up its internal expansion, opening more than 350 new agency offices throughout its international base.

Principal Subsidiaries

Cannock Chase (Netherlands); Dactylo (Netherlands); Vedior Personeelsdiensten (Netherlands); VediorBis (France); Abraxas (U.K.); Select Appointments (U.K.); Sesa Select (Argentina); Accountech (Australia); Parkhouse Industrial (Australia); ASB Interim (Belgium); Vedior Interim (Belgium); ATS Reliance (Canada); AYS (Czech Republic); Office Help (Finland); Soprate (France); FAA (Germany); Vedior Personal Dienstleistungen (Germany); Select Interservices (Greece); Hughes Castell (Hong Kong); CSSL (India); Vedior Lavoro Temporaneo (Italy); Fairplace Japan; Rowlands International (Luxembourg); Viawerk (Netherlands); Sapphire Technologies (New Zealand); Teleresources (Norway); Vedior Psico Forma (Portugal); Vedior Psico Imprego (Portugal); Only the Best (South Africa); Vedior Laborman (Spain); Swissjobs (Switzerland); Kinsey Craig (U.K.); Fairplace Consulting (U.K.); Accountants Inc. (U.S.); Lawtemps (U.S.); DB Concepts (U.S.).

Principal Competitors

Manpower, Inc.; Adecco; Randstad Holdings N.V.; Interim Services; Rentokil Initial; Kelly Services, Inc.; TAC Worldwide.

Further Reading

Smit, Barbara, and Masters, Charles, "Vendex Takeover Is Negro's Legacy," *European*, January 9, 1997, p. 17.
——, "Vedior Sheds Cleaning Division," *Reuters*, May 20, 1999.
——, "Vedior Is Voorzichtig Optimistisch over 2000," *De Telegraaf-I*, May 27, 2000.
——, "Vedior Zet Expansie Op Heel Laag Ppitje," *De Telegraaf-I*, May 3, 2000.

—M. L. Cohen

VENATOR GROUP

Venator Group Inc.

112 West 34th Street
New York, New York 10120
U.S.A.
Telephone: (212) 720-3700
Fax: (212) 553-2018
Web site: http://www.venatorgroup.com

Public Company
Incorporated: 1905 as F.W. Woolworth & Co.; 1998 as
Venator Group Inc.
Employees: 47,000
Sales: $8.09 billion (1996)
Stock Exchanges: New York
Ticker Symbol: Z
NAIC: 44821 Shoe Stores; 44811 Men's Clothing Stores;
44812 Women's Clothing Stores; 44813 Children's and
Infants' Clothing Stores; 44815 Clothing Accessories
Stores; 551112 Offices of Other Holding Companies

Venator Group Inc., known until 1998 as the Woolworth
Corporation, is a diversified multinational retailer with stores
and support operations in North America, Europe, Australia,
and Asia. Since Woolworth's establishment in 1879, it has been
involved in general merchandising; in its new incarnation as
Venator, however, the company focuses on the retailing of
athletic footwear and apparel. Venator's best-performing specialty chains are the various Foot Locker athletic footwear and
apparel concepts and the Northern Reflections specialty apparel
format and its spinoffs.

Origins as the First Five-and-Ten Store

The history of Venator may be traced through that of Woolworth and that company's founder, Frank Winfield Woolworth,
who parlayed the idea of the five-and-ten cent store into an
international retailing empire. Born in 1852, in Rodman, New
York, Woolworth moved to Watertown, New York, in 1873
where he apprenticed and then clerked with Augsbury &
Moore, a wholesaler and dry goods store. Wanting more money,

Woolworth soon left Augsbury & Moore for A. Bushnell &
Company, a local dry goods and carpet store. His new employer, however, found him a poor salesman and lowered his
wages from $10 to $8 a week. In response, Woolworth
overworked himself, had a complete breakdown, and spent six
months convalescing.

When Woolworth recovered in 1876, he returned to his
former employer William Moore, whose business was now
called Moore & Smith. There he concentrated on window displays. In 1878, Moore & Smith found itself with high debt and
excess inventory. To raise money, the store held a five-cent sale.
Smith and Woolworth laid a group of goods such as tin pans,
washbasins, button-hooks, and dippers, along with surplus inventory, on a counter over which they hung a sign reading:
"Any Article on This Counter, 5¢." After the sale, Frank
Woolworth was convinced a five-cent strategy could work on a
broader basis.

In 1879, Woolworth left Moore & Smith. On February 22nd
of that year, he opened his first "Great 5¢ Store" in Utica, New
York. At first business was good, but as the five-cent novelty
faded, the store's poor location became a handicap and he
closed it in early June. Still, he had repaid Moore & Smith's
loan of $315.41, which he had used for his initial inventory, and
had made $252.44 in new capital.

On June 21, 1879, Woolworth opened his second Great 5¢
Store in Lancaster, Pennsylvania. This time he had three windows on a main street and $410 worth of goods. The store was a
success. The first day he sold 31 percent of stock. In succeeding
months, he changed the store's name, first to Five-and-Ten, and
later to Woolworth's. The additional ten-cent items allowed him
to search out further bargains.

Woolworth soon began opening new outlets. Some stores
succeeded, while others failed. By the mid-1880s, there were
seven Woolworth's in New York and Pennsylvania. Most were
run by partner-managers. These men—Woolworth's brother,
Charles Sumner Woolworth; his cousin, Seymour Horace
Knox; former employer, W.H. Moore; and Fred M. Kirby—ran
the stores in which they held a 50 percent interest. Frank Woolworth ran the initial store and took care of purchasing.

Company Perspectives:

It takes a sharp focus to succeed in the competitive world of specialty retailing. At Venator Group we are creating a results-driven organization that balances strategic growth, superior merchandising and thoughtful expense management with a common set of values that each business can embrace to drive future growth. These values commit us to: 1) deliver on our commitments to our shareholders; 2) provide the customer the most wanted product and services first; 3) insist on superior execution in every aspect of our performance; 4) approach every transaction with integrity; 5) create a sustainable competitive advantage by valuing organizational development; and 6) develop strong relationships with our manufacturers. By adhering to these values, we emerge at the start of a new millennium a highly focused athletic organization, competitively positioned to improve our profitability and extend our global reach as the world's leading retailer of athletic footwear and apparel.

In succeeding years, these partner-managers bought out Frank Woolworth's shares and began opening chains on their own. Woolworth continued opening stores. After 1888, he did so completely with his own capital. In these new stores, he entered into a profit-sharing agreement with managers.

While Woolworth owed much of his success to low prices, his treatment of the customer was also important. In the 1870s and 1880s, patrons usually had to ask for goods held behind the counter, and prices varied according to the customer; it was considered impolite to enter a store without buying. Woolworth changed all that. His merchandise sat on counters for everyone to see. His price was the same for everyone. He encouraged people to enter the store even if they were just looking.

Another reason for Woolworth's success was the decline in wholesale prices during the first 12 years of Woolworth's existence. This led to wider availability of goods in the five and ten cent price range, wider margins, and higher profits. As operations grew, Woolworth found he needed a New York City office from which he could govern his stores. In July 1886, he took an office on Chambers Street. Soon after, he began writing a daily letter that went out to all store managers.

In 1888, Frank Woolworth contracted typhoid. Until then, he had handled everything from accounting to ordering to inspecting stores; however, after two months in bed, he realized the importance of delegating authority. With that in mind, he chose Carson C. Peck to run day-to-day operations. Peck had been a fellow clerk at A. Bushnell & Co. and a partner-manager in Woolworth's Utica, New York, store. He became Woolworth's first general manager.

Freed of day-to-day operations, Woolworth made his first European buying trip in 1890. On his return, U.S. consumers flocked to his stores to obtain pottery from England and Scotland, Christmas decorations from Germany, and other goods from the great commercial fairs of Europe.

The same year, Woolworth established the "approved list." On the approved list were goods that Woolworth would reorder for his managers. This system allowed managers the leeway to adjust stock for local preferences while at the same time benefiting from the chain's buying power. In 1897, Woolworth opened his first Canadian store, in Toronto, Ontario. Three years later, there were 59 Woolworth's with sales of $5 million.

Tremendous Growth in Early 20th Century

By 1904, Woolworth was opening stores at a fantastic rate. He opened some stores from scratch. Others he converted from small chains he bought. In 1905 he incorporated as F.W. Woolworth & Co. At this point, Woolworth had $10 million in sales and 120 stores. In 1909, Woolworth sent three associates overseas to open the first of what was to be a hugely successful group of English stores, known as Three and Sixpence stores. In 1910, he appointed the first resident buyer in Germany, and, in 1911, he opened his first overseas warehouse at Fuerth, Germany.

At this point competition began to increase from such retailers as J.G. McCrory and S.S. Kresge Company. Also, many former partner-managers had chains of their own. In 1912, Woolworth saw the opportunity to create a huge new entity. He merged with five other retailers: W.H. Moore, C.S. Woolworth, F.M. Kirby, S.H. Knox, and E.P. Charlton. All were former partner-managers except for Earle Perry Charlton, who had built a chain of his own west of the Rocky Mountains. F.W. Woolworth & Co. became the publicly traded F.W. Woolworth Co., a nationwide retailer with 596 stores and $52 million in sales. Frank Woolworth was chief stockholder and president. The new retailing behemoth took residence in the 60-story neogothic Woolworth building in New York City. Frank Woolworth's office, within the $13.5 million "Skyline Queen," was a replica of Napoleon Bonaparte's Empire Room.

In 1915, Carson Peck died. Peck had been supervising day-to-day operations since 1888. Woolworth assumed Peck's duties, but the strain proved to be too much. On April 8, 1919, Woolworth himself died. To succeed him as president, the board named Hubert T. Parson, Woolworth's first bookkeeper and later a company director and secretary-treasurer. The board also named Charles Sumner Woolworth, F.W. Woolworth's brother, chairman of the board.

Expansion continued under Parson. The company sent its first buyers to Japan in 1919. In 1924, it opened stores in Cuba. Woolworth inaugurated a German operating subsidiary in 1926, and, in 1927, opened its first German store. By the company's 50th anniversary in 1929, there were 2,247 Woolworth stores in the United States, Canada, Cuba, England, and Germany. Sales topped $303 million. In the United States, F.W. Woolworth was far and away the biggest five-and-ten retailer. Its 2,100 U.S. stores had 1929 sales of $273 million. By comparison, J.G. McCrory had about 220 stores with $40 million in sales, and S.S. Kresge had about 500 stores with $147 million in sales.

The Great Depression caused the first decline in the company's sales since 1883, reaching a low of $250 million in 1932. In 1931, the company sold off part of its British operations, allowing that subsidiary to become a public company.

Key Dates:

1879: Frank Woolworth opens his first "Great 5¢ Store" in Utica, New York.
1905: Woolworth incorporates his business as F.W. Woolworth & Co.
1912: F.W. Woolworth & Co. becomes the publicly traded F.W. Woolworth Co.; the company moves into the Woolworth Building.
1926: Woolworth inaugurates its German operating subsidiary.
1960: Sales surpass the $1 billion mark.
1962: Woolworth's opens the first Woolco.
1965: The company purchases G.R. Kinney Corporation.
1972: Woolworth and Woolco are consolidated in one division.
1974: The Kinney shoe division opens the first Foot Locker stores.
1982: Kinney's Canadian operation starts Lady Foot Locker.
1993: Woolco's operations are sold to Wal-Mart.
1997: Woolworth's closes the last of its five-and-dime stores in the United States.
1999: Woolworth's changes its name to Venator Group.

In 1932, Hubert Parsons retired and Byron D. Miller became the company's third president. Miller had worked his way up in the company and had helped start Woolworth's U.K. operations. Among Miller's first acts was to raise the ten cent price ceiling to 20 cents. Woolworth was the last five-and-ten chain to raise its prices. After three years in office, Miller retired and Charles Deyo became president. On taking office in 1935, Deyo and the board of directors removed all arbitrary price limits.

Sales turned upward during the late 1930s, but World War II posed new problems. Nearly half of Woolworth's male employees entered the Armed Forces, as did many female employees. During the war, women managed 500 stores. Demand expanded. Supplies were limited, but consumers tolerated substitutions, and because the war meant labor shortages, consumers also tolerated less service.

Prolonged Slump Following World War II

In 1946, Alfred Cornwell succeeded Deyo as president, while Deyo remained on as CEO. Under Deyo and Cornwell, Woolworth had difficulties adapting to the postwar rush of discount houses, supermarkets, and shopping centers. According to a 1965 *Dun's Review* article, "Woolworth was mired in a depression mentality. It was keeping costs down and prices low at a time when customers wanted service and when prosperity made prices a secondary consideration."

The situation began to deteriorate, and, in 1953, earnings hit a five-year low of $29.8 million. Concerned with what was happening, three board members—Allan P. Kirby, Seymour H. Knox, and Fremont C. Peck—forced Woolworth to create a new forward-looking finance and policy committee to combat what they saw as the management's overly conservative tendencies. Woolworth's British operation was having similar problems. Consumers were abandoning the stores for supermarkets and rivals such as Marks & Spencer, British Home Stores, and Littlewoods. In response, Woolworth increased the number of stores in England but did little to upgrade the existing outlets.

In 1954, James T. Leftwich became president. Leftwich addressed some of Woolworth's problems and spent $110 million to expand, modernize, and move stores. In 1956, Woolworth opened two stores in Mexico City, and, in 1957, began operations in Puerto Rico. Much was left to be done, however, under the leadership of Robert C. Kirkwood, who took over as president in 1958.

Under Kirkwood, Woolworth raised price limits and added profitable soft goods such as clothing and fabrics. Kirkwood also introduced self-service, opened hundreds of new stores, enlarged or relocated hundreds of others, and pushed Woolworth into shopping centers. Further, he increased advertising, instituted formal job training, and shortened hours and improved benefits for traditionally underpaid sales people, a move that reduced costly employee turnover from 43 percent to 19 percent.

Yet while Kirkwood was rejuvenating Woolworth, competitors such as Kresge and W.T. Grant had already overhauled their stores and were moving into new lines and new locations. Each was able to surpass Woolworth in earnings growth. In fact, while Woolworth sales surpassed $1 billion for the first time in 1960, U.S. earnings dropped from $14 million in 1960 to $12.6 million in 1963. It was only the return from British Woolworth that enabled consolidated earnings to keep moving upward. British stockholders later accused the U.S. board of milking the English operation without infusing the proper amount of capital.

Diversifying in the 1960s and 1970s

Woolworth and Kresge both sought new types of stores that would better fit the changing retail environment. In 1962, Woolworth opened the first Woolco, and S.S. Kresge opened the first Kmart. Each offered the services of a full-line department store and was very large—in some locations, more than 100,00 square feet. Woolworth had 17 Woolco stores by 1965, and as the 1960s continued, Woolworth expanded, diversified, and modernized. In 1965, it acquired the G.R. Kinney Corporation for $39 million. Founded by George Romanta Kinney in 1894, Kinney had 584 family shoe stores in 45 states. The same year, Lester A. Burcham became president of Woolworth. Under Burcham, Woolworth expanded operations into Spain and established a buying office in Tokyo. Two years later, it opened the first Woolco in England.

In 1968, sales topped $2 billion, and, in 1969, Woolworth acquired Williams the Shoemen, an Australian shoe store chain that has since become a dominant force in Australian shoe retailing with more than 460 stores ranging from high fashion to athletic and family footwear. Also in 1969, Woolworth acquired Richman Brothers Company, a manufacturer and retailer of men's and boys' clothing. Finally, as part of a 90th anniversary celebration, Woolworth replaced the old "Diamond W" logo with a modern looking white "W" on a light blue field.

Yet Woolworth was still not growing at the rate of its competitors. By 1970, sales at Kresge were running essentially neck and neck with Woolworth. One problem was British Woolworth. In 1965, Woolworth's 52.7 percent-owned subsidiary, F.W. Woolworth Ltd., had contributed 50 percent of the parent company's profits, but during the late 1960s it began a steep decline. The reasons included a lack of investment, a devaluation of the pound, and an increase in employment taxes. By 1969, the British subsidiary was contributing just 30 percent of profits. In an effort to gain market share, British management cut prices. Sales grew, but profits fell.

John S. Roberts, who became Woolworth's president in 1970, also needed to address problems at Woolco, which was performing at nowhere near the rate of Kmart. His solution was to consolidate Woolworth and Woolco in one division in 1972. Rather than providing economies, however, the consolidation only blurred the identity of each chain. Woolworth's 1973 sales were $3.7 billion; Kresge's were $4.6 billion, 90 percent of which was generated by Kmart. A positive event occurred, however, in 1974, when the Kinney shoe division opened the first two Foot Locker stores, athletic-shoe retailers that would later prove highly profitable.

With stock prices on the wane, the board recognized the need for change, and, in 1975, named outsider Edward F. Gibbons president. Gibbons in turn named W. Robert Harris the first president of the U.S. Woolworth and Woolco Division. In 1978, consolidated annual sales topped $6 billion, of which Kinney, growing at a rate of 18 to 20 percent a year, contributed $800 million. Also in 1978, Harris became president and Gibbons became chief executive officer.

Juggling of Store Lineup in 1980s and Early 1990s

While Woolco continued its sluggish growth and Woolworth stores suffered neglect, F.W. Woolworth Co. continued diversifying. In 1979, Woolworth opened the first J. Brannam, a men's clothing store whose name stood for "just brand names." J. Brannam was a quick moneymaker and often stood within or beside otherwise lackluster Woolco department stores. No matter how much the management tinkered, the problems of Woolco refused to go away. After the stores lost $19 million in 1981, Harris and Gibbons hired Bruce G. Albright to revive the ailing chain. Albright, who had come from competitor Dayton Hudson's Target stores, had a plan to revive Woolco, but company projections still saw the stores losing money. After Woolco lost $21 million during the first six months of 1982, Gibbons decided to shut down all 336 Woolcos in the United States, shrinking the $7.2 billion company 30 percent and laying off 25,000 employees. Closing costs were estimated at $325 million.

In the fall of 1982, Woolworth disclosed plans to sell its interest in British Woolworth to a syndicate of English investors, for $279 million. One analyst, quoted in *Business Week*, October 11, 1982, blamed British Woolworth's failure on the U.S. parent, saying, "The American Woolworth has been milking the British unit for years, insisting on high dividend payout that has forced it to scrimp on investment and to take on more and more debt."

Analysts, however, were pleased with the company that remained. Left were the profitable, but shaky, 1,300 variety stores, Richman Brothers, and Kinney Shoe Corporation—a $1.1 billion division that had done well with Kinney, Foot Locker, a women's clothing store known as Susie's Casuals, and the newly created and profitable J. Brannam. Woolco's closing, however, left 28 of the 41 J. Brannam outlets homeless.

Edward F. Gibbons died suddenly in October 1982. Contrary to expectations and much to the chagrin of younger talent, the board named company veteran John W. (Bud) Lynn chief executive officer. As a variety store man, Lynn paid close attention to Woolworth's. He changed merchandise, reducing the number of high-priced items such as appliances and dresses and expanding basic lines like candy, and health and beauty aids. He arranged stores in arrow patterns to cut down on unprofitable corners.

Lynn pushed the company to adopt a set of strategic priorities that angled Woolworth away from money-losing businesses and toward specialty retailing. Kinney's Canadian operation had started the remarkably successful Lady Foot Locker in 1982, and in 1983 Woolworth paid $27 million for Holtzman's Little Folk Shop, a full-price children's clothing merchandiser and its subsidiary, Kids Mart, a discount operation.

Lynn retired in 1987, and the board named Harold Sells as the new chief executive officer. Sells continued to push Woolworth's profitable mall-based specialty operations. Managers sought out new ideas for stores, and those that the company liked were tried. If the stores were profitable, Woolworth's opened more. If they were not profitable, the company tried another idea at the same location.

In 1990, Woolworth opened 896 stores and closed 351. Many of the new ventures were specialty stores, such as Kinneys, Kids Marts, Foot Lockers, and Lady Foot Lockers. The latter two sold a full 20 percent of all brand-name athletic footwear in the United States in the late 1980s. The 40 types of specialty stores included After Thoughts, seller of costume jewelry and handbags; Champs, seller of athletic goods and apparel; and Woolworth Express, seller of the fastest-moving goods of a traditional Woolworth.

In 1993, Sells retired and was replaced as by CFO William Lavin, who quickly made moves toward the elimination of the company's general merchandise stores in favor of an exclusive focus on specialty formats. Four hundred Woolworth's were closed in the United States, and 122 Woolco stores in Canada were sold to Wal-Mart, terminating Woolco altogether. Woolworth also sold 300 underperforming Kinney outlets and liquidated the 286-store Richman Brothers/Anderson-Little men's and women's clothing stores. Along with the nearly 1,000 stores, about 13,000 jobs were eliminated. As a result of these moves, the company recorded a $558 million charge resulting in a net 1993 loss of $495 million.

These radical moves were barely complete when an accounting scandal arose in early 1994, revolving around alleged false reporting of quarterly results during 1993. Several lawsuits were filed which were eventually combined into a class-action lawsuit. This suit appeared to be settled by mid-1997 when Woolworth agreed to make undisclosed cash payments to affected shareholders. Later in 1994, Lavin was forced out, and Roger Farah became chairman and CEO in December 1994.

Rebuilding in the Late 1990s

Farah, a longtime department store manager who had most recently been president of R.H. Macy & Co., took over a Woolworth in shambles. Thanks to dwindling profits, by early 1995, the company was nearly out of cash, and short-term debt had swelled to $853 million. Consequently, Farah's first task was to improve cash flow in 1995. To do so, he broke Woolworth's string of 83 straight years of dividends; restructured company debt, reducing total debt by $475 million and shifting $290 million of short-term debt to longer-term financing; reduced operating spending by $100 million; wrote off $241 million of inventory; and began to sell off nonstrategic chains and real estate. Early in 1995, Woolworth sold the Rx Place chain of pharmacies for $37 million and the 331 Kids Mart/ Little Folks children's clothing stores to the LFS Acquisition investor group for $15 million. Two other Canadian chains, Karuba and Canary Island, were also closed during the year. The various charges incurred as a result of these actions led to a net loss of $164 million.

In 1996, Woolworth continued to restructure. Short-term debt was eliminated altogether, and total debt was reduced an additional $116 million. Another $100 million in operating spending was eliminated, and $222 million in cash was generated from the disposal of additional nonstrategic chains and real estate. Among the divestments were the Accessory Lady chain in the United States; the Silk & Satin lingerie chain in Canada; the Lady Plus apparel chain, the Rubin jewelry chain, the Moderna shoe store chain, and the New Yorker Süud jeans business, all in Germany; and the Gallery shoe store chain in Australia. All told, 1,443 unproductive stores were disposed of in 1995 and 1996.

In the midst of these moves, institutional investor Greenway Partners forced to a vote a shareholder proposal to spin off Woolworth's Athletic Group, which included the profitable and growing Foot Locker and Champs chains. However, the plan was soundly defeated. Unlike his predecessor, Farah was not ready to give up on the neglected Woolworth's chain. To better monitor and plan sales, point-of-sale equipment was installed at all locations in 1995, and purchasing, pricing policies, and promotional strategies were all centralized. He assembled a management team of veterans of successful high volume specialty stores and streamlined merchandising systems.

In 1996, the chain began testing new formats featuring higher-quality (and higher-priced) merchandise, with more brand names. Based on customer surveys, the prototype stores were aimed at the time-pressed and budget-minded working woman looking for products for herself, her home, and her family. So, rather than carrying everything from hamsters to beach chairs, the product mix included more cosmetics and housewares. The antiquated lunch counters were replaced by small coffee bars. The three-store 1996 test was successful enough to justify an expansion of the test to 13 more stores in 1997.

Overall, Woolworth's fortunes improved in the late 1990s, as the company posted a net profit of $169 million in 1996. The company appeared to be on track with the paring back of its unwieldy portfolio of retail formats. Farah began piecing together a sporting goods conglomerate on the foundation of Foot Locker and Champs Sports, acquiring the operations of Sporting Goods, Athletic Fibers, and Eastbay Inc., a Wausau, Wisconsin-based catalog company specializing in athletic footwear. Woolworth and Eastbay planned to develop catalogs for such Woolworth retail brands as Foot Locker and Champs.

Nevertheless, in a telling psychological blow, Woolworth was replaced by Wal-Mart on the Dow Jones Industrial Average in 1997. The chain experienced a $24 million operating loss for the first quarter as compared to a loss of $37 million for all of 1996. Unable to withstand such hemorrhaging long enough to turn the chain around, Woolworth announced on July 17, 1997, that it would close its more than 400 five-and-dime stores in the United States, lay off about 9,200 Woolworth's workers (about 11 percent of the company's workforce), and take a $223 million charge for the discontinued operations. The company planned to convert about 100 of the Woolworth's locations to Foot Locker, Champs Sports, and other specialty formats. Although the Woolworth's chain had seen the final chapter written on its history in the United States, the chain's saga would continue in Mexico and Germany, where about 700 of the five-and-dimes still operated. The German stores were sold off in 1998.

The company also announced that it planned to change its name, according to company literature, "to better reflect its global specialty retailing formats." The new corporate name, the Venator Group, inspired by the Latin word for sportsman, was intended to describe "a global team of retailers . . . invigorated by the challenge of winning in the world's marketplace." In preparation for the change, the company spent more than $130 million to streamline merchandising and back office operations. Over the next three years, it went on to spend another $149 million to redesign the architecture of its information systems for the development of an integrated global retailing approach. In the United States, the Venator Group established 719 such stores and remodeled 582 in 1998. It simultaneously debuted its web site, which featured virtual stores selling athletic footwear, equipment, apparel and accessories from the various Foot Lockers, Champs Sports, and Eastbay lines.

Unfortunately the retailing environment for athletic footwear had become difficult during this time, as consumer tastes shifted to street shoes, fleece, and denim. Foot Locker, as the largest athletic specialty store, while not alone in missing the shift, was more affected by it than its smaller competitors. The Venator Group, under the direction of president and chief executive officer Dale Hilpert since late 1999, responded by expanding its catalog and e-commerce interests, by exiting eight of its non-core businesses, and by closing stores and slashing jobs. The cutbacks continued into January 2000 when Venator announced the closing of 123 Foot Locker, Lady Foot Locker, and Kids Foot Locker stores, 27 Champs Sports units, and 208 Northern Group stores. Venator also began to consolidate the managements of Kids and Lady Foot Lockers concepts into one organization and to reduce expenses and workforce.

By the second half of 1999, Venator Group began to generate significant same-store sales gains, fueled by growth in the high-end footwear category. The company experienced a small increase in comparable-store sales, and its athletic stores gained in market share in 1999. In addition, the direct-to-customer business enacted via Footlocker.com enjoyed a 21.9 percent increase in business that year. By spring 2000, shoe sales throughout the industry were showing signs of rebounding. With 17 percent of the $14 billion U.S. athletic footwear market, 3,700 athletic retail stores in 14 countries, $3.8 billion in annual sales, and significant opportunities in the global market, the Venator Group was looking forward to gaining market share through increased productivity at its retail stores and through its catalog and Internet businesses.

Principal Operating Units

Global Athletic Group; Northern Group.

Principal Competitors

The Sports Authority, Inc.; The Finish Line, Inc.; Just For Feet, Inc.

Further Reading

"Arsenal Mall in Watertown," *Chain Store Age Executive*, July 1998, p.1.

Berman, Phyllis, and Caroline Waxler, "Woolworth's Woes," *Forbes*, August 14, 1995, pp. 47–48.

Biesada, Alexandra, "Dumping on the Dime Store," *Financial World*, October 30, 1990, p. 62.

Bird, Laura, "Hamsters Get Heave-Ho in New Five-and-Tens," *Wall Street Journal*, September 26, 1996, pp. B1, B10.

——, "Woolworth Corp. to Post a Charge and Cut 9,200 Jobs," *Wall Street Journal*, July 18, 1997, p. C16.

——, "Woolworth Is Hoping to Score in Sportswear," *Wall Street Journal*, March 12, 1997, pp. B1, B6.

Bongiorno, Lori, "Lost in the Aisles at Woolworth's," *Business Week*, October 30, 1995, pp. 76, 78.

Gill, Penny, "Sells: Key Player in Woolworth Renaissance," *Stores*, May 1991, p. 24.

Miller, Annetta, "A Dinosaur No More: Woolworth Corp. Leaves Dime Stores Far Behind," *Newsweek*, January 4, 1993, pp. 54–55.

Nichols, John P., *Skyline Queen and the Merchant Prince*, New York: Pocket Books, 1973.

100th Anniversary, 1879–1979, New York: F.W. Woolworth Co., 1979.

Saporito, Bill, "Woolworth to Rule the Malls," *Fortune*, June 5, 1989, p. 145.

Winkler, John K., *Five and Ten: The Fabulous Life of F.W. Woolworth*, Freeport, N.Y.: Books for Libraries Press, 1970 (reprint of 1940 edition).

Woolworth's First 75 Years: The Story of Everybody's Store, New York: F.W. Woolworth Co., 1954.

Young, Vicki M., "Venator Accused of Ageism," *HFN*, July 12, 1999, p. 8.

Zinn, Laura, "Why 'Business Stinks' at Woolworth," *Business Week*, November 25, 1991, pp. 72, 76.

—Jordan Wankoff
—updated by David E. Salamie and Carrie Rothburd

Verlagsgruppe Georg von Holtzbrinck GmbH

Gänsheidestrasse 26
D-70184 Stuttgart
Germany
Telephone: (49)(711) 2150-0
Fax: (49)(711) 2150-269
Web site: http://www.holtzbrinck.com/

Private Company
Incorporated: 1948 as Stuttgarter Hausbücherei
Employees: 11,500
Sales: DM 4.14 billion ($2.11 billion) (1999)
NAIC: 51113 Book Publishers; 51112 Periodical
 Publishers; 51111 Newspaper Publishers; 323119
 Other Commercial Printing; 323121 Tradebinding and
 Related Work; 551112 Offices of Other Holding
 Companies

Verlagsgruppe Georg von Holtzbrinck GmbH is the holding company for Germany's fourth largest publishing and media conglomerate. More than 80 companies active in the fields of book publishing, magazine and newspaper publishing, book printing, and new media belong to the group. The British Macmillan Ltd., the German publishing houses S. Fischer and Rowohlt, and the U.S. St. Martin's Press are some of the most prominent members of the Holtzbrinck family of publishers. Periodicals published by the Holtzbrinck group include the German business and investment magazines *Wirtschaftswoche* and *DM*, Germany's only daily business and finance newspaper *Handelsblatt*, the German weekly newspaper *DIE ZEIT,* and the German daily newspaper *Der Tagesspiegel*. In *Scientific American* and *nature*, Holtzbrinck owns two of the world's leading science magazines, while through the Verlagsgruppe Handelsblatt, Holtzbrinck has a 49 percent stake in *The Wall Street Journal Europe*. The group also owns business databases, online services, TV production companies, and 27.4 percent of Germany's business TV channel n-tv. Holtzbrinck's Internet holdings are organized under the umbrella of the holtzbrinck networXs AG. The Verlagsgruppe Georg von Holtzbrinck is owned by the three heirs of the founder.

1948–71: Book Club Grows into Publishing Group

Georg von Holtzbrinck, the founder of the publishing group, was born in 1909. After graduating from law school, he became involved in the book trade. In 1937 he took over the Bibliothek der Unterhaltung und des Wissens (Library of Entertainment and Knowledge), a German book club founded in 1876 and based in Stuttgart. In 1948 Holtzbrinck transformed the firm into the Stuttgarter Hausbücherei, which became the breeding ground for his empire. The book club's name was changed again in 1959 to Deutscher Bücherbund.

Holtzbrinck next ventured into book publishing, acquiring the renowned S. Fischer Verlag in 1963. Fischer was founded in Berlin in 1886 and after World War II had been re-established in Frankfurt am Main. Such famous European authors of contemporary literature as Theodor Fontane, Henrik Ibsen, Thomas Mann, Virginia Woolf, Sigmund Freud, Thornton Wilder, Boris Pasternak, Arthur Miller, Nadine Gordimer, and more were published by S. Fischer. Moreover, its paperback publishing arm, the Fischer Bücherei, included an extensive range of works in literature, entertainment, and science, as well as encyclopedias and the collected works of respected authors.

Between 1968 and 1971 Holtzbrinck bought stakes in more book publishing houses and ventured into the realm of periodicals. On the book side, he bought a 49 percent stake in Munich-based Kindler Verlag, publisher of large encyclopedias, biographies, art books, and books on politics and current events; a 26 percent share in the Ernst Rowohlt Verlag based near Hamburg, the publisher of such well-known authors as Hemingway, Updike, and Sartre, and which owned a majority share in the printing firm Clausen & Bosse; and 46 percent in Droemer Knaur, another Munich-based book publisher with a reputation for high quality fiction, contemporary nonfiction and political subjects, popular science, and lavishly illustrated titles.

In 1968 Holtzbrinck bought into the periodicals market with a 50 percent stake in the Verlagsgruppe Handelsblatt, which was founded in 1946, based on a license the British military government issued to publish in Dusseldorf a daily newspaper on business and finance. Holtzbrinck also invested in the Saarbrücker Zeitung, the only daily newspaper in the German

Company Perspectives:

Since its founding 1971 the publishing group has followed and further developed company principles that are the guidelines for all its strategic and operative activities. Among these guidelines are an absolute orientation on quality and the extensive concentration on upper-level target groups; a profit orientation that must nonetheless not compromise quality and long-term stability; solid financing that ensures the independence of the family business; and disciplined self-restriction on the part of the family members in regards to money and influence. The publishing group is organized in a decentralized manner with minimal hierarchy. The different companies, which are managed close to the actual markets by local managers, are thereby able to profit from the advantages of a flexible mid-sized company as well as the financial resources and expertise of a big player.

State Saarland, when the paper was reprivatized in 1970. To organize all of Holtzbrinck's holdings under one umbrella, the management holding company Verlagsgruppe Georg von Holtzbrinck was founded in 1971.

1972–83: The Book and Newspaper Conglomerate Grows

By 1980 the Holtzbrinck group owned 100 percent of the publishers Droemer and Kindler and 80 percent of the Verlagsgruppe Handelsblatt. The latter was on its way to becoming the leading publisher of business periodicals and information in Germany. After it merged with its main competitor *Industriekurier* in 1970, the *Handelsblatt* became Germany's number one daily business and finance newspaper.

Ongoing efforts to improve editorial content also helped push up circulation. In the late 1960s the *Handelsblatt* had a circulation of about 30,000 on trading days. By the mid-1980s it circulated more than 100,000 copies. Verlagsgruppe Handelsblatt also published Germany's only weekly business magazine, *Wirtschaftswoche,* which grew out of a predecessor, *Der Deutsche Volkswirt (German Economist),* founded in 1926. In 1977 Verlagsgruppe Handelsblatt bought the monthly magazine *DM* which was redesigned as a business magazine targeting private investors and consumers. Two years later Holtzbrinck acquired 25 percent of the daily paper *Südkurier,* which covered the southern German areas around Lake Constance, the Black Forest, and the Upper Rhine, and a 40 percent stake in the Ulm-based printing operation Franz Spiegel Buch GmbH.

Until he died in 1983 Georg von Holtzbrinck managed his conglomerate from a hilltop headquarters in Stuttgart. Before his death, the founder gave equal shares in his enterprise to each of his three children: Monika Schoeller, who had been CEO of the S. Fischer Verlag since 1974, Dieter von Holtzbrinck, who was responsible for the Verlagsgruppe Handelsblatt, and Stefan von Holtzbrinck, a son from an extramarital relationship whom father Georg later adopted in 1975. The only exception to the equal shares was the Verlagsgruppe Handelsblatt, in which Dieter von Holtzbrinck received a majority stake of 55 percent. To protect

the company's independence as a family business, three family trusts were set up. Each trust was headed by two directors, one of them from outside the Holtzbrinck family. The six directors then formed a supervisory board and elected a seventh director who was also required to be from outside the family.

Holtzbrinck Goes English in 1986

After his father died, Dieter von Holtzbrinck was elected the new CEO by the supervisory board. After having graduated with a university degree in economics, Dieter von Holtzbrinck left the small world he grew up in and went to New York City for a few years. There, working for McGraw Hill, he got his first experience in book publishing. In 1970 he joined the management team of the Handelsblatt Verlagsgruppe in Dusseldorf; ten years later he was the group CEO. When Dieter von Holtzbrinck took over the company he decided to make some major changes. He did not believe the book club business had a future and thus sold the Deutsche Büchergemeinschaft for DM 250 million to Leo Kirch, another German media giant, in 1989. He then extended the range of the company's business publications by offering information services. In 1986 he took over the business information database GENIOS and integrated it into the Verlagsgruppe Handelsblatt. Holtzbrinck also bought a majority share of the Swiss economic research institute Prognos AG in 1990.

At the same time, Dieter von Holtzbrinck was the driving force behind the Holtzbrinck group's expansion into the English language marketplace. Like his father, he favored high quality publishing over pulp and tabloids publishing, long-term profitability over short-term gains, and the independence of his publishers from strict management at Stuttgart headquarters. This business policy made the Holtzbrinck company attractive to publishers who were looking for a strong financial partner but were not willing to give up their independence as entrepreneurs completely. In 1986 Holtzbrinck acquired *Scientific American*, the oldest magazine in the United States, for $52.6 million. The scholarly magazine had experienced a significant decrease in ad sales and circulation, and several big publishers bid for the reputable publication, among them Time Inc., The Economist Newspapers Ltd., and British Printing and Communications Corp. (BPC). Although BPC offered $61 million, Scientific American's board of directors went for Holtzbrinck's offer, which included an agreement not to make any changes in management. Other acquisitions in the scientific field followed: W.H. Freeman, a college and science book publisher, Hanley & Belfus, a publisher of medical titles, and undergraduate college textbook publisher Worth. Another Holtzbrinck acquisition in the United States was Henry Holt & Co., one of the oldest American publishers.

In October 1994, 77-year old New York publisher Roger W. Straus sold his business Farrar, Straus & Giroux to Holtzbrinck. Farrar, Straus & Giroux had built an impressive author portfolio, including international bestselling authors such as Susan Sontag, Tom Wolfe, and Scott Turow, and 19 Nobel price laureates such as Nadine Gordimer and Derek Walcott. In addition to literary fiction, the company also published nonfiction and books for children. All told, Holtzbrinck invested some DM 550 million in American acquisitions between 1985 and 1999.

Another major deal was sealed in 1995 when for DM 600 million Holtzbrinck acquired a 71.1 percent stake in Macmillan

& Co. Ltd., the renowned British publishing group with $385 million annual sales. The deal included the U.S. publisher St. Martin's Press based in New York, one of the ten largest general publishers in the United States and the division that generated over 40 percent of Macmillan's revenues. Macmillan was a 150-year-old family business and the largest independent publishing group in Great Britain with over 2,000 employees and subsidiaries in about 20 countries including Australia, South Africa, Mexico, Japan, and India. The Macmillan shares had been put for sale when the family's trustees were required to spread out ownership of the family estate. Macmillan published general fiction and nonfiction, academic and professional reference books, and the international science magazine *Nature*.

Because Macmillan's management put a high value on high quality publishing, a decentralized organization and independence of its subsidiaries, Holtzbrinck and Macmillan were a perfect match. Holtzbrinck's majority in Macmillan pushed the group's foreign sales up from 12 to 30 percent of the total DM 2.2 billion. After the acquisition, Holtzbrinck's management structure was changed to reflect the importance of the deal. Beginning in January 1996 the supervisory board of the Holtzbrinck group was enlarged to include two Macmillan managers. One of Macmillan's most prestigious projects to date was completed in the same year. After beginning work on the project in 1982, the *Dictionary of Art*, a 34-volume reference in art history to which no fewer than 6,800 scholars had contributed, was published in 1996.

In the midst of such global expansion, Holtzbrinck faced some serious challenges on the homefront, when the German media group Axel Springer called for an investigation into Holtzbrinck and the German Kirch Group. German law at that time did not allow a private television station to be owned or dominated by a single party. Holtzbrinck had invested in the first private German

TV channel, called Sat.1, and later sold its shares to Kirch. In short, Axel Springer accused Dieter von Holtzbrinck of acting as a front for media mogul Leo Kirch. Springer accused Kirch and Holtzbrinck of having a secret agreement that gave Holtzbrinck's voting rights to Kirch; of planning that Sat.1 productions should be almost exclusively produced by Kirch subsidiary PKS and Holtzbrinck subsidiary AVE; and of agreeing that Kirch would reimburse Holtzbrinck for possible losses from Sat.1 activities. The LPR, a state agency overseeing the private media, conducted an investigation, but the whole situation eased in 1997 when a new German law went into effect allowing media groups to own a majority share in private TV stations. By then, Holtzbrinck's shares in Sat.1 were sold to Leo Kirch and its 14.5 percent share of the infotainment TV channel VOX were sold to the Bertelsmann Group.

The Late 1990s: New Media, New Management

The second half of the 1990s brought more major acquisitions in the field of print media. In February 1995 Dietrich Herbst, CEO of Frankfurt-based schoolbook publisher Verlag Moritz Diesterweg, with a nine percent market share in Germany, announced that he would join the Holtzbrinck group. In December 1995 the owner of one of the largest trade book publishers in Switzerland, Rudolf Streit-Scherz, announced that he too would sell his Scherz Verlag to the Holtzbrinck group by July 1996. Also in 1996 Holtzbrinck bought the highly respected German weekly newspaper *DIE ZEIT* for DM 140 million. In early 1999 Holtzbrinck merged some of its publishing arms with the Augsburg-based publisher Weltbild, originally a magazine publisher owned by the Catholic Church whose annual sales skyrocketed in the late 1990s and passed the DM 1 billion mark in 1998 for the first time. The new holding company was called Verlagsgruppe Droemer Weltbild in which both partners held 50 percent. While Holtzbrinck was interested in getting access to Weltbild's distribution channels (over 100 Weltbild book store outlets and a 3.5 million customer mail-order database), Weltbild was interested in getting access to Holtzbrinck's list of high quality titles. In November 1998 German publisher of American author Don DeLillo and owner of German publishing house Kiepenheuer & Witsch, Reinhold Neven, announced that Holtzbrinck would become a minority shareholder of his firm.

By the end of 1998 Holtzbrinck's sales were twice as high as those of a decade earlier: DM 3.64 billion with gross profits of about DM 300 million. Germany's *Managermagazin* noted that no other German media group had grown so fast. The acquisition of *DIE ZEIT* had pushed up the Holtzbrinck group from number seven to number four in total sales among German publishers. Holtzbrinck dominated the German book market and the market for business information. However, new acquisitions and the cost of integrating them into the group had cost Holtzbrinck DM 1.39 billion between 1991 and 1997. The Berlin newspaper *Tagesspiegel*, a Holtzbrinck acquisition from 1993, kept struggling in the red, and Dieter von Holtzbrinck did not expect the newspaper to break even much before 2005. Since it had been taken over by Holtzbrinck, *DIE ZEIT* lost five percent of its almost 500,000 readers. The book business was sluggish, and intensified competition put pressure on profit margins. Even in business-publishing, Holtzbrinck's cash cow, competitors were challenging the group's leading position. German publisher Gruner + Jahr, together with Brisith publisher Pearson, was planning to publish a German version of the *Financial Times*.

In addition, Holtzbrinck headquarters found itself understaffed to deal with its new holdings; for years it had been run by around 50 people (four executive managers, a dozen controllers, and administrative assistants), and suddenly that staff was overseeing about 50 subsidiaries with more than 10,000 employees. Thus, in January 1999 four vice-executive manager positions were filled in Stuttgart, more support staff was hired, and tasks were reallocated. In the United States Holtzbrinck invested $57 million in information technology and distribution, including a $30 million automated distribution center in Gordonsville, Virginia, which cut shipping and return processing time down to less than a week.

To defend its leading position in the profitable market for business information Holtzbrinck partnered with long-term American affiliate Dow Jones & Company to plan a new weekly business title. In 1994 Verlagsgruppe Handelsblatt and Dow Jones had taken over German business news agency Vereinigte Wirtschaftsdienste (VWD) and Czech publisher Economia. Since November 1995 the two companies had coordinated their strategies and cooperated in marketing of advertising and their electronic databases Genios and Dow Jones News Retrieval. In June 1999 Holtzbrinck and Dow Jones announced a strategic alliance and swapped shares of their business newspapers. Holtzbrinck assumed 49 percent of the *Wall Street Journal Europe,* while Dow Jones received 22 percent of *Handelsblatt*. While Holtzbrinck's goal was to open up new European markets to the *Handelsblatt,* Dow Jones aimed at broadening the German readership for the *Wall Street Journal Europe*. While both periodicals were expected to stay independent, an intensification of the exchange of content, and cooperation in ad sales and distribution was planned.

Holtzbrinck's New Media department, founded in 1995, included computer book, software, and CD-ROM publisher Systhema Verlag; the American Voyager Company; and various radio and TV shareholdings. In April 2000 all of Holtzbrinck's Internet shareholdings were organized into a new holding company, the holtzbrinck networXs AG, with headquarters in Munich. The new company included shares of 25 percent or more in Infoseek Germany, Booxtra, Xipolis, e-fellows, Jobline, Newtron, The Motley Fool Germany, and Immowelt. Holtzbrinck planned to go public by 2001 and extend its Internet holdings to about 30.

After some changes in Holtzbrinck's management Dieter von Holtzbrinck remained responsible for group strategy. He told German *managermagazin* that he had never been a fond of the shareholder value principle, believing that striving for profits must remain second to quality and long-term stability. To ensure the necessary stream of new talent for his expanding group that would uphold his standards of quality, Holtzbrinck educated 15 would-be business journalists a year at his own school, the Georg-von-Holtzbrinck-Schule für Wirtschaftsjournalisten in Dusseldorf, as well as about 100 young multimedia specialists annually in another special training firm, Munich-based Activ-Consult. In the meantime, Holtzbrinck's potential successor, stepbrother Stefan von Holtzbrinck, was preparing to join Stuttgart headquarters, as CEO of Holtzbrinck subsidiary Macmillan Magazines.

Principal Subsidiaries

Verlagsgruppe Handelsblatt GmbH; S.Fischer Verlag GmbH; Fischer Taschenbuch Verlag GmbH; Rohwolt Verlag GmbH; Rohwolt Tachenbuch Verlag GmbH; Zeitverlag Gerd Bucerius GmbH & Co.; Verlag Der Tagesspiegel GmbH; AVE Gesellschaft für Fernsehproduktion mbH; AVE Gesellschaft für Hörfunkbeteiligungen mbH; Clausen & Bosse GmbH; holtzbrinck networXs AG; Franz Spiegel Buch GmbH (66.5%); Verlagsgruppe Droemer Weltbild Verwaltungsgesellschaft mbH (50%); Verlag Kiepenheuer & Witsch GmbH & Co. KG (45%); n-tv Nachrichtenfernsehen (27.8%); Henry Holt & Company, Inc. (United States); Farrar, Straus & Giroux, Inc. (United States); Scientific American, Inc. (United States); Macmillan Limited (United Kingdom); St. Martin's Press, Inc. (United States); The Wall Street Journal Europe (Belgium; 49%); Prognos AG (Switzerland).

Principal Competitors

Axel Springer Verlag AG; Bertelsmann AG; WAZ Gruppe; Kirch Gruppe AG.

Further Reading

Auffermann, Verena, ''Fuß in der Tür—Holtzbrinck beteiligt sich am Kiepenheuer & Witsch Verlag,'' *Süddeutsche Zeitung,* November 3, 1998.

Boldt, Klaus, ''Der Mann hinter der Zeit,'' *managermagazin* (online edition), April 1999.

''Der Club der heimlichen Herrscher,'' *Werben und Verkaufen,* April 11, 1997, p. 34.

''Die Holtzbrinck-Gruppe will die Wochenzeitung 'Die Zeit' kaufen,'' *Frankfurter Allgemeine Zeitung,* April 27, 1996, p. 16.

''Die Medienriesen von Rhein und Ruhr,'' *Werben und Verkaufen,* October 29, 1993, p. 78.

Herrera, Stephan, ''Where's Holtzbrinck?,'' *Forbes,* June 1, 1998, p. 88.

''Holtzbrinck und Weltbild ruecken zusammen,'' *Frankfurter Allgemeine Zeitung,* September 26, 1998, p. 19.

''It's Official: FSG to Join Holtzbrinck,'' *Publishers Weekly,* November 7, 1994, p. 13.

Lottman, Herbert R., ''How Dieter von Holtzbrinck Manages His World Group—By Leaving Publishers Alone,'' *Publishers Weekly,* December 4, 1995, p. 40.

Milliot, Jim, ''Sargent, Grisebach Rise at Von Holtzbrinck,'' *Publishers Weekly,* February 2, 1998, p. 16.

Olden, Christian, ''Holtzbrinck mit 'Tagesspiegel','' *HORIZONT,* August 28, 1992, p. 6.

Ott, Klaus, ''Ziehen Kirch und Holtzbrinck an einem Strang?,'' *Süddeutsche Zeitung,* August 12, 1993.

Pauker, Manuela, ''Der stille Riese schlaeft nicht,'' *Werben und Verkaufen,* April 12, 1996, p. 10.

Richardson, Jean, ''Holtzbrinck Buys Out Macmillan Family,'' *Publishers Weekly,* October 25, 1999, p. 12.

''Science Field Undergoes Metamorphosis,'' *Folio: The Magazine for Magazine Management,* September 1986, p. 63.

''Selling by the Book,'' *Mergers & Acquisitions International,* April 24, 1995, p. 13.

Spiegel, Hubert, ''Die Sehnsucht der Giganten,'' *Frankfurter Allgemeine Zeitung,* October 6, 1998. p. 1.

Barber, Tony, and Richard Waters, ''Dow Jones in Share Swap with German Group,'' *Financial Times,* June 2, 1999, p. 24.

—Evelyn Hauser

WACKER

Wacker-Chemie GmbH

Hanns-Seidel-Platz 4
D-81737 München
Germany
Telephone: (49)(89) 6279-01
Fax: (49) (89) 6279-1770
Web site: http://www.wacker.com

Jointly Owned by Hoechst AG and Dr. Alexander
Wacker Familiengesellschaft mbH
Incorporated: 1914
Employees: 16,220
Sales: DM 4.86 billion ($2.48 billion) (1999)
NAIC: 325211 Plastics Material and Resin
  Manufacturing; 325212 Synthetic Rubber
  Manufacturing; 334413 Semiconductor and Related
  Device Manufacturing; 325199 All Other Basic
  Organic Chemical Manufacturing; 325188 All Other
  Basic Inorganic Chemical Manufacturing

Wacker-Chemie GmbH is a worldwide leader in the manufacture of specialty chemicals. It is the world's second largest manufacturer of silicone carbide and number three among the manufacturers of silicone wafers for integrated circuits. Headquartered in Munich, Germany, the company also produces basic organic and inorganic chemicals and materials including catalysts, polymers, and sealants. About one-third of Wacker's sales come from its semiconductor's division; a quarter is generated by the polymers division; 37 percent derive from the silicones division; and about five percent come from the materials division. Wacker-Chemie has over 60 subsidiaries around the world, with manufacturing plants throughout Europe, the United States, and Asia. Descendants of the Wacker family own 50 percent of the company.

The Late 1800s: Wacker and Schuckert
Start a Business

The origins of Wacker Chemie may be traced to Alexander Wacker, who was born in 1846 in the German city of Heidel-

berg. As a young man Wacker hoped to attend a university but ended up apprenticing as a clerk in the textile industry. The business skills he learned there would prove an important asset when he met Sigmund Schuckert in 1877.

Schuckert, a gifted mechanic, had invented a flat ring dynamo machine that transformed water power into electricity. Together, Wacker and Schuckert started a business partnership at Schuckert's Nuremberg workshop. While Schuckert ran the workshop, Alexander Wacker oversaw the business, which employed 12 assistants and three apprentices. As a result of Wacker's successful marketing efforts, S. Schuckert & Co. grew rapidly. By 1885 the company employed 46 clerks and 228 workers. The company's dynamos powered Munich's first electric tram line which started service in 1886.

Along with such dynamic growth came financial pressures, and Alexander Wacker decided to take the company to the next level. In 1892 he reorganized the company as the Elektrizitäts AG, vormals Schuckert & Co. The same year his partner Sigmund Schuckert retired, and Wacker became managing director. Within only ten years, the so-called "Schuckertwerke" had earned a worldwide reputation. By 1902 the company had 7,413 workers and 1,082 clerks on its payroll. Its employees worked in 36 branches and technical offices in Germany. In addition to that, the Elektrizitäts AG set up a worldwide sales network.

In 1902 Wacker started a new venture of his own. Backed with financial support from a friend, he bought out the electrochemical side of the Schuckert business, specifically its carbide factories. Together with three business partners—Bosnian Bosnische Elektrizitäts AG, Swiss Lonza AG, and Norwegian Aktieselkabet Hafslund—he formed a new company for the production of carbide. One year later Wacker transformed the electrochemical laboratory he had founded before the turn of the century into the Consortium für elektrochemische Industrie, an independent limited liability company. The Consortium became the central research lab for the new group of chemical companies which were all shareholders in the facility. Alexander Wacker defined its goal as the development of technologies for the industrial use of acetylene, which made him a pioneer in acetylene chemistry. Acetylene would become one of the most important basic chemicals until well into the 1960s when its

Company Perspectives:

Wacker-Chemie's Policy for Quality, Safety and Environmental Protection: All our employees share the responsibility for quality, safety and environmental protection, as well as for ongoing improvements in these areas. We guarantee the safe handling of products and residues in our manufacturing processes. We minimize resource and energy consumption, emissions and waste. Worldwide, we supply only products where transport, application and disposal are safe and environmentally compatible. We are continually expanding our knowledge about the environmental compatibility of our traditional and new products, taking measures that incorporate any new insights into environmental protection and safety. We intend to convince suppliers to adopt our standards for quality, safety and environmental protection. We insist that all contractual partners working at Wacker-Chemie locations adhere to our guidelines. We attach utmost importance to ongoing safety improvements at our production sites, particularly plant and workplace safety and health safeguards. We take proactive measures to eliminate potential risks. We practice effective risk management. We create and promote a climate of mutual trust through open, continuous dialog with our employees, customers and suppliers, as well as with our neighbors, the authorities and the general public.

place was taken by petrolchemistry. The Consortium was a breeding ground for numerous patents.

Around 1907, Alexander Wacker took the next steps in his career as a businessman. He tested Bavarian rivers for their potential as an energy source in order to secure a supply of sustainable energy for the energy-intensive production of basic chemicals. He also researched the best location for a new carbide plant. Finally, he purchased a property in the Burghausen forest on the banks of the Bavarian river Salzach. Two months after Germany declared war on Russia, in 1914, Alexander Wacker registered the first enterprise of his own under the name Dr. Alexander Wacker, Gesellschaft für elektrochemische Industrie KG, eventually shortened to Wacker-Chemie.

Finally, at age 70, he completed what he had dreamed of for most of his life. In December 1916 Wacker-Chemie started the first mass production of the basic chemicals acetaldehyde, acetic acid, and acetone in the plant in the Bavarian city of Burghausen. That same year, company headquarters were moved to Munich. At that time Wacker-Chemie employed 403 workers and 51 clerks.

Acetone was one of the chemicals most urgently needed by Germany's war economy, so the plant went into operation without its own power supply. Power was provided by nearby Reichenhall by means of Bavaria's first high-voltage power line. The first tank full of acetone was shipped from the Burghausen plant in January 1917. In 1918 the Burghausen plant started producing tetrachloroethane and trichloroethylene, and Wacker's research lab was also moved to Munich. The

same year Elektrobosna and Aktieselskabet Hafslund withdrew from the partnership business. In 1919, during the first year of peace after World War I, Wacker-Chemie began the production of acetic ester, oxybutyric aldehyde, crotonaldehyde, butanol and butyl acetate.

Early Successes through 1939

The 1920s brought economic turmoil to Germany and the world. In 1923 a new currency, the Rentenmark, was introduced in Germany after hyperinflation had hit its peak. The second severe economic downturn came with the stock market crash in 1929 followed by the Great Depression. However, for Wacker-Chemie the 1920s were a decade of dynamic growth. In 1920 the production of ethyl acetate began in the Burghausen plant. A year later a new technology for acetylene purification was implemented and chlorine-alkali electrolysis with diaphragm cells made the production of chlorinated hydrocarbons possible. In 1922 Wacker-Chemie produced shellac, its first synthetic, and started developing pesticides as well. This was also the year that Alexander Wacker died, at age 75.

Over the following years Wacker-Chemie continued to expand its product range, introducing low-carbon ferroaloys, polyvinyl alcohol, actetic anhydride from actetic acid, Wacker acetate silk from acetyl cellulose, and vinyl acetate. Wacker's copper oxychloride-based "Kupferkalk" turned out to be a powerful fungicide for infested hop crops and vineyards. Wacker-Chemie also played a role in the development of stainless steels as Germany's only producer of calcium-silicon alloys and low-carbon ferrochromium. Another important product for Wacker-Chemie during this time was carbide as an end product, for example welding carbide.

The 1920s were also successful years for the Consortium. In 1922 it registered a patent for a technology to produce anhydride from cellulose acetate, or ketene. Another field for research was in the usefulness of chlorine products as pesticides. In 1924 researchers at the Consortium discovered polyvinyl alcohol, which led to the production of the first solely synthetic fiber called Polyviol. In 1928 the Consortium published for the first time results of their work on the polymerization of vinyl chloride and started intense testing the year after.

During this time Wacker-Chemie significantly expanded its production infrastructure. The necessary financial boost came from a new business partner, Farbwerke Hoechst AG, which acquired 50 percent of Wacker's share capital in 1921. In 1922 Wacker's own water-power station—the "Alzwerke"—delivered electricity for the first time to the Burghausen plant. The war had delayed the project which at times employed as many as 3,000 workers. In the same year the company's own railway station was opened. The Burghausen plant was expanded, three new production plants were acquired or built and a share was bought in Wacker's Bavarian distribution partner Christian Dederer GmbH. In 1924 Wacker obtained a lease on a salt mine for 30 years which secured the supply of rock salt for chlorine electrolysis.

By 1930 Wacker's Burghausen plant had grown into a significant chemical production complex. However, because the economy was still depressed, Wacker's workforce was cut by ten

Key Dates:

1914: Alexander Wacker, Gesellschaft für elektrochemische Industrie KG is founded.

1921: Farbwerke Hoechst AG acquires 50 percent of Wacker's share capital.

1933: Silicon carbide producer Elektroschmelzwerk Kempten is acquired.

1938: PVC production begins in Burghausen.

1943–44: Consortium and headquarters laboratories are completely destroyed during bombings.

1947: Eastern German production plants Mückenberg and Tschechnitz are expropriated and nationalized; research on silicones starts in Burghausen.

1953: Wacker becomes limited liability private company and is renamed Wacker-Chemie GmbH.

1955: First facility for mass production of silanes and silicones is built.

1965: Wacker-Chemie acquires Monosilicon and establishes American subsidiary Wacker Chemicals Corp.

1969: Carbide production in Burghausen is terminated.

1987: Wacker-Chemie is the world's third largest producer of silicone.

1998: Hoechst announces plans to sell its 50 percent share in Wacker-Chemie.

percent and work hours were shortened. In 1933 Wacker-Chemie acquired Elektroschmelzwerk Kempten, a silicon carbide producer, and new production lines were opened almost every year. The highlight for Wacker-Chemie research was the development of a suspension technology for the production of polyvinyl chloride (PVC) which opened a new chapter in the history of plastics. In 1938 PVC Wacker-Chemie started PVC production in Burghausen. Other Wacker products of that time included synthetic belt drives, medical sutures, shatter-proof glass, and Drawinella, the first acetate staple fiber similar to wool.

The Reconstruction Years through 1959

By 1939, the year Hitler attacked Poland and World War II began, Wacker-Chemie had 4,125 employees and was generating 75 million marks in sales. Basic chemicals were needed during the war, and Wacker-Chemie once more expanded its production capacities. However, when the Western Allies intensified the war against Germany, Wacker-Chemie suffered significant setbacks. First of all, the Consortium and laboratories at its headquarters were completely destroyed by bombings in 1943 and 1944. In 1945 Wacker-Chemie came under American administration. Three anti-Nazi activists were killed at Wacker's Burghausen just before the surrender to the Allies, and two managing directors were arrested after the surrender. Nearly all of Wacker's production facilities were closed down between May and October 1945. Two of Wacker's production plants, the salt mine and the Alzwerke power plant, were split from the company in order to prevent too great a concentration of economic power. Most significant of all, after the facilities in Burghausen were dismantled by the Soviets, Wacker's two

eastern German production plants were expropriated and nationalized. Those two plants in Mückenberg and Tschechnitz accounted for two-thirds of Wacker's total output. In the first postwar years, it did not seem likely that Wacker-Chemie would be able to survive—but it did.

In 1947, when research started again in Burghausen, Wacker-Chemie opened the silicon chapter of its history. Three years later, the research had turned out to be so promising that an experimental production facility was established. That facility produced silanes—the first preliminary ingredient for silicones—as well as the first silicon products such as a silicone-insulated high-voltage motor. In 1951 the range of Wacker-Chemie silicon products was expanded to include impregnating agents for textiles, release and antifoam agents, pastes, and emulsions. In 1953 Wacker Chemie produced the first hyperpure silicon for semiconductors as well as the first silicon rubber. In 1955, the year when the Federal Republic of Germany regained sovereignty and the last prisoners were returning from Russia, Wacker-Chemie started building its first facility for the mass production of silanes and silicones.

In 1953 a law was passed that gave 51 percent of Wacker-Chemie to Alexander Wacker's heirs while 49 percent remained the property of Farbwerke Hoechst AG. At the company's first regular business meeting, on April 8, 1953, the company was transformed into a limited liability private company, and its name changed to Wacker-Chemie GmbH. In 1958 the share ratio between the Wacker family and Farbwerke Hoechst was changed again to 50 percent each. By the end of the 1950s the number of Wacker employees exceeded the prewar number.

Rapid Growth through 1979

The German economy boomed in the 1960s and so did the German plastics industry. It was during the same time period that polyvinyl plastics based on carbide were succeeded by more economical petrochemical-based materials. In 1960 a new Wacker plant in Cologne started operation. It was the first production line that used ethylene instead of carbide acetylene to make acetaldehyde. Three years later the acetylene-based production of acetaldehyde at the Burghausen plant was closed down. In 1965 Wacker Chemie, Farbwerke Hoechst, and Marathon Oil agreed to built a petrochemical refinery in Burghausen. The refinery began deliveries of ethylene and petrochemical acetylene three years later. Finally, on May 9, 1969, the carbide production in Burghausen, which had significantly contributed to the early success of Wacker-Chemie, was closed down. Other production lines that were shut down during the 1960s included chemical purification equipment, the cellulose acetate fiber Drawinella, and hexachlorethane. At the same time, demand for silicon products was on the rise. Beginning in 1961, hyperpure silicon was produced regularly and semiconductor production was expanded in Burghausen. In 1960 Wacker's hyperpure silicon was sold to the United States for the first time. In 1965 Wacker-Chemie acquired Monosilicon, a manufacturer of hyperpure silicon based in Los Angeles and established its American subsidiary Wacker Chemicals Corp. based in New York.

Three years later Wacker's German silicon activities were organized under the new Wacker-Chemitronic Gesellschaft für

Elektronik Grundstoffe GmbH in Burghausen. Another important step for Wacker-Chemie in the 1960s was the acquisition of the Stetten salt mine, which secured the supplies of rock salt needed for the chemical processes at the Wacker plants.

The 1970s marked the beginning of massive international expansion for Wacker Chemie. Initiated by two of Wacker's top executives—CEO Ekkehard Maurer and marketing director Hans Denis—the company started establishing numerous foreign subsidiaries around the world. Wacker-Mexicana S.A. was set up in 1971 and followed by Wormerveer-based Wacker-Chemie Nederland B.V. in the Netherlands and Vienna-based Wacker-Chemie Ges. m.b.H. Salzburg in Austria in 1972. In 1973 marketing subsidiaries Wacker-Chemie (Schweiz) AG in Liestal and Wacker-Chemie S.A. in Brussels were set up. Subsidiaries in Denmark, Great Britain, Brazil, and Spain were founded between 1975 and 1978. Moreover, in 1978 Wacker-Chemie founded two more companies in the United States: Wacker Siltronic Corporation based in Portland, Oregon, and silicon carbide producer ESK Corporation based in Hennepin, Illinois. In 1979 Wacker bought a share in the Canadian firm Henley Chemicals Ltd. located in Ontario, which had represented Wacker in Canada.

The 1980s and Beyond

With personal computers and other electronics products based on microchips flooding the world, silicon was Wacker's flagship product in the 1980s. In 1980 a brand-new silicon factory was opened at Wacker Siltronic in Portland, Oregon; another began production in Sao Paulo, Brazil, the following year. In 1985 the first Wacker plant started making silicone in Japan, and by 1987 Wacker-Chemie was the third largest producer of silicone in the world. In 1988 the silicone division contributed DM 713 million or 26.5 percent to Wacker's total sales. Besides the well-known silicon wafers used in the microelectronics industry, Wacker-Chemie made over 1,500 silicon products used in the construction, transportation, pharmaceutical, cosmetics, paper, textile, and many other industries in the from of fluids, resins, or elastomers. These products were made in the most sophisticated production facility of its kind in Europe, in Burghausen, where all production stages were carried out under one roof, as well as in the United States, Mexico, Brazil, Australia and Japan.

During the 1980s Wacker's network of worldwide subsidiaries was expanded significantly into Italy, Portugal, Greece, Sweden, Finland, Singapore, and South Africa. In 1988 the company was reorganized into five business divisions: vinyl acetate, polymers and organic chemicals; silicones, silanes and silicas; PVC and chlorine derivatives; semiconductors; and materials. Each division was headed by a director with worldwide responsibility. Wacker's sales passed the DM 3 billion mark for the first time in 1988; 14,000 people worldwide were on the company's payroll. In 1995 Peter-Alexander Wacker joined the company's management board. The great grandson of Wacker Chemie's founder was the first Wacker family member since the 1960s to join the top management team.

In the late 1990s, Wacker Chemie's semiconductor division suffered during the Asian economic crisis; in 1998 Wacker's profits decreased by two-thirds. Despite this setback, Wacker continued to pursue a vivid globalization strategy. In 1998 Wacker-Chemie entered a joint venture with India's largest silicone manufacturer, Metroark. In the same year the company launched two joint ventures with Air Products and Chemicals: emulsions producer Air Products Polymers L.P. (APP) and redispersible powders producer Wacker Polymer Systems L.P. (WPS). A new production facility for silicone wafers in Singapore began production in 1999; technical service centers were also opened in Sao Paulo and Shanghai. In spring 2000 Wacker announced that it would sell its two PVC joint ventures with Celanese, Vinnolit Kunststoff GmbH, and Vintron GmbH, which concluded the company's divestment strategy in the field of inorganic chemicals.

To secure future growth Wacker-Chemie worked in five strategic areas, including biologically-produced building blocks for the life sciences such as cysteine and cyclodextrin, a new production process for actetic acid from cheap raw materials, new materials for hard discs, a pilot line for the mass production of 300-mm hyperpure silicone wafers, and ceramics materials for the auto industry. In 1998 partner Hoechst announced that the company was planning to sell its 50 percent share in connection with the merger of Hoechst AG and Rhone-Poulenc to form Aventis S.A. Since then Wacker-Chemie continued to look for a new solution that would ensure the financial resources necessary to secure Wacker's future growth.

Principal Subsidiaries

Wacker-Chemie GmbH, Werk Burghausen (Germany); Elektroschmelzwerk Kempten GmbH (Germany; 99.67%); Wacker Polymer Systems GmbH & Co. KG (Germany; 80%); Wacker Siltronic Gesellschaft für Halbleitermaterialien AG (Germany); Wacker Siltronic Singapore Pte. Ltd. (80%); Wacker Siltronic Corporation; Wacker Asahikasei Silicone Co., Ltd. (Japan); Céramiques & Composites S.A. (France); Wacker Metroark Chemicals Limited (India; 51%); Wacker Mexicana, S.A. de C.V. (Mexico); Elektroschmelzwerk Delfzijl B.V. (Netherlands; 99.67%); Wacker Biochem Corporation; Wacker Engineered Ceramics, Inc.; Wacker Polymer Systems L.P.; Wacker Chemicals Holding International B.V. (Netherlands); Wacker Chemical Holding Corp.; Kelmar Industries (80%).

Principal Divisions

Semiconductors; Polymers; Silicones; Materials.

Principal Competitors

Dow Corning Corp.; General Electric Company; Compagnie de Saint-Gobain S.A.

Further Reading

"Air Products, Wacker-Chemie Launch Venture," *Adhesives Age*, December 1998, p. 38.

Alperowicz, Natasha, "Wacker-Chemie Confirms Huls Deal," *Chemical Week*, December 9, 1998, p. 17.

——, "Wacker Forms Silicones Joint Venture," *Chemical Week*, November 4, 1998, p. 26.

Chapman, Peter "Wacker Building US Facility to Enter Cyclodextrin Market," *Chemical Market Reporter*, March 24, 1997, p. 1.

Hume, Claudia, "Wacker Family Negotiates Purchase of Hoechst's 50% Stake," *Chemical Week*, November 10, 1999, p. 24.

Milmo, Sean, "Wacker Targets Biochemistry for Rapid Growth," *Chemical Market Reporter*, November 8, 1999.

"75 Years Wacker: Pictorial Chronology of a Company," (special issue) *Werk + Wirken*, Munich: Wacker-Chemie GmbH, 1989, 96 p.

"Wacker; Chemische Spaltung," *Focus*, May 31, 1999, p. 254.

"Wacker erhöht die Investitionen in Sachsen," *Frankfurter Allgemeine Zeitung*, March 27, 1998, p. 20.

"Wacker Negotiates Silicon Carbide Divestment," *Chemical Week*, April 19, 2000, p. 8.

—Evelyn Hauser

Wal-Mart de Mexico, S.A. de C.V.

Blvd. Manuel Avila Camacho 647
Colonia Periodistas
11220 Mexico, DF
Mexico
Telephone: 52-5-387-9200
Fax: 52-5-387-9209

Public Company
Incorporated: 1984 as Cifra, S.A. de C.V.
Employees: 70,997
Sales: $6.40 billion (1999)
Stock Exchanges: OTC
Ticker Symbol: WMMVY
NAIC: 45211 Department Stores; 45299 All Other
    General Merchandise Stores; 45291 Warehouse Clubs
    and Superstores; 44814 Family Clothing Stores;
    72211 Full-Service Restaurants; 551112 Offices of
    Other Holding Companies

Wal-Mart de Mexico, S.A. de C.V., formerly known as Cifra, S.A. de C.V., is the largest retailer in Mexico, operating 460 units under a number of different banners. Wal-Mart de Mexico's two principal retail chains—in terms of their contribution to the company's annual sales totals—are Sam's Club stores and Bodega Aurrera stores, both of which operate as warehouse-style concepts. Combined, the two chains account for 49 percent of the $6.4 billion the company collected in sales in 1999. Aside from the 34 Sam's Club stores and the 69 Bodega Aurrera stores, the company's business formats include: 27 Wal-Mart Supercenters, 38 Superama supermarkets, 51 Suburbia discount apparel stores, 38 medium-sized, general merchandise Aurrera stores, and 205 Vips restaurants. Wal-Mart Stores, Inc. owns 60 percent of Wal-Mart de Mexico.

Origins

Cifra, Wal-Mart de Mexico's predecessor, was founded in 1958 by Jerónimo Arango. The son of a Spanish immigrant to Mexico who prospered in the textile business, Arango spent his youth studying art and literature at several American universities and traveling in Spain, Mexico, and the United States. While in New York City he saw a crowd waiting patiently for the opportunity to enter E.J. Korvette, then a pioneering Fifth Avenue discount department store. Impressed by Korvette's success, he persuaded his father to lend him the equivalent in pesos of $240,000 so that he could organize a similar venture with his two brothers, Placido and Manuel. Called Aurrera Bolívar, this discount store was opened in downtown Mexico City in 1958.

Like the Korvette store, Aurrera Bolívar immediately drew the public, and—also like Korvette's—it attracted the hostility of established retailers, who felt threatened by competition engendered by Aurrera Bolívar's low prices. In fact, the store was selling household goods and clothing at 20 percent below manufacturers' list prices, while established retailers were marking them up by 40 to 45 percent. Soon the brothers had to locate alternate sources of goods as far away as Guadalajara and Monterrey because the Arangos' suppliers were threatened with boycott by angry rivals. Nevertheless, Aurrera reportedly won sympathy by publicizing its competitors' tactics during its sponsorship of the popular television show, ''The 64,000 Peso Question.'' By 1965 eight Aurrera stores were in existence, drawing $16 million in sales. The company's first Superama supermarket opened in 1960 and the first Vip restaurant opened in 1964.

In 1965 Jewel Cos. of Chicago organized a joint venture with the Arango brothers to start new stores, and a year later Jewel acquired a 49 percent stake in the business for about US $20 million. While Manuel and Placido Arango took their part of the money and left the business to establish other enterprises, Jerónimo studied modern retailing at Jewel headquarters in Chicago. In 1970 he opened the first of the firm's Bodega Aurrera discount warehouse stores and Suburbia department stores. Aurrera S.A. became publicly owned in 1976, the year it opened its first hypermarket, and was so successful that by 1981 Jewel's Mexican operations accounted for nearly one-third of its income. Jewel's stake had dropped to 41.7 percent of the outstanding shares by 1980 and eventually would fall to 36.1 percent.

Hard times came in 1982, when the peso collapsed because of huge foreign debt, touching off an inflationary crisis and a severe recession that lasted for years. But Arango was confident enough of the future to buy back Jewel's share in the business

Company Perspectives:

We are the most important retailer in Mexico. Wal-Mart Stores, Inc., our majority shareholder, is the largest retailer in the world. Our leadership is the result of a series of operating and commercial practices aimed at a timely and efficient satisfaction of our customers' needs, thus creating value for them and for our shareholders.

(which he renamed Cifra in 1984) from its successor, American Stores Co., for about $53.4 million. He kept all existing stores open and retained the employees, although they were expected to work longer hours and those who left were not replaced.

Cifra's emphasis on discounting helped sustain the company during these dark years. Located in the poorer neighborhoods of Mexico City, the Bodega Aurrera stores, for example, stocked all types of nonperishable goods to the ceiling and offered prices as low as half those of other retailers. By the end of 1989 Cifra was in its best financial shape ever. It had grown in sales by 20 percent or more in every year of the decade. Its sales in 1989 were about $550 million, and its stock more than tripled in value during the year.

Joint Venture and Subsequent Expansion: Early 1990s

In 1990 Cifra's sales grew by 26 percent, and between 1990 and 1991 its stock shot up almost fivefold. At the end of 1991 there were 38 Almacenes Aurrera self-service department stores, selling general merchandise, clothing, and supermarket items. The high-income Superama chain consisted of 34 freestanding community supermarkets. Next came the 29 Bodega Aurrera discount warehouse stores and the 29 Suburbia family-oriented department stores, selling discount clothing and dry goods. The Vips restaurant operations consisted of 59 cafeterias, 15 El Porton restaurants (initiated in 1978), and four more specialized restaurants. Gran Bazar was the name for Cifra's hypermarkets, and Sigla for its real estate interests in opening new shopping centers.

In May 1992 Cifra announced that it intended to invest $211 million to open 12 new stores during the year and another $68 million to renovate 78 existing ones. The restaurants were modernized to attract new and younger customers. In addition, an investment of $80 million was to be made in such technological developments as information and point-of-sale systems, satellite-based communications, and complex data processing units. By this time, the implementation of a computerized inventory-control system had made the company the leader in the industry for inventory management. Its point-of-sale systems allowed it to collect, analyze, and make use of vast amounts of data concerning consumer preferences and the effects of price changes. Cifra's sales per square foot were almost twice as high in 1992 as those of its competitors, and its liquidity in cash and equivalents as well as its inventory turnover were the highest in the industry.

Cifra's growth remained impressive in 1992. A total of 23 units were built that year. Sales rose by 20.7 percent to $3.7 billion. Operating profits increased by 32 percent during 1992. As much as 31 percent of the company's earnings came from

interest income on its considerable cash surplus. An investor buying $1 of Cifra B shares at the start of 1988 had seen his investment reach $39.46 at the end of 1992. Sales in fiscal 1993 rose to $4.6 billion and were the best per square foot in Mexico.

Cifra formed two joint ventures with Wal-Mart in 1991. One, Commercializadora Mexico-Americana, promoted trade between Mexico and the United States. The other, Club Aurrera, was directed at small businesses and their employees and was patterned on Wal-Mart's Sam's Club. In fact, after a short period of time the Club Aurrera stores were renamed Sam's Club. The first Club Aurrera opened late in 1991 and three more were opened in 1992. This joint venture was serving many customers wishing to buy in quantity. Like Sam's Club, Club Aurrera members-only stores typically offered just one brand of an item stacked to the rafters in cartons. The customer base was expected to include restaurants, discos, and clubs.

In May 1992 the joint venture of Cifra and Wal-Mart was expanded to oversee all of the new Almacenes Aurrera, Superama, Bodega, and Gran Bazar stores. The rationale behind this move was that Wal-Mart's technology and marketing know-how would fuel Cifra's growth to otherwise unattainable levels. One analyst also noted that it precluded the prospect of Wal-Mart forming links with another Mexican retailer or opening stores in Mexico on its own.

By June 1994 there were three Almacenes Aurrera stores, 18 Bodega stores, three Superama Supermarkets, two Suburbia stores, 11 Vips restaurants, ten Sam's Clubs, and three Wal-Mart Supercenters combination stores. Wal-Mart had built three Supercenters in 1993 and early 1994, one of which, with 244,000 square feet, became the largest Wal-Mart Supercenter in the world. In addition, a revision of the agreement added the field of collaboration to Cifra's restaurant and clothing store divisions, previously excluded.

Wal-Mart's expertise was considered especially important in the creation of regional distribution centers. Because Cifra had concentrated on the Mexico City metropolitan area, it was relatively inexperienced in the efficient delivery of supplies to other cities, including Guadalajara, León, and Monterrey to the north and west and Villahermosa and Mérida to the south and east. During this time, the collaboration between Cifra and Wal-Mart was managed primarily by Mexican nationals in Mexico. Wal-Mart was contributing a few dozen Mexican expatriates to help out, but their roles were shifting increasingly to Mexican citizens as skills were passed on to local personnel, according to Bob Martin, president and chief executive officer of Wal-Mart International.

A prototype Almacenes Aurrera was erected in the Mexico City suburb of Las Auguilas. Executed by Fitch Inc. of Worthington, Ohio, the store featured white walls and color codes for the major merchandise categories. New fixtures allowed more prominent opportunities for display and highlighting than in the past, with red—Aurrera's signature color—drawing attention to new merchandise, sales items, and other promotions. Freestanding archways in the back corners were intended to draw customers to the perimeter. The parqueteria, an outside bottle return, bag check, and security checkpoint standard in Mexico, was sheltered to shield shoppers from the elements.

The creation of the North American Free Trade Agreement (NAFTA) at the beginning of 1994 deepened the collaboration

Key Dates:

1958: The first Aurrera store opens in Mexico City.
1960: Superama retail concept is launched.
1964: Vips restaurants are established.
1970: Two more retail concepts, Suburbia and Bodega Aurrera, begin operating.
1977: The company, then known as Cifra, completes initial public offering of stock.
1991: Cifra and Wal-Mart Stores, Inc. sign joint venture agreement.
1997: Wal-Mart Stores acquires majority interest in Cifra, creating Wal-Mart de Mexico.

between Cifra and Wal-Mart. In January 1994 the joint venture was extended to include all future Suburbia stores and Vip restaurants. In October 1994 Cifra and Wal-Mart announced a 50–50 joint venture with Dillard Department Stores, Inc. to build and operate Dillard's stores in Mexico. The first Dillard's store was expected to open in Monterrey in late 1995.

In late 1994 Cifra was reportedly planning to invest heavily in the expansion of its store and restaurant chains. By that time the Cifra empire, by itself and in combination with Wal-Mart, consisted of 35 Almacenes Aurrera, 58 Bodegas Aurrera, 36 Supcramas, 33 Suburbias, 22 Sam's Clubs, and 11 Wal-Mart stores, in addition to 114 Vips cafeterias and restaurants.

The mid-1990s presented some challenges for Cifra. The company's financial reportings for 1993 proved disappointing to many analysts, and the company's stock was trading at about 28 times estimated 1994 earnings, although a cost-cutting campaign helped the company's operating profits to climb 23 percent during the first quarter of 1994. A blow was then dealt to all publicly traded Mexican companies in 1994, when the value of shares on the Bolsa stock exchange experienced a sharp drop. Mexican stocks ended the year down by 44 percent. Finally, the devaluation of the peso in December 1994 triggered a financial panic, and during the first half of January 1995 Mexican stocks dropped another 28 percent. Wal-Mart and Cifra announced during the month that plans to open 24 new stores in Mexico during 1995 were "temporarily on hold" due to the country's economic conditions. Cifra representatives noted, however, that this decision did not affect the long-term growth strategy of the joint venture, nor did it change the level of commitment by both partners in the association. Moreover, analysts noted that one point in favor of Cifra's future was its lack of foreign currency debt.

Wal-Mart Stores Majority Shareholder in Cifra in 1997

Any suspicions that the mid-1990s economic crisis in Mexico might weaken the partnership between Wal-Mart and Cifra were thoroughly eliminated during the latter half of the 1990s. From Wal-Mart's perspective, the Mexican market ranked as one of the company's fast-growing international markets during the late 1990s, a segment of the company's business that was becoming increasingly important as domestic markets began to suffer from an oversaturation of stores. Wal-Mart's commitment to expansion in Mexico was evinced in a landmark transaction in 1997, one that marked a turning point in the history of Cifra. In June 1997, Wal-Mart announced that it was acquiring a 51 percent interest in Cifra in a $1.2 billion deal. The merger agreement was completed in September 1997, giving the $105 billion discount chain control over the stores formerly controlled by the six-year-old joint venture and the stores and restaurants owned solely by Cifra. The new entity was renamed Wal-Mart de Mexico, S.A. de C.V.

With all of the businesses consolidated under one corporate banner, Wal-Mart's expansion efforts in Mexico became decidedly more aggressive. The merger allowed Wal-Mart to use the cash flow produced by Cifra's other businesses to finance the expansion of Sam's Club and the company's supercenters in Mexican markets. In addition, the union strengthened Wal-Mart's ability to expand into smaller markets and broaden its operating territory beyond central Mexico. By the end of the decade, Wal-Mart de Mexico consisted of approximately 460 units, with 34 Sam's Club warehouse stores and 69 Bodega Aurrera stores accounting for 49 percent of the company's $6.4 billion in annual sales. As the company formulated plans for the future, with the massive consolidation efforts under way until the conclusion of the 1990s, expansion was expected to continue throughout Mexico. Supported by the considerable financial resources of Wal-Mart Stores, which increased its stake in Wal-Mart de Mexico to 60 percent in April 2000, the company figured to be the dominant retailer in Mexico during the 21st century.

Principal Subsidiaries

Controladora de Tiendas de Descuento; Cifra-Mart; Wal-Mart Holding Company Mexico; Comercializadora Mexico-Americana.

Principal Competitors

Controladora Comercial Mexicana, S.A. de C.V.; Grupo Gigante, S.A. de C.V.; Organizacion Soriana, S.A. de C.V.

Further Reading

"Cifra: Aiming To Be a Mexican Wal-Mart," *Euromoney,* May 1993, pp. 107–08.

"Cifra, SA," *Latin Finance,* November 1992, pp. 33–34.

"Merger of Merchandising Magnates," *Business Mexico,* June 1994, pp. 22–24.

Millman, Joel, "The Merchant of Mexico," *Forbes,* August 5, 1991, pp. 80–81.

Moffett, Matt, "Mexican Retailers Jockey for Position, Hoping To Win Big as Nation Recovers," *Wall Street Journal,* August 26, 1991, p. A4.

Sandler, Linda, "Retailer Cifra Lights Up Mexican Stock Market, But Its Spectacular Run-Up Raises Caution Flag," *Wall Street Journal,* September 9, 1991, p. C6.

Seckler, Valerie, "Wal-Mart's Mexican Evolution," *WWD,* June 4, 1997, p. 19.

Torres, Craig, "Mexican Retailer Cifra, with a High Multiple and Disappointing Results, Falls into Disfavor," *Wall Street Journal,* February 23, 1994, p. C2.

Zwiebach, Elliot, "Cifra, Wal-Mart Consolidate Mexican Venture," *Supermarket News,* June 9, 1997, p. 4.

—Robert Halasz
—updated by Jeffrey L. Covell

Washington Football, Inc.

21300 Redskins Park Drive
Ashburn, Virginia 20147
U.S.A.
Telephone: (703) 478-8900
Fax: (703) 729-7605
Web site: http://www.redskins.com

Private Company
Incorporated: 1937
Employees: 100 (1998, est.)
Sales: $151.8 million (1999)
NAIC: 711211 Sports Teams and Clubs; 71131
     Promoters of Performing Arts, Sports, and Similar
     Events with Facilities

Washington Football, Inc. is the corporate entity that owns the Washington Redskins, a National Football League (NFL) franchise that dates back to 1932. After it moved to Washington, D.C. in 1937, the team built a solid fan base that has followed it with persistent loyalty through even its bleakest years. The Redskins have always been privately owned—both individually and by investment groups or other individual or majority-share owners—most notably by Jack Kent Cooke, who gained sole control in 1988. Two years after Cooke's death in 1997, a group of investors led by Snyder Communications' CEO Daniel Snyder purchased the team and its home base, Jack Kent Cooke Stadium. Snyder and his group renamed the stadium FedEx Field. The rich legacy of Redskin football itself insures that at least the team's name will stick, despite efforts by some Native Americans to force the owners to change it. The history of Washington Football, Inc. cannot really be divorced from the Redskins' fortunes on the gridiron.

1932–1969: The Marshall Era

George Preston Marshall (1897–1969), a native of Grafton, Virginia, was heir to a successful laundry business in Washington. Before he decided to sell it in 1948, he had nurtured it from two units into a very successful, 57-outlet chain.

Marshall had a showman's flare. In fact, he had tried to carve out a theatrical career in New York beginning in 1914, but he never met with success. Frustrated, he turned his talents to promoting entertainment, and that soon took him into the sports arena. In 1932, with an appetite for more direct involvement in professional athletics, Marshall and three others bought an available National Football League (NFL) franchise—the Boston Braves—for just $1,500.

Marshall and his fellow investors had no real luck in Bean Town, however. They could not get sports writers to give their team sufficient coverage, nor could they begin to fill Fenway Park when the team, renamed the Redskins, moved there in 1933. In Boston, even success on the field did not seem to help pique interest all that much. For example, in 1936 head coach Ray Flaherty led the team to the NFL's Eastern Division title. The accomplishment did not raise attendance much, however; nor did it stop the decision in 1937 to move the franchise to the nation's capital. In 1935, the Redskins played to fewer spectators in their last home game than they would draw at their first practice in Washington, D.C. two years later when they relocated there.

By the time the Redskins got to Washington, Marshall had become an outspoken figure in professional football—an incessant talker and ballyhoo artist whose love of spectacle led him to mount legendary half-time extravaganzas. He was a notable character, and something of an eccentric. He loved trains and refused to drive cars, although he did have a chauffeur drive him to games. At the games, invariably, he would wear a raccoon coat. He was also a notorious tightwad, paying his players as little as he could—even stellar players such as Sammy Baugh. He loved football, though, and he repeatedly insisted that football was the real national pastime, not baseball, which he loved to debunk.

Sadly, Marshall also participated in the racist practices which were common in the NFL at the time. For twenty-four years, he refused to sign a single African American player. Because he had become the sole owner of the Redskins in 1935, he was able to get away with the practice. Besides, his team had tremendous support from fans in Washington and the surrounding area, and even from supporters in the upper tier of Southeastern states. In fact, Marshall promoted the Redskins as a

Company Perspectives:

When the Washington Redskins elected to seek a partner for our stadium name, our goal was to join forces with a globally recognized brand that understood the potential power of the relationship. FedEx was always our number one choice and clearly meets that goal. We also sought a partner that shares our long-term vision of what the Washington Redskins stand for in the community. There will be many examples of these standards in the years to come.

regional team, and in the late 1930s developed a strong rivalry with the Chicago Bears that was fraught with sectionalist undertones. That was during the Baugh dynasty, when the Redskins played in Griffith Stadium, which boasted a seating capacity of only 36,000.

The Baugh era was one of the Redskins' greatest. In a six-season period ending in 1945, the Redskins won 2 NFL championships and 3 Eastern Division titles while compiling a winning percentage of 73.5, the best in the franchise's history. The team's fortunes soon began to wane, however, and Baugh continued to pile up impressive individual statistics but never again played on a championship team. He retired in 1952, after 16 seasons with the Redskins.

Aging stars and poor recruitment plagued the Redskins in the 1950s and 1960s. In fact, during those two decades they managed winning seasons in just three years: 1953, 1956, and 1969. It was a poor statistic, considering that many of the team's players and coaches ended up in the NFL Hall of Fame: Vince Lombardi, Otto Graham, Sammy Baugh, Sonny Jurgensen, Charley Taylor, and Bobby Mitchell.

Mitchell, who came to the Redskins in a 1961 trade with the Cleveland Browns, was the first African American to play on the team. Marshall had finally relented, not from a change of heart—he was a bigot to the end of his life—but because Interior Secretary Stewart Udall threatened to block the Redskins from playing in the new D.C. Stadium that the federal government had paid for. Later named RFK Stadium, the facility could seat 54,000 fans, which was a compelling reason for Marshall to accede to Udall's demands that he integrate the team.

Some apologists have argued that Marshall's racism was based more on policy than anything else. He had worked diligently to make the Redskins the south's team, and many claimed that his racist business practices were simply products of catering to the views many held in the South regarding integration. He had even instructed his coaches, whenever possible, to draft players from southern universities, and he saw to it that the Redskins' games were broadcast over a network of radio stations in several southeastern cities. Clever strategy perhaps, but it was still believed that he himself held racist views, regardless of the above. For example, when Marshall died in 1969, his will included a provision that none of the funds he provided for child welfare were to go to integrated programs.

Despite Marshall's bigoted views, his fellow NFL franchise owners admired him. They voted him into the NFL Hall of Fame as a charter member, not just for his celebrated halftime shows and broadcast innovations in radio and television, but for his genuine contributions to the game, including the revision of some of its rules.

In one sense, the Marshall era ended in 1964, when effective control of the Redskins passed from Marshall to Edward Bennet Williams, a Washington attorney. Although Marshall still owned 52 percent of the organization's stock, he was suffering from heart disease, an aneurysm, diabetes, and emphysema. Williams and two others—Leo DeOrsey and Milton King—were named permanent conservators of Marshall's estate, and when DeOrsey died in 1965, Williams became president of the Redskins. This occurred despite the fact that Williams' share of the ownership was considerably less than the 25 percent owned by the franchise's future majority owner, Jack Kent Cooke.

Although the change of guard brought no immediate change in the Redskins' fortunes on the field, Williams tried to restore some of the team's lost glory with some surprise moves. One such move was a trade with the Philadelphia Eagles that brought veteran quarterback Sonny Jurgensen to the team in 1964. In 1969, Williams also talked the great Vince Lombardi into coming out of retirement to coach the team. Jurgensen, although compiling impressive statistics, did not manage to quarterback the Redskins to a winning season until Lombardi took over the coaching reins. In 1969, with 7 wins, 5 losses and 2 ties, the Redskins achieved their first winning season in 13 years.

1970–1990: On the Path to Glory

Hopes for a new winning dynasty dimmed, however, when cancer took the life of Vince Lombardi in 1970. For Jurgensen, Lombardi had been the ideal coach, and he felt the loss greatly. Jurgensen played under Lombardi's regular successor, coach George Allen, until he retired in 1975. Despite being plagued by injures and playing hurt, he continued to set NFL records until his retirement, leading the Redskins into the playoffs each year and into the Super Bowl in 1972. The team had returned to its winning ways.

Allen worked hard to rebuild the Redskins in the early 1970s. Its offense clicked with Jurgensen's passing, but its defense was one of the most porous in the NFL, and too often it gave up more points than the offense could score. Allen set out to rectify the problem, trading for veteran players who became known as ''The Over-the-Hill Gang.'' The defense quickly improved and helped the team to consecutive winning seasons.

After Jurgensen's retirement, Allen built the offense around Billy Kilmer and his backup, Joe Theismann. However, Allen's tenure at Washington came to an end in 1977, when he and Williams, who disliked Allen, failed to come to a contract extension agreement. Williams hired Jack Pardee as his new coach and Bobby Beathard as his general manager. By that time, the Redskins' offense was being led by Joe Theismann and the hard-charging and hard-living fullback, John Riggins.

Throughout the 1970s, the franchise posted a 91-52-1 record—its first winning decade since the 1940s—and made the playoffs five times, landing in the Super Bowl once. Yet the best

Key Dates:

1932: Franchise is formed as Boston Braves, with George Preston Marshall as main proprietor.

1933: Team is renamed the Boston Redskins.

1935: Marshall becomes sole owner of franchise.

1936: Under head coach Ray Flaherty, team wins NFL Eastern Division title.

1937: Franchise moves to Washington, D.C., becoming the Washington Redskins, and Sammy Baugh joins team.

1961: Marshall finally integrates his team in a trade that puts Bobby Mitchell on the Redskin roster; Jack Kent Cooke buys 25 percent of team.

1964: Conservators of Marshall's estate headed by E.B. Williams take control of franchise.

1969: Marshall dies; Cooke becomes principal owner of Redskins stock but NFL cross-ownership rules prevent him from managing the franchise.

1970: Coach Vince Lombardi dies and is succeeded by George Allen.

1981: John Cooke becomes executive vice president and Joe Gibbs replaces Jack Pardee as head coach.

1988: Jack Kent Cooke gains total control of Redskins.

1991: Redskins win Super Bowl XXVI by beating the Buffalo Bills, 37–24.

1993: Coach Joe Gibbs retires.

1997: Redskins owner Jack Kent Cooke dies.

1999: Group led by Daniel Snyder of Snyder Communications buys team and Jack Kent Cooke Stadium.

was still to come in the 1980s, when, under the control of Jack Kent Cooke and the coaching of Joe Gibbs, the team managed to get into three Super Bowls, winning two of them.

Cooke's management of the Redskins began in 1979, when, in a $42 million divorce settlement, he sold the Los Angeles Lakers and his interest in other professional teams and moved from California to Virginia. At the time, he owned 85 percent of the Redskins' stock, and since he no longer owned other professional teams, he was able to take direct control of the Redskins as majority owner.

Cooke set much store in Beathard's strategies and usually supported him, often over the objections of Jack Pardee, who feuded with Beathard. In early 1981, after the Redskins compiled a poor 3–7 record, Cooke fired Pardee. The team's performance was partly explained by the loss of its running game—the result of a breakdown in negotiations with Riggins—but Pardee paid the price. With the urging of Beathard, Cooke hired Joe Gibbs, the unheralded offensive coordinator of the San Diego Chargers. Gibbs became the 17th head coach in the franchise's history. At the same time, John Cooke, Jack Kent Cooke's son, began serving as the franchise's executive vice-president and took charge of the day-to-day operations of the Redskins.

Gibbs inherited a team that needed some mending, but one that also boasted some very talented players, including Art

Monk, one of the game's greatest wide receivers. He also cajoled Riggins into returning to the team, although he harbored the hope that he could trade "fruitcake" Riggins at the first opportunity. But Riggins bargained for and got a no-trade clause, which meant that he could not become a pawn in Gibbs' rebuilding game plans. As it turned out, Gibbs later credited Riggins with having made him famous.

After a shaky 1981 season, the Redskins hit their stride, particularly the offensive unit. In 1982, the tough charge and blocking of the offensive line, "The Hogs," gave the team the aggressive lift it needed to win, reversing its poor showing of the previous year. It crowned its "miracle season" with a 27–17 victory over the Miami Dolphins in Super Bowl XVII. Another trip to the Super Bowl followed in 1983. Although the Redskins lost to the Oakland Raiders, it was a record year for the team. The Redskins had piled up 541 overall points, which remained a NFL record at the century's end. Joe Theismann also had the best season of his career, passing for 3,714 yards and 29 touchdowns. Riggins, too, logged his best year, running for a team record of 1,347 yards, a mark that lasted until 1996.

Although the Redskins continued to win, by the end of the 1985 season it was clear that some more rebuilding of the team was necessary. The Redskins had a 10–6 record and missed the playoffs that year, in part because of injuries to Theismann and the diminished running ability of Riggins. Age also took its toll, ending the playing careers of both men.

Over the next couple of years, Jay Schroeder quarterbacked the Redskins. In 1986 he led the team to a 12–4 record but failed to get to the Super Bowl when the team's nemesis, the New York Giants, shut them out in the conference championship game, 17–0. In 1987, however, Schroeder was hurt in the first game of the season and was replaced by his backup, Doug Williams. Competition for the starting position followed. After a players' strike delayed the showdown, Williams emerged with the laurels and led the team to a 42–10 championship victory over the Denver Broncos in the Super Bowl.

The last couple of years of the 1980s saw some important changes for the Redskins. Among other things, in 1988 Jack Kent Cooke gained sole ownership of the franchise after buying the outstanding 15 percent share from co-owner Williams. At the time, Williams was dying of cancer. The following year, Bobby Beathard resigned, ceding his general manager's job to Charley Casserly. The team was also undergoing some changes—not all good—and in 1988, faltered after Williams suffered acute appendicitis. The Redskins went on to record their only losing season in Gibbs' 12-year tenure as head coach.

The Redskins rebounded the next year, however, when Mark Rypien won the starting quarterback job from an unhappy Doug Williams and led the team to a 10–6 mark. It was not good enough to get the team into the 1989 playoffs, but it offered a new promise that would be fulfilled two years later when the Redskins once again slugged their way into the Super Bowl.

1990–2000: From Glory to Hope in a Transitional Decade

1990 marked a winning season, but the Redskins once again failed to make the playoffs. The talent was certainly there, but personnel changes made in the final years of the previous decade had left the team fragmented. Gibbs needed something to make them gel. That "something" was unwittingly provided in 1991 by the head coach of the Philadelphia Eagles, Buddy Ryan, who unmercifully taunted the Redskins when his players badly mauled the Washington team in an early season game—what became known as the "Body Bag Game." Gibbs used Ryan's well-publicized jeering to motivate his team and draw his players together. The result was a trip to Super Bowl XXVI and another national championship, claimed in a 37–24 victory over the Buffalo Bills. It would be the team's last hurrah of the decade, though.

A year and half later, Gibbs retired, prompting both extensive roster changes and a shakeup of the coaching staff and the management. The team, with the loss of many veteran players, had actually entered a transitional stage before Gibbs' departure. His retirement just sped the process up and resulted in a couple of feeble seasons—the likes of which had not been seen since the 1960s. In 1993, under new head coach Richie Petitbon, the team went into a tail spin, finishing with a miserable 4–12 record. It never fully recovered.

Petitbon was replaced by Norv Turner, an established coach who offered the promise of being able to rebuild a team that seemed to have run out of good players. It was a tough assignment. In 1994 during his first season as head coach, Turner watched his team play its way to a dismal 3–13 record. From that nadir, there was some upward progress and some excitement, particularly after running back Terry Allen joined the team and quarterback Gus Frerotte won the starting role from Heath Shuler. In 1996, with an exciting run of seven straight victories, the team eked out a 9–7 winning season. Hope briefly returned.

But the next year, when Jack Kent Cooke died, the hope gave way to concern for the franchise's future. Cooke succumbed to a heart attack on April 6, 1997, never having seen a game played in the stadium he was then building. He had become almost a legend—famous for his brash profanity and bullying manner. He was a shrewd man who loved the game, and his loss simply put rebuilding on hold.

Then, in 1999, a group of buyers headed by 35-year-old Daniel Snyder, CEO of Snyder Communications, purchased both the team and the new Jack Kent Cooke Stadium from the Cooke family. The price tag was $800 million. Although John Cooke remained with the organization as its president, Snyder took active control of the organization. He renamed the new

stadium FedEx Field, annoying some of the Redskins' fans. But he also won their respect when he did not cave in to pressure from Native American groups to change the name of the team. He also encouraged Vinny Cerrato, the director of player personnel, to buy the talent to build a new Redskin dynasty—another dynasty of winners. By the end of the decade, the refurbishing had begun.

Always on the plus side during attempts to rebuild was the tremendous support of the Redskins' fans. Throughout the Redskins' history, even in their most dismal slumps, Washington's fans kept their diehard loyalty. As a result, the organization cultivated excellent community relations and a deep-rooted philanthropic involvement in its host city's welfare. For example, in 1999, with the sponsorship of the Arthur Anderson Foundation, Washington Football, Inc. organized the Washington Redskins Leadership Council. The council was made up of about 60 community leaders whose mission it was to determine how funds donated by the Washington Redskins could best serve the Greater Washington community. That kind of commitment went way beyond a public relations stratagem; it underscored the strong and persistent bond between Washington's citizens and their adored Redskins, something few NFL teams can match and most can only envy.

Principal Competitors

All of the franchised National Football League organizations in the NFL's two conferences (American and National), especially those located in east coast cities.

Further Reading

Denlinger, Ken, and Paul Attner, *Redskin Country: From Baugh to the Super Bowl,* New York: Leisure Press, 1983.
Elfin, David, John Keim, and Rick Snider, *Hail to RFK!: 35 Seasons of Redskins Memories,* Washington, D.C.: 21st Century Online Publishing, 1996.
Epstein, Noel, ed., *Redskins: A History of Washington's Team,* Washington, D.C.: Washington Post Books, 1997.
Haggerty, James J., *"Hail to the Redskins:" The Story of the Washington Redskins,* Washington, D.C.: Seven Seas Publishers, 1974.
Loverro, Thom, *Washington Redskins: The Authorized History,* Dallas: Taylor Publishing, 1996.
Schaffer, Athena, "NFL Redskins Owner Cooke Dies at Age 84," *Amusement Business,* April 14, 1997.
Slattery, David, *The Washington Redskins,* Virginia Beach, VA: Jordon & Co., 1977.

—John W. Fiero

White & Case LLP

1155 Avenue of the Americas
New York, New York 10036-2787
U.S.A.
Telephone: (212) 819-8200
Fax: (212) 354-8113
Web site: http://www.whitecase.com

Partnership
Founded: 1901
Employees: 2,300 (est.)
Sales: $351.5 million (1998)
NAIC: 54111 Offices of Lawyers

White & Case LLP is one of the largest law firms in the world and in November 1999 ranked fifth among the *International Financial Law Review* list of fastest growing firms in the world, based on its annual growth rate of about 20 percent. Unlike most American-based law firms, White & Case operates numerous overseas offices to meet its clients needs. Sending its associates abroad helped White & Case avoid layoffs in the early 1990s, when many other large law firms released both associates and even partners as a way to deal with the nation's economic slump. According to a spokesperson in White & Case literature: "International practice in the foundation of our firm." The firm counsels clients on taxation, litigation and other means of dispute resolution, acquisitions and mergers, privatization, disputes over intellectual property issues, and virtually all areas of the law. Thus White & Case plays a major role in the increasingly globalized economy of the 21st century.

Origins and Practice through the 1950s

The law firm of White & Case was founded in 1901 by Justin (J.) DuPratt White and George B. Case. White was born and raised in New York; he graduated from Cornell University in 1890 and was admitted to the New York State Bar in 1892. He would go on to become one of Cornell's distinguished alumni, and the university would later establish an honorary chair, known as the J. DuPratt White Professor of Law, at their law school. Case, on the other hand, was a graduate of Yale, where he studied law and also played baseball, reputedly inventing baseball's "squeeze play" during his tenure on the Yale team. Both White and Case were well-connected socially and in business circles, and from the start their firm, which they established in New York City, was regarded as "white shoe," or formal and conservative.

In 1903 the partners gained an important client when they were employed to provide the legal counsel necessarily to establish the Bankers Trust Company. Bankers Trust was founded by J.P. Morgan and other prominent financiers to provide trust services to customers of state and national banks throughout the United States. Bankers Trust, later known as Bankers Trust New York Corporation, would remain the firm's single largest client in the decades ahead. Case, in particular, proved a valuable resource for J.P. Morgan, accompanying him and advising him during 1912 antitrust hearings with the House Banking and Currency subcommittee.

Though they boasted an influential, prosperous clientele, including Bankers Trust and U.S. Steel, White & Case grew slowly in work force during the prewar years. According to *Hubbell's Legal Directory*, the firm consisted of five lawyers in 1913. In 1926 the partnership opened its Paris office. Three years later White & Case had a work force of 14 lawyers. Unlike many businesses that declined or disappeared in the Great Depression of the 1930s, White & Case increased in size to include 21 lawyers by 1940, according to the *Martindale-Hubbell Law Directory*.

Some of the companies represented by White & Case after World War II included Seagram's, Federal Paper Board, Detroit Edison, Heublein, and Lincoln National Life Insurance Company. With the death of White in 1939 and Case in 1955, the firm's key leader for years was Joseph M. Hartfield. Hartfield had been with White and Case since the early days, present on their work force roster in 1913. He was one of the first, and of only a few, Jewish attorneys to work on Wall Street during this time; he was also a colorful character, a flamboyant bachelor, known as the Colonel since his days as a young man in Kentucky. Recalling Hartfield's strengths during his tenure at White & Case, one attorney told author Paul Hoffman that Hartfield "was the best damned business-getter I ever saw." Hartfield died in 1964 at age 82.

Key Dates:

1901: The firm is founded in New York City.
1903: White & Case is hired to help establish the Bankers Trust in New York.
1926: A Paris branch office is opened.
1960: The Paris office commences operations again after being shuttered during World War II.
1971: The firm's London office is opened.
1974: The Washington, D.C. office is opened.
1978: The Hong Kong office is established.
1980: James B. Hurlock is named managing partner.
1998: White & Case helps facilitate the deal in which Bankers Trust is sold to Deutsche Bank AG.

Another key White & Case leader after World War II was Orison S. Marden. A prominent litigator, Marden became the head of the New York City and New York State bar associations, as well as the American Bar Association. In the 1960s Marden served on the committee that founded the Legal Aid Society, and he served as that society's chairman from 1970 to his death in 1975.

In 1960 White & Case expanded its international practice by reopening its office in Paris, which had closed for the duration of World War II. Moreover, in 1967 the firm opened a Brussels office in the home city of the European Community.

Challenges in the 1960s–70s

As it focused on its global expansion program, White & Case faced some challenges on the U.S. front in the 1960s. In September 1968 White & Case accepted National Student Marketing (NSM) Corporation as a new client. Founded in 1966, NSM was a new and rapidly growing company that had been unceremoniously dropped by its previous law firm, Covington and Burling, which alleged that NSM management had lied and acted unethically in their business dealings both before and after its 1968 initial public offering.

White & Case gave a new partner, Marion Jay Epley III, responsibility for NSM in 1969. In what author Joseph C. Goulden called "the most celebrated case ever on the obligation of a securities lawyer," Epley counseled NSM in its acquisition of three companies in 1969. In 1972 the U.S. Securities and Exchange Commission filed a lawsuit against Epley, White & Case, and other defendants for fraud and deceptions in their SEC acquisition filings. Specifically, Epley and White & Case were charged with failing to inform the SEC of NSM's unethical dealings. An out-of-court settlement in 1977 resulted in Epley being banned from any SEC work for six months, while White & Case agreed to various changes in their practice. "The agreement . . . amounted to a rare surrender of internal autonomy by an American law firm," said Goulden, explaining "A federal agency was telling lawyers how to conduct their profession." This was the first time the firm or its lawyers had been disciplined since the firm's founding in 1901. Although the settlement cost White & Case almost $2 million, the damage to its reputation was also significant. Cherovsky, in his 1991 book,

concluded, "It cost the firm far more by way of prestige and standing than dollars expended." In spite of the bad publicity, one White & Case attorney told Goulden, "We keep growing at the same percentage rate every year."

During this time, White & Case had fallen from its status as Wall Street's fourth largest firm to rank 18th, due in part to the NSM scandal. Other challenges to its ranking included the loss of some business; Seagram switched to another firm for its representation, and as Bankers Trust built up its own legal department they needed fewer services from its outside counsel.

In the 1970s White & Case opened new offices in London, Washington, D.C., and Hong Kong, its first Asian office. More women started entering the legal profession in the 1970s, and by 1980 White & Case had two women partners and 27 associates. In early 1981 the firm reported having no African Americans among its attorneys but that summer hired its first, two black female associates.

In the late 1970s, White & Case, along with several other law firms, played an important role in the release of the U.S. hostages in Iran. The crisis occurred during the Carter Administration, when Moslem fundamentalists took over the government of Iran and soon took 52 Americans hostage in the capitol of Teheran. President Carter froze Iranian deposits in American banks, while huge American bank loans to Iranian entities were in danger. In 1980, after Carter failed to gain the release of the American hostages through military force, 12 law firms representing 12 large American banks began negotiations of their own with Iranian government officials and the German lawyers representing Iranian banks. Among the group of 12 law firms, Shearman & Sterling represented Citibank; Milbank Tweed represented Chase Manhattan Bank; and White & Case represented its long term client Bankers Trust. For nine months they labored to find a behind-the-scenes solution to the financial and hostage crisis. President Carter's decision to finally unfreeze the Iranian accounts in American banks, as well as the long, difficult negotiations on the part of the 12 American law firms with the Iranians, eventually resulted in the release of the hostages on January 20, 1981, shortly after President Reagan's inauguration.

Expansion under James Hurlock in the 1980s–90s

Rapid expansion at White & Case ensued in the 1980s; the firm's number of lawyers increased from 169 in 1986 to 304 in 1990, an 80 percent increase in just four years. Meanwhile, the firm's gross revenues rose from $77 million in 1986 to $144 million in 1989. White & Case associate starting salaries rose from $66,000 in 1986 to $83,000 in 1990, part of a general trend as law firms competed for new law school graduates. White & Case recruited most of its new associates from the law schools of Harvard, Columbia, and New York University, according to Cherovsky's study of New York law firms.

Such rapid expansion by White & Case and other large law firm was influenced by two events in the late 1970s. First, the U.S. Supreme Court ruled that professional societies could not restrict advertising because that represented a violation of the First Amendment right to free speech. Soon, more lawyers, dentists, and other professionals began advertising just like other businessmen. Second, the field of legal journalism changed with the start of *The National Law Journal* and *The American Lawyer*. Their articles on law firm management and finances provided crucial data so that experienced lawyers had comparative data about rival law firms, thus leading to a huge increase in lateral hiring, rising salaries, and a loss of law firm collegiality.

Thus White & Case's increased lawyer count was matched by its opening of numerous new offices in the 1980s, many of them overseas. The Singapore and Stockholm offices were opened in 1983, followed by Ankara and Istanbul offices in 1985; Los Angeles in 1986; Tokyo and Miami in 1987; and Jeddah, Saudi Arabia in 1989.

Elected in 1980 as the managing partner at White & Case, James Hurlock oversaw this massive foreign expansion. "His personal success in representing the central bank of Indonesia and later the central banks of Turkey, Gabon, Zaire, Peru, Costa Rica, Panama and Honduras persuaded him to emphasize building up White & Case's overseas branches," wrote Cherovsky, who noted that "Under Hurlock's leadership White & Case has transformed itself into a modern firm. It seeks top talent from all quarters, broader fields of expertise and an expanded client base while it encourages and rewards hard work and business productivity." Cherovsky concluded that "although this approach has placed the firm on the upswing, it still has not regained the standing it once enjoyed."

As more multinational corporations expanded their overseas operations, law firms chose different ways to serve their clients. A few like White & Case opened many overseas branches. Other firms opted to build up their U.S. offices and spend more money for their lawyers to travel abroad, relying on advanced telecommunications and a few key foreign offices. Another strategy was to join alliances or networks of independent law firms.

White & Case continued to cultivate a work force of popular and influential attorneys. In 1989, White & Case hired a new partner, U.S. Attorney from Manhattan Rudy Guliani. Guliani did not stay long at White & Case, however, leaving soon thereafter to join another firm; he was later elected Mayor of New York City.

White & Case's largest client in the early 1990s remained Bankers Trust, although that company's percentage of the law firm's revenues fell from earlier highs of 20 to 25 percent to around ten percent. Other clients included U.S. Steel, Prudential, Aetna, Cigna, General Electric, General Electric Credit Corporation, as well as the governments of Indonesia and Turkey, and Germany's Deutsche Bank, which it counseled in that firm's purchase, for $10.1 billion, of Bankers Trust in 1998.

In spite of the economic downturn in the early 1990s, White & Case continued to grow rapidly. It opened 17 new offices in the 1990s, including facilities in Prague, Helsinki, Bangkok, Saudi Arabia, Hanoi, and Johannesburg, the latter making White & Case the only American law firm with a South African presence. In turn, some of the new foreign offices expanded rapidly. For example, the Bangkok office grew from its inception in 1993 to employ 35 lawyers by March 2000. With the collapse of communism in Eastern Europe and the breakup of the Soviet Union, White & Case offices in those areas grew rapidly. The Warsaw office grew to 36 lawyers between its origin in 1991 and March 2000.

As its worldwide presence increased, White & Case aided in the expansion of the globalized economy and gained new opportunities as local markets began looking outward. For example, from 1998 to 2000 the German legal market went "from an insular business—German law firms often confined their sphere to a single city in Germany—to one that recognizes the legal profession's role in a globalizing profession," according to White & Case's yearly review dated March 2000.

Statistics clarified the huge expansion project at White & Case in the 1990s. The firm tripled its number of attorneys, from 304 in 1990 to 1,025 in 2000. Its gross revenues increased from $144 million in 1989 to $318 million in 1997, which ranked it as the nation's 15th largest law firm, according to *The American Lawyer* of July/August 1998. The firm ranked 16th based on its 1998 gross revenues of $351 million, said *The American Lawyer* in July 1999.

As the economy recovered and then boomed with the startup and rapid growth of many high-tech and Internet companies, White & Case decided to build up its intellectual property (IP) practice, especially after two of its partners left the firm to establish IP practices for rival firms. In 1999, for example, White & Case opened its Palo Alto office to better serve Silicon Valley clients. It also strengthened its IP capabilities in London, where it became "the first full service US law firm to recruit an entire IP department staffed by English-law qualified practitioners," according to the September 1999 issue of *Managing Intellectual Property*.

On April 1, 2000, Managing Partner James Hurlock retired after serving since 1980 as the head of White & Case. Elected unanimously as the new managing partner, Duane Wall promised to continue emphasizing the firm's international practice. Unlike most American law firms, White & Case stationed about half its 1,000 plus lawyers overseas. "Our primary goal remains having the capability to represent clients whenever and wherever they need us, regardless of geographic, cultural or jurisdictional differences," said Wall in the February 23, 2000 *Financial Times*.

White & Case opened new overseas offices in Manama and Beijing in 2000. Although it faced tough competition from other large firms, including London's Clifford Chance with about 3,000 attorneys, White & Case continued to focus on expansion as it headed into a new millennium. Once known as a fairly formal, conservative, Wall Street icon, in going global White & Case had also reportedly loosened up its corporate culture somewhat. Those involved in the process of interviewing prospective new lawyers at White & Case reported being less interested in Ivy League credentials than in a candidate's leadership qualities, foreign language proficiencies, and potential for generating new business for the firm.

Principal Competitors

Shearman & Sterling; Jones, Day, Reavis & Pogue; Clifford Chance; Skadden, Arps, Slate, Meagher & Flom.

Further Reading

Cherovsky, Erwin, ''White & Case,'' in *The Guide to New York Law Firms,* New York: St. Martin's Press, 1991, pp. 217–221.

Eaglesham, Jean, ''Wall Elected Managing Partner of White & Case,'' *Financial Times* (London), February 23, 2000, p. 18.

Fennell, Edward, ''That First Foot and the Right Door,'' *The Times* (London), February 1, 2000.

Forster, Richard, ''New York Firms Seek the World's Business,'' *International Financial Law Review*, December 1997, pp. 36–39.

Goulden, Joseph C., *The Million Dollar Lawyers,* New York: G.P. Putnam's Sons, 1977, pp. 151–188.

Hoffman, Paul, *Lions of the Eighties: The Inside Story of the Powerhouse Law Firms,* Garden City, N.Y.: Doubleday, 1982.

''J. DuPratt White: Rockland County, New York, Legacy,'' *South of the Mountains,* April 1972.

Spar, Debora L., ''Lawyers Abroad: The Internationalization of Legal Practice,'' *California Management Review*, Spring 1997, pp. 8–28.

''US Firm Shakes Up London IP Scene,'' *Managing Intellectual Property*, September 1999, p. 10.

''White & Case: Colombian Government Sues Ecuadorean Bank in Miami to Recover $64 Million in Public Monies That Vanished,'' *Business Wire*, September 9, 1999, p. 1.

''White & Case,'' *Vault.com: The Insider Career Network,* www.vault.com.

—David M. Walden

Winston & Strawn

35 West Wacker Drive
Chicago, Illinois 60601-9703
U.S.A.
Telephone: (312) 558-5600
Fax: (312) 558-5700
Web site: http://www.winston.com

Partnership
Founded: 1853 as Judd & Winston
Employees: 650
Sales: $288 million (1999)
NAIC: 54111 Offices of Lawyers

One of the nation's top 50 law firms, Winston & Strawn serves corporate clients, government agencies, and others in most areas of modern law, from business financing, taxation, and antitrust matters to mergers and acquisitions and litigation. Its clients include Sears, Allstate, American Airlines, Bell Atlantic, Monsanto, and Abbott Laboratories. It serves many international clients in trade issues, privatization, and facilitating private investment in many nations. In addition, the firm lobbies for its clients to help them comply with regulatory agencies and sometimes to help Congress or foreign legislatures write new laws beneficial to clients. Winston & Strawn is one of the two oldest Chicago law firms. It also operates branch offices in New York, Geneva, Paris, and Washington, D.C.

Origins and Early History in Chicago

In 1853 Chicago was still a modest-sized city with a total of only about 30 or 40 lawyers when Frederick Hampden Winston (F.H. Winston) arrived from New York City to begin his Chicago law career. Born in 1830, Winston graduated from the Harvard Law School in 1852 at a time when most lawyers were educated in the apprenticeship system. From 1853 to 1861 Winston was a partner of Norman B. Judd, a prominent Republican who nominated Abraham Lincoln to be the party's 1860 presidential candidate. Winston's second partner was Henry W. Blodgett, who left in 1870 to become a federal judge.

In 1865 the firm gained its oldest client, the Union Stock Yard and Transit Company of Chicago, later renamed F.H. Prince & Company. F.H. Winston also represented three railroads: the Lake Shore and Michigan Southern; the Chicago, Rock Island & Pacific; and the Pittsburgh, Ft. Wayne and Chicago. Thus the early firm served the booming railroad industry as it consolidated after the Civil War and benefited from improved technology such as steel rails, air brakes, and refrigerated cars.

The famous 1871 Chicago fire destroyed much of the city and also many of the early records of the Winston law firm. In any case, the city built the nation's first skyscrapers in the fire's aftermath, and such rebuilding led to increased work for the legal profession in Chicago.

In 1878 Frederick Seymour Winston (F.S. Winston), the son of F.H. Winston, joined the law firm. The city of Chicago made F.S. Winston its assistant corporation counsel in 1881, and the following year he successfully represented the city before the U.S. Supreme Court in a case involving river access. It was the first case argued by a firm attorney before the Supreme Court.

In the late 1800s the law firm provided counsel to many Chicago breweries and continued to represent them until the Prohibition amendment was approved after World War I.

Practice in the Early 20th Century

The key figure in the firm's history after the turn of the century was Silas Hardy Strawn, who was born in Ottawa, Illinois, in 1866. After graduating from high school, he studied law in an Ottawa office and in 1889 began practicing. In 1891 he joined the Chicago law firm and became a leading citizen of the city. He served as the firm's managing partner for 40 of the 52 years he worked there.

In 1913 Strawn became the president of the Chicago Bar Association, one of the nation's largest local bar societies. During World War I, the Chicago Bar Association strongly supported the patriotic cause. For example, Strawn organized and headed a group of lawyers who volunteered to take over without charge unfinished cases of their colleagues who had joined the military.

In 1922 the firm had 22 lawyers, a large number for the time, when Harold A. Smith began his long career there. He later wrote a book about his life, including several cases that he participated in as a member of Winston & Strawn.

In 1927 the American Bar Association (ABA) chose Strawn as its president. Like most elite attorneys in the ABA, Strawn pushed for higher standards in legal education, including more college before entering law school and three years of law school.

During World War II, the law firm represented Montgomery Ward & Company in a controversial case involving the wartime powers of the federal government. In 1944 President Franklin Roosevelt took control of industry, including retail industry, for the wartime effort, closing some of Montgomery Ward's properties under his authority as the U.S. commander-in-chief. Montgomery Ward, under Sewell Avery, who detested interference in his company, was represented by Winston & Strawn when he challenged the seizures in court. Judges refused to rule on the case, deferring to Roosevelt's authority and citing the fact that the properties would be returned to the company when the war was over. The press heavily covered this case, and Avery made the cover of *Time* when he had to be forcibly removed by the National Guard from Montgomery Ward's property.

Post-World War II Developments

In 1951 the firm employed 39 lawyers, but it needed to grow or die. According to Terry Grimm in the Winston & Strawn history video, Tom Reynolds, Jr., one of the firm's key leaders in this early postwar era, believed that the nation's major law firms would consolidate by 2000 into only about 10 or 12 firms of 2,000 lawyers each. Although that did not happen, Reynolds was generally correct in predicting that law firms would become much larger through consolidation.

In the late 1800s Winston & Strawn began representing the Monon Railroad, nicknamed the Hoosier line because most of its tracks were in Indiana. During the Great Depression the line had declared bankruptcy, but in 1946 the government approved a reorganization plan devised with the help of the law firm. Finally in 1956 the government turned the railroad back to the stockholders.

In the mid-1950s it hired its first female attorney, Joy Farnsworth, but she was a rare exception until many more women started attending law school in the 1970s. In 1963 Winston & Strawn opened an office in Paris, but then decided to close it in 1965. During the 1960s, the law firm also represented the American Bar Foundation that held the title to properties used by the foundation, the ABA, and related groups near the University of Chicago.

In 1970 Winston & Strawn opened its Washington, D.C. office to meet its clients' requests, since they had to deal with many new federal laws and regulations passed in the 1960s. For example, President Johnson persuaded Congress to pass the Civil Rights Act, Mass Transit Act, and Equal Opportunity Act in 1964; Medicare and Medicaid in 1965; and the Omnibus Housing Act and the Housing and Urban Development Act in 1968. Both President Johnson and President Nixon implemented various affirmative action programs that resulted in more companies needing additional legal help.

The Law Firm in the Late 20th Century

Many law firms in the late 1970s started to rapidly expand. As mentioned in Winston & Strawn's history video, at that time law firm advertising increased significantly after the U.S. Supreme Court ruled that professional association restrictions on advertising violated the First Amendment's right to free speech. In addition, the *National Law Journal* and the *American Lawyer* began in the late 1970s publishing articles on law firm management and finances. That led to much more lateral hiring of experienced attorneys from rival firms as salaries shot up in the more competitive atmosphere.

This revolution in legal journalism made law firms more ''accountable'' and on balance was a good change, said Duane Kelley in the Winston & Strawn video. Previously, professional legal ethics discouraged virtually any cooperation with journalists or historians, making law firms generally very closed or even secret organizations that seldom shared much information about their attorneys or their clients. Paul Hoffman in his 1982 *Lions of the Eighties* declared, ''What a difference a decade makes! In contrast to the author's research for *Lions in the Street*, no law firm slammed the door in his face, no lawyer stonewalled.''

Winston & Strawn had just 122 lawyers in two offices in 1978. By 1987 the firm had more than doubled in size and added new offices. During this time the firm became more involved in lobbying in order to help its corporate clients deal with the huge government bureaucracy. For example, in 1981 Walter Mondale, at the conclusion of his vice-presidency under Jimmy Carter, joined the law firm. In 1984 Mondale gained the Democratic nomination for president, but he lost to Ronald Reagan in a campaign in which Mondale was assisted by longtime friend and adviser John Reilly, another Winston & Strawn partner.

Winston & Strawn lost some major clients in the 1980s, including Beatrice Companies. Those lost clients definitely hurt the firm, but it survived the crisis, in part by joining with three law firms in a four-year span. In 1989 it merged with New York's Cole & Deitz, a 90-lawyer firm formed in the 1930s whose clients included the predecessor of NetWest Bank, purchased by Fleet Bank. In 1990 Winston & Strawn merged with yet another firm, Bishop, Cook, Purcell & Reynolds, based in

Key Dates:

1853: F.H. Winston and Norman B. Judd form a partnership in Chicago.
1862: Partnership is renamed Winston & Blodgett.
1871: F.H. Winston practices on his own after Blodgett leaves.
1878: F.H. Winston's son F.S. Winston joins his father's practice.
1885: Firm becomes known as Winston & Meagher.
1901: Name changes to Winston, Babcock, Strawn & Shaw.
1903: Firm moves from the Monadnock Building to the First National Bank Building; changes name to Winston, Payne & Strawn.
1917: Winston, Strawn & Shaw becomes the new name.
1948: Firm is renamed Winston, Strawn, Shaw & Black.
1951: Firm now known as Winston, Strawn, Black & Towner.
1959: Law firm becomes Winston, Strawn, Smith & Patterson.
1970: Washington, D.C., office is opened.
1972: Winston & Strawn becomes the firm's name.
1989: Firm merges with Cole & Deitz.
1990: Firm merges with Bishop, Cook, Purcell & Reynolds based in Washington, D.C.
1999: Winston & Strawn is ranked as the nation's 34th largest law firm.

Washington, D.C. That merger added over 75 lawyers who specialized in energy, environmental, international trade, legislative, litigation, and municipal solid waste issues.

Like several other major law firms, Winston & Strawn suffered from the economic downturn of the early 1990s. According to *Chicago* magazine, the firm laid off 44 lawyers between 1991 and 1994. In 1995 Gary L. Fairchild, the firm's former managing partner, was sentenced to two years in federal prison after he pled guilty to tax evasion and fraud charges that resulted in Winston & Strawn and five former clients losing $784,000. Although Fairchild reimbursed his victims, he was also disbarred and served most of his prison sentence.

The firm's reputation was revitalized after these setbacks by James R. Thompson, its new chairman. The former four-term Republican governor of Illinois left politics in 1991 to join Winston & Strawn. Thompson's political ties at both the state and national level and his firm's growing lobbying practice led Steve Rhodes in his *Chicago* profile of "Lord Jim" to refer to Winston & Strawn as a "politically connected blue-chip law firm."

Another politically connected partner was Beryl Anthony, a former Arkansas Democratic congressman who joined Winston & Strawn after he lost his 1992 reelection bid. This was emblematic of the so-called "revolving door." The *Wall Street Journal* reported that 40 percent of the members of Congress defeated in 1992 then accepted positions with large law firms that provided lobbying and consulting to clients who needed

access to government. Members of both major parties participated in this legal but often criticized practice.

The *Washington Post* on December 15, 1997 reported that Winston & Strawn ranked 20th in a listing of the nation's law firm's according to political donations. The firm split its $179,461 in donations evenly between the Democratic and Republican parties. In 1999 the firm was one of the top ten contributors to Democrat Bill Bradley's campaign for the presidential nomination. On the other hand, Winston & Strawn also donated to the Center for Individual Rights, a conservative group that played a key role in opposing affirmative action programs that generally were supported by the Democrats.

Winston & Strawn added two offices in the 1990s. It opened its Geneva, Switzerland office in 1993, a city with few American law offices. Two years later it started its Paris office.

In the late 1990s the federally owned Tennessee Valley Authority hired Winston & Strawn, along with other firms, to win its battle with another government entity, the Department of Energy, in a dispute over who should manufacture tritium, an isotope used in the production of nuclear weapons.

Winston & Strawn in 1998 for the first time employed more than 600 lawyers and "enjoyed the highest grossing year in our history," according to the firm's *Year in Review 1998*. The firm in 1998 also held its first partners conference, attended by over 200 partners who saw a video on the firm's history. The Chicago mayor proclaimed December 9, 1998 as Winston & Strawn Day.

In 1998 the firm also made major strides in the use of modern technology. All its attorneys gained the use of high-speed laptop computers, and the firm launched its internal communications system called SilasNet. A 1997 survey of midlevel associates ranked Winston & Strawn as sixth out of 157 firms in the use of technology.

Dan K. Webb, described by *Business Week* on October 13, 1997 as Winston & Strawn's "biggest rainmaker," attracted clients such as Commonwealth Edison, the Chicago Blackhawks, and Bell Atlantic. Webb also was the attorney for Philip Morris Inc., the world's largest tobacco company, when a Florida jury in July 2000 ruled that it should pay $73.96 billion in punitive damages to thousands of smokers. Webb's clients helped Winston & Strawn rank as the nation's 34th largest law firm, based on its 1997 gross revenue of $212.5 million as reported in the *American Lawyer* in July/August 1998. In July 1999 the same magazine again ranked Winston & Strawn as number 34, based on its 1998 gross revenue of $241.5 million.

Winston & Strawn in 2000 faced many challenges, such as competition from some much larger law firms, managing its own internal growth, and dealing with the steady advance of technology and information science. It also faced the possibility that the ABA could approve of multipractice firms, in which lawyers teamed up with accountants and other professionals, a movement already well underway in Europe.

Principal Competitors

Mayer, Brown & Platt; Sidley & Austin.

Further Reading

Black, John D., *A Century of a Law Firm: Winston, Strawn, Black & Towner: 1853–1953,* Chicago, Winston & Strawn, 1954.

Carter, Terry, "On a Roll(Back)," *American Bar Association Journal,* February 1998, pp. 54–58.

"Contributions from Lawyers, Lobbyists," *Washington Post,* December 15, 1997, p. A25.

"Fairchild Is Sentenced," *Wall Street Journal,* March 22, 1995, p. B6.

Hoffman, Paul, *Lions of the Eighties: The Inside Story of the Powerhouse Law Firms,* Garden City, N.Y.: Doubleday, 1982.

Jacobson, Louis, "They're Going Nuclear in Dixie," *National Journal,* August 15, 1998, pp. 1934–35.

Kogan, Herman, *The First Century: The Chicago Bar Association 1874–1974,* Chicago: Rand McNally & Company, 1974, pp. 123–24.

Mulrenan, Stephen, "Swiss Lawyers Profit from Historical Neutrality," *International Financial Law Review,* December 1998, pp. 21–39.

Reuben, Richard C., "Suing the Firm," *American Bar Association Journal,* December 1995, p. 68.

Rhodes, Steve, "Lord Jim," *Chicago,* April 2000, pp. 82–87.

Rogers, James Grafton, "Silas Hardy Strawn," in *American Bar Leaders: Biographies of the Presidents of the American Bar Association 1878–1928,* Chicago: American Bar Association, 1932, pp. 242–46.

Segal, David, "Lawyers Big Donors to Presidential Candidates," *Washington Post,* July 27, 1999, p. E01.

Shribman, David, "Politics '84—Mondale's Blunt Confidant: Reilly Keeps List of Running Mates," *Wall Street Journal,* June 21, 1984, p. 1.

Silverstein, Ken, "Brotherly Love," *Multinational Monitor,* October 1997, p. 27.

Smith, Harold A., *70 Eventful Years,* self-published, 1969.

"2 Law Firms in Merger," *New York Times,* September 26, 1990, p. C5.

Weimer, De'Ann, "Can Dan Webb Pull Big Tobacco Out of the Fire?," *Business Week,* October 13, 1997, p. 127.

Winston & Strawn: A Retrospective (video), Chicago: Winston & Strawn, 1998.

—David M. Walden

YankeeNets LLC

45 Rockefeller Plaza, 26th Floor
New York, New York 10111
U.S.A.
Telephone: (212) 218-5100
Fax: (212) 218-5111
Web site: http://www.yankeenets.com

Private Company
Incorporated: 1999
Employees: 300
Sales: $241 million (1999)
NAIC: 711211 Sports Teams and Clubs

YankeeNets LLC, a holding company, is the parent of the New York Yankees American League baseball team, the New Jersey Nets National Basketball franchise, and through its affiliate, Puck Holdings, the New Jersey Devils of the National Hockey League. Under this first-of-a-kind arrangement in professional sports, the teams retain organizational independence but share marketing, sponsorship, and advertising opportunities. YankeeNets also oversees all acquisitions, media deals, and long-term financial strategy. The company's revenues come from ticket sales and the sale of broadcasting and media rights. The investor groups owning the Yankees and the Nets each own 50 percent of YankeeNets.

The New York Yankees

On April 22, 1903, the New York Highlanders played their first baseball game, losing to Washington. They beat Washington the next day. The site for the games was a thrown-together, wooden stadium called Hilltop Park, because it stood on one of the highest points in Manhattan. The site gave the team its name. In January of that year, Frank Ferrel and Bill Devery bought the two-year-old Baltimore Orioles franchise for $18,000 and moved the team to New York. Pitcher-manager Clark Griffith headed the team, which was part of the new American League (the former minor Western League). The National League signed a peace treaty with the AL in 1903 that ended a two-year bidding war for players, but it would be ten years before the NL's New York Giants let the Highlanders play games in their park, the Polo Grounds.

The 1913 move to the Polo Grounds coincided with the team officially changing its name to the Yankees. Sportswriter Mark Roth was credited with first calling them ''the Yankees'' in print. The club's trademark pinstripes first appeared on players' uniforms in 1912. In 1915, ownership of the team changed hands, when Col. Jacob Ruppert and Col. Tillinghast L'Hommedieu Huston bought the franchise. In 1919, George Halas, who founded the National Football League, batted .091 as a Yankee outfielder. But 1910–19 was the worst decade in franchise history. The team went through seven managers and had only four seasons of .500 or better.

The 1920s were certainly ''roaring'' for the Yankees. On January 3, 1920, the team bought Babe Ruth from the Boston Red Sox for $125,000 and a $350,000 loan against the mortgage on Fenway Park. The Yankees won three straight American League pennants in 1921–23, beating the Giants in 1923 for the first of 25 World Championships. A Yankee infielder in that series, Hinkey Haines, was the only player ever to win both a World Series and a National Football League championship, which he won in 1927 as quarterback with the New York Giants. The year 1923 also saw the opening of Yankee Stadium. In 1925, Lou Gehrig began his record streak of playing in 2,130 consecutive games; in 1927, Babe Ruth hit 60 home runs during the season; and in 1929, the Yankees became the first team to make numbers a permanent part of the uniform. During the decade, the team won six pennants and three championships.

The Yankees added Joe DiMaggio to the lineup in 1934, buying him from the San Francisco Seals for $50,000 after releasing Babe Ruth, who had 708 career home runs. In 1932, Lou Gehrig became the first player to hit four home runs in a single game, and in 1939, Gehrig ended his playing streak when he took himself out of the lineup because of illness. The team retired his number two months later. The Yankees won five pennants and five championships during the 1930s.

The 1940s saw the deaths of Gehrig and Ruth; Joe DiMaggio's 56-game hitting streak (and hits in 72 of 73 games); new owners (Dan Topping, Del Webb, and Larry MacPhail bought

Key Dates:

1903: New York Highlanders approved as American League franchise
1912: Highlanders wear pinstripe uniforms for first time.
1913: Team renamed the ''Yankees.''
1923: Yankee Stadium opens.
1929: Yankees first team to make numbers a permanent part of the uniform.
1953: Yankees win fifth consecutive World Championship.
1964: CBS purchases Yankees.
1967: New Jersey Americans is one of 11 original teams in American Basketball Association (ABA).
1968: Americans move to New York and change name to Nets.
1973: Limited partnership headed by George Steinbrenner III buys Yankees from CBS.
1976: ABA and NBA merge.
1977: Nets move back to New Jersey.
1982: Colorado Rockies National Hockey League franchise moves to New Jersey to become New Jersey Devils.
1999: New York Yankees and New Jersey Nets merge to create YankeeNets.
2000: YankeeNets affiliate buys New Jersey Devils hockey team.

the team for $2.8 million in 1945); the first night game in Yankee Stadium; and five managers, ending with the appointment of Casey Stengel in 1949. Interestingly, the decade included two of the three men who managed the team for at least ten years: Joe McCarthy, manager from 1931 to 1946 and Stengel (1949–60). The third long-term manager was Miller Huggins, who led the team from 1918 to 1929. During the 1940s, the team won five pennants and four championships.

The Yankees were hot during the 1950s under Stengel. They won eight pennants and six World Series, including a record five straight, even with Joe DiMaggio officially announcing his retirement in 1951. Catcher Yogi Berra won the American League Most Valuable Player award three times (1951, 1954–55), the most for any Yankee; Mickey Mantle made his Major League debut in 1951 and won the Triple Crown in 1956; Don Larson pitched the only perfect game in World Series history (1956).

The team lost the World Series in 1960 and Stengel lost his job, replaced by Ralph Houk. During the 1961 season, the club hit a record 240 homers and Maris broke Ruth's record with 61 home runs. The team won the World Series in 1961 and again in 1962, a season that included the longest game in Yankee history, lasting 22 innings. They won the pennant in 1963–64, marking five straight divisional titles, but would not win another until 1976. In 1964, CBS bought the team, initially paying $11.2 million for 80 percent and then acquiring the rest of the team later. For the first decade since the 1920s, the team's regular season record was below .600 (.552), and Mantle retired before the 1969 season.

In January 1973, CBS sold the club to a limited partnership, headed by George M. Steinbrenner III. The following year

Yankee Stadium began extensive remodeling and Steinbrenner signed a then-record five-year contract with pitcher Catfish Hunter, marking the beginning of free agentry. During the 1970s, Billy Martin began the first of five stints as manager (1975); Reggie Jackson joined the team (1976); and the team won back-to-back World Series in 1977–78. In 1979, team captain Thurman Munson was killed in a plane crash.

The 1980s began with a new record-setting contract signed by Dave Winfield for ten years, and in 1981 the team won the AL pennant. But with a weak pitching staff and 11 manager changes, they never made higher than second place during the rest of the 1980s, and had a losing season in 1989. In 1988, Deion Sanders was a 30th-round draft pick, playing with the team in 1989 before going to the National Football League.

Following losing seasons in 1990–92, Steinbrenner's choice of managers, first Buck Showalter and then Joe Torre, turned things around. The Yankees won three championships in four years (1996, their first since 1981, and 1998–99), including an American League record 114 regular season wins in 1998. In their century of play, the Yankees had the most MVP winners, World Series MVPs, Hall of Famers, and retired team numbers. The 1999 win marked the team's 25th championship, the most championships in major North American professional sports history.

The New Jersey Nets

One of the original 11 teams in the American Basketball Association, the franchise began as the New Jersey Americans. The ABA wanted to place a team in New York City to give the league legitimacy, just as the American League had done with the Highlanders baseball team 65 years earlier. But the basketball team could not find an arena in Manhattan and they ended up in the Teaneck Armory in New Jersey, playing their first game in October 1967.

The following year, owner Arthur Brown moved the team to Commack Arena in New York. He changed the team's name to the New York Nets when a reporter suggested he get a name that rhymed with Mets and Jets. After failing to sign Lew Alcindor (the future Kareem Abdul-Jabbar), Brown sold the franchise to businessman Roy Boe. The new owner moved the team to the Island Garden in West Hempstead, closer to Manhattan. The team made the playoffs for the first time and attendance tripled.

Lou Carnesecca became the Nets' general manager and head coach in 1970 and signed superstar Rick Barry. The following year, Barry was forced to return to the National Basketball Association, but in the offseason, the Nets obtained Julius Erving. ''Dr. J'' became a media sensation and made the team a championship-caliber club. The Nets won the 1974 ABA Championship under head coach Kevin Loughery.

The Nets won their second ABA championship in 1976. That June, the NBA and the ABA merged. The Nets became an NBA team at the cost of $8 million, of which $3.2 million went to the NBA and $4.8 million went to the New York Knicks as compensation for having a competing team in the same area.

Despite the acquisition of Nate "Tiny" Archibald from Kansas City, the Nets collapsed when Boe sold Erving to Philadelphia for $3 million following a salary dispute. After Archibald broke his foot, the team ended the 1976–77 season with a 22–60 record. Following the season, Boe took the team back to New Jersey. In 1978, Boe sold the Nets to a partnership led by Joseph Taub and Alan Cohen, but despite making the NBA Playoffs for the first time that season, the team continued to have lean years, with an aging cast of players.

The 1980–81 season saw a new coach, Larry Brown, the signing of Otis Birdsong, the move to a new arena at the Meadowlands in East Rutherford, New Jersey, and a winning season. In 1984 the Nets won their first playoff series since becoming an NBA team. But their appearance in the playoffs the following year was their last for seven seasons, even with the additions of Derrick Coleman and Drazen Petrovic in 1990.

The team drafted Kenny Anderson for the 1991–92 season and won its first playoff game since 1984. But with coaching changes, injuries, disciplinary problems and the death of Drazen Petrovic, the Nets had up-and-down seasons through the middle of the decade. In 1996, under coach John Calipari, the Nets made a nine player trade with Dallas to create a new, quick nucleus of players that took the team to the playoffs in 1998. But injuries continued to plague the team.

By the late 1990s, Nets owners Katz and Chambers wanted to move the team to Newark, to help revitalize that city with a new arena. Their co-tenants in the Meadowlands Sports Complex, the New Jersey Devils hockey team, wanted to move to Hoboken. Neither team could build an arena without help from the state, and the state wanted to keep them in one arena. Katz and Chambers tried to buy the Devils, but the owner of that team, John McMullen, was not interested.

Things would begin looking up for the Nets in 2000, after becoming part of YankeeNets. They won the number one pick in the draft and, in June, hired Rod Thorn, the NBA's executive vice-president of basketball operations, to become their president.

New Jersey Devils

The 2000 champion of the National Hockey League began life as the Colorado Rockies. In 1982, John McMullen bought the team and moved it to New Jersey. The team won its first Stanley Cup in 1995.

YankeeNets: 1999–2000

In February 1999, George Steinbrenner announced plans to merge the New York Yankees and the New Jersey Nets to create a new sports entity, a 50–50 corporate partnership called YankeeNets LLC. The value of the holding company was $750 million, with the Yankees worth $600 million and the Nets, $150 million. By December, following approval by the National Basketball Association and the major league baseball owners, the deal was completed. Steinbrenner, who owned 57 percent of the Yankees, received $225 million from the partnership for his share of the baseball team.

The decision to merge came about when talks with Cablevision Systems Corp. about purchasing the Yankees for $600 million fell through. Cablevision refused to agree to let Steinbrenner call the shots for the network's basketball (New York Knicks) and hockey (New York Rangers) teams as well as the Yankees.

Steinbrenner decided to create a company of his own that offered year-round sports programming. The Yankees' 12-year, $486 million broadcasting contract with Cablevision's MSG Network (formerly Madison Square Gardens Network) would expire at the end of the baseball season in 2000 and the Nets' contract with Fox Sports New York, which also was owned by Cablevision, would run out after the 2001–2002 season. By merging, the two teams had much greater clout in negotiating a new local television contract, and Steinbrenner began talking about starting his own regional sports cable network. The other factor supporting a merger, and the one that most interested Lewis Katz, the principal owner of the Nets, was the desire for a new baseball stadium and a new basketball arena.

In October 1999, YankeeNets hired Harvey Schiller to become chairman and chief executive officer. Schiller left the presidency of Turner Sports, where he headed up sports programming for TBS and TNT, helped to set up Turner South, a regional sports network owned by Time Warner, and was president of the Atlanta Thrashers hockey team. Before coming to Turner Sports in 1994, Schiller had been secretary general of the U.S. Olympic Committee, commissioner of the Southeastern Conference of collegiate sports, and a military pilot in Vietnam.

2000 and Beyond

In March 2000, YankeeNets sold $200 million in bonds to pay Steinbrenner for his share of the Yankees. This left the company with a total debt of $327 million. With income dependent on ticket sales and media rights, YankeeNets wanted to build new complexes for its teams, parks with far more high-revenue luxury suites than Yankee Stadium had. The company also needed to increase the amount it received for the television rights to broadcast its baseball and basketball games.

Before the end of 1999, John McMullen, owner of the New Jersey Devils National Hockey team, indicated that he would sell the team to YankeeNets. In March 2000, Puck Holdings, an entity affiliated with YankeeNets, announced the acquisition of the Devils for $175 million, pending approval by the National Hockey League. Puck Holdings was formed by Nets owners Lewis Katz and Ray Chambers to buy the hockey team because neither YankeeNets nor the Nets could take on any more debt. That purchase appeared to ensure that the two New Jersey teams would soon be playing in a new arena in Newark.

During the spring, while still considering starting its own sports network, YankeeNets continued negotiating with Cablevision and other networks for a new television rights deal. Cablevision appeared to be offering a contract worth $100 million a year, more than double the $48 million a year received under the current contract with MSG.

Principal Subsidiaries

New York Yankees; New Jersey Nets.

Further Reading

Akasie, Jay, ''Out of His League,'' *Forbes,* September 20, 1999, p. 54.

——, ''Strike Two,'' *Forbes,* April 17, 2000, p. 4.

''The Boss Is About To Decide If He Wants To Be a Media Mogul,'' *Star-Ledger,* May 18, 2000.

Brennan, John, ''YankeeNets Is a Done Deal,'' *Record Online,* December 1, 1999.

Blum, Ronald, ''Schiller Quits Turner, Expected To Join YankeeNets,'' *Associated Press,* October 30, 1999.

Canavan, Tom, ''Devils Agree To Sell to Affiliate of YankeeNets,'' *Associated Press,* March 16, 2000.

——, ''Devils Owner Eyes Sale to YankeeNets,'' *AP Online,* December 23, 1999.

Dottino, Paul, ''Team of the Century,'' *Record* (Bergen Co., N.J.), October 29, 1999, p. W4.

Garrity, Brian, ''Coming Up Short: Despite Lofty Pricetags, Sports Franchises Haven't Quite Made the Investment Banking Big Leagues,'' *Investment Dealers Digest,* June 5, 2000.

Jordan, George E., ''Sports Firm Ends Plan To Build Soccer Stadium in Newark, N.J.,'' *Star-Ledger,* March 24, 2000.

Lentz, Philip, ''Yanks Slam TV Home Run,'' *Crain's New York Business,* May 1, 2000, p. 1.

Machan, Dyan, ''The Boss' Boss,'' *Forbes,* May 15, 2000, p. 156.

Macht, Norman, ''Series Stops Cold in 1904,'' *Baseball Weekly,* August 21, 1994, p. 23.

Mercurio, Stephanie, ''Public Hearing Puts YankeeNets on Track with Newark Arena,'' *Bond Buyer,* April 6, 2000, p. 3.

Moskowitz, Eric, ''Yankee Thrift: Broadcasters Line Up To Line Steinbrenner's Pockets,'' *TheStreet.com,* March 17, 1999.

Most, Doug, ''New Jersey Has Arena Plan To Keep Nets, Devils Teams,'' *Record* (N.J.), December 7, 1999.

''New York Yankees,'' *Sports Network,* March 31, 2000.

Sabino, David, ''The History: Formidable Figures the Yankees' Legacy Is Rich with Dazzling Numbers, and They All Add Up to Greatness,'' *Sports Illustrated,* November 11, 1996, p. 6.

Smith, Stephen A., ''Rod Thorn Brings Credibility to Credibility-Deficient Nets,'' *Philadelphia Inquirer,* June 4, 2000.

''With Corporate Sponsor, This Bud May Be for Yankee Stadium,'' *Washington Post,* March 2, 1999, p. D2.

''YankeeNets Make $200 Million Bond Offering,'' *Fox News Online,* March 9, 2000.

—Ellen D. Wernick

York Research Corporation

280 Park Avenue
Suite 2700W
New York, New York 10017
U.S.A.
Telephone: (212) 557-6200
Fax: (212) 557-5678
Web site: http://www.yorkresearch.com

Public Corporation
Incorporated: 1941
Employees: 35
Sales: $22.53 million (2000)
Stock Exchanges: NASDAQ
Ticker Symbol: YORK
NAIC: 221119 Other Electric Power Generation

York Research Corporation develops, constructs, owns, and operates electric power and thermal generation (cogeneration) facilities alone or in strategic partnerships. These facilities are fueled by natural gas, solar energy, or windpower. A subsidiary that was marketing electricity and accounting for almost all of York's annual revenue of nearly $1 billion a year filed for Chapter 11 bankruptcy protection in 2000. York Research conducts business through a complex web of subsidiaries, partnerships, joint ventures, and affiliates.

York to 1985: Product Safety and Environmental Testing

York Research was incorporated in 1941 and had its quarters in Stamford, Connecticut. In its early days at least some of York's ''research'' appears to have been mundane, indeed, judging from the manual on floor maintenance it prepared for the American Hotel Association in 1950. By fiscal 1960 (the year ended September 30, 1960) the company was doing nearly $500,000 in annual business, and later in the calendar year it acquired Kip Electronics, a manufacturer of special electron tubes. Annual revenue reached $1.76 million in fiscal 1965. The bulk of this revenue appears to have come from the Florida-Hindle Transformer Division, a producer of industrial and electronic transformers, which York sold for stock in 1966 to Transitron Electronics Corp.

York Research then returned to its core business of product safety testing and consulting, plus consulting and testing in the environmental sciences. Among its activities during 1971 was testing the quietness of pumps used in nuclear submarines, testing the fire safety of certain materials used in the nation's mines and in children's sleepwear, and evaluating a number of new products for safety, costs, and reliability prior to their introduction in the marketplace. But in the early 1970s York also became an energy-management enterprise specializing in testing large projects, such as pilot plants to remove sulfur dioxide from power plants and discharge waste water.

York Research's change in focus was due to Robert Beningson, who became chairman and president in 1968. Beningson, an engineer, was also chairman and president of Combustion Equipment Associates Inc., whose major lines of business included environmentally friendly activities such as scrubbers for power plant emissions and recycling municipal garbage. Combustion Equipment Associates owned a majority of York's stock by the end of fiscal 1973. York's operating revenue rose higher than $1 million in fiscal 1972 and $2 million in fiscal 1974. By the end of fiscal 1974 the company, which added a testing laboratory in Denver, was receiving the major part of its revenues from electric utilities.

York Research, in 1978, was divided into the Air Services Division, which typically did studies on air pollution for utilities and the steel industry; a Municipal and Industrial Wastewater Service Division for assistance to wastewater treatment plants; and a Research and Development Division engaged in discovering new uses for refuse-derived materials. In that year Beningson took what amounted to a leave of absence from York to deal with the problems of Combustion Equipment Associates, which went bankrupt in 1981, leaving unpaid some $70 million in debts.

York Research also fell into serious difficulties in this period. Its revenues sank from $3.36 million in fiscal 1979 to $841,000 in fiscal 1981, during which the federal government

Key Dates:

1941: York Research is incorporated in Connecticut.
1970: York is engaged in products testing and pollution control.
1985: York Research acquires a Brooklyn power plant.
1996: Another York plant in Brooklyn is a major provider of steam for New York City's Consolidated Edison Co.
1996: York acquires an energy-marketing subsidiary.
1999: Five power projects are in operation.
2000: York's energy-marketing business files for bankruptcy.

drastically reduced its regulatory activities in the environmental field. During the summer of 1981 the company sold two subsidiaries, a regional operation servicing western states and a unit that concentrated on wastewater and sewage treatment operations. A third subsidiary continued to conduct studies on air pollution for utility, petrochemical, and government clients. Beningson returned to the helm of York Research in 1982.

Operating Cogeneration Power Plants: 1985–99

Toward the end of 1983 York Research's business began to increase as a consequence of the return to more active levels of government regulatory enforcement. The company also raised money by selling its Stamford building and leasing it back. Cogeneration Technologies, Inc., formed in 1984, was acquired in 1985 for $1.2 million in stock. With the purchase York acquired a power plant in a Brooklyn housing complex that was burning natural gas to generate both steam and electricity for the residents. The company also was intending to profit from recent federal legislation requiring utilities to buy power from independent producers at the price that it would have cost the utilities to produce the power themselves.

York Research lost money in fiscal 1986, 1987, and 1988. In the latter year the company had net operating revenues of only $1 million and a net loss of $4.69 million from continuing operations. York raised about $14.6 million in fiscal 1987, however, from a self-underwritten offshore private placement of its common stock, using a substantial portion of these funds for the development of cogeneration projects. This enabled the company to refurbish the power plant, which had a generating capacity of seven megawatts. After signing contracts with Consolidated Edison Co. of New York, Inc. (Con Edison) to supply 36 megawatts of power, York built a new plant on the site. The funds came from a limited partnership—Warbasse-Cogeneration Technologies Partnership, in which Beningson held a 25 percent share—that borrowed $72 million for the project.

In fiscal 1989 York Research moved its headquarters from Stamford to New York City and reported its best year ever, with net income of $3.55 million on revenue of $15.75 million. The results were misleading, however, for most of the revenue was earned not by the cogeneration project but paid by the limited partnership from borrowed funds. Despite its dubious track record, and the fact that the limited partnership—not York—was the

actual owner of the power plants, York attracted the attention of investors by proposing to provide Con Edison with 170 megawatts of additional power over 30 years. Tomen Corp., a Japanese trading company, was expected to provide the limited partnership with $300 million in financing for this project.

York Research's stock was trading at about $19 a share on July 24, 1991, when Tomen announced that it would not be participating in the project. The share price fell to $6.75 in a single day on trading volume more than 20 times normal. Existing holders of York stock were further disturbed to find that Beningson had recently sold 155,000 shares directly or indirectly owned by him at prices as high as $20 a share. They also learned that he had borrowed money from the company at no interest to exercise warrants issued to him by York when he rejoined the company in 1982. Several other company insiders also sold their shares as late as July 15, according to federal filings. Moreover, York had even lost the financing to operate the housing project plant. Aggrieved shareholders, customers, and creditors filed lawsuits seeking hundreds of millions of dollars. By September 1992 short sellers owned about 40 percent of the company's stock.

In spite of its troubles, York Research, in October 1991, won the Con Edison contract, reportedly by offering to sell the power at prices 30 percent below Con Edison's own costs. In April 1992 the company announced that it had found a lender for the project in the Mission Energy subsidiary of Southern California Edison (SCEcorp), the second largest independent power producer in the world. In addition, although skeptics continued to scoff, York, in October 1992, announced that it had purchased 286,000 kilowatts of power generation equipment from Siemens Power Corp. on behalf of the Brooklyn Navy Yard project. The company settled shareholders' lawsuits by issuing warrants for 780,000 shares of company stock.

York broke ground on the 286-megawatt Brooklyn Navy Yard cogeneration plant in 1995. It became operational the next year under a 40-year contract, providing more than 15 percent of Con Edison's total steam in New York City. The facility also was supplying energy to the host navy yard industrial park and to an adjacent wastewater facility. The plant was not owned by York Research but by Brooklyn Navy Yard Cogeneration Partners, L.P., which in turn was owned equally by B-41 Associates L.P., an indirect 75 percent-owned subsidiary of York, and by a subsidiary of Edison Mission Energy.

York Research also was able to complete the 38-megawatt facility supplying all the thermal and electric needs of the Brooklyn housing project (Amalgamated Warbasse Houses, Inc.). It assumed operation of the facility under a long-term operations and maintenance agreement with Warbasse-Cogeneration Technologies Partnership L.P., a limited partnership whose 25 percent general partner was RRR Ventures Ltd., in which Beningson was president and major stockholder.

In 1997 York Research acquired a limited partnership whose significant asset was a 15-year power purchase agreement with Texas Utilities Electric Co. York, in 1999, completed a wind power project in Big Spring, Texas, with a capacity of 34 megawatts and the installation of the largest wind turbines in the United States. In 1999 York also completed work on an adjacent 6.6-megawatt wind energy facility, owned by a partnership of York and Primesouth, Inc. This facility, like the other one, was intended to provide power to Texas Utilities.

In early 1998 InnCOGEN Limited, an indirect Trinidadian subsidiary of York Research, signed a 30-year power purchase agreement with Trinidad and Tobago Electric Commission. This enabled InnCOGEN to begin work on a $100 million, 215-megawatt power plant, fueled by local natural gas, that went into operation in 1999. Financing for this facility, which was constructed by another party, and the Texas facilities was secured in August 1998, when Credit Suisse First Boston agreed to underwrite the issue of $150 million in bonds due in 2007 and yielding 12 percent in annual interest.

North American Energy Conservation: 1996–2000

York Research, in November 1996, acquired 85 percent of North American Energy Conservation, Inc. (NAEC), a broker dealing in electricity and natural gas, from Beningson—who retained the other 15 percent—for $1. As a result, York's revenues shot up from $26.94 million in fiscal 1997 (the year ended February 28, 1997) to $365.13 million in fiscal 1998. North American was selling natural gas wholesale to utilities, producers, and marketing companies, mainly in the Northeast. The wholesale group also was purchasing natural gas for the company's retail group, which was marketing it to industrial and commercial accounts in New York state. In addition, NAEC also was marketing electricity. York's net income was $7.52 million in fiscal 1997 and $12.04 million in fiscal 1998.

York Research's revenues nearly tripled in fiscal 1999, reaching $972.89 million. But almost all of this sum ($966.64 million) was from NAEC's sales rather than from York's power plant projects. In a 1997 article for *Crain's New York Business,* Judy Temes reported that North American was proceeding in the energy brokering business at its peril, since the $600 billion-a-year field was dominated by much bigger players and, in the words of one analyst, was dependent on "razor-thin margins." This proved prophetic, because during the summer of 1998 certain electricity suppliers failed to deliver contracted power to marketers such as North American. As a result, the unit had to meet its own contractual commitments at substantially increased cost.

In September 1998 York Research decided to discontinue North American's electricity marketing following what it described as "unprecedented turmoil" during the summer, which caused electricity prices to rise from the normal $30 per megawatt to as much as $7,000. York registered a loss of about $10.84 million on its electricity marketing operations and a $5.99 million loss for the fiscal year.

North American Energy Conservation incurred further losses during the summer of 1999, which it said were due in part to the failed long-term contracts. The company filed for Chapter 11 bankruptcy in March 2000, causing York's stock to plunge in value by almost half as a result of the news. During the spring of 2000 the stock, which had traded at a high of $12 a share in 1996, fell below $1 a share at times. In April, York sold NAEC's retail natural gas marketing business to Amerada Hess Corp. The company reported revenues of $22.53 million and net income of $3.58 million from its power generating operations in fiscal 2000. It reported a loss of $34.73 million from NAEC's now discontinued operations during the fiscal year.

Principal Subsidiaries

Cogeneration Technologies, Inc.; InnCOGEN Ltd. (Trinidad and Tobago); North American Energy Conservation, Inc.

Principal Competitors

Cogen America Inc.; Indeck Energy Services Inc.; Sithe Energies USA Inc.

Further Reading

"Heard on the Street," *Wall Street Journal,* November 17, 1960, p. 17.

James, Canute, "Trinidad Gets Power Boost," *Journal of Commerce,* November 20, 1998, p. 10A.

Lowenstein, Roger, "Questions Cloud Outlook for York Research As Stock Plummets After Backer Pulls Out," *Wall Street Journal,* July 25, 1991, p. C2.

Messina, Judith, "Coast Partner May Regenerate York," *Crain's New York Business,* March 20, 1995, p. 31.

Power, William, "York Research Could Be Focus of Epic Battle Between Bulls, Bears as 'Short Squeeze' Looms," *Wall Street Journal,* September 2, 1992, p. C2.

"A Refuse Recycler Runs into Trouble," *New York Times,* October 29, 1980, p. D4.

Temes, Judy, "Energy Company Taking the Heat," *Crain's New York Business,* July 27, 1992, p. 4.

——, "Generating Heat," *Crain's New York Business,* June 3, 1991, pp. 1, 25.

——, "Power Producer Gaining Steam from Energy Brokerage Business, *Crain's New York Business,* February 10, 1997, p. 7.

——, "York Gains Vanish in Cloud of Smoke," *Crain's New York Business,* July 29, 1991, p. 39.

"Transitron Acquiring York Unit," *American Metal Market,* October 20, 1966, p. 7.

"York Research Corporation," *Barron's,* October 12, 1992, p. 71.

"York Research Unit Files for Chapter 11; Shares Plummet 46%," *Wall Street Journal,* March 3, 2000, p. A13.

"York Research To Quit Electricity Marketing, Focus on Natural Gas," *Wall Street Journal,* September 9, 1998, p. B2.

—Robert Halasz

INDEX TO COMPANIES

Index to Companies

Listings in this index are arranged in alphabetical order under the company name. Company names beginning with a letter or proper name such as Eli Lilly & Co. will be found under the first letter of the company name. Definite articles (The, Le, La) are ignored for alphabetical purposes as are forms of incorporation that precede the company name (AB, NV). Company names printed in bold type have full, historical essays on the page numbers appearing in bold. Updates to entries that appeared in earlier volumes are signified by the notation (upd.). Company names in light type are references within an essay to that company, not full historical essays. This index is cumulative with volume numbers printed in bold type.

NationsBank Corporation, 6 357; **10** 425–27; **11** 126; **13** 147; **18** 516, 518; **23** 455; **25** 91, 186; **26** 348, 453
NationsRent, **28** 388
Nationwide Cellular Service, Inc., **27** 305
Nationwide Credit, **11** 112
Nationwide Group, **25** 155
Nationwide Income Tax Service, **9** 326
Nationwide Logistics Corp., **14** 504
Nationwide Mutual Insurance Co., **26** 488
NATIOVIE, **II** 234
Native Plants, **III** 43
NATM Buying Corporation, **10** 9, 468
Natomas Co., **IV** 410; **6** 353–54; **7** 309; **11** 271
Natref, **IV** 535
Natronag, **IV** 325
Natronzellstoff-und Papierfabriken AG, **IV** 324
NatTeknik, **26** 333
Natudryl Manufacturing Company, **10** 271
Natural Gas Clearinghouse, **11** 355. *See also* NGC Corporation.
Natural Gas Corp., **19** 155
Natural Gas Pipeline Company, **6** 530, 543; **7** 344–45
Natural Gas Service of Arizona, **19** 411
Natural Wonders Inc., 14 342–44
NaturaLife International, **26** 470
The Nature Company, **10** 215–16; **14** 343; **26** 439; **27** 429; **28** 306
The Nature Conservancy, 26 323; **28** 305–07, 422
Nature's Sunshine Products, Inc., 15 317–19; **26** 470; **27** 353; **33** 145
Nature's Way Products Inc., **26** 315
Natuzzi Group. *See* Industrie Natuzzi S.p.A.
NatWest Bank, **22** 52. *See also* National Westminster Bank PLC.
Naugles, **7** 506
Nautica Enterprises, Inc., 16 61; **18** 357–60; **25** 258; **27** 60
Nautilus International, Inc., **III** 315–16; **13** 532; **25** 40; **30** 161
Nautor Ab, **IV** 302
Navaho Freight Line, **16** 41
Navajo Refining Company, **12** 240
Navale, **III** 209
Navarre Corporation, 22 536; **24** 348–51
Naviera Vizcaina, **IV** 528
Navigation Mixte, **III** 348
Navire Cargo Gear, **27** 269
Navistar International Corporation, I 152, 155, **180–82**, 186, 525, 527; **II** 330; **10** 280, **428–30 (upd.)**; **17** 327; **33** 254. *See also* International Harvester Co.
Navy Exchange Service Command, 31 342–45
Navy Federal Credit Union, 33 315–17
Naxon Utilities Corp., **19** 359
Naylor, Hutchinson, Vickers & Company. *See* Vickers PLC.
NBC **24** 516–17. *See also* National Broadcasting Company, Inc.
NBC Bankshares, Inc., **21** 524
NBC/Computer Services Corporation, **15** 163
NBD Bancorp, Inc., 9 476; **11** 339–41, 466
NBTY, Inc., 31 346–48
NCA Corporation, **9** 36, 57, 171
NCB. *See* National City Bank of New York.

NCB Brickworks, **III** 501; **7** 207
NCC L.P., **15** 139
NCH Corporation, 8 385–87
Nchanga Consolidated Copper Mines, **IV** 239–40
NCNB Corporation, II 336–37; **12** 519; **26** 453
NCR Corporation, I 540–41; **III** 147–52, **150–53**, 157, 165–66; **IV** 298; **V** 263; **6** 250, **264–68 (upd.)**, 281–82; **9** 416; **11** 62, 151, 542; **12** 162, 148, 246, 484; **16** 65; **29** 44; **30** 336–41 (upd.)
NCS. *See* Norstan, Inc.
NCTI (Noise Cancellation Technologies Inc.), **19** 483–84
nCube Corp., **14** 15; **22** 293
ND Marston, **III** 593
NDB. *See* National Discount Brokers Group, Inc.
NDL. *See* Norddeutscher Lloyd.
NEA. *See* Newspaper Enterprise Association.
NEAC Inc., **I** 201–02
Nearly Me, **25** 313
Neatherlin Homes Inc., **22** 547
Nebraska Bell Company, **14** 311
Nebraska Cellular Telephone Company, **14** 312
Nebraska Consolidated Mills Company, **II** 493; **III** 52; **8** 433; **26** 383
Nebraska Furniture Mart, **III** 214–15; **18** 60–61, 63
Nebraska Light & Power Company, **6** 580
Nebraska Power Company, **25** 89
Nebraska Public Power District, 29 351–54
NEBS. *See* New England Business Services, Inc.
NEC Corporation, I 455, 520; **II** 40, 42, 45, 56–57, **66–68**, 73, 82, 91, 104, 361; **III** 122–23, 130, 140, 715; **6** 101, 231, 244, 287; **9** 42, 115; **10** 257, 366, 463, 500; **11** 46, 308, 490; **13** 482; **16** 139; **18** 382–83; **19** 391; **21** 388–91 (upd.); **25** 82, 531
Neches Butane Products Co., **IV** 552
Neckermann Versand AG, **V** 100–02
Nedbank, **IV** 23
Nederland Line. *See* Stoomvaart Maatschappij Nederland.
Nederlander Organization, **24** 439
Nederlands Talen Institut, **13** 544
Nederlandsche Electriciteits Maatschappij. *See* N.E.M.
Nederlandsche Handel Maatschappij, **26** 242
Nederlandsche Heide Maatschappij, **III** 199
Nederlandsche Heidenmaatschappij. *See* Arcadis NV.
Nederlandsche Kunstzijdebariek, **13** 21
Nederlandsche Nieuw Guinea Petroleum Maatschappij, **IV** 491
Nederlandsche Stoomvart Maatschappij Oceaan, **6** 416
Nederlandse Cement Industrie, **III** 701
Nederlandse Crediethbank N.V., **II** 248
Nederlandse Dagbladunie NV, **IV** 610
N.V. Nederlandse Gasunie, I 326; **V** 627, 658–61
Nederlandse Handel Maatschappij, **II** 183, 527; **IV** 132–33
Nederlandse Vliegtuigenfabriek, **I** 54
Nedlloyd Group. *See* Koninklijke Nedlloyd N.V.

Nedsual, **IV** 23; **16** 28
Neeco, Inc., **9** 301
Needham Harper Worldwide, **I** 23, 28, 30–33; **13** 203; **14** 159
Needlecraft, **II** 560; **12** 410
Needleworks, Inc., **23** 66
Neenah Paper Co., **III** 40; **16** 303
Neenah Printing, **8** 360
NEES. *See* New England Electric System.
Neff Corp., 32 352–53
Negromex, **23** 171–72
Neighborhood Restaurants of America, **18** 241
Neilson/Cadbury, **II** 631
Neilman Bearings Co., **13** 78
Neiman-Marcus Co., I 246; **II** 478; **V** 10, 31; **12** 355–57; **15** 50, 86, 291; **17** 43; **21** 302; **25** 177–78; **27** 429
Neisler Laboratories, **I** 400
Neisner Brothers, Inc., **9** 20
Nekoosa Edwards Paper Co., **IV** 282; **9** 261
NEL Equity Services Co., **III** 314
Nelio Chemicals, Inc., **IV** 345
Nelson Bros., **14** 236
Nelson Publications, **22** 442
Nemuro Bank, **II** 291
Nenuco, **II** 567
Neodata, **11** 293
Neos, **21** 438
Neoterics Inc., **11** 65
Neozyme I Corp., **13** 240
Nepera, Inc., **I** 682; **16** 69
Neptun Maritime Oyj, **29** 431
Neptune, **22** 63
NER Auction Group, **23** 148
NERCO, Inc., V 689, **7** 376–79
Nesbitt Thomson, **II** 211
Nesco Inc., **28** 6, 8
Nescott, Inc., **16** 36
Nesher Israel Cement Enterprises Ltd., **II** 47; **25** 266
Neste Oy, IV 435, **469–71**, 519. *See also* Fortum Corporation
Nestlé S.A., I 15, 17, 251–52, 369, 605; **II** 379, 456, 478, 486–89, 521, **545–49**, 568–70; **III** 47–48; **6** 16; **7** 380–84 (upd.); **8** 131, 342–44, 498–500; **10** 47, 324; **11** 15, 205; **12** 480–81; **13** 294; **14** 214; **15** 63; **16** 168; **19** 50–51; **21** 55–56, 219; **22** 78, 80; **23** 219; **24** 388; **25** 21, 85, 366; **28** 308–13 (upd.); **32** 115, 234
NetCom Systems AB, 26 331–33
Netherland Bank for Russian Trade, **II** 183
Netherlands Fire Insurance Co. of Tiel, **III** 308, 310
Netherlands India Steam Navigation Co., **III** 521
Netherlands Insurance Co., **III** 179, 308–10
Netherlands Trading Co. *See* Nederlandse Handel Maatschappij.
NetHold B.V., **31** 330
NetLabs, **25** 117
NetMarket Company, **16** 146
Netron, **II** 390
Netscape Communications Corporation, 15 320–22; **35** 304–07 (upd.)
NetStar Communications Inc., **24** 49; **35** 69
NetStar Inc.,
Nettai Sangyo, **I** 507
Nettingsdorfer, **19** 227
Nettle Creek Corporation, **19** 304

INDEX TO INDUSTRIES

Index to Industries

ACCOUNTING

Andersen Worldwide, 29 (upd.)
Deloitte & Touche, 9
Deloitte Touche Tohmatsu International, 29
(upd.)
Ernst & Young, 9; 29 (upd.)
KPMG International, 33 (upd.)
L.S. Starrett Co., 13
McLane Company, Inc., 13
Price Waterhouse, 9
PricewaterhouseCoopers, 29 (upd.)
Robert Wood Johnson Foundation, 35
Univision Communications Inc., 24

ADVERTISING & OTHER BUSINESS SERVICES

A.C. Nielsen Company, 13
ABM Industries Incorporated, 25 (upd.)
Ackerley Communications, Inc., 9
Adia S.A., 6
Advo, Inc., 6
Aegis Group plc, 6
AHL Services, Inc., 27
American Building Maintenance Industries,
Inc., 6
The American Society of Composers,
Authors and Publishers (ASCAP), 29
Armor Holdings, Inc., 27
Ashtead Group plc, 34
The Associated Press, 13
Barrett Business Services, Inc., 16
Bates Worldwide, Inc., 14; 33 (upd.)
Bearings, Inc., 13
Berlitz International, Inc., 13
Big Flower Press Holdings, Inc., 21
Bozell Worldwide Inc., 25
Bright Horizons Family Solutions, Inc., 31
Broadcast Music Inc., 23
Burns International Security Services, 13
Campbell-Mithun-Esty, Inc., 16
Carmichael Lynch Inc., 28
Central Parking Corporation, 18
Chiat/Day Inc. Advertising, 11
Christie's International plc, 15
Cintas Corporation, 21
Computer Learning Centers, Inc., 26
CORT Business Services Corporation, 26
Cox Enterprises, Inc., 22 (upd.)
Cyrk Inc., 19
Dale Carnegie Training, Inc., 28
D'Arcy Masius Benton & Bowles, Inc., 6;
32 (upd.)
DDB Needham Worldwide, 14
Deluxe Corporation, 22 (upd.)
Dentsu Inc., I; 16 (upd.)
Deutsche Post AG, 29
Earl Scheib, Inc., 32
EBSCO Industries, Inc., 17
Education Management Corporation, 35
Employee Solutions, Inc., 18
Ennis Business Forms, Inc., 21
Equifax Inc., 6; 28 (upd.)
Equity Marketing, Inc., 26
ERLY Industries Inc., 17

Euro RSCG Worldwide S.A., 13
Fallon McElligott Inc., 22
Fiserv, Inc., 33 (upd.)
FlightSafety International, Inc., 29 (upd.)
Florists' Transworld Delivery, Inc., 28
Foote, Cone & Belding Communications,
Inc., I
Gage Marketing Group, 26
Grey Advertising, Inc., 6
Gwathmey Siegel & Associates Architects
LLC, 26
Ha-Lo Industries, Inc., 27
Hakuhodo, Inc., 6
Handleman Company, 15
Havas SA, 33 (upd.)
Hays Plc, 27
Heidrick & Struggles International, Inc., 28
Hildebrandt International, 29
Interep National Radio Sales Inc., 35
International Management Group, 18
Interpublic Group Inc., I
The Interpublic Group of Companies, Inc.,
22 (upd.)
Iron Mountain, Inc., 33
ITT Educational Services, Inc., 33
J.D. Power and Associates, 32
Japan Leasing Corporation, 8
Jostens, Inc., 25 (upd.)
JWT Group Inc., I
Katz Communications, Inc., 6
Katz Media Group, Inc., 35
Kelly Services Inc., 6; 26 (upd.)
Ketchum Communications Inc., 6
Kinko's Inc., 16
Korn/Ferry International, 34
Labor Ready, Inc., 29
Lamar Advertising Company, 27
Learning Tree International Inc., 24
Leo Burnett Company Inc., I; 20 (upd.)
Lintas: Worldwide, 14
Mail Boxes Etc., 18
Manpower, Inc., 30 (upd.)
marchFIRST, Inc., 34
National Media Corporation, 27
New England Business Services, Inc., 18
New Valley Corporation, 17
NFO Worldwide, Inc., 24
Norrell Corporation, 25
Norwood Promotional Products, Inc., 26
The Ogilvy Group, Inc., I
Olsten Corporation, 6; 29 (upd.)
Omnicom Group, I; 22 (upd.)
On Assignment, Inc., 20
1-800-FLOWERS, Inc., 26
Outdoor Systems, Inc., 25
Paris Corporation, 22
Paychex, Inc., 15
Pierce Leahy Corporation, 24
Pinkerton's Inc., 9
PMT Services, Inc., 24
Publicis S.A., 19
Publishers Clearing House, 23
Randstad Holding n.v., 16
RemedyTemp, Inc., 20
Rental Service Corporation, 28

Robert Half International Inc., 18
Ronco, Inc., 15
Saatchi & Saatchi PLC, I
ServiceMaster Limited Partnership, 6
Shared Medical Systems Corporation, 14
Sir Speedy, Inc., 16
Skidmore, Owings & Merrill, 13
SOS Staffing Services, 25
Sotheby's Holdings, Inc., 11; 29 (upd.)
Spencer Stuart and Associates, Inc., 14
Superior Uniform Group, Inc., 30
Sylvan Learning Systems, Inc., 35
Taylor Nelson Sofres plc, 34
TBWA Advertising, Inc., 6
Thomas Cook Travel Inc., 33 (upd.)
Ticketmaster Corp., 13
TMP Worldwide Inc., 30
TNT Post Group N.V., 30
Towers Perrin, 32
Transmedia Network Inc., 20
Treasure Chest Advertising Company, Inc.,
32
TRM Copy Centers Corporation, 18
True North Communications Inc., 23
Tyler Corporation, 23
U.S. Office Products Company, 25
UniFirst Corporation, 21
United News & Media plc, 28 (upd.)
Unitog Co., 19
Vedior NV, 35
The Wackenhut Corporation, 14
Wells Rich Greene BDDP, 6
Westaff Inc., 33
William Morris Agency, Inc., 23
WPP Group plc, 6
Young & Rubicam, Inc., I; 22 (upd.)

AEROSPACE

A.S. Yakovlev Design Bureau, 15
The Aerospatiale Group, 7; 21 (upd.)
Alliant Techsystems Inc., 30 (upd.)
Aviacionny Nauchno-Tehnicheskii
Komplex im. A.N. Tupoleva, 24
Avions Marcel Dassault-Breguet Aviation,
I
B/E Aerospace, Inc., 30
Banner Aerospace, Inc., 14
Beech Aircraft Corporation, 8
The Boeing Company, I; 10 (upd.); 32
(upd.)
British Aerospace plc, I; 24 (upd.)
Canadair, Inc., 16
Cessna Aircraft Company, 8
Cobham plc, 30
Daimler-Benz Aerospace AG, 16
Ducommun Incorporated, 30
Fairchild Aircraft, Inc., 9
G.I.E. Airbus Industrie, I; 12 (upd.)
General Dynamics Corporation, I; 10
(upd.)
Groupe Dassault Aviation SA, 26 (upd.)
Grumman Corporation, I; 11 (upd.)
Gulfstream Aerospace Corporation, 7; 28
(upd.)

ENGINEERING & MANAGEMENT SERVICES

FOOD PRODUCTS

FOOD SERVICES & RETAILERS

HEALTH & PERSONAL CARE PRODUCTS

HEALTH CARE SERVICES

HOTELS

INFORMATION TECHNOLOGY

INSURANCE

LEGAL SERVICES

MANUFACTURING

MATERIALS

MINING & METALS

PAPER & FORESTRY

REAL ESTATE

RETAIL & WHOLESALE

RUBBER & TIRE

TELECOMMUNICATIONS

TEXTILES & APPAREL

NOTES ON CONTRIBUTORS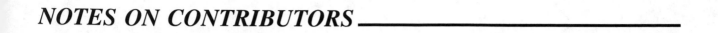

Notes on Contributors

BIANCO, David. Freelance writer, editor, and publishing consultant.

BISCONTINI, Tracey Vasil. Pennsylvania-based freelance writer, editor, and columnist.

BRENNAN, Gerald E. Freelance writer based in California.

BRYNILDSSEN, Shawna. Freelance writer and editor based in Bloomington, Indiana.

COHEN, M. L. Novelist and freelance writer living in Paris.

COVELL, Jeffrey L. Freelance writer and corporate history contractor.

DINGER, Ed. Brooklyn-based freelance writer and editor.

FIERO, John W. Freelance writer, researcher, and consultant.

FUJINAKA, Mariko. Freelance writer and editor based in California.

HAUSER, Evelyn. Freelance writer and marketing specialist based in northern California.

INGRAM, Frederick C. South Carolina-based business writer who has contributed to *GSA Business, Appalachian Trailway News,* the *Encyclopedia of Business,* the *Encyclo-*

pedia of Global Industries, the *Encyclopedia of Consumer Brands,* and other regional and trade publications.

LEMIEUX, Gloria A. Freelance writer and editor living in Nashua, New Hampshire.

MARTIN, Rachel H. Denver-based freelance writer.

MILITE, George A. Philadelphia-based writer specializing in business management issues.

ROTHBURD, Carrie. Freelance technical writer and editor, specializing in corporate profiles, academic texts, and academic journal articles.

SCHULZ, Ana Garcia. St. Louis-based freelance writer.

STANFEL, Rebecca. Freelance writer and editor based in Montana.

SWARTZ, Mark. Brooklyn-based writer.

TRADII, Mary. Freelance writer based in Denver, Colorado.

WALDEN, David M. Freelance writer and historian in Salt Lake City; adjunct history instructor at Salt Lake City Community College.

WERNICK, Ellen. Freelance writer and editor.

WOODWARD, A. Freelance writer.